Microsoft® OFFICE 2013

POST-ADVANCED

Misty E. Vermaat

Contributing Authors
Steven M. Freund
Joy L. Starks
Susan L. Sebok
Mali B. Jones
Philip J. Pratt
Mary Z. Last
Corinne L. Hoisington

CENGAGE
Learning®

SHELLY
CASHMAN
SERIES®

Australia • Brazil • Japan • Korea • Mexico • Singapore • Spain • United Kingdom • United States

Microsoft® Office 2013: Post-Advanced
Misty E. Vermaat

Product Director: Kathleen McMahon

Content Developer: Jon Farnham

Associate Content Developer: Crystal
Parenteau

Product Assistant: Allison Castro

Manufacturing Planner: Julio Esperas

Director of Production: Patty Stephan

Senior Content Project Manager:
Matthew Hutchinson

Development Editors: Lyn Markowicz, Deb
Kaufmann, Amanda Brodkin, Lisa Ruffolo

Senior Brand Manager: Elinor Gregory

Market Development Manager: Kristie Clark

Market Development Manager:
Gretchen Swann

Marketing Coordinator: Amy McGregor

QA Manuscript Reviewers: Jeffrey Schwartz,
John Freitas, Serge Palladino, Susan Pedicini,
Danielle Shaw, Susan Whalen

Art Director: GEX Publishing Services, Inc.

Text Design: Joel Sadagursky

Cover Design: Lisa Kuhn, Curio Press, LLC

Cover Photo: Tom Kates Photography

Compositor: PreMediaGlobal

Copyeditor: Foxxe Editorial

Proofreader: Kim Kosmatka

Indexer: Rich Carlson

For product information and technology assistance, contact us at
Cengage Learning Customer & Sales Support, 1-800-354-9706

For permission to use material from this text or product,
submit all requests online at **cengage.com/permissions**
Further permissions questions can be emailed to
permissionrequest@cengage.com

Library of Congress Control Number: 2013953093

ISBN-13: 978-1-285-16639-1
ISBN-10: 1-285-16639-6

Cengage Learning
20 Channel Center Street
Boston, MA 02210
USA

Cengage Learning is a leading provider of customized learning solutions with
office locations around the globe, including Singapore, the United Kingdom,
Australia, Mexico, Brazil, and Japan. Locate your local office at:
international.cengage.com/region

Cengage Learning products are represented in Canada by Nelson Education, Ltd.

To learn more about Cengage Learning, visit **www.cengage.com**

Purchase any of our products at your local college bookstore or at our
preferred online store at **www.cengagebrain.com**

Printed in the United States of America
1 2 3 4 5 6 7 17 16 15 14

Microsoft OFFICE 2013

POST-ADVANCED

Contents

Microsoft **PowerPoint 2013**

CHAPTER EIGHT
Customizing a Template and Handouts Using Masters

CHAPTER NINE
Modifying a Presentation Using Graphical Elements

Microsoft **Excel 2013**

Microsoft **Access 2013**

Microsoft **Outlook 2013**

CHAPTER FOUR
Creating and Managing Tasks with Outlook

CHAPTER FIVE
Customizing Outlook

Capstone Projects

Preface

The Shelly Cashman Series® offers the finest textbooks in computer education. We are proud that since Microsoft Office 4.3, our series of Microsoft Office textbooks have been the most widely used books in education. With each new edition of our Office books, we make significant improvements based on the software and comments made by instructors and students. For this Microsoft Office 2013 text, the Shelly Cashman Series development team carefully reviewed our pedagogy and analyzed its effectiveness in teaching today's Office student. Students today read less, but need to retain more. They need not only to be able to perform skills, but to retain those skills and know how to apply them to different settings. Today's students need to be continually engaged and challenged to retain what they're learning.

With this Microsoft Office 2013 text, we continue our commitment to focusing on the users and how they learn best.

Objectives of This Textbook

Microsoft Office 2013: Post-Advanced is intended for a third course on Office 2013 applications. This book assumes that students are familiar with the fundamentals and some advanced features of Microsoft Windows 8, Microsoft Word 2013, Microsoft PowerPoint 2013, Microsoft Excel 2013, Microsoft Access 2013, and Microsoft Outlook 2013. These fundamentals are covered in the companion textbooks *Microsoft Office 2013: Introductory* and *Microsoft Office 2013: Advanced*. The objectives of this book are:

- To go beyond the fundamentals and offer an in-depth presentation of Microsoft Word 2013, Microsoft PowerPoint 2013, Microsoft Excel 2013, Microsoft Access 2013, and Microsoft Outlook 2013

- To expose students to practical examples of the computer as a useful tool

- To acquaint students with the proper procedures to create documents, presentations, worksheets, and databases suitable for coursework, professional purposes, and personal use

- To help students discover the underlying functionality of Office 2013 so they can become more productive

- To develop an exercise-oriented approach that allows learning by doing

The Shelly Cashman Approach

A Proven Pedagogy with an Emphasis on Project Planning

Each chapter presents a practical problem to be solved within a project planning framework. The project orientation is strengthened by the use of the Roadmap, which provides a visual framework for the project. Step-by-step instructions with supporting screens guide students through the steps. Instructional steps are supported by the Q&A, Experimental Step, and BTW features.

A Visually Engaging Book that Maintains Student Interest

The step-by-step tasks, with supporting figures, provide a rich visual experience for the student. Call-outs on the screens that present both explanatory and navigational information provide students with information they need when they need to know it.

Supporting Reference Materials (Capstones, Quick Reference)

With the Quick Reference, students can quickly look up information about a single task, such as keyboard shortcuts, and find page references to where in the book the task is illustrated. The Capstone Projects allow students to demonstrate mastery of skills across the Comprehensive content for Word, PowerPoint, Excel, Access, and Outlook.

Integration of the World Wide Web

The World Wide Web is integrated into the Office 2013 learning experience with (1) BTW annotations; (2) BTW, Q&A, and Quick Reference Summary Web pages; and (3) the Learn Online resources for each chapter.

End-of-Chapter Student Activities

Extensive end-of-chapter activities provide a variety of reinforcement opportunities for students to apply and expand their skills through individual and group work. To complete some of these assignments, you will be required to use the Data Files for Students. Visit www.cengage.com/ct/studentdownload for detailed access instructions or contact your instructor for information about accessing the required files.

New to this Edition

Enhanced Coverage of Critical Thinking Skills

A New Consider This element poses thought-provoking questions throughout each chapter, providing an increased emphasis on critical thinking and problem-solving skills. Also, every task in the project now includes a reason *why* the students are performing the task and *why* the task is necessary.

Enhanced Retention and Transference

A new Roadmap element provides a visual framework for each project, showing students where they are in the process of creating each project, and reinforcing the context of smaller tasks by showing how they fit into the larger project.

Integration of Office with Cloud and Web Technologies

A new Lab focuses entirely on integrating cloud and web technologies with Office 2013, using technologies like blogs and online photo editors.

More Personalization

Each chapter project includes an optional instruction for the student to personalize his or her solution, if required by an instructor, making each student's solution unique.

More Collaboration

A new Research and Collaboration project has been added to the Consider This: Your Turn assignment at the end of each chapter.

Instructor Resources

The Instructor Resources include both teaching and testing aids and can be accessed via CD-ROM or at www.cengage.com/login.

Instructor's Manual Includes lecture notes summarizing the chapter sections, figures and boxed elements found in every chapter, teacher tips, classroom activities, lab activities, and quick quizzes in Microsoft Word files.

Syllabus Easily customizable sample syllabi that cover policies, assignments, exams, and other course information.

Figure Files Illustrations for every figure in the textbook in electronic form.

Powerpoint Presentations A multimedia lecture presentation system that provides slides for each chapter. Presentations are based on chapter objectives.

Solutions to Exercises Includes solutions for all end-of-chapter and chapter reinforcement exercises.

Test Bank & Test Engine Test banks include 112 questions for every chapter, featuring objective-based and critical thinking question types, and including page number references and figure references, when appropriate. Also included is the test engine, ExamView, the ultimate tool for your objective-based testing needs.

Data Files for Students Includes all the files that are required by students to complete the exercises.

Additional Activities for Students Consists of Chapter Reinforcement Exercises, which are true/false, multiple-choice, and short answer questions that help students gain confidence in the material learned.

Learn Online

CengageBrain.com is the premier destination for purchasing or renting Cengage Learning textbooks, eBooks, eChapters, and study tools at a significant discount (eBooks up to 50% off Print). In addition, CengageBrain.com provides direct access to all digital products, including eBooks, eChapters, and digital solutions, such as CourseMate and SAM, regardless of where purchased. The following are some examples of what is available for this product on www.cengagebrain.com.

Student Companion Site The Student Companion Site reinforces chapter terms and concepts using true/false questions, multiple choice questions, short answer questions, flash cards, practice tests, and learning games, all available for no additional cost at www.cengagebrain.com.

Microsoft Office 2013 MindTap MindTap is a fully online, highly personalized learning experience built upon Cengage Learning content. MindTap combines student learning tools - readings, multimedia, activities, and assessments - into a singular Learning Path that guides students through their course. Instructors personalize the experience by customizing authoritative Cengage Learning content and learning tools, including the ability to add SAM trainings, assessments, and projects into the Learning Path via a SAM app that integrates into the MindTap framework seamlessly with Learning Management Systems. Available in 2014.

SAM: Skills Assessment Manager Get your students workplace-ready with SAM, the market-leading proficiency-based assessment and training solution for Microsoft Office! SAM's active, hands-on environment helps students master Microsoft Office skills and computer concepts that are essential to academic and career success, delivering the most comprehensive online learning solution for your course!

Through skill-based assessments, interactive trainings, business-centric projects, and comprehensive remediation, SAM engages students in mastering the latest Microsoft Office programs on their own, giving instructors more time to focus on teaching. Computer concepts labs supplement instruction of important technology-related topics and issues through engaging simulations and interactive, auto-graded assessments. With enhancements including streamlined course setup, more robust grading and reporting features, and the integration of fully interactive MindTap Readers containing Cengage Learning's premier textbook content, SAM provides the best teaching and learning solution for your course.

MindLinks MindLinks is a new Cengage Learning Service designed to provide the best possible user experience and facilitate the highest levels of learning retention and outcomes, enabled through a deep integration of Cengage Learning's digital suite into an instructor's Learning Management System (LMS). MindLinks works on any LMS that supports the IMS Basic LTI open standard. Advanced features, including gradebook exchange, are the result of active, enhanced LTI collaborations with industry-leading LMS partners to drive the evolving technology standards forward.

CourseNotes

Cengage Learning's CourseNotes are six-panel quick reference cards that reinforce the most important and widely used features of a software application in a visual and user-friendly format. CourseNotes serve as a great reference tool during and after the course. CourseNotes are available for software applications, such as Microsoft Office 2013. There are also topic-based CourseNotes available, such as Best Practices in Social Networking, Hot Topics in Technology, and Web 2.0. Visit www.cengagebrain.com to learn more!

About Our Covers

The Shelly Cashman Series is continually updating our approach and content to reflect the way today's students learn and experience new technology. This focus on student success is reflected on our covers, which feature real students from The University of Rhode Island using the Shelly Cashman Series in their courses, and reflect the varied ages and backgrounds of the students learning with our books. When you use the Shelly Cashman Series, you can be assured that you are learning computer skills using the most effective courseware available.

Textbook Walk-Through

The Shelly Cashman Series Pedagogy: Project-Based — Step-by-Step — Variety of Assessments

Roadmaps provide a visual framework for each project, showing the students where they are in the process of creating each project.

Step-by-step instructions provide a context beyond the point-and-click. Each step provides information on why students are performing each task and what will occur as a result.

Explanatory callouts summarize what is happening on screen.

Navigational callouts in red show students where to click.

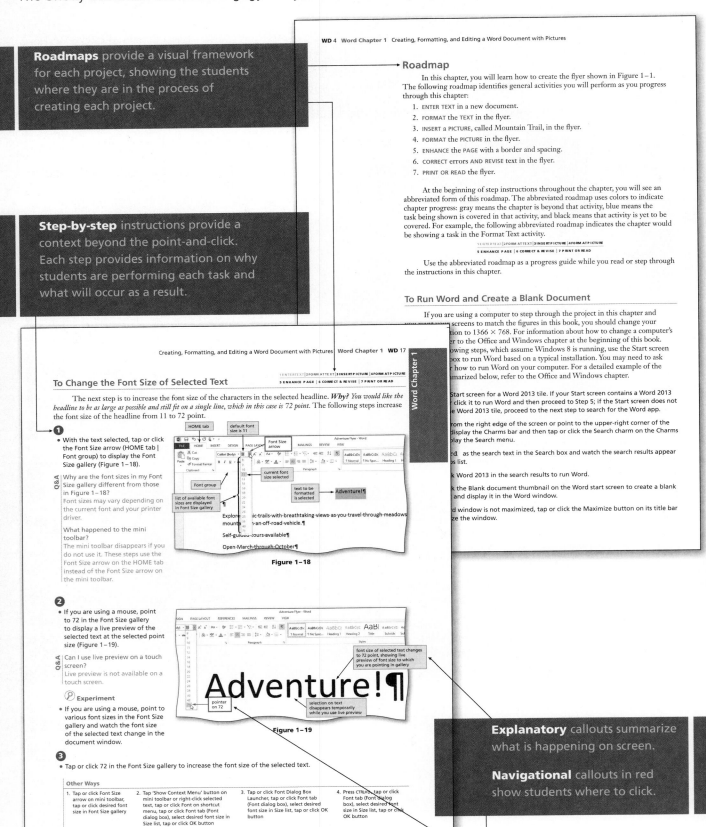

Roadmap

In this chapter, you will learn how to create the flyer shown in Figure 1–1. The following roadmap identifies general activities you will perform as you progress through this chapter:

1. ENTER TEXT in a new document.
2. FORMAT the TEXT in the flyer.
3. INSERT a PICTURE, called Mountain Trail, in the flyer.
4. FORMAT the PICTURE in the flyer.
5. ENHANCE the PAGE with a border and spacing.
6. CORRECT errors AND REVISE text in the flyer.
7. PRINT OR READ the flyer.

At the beginning of step instructions throughout the chapter, you will see an abbreviated form of this roadmap. The abbreviated roadmap uses colors to indicate chapter progress: gray means the chapter is beyond that activity, blue means the task being shown is covered in that activity, and black means that activity is yet to be covered. For example, the following abbreviated roadmap indicates the chapter would be showing a task in the Format Text activity.

1 ENTER TEXT | 2 FORM AT TEXT | 3 INSERT PICTURE | 4 FORM ATP ICTURE
5 ENHANCE PAGE | 6 CORRECT & REVISE | 7 PRINT OR READ

Use the abbreviated roadmap as a progress guide while you read or step through the instructions in this chapter.

To Run Word and Create a Blank Document

If you are using a computer to step through the project in this chapter and you want your screens to match the figures in this book, you should change your resolution to 1366 × 768. For information about how to change a computer's resolution, refer to the Office and Windows chapter at the beginning of this book.

The following steps, which assume Windows 8 is running, use the Start screen or the Search box to run Word based on a typical installation. You may need to ask your instructor how to run Word on your computer. For a detailed example of the procedure summarized below, refer to the Office and Windows chapter.

1. Scroll the Start screen for a Word 2013 tile. If your Start screen contains a Word 2013 tile, tap or click it to run Word and then proceed to Step 5; if the Start screen does not contain the Word 2013 tile, proceed to the next step to search for the Word app.

2. Swipe in from the right edge of the screen or point to the upper-right corner of the screen to display the Charms bar and then tap or click the Search charm on the Charms bar to display the Search menu.

3. Type Word as the search text in the Search box and watch the search results appear in the Apps list.

4. Tap or click Word 2013 in the search results to run Word.

5. Tap or click the Blank document thumbnail on the Word start screen to create a blank document and display it in the Word window.

6. If the Word window is not maximized, tap or click the Maximize button on its title bar to maximize the window.

Word Chapter 1

To Change the Font Size of Selected Text

1 ENTER TEXT | 2 FORM AT TEXT | 3 INSERT PICTURE | 4 FORM ATP ICTURE
5 ENHANCE PAGE | 6 CORRECT & REVISE | 7 PRINT OR READ

The next step is to increase the font size of the characters in the selected headline. *Why? You would like the headline to be as large as possible and still fit on a single line, which in this case is 72 point.* The following steps increase the font size of the headline from 11 to 72 point.

1
- With the text selected, tap or click the Font Size arrow (HOME tab | Font group) to display the Font Size gallery (Figure 1–18).

Q&A Why are the font sizes in my Font Size gallery different from those in Figure 1–18?
Font sizes may vary depending on the current font and your printer driver.

What happened to the mini toolbar?
The mini toolbar disappears if you do not use it. These steps use the Font Size arrow on the HOME tab instead of the Font Size arrow on the mini toolbar.

Figure 1–18

2
- If you are using a mouse, point to 72 in the Font Size gallery to display a live preview of the selected text at the selected point size (Figure 1–19).

Q&A Can I use live preview on a touch screen?
Live preview is not available on a touch screen.

Experiment
- If you are using a mouse, point to various font sizes in the Font Size gallery and watch the font size of the selected text change in the document window.

Figure 1–19

3
- Tap or click 72 in the Font Size gallery to increase the font size of the selected text.

Other Ways

1. Tap or click Font Size arrow on mini toolbar, tap or click desired font size in Font Size gallery	2. Tap 'Show Context Menu' button on mini toolbar or right-click selected text, tap or click Font on shortcut menu, tap or click Font tab (Font dialog box), select desired font size in Size list, tap or click OK button	3. Tap or click Font Dialog Box Launcher, tap or click Font tab (Font dialog box), select desired font size in Size list, tap or click OK button	4. Press CTRL+D, tap or click Font tab (Font dialog box), select desired font size in Size list, tap or click OK button

Q&A boxes anticipate questions students may have when working through the steps and provide additional information about what they are doing right where they need it.

Experiment Steps within the step-by-step instructions encourage students to explore, experiment, and take advantage of the features of the Office 2013 user interface. These steps are not necessary to complete the projects, but are designed to increase confidence with the software and build problem-solving skills.

Consider This boxes pose thought-provoking questions with answers throughout each chapter, promoting critical thought along with immediate feedback.

To Change the Font Size of Selected Text

1 FONT KIE KE | 2 FORM ATTE XT | 3 INSERT PICTURE | 4 FORM ATPICTURE
5 ENHANCE PAGE | 6 CORRECT & REVISE | 7 PRINT OR READ

The next step is to increase the font size of the characters in the selected headline. *Why? You would like the headline to be as large as possible and still fit on a single line, which in this case is 72 point.* The following steps increase the font size of the headline from 11 to 72 point.

1
- With the text selected, tap or click the Font Size arrow (HOME tab | Font group) to display the Font Size gallery (Figure 1–18).

Q&A
Why are the font sizes in my Font Size gallery different from those in Figure 1–18?
Font sizes may vary depending on the current font and your printer driver.

What happened to the mini toolbar?
The mini toolbar disappears if you do not use it. These steps use the Font Size arrow on the HOME tab instead of the Font Size arrow on the mini toolbar.

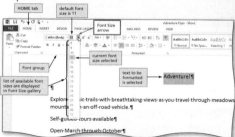

Figure 1–18

2
- If you are using a mouse, point to 72 in the Font Size gallery to display a live preview of the selected text at the selected point size (Figure 1–19).

Q&A
Can I use live preview on a touch screen?
Live preview is not available on a touch screen.

Experiment
- If you are using a mouse, point to various font sizes in the Font Size gallery and watch the font size of the selected text change in the document window.

Figure 1–19

3
- Tap or click 72 in the Font Size gallery to increase the font size of the selected text.

Other Ways

1. Tap or click Font Size arrow on mini toolbar, tap or click desired font size in Font Size gallery	2. Tap 'Show Context Menu' button on mini toolbar or right-click selected text, tap or click Font on shortcut menu, tap or click Font tab (Font dialog box), select desired font size in Size list, tap or click OK button	3. Tap or click Font Dialog Box Launcher, tap or click Font tab (Font dialog box), select desired font size in Size list, tap or click OK button	4. Press CTRL+D, tap or click Font tab (Font dialog box), select desired font size in Size list, tap or click OK button

---

(a) Unformatted Flyer

Figure 1

Font, Font Sizes, and Themes

Characters that appear on the screen are a specific shape and size. The **font**, or typeface, defines the appearance and shape of the letters, numbers, and special characters. In Word, the default font usually is Calibri (shown in Figure 1–14 on 15). You can leave characters in the default font or change them to a different font. **Font size** specifies the size of the characters and is determined by a measurement system called points. A single **point** is about 1/72 of one inch in height. The default font size in Word typically is 11 (Figure 1–14). Thus, a character with a font size of 11 is about 11/72 or a little less than 1/6 of one inch in height. You can increase or decrease the font size of characters in a document.

A document **theme** is a set of unified formats for fonts, colors, and graphics. Word includes a variety of document themes to assist you with coordinating these visual elements in a document. The default theme fonts are Calibri Light for headings and Calibri for body text. By changing the document theme, you quickly can give your document a new look. You also can define your own document themes.

Formatting Marks
With some fonts, the formatting marks will not be displayed properly on the screen. For example, the raised dot that signifies a blank space between words may be displayed behind a character instead of in the blank space, causing the characters to look incorrect.

CONSIDER THIS

How do I know which formats to use in a flyer?
In a flyer, consider the following formatting suggestions.

- **Increase the font size of characters.** Flyers usually are posted on a bulletin board or in a window. Thus, the font size should be as large as possible so that passersby easily can read the flyer. To give the headline more impact, its font size should be larger than the font size of the text in the body copy. If possible, make the font size of the signature line larger than the body copy but smaller than the headline.

- **Change the font of characters.** Use fonts that are easy to read. Try to use only two different fonts in a flyer; for example, use one for the headline and the other for all other text. Too many fonts can make the flyer visually confusing.

- **Change the paragraph alignment.** The default alignment for paragraphs in a document is **left-aligned**, that is, flush at the left margin of the document with uneven right edges. Consider changing the alignment of some of the paragraphs to add interest and variety to the flyer.

- **Highlight key paragraphs with bullets.** A bulleted paragraph is a paragraph that begins with a dot or other symbol. Use bulleted paragraphs to highlight important points in a flyer.

- **Emphasize important words.** To call attention to certain words or lines, you can underline them, italicize them, or bold them. Use these formats sparingly, however, because overuse will minimize their effect and make the flyer look too busy.

- **Use color.** Use colors that complement each other and convey the meaning of the flyer. Vary colors in terms of hue and brightness. Headline colors, for example, can be bold and bright. Signature lines should stand out more than body copy but less than headlines. Keep in mind that too many colors can detract from the flyer and make it difficult to read.

Textbook Walk-Through

Chapter Summary A listing of the tasks completed within the chapter, grouped into major task categories in an outline format.

Apply Your Knowledge This exercise usually requires students to open and manipulate a file that parallels the activities learned in the chapter.

Consider This: Plan Ahead box presents a single master planning guide that students can use as they create documents on their own.

Chapter Summary

In this chapter you have learned to create an Access database, create tables and add records to a database, print the contents of tables, import data, create queries, create forms, create reports, and change database properties. You also have learned how to design a database. The items listed below include all the new Access skills you have learned in this chapter, with tasks grouped by activity.

Database Object Management
Delete a Table or Other Object in the Database (AC 58)
Rename an Object in the Database (AC 58)

Database Properties
Change Database Properties (AC 55)

File Management
Run Access (AC 5)
Create a Database (AC 6)
Create a Database Using a Template (AC 7)
Exit Access (AC 24)
Open a Database from Access (AC 25)
Back Up a Database (AC 56)
Compact and Repair a Database (AC 57)
Close a Database without Exiting Access (AC 57)
Save a Database with Another Name (AC 57)

Form Creation
Create a Form (AC 45)

Import Data
Import an Excel Worksheet (AC 33)

Print Objects
Preview and Print the Contents of a Table (AC 30)

Print the Results of a Query (AC 45)
Print a Report (AC 54)

Query Creation
Use the Simple Query Wizard to Create a Query (AC 40)
Use a Criterion in a Query (AC 43)

Report Creation
Create a Report (AC 48)
Modify Report Column Headings and Resize Columns (AC 50)
Add Totals to a Report (AC 53)

Table Creation
Modify the Primary Key (AC 11)
Define the Remaining Fields in a Table (AC 14)
Save a Table (AC 16)
View the Table in Design View (AC 17)
Change a Field Size in Design View (AC 18)
Close the Table (AC 20)
Resize Columns in a Datasheet (AC 28)
Modify a Table in Design View (AC 37)

Table Update
Add Records to a Table (AC 20)
Add Records to a Table that Contains Data (AC 26)

What decisions will you need to make when creating your next database?
Use these guidelines as you complete the assignments in this chapter and create your own databases outside of this class.

1. Identify the tables that will be included in the database.
2. Determine the primary keys for each of the tables.
3. Determine the additional fields that should be included in each of the tables.
4. Determine relationships between the tables.
   a) Identify the "one" table.
   b) Identify the "many" table.
   c) Include the primary key of the "one" table as a field in the "many" table.
5. Determine data types for the fields in the tables.
6. Determine additional properties for fields.
   a) Determine if a special caption is warranted.
   b) Determine if a special description is warranted.
   c) Determine field sizes.
   d) Determine formats.
7. Identify and remove any unwanted redundancy.
8. Determine a storage location for the database.
9. Determine the best method for distributing the database objects.

CONSIDER THIS

Databases an[d]

How should you submit solutions to questions in the assi[gnments that contain] a ⊕ symbol?
Every assignment in this book contains one or more questions identified [with a symbol that asks] you to think beyond the assigned database. Present your solutions to th[ese questions to your] instructor. Possible formats may include one or more of these options: [write a short answer that] contains the answer; present your answer to the class; discuss your ans[wer with a group; record audio] or video using a webcam, smartphone, or portable media player; or pos[t...]

Apply Your Knowledge

Reinforce the skills and apply the concepts you learne[d]

Adding a Caption, Changing a Data Type, Creating [...]
Note: To complete this assignment, you will be required t[o ...]
www.cengage.com/ct/studentdownload for detailed instruc[...] mation about accessing the required files.

Instructions: Cosmetics Naturally Inc. manufactures and sells beauty and skin care products made with only natural ingredients. The company's products do not contain any synthetic chemicals, artificial fragrances, or chemical preservatives. Cosmetics Naturally has a database that keeps track of its sales representatives and customers. Each customer is assigned to a single sales rep, but each sales rep may be assigned to many customers. The database has two tables. The Customer table contains data on the customers who purchase Cosmetics Naturally products. The Sales Rep table contains data on the sales reps. You will add a caption, change a data type, create two queries, a form, and a report, as shown in Figure 1–83 on the next page.

Perform the following tasks:

1. Start Access, open the Apply Cosmetics Naturally database from the Data Files for Students, and enable the content.
2. Open the Sales Rep table in Datasheet view, add SR # as the caption for the Sales Rep Number field, and resize all columns to best fit the data. Save the changes to the layout of the table and close the table.
3. Open the Customer table in Design view and change the data type for the Postal Code field to Short Text. Change the field size for the field to 5. Save the changes to the table and close the table.
4. Use the Simple Query Wizard to create a query for the Customer table that contains the Customer Number, Customer Name, Amount Paid, Balance, and Sales Rep Number. The query is a detail query. Use the name Customer Query for the query and close the query.
5. Create a simple form for the Sales Rep table. Save the form and use the name Sales Rep for the form. Close the form.
6. Create the report shown in Figure 1–83 for the Customer table. The report includes totals for both the Amount Paid and Balance fields. Be sure the totals appear completely. You might need to expand the size of the total controls. Move the page number so that it is within the margins. Save the report as Customer Financial Report.
7. If requested by your instructor, add your last name to the title of the report, that is, change the title to Customer Financial Report LastName where LastName is your actual last name.
8. Compact and repair the database.
9. Submit the revised database in the format specified by your instructor.
10. ⊕ How would you change the field name of the Balance field in the Customer table to Current Balance?

Continued >

Apply Your Knowledge *continued*

Customer Financial Report				Monday, September 15, 2014
				9:24:56 PM
Customer Number	Customer Name	Amount Paid	Balance	Sales Rep Number
AS24	Ashley's Salon	$1,789.65	$236.99	34
UR23	U R Beautiful	$0.00	$1,235.00	39
		$14,786.17	$5,617.78	

Figure 1–83

Extend Your Knowledge

Extend the skills you learned in this chapter and experiment with new skills. You may need to use Help to complete the assignment.

Using a Database Template to Create a Contacts Database
Note: To complete this assignment, you will be required to use the Data Files for Students. Visit www.cengage.com/ct/studentdownload for detailed instructions or contact your instructor for information about accessing the required files.

Instructions: Access includes both desktop database templates and web-based templates. You can use a template to create a beginning database that can be modified to meet your specific needs. You will use a template to create a Contacts database. The database template includes sample tables, queries, forms, and reports. You will modify the database and create the Contacts Query shown in Figure 1–84.

Perform the following tasks:
1. Start Access.
2. Select the Desktop contacts template in the temp[late] file name Extend Contacts.
3. Enable the content. If requested to do so by your [instructor] Started with Contacts dialog box. Close the Gett[ing]
4. Close the Contact List form.
5. Open the Contacts table in Datasheet view and d[elete the] Attachments field in the table. The Attachments [field]
6. Change the data type for the ID field to Short Te[xt] and change the field size to 4. Change the colum[n] displayed.
7. Save the changes to the Contacts table and close [it.]
8. Use the Simple Query Wizard to create the Con[tacts] query.

Figure 1–[84]

9. Open the Phone Book report in Layout view. Delete the control containing the date. Change the title of the report to Contact Phone List.
10. Save the changes to the report.
11. If requested to do so by your instructor, add your first and last names to the end of the title and save the changes to the report.
12. Submit the revised database in the format specified by your instructor.
13. a. Why would you use a template instead of creating a database from scratch with just the fields you need?
    b. The Attachment data type allows you to attach files to a database record. If you were using this database for a job search, what specific documents might you attach to a Contacts record?

Analyze, Correct, Improve

Analyze a database, correct all errors, and improve the design.

Correcting Errors in the Table Structure
Note: To complete this assignment, you will be required to use the Data Files for Students. Visit www.cengage.com/ct/studentdownload for detailed instructions or contact your instructor for information about accessing the required files.

Instructions: Analyze SciFi Movies is a database containing information on classic science fiction movies that your film professor would like to use for teaching. The Movie table shown in Figure 1–85 contains errors to the table structure. Your professor has asked you to correct the errors and make some improvements to the database. Start Access and open the Analyze SciFi Movies database from the Data Files for Students.

Figure 1–85

1. Correct Movie Number should be the primary key for the Movie table. The ID field should not be a field in the table. The Rating field represents a numerical rating system of one to four to indicate the quality of the movie. Your instructor wants to be able to find the average rating for films directed by a particular director. Only integers should be stored in both the Rating and the Length (Minutes) fields.

2. Improve The default field size for Short Text fields is 255. Changing the field size to more accurately represent the maximum number of characters that can be stored in a field is one way to improve the accuracy of the data. The Movie Number, Director Number, and Awards fields should have a maximum size of 3 characters. The Year Made field should have a maximum field size of 4. The Movie Name and Studio fields should have a maximum field size of 50. If instructed to do so by your instructor, rename the Movie table as Movie Last Name where Last Name is your last name. Submit the revised database in the format specified by your instructor.

3. The Awards field currently has a data type of Short Text, but the only values that will be stored in that field are Yes and No to indicate whether the movie won any awards. What would be a more appropriate data type for this field?

Textbook Walk-Through

STUDENT ASSIGNMENTS

In the Labs

Design, create, modify, and/or use a database following the guidelines, concepts, and skills presented in this chapter. Labs are listed in order of increasing difficulty. Labs 1 and 2, which increase in difficulty, require you to create solutions based on what you learned in the chapter; Lab 3 requires you to create a solution, which uses cloud and web technologies, by learning and investigating on your own from general guidance.

Lab 1: Creating Objects for the Dartt Offsite Services Database

Problem: Dartt Offsite Services is a local company that provides offsite data services and solutions. The company provides remote data backup, disaster recovery planning and services, website backup, and offsite storage of paper documents for small businesses and nonprofit organizations. Service representatives are responsible for communicating data solutions to the client, scheduling backups and other tasks, and resolving any conflicts. The company recently decided to store its client and service rep data in a database. Each client is assigned to a single service rep, but each service rep may be assigned many clients. The database and the Service Rep table have been created, but the Monthly Salary field needs to be added to the table. The records shown in Table 1–6 must be added to the Service Rep table. The company plans to import the Client table from the Excel worksheet shown in Figure 1–86. Dartt would like to finish storing this data in a database and has asked you to help.

	A	B	C	D	E	F	G	H	I	J	K
1	Client Number	Client Name	Street	City	State	Postal Code	Amount Paid	Balance Due	Service Rep Number		
2	BBF32	Babbage CPA Firm	464 Linnell Dr.	Austin	SC	28796	$3,524.00	$567.85	24		
		Thson Veterinary Services					$2,750.00	$1,200.00			
15	WECO5	Walburg Energy Company	12 Polk St.	Walburg	NC	28819	$1,567.45	$1,100.50	24		
16	WSC01	Wood Sports Complex	578 Central Ave.	Walburg	NC	28819	$2,250.00	$1,600.00	24		
17											

Figure 1–86

Note: To complete this assignment, you will be required to use the Data Files for Students. Visit www.cengage.com/ct/studentdownload for detailed information about accessing the required files.

Instructions: Perform the following tasks:
1. Start Access and open the Lab 1 Dartt Offsite Ser
2. Open the Service Rep table in Datasheet view a the table. The field has the Currency data type. Number field.
3. Add the records shown in Table 1–6.
4. Resize the columns to best fit the data. Save the

Table 1–6 Data for Service Rep Table

Service Rep Number	Last Name	First Name	Street	City
21	Kelly	Jenna	25 Paint St.	Kyle
45	Scott	Josh	1925 Pine Rd.	Byron
24	Liu	Mia	265 Marble Dr.	Kyle
37	Martinez	Mike	31 Steel St.	Georgetow

In the Lab Three in-depth assignments in each chapter that require students to apply the chapter concepts and techniques to solve problems. One Lab is devoted entirely to Cloud and Web 2.0 integration.

Consider This: Your Turn exercises call on students to apply creative thinking and problem solving skills to design and implement a solution.

STUDENT ASSIGNMENTS   Word Chapter 1

⊛ Consider This: Your Turn

Apply your creative thinking and problem solving skills to design and implement a solution.

Note: To complete these assignments, you may be required to use the Data Files for Students. Visit www.cengage.com/ct/studentdownload for detailed instructions or contact your instructor for information about accessing the required files.

1: Design and Create a Photography Club Flyer
Personal

Part 1:   As secretary of your school's Photography Club, you are responsible for creating and distributing flyers announcing the club. The flyer should contain two digital pictures appropriately resized; the Data Files for Students contains two pictures called Photography 1 and Photography 2, or you can use your own digital pictures if they are appropriate for the topic of the flyer. The flyer should contain the headline, Photography Club, and this signature line: Questions? Call Emily at (883) 555-0901. The body copy consists of the following text, in any order: Do you love photography? This is the club for you! All skill levels are welcome. Meetings every Tuesday at 5:00 p.m. in the Student Center (room 232). Bring your camera. We look forward to seeing you at our next meeting!

Use the concepts and techniques presented in this chapter to create and format this flyer. Be sure to check spelling and grammar. Submit your assignment and answers to the critical thinking questions in the format specified by your instructor.

Part 2:   ⊛ You made several decisions while creating the flyer in this assignment: where to place text, how to format the text (i.e., font, font size, paragraph alignment, bulleted paragraphs, underlines, italics, bold, color, etc.), which graphics to use, where to position the graphics, how to format the graphics, and which page enhancements to add (i.e., borders and spacing). What was the rationale behind each of these decisions? When you proofread the document, what further revisions did you make and why? How would you recommend distributing this flyer?

2: Design and Create a Hot Air Balloon Rides Flyer
Professional

Part 1:   As a part-time employee at Galaxy Recreations, your boss has asked you to create and distribute flyers announcing hot air balloon rides. The flyer should contain two digital pictures appropriately resized; the Data Files for Students contains two pictures called Hot Air Balloon 1 and Hot Air Balloon 2, or you can use your own digital pictures if they are appropriate for the topic of the flyer. The flyer should contain the headline, Hot Air Balloon Rides, and this signature line: For reservations, call (485) 555-2295. The body copy consists of the following text, in any order: Amazing sights from incredible heights! The experience of a lifetime. Fun for the whole family. No pets. Bring your camera. Open seven days a week from 10:00 a.m. to 4:00 p.m. Book your private tour with Galaxy Recreations today!

Use the concepts and techniques presented in this chapter to create and format this flyer. Be sure to check spelling and grammar. Submit your assignment in the format specified by your instructor.

Part 2:   ⊛ You made several decisions while creating the flyer in this assignment: where to place text, how to format the text (i.e., font, font size, paragraph alignment, bulleted paragraphs, underlines, italics, bold, color, etc.), which graphics to use, where to position the graphics, how to format the graphics, and which page enhancements to add (i.e., borders and spacing). What was the rationale behind each of these decisions? When you proofread the document, what further revisions did you make and why? How would you recommend distributing this flyer?

Continued >

Microsoft® OFFICE 2013

POST-ADVANCED

8 | Using Document Collaboration, Integration, and Charting Tools

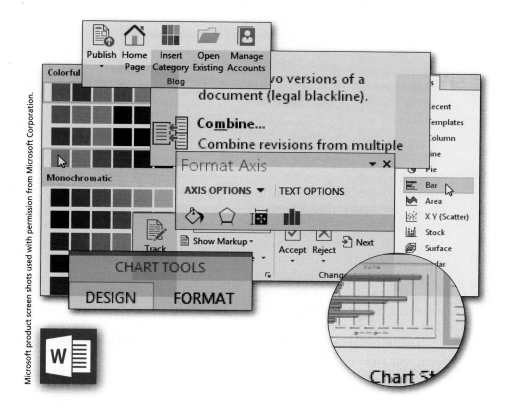

Microsoft product screen shots used with permission from Microsoft Corporation.

Objectives

You will have mastered the material in this chapter when you can:

- Insert, edit, view, and delete comments
- Track changes
- Review tracked changes
- Compare documents
- Combine documents
- Link an Excel worksheet to a Word document
- Break a link

- Create a chart in Word
- Format a Word chart
- View and scroll through side-by-side documents
- Create a new document for a blog post
- Insert a quick table
- Publish a blog post

8 | Using Document Collaboration, Integration, and Charting Tools

Introduction

Word provides the capability for users to work with other users, or **collaborate**, on a document. For example, you can show edits made to a document so that others can review the edits. You also can merge edits from multiple users or compare two documents to determine the differences between them.

From Word, you can interact with other programs and incorporate the data and objects from those programs in a Word document. For example, you can link an Excel worksheet in a Word document or publish a blog post from Word. You also use the charting features of Microsoft Office 2013 in Word.

Project — Memo with Chart

A memo is an informal document that businesses use to correspond with others. Memos often are internal to an organization, for example, to employees or coworkers.

The project in this chapter uses Word to produce the memo shown in Figure 8–1. First, you open an existing document that contains the memo and the Word table. Next, you insert comments and edit the document, showing the changes so that other users can review the changes. The changes appear on the screen with options that allow the author of the document to accept or reject the changes and delete the comments. Then, you chart the Word table using charting features available in several Microsoft Office applications.

In this chapter, you also learn how to link an Excel worksheet to a Word document and create a document for a blog post.

If you are using your finger on a touch screen and are having difficulty completing the steps in this chapter, consider using a stylus. Many people find it easier to be precise with a stylus than with a finger. In addition, with a stylus you see the pointer. If you still are having trouble completing the steps with a stylus, try using a mouse.

INTEROFFICE MEMORANDUM

TO:	MOLLY PADRO
FROM:	ZACH ANDERSON
SUBJECT:	FUND-RAISING RESULTS
DATE:	SEPTEMBER 19, 2014

Our August fund-raiser was a huge success. I would like to thank you and your staff for all of the help before and during the event. Below are a table and chart that summarize the results for our fund-raising efforts this year. In the next few days, you will see a post on our blog, indicating key dates associated with our next fund-raising event.

YTD Fund-Raising Results

Fund-Raising Category	May Event	August Event
Bake Sale	$ 498.50	$ 665.00
Donations	$ 2,200.25	$ 3,241.75
Food Booth	$ 956.25	$ 1,064.50
Gate	$ 4,125.50	$ 5,503.00
Raffle	$ 515.00	$ 795.00
Silent Auction	$ 1,058.95	$ 1,125.51
Vendors	$ 5,025.00	$ 6,470.50

Word table

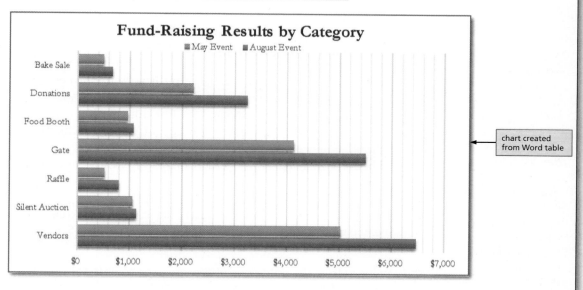

chart created from Word table

Figure 8–1

Roadmap

In this chapter, you will learn how to create the document shown in Figure 8–1 on the previous page. The following roadmap identifies general activities you will perform as you progress through this chapter:

1. INSERT COMMENTS AND TRACK CHANGES in the memo with the table.
2. REVIEW the COMMENTS AND TRACKED CHANGES.
3. LINK an EXCEL WORKSHEET TO a WORD DOCUMENT.
4. CHART a WORD TABLE using Word's CHART TOOLS tab.
5. CREATE AND PUBLISH a BLOG POST.

At the beginning of step instructions throughout the chapter, you will see an abbreviated form of this roadmap. The abbreviated roadmap uses colors to indicate chapter progress: gray means the chapter is beyond that activity, blue means the task being shown is covered in that activity, and black means that activity is yet to be covered. For example, the following abbreviated roadmap indicates the chapter would be showing a task in the 2 REVIEW COMMENTS & TRACKED CHANGES activity.

1 INSERT COMMENTS & TRACK CHANGES	2 REVIEW COMMENTS & TRACKED CHANGES
3 LINK EXCEL WORKSHEET TO WORD DOCUMENT	4 CHART WORD TABLE	5 CREATE & PUBLISH BLOG POST

Use the abbreviated roadmap as a progress guide while you read or step through the instructions in this chapter.

To Run Word and Change Word Settings

One of the few differences between Windows 7 and Windows 8 occurs in the steps to run Word. If you are using Windows 7, click the Start button, type **Word** in the 'Search programs and files' box, click Word 2013, and then, if necessary, maximize the Word window. For a summary of the steps to run Word in Windows 7, refer to the Quick Reference located at the back of this book.

If you are using a computer to step through the project in this chapter and you want your screens to match the figures in this book, you should change your screen's resolution to 1366×768. For information about how to change a computer's resolution, refer to the Office and Windows chapter at the beginning of this book.

The following steps run Word, display formatting marks, and change the zoom to page width.

1 Scroll the Start screen for a Word 2013 tile. If your Start screen contains a Word 2013 tile, tap or click it to run Word and then proceed to Step 5; if the Start screen does not contain the Word 2013 tile, proceed to the next step to search for the Word app.

2 Swipe in from the right edge of the screen or point to the upper-right corner of the screen to display the Charms bar and then tap or click the Search charm on the Charms bar to display the Search menu.

3 Type **Word** as the search text in the Search box and watch the search results appear in the Apps list.

4 Tap or click Word 2013 in the search results to run Word.

5 Tap or click the Blank document thumbnail on the Word start screen to create a blank document and display it in the Word window.

6 If the Word window is not maximized, tap or click the Maximize button on its title bar to maximize the window.

7 If the Print Layout button on the status bar is not selected, tap or click it so that your screen is in Print Layout view.

8 If the 'Show/Hide ¶' button (HOME tab | Paragraph group) is not selected already, tap or click it to display formatting marks on the screen.

9 To display the page the same width as the document window, if necessary, tap or click the Page Width button (VIEW tab | Zoom group).

Reviewing a Document

Word provides many tools that allow users to **collaborate** on a document. One set of collaboration tools within Word allows you to track changes in a document and review the changes. That is, one computer user can create a document and another user(s) can make changes and insert comments in the same document. Those changes then appear on the screen with options that allow the originator (author) to accept or reject the changes and delete the comments. With another collaboration tool, you can compare and/or merge two or more documents to determine the differences between them.

To illustrate Word collaboration tools, this section follows these general steps:

1. Open a document to be reviewed.
2. Insert comments in the document for the originator (author).
3. Track changes in the document.
4. View and delete the comments.
5. Accept and reject the tracked changes. For illustration purposes, you assume the role of originator (author) of the document in this step.
6. Compare the reviewed document to the original to view the differences.
7. Combine the original document with the reviewed document and with another reviewer's suggestions.

To Open a Document and Save It with a New File Name

Assume your coworker has created a draft of a memo and is sending it to you for review. The file, called Fund-Raising Results Memo Draft, is located on the Data Files for Students. Visit www.cengage.com/ct/studentdownload for detailed instructions or contact your instructor for information about accessing the required files. To preserve the original memo, you save the open document with a new file name. The following steps save an open document with a new file name.

1 Tap or click FILE on the ribbon to open the Backstage view and then, if necessary, tap or click the Open tab to display the Open gallery.

2 Navigate to the Data Files for Students and then open the file called Fund-Raising Results Memo Draft.

3 Tap or click FILE on the ribbon to open the Backstage view and then tap or click the Save As tab to display the Save As gallery.

4 To save on a hard disk or other storage media on your computer, proceed to Step 4a. To save on SkyDrive, proceed to Step 4b.

4a Tap or click Computer in the left pane, if necessary, to display options in the right pane related to saving on your computer.

BTW
The Ribbon and Screen Resolution
Word may change how the groups and buttons within the groups appear on the ribbon, depending on the computer's screen resolution. Thus, your ribbon may look different from the ones in this book if you are using a screen resolution other than 1366 × 768.

4b Tap or click SkyDrive in the left pane to display SkyDrive saving options or a Sign In button. If your screen displays a Sign In button, tap or click it and then sign in to SkyDrive.

5 Tap or click the Browse button in the right pane to display the Save As dialog box associated with the selected save location (i.e., Computer or SkyDrive).

6 Type **Fund-Raising Results Memo with Comments and Tracked Changes** in the File name box to change the file name. Do not press the ENTER key after typing the file name because you do not want to close the dialog box at this time.

7 Navigate to the desired save location (in this case, the Word folder in the CIS 101 folder [or your class folder] on your computer or SkyDrive).

8 Tap or click the Save button (Save As dialog box) to save the file in the selected folder on the selected save location with the entered file name.

If requested by your instructor, change the name, Molly Padro, in the memo to your name.

To Insert a Comment

1 INSERT COMMENTS & TRACK CHANGES | 2 REVIEW COMMENTS & TRACKED CHANGES
3 LINK EXCEL WORKSHEET TO WORD DOCUMENT | 4 CHART WORD TABLE | 5 CREATE & PUBLISH BLOG POST

Reviewers often use comments to communicate suggestions, tips, and other messages to the author of a document. A **comment** is a note inserted in a document. Comments do not affect the text of the document.

After reading through the memo, you have two comments for the originator (author) of the document. The following steps insert a comment in the document. *Why? You insert a comment that requests that the author insert a graph in the document.*

1

- Position the insertion point at the location where the comment should be located (in this case, in the third sentence of the memo immediately to the left of the t in the word, table).

- Display the REVIEW tab (Figure 8–2).

- If the 'Display for Review' box (REVIEW tab | Tracking group) does not show All Markup, tap or click the 'Display for Review' arrow

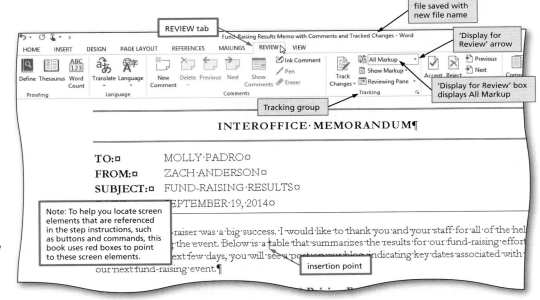

Figure 8–2

(REVIEW tab | Tracking group) and then tap or click All Markup on the Display for Review menu to instruct Word to display the document with all proposed edits shown as markup.

 What are the other Display for Review options?

If you tap or click the 'Display for Review' arrow, several options appear. Simple Markup means Word incorporates proposed changes in the document and places a vertical line near the margin of the line containing the proposed change or a comment balloon at the location of a user comment. All Markup means that all proposed changes are highlighted and all comments appear in full. No Markup shows the proposed edits as part of the final document, instead of as markup. Original shows the document before changes.

2

- Tap or click the 'Insert a Comment' button (REVIEW tab | Comments group) to display a comment balloon in the markup area in the document window and place comment marks around the commented text in the document window.

- Change the zoom so that the entire document and markup area are visible in the document window (Figure 8–3).

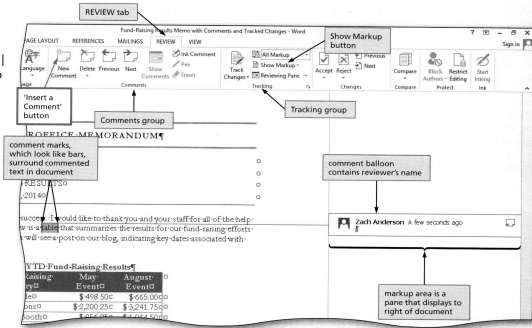

Figure 8–3

Q&A What if the markup area does not appear with the comment balloon?

The balloons setting has been turned off. Tap or click the Show Markup button (REVIEW tab | Tracking group) and then if a check mark does not appear to the left of Comments on the Show Markup menu, tap or click Comments. If comments still do not appear, tap or click the Show Markup button again, tap or point to Balloons on the Show Markup menu, and then tap or click 'Show Only Comments and Formatting in Balloons' on the Balloons submenu, which is the default setting.

Why do comment marks surround selected text?

A comment is associated with text. If you do not select text on which you wish to comment, Word automatically selects the text to the right or left of the insertion point for the comment.

3

- In the comment balloon, type the following comment text: **Add a graph of the data below the table.**

- If necessary, scroll to the right so that the entire comment is visible on the screen (Figure 8–4).

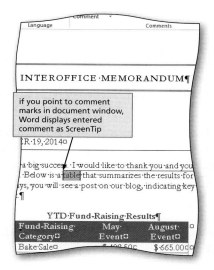

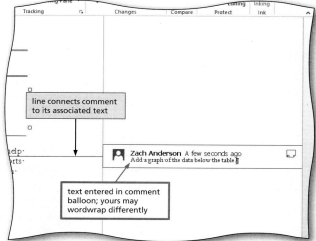

Figure 8–4

Other Ways

1. Press CTRL+ALT+M

To Insert Another Comment

The second comment you want to insert in the document is to request that the blog post also contain a calendar. Because you want the comment associated with several words, you select the text before inserting the comment. The following steps insert another comment in the document.

1 Select the text where the comment should be located (in this case, the text, post on our blog, in the last sentence of the memo).

2 Tap or click the 'Insert a Comment' button (REVIEW tab | Comments group) to display another comment balloon in the markup area in the document window.

3 In the new comment balloon, type the following comment text: **Suggest posting a calendar on the blog.** (Figure 8–5).

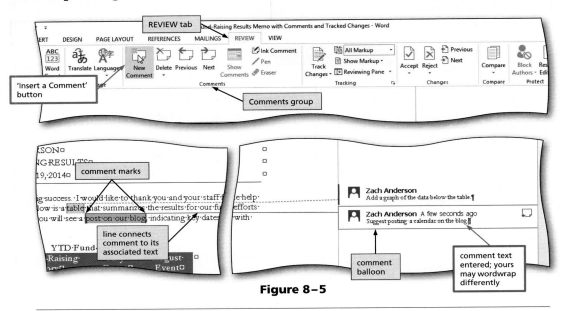

Figure 8–5

To Change Reviewer Information

Word uses predefined settings for the reviewer's initials and/or name that appears in the document window, the comment balloon, and the Reviewing task pane. If the reviewer's name or initials are not correct, you would change them by performing the following steps.

1a. Tap or click the Change Tracking Options Dialog Box Launcher (REVIEW tab | Tracking group) to display the Track Changes Options dialog box. Tap or click the 'Change User Name' button (Track Changes Options dialog box) to display the Word Options dialog box.

   or

1b. Open the Backstage view and then tap or click Options to display the Word Options dialog box. If necessary, tap or click General in the left pane.

2. Enter the correct name in the User name text box (Word Options dialog box), and enter the correct initials in the Initials text box.

3. Tap or click the OK button to change the reviewer information. If necessary, tap or click the OK button in the Track Changes Options dialog box.

To Edit a Comment in a Comment Balloon

You modify comments in a comment balloon by tapping or clicking inside the comment balloon and editing the same way you edit text in the document window. In this project, you change the word, graph, to the word, chart, in the first comment. The following steps edit a comment in a balloon.

1 Tap or click the first comment balloon to select it.

Q&A How can I tell if a comment is selected?
A selected comment appears surrounded by a rectangle and contains a Reply button to the right of the comment.

2 Position the insertion point at the location of the text to edit (in this case, to the left of the g in graph in the first comment) (Figure 8–6).

BTW
Q&As
For a complete list of the Q&As found in many of the step-by-step sequences in this book, visit the Q&A resource on the Student Companion Site located on www.cengagebrain.com. For detailed instructions about accessing available resources, visit www.cengage.com/ct/studentdownload or contact your instructor for information about accessing the required files.

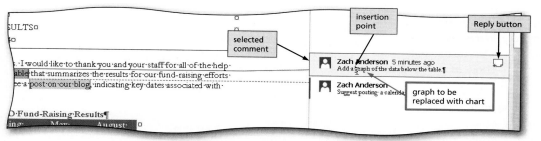

Figure 8–6

3 Replace the word, graph, with the word, chart, to edit the comment (shown in Figure 8–7).

To Reply to a Comment

1 INSERT COMMENTS & TRACK CHANGES | 2 REVIEW COMMENTS & TRACKED CHANGES
3 LINK EXCEL WORKSHEET TO WORD DOCUMENT | 4 CHART WORD TABLE | 5 CREATE & PUBLISH BLOG POST

Sometimes, you want to reply to an existing comment. *Why? You may want to respond to a question by another reviewer or provide additional information to a previous comment you inserted.* The following steps reply to the first comment you inserted in the document.

1
- If necessary, tap or click the comment to which you wish to reply so that the comment is selected (in this case, the first comment).

2
- Tap or click the Reply button in the selected comment to display a reply comment for the selected comment.

3
- In the new indented comment, type the following comment text:
Suggest using horizontal bars to plot the categories. (Figure 8–7).

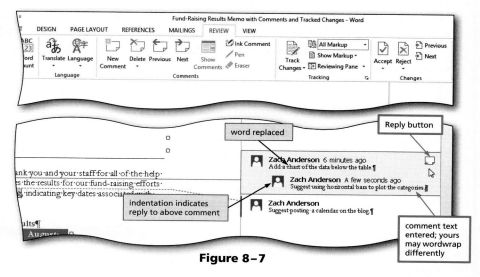

Figure 8–7

Other Ways

1. Tap or click 'Insert a Comment' button (REVIEW tab | Comments group)　　　　2. Press CTRL+ALT+M

To Customize the Status Bar

You can customize the items that appear on the status bar. Recall that the status bar presents information about a document, the progress of current tasks, the status of certain commands and keys, and controls for viewing. Some indicators and buttons appear and disappear as you type text or perform certain commands. Others remain on the status bar at all times.

The following steps customize the status bar to show the Track Changes indicator. *Why? The TRACK CHANGES indicator does not appear by default on the status bar.*

1

- If the status bar does not show a desired item (in this case, the TRACK CHANGES indicator), press and hold or right-click anywhere on the status bar to display the Customize Status Bar menu.

2

- Tap or click the item on the Customize Status Bar menu that you want to show (in this case, Track Changes) to place a check mark beside the item, which also immediately may show as an indicator on the status bar (Figure 8–8).

Q&A Can I show or hide any of the items listed on the Customize Status Bar menu?
Yes, tap or click the item to display or remove its check mark.

- Tap or click anywhere outside of the Customize Status Bar menu or press the ESC key to remove the menu from the screen.

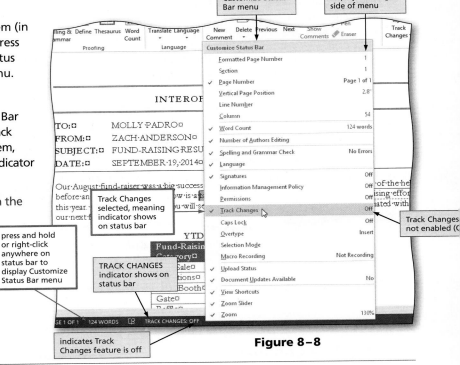

Figure 8–8

To Enable Tracked Changes

When you edit a document that has the track changes feature enabled, Word marks all text or graphics that you insert, delete, or modify and refers to the revisions as **markups** or **revision marks**. An author can identify the changes a reviewer has made by looking at the markups in a document. The author also has the ability to accept or reject any change that a reviewer has made to a document.

The following step enables tracked changes. *Why? To track changes in a document, you must enable (turn on) the track changes feature.*

1

- If the TRACK CHANGES indicator on the status bar shows that the track changes feature is off, tap or click the TRACK CHANGES indicator on the status bar to enable the track changes feature (Figure 8–9).

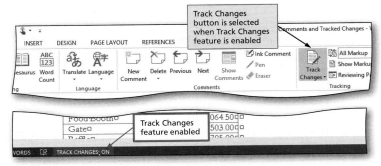

Figure 8–9

Other Ways

1. Tap or click Track Changes button (REVIEW tab | Tracking group)
2. Tap or click Track Changes arrow (REVIEW tab | Tracking group), tap or click Track Changes
3. Press CTRL+SHIFT+E

To Track Changes

You have four suggested changes for the current document:

1. Insert the words, and chart, after the word, table, in the third sentence so that it reads: ... a table and chart that ...
2. Delete the letter, s, at the end of the word, summarizes.
3. Insert the word, upcoming, before the word, next, in the last sentence so that it reads: ... our upcoming next fund-raising event.
4. Change the word, big, to the word, huge, in the first sentence so that it reads: ... a huge success.

The following steps track these changes as you enter them in the document. *Why? You want edits you make to the document to show so that others can review the edits.*

1

- Position the insertion point immediately to the left of the word, that, in the third sentence of the memo to position the insertion point at the location for the tracked change.

- Type **and chart** and then press the SPACEBAR to insert the typed text as a tracked change (Figure 8–10).

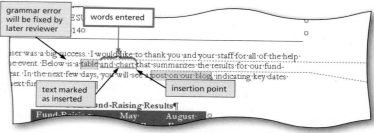

Figure 8–10

Q&A Why is the inserted text in color and underlined?
When the track changes feature is enabled, Word marks (signals) all text inserts by underlining them and changing their color, and marks all deletions by striking through them and changing their color.

When I scroll left, I see a vertical bar in the margin. What is the bar?
The bar is called a changed line (shown in Figure 8–16 on page WD 486), which indicates a tracked change is on the line to the right of the bar.

2

- In the same sentence, delete the s at the end of the word, summarizes (so that it reads, summarize), to mark the letter for deletion (Figure 8–11).

Figure 8–11

3

- In the next sentence, position the insertion point immediately to the left of the word, next. Type **upcoming** and then press the SPACEBAR to insert the typed text as a tracked change.

- In the first sentence, double-tap or double-click the word, big, to select it.

- Type **huge** as the replacement text, which tracks a deletion and an insertion change (Figure 8–12).

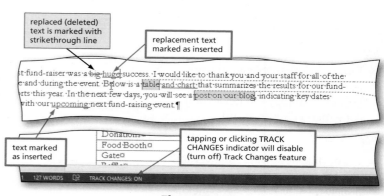

Figure 8–12

Q&A Can I see the name of the person who tracked a change?
 If you are using a mouse, you can point to a tracked change in the document window; Word then will display a ScreenTip that identifies the reviewer's name and the type of change made by that reviewer.

To Change How Markups and Comments Are Displayed

The tracked changes entered in the previous steps appeared inline instead of in markup balloons. Inline means that the inserts are underlined and the deletions are shown as strikethroughs. The default Word setting displays comments and formatting changes in balloons and all other changes inline. If you wanted all changes and comments to appear in balloons or all changes and comments to appear inline, you would perform the following steps.

1. Tap or click the Show Markup button (REVIEW tab | Tracking group) to display the Show Markup menu and then tap or point to Balloons on the Show Markup menu.

2. If you want all revisions and comments to appear in balloons, tap or click 'Show Revisions in Balloons' on the Balloons submenu. If you want all revisions and comments to appear inline, tap or click 'Show All Revisions Inline' on the Balloons submenu. If you want to use the default Word setting, tap or click 'Show Only Comments and Formatting in Balloons' on the Balloons submenu.

To Disable Tracked Changes

When you have finished tracking changes, you should disable (turn off) the track changes feature so that Word stops marking your revisions. You follow the same steps to disable tracked changes as you did to enable them; that is, the indicator or button or keyboard shortcut functions as a toggle, turning the track changes feature on or off each time the command is issued. The following step disables tracked changes.

1 To turn the track changes feature off, tap or click the TRACK CHANGES indicator on the status bar (shown in Figure 8–12 on the previous page), or tap or click the Track Changes button (REVIEW tab | Tracking group), or press CTRL+SHIFT+E.

To Use the Reviewing Task Pane

1 INSERT COMMENTS & TRACK CHANGES | 2 REVIEW COMMENTS & TRACKED CHANGES
3 LINK EXCEL WORKSHEET TO WORD DOCUMENT | 4 CHART WORD TABLE | 5 CREATE & PUBLISH BLOG POST

Word provides a Reviewing task pane that can be displayed either at the left edge (vertically) or the bottom (horizontally) of the screen. **Why?** *As an alternative to reading through tracked changes in the document window and comment balloons in the markup area, some users prefer to view tracked changes and comments in the Reviewing task pane.* The following steps display the Reviewing task pane on the screen.

1
- Tap or click the Reviewing Pane arrow (REVIEW tab | Tracking group) to display the Reviewing Pane menu (Figure 8–13).

2
- Tap or click 'Reviewing Pane Vertical' on the Reviewing Pane menu to display the Reviewing task pane on the left side of the Word window.

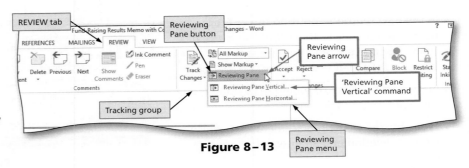

Figure 8–13

Q&A What if I tap or click the Reviewing Pane button instead of the button arrow?
Word displays the Reviewing task pane in its most recent location, that is, either vertically on the left side of the screen or horizontally on the bottom of the screen.

3

- Tap or click the Show Markup button (REVIEW tab | Tracking group) to display the Show Markup menu.

- Tap or point to Balloons on the Show Markup menu to display the Balloons submenu (Figure 8–14).

Q&A Why display the Balloons submenu? Because the Reviewing task pane shows all comments, you do not need the markup area to display comment balloons. Thus, you will display all revisions inline.

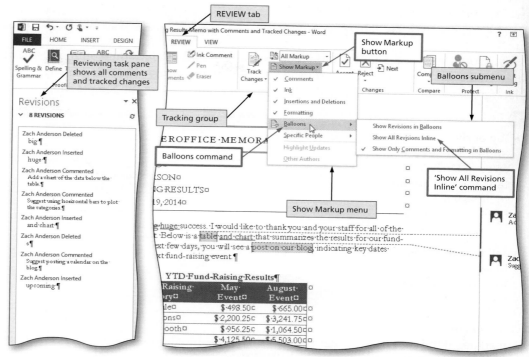

Figure 8–14

4

- Tap or click 'Show All Revisions Inline' on the Balloons submenu to remove the markup area from the Word window and place all markups inline (Figure 8–15).

Q&A Can I edit revisions in the Reviewing task pane? Yes. Simply tap or click in the Reviewing task pane and edit the text the same way you edit in the document window.

5

- Tap or click the Close button in the Reviewing task pane to close the task pane.

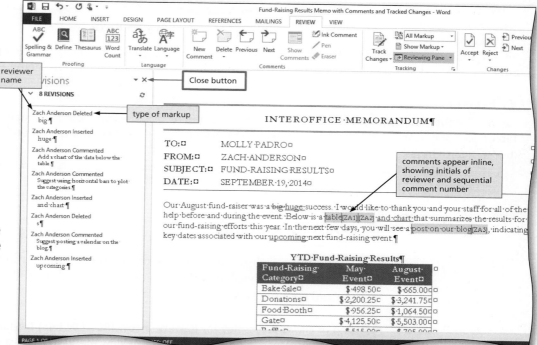

Figure 8–15

 Q&A Can I also tap or click the Reviewing Pane button on the ribbon to close the task pane?
Yes.

To Display Tracked Changes and Comments as Simple Markup

Word provides a Simple Markup option instead of the All Markup option for viewing tracked changes and comments. *Why? Some users feel the All Markup option clutters the screen and prefer the cleaner look of the Simple Markup option.* The following step displays tracked changes using the Simple Markup option.

1

- Tap or click the 'Display for Review' arrow (REVIEW tab | Tracking group) to display the Display for Review menu.

- Tap or click Simple Markup on the Display for Review menu to show a simple markup instead of all markups in the document window (Figure 8–16).

Q&A

What if the comments appear in the markup area instead of as icons in the document?

Be sure the Show Comments button (REVIEW tab | Comments group) is not selected. When the Show Comments button is selected, the comments appear in the markup area to the right of the document.

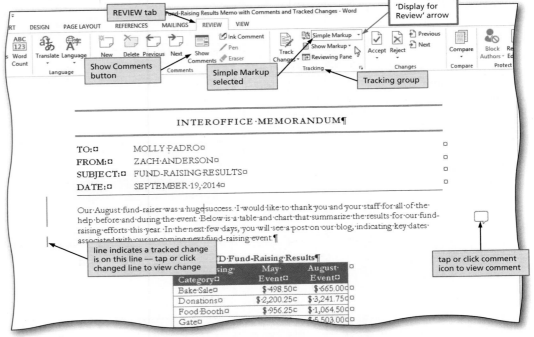

Figure 8–16

Experiment

- Tap or click the comment icon to display the comments. Tap or click the comment icon again to hide the comments. Tap or click one of the changed lines to display the tracked changes. Tap or click one of the changed lines to hide the tracked changes.

To Show All Markup

You prefer to show all markup where comments appear in the markup area and have tracked changes visible in the document window. The following steps show all markup and comments in balloons.

1 Tap or click the 'Display for Review' arrow (REVIEW tab | Tracking group) and then tap or click All Markup on the Display for Review menu to instruct Word to display the document with all proposed edits shown as markup.

2 Tap or click the Show Markup button (REVIEW tab | Tracking group) to display the Show Markup menu, tap or point to Balloons on the Show Markup menu, and then tap or click 'Show Only Comments and Formatting in Balloons', so that the markup area reappears with the comment balloons.

TO PRINT MARKUPS

When you print a document with comments and tracked changes, Word chooses the zoom percentage and page orientation that will best show the comments on the printed document. You can print the document with its markups, which looks similar to how the Word window shows the markups on the screen, or you can print just the list of the markups. If you wanted to print markups, you would perform the following steps.

1. Open the Backstage view and then tap or click the Print tab in the Backstage view to display the Print gallery.
2. Tap or click the first button in the Settings area to display a list of options specifying what you can print. To print the document with the markups, if necessary, place a check mark to the left of Print Markup. To print just the markups (without printing the document), tap or click 'List of Markup' in the Document Info area.
3. Tap or click the Print button.

To Save an Existing Document with the Same File Name

You are finished reviewing the document and have performed several steps since the last save. Thus, you should save the document again, as described in the following step.

1 Tap or click the Save button on the Quick Access Toolbar to save the document again with the same file name, Fund-Raising Results Memo with Comments and Tracked Changes.

Reviewing Tracked Changes and Comments

After tracking changes and entering comments in a document, you send the document to the originator for his or her review. For demonstration purposes in this chapter, you assume the role of originator and review the tracked changes and comments in the document.

To do this, be sure the markups are displayed on the screen. Tap or click the Show Markup button (REVIEW tab | Tracking group) and verify that Comments, 'Insertions and Deletions', and Formatting each have a check mark beside them. Ensure the 'Display for Review' box (REVIEW tab | Tracking group) shows All Markup; if it does not, tap or click the 'Display for Review' arrow (REVIEW tab | Tracking group) and then tap or click All Markup on the Display for Review menu. This option shows the final document with tracked changes.

If you wanted to see how a document would look if you accepted all the changes, without actually accepting them, tap or click the 'Display for Review' arrow (REVIEW tab | Tracking group) and then tap or click No Markup on the Display for Review menu. If you print this view of the document, it will print how the document will look if you accept all the changes. If you wanted to see how the document looked before any changes were made, tap or click the 'Display for Review' arrow (REVIEW tab | Tracking group) and then tap or click Original on the Display for Review menu. When you have finished reviewing the various options, if necessary, tap or click the 'Display for Review' arrow (REVIEW tab | Tracking group) and then tap or click All Markup on the Display for Review menu.

BTW
Limiting Authors
If you wanted to restrict formatting or editing, you would tap or click the Restrict Editing button (REVIEW tab | Protect group) to display the Restrict Editing task pane. To restrict formatting, select the 'Limit formatting to a selection of styles' check box, tap or click the Settings link, select the styles to allow and disallow (Formatting Restrictions dialog box), and then tap or click the OK button. To restrict editing, select the 'Allow only this type of editing in the document' check box, tap or click the box arrow, and then select the desired editing restriction. To restrict formatting or editing to certain authors, select part of the document and select the users who are allowed to edit the selected areas, and then tap or click the 'Yes, Start Enforcing Protection' button. To block authors from making changes to selected text, tap or click the Block Authors button (REVIEW tab | Protect group) and then select the authors to block in the list.

To View Comments

The next step is to read the comments in the marked-up document using the REVIEW tab. *Why? You could scroll through the document and read each comment that appears in the markup area, but you might overlook one or more comments using this technique. Thus, it is more efficient to use the REVIEW tab.* The following step views comments in the document.

1

- Position the insertion point at the beginning of the document, so that Word begins searching for comments from the top of the document.

- Tap or click the Next Comment button (REVIEW tab | Comments group), which causes Word to locate and select the first comment in the document (Figure 8–17).

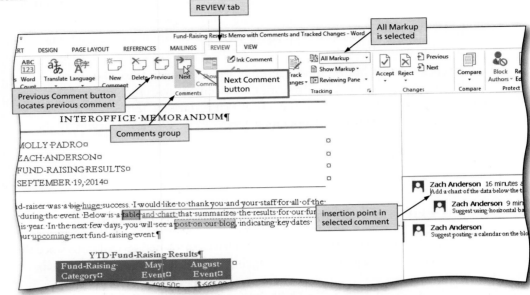

Figure 8–17

To Delete a Comment

The following step deletes a comment. *Why? You have read the comment and want to remove it from the document.*

1

- Tap or click the Delete Comment button (REVIEW tab | Comments group) to remove the comment balloon from the markup area (Figure 8–18).

Q&A

What if I accidentally tap or click the Delete Comment arrow?
Tap or click Delete on the Delete Comment menu.

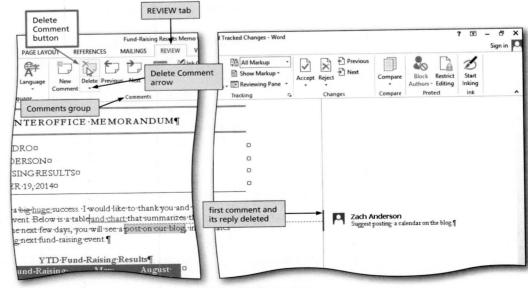

Figure 8–18

Other Ways

1. Tap 'Show Context Menu' button on mini toolbar or right-click comment, tap or click Delete Comment on shortcut menu

TO MARK COMMENTS AS DONE

Instead of deleting comments, some users prefer to leave them in the document but mark them as done. When you mark a comment as done, it changes color. If you wanted to mark a comment as done, you would perform the following steps.

1. Press and hold the comment and then tap the 'Show Context Menu' button on the mini toolbar or right-click the comment to display a shortcut menu.
2. Tap or click 'Mark Comment Done' on the shortcut menu.

To Delete All Comments

1 INSERT COMMENTS & TRACK CHANGES | 2 REVIEW COMMENTS & TRACKED CHANGES
3 LINK EXCEL WORKSHEET TO WORD DOCUMENT | 4 CHART WORD TABLE | 5 CREATE & PUBLISH BLOG POST

The following steps delete all comments at once. *Why? Assume you now want to delete all the comments in the document at once because you have read them all.*

- Tap or click the Delete Comment arrow (REVIEW tab | Comments group) to display the Delete Comment menu (Figure 8–19).

- Tap or click 'Delete All Comments in Document' on the Delete Comment menu to remove all comments from the document, which also closes the markup area (shown in Figure 8–20).

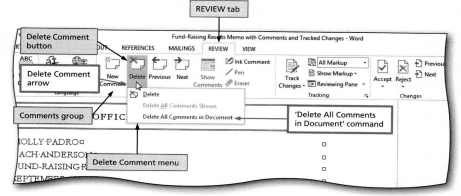

Figure 8–19

To Review Tracked Changes

1 INSERT COMMENTS & TRACK CHANGES | 2 REVIEW COMMENTS & TRACKED CHANGES
3 LINK EXCEL WORKSHEET TO WORD DOCUMENT | 4 CHART WORD TABLE | 5 CREATE & PUBLISH BLOG POST

The next step is to review the tracked changes in the marked-up document using the REVIEW tab. *Why? As with the comments, you could scroll through the document and point to each markup to read it, but you might overlook one or more changes using this technique. A more efficient method is to use the REVIEW tab to review the changes one at a time, deciding whether to accept, modify, or delete each change.* The following steps review the changes in the document.

1

- Position the insertion point at the beginning of the document, so that Word begins the review of tracked changes from the top of the document.

- Tap or click the Next Change button (REVIEW tab | Changes group), which causes Word to locate and select the first markup in the document (in this case, the deleted word, big) (Figure 8–20).

Q&A What if my document also had contained comments?

When you tap or click the Next Change button (REVIEW tab | Changes group), Word locates the next tracked change or comment, whichever appears first.

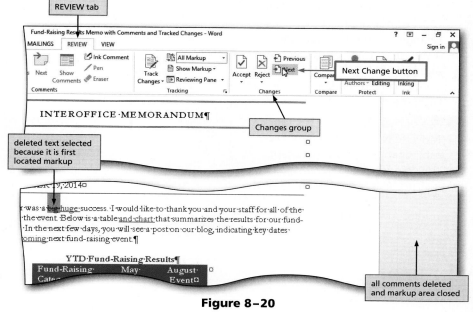

Figure 8–20

2

- Because you agree with this change, tap or click the 'Accept and Move to Next' button (REVIEW tab | Changes group) to accept the deletion of the word, big, and instruct Word to locate and select the next markup (in this case, the inserted word, huge) (Figure 8–21).

Q&A

What if I accidentally tap or click the 'Accept and Move to Next' arrow (REVIEW tab | Changes group)?
Tap or click 'Accept and Move to Next' on the Accept and Move to Next menu.

What if I wanted to accept the change but not search for the next tracked change?
You would tap or click the 'Accept and Move to Next' arrow and then tap or click 'Accept This Change' on the Accept and Move to Next menu.

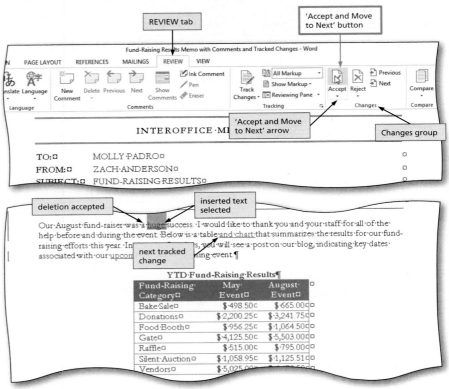

Figure 8–21

3

- Tap or click the 'Accept and Move to Next' button (REVIEW tab | Changes group) to accept the insertion of the word, huge, and instruct Word to locate and select the next markup (in this case, the inserted words, and chart).

- Tap or click the 'Accept and Move to Next' button (REVIEW tab | Changes group) to accept the insertion of the words, and chart, and instruct Word to locate and select the next markup (in this case, the deleted letter s).

- Tap or click the 'Accept and Move to Next' button (REVIEW tab | Changes group) to accept the deletion of the letter s, and instruct Word to locate and select the next markup (in this case, the inserted word, upcoming) (Figure 8–22).

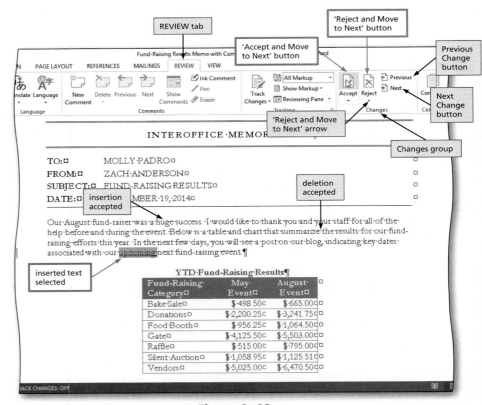

Figure 8–22

- Because you do not agree with this change, tap or click the 'Reject and Move to Next' button (REVIEW tab | Changes group) to reject the marked deletion, and instruct Word to locate and select the next markup. If you are using a touch screen, also tap 'Reject and Move to Next' on the Reject and Move to Next menu.

Q&A

If I am using a mouse, what if I accidentally click the 'Reject and Move to Next' arrow (REVIEW tab | Changes group)?
Click 'Reject and Move to Next' on the Reject and Move to Next menu.

What if I wanted to reject the change but not search for the next tracked change?
You would tap or click the 'Reject and Move to Next' arrow (REVIEW tab | Changes group) and then tap or click Reject Change on the Reject and Move to Next menu.

What if I did not want to accept or reject a change but wanted to locate the next tracked change?
You would tap or click the Next Change button (REVIEW tab | Changes group) to locate the next tracked change or comment. Likewise, to locate the previous tracked change or comment, you would tap or click the Previous Change button (REVIEW tab | Changes group).

5

- Tap or click the OK button in the dialog box that appears, which indicates the document contains no more comments or tracked changes.

Other Ways

1. Tap 'Show Context Menu' button on mini toolbar or right-click comment or tracked change, tap or click desired command on shortcut menu

To Accept or Reject All Tracked Changes

If you wanted to accept or reject all tracked changes in a document at once, you would perform the following step.

1. To accept all tracked changes, tap or click the 'Accept and Move to Next' arrow (REVIEW tab | Changes group) to display the Accept and Move to Next menu and then tap or click 'Accept All Changes' on the menu to accept all changes in the document and continue tracking changes or tap or click 'Accept All Changes and Stop Tracking' to accept all changes in the document and stop tracking changes.

or

1. To reject all tracked changes, tap or click the 'Reject and Move to Next' arrow (REVIEW tab | Changes group) to display the Reject and Move to Next menu and then tap or click 'Reject All Changes' on the menu to reject all changes in the document and continue tracking changes or tap or click 'Reject All Changes and Stop Tracking' to reject all changes in the document and stop tracking changes.

Changing Tracking Options

If you wanted to change the color and markings reviewers use for tracked changes and comments or change how balloons are displayed, use the Advanced Track Changes Options dialog box (Figure 8–23 on the next page). To display the Advanced Track Changes Options dialog box, tap or click the Change Tracking Options Dialog Box Launcher (REVIEW tab | Tracking group) and then tap or click the Advanced Options button (Track Changes Options dialog box).

BTW

Document Inspector
If you wanted to ensure that all comments were removed from a document, you could use the document inspector. Open the Backstage view, display the Info gallery, tap or click the 'Check for Issues' button, and then tap or click Inspect Document. Place a check mark in the 'Comments, Revisions, Versions, and Annotations' check box and then tap or click the Inspect button (Document Inspector dialog box). If any comments are located, tap or click the Remove All button.

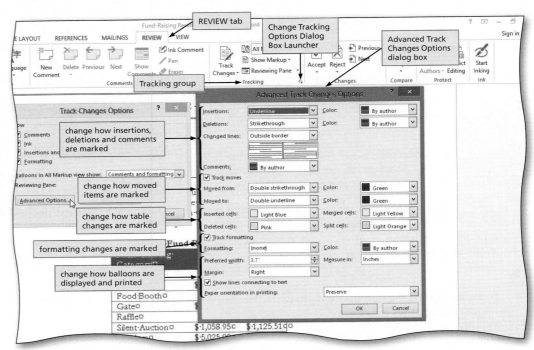

Figure 8–23

To Save an Active Document with a New File Name and Close the File

The current file name is Fund-Raising Results Memo with Comments and Tracked Changes. Because you would like to keep the document with comments and tracked changes, as well as the current one, you will save the current document with a new file name. The following steps save the active document with a new file name.

1 Tap or click FILE on the ribbon to open the Backstage view and then tap or click the Save As tab to display the Save As gallery.

2 To save on a hard disk or other storage media on your computer, proceed to Step 2a. To save on SkyDrive, proceed to Step 2b.

2a Tap or click Computer in the left pane, if necessary, to display options in the right pane related to saving on your computer.

2b Tap or click SkyDrive in the left pane to display SkyDrive saving options or a Sign In button. If your screen displays a Sign In button, tap or click it and then sign in to SkyDrive.

3 Tap or click the Browse button in the right pane to display the Save As dialog box associated with the selected save location (i.e., Computer or SkyDrive).

4 Type `Fund-Raising Results Memo Reviewed` in the File name box to change the file name. Do not press the ENTER key after typing the file name because you do not want to close the dialog box at this time.

5 Navigate to the desired save location (in this case, the Word folder in the CIS 101 folder [or your class folder] on your computer or SkyDrive).

6 Tap or click the Save button (Save As dialog box) to save the memo in the selected folder on the selected save location with the entered file name.

To Compare Documents

With Word, you can compare two documents to each other. ***Why?*** *Comparing documents allows you easily to identify any differences between two files because Word displays the differences between the documents as tracked changes for your review. By comparing files, you can verify that two separate files have the same or different content. If no tracked changes are found, then the two documents are identical.*

Assume you want to compare the original Fund-Raising Results Memo Draft document with the Fund-Raising Results Memo Reviewed document so that you can identify the changes made to the document. The following steps compare two documents.

1

- If necessary, display the REVIEW tab.

- Tap or click the Compare button (REVIEW tab | Compare group) to display the Compare menu (Figure 8–24).

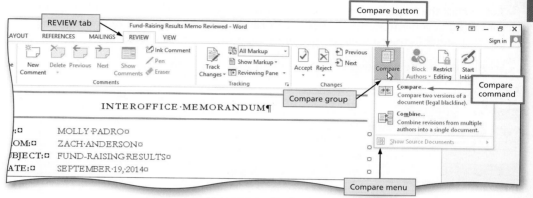

Figure 8–24

2

- Tap or click Compare on the Compare menu to display the Compare Documents dialog box.

- Tap or click the Original document arrow (Compare Documents dialog box) and then tap or click the file, Fund-Raising Results Memo Draft, in the Original document list to select the first file to compare and place the file name in the Original document box.

Q&A What if the file is not in the Original document list?
Tap or click the Open button to the right of the Original document arrow, locate the file, and then tap or click the Open button (Open dialog box).

- Tap or click the Revised document arrow (Compare Documents dialog box) and then tap or click the file, Fund-Raising Results Memo Reviewed, in the Revised document list to select the second file to compare and place the file name in the Revised document box.

Q&A What if the file is not in the Revised document list?
Tap or click the Open button to the right of the Revised document arrow, locate the file, and then tap or click the Open button (Open dialog box).

- If a More button appears in the dialog box, tap or click it to expand the dialog box, which changes the More button to a Less button.

- If necessary, in the Show changes in area, tap or click New document so that tracked changes are marked in a new document. Ensure that all your settings in the expanded dialog box (below the Less button) match those in Figure 8–25.

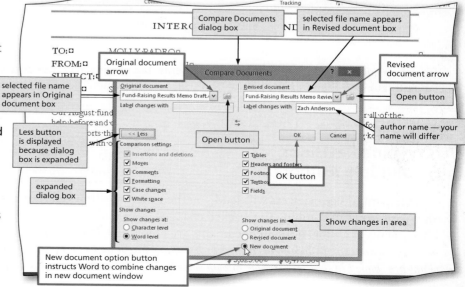

Figure 8–25

3

- Tap or click the OK button to open a new document window and display the differences between the two documents as tracked changes in a new document window; if the Reviewing task pane appears on the screen, tap or click its Close button (Figure 8–26).

 Q&A What if the original and source documents do not appear on the screen with the compared document?
Tap or click the Compare button (REVIEW tab | Compare group) to display the Compare menu, tap or point to 'Show Source Documents' on the Compare menu, and then tap or click Show Both on the Show Source Documents submenu.

Experiment

- Tap or click the Next Change button (REVIEW tab | Changes group) to display the first tracked change in the compared document. Continue tapping or clicking the Next Change or Previous Change buttons. You can accept or reject changes in the compared document using the same steps described earlier in the chapter.

- Scroll through the windows and watch them scroll synchronously.

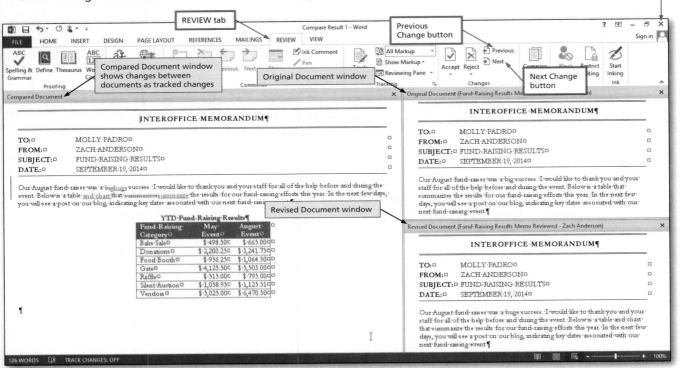

Figure 8–26

4

- When you have finished comparing the documents, tap or click the Close button in the document window (shown in Figure 8–26), and then tap or click the Don't Save button when Word asks if you want to save the compare results.

To Combine Revisions from Multiple Authors

1 INSERT COMMENTS & TRACK CHANGES | 2 REVIEW COMMENTS & TRACKED CHANGES
3 LINK EXCEL WORKSHEET TO WORD DOCUMENT | 4 CHART WORD TABLE | 5 CREATE & PUBLISH BLOG POST

Often, multiple reviewers will send you their markups (tracked changes) for the same original document. Using Word, you can combine the tracked changes from multiple reviewers' documents into a single document, two documents at a time, until all documents are combined. *Why? Combining documents allows you to review all markups from a single document, from which you can accept and reject changes and read comments. Each reviewer's markups are shaded in a different color to help you visually differentiate among multiple reviewers' markups.*

Assume you want to combine the original Fund-Raising Results Memo Draft document with the Fund-Raising Results Memo with Comments and Tracked Changes document and also with a document called Fund-Raising Results Memo - Review by L Jones, which is on the Data Files for Students. Visit www.cengage.com/ct/studentdownload for detailed instructions or contact your instructor for information about accessing the required files. The file by L Jones identifies another grammar error in the memo. The following steps combine these three documents, two at a time.

1

- Tap or click the Compare button (REVIEW tab | Compare group) to display the Compare menu (Figure 8–27).

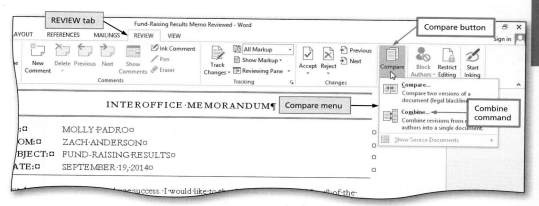

Figure 8–27

2

- Tap or click Combine on the Compare menu to display the Combine Documents dialog box.

- Tap or click the Original document arrow (Combine Documents dialog box) and then tap or click the file, Fund-Raising Results Memo Draft, in the Original document list to select the first file to combine and place the file name in the Original document box.

Q&A What if the file is not in the Original document list?
Tap or click the Open button to the right of the Original document arrow, locate the file, and then tap or click the Open button (Open dialog box).

- Tap or click the Revised document arrow (Combine Documents dialog box) and then tap or click the file, Fund-Raising Results Memo with Comments and Tracked Changes, in the Revised document list to select the second file to combine and place the file name in the Revised document box.

Q&A What if the file is not in the Revised document list?
Tap or click the Open button to the right of the Revised document arrow, locate the file, and then tap or click the Open button (Open dialog box).

- If a More button appears in the dialog box, tap or click it to expand the dialog box, which changes the More button to a Less button.

- In the Show changes in area, if necessary, tap or click Original document so that tracked changes are marked in the original document (Fund-Raising Results Memo Draft). Ensure that all your settings in the expanded dialog box (below the Less button) match those in Figure 8–28.

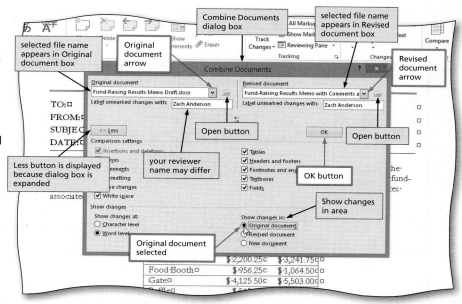

Figure 8–28

- Tap or click the OK button to combine the Fund-Raising Results Memo Draft document with the Fund-Raising Results Memo with Comments and Tracked Changes document and display the differences between the two documents as tracked changes in the original document.

- Tap or click the Compare button again (REVIEW tab | Compare group) and then tap or click Combine on the Compare menu to display the Combine Documents dialog box.

- Locate and display the file name, Fund-Raising Results Memo Draft, in the Original document text box (Combine Documents dialog box) to select the first file and place the file name in the Original document box.

- Tap or click the Open button to the right of the Revised document box arrow (Combine Documents dialog box) to display the Open dialog box.

- Locate the file name, Fund-Raising Results Memo - Review by L Jones, in the Data Files for Students and then tap or click the Open button (Open dialog box) to display the selected file name in the Revised document box (Combine Documents dialog box).

- If a More button appears in the Combine Documents dialog box, tap or click it to expand the dialog box.

- If necessary, in the 'Show changes in' area, tap or click Original document so that tracked changes are marked in the original document (Fund-Raising Results Memo Draft). Ensure that all your settings in the expanded dialog box (below the Less button) match those in Figure 8–29.

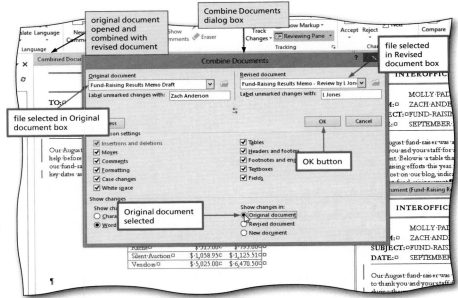

Figure 8–29

- Tap or click the OK button to combine the Fund-Raising Results Memo - Review by L Jones document with the currently combined document and display the differences among the three documents as tracked changes in the original document (Figure 8–30).

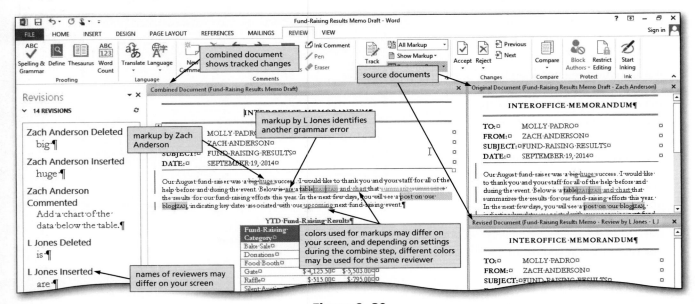

Figure 8–30

What if my screen does not display the original and source documents?
Tap or click the Compare button (REVIEW tab | Compare group) to display the Compare menu, tap or point to 'Show Source Documents' on the Compare menu, and then tap or click Show Both on the Show Source Documents submenu.

🔎 **Experiment**

- Tap or click the Next Change button (REVIEW tab | Changes group) to display the first tracked change in the combined document. Continue tapping or clicking the Next Change or Previous Change buttons. You can accept or reject changes in the combined document using the same steps described earlier in the chapter.

To Show Tracked Changes and Comments by a Single Reviewer

1 INSERT COMMENTS & TRACK CHANGES | 2 REVIEW COMMENTS & TRACKED CHANGES
3 LINK EXCEL WORKSHEET TO WORD DOCUMENT | 4 CHART WORD TABLE | 5 CREATE & PUBLISH BLOG POST

Why? *Instead of looking through a document for a particular reviewer's markups, you can show markups by reviewer. The following steps show the markups by the reviewer named L Jones.*

1

- Tap or click the Show Markup button (REVIEW tab | Tracking group) to display the Show Markup menu and then tap or point to Specific People on the Show Markup menu to display the Specific People submenu (Figure 8–31).

 What if my Specific People submenu differs?
Your submenu may have additional, different, or duplicate reviewer names or colors, depending on your Word settings.

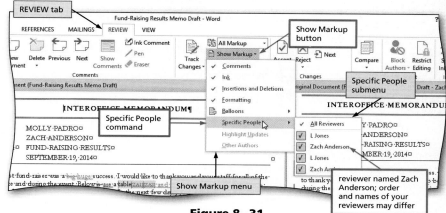

Figure 8–31

2

- Tap or click Zach Anderson on the Reviewers submenu to hide the selected reviewer's markups and leave other markups on the screen.

 Are the Zach Anderson reviewer markups deleted?
No. They are hidden from view.

3

- If necessary, repeat Steps 1 and 2 to hide the second occurrence of reviewer markups for Zach Anderson (Figure 8–32).

🔎 **Experiment**

- Practice hiding and showing reviewer markups in this document.

4

- Redisplay all reviewer comments by tapping or clicking the Show Markup button (REVIEW tab | Tracking group), tapping or pointing to Specific People, and then tapping or clicking All Reviewers on the Specific People submenu.

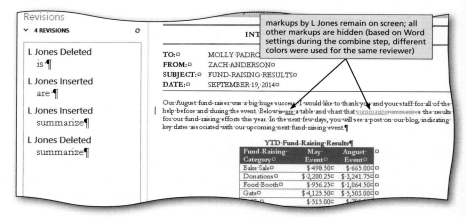

Figure 8–32

BTW
Locating Comments by Reviewer
You can find a comment from a specific reviewer through the Go To dialog box. Tap or click the Find arrow (HOME tab | Editing group) and then tap or click Go To or press CTRL+G to display the Go To sheet in the Find and Replace dialog box. Tap or click Comment in the Go to what list (Find and Replace dialog box). Select the reviewer whose comments you wish to find and then tap or click the Next button.

To Customize the Status Bar

You are finished working with tracked changes in this chapter. The following steps remove the TRACK CHANGES indicator from the status bar.

1 Press and hold or right-click anywhere on the status bar to display the Customize Status Bar menu.

2 Remove the check mark to the left of Track Changes on the Customize Status Bar menu, which removes the TRACK CHANGES indicator from the status bar.

3 Tap or click anywhere outside of the Customize Status Bar menu, or press the ESCAPE key, to remove the Customize Status Bar menu from the screen.

To Close the Document without Saving It

The next step is to close the combined document without saving it.

1 Open the Backstage view and then tap or click Close.

2 When Word displays the dialog box, tap or click the Don't Save button.

3 Close any other open Word documents.

Break Point: If you wish to take a break, this is a good place to do so. You can exit Word now. To resume at a later time, run Word and continue following the steps from this location forward.

Linking an Excel Worksheet to a Word Document

With Microsoft Office, you can copy part or all of a document created in one Office program to a document created in another Office program. The item being copied is called the **object**. For example, you could copy an Excel worksheet (the object) that is located in an Excel workbook (the source file) to a Word document (the destination file). That is, an object is copied from a source to a destination.

You can use one of three techniques to copy objects from one program to another: copy and paste, embed, or link.

- **Copy and paste:** When you copy an object and then paste it, the object becomes part of the destination document. You edit a pasted object using editing features of the destination program. For example, when you select an Excel worksheet in an Excel workbook, tap or click the Copy button (HOME tab | Clipboard group) in Excel, and then tap or click the Paste button (HOME tab | Clipboard group) in Word, the Excel worksheet becomes a Word table.

- **Embed:** When you embed an object, like a pasted object, it becomes part of the destination document. The difference between an embedded object and a pasted object is that you edit the contents of an embedded object using the editing features of the source program. The embedded object, however, contains static data; that is, any changes made to the object in the source program are not reflected in the destination document. If you embed an Excel worksheet in a Word document, the Excel worksheet remains as an Excel worksheet in the Word document. When you edit the Excel worksheet from within the Word document, you will use Excel editing features.

- **Link:** A linked object, by contrast, does not become a part of the destination document even though it appears to be a part of it. Rather, a connection is established between the source and destination documents so that when you open the destination document, the linked object appears as part of it. When you edit a linked object, the source program runs and opens the source document that contains the linked object. For example, when you edit a linked worksheet, Excel runs and displays the Excel workbook that contains the worksheet; you then edit the worksheet in Excel. Unlike an embedded object, if you open the Excel workbook that contains the Excel worksheet and then edit the Excel worksheet, the linked object will be updated in the Word document, too.

How do I determine which method to use: copy/paste, embed, or link?

- If you simply want to use the object's data and have no desire to use the object in the source program, then copy and paste the object.

- If you want to use the object in the source program but you want the object's data to remain static if it changes in the source file, then embed the object.

- If you want to ensure that the most current version of the object appears in the destination file, then link the object. If the source file is large, such as a video clip or a sound clip, link the object to keep the size of the destination file smaller.

The steps in this section show how to link an Excel worksheet (the object), which is located in an Excel workbook (the source file), to a Word document (the destination file). The Word document is similar to the same memo used in the previous section, except that all grammar errors are fixed and it does not contain the table. To link the worksheet to the memo, you will follow these general steps:

1. Run Excel and open the Excel workbook that contains the object (worksheet) you want to link to the Word document.
2. Select the object (worksheet) in Excel and then copy the selected object to the Clipboard.
3. Switch to Word and then link the copied object to the Word document.

Note: The steps in this section assume you have Microsoft Excel installed on your computer. If you do not have Excel, read the steps in this section without performing them.

To Open a Document

The first step in this section is to open the memo that is to contain the link to the Excel worksheet object. The memo file, named Fund-Raising Memo without Table, is located on the Data Files for Students. Visit www.cengage.com/ct/studentdownload for detailed instructions or contact your instructor for information about accessing the required files. The following steps open a document.

1 Tap or click FILE on the ribbon to open the Backstage view and then, if necessary, tap or click the Open tab to display the Open gallery.

2 Navigate to the Data Files for Students and then open the file called Fund-Raising Results Memo without Table.

BTW
Linked Objects
When you open a document that contains linked objects, Word displays a dialog box asking if you want to update the Word document with data from the linked file. Tap or click the Yes button only if you are certain the linked file is from a trusted source; that is, you should be confident that the source file does not contain a virus or other potentially harmful program before you instruct Word to link the source file to the destination document.

Excel Basics

The Excel window contains a rectangular grid that consists of columns and rows. A column letter above the grid identifies each column. A row number on the left side of the grid identifies each row. The intersection of each column and row is a cell. A cell is referred to by its unique address, which is the coordinates of the intersection of a column and a row. To identify a cell, specify the column letter first, followed by the row number. For example, cell reference A1 refers to the cell located at the intersection of column A and row 1 (Figure 8–33).

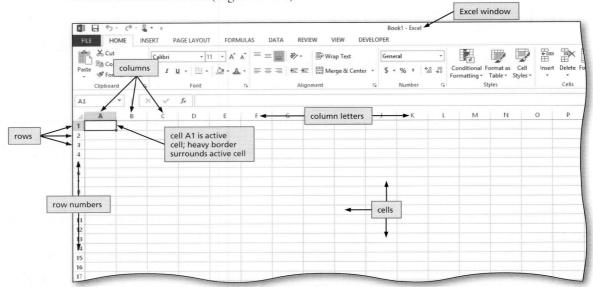

Figure 8–33

To Run Excel and Open an Excel Workbook

The Excel worksheet to be linked to the memo is in an Excel workbook called Fund-Raising Results in Excel, which is located on the Data Files for Students. Visit www.cengage.com/ct/studentdownload for detailed instructions or contact your instructor for information about accessing the required files.

The following steps run Excel and open a workbook. (Do not exit Word or close the open Word document before starting these steps.)

1 Display the Windows Start screen and then scroll the Start screen for an Excel 2013 tile. If your Start screen contains an Excel 2013 tile, tap or click it to run Excel and then proceed to Step 5; if the Start screen does not contain the Excel 2013 tile, proceed to the next step to search for the Excel app.

2 Swipe in from the right edge of the screen or point to the upper-right corner of the screen to display the Charms bar and then tap or click the Search charm on the Charms bar to display the Search menu.

3 Type **Excel** as the search text in the Search box and watch the search results appear in the Apps list.

4 Tap or click Excel 2013 in the search results to run Excel.

5 Tap or click 'Open Other Workbooks' in the left pane of the Excel start screen, navigate to the Data Files for Students, and then tap or click the file called Fund-Raising Results in Excel (Open dialog box).

6 Tap or click the Open button to open the selected file and display the opened workbook in the Excel window.

To Link an Excel Worksheet to a Word Document

The following steps link an Excel worksheet to a Word document. *Why? You want to copy the Excel worksheet to the Clipboard and then link the Excel worksheet to the Word document.*

1

- In the Excel window, drag through the cells in the range A1 through C8 to select them.

- In the Excel window, if you are using a touch screen, tap the Copy button (HOME tab | Clipboard group) and then tap Copy on the Copy menu; if you are using a mouse, click the Copy button (HOME tab | Clipboard group) to copy the selected cells to the Clipboard (Figure 8–34).

Q&A
If I am using a mouse, what if I click the Copy arrow by mistake?
Click Copy on the Copy menu.

What is the dotted line around the selected cells?
Excel surrounds copied cells with a moving marquee to help you visually identify the copied cells.

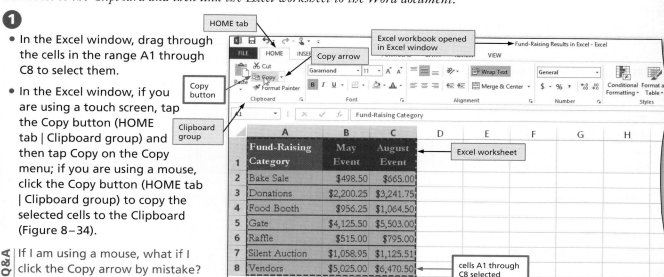

Figure 8–34

2

- Tap or click the Word app button on the taskbar switch to Word and display the open document in the Word window.

- Position the insertion point on the paragraph mark below the table title.

- In Word, tap or click the Paste arrow (HOME tab | Clipboard group) to display the Paste gallery.

Q&A
What if I accidentally tap or click the Paste button instead of the Paste arrow?
Tap or click the Undo button on the Quick Access Toolbar and then tap or click the Paste arrow.

- If you are using a mouse, point to the 'Link & Keep Source Formatting' button in the Paste gallery to display a live preview of that paste option (Figure 8–35).

Experiment

- If you are using a mouse, point to the various buttons in the Paste gallery to display a live preview of each paste option.

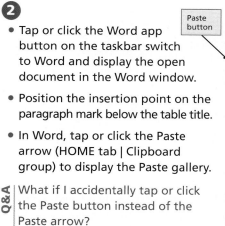
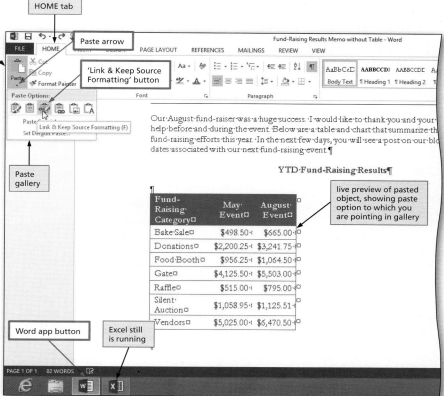

Figure 8–35

• Tap or click the 'Link & Keep Source Formatting' button in the Paste gallery to paste and link the object at the location of the insertion point in the document.

Q&A

What if I wanted to copy an object instead of link it?

To copy an object, you would tap or click the 'Keep Source Formatting' button in the Paste gallery. To convert the object to a picture so that you can use tools on Word's PICTURE TOOLS tab to format it, you would tap or click the Picture button in the Paste gallery.

• Select and then center the linked Excel table using the same technique you use to select and center a Word table.

• Resize the linked Excel table until the table is approximately the same size as Figure 8–36.

Q&A

What if I wanted to delete the linked worksheet?

You would select the linked worksheet and then press the DELETE key.

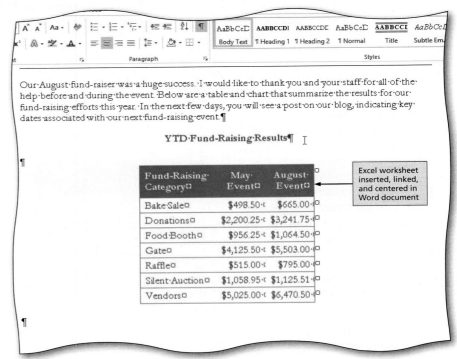

Our August fund-raiser was a huge success. I would like to thank you and your staff for all of the help before and during the event. Below are a table and chart that summarize the results for our fund-raising efforts this year. In the next few days, you will see a post on our blog, indicating key dates associated with our next fund-raising event.¶

YTD Fund-Raising Results¶

Fund-Raising Category	May Event	August Event
Bake Sale	$498.50	$665.00
Donations	$2,200.25	$3,241.75
Food Booth	$956.25	$1,064.50
Gate	$4,125.50	$5,503.00
Raffle	$515.00	$795.00
Silent Auction	$1,058.95	$1,125.51
Vendors	$5,025.00	$6,470.50

Excel worksheet inserted, linked, and centered in Word document

Figure 8–36

Other Ways

1. Tap or click Paste arrow (HOME tab | Clipboard group), tap or click Paste Special, tap or click Paste link (Paste Special dialog box), tap or click 'Microsoft Excel Worksheet Object' in As list, tap or click OK button

2. To link an entire source file, tap or click Object button (INSERT tab | Text group), tap Object on Object menu if using a touch screen, tap or click Create from File tab (Object dialog box), locate file, tap or click 'Link to file' check box, tap or click OK button

TO EMBED AN EXCEL WORKSHEET IN A WORD DOCUMENT

If you wanted to embed an Excel worksheet in a Word document, instead of link it, you would perform the following steps.

BTW

Editing Embedded Objects

If you wanted to edit an embedded object in the Word document, you would double-tap or double-click the object to display the source program's interface in the destination program. For example, double-tapping or double-clicking an embedded Excel worksheet in a Word document displays the Excel ribbon in the Word window. To redisplay the Word ribbon in the Word window, double-tap or double-click outside of the embedded object.

1. Run Excel.

2. In Excel, select the worksheet cells to embed. If you are using a touch screen, tap the Copy button (HOME tab | Clipboard group) and then tap Copy on the Copy menu; if you are using a mouse, click the Copy button (HOME tab | Clipboard group) to copy the selected cells to the Clipboard.

3. Switch to Word. In Word, tap or click the Paste arrow (HOME tab | Clipboard group) to display the Paste gallery and then tap or click Paste Special in the Paste gallery to display the Paste Special dialog box.

4. Select the Paste option button (Paste Special dialog box), which indicates the object will be embedded.

5. Select 'Microsoft Excel Worksheet Object' as the type of object to embed.

6. Tap or click the OK button to embed the contents of the Clipboard in the Word document at the location of the insertion point.

TO EDIT A LINKED OBJECT

At a later time, you may find it necessary to change the data in the Excel worksheet. Any changes you make to the Excel worksheet while in Excel will be reflected in the Excel worksheet in the Word document because the objects are linked to the Word document. If you wanted to edit a linked object, such as an Excel worksheet, you would perform these steps.

1. In the Word document, press and hold the linked Excel worksheet and then tap the 'Show Context Menu' button on mini toolbar or right-click the linked Excel worksheet, tap or point to 'Linked Worksheet Object' on the shortcut menu, and then tap or click Edit Link on the Linked Worksheet Object submenu to run Excel and open the source file that contains the linked worksheet.

2. In Excel, make changes to the Excel worksheet.

3. Tap or click the Save button on the Quick Access Toolbar to save the changes.

4. Exit Excel.

5. If necessary, redisplay the Word window.

6. If necessary, to update the worksheet with the edited Excel data, tap or click the Excel worksheet in the Word document and then press the F9 key, or press and hold the linked object and then tap the 'Show Context Menu' button on the mini toolbar, or right-click the linked object and then tap or click Update Link on the shortcut menu to update the linked object with the revisions made to the source file.

BTW
Opening Word Documents with Links
When you open a document that contains a linked object, Word attempts to locate the source file associated with the link. If Word cannot find the source file, open the Backstage view, display the Info tab, then tap or click 'Edit Links to Files' at the bottom of the right pane to display the Links dialog box. Next, select the appropriate source file in the list (Links dialog box), tap or click the Change Source button, locate the source file, and then tap or click the OK button.

To Break a Link

1 INSERT COMMENTS & TRACK CHANGES | 2 REVIEW COMMENTS & TRACKED CHANGES

3 LINK EXCEL WORKSHEET TO WORD DOCUMENT | 4 CHART WORD TABLE | 5 CREATE & PUBLISH BLOG POST

Why? *You can convert a linked or embedded object to a Word object by breaking the link. That is, you break the connection between the source file and the destination file.* When you break a linked object, such as an Excel worksheet, the linked object becomes a Word object, a Word table in this case. The following steps break the link to the Excel worksheet.

- If you are using a touch screen, press and hold the linked object and then tap the 'Show Context Menu' button on the mini toolbar; if you are using a mouse, right-click the linked object (the linked Excel worksheet, in this case) to display a shortcut menu.

- Tap or point to 'Linked Worksheet Object' on the shortcut menu to display the Linked Worksheet Object submenu (Figure 8–37).

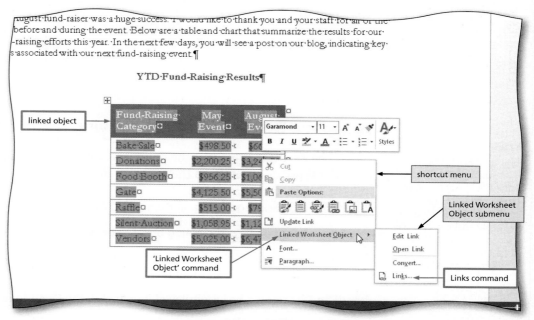

Figure 8–37

• Tap or click Links on the Linked Worksheet Object submenu to display the Links dialog box.

• If necessary, tap or click the source file listed in the dialog box to select it (Links dialog box).

• Tap or click the Break Link button, which displays a dialog box asking if you are sure you want to break the selected links (Figure 8–38).

• Tap or click the Yes button in the dialog box to remove the source file from the list (break the link).

Q&A

How can I verify the link is broken?

Press and hold the table and then tap the 'Show Context Menu button' or right-click the table in the Word document to display a shortcut menu. If the shortcut menu does not contain a 'Linked Worksheet Object' command, a link does not exist for the object. Or, when you double-tap or double-click the table, Excel should not open an associated workbook.

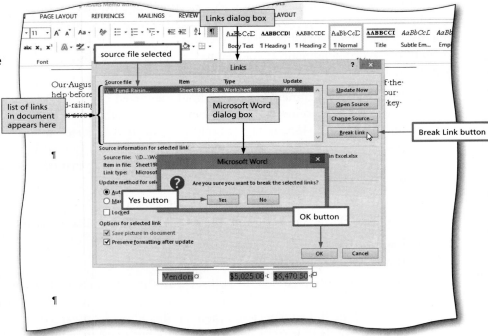

Figure 8–38

Other Ways

1. Select link, press CTRL+SHIFT+F9

CONSIDER THIS

Why would you break a link?

If you share a Word document that contains a linked object, such as an Excel worksheet, users will be asked by Word if they want to update the links when they open the Word document. If users are unfamiliar with links, they will not know how to answer the question. Further, if they do not have the source program, such as Excel, they may not be able to open the Word document. When sharing documents, it is recommended you convert links to a regular Word object; that is, break the link.

BTW

BTWs

For a complete list of the BTWs found in the margins of this book, visit the BTW resource on the Student Companion Site located on www.cengagebrain.com. For detailed instructions about accessing available resources, visit www.cengage.com/ct/studentdownload or contact your instructor for information about accessing the required files.

To Close a Document without Saving It and Exit Excel

The next step is to close the document without saving it. The following steps close the Word document and the Excel window.

1 Open the Backstage view and then tap or click Close.

2 When Word displays the dialog box, tap or click the Don't Save button.

3 Press and hold or right-click the Excel app button on the taskbar and then tap or click Close window on the shortcut menu.

4 If an Excel dialog box is displayed, tap or click the Don't Save button.

Charting a Word Table

Several Office applications, including Word, enable you to create charts from data. In the following pages, you will insert and format a chart of the Fund-Raising Results Word table using the CHART TOOLS tab in Word. You will follow these general steps to insert and then format the chart:

1. Create a chart of the table.
2. Remove a data series from the chart.
3. Apply a chart style to the chart.
4. Change the colors of the chart.
5. Add a chart element.
6. Edit a chart element.
7. Format chart elements.
8. Add an outline to the chart.

To Open a Document

The next step is to open the Fund-Raising Results Memo file that contains the final wording so that you can create a chart of its Word table. This file, called Fund-Raising Results Memo with Table, is located on the Data Files for Students. Visit www.cengage.com/ct/studentdownload for detailed instructions or contact your instructor for information about accessing the required files. The following steps open a document.

1 Tap or click FILE on the ribbon to open the Backstage view and then, if necessary, tap or click the Open tab to display the Open gallery.

2 Navigate to the Data Files for Students and then open the file called Fund-Raising Results Memo with Table.

To Chart a Table

1 INSERT COMMENTS & TRACK CHANGES | 2 REVIEW COMMENTS & TRACKED CHANGES
3 LINK EXCEL WORKSHEET TO WORD DOCUMENT | 4 CHART WORD TABLE | 5 CREATE & PUBLISH BLOG POST

The following steps insert a default chart and then copy the data to be charted from the Word table in the Word document to a chart spreadsheet. *Why? To chart a table, you fill in or copy the data into a chart spreadsheet that automatically opens after you insert the chart.*

- Center the paragraph mark below the table so that the inserted chart will be centered. Leave the insertion point on this paragraph mark because the chart will be inserted at the location of the insertion point.

- Display the INSERT tab.

- Tap or click the 'Add a Chart' button (INSERT tab | Illustrations group) to display the Insert Chart dialog box.

- Tap or click Bar in the left pane (Insert Chart dialog box) to display the available types of bar charts in the right pane.

- Tap or click the various types of charts in the left pane and watch the subtypes appear in the right pane. When finished experimenting, tap or click Bar in the left pane.

- If necessary, tap or click Clustered Bar in the right pane to select the chart type (Figure 8–39).

🔍 **Experiment**

- Tap or click the various types of bar charts in the right pane and watch the graphic change in the right pane. When finished experimenting, tap or click Clustered Bar in the right pane.

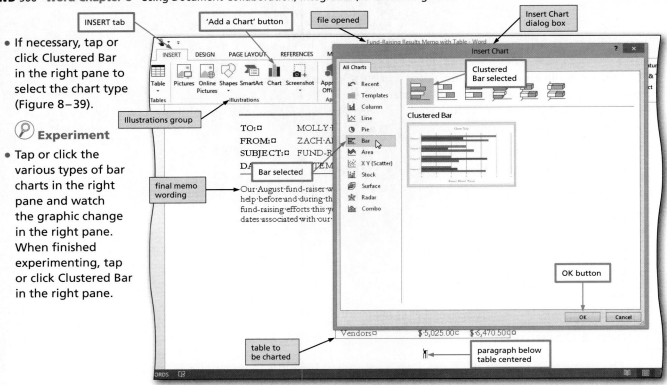

Figure 8–39

2

- Tap or click the OK button so that Word creates a default clustered bar chart in the Word document at the location of the insertion point (Figure 8–40).

Q&A
What are the requirements for the format of a table that can be charted? The chart spreadsheet window shows the layout for the selected chart type. In this case, the categories are in the rows and the series are in the columns. Notice the categories appear in the chart in reverse order.

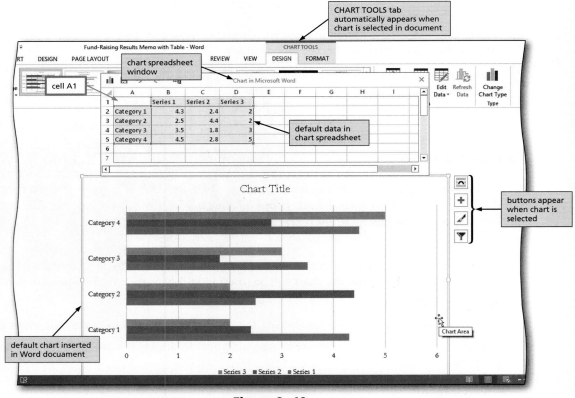

Figure 8–40

3

- In the Word document, select the table to be charted.

- Tap or click the Copy button (HOME tab | Clipboard group) to copy the selected table to the Clipboard (Figure 8–41).

Q&A Instead of copying table data to the chart spreadsheet, could I type the data directly into the spreadsheet? Yes. If the chart spreadsheet window does not appear, tap or click the Edit Data arrow (CHART TOOLS DESIGN tab | Data group) and then tap or click Edit Data on the menu. You also can tap or click the 'Edit Data in Microsoft Excel' button to use Excel to enter the data (if Excel is installed on your computer), or tap or click the Edit Data arrow (CHART TOOLS DESIGN tab | Data group) and then tap or click 'Edit Data in Excel 2013' on the Edit Data menu.

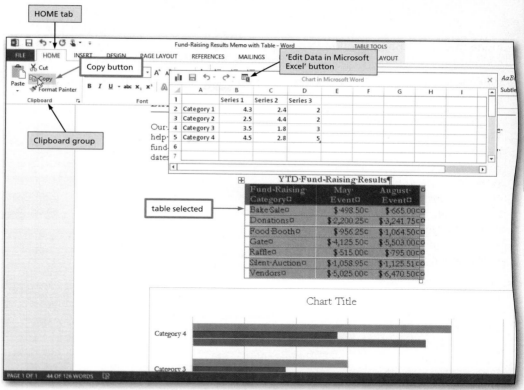

Figure 8–41

4

- In the chart spreadsheet window, tap or click the Select All button (upper-left corner of worksheet) to select the entire worksheet.

- Press and hold or right-click the selected worksheet to display a mini toolbar or shortcut menu (Figure 8–42).

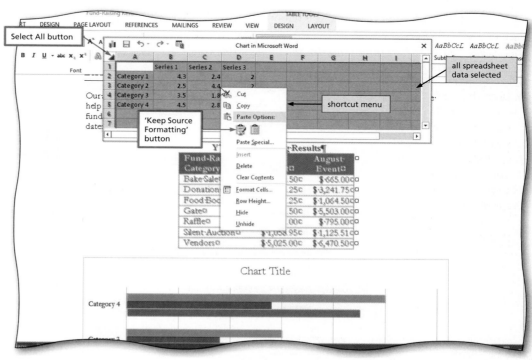

Figure 8–42

- In the chart spreadsheet window, tap the Paste button or click the 'Keep Source Formatting' button to paste the contents of the Clipboard starting in the upper-left corner of the worksheet.

- When Word displays a dialog box indicating that the pasted contents are a different size from the selection, tap or click the OK button.

Q&A

Why did Word display this dialog box?

The source table contains three columns, and the target worksheet has four columns. In the next section, you will delete the fourth column from the chart spreadsheet.

- Resize the chart worksheet window by dragging its window edges and move it by dragging its title bar so it appears as shown in Figure 8–43. Notice that the chart in the Word window automatically changes to reflect the new data in the chart worksheet (Figure 8–43).

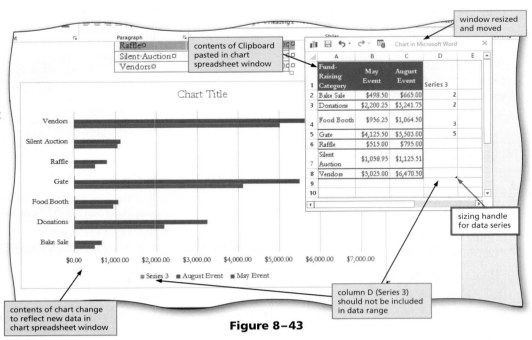

Figure 8–43

To Remove a Data Series from the Chart

1 INSERT COMMENTS & TRACK CHANGES | 2 REVIEW COMMENTS & TRACKED CHANGES
3 LINK EXCEL WORKSHEET TO WORD DOCUMENT | 4 CHART WORD TABLE | 5 CREATE & PUBLISH BLOG POST

The following steps remove the data in column D from the chart, which is plotted as Series 3 (shown in Figure 8–43). **Why?** *By default, Word selects the first four columns in the chart spreadsheet window. The chart in this project covers only the first three columns: the fund-raising categories and two data series — May Event and August Event.*

1

- Drag the sizing handle in cell D8 of the chart spreadsheet leftward so that the selection ends at cell C8; that is the selection should encompass cells A1 through C8 (Figure 8–44).

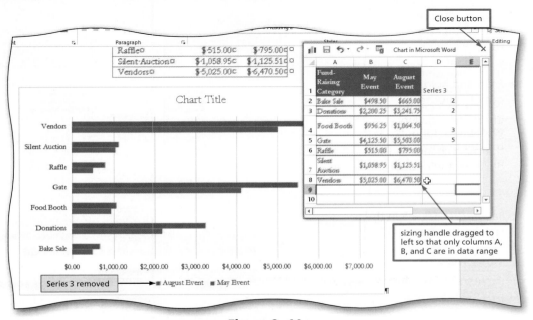

Figure 8–44

Q&A

How would I add a data series?

Add a column of data to the chart spreadsheet. Drag the sizing handle outward to include the series, or you could tap or click the Select Data button (CHART TOOLS DESIGN tab | Data group), tap or click the Add button (Select Data Source dialog box), tap or click the Select Range button (Edit Series dialog box), drag through the data range in the worksheet, and then tap or click the OK button.

How would I add or remove data categories?

Follow the same steps to add or remove data series, except work with spreadsheet rows instead of columns.

● Close the chart spreadsheet window by tapping or clicking its Close button.

Other Ways

1. Tap or click Select Data button (CHART TOOLS DESIGN tab | Data group), tap or click series to remove (Select Data Source dialog box), tap or click Remove button, tap or click OK button

To Apply a Chart Style

1 INSERT COMMENTS & TRACK CHANGES | 2 REVIEW COMMENTS & TRACKED CHANGES
3 LINK EXCEL WORKSHEET TO WORD DOCUMENT | 4 CHART WORD TABLE | 5 CREATE & PUBLISH BLOG POST

The next step is to apply a chart style to the chart. *Why? Word provides a Chart Styles gallery, allowing you to change the chart's format to a more visually appealing style.* The following steps apply a chart style to a chart.

1

● Display the CHART TOOLS DESIGN tab.

● Tap or click the chart to select it.

● If you are using a mouse, point to Style 5 in the Chart Styles gallery (CHART TOOLS DESIGN tab | Chart Styles group) to display a live preview of that style applied to the graphic in the document (Figure 8–45).

 **Experiment**

● If you are using a mouse, point to various styles in the Chart Styles gallery and watch the style of the chart change in the document window.

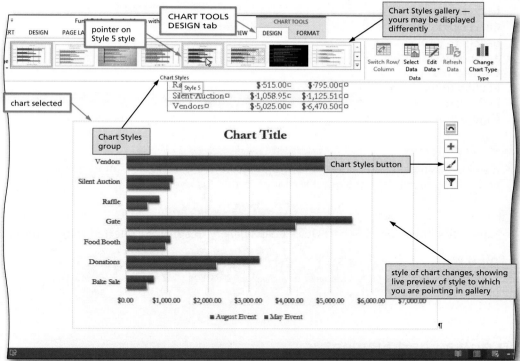

Figure 8-45

2

● Tap or click Style 5 in the Chart Styles gallery (CHART TOOLS DESIGN tab | Chart Styles group) to apply the selected style to the chart.

Other Ways

1. Tap or click Chart Styles button attached to chart, tap or click STYLE tab, tap or click desired style

To Change Colors of a Chart

The following steps change the colors of the chart. *Why? Word provides a predefined variety of colors for charts. You select one that best matches the colors already used in the letter.*

1

- With the chart selected, tap or click the 'Chart Quick Colors' button (CHART TOOLS DESIGN tab | Chart Styles group) to display the Chart Quick Colors gallery.

Q&A

What if the chart is not selected?
Tap or click the chart to select it.

- If you are using a mouse, point to Color 4 in the Chart Quick Colors gallery to display a live preview of the selected color applied to the chart in the document (Figure 8–46).

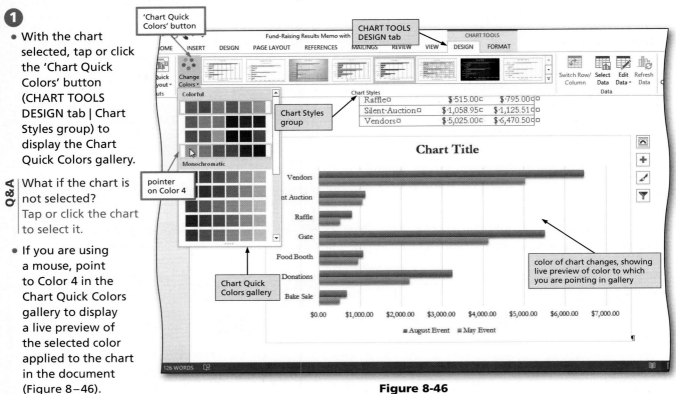

Figure 8-46

Experiment

- If you are using a mouse, point to various colors in the Chart Quick Colors gallery and watch the colors of the graphic change in the document window.

2

- Tap or click Color 4 in the Chart Quick Colors gallery to apply the selected color to the chart.

Other Ways

1. Tap or click Chart Styles button attached to chart, tap or click COLOR tab, tap or click desired style

To Add a Chart Element

The following steps add minor vertical gridlines to the chart. *Why? You want to add more vertical lines to the chart so that it is easier to see the dollar values associated with each bar length.*

1

- With the chart selected, tap or click the 'Add Chart Element' button (CHART TOOLS DESIGN tab | Chart Layouts group) to display the Add Chart Element gallery and then tap or point to Gridlines to display the Gridlines submenu (Figure 8–47).

Experiment

- If you are using a mouse, point to various elements in the Add Chart Element gallery so that you can see the other types of elements you can add to a chart. When finished, point to Gridlines.

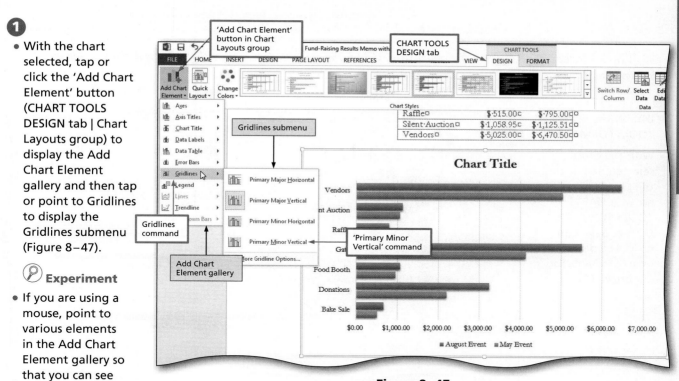

Figure 8–47

2

- Tap or click 'Primary Minor Vertical' on the Gridline submenu to add vertical minor gridlines to the chart (Figure 8–48).

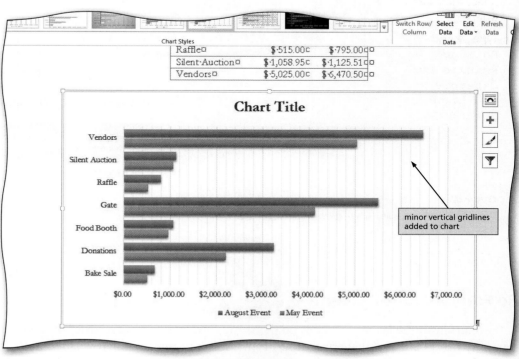

Figure 8–48

To Select a Chart Element and Edit It

The following steps change the chart title. *Why? You want to change the title from the default to a more meaningful name.*

1

- Display the CHART TOOLS FORMAT tab.

- With the chart selected, tap or click the Chart Elements arrow (CHART TOOLS FORMAT tab | Current Selection group) to display the Chart Elements list (Figure 8–49).

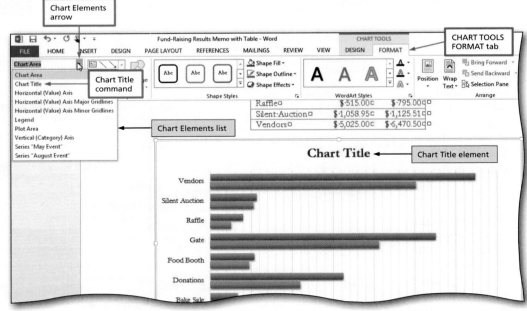

Figure 8–49

2

- Tap or click Chart Title in the Chart Elements list to select the chart's title.

- Type **Fund-Raising Results by Category** as the new title (Figure 8–50).

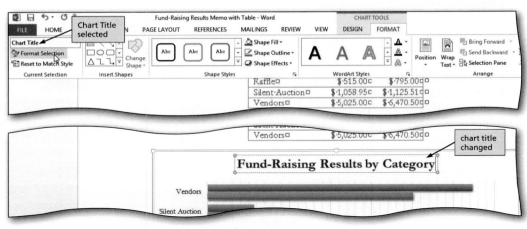

Figure 8–50

Other Ways

1. Tap or click the chart element in the chart to select the element

To Format Chart Elements

Currently, the category names on the vertical axis are in reverse order of the row labels in the table; that is, category names are in alphabetical order from bottom to top and the row labels in the table are in alphabetical order from top to bottom. Also, the numbers across the bottom display with no cents following the dollar values. The following steps format axis elements. *Why? You want the categories to display in the same order as the table, the numbers to display as whole numbers, and the legend to appear at the top of the chart.*

1

- If necessary, select the chart by tapping or clicking it.

- With the chart selected, tap or click the Chart Elements arrow (CHART TOOLS FORMAT tab | Current Selection group) to display the Chart Elements list and then tap or click 'Vertical (Category) Axis'.

- Tap or click the Chart Elements button attached to the right of the chart to display the CHART ELEMENTS gallery.

- Tap or point to and then click the Axes arrow in the CHART ELEMENTS gallery to display the Axes fly-out menu (Figure 8–51).

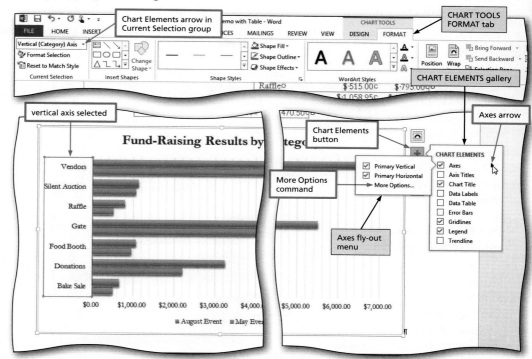

Figure 8–51

2

- Tap or click More Options on the Axes fly-out menu to display the Format Axis task pane.

- If necessary, tap or click AXIS OPTIONS to expand the section.

- If necessary, tap or click the Chart Elements arrow (CHART TOOLS FORMAT tab | Current Selection group) to display the Chart Elements list and then tap or click 'Vertical (Category) Axis'.

- Place a check mark in the 'Categories in reverse order' check box so that the order of the categories in the chart matches the order of the categories in the table (Figure 8–52).

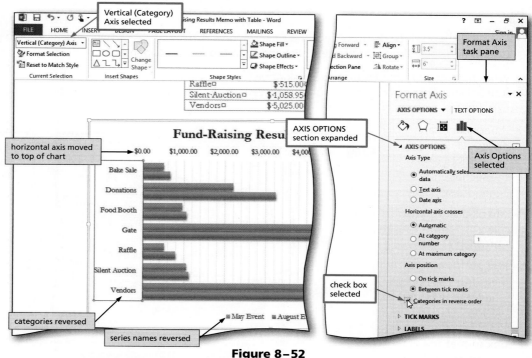

Figure 8–52

Q&A Why did the horizontal axis move from the bottom of the chart to the top?

When you reverse the categories, the horizontal axis automatically moves from the bottom of the chart to the top of the chart. Notice that the series names below the chart also are reversed.

3

- With the chart selected, tap or click the Chart Elements arrow (CHART TOOLS FORMAT tab | Current Selection group) to display the Chart Elements list and then tap or click 'Horizontal (Value) Axis'.

- If necessary, tap or click LABELS and NUMBER at the bottom of the Format Axis task pane to expand the sections in the task pane.

- If necessary, scroll the task pane to display the entire LABELS and NUMBER sections.

- In the LABELS section, tap or click the Label Position arrow and then tap or click High to move the axis to the bottom of the chart.

- In the NUMBER section, change the value in the Decimal places text box to 0 (the number zero) and then press the ENTER key (Figure 8–53).

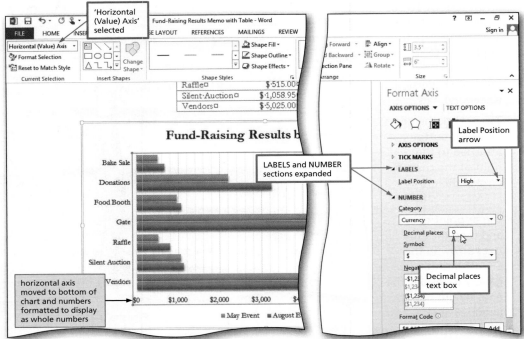

Figure 8–53

4

- With the chart selected, tap or click the Chart Elements arrow (CHART TOOLS FORMAT tab | Current Selection group) to display the Chart Elements list and then tap or click Legend.

Q&A | What happened to the Format Axis task pane?
It now is the Format Legend task pane. The task pane title and options change, depending on the element you are using or formatting.

- If necessary, tap or click LEGEND OPTIONS to expand the section in the Legend task pane.

- Tap or click Top to select the option button.

- Remove the check mark from the 'Show the legend without overlapping the chart' check box so that the legend drops down into the chart a bit (Figure 8–54).

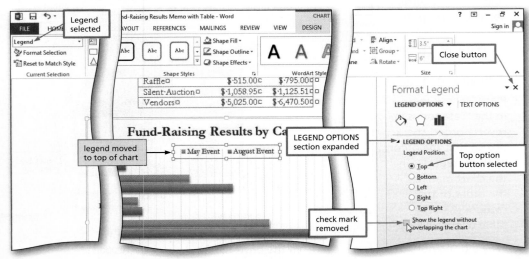

Figure 8–54

5
- Drag the legend up slightly so that it rests on top of the vertical lines in the chart.
- Close the task pane by tapping or clicking its close button.

To Add an Outline to a Chart

1 INSERT COMMENTS & TRACK CHANGES | 2 REVIEW COMMENTS & TRACKED CHANGES
3 LINK EXCEL WORKSHEET TO WORD DOCUMENT | 4 CHART WORD TABLE | 5 CREATE & PUBLISH BLOG POST

The following steps add an outline to the chart with a shadow. *Why? You want a border surrounding the chart.*

1
- With the chart selected, tap or click the Chart Elements arrow (CHART TOOLS FORMAT tab | Current Selection group) to display the Chart Elements list and then tap or click Chart Area.
- Tap or click the Shape Outline arrow (CHART TOOLS FORMAT tab | Shape Styles group) to display the Shape Outline gallery.

2
- Tap or click 'Blue, Accent 1' (fifth color, first row) in the Shape Outline gallery to change the outline color.
- Tap or click the Shape Outline arrow (CHART TOOLS FORMAT tab | Shape Styles group) again and then tap or point to Weight in the Shape Outline gallery to display the Weight gallery (Figure 8–55).

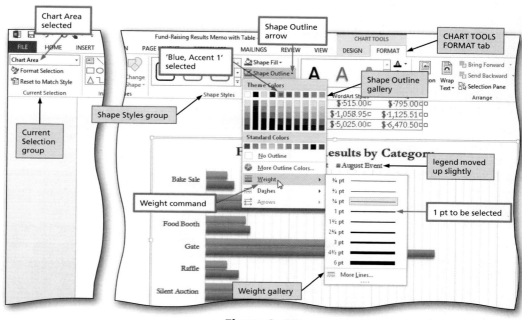

Figure 8–55

3
- Tap or click 1 pt in the Weight gallery to apply the selected weight to the outline.
- Tap or click the Shape Effects button (CHART TOOLS FORMAT tab | Shape Styles group) and then tap or point to Shadow in the Shape Effects gallery to display the Shadow gallery (Figure 8–56).

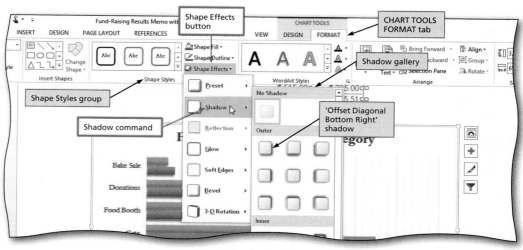

Figure 8–56

4
- Tap or click 'Offset Diagonal Bottom Right' in the Shadow gallery to apply the selected shadow to the outline.

To Save an Active Document with a New File Name and Close the File

You are finished charting the Word table with a clustered chart. Thus, the following steps save the document.

1 Open the Backstage view and then tap or click the Save As tab to display the Save As gallery.

2 Navigate to the desired save location and save the document with the file name, Fund-Raising Results Memo with Table and Clustered Chart.

To Change a Chart Type

1 INSERT COMMENTS & TRACK CHANGES | 2 REVIEW COMMENTS & TRACKED CHANGES
3 LINK EXCEL WORKSHEET TO WORD DOCUMENT | 4 CHART WORD TABLE | 5 CREATE & PUBLISH BLOG POST

The following steps change the chart type. *Why? After reviewing the document, you would like to see how the chart looks as a 3-D clustered bar chart.*

1

- Display the CHART TOOLS DESIGN tab.

- Tap or click the 'Change Chart Type' button (CHART TOOLS DESIGN tab | Type group) to display the Change Chart Type dialog box.

- Tap or click '3-D Clustered Bar' (Change Chart Type dialog box) in the right pane to change the chart type (Figure 8–57).

🔎 **Experiment**

- If you are using a mouse, point to the chart preview in the dialog box to see in more detail how the chart will look in the document.

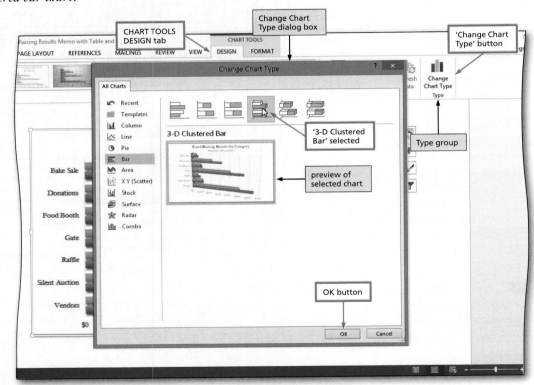

Figure 8–57

2

- Tap or click the OK button to change the chart type (Figure 8–58).

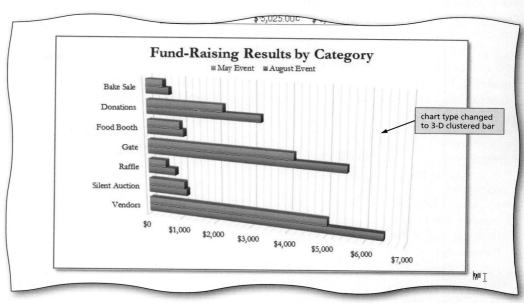

Figure 8–58

To Save an Active Document with a New File Name and Close the File

You would like to save the document with the 3-D clustered chart with a different file name. Thus, the following steps save the document.

1 Open the Backstage view and then tap or click the Save As tab to display the Save As gallery.

2 Navigate to the desired save location and save the document with the file name, Fund-Raising Results Memo with Table and 3-D Clustered Chart.

TO CHART A WORD TABLE USING MICROSOFT GRAPH

In previous versions of Word, you charted Word tables using an embedded program called Microsoft Graph, or simply Graph. When working with the chart, Graph has its own menus and commands because it is a program embedded in Word. Using Graph commands, you can modify the appearance of the chart after you create it. If you wanted to create a chart using the legacy Graph program, you would perform these steps.

1. Select the rows and columns or table to be charted.
2. Display the INSERT tab.
3. Tap or click the Object button (INSERT tab | Text group) to display the Object dialog box.
4. If necessary, tap or click the Create New tab (Object dialog box).
5. Scroll to and then select 'Microsoft Graph Chart' in the Object type list to specify the object being inserted.
6. Tap or click the OK button to start the Microsoft Graph program, which creates a chart of the selected table or selected rows and columns.

To View and Scroll through Documents Side by Side

1 INSERT COMMENTS & TRACK CHANGES | 2 REVIEW COMMENTS & TRACKED CHANGES
3 LINK EXCEL WORKSHEET TO WORD DOCUMENT | 4 CHART WORD TABLE | 5 CREATE & PUBLISH BLOG POST

Word provides a way to display two documents side by side, each in a separate window. By default, the two documents scroll synchronously, that is, together. If necessary, you can turn off synchronous scrolling so that you can scroll through each document individually. The following steps display documents side by side. *Why? You would like to see the how the document with the clustered chart looks alongside the document with the 3-D clustered chart.*

1

- Position the insertion point at the top of the document because you want to begin viewing side by side from the top of the documents.

- Open the file called Fund-Raising Results Memo with Table and Clustered Chart so that both documents are open in Word.

- Display the VIEW tab (Figure 8–59).

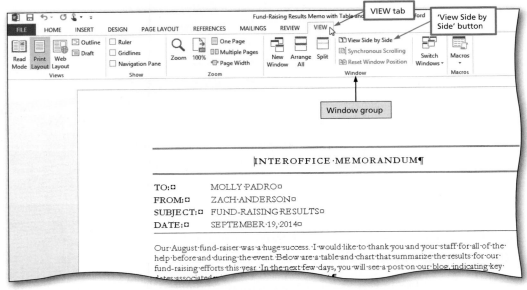

Figure 8–59

2

- Tap or click the 'View Side by Side' button (VIEW tab | Window group) to display each open window side by side (Figure 8–60).

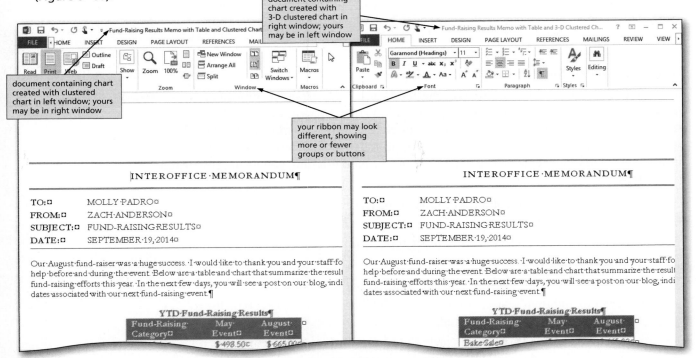

Figure 8–60

• If necessary, adjust the zoom to fit the memo contents in each window.

• Scroll to the bottom of one of the windows and notice how both windows (documents) scroll together (Figure 8–61).

Q&A Can I scroll through one window separately from the other?
By default, synchronous scrolling is active when you display windows side by side. If you want to scroll separately through the windows, simply turn off synchronous scrolling.

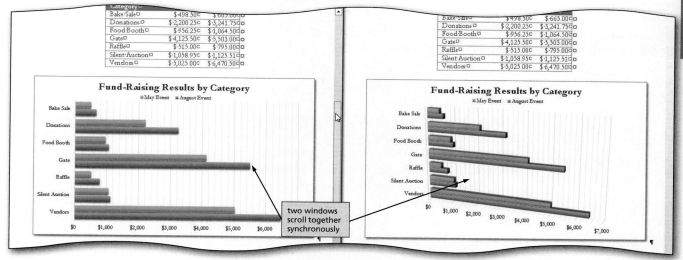

Figure 8–61

• If necessary, display the VIEW tab (in either window).

• Tap or click the Synchronous Scrolling button (VIEW tab | Window group) to turn off synchronous scrolling.

⑤

• Scroll to the top of the window on the right and notice that the window on the left does not scroll because you turned off synchronous scrolling (Figure 8–62).

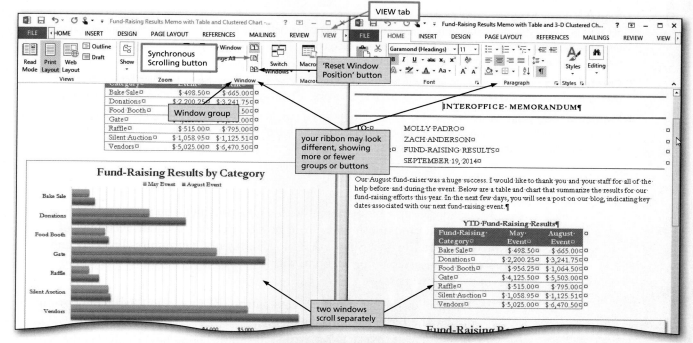

Figure 8–62

Q&A What is the purpose of the 'Reset Window Position' button?
It repositions the side-by-side windows so that each consumes the same amount of screen space.

6

- In either window, tap or click the 'View Side by Side' button (VIEW tab | Window group) to turn off side-by-side viewing and display each window in the full screen.

- Close each open Word document, saving them if prompted.

Break Point: If you wish to take a break, this is a good place to do so. You can exit Word now. To resume at a later time, run Word and continue following the steps from this location forward.

Creating a Blog Post

A **blog**, short for **weblog**, is an informal website consisting of date- or time-stamped articles, or **posts**, in a diary or journal format, usually listed in reverse chronological order. Blogs reflect the interests, opinions, and personalities of the author, called the **blogger**, and sometimes of the website visitors as well.

Blogs have become an important means of worldwide communications. Businesses create blogs to communicate with employees, customers, and vendors. Teachers create blogs to collaborate with other teachers and students, and home users create blogs to share aspects of their personal life with family, friends, and others.

This section of the chapter creates a blog post and then publishes it to a registered blog account at WordPress, which is a blogging service on the web. The blog relays current events for the Yellville Community Center. This specific blog post is a communication about the fund-raisers.

CONSIDER THIS

What should you consider when creating and posting on a blog?

When creating a blog post, you should follow these general guidelines:

1. **Create a blog account on the web.** Many websites exist that allow users to set up a blog free or for a fee. Blogging services that work with Word 2013 include Blogger, SharePoint blog, Telligent Community, TypePad, and WordPress. For illustration purposes in this chapter, a free blog account was created at WordPress.com.

2. **Register your blog account in Word.** Before you can use Word to publish a blog post, you must register your blog account in Word. This step establishes a connection between Word and your blog account. The first time you create a new blog post, Word will ask if you want to register a blog account. You can tap or click the Register Later button if you want to learn how to create a blog post without registering a blog account.

3. **Create a blog post.** Use Word to enter the text and any graphics in your blog post. Some blogging services accept graphics directly from a Word blog post. Others require that you use a picture hosting service to store pictures you use in a blog post.

4. **Publish a blog post.** When you publish a blog post, the blog post in the Word document is copied to your account at the blogging service. Once the post is published, it appears at the top of the blog webpage. You may need to tap or click the Refresh button in the browser window to display the new post.

To Register a Blog Account

Once you set up a blog account with a blog provider, you must register it in Word so that you can publish your Word post on the blog account. Examples of blog providers are Blogger, SharePoint blog, Telligent Community, TypePad, and WordPress. To register a blog account, with WordPress for example, you would perform the following steps.

1. Tap or click the Manage Accounts button (BLOG POST tab | Blog group) to display the Blog Accounts dialog box.

2. Tap or click the New button (Blog Accounts dialog box) to display the New Blog Account dialog box.

3. Tap or click the Blog arrow (New Blog Account dialog box) to display a list of blog providers and then select your provider in the list.

4. Tap or click the Next button to display the New [Provider] Account dialog box (i.e., a New WordPress Account dialog box would appear if you selected WordPress as the provider).

5. In the Blog Post URL text box, replace the <Enter your blog URL here> text with the web address for your blog account. (Note that your dialog box may differ, depending on the provider you select.)

Q&A What is a URL?

A URL (Uniform Resource Locator), often called a web address, is the unique address for a webpage. For example, the web address for a WordPress blog account might be smith.wordpress.com; in that case, the complete blog post URL would read as http://smith.wordpress.com/xhlrpc.php in the text box.

6. In the Enter account information area, enter the user name and password you use to access your blog account.

Q&A Should I tap or click the Remember Password check box?

If you do not select this check box, Word will prompt you for a password each time you publish to the blog account.

7. If your blog provider does not allow pictures to be stored, tap or click the Picture Options button, select the correct option for storing your posted pictures, and then tap or click the OK button (Picture Options dialog box).

8. Tap or click the OK button to register the blog account.

9. When Word displays a dialog box indicating the account registration was successful, tap or click the OK button.

To Create a Blank Document for a Blog Post

1 INSERT COMMENTS & TRACK CHANGES | 2 REVIEW COMMENTS & TRACKED CHANGES

3 LINK EXCEL WORKSHEET TO WORD DOCUMENT | 4 CHART WORD TABLE | 5 CREATE & PUBLISH BLOG POST

The following steps create a new blank Word document for a blog post. *Why? Word provides a blog post template you can use to create a blank blog post document.*

1

- Open the Backstage view.

- Tap or click the New tab in the Backstage view to display the New gallery.

- Tap or click the Blog post thumbnail to select the template and display it in a preview window (Figure 8–63).

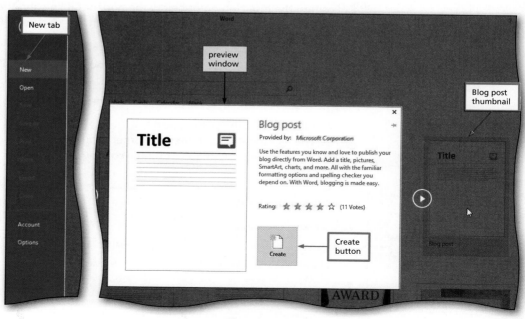

Figure 8–63

2

- Tap or click the Create button in the preview window to create a new document based on the selected template (Figure 8–64).

Q&A

What if a Register a Blog Account dialog box appears?

Tap or click the Register Later button to skip the registration process at this time. Or, if you have a blog account, you can tap or click the Register Now button and follow the instructions to register your account.

Why did the ribbon change?

When creating a blog post, the ribbon in Word changes to display only the tabs required to create and publish a blog post.

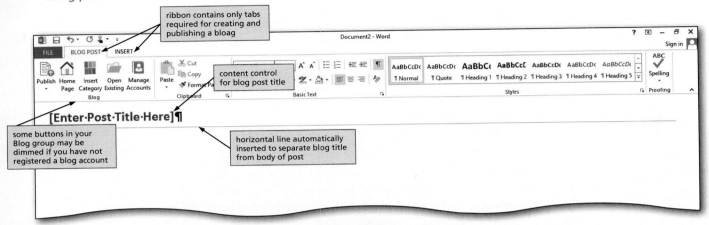

Figure 8–64

To Enter Text

The next step is to enter the blog post title and text in the blog post. The following steps enter text in the blog post.

1 Tap or click the 'Enter Post Title Here' content control and then type **Fund-Raiser Update** as the blog title.

2 Position the insertion point below the horizontal line and then type these three lines of text, pressing the ENTER key at end of each line (Figure 8–65):

Our latest fund-raiser was a huge success!

Thank you to everyone who helped before and during the event!

See the following calendar for key dates for our next event. We hope we can count on you again.

Q&A

Can I format text in the blog post?

Yes, you can use the Basic Text and other groups on the ribbon to format the post. You also can check spelling using the Proofing group.

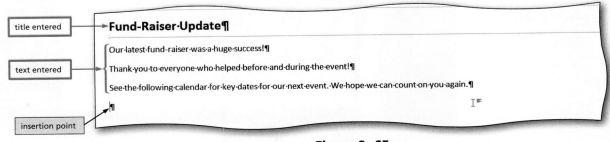

Figure 8–65

To Insert a Quick Table

Word provides several quick tables, which are preformatted table styles that you can customize. Calendar formats are one type of quick table. The following steps insert a calendar in the blog. *Why? You will post the upcoming key fund-raiser dates in the calendar.*

1

- Display the INSERT tab.

- With the insertion point positioned as shown in Figure 8–65, tap or click the 'Add a Table' button (INSERT tab | Tables group) to display the Add a Table gallery.

- Tap or point to Quick Tables in the Add a Table gallery to display the Quick Tables gallery (Figure 8–66).

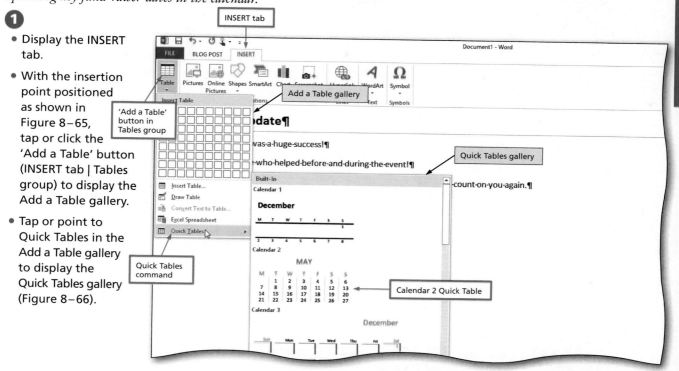

Figure 8–66

2

- Tap or click Calendar 2 in the Quick Tables gallery to insert the selected Quick Table in the document at the location of the insertion point (Figure 8–67).

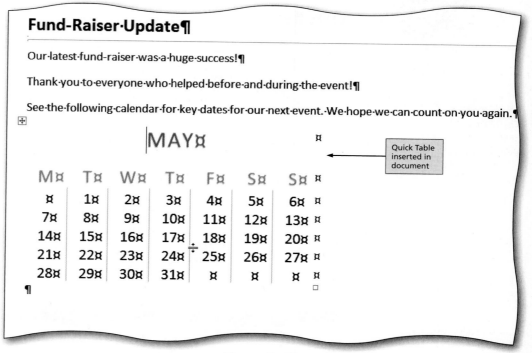

Figure 8–67

To Edit and Format a Table

The calendar in the blog post should show the month of October with a first day of the month starting on Wednesday. The following steps edit the table and apply a quick style.

1 Change the month in the first cell of the table from May to October.

2 Edit the contents of the cells in the table so that the first day of the month starts on a Wednesday and the 31 (the last day of the month) is on a Friday.

3 Enter the text in the appropriate cells for October 1, 7, 16, 22, and 25, as shown in Figure 8–68.

4 If necessary, display the TABLE TOOLS DESIGN tab.

5 Remove the check mark from the First Column check box (TABLE TOOLS DESIGN tab | Table Style Options group) because you do not want the first column in the table formatted differently.

6 Apply the 'Grid Table 1 Light - Accent 5' table style to the table.

7 If necessary, left-align the heading and resize the table column widths to 0.8".

8 Make any other necessary adjustments so that the table appears as shown in Figure 8–68.

BTW
Certification
The Microsoft Office Specialist (MOS) program provides an opportunity for you to obtain a valuable industry credential — proof that you have the Word 2013 skills required by employers. For more information, visit the Certification resource on the Student Companion Site located on www .cengagebrain.com. For detailed instructions about accessing available resources, visit www.cengage.com/ ct/studentdownload or contact your instructor for information about accessing the required files.

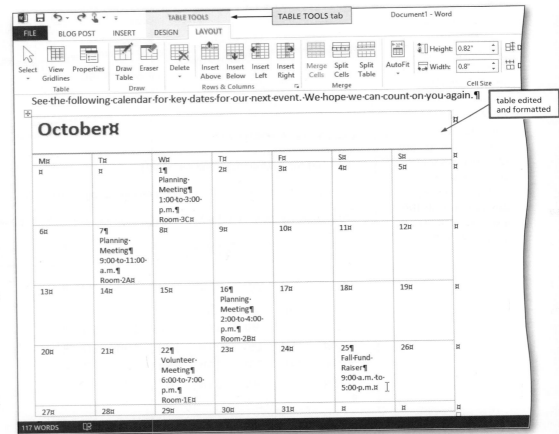

Figure 8–68

To Save an Active Document with a New File Name and Close the File

You are finished entering and formatting the content of the blog post. Thus, the following steps save the blog post.

1 Tap or click FILE on the ribbon to open the Backstage view and then tap or click the Save As tab to display the Save As gallery.

2 Navigate to the desired save location and save the document with the file name, Fund-Raising Blog.

BTW
Deleting Blog Posts
If you want to delete a blog post from your blog account, sign in to your blog account and then follow the instructions from your blog provider to delete a post from your blog.

Note: If you have not registered a blog account, read the next series of steps without performing them.

To Publish a Blog Post

1 INSERT COMMENTS & TRACK CHANGES | 2 REVIEW COMMENTS & TRACKED CHANGES
3 LINK EXCEL WORKSHEET TO WORD DOCUMENT | 4 CHART WORD TABLE | 5 CREATE & PUBLISH BLOG POST

The following step publishes the blog post. **Why?** *Publishing the blog post places the post at the top of the webpage associated with this blog account.*

1

- Display the BLOG POST tab.

- Tap or click the Publish button (BLOG POST tab | Blog group), which causes Word to display a brief message that it is contacting the blog provider and then display a message on the screen that the post was published (Figure 8–69).

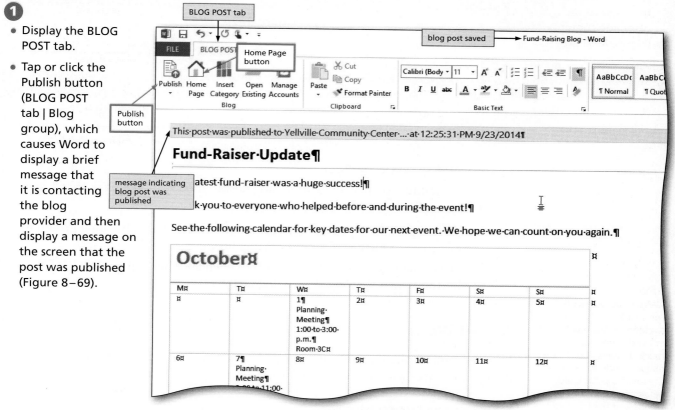

Figure 8–69

To Display a Blog Webpage in a Browser Window

1 INSERT COMMENTS & TRACK CHANGES | 2 REVIEW COMMENTS & TRACKED CHANGES
3 LINK EXCEL WORKSHEET TO WORD DOCUMENT | 4 CHART WORD TABLE | 5 CREATE & PUBLISH BLOG POST

The step on the next page displays the current blog account's webpage in a browser window. **Why?** *You can view a blog account associated with Word if you want to verify a post was successful.*

1

- Tap or click the Home Page button (BLOG POST tab | Blog group) (shown in Figure 8–69 on the previous page), which runs the default browser (Internet Explorer, in this case) and displays the webpage associated with the registered blog account in the browser window. You may need to tap or click the Refresh button in your browser window to display the most current webpage contents (Figure 8–70).

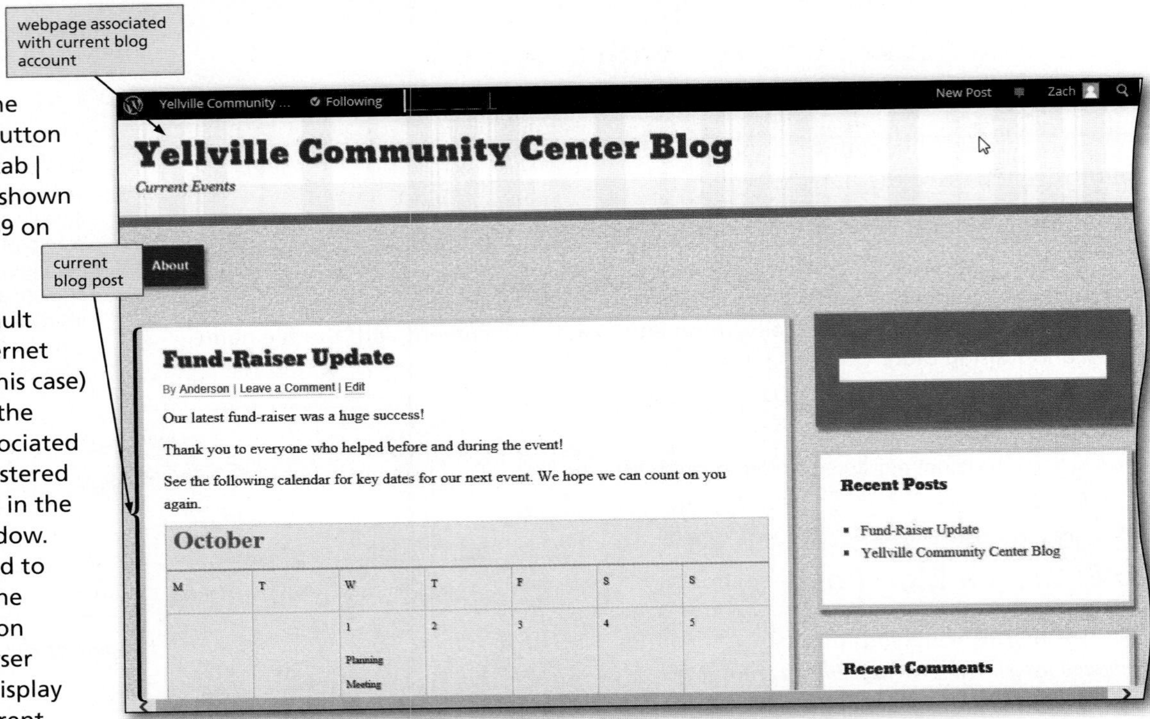

webpage associated with current blog account

current blog post

Figure 8–70

Q&A

What if the wrong webpage is displayed?

You may have multiple blog accounts registered with Word. To select a different blog account registered with Word, switch back to Word, tap or click the Manage Accounts button (BLOG POST tab | Blog group), tap or click the desired account (Blog Accounts dialog box), and then tap or click the Close button. Then, repeat Step 1.

TO OPEN AN EXISTING BLOG POST

If you wanted to open an existing blog post to modify or view it in Word, you would perform the following steps.

1. Tap or click the Open Existing button (BLOG POST tab | Blog group) to display the Open Existing Post dialog box.
2. Select the title of the post you wish to open and then tap or click the OK button (Open Existing Post dialog box).

To Exit Word

You are finished with the project in this chapter. Thus, the following steps close the open browser window and exit Word.

1 Close your browser window.

2 Exit Word.

BTW
Quick Reference
For a table that lists how to complete the tasks covered in this book using touch gestures, the mouse, ribbon, shortcut menu, and keyboard, see the Quick Reference Summary at the back of this book, or visit the Quick Reference resource on the Student Companion Site located on www.cengagebrain.com. For detailed instructions about accessing available resources, visit www.cengage.com/ct/studentdownload or contact your instructor for information about accessing the required files.

Chapter Summary

In this chapter, you have learned how to insert comments, track changes, review tracked changes, compare documents and combine documents, link or embed an Excel worksheet to a Word document, chart a table and format the chart, and create and publish a blog post. The items listed below include all the new Word skills you have learned in this chapter, with the tasks grouped by activity.

Enter and Edit Text
Insert a Comment (WD 478)
Reply to a Comment (WD 481)
Enable Tracked Changes (WD 482)
Track Changes (WD 483)
Disable Tracked Changes (WD 484)
Use the Reviewing Task Pane (WD 484)
Display Tracked Changes and Comments
    as Simple Markup (WD 486)
Show All Markup (WD 486)
View Comments (WD 488)
Delete a Comment (WD 488)
Mark Comments as Done (WD 489)
Delete All Comments (WD 489)
Review Tracked Changes (WD 489)
Accept or Reject All Tracked Changes (WD 491)
Compare Documents (WD 493)
Combine Revisions from Multiple Authors (WD 494)
Show Tracked Changes and Comments by a Single
    Reviewer (WD 497)
Link an Excel Worksheet to a Word
    Document (WD 501)
Embed an Excel Worksheet in a Word
    Document (WD 502)
Edit a Linked Object (WD 503)
Break a Link (WD 503)

File Management
Print Markups (WD 487)

Word Settings
Change Reviewer Information (WD 480)
Customize the Status Bar (WD 482)
Change How Markups and Comments Are
    Displayed (WD 484)
View and Scroll through Documents Side
    by Side (WD 518)

Work with Blogs
Register a Blog Account (WD 520)
Create a Blank Document for a Blog Post (WD 521)
Publish a Blog Post (WD 525)
Display a Blog Webpage in a Browser
    Window (WD 525)
Open an Existing Blog Post (WD 526)

Work with Charts
Chart a Table (WD 505)
Remove a Data Series from a Chart (WD 508)
Apply a Chart Style (WD 509)
Change Colors of a Chart (WD 510)
Add a Chart Element (WD 510)
Select a Chart Element and Edit It (WD 512)
Format Chart Elements (WD 512)
Add an Outline to a Chart (WD 515)
Change a Chart Type (WD 516)
Chart a Word Table Using Microsoft
    Graph (WD 517)

Work with Tables
Insert a Quick Table (WD 523)

What decisions will you need to make when creating documents to share or publish?
Use these guidelines as you complete the assignments in this chapter and create your own shared documents outside of this class.

1. If sharing documents, be certain received files and copied objects are virus free.

    a) Do not open files created by others until you are certain they do not contain a virus or other malicious program (malware).

    b) Use an antivirus program to verify that any files you use are free of viruses and other potentially harmful programs.

2. If necessary, determine how to copy an object.

    a) Your intended use of the Word document will help determine the best method for copying the object: copy and paste, embed, or link.

3. Enhance a document with appropriate visuals.

    a) Use visuals to add interest, clarify ideas, and illustrate points. Visuals include tables, charts, and graphical images (i.e., pictures or clip art).

4. If desired, post communications on a blog.

CONSIDER THIS: PLAN AHEAD

✹ **How should you submit solutions to questions in the assignments identified with a** ✹ **symbol?**
Every assignment in this book contains one or more questions identified with a ✹ symbol. These questions require you to think beyond the assigned document. Present your solutions to the questions in the format required by your instructor. Possible formats may include one or more of these options: write the answer; create a document that contains the answer; present your answer to the class; discuss your answer in a group; record the answer as audio or video using a webcam, smartphone, or portable media player; or post answers on a blog, wiki, or website.

Apply Your Knowledge

Reinforce the skills and apply the concepts you learned in this chapter.

Working with Comments and Tracked Changes

Note: To complete this assignment, you will be required to use the Data Files for Students. Visit www.cengage.com/ct/studentdownload for detailed instructions or contact your instructor for information about accessing the required files.

Instructions: Run Word. Open the document Apply 8-1 Near Field Communications Draft from the Data Files for Students. The document includes two paragraphs of text that contain tracked changes and comments. You are to insert additional tracked changes and comments, accept and reject tracked changes, and delete comments.

Perform the following tasks:

1. If necessary, customize the status bar so that it displays the TRACK CHANGES indicator.

2. Enable (turn on) tracked changes.

3. If requested by your instructor, change the user name and initials so that your name and initials are displayed in the tracked changes and comments.

4. Use the REVIEW tab to navigate to the first comment. Follow the instruction in the comment. Be sure tracked changes are on when you add the required text to the document.

5. When you have finished making the change, reply to the comment with a new comment that includes a message stating you completed the requested task. Mark the comment as done. How does a comment marked as done differ from the other comments? What color are the WU markups? What color are your markups?

6. Navigate to the remaining comments and read through each one.

7. Insert the following comment for the word, wristbands, in the last sentence of the first paragraph: Should this be two words?

8. With tracked changes on, change the word, items, in the third sentence to the word, objects.

9. Edit the comment entered in Step 7 to add this sentence: Be sure to look it up in the dictionary or a dictionary app.

10. Print the document with tracked changes.

11. Print only the tracked changes.

12. Save the document with the file name, Apply 8-1 Near Field Communications Reviewed (Figure 8–71).

13. Show only your tracked changes in the document. Show all users' tracked changes in the document.

14. Reject the insertion of the words, that are, in the first sentence.

15. Delete the comment that begins with the words, Reject the tracked change…

16. Insert the word, successful, as a tracked change at the beginning of the second paragraph as instructed in the comment.

17. Accept all the remaining edits in the document.

18. Delete all the remaining comments.

19. Disable (turn off) tracked changes. Remove the TRACK CHANGES indicator from the status bar.

20. If requested by your instructor, add your name on a line below the second paragraph. Save the modified file with a new file name, Apply 8-1 Near Field Communications Final. Submit the documents in the format specified by your instructor.

21. ✱ Answer the questions posed in #5. How would you change the color of your tracked changes?

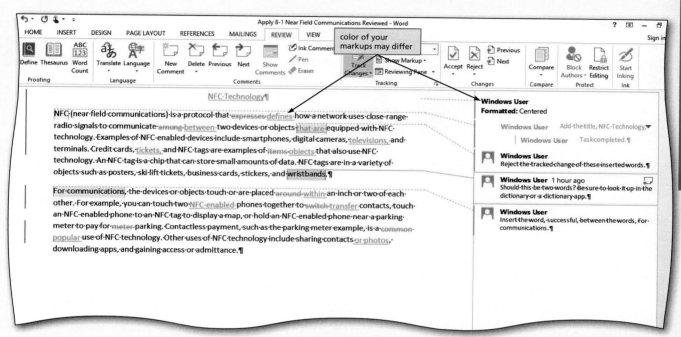

Figure 8–71

Extend Your Knowledge

Extend the skills you learned in this chapter and experiment with new skills. You may need to use Help to complete the assignment.

Using Microsoft Graph to Create a Chart

Note: To complete this assignment, you will be required to use the Data Files for Students. Visit www.cengage.com/ct/studentdownload for detailed instructions or contact your instructor for information about accessing the required files.

Instructions: Run Word. Open the document Extend 8-1 Library Seminar Attendees Memo Draft from the Data Files for Students. You will use Microsoft Graph to chart the table in the memo (Figure 8–72 on the next page).

Continued >

Extend Your Knowledge *continued*

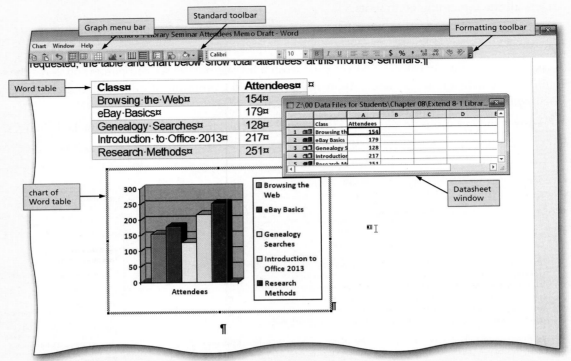

Figure 8–72

Perform the following tasks:

1. Search the web to learn about Microsoft Graph. What is Microsoft Graph?

2. Select the table in the memo to be charted and then follow the steps on page WD 517 to insert a Microsoft Graph chart. Close the Datasheet window.

3. Tap or click the Help on the menu bar in the Graph window and then tap or click 'Microsoft Graph Help' to open the Graph Help window. Browse through the help information to learn how to use Graph.

4. Tap or click the By Column button on the Standard toolbar to plot the data by column instead of by row. What text appears along the horizontal axis now?

5. Move the legend to the bottom of the chart.

6. Change the chart type to a bar chart.

7. Display the categories on the category axis in reverse order, leaving the value axis at the bottom. (*Hint*: Select the Scale tab in Format Axis dialog box and then place check marks in all three check boxes.) If necessary, also change the number of tick marks between items to show all classes.

8. Change the color of the chart area.

9. Change the color of the series "Attendees," which changes the color of the bars.

10. If they are not displayed already, display value axis gridlines.

11. If necessary, drag the chart to center it below the table.

12. If requested by your instructor, change the name at the top of the memo to your name. Save the modified file with a new file name, Apply 8-1 Library Seminar Attendees Memo Final. Submit the documents in the format specified by your instructor.

13. ✺ Answer the question posed in #4. Do you prefer using Microsoft Graph or the CHART TOOLS tab to create a chart in Word? Why?

Analyze, Correct, Improve

Analyze a document, correct all errors, and improve it.

Editing and Formatting a Quick Table and a Chart

Note: To complete this assignment, you will be required to use the Data Files for Students. Visit www.cengage.com/ct/studentdownload for detailed instructions or contact your instructor for information about accessing the required files.

Instructions: Run Word. Open the document Analyze 8-1 Home Plans Memo Draft from the Data Files for Students. The document is a memo that is missing a table and whose chart is not formatted properly. You are to insert, format, and edit a Quick Table and edit a chart.

Perform the following tasks:

1. Correct In the letter, correct the following items:

a. Above the chart and below the Home Plan Breakdown title, insert the Tabular List Quick Table (Figure 8–73). Change the values in the header row and first six table rows as follows: Header row, first column: Style; Header row, second column: Plans; first data row, first column: Colonial; first data row, second column: 1,728; second data row, first column: Contemporary; second data row, second column: 2,582; third data row, first column: European; third data row, second column: 4,820; fourth data row, first column: Ranch; fourth data row, second column: 3,928; fifth data row, first column: Tudor; fifth data row, second column: 1,882; sixth data row, first column: Victorian; sixth data row, second column: 2,058. Delete the last two rows in the table.

b. Select the chart and then display the chart spreadsheet window. Edit the contents of the chart spreadsheet window to match the table in the document.

c. Resize the chart so that all data is readable.

d. Delete the legend.

e. Change the chart type to a type other than line.

f. Format the numbers on the vertical axis to show a comma separator.

g. Change the color of the data series.

h. Add a chart title, category (x) axis title, and horizontal (value) axis title. Add color to each of these titles.

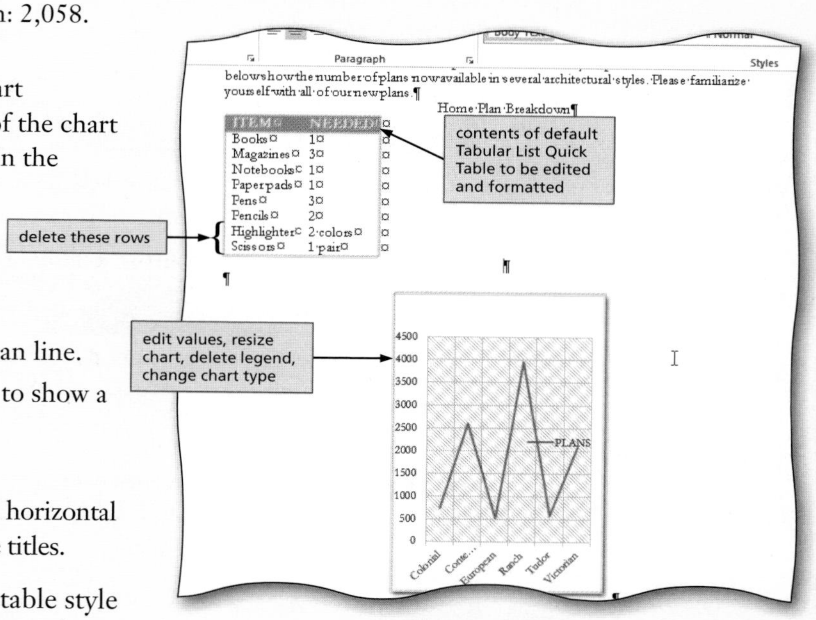

2. Improve Enhance the letter by applying a table style of your choice to the table, centering the table, right-aligning the number values in the table, and resizing columns as appropriate. Apply a chart style of your choice to the chart. Make any other adjustments you deem appropriate to the letter. If requested by your instructor, change the name of the sales manager to your name. Save the modified document with the file name, Analyze 8-1 Home Plans Memo Final, and then submit it in the format specified by your instructor.

3. ✳ Would you prefer to edit the chart values in Excel instead of the chart spreadsheet window? Why or why not?

Figure 8–73

In the Labs

Design and/or create a document using the guidelines, concepts, and skills presented in this chapter. Labs 1 and 2, which increase in difficulty, require you to create solutions based on what you learned in the chapter; Lab 3 requires you to create a solution, which uses cloud and web technologies, by learning and investigating on your own from general guidance.

Lab 1: Creating a Memo with an Excel Table and Chart

Note: To complete this assignment, you will be required to use the Data Files for Students. Visit www.cengage.com/ct/studentdownload for detailed instructions or contact your instructor for information about accessing the required files.

Problem: Your supervisor has asked you to prepare a memo that contains an Excel table and a chart comparing current and projected school enrollments. (*Note:* If you do not have Excel on your computer, create the table using Word instead of importing it from Excel.) You prepare the document shown in Figure 8–74.

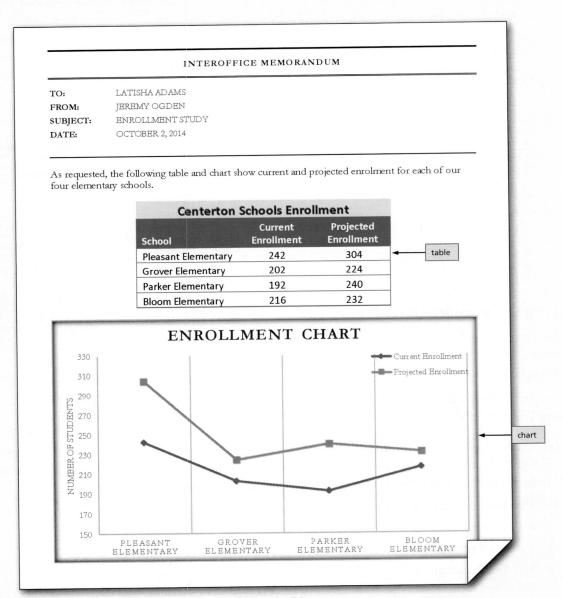

Figure 8–74

Perform the following tasks:

1. Use the Memo (elegant) template to create a new memo and then enter all text in the memo, as shown in the figure. Delete the row containing the cc in the header. Remove the first line indent from the paragraphs below the header. (*Hint*: Use the Paragraph Settings Dialog Box Launcher.)

2. Link the worksheet in the Lab 8-1 School Enrollment in Excel workbook, which is on the Data Files for Students, to the Word memo below the paragraph. If you do not have Excel on your computer, create the table in Word. Change the column width to AutoFit Contents. Center the table.

3. Break the link between the Excel table in the Word document and the Excel worksheet in the Excel workbook. If necessary, resize the table so that it looks like the one in Figure 8–74.

4. Insert a Line with Markers chart, centered below the table.

   a. Copy the rows from the table to the chart spreadsheet window. Remove the Series 3 data series from the chart spreadsheet.

   b. Apply the Style 11 chart style to the chart.

   c. Change the colors to Color 2.

   d. Add a vertical axis title, NUMBER OF STUDENTS.

   e. Change the chart title to ENROLLMENT CHART.

   f. Move the legend so that it appears at the top, right of the chart. Remove the check mark from the 'Show the legend without overlapping the chart' check box. If necessary, position the legend as shown in the figure.

   g. Format the vertical axis so that its minimum value (starting point) is 150.

   h. Adjust spacing above and below paragraphs as necessary so that all of the memo contents fit on a single page.

5. If requested by your instructor, change the name at the top of the memo from Latisha Adams to your name.

6. Save the document with Lab 8-1 School Enrollment Projections as the file name and then submit it in the format specified by your instructor.

7. ☀ This lab instructed you to remove the first line indent from the paragraphs in the memo. Why do you think this was requested?

Lab 2: **Working with Comments and Tracked Changes**

Note: To complete this assignment, you will be required to use the Data Files for Students. Visit www.cengage.com/ct/studentdownload for detailed instructions or contact your instructor for information about accessing the required files.

Problem: Your supervisor has asked you to prepare a draft of a memo, showing all tracked changes and comments. You mark up the document shown in Figure 8–75.

Perform the following tasks:

1. Open the document Lab 8-2 ATM Safety Draft from the Data Files for Students.

2. Insert the comments and track all changes shown in Figure 8–75 on the next page.

3. Save the document with the file name, Lab 8-2 ATM Safety Draft with Markups.

4. Make the changes indicated in the comments and then delete the comments in the document.

5. Accept all tracked changes in the document.

6. Save the document with the file name, Lab 8-2 ATM Safety Final.

Continued >

In the Labs *continued*

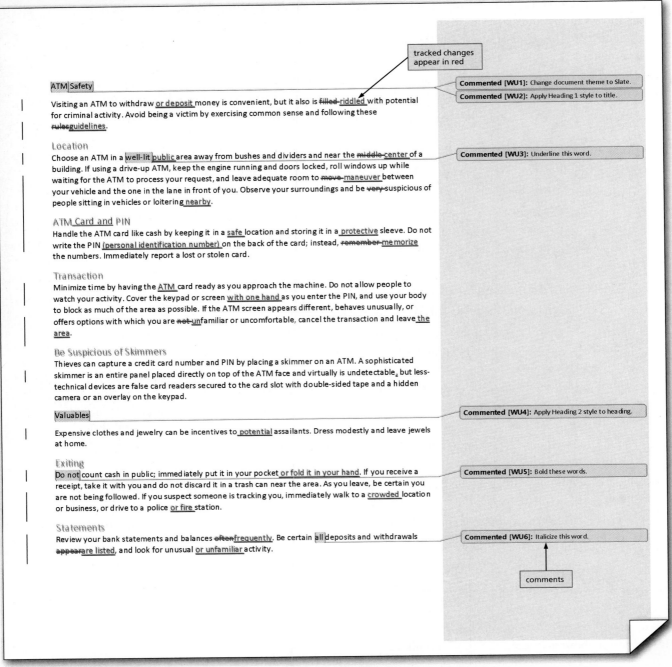

Figure 8–75

7. Compare the Lab 8-2 ATM Safety Draft file (original document) with the Lab 8-2 ATM Safety Final file (revised document). Save the compare result with the file name, Lab 8-2 Safety Compared.

8. Close all windows and then open the Lab 8-2 ATM Safety Compared file. Print the document with markups. Use the REVIEW tab to review each change. Close the document without saving.

9. ✸ How could you determine if two documents contained the same content?

Lab 3: Expand Your World: Cloud and Web Technologies
Creating a Blog Account Using a Blogger Service

Problem: You would like to create a blog account so that you can use Word for blog posts. You research a variety of blogging services and select one for use (Figure 8–76).

Note: You will use a blog account, many of which you can create at no cost, to complete this assignment. If you do not want to create a blog account, read this assignment without performing the instructions.

Instructions: Perform the following tasks:

1. Run a browser. Research these blogging services: Blogger, SharePoint blog, Telligent Community, TypePad, and WordPress.

2. Navigate to the blogger service with which you want to set up an account and then follow the instructions to set up an account.

3. Set up your blog in the blogger service.

4. In Word, register your blog account (see instructions on page WD 520 and WD 521).

5. Create a blog post in Word and then publish your blog post to your account.

6. ✺ Which blogger service did you select and why? Would you recommend this blogger service? Why or why not?

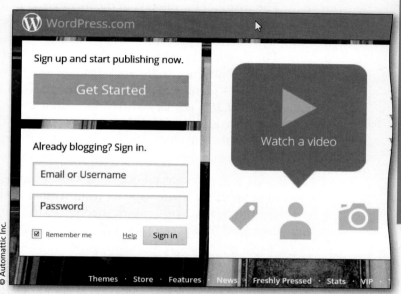

Figure 8–76

© Automattic Inc.

Consider This: Your Turn

Apply your creative thinking and problem solving skills to design and implement a solution.

1: Create a Memo for a Side Job

Personal

Part 1: You and a friend have decided to wash, wax, and detail cars to earn extra cash while attending school. To advertise your services on campus, you need to write a memo to the office of career development that outlines prices of your services. Write the memo to Julio Martinez. Use today's date. The memo should contain a table and chart as specified below.

The wording for the text in the memo is as follows: Jon and Jim at Two Friends Cleaning Services wash, wax, and detail all sizes of cars, pick-up trucks, vans, and SUVs. The table and chart below show prices of our services.

The data for the table is as follows: compact car – wash $8.50, wax $40.00, detailing $55.00; mid-sized car – wash $10.50, wax $50.00, detailing $62.50; full-sized car – wash $12.50, wax $60.00, detailing $70.00; pick-up truck/van/SUV – wash $15.50, wax $70.00, detailing $82.50. Create a chart of all table data.

Use the concepts and techniques presented in this chapter to create and format the memo and its text, table, and chart. Be sure to check the spelling and grammar of the finished memo. Submit your assignment in the format specified by your instructor.

Part 2: ✺ You made several decisions while creating the memo in this assignment: whether to use a memo template or create a memo from scratch, and how to organize and format the memo, table, and chart (fonts, font sizes, colors, shading, styles, etc.). What was the rationale behind each of these decisions? When you proofread the document, what further revisions did you make and why?

Continued >

Consider This: Your Turn *continued*

2: Create a Memo Showing First Quarter Sales

Professional

Part 1: As assistant to the manager of a party supply store, you have been asked to create a memo showing the first quarter sales figures for the top four items. You are to write the memo to all sales staff with a subject of First Quarter Sales. Use today's date. The memo should contain a table and chart as specified below.

The wording for the text in the memo is as follows: Sales figures for the first quarter have been compiled. The table and chart below show sales for the first quarter for the top four items sold.

The data for the table is as follows: decorations – January $10,210.32, February $12,291.28, March $11,382.99; gift wrap/bags – January $7,218.31, February $10,887.19, March $6,485.21; greeting cards – January $1,986.23, February $3,798.25, March $2,669.47; and paper products – January $5,002.36, February $7,652.54, March $6,795.33. Create a chart of all table data.

Use the concepts and techniques presented in this chapter to create and format the memo and its text, table, and chart. Be sure to check the spelling and grammar of the finished memo. Submit your assignment in the format specified by your instructor.

Part 2: ☀ You made several decisions while creating the memo in this assignment: whether to use a memo template or create a memo from scratch, and how to organize and format the memo, table, and chart (fonts, font sizes, colors, shading, styles, etc.). What was the rationale behind each of these decisions? When you proofread the document, what further revisions did you make and why?

3: Create a Memo about Travel Expenses

Research and Collaboration

Your employer has asked you and two of your coworkers to research the flight, hotel, and rental car expenses for a six-day business trip from the home office in Chicago, Illinois, to a conference in Orlando, Florida. Form a three-member team to research the expenses for at least four options in each area (flight, hotel, and rental car). Each team member should research one area. As a group, create a memo that contains a table and chart presenting your findings.

Use the concepts and techniques presented in this chapter to create and format the memo and its text, table, and chart. If requested by your instructor, use team members' names in the memo. Be sure to check the spelling and grammar of the finished memo. Submit your team assignment in the format specified by your instructor.

Part 2: ☀ You made several decisions while creating the memo in this assignment: text to use, whether to use a memo template or create a memo from scratch, and how to organize and format the memo, table, and chart (fonts, font sizes, colors, shading, styles, etc.). What was the rationale behind each of these decisions? When you proofread the document, what further revisions did you make and why?

Learn Online

Reinforce what you learned in this chapter with games, exercises, training, and many other online activities and resources.

Student Companion Site Reinforcement activities and resources are available at no additional cost on www.cengagebrain.com. Visit www.cengage.com/ct/studentdownload for detailed instructions about accessing the resources available at the Student Companion Site.

SAM **SAM** Put your skills into practice with SAM! If you have a SAM account, go to www.cengage .com/sam2013 to access SAM assignments for this chapter.

9 Creating a Reference Document with a Table of Contents and an Index

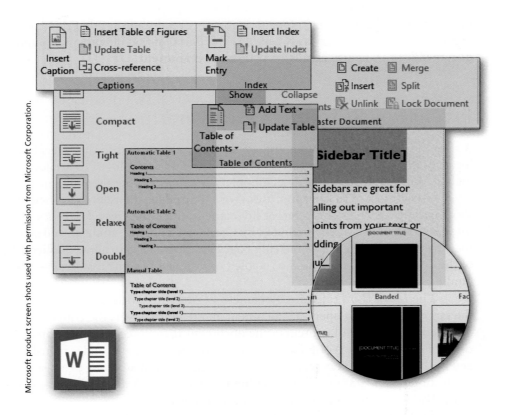

Microsoft product screen shots used with permission from Microsoft Corporation.

Objectives

You will have mastered the material in this chapter when you can:

- Insert a screenshot
- Add and modify a caption
- Create a cross-reference
- Insert and link text boxes
- Compress pictures
- Work in Outline view
- Work with a master document and subdocuments

- Insert a cover page
- Create and modify a table of contents
- Use the Navigation Pane
- Create and update a table of figures
- Build, modify, and update an index
- Create alternating footers
- Add bookmarks

9 | Creating a Reference Document with a Table of Contents and an Index

Introduction

During the course of your academic studies and professional activities, you may find it necessary to compose a document that is many pages or even hundreds of pages in length. When composing a long document, you must ensure that the document is organized so that a reader easily can locate material in that document. Sometimes a document of this nature is called a **reference document**.

Project — Reference Document

A reference document is any multipage document organized so that users easily can locate material and navigate through the document. Examples of reference documents include user guides, term papers, pamphlets, manuals, proposals, and plans.

The project in this chapter uses Word to produce the reference document shown in Figure 9–1. This reference document, titled the *Learn Word*, is a multipage information guide that is distributed by Gardner College to students and staff. Notice that the inner margin between facing pages has extra space to allow duplicated copies of the document to be bound (i.e., stapled or fastened in some manner) — without the binding covering the words.

The *Learn Word* reference document begins with a title page designed to entice the target audience to open the document and read it. Next is the copyright page, followed by the table of contents. The document then describes how to insert four types of graphics in a Word document: clip art, picture, shape, and screenshot. The end of this reference document has a table of figures and an index to assist readers in locating information contained within the document. A miniature version of the *Learn Word* reference document is shown in Figure 9–1.

The section of the *Learn Word* reference document that is titled, Inserting Various Types of Graphics in a Word Document, is a draft document that you will modify. The draft document is located on the Data Files for Students. Visit www.cengage.com/ct/studentdownload for detailed instructions or contact your instructor for information about accessing the required files. After editing the content, you will incorporate a final version in the reference document.

If you are using your finger on a touch screen and are having difficulty completing the steps in this chapter, consider using a stylus. Many people find it easier to be precise with a stylus than with a finger. In addition, with a stylus you see the pointer. If you still are having trouble completing the steps with a stylus, try using a mouse.

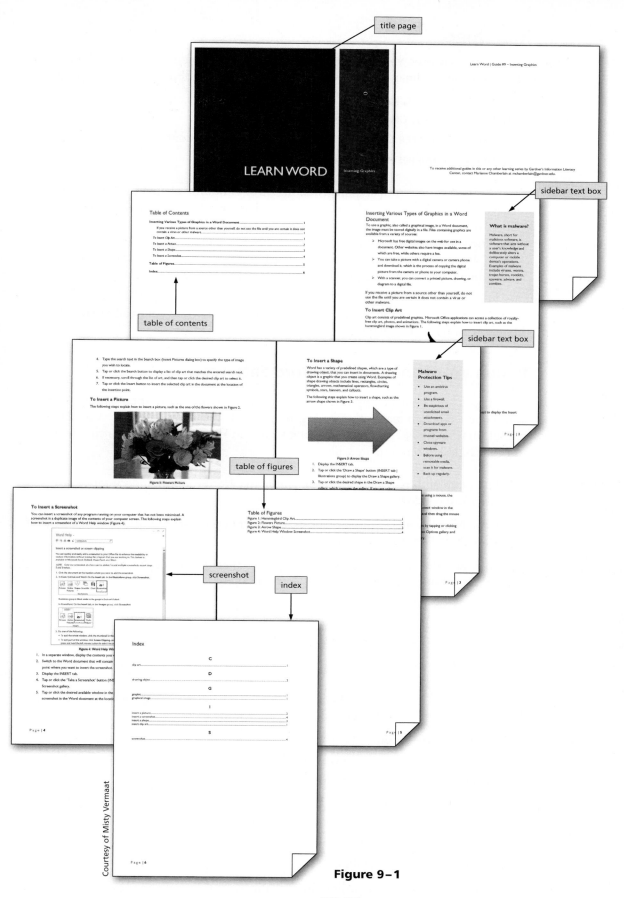

Figure 9–1

Roadmap

In this chapter, you will learn how to create the document shown in Figure 9–1. The following roadmap identifies general activities you will perform as you progress through this chapter:

1. MODIFY a draft of a REFERENCE DOCUMENT.
2. CREATE a MASTER DOCUMENT for the reference document.
3. ORGANIZE the REFERENCE DOCUMENT.

At the beginning of step instructions throughout the chapter, you will see an abbreviated form of this roadmap. The abbreviated roadmap uses colors to indicate chapter progress: gray means the chapter is beyond that activity, blue means the task being shown is covered in that activity, and black means that activity is yet to be covered. For example, the following abbreviated roadmap indicates the chapter would be showing a task in the 2 CREATE MASTER DOCUMENT activity.

1 MODIFY REFERENCE DOCUMENT | **2 CREATE MASTER DOCUMENT** | 3 ORGANIZE REFERENCE DOCUMENT

Use the abbreviated roadmap as a progress guide while you read or step through the instructions in this chapter.

To Run Word and Change Word Settings

If you are using a computer to step through the project in this chapter and you want your screens to match the figures in this book, you should change your screen's resolution to 1366×768. The following steps run Word, display formatting marks, and change the zoom to page width.

1 Run Word and create a blank document in the Word window. If necessary, maximize the Word window.

2 If the Print Layout button on the status bar is not selected, tap or click it so that your screen is in Print Layout view.

3 To display the page the same width as the document window, if necessary, tap or click the Page Width button (VIEW tab | Zoom group).

One of the few differences between Windows 7 and Windows 8 occurs in the steps to run Word. If you are using Windows 7, click the Start button, type **Word** in the 'Search programs and files' box, click Word 2013, and then, if necessary, maximize the Word window. For a summary of the steps to run Word in Windows 7, refer to the Quick Reference located at the back of this book.

Preparing a Document to Be Included in a Reference Document

Before including the Inserting Various Types of Graphics Draft document in a longer document, you will make several modifications to the document:

1. Insert a screenshot.
2. Add captions to the images in the document.
3. Insert references to the figures in the text.
4. Mark an index entry.
5. Insert text boxes that contain information about malware.
6. Compress the pictures.
7. Change the bullet symbol.

The following pages outline these changes.

How should you prepare a document to be included in a longer document?

Ensure that reference elements in a document, such as captions and index entries, are formatted properly and entered consistently.

- **Captions:** A **caption** is text that appears outside of an illustration, usually below it. If the illustration is identified with a number, the caption may include the word, Figure, along with the illustration number (i.e., Figure 1). In the caption, separate the figure number from the text of the figure by a space or punctuation mark such as a period or colon (Figure 1: Hummingbird Clip Art Image).

- **Index Entries:** If your document will include an index, read through the document and mark any terms or headings that you want to appear in the index. Include any term that the reader may want to locate quickly. Omit figures from index entries if the document will have a table of figures; otherwise, include figures in the index if appropriate.

To Open a Document from Word and Then Save It with a New File Name

The draft document that you will insert in the reference document is called Inserting Various Types of Graphics Draft. To preserve the original draft document, you create a file from the original document. The draft document is located on the Data Files for Students. Visit www.cengage.com/ct/studentdownload for detailed instructions or contact your instructor for information about accessing the required files. To preserve the contents of the original draft, you save it with a new file name. The following steps open the draft file and save it with a new file name.

1 Open the Backstage view and then tap or click the Open tab to display the Open gallery.

2 Navigate to the location of the file to be opened (in this case, the Data Files for Students folder).

3 Tap or click the file name, Inserting Various Types of Graphics Draft, to select it.

4 Tap or click the Open button (Open dialog box) to open the selected file.

5 Open the Backstage view and then tap or click the Save As tab to display the Save As gallery.

6 Display the Save As dialog box and then type `Inserting Various Types of Graphics Final` in the File name box to change the file name. Do not press the ENTER key after typing the file name because you do not want to close the dialog box at this time.

7 Navigate to the desired save location (in this case, the Word folder in the CIS 101 folder [or your class folder] on your computer or SkyDrive).

8 Tap or click the Save button (Save As dialog box) to save the document in the selected folder on the selected save location with the entered file name.

9 If the 'Show/Hide ¶' button (HOME tab | Paragraph group) is selected, tap or click it to hide formatting marks.

Q&A What if some formatting marks still appear after tapping or clicking the 'Show/Hide ¶' button?

Open the Backstage view, tap or click Options in the left pane in the Backstage view to display the Word Options dialog box, tap or click Display in the left pane (Word Options dialog box), remove the check mark from the Hidden text check box, and then tap or click the OK button.

BTW
Protected View
To keep your computer safe from potentially dangerous files, Word may automatically open certain files in a restricted mode, called Protected view. To see the Protected view settings, tap or click FILE on the ribbon to open the Backstage view, tap or click Options to display the Word Options dialog box, tap or click Trust Center in the left pane (Word Options dialog box), tap or click the 'Trust Center Settings' button in the right pane to display the Trust Center dialog box, and then tap or click Protected View in the left pane to show the current Protected view settings.

BTW
The Ribbon and Screen Resolution
Word may change how the groups and buttons within the groups appear on the ribbon, depending on the computer's screen resolution. Thus, your ribbon may look different from the ones in this book if you are using a screen resolution other than 1366 × 768.

10 Display the VIEW tab and then tap or click the Multiple Pages button (VIEW tab | Zoom group) to see all three pages of the document at once (Figure 9–2).

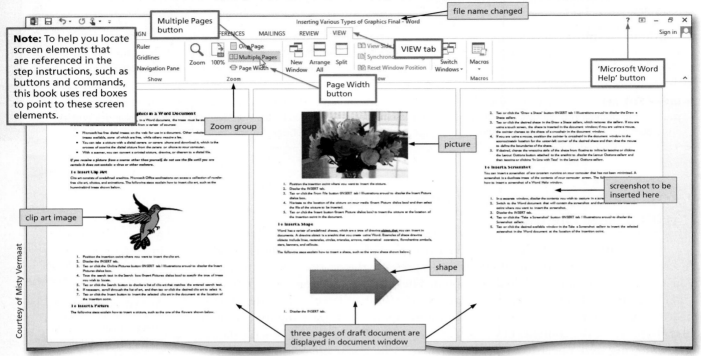

Figure 9–2

11 When you have finished viewing the document, tap or click the Page Width button (VIEW tab | Zoom group) to display the document as wide as possible in the document window.

To Insert a Screenshot

1 MODIFY REFERENCE DOCUMENT | 2 CREATE MASTER DOCUMENT | 3 ORGANIZE REFERENCE DOCUMENT

A **screenshot** is a duplicate image of the contents of your computer or mobile device's screen. The current document is missing a screenshot of a Word Help window. To insert a screenshot, you first must display the screen of which you want a screenshot in a window on your computer or mobile device. *Why? From within Word, you can insert a screenshot of any program running on your computer, provided the program has not been minimized.* The following steps insert a screenshot in a document.

1

• Display the contents you want to capture in a screenshot (in this case, tap or click the 'Microsoft Word Help' button on the title bar to open the Help window, type **screenshots** in the 'Search online help' text box, tap or click the 'Search online help' button, tap or click the 'Insert a screenshot or clipping' link to display the associated help information. If necessary, resize the Word Help window. (Figure 9–3).

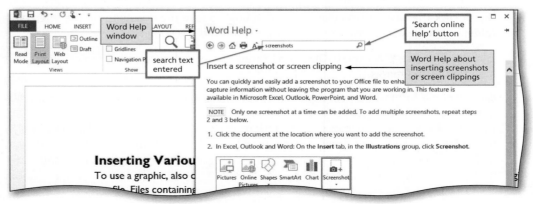

Figure 9–3

2

- In the Word window, position the insertion point in the document where the screenshot should be inserted (in this case, on the centered blank line above the numbered list in the To Insert a Screenshot section at the bottom of the document).

- Display the INSERT tab.

- Tap or click the 'Take a Screenshot' button (INSERT tab | Illustrations group) to display the Take a Screenshot gallery (Figure 9–4).

Q&A What is a screen clipping?
A screen clipping is a section of a window. When you select Screen Clipping in the Take a Screenshot gallery, the window turns opaque so that you can drag through the part of the window to be included in the document.

Why does my Take a Screenshot gallery show more windows?
You have additional programs running in windows on your desktop.

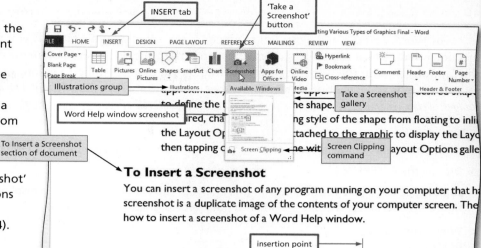

Figure 9–4

3

- Tap or click the Word Help window screenshot in the Take a Screenshot gallery to insert the selected screenshot in the Word document at the location of the insertion point.

- Tap or click the Shape Height and Shape Width box down arrows (PICTURE TOOLS FORMAT tab | Size group) as many times as necessary to resize the screenshot to approximately 5" tall by 4.76" wide (Figure 9–5).

Q&A What if my text appears on a separate page from the screenshot?
Depending on settings, the text may move to the next page.

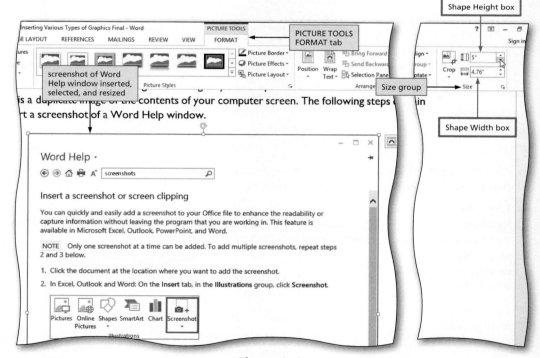

Figure 9–5

To Add a Caption

In Word, you can add a caption to an equation, a figure, and a table. If you move, delete, or add captions in a document, Word renumbers remaining captions in the document automatically. In this reference document, the captions contain the word, Figure, followed by the figure number, a colon, and a figure description. The following steps add a caption to a graphic, specifically, the screenshot. *Why? The current document contains four images: a clip art image, a picture, a shape, and a screenshot. All of these images should have captions.*

①

- If the screenshot is not selected already, tap or click it to select the graphic for which you want a caption.

- Display the REFERENCES tab.

- Tap or click the Insert Caption button (REFERENCES tab | Captions group) to display the Caption dialog box with a figure number automatically assigned to the selected graphic (Figure 9–6).

Why is the figure number a 1?
No other captions have been assigned in this document yet. When you insert a new caption, or move or delete items containing captions, Word automatically updates caption numbers throughout the document.

What if the Caption text box has the label Table or Equation instead of Figure?
Tap or click the Label arrow (Caption dialog box) and then tap or click Figure in the Label list.

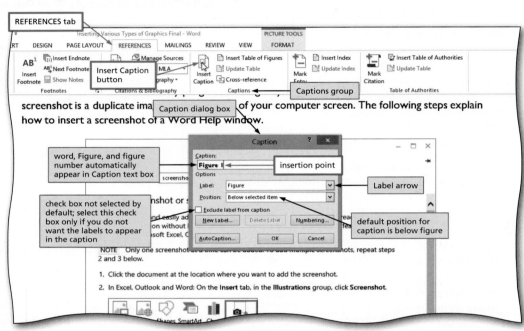

Figure 9–6

②

- Press the COLON (:) key and then press the SPACEBAR in the Caption text box (Caption dialog box) to place separating characters between the figure number and description.

- Type **Help Window Screenshot** as the figure description (Figure 9–7).

Can I change the format of the caption number?
Yes, tap or click the Numbering button (Caption dialog box), adjust the format as desired, and then tap or click the OK button.

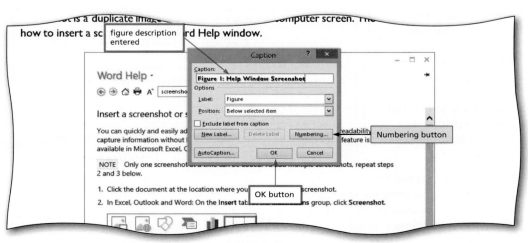

Figure 9–7

③

- Tap or click the OK button to insert the caption below the selected graphic.

- If necessary, scroll to display the caption in the document window (Figure 9–8).

How do I change the position of a caption?
Tap or click the Position arrow (Caption dialog box) and then select the desired position of the caption.

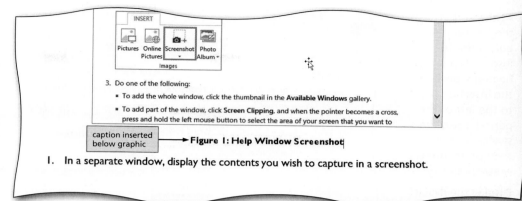

Figure 9–8

Caption Numbers

Each caption number contains a field. In Word, recall that a **field** is a placeholder for data that can change in a document. Examples of fields you have used in previous projects are page numbers, merge fields, IF fields, and the current date. You update caption numbers using the same technique used to update any other field. That is, to update all caption numbers, select the entire document and then press the F9 key, or press and hold or right-click the field and then tap or click Update Field on the shortcut menu. When you print a document, Word updates the caption numbers automatically, regardless of whether the document window displays the updated caption numbers.

To Hide White Space

White space is the space displayed in the margins at the top and bottom of pages (including any headers and footers) and also space between pages. To make it easier to see the text in this document as you scroll through it, the following step hides white space.

① If you are using a touch screen, double-tap in the space between pages; if you are using a mouse, position the pointer in the document window in the space between the pages and then double-click when the pointer changes to a 'Hide White Space' button to hide white space.

BTW
Captions
If a caption appears with extra characters inside curly braces ({ }), Word is displaying field codes instead of field results. Press ALT+F9 to display captions correctly as field results. If Word prints fields codes for captions, tap or click FILE on the ribbon to open the Backstage view, tap or click Options in the Backstage view to display the Word Options dialog box, tap or click Advanced in the left pane (Word Options dialog box), scroll to the Print section in the right pane, remove the check mark from the 'Print field codes instead of their values' check box, tap or click the OK button, and then print the document again.

To Create a Cross-Reference
1 MODIFY REFERENCE DOCUMENT | 2 CREATE MASTER DOCUMENT | 3 ORGANIZE REFERENCE DOCUMENT

The next step in this project is to add a reference to the new figure. *Why? In reference documents, the text should reference each figure specifically and, if appropriate, explain the contents of the figure.*

Because figures may be inserted, deleted, or moved, you may not know the actual figure number in the final document. For this reason, Word provides a method of creating a **cross-reference**, which is a link to an item, such as a heading, caption, or footnote in a document. By creating a cross-reference to the caption, the text that mentions the figure will be updated whenever the caption to the figure is updated. The steps on the next page create a cross-reference.

1

- At the end of the last sentence below the To Insert a Screenshot heading, position the insertion point to the left of the period, press the SPACEBAR, and then press the LEFT PARENTHESIS key.

- Display the INSERT tab.

- Tap or click the 'Insert Cross-reference' button (INSERT tab | Links group) to display the Cross-reference dialog box (Figure 9–9).

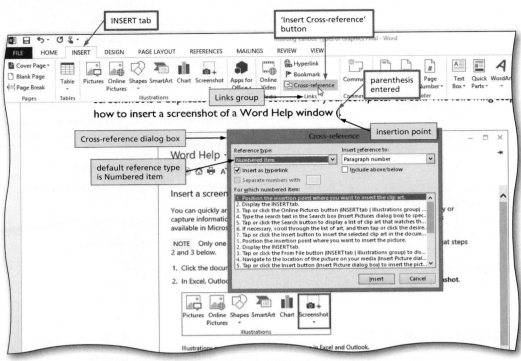

Figure 9–9

2

- Tap or click the Reference type arrow (Cross-reference dialog box) to display the Reference type list; scroll to and then tap or click Figure, which displays a list of figures from the document in the For which caption list (which, at this point, is only one figure).

- If necessary, tap or click 'Figure 1: Help Window Screenshot' in the For which caption list to select the caption to reference.

- Tap or click the 'Insert reference to' arrow and then tap or click 'Only label and number' to instruct Word that the cross-reference in the document should list just the label, Figure, followed by the figure number (Figure 9–10).

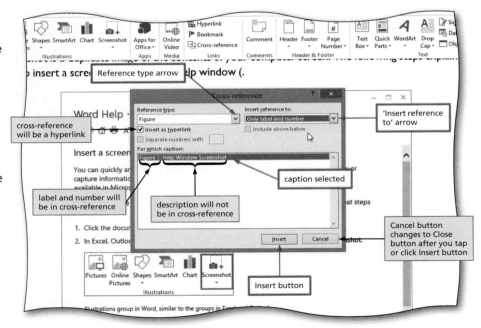

Figure 9–10

3

- Tap or click the Insert button to insert the cross-reference in the document at the location of the insertion point.

Q&A

What if my cross-reference is shaded in gray?

The cross-reference is a field. Depending on your Word settings, fields may appear shaded in gray to help you identify them on the screen.

4

- Tap or click the Close button (Cross-reference dialog box).

- Press the RIGHT PARENTHESIS key to close off the cross-reference (Figure 9–11).

Q&A

How do I update a cross-reference if a caption is added, deleted, or moved?

In many cases, Word automatically updates a cross-reference in a document if the item to which it refers changes. To update a cross-reference manually, select the cross-reference and then press the F9 key, or press and hold or right-click the cross-reference and then tap or click Update Field on the shortcut menu.

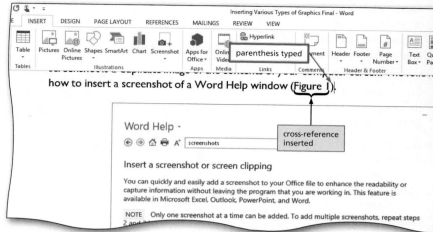

Figure 9–11

Other Ways

1. Tap or click 'Insert Cross-reference' button (REFERENCES tab | Captions group)

To Go to an Object

1 MODIFY REFERENCE DOCUMENT | 2 CREATE MASTER DOCUMENT | 3 ORGANIZE REFERENCE DOCUMENT

Often, you would like to bring a certain page, graphic, or other part of a document into view in the document window. Although you could scroll through the document to find a desired page, graphic, or part of the document, Word enables you to go to a specific location via the Go To sheet in the Find and Replace dialog box.

The following steps go to a graphic. ***Why?*** *The next step in this chapter is to add a caption to another graphic in the document, so you want to display the graphic in the document window.*

1

- Display the HOME tab.

- Tap or click the Find arrow (HOME tab | Editing group) to display the Find menu (Figure 9–12).

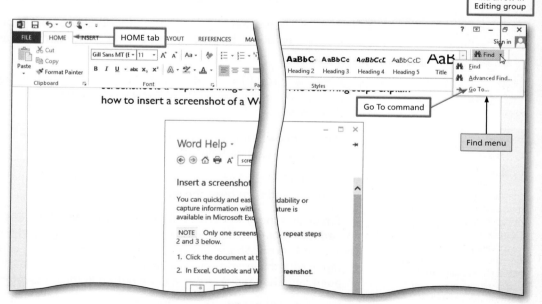

Figure 9–12

2

- Tap or click Go To on the Find menu to display the Find and Replace dialog box.

- Scroll through the Go to what list and then tap or click Graphic to select it.

- Tap or click the Previous button to display the previous graphic in the document window (which is the arrow shape, in this case) (Figure 9–13).

3

- Tap or click Close button to close the dialog box.

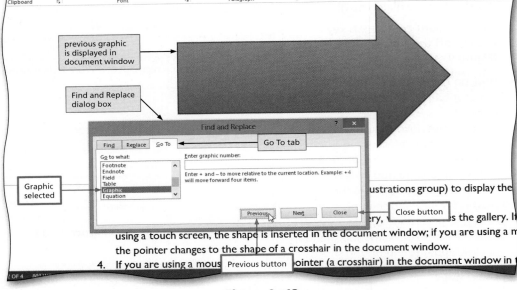

Figure 9–13

Other Ways

1. Press CTRL+G

To Add Captions and Create Cross-References

The previous steps added a caption to the screenshot graphic and then created a cross-reference to that caption. The following steps add captions to the remaining three graphics in the document (that is, the shape, the picture, and the clip art).

1 Tap or click the arrow shape to select the graphic for which you want to add a caption.

2 Tap or click the Insert Caption button (REFERENCES tab | Captions group) to display the Caption dialog box with a figure number automatically assigned to the selected graphic.

3 Press the COLON (:) key and then press the SPACEBAR in the Caption text box (Caption dialog box) to place separating characters between the figure number and description.

4 Type **Arrow Shape** as the figure description and then tap or click the OK button to insert the caption below the selected graphic.

5 At the end of the last sentence above the graphic, change the word, below, to the word, in, and then press the SPACEBAR.

6 Tap or click the 'Insert Cross-reference' button (INSERT or REFERENCES tab | Links or Captions group) to display the Cross-reference dialog box, if necessary, tap or click 'Figure 1: Arrow Shape' in the For which caption list to select the caption to reference, tap or click the Insert button to insert the cross-reference at the location of the insertion point, and then tap or click the Close button in the Cross-reference dialog box.

Q&A Why did I not need to change the settings for the reference type and reference to in the dialog box?
Word retains the previous settings in the dialog box.

BTW
Q&As
For a complete list of the Q&As found in many of the step-by-step sequences in this book, visit the Q&A resource on the Student Companion Site located on www.cengagebrain.com. For detailed instructions about accessing available resources, visit www.cengage.com/ct/studentdownload or contact your instructor for information about accessing the required files.

7 Tap or click the Find arrow (HOME tab | Editing group) to display the Find menu and then tap or click Go To on the Find menu to display the Go To dialog box. With Graphic selected in the Go to what list, tap or click the Previous button to display the previous graphic in the document window (which is the flowers picture in this case). Tap or click the Close button to close the dialog box.

8 Repeat Steps 1 though 7 to add the caption, Flowers Picture, to the picture of the flowers and the caption, Hummingbird Clip Art, to the clip art of the hummingbird. Also add a cross-reference at the end of the sentences above each image (Figure 9–14).

9 Close the Cross-reference dialog box.

BTW
Touch Screen Differences
The Office and Windows interfaces may vary if you are using a touch screen. For this reason, you might notice that the function or appearance of your touch screen differs slightly from this chapter's presentation.

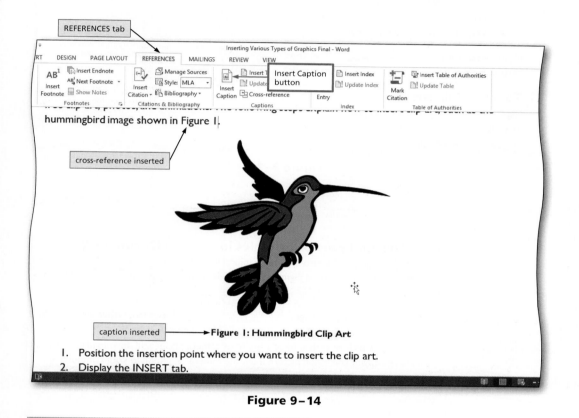

Figure 9–14

To Mark an Index Entry

1 MODIFY REFERENCE DOCUMENT | 2 CREATE MASTER DOCUMENT | 3 ORGANIZE REFERENCE DOCUMENT

The last page of the reference document in this project is an index, which lists important terms discussed in the document along with each term's corresponding page number. For Word to generate the index, you first must mark any text you wish to appear in the index. **Why?** *When you mark an index entry, Word creates a field that it uses to build the index.* Index entry fields are hidden and are displayed on the screen only when you show formatting marks, that is, when the 'Show/Hide ¶' button (HOME tab | Paragraph group) is selected.

In this document, you want the words, graphical image, in the first sentence below the Inserting Various Types of Graphics in a Word Document heading to be marked as an index entry. The steps on the next page mark an index entry.

1

- Select the text you wish to appear in the index (the words, graphical image, in the first sentence of the document in this case).

- Tap or click the Mark Entry button (REFERENCES tab | Index group) to display the Mark Index Entry dialog box (Figure 9–15).

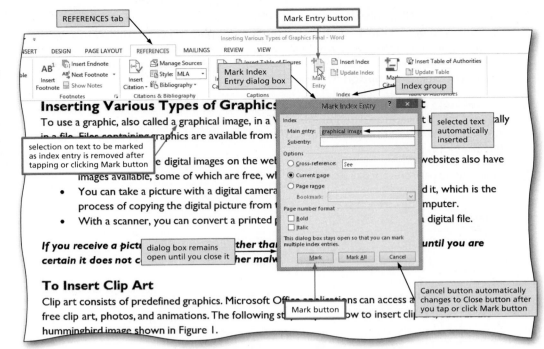

Figure 9–15

2

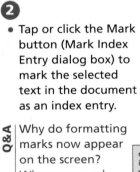

- Tap or click the Mark button (Mark Index Entry dialog box) to mark the selected text in the document as an index entry.

Q&A Why do formatting marks now appear on the screen?
When you mark an index entry, Word automatically shows formatting marks (if they are not showing already) so that you can see the index entry field. Notice that the marked index entry begins with the letters, XE.

- Tap or click the Close button in the Mark Index Entry dialog box to close the dialog box (Figure 9–16).

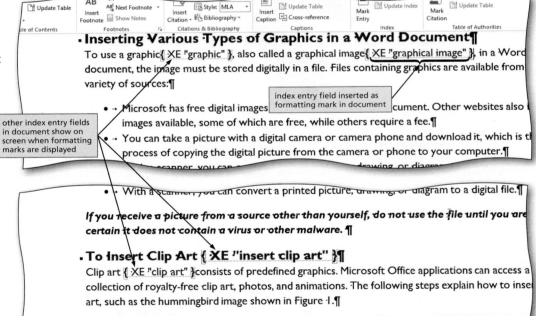

Figure 9–16

Q&A How could I see all index entries marked in a document?
With formatting marks displaying, you could scroll through the document, scanning for all occurrences of XE, or you could use the Navigation Pane (that is, place a check mark in the 'Open the Navigation Pane' check box (VIEW tab | Show group)) to find all occurrences of XE.

Other Ways

1. Select text, press ALT+SHIFT+X

TO MARK MULTIPLE INDEX ENTRIES

Word leaves the Mark Index Entry dialog box open until you close it, which allows you to mark multiple index entries without having to reopen the dialog box repeatedly. To mark multiple index entries, you would perform the following steps.

1. With the Mark Index Entry dialog box displayed, tap or click in the document window; scroll to and then select the next index entry.
2. If necessary, tap or click the Main entry text box (Mark Index Entry dialog box) to display the selected text in the Main entry text box.
3. Tap or click the Mark button.
4. Repeat Steps 1 through 3 for all entries. When finished, tap or click the Close button in the Mark Index Entry dialog box.

To Hide Formatting Marks

To remove the clutter of index entry fields from the document, you should hide formatting marks. The following step hides formatting marks.

1 If the 'Show/Hide ¶' button (HOME tab | Paragraph group) is selected, tap or click it to hide formatting marks.

Q&A What if the index entries still appear after tapping or clicking the 'Show/Hide ¶' button? Open the Backstage view, tap or click Options in the left pane in the Backstage view to display the Word Options dialog box, tap or click Display in the left pane (Word Options dialog box), remove the check mark from the Hidden text check box, and then tap or click the OK button.

To Change Paragraph Spacing in a Document

1 MODIFY REFERENCE DOCUMENT | 2 CREATE MASTER DOCUMENT | 3 ORGANIZE REFERENCE DOCUMENT

In Word, you easily can expand or condense the amount of space between lines in all paragraphs in a document. The following steps expand paragraph spacing. **Why?** *You feel the document text would be easier to read if the paragraphs were more open.*

1
- Display the DESIGN tab.
- Tap or click the Paragraph Spacing button (DESIGN tab | Document Formatting group) to display the Paragraph Spacing gallery (Figure 9–17).

Experiment
- If you are using a mouse, point to various spacing commands in the Paragraph Spacing gallery and watch the paragraphs conform to that spacing.

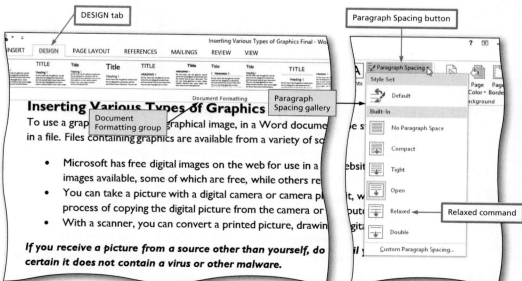

Figure 9–17

2
- Tap or click Relaxed in the Paragraph Spacing gallery to expand the spacing of paragraphs in the document.

To Show White Space

For the remainder of creating this project, you would like to see headers, footers, and margins. Thus, you should show white space. The following step shows white space.

 If you are using a touch screen, double-tap the page break notation; if you are using a mouse, position the pointer in the document window on the page break and then double-click when the pointer changes to a 'Show White Space' button to show white space.

To Insert a Sidebar Text Box

1 MODIFY REFERENCE DOCUMENT | 2 CREATE MASTER DOCUMENT | 3 ORGANIZE REFERENCE DOCUMENT

A **sidebar text box** is a text box that runs across the top or bottom of a page or along the edge of the right or left of a page. The following steps insert a built-in sidebar text box. *Why? Sidebar text boxes take up less space on the page than text boxes positioned in the middle of the page.*

● Be sure the insertion point is near the top of page 1 of the document, as shown in Figure 9–18.

Q&A Does the insertion point need to be at the top of the page?
The insertion point should be close to where you want to insert the text box.

● Display the INSERT tab.

● Tap or click the 'Choose a Text Box' button (INSERT tab | Text group) to display the Choose a Text Box gallery.

Experiment

● Scroll through the Choose a Text Box gallery to see the variety of available text box styles.

● Scroll to display Grid Sidebar in the Choose a Text Box gallery (Figure 9–18).

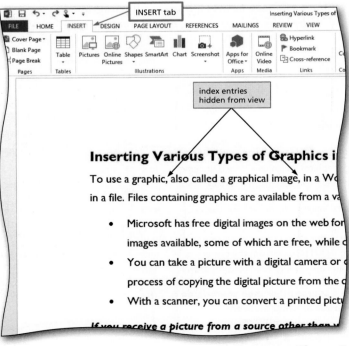
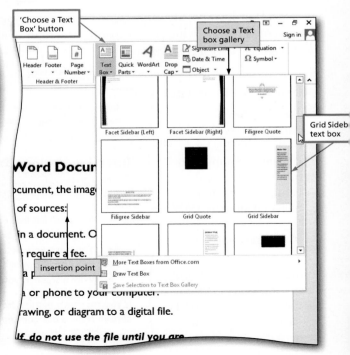

Figure 9–18

2

- Tap or click Grid Sidebar in the Choose a Text Box gallery to insert that text box style in the document (Figure 9–19).

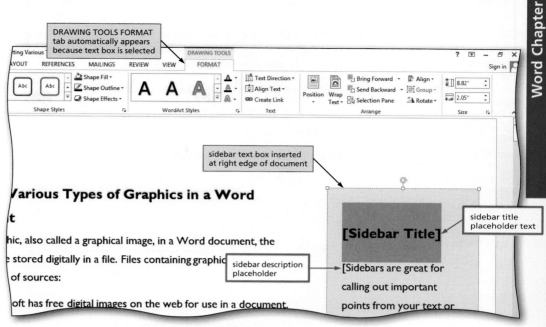

Figure 9–19

Other Ways

1. Tap or click 'Explore Quick Parts' button (INSERT tab | Text group), tap or click 'Building Blocks Organizer' on Explore Quick Parts menu, select desired text box name in Building blocks list, tap or click Insert button

To Enter and Format Text in the Sidebar Text Box

The next step is to enter the text in the sidebar text box. The following steps enter text in the text box.

1 If necessary, tap or click the sidebar title placeholder in the text box to select it.

2 Type **What is malware?**

3 Tap or click the sidebar description placeholder and then type the following paragraph: **Malware, short for malicious software, is software that acts without a user's knowledge and deliberately alters a computer or mobile device's operations. Examples of malware include viruses, worms, trojan horses, rootkits, spyware, adware, and zombies.**

4 Press the ENTER key. Change the font size to 14 point and bold the text. Type **Malware Protection Tips** and then press the ENTER key.

5 Change the font size to 11 point and remove the bold format from the text. Tap or click the Bullets button (HOME tab | Paragraph group) to bullet the list. Tap or click the Decrease Indent button (HOME tab | Paragraph group) to move the bullet symbol left one-half inch. Type **Use an antivirus program.**

6 Press the ENTER key. Type **Use a firewall.**

7 Press the ENTER key. Type **Be suspicious of unsolicited email attachments.**

8 Press the ENTER key. Type **Download apps or programs from trusted websites.**

9 Press the ENTER key. Type **Close spyware windows.**

BTW
Building Blocks
Many of the objects that you can insert through the Building Blocks gallery are available as built-in objects in galleries on the ribbon. Some examples are cover pages in the Add a Cover Page gallery (INSERT tab | Pages group), equations in the Insert an Equation gallery (INSERT tab | Symbols group), footers in the Add a Footer gallery (INSERT tab | Header & Footer group), headers in the Add a Header gallery (INSERT tab | Header & Footer group), page numbers in the Add Page Numbers gallery (INSERT tab | Header & Footer group), text boxes in the Choose a Text Box gallery (INSERT tab | Text group), and watermarks in the Watermark gallery (DESIGN tab | Page Background group).

BTW
Deleting Building Blocks
To delete an existing building block, tap or click the 'Explore Quick Parts' button (INSERT tab | Text group) to display the Explore Quick Parts menu, tap or click 'Building Blocks Organizer' on the Explore Quick Parts menu to display the Building Blocks Organizer dialog box, select the building block to delete (Building Blocks Organizer dialog box), tap or click the Delete button, tap or click the Yes button in the dialog box that appears, and then close the Building Blocks Organizer dialog box.

10 Press the ENTER key. Type **Before using removable media, scan it for malware.** If necessary, drag the bottom of the text box down to make it longer so that all of the entered text is visible.

11 Press the ENTER key. Type **Back up regularly.**

12 Tap or click the One Page button (VIEW tab | Zoom group) so that you can see all of the entered text at once (Figure 9–20).

13 Change the zoom to page width.

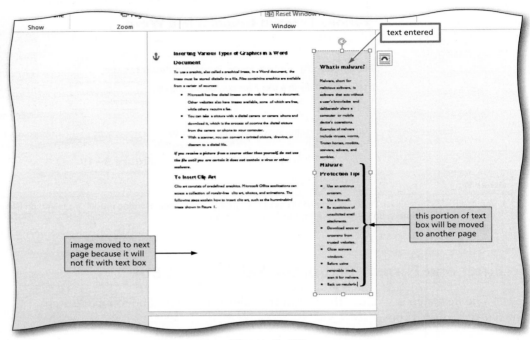

Figure 9–20

To Use the Navigation Pane to Go to a Page

Instead of one long text box, this project splits the text box across the top of two pages, specifically, the first and third pages of this document. The following steps use the Navigation Pane to display page 3 in the document window so that you can insert another text box on that page.

1 Display the VIEW tab. Place a check mark in the 'Open the Navigation Pane' check box (VIEW tab | Show group) to display the Navigation Pane at the left edge of the Word window.

2 Tap or click the PAGES tab in the Navigation Pane to display thumbnail images of the pages in the document.

3 Scroll to and then tap or click the thumbnail of the third page in the Navigation Pane to display the top of the selected page in the top of the document window.

4 Position the insertion point near the bottom of the third page at the approximate location for the sidebar text box (Figure 9–21).

5 Leave the Navigation Pane open for use in the next several steps.

BTW
Field Codes
If your index, table of contents, or table of figures displays odd characters inside curly braces ({ }), then Word is displaying field codes instead of field results. Press ALT+F9 to display the index or table correctly.

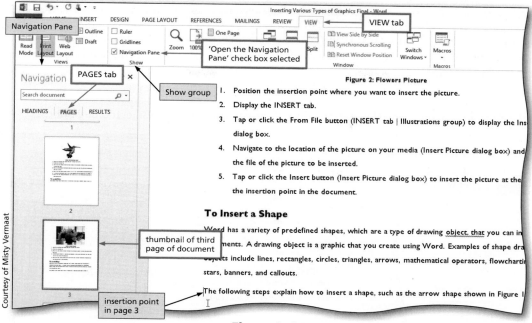

Courtesy of Misty Vermaat

Figure 9–21

To Insert Another Sidebar Text Box

The following steps insert a Grid Sidebar text box building block on the third page in the document.

① Ensure that the insertion point is near the bottom of the third page in the document.

Q&A Why position the insertion point near the bottom of the page?
The content of the first and second text boxes will be shared, which means the content currently at the top of page three may move to page two after you link the text boxes. You want to ensure the text box will be positioned on the third page after linking the two text boxes together. If the text box moves to the second page, you can drag it back to the third page.

② Display the INSERT tab.

③ Tap or click the 'Choose a Text Box' button (INSERT tab | Text group) to display the Choose a Text Box gallery and then locate and select Grid Sidebar in the Choose a Text Box gallery to insert that text box style in the document.

④ Press the DELETE key four times to delete the current contents from the text box (Figure 9–22).

Courtesy of Misty Vermaat

Figure 9–22

BTW
BTWs
For a complete list of the BTWs found in the margins of this book, visit the BTW resource on the Student Companion Site located on www.cengagebrain.com. For detailed instructions about accessing available resources, visit www.cengage.com/ct/studentdownload or contact your instructor for information about accessing the required files.

To Link Text Boxes

Word allows you to link two separate text boxes. *Why? You can flow text from one text box into the other.* To link text boxes, the second text box must be empty, which is why you deleted the contents of the text box in the previous steps. The following steps link text boxes.

- Tap or click the thumbnail of the first page in the Navigation Pane to display the top of the selected page in the document window.

- Tap or click the text box on the first page to select it.

- If necessary, display the DRAWING TOOLS FORMAT tab.

- Tap or click the Create Link button (DRAWING TOOLS FORMAT tab | Text group), which changes the pointer to the shape of a cup if you are using a mouse.

- If you are using a mouse, move the pointer in the document window to see its new shape (Figure 9–23).

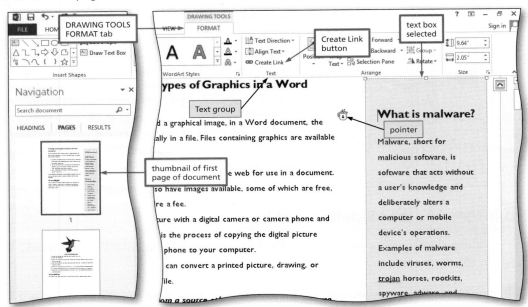

Figure 9–23

- Scroll through the document to display the second text box on the third page in the document window.

Q&A Can I use the Navigation Pane to go to the second text box?
No. If you tap or click in the Navigation Pane, the link process will stop and the pointer will return to its default shape.

- If you are using a mouse, position the pointer in the empty text box, so that the pointer shape changes to a pouring cup (Figure 9–24).

Figure 9–24

Courtesy of Misty Vermaat

3

- If you are using a mouse, click the empty text box to link it to the first text box. If you are using a touch screen, you will need to use a stylus to tap the empty text box.

- Use the Navigation Pane to display the first page in the document window.

- If necessary, scroll to display the first text box in the document window and then select the text box.

- Resize the text box by dragging its bottom-middle sizing handle until the amount of text that is displayed in the text box is similar to Figure 9–25.

Q&A

How would I remove a link?
Select the text box in which you created the link and then tap or click the Break Link button (DRAWING TOOLS FORMAT tab | Text group).

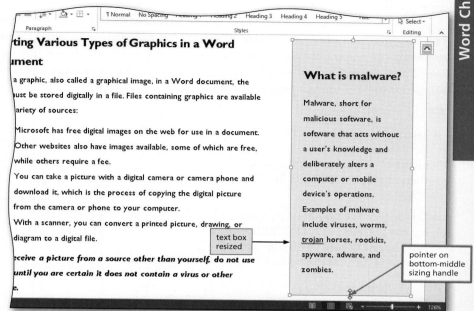

Figure 9–25

4

- Use the Navigation Pane to display the third page in the document window.

- If necessary, scroll to display the second text box in the document window and then select the text box.

- Resize the text box by dragging its bottom-middle sizing handle until the amount of text that is displayed in the text box is similar to Figure 9–26.

- If necessary drag the entire text box to position it as shown in Figure 9–26.

- If necessary, insert a page break to the left of the To Insert a Shape heading so that the heading begins at the top of third page.

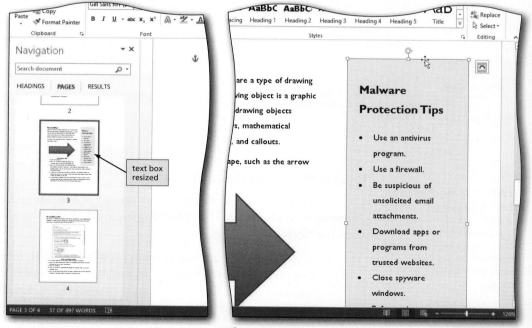

Figure 9–26

To Compress Pictures

1 MODIFY REFERENCE DOCUMENT | 2 CREATE MASTER DOCUMENT | 3 ORGANIZE REFERENCE DOCUMENT

If you plan to email a Word document that contains pictures or graphics or post it for downloading, you may want to reduce its file size to speed up file transmission time. *Why? Pictures and other graphics in Word documents can increase the size of these files.* In Word, you can compress pictures, which reduces the size of the Word document. Compressing the pictures in Word does not cause any loss in their original quality. The following steps compress pictures in a document.

- Tap or click a picture in the document to select it, such as the image of the hummingbird, and then display the PICTURE TOOLS FORMAT tab.

- Tap or click the Compress Pictures button (PICTURE TOOLS FORMAT tab | Adjust group) to display the Compress Pictures dialog box.

- If the 'Apply only to this picture' check box (Compress Pictures dialog box) contains a check mark, remove the check mark so that all pictures in the document are compressed.

- If necessary, tap or click 'Print (220 ppi): excellent quality on most printers and screens' in the Target output area to specify how images should be compressed (Figure 9–27).

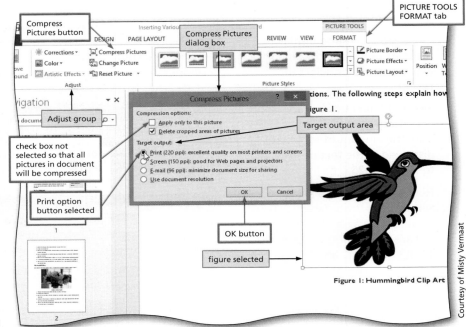

Figure 9–27

- Tap or click the OK button to compress all pictures in the document.

Q&A Can I compress a single picture?

Yes. Select the picture and then place a check mark in the 'Apply only to this picture' check box (Compress Pictures dialog box).

Other Ways

1. Tap or click the Tools button in the Save As dialog box, tap or click Compress Pictures on Tools menu, select options (Compress Pictures dialog box), tap or click OK button

---

BTW
Compressing Pictures
Selecting a lower ppi (pixels per inch) in the Target output area (Compress Picture dialog box) creates a smaller document file, but also lowers the quality of the images.

TO SAVE PICTURES IN OTHER FORMATS

You can save any graphic in a document as a picture file for use in other documents or programs. If you wanted to save a graphic in a Word document, you would perform these steps.

1. If you are using a touch screen, press and hold to display a mini toolbar and then tap the 'Show Context Menu' button on the mini toolbar to display a shortcut menu; if you are using a mouse, right-click the graphic to display a shortcut menu.

2. Tap or click 'Save as Picture' on the shortcut menu to display the File Save dialog box.

3. Navigate to the location you want to save the graphic.

4. Tap or click the 'Save as type' arrow (File Save dialog box) and then select the graphic type for the saved graphic.
5. Tap or click the Save button (File Save dialog box) to save the graphic in the specified location using the specified graphic type.

To Change the Symbol Format in a Bulleted List

1 MODIFY REFERENCE DOCUMENT | 2 CREATE MASTER DOCUMENT | 3 ORGANIZE REFERENCE DOCUMENT

The following steps change the symbol in a bulleted list. *Why? The project in this chapter uses an arrow-type bullet symbol for the bulleted list instead of the default round bullet symbol.* Word provides several predefined bullet symbols for use in bulleted lists.

1

- Navigate to the first page and then select the bulleted list for which you want to change the bullet symbol (in this case, the three bulleted paragraphs on the first page).

- Tap or click the Bullets arrow (HOME tab | Paragraph group) to display the Bullets gallery (Figure 9–28).

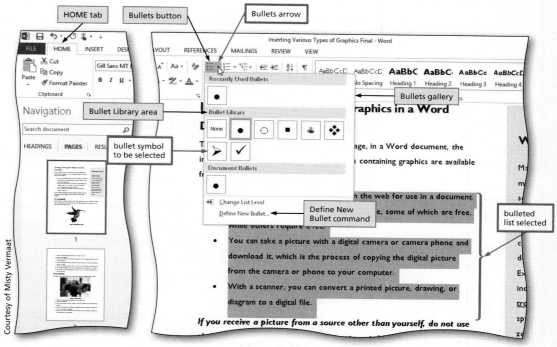

Courtesy of Misty Vermaat

Figure 9–28

2

- Tap or click the desired bullet symbol in the Bullet Library area to change the bullet symbol on the selected bulleted list (Figure 9–29).

Q&A
Can I select any bullet symbol in the Bullet Library area?
Yes. You also can tap or click 'Define New Bullet' in the Bullets gallery if the bullet symbol you desire is not shown in the Bullet Library area.

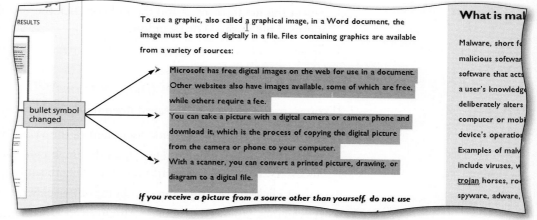

Figure 9–29

3

- Tap or click anywhere to remove the selection from the text.

BTW
Bullets
You can select from a variety of other bullet symbols or change the font attributes of a bullet by tapping or clicking 'Define New Bullet' in the Bullets gallery and then tapping or clicking the Symbol button or Font button in the Define New Bullet dialog box. You also can change the level of a bullet by tapping or clicking the 'Change List Level' command in the Bullets gallery.

To Save an Existing Document with the Same File Name

You are finished modifying the document and have performed several steps since the last save. Thus, you should save the document again, as described in the following step.

1 Tap or click the Save button on the Quick Access Toolbar to save the document again with the same file name, Inserting Various Types of Graphics Final.

To Close a Document

The following steps close the open Word document and the Word Help window.

1 Close the Navigation Pane.

2 Open the Backstage view and then tap or click Close to close the open document.

3 If necessary, display the Word Help window and close it.

To Recover Unsaved Documents (Draft Versions)

If you accidently exit Word without saving a document, you may be able to recover the unsaved document, called a **draft version**, in Word. If you wanted to recover an unsaved document, you would perform these steps.

1. Run Word and create a blank document in the Word window.
2. Open the Backstage view and then, if necessary, tap or click the Open tab to display the Open gallery. Scroll to the bottom of the Recent Documents list. Tap or click the 'Recover Unsaved Documents' button to display an Open dialog box that lists unsaved files retained by Word.

   or

2. Open the Backstage view and then, if necessary, tap or click the Info tab to display the Info gallery. Tap or click the Manage Versions button to display the Manage Versions menu. Tap or click 'Recover Unsaved Documents' on the Manage Versions menu to display an Open dialog box that lists unsaved files retained by Word.
3. Select the file to recover and then tap or click the Open button to display the unsaved file in the Word window.
4. To save the document, tap or click the Save As button on the Message Bar.

To Delete All Unsaved Documents (Draft Versions)

If you wanted to delete all unsaved documents, you would perform these steps.

1. Run Word and create a blank document in the Word window.
2. If necessary, open a document. Open the Backstage view and then, if necessary, tap or click the Info tab to display the Info gallery.
3. Tap or click the Manage Versions button to display the Manage Versions menu.
4. If available, tap or click 'Delete All Unsaved Documents' on the Manage Versions menu.
5. When Word displays a dialog box asking if you are sure you want to delete all copies of unsaved files, tap or click the Yes button to delete all unsaved documents.

Break Point: If you wish to take a break, this is a good place to do so. You can exit Word now. To resume at a later time, run Word and continue following the steps from this location forward.

Working with a Master Document

When you are creating a document that includes other files, you may want to create a master document to organize the documents. A **master document** is simply a document that contains links to one or more other documents, each of which is called a **subdocument**. In addition to subdocuments, a master document can contain its own text and graphics.

In this project, the master document file is named Learn Word – Guide #9. This master document file contains a link to one subdocument: Inserting Graphical Images Final. The master document also contains other items: a title page, a copyright page, a table of contents, a table of figures, and an index. The following pages create this master document and insert the necessary elements in the document to create the finished Learn Word - Guide #9 document.

To Change the Document Theme

The first step in creating this master document is to change its document theme to Dividend. The following steps change the document theme.

1 If necessary, run Word and create a new blank document.

2 Tap or click DESIGN on the ribbon to display the DESIGN tab.

3 Tap or click the Themes button (DESIGN tab | Document Formatting group) to display the Themes gallery.

4 Tap or click Dividend in the Themes gallery to change the document theme to the selected theme.

Outlines

To create a master document, Word must be in Outline view. You then enter the headings of the document as an outline using Word's built-in heading styles. In an outline, the major heading is displayed at the left margin with each subordinate, or lower-level, heading indented. In Word, the built-in Heading 1 style is displayed at the left margin in outline view. Heading 2 style is indented below Heading 1 style, Heading 3 style is indented further, and so on. (Outline view works similarly to multilevel lists.)

You do not want to use a built-in heading style for the paragraphs of text within the document because when you create a table of contents, Word places all lines formatted using the built-in heading styles in the table of contents. Thus, the text below each heading is formatted using the Body Text style.

Each heading should print at the top of a new page. Because you might want to format the pages within a heading differently from those pages in other headings, you insert next page section breaks between each heading.

To Switch to Outline View

The following steps switch to Outline view. **Why?** *To create a master document, Word must be in Outline view.*

1

• Display the VIEW tab (Figure 9–30).

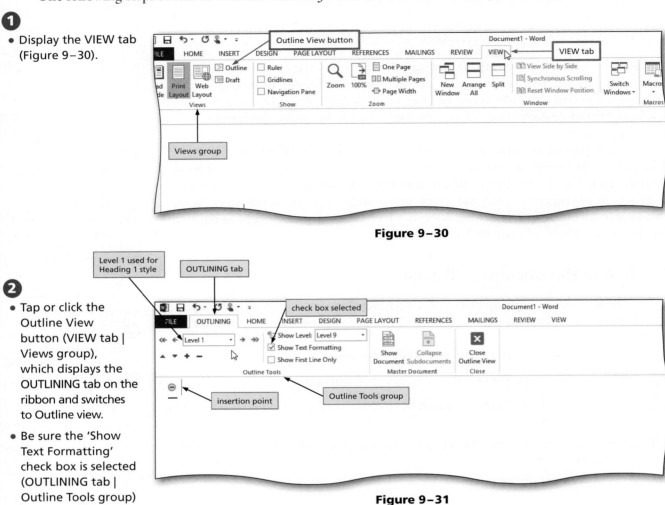

Figure 9–30

2

• Tap or click the Outline View button (VIEW tab | Views group), which displays the OUTLINING tab on the ribbon and switches to Outline view.

• Be sure the 'Show Text Formatting' check box is selected (OUTLINING tab | Outline Tools group) (Figure 9–31).

Figure 9–31

To Add Entries in Outline View

The Learn Word – Guide #9 document contains these three major headings: Inserting Various Types of Graphics in a Word Document, Table of Figures, and Index. The heading, Inserting Various Types of Graphics in a Word Document, is not entered in the outline. **Why not?** *It is part of the subdocument inserted in the master document.*

The first page of the outline (the copyright page) does not contain a heading; instead it contains three paragraphs of body text, which you enter directly in the outline. The Inserting Various Types of Graphics in a Word Document content is inserted from the subdocument. You will instruct Word to create the content for the Table of Figures and Index later in this chapter. The following steps create an outline that contains headings and body text to be used in the master document.

1

- Tap or click the 'Demote to Body Text' button (OUTLINING tab | Outline Tools group), so that you can enter the paragraphs of text for the copyright page.

- Type `Learn Word | Guide #9 – Inserting Graphics` as the first paragraph in the outline and then press the ENTER key.

- Type `To receive additional guides in this or any other learning series by Gardner's Information Literacy Center, contact Marianne Chamberlain at mchamberlain@gardner.edu.` as the second paragraph in the outline and then press the ENTER key.

If requested by your instructor, change the name, Marianne Chamberlain, on the copyright page to your name.

 Q&A Why is only my first line of text in the paragraph displayed?
Remove the check mark from the 'Show First Line Only' check box (OUTLINING tab | Outline Tools group).

- If you are using a touch screen, press and hold the hyperlink and then tap the 'Show Context Menu' button on the mini toolbar; if you are using a mouse, right-click the hyperlink (in this case, the email address) to display a shortcut menu.

- Tap or click Remove Hyperlink on the shortcut menu.

- Tap or click the third Body Text style bullet and then type `Copyright 2014` as the third paragraph and then press the ENTER key.

- Tap or click the 'Promote to Heading 1' button (OUTLINING tab | Outline Tools group) because you are finished entering body text and will enter the remaining headings in the outline next (Figure 9–32).

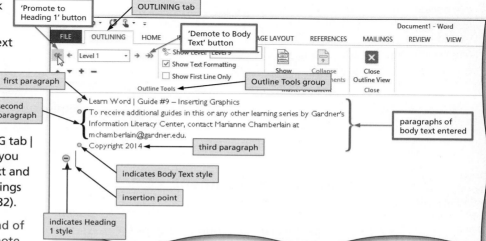

Figure 9–32

 Q&A Could I press SHIFT+TAB instead of tapping or clicking the 'Promote to Heading 1' button?
Yes.

2

- Display the PAGE LAYOUT tab.

- Tap or click the 'Insert Page and Section Breaks' button (PAGE LAYOUT tab | Page Setup group) and then tap or click Next Page in the Section Breaks area in the Insert Page and Section Breaks gallery because you want to enter a next page section break before the next heading.

3

- Type `Table of Figures` and then press the ENTER key.

- Repeat Step 2.

4

- Type `Index` as the last entry (Figure 9–33).

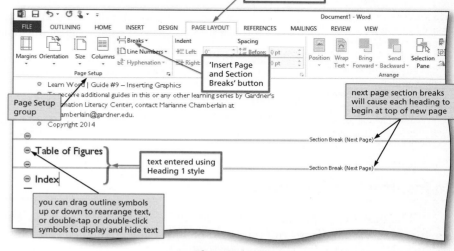

Figure 9–33

 Q&A Why do the outline symbols contain a minus sign?
The minus sign means the outline level does not have any subordinate levels. If an outline symbol contains a plus sign, it means the outline level has subordinate levels.

To Show First Line Only

Users often instruct Word to display just the first line of each paragraph of body text. *Why? When only the first line of each paragraph is displayed, the outline often is more readable.* The following step displays only the first line of body text paragraphs.

1

- Display the OUTLINING tab.

- Place a check mark in the 'Show First Line Only' check box (OUTLINING tab | Outline Tools group), so that Word displays only the first line of each paragraph (Figure 9–34).

Q&A

How would I redisplay all lines of the paragraphs of body text?
Remove the check mark from the 'Show First Line Only' check box (OUTLINING tab | Outline Tools group).

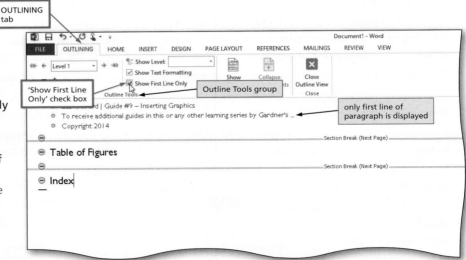

Figure 9–34

BTW
Distributing a Document
Instead of printing and distributing a hard copy of a document, you can distribute the document electronically. Options include sending the document via email; posting it on cloud storage (such as SkyDrive) and sharing the file with others; posting it on a social networking site, blog, or other website; and sharing a link associated with an online location of the document. You also can create and share a PDF or XPS image of the document, so that users can view the file in Acrobat Reader or XPS Viewer instead of in Word.

To Save a Document

The next step is to save the master document because you have performed many steps thus far. The following steps save a document.

1 Open the Backstage view and then tap or click the Save As tab to display the Save As gallery.

2 Display the Save As dialog box and then type `Learn Word - Guide #9` in the File name box to change the file name. Do not press the ENTER key after typing the file name because you do not want to close the dialog box at this time.

3 Navigate to the desired save location (in this case, the Word folder in the CIS 101 folder [or your class folder] on your computer or SkyDrive).

4 Tap or click the Save button (Save As dialog box) to save the document in the selected folder on the selected save location with the entered file name.

To Insert a Subdocument

The next step is to insert a subdocument in the master document. The subdocument to be inserted is the Inserting Various Types of Graphics Final file, which you created earlier in the chapter. Word places the first line of text in the subdocument at the first heading level in the master document. *Why? The first line in the subdocument was defined using the Heading 1 style.* The following steps insert a subdocument in a master document.

①

- Display the HOME tab. If formatting marks do not appear, tap or click the 'Show/Hide ¶' button (HOME tab | Paragraph group).

- Position the insertion point where you want to insert the subdocument (on the section break above the Table of Figures heading).

- Display the OUTLINING tab. Tap or click the Show Document button (OUTLINING tab | Master Document group) so that all commands in the Master Document group appear.

- Tap or click the Insert Subdocument button (OUTLINING tab | Master Document group) to display the Insert Subdocument dialog box.

- Locate and select the Inserting Various Types of Graphics Final file (Insert Subdocument dialog box) (Figure 9–35).

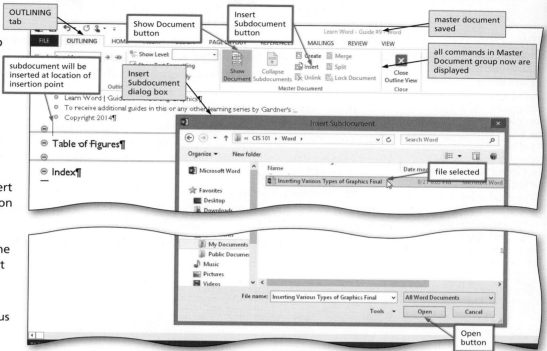

Figure 9–35

②

- Tap or click the Open button (Insert Subdocument dialog box) to insert the selected file as a subdocument.

- If Word displays a dialog box about styles, tap or click the 'No to All' button.

- Press CTRL+HOME to position the insertion point at the top of the document (Figure 9–36).

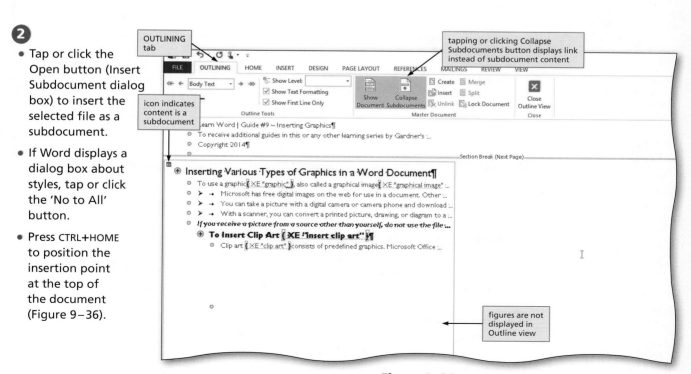

Figure 9–36

Master Documents and Subdocuments

When you open the master document, the subdocuments initially are collapsed; that is, they are displayed as hyperlinks (Figure 9–37). To work with the contents of a master document after you open it, switch to Outline view and then expand the subdocuments by tapping or clicking the Expand Subdocuments button (OUTLINING tab | Master Document group).

You can open a subdocument in a separate document window and modify it. To open a collapsed subdocument, tap or click the hyperlink. To open an expanded subdocument, double-tap or double-click the subdocument icon to the left of the document heading (shown in Figure 9–37).

If, for some reason, you wanted to remove a subdocument from a master document, you would expand the subdocuments, tap or click the subdocument icon to the left of the subdocument's first heading, and then press the DELETE key. Although Word removes the subdocument from the master document, the subdocument file remains on the storage media.

Occasionally, you may want to convert a subdocument to part of the master document — breaking the connection between the text in the master document and the subdocument. To do this, expand the subdocuments, tap or click the subdocument icon, and then tap or click the Remove Subdocument button (OUTLINING tab | Master Document group).

BTW
Locked Subdocuments
If a lock icon is displayed next to a subdocument's name, either the master document is collapsed or the subdocument is locked. If the master document is collapsed, simply tap or click the Expand Subdocuments button (OUTLINING tab | Master Document group). If the subdocument is locked, you will be able to display the contents of the subdocument but will not be able to modify it.

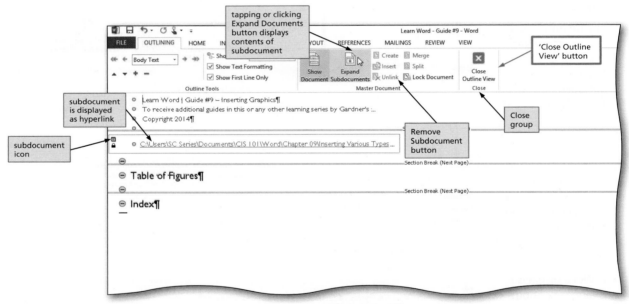

Figure 9–37

To Hide Formatting Marks

To remove the clutter of index entry fields from the document, you should hide formatting marks. The following step hides formatting marks.

1 Display the HOME tab. If the 'Show/Hide ¶' button (HOME tab | Paragraph group) is selected, tap or click it to hide formatting marks.

To Exit Outline View

The following step exits Outline view. *Why? You are finished organizing the master document.*

1

- Display the OUTLINING tab.

- Tap or click the 'Close Outline View' button (shown in Figure 9–37) (OUTLINING tab | Close group) to redisplay the document in Print Layout view, which selects the Print Layout button on the status bar.

- If necessary, press CTRL+HOME to display the top of the document (Figure 9–38).

Experiment

- Scroll through the document to familiarize yourself with the sections. When finished, display the top of the subdocument in the document window.

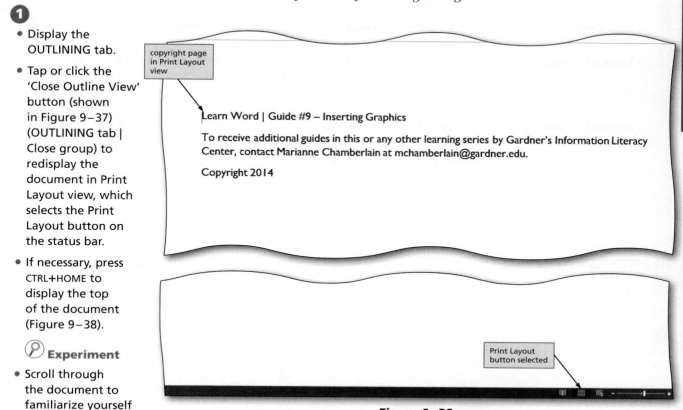

Figure 9–38

To Save an Existing Document with the Same File Name

The following step saves the master document again with the same file name.

1 Tap or click the Save button on the Quick Access Toolbar to save the document again with the same file name, Learn Word - Guide #9.

Organizing a Reference Document

Reference documents are organized and formatted so that users easily can navigate through and read the document. The reference document in this chapter includes the following elements: a copyright page, a title page, a table of contents, a table of figures, an index, alternating footers, and a gutter margin. This section illustrates the tasks required to include these elements.

What elements are common to reference documents?

Reference documents often include a title page, a table of contents, a table of figures or list of tables (if one exists), and an index.

- **Title Page.** A title page should contain, at a minimum, the title of the document. Some also contain the author, a subtitle, an edition or volume number, and the date written.

- **Table of Contents.** The table of contents should list the title (heading) of each chapter or section and the starting page number of the chapter or section. You may use a leader character, such as a dot or hyphen, to fill the space between the heading and the page number. Sections preceding the table of contents are not listed in it — only list material that follows the table of contents.

- **Table of Figures or List of Tables.** If you have multiple figures or tables in a document, consider identifying all of them in a table of figures or a list of tables. The format of the table of figures or list of tables should match the table of contents.

- **Index.** The index usually is set in two columns or one column. The index can contain any item a reader might want to look up, such as a heading or a key term. If the document does not have a table of figures or list of tables, also include figures and tables in the index.

To Insert a Cover Page

Word has many predefined cover page formats that you can use for the title page in a document. The following steps insert a cover page. *Why? The reference document in this chapter includes a title page.*

1

- Display the INSERT tab.

- Tap or click the 'Add a Cover Page' button (INSERT tab | Pages group) to display the Add a Cover Page gallery (Figure 9–39).

Experiment

- Scroll through the Add a Cover Page gallery to see the variety of available predefined cover pages.

Q&A
Does it matter where I position the insertion point before inserting a cover page?
No. By default, Word inserts the cover page as the first page in a document.

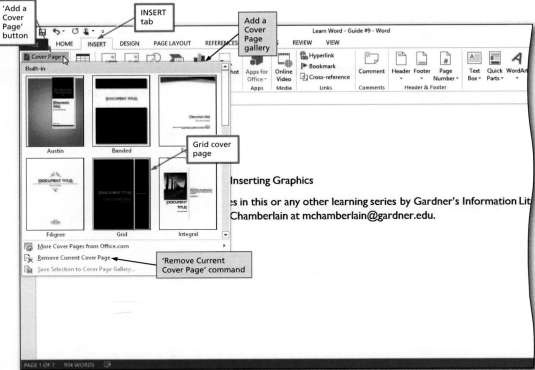

Figure 9–39

②

- Tap or click Grid in the Add a Cover Page gallery to insert the selected cover page as the first page in the current document.

- Display the VIEW tab. Tap or click the One Page button (VIEW tab | Zoom group) to display the entire cover page in the document window (Figure 9–40).

Q&A

Does the cover page have to be the first page?

No. You can press and hold or right-click the desired cover page and then tap or click the desired location on the submenu.

How would I delete a cover page?

You would tap or click the 'Add a Cover Page' button (INSERT tab | Pages group) and then tap or click 'Remove Current Cover Page' in the Add a Cover Page gallery.

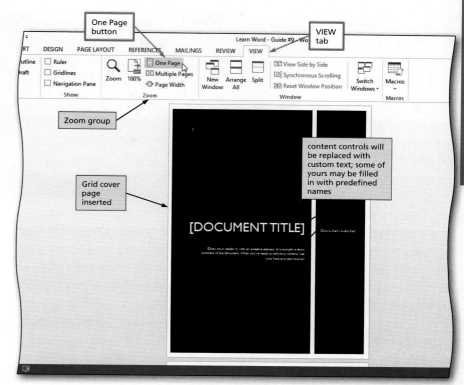

Figure 9–40

③

- Change the zoom back to page width.

Other Ways

1. Tap or click 'Explore Quick Parts' button (INSERT tab | Text group), tap or click 'Building Blocks Organizer', select desired cover page building block (Building Blocks Organizer dialog box), tap or click Insert button, tap or click Close button

---

To Enter Text in Content Controls

The next step is to select content controls on the cover page and replace their instructions or text with the title page information. Keep in mind that the content controls present suggested text. Depending on settings on your computer or mobile device, some content controls already may contain customized text, which you will change. You can enter any appropriate text in any content control. The following steps enter title page text on the cover page.

① Tap or click the DOCUMENT TITLE content control and then type **LEARN WORD** as the title.

② Tap or click the Document subtitle content control and then type **Inserting Graphics** as the subtitle.

③ Tap or click the content control that begins with the instruction, Draw your reader in with an engaging abstract. Type **A series of guides designed to strengthen your information literacy skills.** in the content control. (Figure 9–41 on the next page).

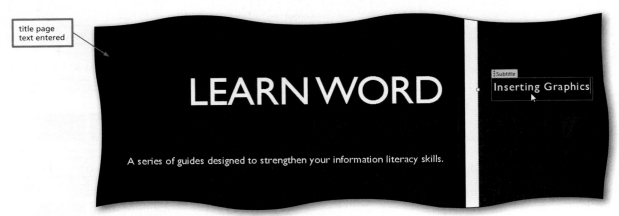

title page text entered

Subtitle
Inserting Graphics

A series of guides designed to strengthen your information literacy skills.

Figure 9–41

To Center Text

The next step is to center the text on the copyright page. The following steps center text.

1 Scroll to display the copyright page text in the document window.

2 Select the text on the copyright page and then center it.

3 Deselect the text.

To Insert a Continuous Section Break and Change the Margins in the Section

The margins on the copyright page are wider than the rest of the document. To change margins for a page, the page must be in a separate section. The next steps insert a continuous section break and then change the margins.

1 Position the insertion point at the location for the section break, in this case, to the left of L in Learn on the copyright page.

2 Display the PAGE LAYOUT tab. Tap or click the 'Insert Page and Section Breaks' button (PAGE LAYOUT tab | Page Setup group) to display the Insert Page and Section Breaks gallery.

3 Tap or click Continuous in the Insert Page and Section Breaks gallery to insert a continuous section break to the left of the insertion point.

4 Tap or click the Adjust Margins button (PAGE LAYOUT tab | Page Setup group) to display the Adjust Margins gallery and then tap or click Wide in the Adjust Margins gallery to change the margins on the copyright page to the selected settings (Figure 9–42).

BTW
Quick Reference
For a table that lists how to complete the tasks covered in this book using touch gestures, the mouse, ribbon, shortcut menu, and keyboard, see the Quick Reference Summary at the back of this book, or visit the Quick Reference resource on the Student Companion Site located on www.cengagebrain.com. For detailed instructions about accessing available resources, visit www.cengage.com/ct/studentdownload or contact your instructor for information about accessing the required files.

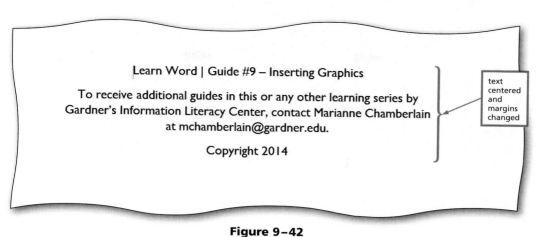

Figure 9–42

To Adjust Vertical Alignment on a Page

You can instruct Word to center the contents of a page vertically using one of two options: place an equal amount of space above and below the text on the page, or evenly space each paragraph between the top and bottom margins. The following steps vertically center text on a page. *Why? The copyright page in this project evenly spaces each paragraph on a page between the top and bottom margins, which is called justified vertical alignment.*

1

- Tap or click the Page Setup Dialog Box Launcher (PAGE LAYOUT tab | Page Setup group) to display the Page Setup dialog box.

- Tap or click the Layout tab (Page Setup dialog box) to display the Layout sheet.

- Tap or click the Vertical alignment arrow and then tap or click Justified (Figure 9–43).

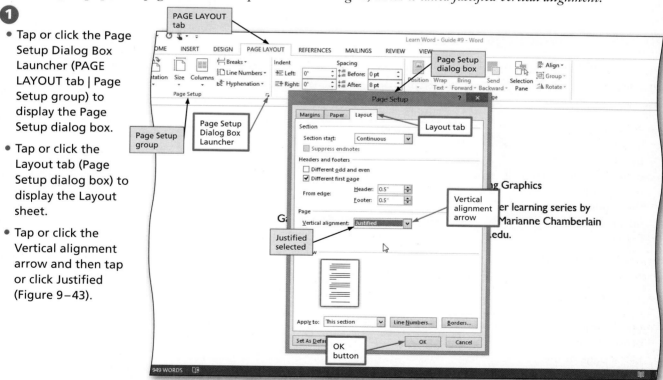

Figure 9–43

- Tap or click the OK button to justify the text in the current section.
- To see the entire justified page, display the VIEW tab and then tap or click the One Page button (VIEW tab | Zoom group) (Figure 9–44).

- Change the zoom back to page width.

Q&A

What are the other vertical alignments?

Top, the default, aligns contents starting at the top margin on the page. Center places all contents centered vertically on the page, and Bottom places contents at the bottom of the page.

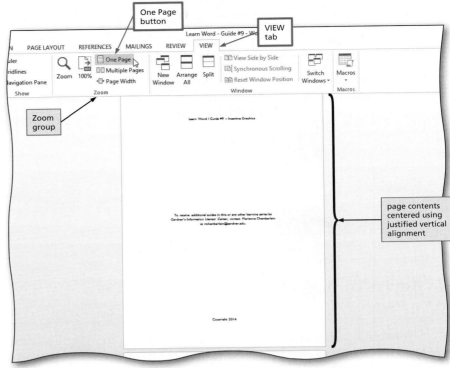

Figure 9–44

To Insert a Blank Page

1 MODIFY REFERENCE DOCUMENT | 2 CREATE MASTER DOCUMENT | 3 ORGANIZE REFERENCE DOCUMENT

The following step inserts a blank page. *Why? In the reference document in this chapter, the table of contents is on a page between the copyright page and the first page of the subdocument.*

- Position the insertion point to the left of the word, Inserting, on the first page of the subdocument (as shown in Figure 9–45).
- Display the INSERT tab.
- Tap or click the 'Add a Blank Page' button (INSERT tab | Pages group) to insert a blank page at the location of the insertion point.
- If necessary, scroll to display the blank page in the document window (Figure 9–45).

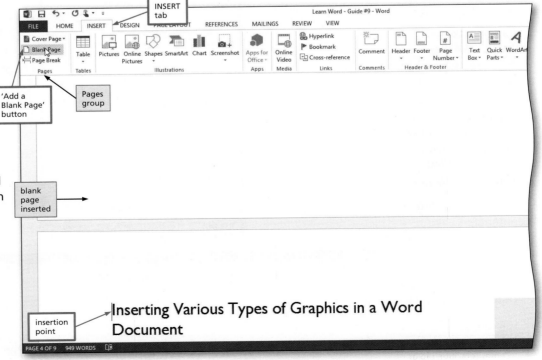

Inserting Various Types of Graphics in a Word Document

Figure 9–45

To Create a Table of Contents

1 MODIFY REFERENCE DOCUMENT | 2 CREATE MASTER DOCUMENT | **3 ORGANIZE REFERENCE DOCUMENT**

A table of contents lists all headings in a document and their associated page numbers. When you use Word's built-in heading styles (for example, Heading 1, Heading 2, and so on), you can instruct Word to create a table of contents from these headings. In the reference document in this chapter, the heading of each section uses the Heading 1 style, and subheadings use the Heading 2 style.

The following steps use a predefined building block to create a table of contents. *Why? Using Word's predefined table of contents formats can be more efficient than creating a table of contents from scratch.*

1

- Position the insertion point at the top of the blank page 3, which is the location for the table of contents. (If necessary, show formatting marks so that you easily can see the paragraph mark at the top of the page.)

- Ensure that formatting marks do not show.

Q&A Why should I hide formatting marks?
Formatting marks, especially those for index entries, sometimes can cause wrapping to occur on the screen that will be different from how the printed document will wrap. These differences could cause a heading to move to the next page. To ensure that the page references in the table of contents reflect the printed pages, be sure that formatting marks are hidden when you create a table of contents.

- Display the REFERENCES tab.

- Tap or click the 'Table of Contents' button (REFERENCES tab | Table of Contents group) to display the Table of Contents gallery (Figure 9–46).

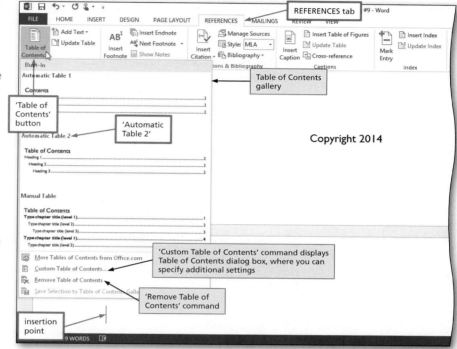

Figure 9–46

2

- Tap or click 'Automatic Table 2' in the Table of Contents gallery to insert the table of contents at the location of the insertion point (Figure 9–47). If necessary, scroll to see the table of contents.

Q&A How would I delete a table of contents?
You would tap or click the 'Table of Contents' button (REFERENCES tab | Table of Contents group) and then tap or click 'Remove Table of Contents' in the Table of Contents gallery.

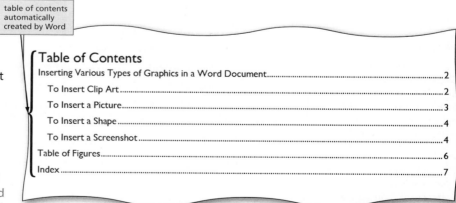

Table of Contents

Figure 9–47

Other Ways

1. Tap or click 'Table of Contents' button (REFERENCES tab | Table of Contents group), tap or click 'Custom Table of Contents', select table of contents options (Table of Contents dialog box), tap or click OK button

2. Tap or click 'Explore Quick Parts' button (INSERT tab | Text group), tap or click 'Building Blocks Organizer', select desired table of contents building block (Building Blocks Organizer dialog box), tap or click Insert button, tap or click Close button

To Insert a Continuous Section Break and Change the Starting Page Number in the Section

The table of contents should not be the starting page number; instead, the subdocument should be the starting page number in the document. To change the starting page number, the page must be in a separate section. The following steps insert a continuous section break and then change the starting page number for the table of contents.

1 Position the insertion point at the location for the section break, in this case, to the left of I in Inserting Various Types of Graphics in a Word Document.

2 Display the PAGE LAYOUT tab. Tap or click the 'Insert Page and Section Breaks' button (PAGE LAYOUT tab | Page Setup group) to display the Insert Page and Section Breaks gallery.

3 Tap or click Continuous in the Insert Page and Section Breaks gallery to insert a continuous section break to the left of the insertion point.

4 Position the insertion point in the table of contents.

5 Display the INSERT tab. Tap or click the 'Add Page Numbers' button (INSERT tab | Header & Footer group) to display the Add Page Numbers menu and then tap or click 'Format Page Numbers' on the Add Page Numbers menu to display the Page Number Format dialog box.

6 Tap or click the Start at down arrow (Page Number Format dialog box) until 0 is displayed in the Start at box (Figure 9–48).

7 Tap or click the OK button to change the starting page for the current section.

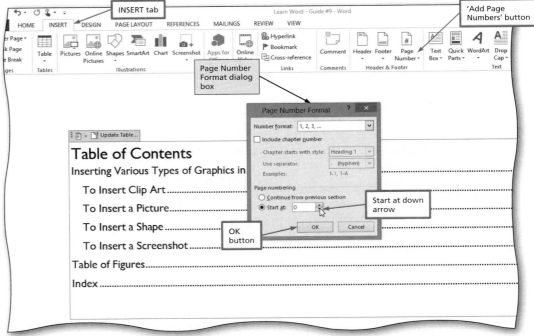

Figure 9–48

BTW
Advanced Layout Options
You can adjust Word's advanced layout options by tapping or clicking FILE on the ribbon to open the Backstage view, tapping or clicking Options in the Backstage view to display the Word Options dialog box, tapping or clicking Advanced in the left pane (Word Options dialog box), sliding or scrolling to the Layout options for area in the right pane, placing a check mark in the desired settings, and then tapping or clicking the OK button.

To Update Page Numbers in a Table of Contents

When you change a document, you should update the associated table of contents. The following steps update the page numbers in the table of contents. *Why? The starting page number change will affect the page numbers in the table of contents.*

- If necessary, tap or click the table of contents to select it.

Q&A If I am using a mouse, why does the ScreenTip say 'CTRL+Click to follow link'?
Each entry in the table of contents is a link. If you hold down the CTRL key while clicking an entry in the table of contents, Word will display the associated heading in the document window.

- Tap or click the Update Table button that is attached to the table of contents to display the Update Table of Contents dialog box.

- Ensure the 'Update page numbers only' option button is selected because you want to update only the page numbers in the table of contents (Figure 9–49).

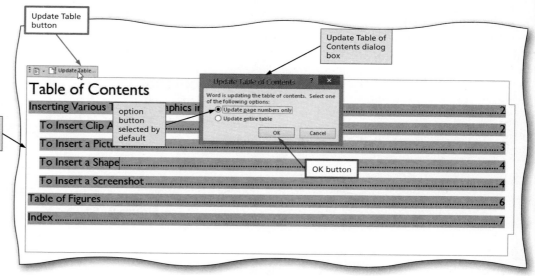

Figure 9–49

- Tap or click the OK button (Update Table of Contents dialog box) to update the page numbers in the table of contents.

- Tap or click outside the table of contents to remove the selection from the table (Figure 9–50).

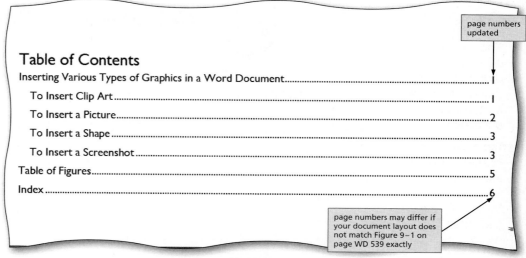

Figure 9–50

Other Ways

1. Select table, tap or click Update Table button (REFERENCES tab | Table of Contents group)   2. Select table, press F9 key

To Find a Format

The subdocument contains a sentence of text formatted as bold italic. To find this text in the document, you could scroll through the document until it is displayed on the screen. A more efficient way is to find the bold, italic format using the Find and Replace dialog box. The following steps find a format. *Why? You want to add the text to the table of contents.*

- If necessary, display the HOME tab.

- Tap or click the Find arrow (HOME tab | Editing group) to display the Find menu (Figure 9–51).

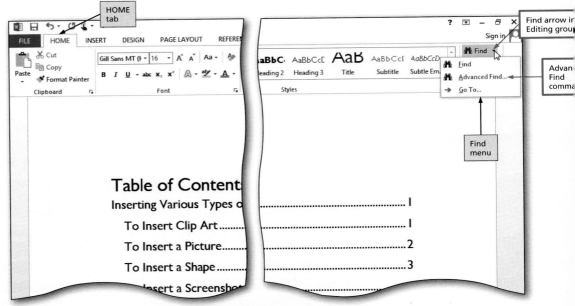

Figure 9–51

2

- Tap or click Advanced Find on the Find menu to display the Find and Replace dialog box.

- If Word displays a More button in the Find and Replace dialog box, tap or click it so that it changes to a Less button and expands the dialog box.

- Tap or click the Format button (Find and Replace dialog box) to display the Format menu (Figure 9–52).

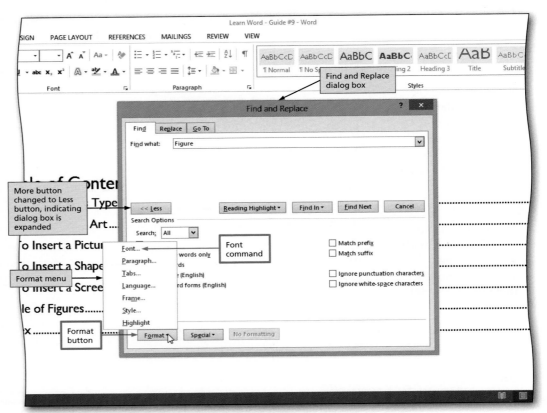

Figure 9–52

- Tap or click Font on the Format menu to display the Find Font dialog box. If necessary, tap or click the Font tab (Find Font dialog box) to display the Font sheet.

- Tap or click Bold Italic in the Font style list because that is the format you want to find (Figure 9–53).

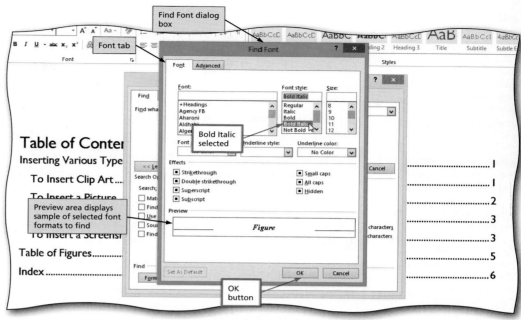

Figure 9–53

- Tap or click the OK button to close the Find Font dialog box.

- Be sure no text is in the Find what text box (or tap or click the Find what arrow and then click [Formatting Only]).

- Be sure all check boxes in the Search Options area are cleared.

- When the Find and Replace dialog box is active again, tap or click its Find Next button to locate and highlight in the document the first occurrence of the specified format (Figure 9–54).

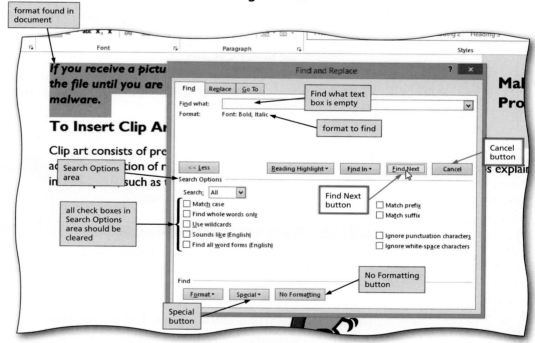

Figure 9–54

Q&A How do I remove a find format?

You would tap or click the No Formatting button in the Find and Replace dialog box.

- Tap or click the Cancel button (Find and Replace dialog box) because the located occurrence is the one you wanted to find.

Q&A Can I search for (find) special characters such as page breaks?

Yes. To find special characters, you would tap or click the Special button in the Find and Replace dialog box.

Other Ways

1. Press CTRL+F

BTW
Find and Replace
The expanded Find and Replace dialog box allows you to specify how Word locates search text. For example, selecting the Match case check box instructs Word to find the text exactly as you typed it, and selecting the 'Find whole words only' check box instructs Word to ignore text that contains the search text (i.e., the word, then, contains the word, the). If you select the Use wildcard check box, you can use wildcard characters in a search. For example, with this check box selected, the search text of *ing would search for all words that end with the characters, ing.

To Format Text as a Heading

The following steps format a paragraph of text as a Heading 3 style. Occasionally, you may want to add a paragraph of text, which normally is not formatted using a heading style, to a table of contents. One way to add the text is to format it as a heading style.

1 With the paragraph still selected (shown in Figure 9–54), if necessary, display the HOME tab.

2 Tap or click Heading 3 in the Styles gallery to apply the selected style to the current paragraph in the document. Tap or click outside the paragraph to deselect it (Figure 9–55).

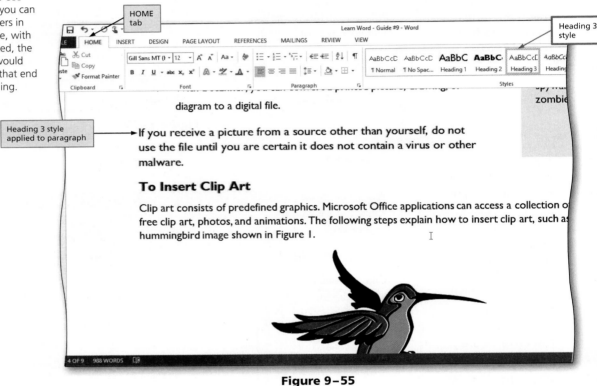

Figure 9–55

BTW
Replace Formats
You can tap or click the Replace tab (Find and Replace dialog box) to find and replace formats. Follow the steps on the previous two pages to enter the format to find in the Find what text box and then follow the same steps to enter the format to replace in the Replace with text box. Next, tap or click the Replace or Replace All button to replace the next occurrence of the format or all occurrences of the format in the document.

To Retain Formatting when Adding Text to the Table of Contents

If you wanted to retain formatting of text when adding it to the table of contents, you would perform the following steps.

1. Position the insertion point in the paragraph of text that you want to add to the table of contents.

2. Tap or click the Add Text button (REFERENCES tab | Table of Contents group) to display the Add Text menu.

3. Tap or click the desired level on the Add Text menu, which adds the format of the selected style to the selected paragraph and adds the paragraph of text to the table of contents.

To Update the Entire Table of Contents

1 MODIFY REFERENCE DOCUMENT | 2 CREATE MASTER DOCUMENT | 3 ORGANIZE REFERENCE DOCUMENT

The following steps update the entire table of contents. ***Why?*** *The text changed to the Heading 3 style should appear in the table of contents.*

- Display the table of contents in the document window.

- Tap or click the table of contents to select it.

- Tap or click the Update Table button that is attached to the table of contents to display the Update Table of Contents dialog box.

- Tap or click the 'Update entire table' option button (Update Table of Contents dialog box) because you want to update the entire table of contents (Figure 9–56).

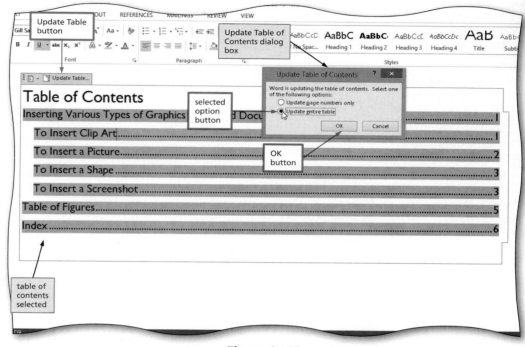

Figure 9–56

- Tap or click the OK button (Update Table of Contents dialog box) to update the entire table of contents (Figure 9–57).

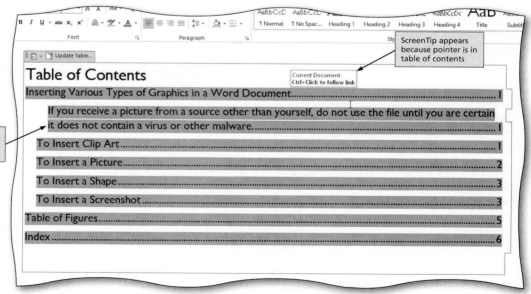

Figure 9–57

Other Ways

1. Select table, tap or click Update Table button (REFERENCES tab | Table of Contents group)

2. Select table, press F9 key

To Change the Format of a Table of Contents

You can change the format of the table of contents to any of the predefined table of contents styles or to custom settings. The following steps change the table of contents format. **Why?** *In this table of contents, you specify the format, page number alignment, and tab leader character.*

- Display the REFERENCES tab.

- Tap or click the 'Table of Contents' button (REFERENCES tab | Table of Contents group) to display the Table of Contents gallery (Figure 9–58).

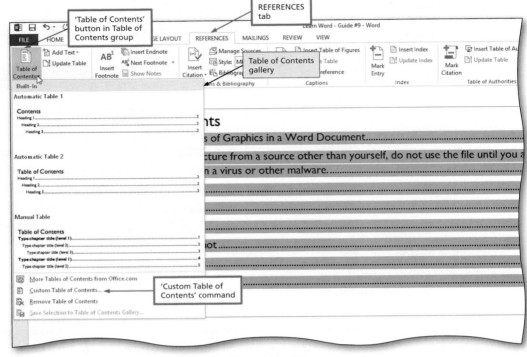

Figure 9–58

- Tap or click 'Custom Table of Contents' in the Table of Contents gallery to display the Table of Contents dialog box.

- Tap or click the Formats arrow (Table of Contents dialog box) and then tap or click Simple to change the format style for the table of contents.

- Place a check mark in the 'Right align page numbers' check box so that the page numbers appear at the right margin in the table of contents.

- Tap or click the Tab leader arrow and then tap or click the first leader type in the list so that the selected leader characters appear between the heading name and the page numbers in the table of contents (Figure 9–59).

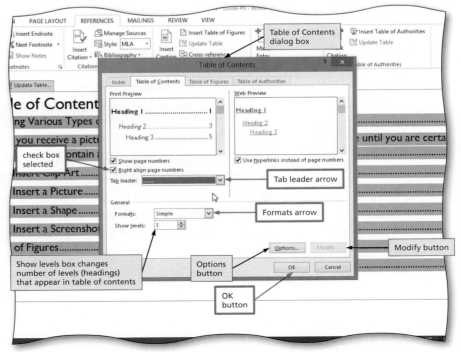

Figure 9–59

3

- Tap or click the OK button to modify the table of contents according to the specified settings. When Word displays a dialog box asking if you want to replace the selected table of contents, tap or click the Yes button (Figure 9–60).

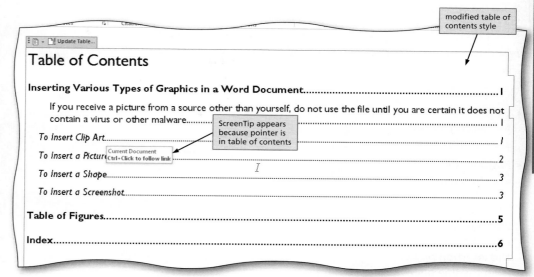

Figure 9–60

To Use the Navigation Pane to Go to a Heading in a Document

1 MODIFY REFERENCE DOCUMENT | 2 CREATE MASTER DOCUMENT | 3 ORGANIZE REFERENCE DOCUMENT

When you use Word's built-in heading styles in a document, you can use the Navigation Pane to go to headings in a document quickly. *Why? When you tap or click a heading in the Navigation Pane, Word displays the page associated with that heading in the document window.* The following step uses the Navigation Pane to display an associated heading in the document window.

1

- Display the VIEW tab. Place a check mark in the 'Open the Navigation Pane' check box (VIEW tab | Show group) to display the Navigation Pane at the left edge of the Word window.

- If necessary, tap or click the HEADINGS tab in the Navigation Pane to display the text that is formatted using Heading styles.

- Tap or click the Table of Figures heading in the Navigation Pane to display the top of the selected page in the top of the document window (Figure 9–61).

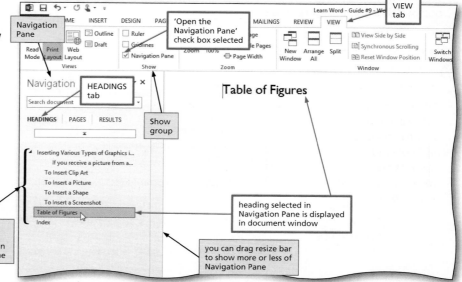

Figure 9–61

Q&A What if all of the headings are not displayed?

Press and hold or right-click a heading in the Navigation Pane and then tap or click Expand All on the shortcut menu to ensure that all headings are displayed. If a heading still is not displayed, verify that the heading is formatted with a heading style. To display or hide subheadings below a heading in the Navigation Pane, tap or click the triangle to the left of the heading. If a heading is too wide for the Navigation Pane, you can point to the heading to display a ScreenTip that shows the complete title.

To Create a Table of Figures

The following steps create a table of figures. *Why? At the end of the reference document is a table of figures, which lists all figures and their corresponding page numbers. Word generates this table of figures from the captions in the document.*

1

- Ensure that formatting marks are not displayed.

- Position the insertion point at the end of the Table of Figures heading and then press the ENTER key, so that the insertion point is on the line below the heading.

- Display the REFERENCES tab.

- Tap or click the 'Table of Figures Dialog' button (REFERENCES tab | Captions group) to display the Table of Figures dialog box.

- Be sure that all settings in your dialog box match those in Figure 9–62.

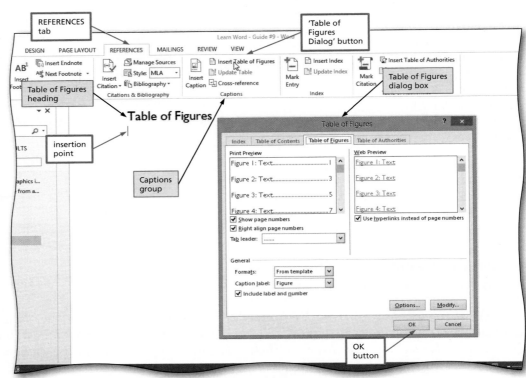

Figure 9–62

2

- Tap or click the OK button (Table of Figures dialog box) to create a table of figures at the location of the insertion point (Figure 9–63).

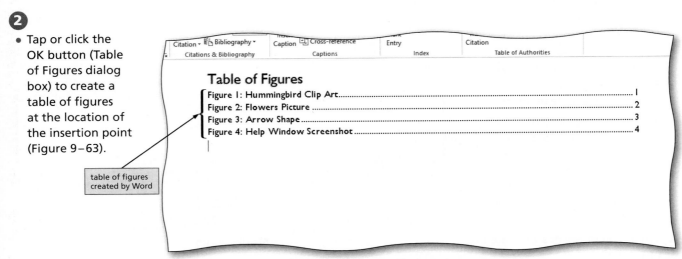

Figure 9–63

To Change the Format of the Table of Figures

If you wanted to change the format of the table of figures, you would perform the following steps.

1. Tap or click the table of figures to select it.
2. Tap or click the 'Table of Figures Dialog' button (REFERENCES tab | Captions group) to display the Table of Figures dialog box.
3. Change settings in the dialog box as desired.
4. Tap or click the OK button (Table of Figures dialog box) to apply the changed settings.
5. Tap or click the OK button when Word asks if you want to replace the selected table of figures.

To Edit a Caption and Update the Table of Figures

1 MODIFY REFERENCE DOCUMENT | 2 CREATE MASTER DOCUMENT | **3 ORGANIZE REFERENCE DOCUMENT**

The following steps change the Figure 4 caption and then update the table of figures. *Why? When you modify captions in a document or move illustrations to a different location in the document, you will have to update the table of figures.*

- Tap or click the heading, To Insert a Screenshot, in the Navigation Pane to display the selected heading in the document window. (If this heading is not at the top of page 7, insert a page break to position the heading at the top of a new page.)

- Insert the text, Word, in the Figure 4 caption so that it reads: Word Help Window Screenshot (Figure 9–64).

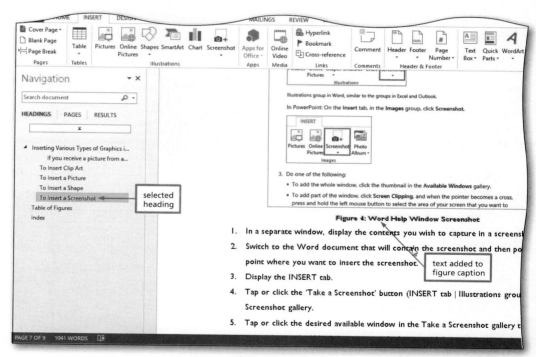

Figure 9–64

BTW
Table of Contents Styles
If you wanted to change the level associated with each style used in a table of contents, tap or click the Options button in the Table of Contents dialog box (shown in Figure 9–59 on page WD 580), enter the desired level number in the text box beside the appropriate heading or other styled item, and then tap or click the OK button. To change the formatting associated with a style, tap or click the Modify button in the Table of Contents dialog box.

2

- Tap or click the heading, Table of Figures, in the Navigation Pane to display the Table of Figures heading in the document window.

- Tap or click the table of figures to select it.

- Tap or click the 'Update Table of Figures' button (REFERENCES tab | Captions group) to display the Update Table of Figures dialog box.

- Tap or click 'Update entire table' (Update Table of Figures dialog box), so that Word updates the contents of the entire table of figures instead of updating only the page numbers (Figure 9–65).

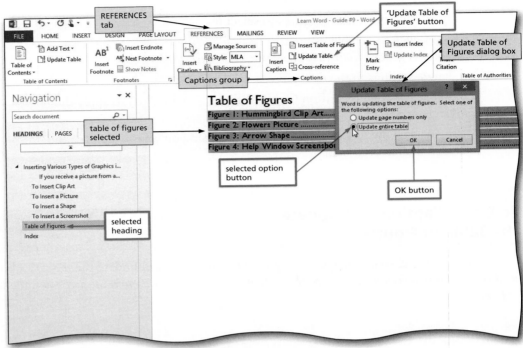

Figure 9–65

3

- Tap or click the OK button to update the table of figures and then tap or click outside the table to deselect it (Figure 9–66).

 Are the entries in the table of figures links?

Yes. As with the table of contents, if you are using a mouse, you can CTRL+click any entry in the table of figures and Word will display the associated figure in the document window.

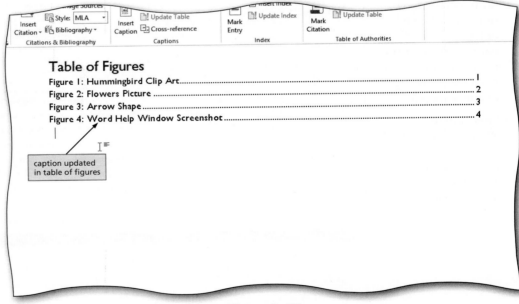

Figure 9–66

Other Ways

1. Select table of figures, press F9 key

To Build an Index

1 MODIFY REFERENCE DOCUMENT | 2 CREATE MASTER DOCUMENT | 3 ORGANIZE REFERENCE DOCUMENT

The reference document in this chapter ends with an index. Earlier, this chapter showed how to mark index entries. *Why? For Word to generate the index, you first must mark any text you wish to appear in the index.*

Once all index entries are marked, Word can build the index from the index entry fields in the document. Recall that index entry fields begin with XE, which appears on the screen when formatting marks are displayed. When index entry fields show on the screen, the document's pagination probably will be altered because of the extra text in the index entries. Thus, be sure to hide formatting marks before building an index. The following steps build an index.

- Tap or click the heading, Index, in the Navigation Pane to display the Index heading in the document window.
- Tap or click to the right of the Index heading and then press the ENTER key, so that the insertion point is on the line below the heading.
- Ensure that formatting marks are not displayed.
- Tap or click the Insert Index button (REFERENCES tab | Index group) to display the Index dialog box.
- If necessary, tap or click the Formats arrow in the dialog box and then tap or click Classic in the Formats list to change the index format.
- Place a check mark in the 'Right align page numbers' check box.
- Tap or click the Tab leader arrow and then tap or click the first leader character in the list to specify the leader character to be displayed between the index entry and the page number.
- Tap or click the Columns down arrow until the number of columns is 1 to change the number of columns in the index (Figure 9–67).

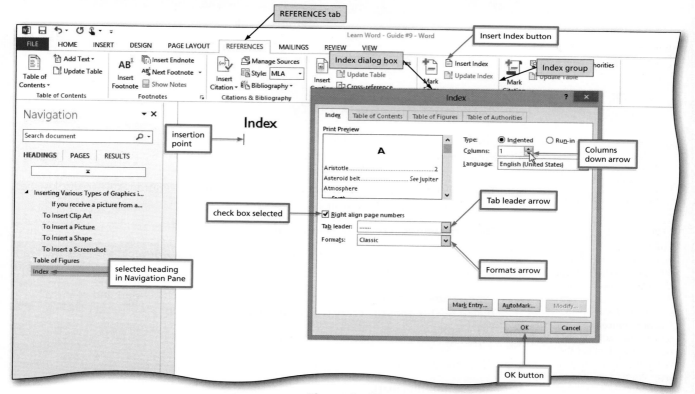

Figure 9–67

2

- Tap or click the OK button (Index dialog box) to create an index at the location of the insertion point (Figure 9–68).

Q&A

How would I change the language used in the index?

Tap or click the Language arrow (Index dialog box) and then tap or click the desired language.

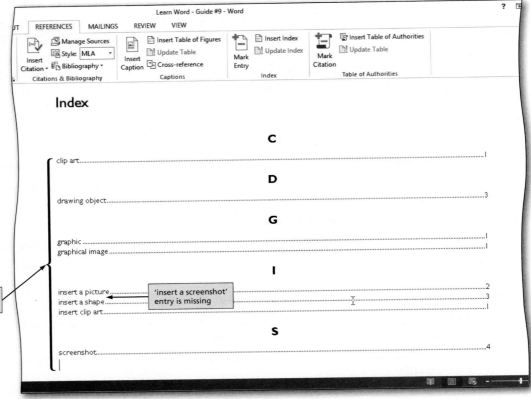

Figure 9–68

To Mark Another Index Entry

Notice in Figure 9–68 that the 'insert a screenshot' index entry is missing. The following steps mark an index entry in the Insert a Screenshot section.

1 Tap or click the heading, To Insert a Screenshot, in the Navigation Pane to display the selected heading in the document window.

2 Select the words, Insert a Screenshot, in the heading.

3 Tap or click the Mark Entry button (REFERENCES tab | Index group) to display the Mark Index Entry dialog box.

4 Type **insert a screenshot** in the Main entry text box (Mark Index Entry dialog box) so that the entry is all lowercase (Figure 9–69).

5 Tap or click the Mark button to mark the entry.

6 Close the dialog box.

7 Hide formatting marks.

BTW
Index Files
Instead of marking index entries in a document, you can create a concordance file that contains all index entries you wish to mark. A **concordance file** contains two columns: the first column identifies the text in the document you want Word to mark as an index entry, and the second column lists the index entries to be generated from the text in the first column. To mark entries in the concordance file, tap or click the AutoMark button in the Index and Tables dialog box.

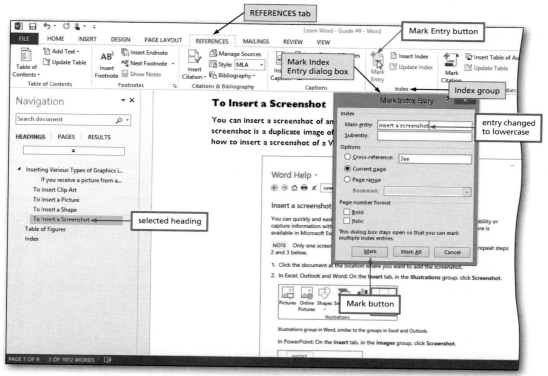

Figure 9–69

TO EDIT AN INDEX ENTRY

At some time, you may want to change an index entry after you have marked it. For example, you may forget to lowercase the entry for the headings. If you wanted to change an index entry, you would perform the following steps.

1. Display formatting marks.
2. Locate the XE field for the index entry you wish to change (i.e., { XE "Insert a Screenshot" }).
3. Change the text inside the quotation marks (i.e., { XE "insert a screenshot" }).
4. Update the index as described in the steps on the next page.

TO DELETE AN INDEX ENTRY

If you wanted to delete an index entry, you would perform the following steps.

1. Display formatting marks.
2. Select the XE field for the index entry you wish to delete (i.e., { XE "insert a screenshot" }).
3. Press the DELETE key.
4. Update the index as described in the steps on the next page.

BTW

Navigation Pane
You can drag any heading in the Navigation Pane to reorganize document content. For example, you could drag the 'To Insert a Screenshot' heading upward in the Navigation Pane so that its content appears earlier in the document.

To Update an Index

The following step updates an index. *Why? After marking a new index entry, you must update the index.*

- Tap or click the heading, Index, in the Navigation Pane to display the selected heading in the document window.
- In the document window, tap or click the index to select it.
- If necessary, display the REFERENCES tab.
- Tap or click the Update Index button (REFERENCES tab | Index group) to update the index (Figure 9–70).

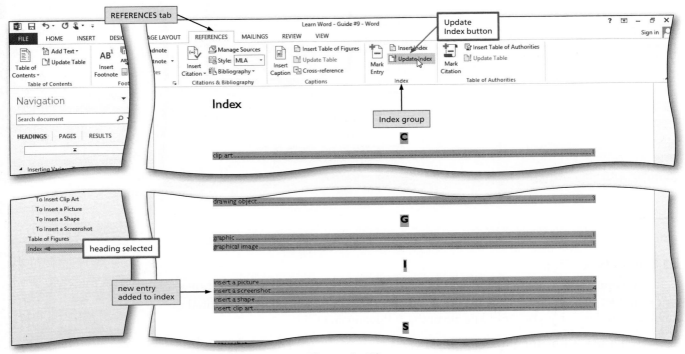

Figure 9–70

Other Ways

1. Select index, press F9 key

TO CHANGE THE FORMAT OF THE INDEX

If you wanted to change the format of the index, you would perform the following steps.

1. Tap or click the index to select it.
2. Tap or click the Insert Index button (REFERENCES tab | Index group) to display the Index dialog box.
3. Change settings in the dialog box as desired. If you want to modify the style used for the index, tap or click the Modify button.
4. Tap or click the OK button (Index dialog box) to apply the changed settings.
5. Tap or click the OK button when Word asks if you want to replace the selected index.

TO DELETE AN INDEX

If you wanted to delete an index, you would perform the following steps.

1. Tap or click the index to select it.
2. Press SHIFT+F9 to display field codes.
3. Drag through the entire field code, including the braces, and then press the DELETE key.

Table of Authorities

In addition to creating an index, table of figures, and table of contents, you can use Word to create a table of authorities. Legal documents often include a **table of authorities** to list references to cases, rules, statutes, etc. To create a table of authorities, mark the citations first and then build the table of authorities.

The procedures for marking citations, editing citations, creating the table of authorities, changing the format of the table of authorities, and updating the table of authorities are the same as those for indexes. The only difference is you use the buttons in the Table of Authorities group on the REFERENCES tab instead of the buttons in the Index group.

BTW
Table of Authorities
See pages WD 723 through WD 726 in the Supplementary Word Tasks section of Chapter 11 for additional instructions related to creating a table of authorities.

To Create Alternating Footers Using a Footer Building Block

1 MODIFY REFERENCE DOCUMENT | 2 CREATE MASTER DOCUMENT | **3 ORGANIZE REFERENCE DOCUMENT**

The *Learn Word* documents are designed so that they can be duplicated back-to-back. That is, the document prints on nine separate pages. When they are duplicated, however, pages one and two are printed on opposite sides of the same sheet of paper. ***Why?*** *Back-to-back duplicating saves resources because it enables the nine-page document to use only five sheets of paper.*

In many books and documents that have facing pages, the page number is always on the same side of the page — often on the outside edge. In Word, you accomplish this task by specifying one type of header or footer for even-numbered pages and another type of header or footer for odd-numbered pages. The following steps create alternating footers beginning on the fourth page of the document (the beginning of the subdocument).

1

- If necessary, hide formatting marks.
- Use the Navigation Pane to display the page with the heading, Inserting Various Types of Graphics in a Word Document.
- Display the INSERT tab.
- Tap or click the 'Add a Footer' button (INSERT tab | Header & Footer group) and then tap or click Edit Footer to display the footer area.
- Be sure the 'Link to Previous' button (HEADER & FOOTER TOOLS DESIGN tab | Navigation group) is not selected.
- Place a check mark in the 'Different Odd & Even Pages' check box (HEADER & FOOTER TOOLS DESIGN tab | Options group), so that you can enter a different footer for odd and even pages.
- If necessary, tap or click the Show Next button (HEADER & FOOTER TOOLS DESIGN tab | Navigation group) to display the desired footer page (in this case, the Odd Page Footer – Section 4).

2

- Tap or click the 'Insert Alignment Tab' button (HEADER & FOOTER TOOLS DESIGN tab | Position group) to display the Alignment Tab dialog box.

- Tap or click Right (Alignment Tab dialog box) because you want to place a right-aligned tab stop in the footer (Figure 9–71).

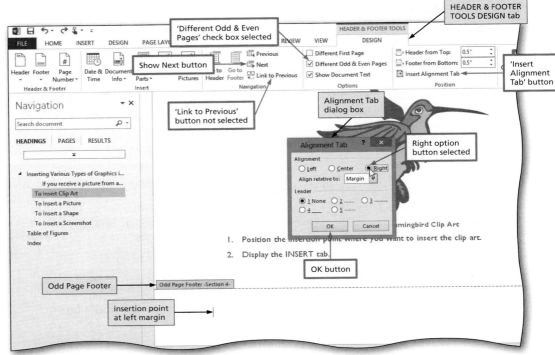

Figure 9–71

3

- Tap or click the OK button to align the paragraph and insertion point in the footer at the right margin.

- Tap or click the 'Add Page Numbers' button (HEADER & FOOTER TOOLS DESIGN tab | Header & Footer group) to display the Add Page Numbers gallery.

- Tap or point to Current Position in the Add Page Numbers gallery to display the Current Position gallery (Figure 9–72).

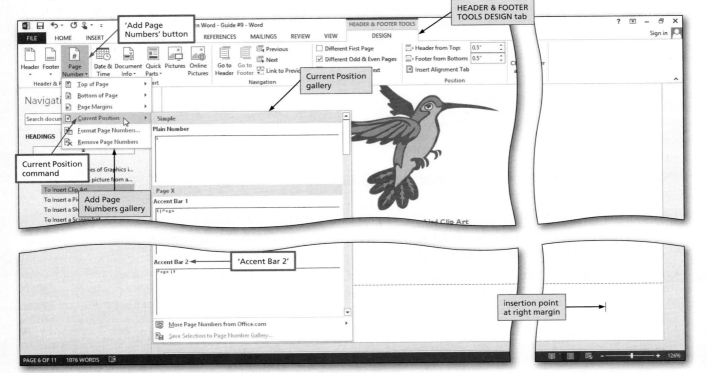

Figure 9–72

4

- Tap or click 'Accent Bar 2' in the Current Position gallery to insert the selected page number in the footer (Figure 9–73).

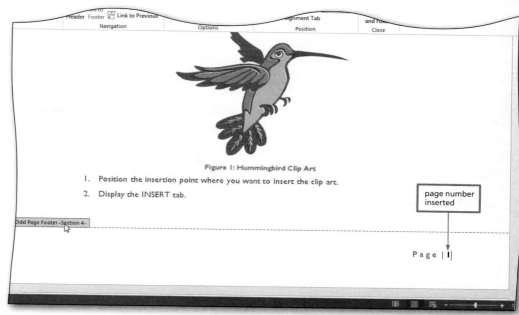

Figure 9–73

5

- Tap or click the Show Next button to display the next footer, in this case, Even Page Footer -Section 4-.

- Be sure the 'Link to Previous' button (HEADER & FOOTER TOOLS DESIGN tab | Navigation group) is not selected.

- Tap or click the 'Add Page Numbers' button (HEADER & FOOTER TOOLS DESIGN tab | Header & Footer group) to display the Add Page Numbers gallery.

- Tap or point to Current Position in the Add Page Numbers gallery to display the Current Position gallery.

- Tap or click 'Accent Bar 2' in the Current Position gallery to insert the selected page number in the footer (Figure 9–74).

Q&A Can I create alternating headers? Yes. Follow the same basic procedure, except insert a header building block or header text.

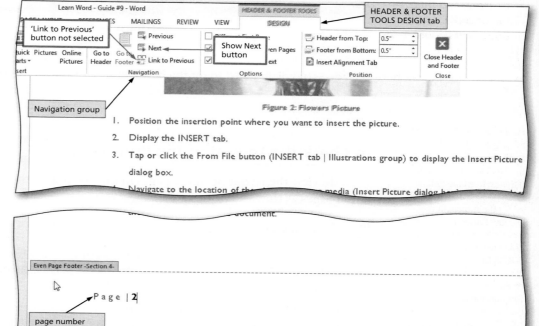

Figure 9–74

To Set a Gutter Margin

The reference document in this chapter is designed so that the inner margin between facing pages has extra space. *Why? Extra space on facing pages allows printed versions of the documents to be bound (such as stapled) — without the binding covering the words.* This extra space in the inner margin is called the **gutter margin**. The following steps set a three-quarter-inch left and right margin and a one-half-inch gutter margin.

- Display the PAGE LAYOUT tab.

- Tap or click the Adjust Margins button (PAGE LAYOUT tab | Page Setup group) and then tap or click Custom Margins in the Adjust Margins gallery to display the Page Setup dialog box.

- Type .75 in the Left box, .75 in the Right box, and .5 in the Gutter box (Page Setup dialog box).

- Tap or click the Apply to arrow and then tap or click Whole document (Figure 9–75).

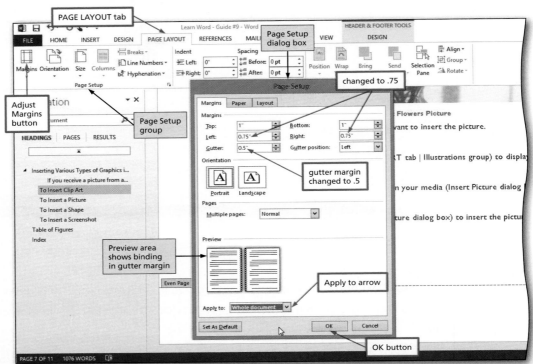

Figure 9–75

- Tap or click the OK button (Page Setup dialog box) to set the new margins for the entire document.

BTW
Header and Footer Margins
If you want the margin of the header or footer to be different from the default of one-half inch, you would adjust the margin in the 'Header Position from Top' or 'Footer Position from Bottom' boxes (HEADER & FOOTER TOOLS DESIGN tab | Position group) or in the Layout sheet of the Page Setup dialog box through the Page Setup Dialog Box Launcher (PAGE LAYOUT tab | Page Setup group). You also can specify alignment of items in the header or footer by tapping or clicking the 'Insert Alignment Tab' button (HEADER & FOOTER TOOLS DESIGN tab | Position group) and then tapping or clicking the desired alignment in the Alignment Tab dialog box.

To Check the Layout of the Printed Pages

To view the layout of all the pages in the document, the following steps display all the pages as they will print.

1 Open the Backstage view.

2 Tap or click the Print tab to display all pages of the document in the right pane, as shown in Figure 9–76. (If all pages are not displayed, change the Zoom level to 10%.)

Q&A Why do blank pages appear in the middle of the document?
When you insert even and odd headers or footers, Word may add pages to fill the gaps.

3 Close the Backstage view.

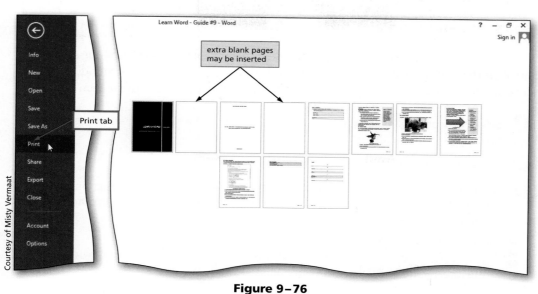

Figure 9–76

BTW
Set Print Scaling
If you wanted to ensure a document prints on a certain paper size, you can scale the document by opening the Backstage view, tapping or clicking the Print tab to display the Print gallery, tapping or clicking the bottom option in the Settings area (Print gallery), tapping or pointing to 'Scale to Paper Size', and then tapping or clicking the desired paper size before printing the document.

To Switch to Draft View

1 MODIFY REFERENCE DOCUMENT | 2 CREATE MASTER DOCUMENT | **3 ORGANIZE REFERENCE DOCUMENT**

To adjust the blank pages automatically inserted in the printed document by Word, you change the continuous section break at the top of the document to an odd page section break. The following step switches to Draft view. **Why?** *Section breaks are easy to see in Draft view.*

1

- Display the VIEW tab. Tap or click the Draft View button (VIEW tab | Views group) to switch to Draft view.

- Scroll to the top of the document and notice how different the document looks in Draft view (Figure 9–77).

Q&A

What happened to the graphics, footers, and other items?
They do not appear in Draft view because Draft view is designed to make editing text in a document easier.

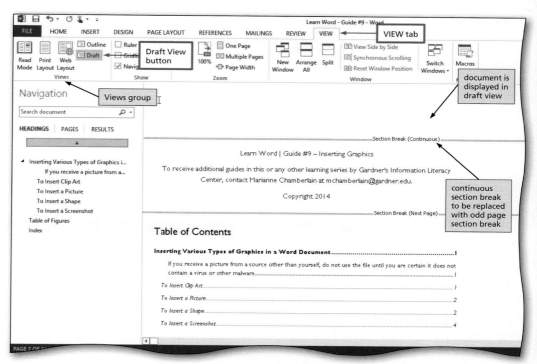

Figure 9–77

BTW
Different First Page
If you wanted only the first page of a document to have a different header or footer, you could place a check mark in the 'Different First Page' check box (HEADER & FOOTER TOOLS DESIGN tab | Options group). Doing so instructs Word to create a First Page Header or First Page Footer that can contain content that differs from the rest of the headers or footers.

To Insert an Odd Page Section Break

To fix the extra pages in the printed document, replace the continuous section break at the end of the title page with an odd page section break. With an odd page section break, Word starts the next section on an odd page instead of an even page.

1 Select the continuous section break at the bottom of the title page and then press the DELETE key to delete the selected section break.

2 If necessary, display the PAGE LAYOUT tab.

3 To insert an odd page section break, tap or click the 'Insert Page and Section Breaks' button (PAGE LAYOUT tab | Page Setup group) and then tap or click Odd Page in the Section Breaks area in the Insert Page and Section Breaks gallery (Figure 9–78).

Q&A Can I insert even page section breaks?
Yes. To instruct Word to start the next section on an even page, tap or click Even Page in the Insert Page and Section Breaks gallery.

4 Tap or click the Print Layout button on the status bar to switch to Print Layout view.

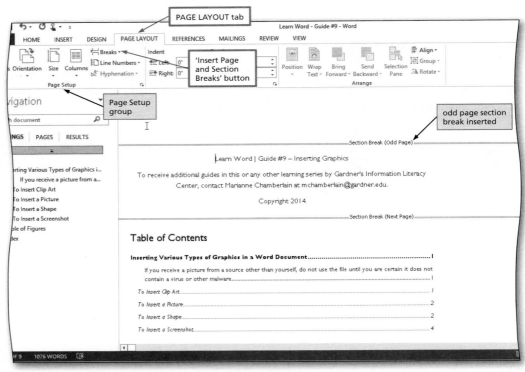

Figure 9–78

To Add a Bookmark

1 MODIFY REFERENCE DOCUMENT | 2 CREATE MASTER DOCUMENT | 3 ORGANIZE REFERENCE DOCUMENT

A **bookmark** is an item in a document that you name for future reference. The next steps add bookmarks. *Why? Bookmarks assist users in navigating through a document online. For example, you could bookmark the headings in the document, so that users easily could jump to these areas of the document.*

- Use the Navigation Pane to display the To Insert Clip Art heading in the document window and then select the heading.

- Display the INSERT tab.

- Tap or click the 'Insert a Bookmark' button (INSERT tab | Links group) to display the Bookmark dialog box.

- Type `ClipArt` in the Bookmark name text box (Figure 9–79).

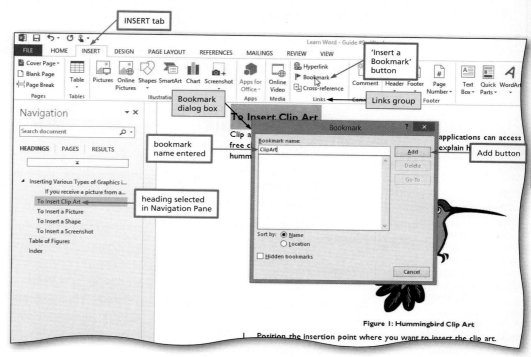

Figure 9–79

Q&A What are the rules for bookmark names?

Bookmark names can contain only letters, numbers, and the underscore character (_). They also must begin with a letter and cannot contain spaces.

- Tap or click the Add button (Bookmark dialog box) to add the bookmark name to the list of existing bookmarks in the document.

- Repeat Steps 1 and 2 for these headings in the document: To Insert a Picture, To Insert a Shape, and To Insert a Screenshot (use bookmark names Picture, Shape, and Screenshot).

To Go to a Bookmark

Once you have added bookmarks, you can jump to them by performing these steps.

1. Tap or click the 'Insert a Bookmark' button (INSERT tab | Links group) to display the Bookmark dialog box (Figure 9–79).

2. Tap or click the bookmark name in the Bookmark name list (Bookmark dialog box) and then tap or click the Go To button.

or

1. Press the F5 key to display the Go To sheet in the Find and Replace dialog box.

2. Tap or click Bookmark in the list (Find and Replace dialog box), select the bookmark name, and then tap or click the Go To button.

BTW
Link to Graphic
If you wanted to link a graphic in a document to a webpage, you would tap or click the 'Add a Hyperlink' button (INSERT tab | Links group), enter the web address in the Address text box (Insert Hyperlink dialog box), and then tap or click the OK button. To display the webpage associated with the graphic, tap or CTRL+click the graphic.

TO INSERT A HYPERLINK

Instead of or in addition to bookmarks in online documents, you can insert hyperlinks that link one part of a document to another. If you wanted to insert a hyperlink that links to a heading or bookmark in the document, you would follow these steps.

1. Select the text to be a hyperlink.
2. Tap or click the 'Add a Hyperlink' button (INSERT tab | Links group) to display the Insert Hyperlink dialog box.
3. In the Link to bar (Insert Hyperlink dialog box), tap or click 'Place in This Document', so that Word displays all the headings and bookmarks in the document.
4. Tap or click the heading or bookmark to which you want to link.
5. Tap or click the OK button.

BTW

Conserving Ink and Toner

If you want to conserve ink or toner, you can instruct Word to print draft quality documents by tapping or clicking FILE on the ribbon to open the Backstage view, tapping or clicking Options in the Backstage view to display the Word Options dialog box, tapping or clicking Advanced in the left pane (Word Options dialog box), sliding or scrolling to the Print area in the right pane, placing a check mark in the 'Use draft quality' check box, and then tapping or clicking the OK button. Then, use the Backstage view to print the document as usual.

To Save and Print a Document and Then Exit Word

The reference document for this project now is complete. Save the document, print it, and then exit Word.

1 Save the document with the same file name.

2 If requested by your instructor, print the finished document (shown in Figure 9–1 on page WD 539). Another option is to save the document as a PDF file and submit the PDF in the format requested by your instructor.

3 Exit Word.

Chapter Summary

In this chapter, you have learned how to insert a screenshot, add captions, create cross-references, use the Building Blocks Organizer, work with master documents and subdocuments, and create a table of contents, a table of figures, and an index. The items listed below include all the new Word skills you have learned in this chapter, with the tasks grouped by activity.

Enter and Edit Text
Switch to Outline View (WD 562)
Add Entries in Outline View (WD 562)
Show First Line Only (WD 564)
Insert a Subdocument (WD 564)
Exit Outline View (WD 567)
Insert a Cover Page (WD 568)
Insert a Blank Page (WD 572)
Find a Format (WD 576)
Use the Navigation Pane to Go to a Heading in a Document (WD 581)
Switch to Draft View (WD 593)
Add a Bookmark (WD 594)
Go to a Bookmark (WD 595)
Insert a Hyperlink (WD 596)

Format a Page
Change Paragraph Spacing in a Document (WD 551)
Adjust Vertical Alignment on a Page (WD 571)
Create Alternating Footers Using a Footer Building Block (WD 589)
Set a Gutter Margin (WD 592)

Reference Settings
Add a Caption (WD 544)
Create a Cross-Reference (WD 545)
Mark an Index Entry (WD 549)
Mark Multiple Index Entries (WD 551)
Create a Table of Contents (WD 573)
Update Page Numbers in a Table of Contents (WD 575)

What decisions will you need to make when creating reference documents?

Use these guidelines as you complete the assignments in this chapter and create your own reference documents outside of this class.

1. Prepare a document to be included in a longer document.

   a) If a document contains multiple illustrations (figures), each figure should have a caption and be referenced from within the text.

   b) All terms in the document that should be included in the index should be marked as an index entry.

2. Include elements common to a reference document such as a title page, a table of contents, and an index.

   a) The title page entices passersby to take a copy of the document.

   b) A table of contents at the beginning of the document and an index at the end helps a reader locate topics within the document.

   c) If a document contains several illustrations, you also should include a table of figures.

3. Prepare the document for distribution, including gutter margins for binding, bookmarks, and hyperlinks as appropriate.

CONSIDER THIS: PLAN AHEAD

How should you submit solutions to questions in the assignments identified with a  symbol?

Every assignment in this book contains one or more questions identified with a ✹ symbol. These questions require you to think beyond the assigned document. Present your solutions to the questions in the format required by your instructor. Possible formats may include one or more of these options: write the answer; create a document that contains the answer; present your answer to the class; discuss your answer in a group; record the answer as audio or video using a webcam, smartphone, or portable media player; or post answers on a blog, wiki, or website.

CONSIDER THIS

Apply Your Knowledge

Reinforce the skills and apply the concepts you learned in this chapter.

Working with Outline View

Note: To complete this assignment, you will be required to use the Data Files for Students. Visit www.cengage.com/ct/studentdownload for detailed instructions or contact your instructor for information about accessing the required files.

Instructions: Run Word. Open the document, Apply 9-1 Information Literacy Outline Draft, from the Data Files for Students. The document is an outline for a paper. You are to modify the outline in Outline view. The final outline is shown in Figure 9–80.

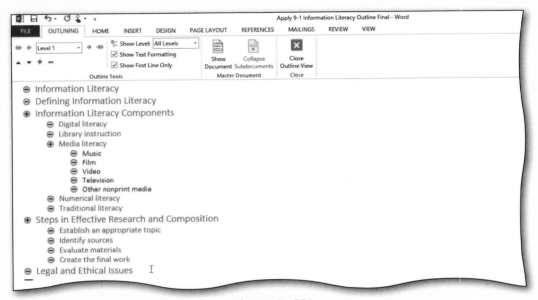

Figure 9–80

Perform the following tasks:

1. If necessary, switch to Outline view.
2. Move the item on the third line, Information Literacy, up two lines so that it is at the top of the outline.
3. In the Information Literacy Components section, move the item, Library instruction, down one line.
4. Practice collapsing and expanding by collapsing the Information Literacy Components item and then expanding the Information Literacy Components item.
5. Demote the five items in the outline below the item, Media literacy (Music, Film, Video, Television, and Other nonprint media) so that they are Level 3 instead of Level 2.
6. Promote the item, Identify sources, so that it is Level 2 instead of Level 3.
7. Change the word, Reading, in the Steps in Effective Reading and Composition item to the word, Research, so that it reads: Steps in Effective Research and Composition.
8. Insert an item, called Traditional literacy, as a Level 2 item below the Numerical literacy item.
9. Delete the item called Review media.
10. Promote the item, Legal and Ethical Issues, to Heading 1 (Level 1).
11. Remove the check mark in the 'Show Text Formatting' check box (OUTLINING tab | Outline Tools group). Place the check mark in the check box again. What is the purpose of this check box?

12. Close Outline view. How does the document differ when displayed in Print Layout view?

13. If requested by your instructor, add your name at the end of the first line of the outline. Save the modified file with a new file name, Apply 9-1 Information Literacy Outline Final. Submit the document in the format specified by your instructor.

14. ✷ Answer the questions posed in #11 and #12. What are two different ways to expand and collapse items in an outline, to move items up and down an outline, and to demote and promote items in an outline?

Extend Your Knowledge

Extend the skills you learned in this chapter and experiment with new skills. You may need to use Help to complete the assignment.

Working with Screenshots

Note: To complete this assignment, you will be required to use the Data Files for Students. Visit www.cengage.com/ct/studentdownload for detailed instructions or contact your instructor for information about accessing the required files.

Instructions: Run Word. Open the document, Extend 9-1 Word Screenshots Draft, from the Data Files for Students. You will insert a screenshot and a screen clipping in the document.

Perform the following tasks:

1. Use Help to expand your knowledge about screenshots, screen clippings, saving images, and print scaling.

2. Change the page from portrait to landscape orientation.

3. Run Word again and create a blank document so that you have two separate Word windows open. Switch to the Word window with the Extend 9-1 Word Screenshots Draft file open. Insert a screenshot, centered on the blank line below the first paragraph.

4. Insert a screen clipping of the ribbon, centered on the blank line below the second paragraph.

5. Save the Word screenshot as a JPEG file with the name, Extend 9-1 Word Screenshot.

6. Save the screen clipping of the ribbon as a JPEG file with the file name, Extend 9-1 Word Ribbon Screen Clipping.

7. Add a border or shadow to the screenshot and the screen clipping.

8. Add these callouts to the screenshot: Quick Access Toolbar, ribbon, status bar.

9. Add these callouts to the screen clipping: tab, group, button (Figure 9–81).

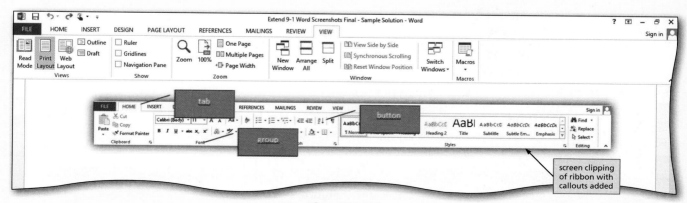

Figure 9–81

Continued >

Extend Your Knowledge *continued*

10. Print the document so that it fits on a single page; that is, make sure it is scaled to the paper size.

11. Locate the saved JPEG files and then double-tap or double-click them. In what program did they open?

12. If requested by your instructor, add a text box to the Word screen with your name in it. Save the modified file with a new file name, Extend 9-1 Word Screenshots Final. Submit the documents in the format specified by your instructor.

13. ✳ Answer the question posed in #11. How did you print the document so that it fits on a single page? What changes could you make to the document so that it all fits on a single page when you view it on the screen?

Analyze, Correct, Improve

Analyze a document, correct all errors, and improve it.

Formatting a Reference Document

Note: To complete this assignment, you will be required to use the Data Files for Students. Visit www.cengage.com/ct/studentdownload for detailed instructions or contact your instructor for information about accessing the required files.

Instructions: Run Word. Open the document, Analyze 9-1 Operating Systems Draft, from the Data Files for Students. The document is a reference document whose elements are not formatted properly (Figure 9–82). You are to edit, modify, and update the table of contents and index; insert and delete section breaks; change bullet symbols; and add and delete bookmarks. Open the Navigation Pane so that you can use it to go to specific headings and pages as referenced in this exercise.

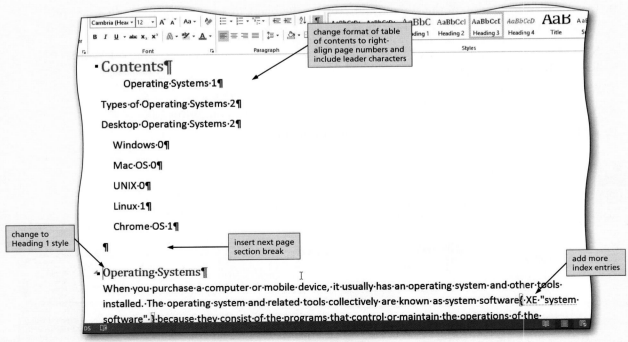

Figure 9–82

Perform the following tasks:

1. Correct In the reference document, correct the following items:

a. Change the title, ALL ABOUT COMPUTER OPERATING SYSTEMS, on the cover page to a color that is easier to see.

b. Insert a next page section break between the table of contents and the Operating Systems heading. Change the Operating Systems heading from a Heading 3 style to a Heading 1 style.

c. Insert a page number in the section starting with the Operating Systems heading. Change the starting page number of the page with the Operating Systems heading to 1. Update the table of contents. Change the format of the table of contents to Automatic Table 2.

d. Notice the page numbers are not correct at the end of the table of contents because an extra section break is in the document. Switch to Draft view and then delete the next page section break above the Windows heading. Switch back to Print Layout view. Update the table of contents again. If necessary, adjust starting page numbers again and then update the table of contents again.

e. Change the format of the Index heading to Heading 1. Update the table of contents again. Change the format of the index to a format other than From template. Right-align the page numbers and place a tab leader character between the index entries and the page numbers.

f. The document currently contains eight index entries. Read through the document and mark at least 15 more entries. Lowercase the C in the Client operating systems index entry so that it reads: client operating systems. Update the index.

2. Improve Enhance the document by changing the bullet symbol in both bulleted lists to one other than the dot symbol. Insert a bookmark for each heading in the document. Use the Go To command to practice locating bookmarks in the document. Delete the bookmark for the Index heading. Make any other adjustments you deem appropriate to the reference document. If requested by your instructor, change the name on the title page to your name. Save the modified document with the file name, Analyze 9-1 Operating Systems Final, and then submit it in the format specified by your instructor.

3. ✴ Do you prefer working in Draft view or Print Layout view? Why?

In the Labs

Design and/or create a document using the guidelines, concepts, and skills presented in this chapter. Labs 1 and 2, which increase in difficulty, require you to create solutions based on what you learned in the chapter; Lab 3 requires you to create a solution, which uses cloud and web technologies, by learning and investigating on your own from general guidance.

Lab 1: Creating a Reference Document with a Cover Page, a Table of Contents, and an Index

Note: To complete this assignment, you will be required to use the Data Files for Students. Visit www.cengage.com/ct/studentdownload for detailed instructions or contact your instructor for information about accessing the required files.

Problem: As a part-time assistant at Learning Computers Institute you have been asked to prepare a guide briefly describing input, output, and storage. A miniature version of this document is shown in Figure 9–83 on the next page. A draft of the body of the document is on the Data Files for Students.

Continued >

In the Labs *continued*

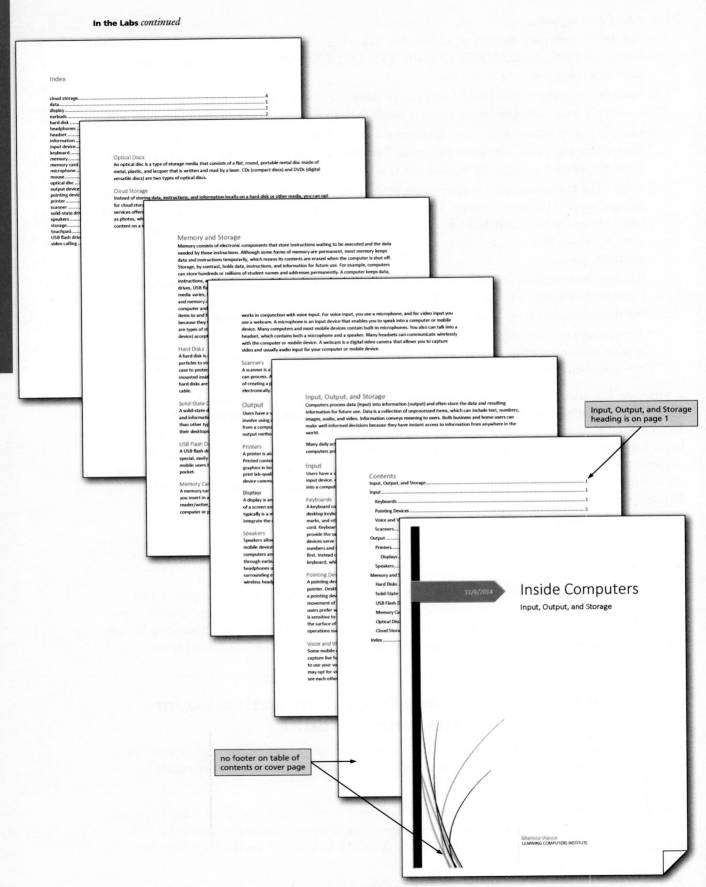

Figure 9–83

Perform the following tasks:

1. Open the document, Lab 9-1 Input Output Storage Draft, from the Data Files for Students. Save the document with a new file name, Lab 9-1 Input Output Storage Final.

2. Create a title page by inserting the Whisp style cover page. Use the following information on the title page: title – Inside Computers; subtitle – Input, Output, and Storage; date – *use today's date*; author – *use your name*; company name – Learning Computers Institute.

3. Insert a blank page between the title page and the Input, Output, and Storage heading.

4. Create a table of contents on the blank page using the Automatic Table 1 style. Insert a continuous section break at the end of the table of contents. Insert the Banded built-in footer starting on the page with the section titled Input, Output, and Storage. Update the table of contents.

5. Mark the following terms in the document as index entries: Data, Information, input device, keyboard, pointing device, mouse, touchpad, video calling, microphone, headset, scanner, output device, printer, display, Speakers, earbuds, headphones, Memory, Storage, hard disk, solid-state drive, USB flash drive, memory card, optical disc, and Cloud storage. Lowercase the first letter in the index entries for the words, Data, Information, Speakers, Memory, Storage, and Cloud storage so that the entire entry appears in lowercase letters in the index.

6. On a separate page at the end of the document, insert the word Index formatted in the Heading 1 style and then build an index for the document. Remember to hide formatting marks prior to building the index. Use the From template format using one column, with right-aligned page numbers and leader characters. Update the table of contents so that it includes the index.

7. Save the document again and then submit it in the format specified by your instructor.

8. ✳ If you wanted the index entries to appear in bold in the index but remain not bold in the document, what steps would you take to accomplish this?

Lab 2: Using a Master Document and Subdocument for a Reference Document

Note: To complete this assignment, you will be required to use the Data Files for Students. Visit www.cengage.com/ct/studentdownload for detailed instructions or contact your instructor for information about accessing the required files.

Problem: Your supervisor at your part-time job has asked you to prepare a guide about the history of the Internet and how the Internet works. A miniature version of this document is shown in Figure 9–84 on the next page. The document is a master document with one subdocument. The subdocument is on the Data Files for Students.

Perform the following tasks:

1. Open the file Lab 9-2 Internet Subdocument Draft, from the Data Files for Students. Save the document with the file name, Lab 9-2 Internet Subdocument Final.

2. Add the following captions to the figures: first figure – Figure 1: Popular Broadband Internet Service Technologies; second figure – Figure 2: Data Usage Examples; third figure – Figure 3: IPv4 and IPv6 Addresses and Domain Name for Google's Website.

3. Replace the occurrences of XX in the document with cross-references to the figure captions.

4. Insert a Retrospect Sidebar text box on the first page. Enter this text in the text box: `Who owns the Internet?` Select the description placeholder and then type: `No single person, company, or government agency owns the Internet. Each organization on the Internet is responsible only for maintaining its own network.` Press the ENTER key. Type: `What is the W3C?` Press the ENTER key.

Continued >

In the Labs *continued*

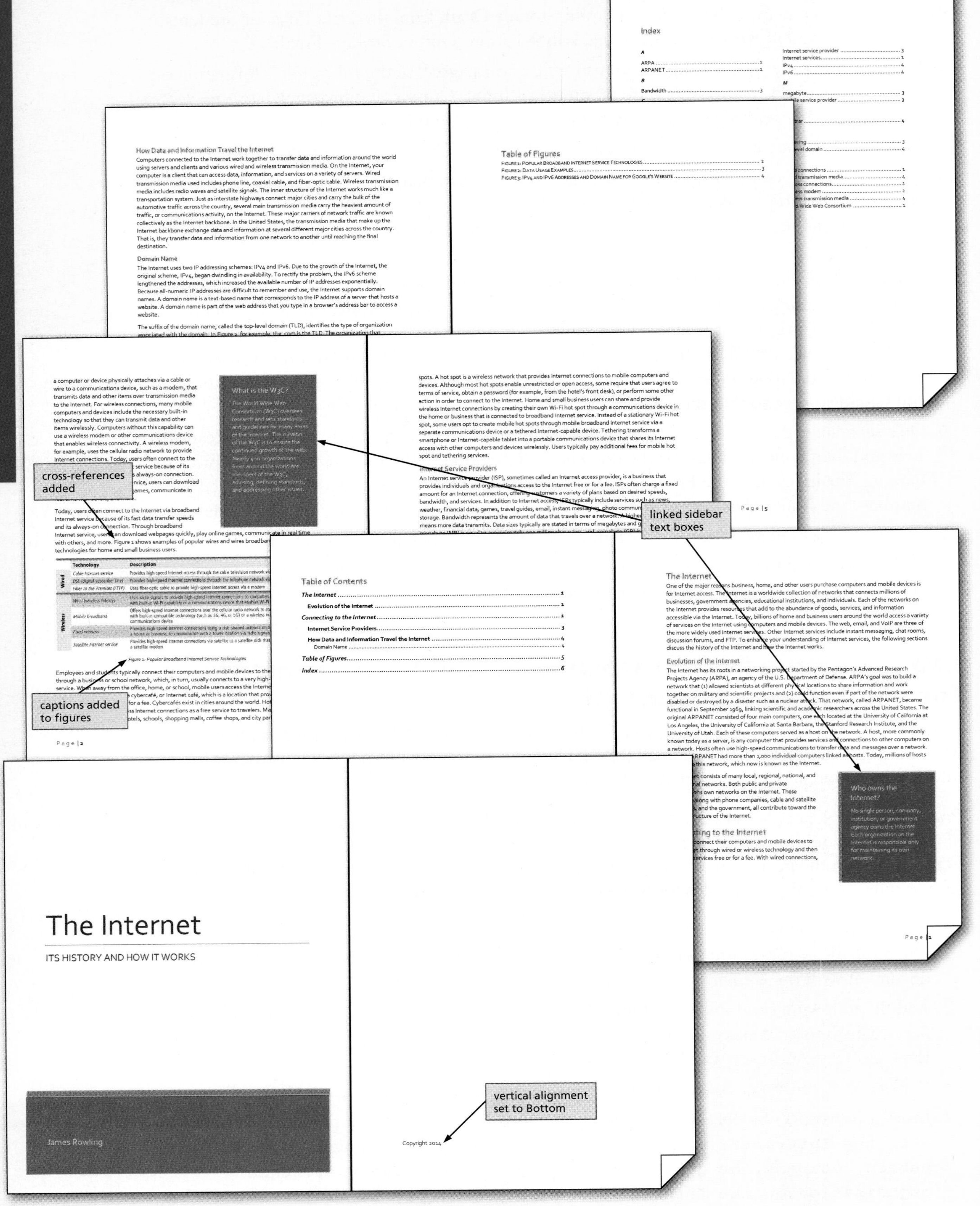
Index
Table of Figures
Table of Contents
What is the W3C?
Who owns the Internet?
The Internet
ITS HISTORY AND HOW IT WORKS
James Rowling
Copyright 2014
cross-references added
linked sidebar text boxes
captions added to figures
vertical alignment set to Bottom

Figure 9–84

Type: `The World Wide Web Consortium (W3C) oversees research and sets standards and guidelines for many areas of the Internet. The mission of the W3C is to ensure the continued growth of the web. Nearly 400 organizations from around the world are members of the W3C, advising, defining standards, and addressing other issues.` Format the second question the same as the first.

5. On the next page, insert another Retrospect Sidebar text box and then delete the contents of the second text box. Link the two text boxes together. Resize each text box so that each one contains just one question and answer. Move the first text box to the bottom of the first page and the second text box to the top of the second page. Save and close the document.

6. Create a new document. In Outline view, type `Copyright 2014` as the first line formatted as Body Text, and the remaining lines containing the headings Table of Figures and Index. Insert a next page section break between each line.

7. Save the master document with the file name, Lab 9-2 Internet Master Document.

8. Between the Copyright line and Table of Figures headings, insert the subdocument named Lab 9-2 Internet Subdocument Final.

9. Switch to Print Layout view.

10. Create a cover page by inserting the Retrospect style cover page. Use the following information on the title page: title – The Internet; subtitle – ITS HISTORY AND HOW IT WORKS; author – *use your name*. Delete the company name and company address placeholders.

11. Format the copyright page with a vertical alignment of Bottom.

12. Insert a blank page between the copyright page and the heading, The Internet.

13. Create a table of contents on the blank page using the Distinctive style, right-aligned page numbers, and dots for leader characters.

14. At the end of the document, format the Table of Figures heading using the Heading 1 style. Then, add a table of figures below the heading using the Formal format with right-aligned page numbers and a tab leader character.

15. Build an index for the document. Remember to hide formatting marks prior to building the index. Use the Formal format in two columns with right-aligned page numbers.

16. Beginning on the fourth page (with the heading, The Internet), create alternating footers. Insert a right tab for the odd page footer. Align left the even page footer. Insert the Accent Bar 2 page number style. The cover page, copyright page, or table of contents should not contain the footer.

17. Resize Figure 2 so that it fits at the bottom of page 3, and resize Figure 3 so that the body text ends on page 4.

18. For the entire document, set the left and right margins to .75" (Moderate) and set a gutter margin of .5".

19. Insert a bookmark for each Heading 2 in the document.

20. Compress the pictures in the document.

21. Update the table of contents, table of figures, and index.

22. Make any additional adjustments so that the document looks like Figure 9–84.

23. Save the document again and then submit it in the format specified by your instructor. If requested by your instructor, print the document back to back.

24. ✳ If you added a figure in the Evolution of the Internet section, how would you renumber the remaining figures in the document?

Continued >

In the Labs *continued*

Lab 3: Expand Your World: Cloud and Web Technologies Using an Online Photo Editor

Note: To complete this assignment, you will be required to use the Data Files for Students. Visit www.cengage.com/ct/studentdownload for detailed instructions or contact your instructor for information about accessing the required files.

Problem: Assume you have a digital photo that you want to edit before including it in a Word document.

Instructions: Perform the following tasks:

1. Run a browser. Search for the text, online photo editor, using a search engine. Visit several of the online photo editors and determine which you would like to use to edit a photo. Navigate to the desired online photo editor.

2. In the photo editor, open the image called Balloon from the Data Files for Students (Figure 9–85). Use the photo editor to enhance the image. Apply at least five enhancements. Which enhancements did you apply?

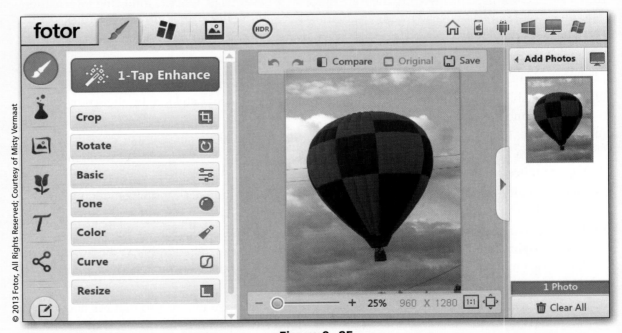

Figure 9–85

3. If requested by your instructor, add your name as a text element to the photo.

4. Save the photo with the file name, Lab 9-3 Revised Balloon. In what format did the online photo editor save the file? Submit the photo in the format specified by your instructor.

5. ✳ Answer the questions posed in #2 and #4. Which online photo editors did you evaluate? Which one did you select to use, and why? Do you prefer using the online photo editor or Word to enhance images?

Consider This: Your Turn

Apply your creative thinking and problem solving skills to design and implement a solution.

Note: To complete these assignments, you may be required to use the Data Files for Students. See the inside back cover of this book for instructions on downloading the Data Files for Students, or contact your instructor for information about accessing the required files.

1: Create a Reference Document about File and Disk Manager Tools

Personal

Part 1: In your Introduction to Computers class, you have been asked to create a reference document that discusses various file and disk manager tools. You decide to use master documents and subdocuments. The subdocument you created is a file named, Your Turn 9-1 - File and Disk Manager Draft, located on the Data Files for Students. In this subdocument, mark at least 20 terms as index entries. Insert at least three screenshots of various file and disk manager tools on your computer or mobile device and then add captions to the screenshot images. Compress the images and then save the subdocument file using a different file name. Create a master document that contains the subdocument file. The master document also should have a title page (cover page), a table of contents, a table of figures, and an index. Format the document with a footer that contains a page number. Use the concepts and techniques presented in this chapter to organize and format the document. Submit your assignment in the format specified by your instructor.

Part 2: ✸ You made several decisions while creating the reference document in this assignment: which terms to mark as index entries, which screenshot images to include, what text to use for captions, and how to organize and format the subdocument and master document (table of contents, table of figures, index, etc.). What was the rationale behind each of these decisions? When you proofread the document, what further revisions did you make and why?

2: Create a Reference Document about Productivity Office Applications

Professional

Part 1: As an assistant at a local computer store, your supervisor has asked you to create a reference document that discusses types of productivity office applications. You decide to use master documents and subdocuments. The subdocument you created is a file named, Your Turn 9-2 - Productivity Office Applications Draft, located on the Data Files for Students. In this subdocument, mark at least 20 terms as index entries. Insert at least three screenshots of various productivity applications on your computer or mobile device and then add captions to the screenshot images. Compress the images and then save the subdocument file using a different file name. Create a master document that contains the subdocument file. The master document also should have a title page (cover page), a table of contents, a table of figures, and an index. Format the document with a footer that contains a page number. Use the concepts and techniques presented in this chapter to organize and format the document. Submit your assignment in the format specified by your instructor.

Part 2: ✸ You made several decisions while creating the reference document in this assignment: which terms to mark as index entries, which screenshot images to include, what text to use for captions, and how to organize and format the subdocument and master document (table of contents, table of figures, index, etc.). What was the rationale behind each of these decisions? When you proofread the document, what further revisions did you make and why?

Continued >

Consider This: Your Turn *continued*

3: Create a Reference Document about Local Entertainment

Research and Collaboration

Part 1: As coworkers at the village hall, your team has been asked to create a reference document that discusses local community events and activities. You decide to use master documents and subdocuments. Each team member should research three events or activities and create a subdocument that presents these events and activities under separate headings. Each subdocument should contain at least one figure. For the figures, you can use screenshots, digital photos, or scanned images. As a group, create the master document that includes the three subdocuments. The master document also should have a title page (cover page), a table of contents, a table of figures, and an index.

Use the concepts and techniques presented in this chapter to organize and format the document. Be sure to check the spelling and grammar of the finished document. Submit your team assignment in the format specified by your instructor.

Part 2: ✳ You made several decisions while creating the reference document in this assignment: text to use, which terms to mark as index entries, which images to include, and how to organize and format the subdocuments and master document (table of contents, table of figures, index, etc.). What was the rationale behind each of these decisions? When you proofread the document, what further revisions did you make and why?

Learn Online

Reinforce what you learned in this chapter with games, exercises, training, and many other online activities and resources.

Student Companion Site Reinforcement activities and resources are available at no additional cost on www.cengagebrain.com. Visit www.cengage.com/ct/studentdownload for detailed instructions about accessing the resources available at the Student Companion Site.

SAM Put your skills into practice with SAM! If you have a SAM account, go to www.cengage.com/sam2013 to access SAM assignments for this chapter.

10 | Creating a Template for an Online Form

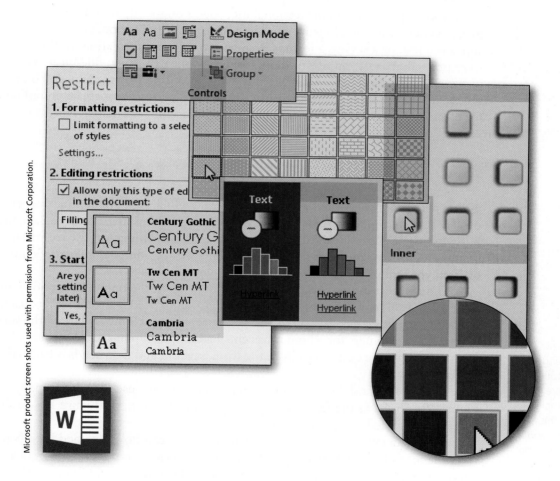

Objectives

You will have mastered the material in this chapter when you can:

- Save a document as a template
- Change paper size
- Change page color
- Insert a borderless table in a form
- Show the DEVELOPER tab
- Insert plain text, drop-down list, check box, rich text, combo box, and date picker content controls

- Edit placeholder text
- Change properties of content controls
- Insert and format a rectangle shape
- Customize a theme
- Protect a form
- Open a new document based on a template
- Fill in a form

10 | Creating a Template for an Online Form

Introduction

During your personal and professional life, you undoubtedly have filled in countless forms. Whether a federal tax form, a time card, a job application, an order, a deposit slip, a request, or a survey, a form is designed to collect information. In the past, forms were printed; that is, you received the form on a piece of paper, filled it in with a pen or pencil, and then returned it manually. With an **online form**, you use a computer to access, fill in, and then return the form. In Word, you easily can create an online form for electronic distribution; you also can fill in that same form using Word.

Project — Online Form

Today, people are concerned with using resources efficiently. To minimize paper waste, protect the environment, enhance office efficiency, and improve access to data, many businesses have moved toward a paperless office. Thus, online forms have replaced many paper forms. You access online forms on a website, on your company's intranet, or from your inbox if you receive the form via email.

The project in this chapter uses Word to produce the online form shown in Figure 10–1. Happy Homes is a cleaning service interested in customer feedback. Instead of sending a survey via the postal service, Happy Homes will send the survey via email to customers for whom it has email addresses. Upon receipt of the online form (a survey), the customer fills in the form, saves it, and then sends it back via email to Happy Homes.

Figure 10–1a shows how the form is displayed on a user's screen initially, Figure 10–1b shows the form partially filled in by one user, and Figure 10–1c shows how this user filled in the entire form.

The data entry area of the form contains three text boxes (named First Name, Last Name, and Other Services Used), one drop-down list box (named Frequency of Service Use), five check boxes (named Standard Cleaning, Green Cleaning, Window Washing, Carpet Cleaning, and Other Services Used), a combination text box/drop-down list box (named Cleaning Staff Rating), and a date picker (named Today's Date).

The form is designed so that it fits completely within a Word window that is set at a page width zoom and has the ribbon collapsed, which prevents a user from having to scroll while filling in the form. The data entry area of the form is enclosed by a rectangle that has a shadow on its top and right edges. The line of text above the data entry area is covered with the color gray, giving it the look of text that has been marked with a gray highlighter pen.

If you are using your finger on a touch screen and are having difficulty completing the steps in this chapter, consider using a stylus. Many people find it easier to be precise with a stylus than with a finger. In addition, with a stylus you see the pointer. If you still are having trouble completing the steps with a stylus, try using a mouse.

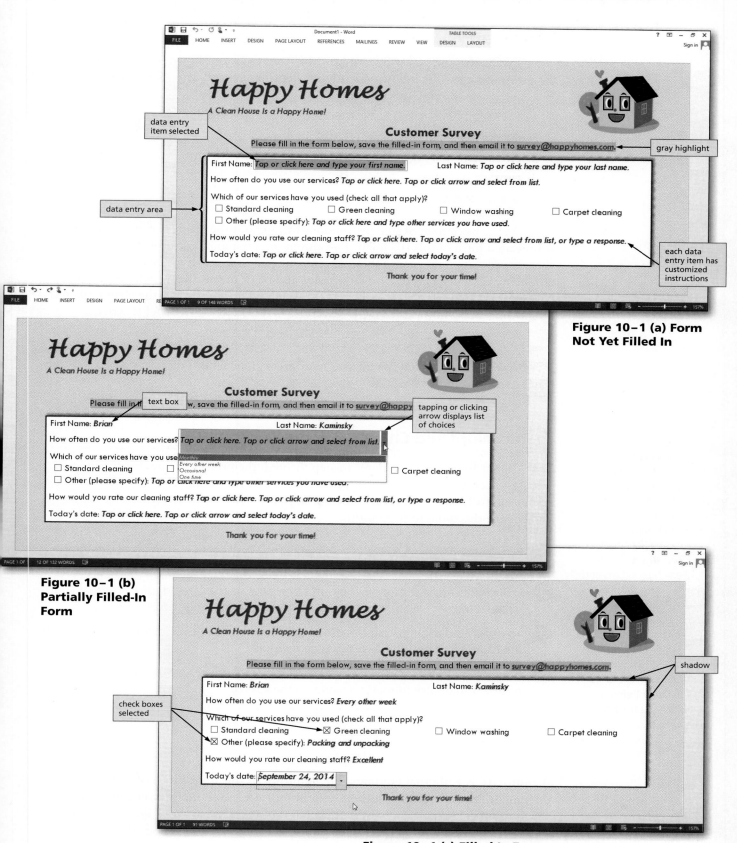

Figure 10–1 (a) Form Not Yet Filled In

Figure 10–1 (b) Partially Filled-In Form

Figure 10–1 (c) Filled-In Form

Roadmap

In this chapter, you will learn how to create the form shown in Figure 10–1 on the previous page. The following roadmap identifies general activities you will perform as you progress through this chapter:

1. SAVE a DOCUMENT as a TEMPLATE.
2. SET FORM FORMATS FOR the TEMPLATE.
3. ENTER TEXT, GRAPHICS, AND CONTENT CONTROLS in the form.
4. PROTECT the FORM.
5. USE the FORM.

At the beginning of step instructions throughout the chapter, you will see an abbreviated form of this roadmap. The abbreviated roadmap uses colors to indicate chapter progress: gray means the chapter is beyond that activity, blue means the task being shown is covered in that activity, and black means that activity is yet to be covered. For example, the following abbreviated roadmap indicates the chapter would be showing a task in the 2 SET FORM FORMATS FOR TEMPLATE activity.

1 SAVE DOCUMENT TEMPLATE | **2 SET FORM FORMATS FOR TEMPLATE**

3 ENTER TEXT, GRAPHICS, & CONTENT CONTROLS | 4 PROTECT FORM | 5 USE FORM

Use the abbreviated roadmap as a progress guide while you read or step through the instructions in this chapter.

To Run Word and Change Word Settings

One of the few differences between Windows 7 and Windows 8 occurs in the steps to run Word. If you are using Windows 7, click the Start button, type **Word** in the 'Search programs and files' box, click Word 2013, and then, if necessary, maximize the Word window. For a summary of the steps to run Word in Windows 7, refer to the Quick Reference located at the back of this book.

If you are using a computer to step through the project in this chapter and you want your screens to match the figures in this book, you should change your screen's resolution to 1366 × 768. The following steps run Word, display formatting marks, and change the zoom to page width.

1 Run Word and create a blank document in the Word window. If necessary, maximize the Word window.

2 If the Print Layout button on the status bar is not selected, tap or click it so that your screen is in Print Layout view.

3 To display the page the same width as the document window, if necessary, tap or click the Page Width button (VIEW tab | Zoom group).

4 If the 'Show/Hide ¶' button (HOME tab | Paragraph group) is not selected already, tap or click it to display formatting marks on the screen.

Saving a Document as a Template

A **template** is a file that contains the definition of the appearance of a Word document, including items such as default font, font size, margin settings, and line spacing; available styles; and even placement of text. Every Word document you create is based on a template. When you select the Blank document thumbnail on the Word start screen or in the New gallery of the Backstage view, Word creates a document based on the Normal template. Word also provides other templates for more specific types of documents, such as memos, letters, and resumes, some of which you have used in previous chapters. Creating a document based on these templates can improve your productivity because Word has defined much of the document's appearance for you.

In this chapter, you create an online form. If you create and save an online form as a Word document, users will be required to open that Word document to display the form on the screen. Next, they will fill in the form. Then, to preserve the content of the original form, they will have to save the form with a new file name. If they accidentally tap or click the Save button on the Quick Access Toolbar during the process of filling in the form, Word will replace the original blank form with a filled-in form.

If you create and save the online form as a template instead, users will open a new document window that is based on that template. This displays the form on the screen as a brand new Word document; that is, the document does not have a file name. Thus, the user fills in the form and then taps or clicks the Save button on the Quick Access Toolbar to save his or her filled-in form. By creating a Word template for the form, instead of a Word document, the original template for the form remains intact when the user taps or clicks the Save button.

> **BTW**
> **The Ribbon and Screen Resolution**
> Word may change how the groups and buttons within the groups appear on the ribbon, depending on the computer's screen resolution. Thus, your ribbon may look different from the ones in this book if you are using a screen resolution other than 1366 × 768.

To Save a Document as a Template

1 SAVE DOCUMENT TEMPLATE | 2 SET FORM FORMATS FOR TEMPLATE
3 ENTER TEXT, GRAPHICS, & CONTENT CONTROLS | 4 PROTECT FORM | 5 USE FORM

The following steps save a new blank document as a template. **Why?** *The template will be used to create the online form shown in Figure 10–1 on page WD 611.*

1

- With a new blank document in the Word window, open the Backstage view and then tap or click the Export tab in the left pane of the Backstage view to display the Export gallery.

- Tap or click 'Change File Type' in the Export gallery to display information in the right pane about various file types that can be opened in Word.

- Tap or click Template in the right pane to specify the file type for the current document (Figure 10–2).

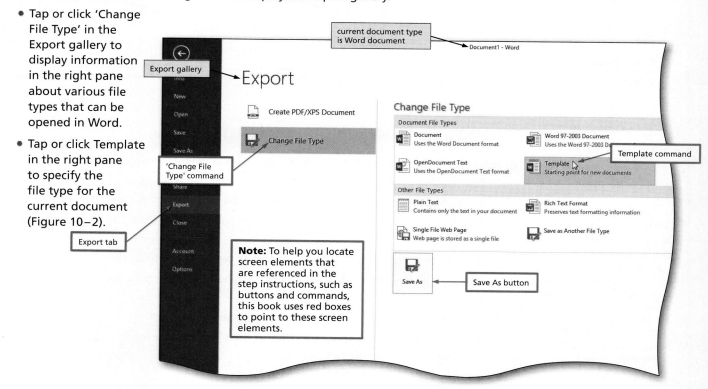

Figure 10–2

• Tap or click the Save As button to display the Save As dialog box with the file type automatically changed to Word Template.

Q&A How does Word differentiate between a saved Word template and a saved Word document?

Files typically have a file name and a file extension. The file extension identifies the file type. The source program often assigns a file type to a file. A Word document has an extension of .docx, whereas a Word template has an extension of .dotx. Thus, a file named July Report.docx is a Word document, and a file named Fitness Form.dotx is a Word template.

• Type **Customer Survey** in the File name box to change the file name.

• Navigate to the desired save location (in this case, the Word folder in the CIS 101 folder [or your class folder]) (Figure 10–3).

3

• Tap or click the Save button (Save As dialog box) to save the document as a Word template with the entered file name in the specified location.

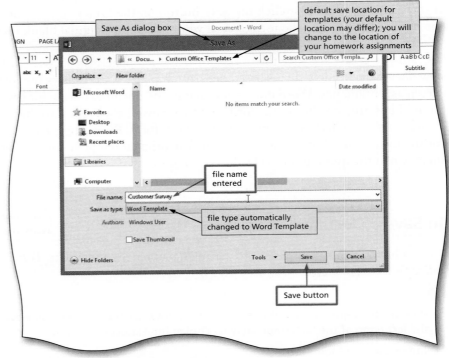

Figure 10–3

Other Ways

1. Press F12, change document type to Word Template   2. Open Backstage view, tap or click Save As, change document type to Word Template

---

Changing Document Settings

To enhance the look of the form, you change several default settings in Word:

1. Display the page as wide as possible in the document window to maximize the amount of space for text and graphics on the form, called page width zoom.

2. Change the size of the paper so that it fits completely within the document window.

3. Adjust the margins so that as much text as possible will fit in the document.

4. Change the document theme to Slice and the theme fonts to the Tw Cen MT font set.

5. Change the page color to a shade of green with a pattern.

The first item was completed earlier in the chapter. The following pages make the remaining changes to the document.

BTW
Touch Screen Differences
The Office and Windows interfaces may vary if you are using a touch screen. For this reason, you might notice that the function or appearance of your touch screen differs slightly from this chapter's presentation.

To Change Paper Size

For the online form in this chapter, all edges of the paper appear in the document window. Currently, only the top, left, and right edges are displayed in the document window. The following steps change paper size. **Why?** *To display all edges of the document in the document window in the current resolution, change the height of the paper from 11 inches to 4 inches.*

• Display the PAGE LAYOUT tab.

• Tap or click the 'Choose Page Size' button (PAGE LAYOUT tab | Page Setup group) to display the Choose Page Size gallery (Figure 10–4).

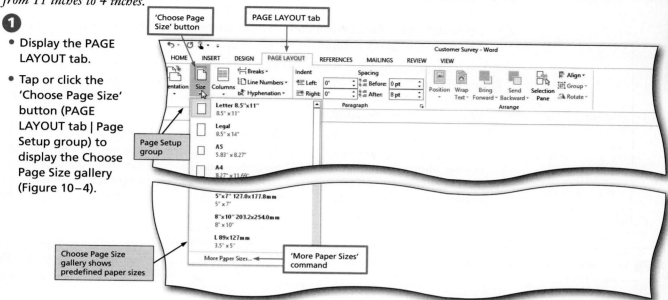

Figure 10–4

• Tap or click 'More Paper Sizes' in the Choose Page Size gallery to display the Paper sheet in the Page Setup dialog box.

• In the Height box (Page Setup dialog box), type **4** as the new height (Figure 10–5).

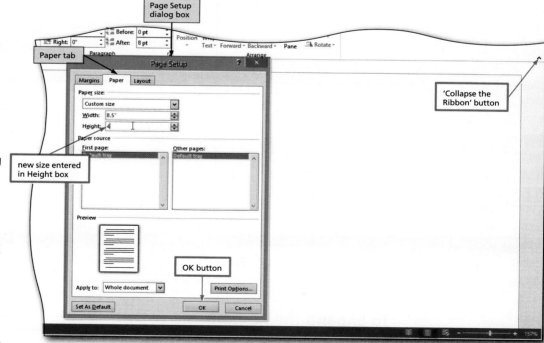

• Tap or click the OK button to change the paper size to the entered measurements, which, in this case, are 8.5 inches wide by 4 inches tall.

Figure 10–5

To Collapse the Ribbon

To display more of a document or other item in the Word window, you can collapse the ribbon, which hides the groups on the ribbon and displays only the main tabs. For the online form to fit entirely in the Word window, you collapse the ribbon. The following step collapses the ribbon so that you can see how the form fits in the document window.

1 Tap or click the 'Collapse the Ribbon' button on the ribbon (shown in Figure 10–5 on the previous page) to collapse the ribbon (Figure 10–6).

Q&A What happened to the 'Collapse the Ribbon' button?
The 'Pin the ribbon' button replaces the 'Collapse the Ribbon' button when the ribbon is collapsed. You will see the 'Pin the ribbon' button only when you expand a ribbon by tapping or clicking a tab.

What if the height of my document does not match the figure?
You may need to show white space. To do this, if you are using a mouse, position the pointer above the top of the page below the ribbon and then double-click when the pointer changes to a 'Show White Space' button; if you are using a touch screen, double-tap below the page. Or, your screen resolution may be different; if so, you may need to adjust the page height or width values.

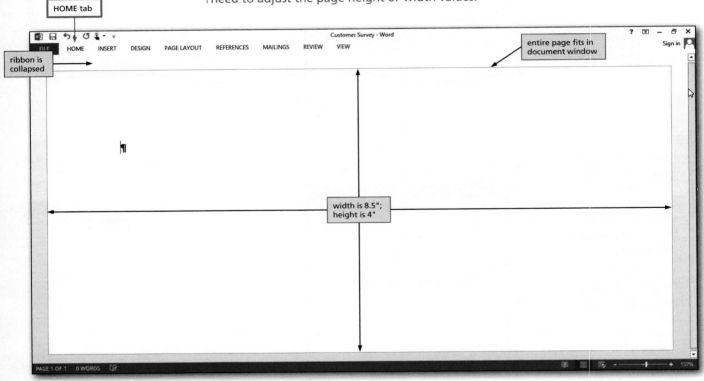

Figure 10–6

To Expand the Ribbon

After you verify that the entire form will fit in the document window, you should expand the ribbon so that you can see the groups while creating the online form. The following steps expand the ribbon.

1 Tap or click HOME on the collapsed ribbon to expand the HOME tab.

2 Tap or click the 'Pin the ribbon' button on the expanded HOME tab to restore the ribbon.

To Set Custom Margins

Recall that Word is preset to use 1-inch top, bottom, left, and right margins. To maximize the space for the contents of the form, this chapter sets the left and right margins to .5 inches, the top margin to .25 inches, and the bottom margin to 0 inches. The following steps set custom margins.

1 Display the PAGE LAYOUT tab. Tap or click the Adjust Margins button (PAGE LAYOUT tab | Page Setup group) to display the Adjust Margins gallery.

2 Tap or click Custom Margins in the Adjust Margins gallery to display the Margins sheet in the Page Setup dialog box.

3 Type **.25** in the Top box (Page Setup dialog box) to change the top margin setting.

4 Type **0** (zero) in the Bottom box to change the bottom margin setting.

Q&A Why set the bottom margin to zero?
This allows you to place form contents at the bottom of the page, if necessary.

5 Type **.5** in the Left box to change the left margin setting.

6 Type **.5** in the Right box to change the right margin setting (Figure 10–7).

7 Tap or click the OK button to set the custom margins for this document.

Q&A What if Word displays a dialog box indicating margins are outside the printable area?
Tap or click the Ignore button because this is an online form that is not intended for printing.

BTW
Quick Reference
For a table that lists how to complete the tasks covered in this book using touch gestures, the mouse, ribbon, shortcut menu, and keyboard, see the Quick Reference Summary at the back of this book, or visit the Quick Reference resource on the Student Companion Site located on www.cengagebrain.com. For detailed instructions about accessing available resources, visit www.cengage.com/ct/studentdownload or contact your instructor for information about accessing the required files.

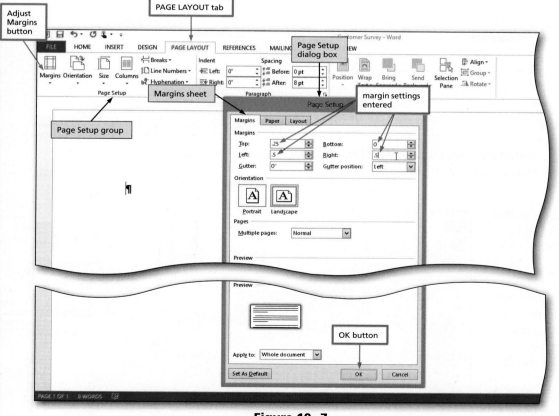

Figure 10–7

To Change the Document Theme and Theme Fonts

The following steps change the document theme colors to Slice and the theme fonts to Tw Cen MT.

1 Display the DESIGN tab. Tap or click the Themes button (DESIGN tab | Document Formatting group) and then tap or click Slice in the Themes gallery to change the document theme.

2 Tap or click the Theme Fonts button (DESIGN tab | Document Formatting group) and then scroll through the Theme Fonts gallery to display the Tw Cen MT font set (Figure 10–8).

3 Tap or click Tw Cen MT in the Theme Fonts gallery to change the font set.

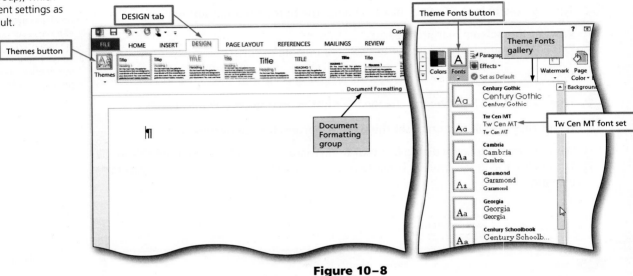

Figure 10–8

1 SAVE DOCUMENT TEMPLATE | 2 SET FORM FORMATS FOR TEMPLATE
3 ENTER TEXT, GRAPHICS, & CONTENT CONTROLS | 4 PROTECT FORM | 5 USE FORM

To Add a Page Color

The following steps change the page color. **Why?** *This online form uses a shade of green for the page color (background color) so that the form is more visually appealing.*

1

- Tap or click the Page Color button (DESIGN tab | Page Background group) to display the Page Color gallery.

- If you are using a mouse, point to 'Dark Green, Accent 3, Lighter 40%' (seventh color in the fourth row) in the Page Color gallery to display a live preview of the selected background color (Figure 10–9).

Experiment

- If you are using a mouse, point to various colors in the Page Color gallery and watch the page color change in the document window.

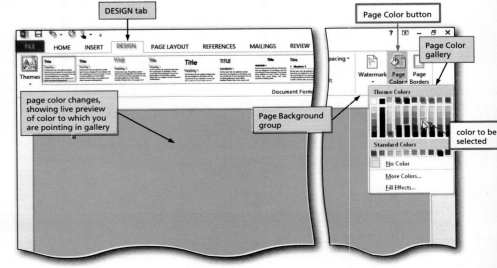

Figure 10–9

2

- Tap or click 'Dark Green, Accent 3, Lighter 40%' to change the page color to the selected color.

Q&A Do page colors print?

When you change the page color, it appears only on the screen. Changing the page color does not affect a printed document.

To Add a Pattern Fill Effect to a Page Color

1 SAVE DOCUMENT TEMPLATE | 2 SET FORM FORMATS FOR TEMPLATE
3 ENTER TEXT, GRAPHICS, & CONTENT CONTROLS | 4 PROTECT FORM | 5 USE FORM

When you changed the page color in the previous steps, Word placed a solid color on the screen. The following steps add a pattern to the page color. *Why? For this online form, the solid background color is a little too bright. To soften the color, you can add a pattern to it.*

1

- Tap or click the Page Color button (DESIGN tab | Page Background group) to display the Page Color gallery (Figure 10–10).

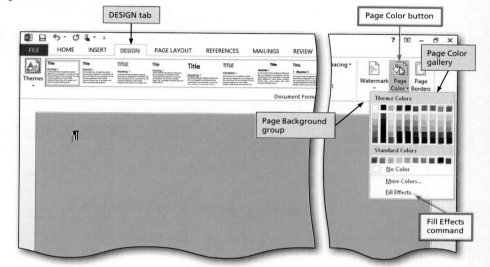

Figure 10–10

2

- Tap or click Fill Effects in the Page Color gallery to display the Fill Effects dialog box.

- Tap or click the Pattern tab (Fill Effects dialog box) to display the Pattern sheet in the dialog box.

- Tap or click the 30% pattern (first pattern in the fifth row) to select it (Figure 10–11).

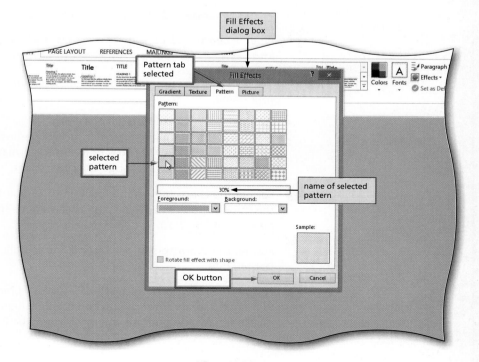

Figure 10–11

- Tap or click the OK button to add the selected pattern to the current page color (Figure 10–12).

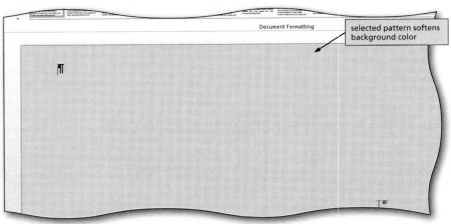

Figure 10–12

Enter Content in the Online Form

The next step in creating the online form in this chapter is to enter the text, graphics, and content controls in the document. The following pages describe this process.

To Enter and Format Text

The following steps enter the text at the top of the online form.

1 Type **Happy Homes** and then press the ENTER key.

2 Type **A Clean House Is a Happy Home!** and then press the ENTER key.

3 Type **Customer Survey** and then press the ENTER key.

4 Type **Please fill in the form below, save the filled-in form, and email it to survey@happyhomes.com.** and then press the ENTER key.

If requested by your instructor, change the name, happyhomes, in the email address to your name.

Q&A Why did the email address change color?
In this document theme, the color for a hyperlink is a shade of blue. When you pressed the ENTER key, Word automatically formatted the hyperlink in this color. Later in this chapter, you will change the color of the hyperlink.

5 Format the characters on the first line to 28-point Lucida Handwriting font, bold, with the color of Dark Blue, Text 2 and then remove space after the paragraph (spacing after should be 0 pt).

6 Format the characters on the second line to italic with the color of Red, Accent 6, Darker 25%.

7 Format the characters on the third line to 16-point bold font with the color of Dark Blue, Text 2, and center the text on the line. Remove space before and after this paragraph (spacing before and after should be 0 pt).

8 Center the text on the fourth line and increase the spacing after this line to 12 point.

9 Position the insertion point on the blank line below the text (Figure 10–13).

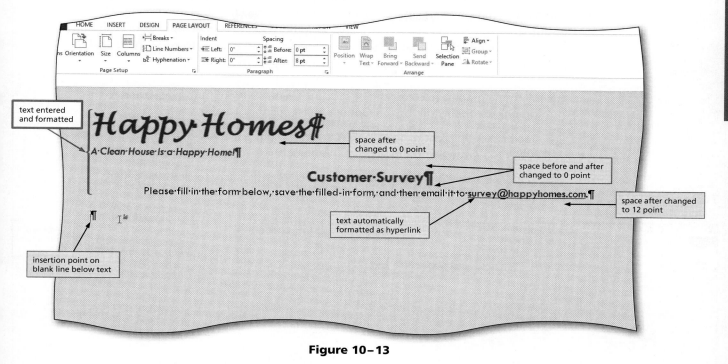

Figure 10–13

To Insert Clip Art and Scale It

The next step is to insert a graphic of a house in the form. Because the graphic's original size is too large, you will reduce its size. The following steps insert and scale a graphic.

1 Display the INSERT tab. Tap or click the Online Pictures button (INSERT tab | Illustrations group) to display the Insert Pictures dialog box.

2 Type **happy house** in the Search box (Insert Pictures dialog box) and then tap or click the Search button to display a list of clip art that matches the entered search text.

3 Tap or click the house clip art that matches the one in Figure 10–14 on the next page (or a similar image) and then tap or click the Insert button to download the image, close the dialog box, and insert the graphic in the document at the location of the insertion point.

Q&A What if I cannot locate the same clip art?
Tap or click the Cancel button and then close the Insert Pictures dialog box. Tap or click the From File button (INSERT tab | Illustrations group) to display the Insert Picture dialog box, navigate to the Happy House file on the Data Files for Students (Insert Picture dialog box), and tap or click the Insert button to insert the picture.

4 With the graphic still selected, use the Shape Height and Shape Width boxes (PICTURE TOOLS FORMAT tab | Size group) to change the graphic height to approximately 1.1" and width to 1.34", respectively (shown in Figure 10–14).

Q&A What if the PICTURE TOOLS FORMAT tab is not the active tab on my ribbon?
Double-tap or double-click the graphic, or tap or click the PICTURE TOOLS FORMAT tab on the ribbon.

To Format a Graphic's Text Wrapping

Word inserted the clip art as an inline graphic, that is, as part of the current paragraph. In this online form, the graphic should be positioned to the right of the company name (shown in Figure 10–1 on page WD 611). Thus, the graphic should be a floating graphic instead of an inline graphic. The text in the online form should not wrap around the graphic. Thus, the graphic should float in front of the text. The following steps change the graphic's text wrapping to In Front of Text.

1 With the graphic selected, tap or click the Layout Options button attached to the graphic to display the Layout Options gallery (Figure 10–14).

2 Tap or click 'In Front of Text' in the Layout Options gallery to change the graphic from inline to floating with the selected wrapping style.

3 Tap or click the Close button in the Layout Options gallery to close the gallery.

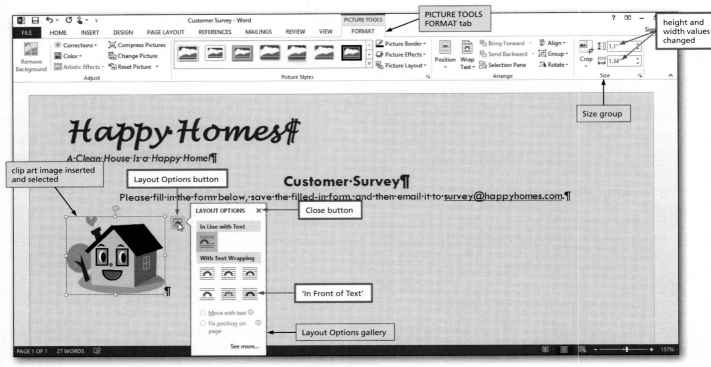

Figure 10–14

BTW
Ordering Graphics
If you have multiple graphics displaying on the screen and would like them to overlap, you can change their stacking order by using the Bring Forward and Send Backward arrows (PICTURE TOOLS FORMAT tab | Arrange group). The 'Bring to Front' command on the Bring Forward menu displays the selected object at the top of the stack, and the 'Send to Back' command on the Send Backward menu displays the selected object at the bottom of the stack. The Bring Forward and Send Backward commands each move the graphic forward or backward one layer in the stack. These commands also are available through the shortcut menu that is displayed when you press and hold or right-click a graphic.

To Move a Graphic

The final step associated with the graphic is to move it so that it is positioned on the right side of the online form. The following steps move a graphic.

1 If necessary, scroll to display the top of the form in the document window.

2 Drag the graphic to the location shown in Figure 10–15.

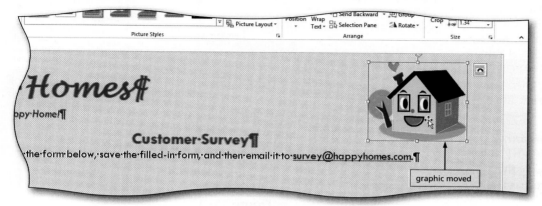

Figure 10–15

To Use a Table to Control Layout

1 SAVE DOCUMENT TEMPLATE | 2 SET FORM FORMATS FOR TEMPLATE
3 ENTER TEXT, GRAPHICS, & CONTENT CONTROLS | 4 PROTECT FORM | 5 USE FORM

The first line of data entry in the form consists of the First Name content control, which begins at the left margin, and the Last Name content control, which begins at the center point of the same line. At first glance, you might decide to set a tab stop at each content control location. This, however, can be a complex task. For example, to place two content controls evenly across a row, you must calculate the location of each tab stop. If you insert a 2 × 1 table instead, Word automatically calculates the size of two evenly spaced columns. Thus, to enter multiple content controls on a single line, insert a table to control layout.

In this online form, the line containing the First Name and Last Name content controls will be a 2 × 1 table, that is, a table with two columns and one row. By inserting a 2 × 1 table, Word automatically positions the second column at the center point. The following steps insert a 2 × 1 table in the form and remove its border. **Why?** *When you insert a table, Word automatically surrounds it with a border. Because you are using the tables solely to control layout, you do not want the table borders visible.*

1

- Position the insertion point where the table should be inserted, in this case, on the blank paragraph mark below the text on the form.

- Display the INSERT tab. Tap or click the 'Add a Table' button (INSERT tab | Tables group) to display the Add a Table gallery (Figure 10–16).

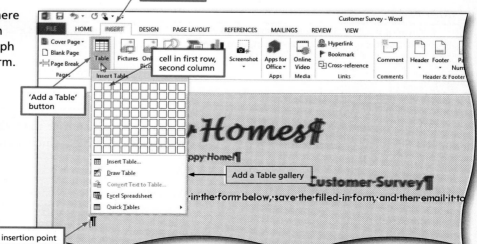

Figure 10–16

2

- Tap or click the cell in the first row and second column of the grid to insert an empty 2 × 1 table at the location of the insertion point.

- Select the table.

Q&A

How do I select a table?

If you are using a mouse, point somewhere in the table and then click the table move handle that appears in the upper-left corner of the table; if you are using a touch screen, tap the Select Table button (TABLE TOOLS LAYOUT tab | Table group) and then tap Select Table on the Select Table menu.

- Tap or click the Borders arrow (TABLE TOOLS DESIGN tab | Borders group) to display the Borders gallery (Figure 10–17).

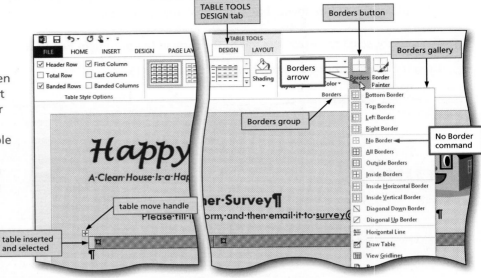

Figure 10–17

3

- Tap or click No Border in the Borders gallery to remove the borders from the table.

4

- Tap or click the first cell of the table to remove the selection (Figure 10–18).

Q&A

My screen does not display the end-of-cell marks. Why not?

Display formatting marks by tapping or clicking the 'Show/Hide ¶' button (HOME tab | Paragraph group).

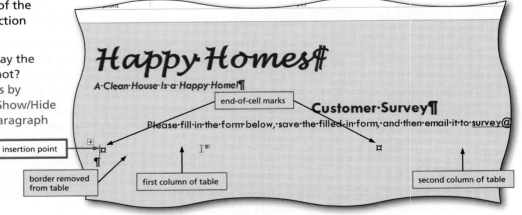

Figure 10–18

Other Ways

1. Tap or click 'Add a Table' button (INSERT tab | Tables group), tap or click Insert Table in Add a Table gallery, enter number of columns and rows, tap or click OK button (Insert Table dialog box)

To Show Table Gridlines

When you remove the borders from a table, you no longer can see the individual cells in the table. To help identify the location of cells, you can display **gridlines**, which show cell outlines on the screen. The following steps show gridlines.

1 If necessary, position the insertion point in a table cell.

2 Display the TABLE TOOLS LAYOUT tab.

3 If gridlines do not show already, tap or click the 'View Table Gridlines' button (TABLE TOOLS LAYOUT tab | Table group) to show table gridlines on the screen (Figure 10–19).

Q&A Do table gridlines print?

No. Gridlines are formatting marks that show only on the screen. Gridlines help users easily identify cells, rows, and columns in borderless tables.

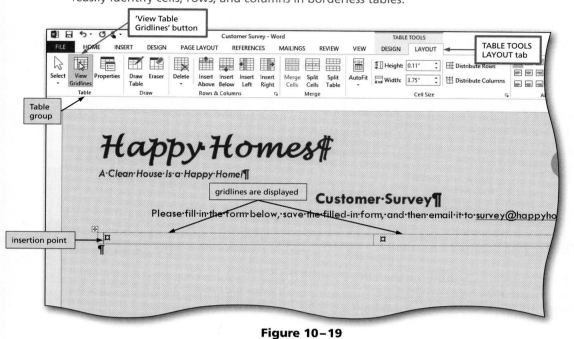

Figure 10–19

Content Controls

To add data entry fields in a Word form, you insert content controls. Word includes nine different content controls you can insert in your online forms. Table 10–1 outlines the use of each of these controls.

Table 10–1 Content Controls		
Type	**Icon**	**Use**
Building Block Gallery		User selects a built-in building block from the gallery.
Check Box		User selects or deselects a check box.
Combo Box		User types text entry or selects one item from a list of choices.
Date Picker		User interacts with a calendar to select a date or types a date in the placeholder.
Drop-Down List		User selects one item from a list of choices.
Picture		User inserts a drawing, a shape, a picture, clip art, or a SmartArt graphic.
Plain Text	Aa	User enters text, which may not be formatted.
Repeating Section		Users can instruct Word to create a duplicate of the content control.
Rich Text	Aa	User enters text and, if desired, may format the entered text.

How do you determine the correct content control to use for each data entry field?

For each data entry field, decide which content control best maps to the type of data the field will contain. The field specifications for the fields in this chapter's online form are listed below:

- The First Name, Last Name, and Other Services Used data entry fields will contain text. The first two will be plain text content controls and the last will be a rich text content control.

- The Frequency of Service Use data entry field must contain one of these four values: Monthly, Every other week, Occasional, One time. This field will be a drop-down list content control.

- The Standard Cleaning, Green Cleaning, Window Washing, Carpet Cleaning, and Other Services Used data entry fields will be check boxes that the user can select or deselect.

- The Cleaning Staff Rating data entry field can contain one of these four values: Excellent, Good, Fair, and Poor. In addition, users should be able to enter their own value in this data entry field if none of these four values is applicable. A combo box content control will be used for this field.

- The Today's Date data entry field should contain only a valid date value. Thus, this field will be a date picker content control.

The following pages insert content controls in the online form.

To Show the DEVELOPER Tab

1 SAVE DOCUMENT TEMPLATE | 2 SET FORM FORMATS FOR TEMPLATE
3 ENTER TEXT, GRAPHICS, & CONTENT CONTROLS | 4 PROTECT FORM | 5 USE FORM

To create a form in Word, you use buttons on the DEVELOPER tab. The following steps display the DEVELOPER tab on the ribbon. *Why? Because it allows you to perform more advanced tasks not required by everyday Word users, the DEVELOPER tab does not appear on the ribbon by default.*

1

- Open the Backstage view (Figure 10–20).

Figure 10–20

2

- Tap or click Options in the left pane of the Backstage view to display the Word Options dialog box.

- Tap or click Customize Ribbon in the left pane (Word Options dialog box) to display associated options in the right pane.

- Place a check mark in the Developer check box in the Main Tabs list (Figure 10–21).

Q&A What are the plus symbols to the left of each tab name?
Tapping or clicking the plus symbol expands to show the groups.

Can I show or hide any tab in this list?
Yes. Place a check mark in the check box to show the tab, or remove the check mark to hide the tab.

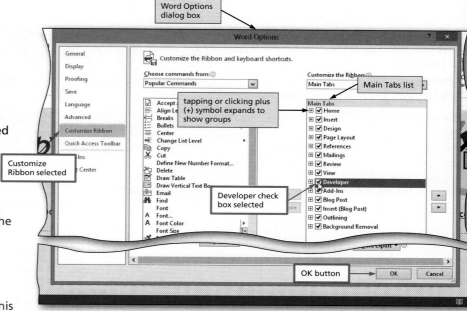

Figure 10–21

3

- Tap or click the OK button to show the DEVELOPER tab on the ribbon (Figure 10–22).

Q&A How do I remove the DEVELOPER tab from the ribbon?
Follow these same steps, except remove the check mark from the Developer check box (Word Options dialog box).

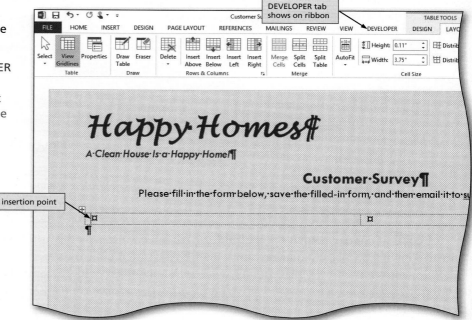

Figure 10–22

To Insert a Plain Text Content Control

1 SAVE DOCUMENT TEMPLATE | 2 SET FORM FORMATS FOR TEMPLATE
3 ENTER TEXT, GRAPHICS, & CONTENT CONTROLS | 4 PROTECT FORM | 5 USE FORM

The first item that a user enters in the Customer Survey is his or her first name. Because the first name entry contains text that the user should not format, this online form uses a plain text content control for the First Name data entry field. The steps on the next page enter the label, First Name:, followed by a plain text content control. *Why? The label, First Name:, is displayed to the left of the plain text content control. To improve readability, a colon or some other character often separates a label from the content control.*

1

- With the insertion point in the first cell of the table as shown in Figure 10–22 on the previous page, type **First Name:** as the label for the content control.
- Press the SPACEBAR (Figure 10–23).

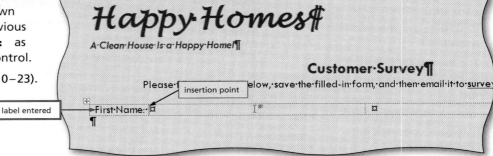

Figure 10–23

2

- Display the DEVELOPER tab.
- Tap or click the 'Plain Text Content Control' button (DEVELOPER tab | Controls group) to insert a plain text content control at the location of the insertion point (Figure 10–24).

Is the plain text content control similar to the content controls that I have used in templates installed with Word, such as in the letter, memo, and resume templates? Yes. The content controls you insert through the DEVELOPER tab have the same functionality as the content controls in the templates installed with Word.

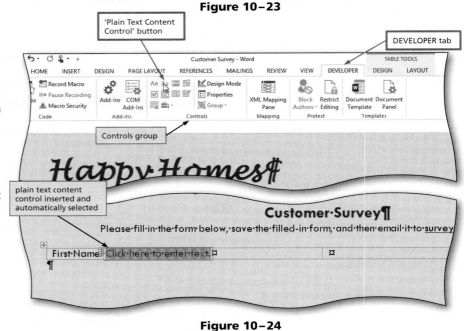

Figure 10–24

To Edit Placeholder Text

1 SAVE DOCUMENT TEMPLATE | 2 SET FORM FORMATS FOR TEMPLATE
3 ENTER TEXT, GRAPHICS, & CONTENT CONTROLS | 4 PROTECT FORM | 5 USE FORM

A content control displays **placeholder text**, which instructs the user how to enter values in the content control. The default placeholder text for a plain text content control is the instruction, Click here to enter text. The following steps edit the placeholder text for the plain text content control just entered. *Why? You can change the wording in the placeholder text so that it is more instructional or applicable to the current form.*

1

- With the plain text content control selected (shown in Figure 10–24), tap or click the Design Mode button (DEVELOPER tab | Controls group) to turn on Design mode, which displays tags at the beginning and ending of the placeholder text (Figure 10–25).

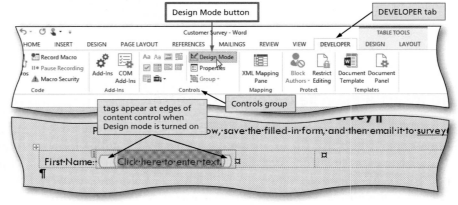

Figure 10–25

2
- Drag through the text to replace in the placeholder text (Figure 10–26).

Figure 10–26

3
- Edit the placeholder text so that it contains the text, Tap or click here and type your first name., as the instruction (Figure 10–27).

Q&A Why did the placeholder text wrap to the next line?

Because of the tags at each edge of the placeholder text, the entered text may wrap in the table cell. Once you turn off Design mode, the placeholder text should fit on a single line. If it does not, you can adjust the font size of the placeholder text to fit.

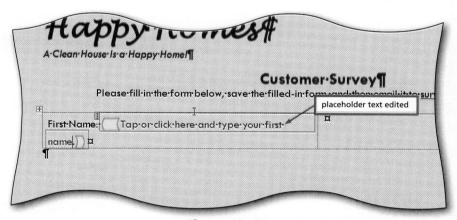

Figure 10–27

4
- Tap or click the Design Mode button (DEVELOPER tab | Controls group) to turn off Design mode (Figure 10–28).

Q&A What if I notice an error in the placeholder text?

Follow these steps to turn on Design mode, correct the error, and then turn off Design mode.

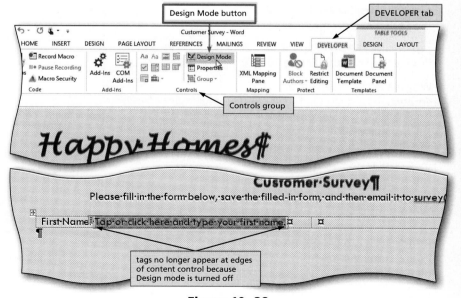

Figure 10–28

To Change the Properties of a Plain Text Content Control

You can change a variety of properties to customize content controls. The following steps change the properties of a plain text content control. *Why? In this form, you assign a tag name to a content control for later identification. You also apply a style to the content control to define how text will look as a user types data or makes selections, and you lock the content control so that a user cannot delete the content control during the data entry process.*

- With the content control selected, tap or click the Control Properties button (DEVELOPER tab | Controls group) to display the Content Control Properties dialog box (Figure 10–29).

Q&A How do I know the content control is selected?
A selected content control is surrounded by an outline. It also may be shaded.

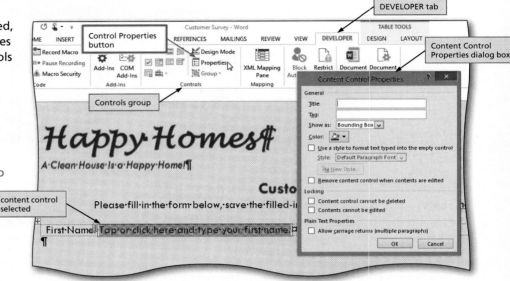

Figure 10–29

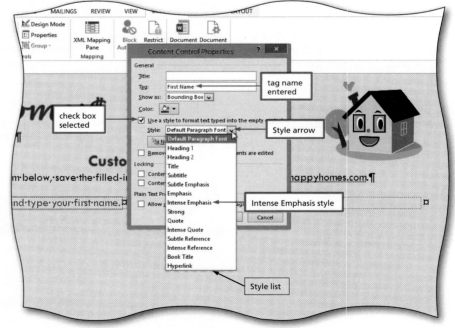

Figure 10–30

- Type **First Name** in the Tag text box (Content Control Properties dialog box).

- Place a check mark in the 'Use a style to format text typed into the empty control' check box so that the Style box becomes active.

- Tap or click the Style arrow to display the Style list (Figure 10–30).

Q&A Why leave the Title text box empty?
When you tap or click a content control in a preexisting Word template, the content control may display an identifier in its top-left corner. For templates that you create, you can instruct Word to display this identifier, called the Title, by changing the properties of the content control. In this form, you do not want the identifier to appear.

What is a bounding box?
A bounding box is a rectangle that surrounds the content control on the form. You can show content controls with a bounding box, with tags, or with no visible markings.

3

- Tap or click Intense Emphasis to select the style for the content control.

- Place a check mark in the 'Content control cannot be deleted' check box so that the user cannot delete the content control (Figure 10–31).

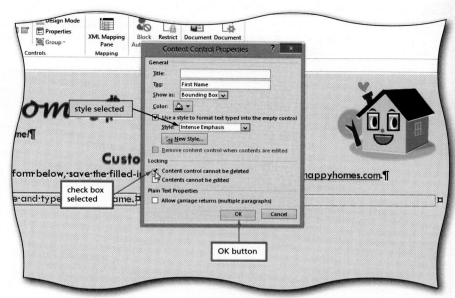

Figure 10–31

4

- Tap or click the OK button to assign the modified properties to the content control (Figure 10–32).

Q&A Why is the placeholder text not formatted to the selected style, Intense Emphasis, in this case? When you apply a style to a content control, as described in these steps, the style is applied to the text the user types during the data entry process. To change the appearance of the placeholder text, apply a style using the HOME tab as described in the next steps.

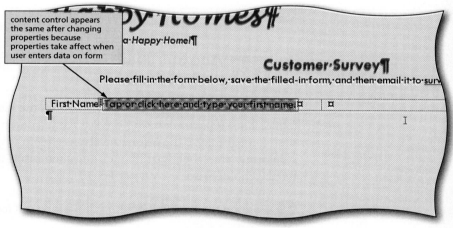

Figure 10–32

To Format Placeholder Text

In this online form, the placeholder text has the same style applied to it as the content control. The following steps format placeholder text.

1 With the placeholder text selected, display the HOME tab.

2 If you are using a mouse, click the Styles gallery down arrow (HOME tab | Styles group) to scroll through the Styles gallery to display the Intense Emphasis style or click the More button (HOME tab | Styles group); if you are using a touch screen, tap the More button (HOME tab | Styles group) to expand the Styles gallery.

3 Tap or click Intense Emphasis in the Styles gallery (even if it is selected already) to apply the selected style to the selected placeholder text (Figure 10–33 on the next page).

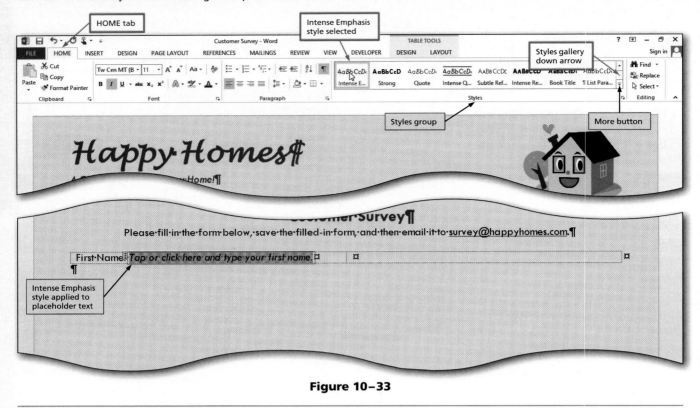

Figure 10–33

To Insert Another Plain Text Content Control and Edit Its Placeholder Text

The second item that a user enters in the Customer Survey is his or her last name. The steps for entering the last name content control are similar to those for the first name, because the last name also is a plain text content control. The following steps enter the label, Last Name:, and then insert a plain text content control and edit its placeholder text.

1 Position the insertion point in the second cell (column) in the table.

2 With the insertion point in the second cell of the table, type **Last Name:** as the label for the content control and then press the SPACEBAR.

3 Display the DEVELOPER tab. Tap or click the 'Plain Text Content Control' button (DEVELOPER tab | Controls group) to insert a plain text content control at the location of the insertion point.

4 With the plain text content control selected, tap or click the Design Mode button (DEVELOPER tab | Controls group) to turn on Design mode (Figure 10–34).

5 If necessary, select the placeholder text to be changed.

6 Edit the placeholder text so that it contains the text, Tap or click here and type your last name., as the instruction.

7 Tap or click the Design Mode button (DEVELOPER tab | Controls group) to turn off Design mode.

BTW
Deleting Content Controls
To delete a content control, select it and then press the DELETE key or tap or click the Cut button (HOME tab | Clipboard group), or press and hold or right-click it and then tap or click Cut on the shortcut menu.

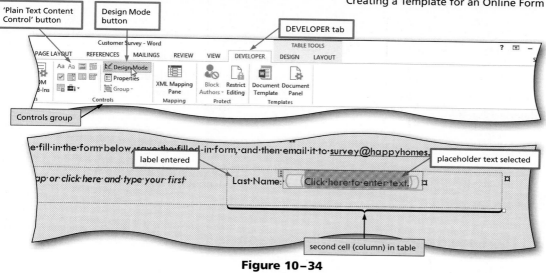

Figure 10–34

To Change the Properties of a Plain Text Content Control

The next step is to change the title, style, and locking properties of the Last Name content control, just as you did for the First Name content control. The following steps change properties of a plain text content control.

1 With the content control selected, tap or click the Control Properties button (DEVELOPER tab | Controls group) to display the Content Control Properties dialog box.

2 Type **Last Name** in the Tag text box (Content Control Properties dialog box).

3 Place a check mark in the 'Use a style to format text typed into the empty control' check box to activate the Style box.

4 Tap or click the Style arrow and then select Intense Emphasis in the list to specify the style for the content control.

5 Place a check mark in the 'Content control cannot be deleted' check box (Figure 10–35).

6 Tap or click the OK button to assign the properties to the content control.

BTW
BTWs
For a complete list of the BTWs found in the margins of this book, visit the BTW resource on the Student Companion Site located on www.cengagebrain.com. For detailed instructions about accessing available resources, visit www.cengage.com/ct/studentdownload or contact your instructor for information about accessing the required files.

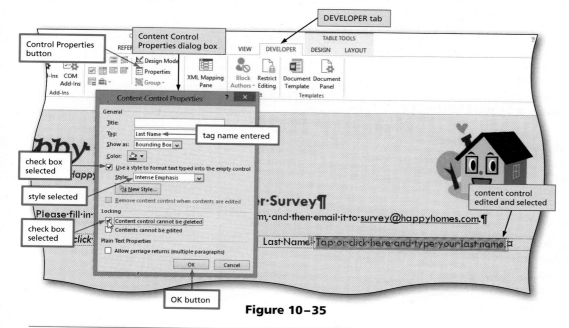

Figure 10–35

To Format Placeholder Text

As with the placeholder text for the first name, the placeholder text for the last name should use the Intense Emphasis style. The following steps format placeholder text.

 With the last name placeholder text selected, display the HOME tab.

2 Locate and select the Intense Emphasis style in the Styles gallery (HOME tab | Styles group) to apply the selected style to the selected placeholder text.

To Increase Space before a Paragraph

The next step in creating this online form is to increase space before a paragraph so that the space below the table is consistent with the space between other elements on the form. The following steps increase space before a paragraph.

1 Position the insertion point on the blank line below the table.

2 Display the PAGE LAYOUT tab.

3 Change the value in the Spacing Before box (PAGE LAYOUT tab | Paragraph group) to 8 pt to increase the space between the table and the paragraph (shown in Figure 10–36).

To Insert a Drop-Down List Content Control

1 SAVE DOCUMENT TEMPLATE | 2 SET FORM FORMATS FOR TEMPLATE
3 ENTER TEXT, GRAPHICS, & CONTENT CONTROLS | 4 PROTECT FORM | 5 USE FORM

In the online form in this chapter, the user selects from one of these four choices for the Frequency of Service Use content control: Monthly, Every other week, Occasional, or One time. The following steps insert a drop-down list content control. **Why?** *To present a set of choices to a user in the form of a drop-down list, from which the user selects one, insert a drop-down list content control. To view the set of choices, the user taps or clicks the arrow at the right edge of the content control.*

1
• With the insertion point positioned on the blank paragraph mark below the First Name content control, using either the ruler or the PAGE LAYOUT tab, change the left indent to 0.06" so that the entered text aligns with the text immediately above it (that is, the F in First).

• Type **How often do you use our services?** and then press the SPACEBAR.

2
• Display the DEVELOPER tab.

• Tap or click the 'Drop-Down List Content Control' button (DEVELOPER tab | Controls group) to insert a drop-down list content control at the location of the insertion point (Figure 10–36).

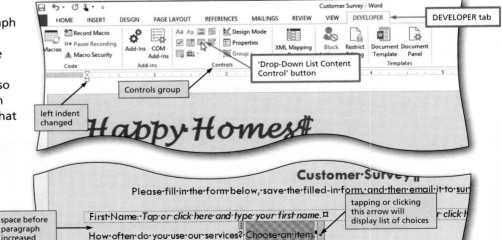

Figure 10–36

To Edit Placeholder Text

The following steps edit the placeholder text for the drop-down list content control.

1 If necessary, display the DEVELOPER tab. With the drop-down list content control selected, tap or click the Design Mode button (DEVELOPER tab | Controls group) to turn on Design mode.

2 Edit the placeholder text so that it contains this instruction, which contains two separate sentences: Tap or click here. Tap or click arrow and select from list.

3 Tap or click the Design Mode button (DEVELOPER tab | Controls group) to turn off Design mode.

To Change the Properties of a Drop-Down List Content Control

1 SAVE DOCUMENT TEMPLATE | 2 SET FORM FORMATS FOR TEMPLATE
3 ENTER TEXT, GRAPHICS, & CONTENT CONTROLS | 4 PROTECT FORM | 5 USE FORM

The following steps change the properties of a drop-down list content control. *Why? In addition to identifying a tag, selecting a style, and locking the drop-down list content control, you can specify the choices that will be displayed when a user taps or clicks the arrow to the right of the content control.*

1

• With the drop-down list content control selected, tap or click the Control Properties button (DEVELOPER tab | Controls group) to display the Content Control Properties dialog box.

• Type **Frequency of Service Use** in the Tag text box (Content Control Properties dialog box).

• Place a check mark in the 'Use a style to format text typed into the empty control' check box to activate the Style box.

• Tap or click the Style arrow and then select Intense Emphasis in the list to specify the style for the content control.

• Place a check mark in the 'Content control cannot be deleted' check box.

• In the Drop-Down List Properties area, tap or click 'Choose an item.' to select it (Figure 10–37).

2

• Tap or click the Remove button (Content Control Properties dialog box) to delete the 'Choose an item.' entry.

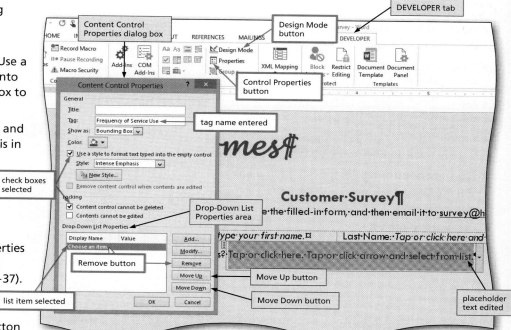

Figure 10–37

Q&A
Why delete the 'Choose an item.' entry?
If you leave it in the list, it will appear as the first item in the list when the user taps or clicks the content control arrow. You do not want it in the list, so you delete it.

Can I delete any entry in a drop-down list using the Remove button?
Yes, select the entry in this dialog box and then tap or click the Remove button. You also can rearrange the order of entries in a list by selecting the entry and then tapping or clicking the Move Up or Move Down buttons.

3

- Tap or click the Add button to display the Add Choice dialog box.

- Type **Monthly** in the Display Name text box (Add Choice dialog box), and notice that Word automatically enters the same text in the Value text box (Figure 10–38).

Q&A What is the difference between a display name and a value?
Often, they are the same, which is why when you type the display name, Word automatically enters the same text in the Value text box. Sometimes, however, you may want to store a shorter or different value. If the display name is long, entering shorter values makes it easier for separate programs to analyze and interpret entered data.

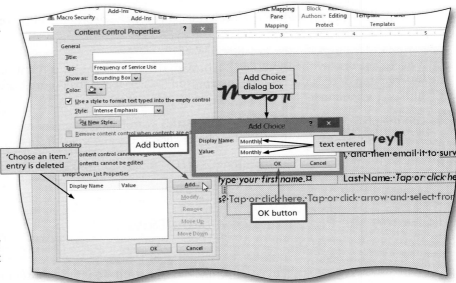

Figure 10–38

4

- Tap or click the OK button (Add Choice dialog box) to add the entered display name and value to the list of choices in the Drop-Down List Properties area (Content Control Properties dialog box).

5

- Tap or click the Add button to display the Add Choice dialog box.

- Type **Every other week** in the Display Name text box.

- Tap or click the OK button to add the entry to the list.

- Tap or click the Add button to display the Add Choice dialog box.

- Type **Occasional** in the Display Name text box.

- Tap or click the OK button to add the entry to the list.

- Tap or click the Add button to display the Add Choice dialog box.

- Type **One time** in the Display Name text box.

- Tap or click the OK button to add the entry to the list (Figure 10–39).

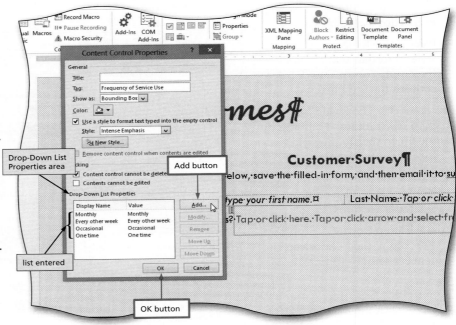

Figure 10–39

6

- Tap or click the OK button (Content Control Properties dialog box) to change the content control properties.

Q&A What if I want to change an entry in the drop-down list?
You would select the drop-down list content control, tap or click the Control Properties button (DEVELOPER tab | Controls group) to display the Content Control Properties dialog box, select the entry to change, tap or click the Modify button, adjust the entry, and then tap or click the OK button.

To Format Placeholder Text

As with the previous placeholder text, the placeholder text for the Frequency of Service Use content control should use the Intense Emphasis style. The following steps format placeholder text.

1 With the Frequency of Service Use placeholder text selected, display the HOME tab.

2 Locate and select the Intense Emphasis style in the Styles gallery (HOME tab | Styles group) to apply the selected style to the selected placeholder text.

3 Press the END key to position the insertion point at the end of the current line and then press the ENTER key to position the insertion point below the Frequency of Service Use content control.

To Enter Text and Use a Table to Control Layout

The next step is to enter the user instructions for the check box content controls and insert a 4 × 1 borderless table so that four evenly spaced check boxes can be displayed horizontally below the check box instructions. The following steps enter text and insert a borderless table.

1 With the insertion point positioned on the paragraph below the Frequency of Service Use content control, tap or click Normal in the Styles gallery (HOME tab | Styles group) to format the current paragraph to the Normal style.

2 Using either the ruler or the PAGE LAYOUT tab, change the left indent to 0.06" so that the entered text aligns with the text immediately above it (that is, the H in How).

3 Type **Which of our services have you used (check all that apply)?** as the instruction.

4 Tap or click the 'Line and Paragraph Spacing' button (HOME tab | Paragraph group) and then tap or click 'Remove Space After Paragraph' so that the check boxes will appear one physical line below the instructions.

5 Press the ENTER key to position the insertion point on the line below the check box instructions.

6 Display the INSERT tab. Tap or click the 'Add a Table' button (INSERT tab | Tables group) to display the Add a Table gallery and then tap or click the cell in the first row and fourth column of the grid to insert an empty 4 × 1 table at the location of the insertion point.

7 Select the table.

8 Tap or click the Borders arrow (TABLE TOOLS DESIGN tab | Borders group) to display the Borders gallery and then tap or click No Border in the Borders gallery to remove the borders from the table.

9 Tap or click the first cell of the table to remove the selection (shown in Figure 10–40 on the next page).

BTW
Certification
The Microsoft Office Specialist (MOS) program provides an opportunity for you to obtain a valuable industry credential — proof that you have the Word 2013 skills required by employers. For more information, visit the Certification resource on the Student Companion Site located on www .cengagebrain.com. For detailed instructions about accessing available resources, visit www.cengage.com/ ct/studentdownload or contact your instructor for information about accessing the required files.

To Insert a Check Box Content Control

The following step inserts the first check box content control. *Why? In the online form in this chapter, the user can select up to five check boxes: Standard cleaning, Green cleaning, Window washing, Carpet cleaning, and Other.*

1

- Position the insertion point at the location for the check box content control, in this case, the leftmost cell in the 4 × 1 table.
- Display the DEVELOPER tab.
- Tap or click the 'Check Box Content Control' button (DEVELOPER tab | Controls group) to insert a check box content control at the location of the insertion point (Figure 10–40).

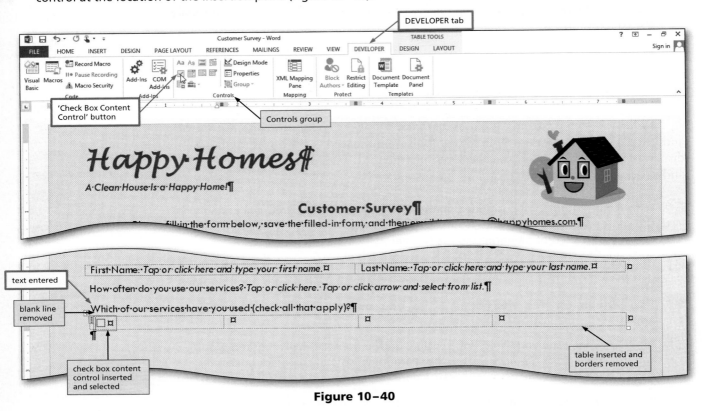

Figure 10–40

To Change the Properties of a Check Box Content Control

The next step is to change the title and locking properties of the content control. The following steps change properties of a check box content control.

1 With the content control selected, tap or click the Control Properties button (DEVELOPER tab | Controls group) to display the Content Control Properties dialog box.

2 Type **Standard Cleaning** in the Tag text box (Content Control Properties dialog box).

3 Tap or click the Show as arrow and then select None in the list, because you do not want a border surrounding the check box content control.

4 Place a check mark in the 'Content control cannot be deleted' check box (Figure 10–41).

5 Tap or click the OK button to assign the properties to the selected content control.

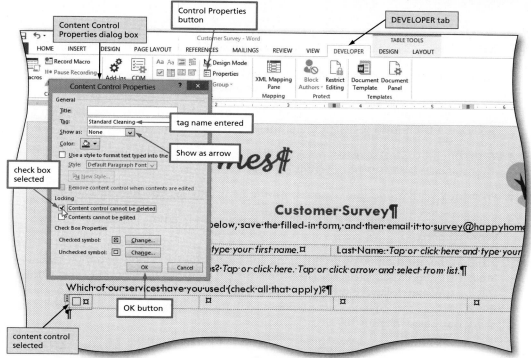

Figure 10–41

To Add a Label to a Check Box Content Control

The following steps add a label to the right of a check box content control.

1 With content control selected, press the END key twice to position the insertion point after the inserted check box content control.

2 Press the SPACEBAR and then type **Standard cleaning** as the check box label (Figure 10–42).

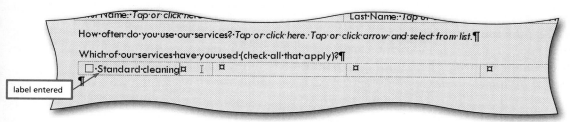

Figure 10–42

To Insert Additional Check Box Content Controls

The following steps insert the remaining check box content controls and their labels.

1 Press the TAB key to position the insertion point in the next cell, which is the location for the next check box content control.

2 Tap or click the 'Check Box Content Control' button (DEVELOPER tab | Controls group) to insert a check box content control at the location of the insertion point.

3 With the content control selected, tap or click the Control Properties button (DEVELOPER tab | Controls group) to display the Content Control Properties dialog box.

4 Type `Green Cleaning` in the Tag text box (Content Control Properties dialog box).

5 Tap or click the Show as arrow and then select None in the list because you do not want a border surrounding the check box content control.

6 Place a check mark in the 'Content control cannot be deleted' check box and then tap or click the OK button to assign the properties to the selected content control.

7 With content control selected, press the END key twice to position the insertion point after the inserted check box content control.

8 Press the SPACEBAR and then type `Green cleaning` as the check box label.

9 Repeat Steps 1 through 8 for the Window washing and Carpet cleaning check box content controls.

10 Position the insertion point on the blank line below the 4 × 1 table and then repeat Steps 1 through 8 for the Other check box content control, which has the label, Other (please specify):, followed by the SPACEBAR. If necessary, using either the ruler or the PAGE LAYOUT tab, change the left indent so that check box above is aligned with the check box below (Figure 10–43).

check box content controls and labels inserted

insertion point

Figure 10–43

To Insert a Rich Text Content Control

1 SAVE DOCUMENT TEMPLATE | 2 SET FORM FORMATS FOR TEMPLATE

3 ENTER TEXT, GRAPHICS, & CONTENT CONTROLS | 4 PROTECT FORM | 5 USE FORM

The next step is to insert the content control that enables users to type in any other types of services they have used. The difference between a plain text and rich text content control is that the users can format text as they enter it in the rich text content control. The following step inserts a rich text content control. *Why? Because you want to allow users to format the text they enter in the Other Services Used content control, you use the rich text content control.*

- If necessary, position the insertion point at the location for the rich text content control (shown in Figure 10–43).

- Tap or click the 'Rich Text Content Control' button (DEVELOPER tab | Controls group) to insert a rich text content control at the location of the insertion point (Figure 10–44).

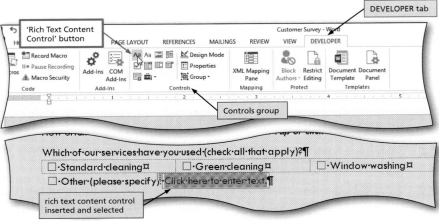

'Rich Text Content Control' button

DEVELOPER tab

Controls group

rich text content control inserted and selected

Figure 10–44

To Edit Placeholder Text

The following steps edit placeholder text for the rich text content control.

1 With the rich text content control selected, tap or click the Design Mode button (DEVELOPER tab | Controls group) to turn on Design mode.

2 If necessary, scroll to display the content control in the document window.

3 Edit the placeholder text so that it contains the text, Tap or click here and type other services you have used., as the instruction.

4 Tap or click the Design Mode button (DEVELOPER tab | Controls group) to turn off Design mode. If necessary, scroll to display the top of the form in the document window.

To Change the Properties of a Rich Text Content Control

In the online form in this chapter, you change the same three properties for the rich text content control as for the plain text content control. That is, you enter a tag name, specify the style, and lock the content control. The following steps change the properties of the rich text content control.

1 With the content control selected, tap or click the Control Properties button (DEVELOPER tab | Controls group) to display the Content Control Properties dialog box.

2 Type **Other Services Used** in the Tag text box (Content Control Properties dialog box).

3 Place a check mark in the 'Use a style to format text typed into the empty control' check box to activate the Style box.

4 Tap or click the Style arrow and then select Intense Emphasis in the list to specify the style for the content control.

5 Place a check mark in the 'Content control cannot be deleted' check box (Figure 10–45).

6 Tap or click the OK button to assign the properties to the content control.

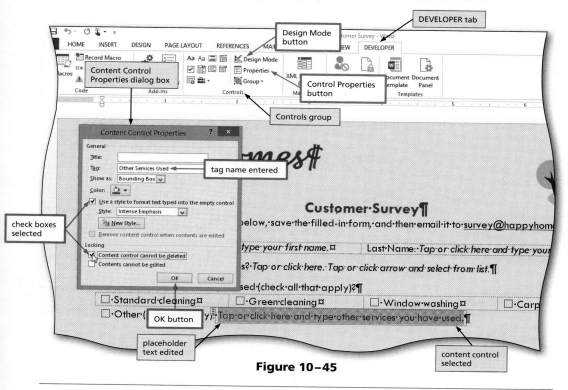

Figure 10–45

To Format Placeholder Text and Add Space before a Paragraph

The placeholder text for the Other Services Used text entry should use the Intense Emphasis style, and the space below the check boxes should be consistent with the space between other elements on the form. The next steps format placeholder text and increase space before a paragraph.

1 With the Other Services Used placeholder text selected, display the HOME tab.

2 Locate and select the Intense Emphasis style in the Styles gallery (HOME tab | Styles group) to apply the selected style to the selected placeholder text.

3 Press the END key to position the insertion point on the paragraph mark after the Other Services Used content control and then press the ENTER key to position the insertion point below the Other Services Used content control.

4 If necessary, display the HOME tab. With the insertion point positioned on the paragraph below the Other Services Used content control, tap or click Normal in the Styles gallery (HOME tab | Styles group) to format the current paragraph to the Normal style.

5 Using either the ruler or the PAGE LAYOUT tab, change the left indent to 0.06" so that the entered text aligns with the text two lines above it (that is, the W in Which).

6 Display the PAGE LAYOUT tab. Change the value in the Spacing Before box (PAGE LAYOUT tab | Paragraph group) to 8 pt to increase the space between the Other Services Used check box and the paragraph.

To Insert a Combo Box Content Control

1 SAVE DOCUMENT TEMPLATE | 2 SET FORM FORMATS FOR TEMPLATE
3 ENTER TEXT, GRAPHICS, & CONTENT CONTROLS | 4 PROTECT FORM | 5 USE FORM

In Word, a combo box content control allows a user to type text or select from a list. The following steps insert a combo box content control. ***Why?*** *In the online form in this chapter, users can type their own entry in the Cleaning Staff Rating content control or select from one of these four choices: Excellent, Good, Fair, or Poor.*

1

• With the insertion point positioned on the blank paragraph mark, type **How would you rate our cleaning staff?** and then press the SPACEBAR.

2

• Display the DEVELOPER tab.

• Tap or click the 'Combo Box Content Control' button (DEVELOPER tab | Controls group) to insert a combo box content control at the location of the insertion point (Figure 10–46).

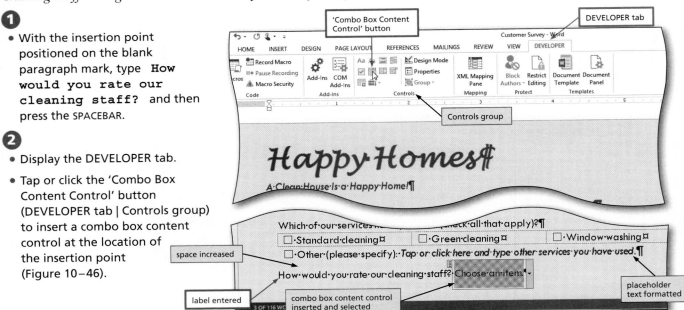

Figure 10–46

To Edit Placeholder Text

The following steps edit the placeholder text for the combo box content control.

① With the combo box content control selected, tap or click the Design Mode button (DEVELOPER tab | Controls group) to turn on Design mode.

② If necessary, scroll to page 2 to display the combo box content control.

Q&A Why did the content control move to another page?
Because Design mode displays tags, the content controls and placeholder text are not displayed in their proper positions on the screen. When you turn off Design mode, the content controls will return to their original locations and the extra page should disappear.

③ Edit the placeholder text so that it contains this instruction, which contains two sentences (Figure 10–47): Tap or click here. Tap or click arrow and select from list, or type a response.

④ Tap or click the Design Mode button (DEVELOPER tab | Controls group) to turn off Design mode.

⑤ Scroll to display the top of the form in the document window.

BTW

Q&As
For a complete list of the Q&As found in many of the step-by-step sequences in this book, visit the Q&A resource on the Student Companion Site located on www.cengagebrain.com. For detailed instructions about accessing available resources, visit www.cengage.com/ct/studentdownload or contact your instructor for information about accessing the required files.

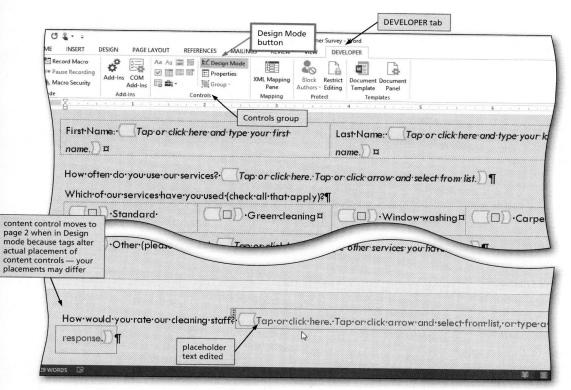

Figure 10–47

To Change the Properties of a Combo Box Content Control

You follow similar steps to enter the list for a combo box content control as you do for the drop-down list content control. The next steps change the properties of a combo box content control. *Why? You enter the tag name, specify the style for typed text, and enter the choices for the drop-down list.*

1

- With content control selected, tap or click the Control Properties button (DEVELOPER tab | Controls group) to display the Content Control Properties dialog box.

- Type **Cleaning Staff Rating** in the Tag text box (Content Control Properties dialog box).

- Place a check mark in the 'Use a style to format text typed into the empty control' check box to activate the Style box.

- Tap or click the Style arrow and then select Intense Emphasis in the list to specify the style for the content control.

- Place a check mark in the 'Content control cannot be deleted' check box.

- In the Drop-Down List Properties area, tap or click 'Choose an item.' to select it (Figure 10–48).

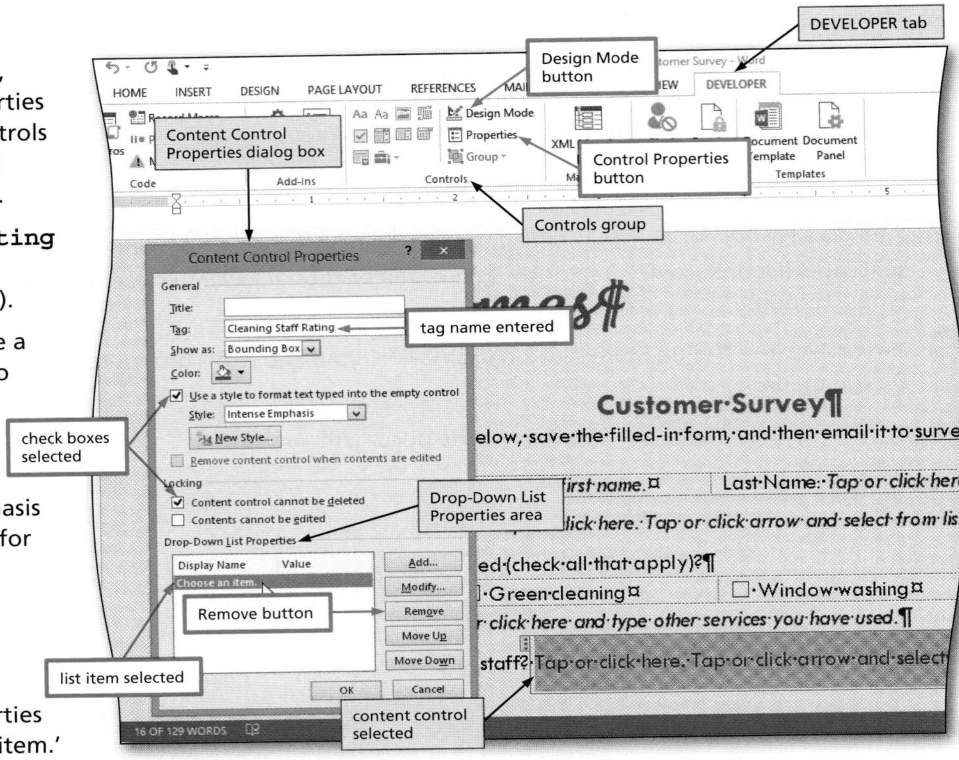

Figure 10–48

2

- Tap or click the Remove button (Content Control Properties dialog box) to delete the selected entry.

3

- Tap or click the Add button to display the Add Choice dialog box.

- Type **Excellent** in the Display Name text box (Add Choice dialog box).

- Tap or click the OK button to add the entered display name to the list of choices in the Drop-Down List Properties area (Content Control Properties dialog box).

- Tap or click the Add button and add **Good** to the list.

- Tap or click the Add button and add **Fair** to the list.

- Tap or click the Add button and add **Poor** to the list (Figure 10–49).

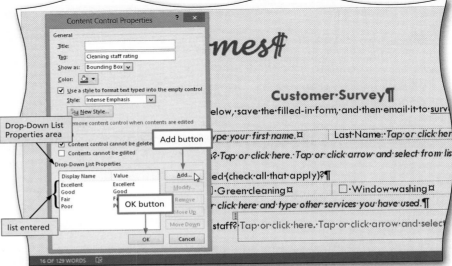

Figure 10–49

4

- Tap or click the OK button (Content Control Properties dialog box) to change the content control properties.

Q&A How do I make adjustments to entries in the list?
Follow the same procedures as you use to make adjustments to entries in a drop-down list content control (see page WD 636).

To Format Placeholder Text

As with the previous placeholder text, the placeholder text for the Cleaning Staff Rating should use the Intense Emphasis style. The following steps format placeholder text.

1 With the Cleaning Staff Rating placeholder text selected, display the HOME tab.

2 Locate and select the Intense Emphasis style in the Styles gallery (HOME tab | Styles group) to apply the selected style to the selected placeholder text.

3 Press the END key to position the insertion point at the end of the current line and then press the ENTER key to position the insertion point below the Cleaning Staff Rating content control.

4 Tap or click Normal in the Styles list (HOME tab | Styles group) to format the current paragraph to the Normal style.

5 Using either the ruler or the PAGE LAYOUT tab, change the left indent to 0.06" so that the entered text aligns with the text above it (that is, the H in How).

To Insert a Date Picker Content Control

1 SAVE DOCUMENT TEMPLATE | **2** SET FORM FORMATS FOR TEMPLATE
3 ENTER TEXT, GRAPHICS, & CONTENT CONTROLS | **4** PROTECT FORM | **5** USE FORM

To assist users with entering dates, Word provides a date picker content control, which displays a calendar when the user taps or clicks the arrow to the right of the content control. Users also can enter a date directly in the content control without using the calendar. The following steps enter the label, Today's Date:, and a date picker content control. *Why? The last item that users enter in the Customer Survey is today's date.*

1

- With the insertion point below the Cleaning Staff Rating content control, type **Today's date:** as the label for the content control and then press the SPACEBAR.

2

- Display the DEVELOPER tab.

- Tap or click the 'Date Picker Content Control' button (DEVELOPER tab | Controls group) to insert a date picker content control at the location of the insertion point (Figure 10–50).

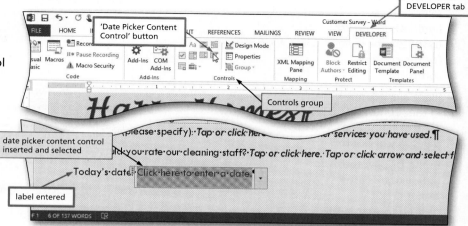

Figure 10–50

To Edit Placeholder Text

The following steps edit the placeholder text for the date picker content control.

1 With the date picker content control selected, tap or click the Design Mode button (DEVELOPER tab | Controls group) to turn on Design mode.

2 If necessary, scroll to page 2 to display the date picker content control.

3 Edit the placeholder text so that it contains this instruction, which contains two sentences: Tap or click here. Tap or click arrow and select today's date.

4 Tap or click the Design Mode button (DEVELOPER tab | Controls group) to turn off Design mode.

5 If necessary, scroll to display the top of the form in the document window.

To Change the Properties of a Date Picker Content Control

1 SAVE DOCUMENT TEMPLATE | 2 SET FORM FORMATS FOR TEMPLATE
3 ENTER TEXT, GRAPHICS, & CONTENT CONTROLS | 4 PROTECT FORM | 5 USE FORM

The following steps change the properties of a date picker content control. **Why?** *In addition to identifying a tag name for a date picker content control, specifying a style, and locking the control, you will specify how the date will be displayed when the user selects it from the calendar.*

1

• With the content control selected, tap or click the Control Properties button (DEVELOPER tab | Controls group) to display the Content Control Properties dialog box.

• Type **Today's Date** in the Tag text box.

• Place a check mark in the 'Use a style to format text typed into the empty control' check box to activate the Style box.

• Tap or click the Style arrow and then select Intense Emphasis in the list to specify the style for the content control.

• Place a check mark in the 'Content control cannot be deleted' check box.

• In the Display the date like this area, tap or click the desired format in the list (Figure 10–51).

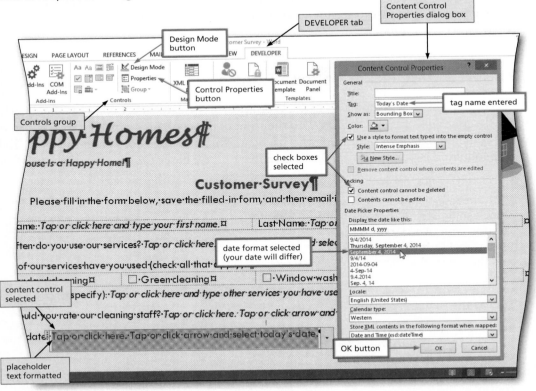

Figure 10–51

2

• Tap or click the OK button to change the content control properties.

To Format Placeholder Text

As with the previous placeholder text, the placeholder text for today's date should use the Intense Emphasis style. The following steps format placeholder text.

1 With the today's date placeholder text selected, display the HOME tab.

2 Locate and select the Intense Emphasis style in the Styles gallery (HOME tab | Styles group) to apply the selected style to the selected placeholder text.

3 Press the END key to position the insertion point at the end of the current line and then press the ENTER key to position the insertion point below the Today's Date content control.

4 Tap or click Normal in the Styles gallery (HOME tab | Styles group) to format the current paragraph to the Normal style.

To Enter and Format Text

The following steps enter and format the line of text at the bottom of the online form.

1 Be sure the insertion point is on the line below the Today's Date content control.

2 Center the paragraph mark.

3 Format the text to be typed with the color of Red, Accent 6, Darker 25%.

4 Type **Thank you for your time!**

5 Change the space before the paragraph to 12 point (Figure 10–52).

6 If the text flows to a second page, reduce spacing before paragraphs in the form so that all lines fit on a single page.

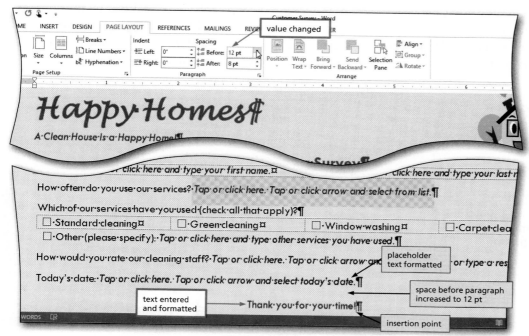

Figure 10–52

To Hide Gridlines and Formatting Marks

Because you are finished with the tables in this form and will not enter any additional tables, you will hide the gridlines. You also are finished with entering and formatting text on the screen. To make the form easier to view, you hide the formatting marks, which can clutter the screen. The following steps hide gridlines and formatting marks.

1 If necessary, position the insertion point in a table cell.

2 Display the TABLE TOOLS LAYOUT tab. If gridlines are showing, tap or click the 'View Table Gridlines' button (TABLE TOOLS LAYOUT tab | Table group) to hide table gridlines.

3 Display the HOME tab. If the 'Show/Hide ¶' button (HOME tab | Paragraph group) is selected, tap or click it to remove formatting marks from the screen.

To Save an Existing Template with the Same File Name

You have made several modifications to the template since you last saved it. Thus, you should save it again. The following step saves the template again.

1 Tap or click the Save button on the Quick Access Toolbar to overwrite the previously saved file.

Break Point: If you wish to take a break, this is a good place to do so. You can exit Word now. To resume at a later time, run Word, open the file called Customer Survey, and continue following the steps from this location forward.

To Draw a Rectangle

1 SAVE DOCUMENT TEMPLATE | 2 SET FORM FORMATS FOR TEMPLATE
3 ENTER TEXT, GRAPHICS, & CONTENT CONTROLS | 4 PROTECT FORM | 5 USE FORM

The next step is to emphasize the data entry area of the form. The data entry area includes all the content controls in which a user enters data. The following steps draw a rectangle around the data entry area, and subsequent steps format the rectangle. *Why? To call attention to the data entry area of the form, this chapter places a rectangle around the data entry area, changes the style of the rectangle, and then adds a shadow to the rectangle.*

1

- Position the insertion point on the last line in the document (shown in Figure 10–52 on the previous page).
- Display the INSERT tab.
- Tap or click the 'Draw a Shape' button (INSERT tab | Illustrations group) to display the Draw a Shape gallery (Figure 10–53).

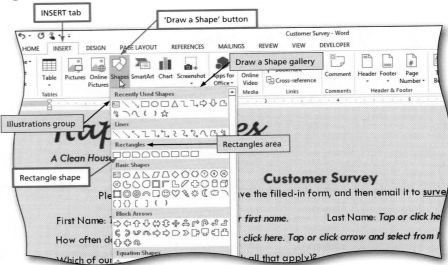

Figure 10–53

- Tap or click the rectangle shape in the Rectangles area of the Draw a Shape gallery, which removes the gallery. If you are using a touch screen, the shape is inserted in the document window; if you are using a mouse, the pointer changes to the shape of a crosshair in the document window.

- If you are using a mouse, position the pointer (a crosshair) in the approximate location for the upper-left corner of the desired shape (Figure 10–54).

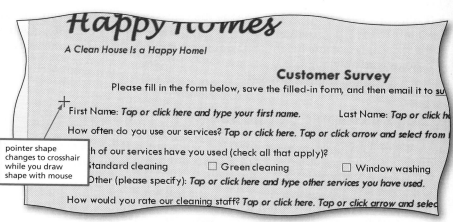

Figure 10–54

3

- If you are using a mouse, drag the pointer downward and rightward to form a rectangle around the data entry area, as shown in Figure 10–55.

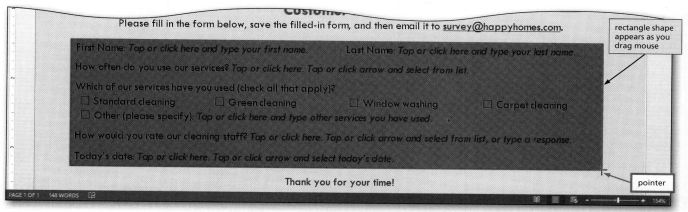

Figure 10–55

4

- If you are using a mouse, release the mouse button to draw the rectangle shape on top of the data entry area (Figure 10–56).

Q&A | What happened to all the text in the data entry area?
When you draw a shape in a document, Word initially places the shape in front of, or on top of, any text in the same area. You can change the stacking order of the shape so that it is displayed behind the text. Thus, the next steps move the shape behind text.

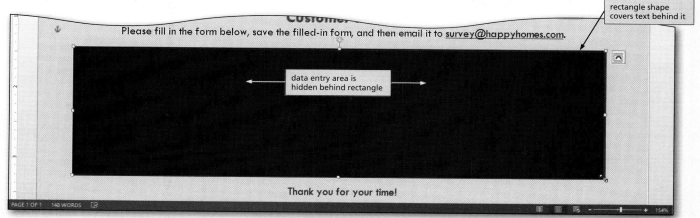

Figure 10–56

5

- If you are using a touch screen, change the values in the Shape Height and Shape Width boxes (DRAWING TOOLS FORMAT tab | Size group) to 1.82" and 7.39" (shown in Figure 10–58); if you are using a mouse, verify your shape is the same approximate height and width and, if necessary, change the values in the Shape Height and Shape Width boxes accordingly.

To Send a Graphic behind Text

1 SAVE DOCUMENT TEMPLATE | 2 SET FORM FORMATS FOR TEMPLATE
3 ENTER TEXT, GRAPHICS, & CONTENT CONTROLS | 4 PROTECT FORM | 5 USE FORM

The following steps send a graphic behind text. **Why?** *You want the rectangle shape graphic to be positioned behind the data entry area text, so that you can see the text in the data entry area along with the shape.*

1

- If necessary, display the DRAWING TOOLS FORMAT tab.
- With the rectangle shape selected, tap or click the Layout Options button attached to the graphic to display the Layout Options gallery (Figure 10–57).

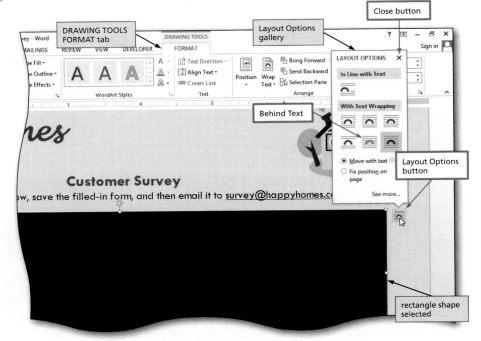

Figure 10–57

2

- Tap or click Behind Text in the Layout Options gallery to position the rectangle shape behind the text (Figure 10–58).

Q&A

What if I want a shape to cover text?

You would tap or click 'In Front of Text' in the Layout Options gallery.

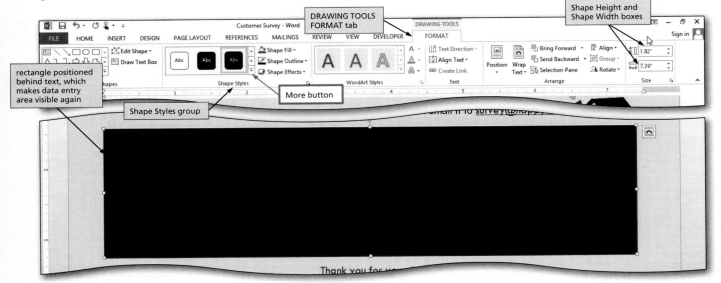

Figure 10–58

3

- Tap or click the Close button in the Layout Options gallery to close the gallery.

Other Ways

1 Tap or click Wrap Text button (DRAWING TOOLS FORMAT tab | Arrange group), select desired option	2. Tap 'Show Context Menu' button on mini toolbar or right-click object, tap or point to Wrap Text on shortcut menu, tap or click desired option

To Apply a Shape Style

The next step is to apply a shape style to the rectangle, so that the text in the data entry area is easier to read. The following steps apply a style to the rectangle shape.

1 With the shape still selected, tap or click the More button in the Shape Styles gallery (DRAWING TOOLS FORMAT tab | Shape Styles group) (shown in Figure 10–58) to expand the Shape Styles gallery.

2 If you are using a mouse, point to 'Colored Outline - Dark Blue, Accent 1' in the Shape Styles gallery (second effect in first row) to display a live preview of that style applied to the rectangle shape in the form (Figure 10–59).

3 Tap or click 'Colored Outline - Dark Blue, Accent 1' in the Shape Styles gallery to apply the selected style to the selected shape.

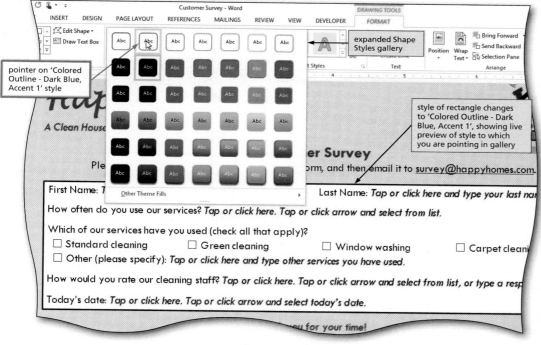

Figure 10–59

BTW

Formatting Shapes
Like other drawing objects or pictures, shapes can be formatted or have styles applied. You can change the fill in a shape by tapping or clicking the Shape Fill arrow (DRAWING TOOLS FORMAT tab | Shape Styles group), add an outline or border to a shape by tapping or clicking the Shape Outline arrow (DRAWING TOOLS FORMAT tab | Shape Styles group), and apply an effect such as shadow or 3-D effects by tapping or clicking the Shape Effects arrow (DRAWING TOOLS FORMAT tab | Shape Styles group).

To Add a Shadow to a Shape

The next steps add a shadow to the rectangle shape. *Why? To further offset the data entry area of the form, this online form has a shadow on the outside top and right edges of the rectangle shape.*

- With the shape still selected, tap or click the Shape Effects button (DRAWING TOOLS FORMAT tab | Shape Styles group) to display the Shape Effects menu.

- Tap or point to Shadow on the Shape Effects menu to display the Shadow gallery.

- If you are using a mouse, point to 'Offset Diagonal Top Right' in the Outer area in the Shadow gallery to display a live preview of that shadow effect applied to the selected shape in the document (Figure 10–60).

Experiment

- If you are using a mouse, point to various shadows in the Shadow gallery and watch the shadow on the selected shape change.

- Tap or click 'Offset Diagonal Top Right' in the Shadow gallery to apply the selected shadow to the selected shape.

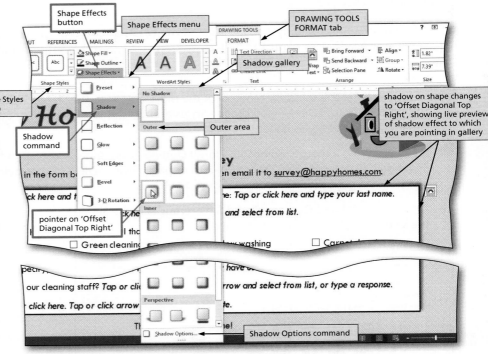

Figure 10–60

Q&A Can I change the color of a shadow?
Yes. Tap or click Shadow Options in the Shadow gallery.

To Highlight Text

To emphasize text in an online document, you can highlight it. **Highlighting** alerts a reader to online text's importance, much like a highlighter pen does on a printed page. Word provides 15 colors you can use to highlight text, including the traditional yellow and green, as well as some nontraditional highlight colors such as gray, dark blue, and dark red. The following steps highlight the fourth line of text in the color gray. *Why? You want to emphasize the line of text on the form that contains instructions related to completing the form.*

- Select the text to be highlighted, which, in this case, is the fourth line of text.

Q&A Why is the selection taller than usual?
Earlier in this project you increased the space after this paragraph. The selection includes this vertical space.

- If necessary, display the HOME tab.

- Tap or click the 'Text Highlight Color' arrow (HOME tab | Font group) to display the Text Highlight Color gallery.

Q&A The Text Highlight Color gallery did not appear. Why not?
If you are using a mouse, you clicked the 'Text Highlight Color' button instead of the 'Text Highlight Color' arrow. Click the Undo button on the Quick Access Toolbar and then repeat Step 1.

What if the icon on the 'Text Highlight Color' button already displays the color I want to use?
If you are using a mouse, you can click the 'Text Highlight Color' button instead of the arrow.

2

- If you are using a mouse, point to Gray-25% in the Text Highlight Color gallery to display a live preview of this highlight color applied to the selected text (Figure 10–61).

🔍 **Experiment**

- If you are using a mouse, point to various colors in the Text Highlight Color gallery and watch the highlight color on the selected text change.

- Tap or click Gray-25% in the Text Highlight Color gallery to highlight the selected text in the selected highlight color.

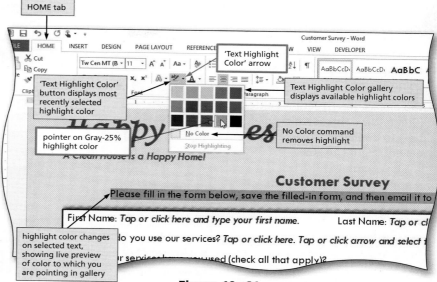

Figure 10–61

Q&A | How would I remove a highlight from text?

Select the highlighted text, tap or click the 'Text Highlight Color' arrow, and then tap or click No Color in the Text Highlight Color gallery.

Other Ways

1. Tap or click 'Text Highlight Color' arrow (HOME tab | Font group), select desired color, select text to be highlighted in document, select any additional text to be highlighted, tap or click 'Text Highlight Color' button to turn off highlighting

To Customize a Theme Color and Save It with a New Theme Name

1 SAVE DOCUMENT TEMPLATE | 2 SET FORM FORMATS FOR TEMPLATE
3 ENTER TEXT, GRAPHICS, & CONTENT CONTROLS | 4 PROTECT FORM | 5 USE FORM

The final step in formatting the online form in this chapter is to change the color of the hyperlink. A document theme has 12 predefined colors for various on-screen objects including text, backgrounds, and hyperlinks. You can change any of the theme colors. The following steps customize the Slice theme, changing its designated theme color for hyperlinks. *Why? You would like the hyperlink to be red, to match the 'thank you' line on the form.*

- Display the DESIGN tab.

- Tap or click the Theme Colors button (DESIGN tab | Document Formatting group) to display the Theme Colors gallery (Figure 10–62).

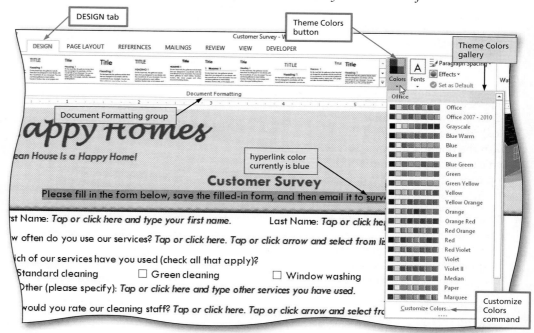

Figure 10–62

2

- Tap or click Customize Colors in the Theme Colors gallery to display the Create New Theme Colors dialog box.

- Tap or click the Hyperlink button (Create New Theme Colors dialog box) to display the Theme Colors gallery (Figure 10–63).

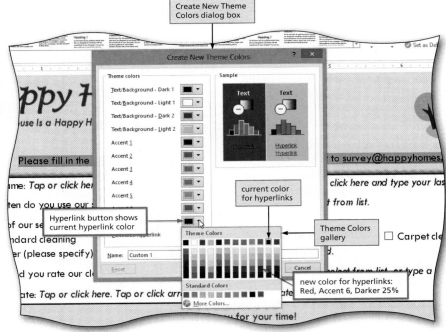

Figure 10–63

3

- Tap or click 'Red, Accent 6, Darker 25%' in the Hyperlink column (tenth color in fifth row) as the new hyperlink color.

- Type **Customer Survey** in the Name text box (Figure 10–64).

Q&A What if I wanted to reset all the original theme colors?
You would tap or click the Reset button (Create New Theme Colors dialog box) before tapping or clicking the Save button.

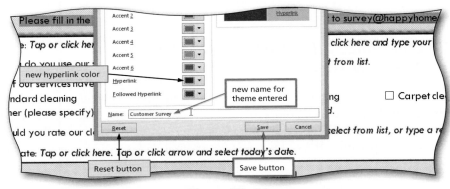

Figure 10–64

4

- Tap or click the Save button (Create New Theme Colors dialog box) to save the modified theme with the name, Customer Survey, which will be positioned at the top of the Theme Colors gallery for future access (Figure 10–65).

Q&A What if I do not enter a name for the modified theme?
Word assigns a name that begins with the letters, Custom, followed by a number (i.e., Custom8).

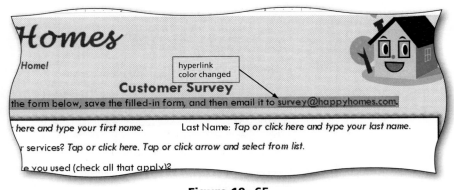

Figure 10–65

Other Ways

1. Make changes to theme colors, fonts, and/or effects; tap or click Themes button (DESIGN tab | Document Formatting group), tap or click 'Save Current Theme' in Themes gallery

To Protect a Form

When you **protect a form**, you are allowing users to enter data only in designated areas — specifically, the content controls. The following steps protect the online form. *Why? To prevent unwanted changes and edits to the form, it is crucial that you protect a form before making it available to users.*

1

- Display the DEVELOPER tab.

- Tap or click the Restrict Editing button (DEVELOPER tab | Protect group) to display the Restrict Editing task pane (Figure 10–66).

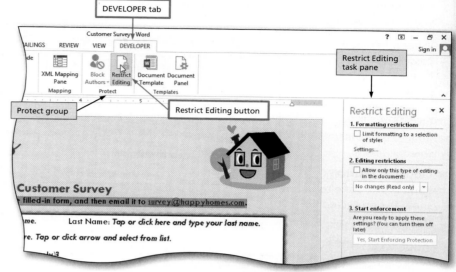

Figure 10–66

2

- In the Editing restrictions area, place a check mark in the 'Allow only this type of editing in the document' check box and then tap or click its arrow to display a list of the types of allowed restrictions (Figure 10–67).

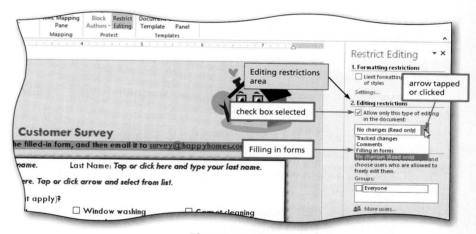

Figure 10–67

3

- Tap or click 'Filling in forms' in the list to instruct Word that the only editing allowed in this document is to the content controls.

- In the Start enforcement area, tap or click the 'Yes, Start Enforcing Protection' button, which displays the Start Enforcing Protection dialog box (Figure 10–68).

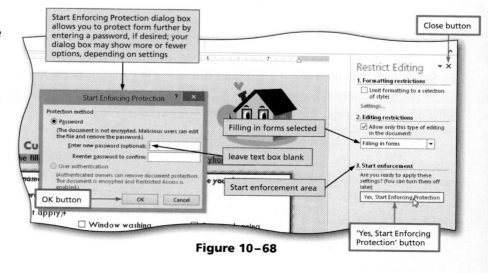

Figure 10–68

4

- Tap or click the OK button (Start Enforcing Protection dialog box) to protect the document without a password.

Q&A

What if I enter a password?

If you enter a password, only a user who knows the password will be able to unprotect the document.

- Close the Restrict Editing task pane to show the protected form (Figure 10–69).

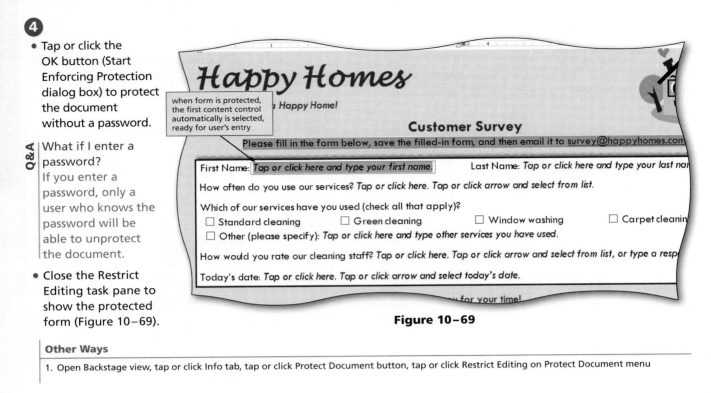

when form is protected, the first content control automatically is selected, ready for user's entry

Happy Homes

a Happy Home!

Customer Survey

Please fill in the form below, save the filled-in form, and then email it to survey@happyhomes.com

First Name: *Tap or click here and type your first name.*   Last Name: *Tap or click here and type your last nan*

How often do you use our services? *Tap or click here. Tap or click arrow and select from list.*

Which of our services have you used (check all that apply)?
☐ Standard cleaning   ☐ Green cleaning   ☐ Window washing   ☐ Carpet cleanin

☐ Other (please specify): *Tap or click here and type other services you have used.*

How would you rate our cleaning staff? *Tap or click here. Tap or click arrow and select from list, or type a resp*

Today's date: *Tap or click here. Tap or click arrow and select today's date.*

u for your time!

Figure 10–69

Other Ways

1. Open Backstage view, tap or click Info tab, tap or click Protect Document button, tap or click Restrict Editing on Protect Document menu

---

Protecting Documents

In addition to protecting a form so that it only can be filled in, Word provides several other options in the Restrict Editing task pane.

TO SET FORMATTING RESTRICTIONS

If you wanted to restrict users from making certain types of formatting changes to a document, you would perform the following steps.

1. Tap or click the Restrict Editing button (DEVELOPER tab | Protect group) to display the Restrict Editing task pane.
2. Place a check mark in the 'Limit formatting to a selection of styles' check box in the Formatting restrictions area.
3. Tap or click the Settings link and then select the types of formatting you want to allow (Formatting Restrictions dialog box).
4. Tap or click the OK button.
5. Tap or click the 'Yes, Start Enforcing Protection' button, enter a password if desired, and then tap or click the OK button (Start Enforcing Protection dialog box).

TO SET EDITING RESTRICTIONS TO TRACKED CHANGES OR COMMENTS OR NO EDITS

If you wanted to restrict users' edits to allow only tracked changes, allow only comments, or not allow any edits (that is, make the document read only), you would perform the following steps.

1. Tap or click the Restrict Editing button (DEVELOPER tab | Protect group) to display the Restrict Editing task pane.
2. Place a check mark in the 'Allow only this type of editing in the document' check box in the Editing restrictions area, tap or click the arrow, and then tap or click the desired option — that is, Tracked changes, Comments, or No changes (Read only) — to specify the types of edits allowed in the document.
3. Tap or click the 'Yes, Start Enforcing Protection' button, enter a password if desired, and then tap or click the OK button (Start Enforcing Protection dialog box).

To Hide the DEVELOPER Tab

You are finished using the commands on the DEVELOPER tab. Thus, the following steps hide the DEVELOPER tab from the ribbon.

1 Open the Backstage view and then tap or click Options in the left pane of the Backstage view to display the Word Options dialog box.

2 Tap or click Customize Ribbon in the left pane (Word Options dialog box).

3 Remove the check mark from the Developer check box in the Main Tabs list.

4 Tap or click the OK button to hide the DEVELOPER tab from the ribbon.

To Hide the Ruler

You are finished using the ruler. Thus, the following steps hide the ruler.

1 Display the VIEW tab.

2 If the ruler is displayed on the screen, remove the check mark from the View Ruler check box (VIEW tab | Show group).

To Collapse the Ribbon

The following step collapses the ribbon so that when you test the form in the next steps, the ribbon is collapsed.

1 Tap or click the 'Collapse the Ribbon' button on the ribbon (shown in Figure 10–5 on page WD 615) to collapse the ribbon.

To Save the Template Again and Exit Word

The online form template for this project now is complete. Thus, the following steps save the template and exit Word.

1 Tap or click the Save button on the Quick Access Toolbar to overwrite the previously saved file.

2 Exit Word.

Working with an Online Form

When you create a template, you use the Open command in the Backstage view to open the template so that you can modify it. After you have created a template, you then can make it available to users. Users do not open templates with the Open command in Word. Instead, a user creates a new Word document that is based on the template, which means the title bar displays the default file name, Document1 (or a similar name) rather than the template name. When Word creates a new document that is based on a template, the document window contains any text and formatting associated with the template. If a user accesses a letter template, for example, Word displays the contents of a basic letter in a new document window.

BTW
Highlighter
If you tap or click the 'Text Highlight Color' button (HOME tab | Font group) without first selecting any text, the highlighter remains active until you turn it off. This allows you to continue selecting text that you want to be highlighted. To deactivate the highlighter, tap or click the 'Text Highlight Color' button (HOME tab | Font group) and then tap or click Stop Highlighting on the Text Highlight Color menu, or press the ESC key.

BTW
Password-Protecting Documents
You can save documents with a password to keep unauthorized users from accessing files. To do this, type the password in the Start Enforcing Protection dialog box (shown in Figure 10–68 on page WD 655); or open the Backstage view, tap or click Save As, display the Save As dialog box, tap or click the Tools button (Save As dialog box), tap or click General Options on the Tools menu, type the password in the appropriate text box (General Options dialog box), type the password again (Confirm Password dialog box), and then tap or click the OK button and Save button (Save As dialog box). As you type a password in the text box, Word displays a series of dots instead of the actual characters so that others cannot see your password as you type it.
Be sure to keep the password confidential. Choose a password that is easy to remember and that no one can guess. Do not use any part of your first or last name, Social Security number, birthday, and so on. Use a password that is at least six characters long, and if possible, use a mixture of numbers and letters.

To Use File Explorer to Create a New Document That Is Based on a Template

When you save a template on storage media, as instructed earlier in this chapter, a user can create a new document that is based on the template through File Explorer. *Why? This allows the user to work with a new document instead of risking the chance of altering the original template.* The following steps create a new Word document that is based on the Customer Survey template.

1

- Tap or click the File Explorer app button on the Windows taskbar to open the File Explorer window.

- Navigate to the location of the saved template (in this case, the Chapter 10 folder in the Word folder in the CIS 101 folder [or your class folder]) (Figure 10–70).

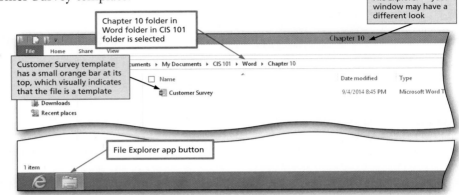

Figure 10–70

2

- Double-tap or double-click the Customer Survey file in the File Explorer window, which runs Word and creates a new document that is based on the contents of the selected template (Figure 10–71).

Q&A

Why did my background page color disappear?

If the background page color does not appear, open the Backstage view, tap or click Options to display the Word Options dialog box, tap or click Advanced in the left pane (Word Options dialog box), scroll to the Show document content section, place a check mark in the 'Show background colors and images in Print Layout view' check box, and then tap or click the OK button.

Why does my ribbon only show three tabs: FILE, TOOLS, and VIEW?

Your screen is in Read mode. Tap or click the VIEW tab and then tap or click Edit Document to switch to Print Layout view.

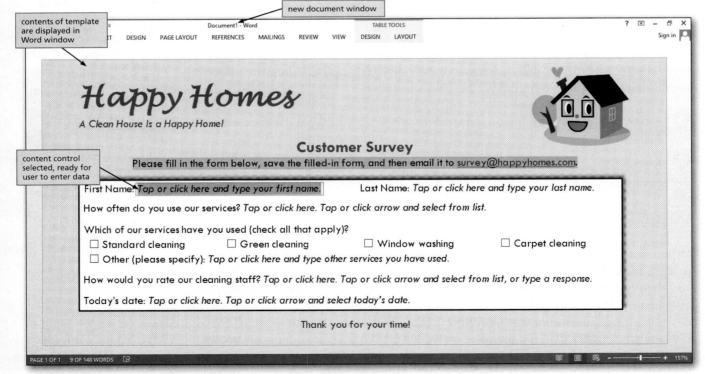

Figure 10–71

To Fill In a Form and Save It

The next step is to enter data in the form. To advance from one content control to the next, a user can tap or click the content control or press the TAB key. To move to a previous content control, a user can tap or click it or press SHIFT+TAB. The following steps fill in the Customer Survey form. **Why?** *You want to test the form to be sure it works as you intended.*

1

- With the First Name content control selected, type **Brian** and then press the TAB key.
- Type **Kaminsky** in the Last Name content control.

  If requested by your instructor, use your first and last name instead of the name, Brian Kaminsky.

- Press the TAB key to select the Frequency of Service Use content control and then tap or click its arrow to display the list of choices (shown in Figure 10–1b on page WD 611).
- Tap or click 'Every other week' in the list.
- Tap or click the Green cleaning and Other check boxes to select them.
- Type **Packing and unpacking** in the Other Services Used content control.
- Tap or click the Cleaning Staff Rating content control and then tap or click its arrow to display the list of choices (Figure 10–72).

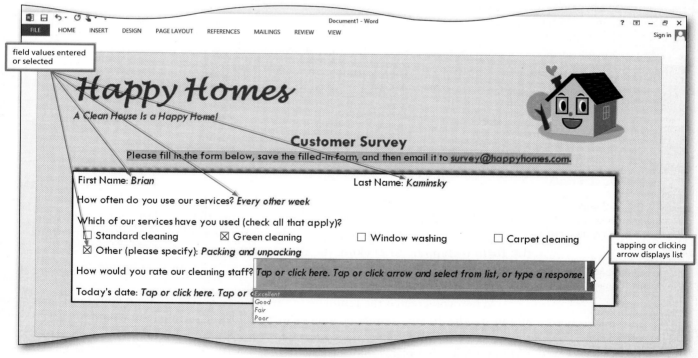

Figure 10–72

BTW
Internet Explorer vs. Windows Explorer
Internet Explorer is a browser included with the Windows operating system. File Explorer is a file manager that is included with the Windows operating system. It enables you to perform functions related to file management, such as displaying a list of files, organizing files, and copying files.

2

- Select Excellent in the list.
- Tap or click the Today's date arrow to display the calendar (Figure 10–73).

3

- Tap or click September 24, 2014 in the calendar to complete the data entry (shown in Figure 10–1c on page WD 611).

4

- Tap or click the Save button on the Quick Access Toolbar and then save the file on your storage media with the file name, Kaminsky Survey. If Word asks if you want to also save changes to the document template, tap or click the No button.

  If requested by your instructor, use your last name in the file name instead of the name, Kaminsky.

Q&A Can I print the form?
You can print the document as you print any other document. Keep in mind, however, that the colors used were designed for viewing online. Thus, different color schemes would have been selected if the form had been designed for a printout.

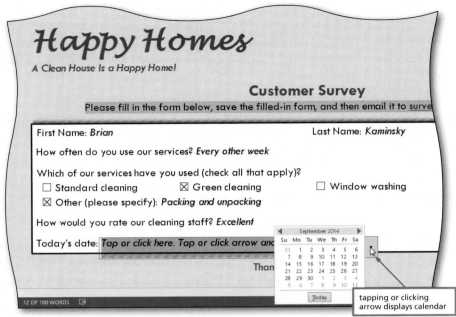

Figure 10–73

BTW
Protected Documents
If you open an existing form that has been protected, Word will not allow you to modify the form's appearance until you unprotect it. To unprotect a form (or any protected document), display the Restrict Formatting and Editing task pane by tapping or clicking the Restrict Editing button (DEVELOPER tab | Protect group) or opening the Backstage view, displaying the Info gallery, tapping or clicking the Protect Document button, and tapping or clicking Restrict Editing on the Protect Document menu. Then, tap or click the Stop Protection button in the Restrict Editing task pane and close the task pane. If a document has been protected with a password, you will be asked to enter the password when you attempt to unprotect the document.

Working with Templates

If you want to modify the template, open it by tapping or clicking the Open command in the Backstage view, tapping or clicking the template name, and then tapping or clicking the Open button in the dialog box. Then, you must **unprotect the form** by tapping or clicking the Restrict Editing button (DEVELOPER tab | Protect group) and then tapping or clicking the Stop Protection button in the Restrict Editing task pane.

When you created the template in this chapter, you saved it on your local storage media. In environments other than an academic setting, you would not save the template on your own storage media; instead, you would save the file in the Custom Office Templates folder (shown in Figure 10–3 on page WD 614). When you save a template in the Custom Office Templates folder, you can locate the template by opening the Backstage view, tapping or clicking the New tab to display the New gallery, and then tapping or clicking the PERSONAL tab in the New gallery, which displays the template in the New gallery (Figure 10–74).

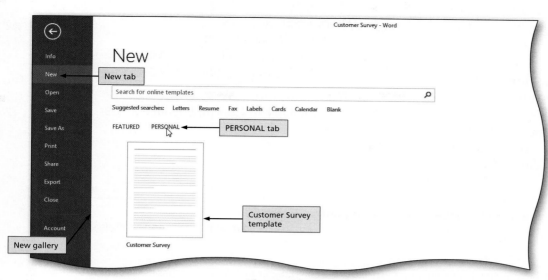

Figure 10–74

BTW
Linking a Form to a Database
If you want to use or analyze the data that a user enters into a form in an Access database or an Excel worksheet, you could save the form data in a comma-delimited text file. This file separates each data item with a comma and places quotation marks around text data items. Then, you can use Access or Excel to import the comma-delimited text file for use in the respective program. To save form data, open the Backstage view, tap or click Save As in the Backstage view, and then display the Save As dialog box. Tap or click the Tools button (Save As dialog box) and then tap or click Save Options on the Tools menu to display the Word Options dialog box. Tap or click Advanced in the left pane (Word Options dialog box), scroll to the Preserve fidelity when sharing this document area in the right pane, place a check mark in the 'Save form data as delimited text file' check box, and then tap or click the OK button. Next, be sure the file type is Plain Text (Save As dialog box) and then tap or click the Save button to save the file as a comma-delimited text file. You can import the resulting comma-delimited file in an Access database or an Excel worksheet. To convert successfully, you should use the legacy controls (i.e., text form field, check box form field, etc.), which are available through the Legacy Tools button (DEVELOPER tab | Controls group). To use Word 2013 content controls, use the 'XML Mapping Pane' button (DEVELOPER tab | Mapping group) and refer to pages WD 726 and WD 727 in the Supplementary Word Tasks section in Chapter 11 for instructions about working with XML.

To Exit Word

The following steps exit Word and close the File Explorer window.

1 Exit Word. (If Word asks if you want to save the modified styles, tap or click the Don't Save button.)

2 If the File Explorer window still is open, close it.

Chapter Summary

In this chapter, you have learned how to create an online form. Topics covered included saving a document as a template, changing paper size, using a table to control layout, showing the DEVELOPER tab, inserting content controls, editing placeholder text, changing properties of content controls, and protecting a form. The items listed below include all the new Word skills you have learned in this chapter, with the tasks grouped by activity.

Create a Template
Insert a Plain Text Content Control (WD 627)
Edit Placeholder Text (WD 628)
Change the Properties of a Plain Text Content Control (WD 630)
Insert a Drop-Down List Content Control (WD 634)
Change the Properties of a Drop-Down List Content Control (WD 634)
Insert a Check Box Content Control (WD 638)
Insert a Rich Text Content Control (WD 640)
Insert a Combo Box Content Control (WD 642)
Change the Properties of a Combo Box Content Control (WD 644)
Insert a Date Picker Content Control (WD 645)
Change the Properties of a Date Picker Content Control (WD 646)

Enter and Edit Text
Fill In a Form and Save It (WD 659)

File Management
Save a Document as a Template (WD 613)
Protect a Form (WD 655)
Use File Explorer to Create a New Document That Is Based on a Template (WD 658)

Format a Page
Change Paper Size (WD 615)
Add a Page Color (WD 618)
Add a Pattern Fill Effect to a Page Color (WD 619)
Customize a Theme Color and Save It with a New Theme Name (WD 653)

Format Text
 Highlight Text (WD 652)

Word Settings
 Collapse the Ribbon (WD 616)
 Expand the Ribbon (WD 616)
 Show the DEVELOPER Tab (WD 626)
 Set Formatting Restrictions (WD 656)
 Set Editing Restrictions to Tracked Changes or
  Comments or No Edits (WD 656)

Work with Graphics
 Draw a Rectangle (WD 648)
 Send a Graphic behind Text (WD 650)
 Add a Shadow to a Shape (WD 652)

Work with Tables
 Use a Table to Control Layout (WD 623)

CONSIDER THIS: PLAN AHEAD

What decisions will you need to make when creating online forms?
Use these guidelines as you complete the assignments in this chapter and create your own online forms outside of this class.

1. Design the form.

  a) To minimize the time spent creating a form while using a computer or mobile device, consider sketching the form on a piece of paper first.

  b) Design a well-thought-out draft of the form — being sure to include all essential form elements, including the form's title, text and graphics, data entry fields, and data entry instructions.

2. For each data entry field, determine its field type and/or list of possible values that it can contain.

3. Save the form as a template, instead of as a Word document, to simplify the data entry process for users of the form.

4. Create a functional and visually appealing form.

  a) Use colors that complement one another.

  b) Draw the user's attention to important sections.

  c) Arrange data entry fields in logical groups on the form and in an order that users would expect.

  d) Data entry instructions should be succinct and easy to understand.

  e) Ensure that users can enter and edit data only in designated areas of the form.

5. Determine how the form data will be analyzed.

  a) If the data entered in the form will be analyzed by a program outside of Word, create the data entry fields so that the entries are stored in separate fields that can be shared with other programs.

6. Test the form, ensuring it works as you intended.

  a) Fill in the form as if you are a user.

  b) Ask others to fill in the form to be sure it is organized in a logical manner and is easy to understand and complete.

  c) If any errors or weaknesses in the form are identified, correct them and test the form again.

7. Publish or distribute the form.

  a) Not only does an online form reduce the need for paper, it saves the time spent making copies of the form and distributing it.

  b) When the form is complete, post it on social media, the web, or your company's intranet, or email it to targeted recipients.

CONSIDER THIS

How should you submit solutions to questions in the assignments identified with a ✳ symbol?
Every assignment in this book contains one or more questions identified with a ✳ symbol. These questions require you to think beyond the assigned document. Present your solutions to the questions in the format required by your instructor. Possible formats may include one or more of these options: write the answer; create a document that contains the answer; present your answer to the class; discuss your answer in a group; record the answer as audio or video using a webcam, smartphone, or portable media player; or post answers on a blog, wiki, or website.

Apply Your Knowledge

Reinforce the skills and apply the concepts you learned in this chapter.

Filling In an Online Form

Note: To complete this assignment, you will be required to use the Data Files for Students. Visit www.cengage.com/ct/studentdownload for detailed instructions or contact your instructor for information about accessing the required files.

Instructions: In this assignment, you access a template through File Explorer. The template is located on the Data Files for Students. The template contains an online form (Figure 10–75). You are to fill in the form.

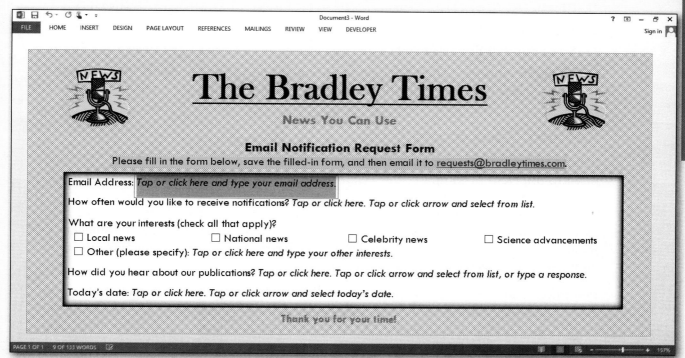

Figure 10–75

Perform the following tasks:

1. Run File Explorer. Double-tap or double-click the Apply 10-1 Bradley Times Survey template in File Explorer.

2. When Word displays a new document based on the Apply 10-1 Bradley Times Survey template, if necessary, collapse the ribbon, hide formatting marks, and change the zoom to page width. Your screen should look like Figure 10–75.

3. With the Email Address content control selected, type `avery@earth.net` or, if requested by your instructor, enter your email address.

4. Tap or click the Notifications content control and then tap or click the arrow. Tap or click Weekly in the list.

5. Tap or click the Local news and Science advancements check boxes to select them.

6. Tap or click the Other check box. If necessary, tap or click the Other text box and then type `Health news` in the text box.

7. Tap or click the 'Hear About Publications' content control to select it. Tap or click the 'Hear About Publications' arrow and then review the list. Press the ESC key because none of these choices answers the question. Type `Friend` as the response.

Continued >

Apply Your Knowledge *continued*

8. Tap or click the Today's Date content control and then click the arrow to display a calendar. If necessary, scroll to display the calendar for October 2014. Tap or click 'October 21, 2014', (or today's date, if requested by your instructor) in the calendar.

9. Save the modified file with a new file name, Apply 10-1 Avery Survey (or, if requested by your instructor, replace the name, Avery, with your name). Submit the document in the format specified by your instructor. Close the document.

10. Open the Apply 10-1 Bradley Times Survey template from the Data Files for Students.

11. Unprotect the Apply 10-1 Bradley Times Survey template.

12. Save the template with a new name, Apply 10-1 Bradley Times Survey Modified.

13. Change the Today's Date content control to the format d-MMM-yy (i.e., 21-Oct-14).

14. Protect the modified template.

15. Save the modified template. Submit the revised template in the format specified by your instructor.

16. ✳ In this form, what are the options in the Notifications and Hear About Publications lists? What items might you add to those lists? How would you add those items?

Extend Your Knowledge

Extend the skills you learned in this chapter and experiment with new skills. You may need to use Help to complete the assignment.

Working with Picture Content Controls, Grouping Objects, Themes, and Passwords
Note: To complete this assignment, you will be required to use the Data Files for Students. Visit www.cengage.com/ct/studentdownload for detailed instructions or contact your instructor for information about accessing the required files.

Instructions: Run Word. Open the document, Extend 10-1 Baby Contest Form Draft, from the Data Files for Students. You will add a picture content control in a text box and then format the text box, group the graphical images, change the text highlight color, change the shadow color, change the shape fill, change theme colors, reset theme colors, save a modified theme, and protect a form with a password.

Perform the following tasks:

1. Use Help to review and expand your knowledge about these topics: picture content controls, text boxes, grouping objects, shadows, shape fill effects, changing theme colors, and protecting forms with passwords.

2. Add a simple text box to the empty space in the right side of the data entry area. Resize the text box so that it fits completely in the data entry area.

3. In the text box, type the label, Baby Photo:, and then below the label, insert a picture content control. Resize the picture content control so that it fits in the text box and then center both the picture and label in the text box (Figure 10–76). Remove the border from the text box.

4. Change the fill effect in the rectangle shape to a texture of your choice. If necessary, change the font color or style of text in the data entry area so that it is readable on the texture.

5. Group the three graphics at the top of the form together. Move the grouped graphics. Return them to their original location.

6. Change the text highlight color of the third line of text to a color other than yellow. If necessary, change the text color so that you can read the text in the new highlight color.

7. Add a shadow to the rectangle and then change the color of the shadow on the rectangle to a color other than the default.

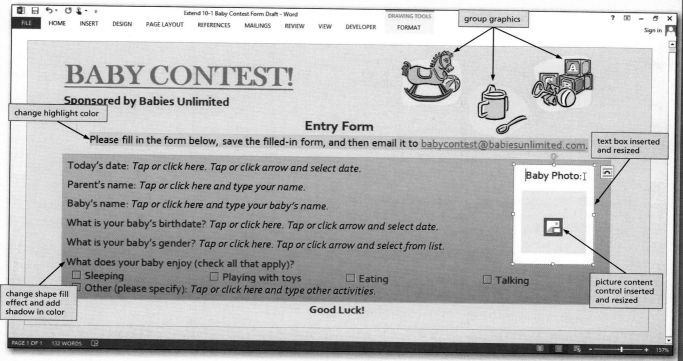

Figure 10–76

8. Change the theme colors for Accent 3. Reset the theme colors before closing the dialog box. Change the theme colors for Accent 1 and Hyperlink. Change theme colors for other items as desired. Save the modified theme colors.

9. Make any necessary formatting changes to the form.

10. Protect the form using the word, baby, as the password.

11. If requested by your instructor, change the sponsoring company name to include your last name. Save the revised document with a new file name, Extend 10-1 Baby Contest Form Modified.

12. Test the form. When filling in the form, use your own baby picture or the picture called Baby Photo on the Data Files for Students for the picture content control. Submit the online form in the format specified by your instructor.

13. ✹ Which texture did you select and why? What is the advantage of grouping graphics? Besides changing the color of the shadow, what other shadow settings can you adjust?

Analyze, Correct, Improve

Analyze a document, correct all errors, and improve it.

Formatting an Online Form

Note: To complete this assignment, you will be required to use the Data Files for Students. Visit www.cengage.com/ct/studentdownload for detailed instructions or contact your instructor for information about accessing the required files.

Instructions: Run Word. Open the document, Analyze 10-1 Harper Survey Draft, from the Data Files for Students. The document is an online form that contains unformatted elements (Figure 10–77 on the next page).

You are to change the graphic's wrapping style; change the page color; change fonts, font sizes, font colors, and text highlight color; remove the table border; edit placeholder text; change content control properties; draw a rectangle and format it; and protect the form.

Continued >

Analyze, Correct, Improve *continued*

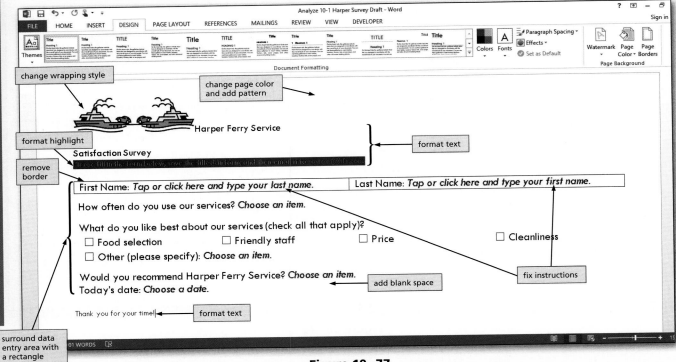

Figure 10–77

Perform the following tasks:

1. Correct In the online form, correct the following items:

a. Change the wrapping style of each graphic from inline to floating. Resize the graphics as necessary. Position one graphic at each edge of the top of the form. Format the graphics as desired.

b. On the third line of text, change the text highlight color so that the text is visible.

c. Change the font, font size, and font color for the first three lines and last line of text. Add font styles as desired. Center these four lines.

d. Remove the border from the 2 × 1 table that surrounds the First Name and Last Name content controls. Show table gridlines.

e. Add blank space between the Recommendation and Today's Date lines at the bottom of the data entry area.

f. Fix the placeholder text for the First Name content control so that it reads: Tap or click here and type your first name. Similarly, fix the placeholder text for the Last Name content control. For the remaining placeholder text, change the instructions so that they are more meaningful.

g. For the content control that lists how often services are used, change the properties as follows: add the tag name, Frequency of Use, and set the locking so that the content control cannot be deleted.

h. In the Recommendation content control, fix the spelling of the option, Maybe.

2. Improve Enhance the online form by changing the page color to a color of your choice (other than white) and then adding a pattern fill effect to the color. Draw a rectangle around the data entry area. Format the rectangle so that it is behind the text. Add a shape style and a shadow to the rectangle. Make any necessary adjustments to the form so that it fits on a single page. Hide table gridlines. Protect the form. If requested by your instructor, change the name, Harper, to your name. Save the modified document with the file name, Analyze 10-1 Harper Survey Modified, test the form, and then submit it in the format specified by your instructor.

3. ✳ Which page color did you choose, and why?

In the Labs

Design and/or create a document using the guidelines, concepts, and skills presented in this chapter. Labs 1 and 2, which increase in difficulty, require you to create solutions based on what you learned in the chapter; Lab 3 requires you to create a solution, which uses cloud and web technologies, by learning and investigating on your own from general guidance.

Lab 1: Creating an Online Form with Plain Text and Drop-Down List Content Controls

Problem: Your uncle owns Ozzie's Creamery and has asked you to prepare an online survey, shown in Figure 10–78.

Perform the following tasks:

1. Save a blank document as a template, called Lab 10-1 Creamery Survey, for the online form.
2. If necessary, change the view to page width.
3. Change the paper size to a width of 8.5 inches and a height of 4 inches.
4. Change the margins as follows: top - 0.25", bottom - 0", left - 0.5", and right - 0.5".
5. Change the document theme to Dividend.
6. Change the page color to Plum, Accent 1, Lighter 50%. Change the fill effect to the Outlined diamond pattern.
7. Enter and format the company name, message, and form title as shown in Figure 10–78 (or with similar fonts). If requested by your instructor, change the creamery name from Ozzie's to

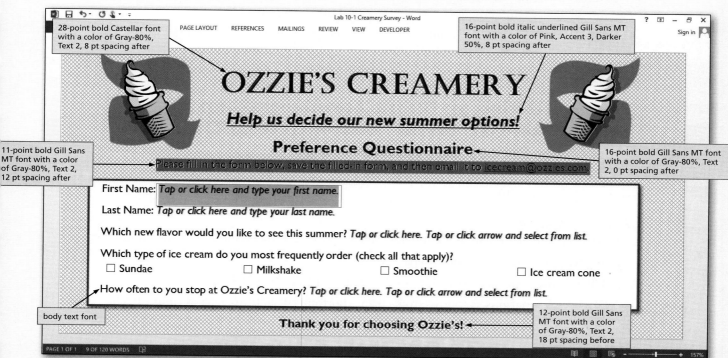

Figure 10–78

Continued >

In the Labs *continued*

your first name. Insert the clip art shown (or a similar image) using the term, ice cream cone, as the search text. Change the wrapping style of the graphics to In Front of Text. If necessary, resize the graphics and position them in the locations shown.

8. Enter the instructions above the data entry area and highlight the line Pink.

9. Customize the colors so that the hyperlink color is Blue-Gray, Accent 6, Darker 50%. Save the modified theme.

10. In the data entry area, enter the labels as shown in Figure 10–78 on the previous page and the content controls as follows: First Name and Last Name are plain text content controls. Summer Flavor is a drop-down list content control with these choices: Blueberry pomegranate, Cinnamon roll, Espresso, Key lime, and Red velvet. Sundae, Milkshake, Smoothie, and Ice cream cone are check boxes. Number of Visits is a drop-down list content control with these choices: Everyday, Several times a week, Once a week, Occasionally through the month, Once a month, A few times a year, and Never.

11. Format the placeholder text to the Intense Emphasis style. Edit the placeholder text of all content controls to match Figure 10–78. Change the properties of the content controls so that each contains a tag name, uses the Intense Emphasis style, and has locking set so that the content control cannot be deleted.

12. Enter the line below the data entry area as shown in Figure 10–78.

13. Adjust spacing above and below paragraphs as necessary so that all contents fit on a single screen.

14. Draw a rectangle around the data entry area. Change the shape style of the rectangle to Colored Outline - Plum, Accent 2. Apply the Offset Diagonal Bottom Right shadow to the rectangle.

15. Protect the form.

16. Save the form again and then submit it in the format specified by your instructor.

17. Access the template through File Explorer. Fill in the form using personal data and then submit the filled-in form in the format specified by your instructor.

18. ✳ If the creamery sold six different types of ice cream instead of four different types, how would you evenly space the six items across the line?

Lab 2: Creating an Online Form with Plain Text, Drop-Down List, Combo Box, Rich Text, Check Box, and Date Picker Content Controls

Problem: You work part-time for Bard's Gym. Your supervisor has asked you to prepare a member survey (Figure 10–79).

Perform the following tasks:

1. Save a blank document as a template, called Lab 10-2 Fitness Survey, for the online form.

2. If necessary, change the view to page width.

3. Change the paper size to a width of 8.5 inches and a height of 4 inches.

4. Change the margins as follows: top - 0.25", bottom - 0", left - 0.5", and right - 0.5".

5. Change the document theme to Droplet.

6. Change the page color to Black, Text 1. Change the fill effect to a 5% pattern.

7. Enter and format the company name, business tag line, and form title as shown in Figure 10–79 (or with similar fonts). If requested by your instructor, change the gym name from

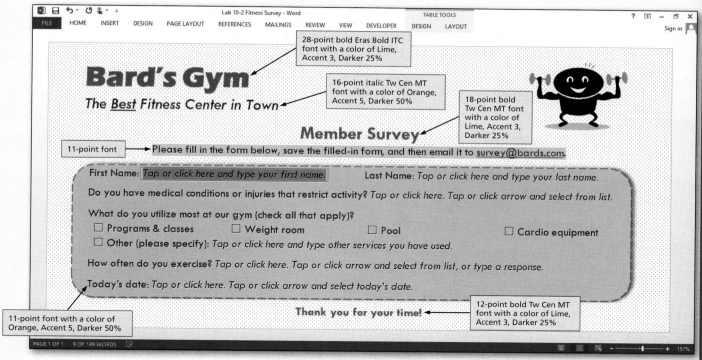

Figure 10–79

Bard's to your last name. Insert the clip art using the text, lifting weights, as the search text. Change the wrapping style of the graphic to In Front of Text. If necessary, resize the graphic and move it to the location shown.

8. Enter the instructions above the data entry area and highlight the line yellow.

9. In the data entry area, enter the labels as shown in Figure 10–79 and the content controls as follows: First Name and Last Name are plain text content controls. Activity Restrictions is a drop-down list content control with these choices: Yes, I have a long-term restriction; Yes, I have a short-term restriction; No; and I am not sure. Programs & classes, Weight room, Pool, Cardio equipment, and Other are check boxes. Other Services is a rich text content control. Exercise Frequency is a combo box content control with these choices: Daily, Three to five times a week, Once to twice a week, Not very often, and Never. Today's date is a date picker content control.

10. Format the placeholder text to Subtle Emphasis. Edit the placeholder text of all content controls to match Figure 10–79. Change the properties of the content controls so that each contains a tag name, uses the Subtle Emphasis style, and has locking specified so that the content control cannot be deleted.

11. Customize the colors so that the hyperlink color is Lime, Accent 3, Darker 50%. Save the modified theme.

12. Enter the line below the data entry area as shown in Figure 10–79.

13. Change the color of labels in the data entry area as shown in the figure.

14. Adjust spacing above and below paragraphs as necessary so that all contents fit on the screen.

15. Draw a Rounded Rectangle around the data entry area. Change the shape style of the rectangle to Subtle Effect - Lime, Accent 3. Change the shape outline to Long Dash. Add an Offset Right shadow.

16. Protect the form.

17. Save the form again and then submit it in the format specified by your instructor.

Continued >

In the Labs *continued*

18. Access the template through File Explorer. Fill in the form using personal data and submit the filled-in form in the format specified by your instructor.

19. ✳ What other question might a gym ask its members? If you were to add this question to the form, how would you fit it so that the form still displays in its entirety on a single page?

Lab 3: Expand Your World: Cloud and Web Technologies
Inserting Online Videos

Note: To complete this assignment, you will be required to use the Data Files for Students. Visit www.cengage.com/ct/studentdownload for detailed instructions or contact your instructor for information about accessing the required files.

Problem: You have created an online form for a library book club and would like to add an online video about e-book readers to the form.

Instructions: Perform the following tasks:

1. Use Help to learn about inserting online videos.

2. Open the document Lab 10-3 Book Club Survey Draft from the Data Files for Students.

3. Display the INSERT tab and then tap or click the Online Video button (INSERT tab | Media group) to display the Insert Video dialog box. Type **e-book reader** in the 'Enter your search term' box (Figure 10–80) and then tap or click the Search button to display a list of videos that match your search criteria.

4. Scroll through the list of videos, tapping or clicking several to see their name, length, and source. Tap or click the View Larger button in the lower-right corner of the video so that you can watch the video. Select an appropriate video and then tap or click the Insert button to insert it on the form. Change the layout to In Front of Text and position the video in the upper-right corner of the form. Resize the video if necessary.

5. Protect the form. Save the form again and then submit it in the format specified by your instructor.

6. Access the template through File Explorer. Test the video.

7. ✳ What options are available in the search results dialog box while you are watching a video? What are some of the sources for the videos in the dialog box? Which video did you insert in the form, and why? How do you play the video inserted on the form? Does the video play where you inserted it on the form? If not, where does it play?

Figure 10–80

Consider This: Your Turn

Apply your creative thinking and problem solving skills to design and implement a solution.

1: Create an Online Form for a School

Personal

Part 1: As an assistant in the adult education center, you have been asked to create an online student survey. Create a template that contains the school name (Holland College), the school's tag line (A Great Place to Learn), and appropriate clip art. The third line should have the text, Seminar Survey. The fourth line should be highlighted and should read: Please fill in the form below, save the filled-in form, and then email it to seminars@hollandcollege.edu. The data entry area should contain the following. First Name and Last Name are plain text content controls within a table. A drop-down list content control with the label, What is your age range?, has these choices: 18-24, 25-40, 41-55, and over 55. The following instruction should appear above these check boxes: What skills have you learned in our seminars (check all that apply)?; the check boxes are Computer, Cooking, Dance, Language, Photography, and Other. A rich text content control has the label, Other (please specify), where students can enter other skills they have learned. A combo box content control with the label, How would you rate our seminars?, has these choices: Excellent, Good, Fair, and Poor. Today's Date is a date picker content control. On the last line, include the text: Thank you for attending our classes!

Use the concepts and techniques presented in this chapter to create and format the online form. Use meaningful placeholder text for all content controls. (For example, the placeholder text for the First Name plain text content control could be as follows: Click here and then type your first name.) Draw a rectangle around the data entry area of the form. Add a shadow to the rectangle. Apply a style to the placeholder text. Assign names, styles, and locking to each content control. Protect the form, test it, and submit it in the format specified by your instructor.

Part 2: ✸ You made several decisions while creating the online form in this assignment: placeholder text to use, graphics to use, and how to organize and format the online form (fonts, font sizes, styles, colors, etc.). What was the rationale behind each of these decisions? When you proofread and tested the online form, what further revisions did you make, and why?

2: Create an Online Form for a Law Office

Professional

Part 1: As a part-time employee at a local law office, you have been asked to create an online client survey. Create a template that contains the firm name (Clark Law), the firm's tag line (Serving You for More than 55 Years), and appropriate clip art. The third line should have the text, Client Survey. The fourth line should be highlighted and should read: Please fill in the form below, save the filled-in form, and then email it to info@clarklaw.com. The data entry area should contain the following. First Name and Last Name are plain text content controls within a table. A drop-down list content control with the label, Which lawyer has been handling your case?, has these choices: Clarissa Door, Gregory Hersher, Diane Lee, and Maria Sanchez. The following instruction should appear above these check boxes: Which category describes your case (check all that apply)?; the check boxes are Adoption, Auto incident, Estate planning, Personal injury, Workers' compensation, and Other. A rich text content control has the label, Other (please specify), where clients can enter other case areas. A combo box content control with the label, How would you rate our services to date?, has these choices: Excellent, Good, Fair, and Poor. Today's Date is a date picker content control. On the last line, include the text: Thank you for your business!

Use the concepts and techniques presented in this chapter to create and format the online form. Use meaningful placeholder text for all content controls. (For example, the placeholder text for the First Name plain text content control could be as follows: Click here and then type your first name.) Draw a rectangle around the data entry area of the form. Add a shadow to the rectangle. Apply a style to the placeholder text. Assign names, styles, and locking to each content control. Protect the form, test it, and submit it in the format specified by your instructor.

Continued >

Consider This: Your Turn *continued*

Part 2: ✺ You made several decisions while creating the online form in this assignment: placeholder text to use, graphics to use, and how to organize and format the online form (fonts, font sizes, styles, colors, etc.). What was the rationale behind each of these decisions? When you proofread and tested the online form, what further revisions did you make, and why?

3: Create an Online Form for a Campus Group
Research and Collaboration

Part 1: Your team will investigate a campus organization, club, or facility that could benefit from an online survey. For example, the fitness center might benefit from knowing time preferences for the racquetball court, or a club might benefit from knowing members' interests for scheduling upcoming events. Once you have made your choice for the online form, determine what information is required for the form to be effective and helpful and then decide which choices to include in the various content controls. Be sure to include at least one of each of the following content controls: plain text, rich text, drop-down list, combo box, picture, check box, and date picker. As a team, select a title, tag line, and appropriate clip art and/or other graphics.

Use the concepts and techniques presented in this chapter to create and format the online form. Decide on the overall design of the form, as well as the fonts, colors, and other visual elements. Each member should design an area of the form. Use meaningful placeholder text for all content controls. Be sure to check the spelling and grammar of the finished form. Protect the form, test it, and submit the team assignment in the format specified by your instructor.

Part 2: ✺ You made several decisions while creating the online form in this assignment: text and instructions to use, placeholder text to use, graphics to use, and how to organize and format the online form (fonts, font sizes, styles, colors, etc.). What was the rationale behind each of these decisions? When you proofread and tested the online form, what further revisions did you make, and why?

Learn Online

Learn Online – Reinforce what you learned in this chapter with games, exercises, training, and many other online activities and resources.

Student Companion Site Reinforcement activities and resources are available at no additional cost on www.cengagebrain.com. Visit www.cengage.com/ct/studentdownload for detailed instructions about accessing the resources available at the Student Companion Site.

SAM Put your skills into practice with SAM! If you have a SAM account, go to www.cengage .com/sam2013 to access SAM assignments for this chapter.

11 | Enhancing an Online Form and Using Macros

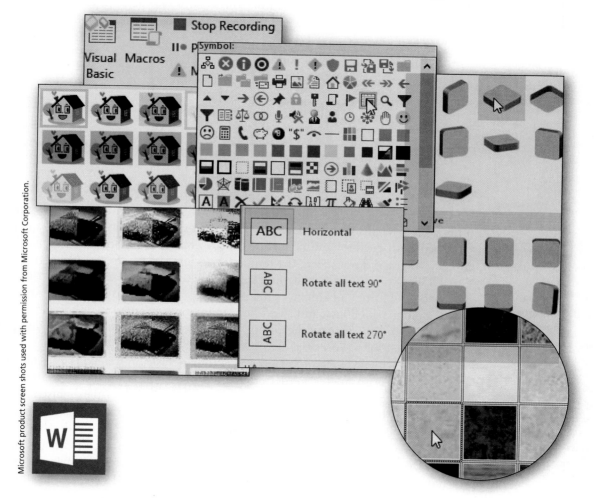

Objectives

You will have mastered the material in this chapter when you can:

- Unprotect a document
- Specify macro settings
- Convert a table to text
- Insert and edit a field
- Create a character style
- Apply and modify fill effects
- Change a shape

- Remove a background from a graphic
- Apply an artistic effect to a graphic
- Insert and format a text box
- Group objects
- Record and execute a macro
- Customize the Quick Access Toolbar
- Edit a macro's VBA code

11 | Enhancing an Online Form and Using Macros

Introduction

Word provides many tools that allow you to improve the appearance, functionality, and security of your documents. This chapter discusses tools used to perform the following tasks:

- Modify text and content controls.
- Enhance with color, shapes, effects, and graphics.
- Automate a series of tasks with a macro.

Project — Online Form Revised

This chapter uses Word to improve the visual appearance of and add macros to the online form created in Chapter 10, producing the online form shown in Figure 11–1a. This project begins with the Customer Survey online form created in Chapter 10. Thus, you will need the online form template created in Chapter 10 to complete this project. (If you did not create the template, see your instructor for a copy.)

    This project modifies the fonts and font colors of the text in the Customer Survey online form and enhances the contents of the form to include a texture fill effect, a picture fill effect, and a text box and picture grouped together. The date in the form automatically displays the computer or mobile device's system date, instead of requiring the user to enter the date.

    This form also includes macros to automate tasks. A **macro** is a set of commands and instructions grouped together to allow a user to accomplish a task automatically. One macro allows the user to hide formatting marks and the ruler by pressing a keyboard shortcut (sometimes called a shortcut key) or tapping or clicking a button on the Quick Access Toolbar. Another macro specifies how the form is displayed initially on a user's Word screen. As shown in Figure 11–1b, when a document contains macros, Word may generate a security warning. If you are sure the macros are from a trusted source and free of viruses, then enable the content. Otherwise, do not enable the content, which protects your computer from potentially harmful viruses or other malicious software.

If you are using your finger on a touch screen and are having difficulty completing the steps in this chapter, consider using a stylus. Many people find it easier to be precise with a stylus than with a finger. In addition, with a stylus you see the pointer. If you still are having trouble completing the steps with a stylus, try using a mouse.

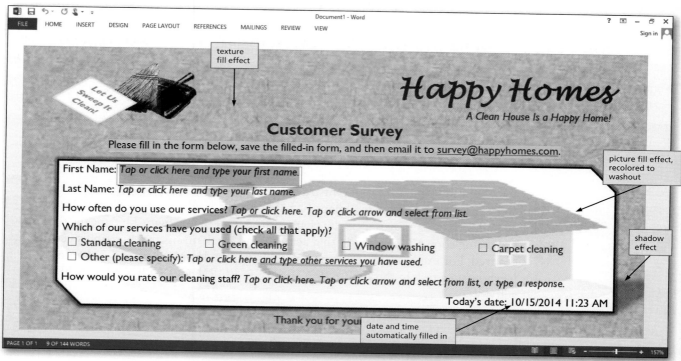

(a) Modified and Enhanced Online Form

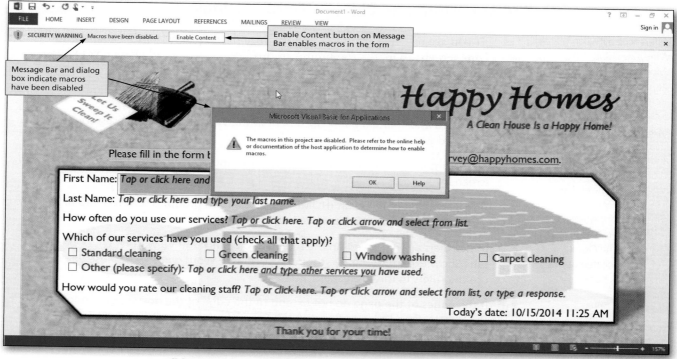

(b) Macros in Online Form Generate Security Warning

Figure 11–1

Roadmap

In this chapter, you will learn how to create the form shown in Figure 11–1 on the previous page. The following roadmap identifies general activities you will perform as you progress through this chapter:

1. SAVE a DOCUMENT AS a MACRO-ENABLED TEMPLATE.
2. MODIFY the TEXT AND FORM CONTENT CONTROLS.
3. ENHANCE the FORM'S VISUAL APPEAL.
4. CREATE MACROS TO AUTOMATE TASKS in the form.

At the beginning of step instructions throughout the chapter, you will see an abbreviated form of this roadmap. The abbreviated roadmap uses colors to indicate chapter progress: gray means the chapter is beyond that activity, blue means the task being shown is covered in that activity, and black means that activity is yet to be covered. For example, the following abbreviated roadmap indicates the chapter would be showing a task in the 2 MODIFY TEXT & FORM CONTENT CONTROLS activity.

1 SAVE DOCUMENT AS MACRO-ENABLED TEMPLATE | 2 MODIFY TEXT & FORM CONTENT CONTROLS
3 ENHANCE FORM'S VISUAL APPEAL | 4 CREATE MACROS TO AUTOMATE TASKS

Use the abbreviated roadmap as a progress guide while you read or step through the instructions in this chapter.

To Run Word and Change Word Settings

If you are using a computer to step through the project in this chapter and you want your screens to match the figures in this book, you should change your screen's resolution to 1366×768. The following steps run Word, display formatting marks, and change the zoom to page width.

1 Run Word and create a blank document in the Word window. If necessary, maximize the Word window.

2 If the Print Layout button on the status bar is not selected, tap or click it so that your screen is in Print Layout view.

3 If the 'Show/Hide ¶' button (HOME tab | Paragraph group) is selected, tap or click it to hide formatting marks because you will not use them in this project.

4 If the rulers are displayed on the screen, tap or click the View Ruler check box (VIEW tab | Show group) to remove the rulers from the Word window because you will not use the rulers in this project.

5 If the edges of the page do not extend to the edge of the document window, display the VIEW tab and then tap or click the Page Width button (VIEW tab | Zoom group).

One of the few differences between Windows 7 and Windows 8 occurs in the steps to run Word. If you are using Windows 7, click the Start button, type **Word** in the 'Search programs and files' box, click Word 2013, and then, if necessary, maximize the Word window. For a summary of the steps to run Word in Windows 7, refer to the Quick Reference located at the back of this book.

BTW
The Ribbon and Screen Resolution
Word may change how the groups and buttons within the groups appear on the ribbon, depending on the computer's screen resolution. Thus, your ribbon may look different from the ones in this book if you are using a screen resolution other than 1366 x 768.

To Save a Macro-Enabled Template

1 SAVE DOCUMENT AS MACRO-ENABLED TEMPLATE | 2 MODIFY TEXT & FORM CONTENT CONTROLS | 3 ENHANCE FORM'S VISUAL APPEAL | 4 CREATE MACROS TO AUTOMATE TASKS

The project in this chapter contains macros. Thus, the first step in this chapter is to open the Customer Survey template created in Chapter 10 (see your instructor for a copy if you did not create the template) and then save the template as a macro-enabled template. *Why? To provide added security to templates, a basic Word template cannot store macros. Word instead provides a specific type of template, called a **macro-enabled template**, in which you can store macros.*

1
- Open the template named Customer Survey created in Chapter 10.

2
- Open the Backstage view, tap or click the Save As tab to display the Save As gallery, navigate to the desired save location, and display the Save As dialog box.

- Type `Customer Survey Modified` in the File name text box (Save As dialog box) to change the file name.

- Tap or click the 'Save as type' arrow to display the list of available file types and then tap or click 'Word Macro-Enabled Template' in the list to change the file type (Figure 11–2).

3
- Tap or click the Save button (Save As dialog box) to save the file using the entered file name as a macro-enabled template.

Q&A
How does Word differentiate between a Word template and a Word macro-enabled template?

A Word template has an extension of .dotx, whereas a Word macro-enabled template has an extension of .dotm. Also, the icon for a macro-enabled template contains an exclamation point.

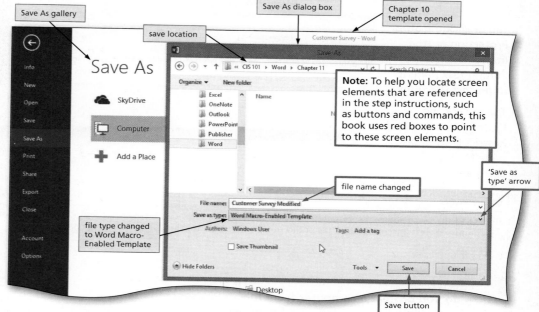

Figure 11–2

To Show the DEVELOPER Tab

Many of the tasks you will perform in this chapter use commands on the DEVELOPER tab. Thus, the following steps show the DEVELOPER tab on the ribbon.

1 Open the Backstage view and then tap or click Options in the left pane of the Backstage view to display the Word Options dialog box.

2 Tap or click Customize Ribbon in the left pane (Word Options dialog box) to display associated options in the right pane.

3 If it is not selected already, place a check mark in the Developer check box in the Main Tabs list.

4 Tap or click the OK button to show the DEVELOPER tab on the ribbon.

BTW
Macro-Enabled Documents
The above steps showed how to create a macro-enabled template. If you wanted to create a macro-enabled document, you would tap or click the 'Save as type' arrow (Save As dialog box), tap or click 'Word Macro-Enabled Document', and then tap or click the Save button.

To Unprotect a Document

The Customer Survey Modified template is protected. Recall that Chapter 10 showed how to protect a form so that users could enter data only in designated areas, specifically, the content controls. The following steps unprotect a document. *Why? Before this form can be modified, it must be unprotected. Later in this project, after you have completed the modifications, you will protect it again.*

1

- Display the DEVELOPER tab.

- Tap or click the Restrict Editing button (DEVELOPER tab | Protect group) to display the Restrict Editing task pane (Figure 11–3).

2

- Tap or click the Stop Protection button in the Restrict Editing task pane to unprotect the form.

- Tap or click the Close button in the Restrict Editing task pane to close the task pane.

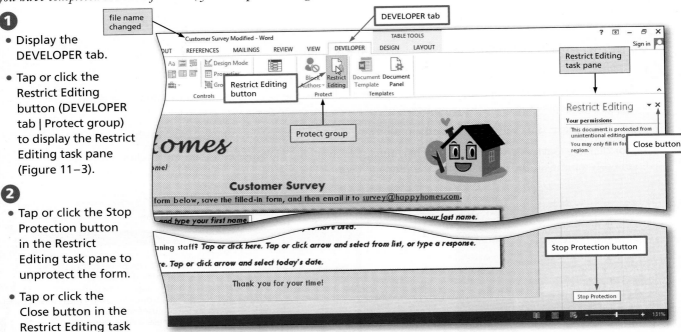

Figure 11–3

Other Ways

1. Tap or click FILE on ribbon, if necessary, tap or click Info tab in Backstage view, tap or click Protect Document button, tap or click Restrict Editing on Protect Document menu, tap or click Stop Protection button in Restrict Editing task pane

CONSIDER THIS

How do you protect a computer from macro viruses?

A **computer virus** is a type of malicious software, or malware, which is a potentially damaging computer program that affects, or infects, a computer or mobile device negatively by altering the way the computer or mobile device works without the user's knowledge or permission. Millions of known viruses and other malicious programs exist. The increased use of networks, the Internet, and email has accelerated the spread of computer viruses and other malicious programs.

- To combat these threats, most computer users run an **antivirus program** that searches for viruses and other malware and destroys the malicious programs before they infect a computer or mobile device. Macros are known carriers of viruses and other malware. For this reason, you can specify a macro setting in Word to reduce the chance your computer will be infected with a macro virus. These macro settings allow you to enable or disable macros. An **enabled macro** is a macro that Word will execute, and a **disabled macro** is a macro that is unavailable to Word.

- As shown in Figure 11–1b on page WD 675, you can instruct Word to display a security warning on a Message Bar if it opens a document that contains a macro(s). If you are confident of the source (author) of the document and macros, enable the macros. If you are uncertain about the reliability of the source of the document and macros, then do not enable the macros.

To Specify Macro Settings in Word

Why? When you open the online form in this chapter, you want the macros enabled. At the same time, your computer should be protected from potentially harmful macros. Thus, you will specify a macro setting that allows you to enable macros each time you open this chapter's online form or any document that contains a macro from an unknown source. The following steps specify macro settings.

1

- Tap or click the Macro Security button (DEVELOPER tab | Code group) to display the Trust Center dialog box.

- If it is not selected already, tap or click the 'Disable all macros with notification' option button (Trust Center dialog box), which causes Word to alert you when a document contains a macro so that you can decide whether to enable the macro(s) (Figure 11–4).

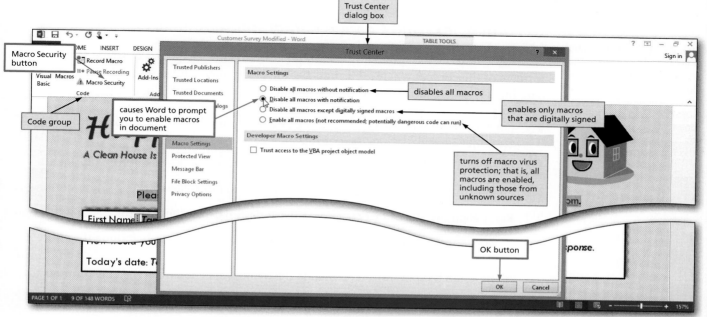

Figure 11–4

2

- Tap or click the OK button to close the dialog box.

Other Ways

1. Tap or click FILE on ribbon, tap or click Options in Backstage view, tap or click Trust Center in left pane (Word Options dialog box), tap or click 'Trust Center Settings' button in right pane, if necessary, tap or click Macro Settings in left pane (Trust Center dialog box), select desired setting, tap or click OK button in each dialog box

---

Modifying Text and Form Content Controls

The form created in Chapter 10 is enhanced in this chapter by performing these steps:

1. Delete the current clip art.
2. Change the document theme.
3. Change the fonts, colors, and alignments of the first four lines of text.
4. Convert the 2 × 1 table containing the First Name and Last Name content controls to text so that each of these content controls is on a separate line.
5. Delete the date picker content control and replace it with a date field.
6. Modify the color of the hyperlink and the check box labels.

The following pages apply these changes to the form.

To Delete a Graphic and Change the Document Theme

BTW
Saving and Resetting Themes
If you have changed the color scheme and font set and want to save this combination for future use, save it as a new theme by tapping or clicking the Themes button (DESIGN tab | Themes group), tapping or clicking 'Save Current Theme' in the Themes gallery, entering a theme name in the File name box (Save Current Theme dialog box), and then tapping or clicking the Save button. If you want to reset the theme template to the default, you would tap or click the Themes button (DESIGN tab | Themes group) and tap or click 'Reset to Theme from Template' in the Themes gallery.

The online form in this chapter has a different clip art and uses the Dividend document theme. The following steps delete the current clip art and change the document theme.

1 Tap or click the happy house clip art to select it and then press the DELETE key to delete the selected clip art.

2 Display the DESIGN tab. Tap or click the Themes button (DESIGN tab | Document Formatting group) and then tap or click Dividend in the Themes gallery to change the document theme.

To Format Text and Change Paragraph Alignment

The next step in modifying the online form for this chapter is to change the formats of the company name, business tag line, form name, form instructions, and date line. The following steps format text and change paragraph alignment.

1 Change the color of the first line of text, Happy Homes, and third line of text, Customer Survey, to 'Plum, Accent 2, Darker 25%'.

2 Right-align the first and second lines of text (company name and business tag line).

3 Change the highlight color on the fourth line of text to Yellow.

4 Right-align the line of text containing the Today's date content control.

5 If necessary, widen the text box surrounding the data entry area to include the entire date placeholder (Figure 11–5).

If requested by your instructor, change the name, happyhomes, in the email address to your name.

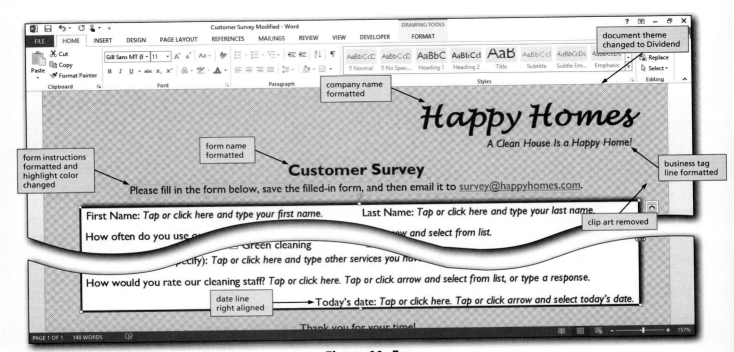

Figure 11–5

To Change the Properties of a Plain Text Content Control

In this online form, the First Name and Last Name content controls are on separate lines. In Chapter 10, you selected the 'Content control cannot be deleted' check box in the Content Control Properties dialog box so that users could not delete the content control accidentally while filling in the form. With this check box selected, however, you cannot move a content control from one location to another on the form. Thus, the following steps change the locking properties of the First Name and Last Name content controls so that you can rearrange them.

1 Display the DEVELOPER tab.

2 Tap or click the First Name content control to select it.

3 Tap or click the Control Properties button (DEVELOPER tab | Controls group) to display the Content Control Properties dialog box.

4 Remove the check mark from the 'Content control cannot be deleted' check box (Content Control Properties dialog box) (Figure 11–6).

5 Tap or click the OK button to assign the modified properties to the content control.

6 Tap or click the Last Name content control to select it and then tap or click the Control Properties button (DEVELOPER tab | Controls group) to display the Content Control Properties dialog box.

7 Remove the check mark from the 'Content control cannot be deleted' check box (Content Control Properties dialog box) and then tap or click the OK button to assign the modified properties to the content control.

BTW
Touch Screen Differences
The Office and Windows interfaces may vary if you are using a touch screen. For this reason, you might notice that the function or appearance of your touch screen differs slightly from this chapter's presentation.

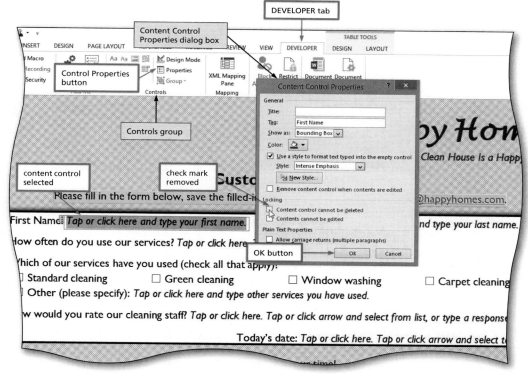

Figure 11–6

To Convert a Table to Text

The First Name and Last Name content controls currently are in a 2 × 1 table. The following steps convert the table to regular text, placing a paragraph break at the location of the second column. *Why? In this online form, these content controls are on separate lines, one below the other. That is, they are not in a table.*

- Position the insertion point somewhere in the table.
- Display the TABLE TOOLS LAYOUT tab.
- Tap or click the 'Convert to Text' button (TABLE TOOLS LAYOUT tab | Data group) to display the Convert Table To Text dialog box.
- Tap or click Paragraph marks (Convert Table To Text dialog box), which will place a paragraph mark at the location of each new column in the table (Figure 11–7).

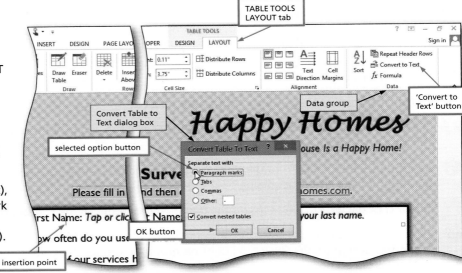

Figure 11–7

2

- Tap or click the OK button to convert the table to text, separating each column with the specified character, a paragraph mark in this case.

Q&A Why did the Last Name content control move below the First Name content control?
The Separate text with area (Convert Table To Text dialog box) controls how the table is converted to text. The Paragraph marks setting converts each column in the table to a line of text below the previous line. The Tabs setting places a tab character where each column was located, and the Commas setting places a comma where each column was located.

- With the First Name and Last Name lines selected, using either the ruler or the PAGE LAYOUT tab, change the left indent to 0.06" so that the text aligns with the text immediately below it (that is, the H in How), as shown in Figure 11–8.

4

- Tap or click anywhere to remove the selection from the text.

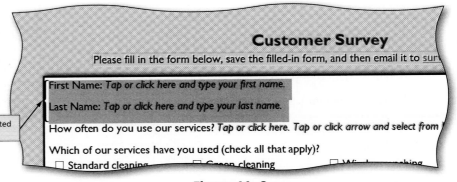

Figure 11–8

To Change the Properties of a Plain Text Content Control

You are finished moving the First Name and Last Name content controls. The following steps reset the locking properties of these content controls.

1 Display the DEVELOPER tab.

2 Tap or click the First Name content control to select it and then tap or click the Control Properties button (DEVELOPER tab | Controls group) to display the Content Control Properties dialog box.

3 Place a check mark in the 'Content control cannot be deleted' check box (Content Control Properties dialog box) and then tap or click the OK button to assign the modified properties to the content control.

4 Repeat Steps 2 and 3 for the Last Name content control.

To Adjust Paragraph Spacing and Resize the Rectangle Shape

With the First Name and Last Name content controls on separate lines, the thank you line moved to a second page, and the rectangle outline in the data entry area now is too short to accommodate the text. The following steps adjust paragraph spacing and extend the rectangle shape downward so that it surrounds the entire data entry area.

1 Position the insertion point in the second line of text on the form (the tag line) and then adjust the spacing after to 0 pt (PAGE LAYOUT tab | Paragraph group).

2 Adjust the spacing after to 6 pt for the First Name and Last Name lines.

3 Adjust the spacing before and after to 6 pt for the line that begins, How often do you use..., and the line that begins, How would you rate...

4 Adjust the spacing before to 6 pt for the thank you line.

5 Scroll to display the entire form in the document window. If necessary, reduce spacing after other paragraphs so that the entire form fits in a single document window.

6 Tap or click the rectangle shape to select it.

7 Position the pointer on the bottom-middle sizing handle of the rectangle shape.

8 Drag the bottom-middle sizing handle downward so that the shape includes the bottom content control, in this case, the Today's Date content control (Figure 11–9). If necessary, resize the other edges of the shape to fit the text.

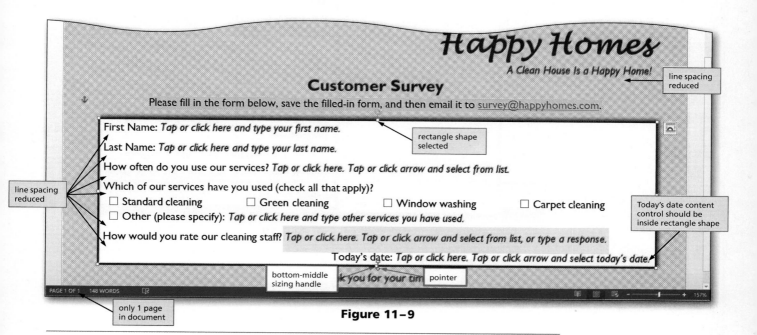

Figure 11–9

To Change the Properties of a Date Picker Content Control

BTW
Document Properties
If you wanted to insert document properties into a document, you would tap or click the 'Explore Quick Parts' button (INSERT tab | Text group) to display the Explore Quick Parts menu, tap or point to Document Property on the Explore Quick Parts menu, and then tap or click the property you want to insert on the Document Property menu. To create custom document properties for a document, open the Backstage view, tap or click the Info tab to display the Info gallery, tap or click the Properties button in the far right pane to display the Properties menu, tap or click Advanced Properties on the Properties menu to display the Document Properties dialog box, tap or click the Custom tab (Document Properties dialog box) to display the Custom sheet, enter the name of the new property in the Name text box, select its type and value in the dialog box, tap or click the Add button to add the property to the document, and then tap or click the OK button to close the dialog box.

In this online form, instead of the user entering the current date, the computer or mobile device's system date will be filled in automatically by Word. Thus, the Today's date content control is not needed and can be deleted. To delete the content control, you first will need to remove the check mark from the 'Content control cannot be deleted' check box in the Content Control Properties dialog box. The following steps change the locking properties of the Today's date content control and then delete the content control.

1 Display the DEVELOPER tab.

2 Tap or click the Today's Date content control to select it.

3 Tap or click the Control Properties button (DEVELOPER tab | Controls group) to display the Content Control Properties dialog box.

4 Remove the check mark from the 'Content control cannot be deleted' check box (Content Control Properties dialog box) (Figure 11–10).

5 Tap or click the OK button to assign the modified properties to the content control.

6 Press and hold and then tap the 'Show Context Menu' button on the mini toolbar or right-click the Today's Date content control to display a shortcut menu; tap or click 'Remove Content Control' on the shortcut menu to delete the selected content control.

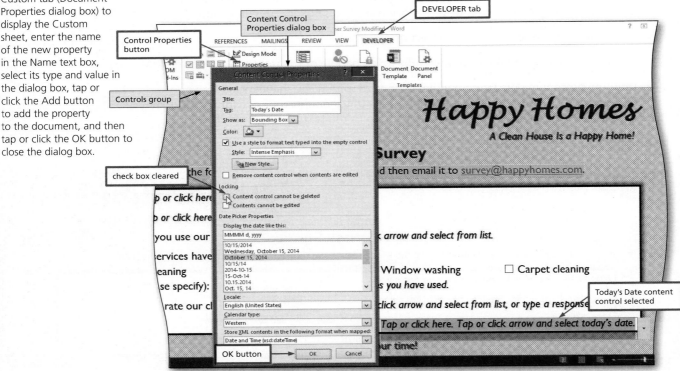

Figure 11–10

To Insert a Date Field

The following steps insert the date and time as a field in the form at the location of the insertion point.
Why? *The current date and time is a field so that the form automatically displays the current date and time. Recall that a field is a set of codes that instructs Word to perform a certain action.*

1

- Display the INSERT tab.

- With the insertion point positioned as shown in Figure 11–11, which is the location for the date and time, tap or click the 'Explore Quick Parts' button (INSERT tab | Text group) to display the Explore Quick Parts menu.

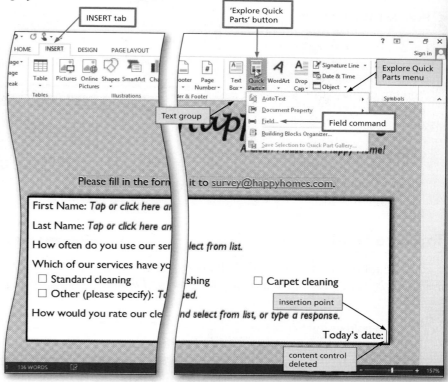

Figure 11–11

2

- Tap or click Field on the Explore Quick Parts menu to display the Field dialog box.

- Scroll through the Field names list (Field dialog box) and then tap or click Date, which displays the Date formats list in the Field properties area.

- Tap or click the date in the format of 10/15/2014 9:45:54 AM in the Date formats list to select a date format — your date and time will differ (Figure 11–12).

Q&A
What controls the date that appears?
Your current computer or mobile device date appears in this dialog box. The format for the selected date shows in the Date formats box. In this case, the format for the selected date is M/d/yyyy h:mm:ss am/pm, which displays the date as month/day/year hours:minutes:seconds AM/PM.

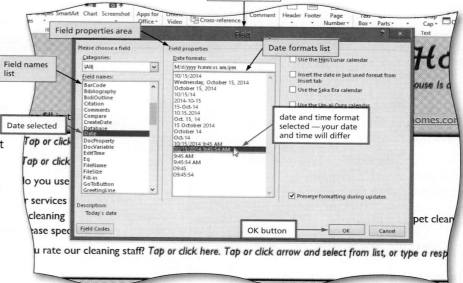

Figure 11–12

3

- Tap or click the OK button to insert the current date and time at the location of the insertion point (Figure 11–13).

Q&A How do I delete a field?
Select it and then press the DELETE key or tap or click the Cut button (HOME tab | Clipboard group), or press and hold or right-click it and then tap the Cut button on the mini toolbar or click Cut on the shortcut menu.

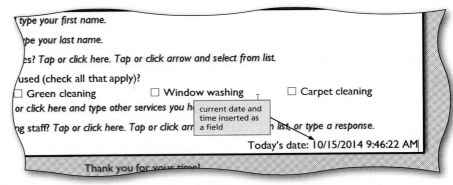

Figure 11–13

Other Ways

1. Tap or click 'Insert Date and Time' button (INSERT tab | Text group), select date format (Date and Time dialog box), place check mark in Update automatically check box, tap or click OK button

---

1 SAVE DOCUMENT AS MACRO-ENABLED TEMPLATE | 2 MODIFY TEXT & FORM CONTENT CONTROLS
3 ENHANCE FORM'S VISUAL APPEAL | 4 CREATE MACROS TO AUTOMATE TASKS

To Edit a Field

The following steps edit the field. *Why? After you see the date and time in the form, you decide not to include the seconds in the time. That is, you want just the hours and minutes to be displayed.*

1

- Press and hold or right-click the date field to display a shortcut menu (Figure 11–14).

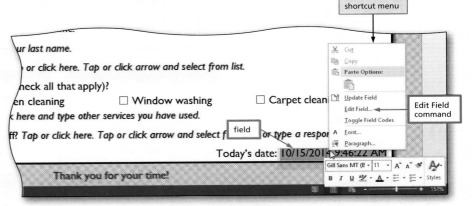

Figure 11–14

2

- Tap or click Edit Field on the shortcut menu to display the Field dialog box.

- If necessary, scroll through the Field names list (Field dialog box) and then tap or click Date to display the Date formats list in the Field properties area.

- Select the desired date format, in this case 10/15/2014 9:47 AM (Figure 11–15).

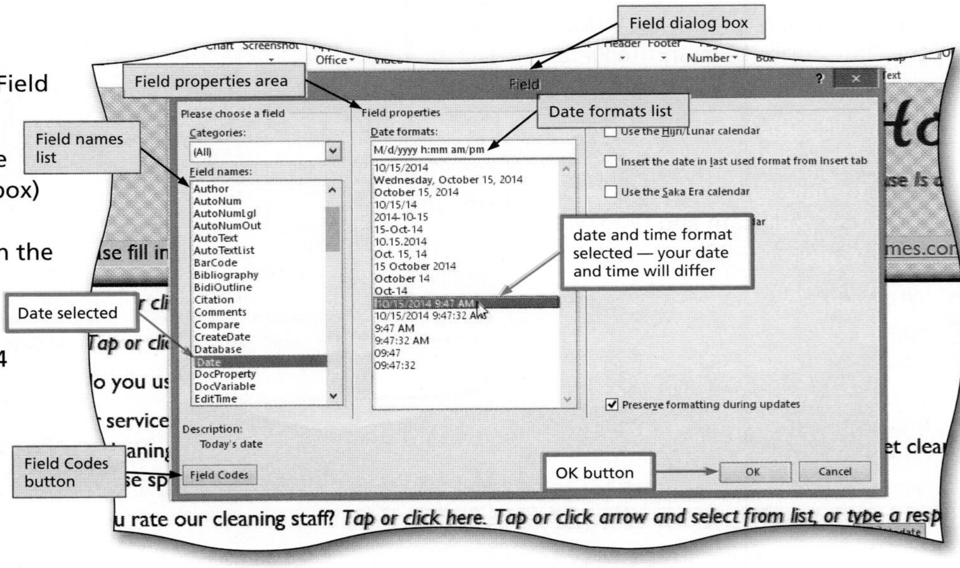

Figure 11–15

3

- Tap or click the OK button to insert the edited field at the location of the insertion point (Figure 11–16).

BTW
Field Formats
If you wanted to create custom field formats, you would tap or click the Field Codes button (Field dialog box) (shown in Figure 11-15) to display advanced field properties in the right pane in the dialog box, tap or click the Options button to display the Field Options dialog box, select the format to apply in the Formatting list, tap or click the 'Add to Field' button, and then tap or click the OK button in each open dialog box.

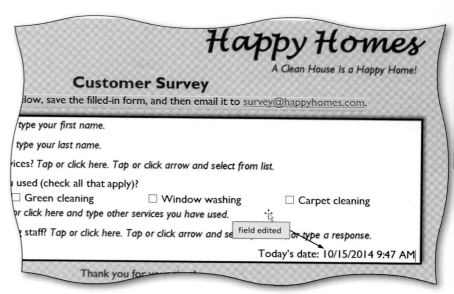

Figure 11–16

To Modify a Style Using the Styles Task Pane

1 SAVE DOCUMENT AS MACRO-ENABLED TEMPLATE | 2 MODIFY TEXT & FORM CONTENT CONTROLS
3 ENHANCE FORM'S VISUAL APPEAL | 4 CREATE MACROS TO AUTOMATE TASKS

The new text highlight color of the form instructions makes it difficult to see the hyperlink. In this online form, the hyperlink should be the same color as the company name so that the hyperlink is noticeable. The following steps modify a style using the Styles task pane. *Why? The Hyperlink style is not in the Styles gallery. To modify a style that is not in the Styles gallery, you can use the Styles task pane.*

1

- Position the insertion point in the hyperlink in the form.
- Display the HOME tab.
- Tap or click the Styles Dialog Box Launcher (HOME tab | Styles group) to display the Styles task pane.
- If necessary, tap or click Hyperlink in the list of styles in the task pane to select it and then tap or click the Hyperlink arrow to display the Hyperlink menu (Figure 11–17).

Q&A What if the style I want to modify is not in the list?
Tap or click the Manage Styles button at the bottom of the task pane (shown in Figure 11–18 on the next page), locate the style, and then tap or click the Modify button in the dialog box.

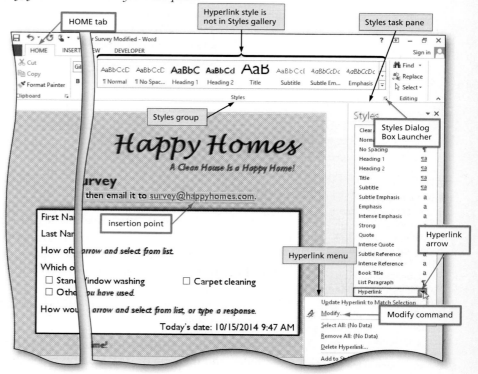

Figure 11–17

2

- Tap or click Modify on the Hyperlink menu to display the Modify Style dialog box.

- Tap or click the Font Color arrow (Modify Style dialog box) to display the Font Color gallery (Figure 11–18).

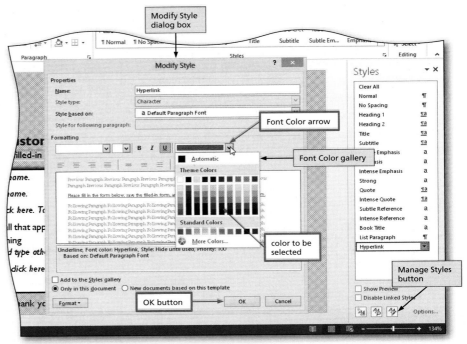

Figure 11–18

3

- Tap or click 'Plum, Accent 2, Darker 25%' (sixth color in fifth row) as the new hyperlink color.

- Tap or click the OK button to close the dialog box. Close the Styles task pane (Figure 11–19).

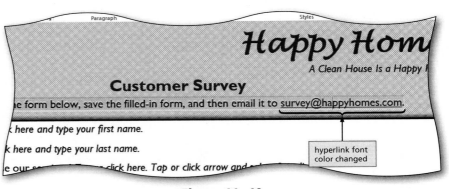

Figure 11–19

BTW
Hidden Styles
Some styles are hidden, which means they do not appear in the Styles task pane. You can display all styles, including hidden styles, by tapping or clicking the Manage Styles button in the Styles task pane (Figure 11–18), which displays the Manage Styles dialog box. Tap or click the Edit tab, if necessary, and then locate the style name in the Select a style to edit list.

To Modify a Style

In this online form, the placeholder text is to be the same color as the company name. Currently, the placeholder text is formatted using the Intense Emphasis style, which uses a light shade of plum as the font color. Thus, the following steps modify the color of the Intense Emphasis style to a darker shade of plum.

1 Scroll through the Styles gallery (HOME tab | Styles group) to locate the Intense Emphasis style.

2 Press and hold or right-click Intense Emphasis in the Styles gallery to display a shortcut menu and then tap or click Modify on the shortcut menu to display the Modify Style dialog box.

3 Tap or click the Font Color arrow (Modify Style dialog box) to display the Font Color gallery (Figure 11–20).

4 Tap or click 'Plum, Accent 2, Darker 25%' (sixth color in fifth row) as the new color.

5 Tap or click the OK button to change the color of the style, which automatically changes the color of every item formatted using this style in the document.

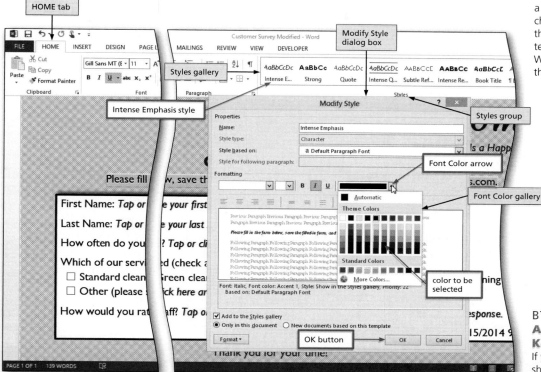

Figure 11–20

BTW

Character vs. Paragraph Styles
In the Styles task pane, character styles display a lowercase letter a to the right of the style name, and paragraph styles show a paragraph mark. With a character style, Word applies the formats to the selected text. With a paragraph style, Word applies the formats to the entire paragraph.

BTW

Assign a Shortcut Key to a Style
If you wanted to assign a shortcut key to a style, you would press and hold or right-click the style name in the Styles gallery (HOME tab | Styles group) or display the Styles task pane and then tap or click the style arrow, tap or click Modify on the menu to display the Modify Style dialog box, tap or click the Format button (Modify Style dialog box), tap or click Shortcut key on the Format menu to display the Customize Keyboard dialog box, press the desired shortcut key(s) (Customize Keyboard dialog box), tap or click the Assign button to assign the shortcut key to the style, tap or click the Close button to close the Customize Keyboard dialog box, and then tap or click the OK button to close the Modify Style dialog box.

To Modify the Default Font Settings

You can change the default font so that the current document and all future documents use the new font settings. That is, if you exit Word, restart the computer, and run Word again, documents you create will use the new default font. If you wanted to change the default font from 11-point Calibri to another font, font style, font size, font color, and/or font effects, you would perform the following steps.

1. Tap or click the Font Dialog Box Launcher (HOME tab | Font group) to display the Font dialog box.
2. Make desired changes to the font settings in the Font dialog box.
3. Tap or click the 'Set As Default' button to change the default settings to those specified in Step 2.
4. When the Microsoft Word dialog box is displayed, select the desired option button and then tap or tap or click the OK button.

To Reset the Default Font Settings

BTW
Advanced Character Attributes
If you wanted to set advanced character attributes, you would tap or click the Font Dialog Box Launcher (HOME tab | Font group) to display the Font dialog box, tap or click the Advanced tab (Font dialog box) to display the Advanced sheet, select the desired Character Spacing or OpenType Features settings, and then tap or click the OK button.

To change the font settings back to the default, you would follow the steps at the bottom of the previous page, using the default font settings when performing Step 2. If you do not remember the default settings, you would perform the following steps to restore the original Normal style settings.

1. Exit Word.
2. Use File Explorer to locate the Normal.dotm file (be sure that hidden files and folders are displayed and include system and hidden files in your search), which is the file that contains default font and other settings.
3. Rename the Normal.dotm file to oldnormal.dotm file so that the Normal.dotm file no longer exists.
4. Run Word, which will recreate a Normal.dotm file using the original default settings.

To Create a Character Style

1 SAVE DOCUMENT AS MACRO-ENABLED TEMPLATE | 2 MODIFY TEXT & FORM CONTENT CONTROLS
3 ENHANCE FORM'S VISUAL APPEAL | 4 CREATE MACROS TO AUTOMATE TASKS

In this online form, the check box labels are to be the same color as the company name. The following steps create a character style called Check Box Labels. *Why? Although you could select each of the check box labels and then format them, a more efficient technique is to create a character style.* If you decide to modify the formats of the check box labels at a later time, you simply change the formats assigned to the style to automatically change all characters in the document based on that style.

- Position the insertion point in one of the check box labels.
- Tap or click the Styles Dialog Box Launcher (HOME tab | Styles group) to display the Styles task pane.
- Tap or click the Manage Styles button in the Styles task pane to display the Manage Styles dialog box (Figure 11–21).

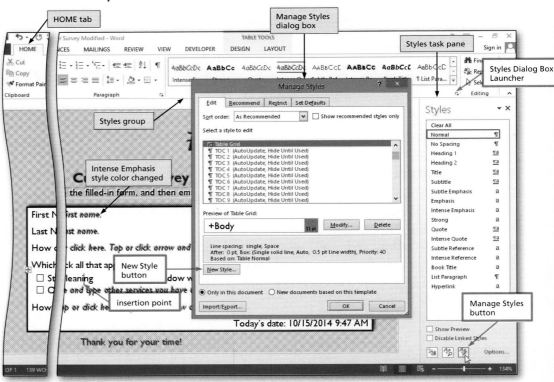

Figure 11–21

- Tap or click the New Style button (Manage Styles dialog box) to display the Create New Style from Formatting dialog box.

- Type **Check Box Labels** in the Name text box (Create New Style from Formatting dialog box) as the name of the new style.

- Tap or click the Style type arrow and then tap or click Character so that the new style does not contain any paragraph formats.

- Tap or click the Font Color arrow to display the Font Color gallery and then tap or click 'Plum, Accent 2, Darker 25%' (sixth color in fifth row) as the new color (Figure 11–22).

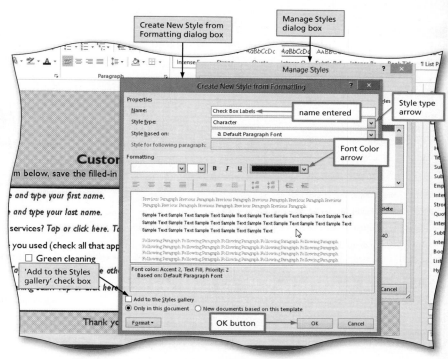

Figure 11–22

- Tap or click the OK button in each open dialog box to create the new character style, Check Box Labels in this case, and insert the new style name in the Styles task pane (Figure 11–23).

Q&A What if I wanted the style added to the Styles gallery?
You would place a check mark in the 'Add to the Styles gallery' check box (Create New Style from Formatting dialog box), shown in Figure 11–22.

Figure 11–23

To Apply a Style

The next step is to apply the Check Box Labels style just created to the check box labels in the form. The following steps apply a style.

1. Drag through the check box label, Standard cleaning, to select it and then tap or click Check Box Labels in the Styles task pane to apply the style to the selected text.

2. Repeat Step 1 for these check box labels (Figure 11–24 on the next page): Green cleaning, Window washing, Carpet cleaning, and Other (please specify).

3. Close the Styles task pane.

4. Tap or click anywhere to remove the selection from the check box label.

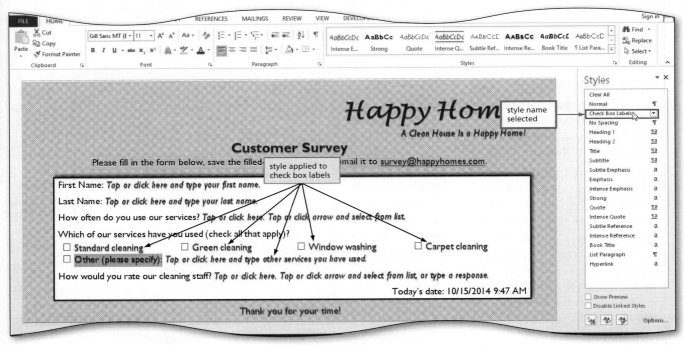

Figure 11–24

To Save an Existing Template with the Same File Name

BTW
Saving Templates
When you save a template that contains building blocks, the building blocks are available to all users who access the template.

You have made several modifications to the template since you last saved it. Thus, you should save it again. The following step saves the template again.

 Tap or click the Save button on the Quick Access Toolbar to overwrite the previously saved file.

Break Point: If you wish to take a break, this is a good place to do so. You can exit Word now. To resume at a later time, run Word, open the file called Customer Survey Modified, and continue following the steps from this location forward.

Enhancing with Color, Shapes, Effects, and Graphics

You will enhance the form created in Chapter 10 by performing these steps:

1. Apply a texture fill effect for the page color.
2. Change the appearance of the shape.
3. Change the color of a shadow on the shape.
4. Fill a shape with a picture.
5. Insert a picture, remove its background, and apply an artistic effect.
6. Insert and format a text box.
7. Group the picture and the text box together.

The following pages apply these changes to the form.

To Use a Fill Effect for the Page Color

Word provides a gallery of 24 predefined textures you can use as a page background. These textures resemble various wallpaper patterns. The following steps change the page color to a texture fill effect. *Why? Instead of a simple color for the background page color, this online form uses a texture for the page color.*

1

- Display the DESIGN tab.

- Tap or click the Page Color button (DESIGN tab | Page Background group) to display the Page Color gallery (Figure 11–25).

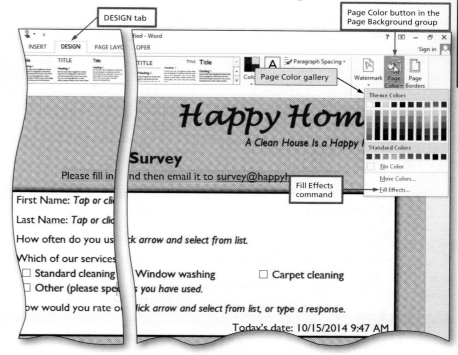

Figure 11–25

2

- Tap or click Fill Effects in the Page Color gallery to display the Fill Effects dialog box.

- Tap or click the Texture tab (Fill Effects dialog box) to display the Texture sheet.

- Scroll to, if necessary, and then tap or click the 'Pink tissue paper' texture in the Texture gallery to select the texture (Figure 11–26).

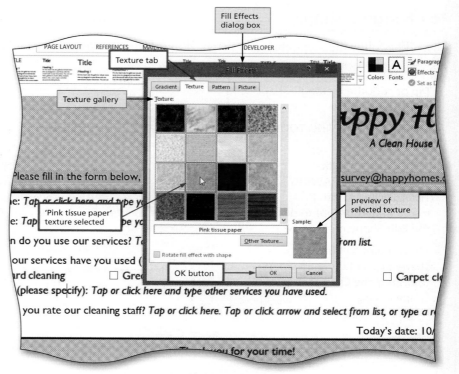

Figure 11–26

3

- Tap or click the OK button to apply the selected texture as the page color in the document (Figure 11–27).

Q&A How would I remove a texture page color?
You would tap or click the Page Color button (DESIGN tab | Page Background group) and then tap or click No Color in the Page Color gallery.

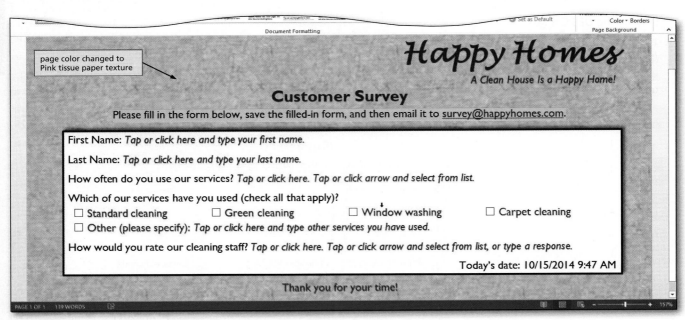

Figure 11–27

To Change a Shape

1 SAVE DOCUMENT AS MACRO-ENABLED TEMPLATE | 2 MODIFY TEXT & FORM CONTENT CONTROLS
3 ENHANCE FORM'S VISUAL APPEAL | 4 CREATE MACROS TO AUTOMATE TASKS

The following steps change a shape. *Why? This online form uses a variation of the standard rectangle shape.*

1

- Tap or click the rectangle shape to select it.

- Display the DRAWING TOOLS FORMAT tab.

- Tap or click the Edit Shape button (DRAWING TOOLS FORMAT tab | Insert Shapes group) to display the Edit Shape menu.

- Tap or point to Change Shape on the Edit Shape menu to display the Change Shape gallery (Figure 11–28).

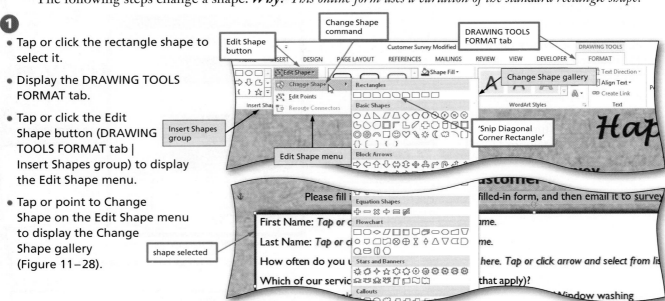

Figure 11–28

2

- Tap or click 'Snip Diagonal Corner Rectangle' in the Rectangles area in the Change Shape gallery to change the selected shape (Figure 11–29).

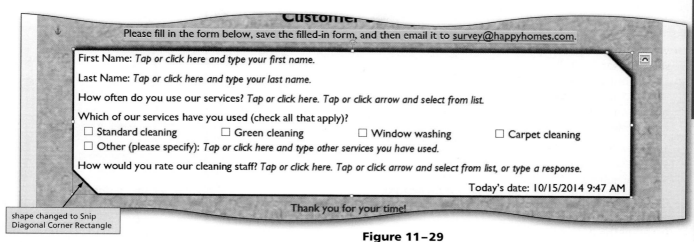

Figure 11–29

To Apply a Glow Shape Effect

The next step is to apply a glow effect to the rectangle shape. You can apply the same effects to shapes as to pictures. That is, you can apply shadows, reflections, glows, soft edges, bevels, and 3-D rotations to pictures and shapes. The following steps apply a shape effect.

1 With the rectangle shape selected, tap or click the Shape Effects button (DRAWING TOOLS FORMAT tab | Shape Styles group) to display the Shape Effects menu.

2 Tap or point to Glow on the Shape Effects menu to display the Glow gallery.

3 If you are using a mouse, point to 'Plum, 5 pt glow, Accent color 1' in the Glow Variations area (first glow in first row) to display a live preview of the selected glow effect applied to the selected shape in the document window (Figure 11–30).

4 Tap or click 'Plum, 5 pt glow, Accent color 1' in the Glow gallery (first glow in first row) to apply the shape effect to the selected shape.

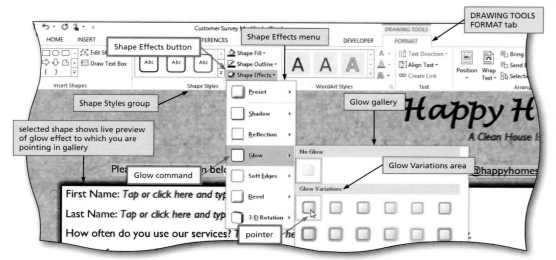

Figure 11–30

To Apply a Shadow Shape Effect

The following steps apply a shadow effect and change its color. *Why? The rectangle in this online form has a shadow that is a similar color to the company tag line.*

- With the rectangle shape still selected, tap or click the Shape Effects button (DRAWING TOOLS FORMAT tab | Shape Styles group) again to display the Shape Effects menu.

- Tap or point to Shadow in the Shape Effects menu to display the Shadow gallery.

- If you are using a mouse, point to 'Perspective Diagonal Upper Right' in the Perspective area at the bottom of the Shadow gallery to display a live preview of that shadow applied to the shape in the document (Figure 11–31).

 **Experiment**

- If you are using a mouse, point to various shadows in the Shadow gallery and watch the shadow on the selected shape change.

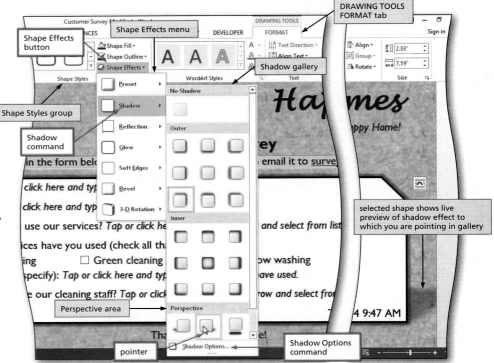

Figure 11–31

2

- Tap or click 'Perspective Diagonal Upper Right' in the Shadow gallery to apply the selected shadow to the selected shape.

- Tap or click the Shape Effects button (DRAWING TOOLS FORMAT tab | Shape Styles group) again to display the Shape Effects menu.

- Tap or point to Shadow in the Shape Effects menu to display the Shadow gallery.

- Tap or click Shadow Options in the Shadow gallery to open the Format Shape task pane.

- Tap or click the Shadow Color button (Format Shape task pane) and then tap or click 'Blue-Gray, Accent 6, Darker 25%' (last color in fifth row) in the Shadow Color gallery to change the shadow color.

- Tap or click the Transparency down arrow as many times as necessary until the Transparency box displays 60% to change the amount of transparency in the shadow (Figure 11–32).

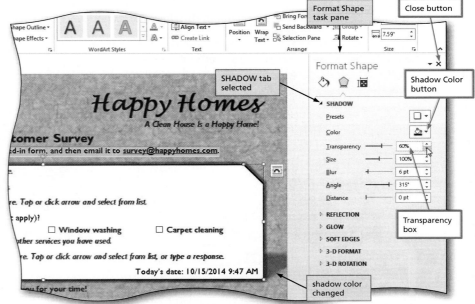

Figure 11–32

3

- Tap or click the Close button to close the Format Shape task pane.

To Fill a Shape with a Picture

The following steps fill a shape with a picture. **Why?** *The rectangle in this online form contains the happy house picture. The picture, called Happy House, is located on the Data Files for Students. Visit www.cengage.com/ct/ studentdownload for detailed instructions or contact your instructor for information about accessing the required files.*

1

- With the rectangle shape still selected, tap or click the Shape Fill arrow (DRAWING TOOLS FORMAT tab | Shape Styles group) to display the Shape Fill gallery (Figure 11–33).

Q&A My Shape Fill gallery did not display. Why not?
If you are using a mouse, you clicked the Shape Fill button instead of the Shape Fill arrow. Repeat Step 1.

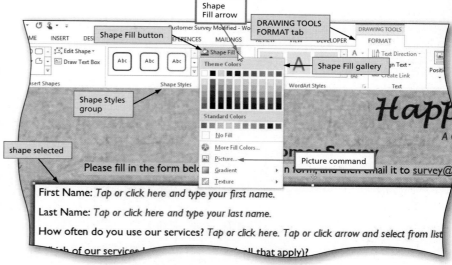

Figure 11–33

2

- Tap or click Picture in the Shape Fill gallery to display the Insert Pictures dialog box.

- Tap or click the Browse button (Insert Pictures dialog box) to display the Insert Picture dialog box. Locate and then select the file called Happy House (Insert Picture dialog box).

- Tap or click the Insert button (Insert Picture dialog box) to fill the rectangle shape with the picture (Figure 11–34).

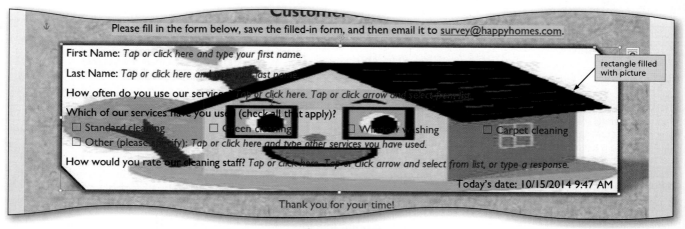

Figure 11–34

To Change the Color of a Picture

The text in the rectangle shape is difficult to read because the picture just inserted is too colorful. You can experiment with adjusting the brightness, contrast, and color of a picture so that the text is readable. In this project, the color is changed to the washout setting so that the text is easier to read. The steps on the next page change the color of the picture to washout.

1 Display the PICTURE TOOLS FORMAT tab.

2 With the rectangle shape still selected, tap or click the Color button (PICTURE TOOLS FORMAT tab | Adjust group) to display the Color gallery.

3 If you are using a mouse, point to Washout in the Recolor area in the Color gallery to display a live preview of the selected color applied to the selected picture (Figure 11–35).

4 Tap or click Washout in the Color gallery to apply the selected color to the selected picture.

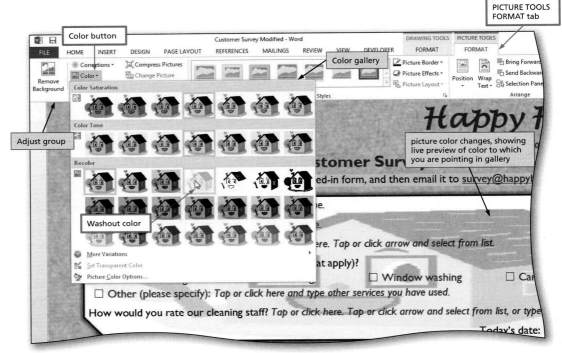

Figure 11–35

To Insert, Change Wrapping Style, and Resize a Picture

The top of the online form in this chapter contains a picture of a whisk broom and dustpan. The picture, called Whisk Broom, is located on the Data Files for Students. Visit www.cengage.com/ct/studentdownload for detailed instructions or contact your instructor for information about accessing the required files.

You will change the wrapping style of the inserted picture so that it can be positioned in front of the text. Because the graphic's original size is too large, you also will resize it. The following steps insert a picture, change its wrapping style, and resize it.

1 Position the insertion point in a location near where the picture will be inserted, in this case, near the top of the online form.

2 Display the INSERT tab. Tap or click the From File button (INSERT tab | Illustrations group) to display the Insert Picture dialog box.

3 Locate and then tap or click the file called Whisk Broom (Insert Picture dialog box) to select the file.

4 Tap or click the Insert button to insert the picture at the location of the insertion point.

5 With the picture selected, tap or click the Wrap Text button (PICTURE TOOLS FORMAT tab | Arrange group) and then tap or click 'In Front of Text' so that the graphic can be positioned on top of text.

6 Change the value in the Shape Height box (PICTURE TOOLS FORMAT tab | Size group) to 1" and the value in the Shape Width box (PICTURE TOOLS FORMAT tab | Size group) to 1.4".

7 If necessary, scroll to display the online form in the document window (Figure 11–36).

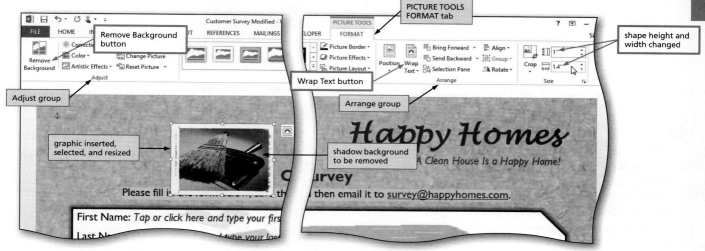

Figure 11–36

To Remove a Background

1 SAVE DOCUMENT AS MACRO-ENABLED TEMPLATE | 2 MODIFY TEXT & FORM CONTENT CONTROLS
3 ENHANCE FORM'S VISUAL APPEAL | 4 CREATE MACROS TO AUTOMATE TASKS

In Word, you can remove a background from a picture. The following steps remove a background. **Why?** *You remove the shadow background from the picture of the whisk broom and dustpan.*

1

- Tap or click the Remove Background button (PICTURE TOOLS FORMAT tab | Adjust group) (shown in Figure 11–36), to display the BACKGROUND REMOVAL tab and show the proposed area to be deleted in purple (Figure 11–37).

Q&A What is the BACKGROUND REMOVAL tab?

You can draw around areas to keep or areas to remove by tapping or clicking the respective buttons on the BACKGROUND REMOVAL tab. If you mistakenly mark too much, use the Delete Mark button. You also can drag

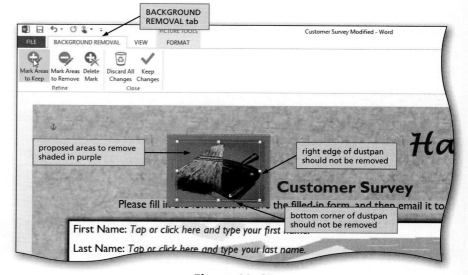

Figure 11–37

the proposed rectangle to adjust the proposed removal area. When finished marking, tap or click the 'Close Background Removal and Keep Changes' button, or to start over, tap or click the 'Close Background Removal and Discard Changes' button.

- Drag the proposed marking lines downward and rightward slightly, as shown in Figure 11–38, so that the entire dustpan shows and the entire shadow background is shaded purple. If necessary, drag the marking lines a few times.

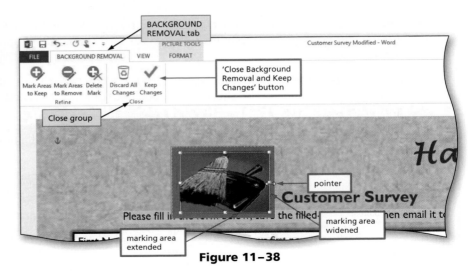

Figure 11–38

- Tap or click the 'Close Background Removal and Keep Changes' button (BACKGROUND REMOVAL tab | Close group) to remove the area shaded purple to close the BACKGROUND REMOVAL tab (Figure 11–39).

Figure 11–39

To Apply an Artistic Effect

1 SAVE DOCUMENT AS MACRO-ENABLED TEMPLATE | 2 MODIFY TEXT & FORM CONTENT CONTROLS
3 ENHANCE FORM'S VISUAL APPEAL | 4 CREATE MACROS TO AUTOMATE TASKS

Word provides several different artistic effects, such as blur, line drawing, and paint brush, that alter the appearance of a picture. The following steps apply an artistic effect to the picture. *Why? You want to soften the look of the picture a bit.*

- With the picture still selected, tap or click the Artistic Effects button (PICTURE TOOLS FORMAT tab | Adjust group) to display the Artistic Effects gallery.

- If you are using a mouse, point to Pastels Smooth (fourth effect in fourth row) in the Artistic Effects gallery to display a live preview of the effect applied to the selected picture in the document window (Figure 11–40).

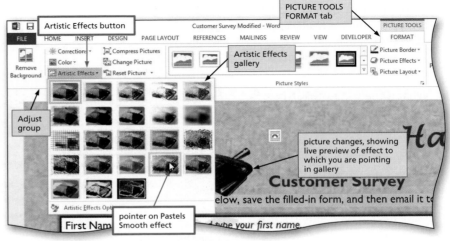

- Tap or click Pastels Smooth in the Artistic Effects gallery to apply the selected effect to the selected picture.

Figure 11–40

To Change the Color of a Graphic and Move the Graphic

In this project, the color of the whisk broom and dustpan is changed to match the colors in the company name. Then, the graphic is to be positioned on the left edge of the form. The following steps change the color of the picture and then move it.

1 With the picture still selected, tap or click the Color button (PICTURE TOOLS FORMAT tab | Adjust group) to display the Color gallery.

2 Tap or click 'Plum, Accent color 1 Light' in the Recolor area in the Color gallery (second color in last row) to apply the selected color to the selected picture.

3 Drag the graphic to the location shown in Figure 11–41.

To Draw a Text Box

1 SAVE DOCUMENT AS MACRO-ENABLED TEMPLATE | 2 MODIFY TEXT & FORM CONTENT CONTROLS
3 ENHANCE FORM'S VISUAL APPEAL | 4 CREATE MACROS TO AUTOMATE TASKS

The picture of the whisk broom and dustpan in this form has a text box with the words, Let Us Sweep It Clean!, positioned near the bottom of the broom. The following steps draw a text box. **Why?** *The first step in creating the text box is to draw its perimeter. You draw a text box using the same procedure as you do to draw a shape.*

1

- Position the insertion point somewhere in the top of the online form.
- Display the INSERT tab.
- Tap or click the 'Choose a Text Box' button (INSERT tab | Text group) to display the Choose a Text Box gallery (Figure 11–41).

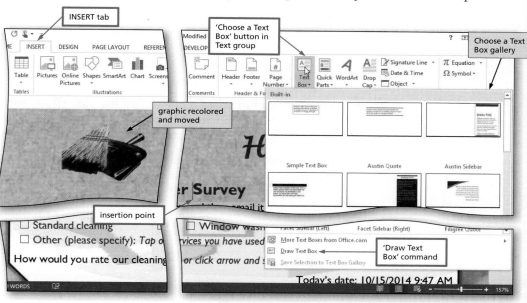

Figure 11–41

2

- Tap or click 'Draw Text Box' in the Text Box gallery, which removes the gallery. If you are using a touch screen, the text box is inserted in the document window; if you are using a mouse, the pointer changes to the shape of a crosshair.
- If you are using a mouse, drag the pointer to the right and downward to form the boundaries of the text box, as shown in Figure 11–42.

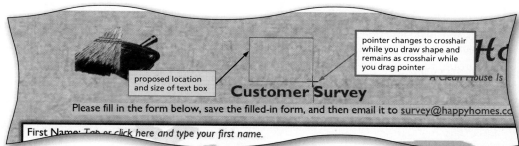

Figure 11–42

- If you are using a mouse, release the mouse button so that Word draws the text box according to your drawing in the document window.

- Verify your shape is the same approximate height and width as the one in this project by changing the values in the Shape Height and Shape Width boxes (DRAWING TOOLS FORMAT tab | Size group) to 0.9" and 0.75", respectively (Figure 11–43).

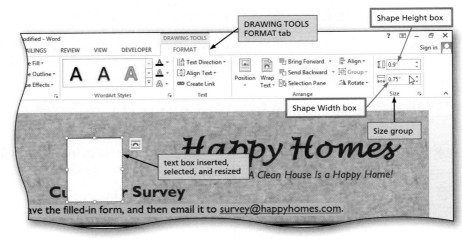

Figure 11–43

To Add Text to a Text Box and Format the Text

The next step is to add the phrase, Let Us Sweep It Clean!, centered in the text box using a text effect. You add text to a text box using the same procedure you do when adding text to a shape. The following steps add text to a text box.

1 Display the HOME tab. With the text box selected, tap or click the Center button (HOME tab | Paragraph group) so that the text you enter is centered in the text box.

2 With the text box selected, tap or click the 'Text Effects and Typography' button (HOME tab | Font group) and then tap or click 'Fill - Blue-Gray, Accent 4, Soft Bevel' (last effect in first row) in the Text Effects gallery to specify the format for the text in the text box.

3 If your insertion point is not positioned in the text box (shape), press and hold or right-click the shape to display a shortcut menu and the mini toolbar and then tap or click Edit Text on the mini toolbar or shortcut menu to place an insertion point centered in the text box.

4 Type `Let Us Sweep It Clean!` as the text for the text box (shown in Figure 11–44). (If necessary, adjust the width of the text box to fit the text.)

To Change Text Direction in a Text Box

1 SAVE DOCUMENT AS MACRO-ENABLED TEMPLATE | 2 MODIFY TEXT & FORM CONTENT CONTROLS
3 ENHANCE FORM'S VISUAL APPEAL | 4 CREATE MACROS TO AUTOMATE TASKS

The following steps change text direction in a text box. **Why?** *The direction of the text in the text box should be vertical instead of horizontal.*

- Display the DRAWING TOOLS FORMAT tab.

- With the shape still selected, tap or click the Text Direction button (DRAWING TOOLS FORMAT tab | Text group) to display the Text Direction gallery (Figure 11–44).

Q&A What if my text box no longer is selected?
Tap or click the text box to select it.

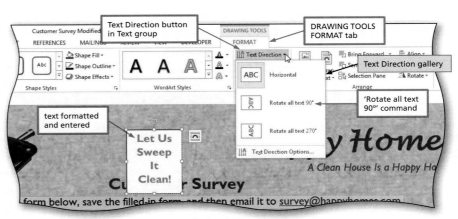

Figure 11–44

2

- Tap or click 'Rotate all text 90°' in the Text Direction gallery to display the text in the text box vertically from top to bottom (Figure 11–45).

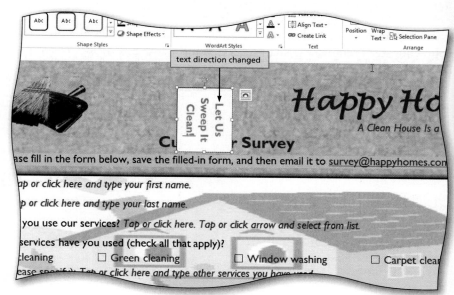

Figure 11–45

Other Ways

1. Tap 'Show Context Menu' button on mini toolbar or right-click text box, tap or click Format Shape on shortcut menu, tap or click TEXT OPTIONS tab (Format Shape task pane), expand TEXT BOX section, tap or click Text direction box, select desired direction, tap or click Close button

To Apply a Shadow Shape Effect to a Text Box

The text box in this online form has an inside shadow that is in the same color as the tag line. The following steps apply a shadow effect and change its color.

1 Move the text box to the left so that it is visible when you change the shadows and colors.

2 With the text box still selected, tap or click the Shape Effects button (DRAWING TOOLS FORMAT tab | Shape Styles group) to display the Shape Effects menu.

3 Tap or point to Shadow in the Shape Effects menu to display the Shadow gallery and then tap or click Inside Center in the Inner area of the Shadow gallery to apply the selected shadow to the selected shape.

4 Tap or click the Shape Effects button (DRAWING TOOLS FORMAT tab | Shape Styles group) again to display the Shape Effects menu.

5 Tap or point to Shadow in the Shape Effects menu to display the Shadow gallery and then tap or click Shadow Options in the Shadow gallery to display the Format Shape task pane.

6 Tap or click the Shadow Color button (Format Shape task pane) and then tap or click 'Blue-Gray, Accent 6, Darker 25%' (last color in fifth row) in the Color gallery to change the shadow color.

7 Change the value in the Transparency box to 60% to change the amount of transparency in the shadow (shown in Figure 11–46 on the next page).

8 Tap or click the Close button to close the Format Shape task pane.

To Change a Shape Outline of a Text Box

You change an outline on a text box (shape) using the same procedure as you do with a picture. The following steps remove the shape outline on the text box. *Why? The text box in this form has no outline.*

1

- With the text box still selected, tap or click the Shape Outline arrow (DRAWING TOOLS FORMAT tab | Shape Styles group) to display the Shape Outline gallery (Figure 11–46).

Q&A
The Shape Outline gallery did not display. Why not?
If you are using a mouse, you clicked the Shape Outline button instead of the Shape Outline arrow. Repeat Step 1.

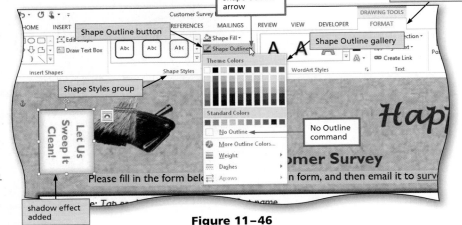

Figure 11–46

Experiment

- If you are using a mouse, point to various colors in the Shape Outline gallery and watch the color of the outline on the text box change in the document.

2

- Tap or click No Outline in the Shape Outline gallery to remove the outline from the selected shape.

Other Ways
1. Tap or click Format Shape Dialog Box Launcher (DRAWING TOOLS FORMAT tab | Shape Styles group); expand LINE section (Format Shape task pane); tap or click No line to remove line, or tap or click Solid line, tap or click Outline color button, and select desired color to change line color; tap or click Close button   2. Tap 'Show Context Menu' button on mini toolbar or right-click text box, tap or click Format Shape on shortcut menu, expand LINE section (Format Shape task pane), tap or click No line to remove line, or tap or click Solid line, tap or click Outline color button, and select desired color to change line color; tap or click Close button

To Apply a 3-D Effect to a Text Box

Word provides 3-D effects for shapes (such as text boxes) that are similar to those it provides for pictures. The following steps apply a 3-D rotation effect to a text box. *Why? In this form, the text box is rotated using a 3-D rotation effect.*

1

- With the text box selected, tap or click the Shape Effects button (DRAWING TOOLS FORMAT tab | Shape Styles group) to display the Shape Effects gallery.

- Tap or point to '3-D Rotation' in the Shape Effects gallery to display the 3-D Rotation gallery.

- If you are using a mouse, point to 'Isometric Top Up' in the Parallel area (third rotation in first row) to display a live preview of the selected 3-D effect applied to the text box in the document window (Figure 11–47).

Experiment

- If you are using a mouse, point to various 3-D rotation effects in the 3-D Rotation gallery and watch the text box change in the document window.

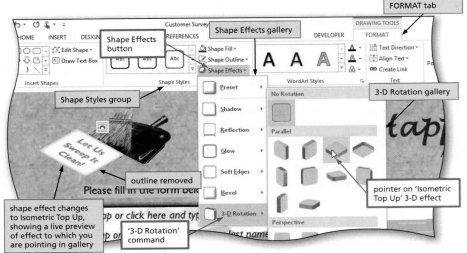

Figure 11–47

2

• Tap or click 'Isometric Top Up' in the 3-D Rotation gallery to apply the selected 3-D effect.

Other Ways

1. Tap or click Format Shape Dialog Box Launcher (DRAWING TOOLS FORMAT tab | Shape Styles group), tap or click TEXT OPTIONS tab (Format Shape task pane), tap or click Text Effects button, if necessary expand 3-D ROTATION SECTION, select desired options, tap or click Close button

2. Tap 'Show Context Menu' button on mini toolbar or right-click text box, tap or click Format Shape on shortcut menu, tap or click TEXT OPTIONS tab (Format Shape task pane), tap or click Text Effects button, if necessary expand 3-D ROTATION SECTION, select desired options, tap or click Close button

---

To Move the Text Box

In this project, the text box is to be positioned near the bristles of the whisk broom graphic. The following step moves the text box.

1 Drag the text box to the location shown in Figure 11–48. (You may need to drag the text box a couple of times to position it as shown in the figure.)

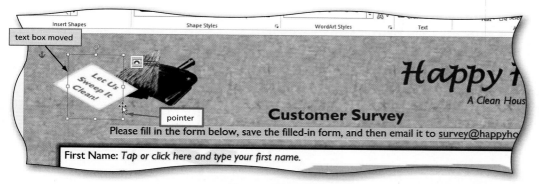

Figure 11–48

To Group Objects

1 SAVE DOCUMENT AS MACRO-ENABLED TEMPLATE | 2 MODIFY TEXT & FORM CONTENT CONTROLS
3 ENHANCE FORM'S VISUAL APPEAL | 4 CREATE MACROS TO AUTOMATE TASKS

When you have multiple graphics, such as pictures, clip art, shapes, and text boxes, positioned on a page, you can group them so that they are a single graphic instead of separate graphics. The following steps group the whisk broom graphic and the text box together. *Why? Grouping the graphics makes it easier to move them because they all move together as a single graphic.*

1

• With the text box selected, hold down the CTRL key while tapping or clicking the whisk broom picture (that is, CTRL+tap or click), so that both graphics are selected at the same time.

Q&A What if I had more than two graphics that I wanted to group? For each subsequent graphic to select, CTRL+tap or click the graphic, which enables you to select multiple objects at the same time.

• Tap or click the Group Objects button (DRAWING TOOLS FORMAT tab | Arrange group) to display the Group Objects menu (Figure 11–49).

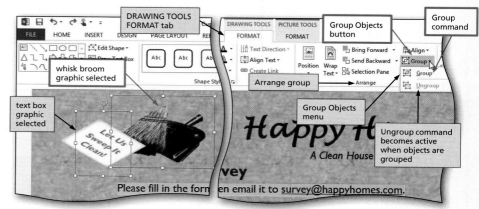

Figure 11–49

2

- Tap or click Group on the Group Objects menu to group the selected objects into a single selected object (Figure 11–50).

Q&A What if I wanted to ungroup grouped objects?
Select the object to ungroup, tap or click the Group Objects button (DRAWING TOOLS FORMAT tab | Arrange group), and then tap or click Ungroup on the Group Objects menu.

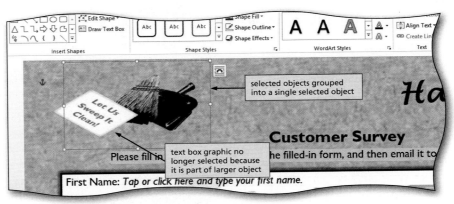

selected objects grouped into a single selected object

text box graphic no longer selected because it is part of larger object

Customer Survey

Please fill in ... he filled-in form, and then email it to

First Name: *Tap or click here and type your first name.*

Figure 11–50

3

- Tap or click outside of the graphic to position the insertion point in the document and deselect the graphic.

To Save an Existing Template with the Same File Name

You have made several modifications to the template since you last saved it. Thus, you should save it again. The following step saves the template again.

1 Tap or click the Save button on the Quick Access Toolbar to overwrite the previously saved file.

Break Point: If you wish to take a break, this is a good place to do so. You can exit Word now. To resume at a later time, run Word, open the file called Customer Survey Modified, and continue following the steps from this location forward.

Using a Macro to Automate a Task

BTW
Naming Macros
If you give a new macro the same name as an existing built-in command in Microsoft Word, the new macro's actions will replace the existing actions. Thus, you should be careful not to name a macro a name reserved for automatic macros (see Table 11–1 on page WD 713) or after any Word commands. To view a list of built-in macros in Word, tap or click the View Macros button (VIEW tab | Macros group) to display the Macros dialog box. Tap or click the Macros in arrow and then tap or click Word commands.

A **macro** consists of a series of Word commands or instructions that are grouped together as a single command. This single command is a convenient way to automate a difficult or lengthy task. Macros often are used to simplify formatting or editing activities, to combine multiple commands into a single command, or to select an option in a dialog box using a shortcut key.

To create a macro, you can use the macro recorder or the Visual Basic Editor. With the macro recorder, Word generates the VBA instructions associated with the macro automatically as you perform actions in Word. If you wanted to write the VBA instructions yourself, you would use the Visual Basic Editor. This chapter uses the macro recorder to create a macro and the Visual Basic Editor to modify it.

The **macro recorder** creates a macro based on a series of actions you perform while the macro recorder is recording. The macro recorder is similar to a video camera: after you start the macro recorder, it records all actions you perform while working in a document and stops recording when you stop the macro recorder. To record a macro, you follow this sequence of steps:

1. Start the macro recorder and specify options about the macro.
2. Execute the actions you want recorded.
3. Stop the macro recorder.

After you record a macro, you can execute the macro, or play it, any time you want to perform the same set of actions.

To Record a Macro and Assign It a Shortcut Key

In Word, you can assign a shortcut key to a macro so that you can execute the macro by pressing the shortcut key instead of using a dialog box to execute it. The following steps record a macro that hides formatting marks and the rulers; the macro is assigned the shortcut key, ALT+H. ***Why?*** *Assume you find that you are repeatedly hiding the formatting marks and rulers while designing the online form. To simplify this task, the macro in this project hides these screen elements.*

1

- Display formatting marks and the rulers on the screen.
- Display the DEVELOPER tab.
- Tap or click the Record Macro button (DEVELOPER tab | Code group) to display the Record Macro dialog box.
- Type **HideScreenElements** in the Macro name text box (Record Macro dialog box).

Q&A Do I have to name a macro?
If you do not enter a name for the macro, Word assigns a default name. Macro names can be up to 255 characters in length and can contain only numbers, letters, and the underscore character. A macro name cannot contain spaces or other punctuation.

- Tap or click the 'Store macro in' arrow and then tap or click 'Documents Based On Customer Survey Modified'.

Q&A What is the difference between storing a macro with the document template versus the Normal template?
Macros saved in the Normal template are available to all future documents; macros saved with the document template are available only with a document based on the template.

- In the Description text box, type this sentence (Figure 11–51): **Hide formatting marks and the rulers.**

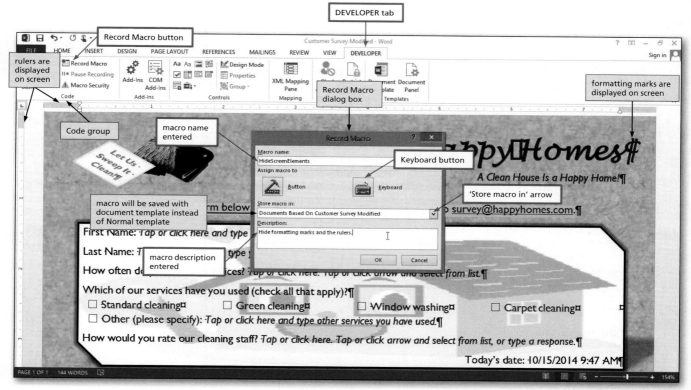

Figure 11–51

2

- Tap or click the Keyboard button to display the Customize Keyboard dialog box.

- Press ALT+H to display the characters ALT+H in the 'Press new shortcut key' text box (Customize Keyboard dialog box) (Figure 11–52).

Q&A Can I type the letters in the shortcut key (ALT+H) in the text box instead of pressing them? No. Although typing the letters places them in the text box, the shortcut key is valid only if you press the shortcut key combination itself.

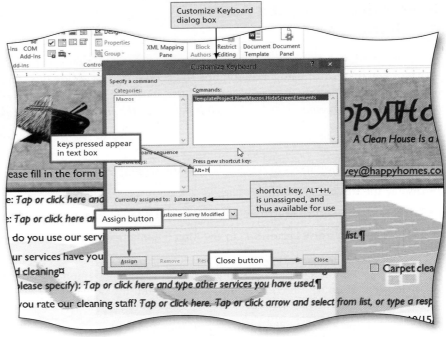

Figure 11–52

3

- Tap or click the Assign button (Customize Keyboard dialog box) to assign the shortcut key, ALT+H, to the macro named, HideScreenElements.

- Tap or click the Close button (Customize Keyboard dialog box), which closes the dialog box, displays a Macro Recording button on the status bar, and starts the macro recorder (Figure 11–53).

Q&A How do I record the macro? While the macro recorder is running, any action you perform in Word will be part of the macro — until you stop or pause the macro.

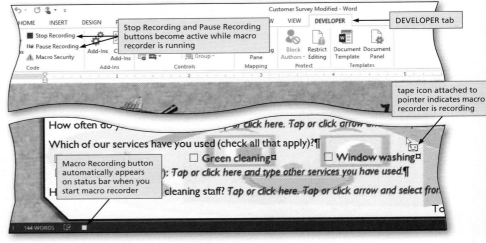

Figure 11–53

What is the purpose of the Pause Recording button (DEVELOPER tab | Code group)? If, while recording a macro, you want to perform some actions that should not be part of the macro, tap or click the Pause Recording button to suspend the macro recorder. The Pause Recording button changes to a Resume Recorder button that you tap or click when you want to continue recording.

4

- Display the HOME tab.

Q&A What happened to the tape icon? While recording a macro, the tape icon might disappear from the pointer when the pointer is in a menu, on the ribbon, or in a dialog box.

- Tap or click the 'Show/Hide ¶' button (HOME tab | Paragraph group) to hide formatting marks.

- Display the VIEW tab. Remove the check mark from the View Ruler check box (VIEW tab | Show group) to hide the rulers (Figure 11–54).

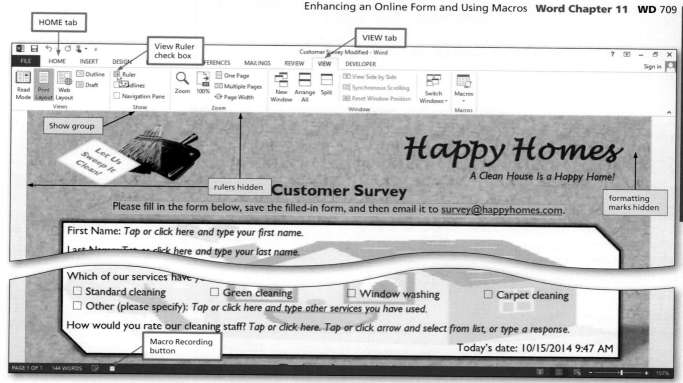

Figure 11–54

5

- Tap or click the Macro Recording button on the status bar to turn off the macro recorder, that is, to stop recording actions you perform in Word.

Q&A

What if I made a mistake while recording the macro?

Delete the macro and record it again. To delete a macro, tap or click the View Macros button (DEVELOPER tab | Code group), select the macro name in the list (Macros dialog box), tap or click the Delete button, and then tap or click the Yes button.

What if I wanted to assign the macro to a button instead of a shortcut key?

You would tap or click the Button button in the Record Macro dialog box (Figure 11–51 on page WD 707) and then follow Steps 4 and 5 above.

Other Ways

1. Tap or click View Macros arrow (VIEW tab | Macros group), tap or click Record Macro on View Macros menu

2. Press ALT+F8, tap or click Create button (Macros dialog box)

To Run a Macro

The next step is to execute, or run, the macro to ensure that it works. Recall that this macro hides formatting marks and the rulers, which means you must be sure the formatting marks and rulers are displayed on the screen before running the macro. Because you created a shortcut key for the macro in this project, the following steps show formatting marks and the rulers so that you can run the HideScreenElements macro using the shortcut key, ALT+H.

1 Display formatting marks on the screen.

2 Display rulers on the screen.

3 Press ALT+H, which causes Word to perform the instructions stored in the HideScreenElements macro, that is, to hide formatting marks and rulers.

BTW

Running Macros

You can run a macro by tapping or clicking the View Macros button (DEVELOPER tab | Code group or VIEW tab | Macros group) or by pressing ALT+F8 to display the Macros dialog box, selecting the macro name in the list, and then tapping or clicking the Run button (Macros dialog box).

To Add a Command and a Macro as Buttons on the Quick Access Toolbar

Word allows you to add buttons to and delete buttons from the Quick Access Toolbar. You also can assign a command, such as a macro, to a button on the Quick Access Toolbar. The following steps add an existing command to the Quick Access Toolbar and assign a macro to a new button on the Quick Access Toolbar. *Why? This chapter shows how to add the New command to the Quick Access Toolbar and also shows how to create a button for the HideScreenElements macro so that instead of pressing the shortcut keys, you can tap or click the button to hide formatting marks and the rulers.*

1

- Tap or click the 'Customize Quick Access Toolbar' button on the Quick Access Toolbar to display the Customize Quick Access Toolbar menu (Figure 11–55).

Q&A
What happens if I tap or click the commands listed on the Customize Quick Access Toolbar menu?
If the command does not have a check mark beside it and you tap or click it, Word places the button associated with the command on the Quick Access Toolbar. If the command has a check mark beside it and you tap or click (deselect) it, Word removes the command from the Quick Access Toolbar.

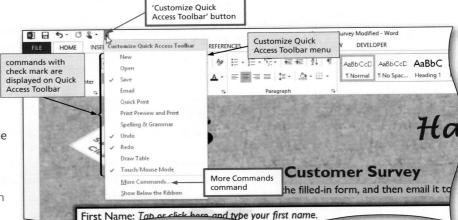

Figure 11–55

2

- Tap or click More Commands on the Customize Quick Access Toolbar menu to display the Word Options dialog box with Quick Access Toolbar selected in the left pane.

- Scroll through the list of popular commands (Word Options dialog box) and then click New to select the command.

- Tap or click the Add button to add the selected command (New, in this case) to the Customize Quick Access Toolbar list (Figure 11–56).

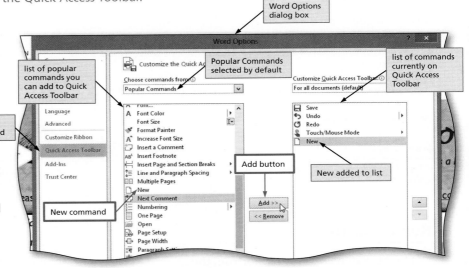

Figure 11–56

3

- Tap or click the 'Choose commands from' arrow to display a list of categories of commands (Figure 11–57).

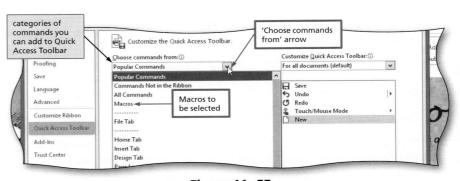

Figure 11–57

4

- Tap or click Macros in the Choose commands from list to display the macro in this document.

- If necessary, tap or click the macro to select it.

- Tap or click the Add button (Word Options dialog box) to display the selected macro in the Customize Quick Access Toolbar list.

- Tap or click the Modify button to display the Modify Button dialog box.

- Change the name in the Display name text box to **Hide Screen Elements** (Modify Button dialog box), which will be the text that appears in the ScreenTip for the button.

- In the list of symbols, tap or click the screen icon as the new face for the button (Figure 11–58).

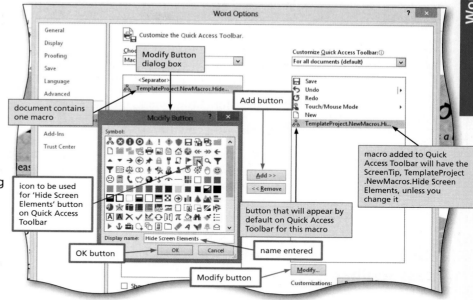

Figure 11–58

5

- Tap or click the OK button (Modify Button dialog box) to change the button characteristics in the Customize Quick Access Toolbar list (Figure 11–59).

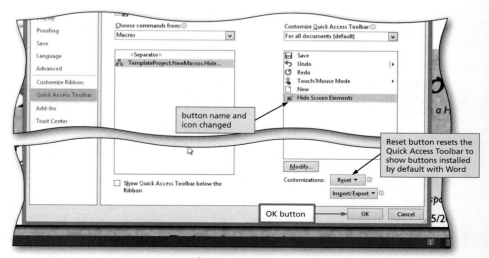

Figure 11–59

6

- Tap or click the OK button (Word Options dialog box) to add the buttons to the Quick Access Toolbar (Figure 11–60).

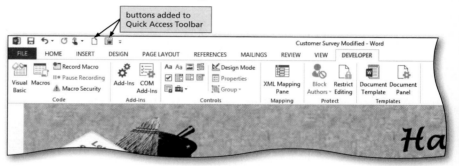

Figure 11–60

Other Ways

1. Press and hold or right-click Quick Access Toolbar, tap or click 'Customize Quick Access Toolbar' on shortcut menu

To Use the New Buttons on the Quick Access Toolbar

The next step is to test the new buttons on the Quick Access Toolbar, that is, the New button and the 'Hide Screen Elements' button, which will execute, or run, the macro that hides formatting marks and the rulers. The following steps use buttons on the Quick Access Toolbar.

1 Tap or click the New button on the Quick Access Toolbar to display a new blank document window. Close the new blank document window.

2 Display formatting marks on the screen.

3 Display rulers on the screen.

4 Tap or click the 'Hide Screen Elements' button on the Quick Access Toolbar, which causes Word to perform the instructions stored in the HideScreenElements macro, that is, to hide formatting marks and the rulers.

To Delete Buttons from the Quick Access Toolbar

1 SAVE DOCUMENT AS MACRO-ENABLED TEMPLATE | 2 MODIFY TEXT & FORM CONTENT CONTROLS
3 ENHANCE FORM'S VISUAL APPEAL | **4 CREATE MACROS TO AUTOMATE TASKS**

The following steps delete the New button and the 'Hide Screen Elements' button from the Quick Access Toolbar. *Why? If you no longer plan to use a button on the Quick Access Toolbar, you can delete it.*

1

- Press and hold or right-click the button to be deleted from the Quick Access Toolbar, in this case the 'Hide Screen Elements' button, to display a shortcut menu (Figure 11–61).

2

- Tap or click 'Remove from Quick Access Toolbar' on the shortcut menu to remove the button from the Quick Access Toolbar.

3

- Repeat Steps 1 and 2 for the New button on the Quick Access Toolbar.

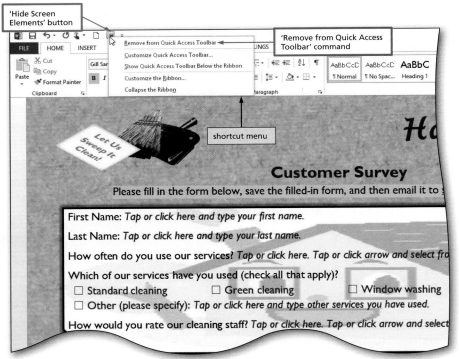

Figure 11–61

To Delete a Macro

If you wanted to delete a macro, you would perform the following steps.

1. Tap or click the View Macros button (DEVELOPER tab | Code group) to display the Macros dialog box.

2. Tap or click the macro to delete and then tap or click the Delete button (Macros dialog box) to display a dialog box asking if you are sure you want to delete the macro. Tap or click the Yes button in the dialog box.

3. Close the Macros dialog box.

Automatic Macros

The previous section showed how to create a macro, assign it a unique name (HideScreenElements) and a shortcut key, and then add a button that executes the macro on the Quick Access Toolbar. This section creates an **automatic macro**, which is a macro that executes automatically when a certain event occurs. Word has five prenamed automatic macros. Table 11–1 lists the name and function of these automatic macros.

Table 11–1 Automatic Macros	
Macro Name	**Event That Causes Macro to Run**
AutoClose	Closing a document that contains the macro
AutoExec	Running Word
AutoExit	Exiting Word
AutoNew	Creating a new document based on a template that contains the macro
AutoOpen	Opening a document that contains the macro

© 2014 Cengage Learning

BTW
Automatic Macros
A document can contain only one AutoClose macro, one AutoNew macro, and one AutoOpen macro. The AutoExec and AutoExit macros, however, are not stored with the document; instead, they must be stored in the Normal template. Thus, only one AutoExec macro and only one AutoExit macro can exist for all Word documents.

The automatic macro you choose depends on when you want certain actions to occur. In this chapter, when a user creates a new Word document that is based on the Customer Survey template, you want to be sure that the zoom is set to page width. Thus, the AutoNew automatic macro is used in this online form.

To Create an Automatic Macro

1 SAVE DOCUMENT AS MACRO-ENABLED TEMPLATE | 2 MODIFY TEXT & FORM CONTENT CONTROLS
3 ENHANCE FORM'S VISUAL APPEAL | 4 CREATE MACROS TO AUTOMATE TASKS

The following steps use the macro recorder to create an AutoNew macro. **Why?** *The online form in this chapter is displayed properly when the zoom is set to page width. Thus, you will record the steps to zoom to page width in the AutoNew macro.*

1
- Display the DEVELOPER tab.

- Tap or click the Record Macro button (DEVELOPER tab | Code group) to display the Record Macro dialog box.

- Type **AutoNew** in the Macro name text box (Record Macro dialog box).

- Tap or click the 'Store macro in' arrow and then click 'Documents Based On Customer Survey Modified'.

- In the Description text box, type this sentence (Figure 11–62): **Specifies how the form initially is displayed.**

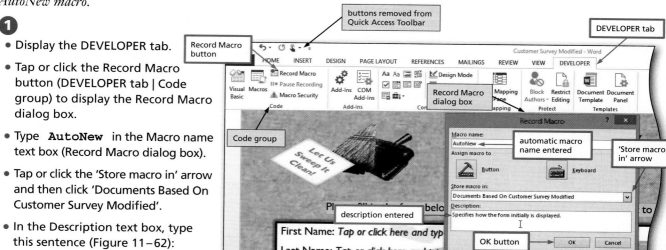

Figure 11–62

- Tap or click the OK button to close the Record Macro dialog box and start the macro recorder.
- Display the VIEW tab.
- Tap or click the Page Width button (VIEW tab | Zoom group) to zoom page width (Figure 11–63).

❸

- Tap or click the Macro Recording button on the status bar to turn off the macro recorder, that is, stop recording actions you perform in Word.

Q&A How do I test an automatic macro?

Activate the event that causes the macro to execute. For example, the AutoNew macro runs whenever you create a new Word document that is based on the template.

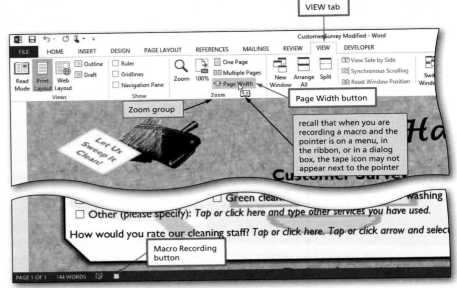

Figure 11–63

To Run the AutoNew Macro

The next step is to execute, or run, the AutoNew macro to ensure that it works. To run the AutoNew macro, you need to create a new Word document that is based on the Customer Survey Modified template. This macro contains instructions to zoom page width. To verify that the macro works as intended, you will change the zoom to 100% before testing the macro. The following steps run a macro.

❶ Use the Zoom Out button on the status bar to change the zoom to 100%.

❷ Save the template with the same file name, Customer Survey Modified.

❸ Tap or click the File Explorer button on the taskbar to open the File Explorer window.

❹ Locate and then double-tap or double-click the file named Customer Survey Modified to display a new document window that is based on the contents of the Customer Survey Modified template, which should be zoomed to page width as shown in Figure 11–1a on page WD 675. (If Word displays a dialog box about disabling macros, tap or click its OK button. If the Message Bar displays a security warning, tap or click the Enable Content button.)

❺ Close the new document that displays the form in the Word window. Tap or click the Don't Save button when Word asks if you want to save the changes to the new document.

❻ Close the File Explorer window.

❼ Change the zoom back to page width.

BTW

VBA

VBA includes many more statements than those presented in this chapter. You may need a background in computer programming if you plan to write VBA code instructions in macros you develop and if the VBA code instructions are beyond the scope of those instructions presented in this chapter.

To Edit a Macro's VBA Code

1 SAVE DOCUMENT AS MACRO-ENABLED TEMPLATE | 2 MODIFY TEXT & FORM CONTENT CONTROLS
3 ENHANCE FORM'S VISUAL APPEAL | **4 CREATE MACROS TO AUTOMATE TASKS**

As mentioned earlier, a macro consists of VBA instructions. To edit a recorded macro, you use the Visual Basic Editor. The following steps use the Visual Basic Editor to add VBA instructions to the AutoNew macro. *Why? In addition to zooming page width when the online form is displayed in a new document window, you would like to be sure that the DEVELOPER tab is hidden and the ribbon is collapsed. These steps are designed to show the basic composition of a VBA procedure and illustrate the power of VBA code statements.*

1

- Display the DEVELOPER tab.

- Tap or click the View Macros button (DEVELOPER tab | Code group) to display the Macros dialog box.

- If necessary, select the macro to be edited, in this case, AutoNew (Figure 11–64).

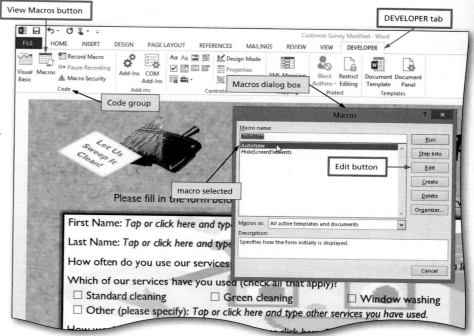

Figure 11–64

2

- Tap or click the Edit button (Macros dialog box) to start the Visual Basic Editor and display the VBA code for the AutoNew macro in the Code window — your screen may look different depending on previous Visual Basic Editor settings (Figure 11–65).

Q&A What if the Code window does not appear in the Visual Basic Editor?

In the Visual Basic Editor, tap or click View on the menu bar and then tap or click Code. If it still does not appear and you are in a network environment, this feature may be disabled for some users.

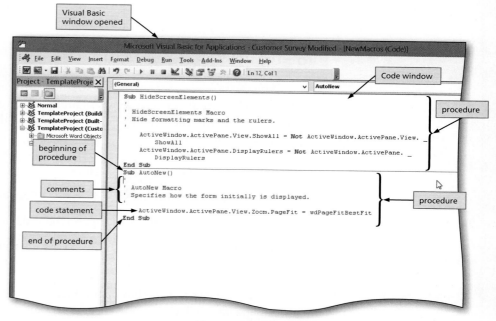

Figure 11–65

What are the lines of text (instructions) in the Code window?

The named set of instructions associated with a macro is called a **procedure**. It is this set of instructions — beginning with the word, Sub, and continuing sequentially to the line with the words, End Sub — that executes when you run the macro. The instructions within a procedure are called **code statements**.

3

- Position the insertion point at the end of the second-to-last line in the AutoNew macro and then press the ENTER key to insert a blank line for a new code statement.

- On a single line, type `Options.ShowDevTools = False` and then press the ENTER key, which enters the VBA code statement that hides the DEVELOPER tab.

Q&A What are the lists that appear in the Visual Basic Editor as I enter code statements?
The lists present valid statement elements to assist you with entering code statements. Because they are beyond the scope of this chapter, ignore them.

- On a single line, type `If Application.CommandBars.Item("Ribbon").Height > 100 Then` and then press the ENTER key, which enters the beginning VBA if statement that determines whether to collapse the ribbon.

- On a single line, press the TAB key, type `ActiveWindow .ToggleRibbon` and then press the ENTER key, which enters the beginning VBA code statement that collapses the ribbon.

- On a single line, press SHIFT+TAB, type `End If` and then press the ENTER key, which enters the beginning VBA code statement that collapses the ribbon (Figure 11–66).

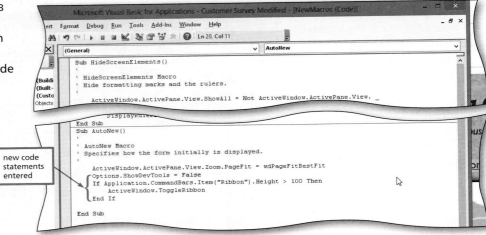

Figure 11–66

4

- Tap or click the Close button on the right edge of the Microsoft Visual Basic window title bar.

To Run the AutoNew Macro

The next step is to execute, or run, the AutoNew macro again to ensure that it works. To be sure the macro works as intended, ensure the DEVELOPER tab is displayed on the ribbon. The AutoNew macro should hide the DEVELOPER tab. The following steps run the automatic macro.

1 If necessary, display the DEVELOPER tab.

2 Save the template with the same file name, Customer Survey Modified.

3 Tap or click the File Explorer button on the taskbar to open the File Explorer window.

4 Locate and then double-tap or double-click the file named Customer Survey Modified to open a new document that is based on the contents of the Customer Survey Modified template, which should be zoomed to page width and display no DEVELOPER tab. (If Word displays a dialog box about disabling macros, tap or click its OK button. If the Message Bar displays a security warning, tap or click the Enable Content button.)

5 Close the new document that displays the form in the Word window. Tap or click the Don't Save button when Word asks if you want to save the changes to the new document.

6 Close the File Explorer window.

VBA

As shown in the steps on pages WD 715 and WD 716, a VBA procedure begins with a Sub statement and ends with an End Sub statement. The Sub statement is followed by the name of the procedure, which is the macro name (AutoNew). The parentheses following the macro name in the Sub statement are required. They indicate that arguments can be passed from one procedure to another. Passing arguments is beyond the scope of this chapter, but the parentheses still are required. The End Sub statement signifies the end of the procedure and returns control to Word.

Comments often are added to a procedure to help you remember the purpose of the macro and its code statements at a later date. Comments begin with an apostrophe (') and appear in green in the Code window. The macro recorder, for example, placed four comment lines below the Sub statement. These comments display the name of the macro and its description, as entered in the Record Macro dialog box. Comments have no effect on the execution of a procedure; they simply provide information about the procedure, such as its name and description, to the developer of the macro.

For readability, code statement lines are indented four spaces. Table 11–2 explains the function of each element of a code statement.

Table 11–2 Elements of a Code Statement

Code Statement Element	Definition	Examples
Keyword	Recognized by Visual Basic as part of its programming language; keywords appear in blue in the Code window	Sub End Sub
Variable	An item whose value can be modified during program execution	ActiveWindow.ActivePane.View.Zoom.PageFit
Constant	An item whose value remains unchanged during program execution	False
Operator	A symbol that indicates a specific action	=

© 2014 Cengage Learning

To Protect a Form Using the Backstage View

You now are finished enhancing the online form and adding macros to it. Because the last macro hid the DEVELOPER tab on the ribbon, you will use the Backstage view to protect the form. The following steps use the Backstage view to protect the online form so that users are restricted to entering data only in content controls.

1 Open the Backstage view and then, if necessary, display the Info gallery.

2 Tap or click the Protect Document button to display the Protect Document menu.

3 Tap or click Restrict Editing on the Protect Document menu to display the Restrict Editing task pane.

4 In the Editing restrictions area, if necessary, place a check mark in the 'Allow only this type of editing in the document' check box, tap or click its arrow, and then select 'Filling in forms' in the list.

5 Tap or click the 'Yes, Start Enforcing Protection' button and then tap or click the OK button (Start Enforcing Protection dialog box) to protect the document without a password.

6 Close the Restrict Editing task pane.

BTW
Setting Exceptions to Editing Restrictions
You can use the Restrict Editing task pane to allow editing in just certain areas of the document, a procedure called adding users excepted from restrictions. To do this, place a check mark in the 'Allow only this type of editing in the document' check box and then change the associated text box to 'No changes (Read only)', which instructs Word to prevent any editing to the document. Next, select the placeholder text for which you want to except users from restrictions and place a check mark in the Everyone check box in the Exceptions (optional) area to instruct Word that the selected item can be edited — the rest of the form will be read only.

To Save an Existing Template with the Same File Name and Exit Word

You have made several modifications to the template since you last saved it. Thus, you should save it again. The following steps save the template again, exit Word, and close the File Explorer window.

1 Tap or click the Save button on the Quick Access Toolbar to overwrite the previously saved file.

2 Exit Word.

3 If the File Explorer window still is open, close it.

Supplementary Word Tasks

If you plan to take the certification exam, you should be familiar with the skills in the following sections.

Adding a Digital Signature to a Document

Some users attach a **digital signature** to a document to verify its authenticity. A digital signature is an electronic, encrypted, and secure stamp of authentication on a document. This signature confirms that the file originated from the signer (file creator) and that it has not been altered.

A digital signature references a digital certificate. A **digital certificate** is an attachment to a file, macro project, email message, or other digital content that vouches for its authenticity, provides secure encryption, or supplies a verifiable signature. Many users who receive online forms enable the macros based on whether they are digitally signed by a developer on the user's list of trusted sources. You can obtain a digital certificate from a commercial certification authority or from your network administrator.

Once a digital signature is added, the document becomes a read-only document, which means that modifications cannot be made to it. Thus, you should create a digital signature only when the document is final. In Word, you can add two types of digital signatures to a document: (1) an invisible digital signature or (2) a signature line.

To Add an Invisible Digital Signature to a Document

An invisible digital signature does not appear as a tangible signature in the document. If the status bar displays a Signatures button, the document has an invisible digital signature. If you wanted to add an invisible digital signature to a document, you would perform the following steps.

1. Open the Backstage view and then, if necessary, display the Info gallery.
2. Tap or click the Protect Document button to display the Protect Document menu and then tap or click 'Add a Digital Signature' on the Protect Document menu to display the Sign dialog box. (If a dialog box appears indicating you need a digital ID, tap or click the OK button and then follow the on-screen instructions. If a dialog box about signature services appears, tap or click its OK button.)
3. Type the purpose of the digital signature in the Purpose for signing this document text box.

4. Tap or click the Sign button to add the digital signature, show the Signatures button on the status bar, and display Marked as Final on a Message Bar.

Q&A How can I view or remove the digital signatures in a document?

Open the Backstage view, if necessary, display the Info tab, and then tap or click the View Signatures button to display the Signatures task pane. To remove a digital signature, tap or click the arrow beside the signature name, tap or click Remove Signature on the menu, and then tap or click the Yes button in the dialog box.

TO ADD A SIGNATURE LINE TO A DOCUMENT

A **digital signature line**, which resembles a printed signature placeholder, allows a recipient of the electronic file to type a signature, include an image of his or her signature, or write a signature using the ink feature on a Tablet PC. Digital signature lines enable organizations to use paperless methods of obtaining signatures on official documents such as contracts. If you wanted to add a digital signature line to a document, you would perform the following steps.

1. Position the insertion point at the location for the digital signature.
2. Display the INSERT tab. Tap or click the 'Add a Signature Line' button (INSERT tab | Text group) to display the Signature Setup dialog box. (If a dialog box appears about signature services, tap or click its OK button.)
3. Type the name of the person who should sign the document in the appropriate text box.
4. If available, type the signer's title and email address in the appropriate text boxes.
5. Place a checkmark in the 'Allow the signer to add comments in the Sign dialog' check box so that the recipient can send a response back to you.
6. Tap or click the OK button (Signature Setup dialog box) to insert a signature line in the document at the location of the insertion point.

Q&A How does a recipient insert his or her digital signature?

When the recipient opens the document, a Message Bar appears that contains a View Signatures button. The recipient can tap or click the View Signatures button to display the Signatures task pane, tap or click the requested signature arrow, and then tap or click Sign on the menu (or double-tap or double-click the signature line in the document) to display a dialog box that the recipient then completes.

Copying and Renaming Styles and Macros

If you have created a style or macro in one document or template, you can copy the style or a macro to another so that you can use it in a second document or template.

TO COPY A STYLE FROM ONE TEMPLATE OR DOCUMENT TO ANOTHER

If you wanted to copy a style from one template or document to another, you would perform the following steps.

1. Open the document or template into which you want to copy the style.
2. If necessary, tap or click the Styles Dialog Box Launcher (HOME tab | Styles group) to display the Styles task pane, tap or click the Manage Styles button at the bottom of the Styles task pane to display the Manage Styles dialog box, and then tap or click the Import/Export button (Manage Styles dialog box) to display Styles sheet in the Organizer dialog box. Or, tap or click the Document Template button (DEVELOPER tab | Templates group) to display the Templates and Add-ins dialog box, tap or click the Organizer button (Templates

BTW
Certification
The Microsoft Office Specialist (MOS) program provides an opportunity for you to obtain a valuable industry credential — proof that you have the Word 2013 skills required by employers. For more information, visit the Certification resource on the Student Companion Site located on www.cengagebrain.com. For detailed instructions about accessing available resources, visit www.cengage.com/ct/studentdownload or contact your instructor for information about accessing the required files.

and Add-ins dialog box) to display the Organizer dialog box, and then, if necessary, tap or click the Styles tab to display the Styles sheet in the dialog box. Notice that the left side of the dialog box displays the style names in the currently open document or template.

3. Tap or click the Close File button (Organizer dialog box) to clear the right side of the dialog box.

Q&A What happened to the Close File button?
It changed to an Open File button.

4. Tap or click the Open File button (Organizer dialog box) and then locate the file that contains the style you wish to copy. Notice that the styles in the located document or template appear on the right side of the dialog box.

5. On the ride side of the dialog box, select the style you wish to copy and then tap or click the Copy button to copy the selected style to the document or template on the left. You can continue to copy as many styles as necessary.

6. When finished copying styles, tap or click the Close button to close the dialog box.

TO RENAME A STYLE

If you wanted to rename a style, you would perform the following steps.

1. Open the document or template that contains the style to rename.

2. If necessary, tap or click the Styles Dialog Box Launcher (HOME tab | Styles group) to display the Styles task pane, tap or click the Manage Styles button at the bottom of the Styles task pane to display the Manage Styles dialog box, and then tap or click the Import/Export button (Manage Styles dialog box) to display the Styles sheet in the Organizer dialog box. Or, tap or click the Document Template button (DEVELOPER tab | Templates group) to display the Templates and Add-ins dialog box, tap or click the Organizer button (Templates and Add-ins dialog box) to display the Organizer dialog box, and then, if necessary, tap or click the Styles tab to display the Styles sheet in the dialog box. Notice that the left side of the dialog box displays the style names in the currently open document or template.

3. Select the style you wish to rename and then tap or click the Rename button (Organizer dialog box) to display the Rename dialog box.

4. Type the new name of the style in the text box and then tap or click the OK button (Rename dialog box).

Q&A Can I delete styles too?
Yes, tap or click the Delete button (Organizer dialog box) to delete any selected styles.

5. When finished renaming styles, tap or click the Close button (Organizer dialog box) to close the dialog box.

TO COPY A MACRO FROM ONE TEMPLATE OR DOCUMENT TO ANOTHER

If you wanted to copy a macro from one template or document to another, you would perform the following steps.

1. Open the document or template into which you want to copy the macro.

2. If necessary, tap or click the View Macros button (DEVELOPER tab | Code group or VIEW tab | Macros group) to display the Macros dialog box, tap or click the Organizer button (Macros dialog box) to display Macro Project Items sheet in the Organizer dialog box. Or, tap or click the Document Template button (DEVELOPER tab | Templates group) to display the Templates and

BTW
Q&As
For a complete list of the Q&As found in many of the step-by-step sequences in this book, visit the Q&A resource on the Student Companion Site located on www.cengagebrain.com. For detailed instructions about accessing available resources, visit www.cengage.com/ct/studentdownload or contact your instructor for information about accessing the required files.

Add-ins dialog box, tap or click the Organizer button (Templates and Add-ins dialog box) to display the Organizer dialog box, and then, if necessary, tap or click the Macro Project Items tab to display the Macro Project Items sheet in the dialog box. Notice that the left side of the dialog box displays the macro names in the currently open document or template.

3. Tap or click the Close File button (Organizer dialog box) to clear the right side of the dialog box.

Q&A What happened to the Close File button?
It changed to an Open File button.

4. Tap or click the Open File button (Organizer dialog box) and then locate the file that contains the macro you wish to copy. Notice that the macros in the located document or template appear on the right side of the dialog box.

5. On the ride side of the dialog box, select the macro you wish to copy and then tap or click the Copy button to copy the selected macro to the document or template on the left. You can continue to copy as many macros as necessary.

6. When finished copying macros, tap or click the Close button (Organizer dialog box) to close the dialog box.

TO RENAME A MACRO

If you wanted to rename a macro, you would perform the following steps.

1. Open the document that contains the macro to rename.

2. If necessary, tap or click the View Macros button (DEVELOPER tab | Code group or VIEW tab | Macros group) to display the Macros dialog box, tap or click the Organizer button (Macros dialog box) to display Macro Project Items sheet in the Organizer dialog box. Or, tap or click the Document Template button (DEVELOPER tab | Templates group) to display the Templates and Add-ins dialog box, tap or click the Organizer button (Templates and Add-ins dialog box) to display the Organizer dialog box, and then, if necessary, tap or click the Macro Project Items tab to display the Macro Project Items sheet in the dialog box. Notice that the left side of the dialog box displays the macro names in the currently open document or template.

3. Select the macro you wish to rename and then tap or click the Rename button (Organizer dialog box) to display the Rename dialog box.

4. Type the new name of the macro in the text box and then tap or click the OK button (Rename dialog box).

Q&A Can I delete macros, too?
Yes, tap or click the Delete button (Organizer dialog box) to delete any selected macros.

5. When finished renaming macros, tap or click the Close button to close the dialog box.

Preparing a Document for Internationalization

Word provides internationalization features you can use when creating documents and templates. Use of features should be determined based on the intended audience of the document or template. By default, Word uses formatting consistent with the country or region selected when installing Windows. In addition to inserting symbols, such as those for currency, and using date and time formats that are recognized internationally or in other countries, you can set the language used for proofing tools and other language preferences.

BTW
BTWs
For a complete list of the BTWs found in the margins of this book, visit the BTW resource on the Student Companion Site located on www.cengagebrain.com. For detailed instructions about accessing available resources, visit www.cengage.com/ ct/studentdownload or contact your instructor for information about accessing the required files.

TO SET THE LANGUAGE FOR PROOFING TOOLS

If you wanted to change the language that Word uses to proof documents or templates, you would perform the following steps.

1. Tap or click the Language button (REVIEW tab | Language group) to display the Language menu.
2. Tap or click 'Set Proofing Language' on the Language menu to display the Language dialog box. (If you want to set this language as the default, tap or click the 'Set As Default' button.)
3. Select the desired language to use for proofing tools and then tap or click the OK button.

TO SET LANGUAGE PREFERENCES

If you wanted to change the language that Word uses for editing, display, Help, and ScreenTips, you would perform the following steps.

1. Tap or click the Language button (REVIEW tab | Language group) to display the Language menu and then tap or click Language Preferences on the Language menu to display the language settings in the Word Options dialog box. Or, open the Backstage view, tap or click Options in the left pane to display the Word Options dialog box, and then tap or click Language in the left pane (Word Options dialog box) to display the language settings.
2. Select language preferences for editing, display and Help, and ScreenTips, and then tap or click the OK button.

Enhancing a Document's Accessibility

Word provides several options for enhancing the accessibility of documents for individuals who have difficulty reading. Some previously discussed tasks you can perform to assist users include increasing zoom and font size, customizing the ribbon, ensuring tab/reading order in tables is logical, and using Read mode. You also can use the accessibility checker to locate and address problematic issues, and you can add alternative text to graphics and tables.

TO USE THE ACCESSIBILITY CHECKER

The accessibility checker scans a document and identifies issues that could affect a person's ability to read the content. Once identified, you can address each individual issue in the document. If you wanted to check accessibility of a document, you would perform the following steps.

1. Open the Backstage view and then, if necessary, display the Info gallery.
2. Tap or click the 'Check for Issues' button to display the Check for Issues menu.
3. Tap or click Check Accessibility on the Check for Issues menu, which scans the document and then displays accessibility issues in the Accessibility Checker task pane.
4. Address the errors and warnings in the Accessibility Checker task pane and then close the task pane.

BTW
Removing Metadata
If you wanted to remove document metadata, such as personal information and comments, you would do the following with the document open in a document window: open the Backstage view, tap or click the Info tab in the Backstage view to display the Info gallery, tap or click the 'Check for Issues' button in the Info gallery to display the Check for Issues menu, tap or click Inspect Document on the Check for Issues menu to display the Document Inspector dialog box, tap or click the Inspect button (Document Inspector dialog box) to instruct Word to inspect the document, review the results (Document Inspector dialog box), and then tap or click the Remove All button(s) for any item that you do not want to be saved with the document. When you have finished removing information, tap or click the Close button to close the dialog box.

To Add Alternative Text to Graphics

For users who have difficulty seeing images on the screen, you can include **alternate text**, also called **alt text**, to your graphics so that these users can see or hear the alternate text when working with your document. Graphics you can add alt text to include pictures, shapes, text boxes, SmartArt graphics, and charts. If you wanted to add alternative text to graphics, you would perform the following steps.

1. Tap or click the Format Shape Dialog Box Launcher (PICTURE TOOLS FORMAT tab | Picture Styles group or DRAWING TOOLS FORMAT tab or SMARTART TOOLS FORMAT tab or CHART TOOLS FORMAT tab | Shape Styles group); or press and hold the object, tap the 'Show Context Menu' button on the mini toolbar, and then tap Format Picture, Format Shape, Format Object, or Format Chart Area on the shortcut menu; or right-click the object and then click Format Picture, Format Shape, Format Object, or Format Chart Area on the shortcut menu to display the Format Picture, Format Shape, or Format Chart Area task pane.

2. Tap or click the 'Layout & Properties' button (Format Picture, Format Shape, or Format Chart Area task pane) and then, if necessary, expand the ALT TEXT section.

3. Type a brief title and then type a narrative description of the picture in the respective text boxes.

4. Close the task pane.

To Add Alternative Text to Tables

For users who have difficulty seeing tables on the screen, you can include alternative text to your tables so that these users can see or hear the alternative text when working with your document. If you wanted to add alternative text to a table, sometimes called a table title, you would perform the following steps.

1. Tap or click the Table Properties button (TABLE TOOLS LAYOUT tab | Table group); or press and hold the table, tap the 'Show Context Menu' button on the mini toolbar, and tap Table Properties on the shortcut menu; or right-click the table and then click Table Properties on the shortcut menu to display the Table Properties dialog box.

2. Tap or click the Alt Text tab (Table Properties dialog box) to display the Alt Text sheet.

3. Type a brief title and then type a narrative description of the table in the respective text boxes.

4. Tap or click the OK button to close the dialog box.

Table of Authorities

Legal documents often include a **table of authorities** to list references to cases, rules, statutes, etc., along with the page number(s) on which the references appear. To create a table of authorities, mark the citations first and then build the table of authorities. The procedures for marking citations, editing citations, creating the table of authorities, changing the format of the table of authorities, and updating the table of authorities are the same as those for indexes. The only difference is that you use the buttons in the Table of Authorities group on the REFERENCES tab instead of the buttons in the Index group.

TO MARK A CITATION

If you wanted to mark a citation, creating a citation entry, you would perform the following steps.

1. Select the long, full citation that you wish to appear in the table of authorities (for example, State v. Smith 220 J.3d 167 (UT, 1997)).
2. Tap or click the Mark Citation button (REFERENCES tab | Table of Authorities group) or press ALT+SHIFT+I to display the Mark Citation dialog box.
3. If necessary, tap or click the Category arrow (Mark Citation dialog box) and then select a new category type.
4. If desired, enter a short version of the citation in the Short citation text box.
5. Tap or click the Mark button to mark the selected text in the document as citation.

Q&A Why do formatting marks now appear on the screen?
When you mark a citation, Word automatically shows formatting marks (if they are not showing already) so that you can see the citation field. The citation entry begins with the letters, TA.

6. Tap or click the Close button in the Mark Citation dialog box.

Q&A How could I see all marked citation entries in a document?
With formatting marks displaying, you could scroll through the document, scanning for all occurrences of TA, or you could use the Navigation Pane (that is, place a check mark in the 'Open the Navigation Pane' check box (VIEW tab | Show group)) to find all occurrences of TA.

TO MARK MULTIPLE CITATIONS

Word leaves the Mark Citation dialog box open until you close it, which allows you to mark multiple citations without having to redisplay the dialog box repeatedly. To mark multiple citations, you would perform the following steps.

1. With the Mark Citation dialog box displayed, tap or click in the document window; scroll to and then select the next citation.
2. If necessary, tap or click the Selected text text box (Mark Citation dialog box) to display the selected text in the Selected text text box.
3. Tap or click the Mark button.
4. Repeat Steps 1 through 3 for all citations you wish to mark. When finished, tap or click the Close button in the dialog box.

TO EDIT A CITATION ENTRY

At some time, you may want to change a citation entry after you have marked it. For example, you may need to change the case of a letter. If you wanted to change a citation entry, you would perform the following steps.

1. Display formatting marks.
2. Locate the TA field for the citation entry you wish to change.
3. Change the text inside the quotation marks.
4. Update the table of authorities as described in the steps at the end of this section.

To Delete a Citation Entry

If you wanted to delete a citation entry, you would perform the following steps.

1. Display formatting marks.
2. Select the TA field for the citation entry you wish to delete.
3. Press the DELETE key, or tap or click the Cut button (HOME tab | Clipboard group), or press and hold or right-click the field and then tap or click Cut on the mini toolbar or shortcut menu.
4. Update the table of authorities as described in the steps at the end of this section.

To Build a Table of Authorities

Once all citations are marked, Word can build a table of authorities from the citation entries in the document. Recall that citation entries begin with TA, and they appear on the screen when formatting marks are displayed. When citation entries show on the screen, the document's pagination probably will be altered because of the extra text in the citation entries. Thus, be sure to hide formatting marks before building a table of authorities. To build a table of authorities, you would perform the following steps.

1. Position the insertion point at the location for the table of authorities.
2. Ensure that formatting marks are not displayed.
3. Tap or click the 'Insert Table of Authorities' button (REFERENCES tab | Table of Authorities group) to display the Table of Authorities dialog box.
4. If necessary, select the category to appear in the table of authorities by tapping or clicking the desired option in the Category list, or leave the default selection of All so that all categories will be displayed in the table of authorities.
5. If necessary, tap or click the Formats arrow (Table of Authorities dialog box) and then select the desired format for the table of authorities.
6. If necessary, tap or click the Tab leader arrow and then select the desired leader character in the list to specify the leader character to be displayed between the marked citation and the page number.
7. If you wish to display the word, passim, instead of page numbers for citations with more than four page references, select the Use passim check box.

Q&A What does the word, passim, mean?
Here and there.

8. Tap or click the OK button (Table of Authorities dialog box) to create a table of authorities using the specified settings at the location of the insertion point.

To Update a Table of Authorities

If you add, delete, or modify citation entries, you must update the table of authorities to display the new or modified citation entries. If you wanted to update a table of authorities, you would perform the following steps.

1. In the document window, tap or click the table of authorities to select it.
2. Tap or click the 'Update Table of Authorities' button (REFERENCES tab | Table of Authorities group) or press the F9 key to update the table of authorities.

To Change the Format of the Table of Authorities

If you wanted to change the format of the table of authorities, you would perform the following steps.

1. Tap or click the table of authorities to select it.
2. Tap or click the 'Insert Table of Authorities' button (REFERENCES tab | Table of Authorities group) to display the Table of Authorities dialog box.
3. Change settings in the dialog box as desired. To change the style of headings, alignment, etc., tap or click the Formats arrow and then tap or click From template; next tap or click the Modify button to display the Style dialog box, make necessary changes and then tap or click the OK button (Style dialog box).
4. Tap or click the OK button (Table of Authorities dialog box) to apply the changed settings.
5. Tap or click the OK button when Word asks if you want to replace the selected category of the table of authorities.

To Delete a Table of Authorities

If you wanted to delete a table of authorities, you would perform the following steps.

1. Tap or click the table of authorities to select it.
2. Press SHIFT+F9 to display field codes.
3. Drag through the entire field code, including the braces, and then press the DELETE key, or tap or click the Cut button (HOME tab | Clipboard group), or press and hold or right-click the field and then tap or click Cut on the mini toolbar or shortcut menu.

Working with XML

You can convert an online form to the XML format so that the data in the form can be shared with other programs, such as Microsoft Access. XML is a popular format for structuring data, which allows the data to be reused and shared. **XML**, which stands for Extensible Markup Language, is a language used to encapsulate data and a description of the data in a single text file, the **XML file**. XML uses **tags** to describe data items. Each data item is called an **element**. Businesses often create standard XML file layouts and tags to describe commonly used types of data.

In Word, you can save a file in a default XML format, in which Word parses the document into individual components that can be used by other programs. Or, you can identify specific sections of the document as XML elements; the elements then can be used in other programs, such as Access. This feature is available only in the stand-alone version of Microsoft Word and in Microsoft Office Professional.

To Save a Document in the Default XML Format

If you wanted to save a document in the XML format, you would perform the following steps.

1. Open the file to be saved in the XML format (for example, a form containing content controls).
2. Open the Backstage view and then tap or click Save As to display the Save As gallery.
3. Navigate to the desired save location and then display the Save As dialog box.
4. Tap or click the 'Save as type' arrow (Save As dialog box), tap or click 'Word XML Document' in the list, and then tap or click the Save button to save the template as an XML document.

Q&A | How can I identify an XML document?
XML documents typically have an .xml extension.

TO ATTACH A SCHEMA FILE

To identify sections of a document as XML elements, you first attach an XML schema to the document, usually one that contains content controls. An **XML schema** is a special type of XML file that describes the layout of elements in other XML files. Word users typically do not create XML schema files. Computer programmers or other technical personnel create an XML schema file and provide it to Word users. XML schema files, often simply called **schema files**, usually have an extension of .xsd. Once the schema is attached, you can use the XML Mapping Pane (DEVELOPER tab | Mapping group) to insert controls from the schema into the document. If you wanted to attach a schema file to a document, such as an online form, you would perform the following steps.

1. Open the file to which you wish to attach the schema, such as an online form that contains content controls.
2. Open the Backstage view and then use the Save As command to save the file with a new file name, to preserve the contents of the original file.
3. Tap or click the Document Template button (DEVELOPER tab | Templates group) to display the Templates and Add-ins dialog box.
4. Tap or click the XML Schema tab (Templates and Add-ins dialog box) to display the XML Schema sheet and then tap or click the Add Schema button to display the Add Schema dialog box.
5. Locate and select the schema file (Add Schema dialog box) and then tap or click the Open button to display the Schema Settings dialog box.
6. Enter the URI and alias in the appropriate text boxes (Schema Settings dialog box) and then tap or click the OK button to add the schema to the Schema Library and to add the namespace alias to the list of available schemas in the XML Schema sheet (Templates and Add-ins dialog box).

Q&A | What is a URI and an alias?
Word uses the URI, also called a **namespace**, to refer to the schema. Because these names are difficult to remember, you can define a namespace alias. In a setting outside of an academic environment, a computer administrator would provide you with the appropriate namespace entry.

7. If necessary, place a check mark in the desired schema's check box.
8. Tap or click the OK button, which causes Word to attach the selected schema to the open document and display the XML Structure task pane in the Word window.

TO DELETE A SCHEMA FROM THE SCHEMA LIBRARY

To delete a schema from a document, you would remove the check mark from the schema name's check box in the XML Schema sheet in the Templates and Add-ins dialog box. If you wanted to delete a schema altogether from the Schema Library, you would do the following.

1. Tap or click the Document Template button (DEVELOPER tab | Templates group) to display the Templates and Add-ins dialog box.
2. Tap or click the XML Schema tab (Templates and Add-ins dialog box) to display the XML Schema sheet and then tap or click the Schema Library button to display the Schema Library dialog box.
3. Tap or click the schema you want to delete in the Select a schema list (Schema Library dialog box) and then tap or click the Delete Schema button.
4. When Word displays the Schema Library dialog box asking if you are sure you wish to delete the schema, tap or click the Yes button.
5. Tap or click the OK button (Schema Library dialog box) and then tap or click the Cancel button (Templates and Add-ins dialog box).

BTW
Quick Reference
For a table that lists how to complete the tasks covered in this book using touch gestures, the mouse, ribbon, shortcut menu, and keyboard, see the Quick Reference Summary at the back of this book, or visit the Quick Reference resource on the Student Companion Site located on www.cengagebrain.com. For detailed instructions about accessing available resources, visit www.cengage.com/ct/studentdownload or contact your instructor for information about accessing the required files.

Chapter Summary

In this chapter, you learned how to enhance the look of text and graphics and automate a series of tasks with a macro. You also learned about several supplementary tasks that you should know if you plan to take the certification exam. The items listed below include all the new Word skills you have learned in this chapter, with the tasks grouped by activity.

Enter and Edit Text
Insert a Date Field (WD 685)
Edit a Field (WD 686)

File Management
Save a Macro-Enabled Template (WD 677)
Unprotect a Document (WD 718)
Add an Invisible Digital Signature to a Document (WD 718)
Add a Signature Line to a Document (WD 719)
Copy a Style from One Template or Document to Another (WD 719)
Copy a Macro from One Template or Document to Another (WD 720)
Save a Document in the Default XML Format (WD 726)
Attach a Schema File (WD 727)
Delete a Schema from the Schema Library (WD 727)

Format a Page
Use a Fill Effect for the Page Color (WD 693)

Format Text
Modify a Style Using the Styles Task Pane (WD 687)
Create a Character Style (WD 690)

Word Settings
Modify the Default Font Settings (WD 689)
Reset the Default Font Settings (WD 690)
Specify Macro Settings in Word (WD 679)
Record a Macro and Assign It a Shortcut Key (WD 707)
Run a Macro (WD 709)
Add a Command and a Macro as Buttons on the Quick Access Toolbar (WD 710)
Delete Buttons from the Quick Access Toolbar (WD 712)
Rename a Macro (WD 721)

Delete a Macro (WD 713)
Create an Automatic Macro (WD 713)
Edit a Macro's VBA Code (WD 715)
Rename a Style (WD 720)
Set the Language for Proofing Tools (WD 722)
Set Language Preferences (WD 722)
Use the Accessibility Checker (WD 722)

Work with Graphics
Change a Shape (WD 694)
Apply a Shadow Shape Effect (WD 696)
Fill a Shape with a Picture (WD 697)
Remove a Background (WD 699)
Apply an Artistic Effect (WD 699)
Draw a Text Box (WD 701)
Change Text Direction in a Text Box (WD 702)
Change a Shape Outline of a Text Box (WD 704)
Apply a 3-D Effect to a Text Box (WD 704)
Group Objects (WD 705)
Add Alternative Text to Graphics (WD 723)

Work with Tables
Convert a Table to Text (WD 682)
Add Alternative Text to Tables (WD 723)

Work with Tables of Authorities
Mark a Citation (WD 724)
Mark Multiple Citations (WD 724)
Edit a Citation Entry (WD 724)
Delete a Citation Entry (WD 725)
Build a Table of Authorities (WD 725)
Update a Table of Authorities (WD 725)
Change the Format of the Table of Authorities (WD 726)
Delete a Table of Authorities (WD 726)

CONSIDER THIS: PLAN AHEAD

What decisions will you need to make when creating macro-enabled and enhanced online forms?
Use these guidelines as you complete the assignments in this chapter and create your own online forms outside of this class.

1. Save the form to be modified as a macro-enabled template, if you plan to include macros in the template for the form.

2. Enhance the visual appeal of a form.

   a) Arrange data entry fields in logical groups on the form and in an order that users would expect.

   b) Draw the user's attention to important sections.

   c) Use colors and images that complement one another.

3. Add macros to automate tasks.

   a) Record macros, if possible.

   b) If you are familiar with computer programming, write VBA code to extend capabilities of recorded macros.

4. Determine how the form data will be analyzed.

   a) If the data entered in the form will be analyzed by a program outside of Word, create the data entry fields so that the entries are stored in a format that can be shared with other programs.

How should you submit solutions to questions in the assignments identified with a ✳ symbol?
Every assignment in this book contains one or more questions identified with a ✳ symbol. These questions require you to think beyond the assigned document. Present your solutions to the questions in the format required by your instructor. Possible formats may include one or more of these options: write the answer; create a document that contains the answer; present your answer to the class; discuss your answer in a group; record the answer as audio or video using a webcam, smartphone, or portable media player; or post answers on a blog, wiki, or website.

Apply Your Knowledge

Reinforce the skills and apply the concepts you learned in this chapter.

Working with Graphics, Shapes, and Fields

Note: To complete this assignment, you will be required to use the Data Files for Students. Visit www.cengage.com/ct/studentdownload for detailed instructions or contact your instructor for information about accessing the required files.

Instructions: Run Word. Open the template, Apply 11-1 Bradley Times Survey, from the Data Files for Students. In this assignment, you add an artistic effect to pictures, group images, change a shape, use a texture fill effect, and insert a date field (Figure 11–67).

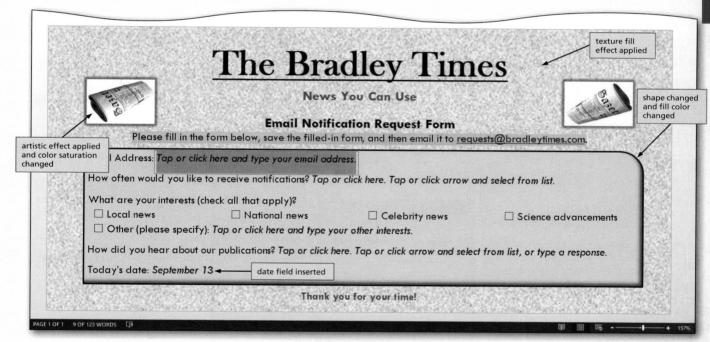

Figure 11–67

Perform the following tasks:

1. Unprotect the template.

2. Apply the Crisscross Etching artistic effect to both of the newspaper images. Change the color saturation of each image to 0%. Apply the following glow effect to each image: Dark Blue, 5 pt glow, Accent color 1.

3. Group the two newspaper images together. Move the grouped images down so that they are positioned just above the instruction line highlighted in yellow.

4. Change the page color to the Newsprint fill effect.

5. Change the shape around the data entry area from Rectangle to Round Single Corner Rectangle.

6. Change the fill color of the rectangle shape to Orange, Accent 5, Lighter 80%.

Continued >

Apply Your Knowledge continued

7. Apply the Inside Diagonal Bottom Right shadow to the rectangle shape.

8. Display the DEVELOPER tab. Change the properties of the date picker content control so that its contents can be deleted and then delete the content control. Insert a date field after the Today's Date: label in the format month day (i.e., September 13). Change the format of the displayed date field to Intense Emphasis. Hide the DEVELOPER tab.

9. If requested by your instructor, change the email address on the form to your email address.

10. Protect the form. Save the modified form using the file name, Apply 11-1 Bradley Times Survey Modified. Submit the revised template in the format specified by your instructor.

11. ✸ If you wanted to change the picture on the form, you could delete the current pictures and then insert new ones, or you could use the Change Picture button (PICTURE TOOLS FORMAT tab | Adjust group)? Which technique would you use and why?

Extend Your Knowledge

Extend the skills you learned in this chapter and experiment with new skills. You may need to use Help to complete the assignment.

Working with Document Security

Note: To complete this assignment, you will be required to use the Data Files for Students. Visit www.cengage.com/ct/studentdownload for detailed instructions or contact your instructor for information about accessing the required files.

Instructions: Run Word. Open the document, Extend 11-1 Credit Card Letter Draft, from the Data Files for Students. You will add a digital signature line, encrypt the document with a password, remove the password, and mark the document as final.

Figure 11–68

Perform the following tasks:

1. Use Help to review and expand your knowledge about these topics: signature lines, passwords, document encryption, and marking the document as final.

2. Add a digital signature line to end of the document (Figure 11–68). Use your personal information in the signature line.

3. Encrypt the document. Be sure to use a password you will remember.

4. Save the revised document with a new file name, Extend 11-1 Credit Card Letter Modified. Then, close the document and reopen it. Enter the password when prompted.

5. Remove the password from the document.

6. Mark the document as final.

7. Submit the document in the format specified by your instructor.

8. ✸ When you encrypted the document, what password did you use? Why did you choose that password? When you marked the document as final, what text appeared on the title bar? What text appeared in the Message Bar? What appeared on the status bar?

Analyze, Correct, Improve

Analyze a document, correct all errors, and improve it.

Formatting an Online Form

Note: To complete this assignment, you will be required to use the Data Files for Students. Visit www.cengage.com/ct/studentdownload for detailed instructions or contact your instructor for information about accessing the required files.

Instructions: Run Word. Open the template, Analyze 11-1 Harper Survey Draft, from the Data Files for Students. In this assignment, you change fill effects and a shape, modify a style, ungroup graphics, and format a text box (Figure 11–69).

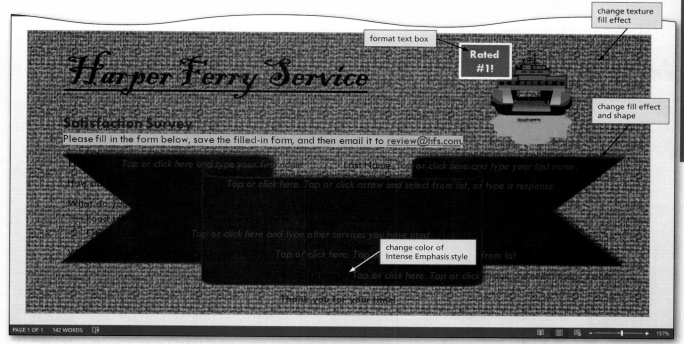

Figure 11–69

Perform the following tasks:

1. Correct In the online form, correct the following items:

    a. Unprotect the template.

    b. Change the page color fill effect to a texture that does not compete with the colors of the text on the form.

    c. Change the shape covering the data entry area to one of the rectangle shapes.

    d. Change the fill effect of the rectangle shape to a color that does not compete with the colors of the data entry instructions.

2. Improve Enhance the online form by changing the color of the Intense Emphasis style from the current color. Ungroup the graphic and text box. Add a glow effect to the graphic. Change the size of the text box so that the text fits on a single line. Change the shape style of the text box to one of your liking. Apply a 3-D rotation effect to the text box. Position the text box in a noticeable location on the form. Protect the form, changing the editing restrictions from Tracked changes to Filling in forms. If requested by your instructor, change the name, Harper, to your name. Save the modified document with the file name, Analyze 11-1 Harper Survey Modified, test the form, and then submit it in the format specified by your instructor.

3. ✺ Which texture fill effect did you choose and why?

In the Labs

Design and/or create a document using the guidelines, concepts, and skills presented in this chapter. Labs 1 and 2, which increase in difficulty, require you to create solutions based on what you learned in the chapter; Lab 3 requires you to create a solution, which uses cloud and web technologies, by learning and investigating on your own from general guidance.

Lab 1: Enhancing the Graphics, Shapes, and Text Boxes on an Online Form

Problem: You created the online form shown in Figure 10–78 on page WD 667 for Ozzie's Creamery. Your uncle has asked you to change the form's appearance and add a text box. You modify the form so that it looks like the one shown in Figure 11–70.

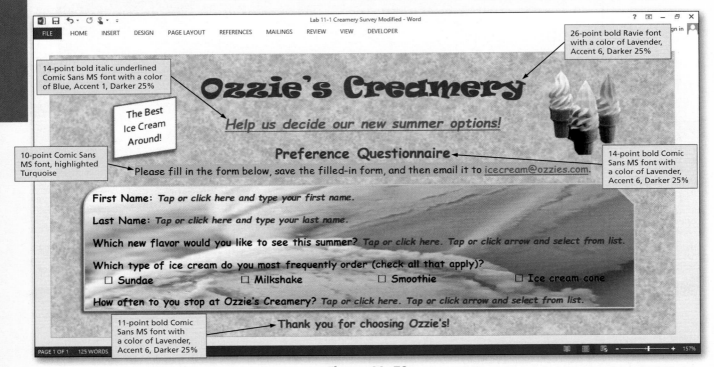

Figure 11–70

Perform the following tasks:

1. Open the template called Lab 10-1 Creamery Survey that you created in Lab 1 of Chapter 10. Save the template with a new file name of Lab 11-1 Creamery Survey Modified. If you did not complete the lab in Chapter 10, see your instructor for a copy. Unprotect the template.

2. Change the document theme to Parallax.

3. Use the Bouquet fill effect for the page color.

4. Modify the formats of the company name, business tag line, form title, user instruction, and thank you lines as shown in Figure 11–70 (or with similar fonts). If requested by your instructor, change the creamery name from Ozzie's to your first name.

5. Use the picture fill effect to place a picture in the rectangle shape. Use the picture called Ice Cream from the Data Files for Students. Change the color of the picture in the rectangle to Red, Accent color 4 Light.

6. Create a character style, with the name Data Entry Labels, for all labels in the data entry that starts with the current format and applies the bold format, uses 10-point Comic Sans MS font, and a color of Black, Text 1, Lighter 5%.

7. Change the shape of the rectangle to Snip and Round Single Corner Rectangle. Change the shape outline color (border) to Pink, Accent 5, Lighter 80%.

8. Apply the Offset Diagonal Bottom Left shadow effect to the rectangle shape. Change the shadow color to Lavender, Accent 6, Darker 25%. Change the transparency of the shadow to 20%.

9. Modify the Intense Emphasis style to the color Lavender, Accent 6, Darker 25% and apply the bold format.

10. Change the clip art on the right with the picture called Ice Cream Cones from the Data Files for Students. Remove the background, as shown in the figure. Apply the Marker artistic effect to the picture. Save the modified image with the file name, Ice Cream Cones Modified.

11. Delete the clip art on the left. Draw a text box that is approximately 0.77" × 0.93" that contains the text, The Best Ice Cream Around!, centered in the text box. Apply the Colored Outline – Lavender, Accent 6 shape style to the text box. Apply the Off Axis 1 Right 3-D rotation to the text box. Add an Offset Diagonal Bottom Left shadow to the text box. Position the text box as shown in the figure.

12. Adjust spacing above and below paragraphs as necessary so that all contents fit on a single screen. Protect the form. Save the form again and submit it in the format specified by your instructor.

13. Access the template through File Explorer. Fill in the form using personal data and submit the filled-in form in the format specified by your instructor.

14. ✹ What is the advantage of creating a style for the data entry labels?

Lab 2: **Enhancing the Look of an Online Form and Adding Macros to the Form**

Problem: You created the online form shown in Figure 10–79 on page WD 669 for Bard's Gym. Your supervisor has asked you to change the form's appearance, add a field, and add some macros. You modify the form so that it looks like the one shown in Figure 11–71.

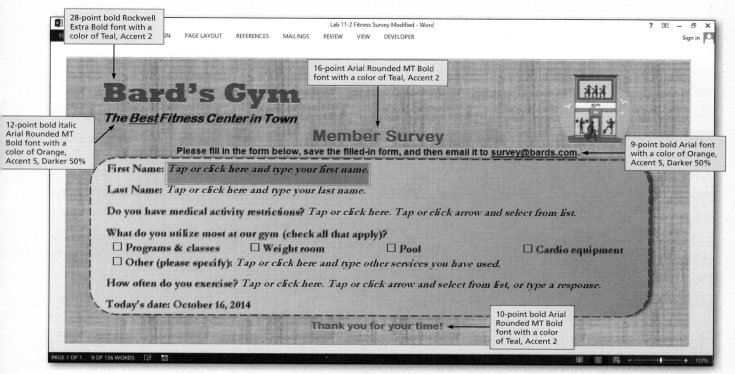

Figure 11–71

Continued >

In the Labs *continued*

Perform the following tasks:

1. Open the template called Lab 10-2 Fitness Survey that you created in Lab 2 of Chapter 10. Save the template as a macro-enabled template with a new file name of Lab 11-2 Fitness Survey Modified. If you did not complete the lab in Chapter 10, see your instructor for a copy. Unprotect the template.

2. Change the document theme to Organic.

3. Use the Papyrus fill effect for the page color.

4. Change the fill color in the rectangle shape to Green, Accent 1, Darker 25%. Apply the From Bottom Right Corner gradient fill effect to the rectangle shape, which lightens the fill color.

5. Modify the formats of the company name, business tag line, form title, user instruction, and thank you line as shown in Figure 11–71 on the previous page (or with similar fonts).

6. Convert the table to text for the 2 × 1 table containing the First Name and Last Name content controls. Change the left indent to 0.06".

7. Remove the Today's Date content control. Insert a date field from the Quick Parts gallery in the format October 16, 2014.

8. Modify the Normal style to include the bold format.

9. Change the text, Do you have medical conditions or injuries that restrict activity?, to the text, Do you have any medical activity restrictions?. Adjust spacing above and below paragraphs as necessary so that all contents fit on a single screen. Adjust the rectangle so that it covers the entire data entry area.

10. Change the current clip art to the one shown in the figure (or a similar image). Change the color of the image to Green, Accent color 1 Light. If necessary, resize the image and position it as shown.

11. Record a macro that hides the formatting marks and the rulers. Name it HideScreenElements. Assign it the shortcut key, ALT+H. Run the macro to test it.

12. Add a button to the Quick Access Toolbar for the macro created in Step 11. Test the button and then delete the button from the Quick Access Toolbar.

13. Create an automatic macro called AutoNew using the macro recorder. The macro should change the view to page width.

14. Edit the AutoNew macro so that it also hides the DEVELOPER tab and the ribbon.

15. Protect the form. Save the form again and submit it in the format specified by your instructor.

16. Access the template through File Explorer. Fill in the form and submit the filled-in form in the format specified by your instructor.

17. ✹ If a recorded macro does not work as intended when you test it, how would you fix it?

Lab 3: Expand Your World: Cloud and Web Technologies
Inserting Online Videos

Problem: You are interested in obtaining a digital ID so that you can digitally sign your documents in Word. You plan to research various digital ID services to determine the one best suited to your needs.

Instructions: Perform the following tasks:

1. Run Word. Open the Backstage view and then, if necessary, display the Info tab. Tap or click the Protect Document button and then tap or click 'Add a Digital Signature' on the Protect Document menu.

2. When Word displays the Get a Digital ID dialog box, tap or click the Yes button, which runs a browser and displays an Office Help window with a list of services that issue digital IDs (Figure 11–72).

3. Tap or click the link beside each service to learn more about each one.

4. Use a search engine to read reviews about these services.

5. Compose a Word document comparing and contrasting the digital ID services suggested by Microsoft. Be sure to cite your sources. In your report, recommend the service you feel best suits your needs.

6. ✳ Which digital ID services did you evaluate? When you read the reviews, were there other services not listed on the Office website? If so, what were their names? Which digital ID service would you recommend? Why?

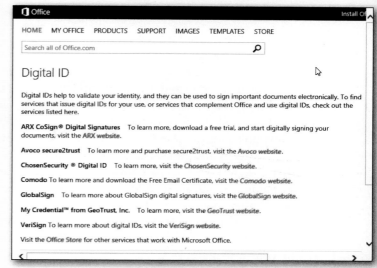

Figure 11–72

Consider This: Your Turn

Apply your creative thinking and problem solving skills to design and implement a solution.

1: Modify an Online Form for a School

Personal

Part 1: You created the student seminar survey online form for Holland College that was defined in Consider This: Your Turn Assignment 1 in Chapter 10 on page WD 671. Your supervisor was pleased with the initial design. You and your supervisor, however, believe the form can be improved by enhancing its appearance. Make the following modifications to the form: Change the school name, tag line, and form title to a different font and color; change the page color to a texture; change the highlight color; and change the font and color of the last line. Change the rectangle shape around the data entry area. In the rectangle, add a picture fill effect using the School Building file on the Data Files for Students (or a similar image) and recolor it using the Washout color. Change the color of the shadow in the rectangle. Delete the existing clip art, replace it with the picture called Tulips on the Data Files for Students (or a similar image), and apply an artistic effect to the picture. Draw a text box with the text, Your opinion counts!, and apply a 3-D effect to the text box.

Specify the appropriate macro security level. Record a macro that hides screen elements and then assign the macro to a button on the Quick Access Toolbar. Record another macro for a task you would like to automate. Add another button to the Quick Access Toolbar for any Word command not on the ribbon.

Use the concepts and techniques presented in this chapter to modify the online form. Be sure to save it as a macro-enabled template. Protect the form, test it, and submit it in the format specified by your instructor.

Part 2: ✳ You made several decisions while creating the online form in this assignment: formats to use (i.e., fonts, font sizes, colors, styles, etc.), graphics to use, which task to automate, and which button to add to the Quick Access Toolbar. What was the rationale behind each of these decisions? When you proofread and tested the online form, what further revisions did you make, and why?

2: Modify an Online Form for a Law Office

Professional

Part 1: You created the client survey online form for Clark Law that was defined in Consider This: Your Turn Assignment 2 in Chapter 10 on page WD 671. Your supervisor was pleased with the initial design. You and your supervisor, however, believe the form can be improved by enhancing its appearance. Make the following modifications to the form: Change the firm name, tag line, and

Continued >

Consider This: Your Turn *continued*

form title to a different font and color; change the page color to a texture; change the highlight color; and change the font and color of the last line. Change the rectangle shape around the data entry area. In the rectangle, add a picture fill effect using the Scales of Justice file on the Data Files for Students (or a similar image) and recolor it using the Washout color. Change the color of the shadow in the rectangle. Delete the existing clip art, replace it with the picture called Courthouse on the Data Files for Students (or a similar image), and apply an artistic effect to the picture. Draw a text box with the text, Your opinion counts!, and apply a 3-D effect to the text box.

Specify the appropriate macro security level. Record a macro that hides screen elements and then assign the macro to a button on the Quick Access Toolbar. Record another macro for a task you would like to automate. Add another button to the Quick Access Toolbar for any Word command not on the ribbon.

Use the concepts and techniques presented in this chapter to modify the online form. Be sure to save it as a macro-enabled template. Protect the form, test it, and submit it in the format specified by your instructor.

Part 2: ✷ You made several decisions while creating the online form in this assignment: formats to use (i.e., fonts, font sizes, colors, styles, etc.), graphics to use, which task to automate, and which button to add to the Quick Access Toolbar. What was the rationale behind each of these decisions? When you proofread and tested the online form, what further revisions did you make, and why?

3: Modify an Online Form for a Campus Group
Research and Collaboration

Part 1: Your team created the online form for a campus group at your school, which was defined in Consider This: Your Turn Assignment 3 in Chapter 10 on page WD 672. Your team was pleased with the initial design but believe the form can be improved by enhancing its appearance. Make the following modifications to the form: Change the school name, tag line, and form title to a different font and color; change the page color to a texture; change the highlight color; and change the font and color of the last line. Change the shape around the data entry area. In the rectangle, add a picture fill effect using an appropriate picture of your choice and recolor it accordingly. Change the color of the shadow in the rectangle. Delete the existing clip art, replace it with a picture of your choice, and apply an artistic effect to the picture. Add a text box to the form and apply a 3-D effect to the text box.

Specify the appropriate macro security level. Record a macro that hides screen elements and then assign the macro to a button on the Quick Access Toolbar. Record another macro for a task you would like to automate. Add another button to the Quick Access Toolbar for any Word command not on the ribbon.

Use the concepts and techniques presented in this chapter to modify the online form. Be sure to save it as a macro-enabled template. Protect the form, test it, and submit it in the format specified by your instructor.

Part 2: ✷ You made several decisions while creating the online form in this assignment: formats to use (i.e., fonts, font sizes, colors, styles, etc.), graphics to use, which task to automate, and which button to add to the Quick Access Toolbar. What was the rationale behind each of these decisions? When you proofread and tested the online form, what further revisions did you make, and why?

Learn Online

Learn Online – Reinforce what you learned in this chapter with games, exercises, training, and many other online activities and resources.

Student Companion Site Reinforcement activities and resources are available at no additional cost on www.cengagebrain.com. Visit www.cengage.com/ct/studentdownload for detailed instructions about accessing the resources available at the Student Companion Site.

SAM Put your skills into practice with SAM! If you have a SAM account, go to www.cengage .com/sam2013 to access SAM assignments for this chapter.

8 | Customizing a Template and Handouts Using Masters

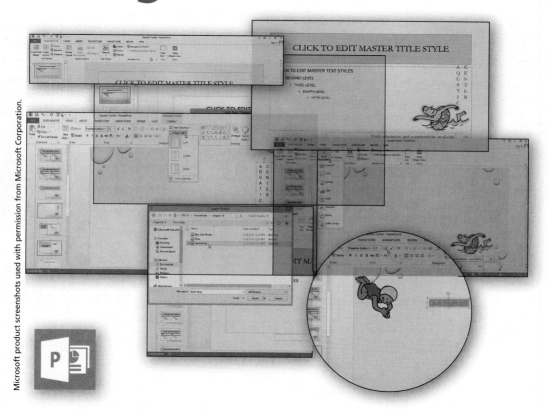

Objectives

You will have mastered the material in this chapter when you can:

- Apply slide and font themes to a slide master

- Change a slide master background

- Add a background style and graphic to a slide master

- Insert a placeholder into a slide layout

- Apply a Quick Style to a placeholder

- Change text direction and character spacing

- Hide background graphics on individual slides

- Apply a fill to a text box and change transparency

- Rename a slide master

- Save a slide master as a template

- Create handouts using the handout master

- Create speaker notes using the notes master

8 | Customizing a Template and Handouts Using Masters

Introduction

BTW

Masters Give a Unique and Uniform Look

Masters are convenient because they allow you to make universal style changes to every slide in your presentation, including ones added later. Using slide masters saves time because you don't have to format every slide or type the same information repeatedly. You can customize the presentation theme and slide layouts, including the background, color, fonts, effects, and placeholder sizes and location.

PowerPoint provides a variety of designs and layouts to meet most presenters' needs. At times, however, you may need a different set of colors, fonts, placeholders, or graphics to display throughout a presentation. PowerPoint allows you to customize the master layouts for slides, handouts, and speaker notes. These masters specify the precise locations and styles of placeholders, pictures, text boxes, and other slide and handout elements.

Once you determine your custom specifications in these masters, you can save the file as a template so that you can reuse these key elements as a starting point for multiple presentations. This unique **template** is a set of special slides you create and then use to create similar presentations. A template consists of a general master slide layout that has elements common to all the slide layouts. One efficient way to create similar presentations is to create a template, save the template, open the template, and then save the slides as a different PowerPoint presentation each time a new presentation is required.

Templates help speed and simplify the process of creating a presentation, so many PowerPoint designers create a template for common presentations they develop frequently. Templates can have a variable number of slide layouts depending upon the complexity of the presentation. A simple presentation can have a few slide layouts; for example, the Aquatic Center presentation will have three slide layouts. A more complex template can have many slide masters and layouts.

Project — Presentation with Customized Slide, Handout, and Notes Masters

BTW

Multiple Slide Masters

You can insert additional slide masters in one file so that one presentation can have two or more different styles. Each slide master has a related set of layout masters. In contrast, however, one presentation can have only one handout master and one notes master.

The community pool has evolved into full-fledged aquatic centers. These facilities offer a wide variety of events and amenities for residents of all ages. Many aquatic centers, including the facility you will feature in this project, feature water slides, wading pools, water aerobics, swimming and diving lessons, lifeguard certification, and birthday parties. The project in this chapter (Figure 8–1) promotes these components. All three slides are created by starting with a template file that contains two basic slide elements: the Aquatic Center's name on a formatted placeholder and an illustration of a man floating. The overall template, called the **slide master** (Figure 8–1a), is formatted with a theme, customized title and text fonts, and customized footer placeholders for the slide layouts. The title slide layout (Figure 8–1b) is used to create Slide 1 (Figure 8–1c), which introduces audiences to the Aquatic Center. Similarly, the blank slide layout (Figure 8–1d) is used for Slide 2 (Figure 8–1e), which promotes the new water slide. The title and content layout (Figure 8–1f on page PPT 476) is used to create the text and graphic on Slide 3 (Figure 8–1g). In addition, the custom handout master

(Figure 8–1h on the next page) is used to create a handout with a diver illustration and header and footer text (Figure 8–1i). Likewise, the custom notes master (Figure 8–1j on page PPT 477) is used to create speaker notes pages (Figures 8–1k, 8–1l, and 8–1m).

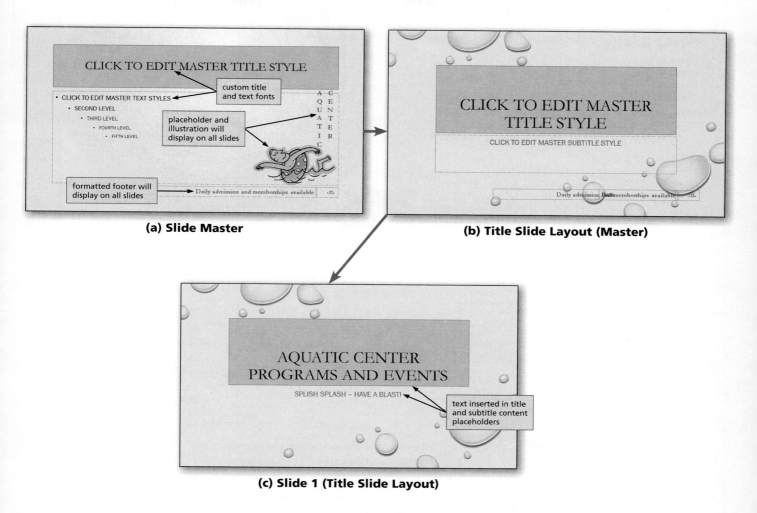

(a) Slide Master

(b) Title Slide Layout (Master)

(c) Slide 1 (Title Slide Layout)

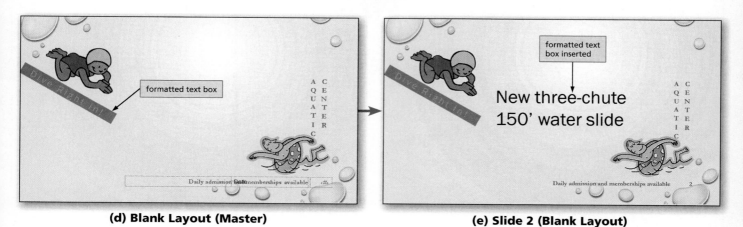

(d) Blank Layout (Master)

(e) Slide 2 (Blank Layout)

Figure 8–1

(f) Title and Content Layout (Master)   **(g) Slide 3 (Title and Content Layout)**

(h) Handout Master

(i) Handout

Figure 8–1 (Continued)

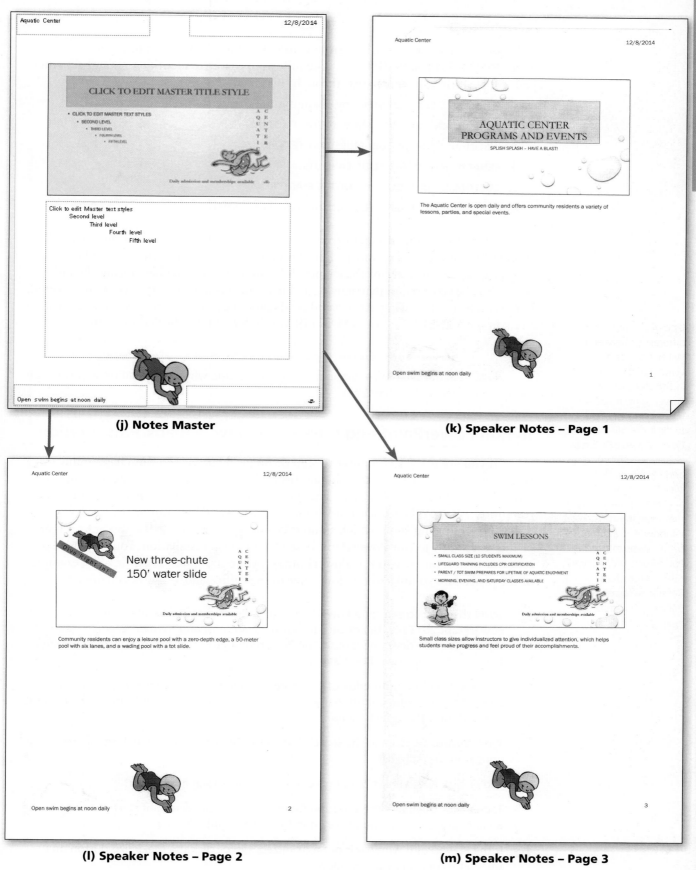

(j) Notes Master

(k) Speaker Notes – Page 1

(l) Speaker Notes – Page 2

(m) Speaker Notes – Page 3

Figure 8–1 (Continued)

Roadmap

In this chapter, you will learn how to create the slides shown in Figure 8–1 on pages PPT 475 through PPT 477. The following roadmap identifies general activities you will perform as you progress through this chapter:

1. CUSTOMIZE SLIDE MASTERS by changing the theme fonts and background.
2. FORMAT and ARRANGE slide master FOOTERS.
3. INSERT and FORMAT GRAPHICS and TEXT BOXES.
4. RENAME and DELETE SLIDE LAYOUTS.
5. CUSTOMIZE HANDOUT and NOTES MASTERS.
6. USE a CUSTOM TEMPLATE to create a new presentation.

At the beginning of step instructions throughout the chapter, you will see an abbreviated form of this roadmap. The abbreviated roadmap uses colors to indicate chapter progress: gray means the chapter is beyond that activity; blue means the task being shown is covered in that activity, and black means that activity is yet to be covered. For example, the following abbreviated roadmap indicates the chapter would be showing a task in the 3 INSERT & FORMAT GRAPHICS & TEXT BOXES activity.

1 CUSTOMIZE SLIDE MASTERS | 2 FORMAT & ARRANGE FOOTERS | **3 INSERT & FORMAT GRAPHICS & TEXT BOXES**
4 RENAME & DELETE SLIDE LAYOUTS | 5 CUSTOMIZE HANDOUT & NOTES MASTERS | 6 USE CUSTOM TEMPLATE

Use the abbreviated roadmap as a progress guide while you read or step through the instructions in this chapter.

To Run PowerPoint and Create and Save a Blank Presentation

If you are using a computer to step through the project in this chapter and you want your screens to match the figures in this book, you should change your screen's resolution to 1366×768. For information about how to change a computer's resolution, refer to the Office and Windows chapter at the beginning of this book.

The following steps, which assume Windows 8 is running, use the Start screen or the search box to run PowerPoint based on a typical installation. You may need to ask your instructor how to run PowerPoint on your computer. For a detailed example of the procedure summarized below, refer to the Office and Windows chapter.

1 Scroll the Start screen for a PowerPoint 2013 tile. If your Start screen contains a PowerPoint 2013 tile, tap or click it to run PowerPoint and then proceed to Step 5; if the Start screen does not contain the PowerPoint 2013 tile, proceed to the next step to search for the PowerPoint app.

2 Swipe in from the right edge of the screen or point to the upper-right corner of the screen to display the Charms bar and then tap or click the Search charm on the Charms bar to display the Search menu.

3 Type **PowerPoint** as the search text in the Search box and watch the search results appear in the Apps list.

4 Tap or click PowerPoint 2013 in the search results to run PowerPoint.

5 Tap or click the Blank Presentation thumbnail on the PowerPoint start screen to create a blank presentation and display it in the PowerPoint window.

6 If the PowerPoint window is not maximized, tap or click the Maximize button on its title bar to maximize the window.

One of the few differences between Windows 7 and Windows 8 occurs in the steps to run PowerPoint. If you are using Windows 7, tap or click the Start button, type **PowerPoint** in the 'Search programs and files' box, tap or click PowerPoint 2013, and then, if necessary, maximize the PowerPoint window. For a summary of the steps to run PowerPoint in Windows 7, refer to the Quick Reference located at the back of this book.

To Save a Presentation with a New File Name

You should save the presentation on your hard disk, SkyDrive, or a location that is most appropriate to your situation.

The following steps assume you already have created folders for storing your files, for example, a CIS 101 folder (for your class) that contains a PowerPoint folder (for your assignments). Thus, these steps save the presentation in the PowerPoint folder in the CIS 101 folder on your desired save location. For a detailed example of the procedure for saving a file in a folder or saving a file on SkyDrive, refer to the Office and Windows chapter at the beginning of this book.

1 Tap or click the Save button on the Quick Access Toolbar, which depending on settings, will display either the Save As gallery in the Backstage view or the Save As dialog box.

2 To save on a hard disk or other storage media on your computer, proceed to Step 2a. To save on SkyDrive, proceed to Step 2b.

2a If your screen opens the Backstage view and you want to save on storage media on your computer, tap or click Computer in the left pane, if necessary, to display options in the right pane related to saving on your computer. If your screen already displays the Save As dialog box, proceed to Step 4.

2b If your screen opens the Backstage view and you want to save on SkyDrive, tap or click SkyDrive in the left pane to display SkyDrive saving options or a Sign In button. If your screen displays a Sign In button, tap or click it and then sign in to SkyDrive.

3 Tap or click the Browse button in the right pane to display the Save As dialog box associated with the selected save location (i.e., Computer or SkyDrive).

4 Type **Aquatic Center** in the File name box to change the file name. Do not press the ENTER key after typing the file name because you do not want to close the dialog box at this time.

5 Navigate to the desired save location (in this case, the PowerPoint folder in the CIS 101 folder [or your class folder] on your computer or SkyDrive).

6 Tap or click the Save button (Save As dialog box) to save the document in the selected folder on the selected save location with the entered file name.

Customizing Presentation Slide Master Backgrounds and Fonts

PowerPoint has many template files with the file extension .potx. Each template file has three masters: slide, handout, and notes. A slide master has at least one layout; you have used many of these layouts, such as Title and Content, Two Content, and Picture with Caption, to create presentations. A **handout master** designates the placement of text, such as page numbers, on a sheet of paper intended to distribute to audience members. A **notes master** defines the formatting for speaker's notes.

Slide Master

If you select a document theme and want to change one of its components on every slide, you can override that component by changing the slide master. In addition, if you want your presentation to have a unique design, you might want to

BTW

The Ribbon and Screen Resolution
PowerPoint may change how the groups and buttons within the groups appear on the ribbon, depending on the computer's screen resolution. Thus, your ribbon may look different from the ones in this book if you are using a screen resolution other than 1366 × 768.

BTW
Q&As
For a complete list of the Q&As found in many of the step-by-step sequences in this book, visit the Q&A resource on the Student Companion Site located on www.cengagebrain.com. For detailed instructions about accessing available resources, visit www.cengage.com/ct/studentdownload or see the inside back cover of this book.

create a slide master rather than attempt to modify a current document theme. A slide master indicates the size and position of text and object placeholders, font styles, slide backgrounds, transitions, and effects. Any change to the slide master results in changing that component on every slide in the presentation. For example, if you change the second-level bullet on the slide master, each slide with a second-level bullet will display this new bullet format.

One presentation can have more than one slide master. You may find two or more slide masters are necessary when your presentation reuses special slide layouts. In this Aquatic Center presentation, for example, one slide will have the title slide to introduce the overall concept, another will have a blank slide to showcase a new water slide, and a third slide will have a title and a bulleted list to give specific information about swim lessons. All slides will have an illustration of a man floating in a swim tube and the words, Aquatic Center, on the slide master.

CONSIDER THIS

Plan the slide master.
Using a new slide master gives you the freedom to specify every slide element. Like an artist with a new canvas or a musician with blank sheet music, your imagination permits you to create an appealing master that conveys the overall look of your presentation.

Before you start developing the master, give your overall plan some careful thought. The decisions you make at this point should be reflected on every slide. A presentation can have several master layouts, but you should change these layouts only if you have a compelling need to change them. Use the concepts you read throughout the chapters in this book to guide your decisions about fonts, colors, backgrounds, art, and other essential slide elements.

To Display a Slide Master

1 CUSTOMIZE SLIDE MASTERS | 2 FORMAT & ARRANGE FOOTERS | 3 INSERT & FORMAT GRAPHICS & TEXT BOXES
4 RENAME & DELETE SLIDE LAYOUTS | 5 CUSTOMIZE HANDOUT & NOTES MASTERS | 6 USE CUSTOM TEMPLATE

To begin developing the Aquatic Center slides, you need to display the slide master. *Why? The slide master allows you to customize the slide components and create a unique design.* The following steps display the slide master.

1
- Tap or click VIEW on the ribbon to display the VIEW tab (Figure 8–2).

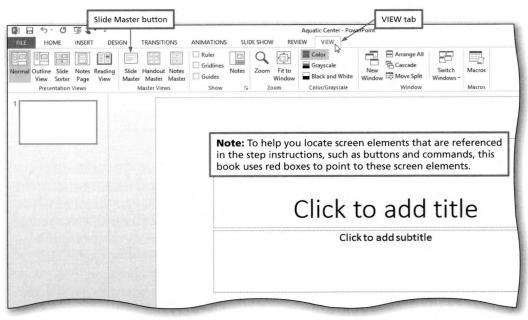

Figure 8–2

- Tap or click the Slide Master button (VIEW tab | Master Views group) to display the SLIDE MASTER tab and the slide thumbnails in the Overview pane.

- If necessary, scroll up and then tap or click the Office Theme Slide Master layout (Figure 8–3).

Q&A

What are all the other thumbnails in the left pane below the slide master?

They are all the slide layouts associated with this slide master. You have used many of these layouts in the presentations you have developed in the exercises in this book.

Why is the layout given this name? The slide layout names begin with the theme applied to the slides. In this case, the default Office Theme is applied. The first slide layout in the list is called the master because it controls the colors, fonts, and objects that are displayed on all the other slides in the presentation.

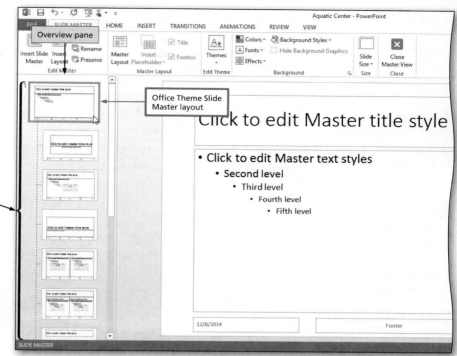

Figure 8–3

To Apply Slide and Font Themes to a Slide Master

1 CUSTOMIZE SLIDE MASTERS | 2 FORMAT & ARRANGE FOOTERS | 3 INSERT & FORMAT GRAPHICS & TEXT BOXES
4 RENAME & DELETE SLIDE LAYOUTS | 5 CUSTOMIZE HANDOUT & NOTES MASTERS | 6 USE CUSTOM TEMPLATE

You can change the look of an entire presentation by applying formats to the slide master in the same manner that you apply these formats to individual slides. In this presentation, you will change the slide theme to Droplet and the font colors to blue and green. *Why? The Droplet theme features water drops along the edges and colors that match the aquatic topic of this presentation.* The following steps apply a theme and change the font theme colors.

- With the slide master displaying, tap or click the Themes button (SLIDE MASTER tab | Edit Theme group) to display the Themes gallery.

- Scroll down to display the Droplet theme in the gallery (Figure 8–4).

Experiment

- If you are using a mouse, point to various themes in the Themes gallery and watch the colors and fonts change on the slide master.

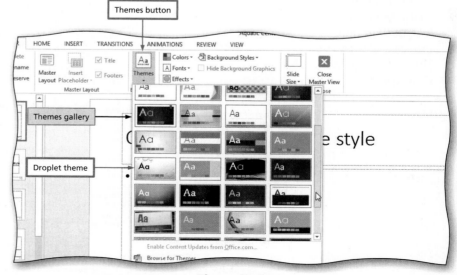

Figure 8–4

2

- Tap or click the Droplet theme to apply this theme to the slide master.

- Tap or click the Theme Colors button (SLIDE MASTER tab | Background group) to display the Theme Colors gallery (Figure 8–5).

3

- Tap or click the Blue color scheme in the Theme Colors gallery to change the slide master colors to Blue.

 Q&A Can I insert another set of slide masters to give other slides in the presentation a unique look?

Yes. PowerPoint allows you to insert multiple masters into an existing presentation.

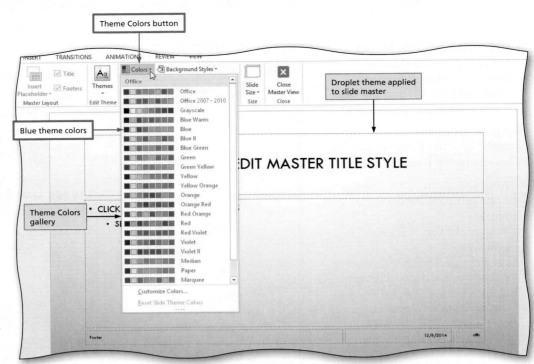

Figure 8–5

To Customize Theme Fonts

1 CUSTOMIZE SLIDE MASTERS | 2 FORMAT & ARRANGE FOOTERS | 3 INSERT & FORMAT GRAPHICS & TEXT BOXES
4 RENAME & DELETE SLIDE LAYOUTS | 5 CUSTOMIZE HANDOUT & NOTES MASTERS | 6 USE CUSTOM TEMPLATE

Each theme has a heading font and a body font applied to it. At times both fonts are the same, and other times, the heading font differs from the body font, but both fonts coordinate with each other. You can customize theme fonts by selecting your own combination of heading and body font and then giving the new theme font set a unique name. ***Why?*** *A particular font may match the tone of the presentation and help convey the message you are presenting.* The following steps apply a new heading and body font to the Droplet theme.

1

- Tap or click the Theme Fonts button (SLIDE MASTER tab | Background group) to display the Theme Fonts gallery (Figure 8–6).

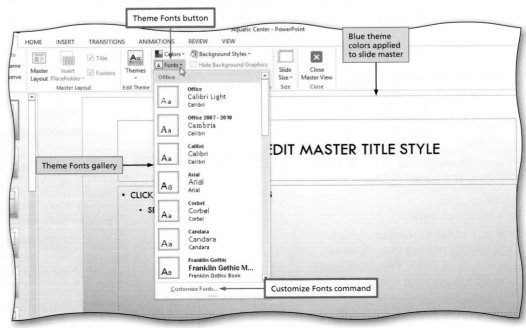

Figure 8–6

- Tap or click Customize Fonts in the Theme Fonts gallery to display the Create New Theme Fonts dialog box.

- Tap or click the Heading font arrow and then scroll to display Garamond in the list (Figure 8–7).

Q&A Can I preview the fonts to see how they are displayed on the slide master?

No preview is available when using the Create New Theme Fonts dialog box. Once you select the font, however, PowerPoint will display text in the Sample box.

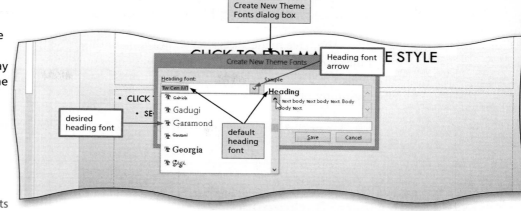

Figure 8–7

- Tap or click Garamond to apply that font as the new heading text font.

- Tap or click the Body font arrow and then scroll to display Franklin Gothic Book in the list (Figure 8–8).

Q&A What if the Garamond or Franklin Gothic Book fonts are not in my list of fonts?

Select fonts that resemble the fonts shown in Figure 8–8.

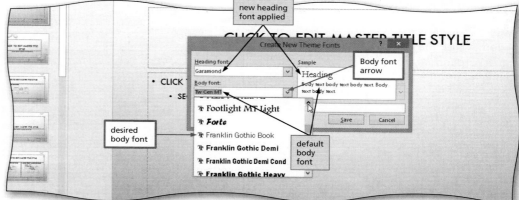

Figure 8–8

- Tap or click Franklin Gothic Book to apply that font as the new body text font.

- Select the text, Custom 1, in the Name text box and then type **Swim** to name the new font set (Figure 8–9).

Q&A Must I name this font set I just created?

No. If you name the set, however, you easily will recognize this combination in your font set if you want to use it in new presentations. It will display in the Custom area of the Fonts gallery.

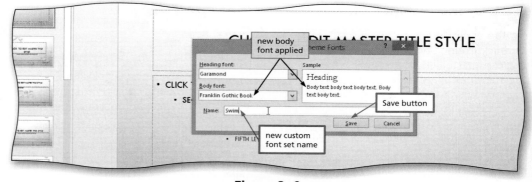

Figure 8–9

- Tap or click the Save button (Create New Theme Fonts dialog box) to save this new font set with the name, Swim, and to display the font changes in the slide master.

To Save an Existing Presentation with the Same File Name

You have made several modifications to the presentation since you last saved it. Thus, you should save it again. The following step saves the presentation again. For an example of the step listed below, refer to the Office and Windows chapter at the beginning of this book.

1 Tap or click the Save button on the Quick Access Toolbar to overwrite the previously saved file.

To Format a Slide Master Background and Apply a Quick Style

1 CUSTOMIZE SLIDE MASTERS | 2 FORMAT & ARRANGE FOOTERS | 3 INSERT & FORMAT GRAPHICS & TEXT BOXES
4 RENAME & DELETE SLIDE LAYOUTS | 5 CUSTOMIZE HANDOUT & NOTES MASTERS | 6 USE CUSTOM TEMPLATE

Once you have applied a theme to the slide master and determined the fonts for the presentation, you can further customize the presentation. *Why? Adding a unique background and customizing the colors can give your presentation a unique look that matches the message you are conveying.* The following steps format the slide master background and then apply a Quick Style.

1
- Tap or click the Background Styles button (SLIDE MASTER tab | Background group) to display the Background Styles gallery (Figure 8–10).

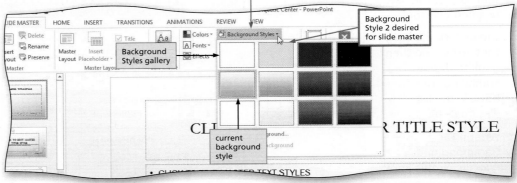

Experiment
- If you are using a mouse, point to various styles in the Background Styles gallery and watch the backgrounds change on the slide master title text placeholder.

Figure 8–10

2
- Tap or click Background Style 2 (second style in first row) to apply this background to the slide master (Figure 8–11).

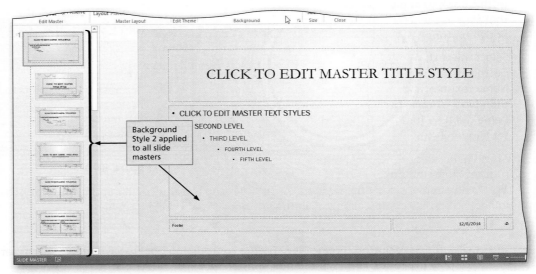

Figure 8–11

3

- Tap or click the slide master title text placeholder to select it.

- Display the HOME tab and then tap or click the Quick Styles button (HOME tab | Drawing group) to display the Quick Styles gallery (Figure 8–12).

 Experiment

- If you are using a mouse, point to various styles in the Quick Styles gallery and watch the background and borders change on the slide master title text placeholder.

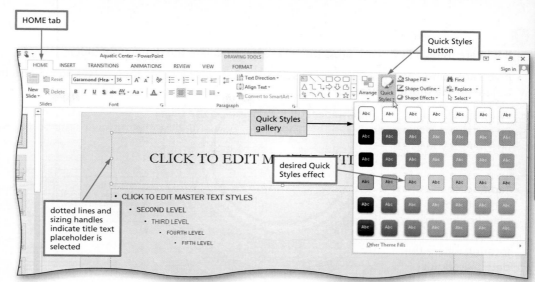

Figure 8–12

4

- Tap or click the Subtle Effect – Turquoise, Accent 2 Quick Style (third style in the fourth row) to apply this style to the title text placeholder (Figure 8–13).

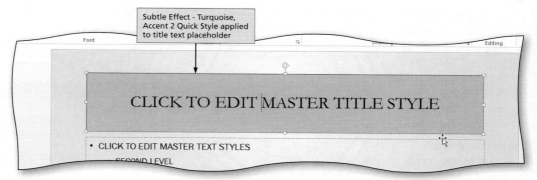

Figure 8–13

To Delete, Move, and Add Text to a Slide Master Footer

1 CUSTOMIZE SLIDE MASTERS | 2 FORMAT & ARRANGE FOOTERS | 3 INSERT & FORMAT GRAPHICS & TEXT BOXES
4 RENAME & DELETE SLIDE LAYOUTS | 5 CUSTOMIZE HANDOUT & NOTES MASTERS | 6 USE CUSTOM TEMPLATE

Slide numbers, the date and time, and footer text can be displayed anywhere on a slide, not just in the default footer placeholder locations. At times you may want to rearrange or delete these slide elements. *Why? These placeholders may interfere with other slide content, or you may not want to display information, such as a page number or the date.* The following steps delete one footer placeholder, move the footer placeholders, and then add footer text.

1

- With the slide master displaying, tap or click the border of the date footer placeholder to select it (Figure 8–14).

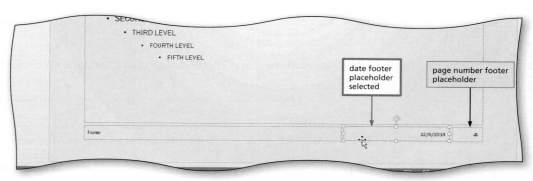

Figure 8–14

2

- If you are using a keyboard, press the DELETE key to delete the date placeholder.

- If you are using a touch screen, tap to select the date placeholder, then press and hold on the placeholder and tap Delete on the shortcut menu.

Q&A What should I do if the placeholder still is showing on the slide?

Be certain you tapped or clicked the placeholder border and not just the text. The border must display as a solid line before you can delete it.

3

- Tap or click the content footer placeholder and then drag it to the location where the date placeholder originally appeared (Figure 8–15).

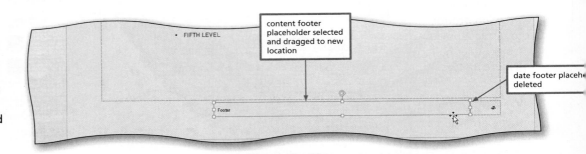

Figure 8–15

4

- Display the INSERT tab, tap or click the Header & Footer button (INSERT tab | Text group), and then place a check mark in the Slide number check box.

- Place a check mark in the Footer check box and then type **Daily admission and memberships available** in the Footer text box.

- Place a check mark in the 'Don't show on title slide' check box (Figure 8–16).

Q&A Can I verify where the footer placeholders will display on the slide layout?

Yes. The black boxes in the bottom of the Preview area indicate the footer placeholders' locations.

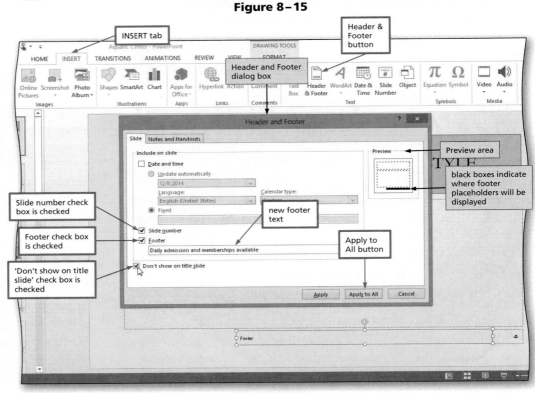

Figure 8–16

5

- Tap or click the 'Apply to All' button (Header and Footer dialog box) to add the slide number and footer text to the slide master.

To Format Slide Master Footer Text

1 CUSTOMIZE SLIDE MASTERS | 2 FORMAT & ARRANGE FOOTERS | 3 INSERT & FORMAT GRAPHICS & TEXT BOXES
4 RENAME & DELETE SLIDE LAYOUTS | 5 CUSTOMIZE HANDOUT & NOTES MASTERS | 6 USE CUSTOM TEMPLATE

You can format footer text using the same font styles and text attributes available to title and subtitle text. **Why?** *Using the same font ensures continuity among the slide elements.* The following steps format the footer text.

1

- Display the HOME tab, select the content footer text, and then tap or click the Font arrow to display the Font gallery (Figure 8–17).

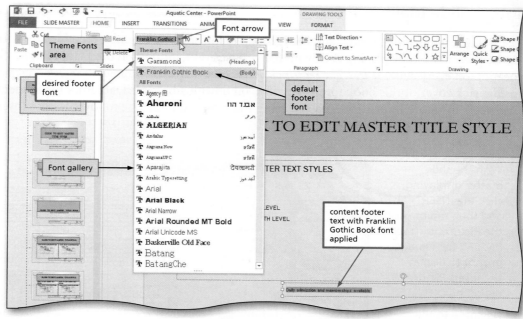

Figure 8–17

2

- Tap or click Garamond in the Theme Fonts section of the Font gallery (HOME tab | Font group) to change the footer font.
- Tap or click the Increase Font Size button several times to increase the font size from 10 to 18 point.
- Change the font color to Blue, Accent 1 (fifth color in the first row).
- Tap or click the Bold button to bold the text.
- Tap or click the Align Right button (HOME tab | Paragraph group) to move the footer text alignment to the right border of the placeholder.
- Use the Format Painter to apply the content footer placeholder formatting to the page number placeholder (Figure 8–18).

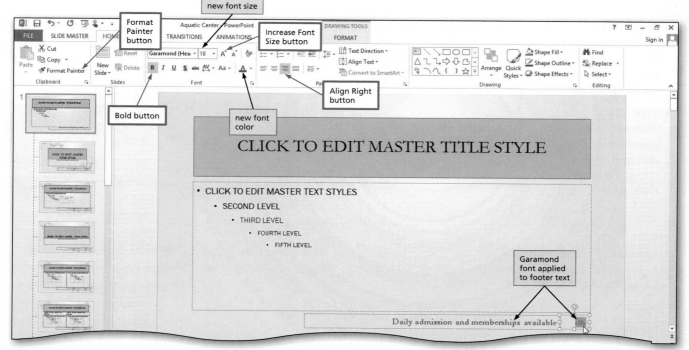

Figure 8–18

To Insert a Background Graphic into a Slide Master

The theme, fonts, footer, and background colors are set. The next step is to draw the viewers' attention to the presentation by placing the Swim Ring illustration, located on the Data Files for Students, in the same location on every slide. *Why? The repetition of this picture creates consistency and helps reinforce the message.* See the inside back cover of this book for instructions on downloading the Data Files for Students, or contact your instructor for more information on accessing the required files. The following steps insert a man floating in a swim ring illustration into the slide master.

1

- With the slide master displaying, click the INSERT tab and then tap or click the Pictures button (INSERT tab | Images group) to display the Insert Picture dialog box.

- Navigate to the location where your data files are stored (in this case, the PowerPoint Chapter 08 folder) and then tap or click Swim Ring to select the file name (Figure 8–19).

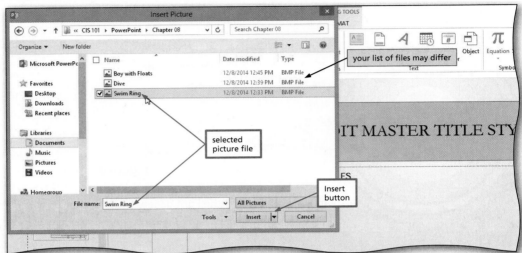

Figure 8–19

What if the picture is not in my data files folder?
Use the same process, but select the device containing the illustration. Another option is to locate this illustration or a similar one on Office.com. You may need to remove the illustration background to call attention to the swimmer.

2

- Tap or click the Insert button (Insert Picture dialog box) to insert the illustration into the slide master.

- Increase the illustration size, as shown in Figure 8–20, and then drag it above the footer placeholders.

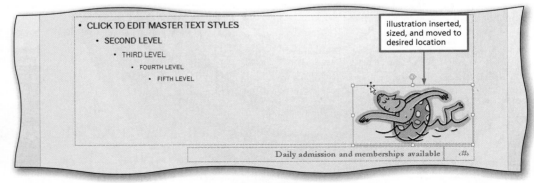

Figure 8–20

Break Point: If you wish to take a break, this is a good place to do so. Be sure to save the Aquatic Center file again and then you can exit PowerPoint. To resume at a later time, run PowerPoint, open the file called Aquatic Center using the steps below, and continue following the steps from this location forward.

TO OPEN A DOCUMENT FROM POWERPOINT

Earlier in this chapter, you saved your presentation using the file name, Aquatic Center. If you exit PowerPoint, you would need to open the Aquatic Center file from the PowerPoint folder in the CIS 101 folder and then continue following the steps in this chapter. For a detailed example of the procedure summarized below, refer to the Office and Windows chapter at the beginning of this book. To open a document from PowerPoint, you would follow these steps:

1. Tap or click FILE on the ribbon to open the Backstage view and then tap or click the Open tab in the Backstage view to display the Open gallery.

2. If the file you wish to open is displayed in the Recent Presentations list, tap or click the file name to open the file and display the opened presentation in the Power-Point window; then, skip the remaining steps. If the file you wish to open is not displayed in the Recent Presentations list, proceed to the next step to locate the file.

3. Tap or click Computer, SkyDrive, or another location in the left pane and then navigate to the location of the file to be opened (in this case, the PowerPoint folder in the CIS 101 folder).

4. Tap or click Aquatic Center to select the file to be opened.

5. Tap or click the Open button (Open dialog box) to open the selected file and display the opened presentation in the PowerPoint window.

Adding and Formatting Placeholders

Each design theme determines where placeholders appear on individual layouts. The slide master has placeholders for bulleted lists, title text, pictures, and other graphical elements. At times, you may find that you need a specific placeholder for a design element not found on any of the slide master layouts. You can add a placeholder in Slide Master view for text, SmartArt, charts, tables, and other graphical elements.

To Insert a Placeholder into a Blank Layout

1 CUSTOMIZE SLIDE MASTERS | 2 FORMAT & ARRANGE FOOTERS | 3 INSERT & FORMAT GRAPHICS & TEXT BOXES
4 RENAME & DELETE SLIDE LAYOUTS | 5 CUSTOMIZE HANDOUT & NOTES MASTERS | 6 USE CUSTOM TEMPLATE

The words, Aquatic Center, will appear on the title slide, but you may desire to add these words to every text slide. *Why? Displaying this text in the same location on all slides helps emphasize the name and also provides a consistent, uniform look to the presentation.* One efficient method of adding this text is to insert a placeholder, type the words, and, if necessary, format the characters. The following steps insert a placeholder into the Blank Layout.

1
- In the Overview pane, scroll down and then tap or click the Blank Layout to display this layout.

- If necessary, display the SLIDE MASTER tab and then tap or click the Insert Placeholder arrow (SLIDE MASTER tab | Master Layout group) to display the Insert Placeholder gallery (Figure 8–21).

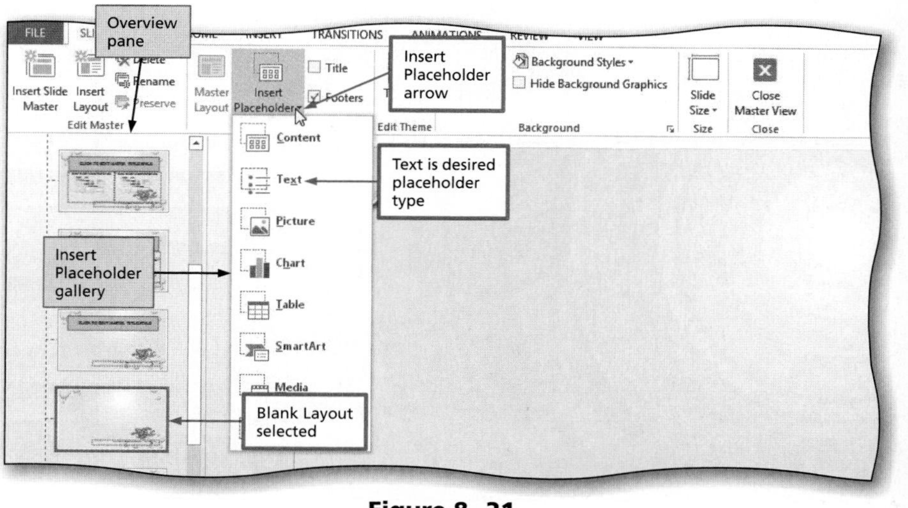

Q&A Why does the Insert Placeholder button on my screen differ from the button shown in Figure 8–21? The image on the button changes based on the type of placeholder content that was last inserted. A placeholder can hold any content, including text, pictures, and tables. If the last type of placeholder inserted was for SmartArt, for example, the Insert Placeholder button would display the SmartArt icon.

Figure 8–21

BTW
BTWs
For a complete list of the BTWs found in the margins of this book, visit the BTW resource on the Student Companion Site located on www.cengagebrain.com. For detailed instructions about accessing available resources, visit www.cengage.com/ct/studentdownload or see the inside back cover of this book.

2

- Tap or click Text in the gallery. If you are using a mouse, the pointer changes to a crosshair.

Q&A Could I have inserted a Content placeholder rather than a Text placeholder?
Yes. The Content placeholder is used for any of the seven types of slide content: text, table, chart, SmartArt, picture, clip art, or media. In this project, you will insert text in the placeholder. If you know the specific kind of content you want to place in the placeholder, it is best to select that placeholder type.

- Position your finger or the pointer at the upper-right area of the layout (Figure 8–22).

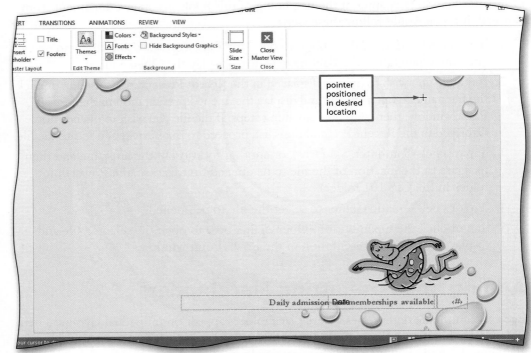

Figure 8–22

3

- Tap or click to insert the new placeholder into the Blank Layout (Figure 8–23).

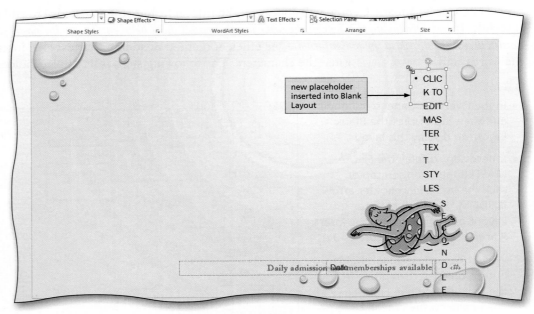

Figure 8–23

To Add and Format Placeholder Text

Now that the text placeholder is positioned, you can add the desired text and then format the characters. You will need to delete the second-, third-, fourth-, and fifth-level bullets in this placeholder. *Why? The placeholders are not used in this presentation.* The following steps add and format the words in the new Blank Layout placeholder.

- Tap or click inside the new placeholder and then select all the text in the placeholder (Figure 8–24).

Figure 8–24

- If you are using a keyboard, press the DELETE key to delete all the selected text in the placeholder. If you are using a touch screen, display the touch keyboard then tap the Backspace key to delete the selected text.

- Display the HOME tab and then tap or click the Bullets button (HOME tab | Paragraph group) to remove the bullet from the placeholder.

- Type **Aquatic Center** in the placeholder.

- Drag the bottom sizing handle down until it is above the Swim Tube illustration, as shown in Figure 8–25.

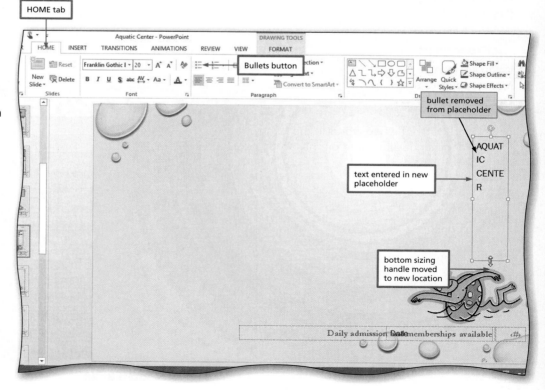

Figure 8–25

3

- Tap or click the Text Direction button (HOME tab | Paragraph group) to open the Text Direction gallery (Figure 8–26).

 Experiment

- If you are using a mouse, point to various directions in the Text Direction gallery and watch the two words in the placeholder change direction on the layout.

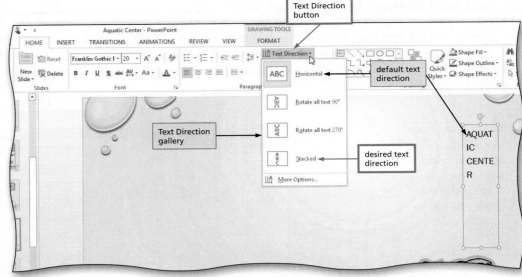

Figure 8–26

4

- Tap or click Stacked to display the text vertically.

- Tap or click the Align Text button (HOME tab | Paragraph group) to display the Align Text gallery (Figure 8–27).

 **Experiment**

- If you are using a mouse, point to the Center and Right icons in the Align Text gallery and watch the two words in the placeholder change alignment on the layout.

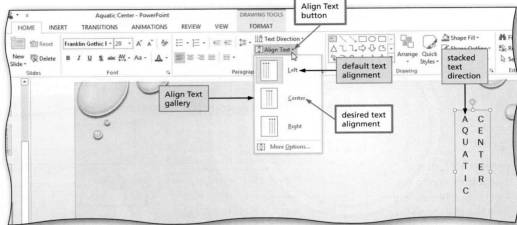

Figure 8–27

5

- Tap or click Center to display the text in the middle of the placeholder (Figure 8–28).

Q&A What is the difference between the Center button in the Paragraph group and the Center button in the Align gallery?

For the Stacked text layout, the Center button in the Paragraph group positions the text between the top and bottom borders of the placeholder. The Center button in the Align gallery centers the text between the left and right borders.

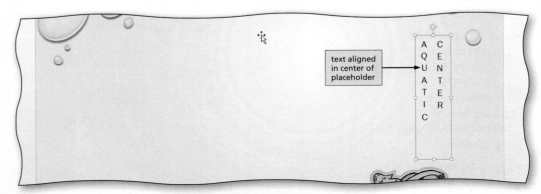

Figure 8–28

- Press and hold or right-click the text in the placeholder to display the mini toolbar and shortcut menu, tap or click the Font arrow on the mini toolbar, and then select Garamond in the Theme Fonts area of the Font gallery.

- Tap or click the Bold button to bold the text.

- Tap or click the Font Color button to change the font color to Blue, Accent 1 (fifth color in the first row) (Figure 8–29).

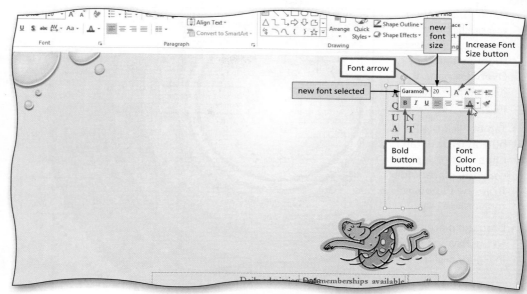

Figure 8–29

To Cut a Placeholder and Paste It into a Slide Master

1 CUSTOMIZE SLIDE MASTERS | 2 FORMAT & ARRANGE FOOTERS | 3 INSERT & FORMAT GRAPHICS & TEXT BOXES
4 RENAME & DELETE SLIDE LAYOUTS | 5 CUSTOMIZE HANDOUT & NOTES MASTERS | 6 USE CUSTOM TEMPLATE

The new formatted placeholder appears only on the Blank Layout. If you selected any other layout in your presentation, such as Two Content or Title Only, this placeholder would not display. This placeholder should appear on all text slides. ***Why?*** *Repeating this placeholder will provide consistency throughout the presentation.* You are not given the opportunity to insert a placeholder into the slide master, but you can paste a placeholder that you copied or cut from another slide. The following steps cut the new placeholder from the Blank Layout and paste it into the slide master.

- With the HOME tab displaying, tap or click the new placeholder border and then tap or click the Cut button (HOME tab | Clipboard group) to delete the placeholder from the layout and copy it to the Clipboard (Figure 8–30).

Q&A
Why did I tap or click the Cut button instead of the Copy button?
Tapping or clicking the Cut button deletes the placeholder. Tapping or clicking the Copy button keeps the original placeholder on the slide, so if you paste the placeholder on the slide master, a second, identical placeholder would display on the Blank Layout.

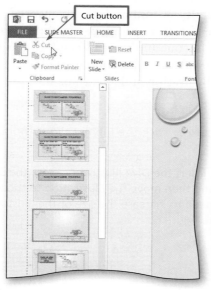
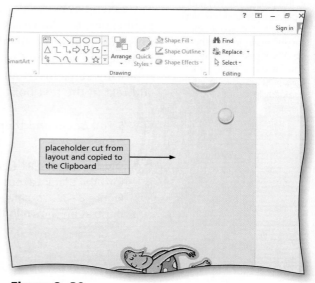

Figure 8–30

2

- Scroll up and then tap or click the Droplet Slide Master thumbnail in the Overview pane to display the slide master.

- Tap or click the Paste button (HOME tab | Clipboard group) to copy the placeholder from the Clipboard to the slide master.

- Drag the placeholder to the location shown in Figure 8–31.

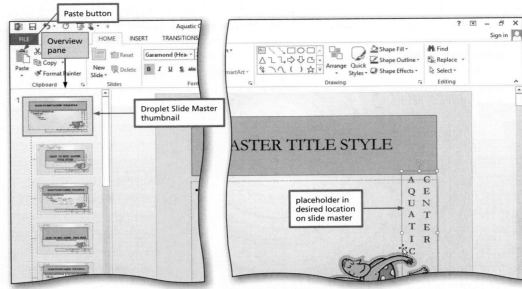

Figure 8–31

Break Point: If you wish to take a break, this is a good place to do so. Be sure to save the Aquatic Center file again and then you can exit PowerPoint. To resume at a later time, run PowerPoint, open the file called Aquatic Center, and continue following the steps from this location forward.

To Insert an Illustration and a Text Box into a Blank Layout

One slide in the completed presentation will feature the Aquatic Center's new events. The content on this slide can vary depending upon the occasion; it might be photographs of children enrolled in swimming classes, teens participating in weekend activities, or adults swimming laps. To ensure continuity when publicizing the Aquatic Center promotions and facilities, you can insert another illustration into the Blank Layout and then add and format a text box. This layout includes the Aquatic Center placeholder you inserted into the slide master. The following steps insert an illustration and a text box into the Blank Layout and then add text in the text box.

1 Scroll down and then tap or click the Blank Layout thumbnail in the Overview pane.

2 Display the INSERT tab, insert the Dive illustration from the Data Files for Students into the Blank Layout and then move the illustration to the location shown in Figure 8–32. You may need to increase the size of the illustration slightly to match the illustration shown in the figure.

3 Display the INSERT tab and then tap or click the Text Box button (INSERT tab | Text group). If you are using a mouse, insert a new text box in a blank area in the center of the slide layout. (If you are using a touch screen, the text box will be inserted automatically.)

4 Type `Dive Right In!` as the text box text, change the font color to Lime, Accent 6 (last color in first row), and then increase the font size to 24 point (Figure 8–32).

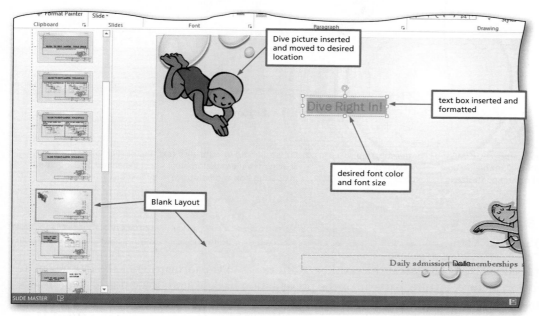

Figure 8–32

To Change Character Spacing

1 CUSTOMIZE SLIDE MASTERS | 2 FORMAT & ARRANGE FOOTERS | 3 INSERT & FORMAT GRAPHICS & TEXT BOXES
4 RENAME & DELETE SLIDE LAYOUTS | 5 CUSTOMIZE HANDOUT & NOTES MASTERS | 6 USE CUSTOM TEMPLATE

Now that the text is added, you can change the spacing between the letters in the placeholder. The amount of space, called **character spacing**, can be increased or decreased from the Normal default in one of four preset amounts: Very Tight, Tight, Loose, or Very Loose. In addition, you can specify a precise amount of space in the Character Spacing tab of the Font dialog box. In this presentation, you will move the text box below the Dive illustration and stretch the letters. *Why? You want to associate the text box with the illustration, so moving them together along the left side of the slide shows the relationship between the female diver and the words in the text box. In addition, the letters in the text box can be stretched to fit the length of the diver.* The following steps increase the character spacing in the text box.

1

- With the text in the new text box selected, tap or click the Character Spacing button (HOME tab | Font group) to display the Character Spacing gallery (Figure 8–33).

 Experiment

- If you are using a mouse, point to the spacing options in the gallery and watch the characters in the placeholder change.

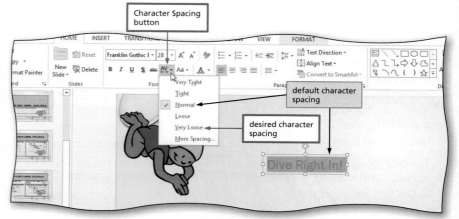

Figure 8–33

2

- Tap or click Very Loose in the gallery to change the character spacing in the text box. If necessary, adjust the size of the text box to fit the text on one line (Figure 8–34).

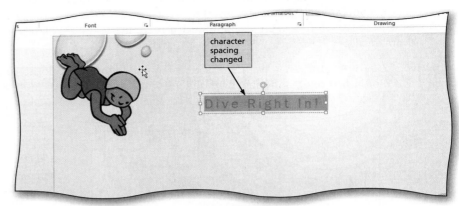

Figure 8–34

Other Ways

1. Tap or click Font dialog box launcher (HOME tab | Font group), tap or click Character Spacing tab (Font dialog box), select Expanded or Condensed in Spacing box and point size in By text box

2. Press and hold or right-click text, tap or click Character Spacing tab (Font dialog box), select Expanded or Condensed in Spacing box and point size in By text box

To Apply a Fill to a Text Box and Increase Transparency

1 CUSTOMIZE SLIDE MASTERS | **2** FORMAT & ARRANGE FOOTERS | **3** INSERT & FORMAT GRAPHICS & TEXT BOXES
4 RENAME & DELETE SLIDE LAYOUTS | **5** CUSTOMIZE HANDOUT & NOTES MASTERS | **6** USE CUSTOM TEMPLATE

Now that the text is added, you can format the text box. A **fill** refers to the formatting of the interior of a shape. The fill can be a color, picture, texture, pattern, or the presentation background. If a color fill is desired, you can increase the transparency so that some of the background color or pattern mixes with the fill color. The following steps apply a green fill to the text box on the Blank Layout and increase the transparency. *Why? The green color is part of the Blue theme colors and also coordinates well with the blue text.*

1

- Tap or click the text inside the Dive Right In text box to remove the selection from the letters.

- Tap or click the Shape Fill arrow (HOME tab | Drawing group) to display the Shape Fill gallery.

 Experiment

- If you are using a mouse, point to various colors in the Shape Fill gallery and watch the placeholder background change.

- Tap or click Blue, Accent 1 (fifth color in the first row) to fill the text box.

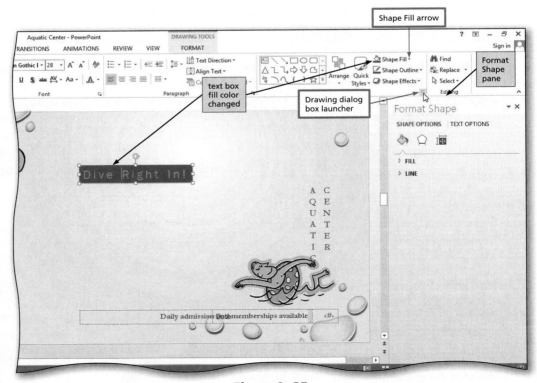

Figure 8–35

- Tap or click the Drawing dialog box launcher (HOME tab | Drawing group) to display the Format Shape pane (Figure 8–35).

- If necessary, tap or click FILL to display the FILL section.

- Tap or click the Transparency slider in the FILL section and drag it to the right until 25% is displayed in the Transparency text box (Figure 8–36).

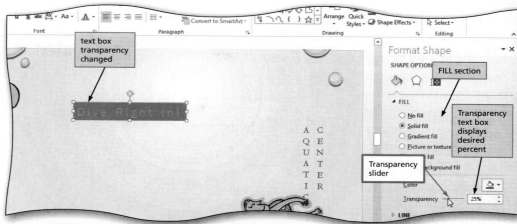

Experiment

- If you are using a mouse, drag the Transparency slider to the left and right, and watch the text box background change.

Figure 8–36

Other Ways

1. Enter percentage in Transparency text box

2. Using mouse, click Transparency up or down arrow

To Change a Text Box Internal Margin

1 CUSTOMIZE SLIDE MASTERS | 2 FORMAT & ARRANGE FOOTERS | 3 INSERT & FORMAT GRAPHICS & TEXT BOXES
4 RENAME & DELETE SLIDE LAYOUTS | 5 CUSTOMIZE HANDOUT & NOTES MASTERS | 6 USE CUSTOM TEMPLATE

Each placeholder and text box has preset internal margins, which are the spaces between the border and the contents of the box. The default left and right margins are 0.1", and the default top and bottom margins are 0.05". In this project, you will drag the text box below the diver illustration, so you want to change the margins. *Why? You want the text to align as closely as possible against the top and bottom borders of the box and the left and right margins to have a slight space between the border and the first and last letters.* The following steps change all four text box margins.

- Tap or click the 'Size & Properties' Shape Option (Format Shape pane).

- If necessary, click TEXT BOX to display the TEXT BOX section.

- Increase the Left margin setting to 0.4".

- Increase the Right margin setting to 0.4".

- Decrease the Top margin setting to 0".

- Decrease the Bottom margin setting to 0" (Figure 8–37).

Q&A Must I change all the margins?

No. You can change one, two, three, or all four internal margins depending upon the placeholder shape and the amount of text entered.

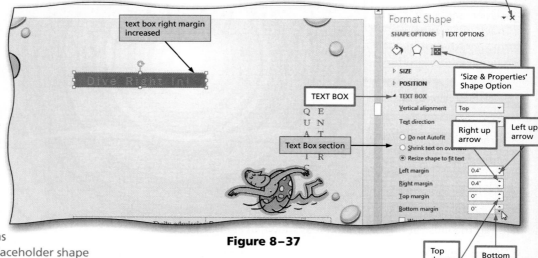

Figure 8–37

- Tap or click the Close button (Format Shape pane).

To Rotate a Picture and a Text Box

Why? *To balance the pictures on the slide, you can move the Dive illustration and the Dive Right In! text box. For a dramatic effect, you can change the orientation of the picture and the placeholder on the slide by rotating them. Dragging the green* **rotation handle** *above a selected object allows you to rotate an object in any direction. The following steps move and rotate the Dive picture and the Dive Right In! text box.*

1
- Tap or click the Dive illustration to select it.

- If you are using a mouse, position the pointer over the rotation handle so that it changes to a Free Rotate pointer (Figure 8–38).

Q&A
I selected the picture, but I cannot see the rotation handle. Why?
The rotation handle may not be visible at the top of the slide layout. Drag the picture downward, and the rotation handle will appear.

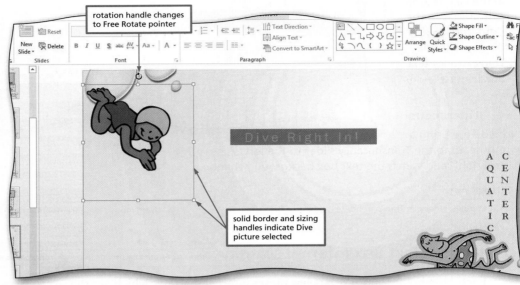

Figure 8–38

2
- Drag the rotation handle counterclockwise so that it is displayed as shown in Figure 8–39.

Q&A
I am using a touch screen and am having difficulty moving the rotation handle. What can I do?
When moving small items on a slide, it may be easier to use a mouse or a stylus instead of attempting to make adjustments using your fingers.

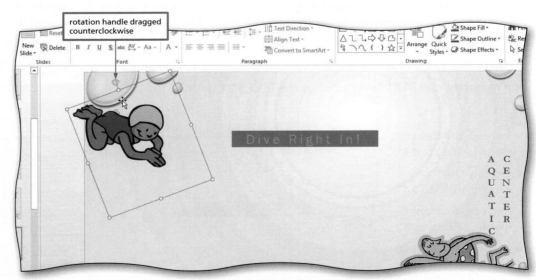

Figure 8–39

3
- Drag the illustration to position it as shown in Figure 8–40.

Q&A
If I am not using a touch screen, can I move the picture in small increments?
Yes. To move or nudge the picture in very small increments, hold down the CTRL key with the picture selected while pressing the UP ARROW, DOWN ARROW, RIGHT ARROW, or LEFT ARROW keys. You cannot perform this action using a touch screen.

- Tap or click the Dive Right In! text box to select it. If you are using a mouse, position the pointer over the rotation handle so that it changes to a Free Rotate pointer.

- Rotate the text box so that it is at the same angle as the diver.

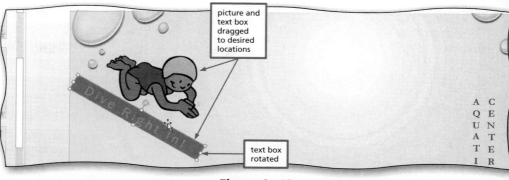

Figure 8–40

- Drag the text box below the diver, as shown in Figure 8–40.

Other Ways

1. For text box, tap or click Rotate button (DRAWING TOOLS FORMAT tab | Arrange group), choose desired rotation

2. For picture, tap or click Rotate button (PICTURE TOOLS FORMAT tab | Arrange group), choose desired rotation

3. For picture, press and hold or right-click picture, tap or click Format Object on shortcut menu, tap or click 3-D ROTATION (Format Picture pane), set rotation to desired angle

4. For text box, press and hold or right-click text box, tap or click Format Shape on shortcut menu, tap or click Effects icon (Format Shape pane), tap or click 3-D ROTATION, set rotation to desired angle

To Hide and Unhide Background Graphics

1 CUSTOMIZE SLIDE MASTERS | 2 FORMAT & ARRANGE FOOTERS | 3 INSERT & FORMAT GRAPHICS & TEXT BOXES
4 RENAME & DELETE SLIDE LAYOUTS | 5 CUSTOMIZE HANDOUT & NOTES MASTERS | 6 USE CUSTOM TEMPLATE

The placeholder, text box, pictures, and other graphical elements are displayed on some slide master layouts and are hidden on others. You have the ability to change the default setting by choosing to hide or unhide the background graphics. The Title Slide Layout, by default, does not hide the background elements. You want to hide the Swim Ring illustration on the title slide. **_Why?_** _You want your audience to focus on the title text and not be distracted by any art on the slide._ The following steps hide the background graphics on the Title Slide Layout, which is the first layout below the Droplet Slide Master in the Overview pane.

- Scroll up, tap or click the Title Slide Layout to display it, and then display the SLIDE MASTER tab (Figure 8–41).

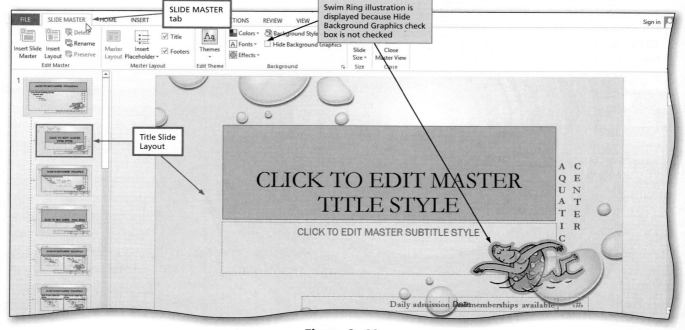

Figure 8–41

2

- Tap or click the Hide Background Graphics check box (SLIDE MASTER tab | Background group) to insert a check mark in it (Figure 8–42).

Q&A

If I decide to unhide the graphics, do I tap or click the same check box to make them appear?
Yes. The Hide Background Graphics check box is a toggle that displays and conceals the graphics.

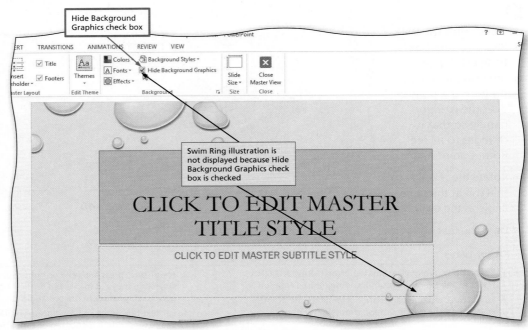

Figure 8–42

To Rename a Slide Master and a Slide Layout

1 CUSTOMIZE SLIDE MASTERS | 2 FORMAT & ARRANGE FOOTERS | 3 INSERT & FORMAT GRAPHICS & TEXT BOXES
4 RENAME & DELETE SLIDE LAYOUTS | 5 CUSTOMIZE HANDOUT & NOTES MASTERS | 6 USE CUSTOM TEMPLATE

Once all the changes are made to a slide master and a slide layout, you may want to rename them with meaningful names that describe their functions or features. The new slide master name will be displayed on the status bar; the new layout name will be displayed in the Slide Layout gallery. The following steps rename the Droplet Slide Master, the Title Slide Layout, the Blank Layout, and the Title and Content Layout. *Why? Renaming the layouts gives meaningful names that reflect the purpose of the design.*

1

- Display the Droplet Slide Master and then tap or click the Rename button (SLIDE MASTER tab | Edit Master group) to display the Rename Layout dialog box.

- Delete the text in the Layout name text box and then type **Aquatic** in the text box (Rename Layout dialog box) (Figure 8–43).

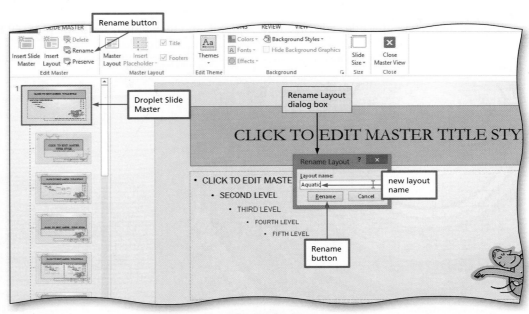

Figure 8–43

2

- Tap or click the Rename button (Rename Layout dialog box) to give the layout the new name, Aquatic Slide Master.

3

- Display the Title Slide Layout, tap or click the Rename button, delete the text in the Layout name text box, and then type **Aquatic Title** as the new layout name (Figure 8–44).

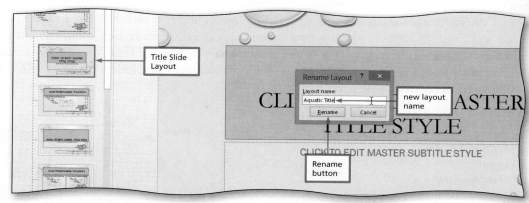

Figure 8–44

4

- Tap or click the Rename button (Rename Layout dialog box) to rename the Title Slide layout.

- Scroll down and then tap or click the Blank Layout to display it, tap or click the Rename button, delete the text in the Layout name text box, and then type **Dive Right In** as the new layout name (Figure 8–45).

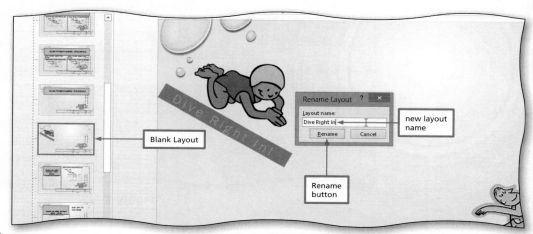

Figure 8–45

5

- Tap or click the Rename button (Rename Layout dialog box).

- Scroll up to display the Title and Content Layout, tap or click the Rename button, delete the text in the Layout name text box, and then type **Miscellaneous** as the new layout name (Figure 8–46).

6

- Tap or click the Rename button (Rename Layout dialog box).

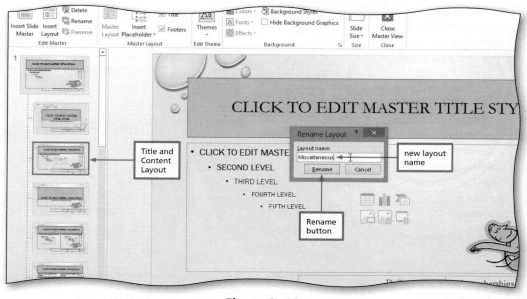

Figure 8–46

PPT 502 PowerPoint Chapter 8 Customizing a Template and Handouts Using Masters

1 CUSTOMIZE SLIDE MASTERS | 2 FORMAT & ARRANGE FOOTERS | 3 INSERT & FORMAT GRAPHICS & TEXT BOXES
4 RENAME & DELETE SLIDE LAYOUTS | 5 CUSTOMIZE HANDOUT & NOTES MASTERS | 6 USE CUSTOM TEMPLATE

To Delete a Slide Layout

You have made many changes to the slide master and two slide layouts. You will use these layouts and the Title and Content Layout, which is now called the Miscellaneous layout, when you close Master view and then add text, graphics, or other content to the presentation in Normal view. You can delete the other layouts in the Overview pane. *Why? You will not use them in this presentation.* The following steps delete slide layouts that will not be used to create the presentation.

- Tap or click the Section Header Layout in the Overview pane to select it (Figure 8–47).

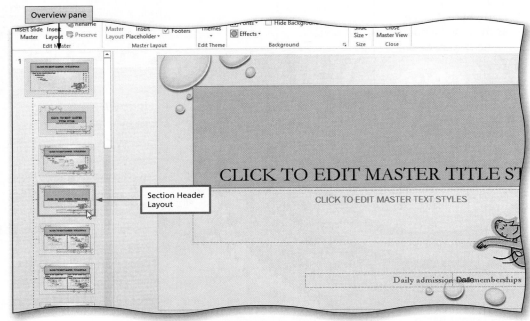

Figure 8–47

2

- If you are using a keyboard, press and hold down the SHIFT key, if necessary scroll down to display the Title Only Layout, and then click the Title Only Layout to select four consecutive layouts. If you are using a touch screen, swipe to the right across each of the three layouts below the Title Only layout to select them (Figure 8–48).

Q&A Why did I select only these four layouts?
The layout below the Title Only Layout is the Dive Right In Layout, and you will use that layout when you create Slide 2 in your presentation.

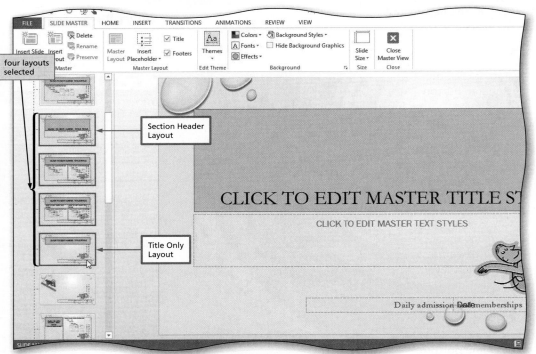

Figure 8–48

3

• Tap or click the Delete button (SLIDE MASTER tab | Edit Master group) to delete the four layouts.

• Tap or click the Content with Caption Layout (the layout below the Dive Right In layout), then select all layouts below it including the last layout, which is the Vertical Title and Text Layout, in the Overview pane (Figure 8–49).

layouts selected

Vertical Title and Text Layout

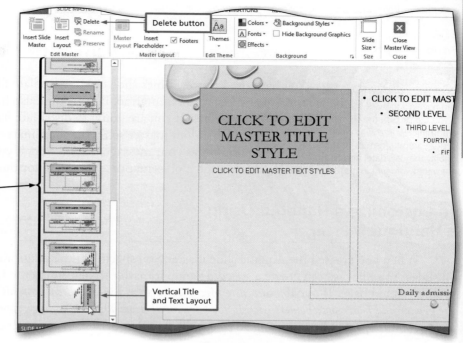

Figure 8–49

4

• Tap or click the Delete button (SLIDE MASTER tab | Edit Master group) to delete the 10 layouts (Figure 8–50).

Q&A Now that I have created this slide master, can I ensure that it will not be changed when I create future presentations?

Yes. Normally a slide master is deleted when a new design template is selected. To keep the original master as part of your presentation, you can preserve it by selecting the thumbnail and then tapping or clicking the Preserve button in the Edit Master group. An icon in the shape of a pushpin is displayed below the slide number to indicate the master is preserved. If you decide to unpreserve a slide master, select this thumbnail and then tap or click the Preserve button.

three layouts will be used to create presentation slides

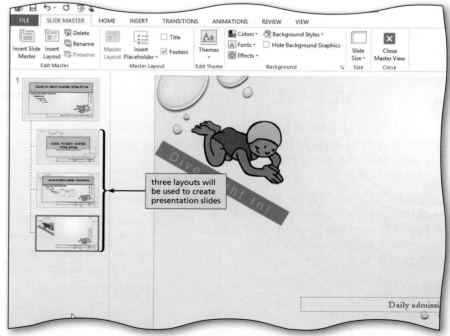

Figure 8–50

Other Ways

1. Tap or click Delete button (HOME tab | Slides group)

2. Press and hold or right-click selected slide, tap or click Delete Layout on shortcut menu

3. Press DELETE key on keyboard

Break Point: If you wish to take a break, this is a good place to do so. You can exit PowerPoint now. To resume at a later time, run PowerPoint and continue following the steps from this location forward.

BTW
Formatting the 'Date and time' Placeholder
The 'Date and time' footer can have a variety of formats. If you tap or click the Update automatically arrow, you can choose among formats that display the day, date, and time in a variety of combinations.

Customizing Handout and Notes Masters

You have used PowerPoint's slide master template file to create unique slide layouts for the Aquatic Center presentation. PowerPoint also has master template files to create handouts and notes. If you are going to distribute handouts to your audience, you can customize the handout master so that it coordinates visually with the presentation slides and reinforces your message. In addition, if you are going to use speaker notes to guide you through a presentation, you can tailor the notes master to fit your needs.

To Customize a Handout Using a Handout Master

1 CUSTOMIZE SLIDE MASTERS | 2 FORMAT & ARRANGE FOOTERS | 3 INSERT & FORMAT GRAPHICS & TEXT BOXES
4 RENAME & DELETE SLIDE LAYOUTS | 5 CUSTOMIZE HANDOUT & NOTES MASTERS | 6 USE CUSTOM TEMPLATE

When you created the Aquatic slide master, you specified the background, fonts, theme, and pictures for all slides. You likewise can create a specific handout master to determine the layout and graphics that will display on the printed page. *Why? You can customize handouts for a your audience's needs by moving, restoring, and formatting the header and footer placeholders; setting the page number orientation; adding graphics; and specifying the number of slides to print on each page.* The following steps use the handout master to create a custom handout.

1
- Display the VIEW tab (Figure 8–51).

Figure 8–51

2
- Tap or click the Handout Master button (VIEW tab | Master Views group) to display the HANDOUT MASTER tab.

- Tap or click the 'Slides Per Page' button (HANDOUT MASTER tab | Page Setup group) to display the Slides Per Page gallery (Figure 8–52).

Q&A Is 6 Slides the default layout for all themes?
Yes. If you have fewer than six slides in your presentation or want to display slide details, then choose a handout layout with 1, 2, 3, or 4 slides per sheet of paper.

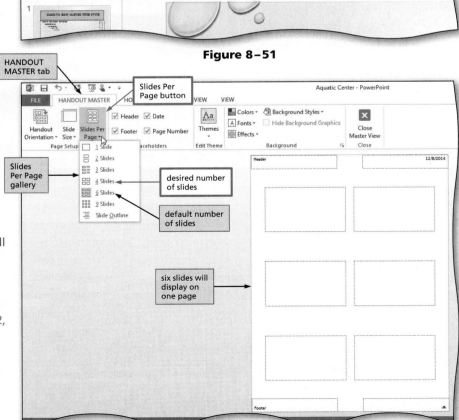

Figure 8–52

3

- Tap or click 4 Slides in the list to change the layout from 6 slides to 4 slides.

- Tap or click the Handout Orientation button (HANDOUT MASTER tab | Page Setup group) to display the Handout Orientation gallery (Figure 8–53).

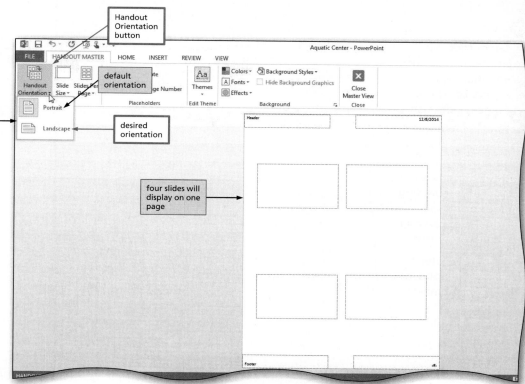

Figure 8–53

4

- Tap or click Landscape in the gallery to display the page layout in landscape orientation (Figure 8–54).

Q&A

How do I decide between portrait and landscape orientation?
If your slide content is predominantly vertical, such as an athlete running or a skyscraper in a major city, consider using the default portrait orientation. If, however, your slide content has long lines of text or pictures of four-legged animals, landscape orientation may be a more appropriate layout.

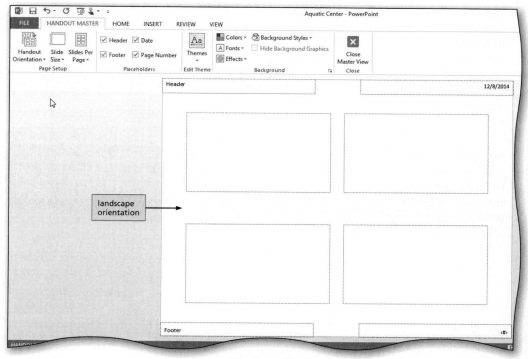

Figure 8–54

5

- Tap or click the Header placeholder and then type **Aquatic Center** as the header text.

- Tap or click the Footer placeholder and then type **New this year: Adult swimming lessons and aqua aerobics!** as the footer text.

- Drag the Footer placeholder above the page number placeholder (Figure 8–55).

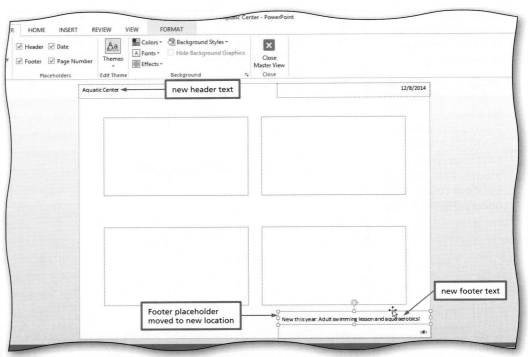

Figure 8–55

6

- Tap or click the Theme Fonts button (HANDOUT MASTER tab | Background group) to display the Theme Fonts gallery (Figure 8–56).

7

- Tap or click Swim in the Custom area of the gallery to apply the Franklin Gothic Book font to the text in the placeholder.

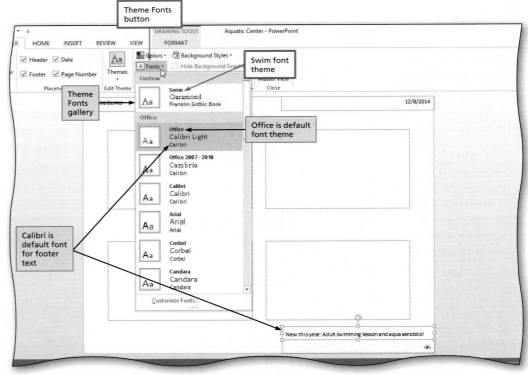

Figure 8–56

8

- Display the INSERT tab, tap or click the Pictures button (INSERT tab | Images group), and then insert the Dive illustration located on the Data Files for Students.

- Rotate the Dive illustration counterclockwise, resize the picture so it is approximately 2.6" × 2.4", and then center it along the upper edge of the handout layout, as shown in Figure 8–57.

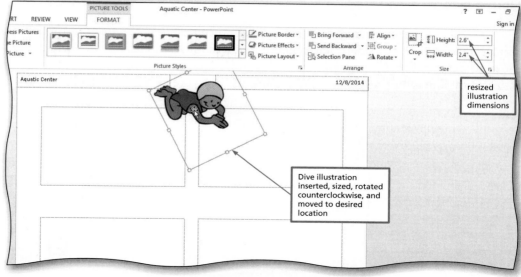

Figure 8–57

9

- Display the INSERT tab, tap or click the 'Header & Footer' button (INSERT tab | Text group), and then place a check mark in the 'Date and time' check box.

- Place a check mark in the Header check box.

- Place a check mark in the Footer check box (Figure 8–58).

10

- Tap or click the 'Apply to All' button (Header and Footer dialog box) to add the header and footer text and date to the handout master.

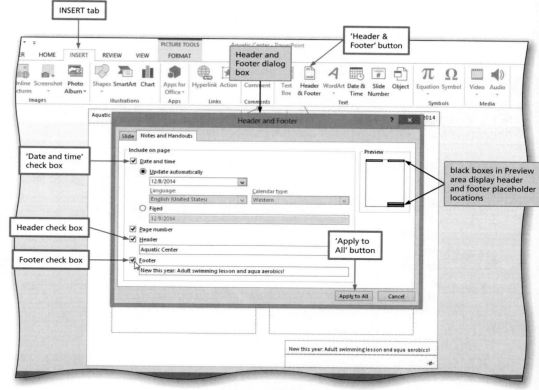

Figure 8–58

Q&A Where will the header and footer display on the handout?

The black boxes in the preview area show where these placeholders are located.

To Customize a Notes Page Using a Notes Master

If you type notes in the Notes pane, you can print them for yourself or for your audience. The basic format found in the Backstage view generally suffices for handouts, but you may desire to alter the layout using the notes master. *Why? You may desire to add graphics and rearrange and format the header, footer, and page number placeholders.* The following steps use the notes master to create a custom handout.

1
- Display the VIEW tab (Figure 8–59).

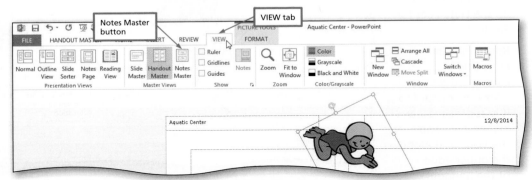

Figure 8–59

2
- Tap or click the Notes Master button (VIEW tab | Master Views group) to display the NOTES MASTER tab.

- Tap or click the Footer placeholder, delete the text, and then type `Open swim begins at noon daily` as the new footer text.

3
- Tap or click the Theme Fonts button to display the Theme Fonts gallery (Figure 8–60).

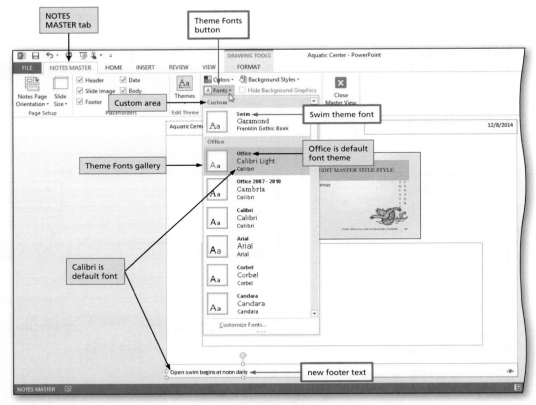

Figure 8–60

4

- Tap or click Swim in the Custom area of the Theme Fonts gallery to apply the Franklin Gothic Book font to the text in the header, footer, date, and page number placeholders.

- Tap or click the 'Notes Page Orientation' button (NOTES MASTER tab | Page Setup group) to display the 'Notes Page Orientation' gallery (Figure 8–61).

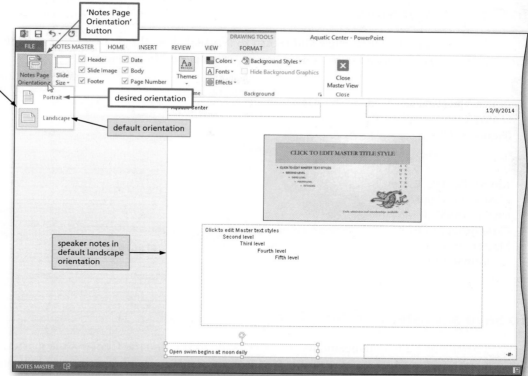

Figure 8–61

 5

- Tap or click Portrait in the gallery to display the page layout in portrait orientation.

- Display the INSERT tab, tap or click the Pictures button, and then insert the Dive illustration located on the Data Files for Students.

- Resize the picture so that it is approximately 2" × 1.85".

- Move the picture so that it is centered between the two footer placeholders, as shown in Figure 8–62.

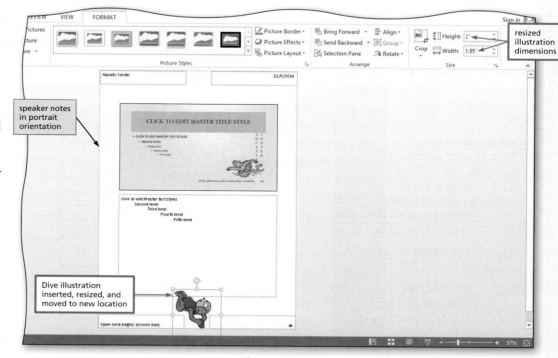

Figure 8–62

To Close Master View

You now can exit Master view and return to Normal view. **Why?** *All the changes to the slide master, handout master, and notes master are complete.* The following steps close Master view.

- Display the NOTES MASTER tab (Figure 8–63).

- Tap or click the 'Close Master View' button (NOTES MASTER tab | Close group) to exit Master view and return to Normal view.

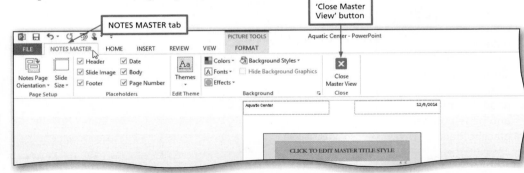

Figure 8–63

To Save a Master as a Template

The changes and enhancements you have made to the Aquatic Center slide master, handout master, and notes master are excellent starting points for future presentations. The background text and graphics allow users to add text boxes, pictures, SmartArt, tables, and other elements depending upon the specific message that needs to be communicated to an audience. Saving a slide master as a template is convenient when you often reuse and modify presentations. **Why?** *You can save your slide layouts as a template to use for a new presentation and use the revised handout and notes masters to print unique pages.* The following steps save the Aquatic masters as a template.

- Open the Backstage view, display the Save As tab, and tap or click the Browse button to display the Save As dialog box.

- Tap or click the 'Save as type' arrow to display the 'Save as type' list (Figure 8–64).

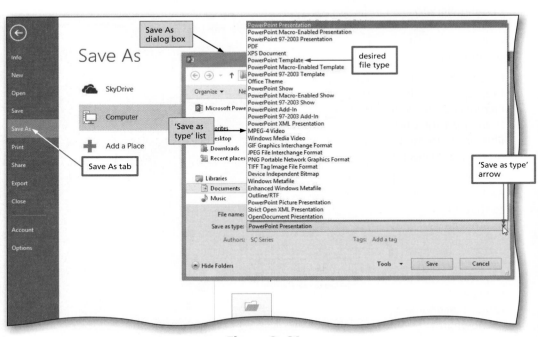

Figure 8–64

2

- Tap or click 'PowerPoint Template' in the 'Save as type' list to change the save as type.

- Type **Aquatic Center Template** in the File name box (Figure 8–65).

3

- Tap or click the Save button (Save As dialog box) to save the Aquatic Center presentation as a template.

4

- Close the Aquatic Center Template file.

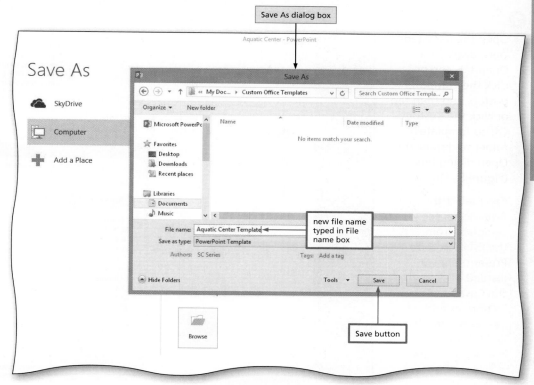

Figure 8–65

Break Point: If you wish to take a break, this is a good place to do so. You can exit PowerPoint now. To resume at a later time, run PowerPoint and continue following the steps from this location forward.

To Open a Template and Save a Presentation

1 CUSTOMIZE SLIDE MASTERS | 2 FORMAT & ARRANGE FOOTERS | 3 INSERT & FORMAT GRAPHICS & TEXT BOXES
4 RENAME & DELETE SLIDE LAYOUTS | 5 CUSTOMIZE HANDOUT & NOTES MASTERS | **6 USE CUSTOM TEMPLATE**

The Aquatic Center Template file you created is a convenient start to a new presentation. The graphical elements and essential slide content are in place; you then can customize the layouts for a specific need, such as a new event or special program. PowerPoint saves templates users create in a folder called 'Custom Office Templates' in the My Documents folder. The steps on the next page open the Aquatic Center Template file and save the presentation with the Aquatic Center name.

1

- Open the Backstage view, display the Open tab, tap or click the Computer button, and then tap or click the Custom Office Templates folder to display the Open dialog box (Figure 8–66).

Q&A Can I select the Aquatic Center Template from the list of Recent Presentations instead of opening the Custom Office Templates folder? Yes. Either technique will locate the desired template.

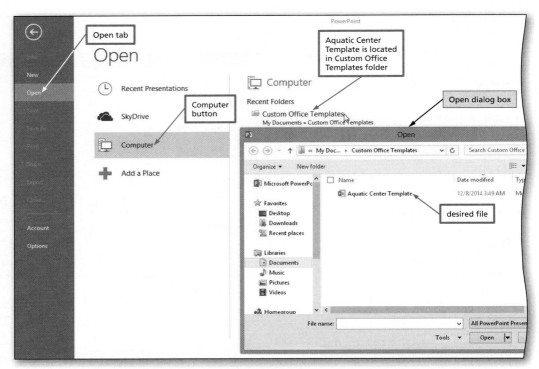

Figure 8–66

2

- Open the file, 'Aquatic Center Template'.

- Open the Backstage view, display the Save As tab, and then navigate to the location where your files are saved.

- Tap or click the 'Save as type' arrow to display the 'Save as type' list, and then tap or click PowerPoint Presentation in the 'Save as type' list to change the save as type.

- Tap or click Aquatic Center in the Save As dialog box to select the file (Figure 8–67).

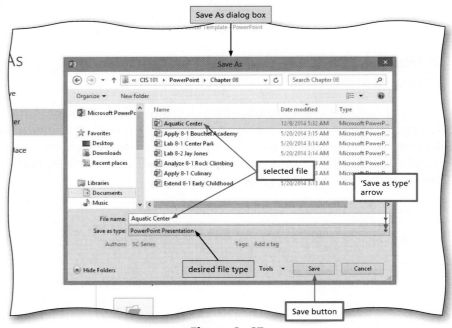

Figure 8–67

3
- Tap or click the Save button (Save As dialog box) to display the Confirm Save As dialog box (Figure 8–68).
- Click the Yes button to replace the file.

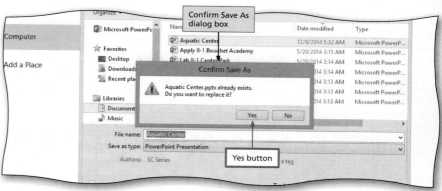

Figure 8–68

To Add Text and Notes to the Title Slide

By default, the title slide layout, which was renamed Aquatic Title, is applied to the first slide. The following steps add text and speaker notes to Slide 1.

1 With the title slide displaying, type **Aquatic Center Programs and Events** as the title text and **Splish Splash – Have a Blast!** as the subtitle text.

2 If necessary, display the Notes pane. Tap or click the Notes pane and type **The Aquatic Center is open daily and offers community residents a variety of lessons, parties, and special events.** (Figure 8–69).

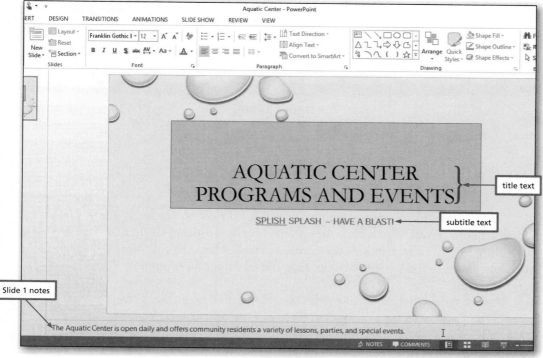

Figure 8–69

To Add Text and Notes to the Blank Layout

The second slide in your presentation will feature the new water slide. The Dive Right In slide layout, which is the new name for the Blank Layout, is designed so that you can add variable slide content below the diver illustration in the upper-left corner. The following steps add a text box and speaker notes to Slide 2. *Why?* *The text box will call attention to the water slide, and the speaker notes contain ideas that a presenter may want to discuss during a presentation.*

1 Insert a slide with the Dive Right In layout and then insert a text box between the two illustrations. Type `New three-chute` as the first line of text box text and then press or tap ENTER. Then type `150' water slide` as the second line of text.

2 Increase the text box font size to 54 point. Size the text box as shown in Figure 8–70 and then drag it to the location shown in the figure.

3 In the Notes pane, type `Community residents can enjoy a leisure pool with a zero-depth edge, a 50-meter pool with six lanes, and a wading pool with a tot slide.` (Figure 8–70).

Figure 8–70

To Add Text, Notes, and an Illustration to the Title and Content Layout

The third slide in your presentation will list details about the swim lessons. The Miscellaneous layout, which is the new name for the Title and Content slide layout, will allow you to insert text into the content placeholder. The following steps insert a slide and add text and a picture to the title and content placeholder.

1 Insert a slide with the Miscellaneous layout and then type `Swim Lessons` as the title text.

2 Type `Small class size (10 students maximum)` as the first content placeholder paragraph.

3 Type `Lifeguard training includes CPR certification` as the second paragraph.

4 Type `Parent / Tot swim prepares for lifetime of aquatic enjoyment` as the third paragraph.

5 Type `Morning, evening, and Saturday classes available` as the fourth paragraph.

6 In the Notes pane, type `Small class sizes allow instructors to give individualized attention, which helps students make progress and feel proud of their accomplishments.`

7 Insert the illustration with the file name, Boy with Floats, located on the Data Files for Students, increase its size to approximately 2.4" × 2.26", and then move the illustration to the lower-left corner of the slide (Figure 8–71).

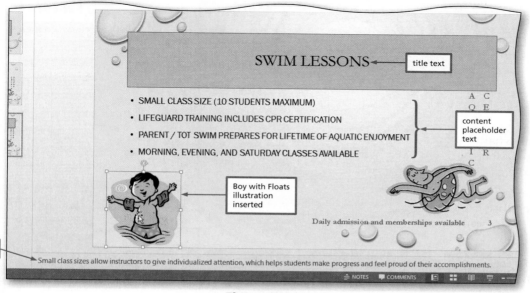

Figure 8–71

To Apply a Fill Color to a Slide

1 CUSTOMIZE SLIDE MASTERS | 2 FORMAT & ARRANGE FOOTERS | 3 INSERT & FORMAT GRAPHICS & TEXT BOXES
4 RENAME & DELETE SLIDE LAYOUTS | 5 CUSTOMIZE HANDOUT & NOTES MASTERS | 6 USE CUSTOM TEMPLATE

Earlier in this project, you formatted the interior of the Dive Right In! text box by applying a fill. In a similar manner, you can apply a fill to an entire slide by selecting a color from the Shape Fill gallery. If desired, you can increase the transparency to soften the color. The following steps apply a fill to Slide 3 and increase the transparency. *Why? Because the Dive Right In! text on Slide 2 is green, you can coordinate the Slide 3 fill color by changing the Slide 3 background to green and decrease the transparency so the letters can be read easily.*

1

- With Slide 3 displaying, press and hold or right-click anywhere on the blue background without a text box or illustration to display the shortcut menu (Figure 8–72).

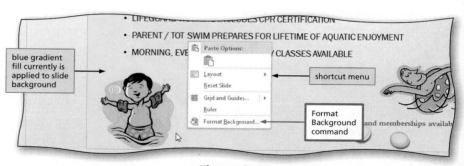

Figure 8–72

2

- Tap or click Format Background on the shortcut menu to display the Format Background pane.

- With the FILL section displaying and the Solid fill option selected, tap or click the Color button to display the Fill Color gallery (Figure 8–73).

Q&A Can I experiment with previewing the background colors?
No live preview feature is available.

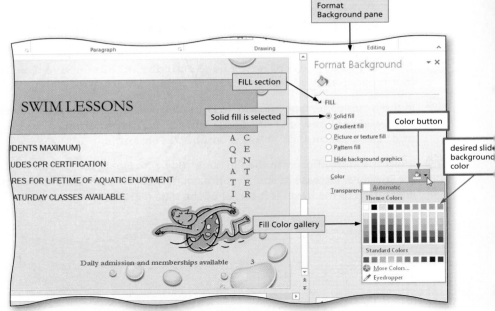

Figure 8–73

3

- Tap or click Lime, Accent 6 (last color in the first row) to change the slide background color.

- Tap or click the Transparency slider in the Fill Color area and drag it to the right until 15% is displayed in the Transparency text box (Figure 8–74).

 **Experiment**

- Drag the Transparency slider to the left and right, and watch the text box background change.

Q&A How can I delete a fill color if I decide not to apply one to my slide?
Any fill effect in the Format Background dialog box is applied immediately. If this dialog box is displayed, tap or click the Reset Background button. If you already have applied the fill color, you must tap or click the Undo button on the Quick Access Toolbar.

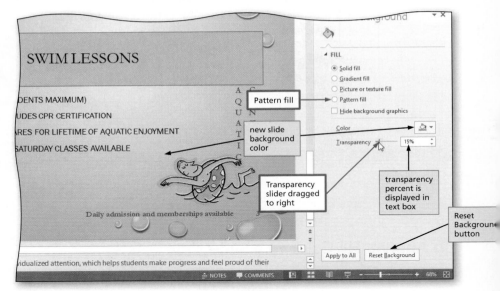

Figure 8–74

Other Ways

1. Enter percentage in Transparency text box
2. Using mouse, click Transparency up or down arrow

To Apply a Pattern to a Slide

1 CUSTOMIZE SLIDE MASTERS | 2 FORMAT & ARRANGE FOOTERS | 3 INSERT & FORMAT GRAPHICS & TEXT BOXES
4 RENAME & DELETE SLIDE LAYOUTS | 5 CUSTOMIZE HANDOUT & NOTES MASTERS | 6 USE CUSTOM TEMPLATE

You add variety to a slide by making a **pattern fill**. This design of repeating horizontal or vertical lines, dots, dashes, or stripes can enhance the visual appeal of one or more slides in the presentation. If you desire to change the colors in the pattern, PowerPoint allows you to select the fill foreground and background colors by clicking the Color button and then choosing the desired colors. The following steps apply a pattern to Slide 3. **Why?** *The dots in this pattern coordinate with the water droplets in the slide background.*

①

- With the Format Background pane displaying, click Pattern fill to display the Pattern gallery and the 5% pattern on Slide 3 (Figure 8–75).

🔍 **Experiment**

- Tap or click various patterns in the Pattern gallery and the 5% pattern on Slide 3.

Q&A How can I delete a pattern if I decide not to apply one to my slide?
If the Format Background pane is displayed, tap or click the Reset Background button. If you already have applied the pattern, you must tap or click the Undo button on the Quick Access Toolbar.

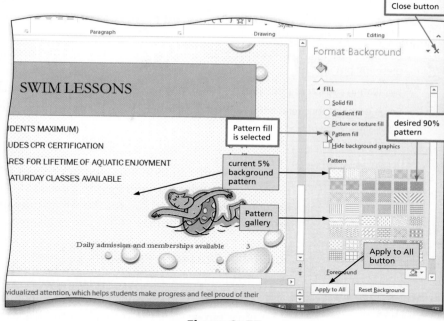

Figure 8–75

②

- Tap or click the 90% pattern (last color in second row) to apply this pattern to the Slide 3 background (Figure 8–76).

Q&A Can I apply this pattern to all the slides in the presentation?
Yes. You would tap or click the 'Apply to All' button in the Format Background pane.

③

- Tap or click the Close button to close the Format Background task pane.

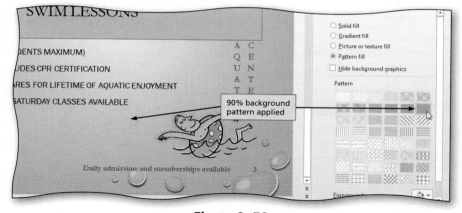

Figure 8–76

To Add a Slide Transition

A final enhancement you will make in this presentation is to apply the Ripple transition to all slides and then change the transition speed and effect option. The following steps apply a transition and effect to the presentation.

① Display the TRANSITIONS tab and then apply the Ripple transition in the Exciting category to all three slides in the presentation.

② Change the transition speed from 01.40 to 04.00.

③ Change the Effect Option from Center to From Top-Left.

Document Properties

PowerPoint helps you organize and identify your files by using **document properties,** which are the details about a file such as the project author, title, and subject. For example, a class name or presentation topic can describe the file's purpose or content.

CONSIDER THIS

Why would you want to assign document properties to a presentation?

Document properties are valuable for a variety of reasons:

- Users can save time locating a particular file because they can view a file's document properties without opening the presentation.
- By creating consistent properties for files having similar content, users can better organize their presentations.
- Some organizations require PowerPoint users to add document properties so that other employees can view details about these files.

The more common document properties are standard and automatically updated properties. **Standard properties** are associated with all Microsoft Office files and include author, title, and subject. **Automatically updated properties** include file system properties, such as the date you create or change a file, and statistics, such as the file size.

TO CHANGE DOCUMENT PROPERTIES

To change document properties, you would follow these steps.

1. Tap or click FILE on the ribbon to open the Backstage view and then, if necessary, tap or click the Info tab in the Backstage view to display the Info gallery.

2. If the property you wish to change is displayed in the Properties list in the right pane of the Info gallery, try to tap or click to the right of the property. If a text box appears to the right of the property, type the text for the property in the text box, and then tap or click the Back button in the upper-left corner of the Backstage view to return to the PowerPoint window. Skip the remaining steps.

3. If the property you wish to change is not displayed in the Properties list in the right pane of the Info gallery or you cannot change it in the Info gallery, tap or click the Properties button in the right pane to display the Properties menu, and then tap or click 'Show Document Panel' on the Properties menu to close the Backstage view and display the Document Information Panel in the PowerPoint presentation window.

Q&A Why are some of the document properties in my Document Information Panel already filled in?

The person who installed Office 2013 on your computer or network may have set or customized the properties.

4. Type the desired text in the appropriate property text boxes.

Q&A What if the property I want to change is not displayed in the Document Information Panel?

Tap or click the Document Properties button in the Document Information Panel and then tap or click Advanced Properties on the menu to display the Properties dialog box. If necessary, tap or click the Summary tab (Properties dialog box) to display the Summary sheet, fill in the appropriate text boxes, and then tap or click the OK button.

5. Tap or click the 'Close the Document Information Panel' button at the right edge of the Document Information Panel so that the panel no longer appears in the PowerPoint presentation window.

Printing a Presentation

After creating a presentation, you may want to print it. Printing a presentation enables you to distribute it to others in a form that can be read or viewed but typically not edited. It is a good practice to save a presentation before printing it, in the event you experience difficulties printing.

BTW

Printing Document Properties

To print document properties, tap or click FILE on the ribbon to open the Backstage view, tap or click the Print tab in the Backstage view to display the Print gallery, tap or click the first button in the Settings area to display a list of options specifying what you can print, tap or click Document Info in the list to specify you want to print the document properties instead of the actual document, and then tap or click the Print button in the Print gallery to print the document properties on the currently selected printer.

BTW

Conserving Ink and Toner

If you want to conserve ink or toner, you can instruct PowerPoint to print draft quality documents by tapping or clicking FILE on the ribbon to open the Backstage view, tapping or clicking Options in the Backstage view to display the PowerPoint Options dialog box, tapping or clicking Advanced in the left pane (PowerPoint Options dialog box), sliding or scrolling to the Print area in the right pane, placing a check mark in the 'Use draft quality' check box, and then tapping or clicking the OK button. Then, use the Backstage view to print the document as usual.

What is the best method for distributing a presentation?

The traditional method of distributing a presentation uses a printer to produce a hard copy. A **hard copy** or **printout** is information that exists on a physical medium such as paper. Hard copies can be useful for the following reasons:

- Some people prefer proofreading a hard copy of a presentation rather than viewing it on the screen to check for errors and readability.

- Hard copies can serve as a backup reference if your storage medium is lost or becomes corrupted and you need to recreate the presentation.

Instead of distributing a hard copy of a presentation, users can distribute the presentation as an electronic image that mirrors the original presentation's appearance. The electronic image of the presentation can be sent as an email attachment, posted on a website, or copied to a portable storage medium such as a USB flash drive. Two popular electronic image formats, sometimes called fixed formats, are PDF by Adobe Systems and XPS by Microsoft. In PowerPoint, you can create electronic image files through the Save As dialog box and the Export, Share, and Print tabs in the Backstage view. Electronic images of presentations, such as PDF and XPS, can be useful for the following reasons:

- Users can view electronic images of presentations without the software that created the original presentation (e.g., PowerPoint). Specifically, to view a PDF file, you use a program called Adobe Reader, which can be downloaded free from Adobe's website. Similarly, to view an XPS file, you use a program called XPS Viewer, which is included in the latest versions of Windows and Internet Explorer.

- Sending electronic presentations saves paper and printer supplies. Society encourages users to contribute to **green computing**, which involves reducing the electricity consumed and environmental waste generated when using computers, mobile devices, and related technologies.

To Print a Presentation

1 CUSTOMIZE SLIDE MASTERS | 2 FORMAT & ARRANGE FOOTERS | 3 INSERT & FORMAT GRAPHICS & TEXT BOXES
4 RENAME & DELETE SLIDE LAYOUTS | 5 CUSTOMIZE HANDOUT & NOTES MASTERS | **6 USE CUSTOM TEMPLATE**

With the completed presentation saved, you may want to print it. *Why? Because this handout is being distributed, you will print a hard copy on a printer.* The following steps print a hard copy of the contents of the saved Aquatic Center presentation.

- Tap or click FILE on the ribbon to open the Backstage view.

- Tap or click the Print tab in the Backstage view to display the Print gallery.

Q&A How can I print multiple copies of my presentation?
Increase the number in the Copies box in the Print gallery.

What if I decide not to print the presentation at this time?
Tap or click the Back button in the upper-left corner of the Backstage view to return to the presentation window.

2

- Verify that the printer listed on the Printer Status button will print a hard copy of the presentation. If necessary, click the Printer Status button to display a list of available printer options and then click the desired printer to change the currently selected printer.

3

- Tap or click the Print button in the Print gallery to print the presentation on the currently selected printer.

- When the printer stops, retrieve the hard copy.

Q&A Do I have to wait until my presentation is complete to print it?
No, you can follow these steps to print a presentation at any time while you are creating it.

What if I want to print an electronic image of a presentation instead of a hard copy?
You would click the Printer Status button in the Print gallery and then select the desired electronic image option, such as Microsoft XPS Document Writer, which would create an XPS file.

Other Ways

1. Press CTRL+P, press ENTER

To Print a Handout Using the Handout Master

The handout master you created has header and footer text using the Franklin Gothic Book font, a revised location for the Footer placeholder, and the Swim Ring illustration in the lower-left corner. The following steps print a handout using the handout master.

- Open the Backstage view and then display the Print gallery.

- Tap or click the 'Full Page Slides' button in the Settings area to display the gallery (Figure 8–77).

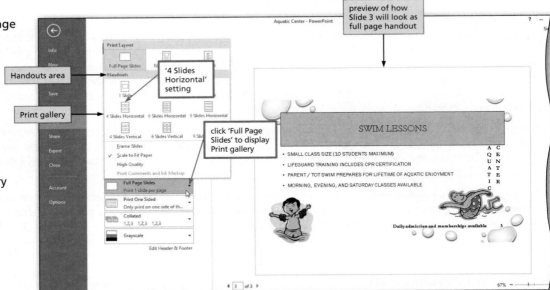

Figure 8–77

- Tap or click '4 Slides Horizontal' in the Handouts area.

- Tap or click Portrait Orientation in the Settings area to display the Orientation gallery (Figure 8–78).

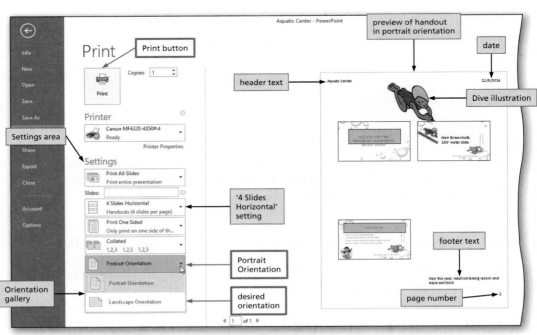

Figure 8–78

4

- Tap or click Landscape Orientation to change the setting.

- Verify that '4 Slides Horizontal' is selected as the option in the Settings area and that the preview of Page 1 shows the header text, date, footer text, page number, Dive illustration, and three slides in landscape orientation.

- Tap or click the Print button in the Print Gallery to print the handout (Figure 8–79).

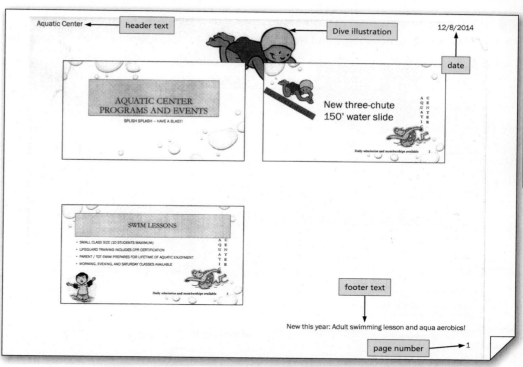

Figure 8–79 Handout in Landscape Orientation

To Print Speaker Notes Using the Notes Master

1 CUSTOMIZE SLIDE MASTERS | 2 FORMAT & ARRANGE FOOTERS | 3 INSERT & FORMAT GRAPHICS & TEXT BOXES
4 RENAME & DELETE SLIDE LAYOUTS | 5 CUSTOMIZE HANDOUT & NOTES MASTERS | **6 USE CUSTOM TEMPLATE**

You also can print speaker notes while the Backstage view is displayed. The custom notes master you created has the same footer as the handout master, revised footer text using the Franklin Gothic Book font, the current date, and the resized Swim Ring illustration in the lower-right corner. The following steps print notes pages using the notes master.

1

- With the Backstage view open, display the Print gallery and then tap or click Notes Pages in the Print Layout area.

- Tap or click Landscape Orientation in the Settings area and then tap or click Portrait Orientation in the gallery to change the setting.

- If necessary, tap or click the Previous Page button to preview Slide 1.

- Verify that the page preview shows the header text, date, speaker notes, revised footer text, diver illustration, and page number in portrait orientation (Figure 8–80).

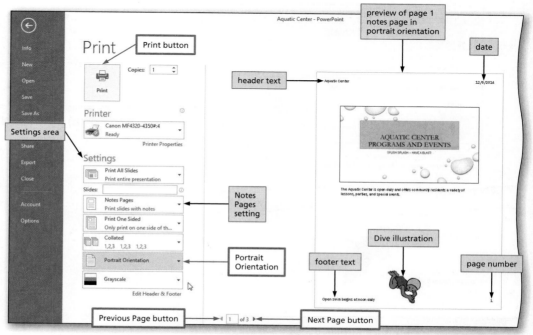

Figure 8–80

- Tap or click the Previous Page and Next Page buttons to display previews of the other pages.
- Tap or click the Print button in the Print gallery to print the notes (Figure 8–81).

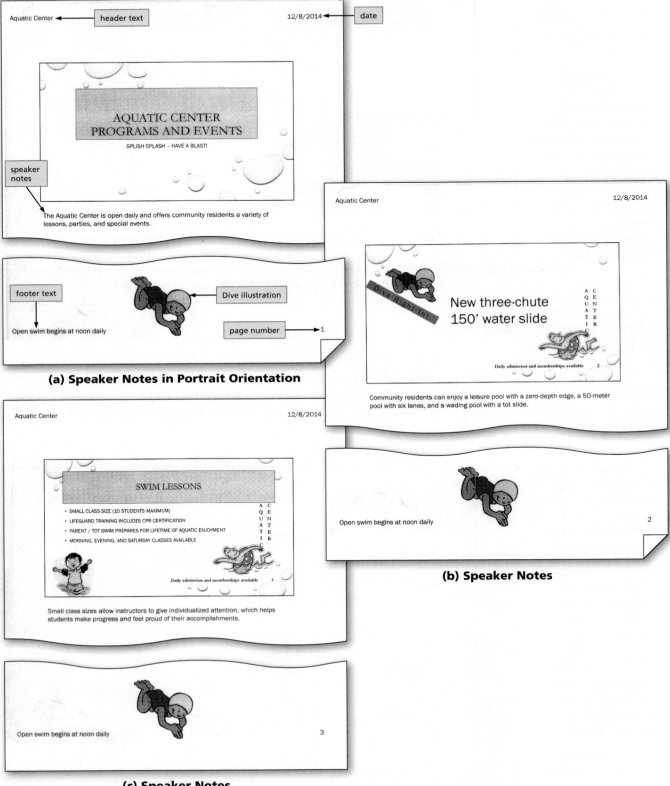

Figure 8–81

To Sign Out of a Microsoft Account

If you are signed in to a Microsoft account and are using a public computer or otherwise wish to sign out of your Microsoft account, you should sign out of the account from the Account gallery in the Backstage view before exiting PowerPoint. Signing out of the account is the safest way to make sure that nobody else can access SkyDrive files or settings stored in your Microsoft account. The following steps sign out of a Microsoft account from PowerPoint. For a detailed example of the procedure summarized below, refer to the Office and Windows chapter at the beginning of this book.

1 If you wish to sign out of your Microsoft account, tap or click FILE on the ribbon to open the Backstage view and then tap or click the Account tab to display the Account gallery.

2 Tap or click the Sign out link, which displays the Remove Account dialog box. If a Can't remove Windows accounts dialog box appears instead of the Remove Account dialog box, click the OK button and skip the remaining steps.

Q&A Why does a Can't remove Windows accounts dialog box appear?
If you signed in to Windows using your Microsoft account, then you also must sign out from Windows, rather than signing out from within PowerPoint. When you are finished using Windows, be sure to sign out at that time.

3 Tap or click the Yes button (Remove Account dialog box) to sign out of your Microsoft account on this computer.

Q&A Should I sign out of Windows after signing out of my Microsoft account?
When you are finished using the computer, you should sign out of your account for maximum security.

4 Tap or click the Back button in the upper-left corner of the Backstage view to return to the presentation.

BTW
Certification
The Microsoft Office Specialist (MOS) program provides an opportunity for you to obtain a valuable industry credential — proof that you have the PowerPoint 2013 skills required by employers. For more information, visit the Certification resource on the Student Companion Site located on www.cengagebrain.com. For detailed instructions about accessing available resources, visit www.cengage.com/ct/studentdownload or see the inside back cover of this book.

To Exit PowerPoint

This project now is complete. The following steps exit PowerPoint. For a detailed example of the procedure summarized below, refer to the Office and Windows chapter at the beginning of this book.

1a If you have one PowerPoint presentation open, tap or click the Close button on the right side of the title bar to close the open document and exit PowerPoint.

1b If you have multiple PowerPoint presentations open, press and hold or right-click the PowerPoint app button on the taskbar and then tap or click 'Close all windows' on the shortcut menu, or press ALT+F4 to close all open presentations and exit PowerPoint.

Q&A Could I press and hold or repeatedly click the Close button to close all open documents and exit PowerPoint?
Yes.

2 If a Microsoft PowerPoint dialog box appears, tap or click the Save button to save any changes made to the presentation since the last save.

BTW
Quick Reference
For a table that lists how to complete the tasks covered in this book using touch gestures, the mouse, ribbon, shortcut menu, and keyboard, see the Quick Reference Summary at the back of this book, or visit the Quick Reference resource on the Student Companion Site located on www.cengagebrain.com. For detailed instructions about accessing available resources, visit www.cengage.com/ct/studentdownload or see the inside back cover of this book.

Chapter Summary

In this chapter you have learned how to customize master slide layouts by changing the slide and font themes, formatting the background and footers, and adding background graphics. You then inserted a placeholder, added and formatted text, applied a fill, and changed the internal margins. Also, you rotated a picture and a placeholder, displayed the background graphics, and renamed and deleted slide layouts. Then you customized the handout and notes masters by adding a picture and changing the layout orientation. You then saved the slide master as a template, opened this template, added slide content, and printed a handout and speaker notes pages. The items listed below include all the new PowerPoint skills you have learned in this chapter.

Change Slide Background Elements

Format a Slide Master Background and Apply a Quick Style (PPT 484)
Insert a Background Graphic into a Slide Master (PPT 488)
Hide and Unhide Background Graphics (PPT 499)
Apply a Fill Color to a Slide (PPT 515)
Apply a Pattern to a Slide (PPT 516)

Create and Use a Template

Save a Master as a Template (PPT 510)
Open a Template and Save a Presentation (PPT 511)

Customize and Print Handouts and Notes Using Masters

Customize a Handout Using a Handout Master (PPT 504)
Customize a Notes Page Using a Notes Master (PPT 508)
Print a Presentation (PPT 519)
Print a Handout Using the Handout Master (PPT 520)
Print Speaker Notes Using the Notes Master (PPT 521)

Customize Slide Masters

Display a Slide Master (PPT 480)
Apply Slide and Font Themes to a Slide Master (PPT 481)
Customize Theme Fonts (PPT 482)
Cut a Placeholder and Paste It into a Slide Master (PPT 493)
Rename a Slide Master and a Slide Layout (PPT 500)
Delete a Slide Layout (PPT 502)
Close Master View (PPT 510)

Insert and Format Placeholders

Delete, Move, and Add Text to a Slide Master Footer (PPT 485)
Format Slide Master Footer Text (PPT 486)
Insert a Placeholder into a Blank Layout (PPT 489)
Add and Format Placeholder Text (PPT 491)
Change Character Spacing (PPT 495)

Insert and Format Text Boxes

Apply a Fill to a Text Box and Increase Transparency (PPT 496)
Change a Text Box Internal Margin (PPT 497)
Rotate a Picture and a Text Box (PPT 498)

What decisions will you need to make when creating your next presentation?

Use these guidelines as you complete the assignments in this chapter and create your own slide show decks outside of this class.

1. **Plan the slide master.** Using a new slide master gives you the freedom to plan every aspect of your slide. Take care to think about the overall message you are trying to convey before you start PowerPoint and select elements for this master.

2. **Develop the slide master prior to creating presentation slides.** You can save time and create consistency when you design and build your master at the start of your PowerPoint session rather than after you have created individual slides.

3. **Decide how to distribute copies of slides.** Some audience members will desire printed copies of your slides. To conserve paper and ink, you may decide to limit the number of copies you print or to post the presentation electronically in a shared location for users to print the presentation if they so choose.

How should you submit solutions to questions in the assignments identified with a ✹ symbol?

Every assignment in this book contains one or more questions identified with a ✹ symbol. These questions require you to think beyond the assigned presentation. Present your solutions to the questions in the format required by your instructor. Possible formats may include one or more of these options: write the answer; create a document that contains the answer; present your answer to the class; discuss your answer in a group; record the answer as audio or video using a webcam, smartphone, or portable media player; or post answers on a blog, wiki, or website.

Apply Your Knowledge

Reinforce the skills and apply the concepts you learned in this chapter.

Applying a Slide Theme to a Slide Master, Creating a New Theme Font, and Changing the Title Layout

Note: To complete this assignment, you will be required to use the Data Files for Students. Visit www.cengage.com/ct/studentdownload for detailed instructions or contact your instructor for information about accessing the required files.

Instructions: Run PowerPoint. Open the presentation, Apply 8-1 Culinary, from the Data Files for Students.

The three slides in this presentation discuss careers available to culinary arts majors. The document you open is a partially formatted presentation. You will apply a slide theme to a slide master, create a new theme font, and change the slide master background. Your presentation should look like Figure 8–82 on the next page.

Perform the following tasks:

1. Display Slide Master view and select the Slide Master thumbnail. Change the document theme to Berlin, the colors to Red Violet, and then create a new Theme Font named Bouchet using Papyrus for the heading font and Verdana for the body font.

2. Select the Title Slide Layout (Figure 8–82a), select the title text, change the color to Pink, Accent 1 (the fifth color in the first Theme Colors row), and then align this text left. Select the subtitle text, change the font size to 32 point, align the text left, bold the text, and then apply the Fill – Indigo, Background 2, Inner Shadow WordArt style (the fifth style in the third row) to the subtitle text. Delete the slide number text box in the pink rectangle shape, type, **Since 1926,** on two lines in the pink rectangle shape, and then change the font size to 24 point. Create a background on the title slide layout by inserting the photo called Wine and Cheese, which is available on the Data Files for Students. Change the transparency to 50%, as shown in Figure 8–82a.

3. Select the Two Content Layout, select the title font and change the font color to Pink, Accent 1 (the fifth color in the first Theme Colors row). Close Slide Master view.

4. On Slide 1, type **Bouchet Academy** as the title and **Culinary Career Education** as the subtitle, as shown in Figure 8–82b.

5. On Slide 2, change the layout to Two Content. Apply the Bevel Rectangle picture style to the two photos (the seventh style in the third row) and move them to the location shown in Figure 8–82c.

6. On Slide 3, change the layout to Two Content. Increase the size of the photo to approximately 4.28" × 4.28", apply the Rotated, White picture style (the third style in the third row), and then move the photo to the location shown in Figure 8–82d.

7. If requested by your instructor, add the name of your high school mascot as the fourth bulleted paragraph on Slide 3.

8. Apply the Split transition and change the duration to 3.25 for all slides.

9. Save the presentation using the file name, Apply 8-1 Bouchet Academy.

10. Submit the revised document in the format specified by your instructor.

11. ✹ In this presentation, you created a new theme font in the Slide Master and named it Bouchet. Why? You also changed the theme colors to Red Violet. How did this improve the presentation?

Continued >

Apply Your Knowledge *continued*

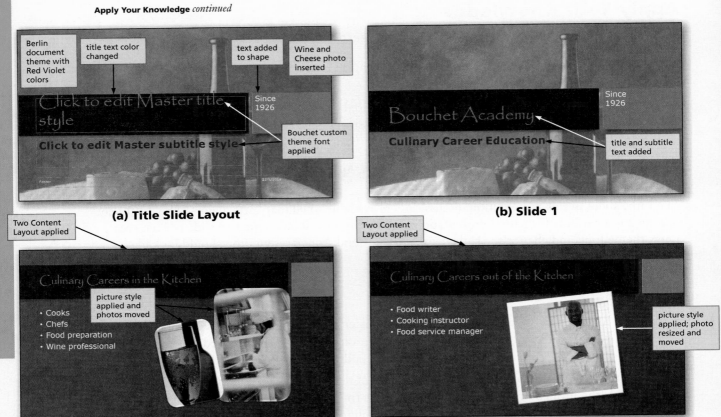

(a) **Title Slide Layout**

(b) **Slide 1**

(c) **Slide 2**

(d) **Slide 3**

Figure 8–82

Extend Your Knowledge

Extend the skills you learned in this chapter and experiment with new skills. You may need to use Help to complete the assignment.

Adding a Background to a Slide Master, Adjusting Footer Content and Placeholders, Inserting and Renaming a Layout, and Applying a Quick Style to a Placeholder

Note: To complete this assignment, you will be required to use the Data Files for Students. Visit www.cengage.com/ct/studentdownload for detailed instructions or contact your instructor for information about accessing the required files.

Instructions: Run PowerPoint. Open the presentation, Extend 8-1 Early Childhood, from the Data Files for Students. You will add a background graphic to the slide master, adjust footer content and placeholders, insert and rename a layout, and apply a style to a placeholder, as shown in Figure 8–83 on page PPT 528.

Perform the following tasks:
1. Display Slide Master view and then select the Slide Master thumbnail. Add the slide number and the Fixed date 12/8/14 to the footer placeholders. *Hint*: You may need to use Help to learn how to insert the date into the footer. Delete the center text placeholder in the footer area. Move the 'Date' footer placeholder to the upper-right area of the slide master. Right-align the 'Date' placeholder text, change the color to Black, Text 1 (the second color in the first Theme Colors row), and then bold this text. Add a background texture fill style by selecting Bouquet from the preset textures (the fifth texture in the fourth row). Customize the theme fonts using Rockwell for the heading font and Arial for the body font, as shown in Figure 8–83a. Name the new font set, Childhood.

2. Select the Title Slide Layout, select the title text and the subtitle text and align the text left. Select the Title and Content Layout and apply the 90% Pattern fill to this layout.

3. Insert a layout and rename it Closing Slide (Figure 8–83b on the next page). Select the title text, change the font color to Purple (the tenth color in the Standard Colors row), and then center this text. Select the title text placeholder, change the fill to Blue, Accent 1 (the fifth color in the Theme Colors row), select the Subtle Effect – Blue, Accent 5 style (the sixth style in the fourth row), and then change the transparency to 75%. Close Slide Master view.

4. On Slide 1 (Figure 8–83c), apply the Soft Edge Oval picture style (the sixth style in the third row) to both photos. Move the photos to the right side of the slide with the photo of the twins positioned on top of the other photo. Move the title and subtitle text placeholders so the left edges are at 5.50" left of center. Move the subtitle text placeholder down so the bottom of the placeholder is at the bottom edge of the slide. Decrease the size of the blocks illustration to approximately 1.04" × 1.87" and move it below the title placeholder.

5. Select the title text, change the font color to Blue, Accent 1 (the fifth color in the first Theme Colors row), bold it, and then apply the Gray – 50%, 18 pt glow, Accent color 3 glow effect to the text (the third effect in the fourth Glow Variations row). Use Format Painter to apply these same attributes to the subtitle text. Use the Smart Guides to position the blocks illustration between the title and subtitle placeholders.

6. On Slide 2 (Figure 8–83d), change the layout to Two Content. Change the title font color to Purple (the last color in the Standard Colors row), and then bold the title text. Use Format Painter to apply this same attribute to the title text on Slide 3. Change the second line of the title text on Slide 2 to 36 point and then use the Format Painter to apply this same attribute to the second line of the title on Slide 3.

7. Convert the bulleted text on Slide 2 to the Step Up Process SmartArt graphic (the second graphic in the first Process row). Change the colors to Colorful Range – Accent Colors 5 to 6 (the fifth color in the Colorful row), change the style to Cartoon (the third style in the first 3-D row), and then increase the size of the SmartArt graphic to approximately 5.75" × 7.5". Insert the photo called Toddler 1, which is available on the Data Files for Students. Move the photo to the right side of the slide using the Smart Guide and apply the Reflected Rounded Rectangle picture style (the fifth style in the first row), as shown in Figure 8–83d.

8. On Slide 3 (Figure 8–83e), convert the bulleted text to the Stacked Venn SmartArt graphic (the second graphic in the last Relationship row). Change the colors to Colorful Range – Accent Colors 5 to 6 (the fifth color in the Colorful row), change the style to Powder (the fourth style in the first 3-D row), and then increase the size of the SmartArt graphic text to 16 point and bold it. Move the graphic to the position shown in the figure. Insert the photo called Toddler 2, which is available on the Data Files for Students. Apply the Perspective Shadow, White picture style (the fourth style in the third row), as shown in Figure 8–83e.

9. On Slide 4 (Figure 8–83f), change the layout to Closing Slide. Create a background by inserting the photo called Children Playing, which is available on the Data Files for Students.

10. If requested by your instructor, add the number of bones you have broken after the word, Skills, in the subtitle placeholder on Slide 1 (Figure 8–83c).

11. Apply the Cube transition in the Exciting category to all slides and then change the duration to 2.50 seconds.

12. Save the presentation using the file name, Extend 8-2 Early Childhood Motor Skills.

13. Submit the revised document in the format specified by your instructor.

14. ✳ In this presentation, you changed the background of some slides to Bouquet. Was this a good choice? Why? In the Slide Master, you inserted a layout and changed the title text placeholder fill color and applied a style. How did this help your presentation?

Continued >

Extend Your Knowledge *continued*

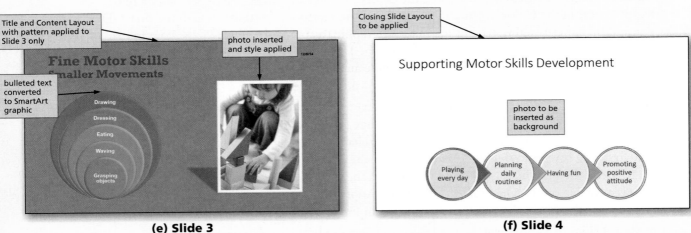

(a) Slide Master

(b) Closing Slide Layout

(c) Slide 1

(d) Slide 2

(e) Slide 3

(f) Slide 4

Figure 8–83

Analyze, Correct, Improve

Analyze a presentation, correct all errors, and improve it.

Changing a Font Theme and Background Style, Deleting a Placeholder and a Graphic, Hiding a Background Graphic on a Slide, and Rotating a Placeholder on a Slide Master

Note: To complete this assignment, you will be required to use the Data Files for Students. Visit www.cengage.com/ct/studentdownload for detailed instructions or contact your instructor for information about accessing the required files.

Instructions: Run PowerPoint. Open the presentation, Analyze 8-1 Rock Climbing, from the Data Files for Students. You are a rock climbing instructor and guide for PEAKS Rock Climbing

Company. Your boss asked you to prepare a presentation with information about your company to hand out to the next group of rock climbing students. Modify the slides by making the indicated corrections and improvements.

1. Correct

a. Display the Slide Master view (Figure 8–84a on the next page) and then select the Slide Master thumbnail. Change the background style from Style 10 to the Granite texture fill (second fill in third row). Change the theme font to Gil Sans MT. Delete the illustration in the lower-right corner of the slide. Close Slide Master view.

b. On Slide 1 (Figure 8–84b), cut the Peaks logo from the upper-left corner of the slide, display Slide Master view, select the Slide Master thumbnail and paste the logo and then move it to the lower-left corner of the Slide Master. Close Slide Master view.

c. On Slide 1 (Figure 8–84b), delete the photo and create a background by inserting the same photo, called Rock Climber, which is available on the Data Files for Students. Center both lines of the title text.

d. On Slide 2 (figure not shown), decrease the size of the photo to approximately 4.87" × 4.94", move it to the right side of the slide, and apply the Moderate Frame, Black picture style to the photo (the fifth style in the second row).

e. On Slide 3 (figure not shown), decrease the size of the text box so that it is not covering the logo. Move the rope photo to the upper-right corner of the slide, and move the shoes photo to the right and down slightly so it is not touching the text box. Apply the Rotated, White picture style to the shoes photo (the third style in the third row).

f. If requested by your instructor, add your mother's maiden name as the last bulleted paragraph on Slide 2.

2. Improve

a. Display the Slide Master view (Figure 8–84a) and select the Slide Master thumbnail. Delete the Date and Time, Slide number, and Footer placeholders because the Granite texture makes them difficult to view. Close Slide Master view.

b. On Slide 1, change the first line of the title font to Gil Sans Ultra Bold. Apply the WordArt style Gradient Fill – Gold, Accent 4, Outline – Accent 4 to the title (the third style in the second row). Change the text outline color to Black, Text 1 (the second color in the first Theme Colors row), and then change the outline weight to 3 pt. Change the second line of the title to Gil Sans Ultra Bold Condensed, and the size to 40 point.

c. Display the Slide Master view. Insert a new layout and rename it, Rotated Title. Move this new layout under the Slide Master. Insert a Picture placeholder in the right side of the slide. Insert a text placeholder in the center of the slide. Change the size of the title text placeholder to 1.45" × 7.5", rotate it left 90 degrees, and then change the shape fill color to Gray-50%, Accent 3 (the seventh color in the first Theme Colors row). Hide the background graphic on this layout and then move the Title placeholder to the left edge of the slide. Change character spacing to Very Loose and center the text. Close Slide Master view.

d. Change the layout on Slide 4 (figure not shown) to Rotated Title. Change the title font to Gil Sans Ultra Bold and change the font color to Dark Red (the first color in the Standard Colors row).

e. On Slides 2, 3, and 5, bold the title text (figures not shown).

f. On Slide 4, change the size of the bulleted text placeholder to approximately 3.12" × 5.2" and, if necessary, move the text placeholder to the left. Increase the size of the photo and move it to the right.

g. Change the Vortex transition to the Doors transition and then change the duration to 4.50 seconds for all slides.

h. Save the presentation using the file name, Analyze 8-1 Peaks Rock Climbing.

i. Submit the revised document in the format specified by your instructor.

Continued >

Analyze, Correct, Improve *continued*

3. ✳ Which errors existed in the starting file? How did changing the fonts and font sizes help? How did creating a background with the rock climber photo on Slide 1 improve the look of the slide?

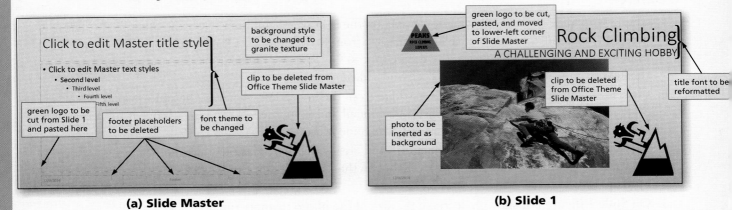

(a) Slide Master   **(b) Slide 1**

Figure 8–84

In the Labs

Design and/or create a presentation using the guidelines, concepts, and skills presented in this chapter. Labs 1 and 2, which increase in difficulty, require you to create solutions based on what you learned in the chapter; Lab 3 requires you to create a solution, which uses cloud and web technologies, by learning and investigating on your own from general guidance.

Lab 1: Deleting Slide Layouts, Rotating a Text Box and a Photo, Renaming a Slide Layout, Adding a Graphic, and Saving a Slide Master as a Template

Problem: You work for the town of Treesville in the parks and recreation division. Your director has decided to run weekly ads in the local newspaper highlighting the summer activities planned at Center Park. He has asked you to set up a template so that he can use it for future presentations about Center Park. He asked you to prepare the first week's ad and the ad for the annual July 4th fireworks event. You decide to do a PowerPoint presentation so that the ads also can run on a kiosk at the library and the town hall. You create the slide master template shown in Figure 8–85a, title slide layout and July 4th layout shown in Figures 8–85b and 8–85d. You create the two ads shown in Figures 8–85c and 8–85e.

Note: To complete this assignment, you will be required to use the Data Files for Students. Visit www.cengage.com/ct/studentdownload for detailed instructions or contact your instructor for information about accessing the required files.

Instructions: Perform the following tasks:
1. Open the presentation, Lab 8-1 Center Park, from the Data Files for Students.
2. Display Slide Master view. Delete all layouts except the Title Slide Layout, Title and Content Layout, and the Blank Layout. Select the Slide Master thumbnail. Create a background by inserting the photo called Park, which is available on the Data Files for Students. Delete all the placeholders except for the center footer text placeholder. Add the text, **Ad for week of:** in the center footer placeholder and change the font color to Black, Text 1. Close Slide Master view.
3. Select the Treesville logo and the WordArt on the Slide 1 and cut and paste it to the slide master. Close Slide Master view and then delete Slide 1. Click in the slide area to add the first slide with the new slide master. Save this file as a template and name it Center Park Template (Figure 8–85a).

4. Save the Center Park Template file as a presentation with the name, Lab 8-1 Treesville Summer Ads (Figures 8–85c and 8–85e).

5. Display Slide Master view and select the Title Slide Layout (Figure 8–85b). Delete all the placeholders except for the center footer placeholder. Insert a Rectangle shape in the lower-center area of the slide, type, **This Week in the Park**, in the shape, change the font size to 32 point, and then align the text to the top of the shape. Resize the shape to 5.93" × 13.33", change the transparency to 55%, and then move the shape so the bottom edge is at the bottom of the slide, as shown in Figure 8–85b. Close Slide Master view.

6. On Slide 1 (Figure 8–85c), change the layout to Title Slide. Insert the two photos called Volleyball and Carnival, and the illustration called Music, which are available on the Data Files for Students. Apply the Soft Edge Oval picture style (sixth style in the fourth row) to the Volleyball and Carnival photos. Insert a text box under the music illustration and type, **Enjoy music with DJ John every evening from 6 - 10 p.m.**, change the font size to 22 point, change the font color to Yellow (the fourth color in the Standard Colors row), and then center the text. Copy and paste this text box two times. Type **Volleyball tournaments!** in the second text box and type **Carnival – Fun for all ages!** in the third text box. Move these text boxes under the respective photos as shown in Figure 8–85c.

7. Display Slide Master view and select the Blank Layout. Insert the photo called Flag, which is available on the Data Files for Students. Adjust the size of the photo to approximately 2.59" × 2.07", rotate it -57 degrees, and then move it to the upper-right area of the slide. Insert a text box and type **Enjoy a day of family fun!** in the text box, increase the font size to 32 point, change the font color to White, Background 1 (the first color in the first Theme Colors row), and then center the text. Rotate the text box -34 degrees and then move it to the location shown in Figure 8–85d. Rename this layout, July 4th. Close Slide Master view.

8. Insert a new slide with the July 4th layout. Insert the two photos called Family and Fireworks, which are available on the Data Files for Students. Apply the Reflected Perspective Right picture style (the second style in the fourth row) to the Family photo and apply the Bevel Perspective Left, White picture

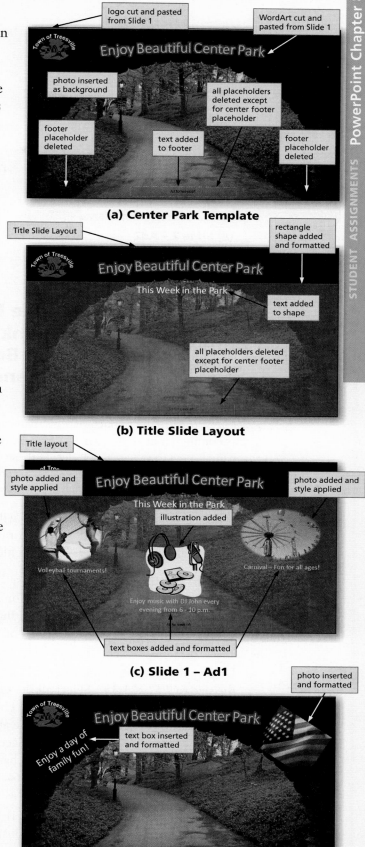

(a) Center Park Template

(b) Title Slide Layout

(c) Slide 1 – Ad1

(d) July 4th Layout – Ad2

Figure 8–85 (Continued)

Continued >

In the Labs *continued*

(e) Slide 2 – Ad2

Figure 8–85

style (the third style in the fourth row) to the Fireworks photo, and then move the photos to the locations shown in Figure 8–85e.

9. If requested by your instructor, add the time you were born after the word, tournaments in the left text box on Slide 1 (Figure 8–85c on the previous page).

10. Submit the document in the format specified by your instructor.

11. ✸ In Step 3, you saved the presentation as a template. Why? How did adding a shape with a transparent background to the title slide layout help your presentation?

Lab 2: Formatting a Slide Master Background, Inserting a Placeholder into a Blank Layout, Rotating a Text Box, Applying a Fill to a Text Box, Changing a Text Box Internal Margin, and Creating Handouts Using the Handout and Notes Masters

Problem: You are the public relations manager for a brand new office design company. There are two events coming up in your town. One is a local business seminar and the other is a job fair. Because your company is new to the area, you decide these events would be beneficial to introduce your company to the local market. You created a presentation with four slides, as shown in Figures 8–86c through 8–86f.

Note: To complete this assignment, you will be required to use the Data Files for Students. Visit www.cengage.com/ct/studentdownload for detailed instructions or contact your instructor for information about accessing the required files.

Instructions: Perform the following tasks:

1. Open the presentation, Lab 8-2 Jay Jones, from the Data Files for Students. Display Slide Master view. Select the Slide Master thumbnail. Create a background by using a solid fill, select the color Orange (the third color in the first Standard Colors row), and then change the transparency to 65%.

2. Display the Blank Layout. Insert a Text Placeholder on the right side of the slide and adjust the size to 7.5" × 1.35". Select all the text in the placeholder, remove the bullet, and type **Jay Jones Office Designers**, change the font to Castellar, increase the font size to 36 point, center this text, and then rotate all text 270 degrees. Apply the shape quick style Light 1 Outline, Colored Fill – Gray-50%, Accent 3 (the fourth style in the third row). Change the text box left internal margin to 0.2" and change the top internal margin to 1". The text should be on two lines as shown in Figure 8–86a. Cut and paste this placeholder to the Slide Master and move it to the right edge of the slide as shown in the figure.

3. With the Slide Master still open, insert the illustration called Logo, which is available on the Data Files for Students. Rotate the illustration left 90 degrees and move it to the top of the new text placeholder, as shown in Figure 8–86a.

4. Display the Title Slide Layout (Figure 8–86b) and delete the title placeholder. Align the subtitle placeholder to the bottom edge of the slide and change the size to 1.36" × 12".

Insert a Picture placeholder in the upper-left corner of the slide, change the size to 6.14" × 12", and then move it to the area shown in Figure 8–86b.

5. Display the Two Content Layout. Change the title font size to 48 point, the color to Purple (the tenth color in the Standard Colors row), and then bold this text. Close Slide Master view.

6. Select Slide 1 and change the layout to Title Slide. Insert the photo called JJ Office, which is available on the Data Files for Students. Select the subtitle text and bold the text. With the subtitle placeholder still selected, use the eyedropper to match the Purple color on the left side of the third floor of the office building, as shown in Figure 8–86c.

7. On Slides 2 through 4 (Figures 8–86d through 8–86f), adjust the sizes of the photos so they are not overlapping the titles or the text on the right side of the slides.

8. If requested by your instructor, type the name of the last TV program you watched as the fifth bulleted paragraph on Slide 4.

9. Apply the Doors transition in the Exciting category and then change the duration to 3.00 seconds for all slides.

10. Open the handout master, change the orientation to landscape. Type **Jay Jones Office Designers** as the header text. Delete the date in the upper-right header text box. Insert the JJ Office photo, change the size to 2.09" × 4.13", and then move it to the lower-right area of the handout master, as shown in Figure 8–86g. Close the Master View.

11. Open the notes master and then type **Jay Jones Office Designers** as the header text. Delete the date in the upper-right header text box. Insert the JJ Office photo, change the size to 1.2" × 2.38", and then move it to the right side of the notes master, as shown in Figure 8–86h. Close the Master View.

12. Save the presentation using the file name, Lab 8-2 Jay Jones Office Designers.

13. Submit the document in the format specified by your instructor.

14. ✷ Why did you add a background to all slides and why did you choose a 65% transparency? Did inserting a text placeholder with the company name and logo help the presentation? How?

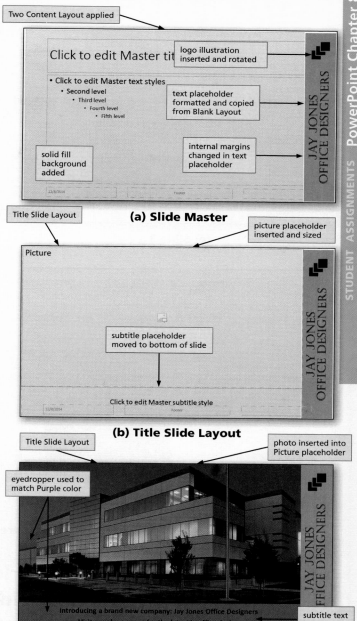

(a) Slide Master

(b) Title Slide Layout

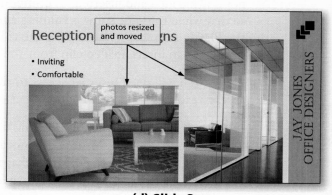

(c) Slide 1

(d) Slide 2

Figure 8–86 (Continued)

Continued >

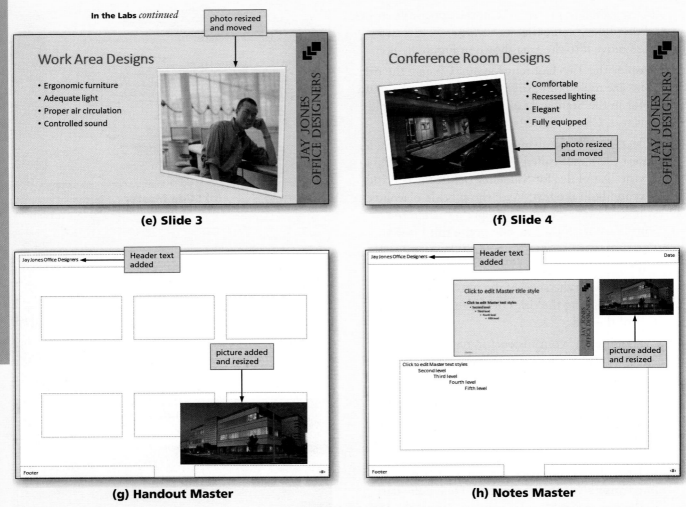

(e) Slide 3   (f) Slide 4

(g) Handout Master   (h) Notes Master

Figure 8–86

Lab 3: Expand Your World: Cloud and Web Technologies
Linking to a YouTube Video

Problem: You have created a presentation and want to play a video from an online website, such as YouTube or a news or sports organization, while running a slide show. Some websites encourage users to share video clips, while others restrict users from performing this process. The videos are not downloaded and inserted, or **embedded**, in the file; instead, they are **linked** to the presentation so that when the slide show is running and an Internet connection is present, the user can click the Play button to begin watching the video. PowerPoint includes commands on the Insert Video dialog box to insert a video clip from YouTube and from other websites.

Note: You will need Internet access to complete this assignment. If you do not have Internet access, read this assignment without performing the instructions.

Instructions: Perform the following tasks:

1. Log on to your Microsoft Windows account. In PowerPoint, open the Aquatic Center presentation you created in this chapter. At the end of the presentation, insert one slide using the Miscellaneous layout and then add the title text, "Swimming Safety Tips" on Slide 4. Save the file with the new filename, Lab 8-3 Aquatic Center with Video.

2. With Slide 4 displaying, tap or click the Insert Video icon in the content placeholder to display the Insert Video dialog box.

3. If necessary, tap or click the YouTube icon in the 'Also insert from' area to display the YouTube search box. Tap or click the YouTube search text box, type `swimming safely` as the search text, and then tap or click the Search button (the magnifying glass) or press the ENTER key. Watch several videos on the website and then select one you desire to link to your PowerPoint presentation.

4. Tap or click the Insert button (Insert Video dialog box) to display the selected clip on Slide 4. Increase the clip size and then add a border and an effect.

5. If requested by your instructor, enter the name of the city or county in which you were born in the Notes pane.

6. ✸ Do videos add to the audience's ability to retain information presented during a presentation? Why did you select this specific video to display on Slide 4?

Consider This: Your Turn

Apply your creative thinking and problem-solving skills to design and implement a solution.

1. Design and Create a Presentation about Tornado Safety Awareness
Personal

Part 1: There have been a lot of tornadoes reported all over the country. Some areas seem to have more tornadoes than others, but they can occur anywhere. Most tornadoes form from thunderstorms when two air masses (warm moist air and cool dry air) meet. A tornado can touch down to the ground from the storm and can produce wind speeds of up to 300 mph. The paths of tornadoes can be as wide as 50 miles. A funnel cloud is a cone-shaped rotating air column that extends down from the thunderstorm; if it touches the ground, it is called a tornado. If you hear about a tornado watch, tornadoes are possible in your area, and you should be alert and listen to the news. If you hear there is a tornado warning, a tornado could be close by and you should seek shelter right away. Your family does not have a plan if a tornado strikes. You decide to do a PowerPoint presentation to share with your family and friends. Information to include in your presentation is how to prepare ahead of time, such as putting together an emergency kit with food and water. You also should discuss what to do during a tornado. Use the concepts and techniques presented in this chapter to prepare a presentation. Select a suitable theme, and use WordArt or SmartArt graphics where appropriate. The presentation can contain photos, illustrations, and videos. You can use photos and illustrations from Office.com if they are appropriate for this topic. Submit your assignment in the format specified by your instructor.

Part 2: ✸ You made several decisions while creating the presentation in this assignment: where to place text, how to format the text (such as font, font size, and colors), which image(s) to use, what shapes, WordArt, and SmartArt graphics to add to the slide master to make the presentation look professional and consistent. What was the rationale behind each of these decisions? When you reviewed the document, what further revisions did you make and why? Where would you recommend showing this slide show?

2. Design and Create a Presentation about Boxing for Fitness
Professional

Part 1: As a personal trainer, you feel it is important to give your clients some variety in their workout routines. You enjoy boxing for fitness. It is a great full-body cardio workout and can be a lot of fun. It is a great way to burn calories. You decide to put together a presentation for the next open house at your fitness center. You want to give your clients and others information about boxing and what they may need to get started. Your fitness center has some of the equipment already such as heavy bags (for hitting), gloves in various sizes, and jump ropes for training.

Continued >

Consider This: Your Turn *continued*

The wraps that are worn under the gloves to cover the knuckles and prevent bruising and scrapes should be purchased by each individual. You also will mention some of the techniques used such as proper stance. You will describe the different punches like jabs, hooks, and uppercuts. The presentation could contain photos, illustrations, and videos. You can use your own photos and videos or use photos and illustrations from Office.com if they are appropriate for this topic. Customize your presentation by creating new layouts in the slide master to add interest to the presentation. Submit your assignment in the format specified by your instructor.

Part 2: ☀ You made several decisions while creating the presentation in this assignment: where to place text, how to format the text (such as font, font size, and colors), which image(s) to use, what shapes, WordArt, and SmartArt graphics to add to the slide master to make the presentation look professional and consistent. What was the rationale behind each of these decisions? When you reviewed the document, what further revisions did you make and why? Where would you recommend showing this slide show?

3. Design and Create a Presentation about Distracted Driving
Research and Collaboration

Part 1: Your criminal justice class is studying the effects of distracted driving. When you are driving any kind of vehicle, you need to have full concentration. Motorists continue to use cell phones despite the fact that the majority of states have banned texting while driving and several states now prohibit use of a phone without a hands-free device. Cell phone usage is not the only distraction while driving. Eating and drinking, applying make-up and nail polish, even listening to the radio or books on tape can distract you while you are driving. Your class has divided into three groups. One group will conduct a survey among students and non-students in the area about use of cell phones or other distracted behavior while driving. Another group will research the statistics from state to state and laws that have been passed regarding distracted driving. Your group will pull all the information together and create a PowerPoint presentation. Use at least three objectives found at the beginning of this chapter to develop the presentation. Print handouts and speaker notes for the class presentation. Customize a template for your school that may be used for other reports like this. You can use your own photos and videos or those available from Office.com if they are appropriate for this topic.

Part 2: ☀ You made several decisions while creating the presentation in this assignment: where to place text, how to format the text (such as font, font size, and colors), which image(s) to use, what shapes, WordArt, and SmartArt graphics to add to the slide master to make the presentation look professional and consistent. What was the rationale behind each of these decisions? When you reviewed the document, what further revisions did you make and why? Where would you recommend showing this slide show?

Learn Online Reinforce what you learned in this chapter with games, exercises, training, and many other online activities and resources.

Student Companion Site Reinforcement activities and resources are available at no additional cost on www.cengagebrain.com. Visit www.cengage.com/ct/studentdownload for detailed instructions about accessing the resources available at the Student Companion Site.

SAM Put your skills into practice with SAM! If you have a SAM account, go to www.cengage .com/sam2013 to access SAM assignments for this chapter.

9 Modifying a Presentation Using Graphical Elements

Microsoft product screenshots used with permission from Microsoft Corporation.

Objectives

You will have mastered the material in this chapter when you can:

- Change a text box outline color, weight, and style
- Set text box formatting as the default for new text boxes
- Apply a gradient, texture, pattern, and effects to a text box
- Convert WordArt to SmartArt
- Reorder SmartArt shapes
- Promote and demote SmartArt text

- Add and remove SmartArt shapes
- Convert a SmartArt graphic to text
- Customize the ribbon
- Combine and subtract shapes
- Create a handout by exporting files to Microsoft Word
- Save the presentation as a picture presentation

9 | Modifying a Presentation Using Graphical Elements

BTW
Identifying Shapes
Most objects in our world are composed of shapes: a circle, square, and triangle. Artists see objects as combinations of these shapes and begin their drawings by sketching these basic forms in proportion to each other. For example, a tree has the form of a circle for the branches and a rectangle for the trunk. A car has the form of a rectangle for the body, a smaller rectangle for the passenger compartment, and four circles for the wheels. Become observant of the relationships between objects in your world as you learn to use PowerPoint's drawing tools.

Introduction

PowerPoint's themes determine the default characteristics of slide objects. Colors, border weights and styles, fills, effects, and other formatting options give the slides a unique character. You can create your own designs for text boxes, shapes, lines, and other slide content, and then reuse these graphical objects throughout the presentation. Once you learn to format one type of object, such as a text box, you can use similar techniques to format other slide objects, such as SmartArt and shapes. One efficient way to create consistent graphical elements is to save your settings as the default. Then, when you insert the same objects later during the presentation design process, they will have the same characteristics as the initial element.

SmartArt graphics have individual layouts, styles, and color schemes. If one of these designs does not meet the specific needs of your slide content, you can modify the graphic by adding shapes, reordering the current shapes, and changing each element's size and location. You also can convert the SmartArt to text or to a shape if SmartArt is not the best method of conveying your ideas to an audience. PowerPoint's myriad formatting options allow you to tailor graphical elements to best fit your unique design needs.

BTW
Using Metaphorical Shapes
Use your imagination to use simple shapes and objects as metaphors. For example, a broken pencil can represent a stressful situation whereas a slice of cake can serve as imagery for a simple task. Make the shape large and bold, and use as few words as possible. Your audience should be able to understand and relate to the images without much explanation on the slides or from the speaker.

Project — Presentation with Customized Text Boxes, SmartArt, and Shapes

The invention of the steam locomotive changed the history of transportation forever. In the early 1800s, trains powered by steam were gaining popularity and replacing carts pulled by horses on wooden or iron rails. Peter Cooper built the first steam engine, called the Tom Thumb, to run on American common-carrier railroads.

Railroad buffs today are restoring steam engines and coaches. Excursions to destinations near and far are extremely popular. The presentation you create in this chapter (Figure 9–1) would be useful to show at visitor centers to promote these trips. All four slides are created by modifying a starting file that has a variety of content. The title slide (Figure 9–1a) contains a text box that is formatted with an outline style, a weight, and a color. These modifications are saved as the default settings for all other text boxes inserted into other slides. The second slide (Figure 9–1b) features a new colorful picture and a formatted text box. The text on Slide 3 (Figure 9–1c) is converted from WordArt to a SmartArt graphic. The layout, style, color, and shapes are changed and enhanced. The final slide (Figure 9–1d) has bulleted text converted from a SmartArt graphic; it also has a steam engine composed of formatted shapes. After the slides are created, you export the file to Microsoft Word to create a handout (Figures 9–1e and 9–1f) and then save the presentation as a picture presentation.

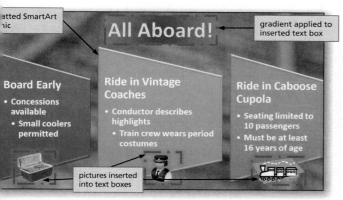

(a) Slide 1

formatted text box

picture changed from original presentation

pattern applied to inserted text box

(b) Slide 2

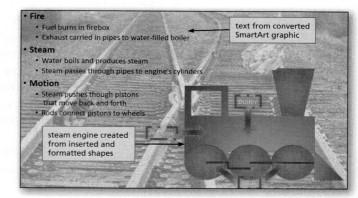

atted SmartArt nic

gradient applied to inserted text box

Board Early
- Concessions available
- Small coolers permitted

pictures inserted into text boxes

(c) Slide 3

- **Fire**
  - Fuel burns in firebox
  - Exhaust carried in pipes to water-filled boiler
- **Steam**
  - Water boils and produces steam
  - Steam passes through pipes to engine's cylinders
- **Motion**
  - Steam pushes though pistons that move back and forth
  - Rods connect pistons to wheels

text from converted SmartArt graphic

steam engine created from inserted and formatted shapes

(d) Slide 4

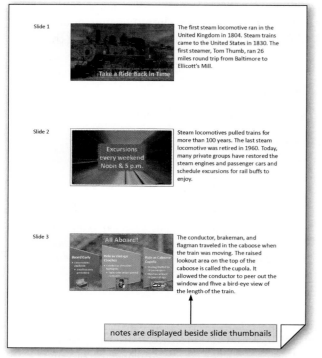

Slide 1 — The first steam locomotive ran in the United Kingdom in 1804. Steam trains came to the United States in 1830. The first steamer, Tom Thumb, ran 26 miles round trip from Baltimore to Ellicott's Mill.

Slide 2 — Steam locomotives pulled trains for more than 100 years. The last steam locomotive was retired in 1960. Today, many private groups have restored the steam engines and passenger cars and schedule excursions for rail buffs to enjoy.

Slide 3 — The conductor, brakeman, and flagman traveled in the caboose when the train was moving. The raised lookout area on the top of the caboose is called the cupola. It allowed the conductor to peer out the window and fhve a bird-eye view of the length of the train.

notes are displayed beside slide thumbnails

(e) Microsoft Word Handout – Page 1

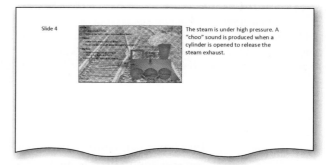

Slide 4 — The steam is under high pressure. A "choo" sound is produced when a cylinder is opened to release the steam exhaust.

(f) Microsoft Word Handout – Page 2

Figure 9–1

Roadmap

In this chapter, you will learn how to create the slides shown in Figure 9–1 on the previous page. The following roadmap identifies general activities you will perform as you progress through this chapter:

1. INSERT and CUSTOMIZE TEXT BOXES by changing the weight, color, and style and by adding an effect, pattern, and fill.
2. CONVERT WORDART TO SMARTART and then FORMAT by changing bullet levels, the layout, and the shape.
3. INSERT and FORMAT SHAPES.
4. DRAW and FORMAT LINES.
5. CUSTOMIZE THE RIBBON by adding a new group and buttons.
6. EXPORT a FILE to Microsoft Word and CREATE a PICTURE PRESENTATION.

At the beginning of step instructions throughout the chapter, you will see an abbreviated form of this roadmap. The abbreviated roadmap uses colors to indicate chapter progress: gray means the chapter is beyond that activity; blue means the task being shown is covered in that activity, and black means that activity is yet to be covered. For example, the following abbreviated roadmap indicates the chapter would be showing a task in the 3 INSERT & FORMAT SHAPES activity.

| 1 INSERT & CUSTOMIZE TEXT BOXES | 2 CONVERT WORDART TO SMARTART & FORMAT | **3 INSERT & FORMAT SHAPES** |

| 4 DRAW & FORMAT LINES | 5 CUSTOMIZE THE RIBBON | 6 EXPORT FILE & CREATE PICTURE PRESENTATION |

Use the abbreviated roadmap as a progress guide while you read or step through the instructions in this chapter.

To Run PowerPoint and Save a File

If you are using a computer to step through the project in this chapter and you want your screens to match the figures in this book, you should change your computer's resolution to 1366×768. The following steps run PowerPoint and then save a file.

1 Run PowerPoint. If necessary, maximize the PowerPoint window.

2 Open the presentation, Train, located on the Data Files for Students.

3 Save the presentation using the file name, Steam Train.

One of the few differences between Windows 7 and Windows 8 occurs in the steps to run PowerPoint. If you are using Windows 7, tap or click the Start button, type **PowerPoint** in the 'Search programs and files' box, tap or click PowerPoint 2013, and then, if necessary, maximize the PowerPoint window. For a summary of the steps to run PowerPoint in Windows 7, refer to the Quick Reference located at the back of this book.

CONSIDER THIS

Choose colors wisely.

Color can create interest in the material on your slides, so you need to think about which colors best support the message you want to share with your audience. The color you add to text boxes signals that the viewer should pay attention to the contents. Orange, red, and yellow are considered warm colors and will be among the first colors your viewers perceive on your slide. Blue and green are considered cool colors, and they often blend into a background and are less obvious than the warm colors.

Formatting Text Boxes

Text boxes can be formatted in a variety of ways to draw attention to slide content. You can apply formatting, such as fill color, gradient, texture, and pattern. You can add a picture; change the outline color, weight, and style; and then set margins and alignment. Once you determine the desired effects for a text box, you can save these settings as a default to achieve consistency and save time. Then, each time you insert another text box, the same settings will be applied.

In the following pages, you will perform these tasks on Slide 1:

1. Insert a text box into Slide 1.
2. Type text into the text box.
3. Change the text box outline color.
4. Change the text box outline weight.
5. Change the text box outline style.
6. Apply a glow effect to the text box.
7. Change the text box text to WordArt.
8. Increase the WordArt font size and center the paragraph in the text box.
9. Set the text box formatting as the default for new text boxes.

Once the text box formatting is complete on Slide 1, you then will perform these tasks on Slide 2:

1. Insert a text box and enter text.
2. Apply a pattern to the text box.
3. Change the text box pattern foreground and background colors.
4. Change the Slide 2 picture.

You also will perform these tasks on Slide 3:

1. Insert a text box and enter text.
2. Apply a gradient to the text box.
3. Align the text box in the center of the slide.

To Insert a Text Box and Text

The default text box is displayed with the Calibri font and has no border, fill, or effects. To begin customizing the Steam Train presentation, you will insert a text box and then type the text that serves as the title to your presentation. The following steps insert a text box and enter text into the text box.

1 Display the INSERT tab, tap or click the Text Box button (INSERT tab | Text group), position the pointer in the grass below the engine's front wheel on Slide 1, and then tap or click to insert the new text box.

2 Type **Take a Ride Back in Time** as the text box text (Figure 9–2 on the next page).

Q&A Do I need to position the text box in the precise location indicated in Figure 9–2? No. You will reposition the text box later in this chapter after you have made the formatting changes.

Can I change the shape of the text box? Yes. By default, a rectangular text box is inserted. If you want to use a different shape, select the text box, display the DRAWING TOOLS FORMAT tab, tap or click the Edit Shape button (DRAWING TOOLS FORMAT tab | Insert Shapes group), point to Change Shape in the list, and then tap or click the desired new shape.

BTW

The Ribbon and Screen Resolution
PowerPoint may change how the groups and buttons within the groups appear on the ribbon, depending on the computer's screen resolution. Thus, your ribbon may look different from the ones in this book if you are using a screen resolution other than 1366 × 768.

BTW

Q&As
For a complete list of the Q&As found in many of the step-by-step sequences in this book, visit the Q&A resource on the Student Companion Site located on www.cengagebrain.com. For detailed instructions about accessing available resources, visit www.cengage.com/ct/studentdownload or see the inside back cover of this book.

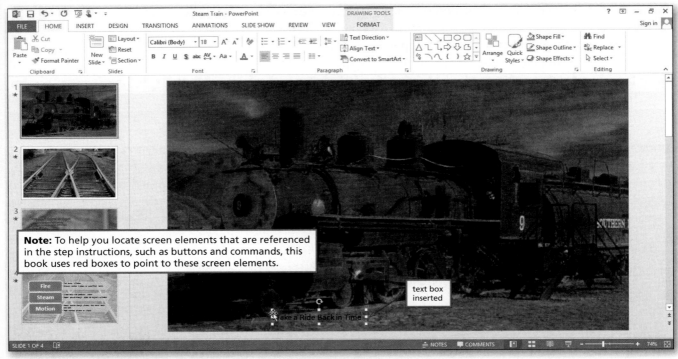

Figure 9–2

To Change a Text Box Outline Weight

1 INSERT & CUSTOMIZE TEXT BOXES | 2 CONVERT WORDART TO SMARTART & FORMAT | 3 INSERT & FORMAT SHAPES
4 DRAW & FORMAT LINES | 5 CUSTOMIZE THE RIBBON | 6 EXPORT FILE & CREATE PICTURE PRESENTATION

The first graphical change you will make to the text box is to increase the thickness of its border, which is called the outline. *Why? This thicker line is a graphical element that helps to call attention to the box.* The weight, or thickness, of the text box border is measured in points. The following steps increase the outline weight.

1

- Tap or click FORMAT on the ribbon to display the DRAWING TOOLS FORMAT tab.

- Tap or click the Shape Outline arrow (DRAWING TOOLS FORMAT tab | Shape Styles group) to display the Shape Outline gallery.

- Tap or click Weight in the Shape Outline gallery to display the Weight list (Figure 9–3).

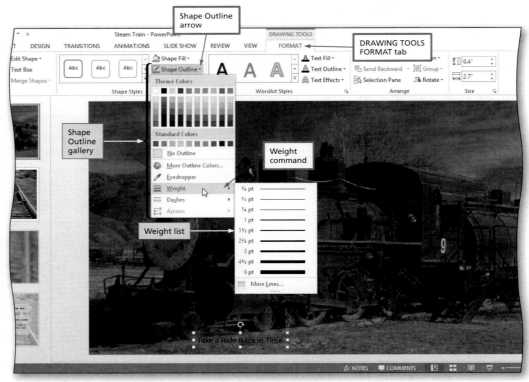

Figure 9–3

2

- If you are using a mouse, point to 6 pt to display a live preview of this outline line weight (Figure 9–4).

Experiment

- If you are using a mouse, point to various line weights on the Weight list and watch the border weights on the text box change.

3

- Tap or click 6 pt to add an outline around the text box.

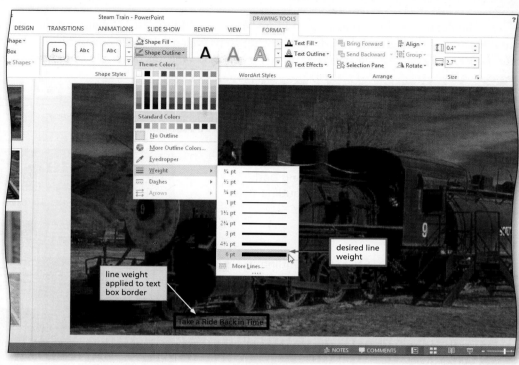

Figure 9–4

To Change a Text Box Outline Color

1 INSERT & CUSTOMIZE TEXT BOXES | 2 CONVERT WORDART TO SMARTART & FORMAT | 3 INSERT & FORMAT SHAPES
4 DRAW & FORMAT LINES | 5 CUSTOMIZE THE RIBBON | 6 EXPORT FILE & CREATE PICTURE PRESENTATION

The default outline color in the Office Theme is black. In this project, you will change the outline color to blue. *Why? The majority of people state that blue is their favorite color. In addition, blue contrasts well with the black-and-white photo in the slide background.* The following steps change the text box outline color.

1

- With the text box still selected, tap or click the Shape Outline arrow (DRAWING TOOLS FORMAT tab | Shape Styles group) to display the Shape Outline gallery.

- If you are using a mouse, point to Blue in the Standard Colors area to display a live preview of that outline color on the text box (Figure 9–5).

Experiment

- If you are using a mouse, point to various colors in the Shape Outline gallery and watch the border colors on the text box change.

2

- Tap or click Blue to change the text box border color.

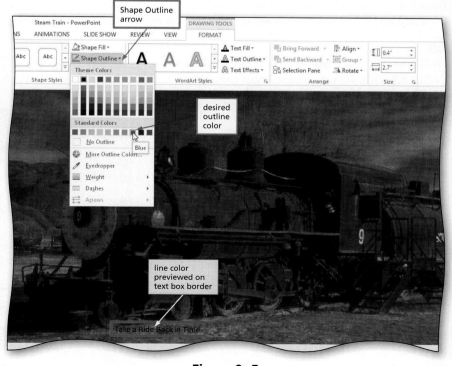

Figure 9–5

To Change a Text Box Outline Style

The default outline style is a solid line. You can add interest by changing the style to dashes, dots, or a combination of dashes and dots. The following steps change the text box outline style to Long Dash Dot. *Why?* *The dashes in this pattern resemble the rails and the dots resemble the shorter railroad ties that anchor the rails.*

- Tap or click the Shape Outline arrow (DRAWING TOOLS FORMAT tab | Shape Styles group) to display the Shape Outline gallery.

- Tap or click Dashes to display the Dashes list.

- If you are using a mouse, point to Long Dash Dot to display a live preview of this outline style (Figure 9–6).

Experiment

- Point to various styles in the Shape Outline gallery and watch the borders on the text box change.

- Tap or click Long Dash Dot to change the text box border style.

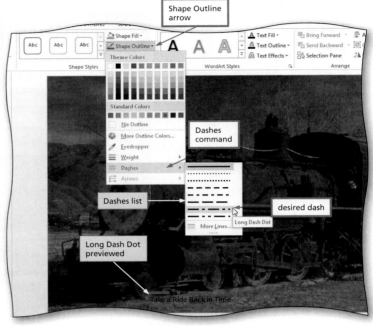

Figure 9–6

To Apply an Effect to a Text Box

PowerPoint provides a variety of visual effects to add to the text box. They include shadow, glow, reflection, and 3-D rotation. The following steps apply a glow effect to the text box. *Why?* *The background photo has a soft texture, so you can coordinate with this soft effect by adding a glow effect to the text box.*

- Tap or click the Shape Effects button (DRAWING TOOLS FORMAT tab | Shape Styles group) to display the Shape Effects gallery.

- Tap or click Glow to display the Glow gallery.

- If you are using a mouse, point to Blue, 18 pt glow, Accent color 1 (first color in the fourth row in the Glow Variations area) to display a live preview of this outline effect (Figure 9–7).

Experiment

- If you are using a mouse, point to various effects in the Glow gallery and watch the glow effects change on the text box.

- Tap or click the Blue, 18 pt glow, Accent color 1 variation to apply the glow effect.

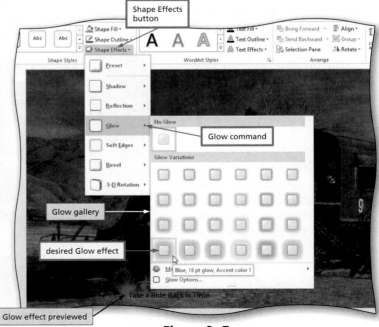

Figure 9–7

To Format Text Box Text

The text box outline color, width, line style, and effect are set, so you now can choose a font and font size that complement the formatting changes. A WordArt style can add visual interest to the text box. The following steps change the text box text to WordArt, change the font size, and center the text in the text box.

1 Select all the text box text, tap or click the WordArt Styles More button (DRAWING TOOLS FORMAT tab | WordArt Styles group) to expand the gallery, and then tap or click Pattern Fill – Blue, Accent 1, Light Downward Diagonal Outline - Accent 1 (fourth letter A in fourth row) to apply this style.

2 Increase the font size to 66 point.

3 Center the text in the text box. If necessary, drag the text box to the location shown in Figure 9–8.

Figure 9–8

BTW

Touch Screen Differences
The Office and Windows interfaces may vary if you are using a touch screen. For this reason, you might notice that the function or appearance of your touch screen differs slightly from this chapter's presentation.

BTW

Line Spacing Measurements
The lower part of each letter rests on an imaginary line called the baseline. The space between the baseline of one row of type and the baseline of the row beneath it is called line spacing. Typically, the line spacing is 120 percent of the font size. For example, if the font size is 10 point, the line spacing is 12 point so that two points of space are displayed between the lines.

To Set Text Box Formatting as the Default

1 INSERT & CUSTOMIZE TEXT BOXES | 2 CONVERT WORDART TO SMARTART & FORMAT | 3 INSERT & FORMAT SHAPES
4 DRAW & FORMAT LINES | 5 CUSTOMIZE THE RIBBON | 6 EXPORT FILE & CREATE PICTURE PRESENTATION

The text box you inserted and formatted has a variety of visual elements that work well with the steam engine picture and overall theme. You can insert text boxes with the same formatting into other slides in the presentation. *Why? To save time and ensure all the formatting changes are applied consistently, you can set the formatting of one text box as the default for all other text boxes you insert into the presentation.* The steps on the next page set the text box on Slide 1 as the default.

1

- Press and hold or right-click the text box outline to display the shortcut menu (Figure 9–9).

2

- Tap or click 'Set as Default Text Box' on the shortcut menu to set the text box formatting as the default for any new text boxes.

Q&A What should I do if the 'Set as Default Text Box' command is not displayed on the shortcut menu? Repeat Step 1 and be certain to tap or click the text box border, not the interior of the box.

Does setting the default text box affect all presentations or just the current one? Only the current presentation is affected.

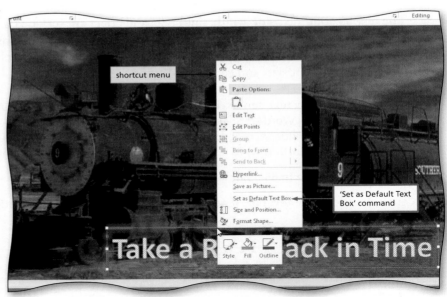

Figure 9–9

To Insert a Formatted Text Box and Enter Text

Any new text boxes you insert will have the same formatting you applied to the Slide 1 text box. You want to emphasize to your presentation viewers that train excursions are offered twice daily, so a text box on Slide 2 is a good place to state this information. The following steps insert a formatted text box into Slide 2 and enter text.

1 Display Slide 2, display the INSERT tab, and then tap or click the Text Box button.

2 Insert the text box into the center of the slide and then type **Excursions** as the first line of the text box text.

3 Press SHIFT+ENTER to insert a line break and then type **every weekend** as the second text box line.

4 Press SHIFT+ENTER to insert a line break and then type **Noon & 5 p.m.** as the third text box line.

5 If necessary, drag the text box to the location shown in Figure 9–10.

Figure 9–10

To Apply a Pattern to a Text Box

Why? *A pattern fill can call attention to a text box.* PowerPoint provides a Pattern gallery, allowing you to change the appearance of the text box with a variety of horizontal and vertical lines, dots, dashes, and stripes. If desired, you can change the default fill foreground and background colors. The following steps apply a pattern to the Slide 2 text box and change the foreground and background colors.

1

- Press and hold or right-click anywhere on the Slide 2 text box to display the shortcut menu (Figure 9–11).

Figure 9–11

2

- Tap or click Format Shape on the shortcut menu to display the Format Shape pane.

- If necessary, tap or click FILL to expand the FILL section. Tap or click Pattern fill to display the Pattern gallery and the 5% pattern on the text box (Figure 9–12).

 Can I experiment with previewing the patterns on the text box?
No, the live preview function is not available.

Can the default pattern gallery color vary?
Yes. You may find that your default color is black rather than the shade of blue shown in the figure.

Figure 9–12

3

- Tap or click the Narrow vertical pattern (third pattern in fourth row) to apply this pattern to the Slide 2 text box.

Q&A How can I delete a pattern if I decide not to apply one to my slide?
If you already have applied the pattern, tap or click the Undo button on the Quick Access Toolbar.

- Scroll down the Format Shape pane and then tap or click the Foreground button to display the color gallery (Figure 9–13).

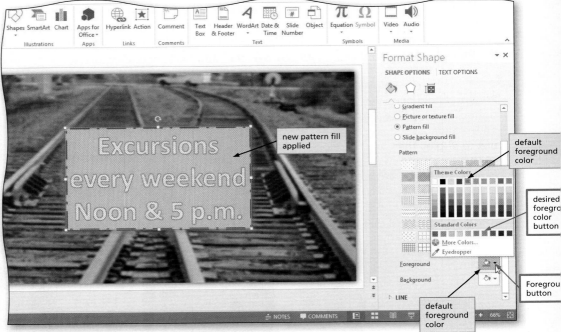

Figure 9–13

Q&A Can the default foreground color vary in the gallery?
Yes. You may find that your default color is black rather than the shade of blue shown in the figure.

4

- Tap or click Light Blue (seventh color in the Standard Colors row) to apply this color to the text box pattern and to display the Pattern gallery with the new foreground color.

- Tap or click the Background button to display a color gallery (Figure 9–14).

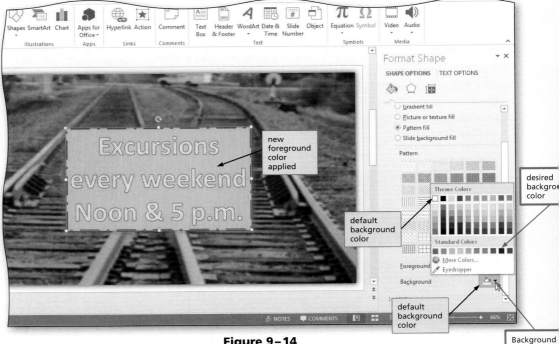

Figure 9–14

⑤

- Tap or click Dark Blue (ninth color in the Standard Colors row) to apply this color to the text box background and to display the Pattern gallery with the new background color (Figure 9–15).

⑥

- Tap or click the Close button to close the Format Shape pane.

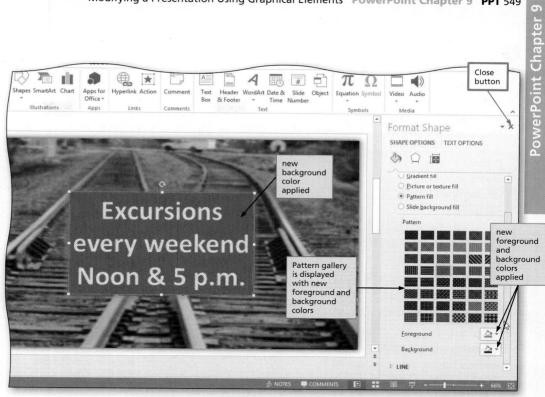

Figure 9–15

To Apply a Gradient Fill to a Text Box

1 INSERT & CUSTOMIZE TEXT BOXES | 2 CONVERT WORDART TO SMARTART & FORMAT | 3 INSERT & FORMAT SHAPES
4 DRAW & FORMAT LINES | 5 CUSTOMIZE THE RIBBON | 6 EXPORT FILE & CREATE PICTURE PRESENTATION

Why? *A gradient fill is another type of format you can apply to create interest in a slide element.* It blends one color into another shade of the same color or another color. PowerPoint provides several preset gradients, or you can create your own custom color mix. The following steps insert a text box into Slide 3 and then apply a gradient fill.

①

- Display Slide 3, display the INSERT tab, and then insert a text box near the top of the slide.

- Type **All Aboard!** as the text box text, and if necessary, drag the text box to the location shown in Figure 9–16.

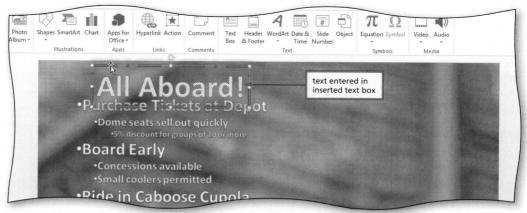

Figure 9–16

2

- Tap or click the DRAWING TOOLS FORMAT tab and then tap or click the Shape Fill arrow (DRAWING TOOLS FORMAT tab | Shape Styles group) to display the Shape Fill gallery.

- Tap or click Gradient to display the Gradient gallery (Figure 9–17).

 **Experiment**

- If you are using a mouse, point to various fills in the Gradient gallery and watch the interior of the text box change.

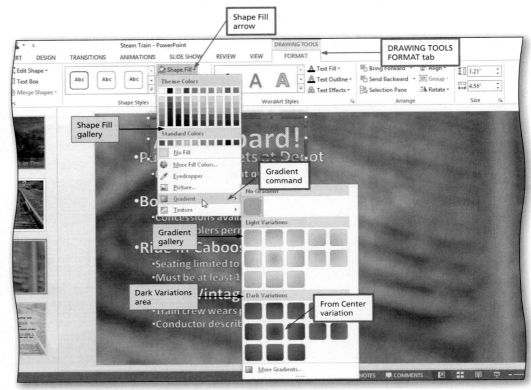

Figure 9–17

3

- Tap or click From Center (second variation in the second row in the Dark Variations area) to apply the gradient fill.

To Center a Text Box

1 INSERT & CUSTOMIZE TEXT BOXES | 2 CONVERT WORDART TO SMARTART & FORMAT | 3 INSERT & FORMAT SHAPES
4 DRAW & FORMAT LINES | 5 CUSTOMIZE THE RIBBON | 6 EXPORT FILE & CREATE PICTURE PRESENTATION

The text box on Slide 3 will serve as the title. You could attempt to center it horizontally on the slide and use the rulers to aid you in this process. You also can use PowerPoint's align feature. **Why?** *Using the Align command is a more efficient method of centering the text box between the left and right edges of the slide.* You can align a slide element horizontally along the left or right sides or in the center of the slide, and you also can align an element vertically along the top, bottom, or middle of the slide. The following steps align the Slide 3 text box horizontally.

1

- With the Slide 3 text box selected, tap or click the Align button (DRAWING TOOLS FORMAT tab | Arrange group) to display the Align menu (Figure 9–18).

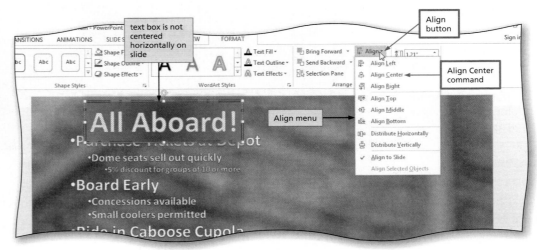

Figure 9–18

2

- Tap or click Align Center to center the text box horizontally on the slide (Figure 9–19).

Q&A Can I position a text box in a precise location on a slide? Yes. With the text box selected, press and hold or right-click a border of the box to display the shortcut menu and then tap or click Format Shape on the shortcut menu to display the Format Shape pane. Tap or click the Size & Properties icon, and then tap or click POSITION and enter Horizontal position and Vertical position measurements. Specify if these measurements should be from the Top Left Corner or the Center of the text box and then tap or click the Close button (Format Shape pane).

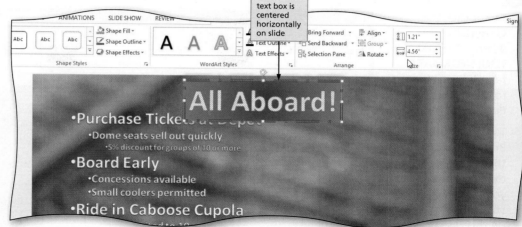

Figure 9–19

To Change a Slide Picture

1 INSERT & CUSTOMIZE TEXT BOXES | 2 CONVERT WORDART TO SMARTART & FORMAT | 3 INSERT & FORMAT SHAPES
4 DRAW & FORMAT LINES | 5 CUSTOMIZE THE RIBBON | 6 EXPORT FILE & CREATE PICTURE PRESENTATION

PowerPoint allows you to change a picture on a slide easily. The following steps change the Slide 2 picture. *Why? The photograph on Slide 2 features crossing train tracks, but the background does not have much contrast or many rich colors. A more dramatic photograph of tracks is located on the Data Files for Students.*

1

- Display Slide 2, tap or click anywhere on the picture except the text box to select the picture, and then tap or click the PICTURE TOOLS FORMAT tab (Figure 9–20).

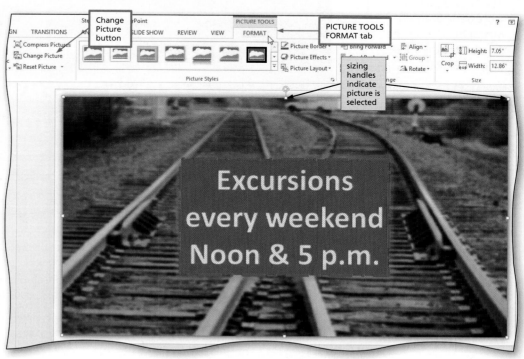

Figure 9–20

2

• Tap or click the Change Picture button (PICTURE TOOLS FORMAT tab | Adjust group) to display the Insert Pictures dialog box.

• Tap or click the Browse button and then navigate to the location where your Data Files for Students are stored (in this case, the PowerPoint folder in the CIS 101 folder [or your class folder] on your computer or SkyDrive).

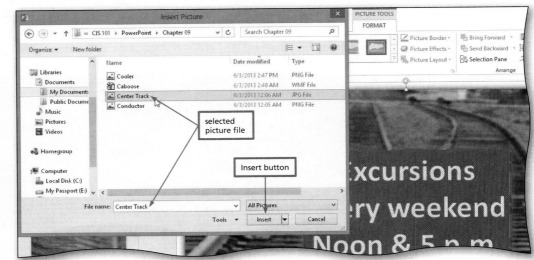

Figure 9–21

• Tap or click Center Track to select the file name (Figure 9–21).

Q&A What if the picture is not in my Data Files for Students folder?
Use the same process, but select the device containing the photograph. Another option is to locate this photograph or a similar one on Office.com.

3

• Tap or click the Insert button (Insert Picture dialog box) to change the Slide 2 picture. If necessary, drag the sizing handles to the borders of the slide (Figure 9–22).

Q&A What if I do not want to use this picture?
Tap or click the Undo button on the Quick Access Toolbar.

Figure 9–22

Break Point: If you wish to take a break, this is a good place to do so. Be sure to save the Steam Train file again and then you can exit PowerPoint. To resume at a later time, run PowerPoint, open the file called Steam Train, and continue following the steps from this location forward.

Manipulating SmartArt

Every SmartArt layout has a unique design and graphical elements. The shapes maximize vertical and horizontal space for text and pictures. When your presentation calls for special design needs or additional shapes, you can change the defaults that specify where each SmartArt element is displayed. You can add, subtract, and reorder shapes; promote and demote text; make a single shape smaller or larger; and change the SmartArt fill, outline, and colors.

In the following pages, you will perform these tasks on Slide 3:

1. Convert WordArt paragraphs to a SmartArt Target List.
2. Reorder two shapes in the SmartArt layout.
3. Reorder two bulleted paragraphs in a shape.
4. Promote and demote bulleted paragraphs.
5. Change the SmartArt layout and style.
6. Resize the entire SmartArt layout and shapes within the layout.
7. Apply pictures to SmartArt shapes.
8. Convert the SmartArt graphic to text.

Use keywords in SmartArt graphics.

Most SmartArt shapes have very limited space for text. You must, therefore, carefully choose each word you are going to display in the graphic. The text you select can serve as keywords, or a speaking outline. If you glance at the SmartArt when you are presenting the slide show in front of an audience, each word should prompt you for the main point you are going to make. These keywords should jog your memory if you lose your train of thought or are interrupted.

To Convert WordArt to SmartArt

1 INSERT & CUSTOMIZE TEXT BOXES | 2 CONVERT WORDART TO SMARTART & FORMAT | 3 INSERT & FORMAT SHAPES
4 DRAW & FORMAT LINES | 5 CUSTOMIZE THE RIBBON | 6 EXPORT FILE & CREATE PICTURE PRESENTATION

The bulleted paragraphs on Slide 3 are formatted as WordArt. Although WordArt can add visual interest, using a graphical element such as SmartArt can be even more effective in helping the audience to grasp essential concepts. *Why? SmartArt diagrams are creative means to show processes, lists, cycles, and other relationships.* PowerPoint suggests layouts that might fit the concept you are trying to present and then easily converts WordArt to SmartArt. The following steps convert WordArt to SmartArt.

1
- Display Slide 3, press and hold or right-click anywhere in the WordArt bulleted list paragraphs to display the shortcut menu, and then tap or click 'Convert to SmartArt' to display the SmartArt gallery.

Q&A Does it matter where I place the cursor?
No. As long as the cursor is placed in the WordArt text, you will be able to convert the paragraphs to SmartArt.

- If you are using a mouse, point to Vertical Block List in the gallery to display a live preview of that layout applied to the WordArt paragraphs (Figure 9–23).

Figure 9–23

**Experiment**
- If you are using a mouse, point to various graphics in the SmartArt gallery and watch the layouts change.

• Tap or click Vertical Block List in the SmartArt gallery to convert the WordArt to that layout.

Q&A How is the text arranged in the Vertical Block List SmartArt layout?
The four first-level paragraphs are in the left column of the graphic and have a larger font size than the eight bulleted second-level paragraphs in the right column.

To Reorder SmartArt Shapes

1 INSERT & CUSTOMIZE TEXT BOXES | 2 CONVERT WORDART TO SMARTART & FORMAT | 3 INSERT & FORMAT SHAPES

4 DRAW & FORMAT LINES | 5 CUSTOMIZE THE RIBBON | 6 EXPORT FILE & CREATE PICTURE PRESENTATION

Now that the SmartArt layout is created, you can modify the graphic. One change you can make is to change the order of the shapes. You decide that two items in the graphic should be displayed in a different order. *Why? The caboose is at the end of a train, so it is fitting that the Ride in Caboose Cupola shape is displayed at the end of the list. You also decide that potential customers would be interested in knowing that the excursion is narrated, so you want to move the information in the second bulleted paragraph in the Ride in Vintage Coaches shape above the fact that the crew will be dressed in period costumes.* PowerPoint provides tools to move shapes and paragraphs in a vertical layout up or down. The following steps reorder the Ride in Caboose Cupola and Ride in Vintage Coaches shapes and the two bulleted paragraphs in the Ride in Vintage Coaches shape.

1
• Position the pointer in the Ride in Vintage Coaches shape and then tap or click to select it and the two bulleted paragraphs (Figure 9–24).

Q&A Are both shapes selected even though the sizing handles are displayed only around the Ride in Vintage Coaches shape?
Yes. The Ride in Vintage Coaches shape is a first-level paragraph, and the two bulleted second-level paragraphs are associated with it. When a first-level paragraph is selected, any related paragraphs also are selected with it.

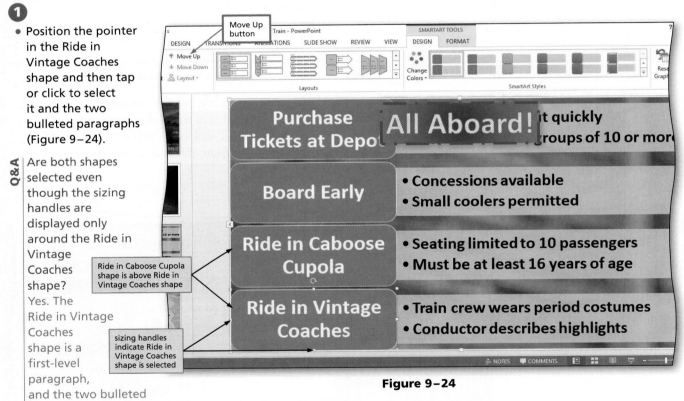

Figure 9–24

- With the SMARTART TOOLS DESIGN tab displaying, tap or click the Move Up button (SMARTART TOOLS DESIGN tab | Create Graphic group) to reorder the Ride in Vintage Coaches shape above the Ride in Caboose Cupola shape.

- Position the pointer in the bulleted paragraph, Train crew wears period costumes (Figure 9–25).

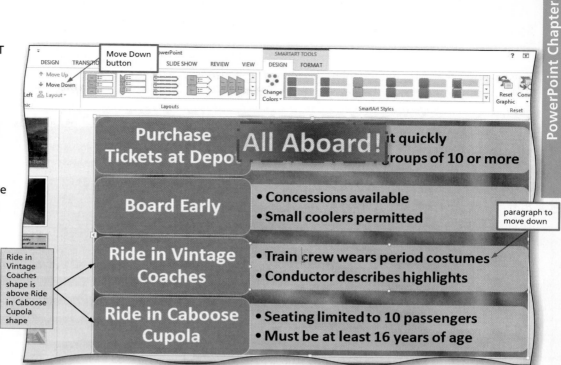

Figure 9–25

- Tap or click the Move Down button (SMARTART TOOLS DESIGN tab | Create Graphic group) to reorder the bulleted paragraph, Train crew wears period costumes, below the bulleted paragraph, Conductor describes highlights.

To Promote a SmartArt Bullet Level

1 INSERT & CUSTOMIZE TEXT BOXES | 2 CONVERT WORDART TO SMARTART & FORMAT | 3 INSERT & FORMAT SHAPES
4 DRAW & FORMAT LINES | 5 CUSTOMIZE THE RIBBON | 6 EXPORT FILE & CREATE PICTURE PRESENTATION

PowerPoint provides tools that allow you to promote and demote bulleted text. These tools function in the same manner as the Increase List Level and Decrease List Level buttons that change the indents for bulleted text.

Another change you want to make on Slide 3 is to promote the bulleted paragraph, 5% discount for groups of 10 or more, to the same level as the bullet above it. *Why? Because this fact may encourage people to attend the excursion.* The following steps promote the second bullet in the Purchase Tickets at Depot shape.

- Select the All Aboard! text box and drag it to the left so that it is positioned over the Purchase Tickets at Depot graphic.

- Position the pointer in the bulleted paragraph, 5% discount for groups of 10 or more, and then display the SMARTART TOOLS DESIGN tab (Figure 9–26).

Figure 9–26

2
- Tap or click the Promote button (SMARTART TOOLS DESIGN tab | Create Graphic group) to decrease the indent of the bulleted paragraph.

To Demote a SmartArt Bullet Level

The two bulleted items in the Board Early shape are second-level paragraphs, but you decide to demote the second paragraph, Small coolers permitted. You also want to demote the paragraph, Train crew wears period costumes. *Why? The fact that passengers are permitted to bring small coolers on board is not as important to emphasize as the fact that concessions are available. In addition, the fact that the crew is wearing costumes is secondary to the point that the excursion is narrated.* The following steps demote the second-level bulleted paragraphs.

1
- Position the pointer in the bulleted paragraph, Small coolers permitted (Figure 9–27).

Figure 9–27

2
- With the SMARTART TOOLS DESIGN tab displaying, tap or click the Demote button (SMARTART TOOLS DESIGN tab | Create Graphic group) to increase the indent of the bulleted paragraph.
- Position the pointer in the bulleted paragraph, Train crew wears period costumes, and then tap or click the Demote button to increase the indent of this paragraph (Figure 9–28).

Figure 9–28

TO ADD A SMARTART BULLET

If you need to add information to a SmartArt shape, you can create a new bulleted paragraph. This text would display below the last bulleted paragraph in the shape. If you wanted to add a SmartArt bullet, you would perform the following steps.

1. Select the SmartArt graphic shape where you want to insert the bulleted paragraph.
2. Tap or click the Add Bullet button (SMARTART TOOLS DESIGN tab | Create Graphic group) to insert a new bulleted paragraph below any bulleted text.

To Change the SmartArt Layout

1 INSERT & CUSTOMIZE TEXT BOXES | 2 CONVERT WORDART TO SMARTART & FORMAT | 3 INSERT & FORMAT SHAPES
4 DRAW & FORMAT LINES | 5 CUSTOMIZE THE RIBBON | 6 EXPORT FILE & CREATE PICTURE PRESENTATION

Once you begin formatting a SmartArt shape, you may decide that another layout better conveys the message you are communicating to an audience. PowerPoint allows you to change the layout easily. Any graphical changes that were made to the original SmartArt, such as moving shapes or promoting and demoting paragraphs, are applied to the new SmartArt layout. The following steps change the SmartArt layout to Trapezoid List. *Why? Most of the shapes and pictures in the presentation are composed of squares and rectangles, so you want to continue using similar shapes. In addition, the Trapezoid List shapes are placed in a consecutive horizontal order, much like the train coaches that are coupled together.*

1

- With the SMARTART TOOLS DESIGN tab displaying, tap or click the More button in the Layouts group to expand the Layouts gallery (Figure 9–29).

Can I select one of the layouts displaying in the Layouts group without expanding the layout gallery?
Yes. At times, however, you may want to display the gallery to view and preview the various layouts.

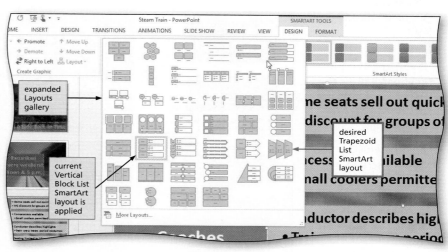

Figure 9–29

2

- If you are using a mouse, point to the Trapezoid List layout (last layout in the fifth row) to display a live preview of this SmartArt layout (Figure 9–30).

Experiment

- If you are using a mouse, point to various layouts in the gallery and watch the SmartArt layouts change.

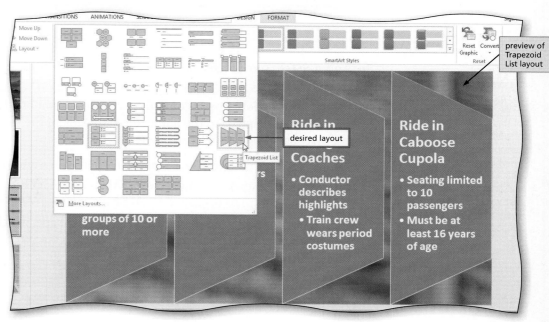

Figure 9–30

Are additional layouts available other than those displayed in the gallery?

Yes. Tap or click More Layouts to display the Choose a SmartArt Graphic dialog box and then select another layout.

3

- Tap or click Trapezoid List to change the layout.

To Remove a SmartArt Shape

1 INSERT & CUSTOMIZE TEXT BOXES | 2 CONVERT WORDART TO SMARTART & FORMAT | 3 INSERT & FORMAT SHAPES
4 DRAW & FORMAT LINES | 5 CUSTOMIZE THE RIBBON | 6 EXPORT FILE & CREATE PICTURE PRESENTATION

Now that the new SmartArt layout is created, you can modify the graphic. One change you can make is to delete elements. You decide to delete the first shape on Slide 2. *Why? The slide contains information about what passengers will experience during the excursion, so the facts about buying tickets and boarding are a different topic.* The following steps remove a SmartArt shape.

1

- Tap or click a border of the left SmartArt shape, Purchase Tickets at Depot, to select the entire shape (Figure 9–31).

2

- If you are using a keyboard, press the DELETE key to delete the left SmartArt shape.

- If you are using a touch screen, press and hold the SmartArt shape and then tap Delete on the shortcut menu.

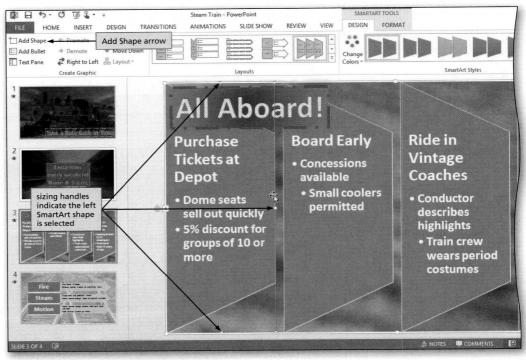

Figure 9–31

BTW

BTWs
For a complete list of the BTWs found in the margins of this book, visit the BTW resource on the Student Companion Site located on www.cengagebrain.com. For detailed instructions about accessing available resources, visit www.cengage.com/ct/studentdownload or see the inside back cover of this book.

TO ADD A SMARTART SHAPE

You may add a new SmartArt shape to the layout if you need to display additional information. PowerPoint gives you the option of adding this shape above or below a selected shape or to the left or the right side of the shape. If you wanted to add a SmartArt shape, you would perform the following steps.

1. Select a SmartArt graphic shape near where you want to insert another shape.

2. Tap or click the Add Shape arrow (SMARTART TOOLS DESIGN tab | Create Graphic group) to display the Add Shape menu.

3. Tap or click the desired location for the new shape, which would be after, before, above, or below the selected shape.

To Resize a SmartArt Graphic by Entering an Exact Measurement

1 INSERT & CUSTOMIZE TEXT BOXES | 2 CONVERT WORDART TO SMARTART & FORMAT | 3 INSERT & FORMAT SHAPES
4 DRAW & FORMAT LINES | 5 CUSTOMIZE THE RIBBON | 6 EXPORT FILE & CREATE PICTURE PRESENTATION

Why? *The All Aboard text box overlaps the left SmartArt shape, so you need to make room for this element at the top of the slide by reducing the size of the entire SmartArt graphic.* You can resize a slide element by dragging the sizing handles or by specifying exact measurements for the height and width. The following steps resize the SmartArt graphic by entering an exact measurement.

1

● If necessary, select the entire SmartArt graphic by tapping or clicking an outer edge of the graphic at the edge of the slide (Figure 9–32).

Q&A How will I know the entire graphic is selected?
You will see the Text pane control and sizing handles around the outer edge of the SmartArt.

Figure 9–32

2

● Display the SMARTART TOOLS FORMAT tab and then change the setting in the Height box to 6" (Figure 9–33).

3

● Drag the SmartArt graphic downward so its lower edge is aligned with the lower edge of the slide.

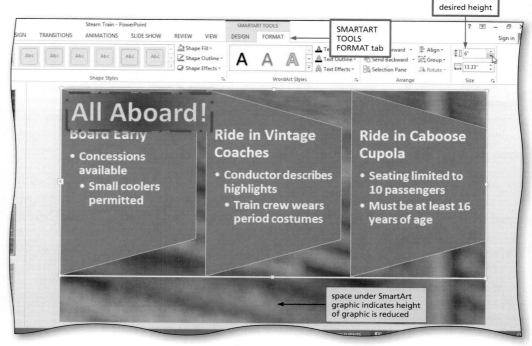

Figure 9–33

Other Ways

1. Press and hold or right-click graphic, tap or click 'Size and Position' on shortcut menu, if necessary tap or click 'Size & Properties' icon (Format Shape pane), if necessary tap or click SIZE, enter graphic height and width values in boxes, close Format Shape pane

To Resize a SmartArt Graphic Shape

The entire SmartArt shape and the text box now are the proper proportions to display together on the slide. In addition to changing the height and width of the SmartArt graphic, you also can change the height and width of one individual SmartArt shape in the graphic. *Why? Passengers who ride the steam train excursions marvel at the vintage coaches and the quality of workmanship they have. To emphasize this unique feature, you want to make the center SmartArt shape larger than the others and deemphasize the Board Early and Ride in Caboose Cupola shapes.* The following steps resize the SmartArt graphic shapes.

1

- Tap or click the left SmartArt shape, Board Early, to select it.

- With the SMARTART TOOLS FORMAT tab displaying, tap or click the Smaller button (SMARTART TOOLS FORMAT tab | Shapes group) once to decrease the shape size (Figure 9–34).

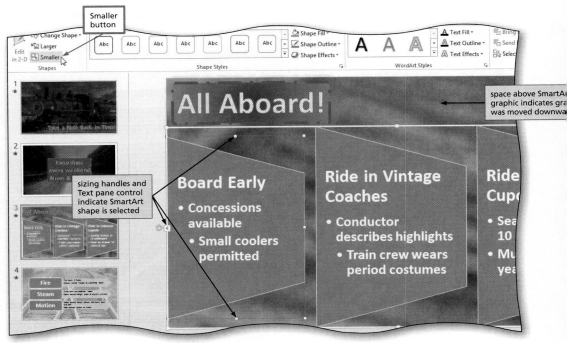

Figure 9–34

2

- Tap or click the right shape, Ride in Caboose Cupola, to select it and then tap or click the Smaller button (Figure 9–35).

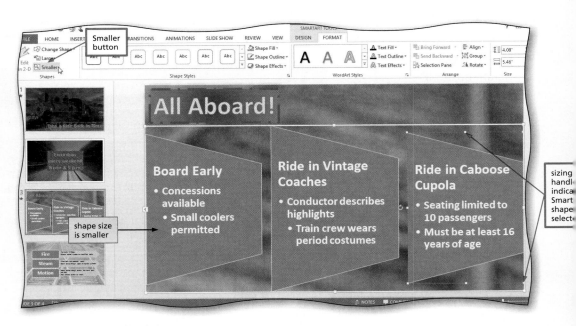

Figure 9–35

3

- Tap or click the center shape, Ride In Vintage Coaches, to select it and then tap or click the Larger button twice (Figure 9–36).

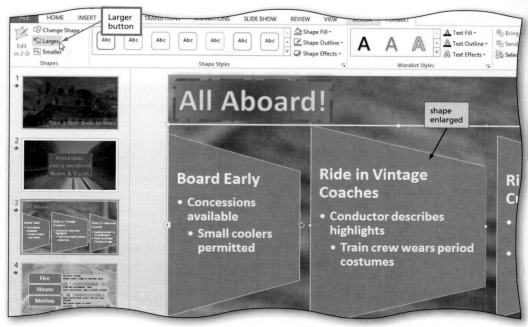

Figure 9–36

Other Ways

1. Press and hold or right-click graphic, tap or click 'Size and Position' on shortcut menu, if necessary tap or click 'Size & Properties' icon (Format Shape pane), if necessary tap or click SIZE, enter graphic height and width values in boxes, close Format Shape pane

---

To Apply a Picture to a Text Box

1 INSERT & CUSTOMIZE TEXT BOXES | 2 CONVERT WORDART TO SMARTART & FORMAT | 3 INSERT & FORMAT SHAPES
4 DRAW & FORMAT LINES | 5 CUSTOMIZE THE RIBBON | 6 EXPORT FILE & CREATE PICTURE PRESENTATION

Sufficient space exists in the lower halves of the three shapes to insert a picture. ***Why?*** *A picture helps to reinforce the written message and also calls attention to the major points being made in each of the three shapes.* For consistency with the slide title, you can insert a text box that has the default formatting and then add a picture. The following steps add a text box and then apply a picture into two SmartArt graphic shapes.

1

- Display the INSERT tab and then insert a text box below the bulleted paragraph, Train crew wears period costumes, in the middle SmartArt shape.

- Display the DRAWING TOOLS FORMAT tab and then tap or click the Shape Fill arrow (DRAWING TOOLS FORMAT tab | Shape Styles group) to display the Shape Fill gallery (Figure 9–37).

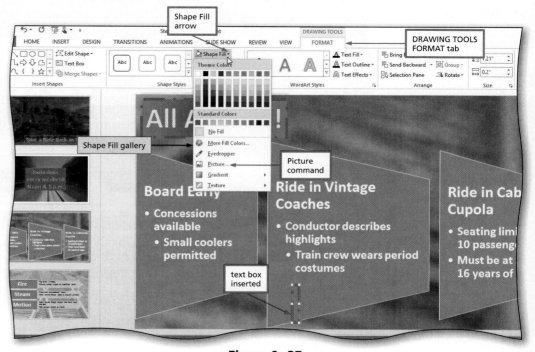

Figure 9–37

• Tap or click Picture in the Shape Fill gallery to display the Insert Pictures dialog box. Tap or click the Browse button and then navigate to the location where your Data Files for Students are stored (in this case, the PowerPoint folder in the CIS 101 folder [or your class folder] on your computer or SkyDrive).

• Tap or click Conductor to select the file name (Figure 9–38).

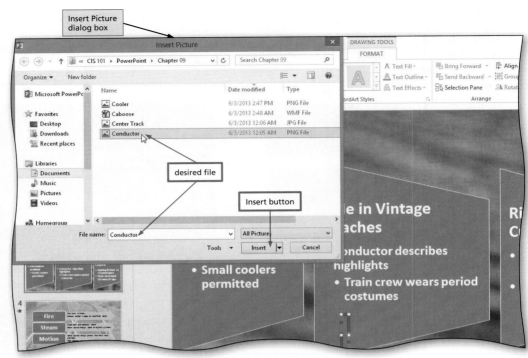

Figure 9–38

• Tap or click the Insert button (Insert Picture dialog box) to insert the Conductor picture into the text box. You will resize the text box in a later step.

• Insert a text box below the bulleted paragraph, Small coolers permitted, in the left SmartArt shape, display the Shape Fill gallery, and then insert the picture, Cooler.

• Insert a text box below the bulleted paragraph, Must be at least 16 years of age, in the right SmartArt shape, display the Shape Fill gallery, and then insert the picture, Caboose.

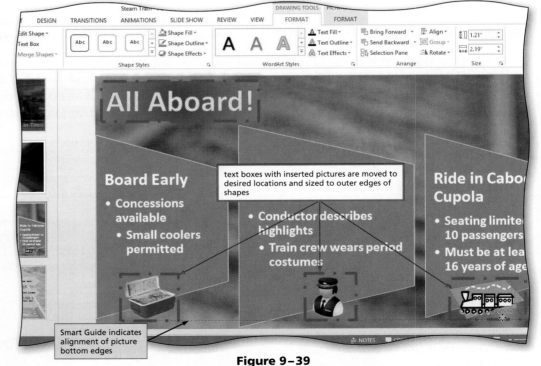

Figure 9–39

• Drag the left and right sizing handles of the boxes to size the three text boxes and then use the Smart Guides to align the lower edges of the pictures, as shown in Figure 9–39.

To Add a SmartArt Style to the Graphic and Change the Color

To enhance the appearance of the rectangles in the Trapezoid List layout, you can add a transparent three-dimensional style that allows some of the background to show through the graphic. You also can add more colors. The following steps add the Inset style and a Colorful range.

1 Select the entire SmartArt graphic, display the SMARTART TOOLS DESIGN tab, and then tap or click the More button in the SmartArt Styles group to expand the SmartArt Styles gallery.

2 Tap or click Inset in the 3-D area (second graphic in first row) to apply this style to the graphic.

3 Tap or click the Change Colors button (SMARTART TOOLS DESIGN tab | SmartArt Styles group) to display the Change Colors gallery.

4 Tap or click Colorful Range – Accent Colors 5 to 6 (fifth graphic in Colorful row) to apply this color variation to the graphic.

5 Select the All Aboard! text box, display the DRAWING TOOLS FORMAT tab, tap or click the Align button (DRAWING TOOLS FORMAT tab | Arrange group), and then tap or click Align Center to center the text box at the top of the slide (Figure 9–40).

Figure 9–40

To Convert a SmartArt Graphic to Text

1 INSERT & CUSTOMIZE TEXT BOXES | 2 CONVERT WORDART TO SMARTART & FORMAT | 3 INSERT & FORMAT SHAPES
4 DRAW & FORMAT LINES | 5 CUSTOMIZE THE RIBBON | 6 EXPORT FILE & CREATE PICTURE PRESENTATION

Passengers often wonder how a steam engine operates, and the SmartArt graphic information on Slide 4 explains the basic principles. In a later portion of this chapter, you will supplement these details with a graphic pointing out the main components of a steam engine. At times, you may decide that SmartArt is not the optimal method of presenting information to an audience and instead want to depict the same concept using text. *Why? The SmartArt's visual elements may detract from the points being made, so the bulleted list might be useful for instructional purposes. In addition, it may take up so much room on the slide that other visual elements may not fit.* PowerPoint allows you to remove the shapes and change the text in the graphic to a bulleted list. The steps on the next page convert the SmartArt graphic to text.

1

- Display Slide 4 and then select the entire SmartArt graphic.

Q&A If one of the SmartArt shapes is selected, how do I select the entire graphic?
Be certain to tap or click the edge of the graphic. You will see sizing handles and the Text pane control when the SmartArt graphic is selected.

- Display the SMARTART TOOLS DESIGN tab and then tap or click the Convert button (SMARTART TOOLS DESIGN tab | Reset group) to display the Convert menu (Figure 9–41).

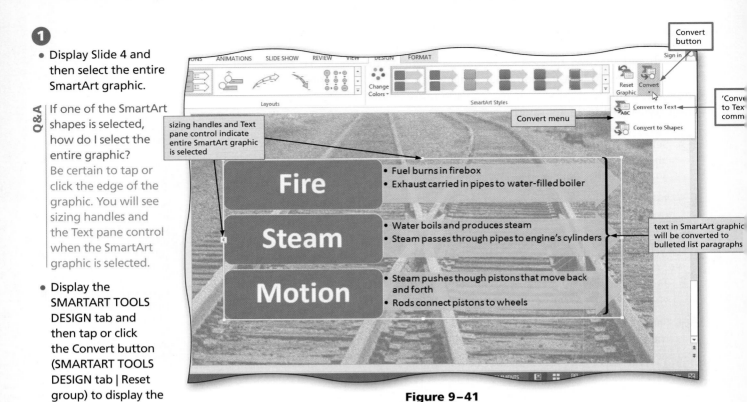

Figure 9–41

2

- Tap or click 'Convert to Text' to display the SmartArt text as nine bulleted list paragraphs (Figure 9–42).

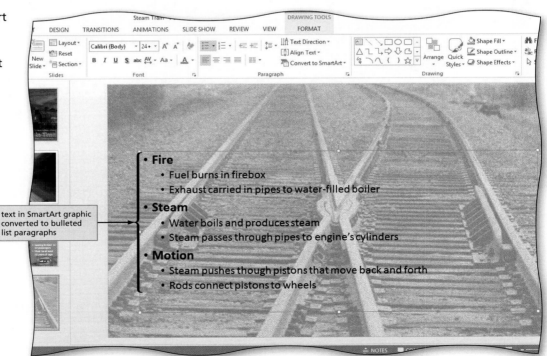

Figure 9–42

3

- Position the bulleted list placeholder in the upper-left corner of the slide (Figure 9–43).

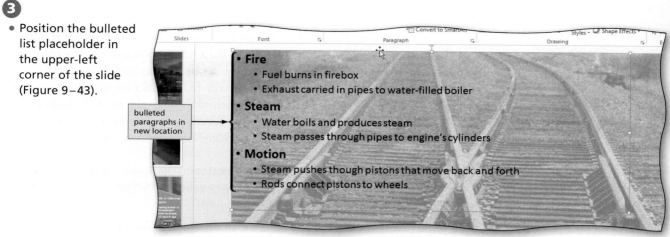

Figure 9–43

To Convert a SmartArt Graphic to Shapes

An alternative to changing a graphic to text is changing a graphic to shapes. In this manner, a shape can be moved, resized, or deleted independently of any other shape in the SmartArt. If you wanted to convert a SmartArt graphic to shapes, you would perform the following steps.

1. Select the entire SmartArt graphic.
2. Tap or click the Convert button (SMARTART TOOLS DESIGN tab | Reset group) to display the Convert menu.
3. Tap or click 'Convert to Shapes'.

BTW

SmartArt in Handouts
SmartArt diagrams are composed of individual vector graphics. Some presenters decide to include these diagrams in a handout but not as part of a presentation so that audience members can study the relationships among the shapes after the presentation has concluded.

> **Break Point:** If you wish to take a break, this is a good place to do so. Be sure to save the Steam Train file again and then you can exit PowerPoint. To resume at a later time, run PowerPoint, open the file called Steam Train, and continue following the steps from this location forward.

Inserting and Modifying Shapes

The items in the Shapes gallery provide a variety of useful shapes you can insert into slides. Diagrams with labels often help audiences identify the parts of an object. Text boxes with clear, large type and an arrow pointing to a precise area of the object work well in showing relationships between components. You also can use items in the Shapes gallery to create your own custom artwork.

A steam engine has several components: They include the firebox, which provides the heat; the boiler, where the water is heated until it forms steam; and the rods, which turn the wheels. These parts can be depicted with a variety of items found in the Shapes gallery. You also want to add text boxes and arrows to identify the components. At times, you may be unable to find a shape in the gallery that fits your specific needs. In those instances, you might find a similar shape and then alter it to your specifications.

BTW

Vector Graphics
Geometric shapes, lines, arrows, and action buttons are vector graphics, which are drawn using mathematical formulas. The size, color, line width, starting and ending points, and other formatting attributes are stored as numeric values and are recalculated when you resize or reformat each shape. Most clip art and video games also use vector graphics.

BTW
Inserting Shapes
The Shapes gallery is displayed on two tabs: the DRAWING TOOLS FORMAT tab (Insert Shapes group) and the HOME tab (Drawing group). Shapes also are available if you display the INSERT tab and then tap or click the Shapes button (Illustrations group).

To Insert Shapes and an Arrow

You can draw parts of the steam engine with shapes located in the Shapes gallery: one rectangle for the rear of the engine, which contains the firebox and also the cab for the engineer and fireman; another rectangle for the boiler; circles for the wheels; a triangle for the pilot, also called the cow catcher, in the front; and a trapezoid for the stack. A cloud shape can represent the exhaust that has moved through the stack. In addition, the Notched Right Arrow shape can be inserted to serve as a leader line for labeling a steam engine part. The following steps insert six shapes and an arrow into Slide 4.

1 With Slide 4 displaying, tap or click the More button in the Shapes gallery (HOME tab | Drawing group) to display the entire Shapes gallery and then tap or click the Rectangle shape (first shape in the Rectangles area).

2 Position the pointer below the last bulleted paragraph and then tap or click to insert the Rectangle shape.

3 Display the Shapes gallery and then tap or click the Oval shape (second shape in the first Basic Shapes row).

4 Position the pointer below the Rectangle and then tap or click to insert the Oval shape.

5 Display the Shapes gallery, tap or click the Trapezoid shape (sixth shape in the first row in the Basic Shapes area), and then insert this shape to the right of the word, forth, in the bulleted list.

6 Display the Shapes gallery, tap or click the Cloud shape (eleventh shape in the third row in the Basic Shapes area), and then insert this shape above the Trapezoid shape.

7 Display the Shapes gallery, tap or click the Right Triangle shape (fourth shape in the first Basic Shapes row), and then insert this shape below the Trapezoid shape.

8 Display the Shapes gallery, tap or click the Notched Right Arrow shape (sixth shape in the second row in the Block Arrows area), and then insert this shape to the right of the Cloud shape (Figure 9–44).

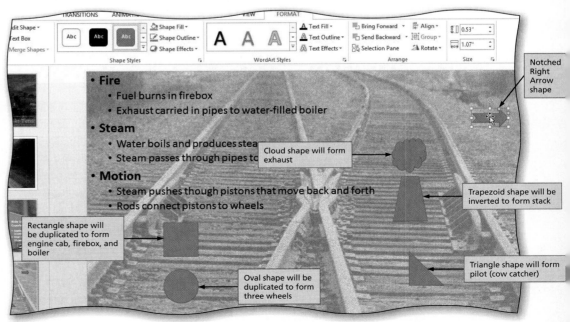

Figure 9–44

To Resize and Move Shapes

The six shapes on Slide 4 are the default sizes, and they need to be proportioned to reflect accurate engine dimensions. If you are not using a touch screen, you can keep the resized shape proportions identical to the original shape by pressing the SHIFT key while tapping or clicking a sizing handle and then dragging the pointer inward or outward to decrease or increase the size. If you do not hold down the SHIFT key, you can elongate the height or the width to draw an object that is not identical to the shape shown in the Shapes gallery. If you want to alter the shape's proportions, drag one of the sizing handles inward or outward. The following steps resize the shapes and arrow.

1 Select the rectangle and then drag the top-center sizing handle upward to the bulleted list and the bottom-center sizing handle downward to the center of the circle.

2 With the rectangle selected, display the HOME tab, tap or click the Copy button (HOME tab | Clipboard group), and then tap or click the Paste button (HOME tab | Clipboard group).

3 Drag the new rectangle to the right and then position the pointer over the rotation handle and turn the rectangle to the right 90 degrees.

4 Drag the triangle to the lower-right side of the new rectangle and then drag the upper-right sizing handle diagonally to the lower left.

5 Drag the trapezoid to the upper-right edge of the new rectangle and then position the pointer over the rotation handle and turn the rectangle 180 degrees.

6 Drag the Cloud to the upper-left side of the Trapezoid.

7 With the HOME tab displaying, tap or click the Oval, tap or click the Copy button and then tap or click the Paste button twice. Position the two new ovals to the right of the first oval.

8 Use the Smart Guides to align the bottom of the ovals and the triangle (Figure 9–45).

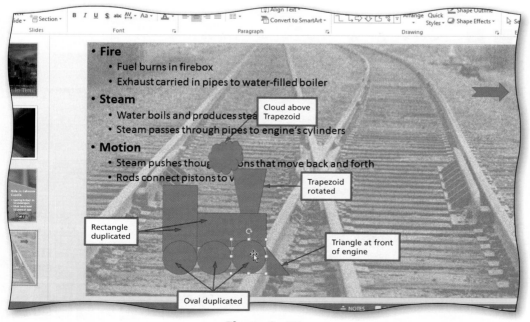

Figure 9–45

To Apply a Fill to a Shape

The shapes on Slide 4 have light blue fill. You can change the shape fill using the same types of fills you used for the text boxes in this presentation. For example, you can apply a gradient, pattern, texture, or picture. *Why? Using similar fills among the slides adds consistency and gives a uniform look to the presentation.* The method of applying these fill effects is similar to the steps you used to format text boxes. The following steps apply fills to the shapes.

1

- Select the two rectangles and the triangle. Display the DRAWING TOOLS FORMAT tab, tap or click the Shape Fill arrow (DRAWING TOOLS FORMAT tab | Shape Styles group) to display the Shape Fill gallery, and then tap or click Gradient to display the Gradient gallery (Figure 9–46).

 Experiment

- If you are using a mouse, point to various gradients in the Gradient gallery and watch the interiors of the three shapes change.

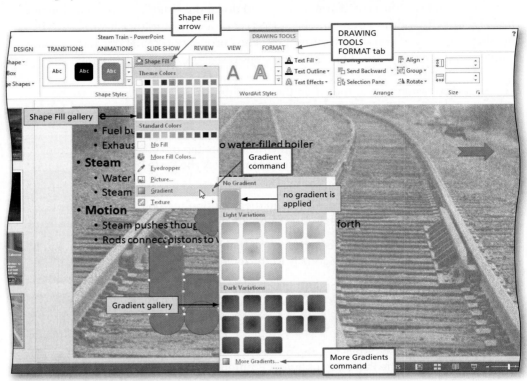

Figure 9–46

2

- Tap or click More Gradients in the Gradient gallery to display the Format Shape pane.

- If necessary, display the FILL section. Tap or click Gradient fill to expand the gradient options and then tap or click the Preset gradients button to display the Preset gradients gallery (Figure 9–47).

Q&A Can I experiment with previewing the gradient colors?
No, the live preview feature is not available.

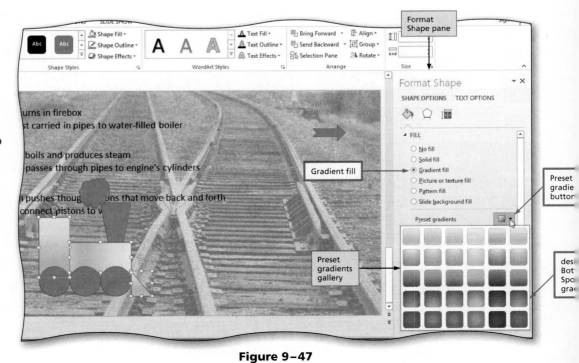

Figure 9–47

❸

- Tap or click Bottom Spotlight - Accent 6 (last color in the fourth row in the Preset gradients gallery) to apply the gradient fill to the three shapes.

Q&A How can I delete a gradient fill if I decide not to apply one to the shape?
If you already have applied the pattern, you must tap or click the Undo button on the Quick Access Toolbar.

❹

- Select the trapezoid and the three wheels, tap or click Gradient fill, and then tap or click the Preset gradients button (Figure 9–48).

Q&A Why did these four shapes fill with the green gradient fill when I tapped or clicked Gradient fill?
PowerPoint recalls the last gradient you selected.

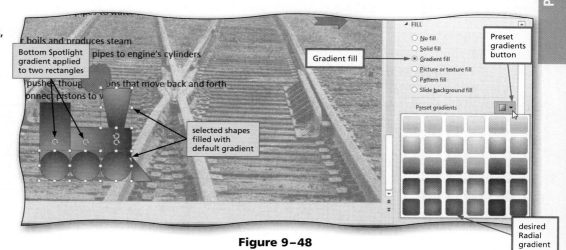

Figure 9–48

❺

- Tap or click Radial Gradient – Accent 3 (third color in the fifth row) to apply this gradient to the shapes.

- Select the cloud and then tap or click 'Picture or texture fill' to display the 'Picture or texture fill' section (Figure 9–49).

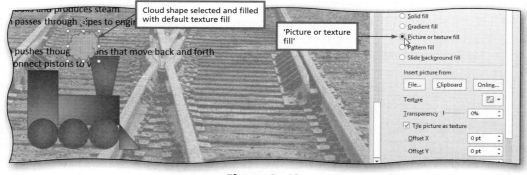

Figure 9–49

Q&A Why did the cloud fill with a texture?
Depending on previous settings for shape fills, PowerPoint may insert a fill or change the Transparency when you click the 'Picture or texture fill' option button.

❻

- Tap or click the Texture button to display the Texture gallery (Figure 9–50).

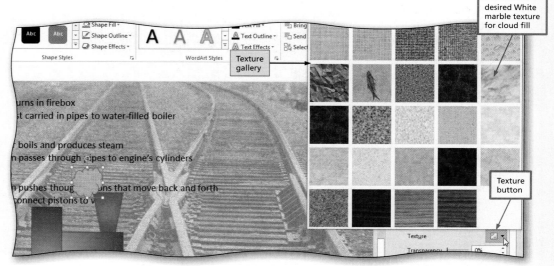

Figure 9–50

7

- Tap or click the White marble texture (fifth texture in the second row) to apply this texture to the cloud.

- If necessary, set the Transparency slider to 0%.

- Scroll down the Format Picture pane and then, if necessary, tap or click LINE to expand the LINE section. Tap or click the Color button to display the Color gallery (Figure 9–51).

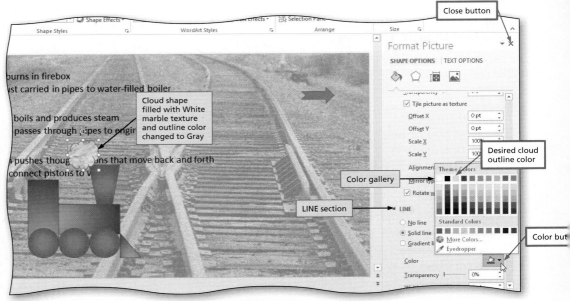

Figure 9–51

8

- Tap or click Gray - 25%, Background 2 (third color in the first Theme Colors row) to apply this color to the cloud edges.

- Tap or click the Close button to close the Format Picture pane.

To Subtract a Shape

1 INSERT & CUSTOMIZE TEXT BOXES | 2 CONVERT WORDART TO SMARTART & FORMAT | 3 INSERT & FORMAT SHAPES
4 DRAW & FORMAT LINES | 5 CUSTOMIZE THE RIBBON | 6 EXPORT FILE & CREATE PICTURE PRESENTATION

The cab you drew does not have a window, but you easily can create one. **Why?** *Your engine will look more accurate with this element.* One method of creating this window is to overlap a new Rectangle shape and the current vertical rectangle shape and then subtract the area of the new rectangle. The result is a blank area that displays the slide background. The following steps insert a Rectangle shape and then subtract this object.

1

- Display the Shapes gallery, select the Rectangle shape in the Rectangles area (first shape), and then insert the shape into the cab portion of the engine.

- Size the shape so that each side is 0.7" and then use the Smart Guides to align the shape, as shown in Figure 9–52.

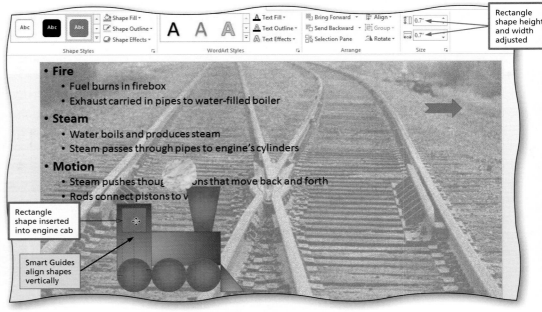

Figure 9–52

- If you are using a keyboard, click the vertical green rectangle to select it, press and hold down the CTRL key, and then click the square to select both shapes.

Q&A Can I perform this step using a touch screen?
No. You will need to use a keyboard to select multiple shapes.

- With the DRAWING TOOLS FORMAT tab displaying, tap or click the Merge Shapes button (DRAWING TOOLS FORMAT tab | Insert Shapes group) to display the Merge Shapes list (Figure 9–53).

Q&A Do I need to select the shapes in this order?
Yes. You first select the shape that you want to keep and then tap or click the shape that you want to delete.

 **Experiment**

- If you are using a mouse, point to the commands in the Merge Shapes list and watch the results of the various merge commands.

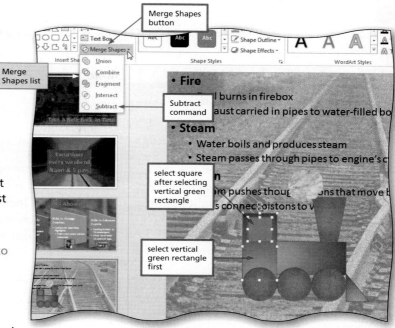

Figure 9–53

- Tap or click Subtract in the Merge Shapes list to delete the green background behind the square shape.

To Merge Shapes

1 INSERT & CUSTOMIZE TEXT BOXES | 2 CONVERT WORDART TO SMARTART & FORMAT | 3 INSERT & FORMAT SHAPES
4 DRAW & FORMAT LINES | 5 CUSTOMIZE THE RIBBON | 6 EXPORT FILE & CREATE PICTURE PRESENTATION

The two rectangles forming the engine have a common vertical line where the two shapes intersect. You can eliminate this line if you merge the shapes. In addition, you can merge the triangular pilot shape with the rectangles. **Why?** *The three elements will appear seamless as part of the main structure of the engine.* The following steps merge the two rectangles and the triangle.

- Select the three green engine shapes (the two rectangles and the triangle). With the DRAWING TOOLS FORMAT tab displaying, tap or click the Merge Shapes button (DRAWING TOOLS FORMAT tab | Insert Shapes group) to display the Merge Shapes list (Figure 9–54).

Q&A How do I select the three engine shapes?
Hold down the CTRL key and then tap or click each shape.

 **Experiment**

- If you are using a mouse, point to the commands in the Merge Shapes list and watch the results of the various merge commands.

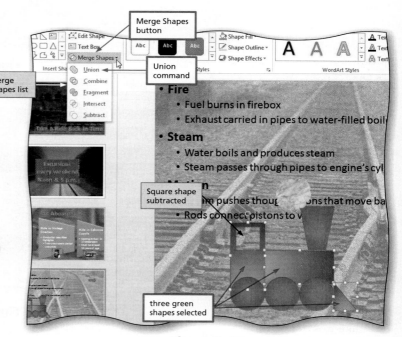

Figure 9–54

● Tap or click Union (DRAWING TOOLS FORMAT tab | Insert Shapes group) to combine the green shapes.

Q&A Why am I using the Union command instead of the Combine command?
The Union command joins the shapes using the formatting of the top shape. The Combine command also joins shapes, but it deletes the area where the two shapes overlap.

To Draw a Line

1 INSERT & CUSTOMIZE TEXT BOXES | 2 CONVERT WORDART TO SMARTART & FORMAT | 3 INSERT & FORMAT SHAPES
4 DRAW & FORMAT LINES | 5 CUSTOMIZE THE RIBBON | 6 EXPORT FILE & CREATE PICTURE PRESENTATION

Why? *The shapes on Slide 4 comprise the main parts of a steam engine. To complete the drawing, you need to add the rods, which connect on one end to the wheels and on the other end to a piston.* Rods can be represented by a line shape. One type of rod is a straight bar, and this type of line is included in the Shapes gallery. Some other lines in the gallery are the Elbow Connector, Curve, Freeform, and Scribble. The lines and connectors have zero, one, or two arrowheads. The following steps draw a straight line without arrowheads and position this shape on Slide 4.

● Display the Shapes gallery and then point to the Line shape (first shape in the Lines area) (Figure 9–55).

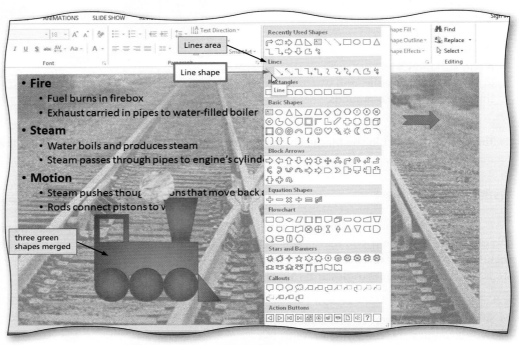

Figure 9–55

● Tap or click the Line shape and then position the pointer on the right wheel to display the points (Figure 9–56).

Q&A What are the dots on the perimeter of the wheel?
The dots are called points. Every shape is formed by a series of points connected with lines that are straight or curved. If desired, you can drag a point to alter the shape's form.

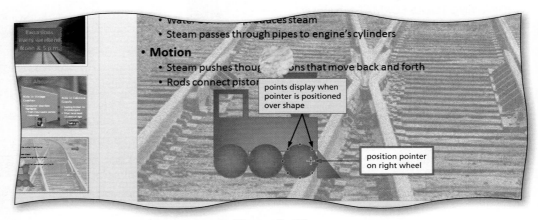

Figure 9–56

3

- Position the pointer on the point at the 3 o'clock position on the right side of the wheel and then tap or click to insert one end of the line on this point.

- Drag the sizing handle at the other end of the line to the center of the middle wheel (Figure 9–57).

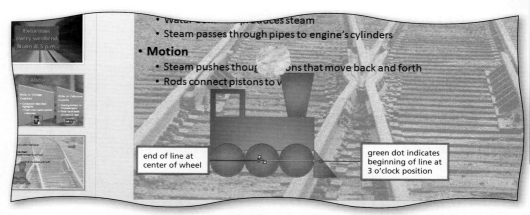

Figure 9–57

To Change a Line Weight and Color

1 INSERT & CUSTOMIZE TEXT BOXES | 2 CONVERT WORDART TO SMARTART & FORMAT | 3 INSERT & FORMAT SHAPES
4 DRAW & FORMAT LINES | **5 CUSTOMIZE THE RIBBON** | 6 EXPORT FILE & CREATE PICTURE PRESENTATION

In this project, you changed a text box and shape outline color and weight. In a similar fashion, you can change line outline formatting. *Why? The line you drew on Slide 4 is thin, and the color does not display well against the wheels' gray background.* You can increase the line thickness and change its color to enhance the shape. The following steps change the line thickness and color.

1

- With the line selected, tap or click the Shape Outline arrow (DRAWING TOOLS FORMAT tab | Shape Styles group) and then tap or click Weight to display the Weight gallery.

- If you are using a mouse, point to 6 pt to see a preview of that weight applied to the line (Figure 9–58).

🔍 **Experiment**

- If you are using a mouse, point to various weights in the Weight gallery and watch the line thickness change.

Figure 9–58

- Tap or click 6 pt in the Weight gallery to apply that weight to the line.

- Tap or click the Shape Outline arrow again. If you are using a mouse, point to Blue-Gray, Text 2 (fourth color in the first Theme Colors area) to see a preview of that color applied to the line (Figure 9–59).

 Experiment

- If you are using a mouse, point to various colors in the Theme Colors gallery and watch the line color change.

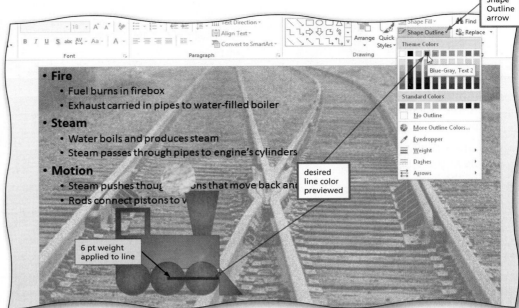

Figure 9–59

- Tap or click Blue-Gray, Text 2 to apply that color to the line.

To Set Line Formatting as the Default

1 INSERT & CUSTOMIZE TEXT BOXES | 2 CONVERT WORDART TO SMARTART & FORMAT | 3 INSERT & FORMAT SHAPES
4 DRAW & FORMAT LINES | 5 CUSTOMIZE THE RIBBON | 6 EXPORT FILE & CREATE PICTURE PRESENTATION

The line you inserted and formatted is one of two rods in the steam engine diagram. You can set these line attributes as the default for the other line you will draw in the presentation. *Why? Setting the default characters saves time when you add other lines because you do not need to repeat all the formatting steps. It also ensures consistency among the line shapes.* The following steps set the line shape on Slide 4 as the default.

- Press and hold or right-click the line to display the shortcut menu (Figure 9–60).

- Tap or click 'Set as Default Line' on the shortcut menu to set the line formatting as the default for any new lines.

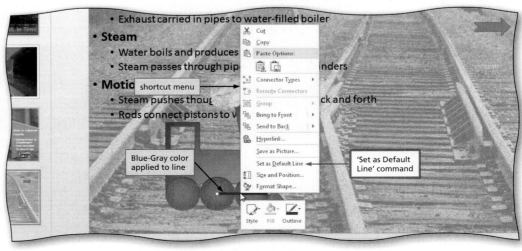

Figure 9–60

To Draw an Additional Line

One more line is needed to connect the left wheel to the center wheel. A line with an elbow is the best shape to use in this instance. ***Why?*** *This shape has two bends, which is the shape of the rear rod. You could, instead, draw this rod using three lines and then connect these shapes, but the elbow already has the required components.* The following steps draw these lines.

1

- Display the Shapes gallery again. If you are using a mouse, point to the Elbow Connector (fourth line in the Lines area) (Figure 9–61).

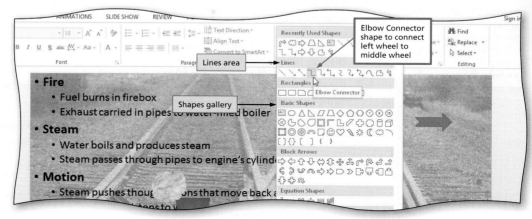

Figure 9–61

2

- Tap or click the Elbow Connector, position the pointer in the center of the left wheel, and then tap or click to insert one end of the line at this location (Figure 9–62).

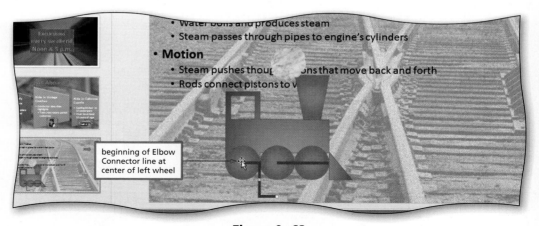

Figure 9–62

3

- Drag the sizing handle at the other end of the line near the center of the middle wheel, slightly below the straight line that connects the right and center wheels (Figure 9–63).

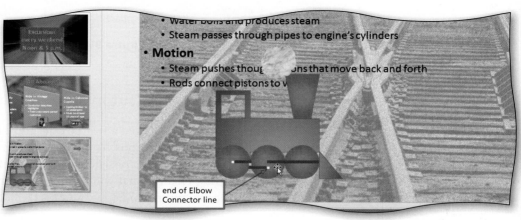

Figure 9–63

To Group and Size the Engine Objects

All the shapes comprising the engine are separate elements on the slide. You will need to move and enlarge the engine on the slide, so you easily can complete these tasks if you group all the components so they no longer are individual pieces. The following steps group all these shapes and then enlarge the entire engine shape.

1 Select all the engine shapes and the cloud and then display the PICTURE TOOLS FORMAT tab.

2 Tap or click the Group button (PICTURE TOOLS FORMAT tab | Arrange group) to display the Group list and then click Group in the list to combine all the shapes.

3 Size the engine object so that it is approximately 6" × 6.5" and then move it to the right side of the slide, as shown in Figure 9–64.

4 Position the pointer after the word, pistons, in the first bulleted list item below the word, Motion. If you are using a touch screen, display the onscreen keyboard.

5 Tap or press SHIFT+ENTER to insert a line break (Figure 9–64).

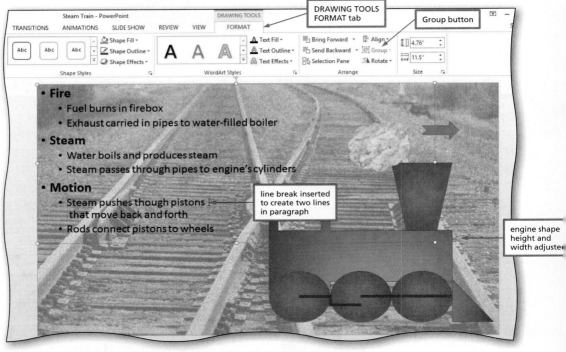

Figure 9–64

To Change a Shape Fill and Outline and Apply Effects

Earlier in this project, you changed a text box outline color, weight, and style. You also applied a glow effect to a text box. You, similarly, can change the outline formatting and effects for a shape. For consistency, you can enhance the arrow by using some of the same formatting changes that you applied to the text box. The following steps change the arrow shape outline and apply an effect.

1 Select the Notched Right Arrow, tap or click the Shape Fill arrow (DRAWING TOOLS FORMAT tab | Shape Styles group), display the Gradient gallery, and then tap or click From Center (second gradient in second row) in the Dark Variations area.

2 Tap or click the Shape Outline arrow (DRAWING TOOLS FORMAT tab | Shape Styles group), display the Weight gallery, and then tap or click 3 pt.

3 Display the Shape Outline gallery again and then tap or click Green (sixth color in the Standard Colors area) to change the shape border color.

4 Display the Shape Outline gallery again, display the Dashes gallery, and then tap or click Square Dot to change the border style.

5 Tap or click the Shape Effects button to display the Shape Effects gallery, display the Glow gallery, and then tap or click the Blue, 8 pt glow, Accent color 1 (first color in the second row in the Glow Variations area) to apply the glow effect (Figure 9–65).

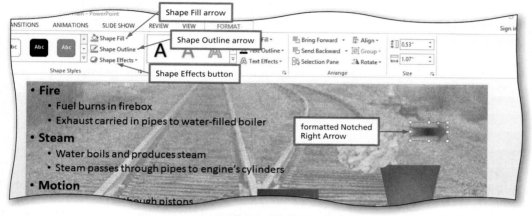

Figure 9–65

BTW
Printing Document Properties
To print document properties, tap or click FILE on the ribbon to open the Backstage view, tap or click the Print tab in the Backstage view to display the Print gallery, tap or click the first button in the Settings area to display a list of options specifying what you can print, tap or click Document Info in the list to specify you want to print the document properties instead of the actual document, and then tap or click the Print button in the Print gallery to print the document properties on the currently selected printer.

To Set Shape Formatting as the Default

1 INSERT & CUSTOMIZE TEXT BOXES | 2 CONVERT WORDART TO SMARTART & FORMAT | 3 INSERT & FORMAT SHAPES
4 DRAW & FORMAT LINES | 5 CUSTOMIZE THE RIBBON | 6 EXPORT FILE & CREATE PICTURE PRESENTATION

The Notched Right Arrow shape you inserted and formatted complements the default text box you inserted on the slides in the presentation. You will use this shape on several parts of Slide 4 to help identify parts of the steam engine, so you can set its formatting as a default. *Why? To save time and ensure all the formatting changes are applied, you can set the formatting of one shape as the default for all other shapes you insert into the presentation.* The following steps set the arrow shape formatting on Slide 4 as the default.

1
- Press and hold or right-click the Notched Right Arrow shape to display the shortcut menu (Figure 9–66).

2
- Tap or click 'Set as Default Shape' on the shortcut menu to set the shape formatting as the default for any new shapes.

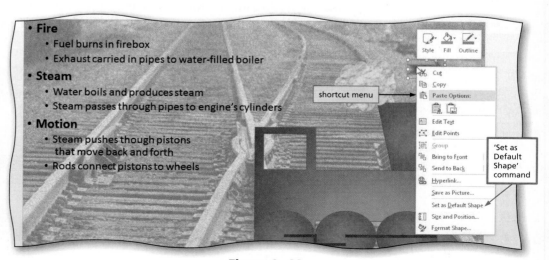

Figure 9–66

Use politically correct language.

Many companies have strict policies in order to prevent harassment in the workplace. These guidelines are developed to protect employees from adverse treatment based on race, religion, national origin, gender, or other personal traits. Keep these policies in mind as you label components on your slides. For example, some females may be offended if you refer to an adult woman as a "girl," or an older athlete may resent being labeled as an "aging" rather than as a "veteran" player.

BTW

Conserving Ink and Toner

If you want to conserve ink or toner, you can instruct PowerPoint to print draft quality documents by tapping or clicking FILE on the ribbon to open the Backstage view, tapping or clicking Options in the Backstage view to display the PowerPoint Options dialog box, tapping or clicking Advanced in the left pane (PowerPoint Options dialog box), sliding or scrolling to the Print area in the right pane, placing a check mark in the 'Use draft quality' check box, and then tapping or clicking the OK button. Then, use the Backstage view to print the document as usual.

To Label the Shapes

The final step in creating Slide 4 is to label the parts of the steam engine. The Notched Right Arrow shape and the text box are formatted as defaults, so the labeling process is easy to accomplish. The following steps insert text boxes and arrows into Slide 4 and then enter text in the text boxes.

1 With Slide 4 displaying, insert a text box into the railroad track on the left side of the engine, type **Rods** in the text box, decrease the font size to 24 point, and move the text box to the bottom edge of the center wheel. Use the Smart Guides to center the text box and the wheel.

2 Insert a text box into the railroad track on the left side of the engine, type **Boiler** in the text box, decrease the font size to 24 point, and move the text box between the engine cab and the stack. Use the Smart Guides to align this text box with the Rods text box.

3 Insert a text box, type **Firebox** in the text box, decrease the font size to 24 point, and move the text box to the left side of the engine. Use the Smart Guides to align the text box in the center of the slide and the center of the engine.

4 Drag the Notched Right arrow to the right of the Firebox text box. Display the DRAWING TOOLS FORMAT tab, tap or click the Bring Forward arrow (DRAWING TOOLS FORMAT tab | Arrange group), and then tap or click 'Bring to Front' to display the arrow on top of the engine.

5 Insert a Notched Right arrow. Rotate the arrow 90 degrees and then drag it below the Boiler text box.

6 Insert a Notched Right arrow. Rotate the arrow so it is pointing to the upper-right corner of the slide and then drag it to the right of the Rods text box.

7 Insert a Notched Right arrow. Rotate the arrow so it is pointing to the upper-left corner of the slide and then drag it to the left of the Rods text box (Figure 9–67).

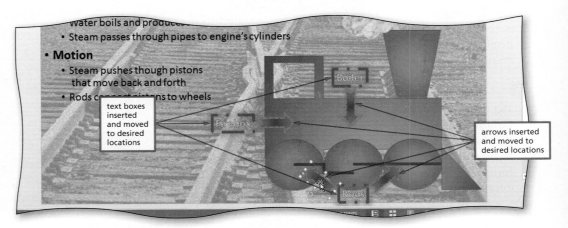

Figure 9–67

To Customize the Ribbon

Many commands available in PowerPoint are not included on any of the tabs on the ribbon. You can, however, add such commands to the ribbon or to the Quick Access Toolbar. *Why? Many of these commands perform tasks you commonly repeat, so it would be convenient to have the buttons accessible in a group on the ribbon.* The following steps customize the ribbon by adding the 'Print Preview and Print' and 'Create Handouts in Microsoft Word' commands to the ribbon and then arranging their order in the group.

1

- With the HOME tab displaying, open the Backstage view and then tap or click Options to display the PowerPoint Options dialog box.

- Tap or click Customize Ribbon in the left pane to display the Customize the Ribbon pane (Figure 9–68).

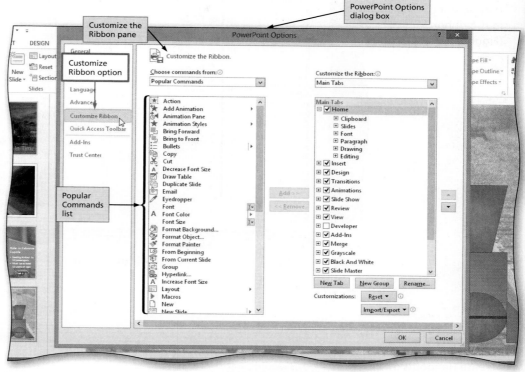

Figure 9–68

2

- Tap or click the 'Choose commands from' arrow to display the 'Choose commands from' list (Figure 9–69).

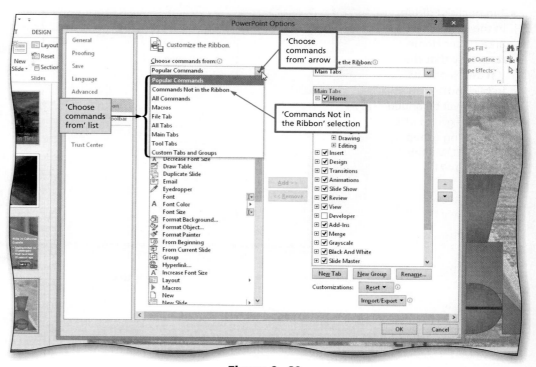

Figure 9–69

- Tap or click 'Commands Not in the Ribbon' in the 'Choose commands from' list to display a list of commands that do not display in the ribbon (Figure 9–70).

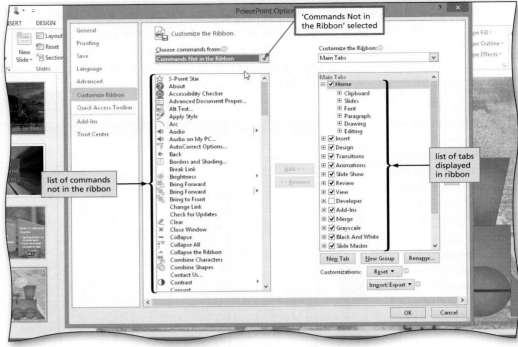

Figure 9–70

- Scroll down and then tap or click 'Create Handouts in Microsoft Word' to select this button.

- Tap or click Editing in the Main Tabs area under Home to specify that the 'Create Handouts in Microsoft Word' button will be added in a new group after the Editing group on the HOME tab (Figure 9–71).

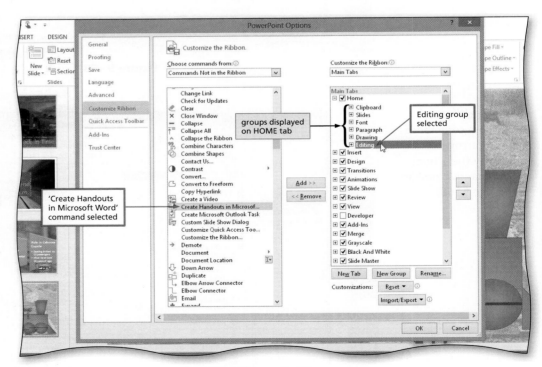

Figure 9–71

5

- Tap or click the New Group button to create a new group.

- Tap or click the Rename button and then type **Handouts** as the new group name in the Display name text box (Rename dialog box) (Figure 9–72).

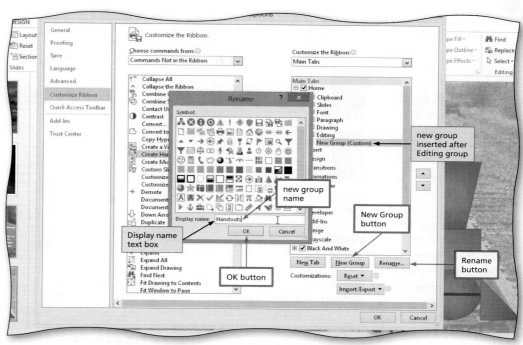

Figure 9–72

6

- Tap or click the OK button (Rename dialog box) to rename the new group.

- Tap or click the Add button to add the 'Create Handouts in Microsoft Word' button to the Handouts group.

- Scroll down, tap or click 'Print Preview and Print' in the list of 'Commands Not in the Ribbon', and then tap or click the Add button to add the button to the Handouts group (Figure 9–73).

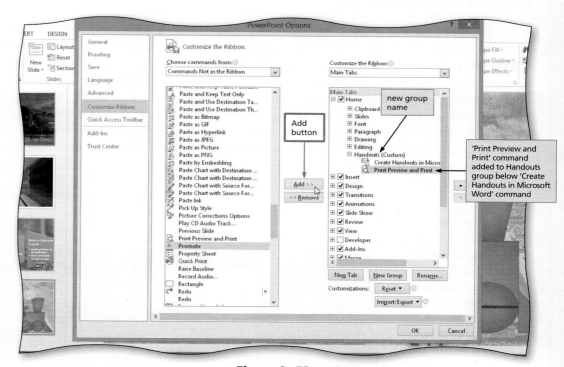

Figure 9–73

- Tap or click the Move Up button (PowerPoint Options dialog box) to move the 'Print Preview and Print' button above the 'Create Handouts in Microsoft Word' button (Figure 9–74).

- Tap or click the OK button to close the PowerPoint Options dialog box and display the two buttons in the new Handouts group on the HOME tab in the ribbon.

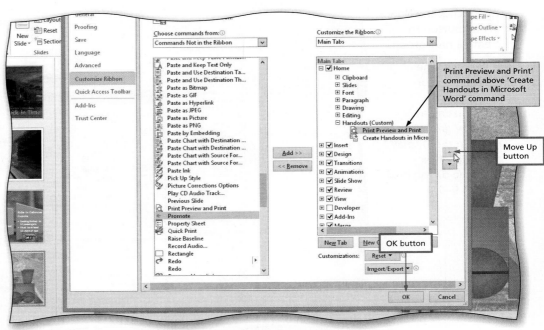

Figure 9–74

To Create a Handout by Exporting a File to Microsoft Word

1 INSERT & CUSTOMIZE TEXT BOXES | 2 CONVERT WORDART TO SMARTART & FORMAT | 3 INSERT & FORMAT SHAPES
4 DRAW & FORMAT LINES | 5 CUSTOMIZE THE RIBBON | 6 EXPORT FILE & CREATE PICTURE PRESENTATION

The handouts you create using Microsoft PowerPoint are useful to distribute to audiences. Each time you need to create these handouts, however, you need to open the file in PowerPoint and then print from the Backstage view. As an alternative, it might be convenient to save, or export, the file as a Microsoft Word document if you are going to be using Microsoft Word to type a script or lecture notes. *Why? The handout can have a variety of layouts; for example, the notes you type in the Notes pane can be displayed to the right of or beneath the slide thumbnails, blank lines can be displayed to the right of or beneath the slide thumbnails, or just an outline can be displayed.* The following steps use the 'Create Handouts in Microsoft Word' button you added to the new Handouts group on the HOME tab to export the presentation to Microsoft Word and then create a handout.

- With the HOME tab displaying, tap or click the 'Create Handouts in Microsoft Word' button (HOME tab | Handouts group) to display the 'Send to Microsoft Word' dialog box (Figure 9–75).

Q&A How would I create this handout if I had not created the Handouts group? You would use the Backstage view.

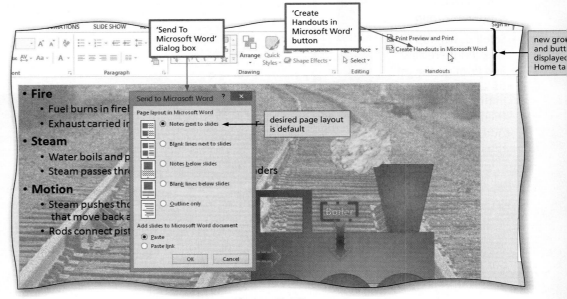

Figure 9–75

- Tap or click the OK button to save the file with the default 'Notes next to slides' layout.
- If the handout does not display in a new Microsoft Word window, tap or click the Microsoft Word program button on the Windows taskbar to see a live preview of the handout. If you print the handouts, they will resemble the pages shown Figure 9–76.

Slide 1

The first steam locomotive ran in the United Kingdom in 1804. Steam trains came to the United States in 1830. The first steamer, Tom Thumb, ran 26 miles round trip from Baltimore to Ellicott's Mill.

Slide 4

The steam is under high pressure. A "choo" sound is produced when a cylinder is opened to release the steam exhaust.

Slide 2

Steam locomotives pulled trains for more than 100 years. The last steam locomotive was retired in 1960. Today, many private groups have restored the steam engines and passenger cars and schedule excursions for rail buffs to enjoy.

Slide 3

The conductor, brakeman, and flagman traveled in the caboose when the train was moving. The raised lookout area on the top of the caboose is called the cupola. It allowed the conductor to peer out the window and fhve a bird-eye view of the length of the train.

(a) Page 1   **(b) Page 2**

Figure 9–76

- Save the presentation using the file name, Steam Engine Word Handout.
- Close the Word file and then exit Word.

Other Ways

1. Open Backstage view, display Export tab, tap or click Create Handouts, tap or click Create Handouts button

---

Work with a buddy.
Although you may believe you create your best work when you work alone, research shows that the work product generally improves when two or more people work together on a creative task. A classmate or team member at work can assist you in many ways. For example, this person can help you gather research for your graphics and bulleted text or provide feedback on the slides' clarity and readability. As you rehearse, a buddy can time your talk and identify the times when the presentation lacks interest. If a buddy attends your actual presentation, he can give objective feedback on the components that worked and those that can use revision for the next time you present the material.

CONSIDER THIS

To Save the Presentation as a Picture Presentation

Why? *If you are going to share your slides with other presenters and do not want them to alter the slide content, you can save each slide as a picture. When they run the slide show, each slide is one complete picture, so the text and shapes cannot be edited. You also can use an individual slide picture as a graphic on another slide or in another presentation.* The following steps save a copy of the presentation as a picture presentation.

1

- Open the Backstage view, display the Export tab, and then tap or click 'Change File Type' to display the 'Change File Type' gallery.

- Tap or click 'PowerPoint Picture Presentation' in the Presentation File Types area (Figure 9–77).

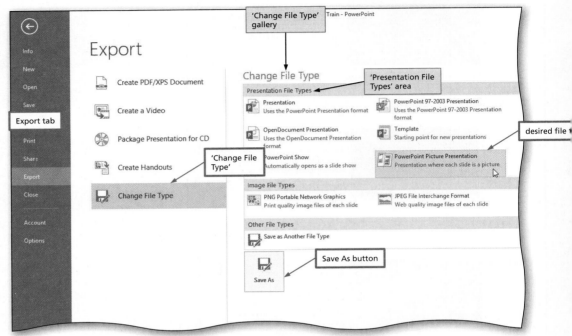

Figure 9–77

2

- Tap or click the Save As button to display the Save As dialog box.

- Type **Steam Train Picture Presentation** in the File name text box (Figure 9–78).

3

- Tap or click the Save button (Save As dialog box) to save the presentation as a picture presentation.

- Tap or click the OK button (Microsoft PowerPoint dialog box).

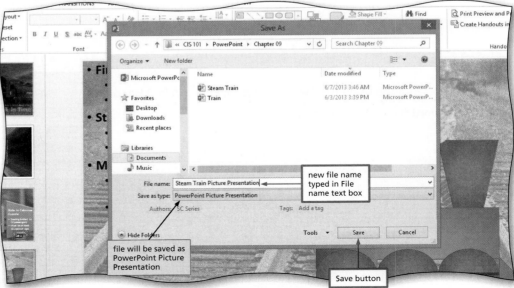

Figure 9–78

To Reset the Ribbon

Why? *Your work with the PowerPoint presentation is complete, so you can delete the group and buttons you added to the ribbon.* The following steps remove the Handouts group and the 'Print Preview and Print' and 'Create Handouts in Microsoft Word' commands from the HOME tab.

- Open the Backstage view, tap or click Options to display the PowerPoint Options dialog box, and then tap or click Customize Ribbon in the left pane to display the Customize the Ribbon pane.

- Tap or click the Reset button (PowerPoint Options dialog box) to display the Reset menu (Figure 9–79).

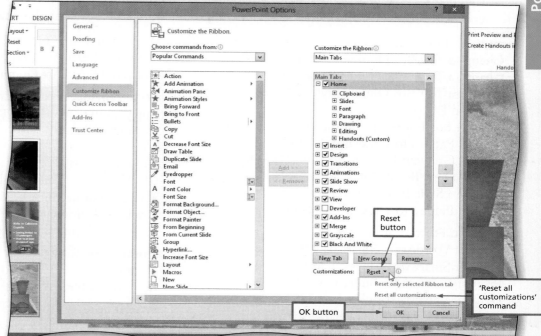

Figure 9–79

- Tap or click 'Reset all customizations'.

- Tap or click the Yes button (Microsoft Office dialog box) to delete all customizations.

- Tap or click the OK button (PowerPoint Options dialog box) to close the dialog box.

Q&A Do I need to remove the group and commands from the ribbon?

No. For consistency, the ribbon is reset after the added group and commands no longer are needed. If you share a computer with others, you should reset the ribbon.

To Save a Presentation and Exit PowerPoint

The presentation now is complete. You should save the presentation and then exit PowerPoint.

1. Save the Steam Train presentation again with the same file name.

2. Exit PowerPoint, closing all open documents.

BTW

Quick Reference
For a table that lists how to complete the tasks covered in this book using touch gestures, the mouse, ribbon, shortcut menu, and keyboard, see the Quick Reference Summary at the back of this book, or visit the Quick Reference resource on the Student Companion Site located on www.cengagebrain.com. For detailed instructions about accessing available resources, visit www.cengage.com/ct/studentdownload or see the inside back cover of this book.

Chapter Summary

In this chapter you have learned how to modify a presentation using text boxes, SmartArt, and shapes. You customized a text box, set it as the default, and then inserted new text boxes and applied formatting, including a texture, gradient, and pattern. You also converted WordArt to SmartArt and then formatted the shapes and bulleted paragraphs. Then you created a diagram from shapes, which had gradients and patterns applied. Finally, you saved the presentation as a picture presentation and exported the file to Microsoft Word to create a handout. The items listed below include all the new PowerPoint skills you have learned in this chapter.

Format Text Boxes and Change a Slide Picture
Change a Text Box Outline Weight (PPT 542)
Change a Text Box Outline Color (PPT 543)
Change a Text Box Outline Style (PPT 544)
Apply an Effect to a Text Box (PPT 544)
Set Text Box Formatting as the Default (PPT 545)
Apply a Pattern to a Text Box (PPT 547)
Apply a Gradient Fill to a Text Box (PPT 549)
Center a Text Box (PPT 550)
Change a Slide Picture (PPT 551)
Apply a Picture to a Text Box (PPT 561)

Create and Format SmartArt
Convert WordArt to SmartArt (PPT 553)
Reorder SmartArt Shapes (PPT 554)
Promote a SmartArt Bullet Level (PPT 555)
Demote a SmartArt Bullet Level (PPT 556)
Add a SmartArt Bullet (PPT 557)
Change the SmartArt Layout (PPT 557)
Remove a SmartArt Shape (PPT 558)
Add a SmartArt Shape (PPT 558)
Resize a SmartArt Graphic by Entering an Exact
    Measurement (PPT 559)

Resize a SmartArt Graphic Shape (PPT 560)
Convert a SmartArt Graphic to Text (PPT 563)
Convert a SmartArt Graphic to Shapes (PPT 565)

Draw and Insert Shapes, Lines, and Arrows
Apply a Fill to a Shape (PPT 568)
Subtract a Shape (PPT 570)
Merge Shapes (PPT 571)
Draw a Line (PPT 572)
Change a Line Weight and Color (PPT 573)
Set Line Formatting as the Default (PPT 574)
Draw an Additional Line (PPT 575)
Set Shape Formatting as the Default (PPT 577)

Customize the Ribbon
Customize the Ribbon (PPT 579)
Reset the Ribbon (PPT 585)

Create Handouts and Save the Presentation
Create a Handout by Exporting a File to Microsoft
    Word (PPT 582)
Save the Presentation as a Picture Presentation
    (PPT 584)

CONSIDER THIS

General Project Guidelines
When creating a PowerPoint presentation, the actions you perform and the decisions you make will affect the appearance and characteristics of the finished document. As you create a presentation with illustrations, such as the project shown in Figure 9–1 on page PPT 539, you should follow these general guidelines:

1. **Choose colors wisely.** The appropriate use of color can add interest and help audience members retain information. Used inappropriately, however, mismatched colors will generate confusion and create an impression of unprofessionalism.

2. **Use keywords in SmartArt graphics.** The words you type into your SmartArt graphic can serve as a prompt of the key points you want to make in the presentation.

3. **Use politically correct language.** When you type words into text boxes, be mindful of the terms you are using to identify the images.

4. **Work with a buddy.** As you develop your slide content and then rehearse the presentation, ask a friend or work associate to assist you with various tasks.

CONSIDER THIS

How should you submit solutions to questions in the assignments identified with a ✳ symbol?
Every assignment in this book contains one or more questions identified with a ✳ symbol. These questions require you to think beyond the assigned presentation. Present your solutions to the questions in the format required by your instructor. Possible formats may include one or more of these options: write the answer; create a document that contains the answer; present your answer to the class; discuss your answer in a group; record the answer as audio or video using a webcam, smartphone, or portable media player; or post answers on a blog, wiki, or website.

Apply Your Knowledge

Reinforce the skills and apply the concepts you learned in this chapter.

Applying an Effect to a Text Box, Inserting and Subtracting Shapes, Resizing a SmartArt Graphic Using Exact Measurements, and Reordering SmartArt Shapes

Note: To complete this assignment, you will be required to use the Data Files for Students. Visit www.cengage.com/ct/studentdownload for detailed instructions or contact your instructor for information about accessing the required files.

Instructions: Run PowerPoint. Open the presentation, Apply 9-1 Sun Corp, from the Data Files for Students.

The two slides in this presentation are for the Sun Corporation's announcement of its new management team. The document you open is a partially formatted presentation. You will apply an effect to a text box, insert and subtract shapes for a logo, reorder SmartArt shapes, and resize SmartArt to an exact measurement. Your presentation should look like Figure 9–80.

Perform the following tasks:

1. On Slide 1, select the title text placeholder and apply the Orange, 18 pt glow, Accent color 1 Glow effect (the first effect in the fourth Glow Variations row). Change the subtitle font to Arial, change the size to 32 point, change the font color to Gray-25%, Background 2, Darker 75% (the third color in the fifth Theme Colors row), bold, italicize, and then underline this text.

2. Insert a rectangle by using the Rectangle shape, (the first shape in the Rectangles row), resize the shape to 2.87" × 2.2", change the shape fill color to Orange, Accent 1, Lighter 40% (the fifth color in the fourth Theme Colors row), and then change the shape outline to No Outline. Move this shape to the left side of the title text placeholder as shown in Figure 9–80a.

3. Create a sun shape by inserting a 24-Point Star (the eleventh shape in the first Stars and Banners row), resize the shape to 1.5" × 1.5", and then copy and paste this shape three times. Move these four sun shapes on top of the rectangle shape that you created in Step 2. Position one at the top, bottom, left, and right, respectively so that about half of the sun shapes are off the edge of the rectangle shape. Use the Smart Guides to help you line them up.

4. Select the rectangle shape, hold down the CTRL key, select the four sun shapes, tap or click the Merge Shapes button, and then tap or click the Subtract command. Figure 9–80a shows the completed logo.

5. On Slide 2, select the shape labeled Sandra Smith on the organization chart and delete it. Select the shape labeled Ann Wilson and Promote up one level, as shown in Figure 9–80b. Change the Organization Chart SmartArt layout to the Picture Organization Chart (the second graphic in the first Hierarchy row) and resize it to 7.5" × 11.5".

(a) Slide 1

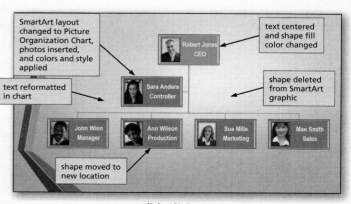

(b) Slide 2

Figure 9–80

Continued >

Apply Your Knowledge continued

6. Insert the photos of the six employees which are available from the Data Files for Students and named, Robert Jones, Sara Anders, John Winn, Sue Mills, Mae Smith, and Ann Wilson. Select the text in the shape labeled, Robert Jones, center this text, and then change the shape fill color to Orange, Accent 1 (the fifth color in the first Theme Colors row). Select all the text in the organization chart, change the font to Arial Narrow, change the font size to 20 point, and then bold this text.

7. Change the colors of the SmartArt graphic to Colorful Range – Accent Colors 2 to 3 (the second color in the Colorful area), and then apply the Cartoon 3-D style (the third style in the 3-D area). Center the SmartArt graphic on the slide as shown in the figure.

8. If requested by your instructor, add your birth year, birth city, and birth state as the second line of the subtitle on Slide 1.

9. Apply the Push transition and change the duration to 4.00 for all slides.

10. Save the presentation using the file name, Apply 9-1 Sun Corp Management.

11. Submit the revised document in the format specified by your instructor.

12. ✳ In this presentation, you created a logo by subtracting shapes. Did this enhance the presentation? How? You changed the layout of the SmartArt organization chart and added photos. How did this help your presentation?

Extend Your Knowledge

Extend the skills you learned in this chapter and experiment with new skills. You may need to use Help to complete the assignment.

Applying a Photo to a Shape, Changing a Text Box Outline Style, Applying a Pattern to a Text Box, Merging Shapes Using Union, and Setting Line Formatting as the Default

Note: To complete this assignment, you will be required to use the Data Files for Students. Visit www.cengage.com/ct/studentdownload for detailed instructions or contact your instructor for information about accessing the required files.

Instructions: Run PowerPoint. Open the presentation, Extend 9-1 Flower Shop, from the Data Files for Students. You will apply a photo to a shape, change text box outlines and fills, insert and merge shapes, and set line formatting as the default. Use Figures 9–81a and 9–81b as a guide.

Perform the following tasks:

1. On Slide 1, insert the Bevel shape (the first shape in the third Basic Shapes row). Resize the shape to approximately 5.26" × 4.51" and apply the tulip photo to the shape, as shown in Figure 9–81a. The photo, named Yellow Tulip, is available on the Data Files for Students. Move the shape so the left edge is approximately 1" from the left side of the slide and then center it vertically on the slide.

2. Insert a text box on the right side of Slide 1, type **Visit the Flower Pot** in the text box, change the font to MV Boli, change the font size to 66 point, apply the Gradient Fill – Gold, Accent 4, Outline – Accent 4 WordArt style (the third style in the second row) to the text, and then center the text. Change the size of the text box to 2.32" × 5.5" so that there are two words on each line, and then align the text in the middle of the text box. Change the border of the text box to the Square Dot dashes and then change the line weight to 3 pt.

3. Insert a second text box on the right side of Slide 1, type `Located outside the bookstore` in the text box, change the font size to 36 point, center the text, and then bold it. Adjust the size of the text box so that the text fits on two lines. Apply the Wide upward diagonal pattern to the text box. Move this text box so it is centered under the first text box. Select both text boxes and Distribute Vertically on the right side of the slide.

4. On Slide 2, change the square shape to a Trapezoid (the fifth shape in the first Basic Shapes row). *Hint:* You may need to use Help to learn how to change a shape. Center the trapezoid shape on top of the blue oval shape, move it down so that the bottom of the trapezoid shape is almost to the bottom of the oval shape, select both shapes, and then select Union under Merge Shapes. Change the shape fill color to Orange, Accent 2, Darker 25% (the sixth color in the fifth Theme Colors row). Select the green oval shape and apply the Walnut texture fill to this shape. Move this shape on top of the flower pot, and then select the flower pot and group these two shapes together. Move the flower pot to the bottom-center area of the slide, as shown in Figure 9–81b.

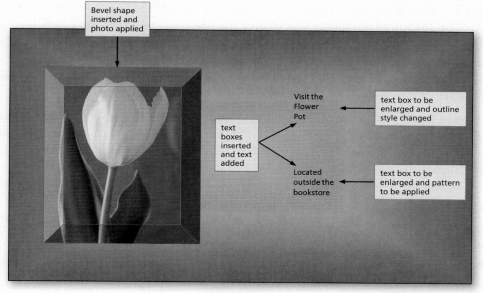

(a) Slide 1

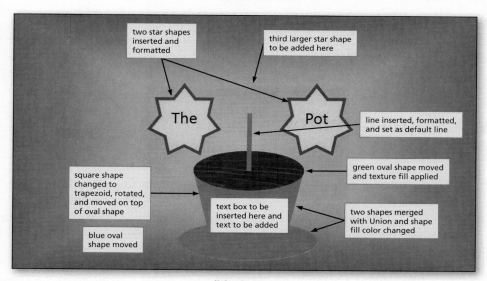

(b) Slide 2

Figure 9–81

Continued >

Extend Your Knowledge *continued*

5. Create a flower shape by inserting a 7-Point Star shape, resize it to approximately 2" × 2", change the shape fill color to Yellow (the fourth color in the Standard Colors row), change the shape outline color to Purple (the last color in the Standard Colors row), and then change the outline weight to 6 pt. Type **The** in the shape, change the font size to 36 point, and then change the font color to Black, Text 1 (the second color in the first Theme Colors row). Duplicate the shape and then type **Pot** in the second shape. Move the two flower shapes to the location shown in Figure 9–81b on the previous page.

6. Select the left flower shape and duplicate it. With the flower shape selected, apply the Lock aspect ratio and then use one of the corner sizing handles to resize the shape to approximately 2.87" × 2.87". *Hint:* You may need to use Help to learn how to apply the Lock aspect ratio. Move this shape above the flower pot to the location indicated in the figure. Type **Flower** in the shape.

7. Insert a line from the bottom-center (yellow area) of the middle flower to the middle of the dark area on the top of the flower pot, change the line color to Green, Accent 6, Darker 25% (the last color in the fifth Theme Colors row), change the weight of the line to 10 pt. Set this line formatting as the default. Insert a line from each of the two small flowers to the dark area on the top of the flower pot. Select all three lines and send them backward. Approximate size and location of the center green line is shown in Figure 9–81b.

8. Insert a text box in the center of the flower pot and type **Open Daily: 9 to 5** on the first line, type **Fresh flowers** on the second line, and then type **Gift ideas** on the third line. Change the font to Arial Narrow, increase the font size as large as possible (approximately 22 points) so the top line does not break, center the text, and then bold it. Increase the width of the text box so the type fits on the flower pot, and if necessary, remove the shape fill and outline from the text box.

9. If requested by your instructor, type your mother's maiden name in place of the text, Gift Ideas, in the text box on Slide 2 (Figure 9–81b).

10. Apply the Blinds transition in the Exciting category to all slides and then change the duration to 3.50 seconds.

11. Save the presentation using the file name, Extend 9-1 The Flower Pot.

12. Submit the revised document in the format specified by your instructor.

13. ✸ In this presentation, you inserted a flower photo into the bevel shape. How did this improve the look of the slide? Why did you use the Lock aspect ratio when changing the size of the flower shape on Slide 2?

Analyze, Correct, Improve

Analyze a presentation, correct all errors, and improve it.

Changing a Background Photo, Applying a Fill to a Shape, Converting WordArt to SmartArt, and Resizing, Changing Line Weight, and Color of a Shape
Note: To complete this assignment, you will be required to use the Data Files for Students. Visit www.cengage.com/ct/studentdownload for detailed instructions or contact your instructor for information about accessing the required files.

Instructions: Run PowerPoint. Open the presentation, Analyze 9-1 Classes, from the Data Files for Students. The principal at the high school you work at asked you to prepare a presentation about the new adult classes that will be offered in the fall. Modify the slides by making the indicated corrections and improvements.

1. Correct

a. The photo used as the background on Slide 1 (Figure 9–82a) is outdated so you will change it to the photo called Classroom, shown in the figure, which is available on the Data Files for Students. Change the transparency to 0%. Delete the copy of the Classroom photo.

b. On Slide 1, increase the size of the top Wavy shape to approximately 2.14" × 8.85", change the border weight to 3 pt, change the shape fill color to Dark Blue (the ninth color in the Standard Colors row), and then change the transparency to 50%. Move this shape to the upper-left corner of the slide. Set this shape formatting as the Default.

c. Insert a Double Wave shape (the eighth shape in the second Stars and Banners row) across the width of the slide and copy and paste the text from the text box at the bottom of the slide into this shape. Change the height of the shape to 1.25". Delete the text box at the bottom of the slide.

d. On Slide 2 (Figure 9–82b), convert the WordArt bulleted text to the Vertical Block List SmartArt graphic (the second graphic in the seventh List row). Change the colors to Colorful Range – Accent Colors 4 to 5 (the fourth colors in the Colorful row). Select the five left shapes labeled with the days of the week, and then tap or click the Smaller button three times.

e. If requested by your instructor, type the name of your high school in place of Eagle Ridge on Slide 1 (Figure 9–82a).

(a) Slide 1

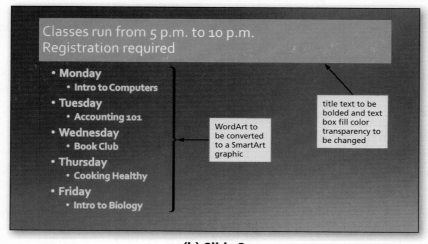

(b) Slide 2

Figure 9–82

Continued >

Analyze, Correct, Improve *continued*

2. Improve

a. On Slide 1, change the border color on the two wavy shapes to Orange, Accent 1 (the fifth color in the first Theme Colors row).

b. Change the font size of the text in the bottom shape to 40 point, apply the Fill – White, Text 1, Shadow WordArt style (the first style in the first row) to the text, and then bold this text. Move this shape to approximately .05" from the bottom of the slide.

c. On Slide 2, bold the title text and with the title text placeholder still selected, change the blue fill color transparency to 50%.

d. Apply the Metallic Scene style to the SmartArt graphic and then visually center the graphic on the slide.

e. Change the Rotate transition to the Conveyor transition and then change the duration to 3.25 seconds for all slides.

f. Save the presentation using the file name, Analyze 9-1 Adult Classes.

g. Submit the revised document in the format specified by your instructor.

3. ✺ Which errors existed in the starting file? How did changing the shape fills and line weights help? How did changing the photo on Slide 1 improve the look of the slide?

In the Labs

Design and/or create a presentation using the guidelines, concepts, and skills presented in this chapter. Labs 1 and 2, which increase in difficulty, require you to create solutions based on what you learned in the chapter; Lab 3 requires you to create a solution, which uses cloud and web technologies, by learning and investigating on your own from general guidance.

Lab 1: Combining Shapes, Changing the Outline Style and Centering a Text Box, Converting a SmartArt Graphic to Text, Promoting a SmartArt Bullet Level, and Applying an Illustration to a Text Box

Problem: You are an instructor at the Dance Studio 9 school of dance. Your school is under new ownership, and the new owner has made some changes including a new name and moving to a new larger location. He asked you to create a new logo with the new name and create a PowerPoint presentation to promote an upcoming dance lesson special. You create the presentation shown in Figures 9–83a through 9–83d on page PPT 594.

Note: To complete this assignment, you will be required to use the Data Files for Students. Visit www.cengage.com/ct/studentdownload for detailed instructions or contact your instructor for information about accessing the required files.

Instructions: Perform the following tasks:

1. Open the presentation, Lab 9-1 Dance, from the Data Files for Students. Customize the Ribbon by adding a group called Nudge to the HOME tab and then adding the Nudge Down, Nudge Left, Nudge Right, and the Nudge Up commands to this new group.

2. Decrease the size of the illustration on Slide 1 to approximately 4.09" × 3.42", apply the Perspective Shadow, White picture style (the fourth style in the third row), change the color to Grayscale, and then change the picture border color to Gold, Accent 3 (the seventh color in the first Theme Colors row). Move the illustration to the upper-right area of the slide, as shown in Figure 9–83a.

3. *Note:* See Figure 9–83d on the next page for illustrations to assist you in creating the logo on Slide 1. Insert a Double Wave shape (the last shape in the second Stars and Banners row), resize to 2" × 4", and rotate the shape slightly to the left. With the shape still selected, copy and paste the shape two times. Select the HOME tab and locate the Nudge Group you added to the ribbon. Select the top shape, tap or click the Nudge Right button, and then the Nudge Down button 16 times each. Select the middle shape, tap or click the Nudge Right button, and then the Nudge Down button eight times each. See the upper-left illustration in Figure 9–83d.

4. Select the three shapes, and then merge them using the Combine command as shown in the upper-right illustration in Figure 9–83d. Add the text `Dance Studio 9` in the combined shape, change the font to Arial, change the font color to Black, Background 1 (the first color in the first Theme Colors row), and then bold this text. Change the shape fill color to White, Text 1, Darker 35% (the second color in the fifth Theme Colors row), as shown in the lower-left illustration in Figure 9–83d.

5. Apply the Triangle Down Transform text effect (the fourth effect in the first Warp row) to the text. Select the shape, and then apply the Olive Green, 11 pt glow, Accent color 4 Glow effect as shown in the lower-right illustration in Figure 9–83d. Apply the Preset 2 shape effect to the shape, resize it to approximately 2.5" × 5", and move the shape to the upper-left area of the Slide 1, as shown in Figure 9–83a.

6. Insert a text box on Slide 1, type `DANCERS OF ALL LEVELS WELCOME`, change the font size to 40 point, bold this text, center it, align the text in the middle of the text box, and then apply the Fill – White, Outline – Accent 2, Hard Shadow – Accent 2 WordArt style (the fourth style in the third row) to the text. Change the text box shape fill color to Black, Background 1, Lighter 25% (the first color in the fourth Theme Colors row), change the text box outline to the Round Dot Dashes, and then change the outline weight to 6 pt.

7. Change the size of the text box to 1.5" × 10", distribute the text box horizontally, and then align it to the bottom of the slide. Press the Nudge Up button 15 times to position the text box, as shown in Figure 9–83a. Copy and paste this text box to Slides 2 and 3, and position them as shown in Figure 9–83b and 9–83c.

8. On Slide 2 (Figure 9–83b), change the title text to, `NEW STUDENT SPECIALS`. Do not change the size of the text box. Change the SmartArt layout to the Vertical Block List (the second layout in the seventh List row). Change the color of the SmartArt graphic to Colored Fill – Accent 3 (the second color in the Accent 3 row), and then apply the Polished style (the first style in the first 3-D row).

9. Select the two left shapes that show the prices, and tap or click the Smaller button three times. Change the font size in these two shapes to 36 point, the font color to Black, Background 1 (the first color in the first Theme Colors row). In the top-right shape, demote the second and fourth bulleted paragraphs. In the bottom-right shape, demote the second bulleted paragraph, and then promote the fourth bulleted paragraph. Change the font size in the top-right and bottom-right shapes to 24 point, as shown in Figure 9–83b.

10. Insert a text box in the right area of the top-right and bottom-right shapes in the SmartArt graphic. In the top text box, insert the illustration called Dancing Shoes. In the bottom text box, insert the illustration called Music. Both illustrations are available from the Data Files for Students.

11. On Slide 3, change the title text to, `FEATURED DANCES`, as shown in Figure 9–83c. Do not change the size of the text box. Convert the SmartArt graphic to text. Change the bulleted list font size to 36 point, and then change the bullets to the Arrow bullets. Change the size of the text box to 3" × 5", and then change the shape fill to Gold, Accent 3 (the seventh color in the Theme Colors row). Change the bulleted list font color to Black, Background 1 (the first color in the first Theme Colors row). Move the bulleted list text box to the area shown in the figure. Apply the Soft Edge Oval picture style (the sixth style in the third row) to the illustration.

Continued >

In the Labs *continued*

12. If requested by your instructor, add the year of your birth after the word Waltz on Slide 3 (Figure 9–83c).

13. Apply the Shape transition in the Subtle category to all slides and then change the duration to 3.00 seconds.

14. Reset the ribbon. Save the presentation using the file name, Lab 9-1 Dance Studio 9. Submit the document in the format specified by your instructor.

15. ✹ Did the design of the new logo enhance the presentation? You added a Dashed Dot border to the title text boxes? Why? Did changing the SmartArt graphic to text help the presentation? Why?

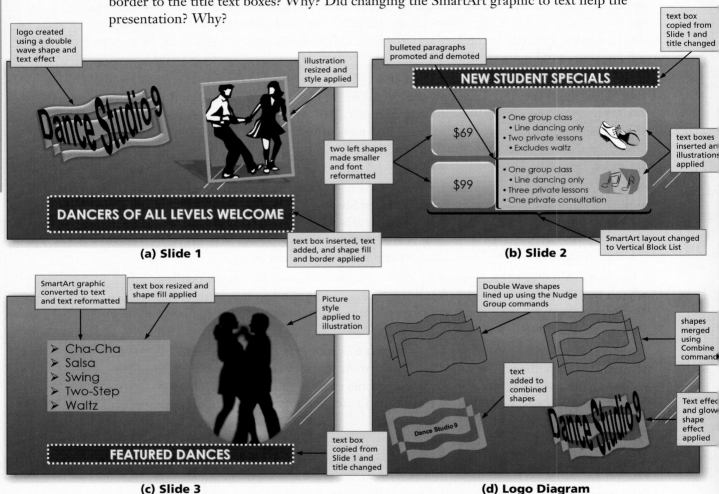

(a) Slide 1

(b) Slide 2

(c) Slide 3

(d) Logo Diagram

Figure 9–83

Lab 2: Changing a Text Box Outline Weight and Style, Changing a Photo, Inserting Shapes and Combining Shapes, Setting Shape and Text Box Formatting as the Default, Reordering SmartArt Shapes, and Creating a Handout by Exporting a File to Microsoft Word

Problem: You are studying the anatomy of the human eye in your biology class. Your instructor has divided the class into several groups. Your group was instructed to prepare a PowerPoint presentation focusing on how we see and some tips on keeping your eyes healthy. One of the members in your group started designing a diagram of the eye using shapes, and asked if you would finish the diagram and add some creative touches to the presentation. You create a presentation with four slides, as shown in Figure 9–84a on the next page through 9–84d on page PPT 597.

Note: To complete this assignment, you will be required to use the Data Files for Students. Visit www.cengage.com/ct/studentdownload for detailed instructions or contact your instructor for information about accessing the required files.

Instructions: Perform the following tasks:

1. Open the presentation, Lab 9-2 Eyes, from the Data Files for Students.

2. On Slide 1, change the photo to Brown Eyes, which is available on the Data Files for Students. Resize the photo to approximately 4" × 6", change the picture style to the Rotated, White picture style, change the picture border color to Blue, Accent 4, Lighter 80% (the eighth color in the second Theme Colors row), and then move the photo to the upper-left area of the slide as shown in Figure 9–84a.

3. Change the title font text to Arial Black, increase the font size to 60 point, and then apply the Gradient Fill – Blue, Accent 4, Outline – Accent 4 WordArt style (the third style in the second row). Drag the left-center sizing handle to the left until the text is on one line, center the text, and then align the text in the middle of the text box. Add the Newsprint texture to the text box shape. Apply the Long Dash Dot Dot dashes outline to the shape, change the color to Blue, Accent 4, Lighter 40% (the eighth color in the fourth Theme Colors row), and then change the shape outline weight to 6 pt. Change the size of the text box to approximately 2" × 10", send it backward, and then move it so that the upper-left corner of the text box is behind the bottom-right edge of the photo, as shown in the figure.

4. On Slide 2, increase the size of the photo to 3.67" × 5.5" and then align the photo vertically on the right area of the slide, as shown in Figure 9–84b.

5. Insert the callout shape, Line Callout 1 (Border and Accent Bar) (second shape in the second Callouts row), change the shape outline color to Yellow (the fourth color in the first Standard Colors row), change the shape outline weight to 2¼ pt. Type a letter in the shape, highlight it, change the font to Arial Narrow, change the font size to 24 point, bold the text, and then change the font color to Yellow. Press and hold or right-click this shape and set it as the default shape.

6. On Slide 2, insert three callout shapes, type the text in each shape, move them to the locations shown, and then select the yellow sizing handle at the end of each line and move it on the eye diagram, as shown in Figure 9–84b. *Note:* For the Iris callout, you can flip the shape horizontally as shown.

7. Slide 3 is the eye diagram you will finish by adding shapes for the cornea and retina. Insert a Moon shape (the tenth shape in the third Basic Shapes row), select No Outline, resize it to 3.44" × 1.54", change the shape fill to White, Text 1 (the second color in the first Theme Colors row), and then duplicate the shape. Select the first shape, Send it to Back, and then move it to the left side of the blue diagram as shown in Figure 9–84c.

8. Select the second moon shape, rotate it horizontally, change the size to 2.94" × 0.76", and then change the shape fill color to Purple, Accent 5 (the ninth color in the first Theme Colors row). Insert a Right Arrow shape (the first shape in the first Block Arrows row), select No Outline, resize it to 0.87" × 1.25", and then change the shape fill color to Purple, Accent 5. Move this arrow shape to the right-center area of the purple moon, select both purple shapes and then merge them using the Union command. Move this purple shape to the inside of the blue circle shape lining it up at the right edge of the green line inside the circle shape, as shown in Figure 9–84c. You will not be able to merge these shapes. You can select the three shapes and then group them in case you need to move the eye diagram on the slide.

Continued >

In the Labs *continued*

9. For the callouts on Slide 3, insert a text box, change the shape fill and shape outline color to Black, Background 1 (the first color in the Theme Colors row), change the font to Arial, change the font size to 20 point, and then bold the text. Change the internal margins to 0.2" for the left and right margins, and 0.1" for the top and bottom margins. Set this text box formatting as the default. Create six text boxes, enter the text shown in the figure, adjust the size of each text box for even line distribution, and then move them to the locations shown in Figure 9–84c.

10. On Slide 3, insert an Arrow line (the second shape in the Lines row), change the shape outline color to Black, Background 1, and then change the weight of the line to 3 pt, and then set it as the default line. Insert a line from each of the six text boxes with the arrow pointing to the respective part on the diagram, as shown in Figure 9–84c. *Note:* Use the zoom to make it easier to position the callouts.

11. On Slide 4, center the title text and then bold it. Convert the WordArt bulleted text to the Varying Width List SmartArt graphic (the fourth graphic in the second List row), change the colors to Colorful Range – Accent Colors 5 to 6 (the fifth color group in the Colorful area), and then apply the Inset 3-D style (the second style in the first 3-D row) to the graphic. Reorder the SmartArt shapes so that the shape with the text, Get regular eye exams, is at the top, as shown in Figure 9–84d.

12. If requested by your instructor, add your eye color after the dash in the Iris callout on Slide 2.

13. Apply the Uncover transition in the Subtle category to all slides and then change the duration to 2.50 seconds.

14. Create a handout in Microsoft Word using the 'Blank lines next to slides' page layout, as shown in Figure 9–84e.

15. Save the presentation using the file name, Lab 9-2 Anatomy of the Eye.

16. Save the presentation as a picture presentation using the file name, Lab 9-2 Amazing Eyes.

17. Submit the document in the format specified by your instructor.

18. ✳ Did formatting the text box on Slide 1 improve the look of the slide? Was saving the formatting as the default for shapes, lines, and text boxes helpful? Why? Do you think your audience will be able to read the callouts on Slides 2 and 3? If not, how could you have improved the formatting?

(a) Slide 1

Figure 9–84 (Continued)

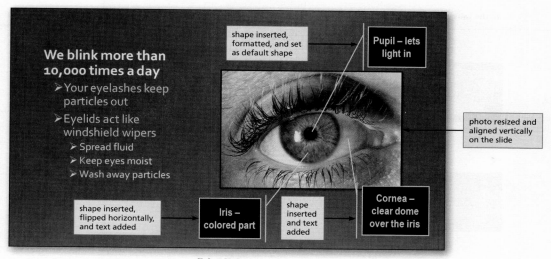

(b) Slide 2

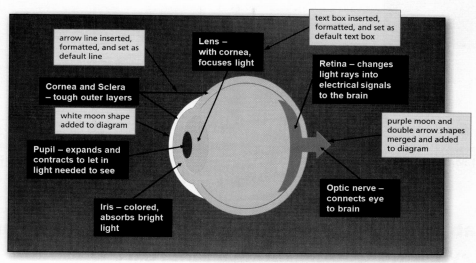

(c) Slide 3

(d) Slide 4

Figure 9–84 (Continued)

Continued >

In the Labs *continued*

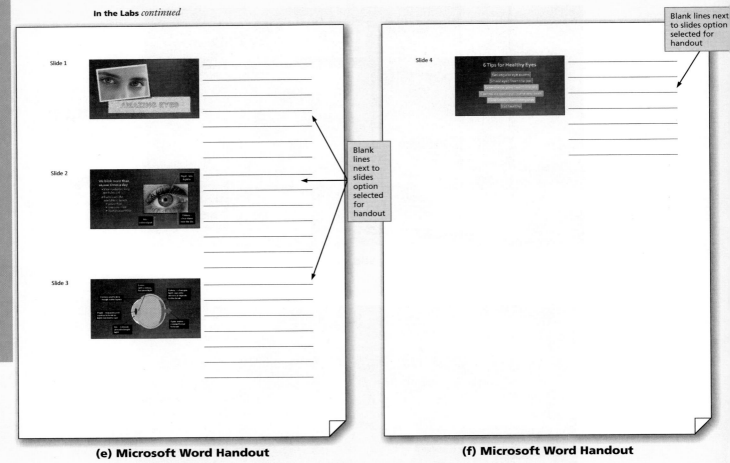

(e) Microsoft Word Handout   **(f) Microsoft Word Handout**

Figure 9–84

Lab 3: Expand Your World: Cloud and Web Technologies
Reviewing Google Images SmartArt

Problem: You want to add SmartArt to the presentation you have created to accompany a speech you are scheduled to deliver in your Earth science class on the topic of tidal waves. You need some ideas, so you browse the images on Google for ideas.

Note: You will need Internet access to complete this assignment. If you do not have Internet access, read this assignment without performing the instructions.

Instructions: Perform the following tasks:
1. In PowerPoint, open the file, Lab 9-3 Tidal Wave, located on the Data Files for Students. View Slides 2 and 3 to familiarize yourself with the content.
2. Open your browser and navigate to Google.com. Tap or click Images at the top of the screen to display the Google Images webpage. Tap or click the Google Images search text box, type **smartart** as the search text, and then tap or click the Search button (the magnifying glass) or press the ENTER key.
3. View several SmartArt images with designs that would be appropriate for the material on Slides 2 and 3 in your Tidal Wave presentation. Select two different designs and then convert the bulleted lists in the slides to these designs.
4. On Slide 1, replace the Student Name text with your name. If requested by your instructor, change the course number to the area code of the town where you were born.

5. Save the presentation with the file name, Lab 9-3 Tidal Wave SmartArt.

6. Submit the revised presentation in the format specified by your instructor.

7. ✹ Which SmartArt images on the Google Images webpage did you use as guides for your presentation? Why did you select these particular examples?

✹ Consider This: Your Turn

Apply your creative thinking and problem-solving skills to design and implement a solution.

1. Design and Create a Presentation about Underwater Hockey

Personal

Part 1:   Most people are familiar with some of the more popular forms of hockey like ice, field, and roller hockey, but not many know about underwater hockey. Like other types of hockey, in underwater hockey two teams try to score goals with a puck or ball, into the opponent's net using a stick. Your son joined an underwater hockey league and has asked you to gather some information and create a presentation that he can use to share with his friends who have expressed an interest in the sport. Sometimes referred to as Octopush or water hockey, the sport is a non-contact sport played around the world beginning in the United Kingdom in the mid-1950s. The goals are set up on the bottom of a swimming pool and two teams with six players at a time play two 10-minute sessions, and four additional team players are ready to play as subs. There is equipment required such as a diving mask, snorkel, fins, a glove, and a short stick (not more than 350mm including the handle), and of course head and ear protection (usually a helmet). When the game starts and the puck is in place in the middle of the pool, players hold their breath and dive to the bottom of the pool to go after the puck and push it to the opponent's goal net. Play stops after a goal is scored, or when a referee calls time for a penalty. The puck is about the same size as an ice hockey puck, but is made of lead and weighs about 3 pounds. Use the concepts and techniques presented in this chapter to prepare a presentation. Select a suitable theme, and use shapes, WordArt, and SmartArt graphics where appropriate. The presentation can contain photos, illustrations, and videos. You can use photos and illustrations from Office.com if they are appropriate for this topic. Submit your assignment in the format specified by your instructor.

Part 2:   ✹ You made several decisions while creating the presentation in this assignment: where to insert text boxes and shapes, what fills to use, how to format the text and text box backgrounds (such as font, font size, and colors), which image(s) to use, and what WordArt and SmartArt graphics to use to make the presentation look professional and consistent. What was the rationale behind each of these decisions? When you reviewed the document, what further revisions did you make and why? Where would you recommend showing this slide show?

2. Design and Create a Presentation about the Writing Process

Professional

Part 1:   Your English composition instructor taught you how to compose an essay using the writing process. This theory stresses that writing is not a linear procedure because a good writer brainstorms ideas, selects one as a topic, performs some prewriting to generate essay details, organizes the major points, writes, and then revises. At any point in the essay, a writer can backtrack to repeat or refine a step. Once a draft is complete, it should be reviewed by a peer. The writer should then take the criticism and revise the rough draft at least once.

You work in your school's Writing Lab, and many students have come to you for help when composing their essays. After explaining the writing process verbally many times, you decide to develop a PowerPoint presentation that depicts this concept to show the students. The presentation should contain SmartArt, text boxes, and shapes to help explain the writing process. You may find examples in your English composition textbook or online. Submit your assignment in the format specified by your instructor.

Continued >

Consider this: Your Turn *continued*

Part 2: ✳ You made several decisions while creating the presentation in this assignment: where to insert text boxes and shapes, what fills to use, how to format the text and text box backgrounds (such as font, font size, and colors), which image(s) to use, and which SmartArt graphics to use to make the presentation look professional and consistent. What was the rationale behind each of these decisions? When you reviewed the document, what further revisions did you make and why? Where would you recommend showing this slide show?

3. Design and Create a Presentation about Clouds
Research and Collaboration

Part 1: In your meteorology class you are studying cloud formations. Clouds are grouped into four categories: Low clouds, middle clouds, high clouds, and vertically-developed clouds. The low clouds form below 6,500 feet and are primarily water droplets but can also contain ice or snow. Stratus clouds usually are a dull gray color and look like a blanket. Stratocumulus clouds are formed when stratus clouds break up. Nimbostratus clouds are darker than stratus clouds and bring rain or snow consistently for long periods of time. Middle clouds form at 6,500 to 20,000 feet and are primarily water droplets, but also can be ice crystals. Altocumulus clouds usually appear as layers of puffy clouds. Altostratus clouds appear as gray flat sheets that cover most of the sky and obscure the sun. High clouds form above 20,000 feet and are primarily ice crystals. Cirrus clouds spread across the sky and have a feathery appearance. Cirrocumulus clouds are wavy and rippled. Cirrostratus clouds spread in a thin sheet and give the sky a white appearance. Vertically-developed clouds grow to heights of more than 39,000 feet. Cumulus clouds look like cotton balls. Cumulonimbus clouds are cumulus clouds that have grown high into the atmosphere with dark bases, and can produce severe storms. Your class will be divided into four groups, and each group will gather information and photos about one category of clouds. Then you will meet to discuss what information to include in the PowerPoint presentation. Use at least three objectives found at the beginning of this chapter to develop the presentation. Some shapes in PowerPoint may help with your presentation, and a few lines, such as Freeform, can be used to draw and illustrate clouds. Print handouts and speaker notes for the class presentation. You can use your own photos and videos or those available from Office.com if they are appropriate for this topic.

Part 2: ✳ You made several decisions while creating the presentation in this assignment: where to insert text boxes and shapes, what fills to use, how to format the text and text box backgrounds (such as font, font size, and colors), which image(s) to use, and what WordArt and SmartArt graphics to use to make the presentation look professional and consistent. What was the rationale behind each of these decisions? When you reviewed the document, what further revisions did you make and why? Where would you recommend showing this slide show?

Learn Online

Reinforce what you learned in this chapter with games, exercises, training, and many other online activities and resources.

Student Companion Site Reinforcement activities and resources are available at no additional cost on www.cengagebrain.com. Visit www.cengage.com/ct/studentdownload for detailed instructions about accessing the resources available at the Student Companion Site.

SAM Put your skills into practice with SAM! If you have a SAM account, go to www.cengage .com/sam2013 to access SAM assignments for this chapter.

10 | Developing a Presentation with Content from Outside Sources

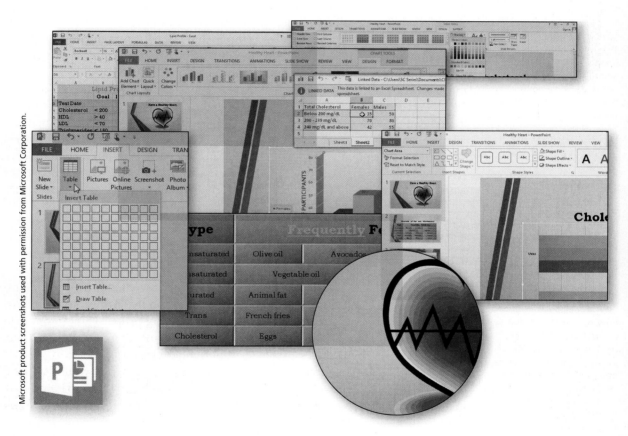

Microsoft product screenshots used with permission from Microsoft Corporation.

Objectives

You will have mastered the material in this chapter when you can:

- Insert an object from a file
- Embed and edit a file
- Draw and format a table
- Resize, split, distribute, and arrange table columns and rows
- Insert and edit a linked Excel worksheet
- Switch chart rows and columns

- Change a chart type
- Apply a chart style
- Apply effects to chart elements
- Display chart elements
- Edit chart data
- Add a hyperlink to a table

10 | Developing a Presentation with Content from Outside Sources

BTW
Using Tables and Charts
Charts and tables can give meaning to the figures and facts you want to emphasize in your presentation. These tools help audiences understand abstract concepts and the relationships between sets of data. Present only one main idea in a chart or table. Overloading your slides with data may confuse your audience and defeat the purpose of these graphical elements.

Introduction

Adding visuals to a presentation could help audience members remember the important facts you want to share. Researchers have found that adding such graphics as tables, charts, graphs, and maps increases retention by more than 50 percent. Audiences also believe that speakers who include visuals in their presentations are more qualified and believable than speakers who do not have accompanying visuals. In addition, studies have shown that meeting times are reduced and decisions are reached more quickly when group members have seen visuals that help them reach a consensus.

PowerPoint has many features that allow you to insert visuals and then modify them directly on the slide. For example, you can embed a Microsoft Word document and then edit its text or replace its graphics. You can link an Excel worksheet with a PowerPoint slide so that when numbers are modified in the slide, the corresponding numbers on the worksheet also are updated. These tools help you work productively and generate slides with graphics that help your audience comprehend and remember your message.

Project — Presentation with Embedded and Linked Files and Formatted Table and Chart

BTW
First Impressions
Take care in designing an opening slide that meets the audience's expectations and generates interest in the remainder of the presentation. The first slide in your presentation sets the tone of your entire presentation. Before you say one word, your audience sees what you have projected on the screen and forms a first impression of whether the speech is going to be interesting, professional, and relevant.

A low-fat diet and exercise are two factors that can prevent and treat many chronic diseases, including heart disease, obesity, diabetes, and hypertension. Many fitness centers include wellness programs that focus on eating properly and monitoring cholesterol levels. They offer classes in meal proportions, nutrition, and cooking, and they also provide blood pressure checks and blood tests.

The presentation you create in this chapter (Figure 10–1) would be useful to show during a nutrition class at your local fitness center. You begin Slide 1 (Figure 10–1a) by inserting a flyer with graphics and text (Figure 10–1b). You then decide to emphasize the healthy aspect of learning to eat properly and monitor blood composition, so you edit the title text by adding the word, Healthy, directly onto the slide. The second slide (Figure 10–1c) includes a chart that you draw and enhance using PowerPoint's tools and graphical features. If you tap or click a cell in the chart when running the presentation, a hyperlinked Adobe PDF file that can be used to track food consumption (Figure 10–1d) displays. You insert the table on Slide 3 (Figure 10–1e) from a Microsoft Excel worksheet (Figure 10–1f) that contains the results of one blood draw. You will update this table with the results of a second blood draw, and these figures also will update the original Excel worksheet. Fitness center members have provided the results of their cholesterol tests, and this data was used to create the chart that is displayed on Slide 4 (Figure 10–1g on page PPT 604) and created in Microsoft Excel (Figure 10–1h). You then obtain the test results from a few more fitness center members, so you update the worksheet data that generated the chart, which, in turn, modifies the chart automatically.

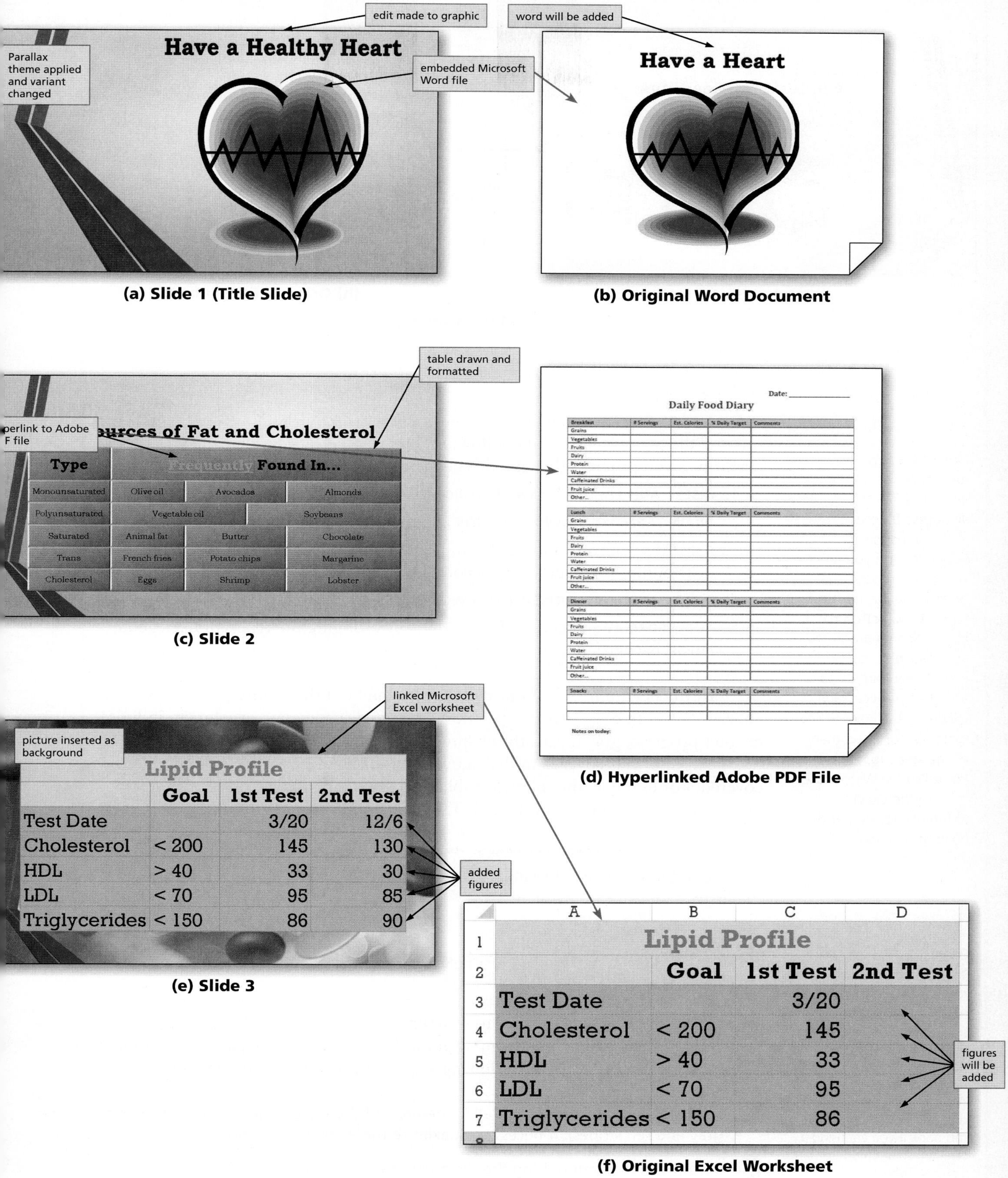
edit made to graphic
word will be added
Parallax theme applied and variant changed
Have a Healthy Heart
embedded Microsoft Word file
Have a Heart
(a) Slide 1 (Title Slide)
(b) Original Word Document
table drawn and formatted
perlink to Adobe F file
urces of Fat and Cholesterol
Type
Frequently Found In...
Monounsaturated
Olive oil
Avocados
Almonds
Polyunsaturated
Vegetable oil
Soybeans
Saturated
Animal fat
Butter
Chocolate
Trans
French fries
Potato chips
Margarine
Cholesterol
Eggs
Shrimp
Lobster
Date:
Daily Food Diary
Breakfast
Lunch
Dinner
Snacks
Servings
Est. Calories
% Daily Target
Comments
Grains
Vegetables
Fruits
Dairy
Protein
Water
Caffeinated Drinks
Fruit juice
Other...
Notes on today:
(c) Slide 2
(d) Hyperlinked Adobe PDF File
linked Microsoft Excel worksheet
picture inserted as background
Lipid Profile
Goal
1st Test
2nd Test
Test Date
Cholesterol
HDL
LDL
Triglycerides
< 200
> 40
< 70
< 150
3/20
145
33
95
86
12/6
130
30
85
90
added figures
(e) Slide 3
A
B
C
D
figures will be added
(f) Original Excel Worksheet

Figure 10–1

(g) Slide 4

(h) Original Excel Chart

Figure 10–1 (Continued)

Roadmap

In this chapter, you will learn how to create the slides shown in Figure 10–1 on this and the previous page. The following roadmap identifies general activities you will perform as you progress through this chapter:

1. INSERT AND EDIT a Microsoft WORD FILE by adding text.
2. DRAW TABLE ROWS AND COLUMNS and then erase lines and split columns and rows.
3. FORMAT a TABLE by adding shading, a gradient fill, and a cell bevel, and then distributing rows and resizing columns and rows.
4. INSERT AND EDIT a LINKED Excel WORKSHEET.
5. COPY, FORMAT and EDIT an Excel CHART by changing the type, colors, legend, labels, background, and data.

At the beginning of step instructions throughout the chapter, you will see an abbreviated form of this roadmap. The abbreviated roadmap uses colors to indicate chapter progress: gray means the chapter is beyond that activity; blue means the task being shown is covered in that activity, and black means that activity is yet to be covered. For example, the following abbreviated roadmap indicates the chapter would be showing a task in the 3 FORMAT TABLE activity.

1 INSERT & EDIT WORD FILE | 2 DRAW TABLE ROWS & COLUMNS | **3 FORMAT TABLE**
4 INSERT & EDIT LINKED WORKSHEET | 5 COPY, FORMAT & EDIT CHART

Use the abbreviated roadmap as a progress guide while you read or step through the instructions in this chapter.

To Run PowerPoint, Choose a Theme and Variant, and Save a File

If you are using a computer to step through the project in this chapter and you want your screens to match the figures in this book, you should change your computer's resolution to 1366×768. The following steps run PowerPoint and then save a file.

1 Run PowerPoint, apply the Parallax theme, and then select the last variant (with the gray and red stripes). If necessary, maximize the PowerPoint window.

2 Save the presentation using the file name, Healthy Heart.

One of the few differences between Windows 7 and Windows 8 occurs in the steps to run PowerPoint. If you are using Windows 7, tap or click the Start button, type **PowerPoint** in the 'Search programs and files' box, tap or click PowerPoint 2013, and then, if necessary, maximize the PowerPoint window. For a summary of the steps to run PowerPoint in Windows 7, refer to the Quick Reference located at the back of this book.

BTW
The Ribbon and Screen Resolution
PowerPoint may change how the groups and buttons within the groups appear on the ribbon, depending on the computer's screen resolution. Thus, your ribbon may look different from the ones in this book if you are using a screen resolution other than 1366×768.

Use powerful words to accompany the text on your slides.
Carefully plan the speech that coordinates with the slides in your presentation. Use examples that substantiate the objects on the slides, and use familiar, precise words and terms that enlighten the audience. Do not include obvious material as filler because audience members will conclude that you are wasting their time with irrelevant information.

Inserting Graphics or Other Objects from a File

PowerPoint allows you to insert many types of objects into a presentation. You can insert clips, pictures, video and audio files, and symbols, and you also can copy and paste or drag and drop objects from one slide to another. At times you may want to insert content created with other Microsoft Office programs, such as a Word flyer, an Excel table or graph, a Paint graphic, or a document created with another Microsoft Windows-based application. The original document is called the **source**, and the new document that contains this object is called the **destination**. When you want to copy a source document object, such as a Word flyer, to a destination document, such as your PowerPoint slide, you can use one of three techniques.

- **Embedding** — An **embedded object** becomes part of the destination slide, but you edit and modify the contents using the source program's commands and features. In this project, for example, you will embed a Word document and then edit the text using Microsoft Word without leaving PowerPoint.

- **Linking** — Similar to an embedded object, a **linked object** also is created in another application and is stored in the **source file**, the original file in which the object was created. The linked object maintains a connection to its source and does not become part of the destination slide. Instead, a connection, or link, made between the source and destination objects gives the appearance that the objects are independent. In reality, the two objects work together so that when one is edited, the other is updated. If the original object is changed, the linked object on the slide also changes. In this project, for example, you will link a Microsoft Excel table and then edit the data using Excel. As the numbers in the table change, the numbers in the linked table on the PowerPoint slide also are updated to reflect those changes.

- **Copying and pasting** — An object that you copy from a source document and then paste in a destination document becomes part of the destination program. Any edits that you make are done using the destination software. When you paste the object, you have the options of embedding or linking the document. For example, if you copy a picture from a Word document, embed it into your slide, and then recolor or remove the background, those changes are made using PowerPoint's commands and do not affect the source object. In contrast, in this project you will copy an Excel chart and then paste it into a slide by linking the two documents. When you modify the object without leaving PowerPoint, any changes you make to the data in PowerPoint will be reflected in the original Excel source document.

The first two techniques described above are termed **object linking and embedding (OLE,** pronounced o-lay). This means of sharing material developed in various sources and then updating the files within a destination program is useful when you deliver presentations frequently that display current data that changes constantly. For example, your PowerPoint presentation may contain a chart reflecting current fitness center enrollment statistics, or you may include a table with the fitness center's membership totals for the previous year.

BTW
Touch Screen Differences
The Office and Windows interfaces may vary if you are using a touch screen. For this reason, you might notice that the function or appearance of your touch screen differs slightly from this chapter's presentation.

BTW
Q&As
For a complete list of the Q&As found in many of the step-by-step sequences in this book, visit the Q&A resource on the Student Companion Site located on www.cengagebrain.com. For detailed instructions about accessing available resources, visit www.cengage.com/ct/ studentdownload or see the inside back cover of this book.

To Insert a File with Graphics and Text

The first object you will add to your presentation is a graphical flyer created in Microsoft Word. This flyer contains artwork and text developed as part of an advertising campaign for a class at the fitness center promoting lowering heart attack risks. You desire to use this document in your slide show. *Why? The heart image and text fit well with the topic of your presentation.* The following steps insert a Microsoft Word file with a graphic and text.

1

- Delete both the title and subtitle placeholders.

- Display the INSERT tab and then tap or click the Object button (INSERT tab | Text group) to display the Insert Object dialog box (Figure 10–2).

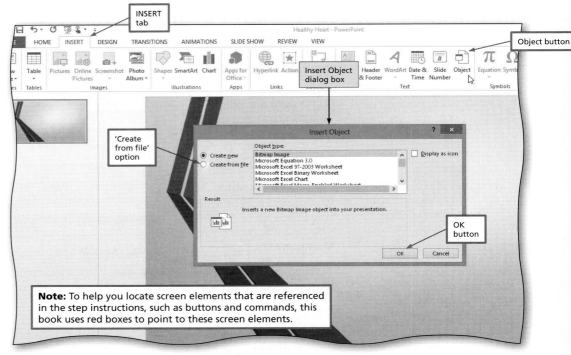

Note: To help you locate screen elements that are referenced in the step instructions, such as buttons and commands, this book uses red boxes to point to these screen elements.

Figure 10–2

2

- Tap or click 'Create from file' (Insert Object dialog box) to display the File box.

- Tap or click the Browse button and then navigate to the location where your Data Files for Students are stored (in this case, the PowerPoint folder in the CIS 101 folder [or your class folder] on your computer or SkyDrive).

- Scroll down and then tap or click Heart Flyer to select the Microsoft Word file (Figure 10–3).

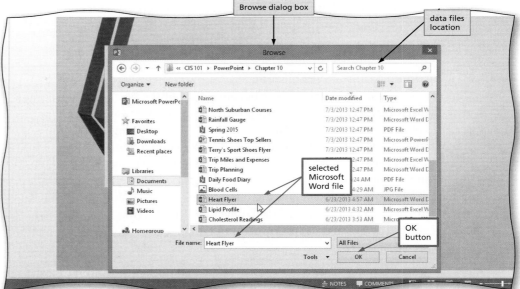

Figure 10–3

What is the difference between the Create new and the 'Create from file' options?

The Create new option opens an application and allows you to develop an original object. In contrast, the 'Create from file' option prompts you to locate a file that already is created and saved so you can modify the object using the program that was used to create it.

3

● Tap or click the OK button (Browse dialog box) to insert the file name into the File box (Insert Object dialog box) (Figure 10–4).

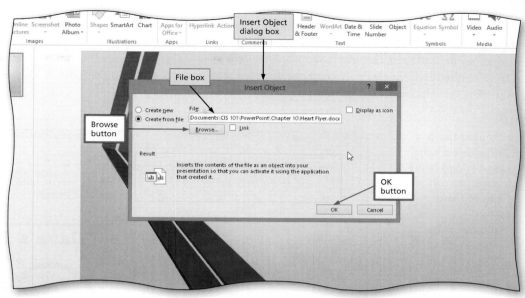

Figure 10–4

4

● Tap or click the OK button (Insert Object dialog box) to display the Heart Flyer contents on Slide 1 (Figure 10–5).

Q&A
Why did several seconds pass before this flyer was displayed on the slide?
PowerPoint takes more time to insert embedded and linked inserted objects than it takes to perform an ordinary cut-and-paste or copy-and-paste action. You must be patient while PowerPoint is inserting the object.

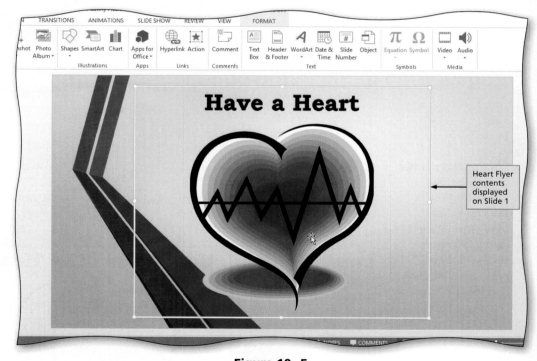

Figure 10–5

BTW
Importing Text Files
In this project you import a Microsoft Word file, but you also can import a text (.txt) file, which has alphanumeric characters with little or no visual formatting. To import a text file, perform the same steps you use to insert the Heart Flyer, but locate a file with the .txt file extension instead of the .docx file extension.

To Edit an Embedded File

The flyer provides an excellent graphic and text to use on Slide 1, but you want to edit the text by adding the word, Healthy. *Why? Adding the word, Healthy, emphasizes the need to adopt an overall lifestyle approach, which leads nicely to your slides that emphasize the benefits of a low-fat diet and regular blood tests.* PowerPoint allows you to edit an embedded file easily by opening the source program, which in this case is Microsoft Word. The following steps edit the Microsoft Word text.

1

- Double-tap or double-click the embedded heart object to run the Microsoft Word program and open the document on Slide 1 (Figure 10–6).

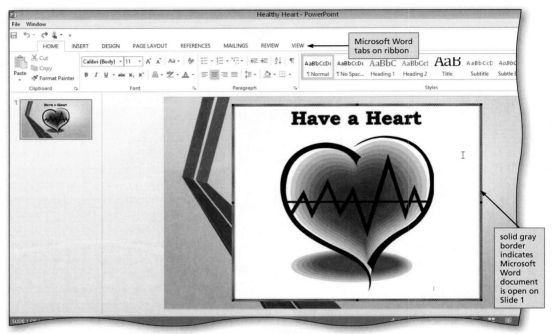

Figure 10–6

2

- Position the pointer directly before the letter H in the word, Heart, type **Healthy** as the insertion text, and then press the SPACE BAR (Figure 10–7).

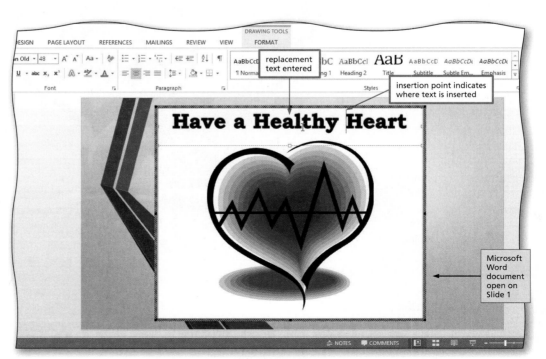

Figure 10–7

3

- Tap or click outside the Word document to close Microsoft Word and display the edited flyer object on Slide 1.

- Display the DRAWING TOOLS FORMAT tab, size the object so that it is approximately 7.5" × 8.2", and then position the object as shown in Figure 10–8.

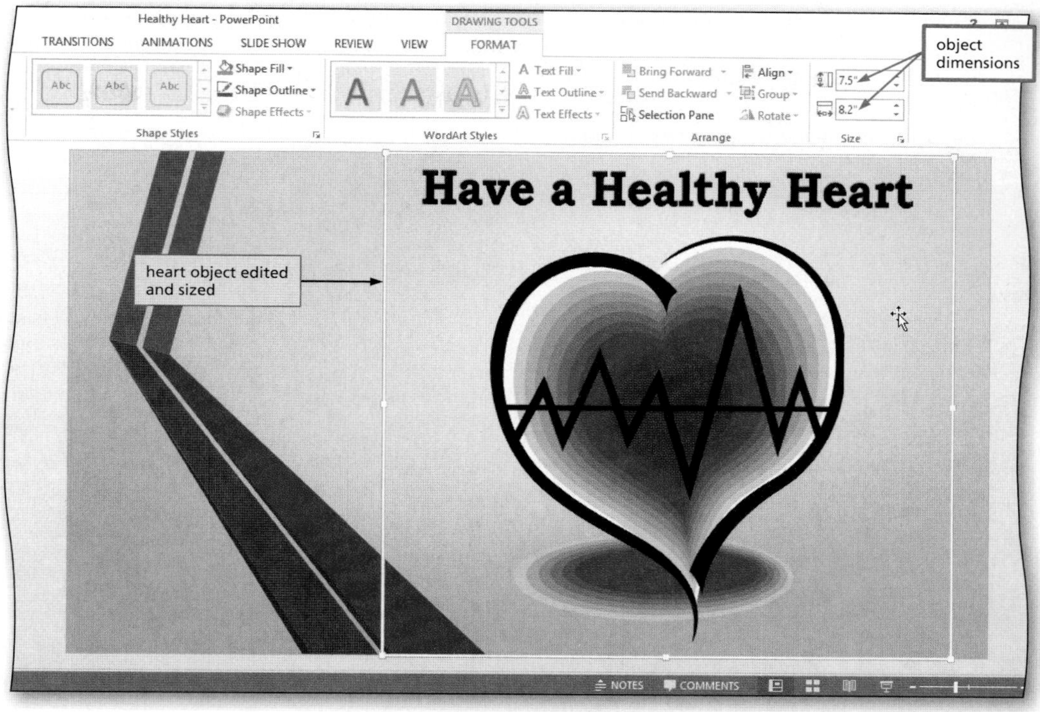

Figure 10–8

Q&A Does PowerPoint take more time to position embedded objects than copied objects?
Yes, you must be patient while PowerPoint responds to your touch, mouse, or arrow key movements.

How can I center the object precisely as shown in Figure 10–8?
If you are using a keyboard, you can use the ARROW keys to move the object in small increments.

Other Ways

1. Press and hold or right-click Word object, tap or click Document Object on shortcut menu, tap or click Edit

Drawing and Adjusting a Table

Tables are useful graphical elements to present data organized in descriptive rows and columns. Each cell created from the intersection of a row and column has a unique location name and contains numeric or textual data that you can edit.

In the following pages, you will perform these tasks on Slide 2:

1. Draw a table.
2. Draw table rows.
3. Draw table columns.
4. Erase a table line.
5. Split a table column and row.
6. Add shading to a table.
7. Add a gradient fill to a table.
8. Add a cell bevel.
9. Distribute table rows.
10. Resize table columns and rows.
11. Center the table.

BTW
Drawing a Table Using a Tablet
In this project, you will create a table using PowerPoint's pencil pointer. This tool allows you to use a mouse and draw rows and columns. On a touch screen, however, the pencil pointer is not available. You may, therefore, use a mouse, stylus, or other pointing device to draw a table. Or, you can create a table by tapping the 'Add a Table' button (INSERT tab | Tables group) and then specifying the desired number of rows and columns.

CONSIDER THIS

Develop tables that are clear and meaningful.
Use a table to present complex material, but be certain the information makes useful comparisons. Tables generally are used to show relationships between sets of data. For example, they may show prices for grades of gasoline in three states, the number of in-state and out-of-state students who have applied for admission to various college programs, or the rushing and passing records among quarterbacks in a particular league. The units of measurement, such as dollars, specific majors, or yards, should be expressed clearly on the slides. The data in the rows and columns should be aligned uniformly. Also, the table labels should be meaningful and easily read.

To Draw a Table

1 INSERT & EDIT WORD FILE | 2 DRAW TABLE ROWS & COLUMNS | 3 FORMAT TABLE
4 INSERT & EDIT LINKED WORKSHEET | 5 COPY, FORMAT & EDIT CHART

PowerPoint allows you to insert a table in several ways. You can tap or click the Table button on the INSERT tab and either tap or click the Insert Table command or drag your finger or pointer to specify the number of rows and columns you need. You also can tap or click the Insert Table button in a content placeholder. Another method that allows flexibility is to draw the entire table. However, you must use a mouse or other pointing device to use the Draw Table command. The following steps draw a table on Slide 2. *Why? This method allows flexibility to draw the outer edges and then add the columns and rows.*

1

- Insert a new slide with the Title Only layout. Type **Sources of Fat and Cholesterol** as the title text.

- Change the title text font to Bookman Old Style and bold this text.

- Display the VIEW tab and then, if necessary, click the Ruler check box (VIEW tab | Show group) to display the horizontal and vertical rulers.

- Display the INSERT tab and then click the Table button (INSERT tab | Tables group) to display the Insert Table gallery (Figure 10–9).

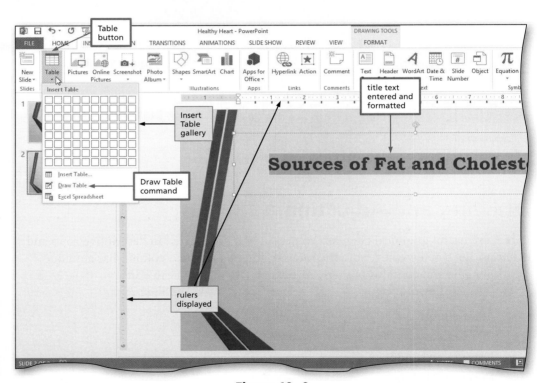

Figure 10–9

• Click Draw Table and then position the pointer, which has the shape of a pencil, in the upper-left area below the slide title.

Q&A If I decide I do not want to draw a table, how can I change the pointer to the block arrow? Press the ESC key.

• Drag the pencil pointer to the lower-right corner of the slide to draw the outer edges of the table (Figure 10–10).

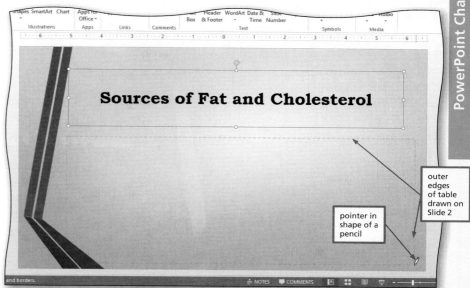

Figure 10–10

• Release the mouse button to create the table frame.

Q&A Must my table be the same size or be positioned in the same location shown in the figure? No. You will resize and reposition the table later in this project.

To Draw Table Rows

1 INSERT & EDIT WORD FILE | 2 DRAW TABLE ROWS & COLUMNS | 3 FORMAT TABLE
4 INSERT & EDIT LINKED WORKSHEET | 5 COPY, FORMAT & EDIT CHART

Once you draw the four sides of the table, you then can use the pointer as a pencil to draw lines for the columns and rows in the positions where you desire them to display. You could, therefore, draw columns having different widths and rows that are spaced in irregular heights. The following steps draw four lines to create five table rows. *Why? The first row will contain the column headings, and the remaining rows will list specific foods that contain the four types of fats: monounsaturated, polyunsaturated, saturated, and trans.* Note that you must use a mouse or other pointing device to draw table rows.

• With the TABLE TOOLS DESIGN tab displaying, click the Draw Table button (TABLE TOOLS DESIGN tab | Draw Borders group) to change the pointer to a pencil and then position the pencil pointer inside the table approximately 1" from the top table edge (Figure 10–11).

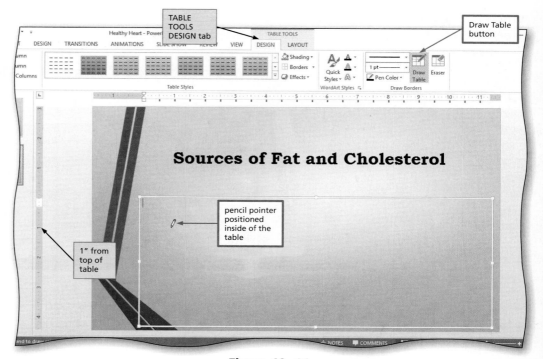

Figure 10–11

2

- Drag the pencil pointer to the right to draw a horizontal line across the entire table and divide the table into two cells (Figure 10–12).

Q&A Should I drag the pencil pointer to the right edge of the table?
No. PowerPoint will draw a complete line when you begin to move the pencil pointer in one direction.

If I drew the line in an incorrect location, how can I erase it?
Press the ESC key or CTRL+Z, tap or click the Undo button on the Quick Access Toolbar, or tap or click the Table Eraser button (TABLE TOOLS DESIGN tab | Draw Borders group) and then tap or click the line.

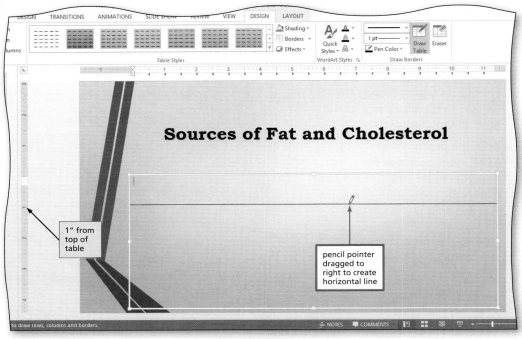

Figure 10–12

3

- Draw three additional horizontal lines, as shown in Figure 10–13.

Q&A How can I get my pencil pointer to reappear if it no longer is displaying?
Click the Draw Table button again.

Do I need to align the lines in the precise positions shown?
No. You will create evenly spaced rows later in this project.

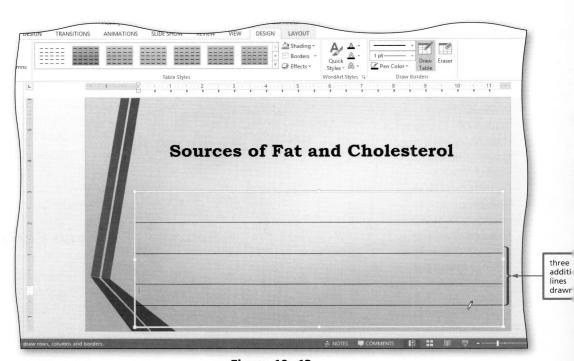

Figure 10–13

To Draw Table Columns

The pencil pointer is useful to draw table columns with varying widths. The two major categories in the table are the type of fats and the specific foods that contain high levels of these fats. The saturated row will be subdivided. *Why? You want to show an additional food item that has a high amount of that particular fat.* The following steps draw six vertical lines to create columns. Note that you must use a mouse or other pointing device to draw table columns.

1

- Position the pencil pointer inside the table approximately 2.5" from the left table edge (Figure 10–14).

Can I change the line color?
Yes. Click the Pen Color button (TABLE TOOLS DESIGN tab | Draw Borders group) and then select a different color.

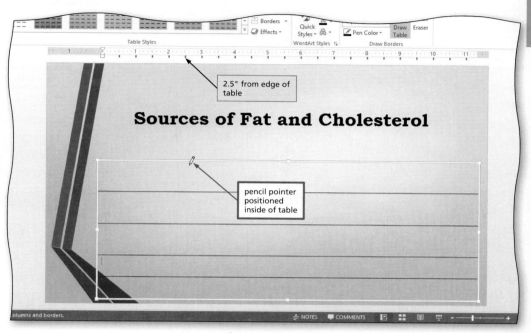

Figure 10–14

2

- Drag the pencil pointer down through all the horizontal lines to draw a vertical line that divides the table into 10 cells.

- Position the pencil pointer inside the second cell in the second row approximately 4.5" from the left table edge (Figure 10–15).

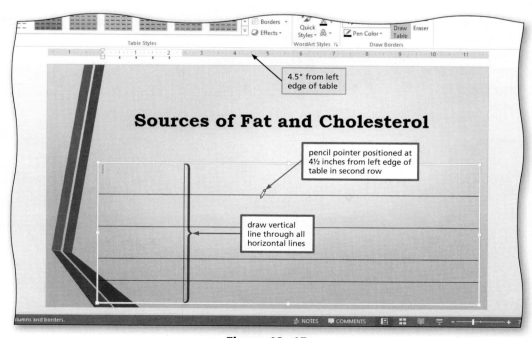

Figure 10–15

• Drag the pencil pointer down slightly to draw a vertical line in only that cell (Figure 10–16).

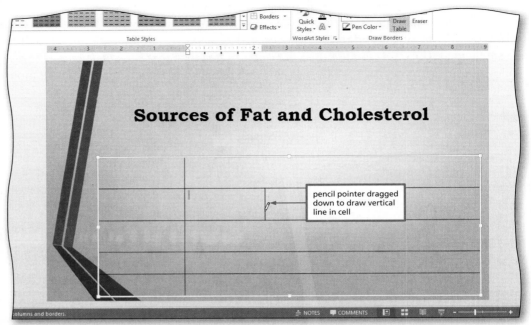

Figure 10–16

• Draw five additional vertical lines, as shown in Figure 10–17.

Q&A Are vertical and horizontal lines the only types of lines I can draw?
No. You also can draw a diagonal line from one corner of a cell to another corner.

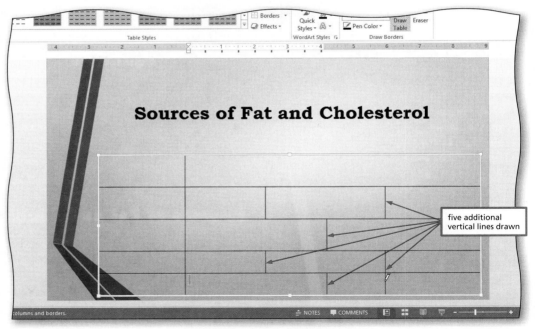

Figure 10–17

BTW
Checking for Accessibility Issues
As you develop tables and other slide elements, you may want to check the presentation for content that people with disabilities may be unable to read. To identify possible accessibility problems, display the Info tab in the Backstage view and notice if the message, Content that people with disabilities find difficult to read, is displayed next to the 'Check for Issues' button. If so, tap or click the 'Check for Issues' button and then tap or click Check Accessibility in the menu. The Accessibility Checker task pane will display issues that you can address.

To Erase a Table Line

PowerPoint supplies an eraser tool that allows you to delete vertical and horizontal lines in a table. This eraser is useful to delete unnecessary column lines. You must use a mouse or other pointing device to use the eraser tool. The following steps use the eraser to delete one vertical line in a row. *Why? You decide to include only two food items in the last row.*

- Click the Table Eraser button (TABLE TOOLS DESIGN tab | Draw Borders group).

- Position the pointer, which has the shape of an eraser, over the third line in the last row (Figure 10–18).

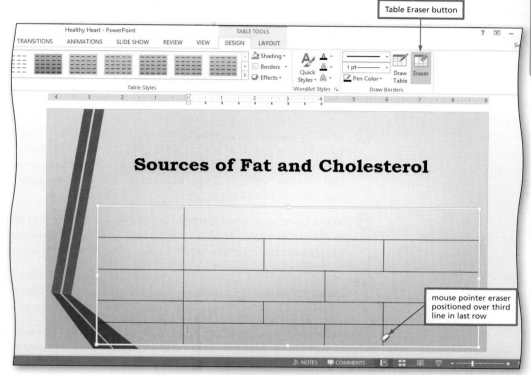

Figure 10–18

- Click the vertical line to erase it (Figure 10–19).

- Press the ESC key and then click inside the cell to change the pointer to the I-beam and display the insertion point.

❸

- Display the VIEW tab and then click the Ruler check box (VIEW tab | Show group) to hide the horizontal and vertical rulers.

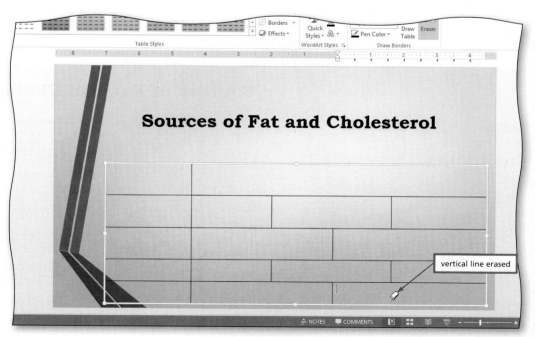

Figure 10–19

BTW
Navigating the Table
In this project, you advance the insertion point to the next cell by pressing the TAB key or by tapping the desired cell. To move to the previous cell, press the SHIFT + TAB keys or tap the desired cell. Press the DOWN ARROW key or tap the desired cell to move to the next row, and press the UP ARROW key or tap the desired cell to move up one row.

To Enter Data in a Table

Four major types of fats are found in food: monounsaturated, polyunsaturated, saturated, and trans. The table you created will list the fat types on the left side of each row and specific foods on the right side. The first row will label the two parts of the table. To place data in a cell, you tap or click the cell and then type text. The following steps enter data in the cells of the empty table.

1 Position the pointer in the upper-left cell of the table, type **Type** in the cell, and then press the TAB key or tap the next cell to advance the insertion point to the next cell.

2 Type **Frequently Found In...** in the upper-right cell and then tap the first cell in the second row or press the TAB key to advance the insertion point to the first cell in the second row.

3 Type **Monounsaturated** and then tap in the next cell or press the TAB key to advance the insertion point to the next cell. Type **Olive oil** and then advance the insertion point to the next cell. Type **Avocados** and advance the insertion point to the next cell. Type **Almonds** and then advance the insertion point to the first column of the third row.

4 In the third row, type **Polyunsaturated** in the first column, **Vegetable oil** in the second column, and **Soybeans** in the third column. Tap or press the TAB key to advance the insertion point to the first column of the fourth row.

5 In the fourth row, type **Saturated** in the first column, **Animal fat** in the second column, **Butter** in the third column, and **Chocolate** in the fourth column. Advance the insertion point to the first column of the fifth row.

6 In the fifth row, type **Trans** in the first column, **French fries** in the second column, and **Margarine** in the third column (Figure 10–20).

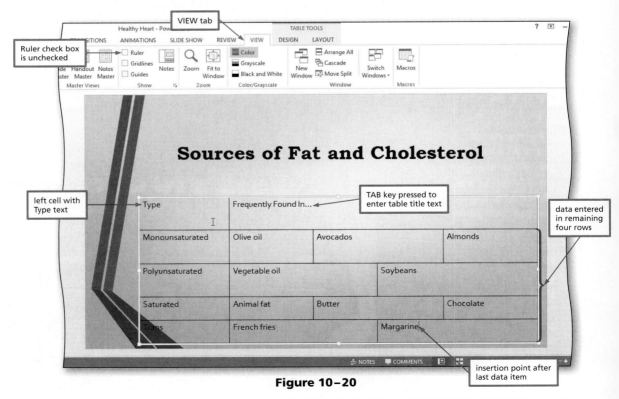

Figure 10–20

To Split a Table Column and Row

You easily can create additional table columns and rows by dividing current cells and rows. The following steps split a column and a row. *Why? You want to add another food in the Trans row. You also decide that it is important to note several foods that have high levels of cholesterol and want this information to be displayed as the last row in the table.*

1

- With the pointer positioned in the French fries cell, tap or click the TABLE TOOLS LAYOUT tab to display the TABLE TOOLS LAYOUT ribbon and then tap or click the Split Cells button (TABLE TOOLS LAYOUT tab | Merge group) to display the Split Cells dialog box (Figure 10–21).

Q&A Are the default numbers in the dialog box always 2 columns and 1 row?

Yes, but you can increase the numbers if you need to divide the cell into more than two halves or need to create two or more rows within one cell.

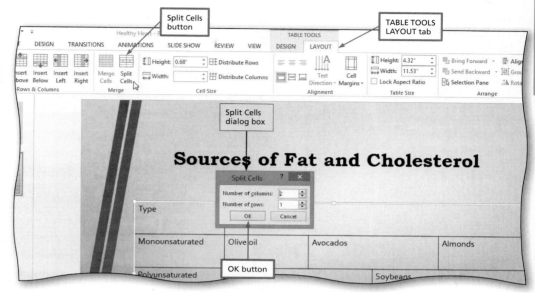

Figure 10–21

2

- Tap or click the OK button (Split Cells dialog box) to create a third cell in the Trans row.

- Tap or click the Select button (TABLE TOOLS LAYOUT tab | Table group) to display the Select menu (Figure 10–22).

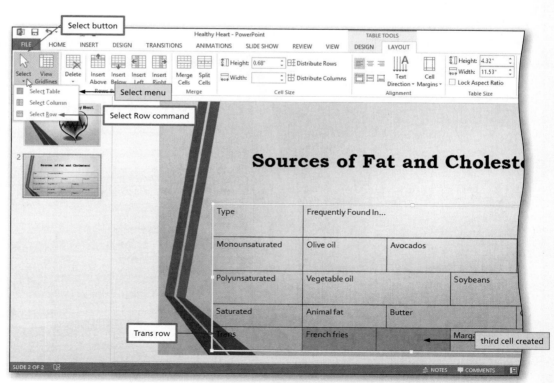

Figure 10–22

3

- Tap or click Select Row in the Select menu to select the Trans row.

- With the TABLE TOOLS LAYOUT tab displaying, tap or click the Split Cells button (TABLE TOOLS LAYOUT tab | Merge group) to display the Split Cells dialog box (Figure 10–23).

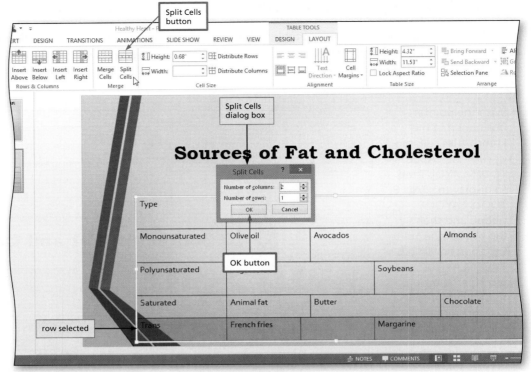

Figure 10–23

4

- Decrease the number of columns from 2 to 1.

- Increase the number of rows from 1 to 2 (Figure 10–24).

Q&A How many rows and columns can I create by splitting the cells? The maximum number varies depending upon the width and height of the selected cell.

5

- Tap or click the OK button (Split Cells dialog box) to create a row below the Trans row.

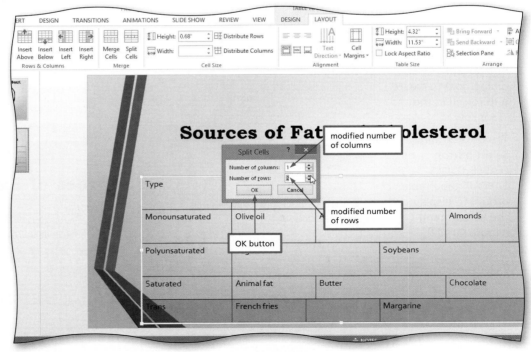

Figure 10–24

Other Ways

1. Right-click table, click Split Cells on shortcut menu, enter number of columns and rows, click OK button

To Enter Additional Data in a Table

With the additional row and column added to the table, you now can add the Cholesterol data in the inserted row and also add another food, Potato chips, to the new cell in the Trans row. The following steps enter data in the new cells.

1 Position the pointer in the first cell of the last row and then type `Cholesterol` in the cell. Advance the insertion point to the adjacent right column cell and then type `Eggs` and `Shrimp` and `Lobster` in the cells in this row.

2 Position the pointer in the new cell in the Trans row and then type `Potato chips` in the cell.

3 Drag the edges of the cells so the cell widths are similar to those in Figure 10–25. Use the Smart Guides to help align the cells vertically.

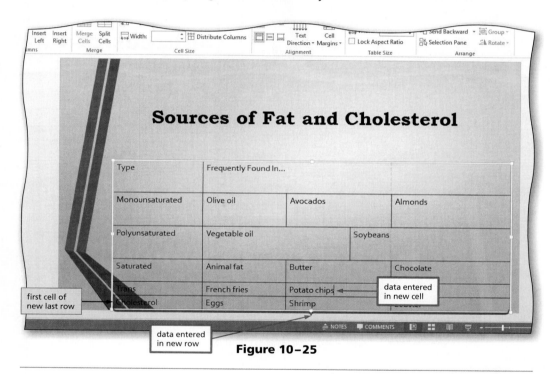

Figure 10–25

Use appropriate colors when formatting graphics you want people to remember.
Studies have shown that men and women differ slightly in their recall of graphics formatted with various colors. Men remembered objects colored with shades of violet, dark blue, olive green, and yellow. Women recalled objects they had seen with dark blue, olive green, yellow, and red hues.

CONSIDER THIS

BTW
Customizing Table Formatting
PowerPoint applies a style to a table automatically based on the theme. To change this format, you can select a style in the Table Styles gallery, which presents several options to give a professional and colorful design and format. You, however, may desire to customize the layout by adding or modifying borders, the background color, or the font. To clear a style from a table, display the TABLE TOOLS DESIGN tab, tap or click the More button in the Table Styles group, and then tap or click Clear Table.

To Add Shading to a Table

You can format the table in several ways, including adding shading to color the background. The following steps add shading to the table. *Why? Shading makes the table more visually appealing and helps distinguish each cell.*

- Tap or click the Select button (TABLE TOOLS LAYOUT tab | Table group) to display the Select menu (Figure 10–26).

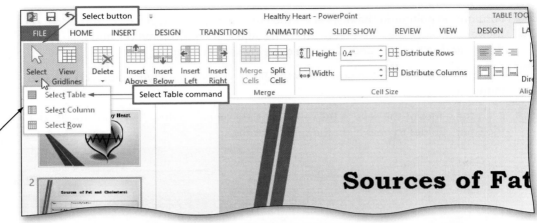

Figure 10–26

- Tap or click Select Table in the Select menu to select the entire table.

- Tap or click the TABLE TOOLS DESIGN tab and then tap or click the Shading arrow (TABLE TOOLS DESIGN tab | Table Styles group) to display the Shading gallery.

- If you are using a mouse, point to Red, Accent 1, Lighter 80% (fifth color in the second Theme Colors row) in the Shading gallery to display a live preview of that color applied to the table in the slide (Figure 10–27).

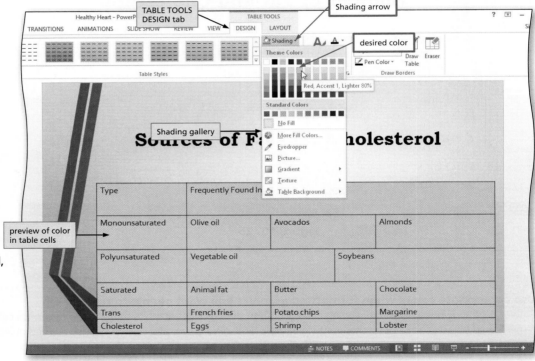

Figure 10–27

Experiment

- If you are using a mouse, point to various colors in the Shading gallery and watch the background of the table change.

- Tap or click Red, Accent 1, Lighter 80% in the Shading gallery to apply the selected color to the table.

To Add a Gradient Fill to a Table

Another enhancement you can make to the table is to add a gradient fill so that one shade of the red color gradually progresses to another shade of the same color. The following steps add a gradient fill to the table. *Why? Using a gradient fill is another method of calling attention to each individual table cell.*

1

- With the table still selected, tap or click the Shading arrow (TABLE TOOLS DESIGN tab | Table Styles group) again to display the Shading gallery.

- Tap or click Gradient to display the Gradient gallery.

- If you are using a mouse, point to Linear Diagonal – Bottom Right to Top Left (last gradient in the last row of the Variations area) to display a live preview of that gradient applied to the table in the slide (Figure 10–28).

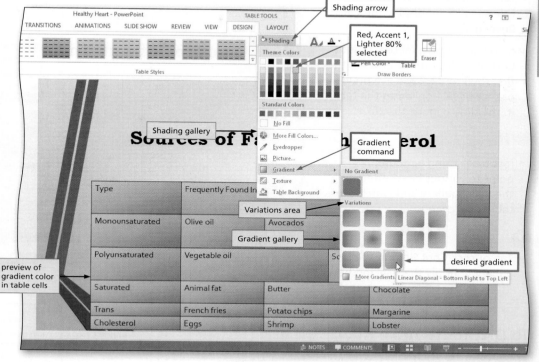

Figure 10–28

 Q&A What if my Gradient gallery shows Light and Dark variations?
Select the last gradient in the Light Variations area.

Experiment

- If you are using a mouse, point to various gradients in the Gradient gallery and watch the background of the table change.

2

- Tap or click Linear Diagonal – Bottom Right to Top Left in the Shading gallery to apply the selected gradient to the table.

To Add a Cell Bevel

Why? Bevels modify the cell edges to give a 3-D effect, which makes each cell stand out. Some bevels give the appearance that the cell is protruding from the table, while others give the effect that the cell is depressed into the table. The steps on the next page add a bevel to the table cells.

1

- With the table still selected, tap or click the Effects button (TABLE TOOLS DESIGN tab | Table Styles group) to display the Effects menu.

- Tap or click Cell Bevel on the Effects menu to display the Cell Bevel gallery.

- If you are using a mouse, point to Cool Slant (rightmost bevel in the first row) to display a live preview of that bevel applied to the table in the slide (Figure 10–29).

 Experiment

- If you are using a mouse, point to various bevel effects in the Bevel gallery and watch the table cells change.

2

- Tap or click Cool Slant in the Bevel gallery to apply the selected bevel effect to the table.

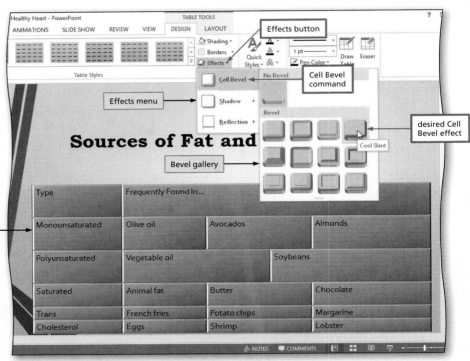

Figure 10–29

To Distribute Table Rows

1 INSERT & EDIT WORD FILE | 2 DRAW TABLE ROWS & COLUMNS | **3 FORMAT TABLE**
4 INSERT & EDIT LINKED WORKSHEET | 5 COPY, FORMAT & EDIT CHART

At times you may desire the row heights to vary. In the Slide 2 table, however, you desire the heights of the rows to be uniform. To make each selected row the same height, you distribute the desired rows. The following steps distribute table rows. *Why? The horizontal lines you drew are not spaced equidistant from each other, and distributing the rows is an efficient manner of creating rows with the same height.*

1

- With the table still selected, display the TABLE TOOLS LAYOUT tab and then select the cells in the second, third, fourth, fifth, and sixth rows (Figure 10–30).

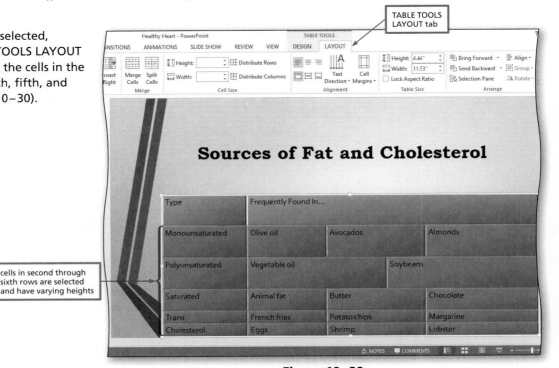

Figure 10–30

2

- Tap or click the Distribute Rows button (TABLE TOOLS LAYOUT tab | Cell Size group) to equally space these five rows vertically (Figure 10–31).

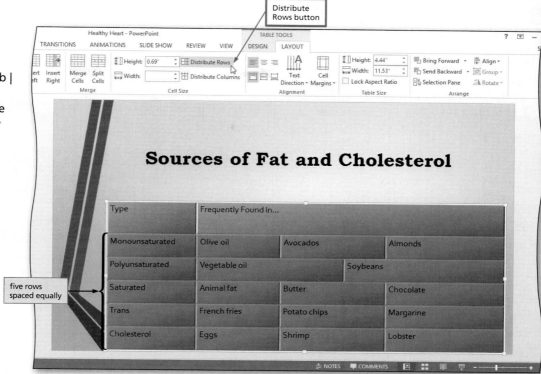

Figure 10–31

To Resize Table Columns and Rows

1 INSERT & EDIT WORD FILE | 2 DRAW TABLE ROWS & COLUMNS | 3 FORMAT TABLE
4 INSERT & EDIT LINKED WORKSHEET | 5 COPY, FORMAT & EDIT CHART

The first table row should have a height taller than the rows beneath it. In addition, the first column of the table should be somewhat narrower than the specific foods listed below the Frequently Found In… heading. *Why?* *You will increase the heading text font size in a later part of this project, so you need to leave sufficient room for these letters. In addition, each cell in the first column has only one word per row.* The following steps resize the table columns and rows.

- With the TABLE TOOLS LAYOUT tab displaying, position the insertion point in the Type cell in the first row.

- Tap or click the Height box (TABLE TOOLS LAYOUT tab | Cell Size group) and set the row height to 1" (Figure 10–32).

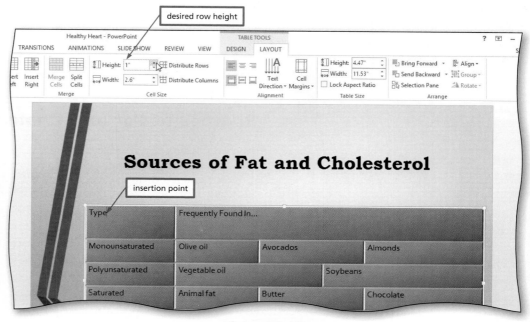

Figure 10–32

2

• Tap or click the Width box (TABLE TOOLS LAYOUT tab | Cell Size group) and set the cell width to 2.3" (Figure 10–33).

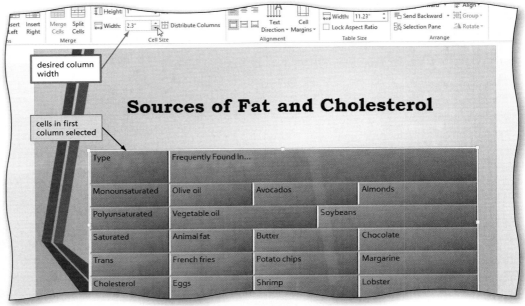

Figure 10–33

To Align Data in Cells

The next step is to change the alignment of the data in all the table cells. In addition to aligning text horizontally in a cell (left, center, or right), you can align it vertically within a cell (top, middle, or bottom). The following steps center data in the table both horizontally and vertically.

1 Select all the table cells and then tap or click the Center button (TABLE TOOLS LAYOUT tab | Alignment group) to center the text horizontally in the cells.

2 Tap or click the Center Vertically button (TABLE TOOLS LAYOUT tab | Alignment group) to center the contents of the cells vertically (Figure 10–34).

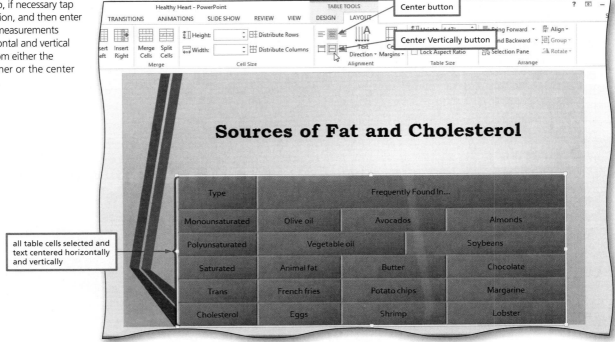

Figure 10–34

To Center a Table

Why? *The table should be positioned an equal distance between the left and right slide edges to balance this object in the slide.* To center the table, you align it in the middle of the slide. The following steps center the table horizontally.

1

- With the insertion point in the table, tap or click the Align button (TABLE TOOLS LAYOUT tab | Arrange group) to display the Align menu (Figure 10–35).

2

- Tap or click Align Center on the Align menu, so PowerPoint adjusts the position of the table evenly between the left and right sides of the slide. Adjust the table vertically on the slide so that it is displayed between the title text placeholder and the bottom edge of the slide.

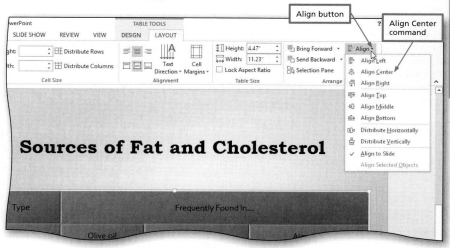

Figure 10–35

To Format Table Data

The final table enhancements are to bold and increase the font size of the text in the first row and to change the font of all the table text. The following steps bold the text in the first row and then increase the font size and also change the font for all the table data.

1 Select the first row, display the HOME tab, and then bold the text and increase the font size to 32 point.

2 Select all the table text and then change the font to Bookman Old Style (Figure 10–36). If necessary, change the width of the columns so the words display with adequate spacing on the left and right sides.

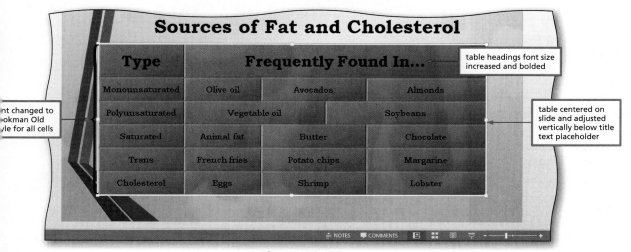

Figure 10–36

Break Point: If you wish to take a break, this is a good place to do so. Be sure to save the Healthy Heart file again and then you can exit PowerPoint. To resume at a later time, run PowerPoint, open the file called Healthy Heart, and continue following the steps from this location forward.

BTW
File Sizes
Files with embedded objects typically have larger file sizes than those with linked objects because the source data is stored in the presentation. In order to keep file sizes manageable, Microsoft recommends inserting a linked object rather than an embedded object when the source file is large or complex.

Inserting a Linked Excel Worksheet

Linked files maintain a connection between the source file and the destination file. When you select the **Link check box** in the Insert Object dialog box, the object is inserted as a linked object instead of an embedded object. Your PowerPoint presentation stores a representation of the original file and information about its location. If you later move or delete the source file, the link is broken, and the object will not be available. Consequently, if you make a presentation on a computer other than the one on which the presentation was created, and the presentation contains linked objects, be certain to include a copy of the source files. The source files must be stored in the exact location as originally specified when you linked them to your presentation.

PowerPoint associates a linked file with a specific application, which PowerPoint bases on the file extension. For example, if you select a source file with the file extension **.docx**, PowerPoint recognizes the file as a Microsoft Word file. Additionally, if you select a source file with the file extension **.xlsx**, PowerPoint recognizes the file as a Microsoft Excel file.

In the following pages, you will insert a linked Excel worksheet, align it on the slide, and then edit three cells.

To Insert a Linked Excel Worksheet

1 INSERT & EDIT WORD FILE | 2 DRAW TABLE ROWS & COLUMNS | 3 FORMAT TABLE
4 INSERT & EDIT LINKED WORKSHEET | 5 COPY, FORMAT & EDIT CHART

The Lipid Profile Excel worksheet contains a table with data corresponding to measurements taken during a blood test. The first column lists four components of blood: total cholesterol, high-density lipoprotein (HDL) cholesterol, low-density lipoprotein (LDL) cholesterol, and triglycerides. The second column lists desired test results. The third column gives the results of one blood test taken on March 20. You can insert the results of a second blood test in the last column. When you insert the Lipid Profile chart, you can specify that it is linked from the PowerPoint slide to the Excel worksheet. *Why?* *Any edits made to specific cells are reflected in both the source and destination files.* The following steps insert and link the Microsoft Excel worksheet.

- Insert a new slide with the Blank layout.

- Tap or click the Format Background button (DESIGN tab | Customize group) to display the Format Background pane. Insert the Blood Cells picture located on your Data Files for Students (in this case, the Power Point folder in the CIS 101 folder [or your class folder] on your computer or SkyDrive) as a background for the new slide (Figure 10–37).

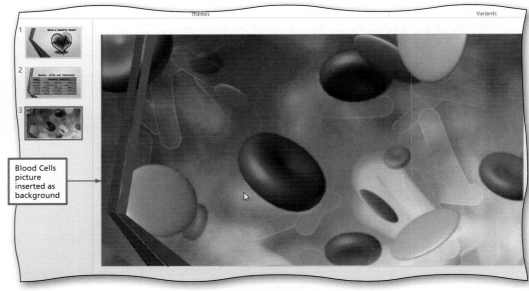

Figure 10–37

2

- Close the Format Background pane.

- Display the INSERT tab and then tap or click the Object button (INSERT tab | Text group) to display the Insert Object dialog box.

- Tap or click 'Create from file' (Insert Object dialog box) to display the File box (Figure 10–38).

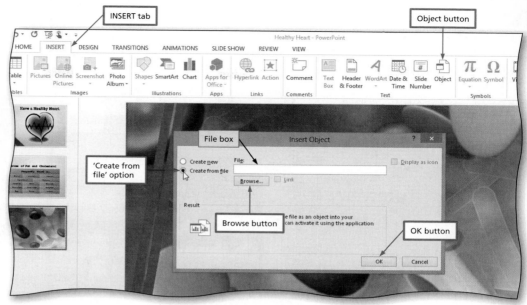

Figure 10–38

3

- Tap or click the Browse button, navigate to the location of your Data Files for Students (in this case, the PowerPoint folder in the CIS 101 folder [or your class folder] on your computer or SkyDrive), and then scroll down and tap or click Lipid Profile to select the file name (Figure 10–39).

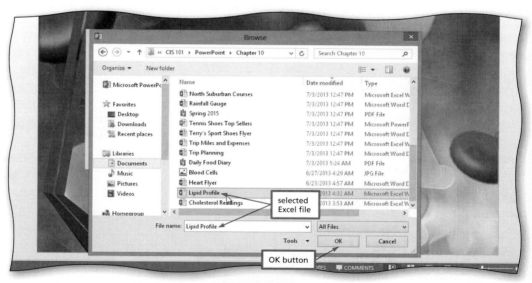

Figure 10–39

4

- Tap or click the OK button (Browse dialog box) to insert the file name into the File box (Insert Object dialog box).

- Tap or click the Link check box (Insert Object dialog box) to select the check box (Figure 10–40).

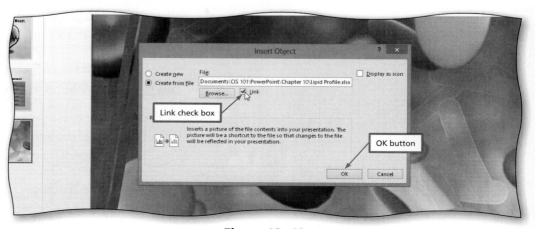

Figure 10–40

5

- Tap or click the OK button (Insert Object dialog box) to insert the Lipid Profile Excel worksheet into Slide 3.

- Display the DRAWING TOOLS FORMAT tab and change the worksheet height to 5.5" (Figure 10–41).

 Why did the worksheet width change when I changed the height measurement?
The worksheet's width and height stay in proportion to each other, so when you change one dimension, the other dimension changes accordingly.

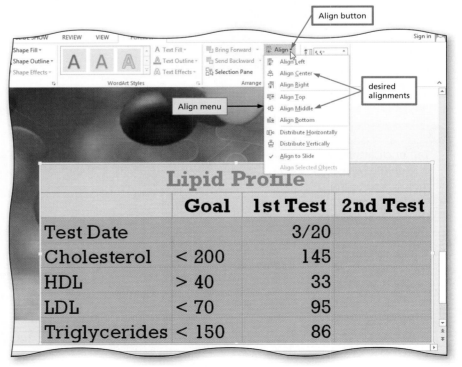

Figure 10–41

To Align a Worksheet

1 INSERT & EDIT WORD FILE | 2 DRAW TABLE ROWS & COLUMNS | 3 FORMAT TABLE
4 INSERT & EDIT LINKED WORKSHEET | 5 COPY, FORMAT & EDIT CHART

Why? *PowerPoint inserts the table on Slide 3 in a location that is not visually appealing, so you want to center it on the slide.* You can drag the table to a location, but you also can have PowerPoint precisely align the object horizontally in the left, center, or right areas of the slide, and vertically in the top, middle, or bottom of the slide. The following steps align the table horizontally and vertically on Slide 3.

1

- With the DRAWING TOOLS FORMAT tab displaying, tap or click the Align button (DRAWING TOOLS FORMAT tab| Arrange group) to display the Align menu (Figure 10–42).

Figure 10–42

2

- Tap or click Align Center on the Align menu to position the worksheet evenly between the left and right edges of the slide.

- Tap or click the Align button again to display the Align menu and then tap or click Align Middle to position the worksheet in the center of the slide (Figure 10–43).

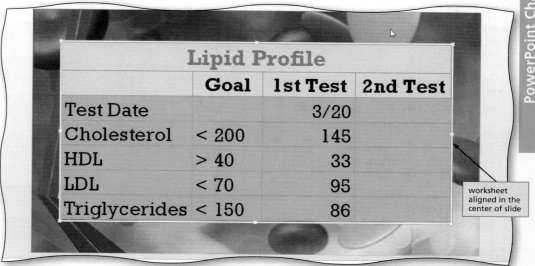

Figure 10–43

To Edit a Linked Worksheet

1 INSERT & EDIT WORD FILE | 2 DRAW TABLE ROWS & COLUMNS | 3 FORMAT TABLE
4 INSERT & EDIT LINKED WORKSHEET | 5 COPY, FORMAT & EDIT CHART

Each table or worksheet cell is identified by a unique address, or **cell reference**, representing the intersection of a column and row. The column letter is first and is followed by the row number. For example, cell B6 is located at the intersection of the second column, B, and the sixth row. Three cells need updating. *Why? You have obtained test results from a blood test taken on December 6 and want to record this information.* The following steps edit cells in the linked table.

1

- Double-tap or double-click the table to open Microsoft Excel and display the worksheet.

- Tap or click the blank Test Date cell below the rightmost column, 2nd Test, to make cell D3 the active cell (Figure 10–44). If you are using a touch screen, display the onscreen keyboard.

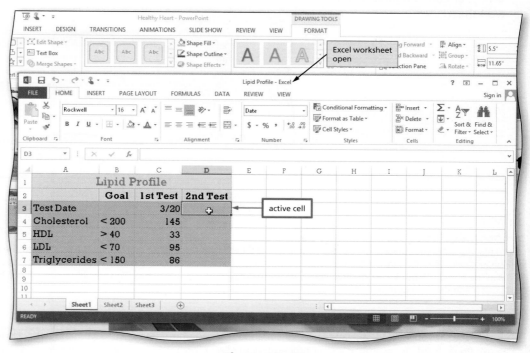

Figure 10–44

- Type `12/6` as the new test date and then tap or press the ENTER key to complete the entry and make cell D4 the active cell.

- Type `130` as the new cholesterol number and then tap or press the ENTER key to complete the entry and make cell D5 the active cell.

- Type `30` as the new HDL number, `85` as the new LDL number, and `90` as the new triglycerides number. Be certain to tap or press the ENTER key to complete the triglycerides entry in cell D7 (Figure 10–45). If you are using a touch screen, hide the onscreen keyboard.

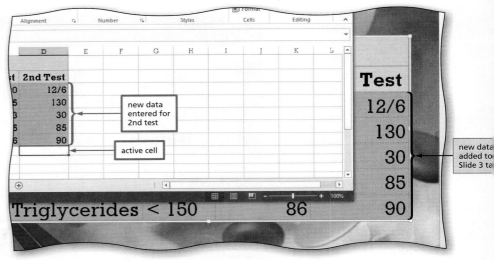

Figure 10–45

- Tap or click the Close button in the upper-right corner of the Microsoft Excel window to quit Excel (Figure 10–46).

- Tap or click the Save button (Microsoft Excel dialog box) to save your edited numbers in the worksheet.

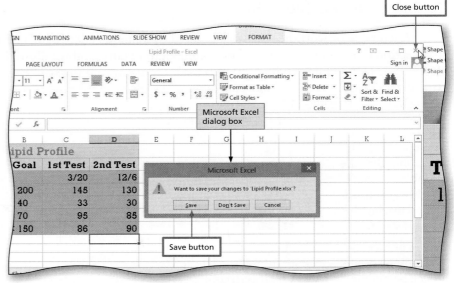

Figure 10–46

BTW
Embedding Fonts
If you plan to show your presentation using a computer other than yours, consider embedding the fonts to ensure that the fonts on your slides will be available. To embed the fonts, display the Save As dialog box, tap or click the Tools button, tap or click Save Options, select the 'Embed fonts in the file' check box in the Preserve fidelity when sharing this presentation area (PowerPoint Options dialog box), and then tap or click the OK button and the Save button.

Break Point: If you wish to take a break, this is a good place to do so. Be sure to save the Healthy Heart file again and then you can exit PowerPoint. To resume at a later time, run PowerPoint, open the file called Healthy Heart, and continue following the steps from this location forward. Note: PowerPoint will prompt you to update the Excel file that you modified.

Copying and Modifying a Linked Excel Chart

The Microsoft Excel table you inserted into Slide 3 is a linked object. You added data to the table using the Microsoft Excel source program, and that change is reflected on the PowerPoint slide and in the original Excel document. Now you will insert and then modify a Microsoft Excel chart on Slide 4. This object will be linked, so any changes you make to the layout, legend, or background will be reflected in the destination object on the slide and in the original Excel worksheet.

In the following pages, you will perform these tasks on Slide 4:

1. Copy a chart from a file.
2. Align the chart.
3. Switch rows and columns.
4. Change the chart type.
5. Apply a style.
6. Display and format axis titles.
7. Format a legend.
8. Display and format chart labels.
9. Display gridlines.
10. Format the background.
11. Edit data.

BTW

Certification
The Microsoft Office Specialist (MOS) program provides an opportunity for you to obtain a valuable industry credential — proof that you have the PowerPoint 2013 skills required by employers. For more information, visit the Certification resource on the Student Companion Site located on www.cengagebrain. com. For detailed instructions about accessing available resources, visit www.cengage. com/ct/studentdownload or see the inside back cover of this book.

To Copy an Excel Chart

1 INSERT & EDIT WORD FILE | 2 DRAW TABLE ROWS & COLUMNS | 3 FORMAT TABLE
4 INSERT & EDIT LINKED WORKSHEET | **5 COPY, FORMAT & EDIT CHART**

The chart you want to insert into your slide show was created in Microsoft Excel. The file consists of two sheets: one for the chart and another for the numbers used to create the chart. The chart is on Sheet1. One method of placing this chart into a PowerPoint presentation is to copy this object from the Excel worksheet and then paste it into a slide. The following steps copy and link a chart from Sheet1 of the Microsoft Excel file using the destination formatting. *Why? Copying and linking allows you to modify the chart content easily. You want to use the destination formatting so the chart uses the Parallax theme colors and styles.*

- Insert a new slide with the Title Only layout. Type **Cholesterol Readings** as the title text, change the font to Bookman Old Style, and then bold this text.

- Tap or click the File Explorer app button on the taskbar to make the File folder window the active window. Navigate to the location where your Data Files for Students are stored (in this case, the PowerPoint folder in the CIS 101 folder [or your class folder] on your computer or SkyDrive). If necessary, scroll down to display the Cholesterol Readings file in the Name list (Figure 10–47).

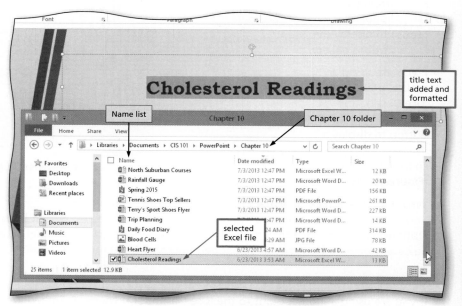

Figure 10–47

2

- Double-tap or double-click the Cholesterol Readings file to run Microsoft Excel and display the chart on Sheet1.

- Tap or click a blank area above the chart legend to select the entire chart and then display the HOME tab.

- Tap or click the Copy button (HOME tab | Clipboard group) to copy the chart to the Office Clipboard (Figure 10–48).

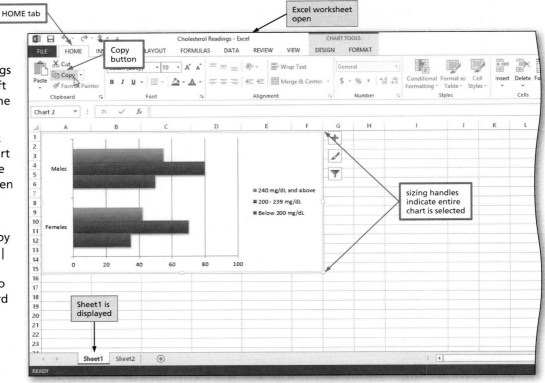

Figure 10–48

3

- Tap or click the PowerPoint app button on the taskbar to make the PowerPoint window the active window. With Slide 4 and the HOME tab displaying, click the Paste arrow (HOME tab | Clipboard group) to display the Paste Options gallery.

- If you are using a mouse, point to the 'Use Destination Theme & Link Data' button to display a live preview of the chart in the slide (Figure 10–49).

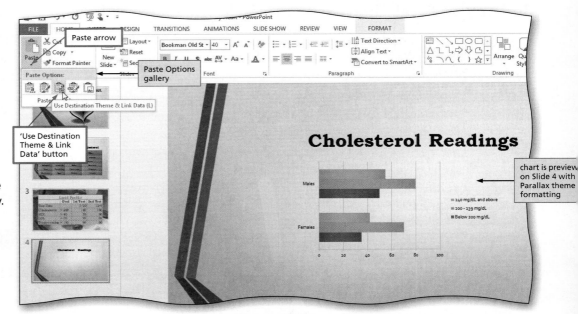

Figure 10–49

 Why did I click the Paste arrow instead of the Paste button?

You want to use the colors and style of Parallax theme (the destination theme), so you need to display the Paste Options gallery to make that choice and to link the chart to the original Excel worksheet. If you had clicked the Paste button, you would have embedded the chart using the Excel worksheet theme (the source theme).

Experiment

- If you are using a mouse, point to the 'Use Destination Theme & Embed Workbook' button in the Paste Options gallery to display a live preview of the chart with the Parallax theme applied.

- Tap or click the 'Use Destination Theme & Link Data' button to paste the chart into Slide 4.

- Display the CHART TOOLS FORMAT tab and then change the chart size to 5.5" × 11.5" (Figure 10–50).

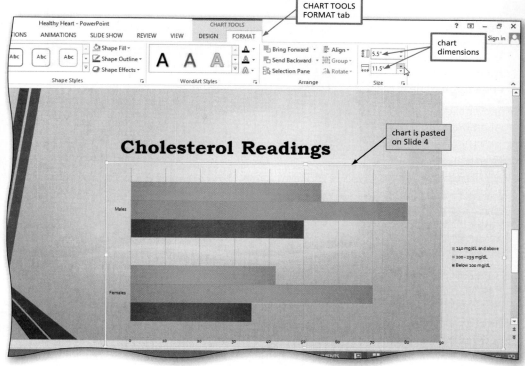

Figure 10–50

Other Ways

1. Press and hold or right-click Excel chart, tap or click Copy, exit Microsoft Excel, tap or click Paste arrow (HOME tab | Clipboard group), tap or click 'Use Destination Theme & Link Data'

To Align a Chart

1 INSERT & EDIT WORD FILE | 2 DRAW TABLE ROWS & COLUMNS | 3 FORMAT TABLE
4 INSERT & EDIT LINKED WORKSHEET | **5 COPY, FORMAT & EDIT CHART**

Why? *You aligned the table on Slide 3 horizontally and vertically. You, likewise, want to align the chart on Slide 4 so that it is displayed in an appropriate location on the slide.* Although you can drag the chart on the slide, you also can use PowerPoint commands to align the object horizontally in the left, center, or right areas of the slide, and vertically in the top, middle, or bottom of the slide. The following steps align the chart horizontally and vertically on Slide 4.

- With the chart selected and the CHART TOOLS FORMAT tab displaying, tap or click the Align button (CHART TOOLS FORMAT tab | Arrange group) to display the Align menu (Figure 10–51).

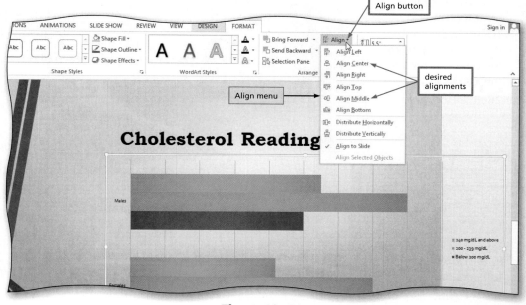

Figure 10–51

2

- Tap or click Align Right on the Align menu to position the chart along the right edge of the slide.

- Tap or click the Align button again to display the Align menu and then tap or click Align Bottom to position the chart at the lower edge of the slide (Figure 10–52).

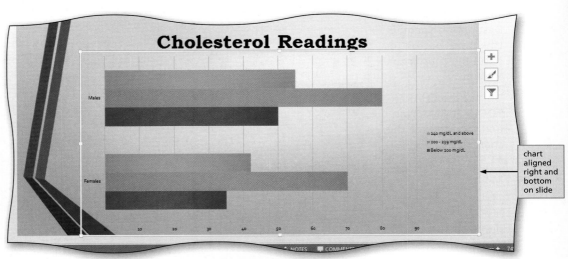

chart aligned right and bottom on slide

Figure 10–52

To Switch Rows and Columns in a Chart

1 INSERT & EDIT WORD FILE | 2 DRAW TABLE ROWS & COLUMNS | 3 FORMAT TABLE
4 INSERT & EDIT LINKED WORKSHEET | 5 COPY, FORMAT & EDIT CHART

Excel created the chart on Slide 4 (Sheet1 in the Excel file) based on the values in the worksheet on Sheet2 of the Excel file. The scale is based on the values in the **y-axis**, which also is called the **vertical axis** or **value axis**. The titles along the **x-axis**, also referred to as the **horizontal axis** or **category axis**, are derived from the top row of the Sheet2 worksheet and are displayed along the left edge of the chart. Each bar in the chart has a specific color to represent one of the three categories of cholesterol levels grouped by males and females. You can switch the data in the chart so that a male and female bar is displayed for each of the three cholesterol levels. *Why? In your presentation to fitness center members, you want to emphasize that males and females often have quite different cholesterol levels.* The following step switches the rows and columns in the chart.

1

- Display the CHART TOOLS DESIGN tab on the ribbon.

- Tap or click the Switch Row/Column button (CHART TOOLS DESIGN tab | Data group) to swap the data charted on the x-axis with the data on the y-axis (Figure 10–53).

Q&A
If the Switch Row/Column button is dimmed, how can I switch the data?
Be certain the Excel worksheet is open. The button is active only when the worksheet is open.

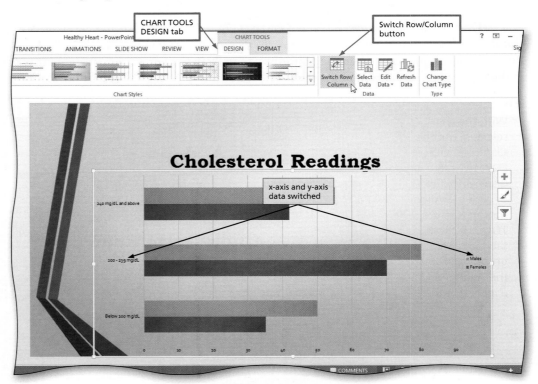

CHART TOOLS DESIGN tab

Switch Row/Column button

x-axis and y-axis data switched

Figure 10–53

To Change the Chart Type

The bar chart represents data horizontally for each of the three cholesterol levels. You can change the chart appearance by selecting another type in the Insert Chart dialog box. The sample charts are divided into a variety of categories, including column, line, pie, and bar. The clustered column type that you want to use in the presentation is located in the Column area, which has seven layouts. The following steps change the chart to a 3-D Clustered Column chart type. *Why? The vertical bars help show the increase and decrease of cholesterol levels, and the 3-D effect adds an interesting visual element.*

- Tap or click the 'Change Chart Type' button (CHART TOOLS DESIGN tab | Type group) to display the Change Chart Type dialog box.

- Tap or click Column in the left pane (Change Chart Type dialog box) to display a Clustered Column thumbnail (Figure 10–54).

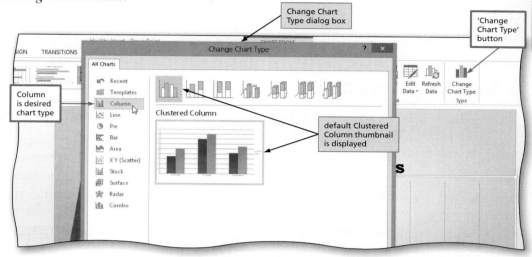

Figure 10–54

- Tap or click the 3-D Clustered Column button (fourth chart) to select this chart type and display a thumbnail with a 3-D effect (Figure 10–55).

Q&A Can I see a larger preview of the chart?
If you are using a mouse, you can point to the chart to enlarge the preview.

3

- Tap or click the OK button (Change Chart Type dialog box) to change the chart type to 3-D Clustered Column.

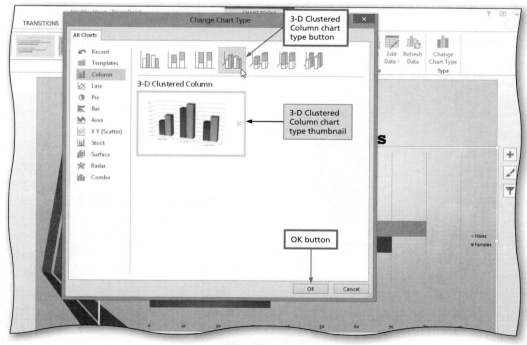

Figure 10–55

To Exclude Data in a Chart

If you have multiple categories (which display in the x-axis) or series (which display in the legend) of data and want to exclude one or more of them from displaying, you can instruct PowerPoint to exclude data elements. If you wanted to exclude a particular category or series, you would perform the following steps.

1. Tap or click the Chart Filters button (funnel icon) on the right side of the chart to display a pane with each data element.
2. Clear the check boxes of the elements you want to exclude on the chart.
3. To display an excluded data element, select the check box.

To Apply a Style to a Chart

Why? You can modify the chart's appearance easily by selecting a predefined style. The styles available in the Chart Styles gallery have a variety of colors and backgrounds and display in both 2-D and 3-D. The following steps apply a style to the chart.

- Tap or click the Chart Style button (paintbrush icon) on the right side of the chart area to display the Chart Style gallery with the STYLE tab displayed.
- If you are using a mouse, scroll down until the eighth style (Style 8) in the Chart Style gallery is displayed and then point to this style to see a live preview on Slide 4 (Figure 10–56).

Experiment

- If you are using a mouse, point to various chart styles and watch the layouts change.

- Tap or click Style 8 in the Chart Style gallery to apply the chart style to the chart.

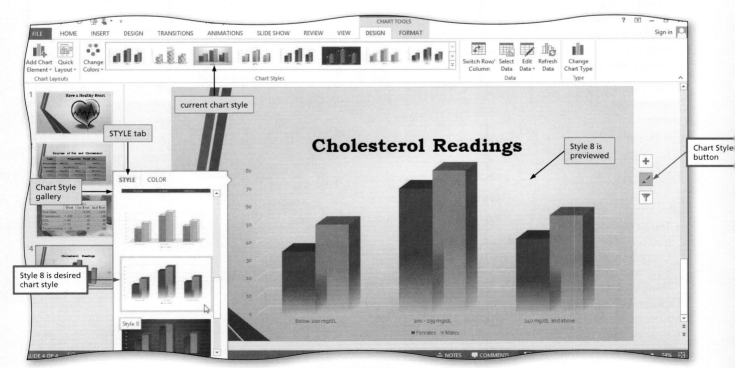

Figure 10–56

To Change Chart Colors

You can modify a chart's colors easily by selecting one of the color groups available in the Chart Color gallery. These colors are grouped in two categories: Colorful and Monochromatic. For a unique look, PowerPoint also allows you create a custom color combination. The following steps change the chart colors. *Why? The two columns in the chart have very similar colors, so you want to distinguish the Males columns from the Females columns by changing to a color scheme with more contrast.*

1

- With the Chart Style gallery still displaying, tap or click the COLOR tab at the top of the pane to display the Chart Color gallery (Figure 10–57).

Q&A Why is a box surrounding the six colors in the first row in the Colorful section?
Those colors are currently applied to the chart.

Experiment

- If you are using a mouse, point to various color groups and watch the chart colors change.

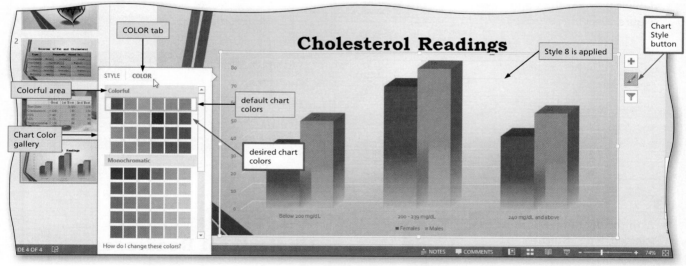

Figure 10–57

2

- Tap or click Color 2 (the second row in the Colorful area) to apply these colors to the chart.

- Tap or click the Chart Style button to the right of the chart to close the Chart Color gallery.

- Press and hold or right-click the Excel app button on the taskbar and then tap or click Close window to exit Excel.

Other Ways
1. Tap or click Change Colors button (CHART TOOLS DESIGN tab | Chart Styles group)

BTW
Quick Reference
For a table that lists how to complete the tasks covered in this book using touch gestures, the mouse, ribbon, shortcut menu, and keyboard, see the Quick Reference Summary at the back of this book, or visit the Quick Reference resource on the Student Companion Site located on www.cengagebrain.com. For detailed instructions about accessing available resources, visit www.cengage.com/ct/studentdownload or see the inside back cover of this book.

To Display and Format Axis Titles

The legend below the chart identifies the colors assigned to each of the bars. You can modify the default legend in a variety of ways, including moving its location, changing the fill and outline, adding an effect, and changing the font. The Chart Elements button on the right side of the chart area allows you to display or hide a chart element. When you click this button, the Chart Elements pane is displayed. A check mark appears in the check box for each chart element that is displayed. You can check and uncheck each chart element to display or hide axes, the chart title, labels, gridlines, and the legend. The following steps display the axis titles and then format the text. *Why? You want your audience to recognize that the y-axis represents the total number of people in the cholesterol sample and the x-axis represents the cholesterol categories.*

- Tap or click the Chart Elements button (plus sign icon) on the right side of the chart area to display the CHART ELEMENTS pane. Tap or click the Axis Titles check box to display the two default titles for the x and y axes (Figure 10–58).

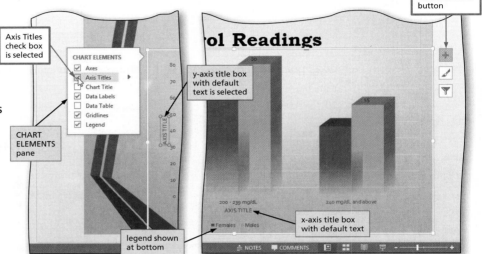

Figure 10–58

- With the default y-axis title box selected, type **Number of Participants** in the text box.
- Select the text and then increase the font size to 18 point and bold the text.

- Tap or click the x-axis title to select it, delete the default text, and then type **Total Cholesterol** as the replacement text.
- Select the text and then increase the font size to 18 point and bold the text (Figure 10–59).

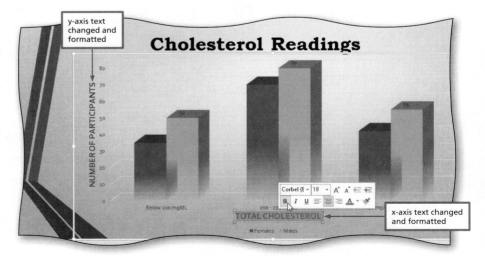

Figure 10–59

Other Ways

1. Tap or click Add Chart Element button (CHART TOOLS DESIGN tab | Chart Layouts group), tap or click Axis Titles

To Move a Chart Legend

1 INSERT & EDIT WORD FILE | 2 DRAW TABLE ROWS & COLUMNS | 3 FORMAT TABLE
4 INSERT & EDIT LINKED WORKSHEET | 5 COPY, FORMAT & EDIT CHART

The legend below the chart identifies the colors assigned to each of the bars. You can modify the default legend in a variety of ways, including moving its location, changing the fill and outline, adding an effect, and changing the font. The following steps move the legend to the left side of the chart. *Why? A blank area is available between the two vertical bars and the left side of the chart, and you believe the legend will be more effective there.*

- With the CHART ELEMENTS pane still displaying, position the pointer over the word, Legend, in the list to display an arrow and then tap or click this arrow to display the Legend menu (Figure 10–60).

- Tap or click Left to display the legend on the left side of the chart.

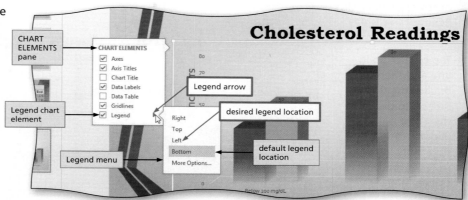

Figure 10–60

Other Ways

1. Tap or click Add Chart Element button (CHART TOOLS DESIGN tab | Chart Layouts group), tap or click Legend arrow

To Format a Chart Legend

1 INSERT & EDIT WORD FILE | 2 DRAW TABLE ROWS & COLUMNS | 3 FORMAT TABLE
4 INSERT & EDIT LINKED WORKSHEET | 5 COPY, FORMAT & EDIT CHART

You can modify the default legend in a variety of ways, including moving its location, changing the fill and outline, adding an effect, and changing the font. The following steps format the legend. *Why? Changing the line color and adding a glow help call attention to the legend.*

- With the CHART ELEMENTS pane still displaying, display the Legend menu (Figure 10–61).

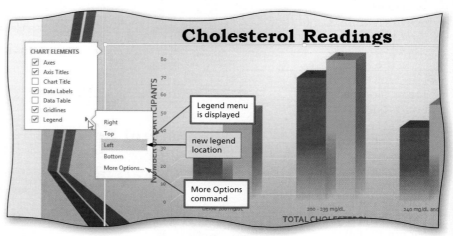

Figure 10–61

- Tap or click More Options to display the Format Legend pane. Tap or click the 'Fill & Line' button and then, if necessary, tap or click BORDER to display the BORDER area.

- Tap or click Solid line and then tap or click the Color button to display the Color gallery (Figure 10–62).

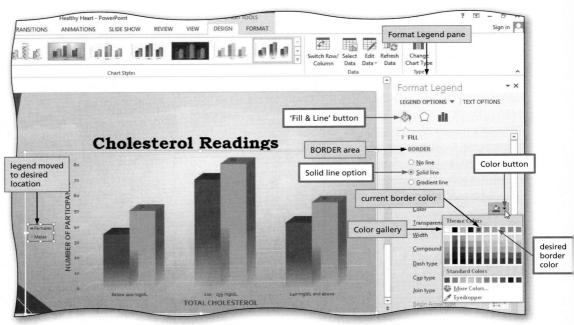

Figure 10–62

- Tap or click Gold, Accent 3 (seventh color in the first Theme Colors row) to change the legend border line color.

- Increase the line width to 1.5 pt (Figure 10–63).

Q&A Is a live preview available?
No, this feature is not offered.

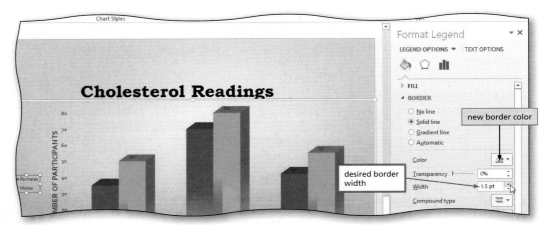

Figure 10–63

- Tap or click the Effects button (Format Legend pane) and then, if necessary, display the GLOW area. Tap or click the Presets button to display the Glow gallery (Figure 10–64).

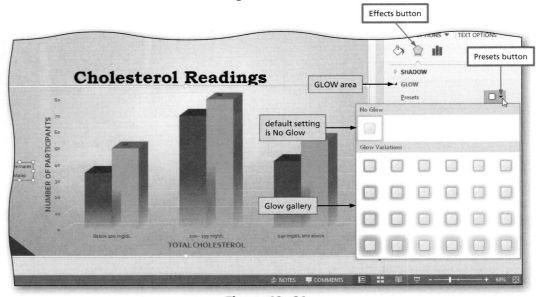

Figure 10–64

- If you are using a mouse, point to Gold, 8 pt glow, Accent color 3 (third variation in the second row) (Figure 10–65).

- Tap or click the Gold, 8 pt glow, Accent color 3 variation to apply this Glow preset to the legend.

- Tap or click the Close button (Format Legend pane).

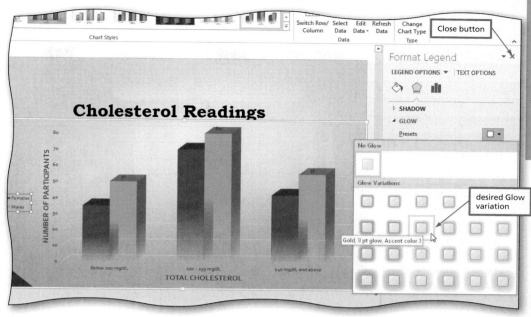

Figure 10–65

Other Ways

1. Press and hold or right-click legend, tap or click Format Legend on shortcut menu

To Format a Chart Background

1 INSERT & EDIT WORD FILE | 2 DRAW TABLE ROWS & COLUMNS | 3 FORMAT TABLE
4 INSERT & EDIT LINKED WORKSHEET | 5 COPY, FORMAT & EDIT CHART

The background area behind and to the left of the chart bars is called the **chart wall**. You can format this portion of the chart by adding a fill, an outline, and effects such as a shadow. The following steps add a gradient fill to the background chart wall. *Why? The gradient adds a visual element and helps call attention to the white gridlines.*

1

- Press and hold or right-click an area of the chart wall to select this chart element and to display a mini toolbar and shortcut menu. If necessary, tap or click the Chart Elements arrow and then tap or click Walls in the list (Figure 10–66).

Q&A

How will I know if this piece of the chart is selected? You will see six small blue circles, each one located at the upper or lower gridline corner.

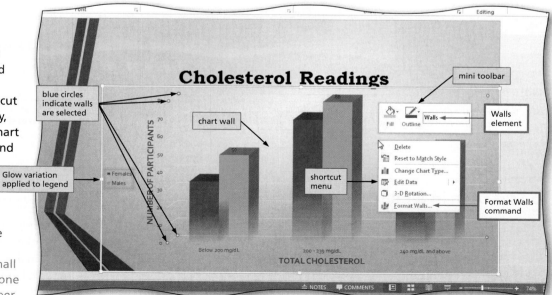

Figure 10–66

- If necessary, display the shortcut menu again. Tap or click Format Walls in the shortcut menu to display the Format Walls pane. If necessary, tap or click FILL to expand the FILL section.

- Tap or click Gradient fill to display options related to gradient colors in the pane. Tap or click the Preset gradients button to display a palette of built-in gradient fill colors (Figure 10–67).

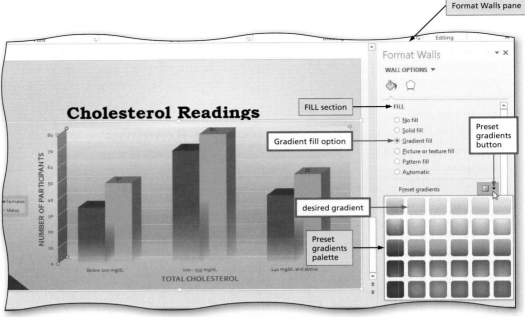

Figure 10–67

- Tap or click Light Gradient – Accent 2 (second gradient in the first row) to apply this gradient to the chart walls (Figure 10–68).

- Tap or click the Close button (Format Walls pane).

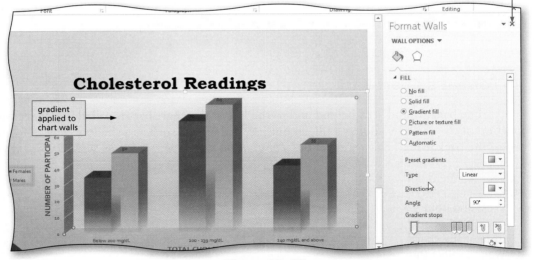

Figure 10–68

Other Ways

1. Tap or click the Chart Elements arrow (CHART TOOLS FORMAT tab | Current Selection group), tap or click Walls, tap or click Format Selection (CHART TOOLS FORMAT tab | Current Selection group), if necessary tap or click Fill & Line button, if necessary tap or click FILL, tap or click Gradient fill (Format Walls pane)

To Edit Data in a Chart

1 INSERT & EDIT WORD FILE | 2 DRAW TABLE ROWS & COLUMNS | 3 FORMAT TABLE
4 INSERT & EDIT LINKED WORKSHEET | 5 COPY, FORMAT & EDIT CHART

The data in Sheet2 of the worksheet is used to create the chart on Slide 4. If you edit this data, the corresponding bars in the chart change height to reflect new numbers. The chart is a linked object, so when you modify the data and close the worksheet, the chart will reflect the changes and the original file stored on your Data Files for Students also will change. The following steps edit three cells in the worksheet. *Why? You have obtained test results from additional fitness center members and want to update your chart and the Excel worksheet with this information.*

1

- Display the CHART TOOLS DESIGN tab and then tap or click the Edit Data button (CHART TOOLS DESIGN tab | Data group) to display Sheet2 of the worksheet.

 Why might I want to tap or click the Edit Data arrow instead of the Edit Data button?
You would be given the option to run Microsoft Excel and then edit the worksheet using that app. More options would be available using Excel. If you simply need to edit data, you can perform that task easily using PowerPoint.

- Tap or click cell B2 (Below 200 mg/dL for Females) to make cell B2 the active cell (Figure 10–69).

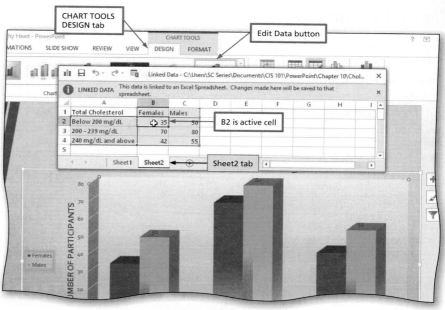

Figure 10–69

2

- Type 40 as the replacement number and then tap cell B3 or press the DOWN ARROW key to make cell B3 (200 – 239 mg / dL for Females) the active cell.

- Type 65 as the replacement number and then tap cell C3 or press the RIGHT ARROW key to make cell C3 (200 – 239 mg / dL for Males) the active cell.

- Type 85 as the replacement number and then press the ENTER key (Figure 10–70).

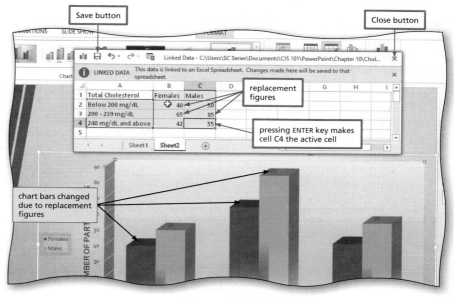

Figure 10–70

3

- Tap or click the Save button on the spreadsheet toolbar to save the data to the Excel spreadsheet.

- Tap or click the Close button on the spreadsheet to close the window.

- Tap or click the slide in a location outside the chart area (Figure 10–71).

Figure 10–71

To Add a Hyperlink to a Table

A hyperlink connects one element on a slide to another slide, presentation, picture, file, webpage, or email address. Presenters use hyperlinks to display these elements to an audience. In this Healthy Heart presentation, you will create a hyperlink from a cell in the table on Slide 2 to an Adobe PDF file. *Why? You want to show your audience a simple form they can use to monitor their food intake each day.* When you tap or click this particular table cell during a slide show, Adobe Acrobat starts and then opens this PDF file. The following steps hyperlink a table cell to a PDF file.

- Display Slide 2 and then place the pointer in the word, Frequently, in the rightmost cell.

- Display the INSERT tab and then tap or click the Hyperlink button (INSERT tab | Links group) to display the Insert Hyperlink dialog box.

- If necessary, tap or click the 'Existing File or Web Page' button in the Link to area.

- If necessary, tap or click the Current Folder button in the Look in area and then navigate to the location where your Data Files for Students are stored (in this case, the PowerPoint folder in the CIS 101 folder [or your class folder] on your computer or SkyDrive).

- Tap or click Daily Food Diary to select this file as the hyperlink (Figure 10–72).

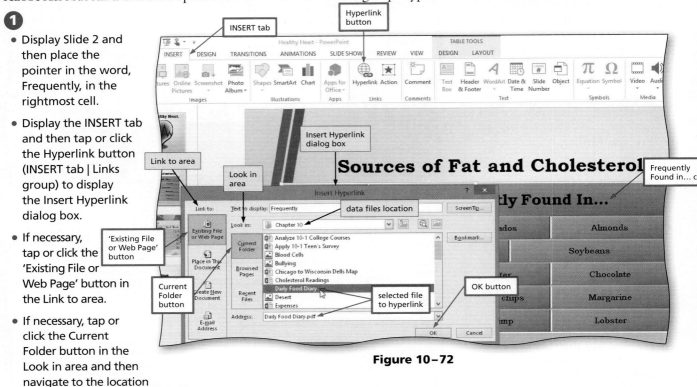

Figure 10–72

- Tap or click the OK button (Insert Hyperlink dialog box) to insert the hyperlink.

To Add a Transition between Slides

The final enhancements you will make in this presentation are to apply a transition, change the transition effect option, and change the transition speed. The following steps apply these transition effects to the presentation.

1. Apply the Doors transition in the Exciting category to all slides.

2. Change the effect option to Horizontal.

3. Change the transition speed from 1.40 to 3.00 seconds.

BTW

Conserving Ink and Toner

If you want to conserve ink or toner, you can instruct PowerPoint to print draft quality documents by tapping or clicking FILE on the ribbon to open the Backstage view, tapping or clicking Options in the Backstage view to display the PowerPoint Options dialog box, tapping or clicking Advanced in the left pane (PowerPoint Options dialog box), sliding or scrolling to the Print area in the right pane, placing a check mark in the 'Use draft quality' check box, and then tapping or clicking the OK button. Then, use the Backstage view to print the document as usual.

To Run, Print, Save, and Exit PowerPoint

The presentation now is complete. You should run the presentation, view the hyperlinked file, print the slides, save the presentation, and then exit PowerPoint.

1 Run the Healthy Heart presentation. When Slide 2 is displayed, tap or click 'FREQUENTLY FOUND IN…' in the table to display the Daily Food Diary document as the hyperlinked file. If the Microsoft Office dialog box is displayed, tap or click the OK button to open the PDF file.

2 Review the contents of the Daily Food Diary document. Swipe in from the left edge of the screen, and then back to the left, or point to the upper-left corner of the screen to display a live preview thumbnail of Slide 2. If the Slide 2 thumbnail is not displayed, point to the PowerPoint app button on the taskbar to see a live preview of Slide 2.

3 Tap or click the thumbnail of Slide 2 to display that slide and then display Slide 3 and Slide 4. End the slide show.

4 Print the Healthy Heart presentation as a handout with two slides per page (Figure 10–73).

5 Save the Healthy Heart presentation again with the same file name.

6 Exit PowerPoint, closing all open documents.

BTW

Printing Document Properties

To print document properties, tap or click FILE on the ribbon to open the Backstage view, tap or click the Print tab in the Backstage view to display the Print gallery, tap or click the first button in the Settings area to display a list of options specifying what you can print, tap or click Document Info in the list to specify you want to print the document properties instead of the actual document, and then tap or click the Print button in the Print gallery to print the document properties on the currently selected printer.

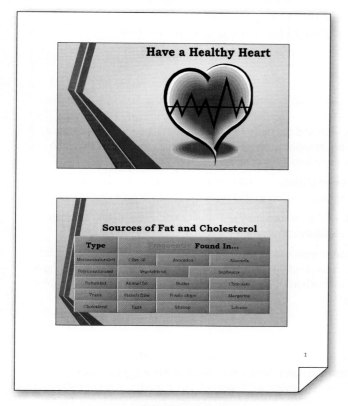

(a) Page 1

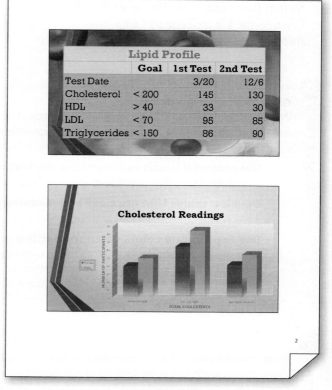

(b) Page 2

Figure 10–73

Chapter Summary

In this chapter you have learned how to develop a presentation using information you inserted from a Microsoft Word flyer and Microsoft Excel chart. These documents were either embedded or linked, and you edited each of them to update words or numbers. You also drew a table and enhanced it, and linked an Adobe PDF file to the table. You altered the Microsoft Excel object by changing the chart type, background, gridlines, and legend. The items listed below include all the new PowerPoint skills you have learned in this chapter.

Align Objects
Center a Table (PPT 625)
Align a Worksheet (PPT 628)
Align a Chart (PPT 633)

Create a Table
Draw a Table (PPT 610)
Draw Table Rows (PPT 611)
Draw Table Columns (PPT 613)
Erase a Table Line (PPT 615)
Split a Table Column and Row (PPT 617)

Edit Objects
Edit an Embedded File (PPT 608)
Edit a Linked Worksheet (PPT 629)
Edit Data in a Chart (PPT 642)

Format a Chart
Switch Rows and Columns in a Chart (PPT 634)
Change the Chart Type (PPT 635)
Apply a Style to a Chart (PPT 636)

Exclude Data in a Chart (PPT 636)
Change Chart Colors (PPT 637)
Display and Format Axis Titles (PPT 638)
Move a Chart Legend (PPT 639)
Format a Chart Legend (PPT 639)
Format a Chart Background (PPT 641)

Format a Table
Add Shading to a Table (PPT 620)
Add a Gradient Fill to a Table (PPT 621)
Add a Cell Bevel (PPT 621)
Distribute Table Rows (PPT 622)
Resize Table Columns and Rows (PPT 623)

Insert Objects
Insert a File with Graphics and Text (PPT 606)
Insert a Linked Excel Worksheet (PPT 626)
Copy an Excel Chart (PPT 631)
Add a Hyperlink to a Table (PPT 644)

CONSIDER THIS

General Project Guidelines

When creating a PowerPoint presentation, the actions you perform and the decisions you make will affect the appearance and characteristics of the finished document. As you create a presentation with illustrations, such as the project shown in Figure 10–1 on pages PPT 603 to PPT 604, you should follow these general guidelines:

1. **Use powerful words to accompany the text on your slides.** The slides are meant to enhance your talk by clarifying main points and calling attention to key ideas. Your speech should use words that explain and substantiate your visuals.

2. **Develop tables that are clear and meaningful.** Tables are extremely useful vehicles for presenting complex relationships. Their design plays an important part in successfully conveying the information to the audience.

3. **Use appropriate colors when formatting graphics you want people to remember.** Numerous studies have shown that appropriate graphics help audiences comprehend and remember the information presented during a speech. Color has been shown to increase retention by as much as 80 percent. When choosing colors for your graphics, use hues that fit the tone and objective of your message.

CONSIDER THIS

How should you submit solutions to questions in the assignments identified with a ✷ symbol?

Every assignment in this book contains one or more questions identified with a ✷ symbol. These questions require you to think beyond the assigned presentation. Present your solutions to the questions in the format required by your instructor. Possible formats may include one or more of these options: write the answer; create a document that contains the answer; present your answer to the class; discuss your answer in a group; record the answer as audio or video using a webcam, smartphone, or portable media player; or post answers on a blog, wiki, or website.

Apply Your Knowledge

Reinforce the skills and apply the concepts you learned in this chapter.

Changing a Chart, Formatting Chart Legends, and Editing a Table

Note: To complete this assignment, you will be required to use the Data Files for Students. Visit www.cengage.com/ct/studentdownload for detailed instructions or contact your instructor for information about accessing the required files.

Instructions: Run PowerPoint. Open the presentation, Apply 10-1 Teen's Survey, from the Data Files for Students.

You conducted a survey of your freshman class to find out how much time they spend on certain activities each day. You also asked if they had ever experienced bullying now or in the past. The document you open is a partially formatted presentation. You will change a chart type, format a chart legend, and add data to a table. Your presentation should look like Figure 10–74.

Perform the following tasks:

1. On Slide 1, apply the Blue, 18 pt glow, Accent color 5 text effect to the title text, and then enlarge the photo to approximately 6.07" × 13.33", move it to the bottom of the slide, and then apply the Soft Edge Rectangle picture style (the sixth style in the first row) as shown in Figure 10–74a.

2. On Slide 2, change the chart type from a bar chart to a 3-D Pie chart, and change the size to approximately 6.5" × 12.23". Increase the chart title font size to 40 point, change the chart colors to Color 4 (the fourth row in the Colorful area), and then change the chart style to Style 7.

3. On Slide 2, change the data labels fill to White, Background 1 (the first color in the first Theme Colors row), change the font size to 14 point, change the font color to Black, Text 1 (the second color in the first Theme Colors row), and then bold this text. Change the legend font size to 18 point, and then bold this text. Distribute the chart vertically and horizontally on the slide, as shown in Figure 10–74b on the next page.

4. Create a background on Slide 3 by inserting the photo called Bullying, which is available on the Data Files for Students, as shown in Figure 10–74c.

(a) Slide 1

Figure 10–74

Continued >

Apply Your Knowledge *continued*

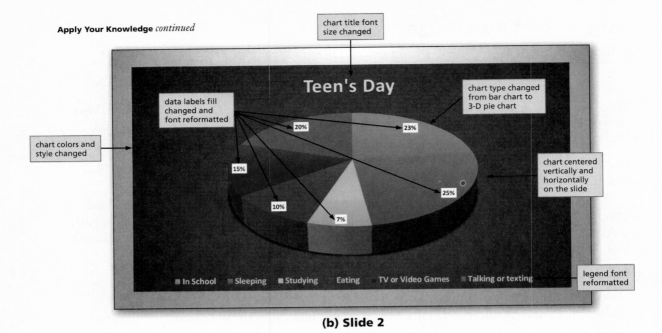

(b) Slide 2

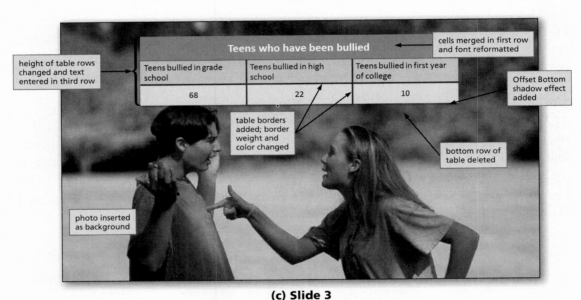

(c) Slide 3
Figure 10–74 (Continued)

5. Merge the three cells in the first row of the chart on Slide 3. Increase the size of the font in the first row to 24 point, bold the text, and then center the text both horizontally and vertically in the cell. Change the height of the first and second rows to 0.8", and then change the height of the third row to 0.6". Delete the bottom row of the table. Insert the numbers in the third row, and then center the numbers. Move the table to the location shown in Figure 10–74c.

6. Apply the Dark Style 2 – Accent 5/Accent 6 table style to the table (the fourth style in the second Dark row). Add all borders to the table, change the border weight to 3 pt, change the pen color to Dark Blue (the ninth color in the Standard Colors row), and then add two vertical lines and one horizontal line. Add the Offset Bottom shadow effect (the second effect in the first Outer row), as shown in the figure.

7. If requested by your instructor, add your birth year after the title of the table on Slide 3.

8. Apply the Peel Off transition (Exciting category) and change the duration to 4.00 for all slides.

9. Save the presentation using the file name, Apply 10-1 Typical Teen's Day.

10. Submit the revised document in the format specified by your instructor.

11. ✸ In this presentation, you changed the chart type on Slide 2 from a bar chart to a pie chart. Why? Did adding a table style to the table on Slide 3 improve the table?

Extend Your Knowledge

Extend the skills you learned in this chapter and experiment with new skills. You may need to use Help to complete the assignment.

Drawing and Formatting Tables

Note: To complete this assignment, you will be required to use the Data Files for Students. Visit www.cengage.com/ct/studentdownload for detailed instructions or contact your instructor for information about accessing the required files. You will need to use a mouse or other pointing device to draw tables.

Instructions: Run PowerPoint. Open the presentation, Extend 10-1 Sodium, from the Data Files for Students. You will format one table and then draw and format a second table, as shown in Figure 10–75 on the next page.

Perform the following tasks:

1. On Slide 1 (Figure 10–75a), delete the first row of the table, which contains the table title, Daily Sodium Levels. To delete this row, place the pointer in that row, tap or click the TABLE TOOLS LAYOUT tab, tap or click the Delete button (TABLE TOOLS LAYOUT tab | Rows & Columns group), and tap or click Delete Rows in the Delete menu.

2. With the table selected, display the TABLE TOOLS DESIGN tab and then click the Pen Weight arrow (TABLE TOOLS DESIGN tab | Draw Borders group). Tap or click 3 pt to change the border weight.

3. Change the pen color by tapping or clicking the Pen Color button (TABLE TOOLS DESIGN tab | Draw Borders group) and then selecting Green (the sixth color in the Standard Colors row).

4. Tap or click the Borders arrow (TABLE TOOLS DESIGN tab | Table Styles group) and then select All Borders in the Borders gallery to apply the new border settings to the entire table.

5. Change the table shading color to Blue-Gray, Accent 3 (the seventh color in the first Theme Colors row), and then apply the From Center Variation gradient (the second gradient in the second variations row in the Light Variations area). Change the table text font to Arial, bold this text, and then center the table horizontally on the lower area of the slide.

6. Display Slide 2 (Figure 10–75b) and then draw a table with five rows and five columns. Distribute the rows and the columns. (*HINT:* To distribute the columns, display the TABLE TOOLS LAYOUT tab and then tap or click the Distribute Columns button [TABLE TOOLS LAYOUT tab | Cell Size group].) Change the line weight to 3 pt and the pen color to Dark Blue (the ninth color in the Standard Colors row). Click the Draw Table button and then click the four main borders of the table to apply the new border settings.

7. Click the first cell in the first row, click the Table Eraser button, and then erase the vertical line between the first and second cells in the first row.

8. Erase the horizontal lines in the first, third, and fourth columns of the second row.

9. Erase the horizontal lines in the first, third, and fourth columns of the fourth row.

10. Enter the data in the table using Figure 10–75b as a guide. Select all text in the table and then change the font to Arial and the font size to 20 point. Center the text both horizontally and vertically in each cell. Select the first row of the table and then bold this text.

Continued >

Extend Your Knowledge *continued*

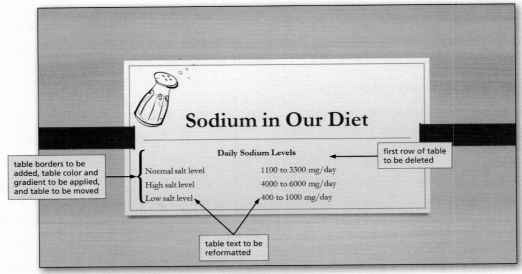

(a) Slide 1

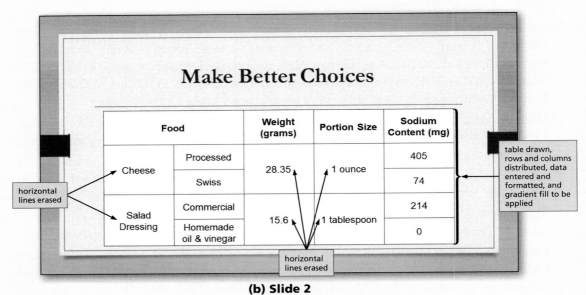

(b) Slide 2

Figure 10–75

11. Select the table on Slide 2, adjust the size of the table to approximately 3.94" × 9.79". Change the shading color to Teal, Accent 2, Lighter 40% (the sixth color in the fourth Theme Colors row), and then apply the Linear Down Gradient (the second gradient in the first Variations row) to the table.

12. If requested by your instructor, replace the word, Our, in the title text of Slide 1 with your grandfather's first name.

13. Apply the Split transition in the Subtle category to all slides and then change the duration to 3.50 seconds.

14. Save the presentation using the file name, Extend 10-1 Sodium in Our Diet.

15. Submit the revised document in the format specified by your instructor.

16. ✷ In this presentation, you added borders to the table on Slide 1. Did these borders help separate the cells and make the data easier to read? On Slide 2, you formatted the table. How did these colors enhance this slide element?

Analyze, Correct, Improve

Analyze a presentation, correct all errors, and improve it.

Editing a Table, Linking a Chart from a File, Changing a Chart, Switching Rows and Columns in a Chart, and Adding a Hyperlink to a Table

Note: To complete this assignment, you will be required to use the Data Files for Students. Visit www.cengage.com/ct/studentdownload for detailed instructions or contact your instructor for information about accessing the required files.

Instructions: Run PowerPoint. Open the presentation, Analyze 10-1 College Courses, from the Data Files for Students. Based on recent enrollment, there is an increase in demand for certain courses, such as psychology and forensic science, and a decrease in enrollment in chemistry classes. You work part time in your school's registration office, and your supervisor has asked you to gather information based on enrollment and to create a PowerPoint presentation. There have been several inquiries about the upcoming Spring semester registration, so your supervisor asked you to add a hyperlink to the Spring Semester PDF file, Spring 2015. Modify the slides by making the indicated corrections and improvements.

1. Correct

   a. Select the table on Slide 1 (Figure 10–76a) and delete the first row. Select the remaining text in the table and center it, and then align it in the middle of each cell. Change the width of the first column to 1.5", and then change the width of the fourth column to 1.7". Change the height of the second row to 1". Change the border line weight to 1 pt and the color to Black, Text 1 (the second color in the first Theme Colors row). Move the table to the lower-left corner of the slide.

   b. Add a hyperlink from the word, Spring, in the second column to the Spring 2015 Adobe PDF file located in the Data Files for Students (Figure 10–76b on the next page).

   c. Display Slide 2 (Figure 10–76c). Copy the chart on Sheet1 in the North Suburban Courses Microsoft Excel file located on the Data Files for Students and then paste it using the 'Use Destination Theme & Link Data' option. Size the chart so that it is 5" × 8.5", align it in the center of the slide, and then move it below the title text placeholder.

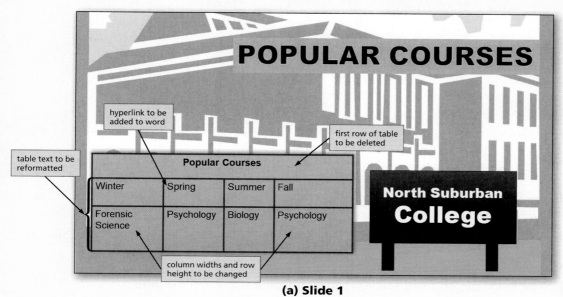

(a) Slide 1

Figure 10–76

Continued >

Analyze, Correct, Improve *continued*

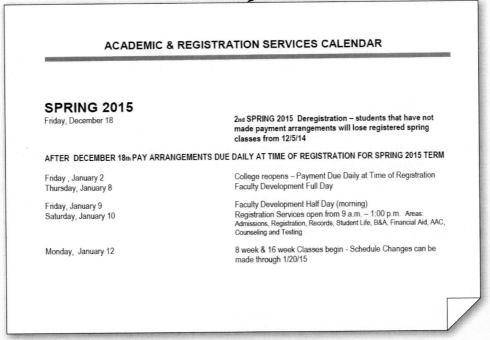

(b) **Hyperlinked Adobe PDF File**

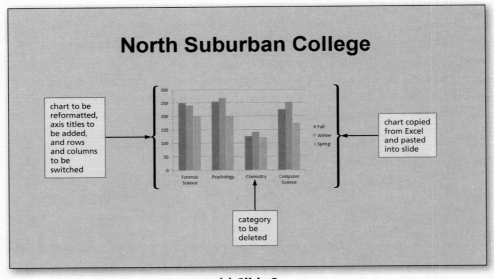

(c) **Slide 2**

Figure 10–76 (Continued)

d. Edit the Winter enrollment data for Psychology from 268 to 260 and the Spring enrollment for Computer Science from 175 to 300 (Figure 10–76d).

e. If requested by your instructor, add your birth year after the word, Fall, in the table on Slide 1.

2. Improve

a. On Slide 1, add the Art Deco cell bevel effect (the fourth effect in the third row in the Bevel area) to all cells in the table.

b. On Slide 2, switch the rows and columns. Delete the Chemistry category so that data for only Forensic Science, Psychology, and Computer Science is displayed.

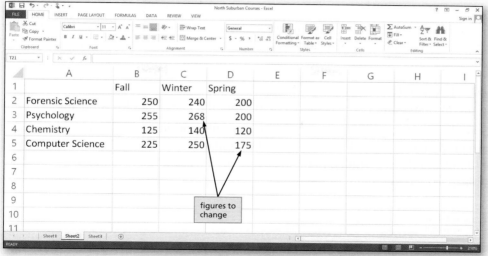

(d) Original Excel Worksheet
Figure 10–76 (Continued)

c. Change the Legend Position to the top of the chart and increase the font size to 16 point.

d. Change the style to Style 4 and the color to Color 4 (the fourth row in the Colorful area).

e. Display the Axis Titles. Select the Horizontal (Category) Axis Title and type **Popular College Courses** as the replacement text. Select the Vertical (Value) Axis Title and type **Enrollment** as the replacement text. Increase the font size to 20 point for both titles.

f. Apply the Top Spotlight – Accent 4 gradient (the fourth gradient in the second row of the Preset gradients) to the Chart Area.

g. Change the transition to the Window transition and then change the duration to 3.25 seconds for all slides.

h. Save the presentation using the file name, Analyze 10-1 North Suburban College.

i. Submit the revised document in the format specified by your instructor.

3. ✹ How did changing the table style on Slide 1 help? How did changing the chart style on Slide 2 improve the look of the slide? Why is linking the Excel file important in this presentation?

In the Labs

Design and/or create a presentation using the guidelines, concepts, and skills presented in this chapter. Labs 1 and 2, which increase in difficulty, require you to create solutions based on what you learned in the chapter; Lab 3 requires you to create a solution, which uses cloud and web technologies, by learning and investigating on your own from general guidance.

Lab 1: Inserting a Graphic from a File, Inserting a Linked Excel Worksheet, Inserting a Linked Word Document, and Entering Data in a Table

Problem: You and your family took a trip to Wisconsin Dells last summer. You also visited Kettle Moraine State Forest. Your travel club asked if you would share the experience of your trip and what your expenses were.

Continued >

In the Labs *continued*

Note: To complete this assignment, you will be required to use the Data Files for Students. Visit www.cengage.com/ct/studentdownload for detailed instructions or contact your instructor for information about accessing the required files.

Instructions: Perform the following tasks:

1. Open the presentation, Lab 10-1 Road Trip, from the Data Files for Students.

2. On Slide 1 (Figure 10–77a), use the Create from file option of the Insert Object dialog box to insert a graphic from the Microsoft PowerPoint file called Chicago to Wisconsin Dells Map from the Data Files for Students (Figure 10–77b). Position the map in the upper-left corner of the slide as shown in the figure.

(a) Slide 1

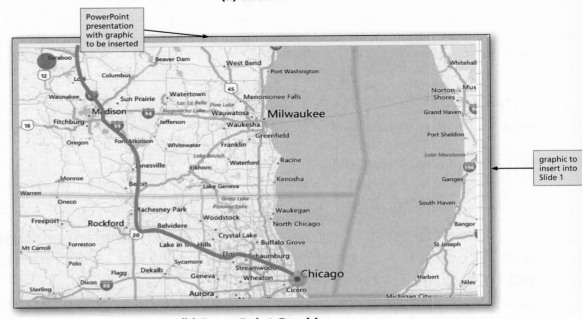

(b) PowerPoint Graphic

Figure 10–77

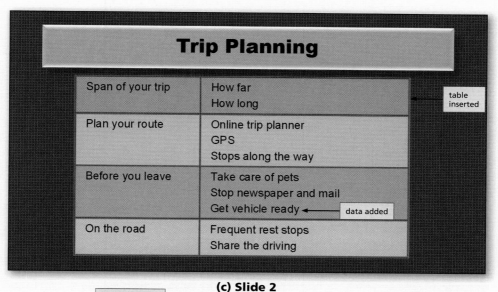

(c) Slide 2

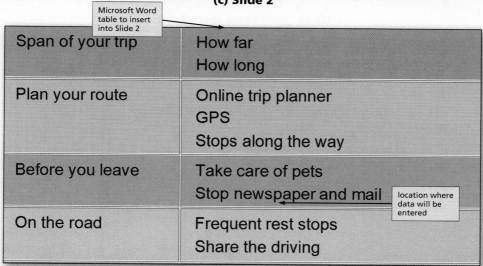

(d) Original Word Document

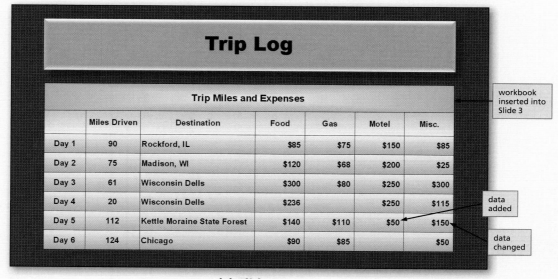

(e) Slide 3
Figure 10–77 (Continued)

Continued >

In the Labs *continued*

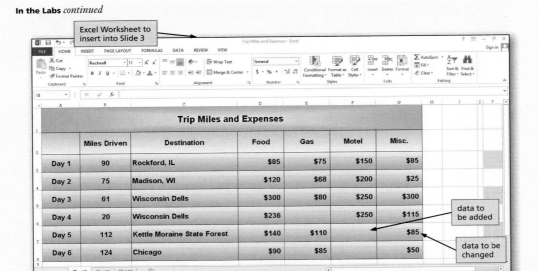

(f) Original Excel Worksheet

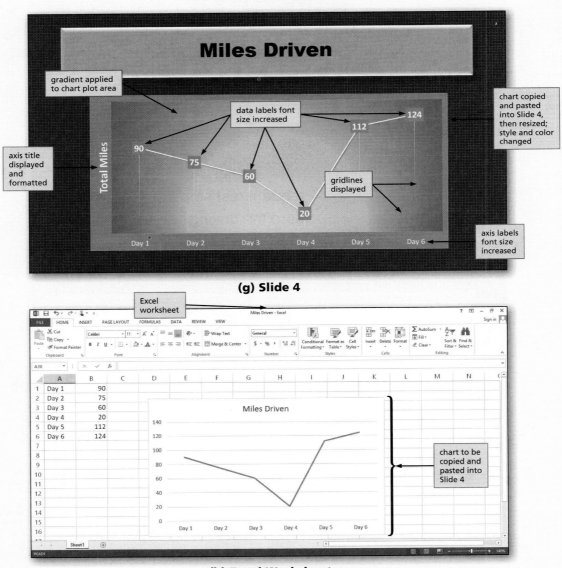

(g) Slide 4

(h) Excel Worksheet

Figure 10–77 (Continued)

3. On Slide 2 (Figure 10–77c on page PPT 655), use the Create from file option of the Insert Object dialog box to insert a table from the Microsoft Word file called Trip Planning (Figure 10–77d), from the Data Files for Students and link it. Change the size of the table to approximately 5.53" × 9.7", move it to the lower area of the slide, and center it as shown in the figure. Double-tap or double-click the table and enter data by typing `Get vehicle ready` in the third row, right column below Stop newspaper and mail, as shown in the figure.

4. On Slide 3 (Figure 10–77e), use the Create from file option of the Insert Object dialog box to insert a table from the Microsoft Excel file, Trip Miles and Expenses (Figure 10–77f), from the Data Files for Students and link it. Change the size of the table to approximately 4.8" × 11.47", center it on the slide, and then move it to the location shown in the figure. For the Kettle Moraine visit, type `$50` for camping fees in the motel column. Highlight the $85 in the seventh row, last column and type `$150` as the replacement text.

5. On Slide 4 (Figure 10–77g), copy and paste the chart in Sheet1 of the Microsoft Excel file, Miles Driven, from the Data Files for Students (Figure 10–77h). Use Destination Theme and Embed Workbook. Increase the size of the chart to approximately 4.5" × 10", position it in the area shown in the figure, and center it on the slide. Change the chart style to Style 12 and the color to Color 10.

6. Display the Primary Vertical Axis Title, highlight it, and then type `Total Miles` as the replacement text. Increase the font size to 24 point. Select the Gridlines check box in the CHART ELEMENTS pane so that the Primary Major Horizontal gridlines are added to the chart. Clear the Chart Title check box in the CHART ELEMENTS pane so that the title is not displayed.

7. Apply the Bottom Spotlight – Accent 4 gradient (the fourth gradient in the fourth row) to the chart Plot Area. Increase the size of the data labels to 20 point, as shown in Figure 10–77g.

8. Increase the size of the Horizontal (Category) Axis labels (Day 1 through Day 6) along the bottom of the chart to 16 point, as shown in the figure.

9. If requested by your instructor, add your home address in the last row, first column of the table on Slide 2.

10. Apply the Doors transition in the Exciting category and then change the duration to 3.75 seconds for all slides.

11. Submit the document in the format specified by your instructor. Save the presentation using the file name, Lab 10-1 Road Trip to Wisconsin Dells.

12. ✸ On Slide 1, you inserted a graphic from another PowerPoint presentation. How did this improve this slide? You increased the size of the labels on Slide 4. What other changes could make the slide more readable?

Lab 2: Inserting a Table from a Word Document, Inserting an Illustration from a Word Document, and Editing an Embedded File

Problem: In your earth science class, you are studying rainfall on earth. There are certain areas that receive a lot of rain and some that hardly get any. In your research you've discovered there is actually a desert in South America that has never had any recorded rainfall. It's known as the driest place on earth. To help you understand how rainfall is recorded, you decide to build your own rainfall gauge and track the rainfall for six months. You create a presentation with four slides, as shown in Figures 10–78a through 10–78d on the next page.

Continued >

In the Labs *continued*

Note: To complete this assignment, you will be required to use the Data Files for Students. Visit www.cengage.com/ct/studentdownload for detailed instructions or contact your instructor for information about accessing the required files.

Instructions: Perform the following tasks:

1. Open the presentation, Lab 10-2 Rainfall, from the Data Files for Students.

2. Display Slide 1 (Figure 10–78a) and then draw a table with five rows and two columns. Change the height of the first row to 0.7", the height of rows two through five to 0.6", and then change the width of both columns to 5".

3. Enter the data in the table using Figure 10–78a as a guide. Select all text in the table and then change the font to Arial and the font size to 24 point. Align all the text in the middle of each cell. Center the text in the first row and bold this text, as shown in Figure 10–78a.

4. Change the color of the table background to Gold, Accent 4 (the eighth color in the first Theme Colors row), and then apply the Linear Down gradient (the second gradient in the first Variations row) to the table. Apply the Convex bevel (the third bevel in the second Bevel row) to the table, as shown in Figure 10–78a.

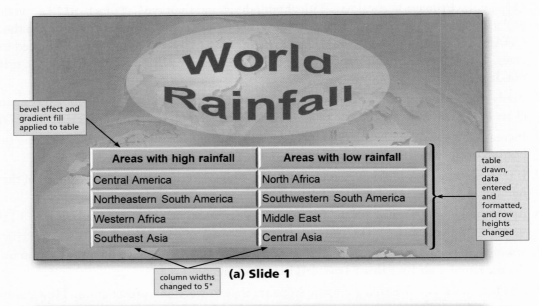

(a) Slide 1

(b) Slide 2
Figure 10–78

(c) Original Word Document

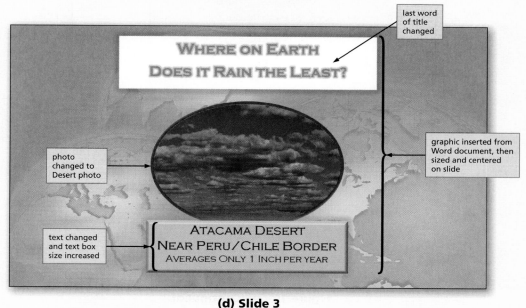

(d) Slide 3

Figure 10–78 (Continued)

5. On Slide 2 (Figure 10–78b), insert and embed the object Microsoft Word file, Most Rainfall Flyer (Figure 10–78c), from the Data Files for Students. Adjust the size of the graphic to approximately 7.82" × 8.08", align the graphic to the center and middle of the slide, as shown in Figure 10–78b.

Continued >

In the Labs *continued*

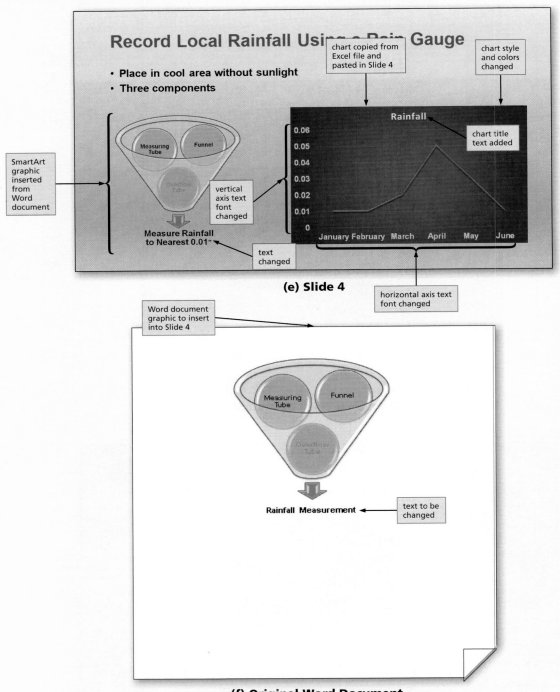

(e) Slide 4

(f) Original Word Document

Figure 10–78 (Continued)

6. On Slide 3 (Figure 10–78d on the previous page), repeat the steps for Slide 2. Select the flyer and replace the last word of the title, Most, with the word, Least. Change the photo in the flyer to the photo called Desert, from the Data Files for Students. Select the text in the text box on the bottom of the flyer, and then type `Atacama Desert, Near Peru/Chile Border,` `Averages only 1 inch per year` as the new text. Increase the size of the text box so that the text fits on three lines as shown in Figure 10–78d. *Note:* To keep this Word document in its original format, do not save this file.

7. On Slide 4 (Figure 10–78e), use the Create from file option of the Insert Object dialog box to insert the rain gauge SmartArt graphic from the Microsoft Word file, Rainfall Gauge

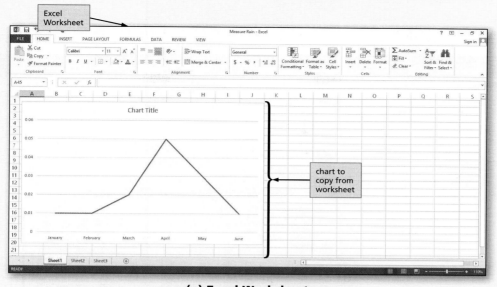

(g) Excel Worksheet
Figure 10–78 (Continued)

(Figure 10–78f), from the Data Files for Students. Highlight the text below the graphic, Rainfall Measurement, type **Measure Rainfall to Nearest 0.01"**, as the replacement text, and then change the font size to 18 point, as shown in Figure 10–78e.

8. On Slide 4, copy the chart on Sheet1 in the Measure Rain Microsoft Excel file (Figure 10–78g), located on the Data Files for Students, and then paste it using the 'Use Destination Theme & Link Data' option. Move the chart to the right side of the slide, as shown in Figure 10–78e.

9. Change the chart style to Style 7, and then change the colors to Color 9 (the fifth row in the Monochromatic area). Highlight the chart title text and type **Rainfall** as the replacement title. Change the Vertical (Value) Axis and the Horizontal (Category) Axis font to Arial, and then change the size to 16 point.

10. If requested by your instructor, type the name of your current pet after the word, components, in the second bulleted paragraph on Slide 4.

11. Apply the Ripple transition in the Exciting category and then change the duration to 2.00 seconds for all slides.

12. Save the presentation using the file name, Lab 10-2 Rainfall Worldwide.

13. Submit the document in the format specified by your instructor.

14. ✹ On Slides 2 and 3, you inserted a graphic from a Microsoft Word flyer and made changes to the graphic, including changing the photo on Slide 3. Was this an effective way to show the countries where there is the most and least amount of rainfall? Could you have used a different chart type to show recorded rainfall on Slide 4?

Lab 3: Expand Your World: Cloud and Web Technologies
Using the PowerPoint Web App to Create and Format SmartArt

Problem: You are using a mobile device or computer at your fitness center that does not have PowerPoint but has Internet access. To make use of time between your personal training session and your nutrition class, you use the PowerPoint Web App and the data in Slide 2 of the Healthy Heart presentation in this chapter to create a SmartArt graphic (Figure 10–79 on the next page). This graphic can be used as a replacement for Slide 2 if you decide to present the same information in an alternate manner.

Continued >

In the Labs *continued*

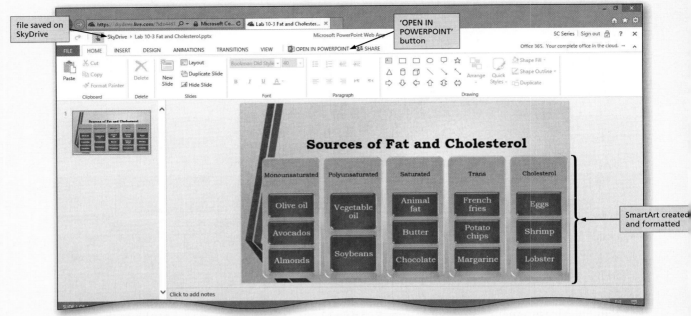

Figure 10–79

Instructions: Perform the following tasks:

1. Run a browser. Navigate to the Office Web Apps website. You will need to sign in to your SkyDrive account.

2. Tap or click the Create button to begin creating a PowerPoint presentation using the PowerPoint Web App. Name the document Lab 10-3 Fat and Cholesterol.

3. Use the Title and Content layout, apply the Parallax theme and then change the variant to Variant 4 (the rightmost variant with the gray and red stripes).

4. To create the SmartArt graphic, tap or click the SmartArt icon in the content placeholder, select the Grouped List design (the eighth design in the third row), and then enter the data from Slide 2 of the Healthy Heart presentation, which is shown in Figure 10–1(c) on page PPT 603.

5. Apply the Polished SmartArt style (the first style in the second row) and change the colors to Colored Fill – Accent 1 (the second color in the Accent 1 row). Change the font of all text to Bookman Old Style and then bold the title text. Use the SmartArt corner sizing handles to increase the graphic's size, as shown in Figure 10–79.

6. Tap or click the 'OPEN IN POWERPOINT' button and then tap or click the Yes button (Microsoft Office dialog box) to open the document in the PowerPoint desktop app. If necessary, sign in to your Microsoft account when prompted.

7. In the PowerPoint desktop app, apply the Cartoon SmartArt style (the third design in the first 3-D row) to the graphic and bold the five column headings (Monounsaturated, Polyunsaturated, Saturated, Trans, and Cholesterol). Save the table on your SkyDrive account with the file name, Lab 10-3 Fat and Cholesterol Modified.

8. Redisplay your SkyDrive account and open the file Lab 10-3 Fat and Cholesterol Modified in the PowerPoint Web App. Select the option to edit the modified document in the PowerPoint Web App.

9. Using either the PowerPoint Web App or the PowerPoint desktop app, submit the Lab 10-3 Fat and Cholesterol document in the format requested by your instructor. Sign out of your SkyDrive account. Sign out of the Microsoft account in PowerPoint.

10. ✸ Which SmartArt features that are available in the PowerPoint desktop app are not available in the PowerPoint Web App? Did the file retain the SmartArt style you applied? Is the information presented more clearly in the Healthy Heart chart or in the SmartArt graphic? Why?

✸ Consider This: Your Turn

Apply your creative thinking and problem-solving skills to design and implement a solution.

1. Design and Create a Presentation about Caffeine Content of Beverages
Personal

Part 1:   Your doctor recently told you to reduce caffeine consumption for health reasons. You have researched the beverages you consume, and you found that the highest amount of caffeine is in brewed coffee that you drink several times a day (8-ounce serving) - 95–200 mg. Other beverages that you consume have high amounts of caffeine as well. They are: hot chocolate (5-ounce serving) - 2–10 mg; cola (12-ounce serving) - 30–50 mg; green tea (8-ounce serving) - 30–50 mg; other teas (5-ounce serving) - 40–100 mg; and energy drinks (8-ounce serving) - 80 mg. You also learned that a 5-ounce serving of decaffeinated coffee has between 2 and 5 mg of caffeine. You decide to create a PowerPoint presentation for your family and friends to share your findings. Use the concepts and techniques presented in this chapter to prepare a presentation. Select a suitable theme, create a table showing caffeine levels, insert a chart, and use WordArt or SmartArt graphics where appropriate. You can use photos and illustrations from Office.com if they are appropriate for this topic. Submit your assignment in the format specified by your instructor.

Part 2:   ✸ You made several decisions while creating the presentation in this assignment: where to place text and how to format the table and chart. What was the rationale behind each of these decisions? When you reviewed the document, what further revisions did you make and why? Where would you recommend showing this slide show?

2. Design and Create a Presentation about Your Shoe Business
Professional

Part 1:   You are the owner of Terry's Tennis Shoes, a small athletic shoe store in your town. Business has been so good that you decided to open another store in a nearby town. You rented a building and hired a manager for the new location. The new manager has hired employees, and you suggested having a meeting with employees from both stores. You decide to put together a PowerPoint presentation for this meeting. Your top-selling shoes for the last six months were: Pink High Top (950 pairs sold), Patterned High Top (1,200 pairs sold), Black High Top (1,750 pairs sold), and Checkered (850 pairs sold). Use the PowerPoint file called Tennis Shoes Top Sellers, which is available on the Data Files for Students, to show these four styles and some of your other top sellers. Insert the file called Terry's Sport Shoes Flyer, located on the Data Files for Students, to show an example of an ad for the store. Select a suitable theme. The presentation could contain other photos and illustrations from Office.com if they are appropriate for this topic. Customize your presentation by creating a table and chart. Submit your assignment in the format specified by your instructor.

Continued >

STUDENT ASSIGNMENTS

Consider This: Your Turn *continued*

Part 2: ✳ You made several decisions while creating the presentation in this assignment: where to place text, how to format the text (such as font, font size, and colors), which image(s) to use, and what type of table and chart you used to make the presentation look professional and consistent. What was the rationale behind each of these decisions? When you reviewed the document, what further revisions did you make and why? Where would you recommend showing this slide show?

3. Design and Create a Presentation about World Energy

Research and Collaboration

Part 1: In your science class you are studying world energy. Energy is required for many essential functions in our everyday living, such as driving vehicles and using electricity. For many years, our energy came from fossil fuels: coal, oil, and gas. Now, other forms are prevalent, including renewables such as hydroelectric, geothermal, solar, wind, and biodiesel. Hydroelectric plants use dams to harness running water to generate energy. Geothermal power comes from ground water heated by molten rock. Solar panels capture and store energy from the sun. Biodiesel fuel can be made from both used and unused sources of vegetable oil and animal fats. Currently, our energy comes from these sources worldwide: Coal/Peat - 27 percent; Oil - 33.2 percent; Gas - 21.1 percent; Renewables - 12.9 percent; Nuclear - 5.8 percent. Your class has divided into three groups. One group will study fossil fuels and another group will study renewables. The third group will pull all the information together and create a PowerPoint presentation. Create a chart using the data furnished above. For just the renewables, you can change the chart type to 'Pie of Pie' or you can create a separate pie chart with approximate percentages of the renewable sources. Use at least three objectives found at the beginning of this chapter to develop the presentation. You can use your own pictures or those available from Office.com if they are appropriate for this topic.

Part 2: ✳ You made several decisions while creating the presentation in this assignment, including where to place text and how to create and format the energy sources data. What was the rationale behind each of these decisions? When you reviewed the document, what further revisions did you make and why? Where would you recommend showing this slide show?

Learn Online

Reinforce what you learned in this chapter with games, exercises, training, and many other online activities and resources.

Student Companion Site Reinforcement activities and resources are available at no additional cost on www.cengagebrain.com. Visit www.cengage.com/ct/studentdownload for detailed instructions about accessing the resources available at the Student Companion Site.

SAM Put your skills into practice with SAM! If you have a SAM account, go to www.cengage.com/sam2013 to access SAM assignments for this chapter.

FILE HOME INSERT DESIGN TRANSITIONS ANIMATIONS SLIDE SHOW REVIEW VIEW

11 | Organizing Slides and Creating a Photo Album

Microsoft product screenshots used with permission from Microsoft Corporation.

Objectives

You will have mastered the material in this chapter when you can:

- Create a section break
- Rename a section
- Reorder a section
- Create a custom slide show
- Create a photo album
- Reorder pictures in a photo album
- Adjust the quality of pictures in a photo album

- Add captions to pictures in a photo album
- Use the Research task pane to look up information
- Change slide orientation
- Set up a custom size slide
- Copy and compress a video file
- Email a presentation
- Create a video from a presentation

11 | Organizing Slides and Creating a Photo Album

Introduction

BTW
Using Photographs
A carefully selected image can convey an engaging message that your audience will remember long after the presentation has ended. One picture can evoke emotions and create a connection between the speaker and the listeners. The adage, "A picture is worth a thousand words," is relevant when audience members view PowerPoint slides.

Sharing photographs and videos has become a part of our everyday lives. We often use digital cameras and visit online social media websites to share our adventures, special occasions, and business activities. The presentations can be organized into sections so that particular slides are shown to specific audiences. For example, one large presentation created for freshmen orientation can be divided into one section for registration, another for financial aid, and a third for campus activities; each section could be shown to different audiences.

In addition, PowerPoint's ability to create a photo album allows you to organize and distribute your pictures by adding interesting layouts, vibrant backgrounds, and meaningful captions. These photo albums can be emailed, published to a website, or turned into a video to distribute to friends and business associates, who do not need PowerPoint installed on their computers to view your file.

Project — Presentation with Sections and a Photo Album

BTW
Designing Postcards
A postcard is an effective means of sending information to a specific audience, according to marketing experts. The size is large enough to support eye-catching images yet small enough to get the message into the readers' hands. Designers recommend using two-thirds of the postcard for a graphic and one-third for text.

Alaska is a travel destination unlike any place in the world. The state's 570,000 square miles are home to moose, bears, bald eagles, blue and humpbacked whales, and hundreds of other species. Visitors enjoy whale watching, fishing, hiking, and relaxing in the state's natural beauty. Float plane trips and rail excursions take travelers deep within the mountains to view wildlife and the trails prospectors traveled more than 100 years ago in search of treasures during the gold rush. Many travel groups plan vacations to Alaska, and they welcome experts and vacationers who share insights and photos of their travels. Members of the Travel Club in your community have asked you to present highlights of your Alaskan vacation that you enjoyed recently.

The presentation you create in this chapter (Figure 11–1) contains photos you took during this trip, which began in Seattle and included stops in Juneau, Skagway, and Ketchikan. You divide the slide show into sections for Lakes (Figure 11–1a), Train Excursion, Glaciers, and Float Plane trip. You then create a photo album, add pictures, make adjustments to brightness and contrast, and add captions (Figures 11–1b and 11–1c). You also create a second photo album with black-and-white images (Figure 11–1d). In addition, you create two slides with a custom size to use as a marketing tool to promote the annual Travel Expo and insert a video file on one of the slides (Figure 11–1e). You then email the meeting announcement file to a member and also convert another file to a video so that Travel Club members who do not have PowerPoint installed on their computers can view a glacier you visited during your vacation.

FILE   HOME   INSERT   DESIGN   TRANSITIONS   ANIMATIONS   SLIDE SHOW   REVIEW   VIEW

text edited for Section Header layout

Photo courtesy of Susan Sebok

(a) Alaskan Adventure Section Slide

photo album title and subtitle text edited and formatted

(b) Photo Album Title Slide

photo enhanced

Photo courtesy of Susan Sebok

(c) Photo Album Slide

black-and-white picture in photo album

caption edited

Photo courtesy of Susan Sebok

(d) Black-and-White Photo Album Slide

custom size slide has portrait orientation

video copied and compressed

Video courtesy of Susan Sebok

(e) Custom Size Slide

Figure 11–1

Roadmap

In this chapter, you will learn how to create the slides shown in Figure 11–1 on the previous page. The following roadmap identifies general activities you will perform as you progress through this chapter:

1. CREATE and ORGANIZE SECTIONS in a presentation.
2. Select specific slides to CREATE a CUSTOM SLIDE SHOW.
3. CREATE a PHOTO ALBUM and ENHANCE photo album ELEMENTS.
4. SPECIFY a CUSTOM SLIDE SIZE and ADD a VIDEO CLIP.
5. SHARE and DISTRIBUTE a PRESENTATION by emailing and creating a video.

At the beginning of step instructions throughout the chapter, you will see an abbreviated form of this roadmap. The abbreviated roadmap uses colors to indicate chapter progress: gray means the chapter is beyond that activity; blue means the task being shown is covered in that activity, and black means that activity is yet to be covered. For example, the following abbreviated roadmap indicates the chapter would be showing a task in the 2 CREATE CUSTOM SLIDE SHOW activity.

1 CREATE & ORGANIZE SECTIONS | 2 CREATE CUSTOM SLIDE SHOW | 3 CREATE PHOTO ALBUM & ENHANCE ELEMENTS | 4 SPECIFY CUSTOM SLIDE SIZE & ADD VIDEO CLIP | 5 SHARE & DISTRIBUTE PRESENTATION

Use the abbreviated roadmap as a progress guide while you read or step through the instructions in this chapter.

To Run PowerPoint and Save a File

If you are using a computer to step through the project in this chapter and you want your screens to match the figures in this book, you should change your computer's resolution to 1366 × 768. The following steps run PowerPoint and then save a file.

1 Run PowerPoint. If necessary, maximize the PowerPoint window.

2 Open the presentation, Alaska, located on the Data Files for Students.

3 Save the presentation using the file name, Alaskan Adventure.

Creating Sections and a Custom Slide Show

Quality PowerPoint presentations are tailored toward specific audiences, and experienced presenters adapt the slides to meet the listeners' needs and expectations. Speakers can develop one slide show and then modify the content each time they deliver the presentation. In the Alaskan Adventure slide show, for example, a speaker may decide to place the slides that showcase spectacular glaciers at the end of the presentation to build suspense. Or, these slides can appear at the beginning of the presentation to generate interest.

You can divide the slides into **sections** to help organize the slides. These sections serve the same function as dividers in a notebook or tabs in a manual: They help the user find required information and move material in a new sequence. In PowerPoint,

One of the few differences between Windows 7 and Windows 8 occurs in the steps to run PowerPoint. If you are using Windows 7, tap or click the Start button, type **PowerPoint** in the 'Search programs and files' box, tap or click PowerPoint 2013, and then, if necessary, maximize the PowerPoint window. For a summary of the steps to run PowerPoint in Windows 7, refer to the Quick Reference located at the back of this book.

BTW
The Ribbon and Screen Resolution
PowerPoint may change how the groups and buttons within the groups appear on the ribbon, depending on the computer's screen resolution. Thus, your ribbon may look different from the ones in this book if you are using a screen resolution other than 1366 × 768.

you can create sections, give them unique names, and then move slides into each section. You then can move one entire section to another part of the slide show or delete the section if it no longer is needed. Each section can be displayed or printed individually.

A **custom show** is an independent set of slides to show to a specific audience. These slides can be in a different order than in the original presentation. For example, you may desire to show a title slide, the last nine slides, and then Slides 2, 5, and 8, in that order. One PowerPoint file can have several custom shows to adapt to specific audiences.

To Insert Slides with a Section Layout

1 CREATE & ORGANIZE SECTIONS | 2 CREATE CUSTOM SLIDE SHOW | 3 CREATE PHOTO ALBUM & ENHANCE ELEMENTS

4 SPECIFY CUSTOM SLIDE SIZE & ADD VIDEO CLIP | 5 SHARE & DISTRIBUTE PRESENTATION

Your presentation will have four sections: Lakes, Train Excursion, Glaciers, and Float Plane. One of PowerPoint's layouts is named Section Header, and it is similar to the Title Slide layout because it has a title and a subtitle placeholder. To ensure consistency and save time, you can create one slide with a Section Header layout and then duplicate and modify it for each section. *Why? You can help your audience understand the organization of your slide show if you have one slide announcing the content of each section.* The following steps insert the four section slides.

- With Slide 1 selected and the HOME tab displaying, tap or click the New Slide arrow (HOME tab | Slides group) to display the Office Theme gallery (Figure 11–2).

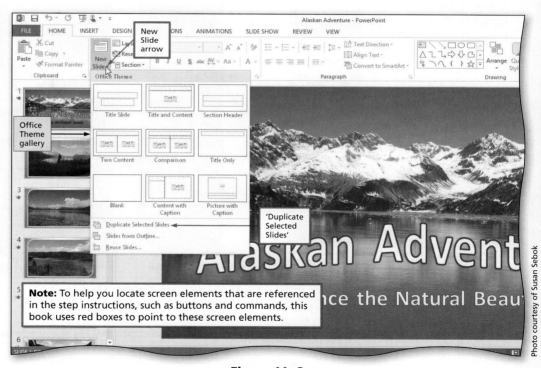

Figure 11–2

Photo courtesy of Susan Sebok

2

- Tap or click 'Duplicate Selected Slides' in the Office Theme gallery to create a new Slide 2 that is a duplicate of Slide 1.

- Tap or click the Slide Layout button (HOME tab | Slides group) to display the Office Theme layout gallery (Figure 11–3).

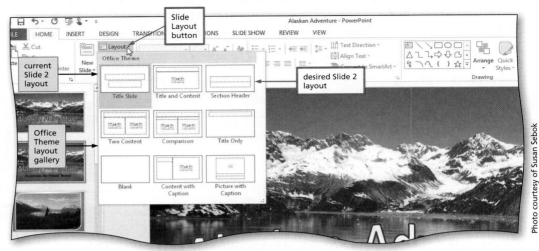

Figure 11–3

3

- Tap or click the Section Header layout to apply that layout to the new Slide 2 (Figure 11–4).

Figure 11–4

Other Ways

1. Press and hold or right-click Slide 1, tap or click Duplicate Slide on shortcut menu; then press and hold or right-click Slide 2, tap or click Layout on shortcut menu

BTW

Touch Screen Differences

The Office and Windows interfaces may vary if you are using a touch screen. For this reason, you might notice that the function or appearance of your touch screen differs slightly from this chapter's presentation.

To Edit the Subtitle

The slide with the Section Header layout should have characteristics similar to the title slide to give the presentation continuity. One method of slightly altering the title slide is to change the text to reflect the next set of slides in the presentation. The following steps edit the subtitle text.

① With Slide 2 displaying, select the words, Natural Beauty, in the subtitle text placeholder and then type `Lakes` as the replacement text.

② Select all the subtitle text, tap or click the Character Spacing button (HOME tab | Font group), and then change the character spacing to Loose.

③ Change the title text font color to Blue (eighth color in the Standard Colors row) (Figure 11–5).

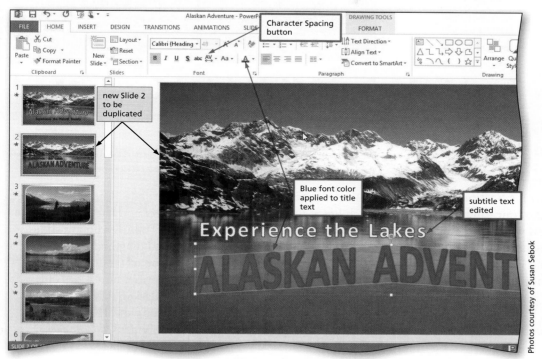

Figure 11–5

Photos courtesy of Susan Sebok

To Duplicate and Edit the Section Slides

Slide 2 is formatted appropriately to display at the beginning of the Lakes section of the slide show. A similar slide should display at the beginning of the Train Excursion, Glaciers, and Float Plane sections. The following steps duplicate Slide 2 and edit the title text.

① With Slide 2 selected and the HOME tab displaying, tap or click the New Slide arrow and then tap or click 'Duplicate Selected Slides'.

② Repeat Step 1 twice to insert two additional duplicate slides.

③ Display Slide 3, select the words, the Lakes, and then type `a Train Excursion` in the subtitle text placeholder.

④ Display Slide 4, select the word, Lakes, and then type `Glaciers` in the subtitle text placeholder.

⑤ Display Slide 5, select the words, the Lakes, and then type `a Float Plane` in the subtitle text placeholder (Figure 11–6 on the next page).

BTW

Q&As
For a complete list of the Q&As found in many of the step-by-step sequences in this book, visit the Q&A resource on the Student Companion Site located on www.cengagebrain.com. For detailed instructions about accessing available resources, visit www.cengage.com/ct/studentdownload or see the inside back cover of this book.

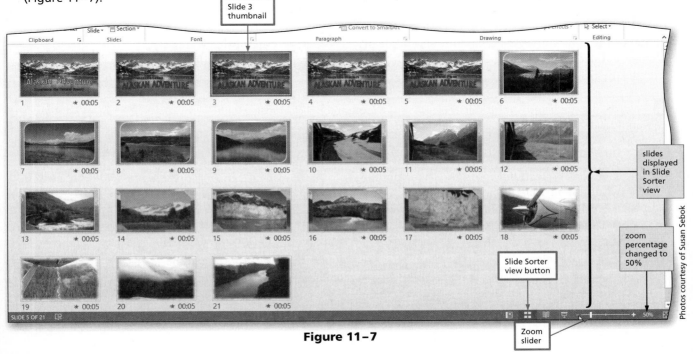

Figure 11–6

Photos courtesy of Susan Sebok

To Arrange Slides in Slide Sorter View

The four slides with a Section Header layout currently are displayed after the title slide. They are followed by 16 slides grouped into four categories, each of which has a distinct photo style or effect and background. The Lakes slides have photos with a rounded diagonal white border and a blue background, Train Excursion slides have photos with a gray border and a mountain background, Glacier photos have snipped diagonal corners and a water background, and Float Plane photos have soft edges and a cloud background. One of the four section slides you formatted should be positioned at the beginning of each category. When the presentation has only a few slides, you easily can drag and drop the slide thumbnails in the Slides pane. Your Alaskan Adventure presentation, however, has 21 slides. The following steps arrange the slides in Slide Sorter view. *Why? To easily arrange the slides, you can change to Slide Sorter view and drag and drop the thumbnails into their desired locations.*

1

- Tap or click the Slide Sorter view button to display the slides in Slide Sorter view and then tap or click the Slide 3 thumbnail (Experience a Train Excursion) to select it.

- Drag the Zoom slider to the left to change the zoom percentage to 50% so that all the slides are displayed (Figure 11–7).

Figure 11–7

2

- Drag the Slide 3 thumbnail between the Slide 9 and Slide 10 thumbnails so that it is positioned in the desired location between these two slides (Figure 11–8).

Photos courtesy of Susan Sebok

Figure 11–8

3

- Release your finger or the mouse button to display the Slide 3 thumbnail in a new location as Slide 9.
- Select the new Slide 3 (Experience Glaciers) and drag it between Slide 13 and Slide 14.
- Select the new Slide 3 (Experience a Float Plane) and drag it between Slide 17 and Slide 18 (Figure 11–9).

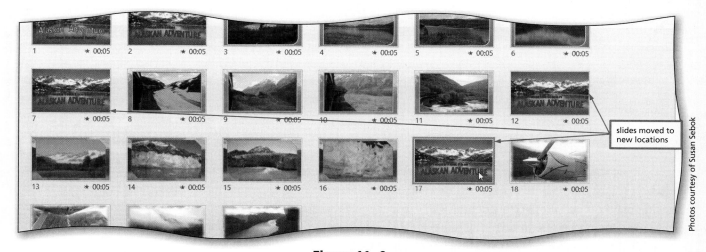

Photos courtesy of Susan Sebok

Figure 11–9

To Create a Section Break

1 CREATE & ORGANIZE SECTIONS | 2 CREATE CUSTOM SLIDE SHOW | 3 CREATE PHOTO ALBUM & ENHANCE ELEMENTS
4 SPECIFY CUSTOM SLIDE SIZE & ADD VIDEO CLIP | 5 SHARE & DISTRIBUTE PRESENTATION

The slides in the presentation are divided into four categories: Lakes, Train Excursion, Glaciers, and Float Plane. You can create a section break to organize slides into a particular group. *Why? At times, you may want to display slides from one particular category or move a section of slides to another part of the presentation.* The steps on the next page create five sections in the presentation.

1

- In Slide Sorter view, position the pointer between Slide 1 and Slide 2 and then tap or click once to display the vertical bar (Figure 11–10).

Q&A I am using a touch screen. When I tap between the slides to display the vertical bar, a shortcut menu also displays with an Add Section button. Can I just tap that button instead of using the HOME tab Section button?
Yes.

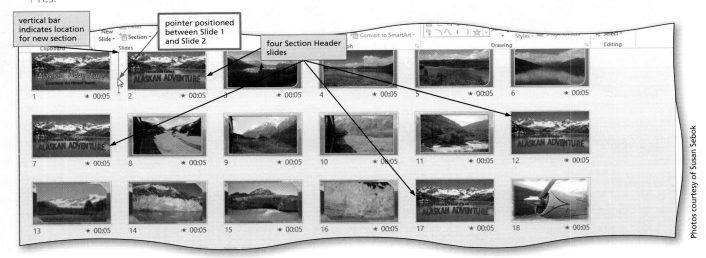

Figure 11–10

2

- With the HOME tab displaying, tap or click the Section button (HOME tab | Slides group) to display the Section menu (Figure 11–11).

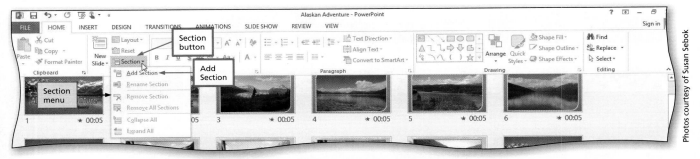

Figure 11–11

3

- Tap or click Add Section in the menu to create a section.
- Position the pointer between Slide 6 and Slide 7, which is the start of the slides with the Train Excursion, and then tap or click once to display the vertical bar (Figure 11–12).

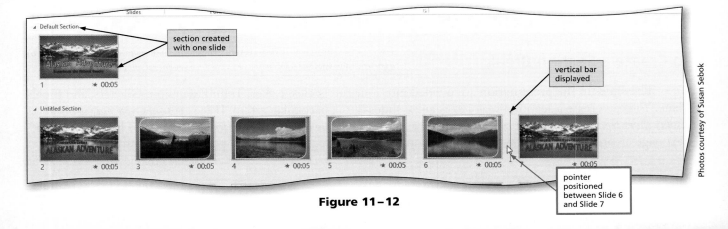

Figure 11–12

4

- Tap or click the Section button (HOME tab | Slides group) to display the Section menu and then tap or click Add Section in the menu to create a section with the name, Untitled Section.

- Position the pointer between Slide 11 and Slide 12, which is the start of the slides with glacier photos (Figure 11–13).

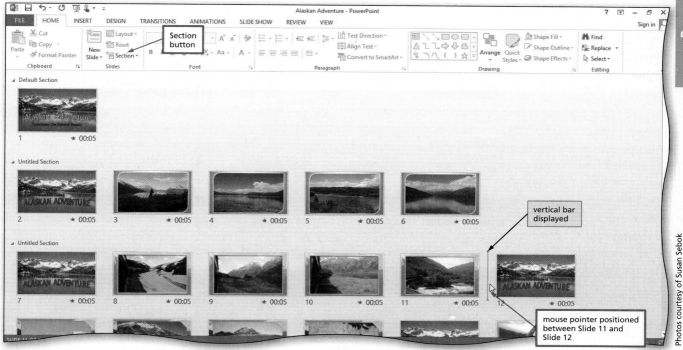

Figure 11–13

5

- Tap or click the Section button and then tap or click Add Section in the menu to create a section with the name, Untitled Section.

- Scroll down to display the final slides in the presentation, position the pointer between Slide 16 and Slide 17, and then create a section (Figure 11–14).

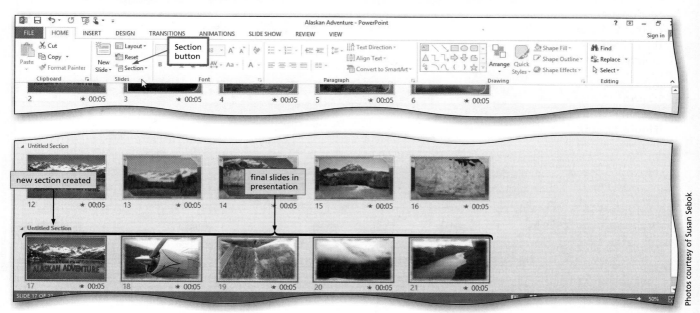

Figure 11–14

To Rename a Section

The default section names, Untitled and Default, do not identify the content of the slides in the group. The following steps rename each of the five sections in the presentation. *Why? Giving each section a unique name helps to categorize the slides easily.*

1

- With the last section featuring the float plane photos selected and the HOME tab displaying, tap or click the Section button (HOME tab | Slides group) to display the Section menu (Figure 11–15).

Q&A If the Float Plane section is not highlighted, how can I select it? Tap or click the divider between the sections. You will know the section is selected when the thumbnails have a red border and the text and slide numbers have a red font color.

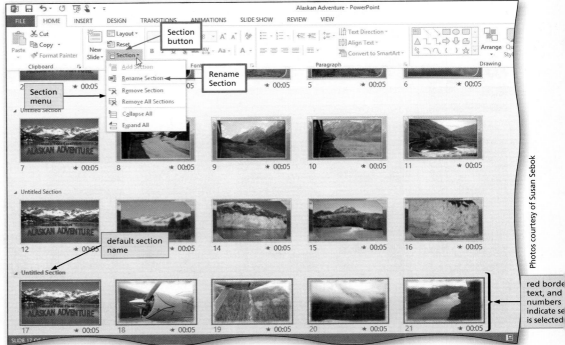

Figure 11–15

2

- Tap or click Rename Section in the menu to display the Rename Section dialog box.

- Type **Float Plane** in the Section name box (Figure 11–16).

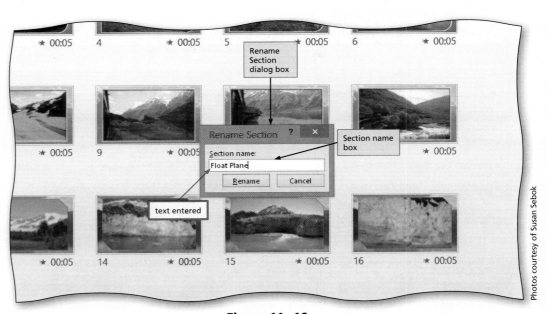

Figure 11–16

3

- Tap or click the Rename button (Rename Section dialog box) to change the section name.

- Tap or click the Untitled Section divider for the Glaciers section (Slide 12 through Slide 16) to select it and then tap or click the Section button (HOME tab | Slides group) to display the Section menu (Figure 11–17).

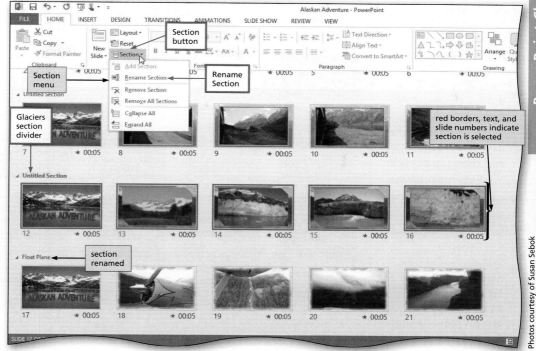

Figure 11–17

4

- Tap or click Rename Section to display the Rename Section dialog box, type **Glaciers** in the Section name box, and then tap or click the Rename button to change the section name.

- Select the divider for the Train Excursion section (Slide 7 through Slide 11), display the Rename Section dialog box, type **Train Excursion** as the new section name, and then tap or click the Rename button (Figure 11–18).

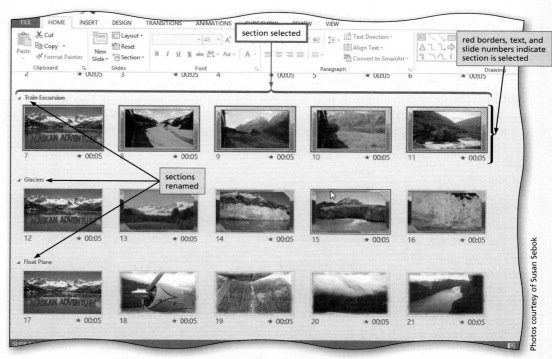

Figure 11–18

5

- Scroll up to display the first two sections, select the divider for the Lakes slides (Slide 2 through Slide 6), display the Rename Section dialog box, type **Lakes** as the new section name, and then tap or click the Rename button.

- Select the Default Section divider for Slide 1, display the Rename Section dialog box, type **Alaskan Adventure Title** as the new section name, and then tap or click the Rename button (Figure 11–19).

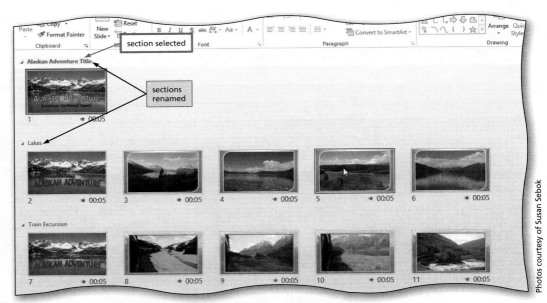

Figure 11–19

Photos courtesy of Susan Sebok

Other Ways

1. Press and hold or right-click section divider, tap or click Rename Section on shortcut menu

To Collapse and Reorder Sections

1 CREATE & ORGANIZE SECTIONS | 2 CREATE CUSTOM SLIDE SHOW | 3 CREATE PHOTO ALBUM & ENHANCE ELEMENTS
4 SPECIFY CUSTOM SLIDE SIZE & ADD VIDEO CLIP | 5 SHARE & DISTRIBUTE PRESENTATION

Why? *Travel Club members have expressed much more interest this year in glaciers than the Train Excursion, so you want to change the order of these two sets of slides in your presentation.* When slides are organized into sections, it is easy to change the order in which the sections display. Because your presentation consists of multiple sections, you can collapse the sections so that only the section titles are displayed. You then can reorder the sections and expand the sections. The following steps collapse the sections, reorder the Glaciers and Train Excursion sections, and expand the sections.

1

- With the first section, Alaskan Adventure Title, selected and the HOME tab displaying, tap or click the Section button (HOME tab | Slides group) to display the Section menu (Figure 11–20).

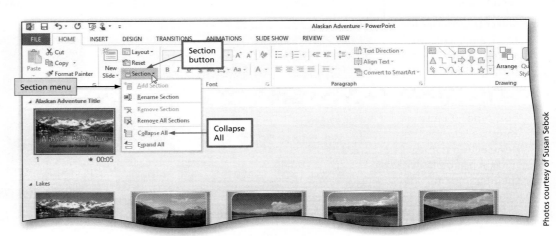

Figure 11–20

Photos courtesy of Susan Sebok

Q&A

Can I remove a section?

Yes. To delete one section, select the title and then tap or click Remove Section in the Section menu. To remove all sections, display the Section menu and then tap or click 'Remove All Sections'.

- Tap or click Collapse All in the Section menu to display only the section names.

- Tap or click the Glaciers section name to select it and then drag the section upward between the Lakes and Train Excursion sections (Figure 11–21).

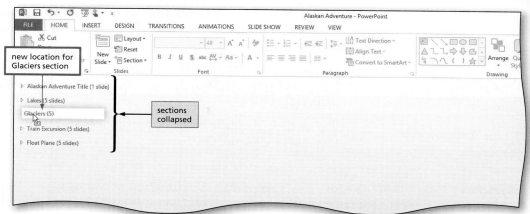

Figure 11–21

- Release your finger or the mouse button to move the Glaciers section between the Lakes and Train Excursion sections.

- Tap or click the Section button (HOME tab | Slides group) to display the Section menu (Figure 11–22).

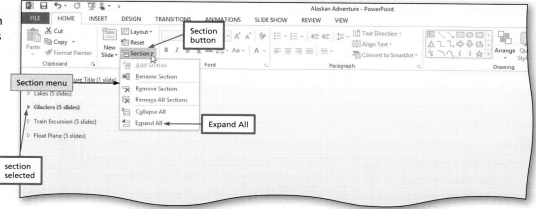

Figure 11–22

- Tap or click Expand All in the Section menu to display all the slides in their corresponding sections (Figure 11–23).

- Run the presentation to display all the slides in the desired order.

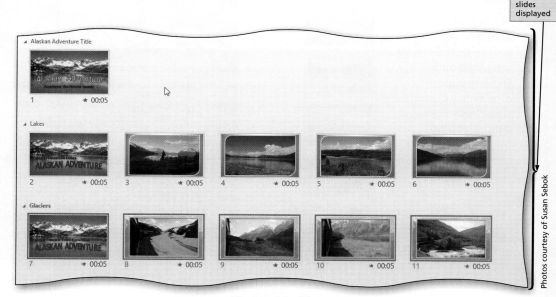

Photos courtesy of Susan Sebok

Figure 11–23

Other Ways

1. Press and hold or right-click section name, tap or click Move Section Up, Move Section Down, Collapse All, or Expand All on shortcut menu

TO SHOW A PRESENTATION WITH MANUAL TIMING

The Alaskan Adventure slides are set to display for specified times. If you desire to override the automatic timings and advance the slides manually, you would perform the following steps.

1. Display the SLIDE SHOW tab and then tap or click the 'Set Up Slide Show' button (SLIDE SHOW tab | Set Up group) to display the Set Up Show dialog box.

2. Tap or click Manually in the Advance slides area (Set Up Show dialog box) and then tap or click the OK button.

Break Point: If you wish to take a break, this is a good place to do so. Be sure to save the Alaskan Adventure file again and then you can exit PowerPoint. To resume at a later time, run PowerPoint, open the file called Alaskan Adventure, and continue following the steps from this location forward.

To Create a Custom Slide Show

1 CREATE & ORGANIZE SECTIONS | 2 CREATE CUSTOM SLIDE SHOW | 3 CREATE PHOTO ALBUM & ENHANCE ELEMENTS
4 SPECIFY CUSTOM SLIDE SIZE & ADD VIDEO CLIP | 5 SHARE & DISTRIBUTE PRESENTATION

Many presenters deliver their speeches in front of targeted audiences. For example, the director of human resources may present one set of slides for new employees, another set for potential retirees, and a third for managers concerned with new regulations and legislation. Slides for all these files may be contained in one file, and the presenter can elect to show particular slides to accompany specific speeches. PowerPoint allows you to create a **custom show** that displays only selected slides. The following steps create a custom show. *Why? You want to create a smaller file in case your speech time at the meeting is less than planned and you need to shorten your talk.*

1

• Tap or click the Normal view button to display the slides in Normal view and then display the SLIDE SHOW tab.

• Tap or click the 'Custom Slide Show' button (SLIDE SHOW tab | Start Slide Show group) to display the Custom Slide Show menu (Figure 11–24).

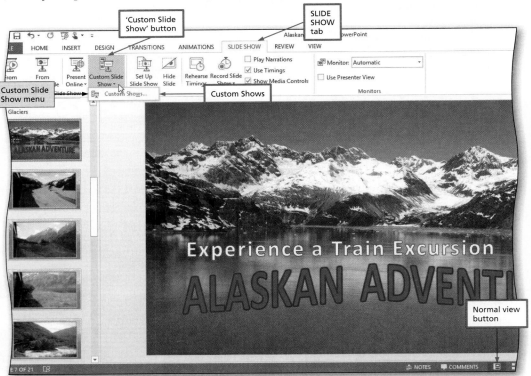

Figure 11–24

Photos courtesy of Susan Sebok

- Tap or click Custom Shows to open the Custom Shows dialog box (Figure 11–25).

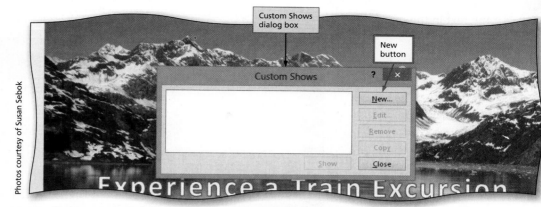

Figure 11–25

- Tap or click the New button (Custom Shows dialog box) to display the Define Custom Show dialog box.

- Tap or click the '1. Alaskan Adventure' check box in the Slides in presentation area to select this slide (Figure 11–26).

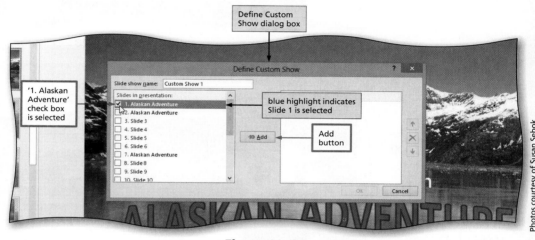

Figure 11–26

- Tap or click the Add button (Define Custom Show dialog box) to add this slide to the Slides in custom show area.

- Scroll down and then tap or click the check boxes for Slide 3, Slide 6, Slide 9, Slide 11, Slide 13, Slide 14, Slide 19, and Slide 21 in the Slides in presentation area.

- Tap or click the Add button (Define Custom Show dialog box) to add these slides to the Slides in custom show area (Figure 11–27).

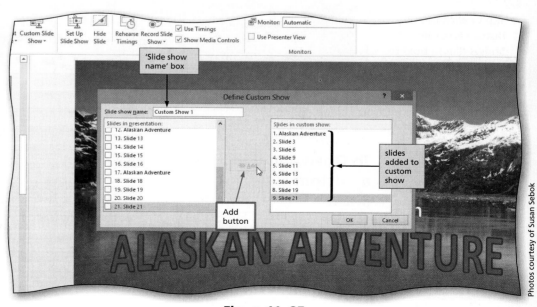

Figure 11–27

5

- Select the text in the 'Slide show name' text box (Define Custom Show dialog box) and then type **Travel Club Favorites** as the new name (Figure 11–28).

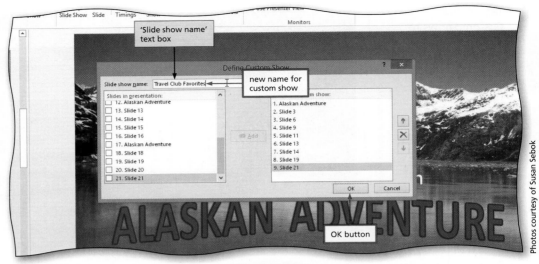

Figure 11–28

 6

- Tap or click the OK button (Define Custom Show dialog box) to create the new Travel Club Favorites custom show and display the Custom Shows dialog box (Figure 11–29).

7

- Tap or click the Close button (Custom Shows dialog box) to close the dialog box.

Figure 11–29

BTW
Hyperlinking Custom Shows
You can hyperlink to a custom show with slides relating to a specific topic in your presentation. Click the Hyperlink button (INSERT tab | Links group), click the 'Place in This Document' button, and then select the custom show in the Select a place in this document list.

To Open and Edit a Custom Slide Show

1 CREATE & ORGANIZE SECTIONS | 2 CREATE CUSTOM SLIDE SHOW | 3 CREATE PHOTO ALBUM & ENHANCE ELEMENTS
4 SPECIFY CUSTOM SLIDE SIZE & ADD VIDEO CLIP | 5 SHARE & DISTRIBUTE PRESENTATION

A PowerPoint file may have several custom slide shows. You can elect to display one of them at anytime depending upon the particular needs of your audience. If you need to reorder the slides, you can change the sequence easily. The following steps open a custom show and edit the slide sequence.

1

- With the SLIDE SHOW tab displaying, tap or click the 'Custom Slide Show' button (SLIDE SHOW tab | Start Slide Show group) to display the Custom Slide Show menu (Figure 11–30).

Q&A Why does 'Travel Club Favorites' display in the Custom Slide Show menu?
The names of any custom shows will be displayed in the menu. If desired, you could click this custom show name to run the slide show and display the selected slides.

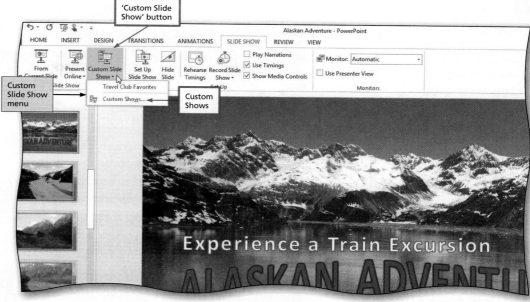

Figure 11–30

Photos courtesy of Susan Sebok

2

- Tap or click Custom Shows to display the Custom Shows dialog box (Figure 11–31).

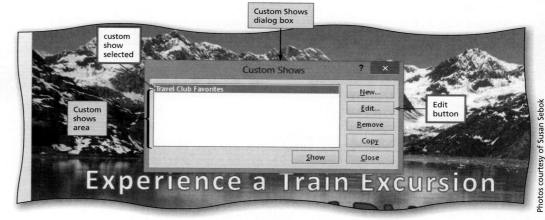

Figure 11–31

Photos courtesy of Susan Sebok

3

- With the Travel Club Favorites custom show selected in the Custom shows area, tap or click the Edit button (Custom Shows dialog box) to display the Define Custom Show dialog box.

- Tap or click Slide 19 in the Slides in custom show area to select it (Figure 11–32).

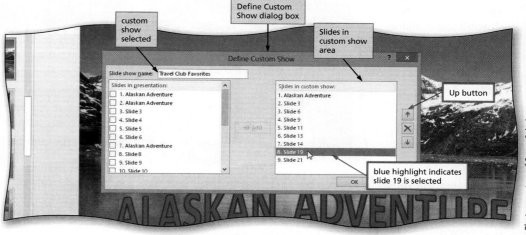

Figure 11–32

Photos courtesy of Susan Sebok

4

• Tap or click the Up button six times to move Slide 19 below Slide 1 as the second slide in the custom show (Figure 11–33).

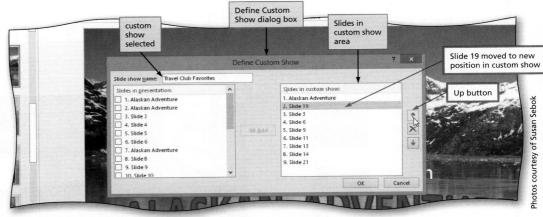

Figure 11–33

5

• Tap or click Slide 21 in the Slides in custom show area to select it and then tap or click the Up button six times to move Slide 21 below Slide 19 as the third slide in the custom show.

• Tap or click Slide 9 in the Slides in custom show area to select it and then tap or click the Down button once to move Slide 9 below Slide 11 as the seventh slide in the custom show (Figure 11–34).

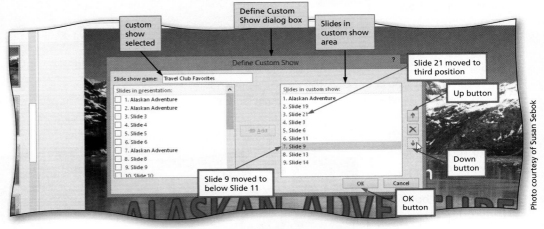

Figure 11–34

Q&A Can I move the slides so they display later in the custom show?

Yes. Select the slide you want to reorder and then tap or click the Down button.

6

• Tap or click the OK button (Define Custom Show dialog box) to create the revised Travel Club Favorites custom show and display the Custom Shows dialog box (Figure 11–35).

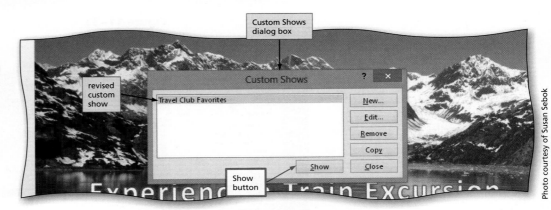

Figure 11–35

7

• Tap or click the Show button (Custom Shows dialog box) to run the Travel Club Favorites custom show.

• When all the slides have displayed, exit the custom show.

• Save the Alaskan Adventure file. Do not close this file because you are going to use it later in this project.

Break Point: If you wish to take a break, this is a good place to do so. You can exit PowerPoint now. To resume at a later time, run PowerPoint, open the file called Alaskan Adventure, and continue following the steps from this location forward.

CONSIDER THIS

Use photographs with sharp focus and contrast.
Clear, sharp pictures provide details that draw an audience into your presentation. High-quality photographs impress your audience and state that you have an eye for detail and take pride in your work. When your slides are projected on a large screen, any imperfection is magnified, so you must take care to select photographs that are in focus and have high contrast.

Creating a Photo Album

A PowerPoint **photo album** is a presentation that contains pictures to share with friends and business colleagues. It can contain a theme, a vibrant background, custom captions, a specific layout, frames around pictures, and boxes. You can enhance the quality of the pictures by increasing or decreasing brightness and contrast, and you can rotate the pictures in 90-degree increments. You also can change color pictures to display in black and white.

You can share your photo album in a variety of ways. You can, for example, email the file, publish it to the web, or print the pictures as handouts.

BTW
Printing in Grayscale
In this project you will convert your photos from color to black and white. If you desire to keep your images in color but want to print in black and white, PowerPoint provides that option. Display the FILE tab, tap or click the Print tab, tap or click the Color button, and then tap or click Grayscale. If you then want to print in color, tap or click the Grayscale button and then tap or click Color.

To Start a Photo Album and Add Pictures

1 CREATE & ORGANIZE SECTIONS | 2 CREATE CUSTOM SLIDE SHOW | 3 CREATE PHOTO ALBUM & ENHANCE ELEMENTS
4 SPECIFY CUSTOM SLIDE SIZE & ADD VIDEO CLIP | 5 SHARE & DISTRIBUTE PRESENTATION

Why? *Once you have gathered files of digital pictures, you can begin building a photo album.* You initially create the album and then later enhance its appearance. The following steps start a photo album and add pictures.

1

• Display the INSERT tab and then tap or click the 'New Photo Album' button (INSERT tab | Images group) to display the Photo Album dialog box (Figure 11–36).

Q&A
Why am I viewing a menu with the 'New Photo Album' and 'Edit Photo Album' commands instead of the Photo Album dialog box?
You mistakenly clicked the 'New Photo Album' arrow instead of the 'New Photo Album' button.

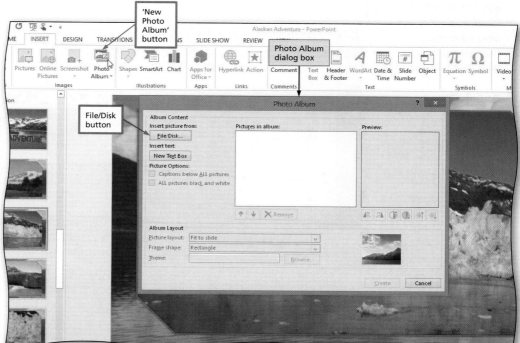

Photo courtesy of Susan Sebok

Figure 11–36

2

- Tap or click the File/Disk button to display the Insert New Pictures dialog box.

- If necessary, navigate to the location where your Data Files for Students are stored (in this case, the PowerPoint Chapter 11 folder in the CIS 101 folder [or your class folder] on your computer or SkyDrive) (Figure 11–37).

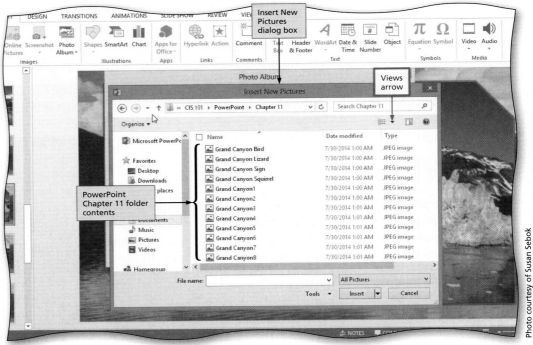

Figure 11–37

3

- If necessary, tap or click the Views arrow on the toolbar (Insert New Pictures dialog box) to display the view settings (Figure 11–38).

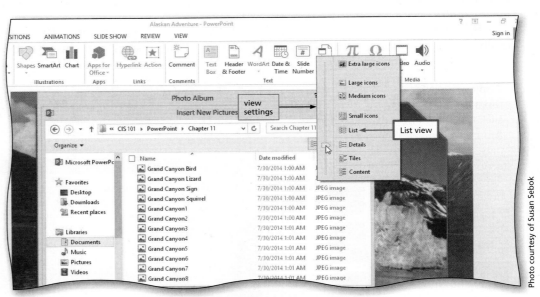

Figure 11–38

4

- Tap or click List in the view settings to change the view setting and display only the picture file names.

- Tap or click Mount Rainier in Background to select the file name, and then select the file names Pike Place Market, Safeco Field View from Water, Safeco Field, Salmon Bake, Seattle Great Wheel, Seattle Map, and Seattle Skyline as additional files to insert (Figure 11–39).

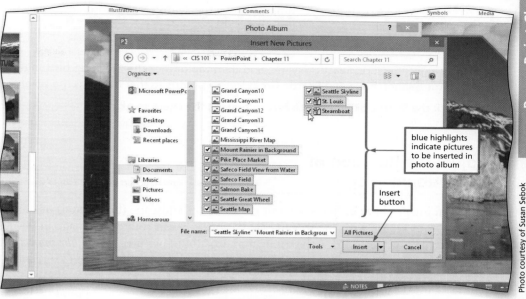

Figure 11–39

Photo courtesy of Susan Sebok

Q&A

If I mistakenly select a file name, how can I remove the selection?
Tap or click the file name again.

I'm having trouble selecting multiple files on the touch screen. What can I do?
You may need to use a mouse in combination with the onscreen keyboard CTRL key, or you can select and insert each file individually.

BTW

Selecting Slides or Other Items
To select sequential or adjacent files or items, select the first item, press and hold down the SHIFT key, and then select the last item. All items between the first and last item will be highlighted. To select nonadjacent files or items, select the first item and then press and hold down the CTRL key. While holding down the CTRL key, select additional items.

5

- Tap or click the Insert button (Insert New Pictures dialog box) to add the pictures to the album.

To Reorder Pictures in a Photo Album

1 CREATE & ORGANIZE SECTIONS | 2 CREATE CUSTOM SLIDE SHOW | 3 CREATE PHOTO ALBUM & ENHANCE ELEMENTS
4 SPECIFY CUSTOM SLIDE SIZE & ADD VIDEO CLIP | 5 SHARE & DISTRIBUTE PRESENTATION

PowerPoint inserted the pictures in alphabetical order, which may not be the desired sequence for your album. You easily can change the order of the pictures in the same manner that you change the slide order in a custom show. The following steps reorder the photo album pictures. *Why? Showing the map of Seattle at the beginning of the presentation orientates your audience members to the geography of the region.*

1

- Tap or click the check box for the seventh picture, Seattle Map, to select it (Figure 11–40).

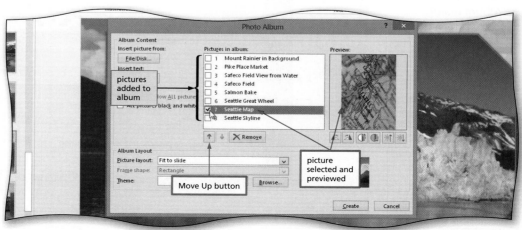

Figure 11–40

Photo courtesy of Susan Sebok

2

- Tap or click the Move Up button six times to move the Seattle Map photo upward so that it now is the first picture (picture 1) in the album.
- Tap or click the Seattle Map check box to remove the check mark.
- Select the eighth picture, Seattle Skyline, and then tap or click the Move Up button once to move this picture between the Salmon Bake and Seattle Great Wheel photos so that it now is the seventh picture.
- Tap or click the Seattle Skyline check box to remove the check mark.

To Adjust the Rotation of a Photo Album Image

1 CREATE & ORGANIZE SECTIONS | 2 CREATE CUSTOM SLIDE SHOW | 3 CREATE PHOTO ALBUM & ENHANCE ELEMENTS
4 SPECIFY CUSTOM SLIDE SIZE & ADD VIDEO CLIP | 5 SHARE & DISTRIBUTE PRESENTATION

Digital images have either a portrait (vertical) or landscape (horizontal) orientation. If a picture is displayed in your album with the wrong orientation, you can rotate the image in 90-degree increments to the left or the right. The following steps rotate a photo album picture. *Why? The map of Seattle is tilted toward the left, and audience members will be able to read the town names more easily if the picture is rotated.*

1

- Tap or click the check box for the first picture, Seattle Map, to select it and display a preview (Figure 11–41).

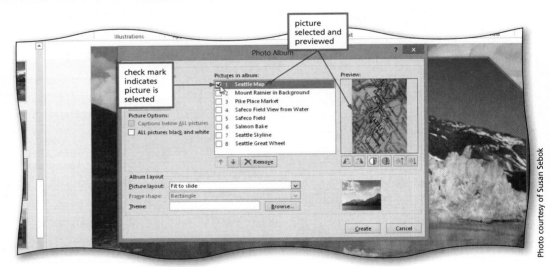

Figure 11–41

2

- Tap or click the 'Rotate Left 90°' button (Photo Album dialog box) to turn the picture to the left (Figure 11–42).

3

- Tap or click the Seattle Map check box to remove the check mark.

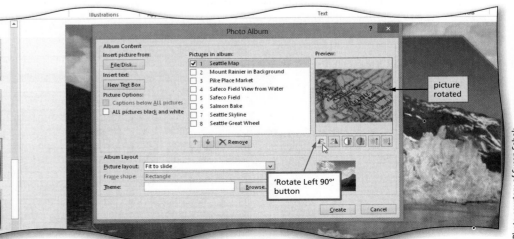

Figure 11–42

To Adjust the Contrast of a Photo Album Image

A picture you insert may need correcting to enhance its visual appeal. You can adjust the difference between the darkest and lightest areas of the picture by increasing or decreasing the contrast. The following steps adjust the contrast of a photo album picture. *Why?* *The Mount Rainier photo shows the mountain peak in the distance, and its prominence would be enhanced if the image had more dark and light areas.*

- Tap or click the check box for the second picture, Mount Rainier in Background, to select it and display a preview (Figure 11–43).

- Tap or click the Increase Contrast button (Photo Album dialog box) four times to change the contrast of this picture.

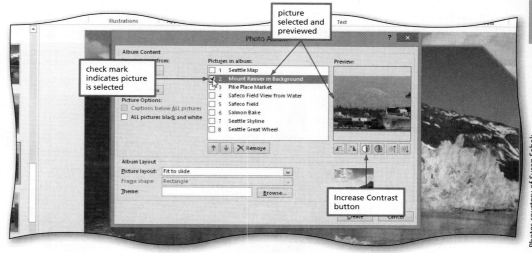

Figure 11–43

To Adjust the Brightness of a Photo Album Image

If a picture in the photo album is too light or too dark, you can adjust its brightness to enhance its appearance. The following step adjusts the brightness of a photo album picture. *Why?* *The Mount Rainier photo is somewhat dark, so increasing the brightness would help the colors stand out on the slide and give more depth to the image.*

- With the Mount Rainier picture selected, tap or click the Increase Brightness button (Photo Album dialog box) two times to intensify the colors in the picture (Figure 11–44).

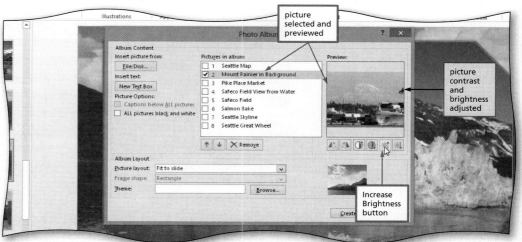

Figure 11–44

Photos courtesy of Susan Sebok

Photos courtesy of Susan Sebok

To Change a Photo Album Layout

PowerPoint inserts each photo album picture so that it fills, or fits, one entire slide. You can modify this layout to display two or four pictures on a slide, display a title, or add white space between the image and the slide edges. You also can add a white or black frame around the perimeter of each picture. The following steps change an album layout. *Why? The photos are spectacular, so you want to display only one on each slide. Adding a frame provides contrast between the photos and the background.*

- With the Photo Album dialog box displayed, tap or click the Picture layout arrow in the Album Layout area (Photo Album dialog box) to display the Picture layout list (Figure 11–45).

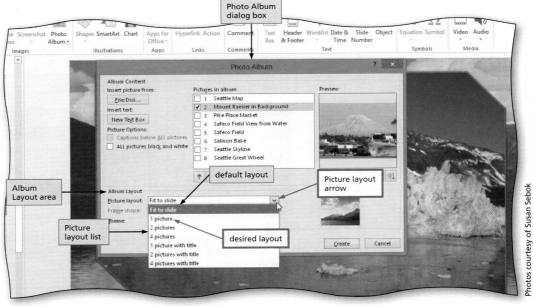

Figure 11–45

- Tap or click 1 picture in the Picture layout list to change the layout so that one picture is displayed on each slide and a rectangular frame is displayed around each picture.

- Tap or click the Frame shape arrow in the Album Layout area (Photo Album dialog box) to display the Frame shape list (Figure 11–46).

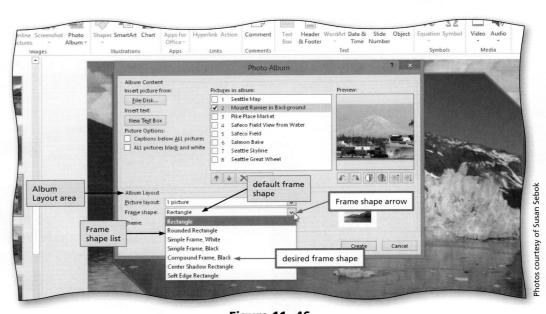

Figure 11–46

- Tap or click 'Compound Frame, Black' in the Frame shape list to add a double black frame around the picture.

To Add a Photo Album Theme

The themes that are used to design a presentation also are available to add to a photo album. These themes determine the colors and fonts that complement each other and increase the visual appeal of the slides. The following steps add a theme to the photo album. *Why? Seattle is known as the Emerald City, so you want to select a theme that has a green background and a simple layout and font that will complement the majestic photos.*

- Tap or click the Browse button in the Album Layout area (Photo Album dialog box) to display the Choose Theme dialog box.

- Tap or click Ion in the theme list to select this theme (Figure 11–47).

- Tap or click the Select button (Choose Theme dialog box) to apply this theme to the presentation.

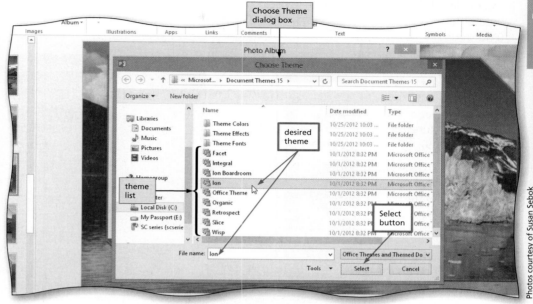

Figure 11–47

Photos courtesy of Susan Sebok

To Add Captions below All Pictures

If you desire a caption below each picture, you can request PowerPoint add this feature to the slides. The file name is displayed as the caption text, but you can edit and add effects to this text. The following step selects the option to add a caption below all pictures in the photo album. *Why? The audience members will see the text on the slide and hear you describe the images. Because they are using these two senses, they should be able to recall the information you are presenting. In addition, absent Travel Club members could view the presentation during their free time and learn the names of the places and objects presented on the slides.*

- In the Picture Options area (Photo Album dialog box), tap or click the 'Captions below ALL pictures' check box to select the check box (Figure 11–48).

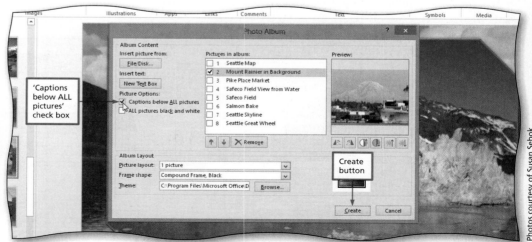

Figure 11–48

Photos courtesy of Susan Sebok

To Create a Photo Album

Once you have inserted the pictures, determined the picture sequence, layout, and frame shape, you are ready to make the photo album. *Why? You have specified all the information PowerPoint needs to create this album.* The following step creates the photo album.

1

- Tap or click the Create button (Photo Album dialog box) to close the dialog box and create a photo album with a title page and nine pictures (Figure 11–49).

Q&A
Why does a particular name display below the Photo Album title? PowerPoint displays the user name that was entered when the program was installed. To see this name, display the Backstage view, tap or click Options to display the PowerPoint Options dialog box, and then view or change the name entered in the User name box in the Personalize your copy of Microsoft Office area.

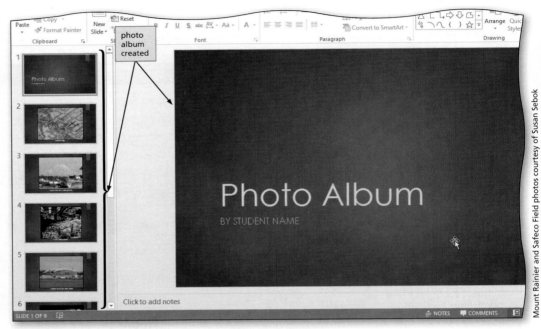

Figure 11–49

To Edit a Photo Album

Once you review the photo album PowerPoint creates, you can modify the contents by adding and deleting pictures, changing the layout and frames, and adding transitions. The following steps edit the photo album. *Why? You want to change the frame style and color, add a text box on a new slide, and add a transition to add interest and to give additional information to your audience members.*

1

- Display the INSERT tab and then tap or click the 'New Photo Album' arrow (INSERT tab | Images group) to display the New Photo Album menu (Figure 11–50).

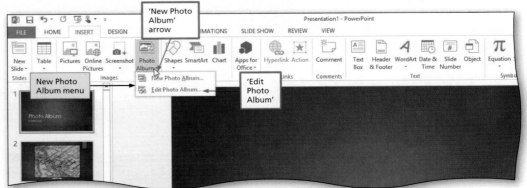

Figure 11–50

Mount Rainier and Safeco Field photos courtesy of Susan Sebok

Mount Rainier and Safeco Field photos courtesy of Susan Sebok

2

- Tap or click 'Edit Photo Album' in the menu to display the Edit Photo Album dialog box.

- Tap or click the Frame shape arrow to display the Frame shape list and then tap or click 'Simple Frame, White' in the list to change the frame from a compound black border to a single white border.

- Tap or click the 'New Text Box' button (Edit Photo Album dialog box) to insert a new slide in the album with the name, Text Box.

- Select the Text Box picture check box and then tap or click the Move Up button once to move this picture upward as the first picture in the Pictures in album list (Figure 11–51).

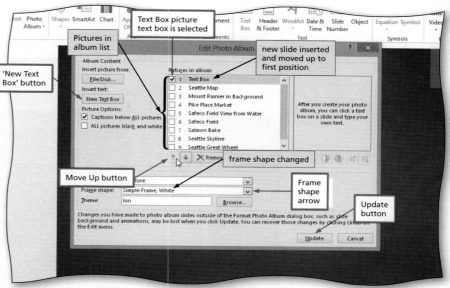

Figure 11–51

Q&A Can I insert a box on one slide that already has a picture?
Yes. Tap or click the Text Box button (INSERT tab | Text group) and then tap or click the slide where you want to insert the box. You then can arrange the box and picture on the slide.

3

- Tap or click the Update button (Edit Photo Album dialog box) to make the changes to the photo album.

- Apply the Gallery transition and then change the duration to 5 seconds for all slides.

To Insert and Format Text in a Photo Album

PowerPoint inserts text into the slides, such as the file name for captions and the user name associated with the Microsoft Office installation as the subtitle text on the title slide. You can revise and format this text by changing the font, font size, color, and any other font styles and effects. The following steps edit text in the photo album.

1 With Slide 1 displaying, select the title text, Photo Album, and then type `Scenic Seattle` as the replacement text.

2 Select the subtitle text, By Student Name, and then type `Explore the Emerald City - The Gateway to Alaska` as the replacement text.

3 Increase the font size of the subtitle text to 24 point.

4 Display Slide 2, select the words, Text Box, and then type `Seattle is the Pacific Northwest's largest city and is a major port for commercial trade. The city is the birthplace of Starbucks, Pearl Jam, and Jimi Hendrix.` as the replacement text.

5 Press the ENTER key two times and then type `Precipitation falls an average of 150 days per year.` as the second paragraph.

6 Display Slide 3, select the caption text, and then type `Seattle is located on an isthmus between Puget Sound and Lake Washington.` as the new caption.

BTW
Resetting Placeholders
You can reset all customization changes to the preset options. Tap or click the Reset button (HOME tab | Slides group) or press and hold or right-click the slide or thumbnail and then tap or click Reset Slide on the shortcut menu. To retain custom formatting changes and move the placeholders to their original locations, tap or click the Layout button (HOME tab | Slides group) or press and hold or right-click the slide or thumbnail and then click Layout on the shortcut menu. Then, reapply the active layout from the Layout gallery.

7 Display Slide 9, select the caption text, and then type **The Space Needle is a major focal point of the skyline.** as the new caption.

8 Display Slide 1 and then run the slide show.

9 Save the presentation with the file name, Seattle Photo Album (Figure 11–52).

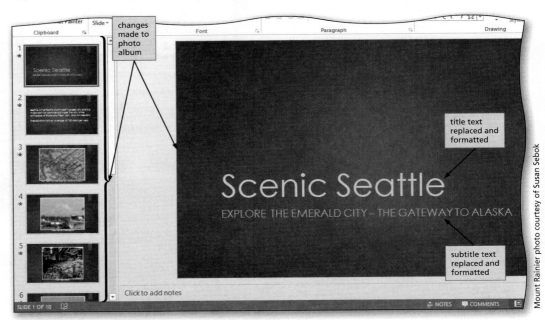

Figure 11–52

To Create Black-and-White Images in a Photo Album

Why? *Black-and-white pictures often generate interest and give a unique version of the color photographs. The series of shades ranging from black to white, or grayscale, provide a different perspective of our world.* The following steps edit a photo album to use black-and-white images.

1
- Display the INSERT tab, tap or click the 'New Photo Album' arrow, and then tap or click 'Edit Photo Album'.

- Tap or click the 'ALL pictures black and white' check box to select the check box (Figure 11–53).

Q&A Can I change the view to see my slides in grayscale or black and white?
Yes. Display the VIEW tab and then tap or click the Grayscale or the 'Black and White' button (Color/Grayscale group). The Grayscale option shows a variety of shades ranging from white to black whereas the Black and White option displays only black-and-white objects.

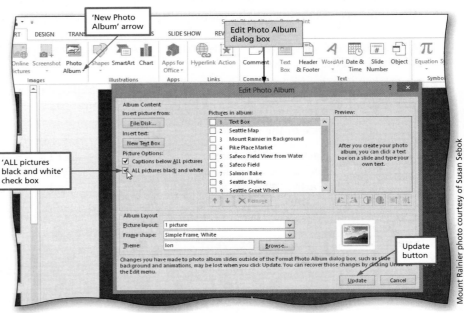

Figure 11–53

2

- Tap or click the Update button (Edit Photo Album dialog box) to change the photographs from color to black-and-white images on the slides.

- Run the slide show.

- Save the presentation with the file name, Seattle Photo Album Black and White.

- Print the presentation as a handout with three slides per page (Figure 11–54).

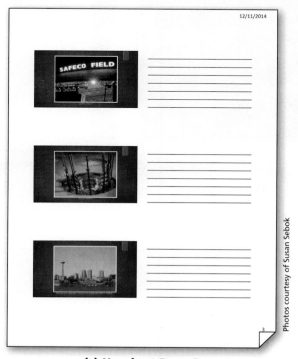

(a) Handout Page 1

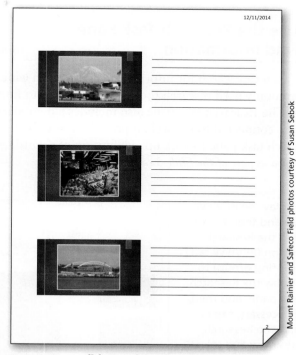

(b) Handout Page 2

(c) Handout Page 3

Photos courtesy of Susan Sebok

(d) Handout Page 4

Photos courtesy of Susan Sebok

Mount Rainier and Safeco Field photos courtesy of Susan Sebok

BTW

Conserving Ink and Toner

If you want to conserve ink or toner, you can instruct PowerPoint to print draft quality documents by tapping or clicking FILE on the ribbon to open the Backstage view, tapping or clicking Options in the Backstage view to display the PowerPoint Options dialog box, tapping or clicking Advanced in the left pane (PowerPoint Options dialog box), sliding or scrolling to the Print area in the right pane, placing a check mark in the 'Use draft quality' check box, and then tapping or clicking the OK button. Then, use the Backstage view to print the document as usual.

Figure 11–54

BTW
Printing Document Properties
To print document properties, tap or click FILE on the ribbon to open the Backstage view, tap or click the Print tab in the Backstage view to display the Print gallery, tap or click the first button in the Settings area to display a list of options specifying what you can print, tap or click Document Info in the list to specify you want to print the document properties instead of the actual document, and then tap or click the Print button in the Print gallery to print the document properties on the currently selected printer.

To Use the Research Task Pane to Find Information

1 CREATE & ORGANIZE SECTIONS | 2 CREATE CUSTOM SLIDE SHOW | 3 CREATE PHOTO ALBUM & ENHANCE ELEMENTS
4 SPECIFY CUSTOM SLIDE SIZE & ADD VIDEO CLIP | 5 SHARE & DISTRIBUTE PRESENTATION

You can search for information regarding a wide variety of topics using PowerPoint's reference materials. A commonly used research tool is the thesaurus to find synonyms for words on your slides or in the Notes pane. The Research task pane also includes a dictionary, encyclopedia, and translation services. In addition, if you are connected to the web, it provides a search engine and other useful websites. The following steps use the Research task pane to look up a definition of a word. *Why? You want to know more about the word, isthmus, which you typed as part of the Slide 3 caption text.*

1

- Display the REVIEW tab and then tap or click the Research button (REVIEW tab | Proofing group) to display the Research task pane, and then, if necessary, tap or click the Research list arrow and select 'All Reference Books' (Figure 11–55).

Q&A Why does my Research task pane look different?
Your computer's settings and Microsoft's website search settings determine the way your Research task pane is displayed.

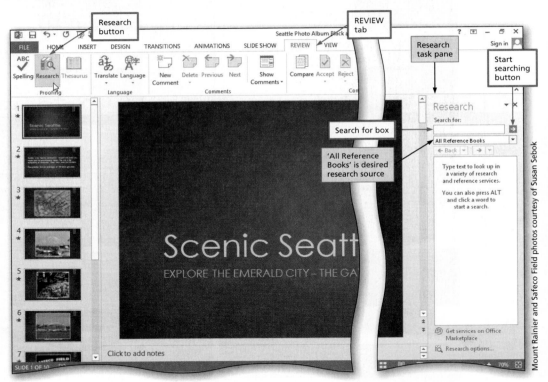

Figure 11–55

Mount Rainier and Safeco Field photos courtesy of Susan Sebok

2

- Type `isthmus` in the Search for box and then tap or click the Start searching button to perform a search for definitions of this word (Figure 11–56).

Q&A

What is Encarta?
It is the name of Microsoft's encyclopedia, which contains thousands of articles, illustrations, photos, and other reference materials.

What should I do if I see the message, No results were found, instead of a list of search results?
If a 'Get services on Office Marketplace' icon is displayed at the bottom of the Research pane, tap or click it, follow instructions to update your services, and then repeat your search.

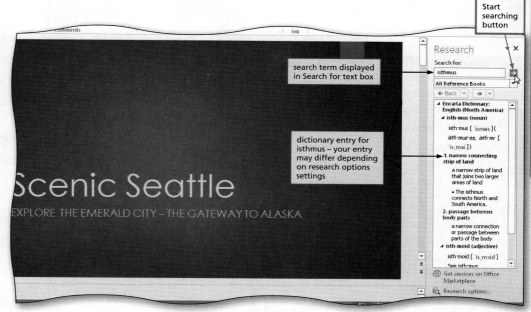

Figure 11–56

3

- Tap or click the Search for arrow in the Research task pane to display a list of search locations (Figure 11–57).

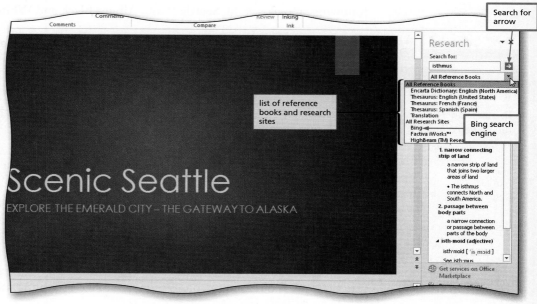

Figure 11–57

4

- Tap or click Bing in the list to perform an Internet search for websites with information about this search term (Figure 11–58).

Q&A

What is Bing?
It is the name of Microsoft's search engine, which is a program that locates websites, webpages, images, videos, news, maps, and other information related to a specific topic.

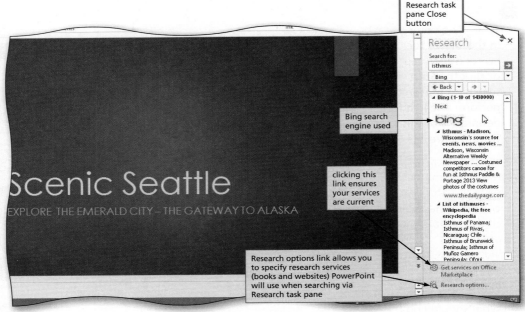

Figure 11–58

5

- Tap or click the Close button in the Research pane.

To Close a Presentation

The second photo album with the black-and-white pictures is complete. The following step closes the Seattle Photo Album Black and White file.

1 With the Backstage view open, tap or click Close to close the open Seattle Photo Album Black and White file without exiting PowerPoint.

Break Point: If you wish to take a break, this is a good place to do so. You can exit PowerPoint now. To resume at a later time, run PowerPoint and continue following the steps from this location forward.

Sharing and Distributing a Presentation

Many people design PowerPoint presentations to accompany a speech given in front of an audience, and they also develop slide shows to share with family, work associates, and friends in a variety of ways. For example, they can print a slide on thick paper and send the document through the mail. They also can email the file or create a video to upload to a website or view on a computer. Video files can become quite large in file size, so PowerPoint allows you to reduce the size by compressing the file.

CONSIDER THIS

Use hyperlinks to show slides with landscape and portrait orientations.

When you are creating your presentation, you have the option to display all your slides in either the default landscape orientation or in portrait orientation. You may, however, desire to have slides with both orientations during a single presentation. Using hyperlinks is one solution to mixing the orientations. Apply a hyperlink to an object on the last slide in one orientation and then hyperlink to another presentation with slides in the other orientation. If you desire to hyperlink to one particular slide in a second presentation, tap or click the Bookmark button in the Insert Hyperlink dialog box and then select the title of the slide you want to use as your link. Once you have displayed the desired slides in the second presentation, create another hyperlink from that presentation back to a slide in your original presentation.

To Change the Slide Orientation

By default, PowerPoint displays slides in landscape orientation, where the width dimension is greater than the height dimension. You can change this setting to specify that the slides display in portrait orientation. ***Why?*** *In portrait orientation, the height dimension is greater than the width dimension, so it is useful to display tall objects, people who are standing, or faces.* The following steps change the slide orientation.

1

- Open the presentation, Travel Expo, located on the Data Files for Students.

- Display the DESIGN tab and then tap or click the Slide Size button (DESIGN tab | Customize group) to display the Slide Size gallery (Figure 11–59).

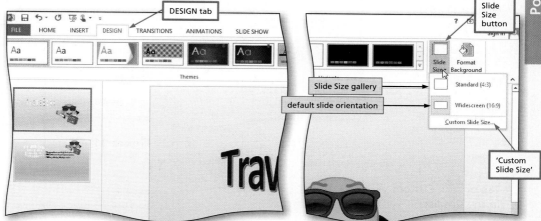

Figure 11–59

2

- Tap or click 'Custom Slide Size' to display the Slide Size dialog box and then tap or click Portrait in the Slides area of the Orientation section to change the slide orientation from Landscape to Portrait (Figure 11–60).

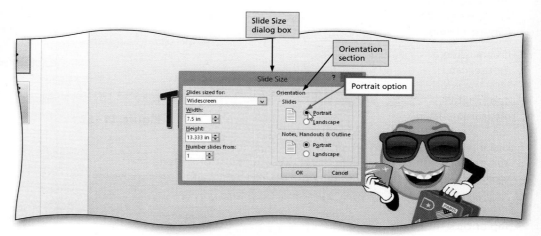

Figure 11–60

To Set Up a Custom Size

Why? *To announce the Travel Expo event and encourage community members to attend, you want to mail postcards to the residents' homes.* To simplify the process, you can create a PowerPoint slide that is the precise measurement of a postcard, print the card on heavy paper stock, and mail the card to club members. You can specify that your PowerPoint slides are a precise dimension. The steps on the next page change the slide size to a custom size.

- With the Slide Size dialog box displaying, tap or click the 'Slides sized for' arrow to display the size list (Figure 11–61).

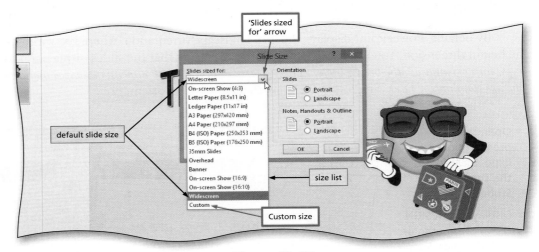

Figure 11–61

- Tap or click Custom in the size list.
- Change the slide width to 5 inches in the Width box.
- Change the slide height to 7 inches in the Height box (Figure 11–62).

Q&A If I am using a mouse, can I type the width and height measurements in the boxes instead of clicking the down arrows repeatedly?

Yes. You also can click and hold down the mouse button instead of repeatedly clicking the arrows until the desired dimensions are displayed.

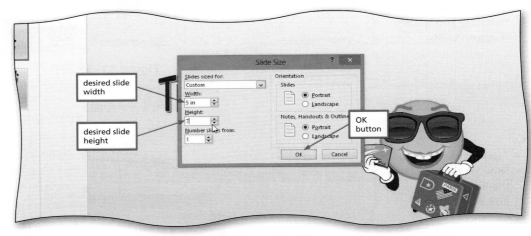

Figure 11–62

- Tap or click the OK button (Slide Size dialog box) to display the Microsoft PowerPoint dialog box (Figure 11–63).

- Tap or click the Ensure Fit button (Microsoft PowerPoint dialog box) to apply the custom sizes and close the dialog box.

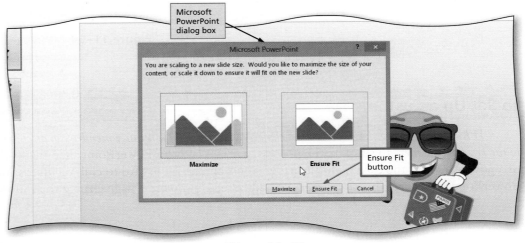

Figure 11–63

To Display Multiple Presentation Windows Simultaneously

1 CREATE & ORGANIZE SECTIONS | 2 CREATE CUSTOM SLIDE SHOW | 3 CREATE PHOTO ALBUM & ENHANCE ELEMENTS
4 SPECIFY CUSTOM SLIDE SIZE & ADD VIDEO CLIP | 5 SHARE & DISTRIBUTE PRESENTATION

Why? *When you are reviewing elements of several presentations, it often is efficient and convenient to open and display them simultaneously on the screen.* The following steps display three open presentations simultaneously.

1

- Open the presentation, Glacier Bay, located on the Data Files for Students and then display the VIEW tab (Figure 11–64).

- If necessary, open the Alaskan Adventure file if you closed it earlier in this project.

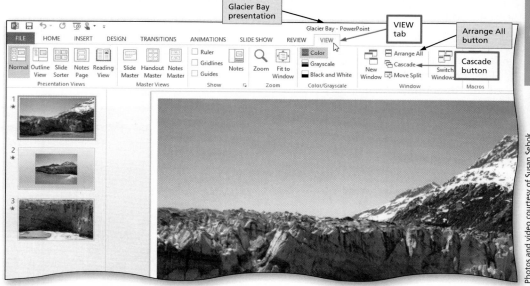

Figure 11–64

Photos and video courtesy of Susan Sebok

2

- Tap or click the Cascade button (VIEW tab | Window group) to display the three open presentations – Glacier Bay, Travel Expo, and Alaskan Adventure – from the upper-left to the lower-right corners of the screen.

Q&A What is the difference between the Cascade button and the Arrange All button?

When you tap or click the Cascade button, the open windows display overlapped, or stacked, on each other. Tapping or clicking the Arrange All button tiles all the open windows side by side on the screen. Each window may display narrower than in Normal view so that all the open windows are visible simultaneously.

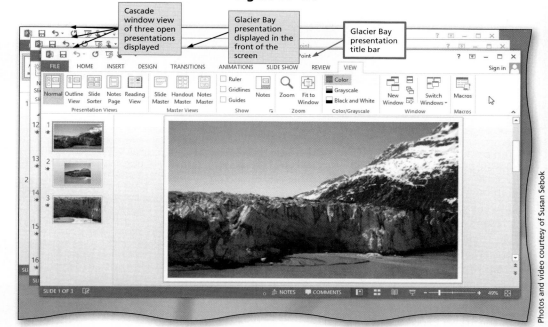

Figure 11–65

Photos and video courtesy of Susan Sebok

- If necessary, tap or click the Glacier Bay presentation title bar to display that presentation in the front of the screen (Figure 11–65).

Q&A The Glacier Bay title bar is not visible on my screen. Can I move the presentation windows so that it is visible?

Yes. You can drag the presentation title bars to arrange the windows.

To Copy a Video File

Why? Slide 2 in the Glacier Bay presentation contains a video clip of the glacier that you want to insert at the bottom of Slide 2 in the Travel Expo file. With multiple presentations open simultaneously on your screen, you can view all the slides quickly and decide which elements of one presentation you desire to copy to another. The following steps copy the video file from Slide 2 of the Glacier Bay presentation to Slide 2 of the Travel Expo presentation.

1

- Tap or click the Slide 2 thumbnail of the Glacier Bay presentation to display that slide.

- Press and hold or right-click the video image in the center of the slide to select it and to display the shortcut menu (Figure 11–66).

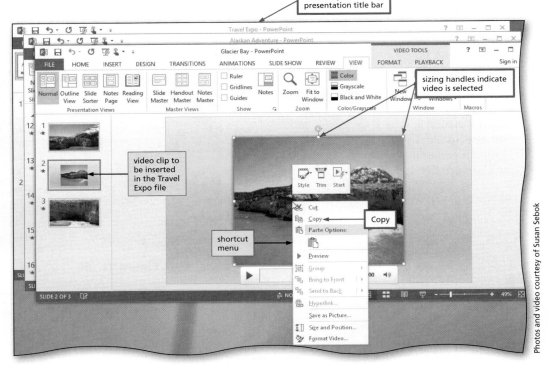

Figure 11–66

2

- Tap or click Copy on the shortcut menu.

- Tap or click the Travel Expo presentation title bar to display that presentation in the front of the screen.

- Tap or click the Slide 2 thumbnail of the Travel Expo presentation to display that slide.

- Press and hold or right-click the slide to display the shortcut menu and then point to the 'Use Destination Theme' button under Paste Options to display a preview of the video clip on that slide (Figure 11–67).

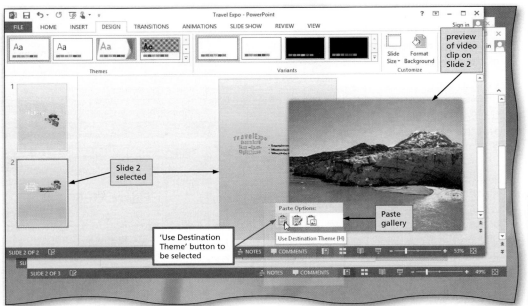

Figure 11–67

3

- Tap or click the 'Use Destination Theme' button in the Paste gallery to insert the video into the slide.

- If necessary, drag the Travel Expo presentation title bar downward so the Glacier Bay title bar is visible (Figure 11–68).

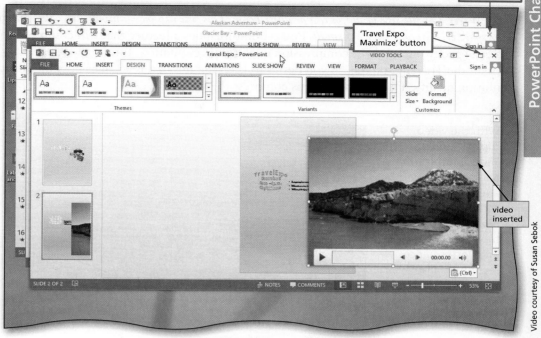

Figure 11–68

Video courtesy of Susan Sebok

4

- Tap or click the 'Glacier Bay Close' button to close that presentation.

- Tap or click the 'Travel Expo Maximize' button to maximize the PowerPoint window.

- Select the video, display the VIDEO TOOLS FORMAT tab, size the video to 3" × 4", and move the clip to the location shown in Figure 11–69.

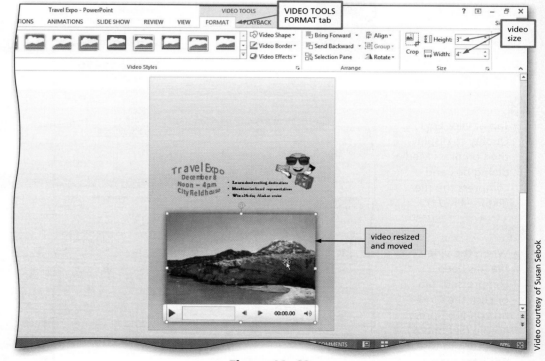

Figure 11–69

Video courtesy of Susan Sebok

To Compress a Video File

Why? *The file size of videos can be quite large. This size can pose a problem if you desire to email a presentation or if the space on a storage device is small.* PowerPoint includes a feature that will compress your file to reduce its size. You can specify one of three compression qualities: Presentation, Internet, or Low. In this project, you are going to email the Travel Expo file, so you desire to keep the file size as small as possible without sacrificing too much resolution quality. The following steps compress the video file.

- With the video clip selected on Slide 2, display the Backstage view and then tap or click the Compress Media button (Info tab | Media Size and Performance section) to display the Compress Media menu (Figure 11–70).

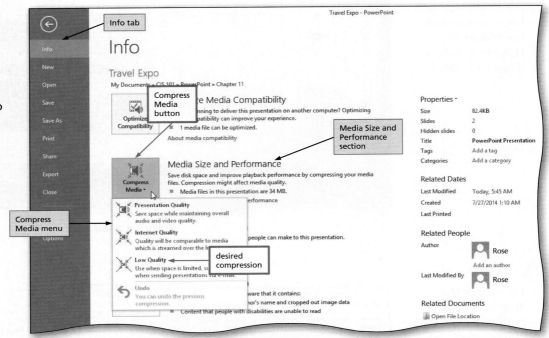

Figure 11–70

- Tap or click Low Quality to display the Compress Media dialog box and compress the file (Figure 11–71).

- When the video file has been compressed, tap or click the Close button (Compress Media dialog box) to return to the Backstage view.

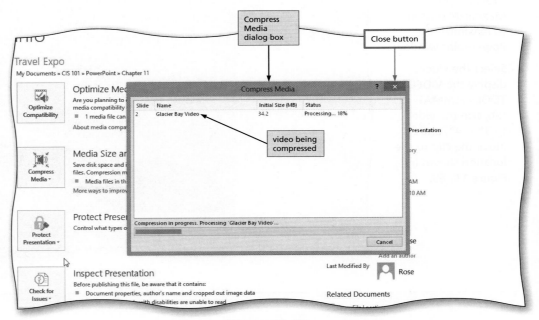

Figure 11–71

To Record Narration

In some situations, you may want your viewers to hear recorded narration that accompanies slides. You can record narration separately and then add this file to the slide. You also can record narration while the slide show is running. To record this narration, you would perform the following steps.

1. Display the SLIDE SHOW tab and then tap or click the 'Record Slide Show' arrow (SLIDE SHOW tab | Set Up group).
2. Tap or click 'Start Recording from Beginning' if you want to begin with the first slide or click 'Start Recording from Current Slide' if you want to begin with the slide that is displaying on your screen.
3. Tap or click the 'Narrations and laser pointer' check box (Record Slide Show dialog box) and, if appropriate, tap or click the 'Slide and animation timings' check box ('Record Slide Show' dialog box) to select or remove the check mark.
4. Tap or click the Start Recording button (Record Slide Show dialog box).
5. When you have finished speaking, press and hold or right-click the slide and then tap or click End Show on the shortcut menu.

To Preview Narration

Once you have recorded narration, you can play the audio to review the sound. To preview this narration, you would perform the following steps.

1. In Normal view, tap or click the sound icon on the slide.
2. Display the AUDIO TOOLS PLAYBACK tab and then tap or click the Play button (AUDIO TOOLS PLAYBACK tab | Preview group).

To Show a Presentation with or without Narration

If you have recorded narration to accompany your slides, you can choose whether to include this narration when you run your slide show. You would perform the following steps to run the slide show either with or without narration.

1. Display the SLIDE SHOW tab and then tap or click the Play Narrations check box (SLIDE SHOW tab | Set Up group) to remove the check from the box.
2. If you have chosen to show the presentation without narration and then desire to allow audience members to hear this recording, tap or click the Play Narrations check box (SLIDE SHOW tab | Set Up group) to check this option.

BTW

Turn Off Slide Timings

If you recorded narration with slide timings, you might decide to play the comments for your audience but want to advance the slides manually. PowerPoint gives you the option to turn slide timings off and then turn them back on without having to recreate them. Tap or click the 'Set Up Slide Show' button (SLIDE SHOW tab | Set Up group) and then tap or click Manually in the Advance slides area (Set Up Show dialog box). To turn the slide timings back on, tap or click 'Using timings, if present' in the Advance slides area (Set Up Show dialog box).

BTW

Certification

The Microsoft Office Specialist (MOS) program provides an opportunity for you to obtain a valuable industry credential — proof that you have the PowerPoint 2013 skills required by employers. For more information, visit the Certification resource on the Student Companion Site located on www.cengagebrain.com. For detailed instructions about accessing available resources, visit www.cengage.com/ct/studentdownload or see the inside back cover of this book.

To Email a Slide Show from within PowerPoint

1 CREATE & ORGANIZE SECTIONS | 2 CREATE CUSTOM SLIDE SHOW | 3 CREATE PHOTO ALBUM & ENHANCE ELEMENTS
4 SPECIFY CUSTOM SLIDE SIZE & ADD VIDEO CLIP | 5 SHARE & DISTRIBUTE PRESENTATION

Why? *Presenters often email their presentations to friends and colleagues to solicit feedback and share their work.* PowerPoint offers a convenient method of emailing a presentation directly within PowerPoint. The steps on the next page create a message, attach a presentation, and send a slide show to Mary Halen.

- With the Backstage view displaying, display the Share gallery.

- Tap or click the Email button to display the Email options (Figure 11–72).

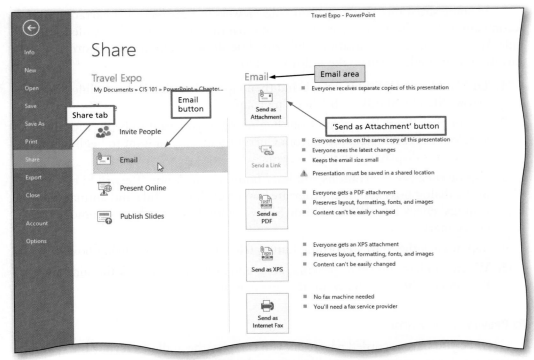

Figure 11–72

- Tap or click the 'Send as Attachment' button in the Email area to open the Travel Expo.pptx – Message (HTML) window in Microsoft Outlook (Figure 11–73).

Q&A Must I use Microsoft Outlook to send this email message?
No, you do not have to have Outlook installed; however, you need to have an email program installed in Windows to send the email. If you don't use Outlook, you could install Windows Live Mail or another email program.

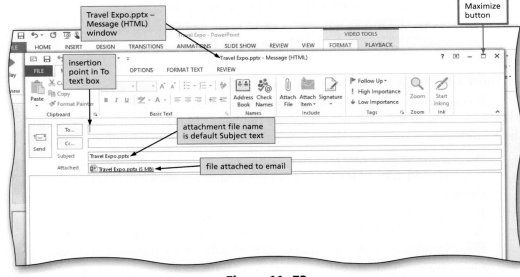

Figure 11–73

- If necessary, tap or click the Maximize button in the Travel Expo.pptx – Message (HTML) window to maximize the window.

- With the insertion point in the To box, type **mary_halen@hotmail.com** to enter the email address of the recipient.

- Tap or click to position the insertion point in the Subject box, select the file name that is displaying, and then type **Upcoming Travel Expo** as the subject.

- Tap in the message area or press the TAB key two times to move the insertion point into the message area.

4

- Type **Miss Halen,** as the greeting line.

- Press the ENTER key to move the insertion point to the beginning of the next line.

- Type **The announcement for our upcoming Travel Expo is attached. I hope you will be able to attend.** to enter the message text.

- Press the ENTER key twice to insert a blank line and move the insertion point to the beginning of the next line. Type **George Alexander** as the signature line (Figure 11–74).

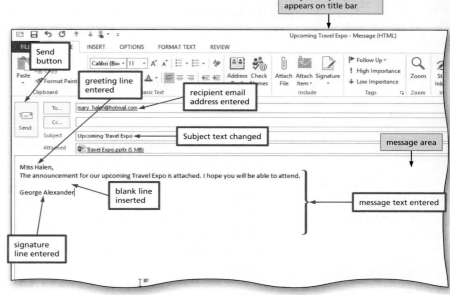

Figure 11–74

Q&A May I type my own name instead of George's name?

Yes. You may desire to have your name on the title slide, or your instructor may request that you substitute your name or provide other identifying information.

5

- Tap or click the Send button in the message header to send the email message and to close the message window.

To Run and Save the Presentation

When you run the Travel Expo presentation, the video will play automatically because the file had that setting in the Glacier Bay presentation. The following steps run the slide show and then save and close the document.

1 Display Slide 1 and then run the presentation.

2 Save the presentation with the file name, Travel Expo Mail.

3 Display the Backstage view and then tap or click Close to close the Travel Expo Mail file without exiting PowerPoint.

BTW

Restricting Permissions

You can allow PowerPoint users to see your presentation but not allow them to change the slide content, copy the slides, or print the presentation. To protect your presentation, display the FILE tab, display the Info tab in the Backstage view, tap or click the Protect Presentation button, tap or click the Restrict Access button, and then tap or click 'Connect to Rights Management Servers and get templates'.

Rehearse, rehearse, rehearse.

Speakers should spend as much time practicing their presentations as they do preparing their PowerPoint slides. Frequently, however, they use the majority of their preparation time designing and tweaking the slides. Audience members expect to see a presenter who is prepared, confident, and enthusiastic. Practicing the presentation helps convey this image. As you rehearse, focus on a strong introduction that grasps the audience's attention and previews the main points of your talk. You have only one chance to make a good first impression, so begin the speech by establishing eye contact with audience members in various parts of the room. Resist the urge to stare at the slides projected on the screen. Your audience came to your presentation to hear you speak, and rehearsing will help you deliver a high-quality talk that exceeds their expectations.

CONSIDER THIS

TO PRESENT A SLIDE SHOW ONLINE

Microsoft's Office Presentation Service feature allows you to share your presentation remotely with anyone having an Internet connection. As you display your slides, they see a synchronized view of your slide show in their web browser,

BTW
**Configuring Slide
Show Resolution**
You can change the
resolution you want to use
to display your presentation.
This feature is valuable when
your computer is connected
to two different monitors,
when you are delivering
your presentation using a
computer other than the one
used to create the slides, or
when the projector does not
support the resolution you
specified when you saved the
presentation. To configure
the resolution, tap or click
the 'Set Up Slide Show'
button (SLIDE SHOW tab |
Set Up group), tap or click
the Resolution arrow (Set Up
Show dialog box), and then
select the new resolution.

even if they do not have PowerPoint installed on their computers. To present your presentation, you would perform the following steps.

1. Tap or click the Present Online arrow (SLIDE SHOW tab | Start Slide Show group) to display the Present Online menu.

2. Tap or click 'Office Presentation Service' to display the Present Online dialog box.

3. Tap or click the CONNECT button to agree to the service terms, if necessary, enter your Windows Live ID email address, tap or click the Next button (Sign in dialog box), enter your Windows Live ID email address and password, and then tap or click the Sign in button (Sign in dialog box).

4. After PowerPoint has connected to the service and completed preparing the presentation, share the presentation link with up to 50 remote viewers and then tap or click the START PRESENTATION button (Present Online dialog box). People visiting the website can view your presentation with any annotations you make.

5. When you have displayed the last slide, tap or click the 'End Online Presentation' button (PRESENT ONLINE tab | Present Online group) and then tap or click the 'End Online Presentation' button (Microsoft PowerPoint dialog box).

To Create a Video

1 CREATE & ORGANIZE SECTIONS | 2 CREATE CUSTOM SLIDE SHOW | 3 CREATE PHOTO ALBUM & ENHANCE ELEMENTS
4 SPECIFY CUSTOM SLIDE SIZE & ADD VIDEO CLIP | 5 SHARE & DISTRIBUTE PRESENTATION

Why? *Watching video files is a common activity with the advent of easy-to-use recording devices and websites that host these files.* You can convert your PowerPoint presentation to a video file and upload it to a website or share the file with people who do not have PowerPoint installed on their computers. The following steps create a video of the Alaskan Adventure presentation.

- Display the Alaskan Adventure file and, if necessary, tap or click the Maximize button in the title bar to maximize the window.

- Display the Backstage view and then display the Export gallery.

- Tap or click the 'Create a Video' button to display the Create a Video section.

- If 'Internet & DVD' is not selected as the screen resolution in the Create a Video section, tap or click the 'Computer & HD Displays' button to display a list of screen resolutions (Figure 11–75).

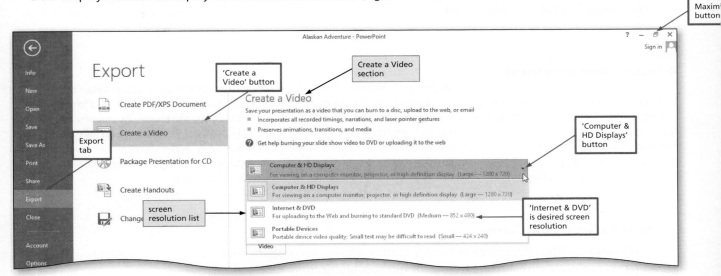

Figure 11–75

2

- If 'Internet & DVD' is not selected as the screen resolution, tap or click the 'Internet & DVD' button to select the Medium (852 × 480) resolution.

- If 'Don't Use Recorded Timings and Narrations' is not selected as the default duration, tap or click the 'Use Recorded Timings and Narrations' button in the Create a Video section to display a list of recording options (Figure 11–76).

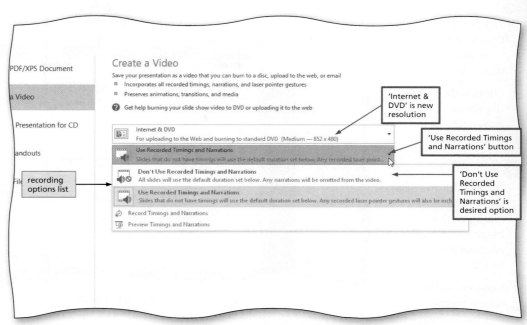

Figure 11–76

3

- Tap or click 'Don't Use Recorded Timings and Narrations' to select that option.

- Change the 'Seconds spent on each slide' time to 10 seconds (Figure 11–77).

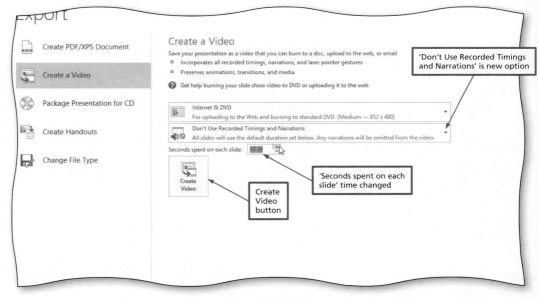

Figure 11–77

BTW

Quick Reference

For a table that lists how to complete the tasks covered in this book using touch gestures, the mouse, ribbon, shortcut menu, and keyboard, see the Quick Reference Summary at the back of this book, or visit the Quick Reference resource on the Student Companion Site located on www.cengagebrain.com. For detailed instructions about accessing available resources, visit www.cengage.com/ct/studentdownload or see the inside back cover of this book.

4

- Tap or click the Create Video button to open the Save As dialog box.

- Change the video file name to Alaskan Adventure Video (Figure 11–78).

5

- Tap or click the Save button (Save As dialog box) to begin creating the Alaskan Adventure Video file.

Q&A Does PowerPoint take a long period of time to create the video?

Yes. It may take several minutes to export the presentation to a video. Windows Media Player will display an error message stating that the file is in use if you attempt to open the video file while it is being created.

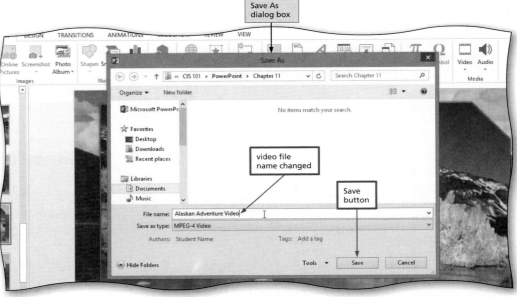

Figure 11–78

6

- When the video has been created, save the presentation again.

BTW
Practice Using Presenter View
One of the new features in PowerPoint 2013 is Presenter view, which allows a speaker to use dual monitors: one that displays what the audience is seeing, and another with controls to aid the presenter. You can rehearse using Presenter view with one monitor so that you are comfortable using the features. Be certain that 'Use Presenter View' is selected (SLIDE SHOW tab | Monitors group) and then press ALT+F5. You will not be able to edit the slides while using Presenter view.

BTW
Printing Selections
When you are developing slides or creating handouts for a particular audience, you may not want to print every slide in your presentation. To print specific slides, select the desired slides in the Thumbnail pane. Then, display the FILE tab, tap or click the Print tab in the Backstage view, tap or click the first button in the Settings area, tap or click Print Selection in the list to specify you want to print the slides you have selected, and then tap or click the Print button in the Print gallery to print these slides.

TO SET UP PRESENTER VIEW

Experienced speakers often deliver a presentation using two monitors: one to display their speaker notes privately, and a second to display the slides and project them on a large screen for the audience to view. PowerPoint's Presenter view supports the use of two monitors connected to one computer so presenters can view the slide currently being projected while viewing the slide thumbnails, seeing a preview of the next slide or animation, reading their speaker notes, viewing the elapsed time, lightening or darkening the audience's screen, or customizing the presentation by skipping the next slide or reviewing a slide previously displayed. A computer must support the use of multiple monitors and must be configured to use this feature. To use Presenter view, you would perform the following step.

1. Display the SLIDE SHOW tab and then tap or click the 'Use Presenter View' check box (SLIDE SHOW tab | Monitors group).

To Run and Print the Presentation

The presentation now is complete. You should run the slide show, print handouts, and then exit PowerPoint.

1 Run the slide show.

2 Print the presentation as a handout with six horizontal slides per page (Figure 11–79).

3 Exit PowerPoint, closing all open documents.

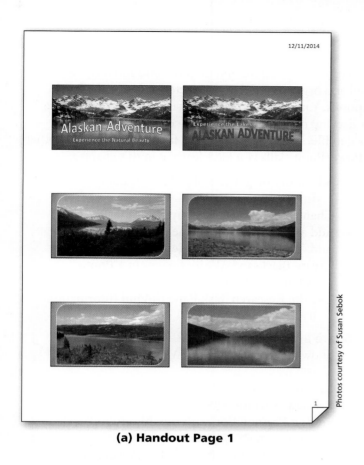

(a) Handout Page 1

(b) Handout Page 2

(c) Handout Page 3

(d) Handout Page 4

Figure 11–79

Chapter Summary

In this chapter you have learned how to organize a presentation into sections and then rename and move entire sections in the file. You then created a photo album, added and organized pictures, selected a theme and layout, adjusted a photo's contrast and brightness, and edited captions. You also changed the images to black and white in a separate photo album. Then, you specified a custom size and modified two slides by changing the slide orientation to portrait and inserting and compressing a video file. You then emailed the file and converted another file to video. The items listed below include all the new PowerPoint skills you have learned in this chapter.

Add and Compress a Video Clip
Display Multiple Presentation Windows Simultaneously (PPT 701)
Copy a Video File (PPT 702)
Compress a Video File (PPT 704)

Create and Organize Sections
Insert Slides with a Section Layout (PPT 669)
Arrange Slides in Slide Sorter View (PPT 672)
Create a Section Break (PPT 673)
Rename a Section (PPT 676)
Collapse and Reorder Sections (PPT 678)

Develop a Photo Album
Start a Photo Album and Add Pictures (PPT 685)
Reorder Pictures in a Photo Album (PPT 687)
Create a Photo Album (PPT 692)
Edit a Photo Album (PPT 692)

Develop and Edit a Custom Slide Show
Create a Custom Slide Show (PPT 680)
Open and Edit a Custom Slide Show (PPT 682)

Enhance Photo Album Elements
Adjust the Rotation of a Photo Album Image (PPT 688)
Adjust the Contrast of a Photo Album Image (PPT 689)

Adjust the Brightness of a Photo Album
Image (PPT 689)
Change a Photo Album Layout (PPT 690)
Add a Photo Album Theme (PPT 691)
Add Captions below All Pictures (PPT 691)
Create Black-and-White Images in a Photo Album (PPT 694)
Use the Research Task Pane to Find Information (PPT 696)

Share and Distribute a Presentation
Show a Presentation with Manual Timing (PPT 680)
Record Narration (PPT 705)
Preview Narration (PPT 705)
Show a Presentation with or without Narration (PPT 705)
Email a Slide Show from within PowerPoint (PPT 705)
Present a Slide Show Online (PPT 707)
Create a Video (PPT 708)
Set Up Presenter View (PPT 710)

Specify a Custom Slide Size
Change the Slide Orientation (PPT 699)
Set Up a Custom Size (PPT 699)

CONSIDER THIS

General Project Guidelines
When creating a PowerPoint presentation, the actions you perform and the decisions you make will affect the appearance and characteristics of the finished document. As you create a presentation with illustrations, such as the project shown in Figure 11–1 on page PPT 667, you should follow these general guidelines:

1. **Use photographs with sharp focus and contrast.** The adage, "A picture is worth a thousand words," is relevant in a PowerPoint presentation. When your audience can see a visual representation of the concept you are describing during your talk, they are apt to understand and comprehend your message. Be certain your pictures are sharp and clear.

2. **Use hyperlinks to show slides with landscape and portrait orientations.** All slides in one presentation must be displayed in either landscape or portrait orientation. If you want to have variety in your slide show or have pictures or graphics that display best in one orientation, consider using hyperlinks to mix the two orientations during your presentation.

3. **Rehearse, rehearse, rehearse.** Outstanding slides lose their value when the presenter is unprepared to speak. Always keep in mind that the visual aspects are meant to supplement a speaker's verbal message. Practice your presentation before different types of audiences to solicit feedback, and use their comments to improve your speaking style.

How should you submit solutions to questions in the assignments identified with a symbol?
Every assignment in this book contains one or more questions identified with a symbol. These questions require you to think beyond the assigned presentation. Present your solutions to the questions in the format required by your instructor. Possible formats may include one or more of these options: write the answer; create a document that contains the answer; present your answer to the class; discuss your answer in a group; record the answer as audio or video using a webcam, smartphone, or portable media player; or post answers on a blog, wiki, or website.

Apply Your Knowledge

Reinforce the skills and apply the concepts you learned in this chapter.

Creating and Reordering Sections and Creating Custom Slide Shows

Note: To complete this assignment, you will be required to use the Data Files for Students. Visit www.cengage.com/ct/studentdownload for detailed instructions or contact your instructor for information about accessing the required files.

Instructions: Run PowerPoint. Open the presentation, Apply 11-1 Tennis, from the Data Files for Students.

The slides in this presentation provide information about tennis lessons at the CHF Racquet Center. The document you open is a partially formatted presentation. You will insert slides, insert section breaks, reorder and rename sections, and create two custom slide shows so that the presentation matches the one shown in Figure 11–80 on the next page.

Perform the following tasks:

1. Select Slide 1 (Figure 11–80c on page PPT 715), create a new Slide 2 that is a duplicate of Slide 1, change the layout to Section Header, and then change the transparency of the background to 35%. Create a new Slide 3 that is a duplicate of Slide 2.

2. On Slide 2, select the title text and then type **Women's Tennis Lessons** as the new title text. On Slide 3, select the title text and then type **Men's Tennis Lessons** as the new title text. Decrease the title text font size to 54 point on Slides 2 and 3.

3. Change the view to Slide Sorter view (Figures 11–80a and 11–80b), select Slide 4, and then add a section break. Rename the section divider, Women's Tennis.

4. Select the Default Section divider (before Slide 1) and rename it, CHF Racquet Center - Tennis.

5. Select Slide 5, add a section break, and then rename it, Men's Tennis. Move the Women's Tennis section header slide to the beginning of the Women's Tennis section, and move the Men's Tennis section header slider to the beginning of the Men's Tennis section.

6. Select Slide 6, add a section break, and then rename it, Mixed Doubles.

7. Select Slide 7, add a section break, and then rename it, Scoring.

8. Reorder the sections by moving the Men's Tennis section before the Women's Tennis section. The slides should now appear in the order shown in Figures 11–80c through 11–80i on pages PPT 715–717.

9. Create a custom slide show called Men's and Women's Tennis Lessons. Include only Slides 2, 3, 4, and 5 in this custom slide show.

10. Create a second custom slide show called Tennis Schedule. Include only Slides 3, 5, and 6 in this custom slide show.

11. If requested by your instructor, add the city where you were born as the second line of the subtitle on Slide 1.

12. Apply the Window transition (Dynamic category) and change the duration to 2.50 for all slides.

13. Save the presentation using the file name, Apply 11-1 Tennis Lessons.

Continued >

Apply Your Knowledge *continued*

14. Submit the revised document in the format specified by your instructor.

15. ✳ In this presentation, you created two new slides (duplicates of the title slide) and used them as section headers. How did this help when creating sections in the presentation? Did changing the background photo transparency for the section header slides make a difference? Why?

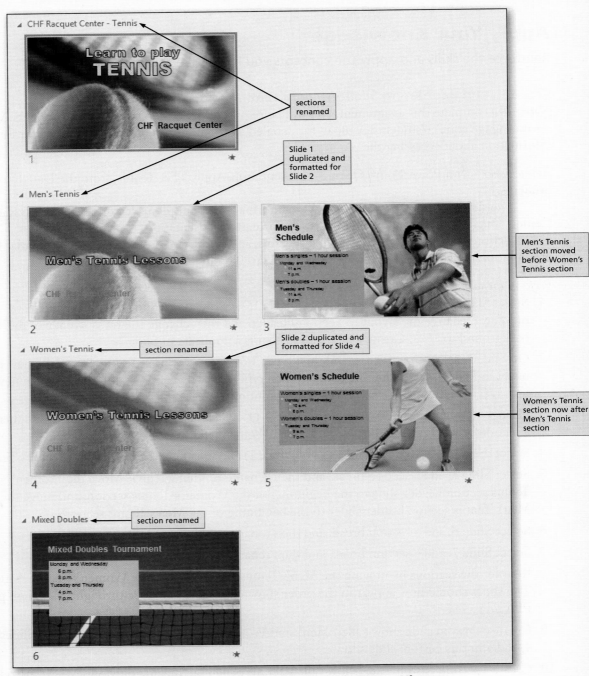

(a) First Six Slides of Presentation in Slide Sorter View

Figure 11–80

(b) Last Slide of Presentation in Slide Sorter View

(c) Slide 1

(d) Slide 2

Figure 11–80 (Continued)

Continued >

Apply Your Knowledge *continued*

(e) Slide 3

(f) Slide 4

(g) Slide 5

Figure 11–80

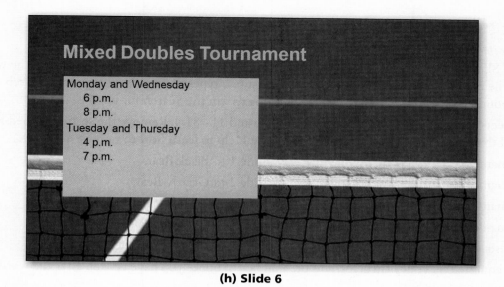

(h) Slide 6

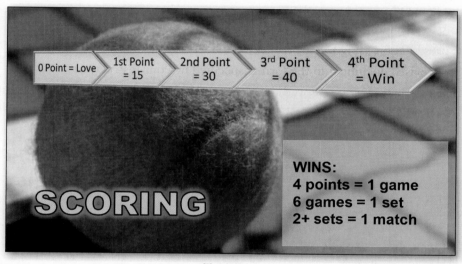

(i) Slide 7

Figure 11–80 (Continued)

Extend Your Knowledge

Extend the skills you learned in this chapter and experiment with new skills. You may need to use Help to complete the assignment.

Formatting Sections and Proofing a Presentation

Note: To complete this assignment, you will be required to use the Data Files for Students. Visit www.cengage.com/ct/studentdownload for detailed instructions or contact your instructor for information about accessing the required files.

Instructions: Run PowerPoint. Open the presentation, Extend 11-1 Bears, from the Data Files for Students. A koala is sometimes mistaken for a bear, but it is actually a marsupial. You will remove the section with the two koala slides (Slides 7 and 8) and proof the presentation shown in Figure 11–81 beginning on the next page through page PPT 720.

Continued >

Extend Your Knowledge *continued*

Perform the following tasks:

1. On Slide 1 (Figure 11–81a), there are only six of the eight living species of bears in the world in the numbered list. Add the names of the last two types of bears by using the Research proofing tool. (*Hint:* Type `8 types of bears` in the Search for box.)

2. Select Slide Sorter View (see Figures 11–81b and 11–81c). Remove the section named Koala and the two slides. (*Hint:* You may need to use Help to learn how to remove a section.)

3. Rename the Untitled Section divider after Slide 1 to Black Bear.

4. Rename the Untitled Section divider after Slide 2 to Grizzly Bear.

5. Rename the Untitled Section divider after Slides 3 and 4 to Giant Panda.

6. Rename the Untitled Section divider after Slides 5 and 6 to Polar Bear.

7. Present the slide show online to your instructor and to two classmates.

8. If requested by your instructor, add the number of bones you have broken after the word pounds on Slide 8.

9. Apply the Peel Off transition in the Exciting category, change the duration to 2.25 seconds, and then apply to all slides.

10. Save the presentation using the file name, Extend 11-1 Bears of the World.

11. Submit the revised document in the format specified by your instructor.

12. ✺ In this presentation, you removed the section with the koalas. Why? Which website did you use to find the names of the two missing bear species for Slide 1? Was it easy to find this information?

(a) Slide 1

Figure 11–81

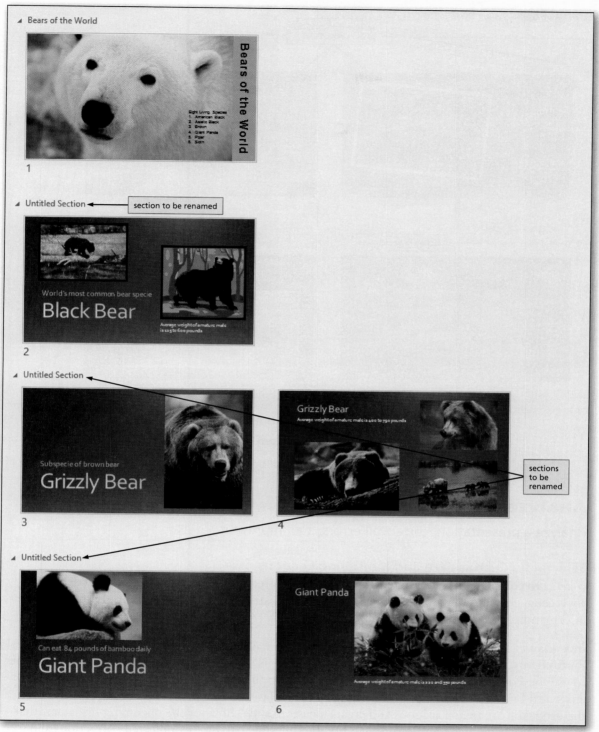

(b) First Six Slides of Presentation in Slide Sorter View
Figure 11–81 (Continued)

Continued >

Extend Your Knowledge *continued*

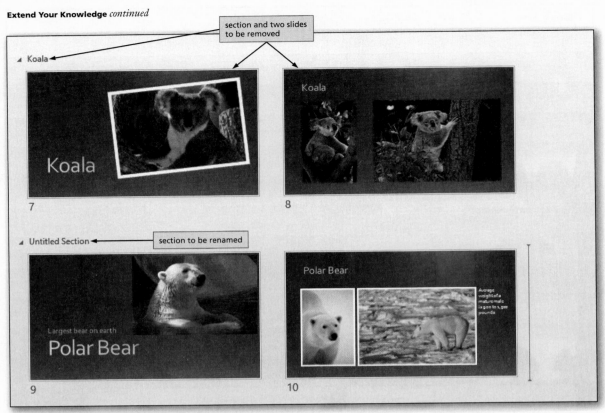

(c) Last Four Slides of Presentation in Slide Sorter View

Figure 11–81 (Continued)

Analyze, Correct, Improve

Analyze a presentation, correct all errors, and improve it.

Selecting a Custom Size and Modifying Sections

Note: To complete this assignment, you will be required to use the Data Files for Students. Visit www.cengage.com/ct/studentdownload for detailed instructions or contact your instructor for information about accessing the required files.

Instructions: Run PowerPoint. Open the presentation, Analyze 11-1 Flowers, from the Data Files for Students. You work for a florist and their specialty is wedding flowers. Your manager asked you to use the PowerPoint presentation that is running on the kiosk in the store and revise it for the city's next business expo. She will be making a presentation and handing out 14" × 8.5" flyers at the expo. You are to add sections and create a custom slide show for the upcoming bridal fair that just features bridal bouquet flowers. Modify the slides by making the indicated corrections and improvements.

1. Correct

    a. On Slide 1, insert a Double Wave shape (the last shape in the Stars and Banners shapes), size it to approximately 1.44" × 2.9", and then apply the Subtle Effect – Green, Accent 6 shape style (the seventh style in the fourth row). Type `Izabella's Flowers` on the first line, change the font to Lucida Calligraphy, and then change the point size to 20 point. Type `100 Main Street` on the second line, type `Open 7 days` on the third line, and type `10 a.m. to 6 p.m.` on the fourth line. Select the second, third, and fourth lines of text, change the font to Arial, and then change the font size to 14 point. Rotate the shape to the left and then move it to the upper-left corner of the slide, as shown in Figure 11–82a on the next page.

b. Select Slide 2 and create a new Slide 3 that is a duplicate of Slide 2. On Slide 2, delete the three small photos and leave the large center photo. Reduce the size of the heart shape to approximately 2.65" × 2.86", rotate it to the right (rotation should be 370 degrees), and then move it to the upper-right corner of the slide. Copy and paste the Double Wave shape from Slide 1 to the upper-left corner of Slide 2.

c. With Slide 2 still selected, use the Research proofing tool to look up `popular bridal flowers` and add at least three or four more flower names to the purple square shape in the lower-right corner of the slide. Change the font for all the text in the purple shape to Arial.

d. Select Slide 3 and reduce the size of the heart shape to approximately 2.65" × 2.86", and if necessary, move the heart shape so that it is not hanging off the edge of the slide. Delete the purple square shape in the lower-right corner of the slide.

e. Display the slides in Slide Sorter view (see Figure 11–82a). Select Slide 2 and add a section break. Select the section divider and rename the section `Bride's Flowers` as the new section divider. Select Slide 4 and add a section break. Select the section divider and rename the section `Other Wedding Flowers`, as shown in Figure 11–82a.

f. With the Slide Sorter view still displayed, move the Other Wedding Flowers section before the Bride's Flowers section. (Not shown in the figure.)

g. Create a custom slide show called Bride's Flowers. Include only Slides 1, 6, and 7 in this custom slide show.

h. If requested by your instructor, add your mother's middle name in place of the word, Izabella, in the shape on Slide 6.

2. Improve

a. Rename the Default section divider, Izabella's Flowers.

b. On Slide 2, reduce the size of the heart shape to approximately 2.52" × 2.97" and move the shape to the upper-left corner of the slide (not shown in the figure).

c. On Slide 6, select the purple shape in the lower-right corner of the slide, and increase the font size to 28 point. If necessary, increase the size of the shape and move the shape up and slightly to the left on the slide (not shown in figure). Apply the Metal Frame picture style to the photo on the slide (the third style in the first row).

d. Change the size of the slides to a custom width of 14" and a height of 8.5". (*Hint:* Click the Maximize button [Microsoft PowerPoint dialog box] to adjust the slide content.)

e. Change the transition from Curtains to Glitter (Exciting category), change the duration to 3.25 seconds, and then apply to all slides.

f. Save the presentation using the file name, Analyze 11-1 Wedding Flowers.

g. Submit the revised document in the format specified by your instructor.

3. ✻ Which errors existed in the starting file? When you created the custom slide show for Bride's Flowers, do you think the correct slides were included? Would you have selected different slides? Why or why not?

Continued >

Analyze, Correct, Improve *continued*

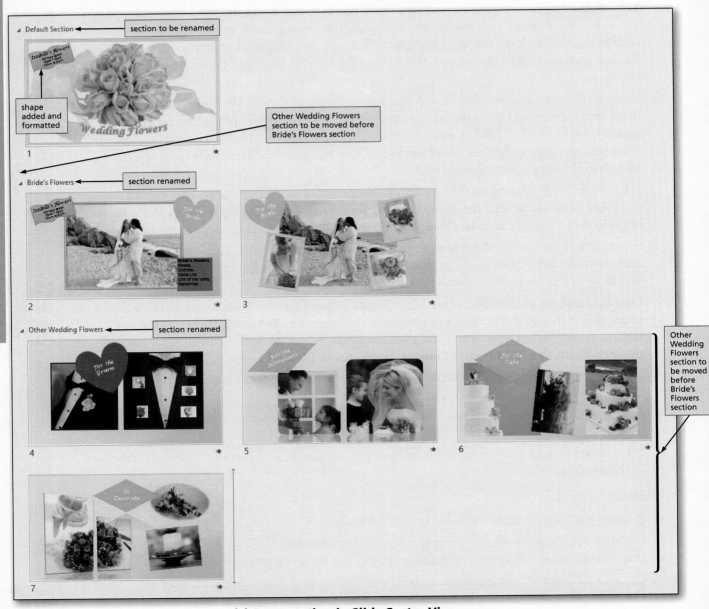

(a) Presentation in Slide Sorter View

Figure 11–82

(b) Slide 2

(c) Slide 3

Figure 11–82 (Continued)

In the Labs

Design and/or create a presentation using the guidelines, concepts, and skills presented in this chapter. Labs 1 and 2, which increase in difficulty, require you to create solutions based on what you learned in the chapter; Lab 3 requires you to create a solution, which uses cloud and web technologies, by learning and investigating on your own from general guidance.

Lab 1: Working with Multiple Presentation Windows Simultaneously, Setting Manual Timing, and Creating a Video

Problem: While attending school, you work for River Ridge, a canoe and kayak outfitter located on the beautiful Watson River near your college campus. You are preparing a presentation for the outdoor adventure club on campus. River Ridge won a special award for the Best Guided Kayak Adventure. You will be working with two PowerPoint presentations. One has all the information about canoe and kayak trips and the other one shows the award that River Ridge won. You will create a video of your final combined presentation.

Note: To complete this assignment, you will be required to use the Data Files for Students. Visit www.cengage.com/ct/studentdownload for detailed instructions or contact your instructor for information about accessing the required files.

Instructions: Perform the following tasks:
1. Open the presentation, Lab 11-1 Canoe and Kayak Trips, from the Data Files for Students, and remove all sections. Insert a new blank slide after Slide 5.
2. Open the presentation, Lab 11-1 River Ridge Award, from the Data Files for Students, and then cascade the two open document windows on the screen.
3. Copy and paste the explosion shape from the upper-right corner of Slide 1 on the River Ridge Award presentation to the upper-right corner of Slide 1 on the Canoe and Kayak Trip presentation. Select the new Slide 6 of this presentation (Figure 11–83f on page PPT 726).
4. Select Slide 2 of the River Ridge Award presentation. Select the award illustration, the photo, and the text box, copy these three items, and then paste them on Slide 6 of the Canoe and Kayak Trip presentation. Close the award presentation without saving changes.
5. The slides now should appear in the order shown in Figures 11-83a through 11-83f.
6. Set up the slide show to advance slides manually. Use Presenter View when you run the slide show.
7. If requested by your instructor, add the name of your grade school or high school as the last line in the text box on Slide 5.
8. Apply the Ripple transition in the Exciting category, change the duration to 2.50 seconds, and then apply to all slides.
9. Create a video of the Lab 11-1 River Ridge Canoe and Kayak Trips presentation and name it Lab 11-1 River Ridge Canoe and Kayak Trips Video.
10. Save the presentation using the file name, Lab 11-1 River Ridge Canoe and Kayak Trips. Submit the document and the video in the format specified by your instructor.
11. ✷ On Slide 6, you copied the illustration, photo, and a text box from another presentation. What did this add to your presentation?

shape copied and pasted from other presentation

(a) Slide 1

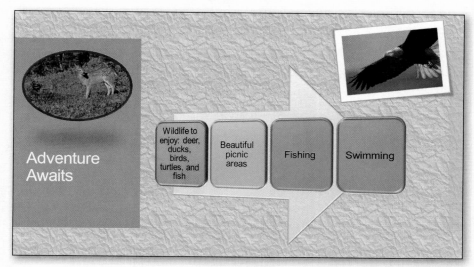

(b) Slide 2

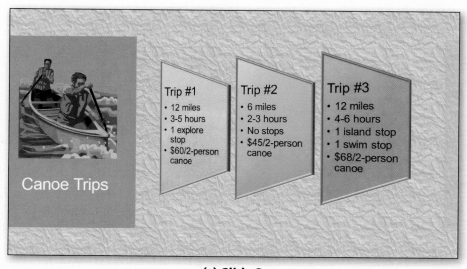

(c) Slide 3

Figure 11–83 (Continued)

Continued >

In the Labs *continued*

(d) Slide 4

(e) Slide 5

(f) Slide 6

Figure 11–83 (Continued)

Lab 2: Creating Photo Albums in Color and Black-and-White, Adding Captions, Reordering Photos, Adjusting Rotation of an Image, Adjusting Brightness and Contrast of an Image, Copying and Compressing a Video File, and Recording a Narration

Problem: Your geology class took a trip to Arizona to see the Grand Canyon. You decide to create a photo album to share your experiences. To add interest to the color photo album, your instructor gave you a short video he took of the Grand Canyon. You will copy the video into your color photo album. You create a presentation shown in Figures 11–84a on page PPT 729 through 11–84d on page PPT 732.

Note: To complete this assignment, you will be required to use the Data Files for Students. Visit www.cengage.com/ct/studentdownload for detailed instructions or contact your instructor for information about accessing the required files.

Instructions, Part 1: Perform the following tasks:

1. Insert a new photo album.
2. Insert the Grand Canyon1, Grand Canyon2, Grand Canyon3, Grand Canyon4, Grand Canyon5, Grand Canyon6, Grand Canyon7, and Grand Canyon8 photos from the Data Files for Students.
3. Do not create the album (tap or click the Create button in the Photo Album dialog box) until you are asked to do so.
4. Select the Grand Canyon3 photo in the album and move it above the Grand Canyon2 photo.
5. Select the GrandCanyon7 photo in the album and move it below the Grand Canyon8 photo.
6. Change the GrandCanyon1 layout to '2 pictures', select the 'Captions below ALL pictures' option, and then select the 'Simple Frame, White' frame shape.
7. Select the Facet theme for the photo album. Create the photo album. Save the presentation using the file name, Lab 11-2 Grand Canyon Color Album.
8. Change the theme to Berlin for the color photo album, and keep the orange variant (the first variant).
9. On Slide 1, change the title to `Grand Canyon` and then, if necessary, enter your name in the subtitle placeholder. The slide should appear as shown in Figure 11–84a.
10. On Slide 2, type the caption of the left photo as `Established in 1919` and then type `You have to see it to believe it!` as the caption of the right photo. The slide should appear as shown in Figure 11–84b.
11. On Slide 3, type the caption of the left photo as `One South Rim view` and then type `Another great view` as the caption of the right photo. The slide should appear as shown in Figure 11–84c.
12. On Slide 4, type the caption of the left photo as `Colorado River runs through it` and then type `Colorado River traces a course` as the caption of the right photo. The slide should appear as shown in Figure 11–84d.
13. Edit the photo album using the Photo Album arrow (INSERT tab | Images group). Remove the two photos Grand Canyon8 and Grand Canyon7. Insert the Grand Canyon Bird, Grand Canyon Lizard, Grand Canyon Sign, and Grand Canyon Squirrel photos. Rotate the Grand Canyon Sign photo clockwise. Tap or click the Update button. Slides 5 and 6 should appear as shown in Figures 11–84e and 11–84f.
14. Insert a new slide after Slide 6 and select the Title Only layout. Type `Grand Canyon Live` as the title text placeholder text.

Continued >

In the Labs *continued*

15. Open the Grand Canyon Video presentation located on the Data Files for Students and then cascade the two open document windows on the screen. Copy the video and paste it into Slide 7 of the Lab 11-2 Grand Canyon Color Album as shown in Figure 11–84g on page PPT 731. Change the video to Start Automatically, and apply the Reflected Bevel, White video style to the video (the fourth style in the first Intense row). Close the Grand Canyon Video presentation. Maximize the Lab 11-2 Grand Canyon Color Album presentation.

16. Apply the Gallery transition, change the duration to 2.50 seconds, and then apply to all slides.

17. Set up the presentation to run in Presenter view. The slides should appear as shown in Figures 11–84a through 11–84g.

18. Compress the media file in the presentation to Presentation Quality and then email this presentation to your instructor.

Instructions Part 2: Perform the following tasks:

1. Start a new photo album.

2. Insert the Grand Canyon9, Grand Canyon10, Grand Canyon11, Grand Canyon12, Grand Canyon13, and Grand Canyon14 photos from the Data Files for Students.

3. Do not create the album until you are asked to do so.

4. Select the 'ALL pictures black-and-white' picture option, the 2 pictures option layout, the Compound Frame Black Frame shape, and the Slice Theme.

5. Select the Grand Canyon9 picture in the album and increase the contrast of the picture two times.

6. Select the Grand Canyon11 picture in the album and decrease the brightness of the picture two times.

7. Create the photo album. The slides should appear as shown in Figures 11-84h through 11-84k on page PPT 732 when this lab is complete.

8. Select Slide 1. Type **Grand Canyon** as the title text. If necessary, add your name in place of the subtitle text.

9. Select Slide 2. Record the slide show from the current slide. Note: The following steps contain narration that you will read while progressing through the slides. Read the following narration: **"Join us as we explore the Grand Canyon."** for this slide.

10. Advance to Slide 3 and then read the following narration: **"Breathtaking views and the Colorado river runs through it."** for this slide.

11. Advance to Slide 4 and then read the following narration: **"It's hard to look at the Grand Canyon and not be curious about geology."** for this slide.

12. Stop the presentation so that the recording session ends.

13. Display Slide 1 and then run the slide show to view the presentation and to hear the narration you just recorded.

14. Apply the Fade transition, change the duration to 3.00 seconds, and then apply to all slides.

15. Save the presentation using the file name, Lab 11-2 Grand Canyon Narration.

16. Submit the revised document in the format specified by your instructor.

17. If requested by your instructor, type the year you started college after your name on Slide 1.

18. ✺ When you created the color and black-and-white photo albums of Grand Canyon photos, you set up the album with two photos per slide. Do you think it would have been better to do one photo per slide? Why? Do you think adding captions to the color album was effective? In the black-and-white photo album, you used the Slice design with the blue variant. Was this a good choice? Why?

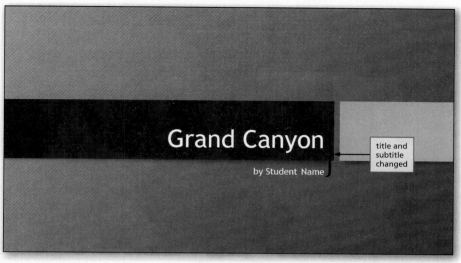

(a) Slide 1

(b) Slide 2

(c) Slide 3

Figure 11–84 (Continued)

Continued >

In the Labs *continued*

(d) Slide 4

(e) Slide 5

(f) Slide 6

Figure 11–84 (Continued)

Video courtesy of Susan Sebok

(g) Slide 7

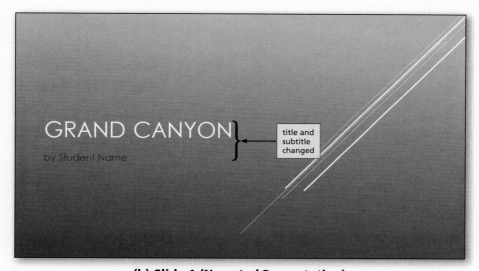

(h) Slide 1 (Narrated Presentation)

Photos courtesy of Susan Sebok

(i) Slide 2 (Narrated Presentation)

Figure 11–84 (Continued)

Continued >

In the Labs *continued*

(j) Slide 3 (Narrated Presentation)

(k) Slide 4 (Narrated Presentation)

Figure 11–84 (Continued)

Lab 3: Expand Your World: Cloud and Web Technologies
Exploring Apps for Office

Problem: You use apps on your phone and tablet regularly to look up a variety of information. You see that you can use apps not only in PowerPoint, but in other Office apps. You would like to investigate some of the apps available for PowerPoint to determine which ones would be helpful for you to use.

Note: You will be required to use your Microsoft Account to complete this assignment. If you do not have a Microsoft account and do not want to create one, read this assignment without performing the instructions.

Instructions: Perform the following tasks:

1. Use Help to learn about Apps for Office. If necessary, sign in to your Windows account.

2. If you are not signed in already, sign in to your Microsoft Account in PowerPoint.

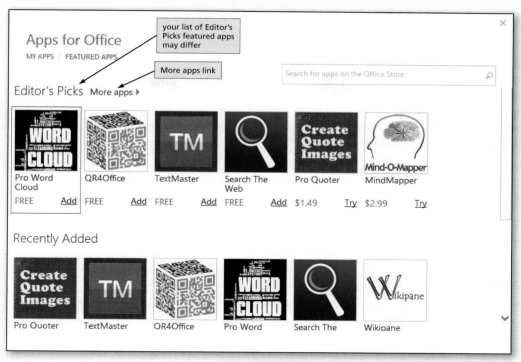

Figure 11–85

3. Display the INSERT tab and then tap or click the 'Insert an App' button (INSERT tab | Apps group) to display the Apps for Office dialog box. (If a menu is displayed, tap or click the See All link to display the Apps for Office dialog box.) On the FEATURED APPS tab, view the Editor's Picks apps (Figure 11–85). Your list of Editor's Picks featured apps may differ.

4. Tap or click the More apps link to visit the online Office Store. View the apps that will work with PowerPoint 2013. Locate a free app that you feel would be helpful to you while you use PowerPoint, tap or click the Add button, and then follow the instructions to add the app to PowerPoint.

5. In PowerPoint, tap or click the 'Insert an App' button (INSERT tab | Apps group) to display the Apps for Office dialog box. Tap or click the app you added and then tap or click the Insert button to add the app. Tap or click the 'Insert an App' arrow (INSERT tab | Apps group) to see the added app in the list.

6. Practice using the app.

7. ✸ Which apps are available for PowerPoint in the online Office Store? What were their costs to download? Which app did you download and why? Does the app work as you intended? Would you recommend the app to others?

Consider This: Your Turn

Apply your creative thinking and problem-solving skills to design and implement a solution.

1. Design and Create a Presentation about Stand-Up Paddleboarding (SUP)
Personal

Part 1: Your part-time job at River Ridge has been a fulfilling experience. The company received special recognition when it was awarded the Best Kayak Adventure of 2014. You have been a guide on many canoe and kayak trips. You also have become skilled at paddleboarding and have

Continued >

Consider This: Your Turn *continued*

taught this fun activity to people of all ages. River Ridge is planning to develop a schedule for paddleboarding lessons. Use the concepts and techniques presented in this chapter to prepare a presentation for promoting the business. You can shoot a short video to include in the presentation, search online for photos and videos, or use photos and illustrations from Office.com if they are appropriate for this presentation. Select a suitable theme, create section breaks, record narration, and create a video from the presentation. Change the slide orientation to portrait for a handout. Submit your assignment in the format specified by your instructor.

Part 2: ✹ You made several decisions while creating the presentation in this assignment: where to place text, photos and illustrations, how to divide the presentation into sections, which words to include in your narration, and whether to create a photo album. What was the rationale behind each of these decisions? When you reviewed the document, what further revisions did you make and why? Where would you recommend showing this slide show?

2. Design and Create a Presentation about Your Ice Cream Parlor Business

Professional

Part 1: You are the owner of your town's only ice cream parlor called Ice Cream Creations. It is a small family-owned business that has been serving delicious ice cream desserts for more than 30 years. The business recently has expanded to include homemade candy and added a plant where you make your own ice cream and create new flavors. You decide to put together a PowerPoint presentation for the next Chamber of Commerce meeting. Select a suitable theme, create section breaks, record narration, and create a video from the presentation. Change the slide size to a size suitable for posters to hang in your shop. The presentation could contain photos from a PowerPoint file called Ice Cream Creations available on the Data Files for Students or you can use photos and illustrations from Office.com if they are appropriate for this topic. You can create a photo album with narration showing some of your special ice cream dishes. Submit your assignment in the format specified by your instructor.

Part 2: ✹ You made several decisions while creating the presentation in this assignment: where to place text, photos and illustrations, where to use WordArt, how to divide the presentation into sections, and whether to create a video. What was the rationale behind each of these decisions? When you reviewed the document, what further revisions did you make and why? Where would you recommend showing this slide show?

3. Design and Create a Presentation about Traveling by Steamboat on the Mississippi River

Research and Collaboration

Part 1: You are studying rivers in your geography class and your group has been assigned the topic of traveling by steamboat on the Mississippi River, also called the Mighty Mississippi. Your group has divided into three small groups. One group will gather facts about the history of the river when people could travel by boat on the river in the early 1800s. Another group will look into the history of steamboats, including the different types and when they were first used to travel on the river. The third group will gather photos, illustrations, and videos about steamboat travel on the Mississippi River and develop several itineraries and places to visit along the routes. Your group will put together a PowerPoint presentation using at least three objectives found at the beginning of this chapter. Select a suitable theme, create section breaks, create a custom slide show, record narration, and create a video from the presentation. Three illustrations are available on the Data Files for Students: Steamboat, St. Louis, and Mississippi River Map. You can use your own photos or those available from Office.com if they are appropriate for this topic. Change the slide orientation to portrait for a handout to the class during your group's presentation. You also should create a black-and-white photo album for this topic.

Part 2: ✳ You made several decisions while creating the presentation in this assignment: where to place text, photos and illustrations, where to use WordArt, how to divide the presentation into sections, whether to create a photo album in color or black and white, and the words to use in the script for narration. What was the rationale behind each of these decisions? When you reviewed the document, what further revisions did you make and why? Where would you recommend showing this slide show?

Learn Online

Reinforce what you learned in this chapter with games, exercises, training, and many other online activities and resources.

Student Companion Site   Reinforcement activities and resources are available at no additional cost on www.cengagebrain.com. Visit www.cengage.com/ct/studentdownload for detailed instructions about accessing the resources available at the Student Companion Site.

SAM   Put your skills into practice with SAM! If you have a SAM account, go to www.cengage .com/sam2013 to access SAM assignments for this chapter.

8 | Working with Trendlines, PivotTable Reports, PivotChart Reports, and Slicers

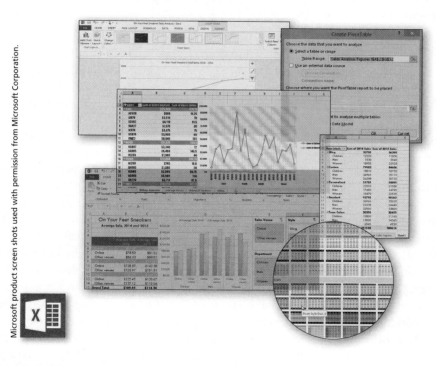

Objectives

You will have mastered the material in this chapter when you can:

- Analyze worksheet data using a trendline
- Create a PivotTable report
- Format a PivotTable report
- Apply filters to a PivotTable report
- Create a PivotChart report
- Format a PivotChart report
- Apply filters to a PivotChart report

- Analyze worksheet data using PivotTable and PivotChart reports
- Create calculated fields
- Create slicers to filter PivotTable and PivotChart reports
- Format slicers
- Analyze PivotTable and PivotChart reports using slicers

8 | Working with Trendlines, PivotTable Reports, PivotChart Reports, and Slicers

Introduction

In both academic and business environments, people are presented with large amounts of data that needs to be analyzed and interpreted. Data is increasingly available from a wide variety of sources, and gathered with much more ease. Analysis of data and interpretation of the results of the analysis are important skills to acquire. Questions can be asked that identify patterns in data, providing businesses and individuals with information that can be used for making decisions about business situations.

Project — On Your Feet Sneakers Sales Analysis

On Your Feet Sneakers is a specialty sneaker shop that provides personalized, detailed, and custom-designed sneakers for adults and children. The store sells five types of sneakers: a standard sneaker that customers can decorate themselves, sneakers customized with team colors, bling sneakers decorated with rhinestones, and two handcrafted sneakers — bling or team color sneakers with name personalization, and a custom-decorated sneaker designed in consultation with the customer. Sales are offered primarily online, and at specialized alternate venues. The company saw a spike in sales in 2012 after some very favorable media coverage. The owner of On Your Feet Sneakers is interested in reviewing sales figures for the past six years. The company owner also has requested that you compare the sales figures for the last two years to examine sales for the different styles, by department, and by sales venue. In this chapter, you will learn how to use the trendline charting feature in Excel to examine data for trends, and to analyze sales data for On Your Feet Sneakers using PivotTable and PivotChart reports. The results of this analysis are shown in Figure 8–1.

A **trendline** (Figure 8–1a) is a visual way to show how two variables relate to each other. Trendlines often are used to represent changes in one set of data over time, but also can represent changes in one set of data with changes in another. Excel can overlay a trendline on certain types of charts.

PivotTable reports, PivotChart reports, and trendlines provide methods to manipulate and visualize data. A **PivotTable report** (Figure 8–1b) is an interactive view of worksheet data that gives users the ability to summarize the data by selecting categories in which to group their data. When using a PivotTable report, you can quickly change selected categories, without needing to manipulate the worksheet itself. You can examine and analyze several complex organizations of the data, and may spot relationships you might not otherwise see. For example, you can look at total sales for each department, broken down by style, and then look at the quarterly sales for certain subgroupings of styles, without having to do complex reorganizations of the data.

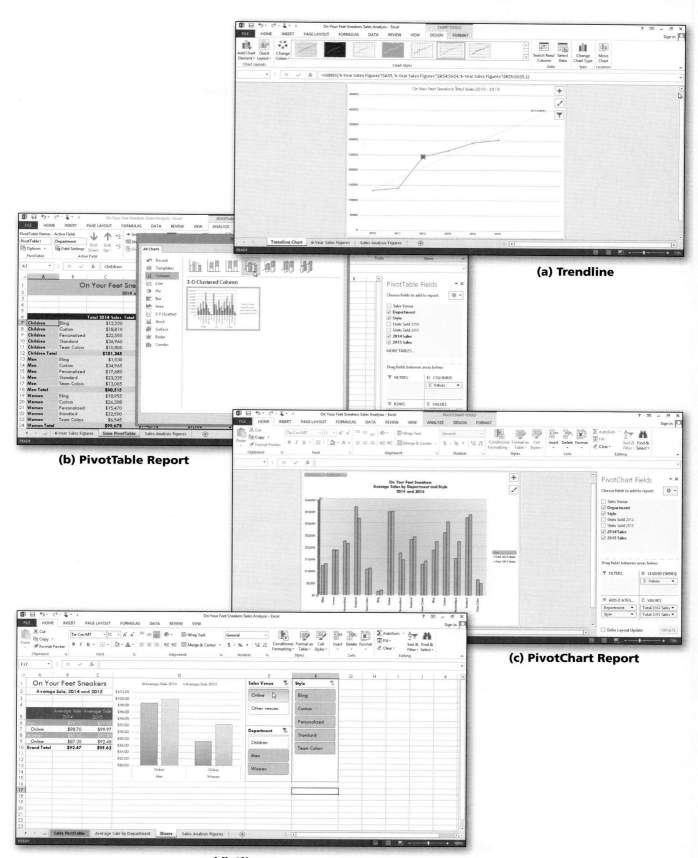

(a) Trendline

(b) PivotTable Report

(c) PivotChart Report

(d) Slicers

Figure 8–1

A **PivotChart report** (Figure 8–1c on the previous page) is an interactive chart that allows users to change the groupings that graphically present data. For example, if On Your Feet Sneakers wanted to view a pie chart showing percentages of total sales for each style, a PivotChart could show that percentage categorized by adult versus children's sales, without having to rebuild the chart from scratch for each view. PivotChart reports are visual representations of PivotTables. When you create a PivotChart report, Excel creates and associates a PivotTable with that PivotChart report.

Slicers (Figure 8–1d on the previous page) are graphic objects that contain buttons you tap or click to filter the data in PivotTables and PivotCharts. Each button clearly identifies the filter it applies, making it easy to interpret the data displayed in the PivotTable report.

Using trendlines, PivotTables, PivotCharts, and slicers, a user with little knowledge of formulas, functions, and ranges can complete powerful what-if analyses of a set of data.

Figure 8–2 illustrates the requirements document for the On Your Feet Sneakers Sales Analysis worksheet. It includes the needs, source of data, calculations, and other facts about the worksheet's development.

Worksheet Title	On Your Feet Sneakers Sales Analysis
Needs	Evaluate two different sets of sales data: 1. Total Sales data for 2010–2015. Provide a visual representation of Sales over the past 6 years, and a forecast for the next 2 years based on the current trend. 2. Sales data for 2014 and 2015 for all sales venues, with details identifying department, style, and number of items sold. For this data, use PivotTables and PivotCharts to look for patterns and anomalies in the sales data, based on different breakouts. Some breakouts of interest include Total Sales and Average Sales for Department and Style, by Sales Venue. 3. Set up slicers to facilitate easy examination of various subgroupings by users with little or no Excel experience.
Source of Data	Data is available in the workbook On Your Feet Sneakers Sales Data.xlsx.
Calculations	In addition to total sales for the various groupings, produce comparisons of average sales for those groupings. Finally, create calculations of the value of the average sales for various combinations.

© 2014 Cengage Learning

Figure 8–2

Roadmap

In this chapter, you will learn how to create and use the workbook shown in Figure 8–1. The following roadmap identifies general activities you will perform as you progress through this chapter:

1. CREATE the LINE CHART and TRENDLINE.
2. CREATE the PIVOTTABLE.
3. CHANGE the LAYOUT and VIEW of the PIVOTTABLE.
4. FILTER the PIVOTTABLE.
5. FORMAT the PIVOTTABLE.
6. CREATE the PIVOTCHART.
7. CHANGE the PIVOTCHART VIEW AND CONTENTS.
8. ADD SLICERS.

At the beginning of step instructions throughout the chapter, you will see an abbreviated form of this roadmap. The abbreviated roadmap uses colors to indicate chapter progress: gray means the chapter is beyond that activity, blue means the task being shown is covered in that activity, and black means that activity is yet to be covered. For example, the following abbreviated roadmap indicates the chapter would be showing a task in the 3 CHANGE LAYOUT & VIEW PIVOTTABLE activity.

1 CREATE LINE CHART & TRENDLINE | 2 CREATE PIVOTTABLE | 3 CHANGE LAYOUT & VIEW OF PIVOTTABLE | 4 FILTER PIVOTTABLE
5 FORMAT PIVOTTABLE | 6 CREATE PIVOTCHART | 7 CHANGE PIVOTCHART VIEW & CONTENTS | 8 ADD SLICERS

Use the abbreviated roadmap as a progress guide while you read or step through the instructions in this chapter.

To Run Excel and Open a Workbook

The following steps, which assume Windows 8 is running, use the Start screen or the search box to run Excel based on a typical installation. You may need to ask your instructor how to run Excel on your computer. For a detailed example of the procedure summarized below, refer to the Office and Windows chapter.

To complete these steps, you will be required to use the Data Files for Students. Visit www.cengage.com/ct/studentdownload for detailed instructions or contact your instructor for information about accessing the required files.

1 Scroll the Start screen for an Excel 2013 tile. If your Start screen contains an Excel 2013 tile, tap or click it to run Excel. Otherwise, search for the Excel app using the Charms bar and then tap or click Excel 2013 in the search results.

2 Tap or click 'Open Other Workbooks' on the Excel start screen.

3 Navigate to the location of the Data Files for Students and the Excel Chapter 8 folder.

4 Double-tap or double-click the file named On Your Feet Sneakers Sales Data to open it.

5 If the Excel window is not maximized, tap or click the Maximize button on its title bar to maximize the window.

6 Save the workbook using the file name, On Your Feet Sneakers Sales Analysis.

Adding a Trendline to a Chart

Using a trendline on certain Excel charts allows you to illustrate how one set of data is changing in relation to another set of data. Trends are most often thought about in terms of how a value changes over time, but trends can also describe the relationship between two variables, such as height and weight. In Excel, you add a trendline to an existing Excel chart; however, not all types of Excel charts can have a trendline added to them. Chart types that do not examine the relationship between two variables, such as pie and doughnut charts, which examine the contribution of different parts to a whole, cannot include trendlines. Excel allows you to add trendlines to several types of charts, such as unstacked 2-D area, bar, column, line, inventory, XY (scatter), and bubble charts.

BTW

The Ribbon and Screen Resolution
Excel may change how the groups and buttons within the groups appear on the ribbon, depending on the computer's screen resolution. Thus, your ribbon may look different from the ones in this book if you are using a screen resolution other than 1366 × 768.

BTW

BTWs
For a complete list of the BTWs found in the margins of this book, visit the BTW resource on the Student Companion Site located on www.cengagebrain.com. For detailed instructions about accessing available resources, visit www.cengage.com/ct/studentdownload or contact your instructor for information about accessing the required files.

How do you determine which trends to analyze?

Before you add a trendline to a chart, you need to determine the data series to analyze. If the chart uses only one data series, Excel uses it automatically. If the chart involves more than one data series, you select the one you want to use as you add a trendline. You then can analyze current or future trends.

To analyze a current trend, make sure you have enough data available for the period you want to analyze. For example, two years of annual sales totals might not provide enough data to analyze sales performance. Five years of annual sales totals or two years of monthly sales totals are more likely to present a trend.

To analyze a future trend, you use a trendline to project data beyond the values of the data set. This process is called forecasting. Forecasting helps predict data values that are outside of a data set. For example, if a data set is for a 10-year period and the data shows a trend in that 10-year period, Excel can predict values beyond that period or estimate what the values may have been before that period.

When you add a trendline to a chart, you can set the number of periods to forecast forward or backward in time. For example, if you have six years of sales data, you can forecast two periods forward to show the trend for eight years: six years of current data and two years of projected data. You also can display information about the trendline on the chart to help guide your analysis. For example, you can display the equation used to calculate the trend and show the **R-squared value**, which is a number from 0 to 1 that measures the strength of the trend. An R-squared value of 1 means the estimated values in the trendline correspond exactly to the actual data.

To Create a 2-D Line Chart

1 CREATE LINE CHART & TRENDLINE | 2 CREATE PIVOTTABLE | 3 CHANGE LAYOUT & VIEW OF PIVOTTABLE | 4 FILTER PIVOTTABLE
5 FORMAT PIVOTTABLE | 6 CREATE PIVOTCHART | 7 CHANGE PIVOTCHART VIEW & CONTENTS | 8 ADD SLICERS

Why? *Line charts are suited to charting a variable, in this case sales, over a number of time periods.* The following steps create a 2-D line chart of the On Your Feet Sneakers sales data. You will add a trendline to the chart shortly.

- If necessary, make 6-Year Sales Figures the active sheet.
- Select cells A4:G5 to select the range to be charted (Figure 8–3).

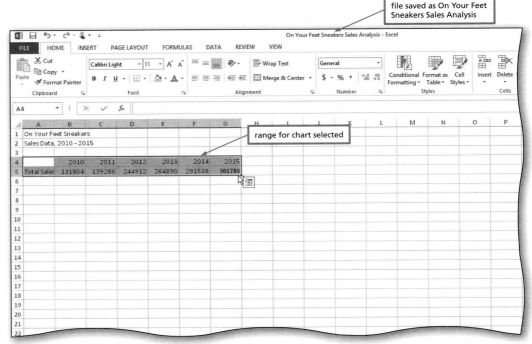

Figure 8–3

2

- Tap or click INSERT on the ribbon to display the INSERT tab.

- Tap or click the 'Insert Line Chart' button (INSERT tab | Charts group) to display the Insert Line Chart gallery (Figure 8–4).

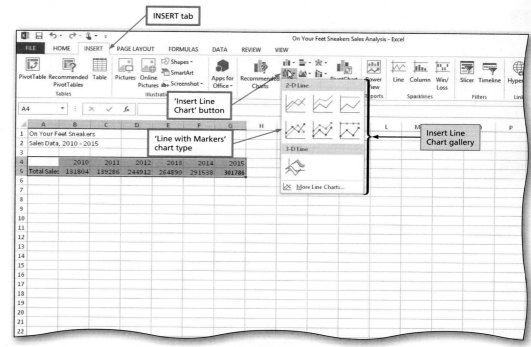

Figure 8–4

3

- Tap or click 'Line with Markers' in the 2-D Line area in the Insert Line Chart gallery to insert a 2-D line chart with data markers (Figure 8–5).

Q&A What are data markers?

A data marker is the symbol in a chart that represents a single value from a worksheet cell. In this case, the data markers are circles that represent the six sales figures.

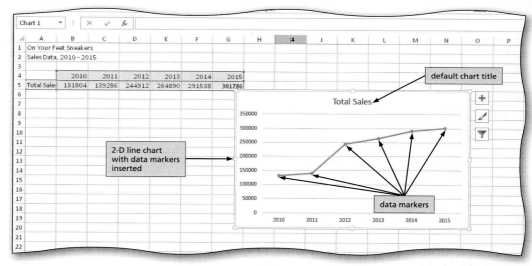

Figure 8–5

Why do the selected cells appear with colored fill?

Excel uses colors to identify chart elements when preparing to create a chart. In this case, the red cell is the chart title, the purple cells are the category axis values, and the blue cells are the value axis values.

4

- Tap or click the Move Chart button (CHART TOOLS DESIGN tab | Location group) to display the Move Chart dialog box.
- Tap or click New sheet (Move Chart dialog box) to select the option button.
- If necessary, double-tap or double-click the default text in the New sheet text box to select the text.
- Type `Trendline Chart` to enter a name for the new chart sheet (Figure 8–6).

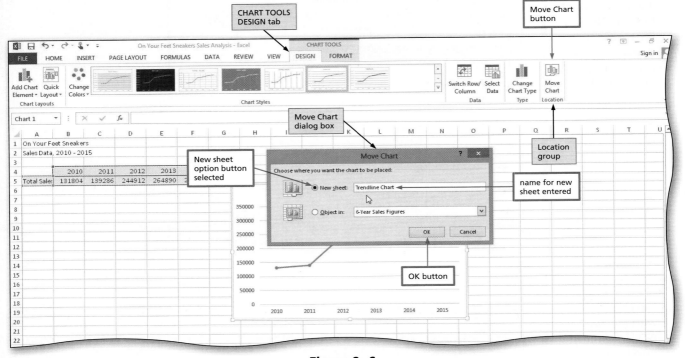

Figure 8–6

5

- Tap or click the OK button (Move Chart dialog box) to move the chart to a new sheet named Trendline Chart.
- Tap or click the default Total Sales chart title to select it.
- Type `On Your Feet Sneakers Total Sales 2010 – 2015` and then press the ENTER key to enter the new chart title.
- Tap or click outside of the chart area to deselect the chart (Figure 8–7).

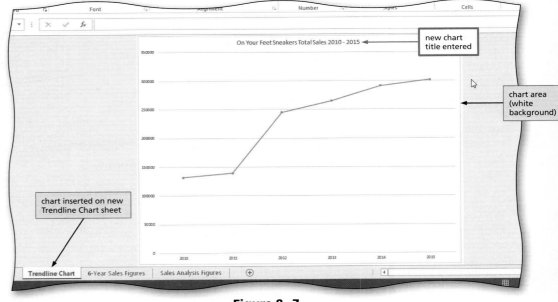

Figure 8–7

Other Ways

1. Tap or click 'Quick Analysis Lens' button, tap or click Charts tab   2. ALT+N, N

To Add a Trendline to a Chart

Why? *You add a trendline to a chart to analyze current and/or future trends.* A trendline must be added to an existing chart. The following steps add a trendline to the On Your Feet Sneakers Total Sales 2010 - 2015 chart and predict the total sales two years beyond the data set in the six-year sales figures worksheet.

1

- Tap or click the chart to select it.

- Tap or click the CHART TOOLS DESIGN tab on the ribbon.

- Tap or click the 'Add Chart Element' button (CHART TOOLS DESIGN tab | Chart Layouts group) to display the Add Chart Element menu.

- Tap or click Trendline to display the Trendline gallery (Figure 8–8).

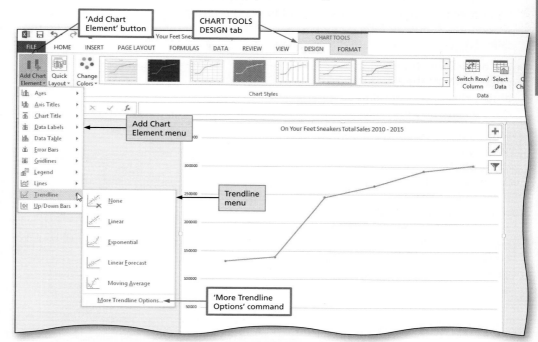

Figure 8–8

2

- Tap or click 'More Trendline Options' in the Trendline gallery to display the Format Trendline task pane.

- If necessary, tap or click the Trendline Options button.

- If necessary, tap or click Linear in the Trendline Options area to select a linear trendline type (Figure 8–9).

Q&A Why should I select the Linear option button in this case? The 2-D line chart you created is a basic straight line, so it is appropriate for a linear trendline, which shows values that are increasing or decreasing at a steady rate.

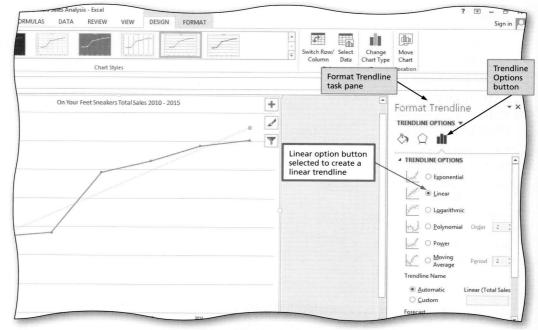

Figure 8–9

- If necessary, scroll down in the Format Trendline task pane until the Forecast area is visible. Drag to select the default value in the Forward text box in the Forecast area.
- Type **2.0** to add a trendline to the chart with a two-period forward forecast.

Q&A | What does it mean to enter a two-period forward forecast?
A two-period forward forecast estimates the total sales for the two time periods (in this case, years) that follow the sales data you used to create the line chart.

- Tap or click the 'Display R-squared value on chart' check box to display the R-squared value on the chart (Figure 8–10).

Q&A | What is the effect of selecting the 'Display R-squared value on chart' check box?
Selecting this check box displays the R-squared value on the chart. The R-squared value is a measure of how well the trendline describes the relationship between total sales and time. The closer the value is to 1, the more accurate the trendline.

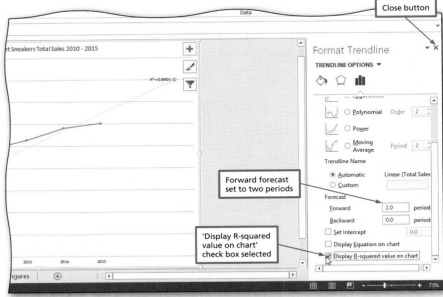

Figure 8–10

- Tap or click the Close button (Format Trendline task pane) to add the trendline with the selected options.
- Tap or click PAGE LAYOUT on the ribbon to display the PAGE LAYOUT tab.
- Use the Themes button (PAGE LAYOUT tab | Themes group) to apply the Circuit theme to the workbook (Figure 8–11).

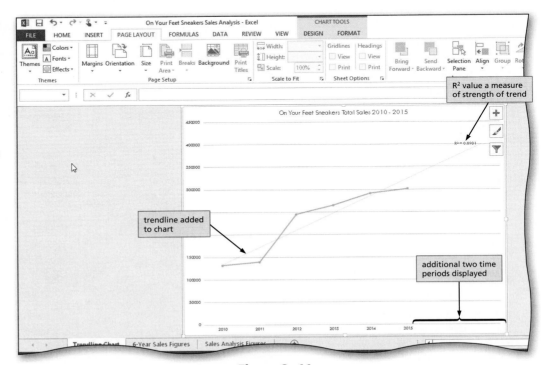

Figure 8–11

Other Ways

1. Press and hold or right-click graphed line, tap or click Add Trendline on shortcut menu

2. Tap or click 'Add Chart Element' button (CHART TOOLS DESIGN tab | Chart Layouts group), tap or click Trendline

More about Trendlines

It is important to take note of the axes when looking at trendlines. Charts with trendlines often are reformatted to start the vertical axis at a number other than zero, particularly when the values on the vertical axis are high. When interpreting a trendline, you should look at the vertical axis to see if it starts at zero. If it does not, be aware that trends represented by the trendline may appear exaggerated. Figure 8–12 shows a chart with a trendline that uses the same data as the chart in Figure 8–11. The difference between the two charts is in the vertical axis, which starts at zero in Figure 8–11 and at 100,000 in Figure 8–12. The difference between the projected values for 2014 and 2015 appears much larger in Figure 8–12 where the axis starts at 100,000. When analyzing, always check the axes to be sure that the differences shown in the chart are not being visually overstated.

BTW

Q&As

For a complete list of the Q&As found in many of the step-by-step sequences in this book, visit the Q&A resource on the Student Companion Site located on www.cengagebrain.com. For detailed instructions about accessing available resources, visit www.cengage .com/ct/studentdownload or contact your instructor for information about accessing the required files.

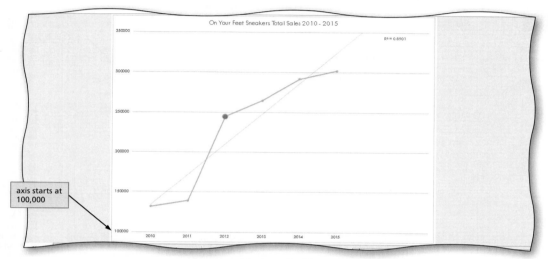

axis starts at 100,000

Figure 8–12

To Change the Format of a Data Point

1 CREATE LINE CHART & TRENDLINE | 2 CREATE PIVOTTABLE | 3 CHANGE LAYOUT & VIEW OF PIVOTTABLE | 4 FILTER PIVOTTABLE
5 FORMAT PIVOTTABLE | 6 CREATE PIVOTCHART | 7 CHANGE PIVOTCHART VIEW & CONTENTS | 8 ADD SLICERS

Why? *When graphing data, you may want to call visual attention to a particular data point or points.* The following steps change the format of the 2012 data point.

1

- Tap or click the 2012 data point twice to select the single point.

- If you are using a touch screen, press and hold the selected data point to display the mini toolbar and then tap 'Show Context Menu' on the mini toolbar to display the shortcut menu.

- If you are using a mouse, right-click the selected data point to display the shortcut menu (Figure 8–13).

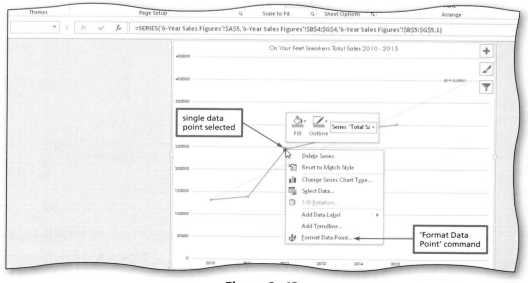

Figure 8–13

2

- Tap or click 'Format Data Point' on the shortcut menu to display the Format Data Point task pane.

- Tap or click the 'Fill & Line' button in the Format Data Point task pane.

- Tap or click MARKER.

- If necessary, tap or click MARKER OPTIONS to expand the section, select the contents of the Size box, and then type **12** as the new size.

- If necessary, tap or click FILL to expand the section, tap or click the Color button, and then select 'Red, Accent 3' (row 1, column 7) (Figure 8–14).

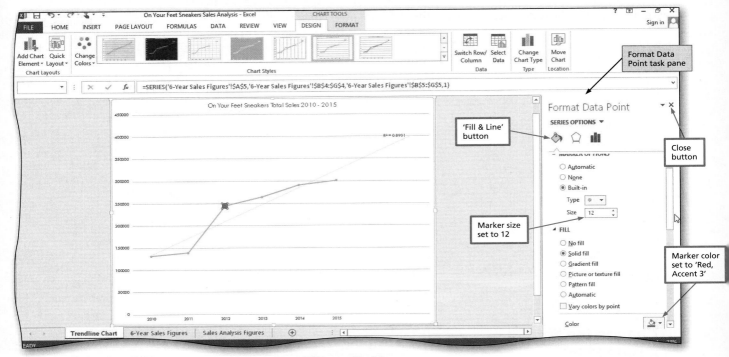

Figure 8–14

3

- Tap or click the Close button (Format Data Point task pane) to change the data point format (Figure 8–15).

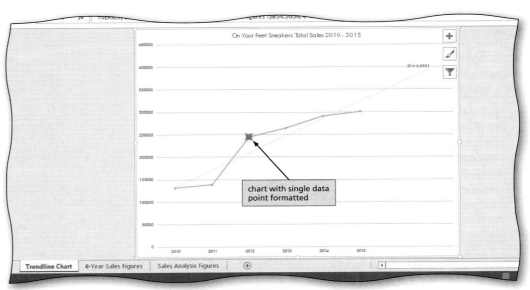

Figure 8–15

Creating and Formatting PivotTable and PivotChart Reports

A PivotTable report is an interactive tool that summarizes worksheet data. When working with data tables or lists of data, each different organization of the data requires a new table or list. In contrast, you can reorganize data and examine summaries in a PivotTable report with a few taps or mouse clicks. PivotTable reports allow you to view different summaries of the data quickly and easily, using just a single table.

When creating a PivotTable report, you can use categories in the data to summarize different groups or totals. PivotTable **fields** are drawn from columns in the worksheet data. PivotTables use two types of fields: data, which contain values that the PivotTable will summarize, and category, which describe the data by categorizing it. Category fields correspond to columns in the original data, and data fields correspond to summary values of original data across categories. You can change row and column groupings quickly to summarize the data in different ways to ask new questions. Reorganizing the table reveals different levels of detail and allows you to analyze specific subgroups.

One PivotTable created in this project is shown in Figure 8–16. It summarizes the On Your Feet Sneakers data to show the total sales and average sales in 2014 and 2015 for each department by style (bling, custom, personalized, standard, or team colors). The filter button in cell A4 filters the results by department, and the filter button in cell B4 filters the results by style. Columns C and D show the values for the total sales in 2014 and 2015, and columns E and F show the values for the average sales in 2014 and 2015.

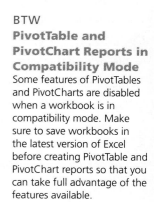

BTW
PivotTable and PivotChart Reports in Compatibility Mode
Some features of PivotTables and PivotCharts are disabled when a workbook is in compatibility mode. Make sure to save workbooks in the latest version of Excel before creating PivotTable and PivotChart reports so that you can take full advantage of the features available.

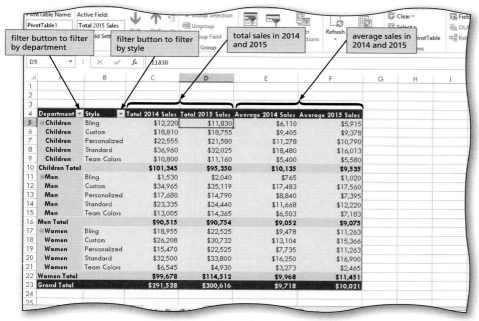

Figure 8–16

How do you determine which fields to use in a PivotTable?
You can create PivotTable and PivotChart reports in almost any configuration of your existing data. To use this powerful tool effectively, you need to create these reports with questions in mind. Look at the categories you can use to describe your data and think about how the various categories can interact. Common questions relate to how the data changes over time, and how the data varies in geographical locations, such as states or regions, different functional groups within an organization, different product groupings, and demographic groupings, such as age and gender.

CONSIDER THIS

You can create PivotTable reports either on the same worksheet as the data to be analyzed or on a new sheet in the same workbook as the sheet containing the data. When you create a PivotTable report, you also can create a PivotChart report. PivotChart reports are interactive charts that also allow you to change the way that data is organized and displayed. PivotCharts always are based on a PivotTable. In fact, they are visual representations of the PivotTable that forms their base.

To Create a Blank PivotTable

1 CREATE LINE CHART & TRENDLINE | 2 CREATE PIVOTTABLE | 3 CHANGE LAYOUT & VIEW OF PIVOTTABLE | 4 FILTER PIVOTTABLE
5 FORMAT PIVOTTABLE | 6 CREATE PIVOTCHART | 7 CHANGE PIVOTCHART VIEW & CONTENTS | 8 ADD SLICERS

Why? *Creating a blank PivotTable allows the user to create a framework within which to use all the data available.* The following steps create a blank PivotTable report using the ribbon.

1
- Tap or click the Sales Analysis Figures sheet tab to make the Sales Analysis Figures sheet active.
- Tap or click cell B3 to select a cell containing data for the PivotTable.
- Tap or click INSERT on the ribbon to display the INSERT tab.

Q&A Do I have to click the first cell with values to be used in the PivotTable?
You can click anywhere in the range that contains the data that will be used in the PivotTable.

- Tap or click the PivotTable button (INSERT tab | Tables group) to display the Create PivotTable dialog box (Figure 8–17).

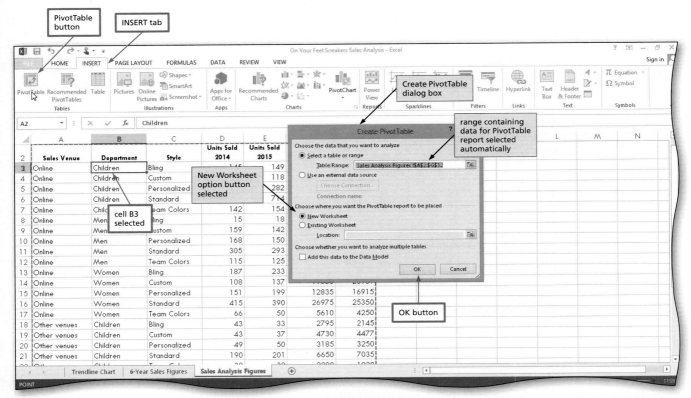

Figure 8–17

②

- Tap or click the OK button (Create PivotTable dialog box) to create a blank PivotTable report on a new worksheet and display the PivotTable Fields task pane (Figure 8–18).

Q&A

Why is the PivotTable blank?
When you create a PivotTable, you first insert the structure. The resulting PivotTable is blank until you add content to it, which you do in the next set of steps.

My PivotTable Fields task pane just disappeared. What happened?
If you tap or click outside of the PivotTable or PivotChart, the task pane no longer will be displayed. To redisplay the pane, tap or click in the PivotTable or PivotChart.

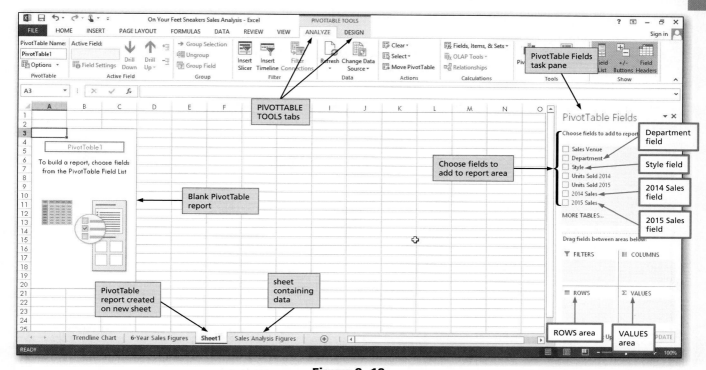

Figure 8–18

Other Ways

1. Tap or click cell in range, press and hold or right-click, tap or click Quick Analysis on shortcut menu, tap or click TABLES tab, select PivotTable

2. Tap or click cell in range, tap or click Recommended PivotTables (INSERT tab | Tables group)

To Add Data to the PivotTable

1 CREATE LINE CHART & TRENDLINE | 2 CREATE PIVOTTABLE | 3 CHANGE LAYOUT & VIEW OF PIVOTTABLE | 4 FILTER PIVOTTABLE
5 FORMAT PIVOTTABLE | 6 CREATE PIVOTCHART | 7 CHANGE PIVOTCHART VIEW & CONTENTS | 8 ADD SLICERS

Why? *Once the blank PivotTable is created, it needs to be populated using any or all of the fields in the PivotTable Fields task pane.* Add data by selecting check boxes in the PivotTable Fields task pane or by dragging fields from the Choose fields to add to report area to the Drag fields between areas below area. Fields added to the VALUES area must contain summary numeric data. Fields added to the COLUMNS area also should contain summary numeric data. As shown in Figure 8–16 on page EX 485, the rows show style by department. The columns include the two data fields, 2014 Sales and 2015 Sales. The next step adds data to the PivotTable.

1

- Drag the Style field from the Choose fields to add to report area to the ROWS area to add the Style field to the PivotTable report.

- Tap or click the Department check box in the Choose fields to add to report list to add the Department field to the ROWS area below the Type field.

Q&A | How did the Department field end up in the ROWS area?
Excel places a checked field in the group it determines is correct for that field. You can drag the field to a different group if you choose.

- Drag the 2014 Sales field to the VALUES area to add the field to column B of the PivotTable.

- Drag the 2015 Sales field to the VALUES area to add the field to column C of the PivotTable (Figure 8–19).

Q&A | What is shown in the PivotTable?
Excel displays the Style and Department fields as rows in the PivotTable. The 2014 Sales and 2015 Sales show as columns.

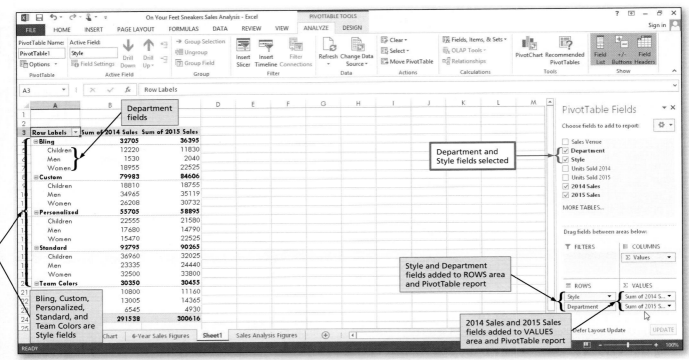

Figure 8–19

Other Ways

1. Tap or click check box for each field name (PivotTable Fields task pane)

To Change the Layout
of a PivotTable

1 CREATE LINE CHART & TRENDLINE | 2 CREATE PIVOTTABLE | 3 CHANGE LAYOUT & VIEW OF PIVOTTABLE | 4 FILTER PIVOTTABLE
5 FORMAT PIVOTTABLE | 6 CREATE PIVOTCHART | 7 CHANGE PIVOTCHART VIEW & CONTENTS | 8 ADD SLICERS

Why change the layout? *You can display a PivotTable in one of three layouts. By default, PivotTable reports are presented in a compact layout. When using multiple row labels, a different layout can make identifying the groups and subgroups easier for the reader.* The following steps change the layout of the PivotTable report to the tabular layout and then add item labels to all rows.

- Tap or click the PIVOTTABLE TOOLS DESIGN tab on the ribbon to display the PIVOTTABLE TOOLS DESIGN tab.

- Tap or click the Report Layout button (PIVOTTABLE TOOLS DESIGN tab | Layout group) to display the Report Layout menu (Figure 8–20).

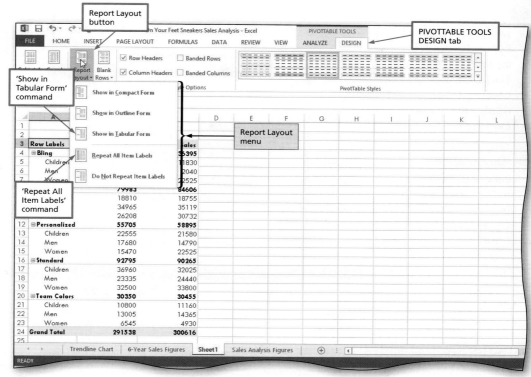

Figure 8–20

- Tap or click 'Show in Tabular Form' to display the PivotTable report in a tabular format (Figure 8–21).

Experiment

- Tap or click all the layout options to review the differences in the layout. When done, tap or click 'Show in Tabular Form' once again.

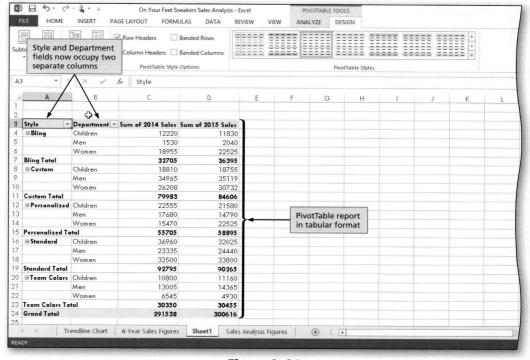

Figure 8–21

- Tap or click the Report Layout button (PIVOTTABLE TOOLS DESIGN tab | Layout group) to display the Report Layout menu.

- Tap or click 'Repeat All Item Labels' (shown in Figure 8–20) to display item (Type) labels for all Department entries (Figure 8–22).

Figure 8–22

To Change the View of a PivotTable Report

1 CREATE LINE CHART & TRENDLINE | 2 CREATE PIVOTTABLE | 3 CHANGE LAYOUT & VIEW OF PIVOTTABLE | 4 FILTER PIVOTTABLE
5 FORMAT PIVOTTABLE | 6 CREATE PIVOTCHART | 7 CHANGE PIVOTCHART VIEW & CONTENTS | 8 ADD SLICERS

Why change the view of a PivotTable report? You can change the view of this data depending on what you want *to analyze.* The PivotTable report in the On Your Feet Sneakers Sales Analysis workbook currently shows the sum of revenue for each year by department and style (Figure 8–22). If you use the sort and summary features in Excel, comparing sales for each department and style would require many steps. With PivotTable reports, this comparison is accomplished quickly. The following step changes the view of the PivotTable to show total sales by style for each department.

- Drag the Style button in the ROWS area in the PivotTable Fields task pane below the Department button to group total sales by the Department field rather than by the Style field (Figure 8–23).

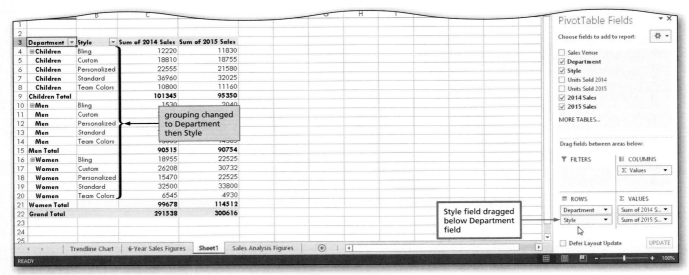

Figure 8–23

Other Ways

1. Tap or click Style button, tap or click Move Down on menu

To Filter a PivotTable Report Using a Report Filter

Why? In a PivotTable report, you can add detail by further categorizing the data to look at a particular subgroup or subgroups. You can use the Sales Venue field to view sales in a particular venue by style and department. Viewing a PivotTable report for only a subset that meets a selection criterion is known as filtering. The following steps add a report filter to change the view of the PivotTable and then filter the PivotTable by Sales Venue.

1

- Drag the Sales Venue field from the Choose field to add to report area to the FILTERS area in the PivotTable Fields task pane to create a report filter in the PivotTable (Figure 8–24).

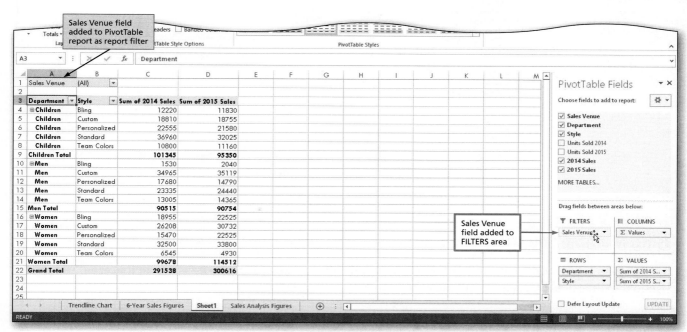

Figure 8–24

2

- Tap or click the filter button in cell B1 to display the filter menu for column B, Sales Venue in this case.

- Tap or click Online on the filter menu to select the Online criterion (Figure 8–25).

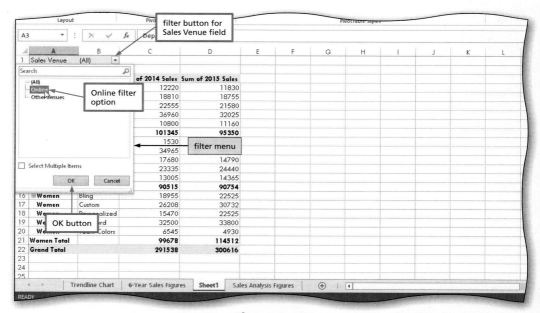

Figure 8–25

3

• Tap or click the OK button to display totals for online sales only (Figure 8–26).

Q&A What is shown now in the PivotTable report?
Now the PivotTable shows total sales for each department and style for online sales only.

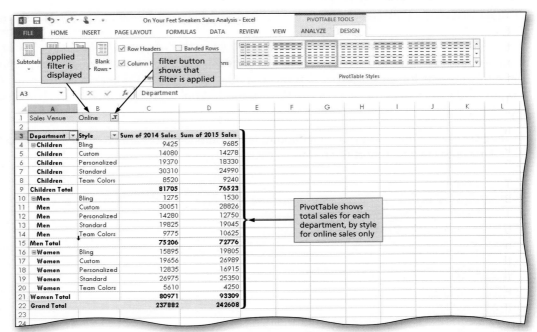

Figure 8–26

To Filter a PivotTable Report Using Multiple Selection Criteria

1 CREATE LINE CHART & TRENDLINE | 2 CREATE PIVOTTABLE | 3 CHANGE LAYOUT & VIEW OF PIVOTTABLE | 4 FILTER PIVOTTABLE
5 FORMAT PIVOTTABLE | 6 CREATE PIVOTCHART | 7 CHANGE PIVOTCHART VIEW & CONTENTS | 8 ADD SLICERS

Why? *You may need to identify a subset that is defined by more than one filter criterion.* The following steps change the filter field and select multiple criteria on which to filter.

1

• Drag the Style button from the ROWS area to the FILTERS area.

• Drag the Sales Venue button from the FILTERS area to the ROWS area below Department (Figure 8–27).

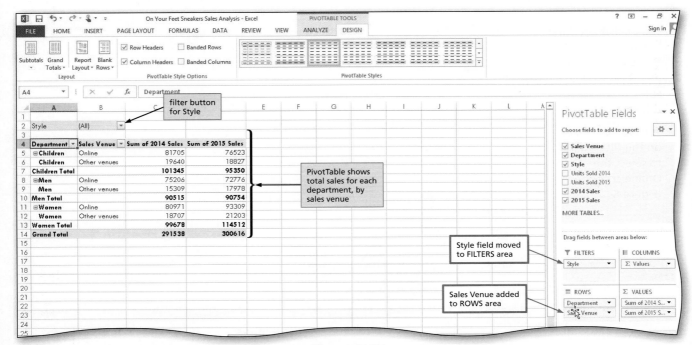

Figure 8–27

2

- Tap or click the filter button in cell B2 to display the filter menu for the Style field.

- Tap or click the 'Select Multiple Items' check box to prepare to select multiple criteria.

- Tap or click the Bling, Standard, and Team Colors check boxes on the filter menu to deselect these criteria and filter on Custom and Personalized only (Figure 8–28).

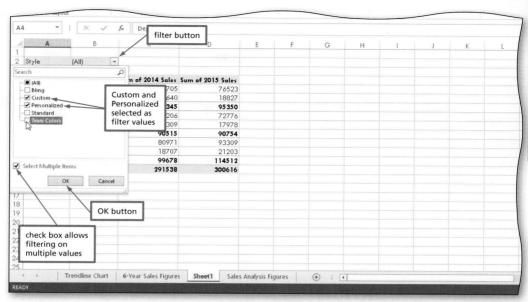

Figure 8–28

3

- Tap or click the OK button to display sales totals for Custom and Personalized styles (Figure 8–29).

Q&A | How do I know which criteria have been selected?
With a filter, you need to click the filter button to see which criteria have been selected.

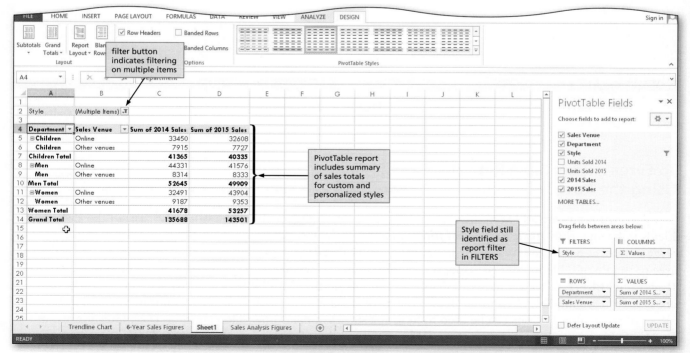

Figure 8–29

To Remove a Report Filter from a PivotTable Report

Why? *When you no longer need to display filtered data in a PivotTable, you can easily remove the filter.* The following step removes the Style report filter from the PivotTable report.

1

- Tap or click the filter button in cell B2 and tap or click the All check box to include all Style criteria in the PivotTable report.
- Tap or click the OK button.
- Drag the Style button out of the PivotTable Fields task pane to remove the field from the PivotTable report (Figure 8–30).

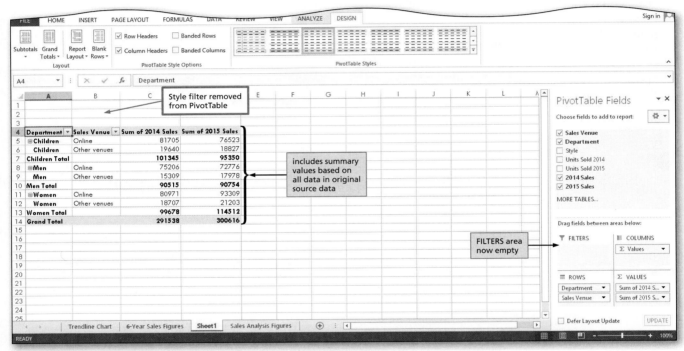

Figure 8–30

To Filter a PivotTable Report Using the Row Label Filter

Report filters are added to the PivotTable report by adding a field to the FILTERS area of the PivotTable Fields task pane. *Why use a Row Label filter?* *In a PivotTable report, you may want to look at a subset of data based on fields that are already in use.* When the field of interest is already part of the PivotTable, included in the ROWS area of the PivotTable Fields task pane, you can use filters associated with those fields in the PivotTable report, **Row Label filters**, to view a subset of data. For example, in the PivotTable in Figure 8–30, the ROWS fields are Department and Sales Venue. Each of these fields has a filter button associated with it in the PivotTable, and either of these filter buttons can be used to look at a subset of data. The following steps use a filter for one of the ROWS fields to restrict data in the PivotTable report to sales of custom and personalized styles.

1

- Drag the Sales Venue button out of the ROWS area in the PivotTable Fields task pane to remove the field from the report.

- Tap or click the Style check box in the Choose fields to add to report list to add the Style field to the ROWS area below the Department field.

- Tap or click the filter button in cell B4 to display the filter menu for the Style field (Figure 8–31).

Q&A I do not have a filter button in cell B4. How do I access the menu? The filter buttons may be hidden. Tap or click the Field Headers button (PIVOTTABLE TOOLS ANALYZE tab | Show group) to turn on the field headers and make the filter buttons visible.

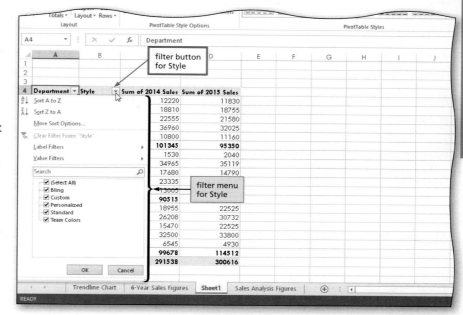

Figure 8–31

Why does cell B4 not appear selected when I use the filter button? Filtering happens independently of cell selection. You do not need to select the cell in which the filter button is located in order to use the filter. In Figure 8–31, for example, the filter button for Style has been clicked while cell A4 is the active, or selected cell.

2

- Tap or click the Bling, Standard, and Team Colors check boxes on the filter menu to leave only the Custom and Personalized styles selected (Figure 8–32).

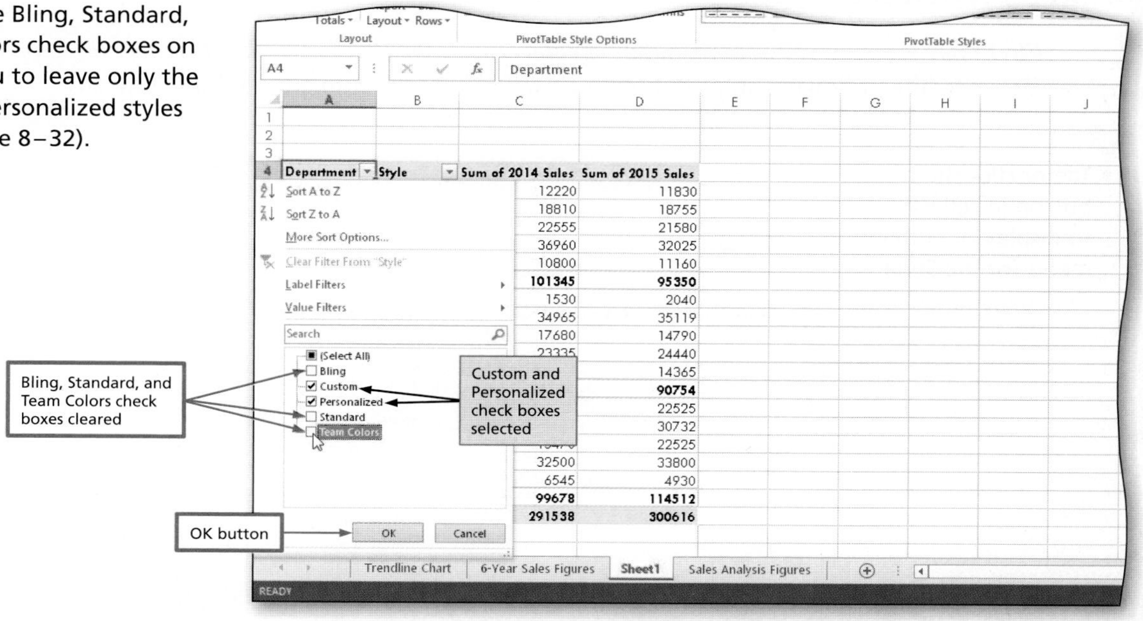

Figure 8–32

3

- Tap or click the OK button to display total sales figures for Custom and Personalized styles only, categorized by department (Figure 8–33).

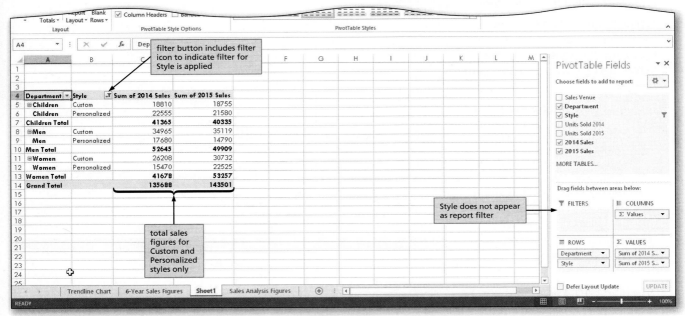

Figure 8–33

To Remove a Row Label Filter from a PivotTable Report

1 CREATE LINE CHART & TRENDLINE | 2 CREATE PIVOTTABLE | 3 CHANGE LAYOUT & VIEW OF PIVOTTABLE | 4 FILTER PIVOTTABLE
5 FORMAT PIVOTTABLE | 6 CREATE PIVOTCHART | 7 CHANGE PIVOTCHART VIEW & CONTENTS | 8 ADD SLICERS

Why? *Once you have reviewed the subset of data, remove the Row Label filter to restore the PivotTable report to reflect all records.* The following steps remove a Row Label filter from a PivotTable report.

1

- Tap or click the filter button in cell B4 to display the filter menu for the Style field (Figure 8–34).

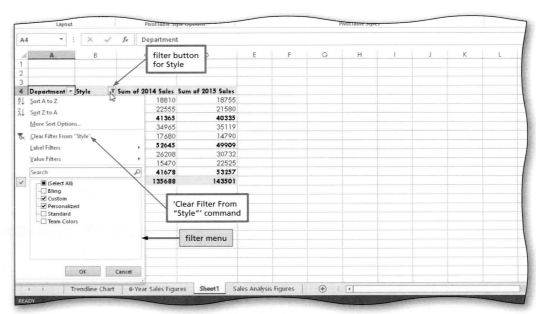

Figure 8–34

- Tap or click 'Clear Filter From "Style"' on the filter menu to display total sales figures for styles in all departments (Figure 8–35).

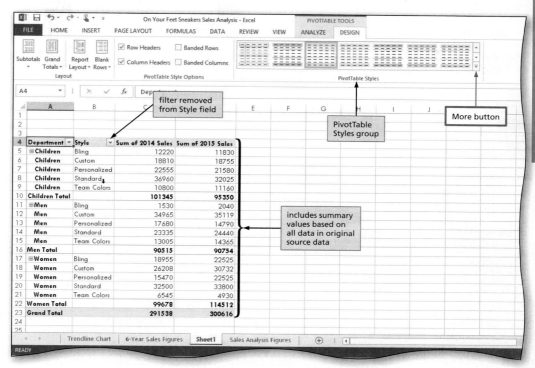

Figure 8–35

Formatting PivotTable Reports

You can use several formatting options to enhance the appearance of PivotTable reports and make the content easier to read. Excel includes a number of preset PivotTable report styles to simplify this task. These styles function in a similar fashion to Excel's table styles. Care should be taken when formatting PivotTable reports, however, because formatting techniques that work for regular tables of data do not behave in the same fashion in PivotTable reports. PivotTable report formatting requires the use of PivotTable styles and field settings.

To Format a PivotTable Report

1 CREATE LINE CHART & TRENDLINE | 2 CREATE PIVOTTABLE | 3 CHANGE LAYOUT & VIEW OF PIVOTTABLE | 4 FILTER PIVOTTABLE
5 FORMAT PIVOTTABLE | 6 CREATE PIVOTCHART | 7 CHANGE PIVOTCHART VIEW & CONTENTS | 8 ADD SLICERS

Why? *PivotTable reports benefit from formatting to enhance their readability.* The following steps format a PivotTable report by applying a PivotTable style and specifying number formats for the fields.

- Double-tap or double-click the Sheet1 sheet tab to select the sheet tab name, type `Sales PivotTable` as the new sheet tab name, and then press the ENTER key to rename the sheet tab.

- Press and hold or right-click the Sales PivotTable sheet tab and then point to Tab Color on the shortcut menu to prepare for changing the color of the sheet tab.

- Tap or click 'Lime, Accent 1' (column 5, row 1) in the Theme Colors area to apply the color to the sheet tab.

- Tap or click cell A7 to select a cell in the PivotTable.

- If necessary, tap or click PIVOTTABLE TOOLS DESIGN on the ribbon to display the PIVOTTABLE TOOLS DESIGN tab.

- Tap or click the More button in the PivotTable Styles gallery (PIVOTTABLE TOOLS DESIGN tab | PivotTable Styles group) to expand the gallery.

- Scroll down until the Dark section of the gallery is visible.

- If you are using a mouse, point to 'Pivot Style Dark 9' PivotTable style (column 2, row 2) in the Dark section of the PivotTable Styles gallery to display a preview of the style in the PivotTable (Figure 8–36).

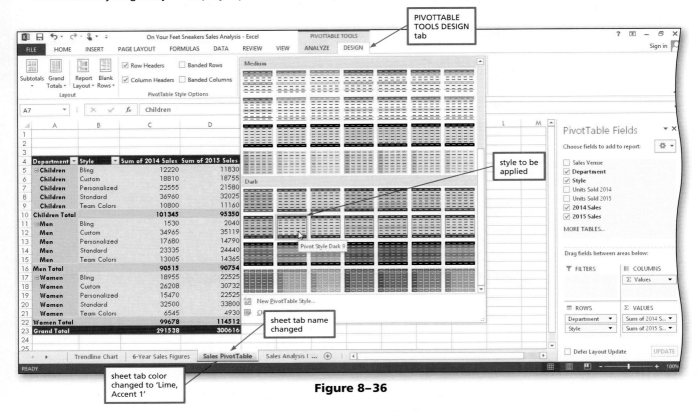

Figure 8–36

2

- Tap or click 'Pivot Style Dark 9' in the PivotTable Styles gallery to apply the style to the PivotTable report.

- Press and hold or right-click cell C6 and then tap or click Number Format on the shortcut menu to display the Format Cells dialog box.

- Tap or click Currency in the Category list (Format Cells dialog box) to select the Currency number format.

- Type 0 in the Decimal places box to specify no decimal places (Figure 8–37).

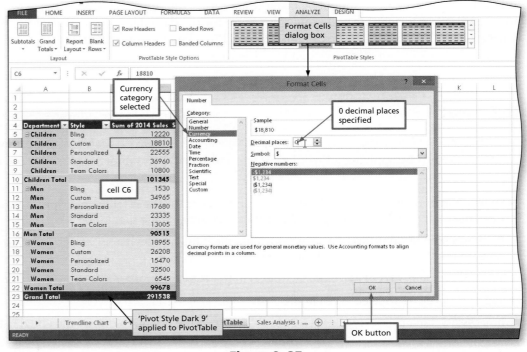

Figure 8–37

3

- Tap or click the OK button to apply the Currency style to all 2014 Sales values in the PivotTable report.

Q&A

Why does the number format change apply to all Sales values? When formatting is applied to a PivotTable field, all field entries are updated to reflect that formatting.

Why is the dollar currency symbol displayed for the Sales values? The dollar currency symbol is included by default.

- Repeat Step 2 with cell D6 selected and then tap or click the OK button (Format Cells dialog box) to apply the Currency style to all 2015 Sales values in the PivotTable report.

- Tap or click cell E24 to deselect the PivotTable report.

- Tap or click the Save button on the Quick Access Toolbar to save the workbook (Figure 8–38).

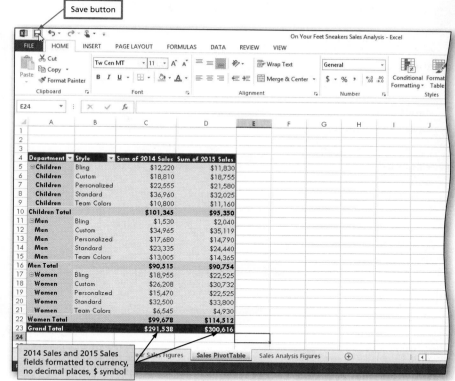

Figure 8–38

How do you choose a particular PivotTable style?

When you plan PivotTables and PivotCharts, consider what information you want to display in each report. As you are developing a report, review the galleries of PivotTable and PivotChart styles to find the best one to display your data. For example, some PivotTable styles include banded rows and columns, which can make it easier to scan and interpret the report.

CONSIDER THIS

To Switch Summary Functions in a PivotTable

1 CREATE LINE CHART & TRENDLINE | 2 CREATE PIVOTTABLE | 3 CHANGE LAYOUT & VIEW OF PIVOTTABLE | 4 FILTER PIVOTTABLE

5 FORMAT PIVOTTABLE | 6 CREATE PIVOTCHART | 7 CHANGE PIVOTCHART VIEW & CONTENTS | 8 ADD SLICERS

Why? *The default summary function in a PivotTable is the SUM function. For some comparisons, using a different summary function will yield more useful measures.* In addition to analyzing total sales by department and style for various groupings, you are also interested in looking at average sales by style and department. In PivotTable reports, you easily can change the function used to summarize data from the original table. Currently, the PivotTable report for On Your Feet Sneakers displays the total sales for each department by style. Average sales by style and by department might be a better measure for comparing the sales. The following steps switch summary functions in a PivotTable.

1

- Press and hold or right-click cell C5 to display the shortcut menu and prepare for changing the summary function for the Sales values.

- Point to 'Summarize Values By' on the shortcut menu to display the Summarize Values By submenu (Figure 8–39).

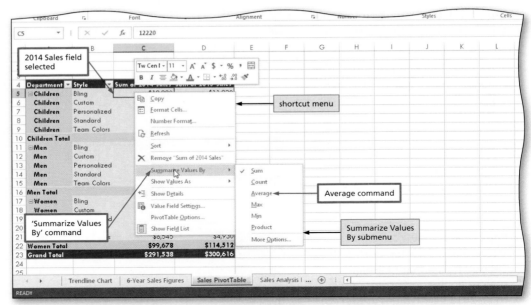

Figure 8–39

2

- Tap or click Average on the Summarize Values By submenu to change the summary function from Sum to Average (Figure 8–40).

Q&A | Why did the column title in cell C4 change?
When you change a summary function, the column heading automatically updates to reflect the new summary function chosen.

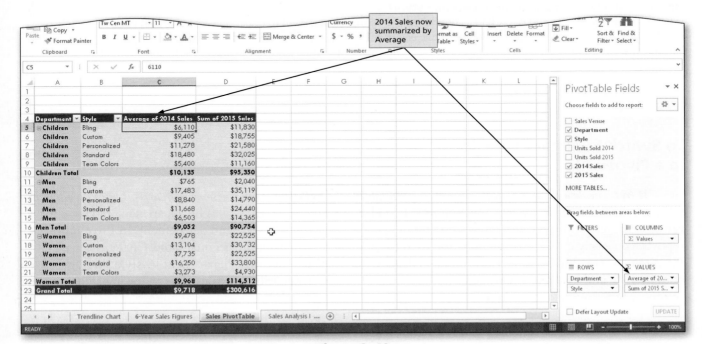

Figure 8–40

3

• Repeat Steps 1 and 2 to change the summary function used in column D from Sum to Average (Figure 8–41).

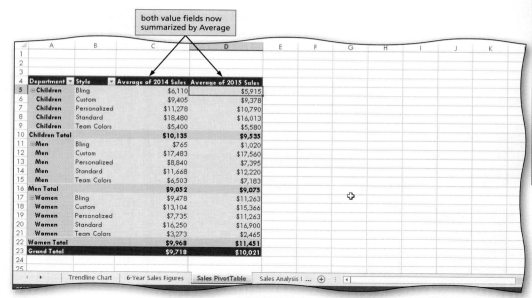

Figure 8–41

More on Summary Functions for PivotCharts and PivotTables

Table 8–1 lists the summary functions Excel provides for analysis of data in PivotChart and PivotTable reports. Summary functions can be selected from the shortcut menu of a cell in the PivotTable report, as was just illustrated when changing the summary function from Sum to Average. Some summary functions do not appear directly on the shortcut menu, but rather are accessed by tapping or clicking More Options on the Summary Functions submenu. Summary functions also can be selected by using the Field Settings button in the Active Field group on the PIVOTTABLE TOOLS ANALYZE tab to access the Value Field Settings dialog box (Figure 8–42a)

Table 8–1 Summary Functions for PivotChart Report and PivotTable Report Data Analysis	
Summary Function	**Description**
Sum	Sum of the values (default function for numeric source data)
Count	Number of data values
Average	Average of the values
Max	Largest value
Min	Smallest value
Product	Product of the values
Count Nums	Number of data values that contain numeric data
StdDev	Estimate of the standard deviation of all of the data to be summarized, used when data is a sample of a larger population of interest
StdDevp	Standard deviation of all of the data to be summarized, used when data is the population of interest
Var	Estimate of the variance of all of the data to be summarized, used when data is a sample of a larger population of interest
Varp	Variance of the data to be summarized, used when data is the population of interest

© 2014 Cengage Learning

or by using the field button in the VALUES area in the PivotTable Fields task pane (Figure 8–42b) to access the 'Value Field Settings' command and the Value Field Settings dialog box.

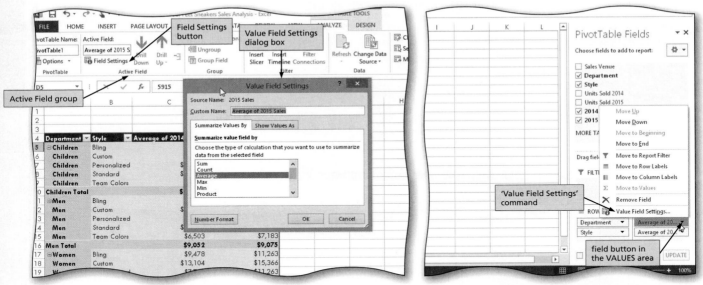

(a) **Value Field Settings Dialog Box**   (b) **PivotTable Fields Task Pane**

Figure 8–42

To Add a Second Value Calculation to a PivotTable Report

1 CREATE LINE CHART & TRENDLINE | 2 CREATE PIVOTTABLE | 3 CHANGE LAYOUT & VIEW OF PIVOTTABLE | 4 FILTER PIVOTTABLE

5 FORMAT PIVOTTABLE | **6 CREATE PIVOTCHART** | 7 CHANGE PIVOTCHART VIEW & CONTENTS | 8 ADD SLICERS

Why? *In addition to changing summary functions, you may need to add new fields to analyze additional or more complex questions.* You have been asked to review and compare both total and average sales for 2014 and 2015. You will need to add value fields and change the summary function to meet this request. The following steps add a second value calculation for each of the two years and use these fields in the PivotTable report.

1

- In the PivotTable Fields task pane, drag the 2014 Sales field to the VALUES area above the 'Average of 2014 Sales' button to add the field to column C of the PivotTable.

- In the VALUES area, tap or click the 'Sum of 2014 Sales' button to display the Sum of 2014 Sales menu (Figure 8–43).

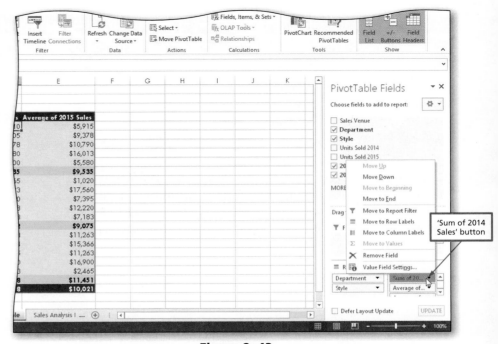

Figure 8–43

- Tap or click 'Value Field Settings' to display the Value Field Settings dialog box.
- Enter **Total 2014 Sales** in the Custom Name text box (Value Field Settings dialog box) to rename the value field (Figure 8–44).

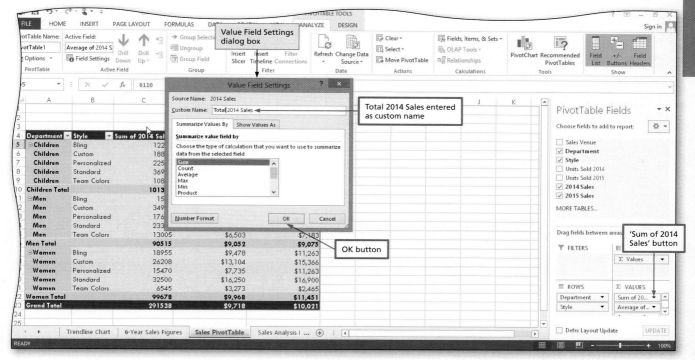

Figure 8–44

- Tap or click the OK button (Value Field Settings dialog box) to apply the custom name to the 2014 Sales field.
- Drag the 2015 Sales field to the VALUES area between the Total 2014 Sales values and the Average of 2014 Sales values to add the field to column D of the PivotTable.
- Tap or click the 'Sum of 2015 Sales' button and then tap or click 'Value Field Settings' to display the Value Field Settings dialog box.
- Enter **Total 2015 Sales** in the Custom Name text box to rename the value field.
- Tap or click the OK button (Value Field Settings dialog box) to apply the custom name.
- Use the Value Field Settings dialog box to customize the names as shown in cells E4 and F4 (shown in Figure 8–45).
- Format the values in columns C and then D to the Currency category, 0 decimal places, and the $ symbol.
- Tap or click the Save button on the Quick Access Toolbar to save the workbook (Figure 8–45).

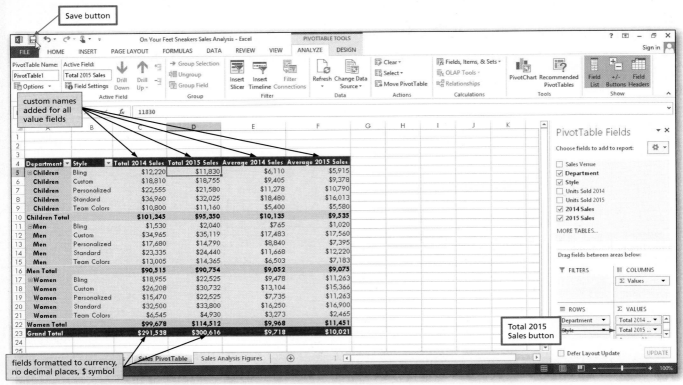

Figure 8–45

To Customize the Display of the Field List and Field Headers in the PivotTable Report

1 CREATE LINE CHART & TRENDLINE | 2 CREATE PIVOTTABLE | 3 CHANGE LAYOUT & VIEW OF PIVOTTABLE | 4 FILTER PIVOTTABLE
5 FORMAT PIVOTTABLE | 6 CREATE PIVOTCHART | 7 CHANGE PIVOTCHART VIEW & CONTENTS | 8 ADD SLICERS

Why? *Customizing the display of the field list and field headers can provide a less-cluttered worksheet.* You can choose which supporting items you display in the PivotTable report and on the worksheet containing the report. You can display or hide the PivotTable Fields task pane, field headers, and buttons. You also can turn off the autofitting of column widths to further customize the columns of the report. The following steps remove the PivotTable Fields task pane and field headers from the report and worksheet and turn off the column autofitting.

- Tap or click the Field List button (PIVOTTABLE TOOLS ANALYZE tab | Show group) to hide the PivotTable Fields task pane.

- Tap or click the Field Headers button (PIVOTTABLE TOOLS ANALYZE tab | Show group) to hide the field headers (Figure 8–46).

Q&A   How can I display the PivotTable Fields task pane and field headers after hiding them?
The Field List, +/- Buttons, and Field Headers buttons (PIVOTTABLE TOOLS ANALYZE tab | Show group) are toggle buttons. Tapping or clicking them again turns the display back on.

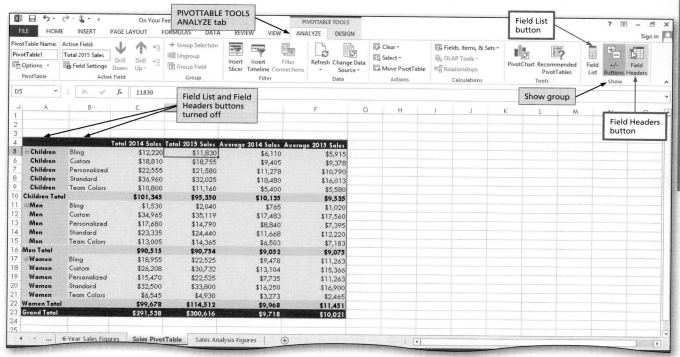

Figure 8–46

2

- Tap or click the PivotTable Options button (PIVOTTABLE TOOLS ANALYZE tab | PivotTable group) to display the PivotTable Options dialog box.

- Tap or click the 'Autofit column widths on update' check box to remove the check mark (Figure 8–47).

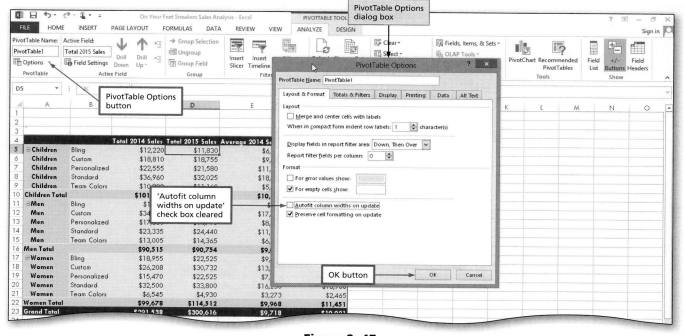

Figure 8–47

3

- Tap or click the OK button (PivotTable Options dialog box) to turn off the autofitting of column widths.

To Customize the Display of the Expand and Collapse Buttons in a PivotTable Report

The Expand and Collapse buttons expand and collapse across categories, reducing the amount of detail visible in the report without removing the field from the report. *Why customize the display of these buttons? In some instances, the report may be more visually appealing without the Expand or Collapse buttons in the report.* The following steps illustrate expanding and collapsing categories using the buttons and shortcut menus, and then suppressing the display of the Expand and Collapse buttons in the report.

1

• Tap or click the Collapse button in cell A5 to collapse the Children style information (Figure 8–48).

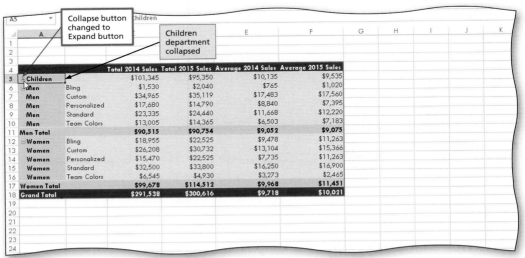

Figure 8–48

2

• Press and hold or right-click cell A12 to display the shortcut menu and then point to Expand/Collapse to display the Expand/Collapse submenu (Figure 8–49).

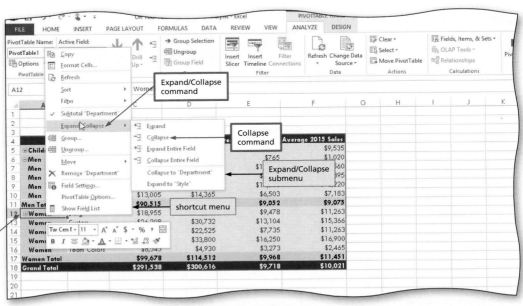

Figure 8–49

- Tap or click Collapse on the Expand/Collapse submenu to collapse the Women department data.
- Tap or click the +/- Buttons button (PIVOTTABLE TOOLS ANALYZE tab | Show group) to hide the Expand and Collapse buttons in the PivotTable (Figure 8–50).

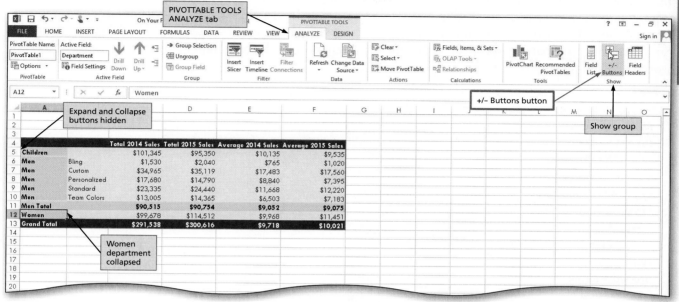

Figure 8–50

- Press and hold or right-click cell A5 and then point to Expand/Collapse on the shortcut menu to display the Expand/Collapse submenu.

- Tap or click 'Expand Entire Field' on the Expand/Collapse submenu to expand the Department field.

- Insert two blank rows above row 1 for the title and subtitle.

- In cell A1, enter the title **On Your Feet Sneakers Sales Report** and then enter the subtitle **2014 and 2015** in cell A2.

- Merge and center the text across A1:F1 and A2:F2. Apply the Title style to cell A1 and the Heading 4 style to cell A2. Apply the fill color 'Lime, Accent 1, Lighter 40%' (column 5, row 4) to cells A1:A2 (Figure 8–51).

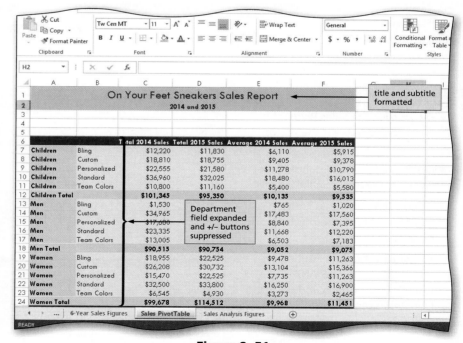

Figure 8–51

Q&A Why not use the existing blank rows for the title and subtitle?
Excel needs the blank rows above a PivotTable to remain blank, for any filters added in the PivotTable Fields task pane. If you enter any content in the existing blank rows, you will not be able to add filters in the PivotTable Fields task pane.

To Update the Contents of a PivotTable Report

When you update cell contents in Excel, you update related tables, formula calculations, and charts. **Why does this not work for PivotTables?** *PivotTables do not update automatically when you change the underlying data for the PivotTable report.* You must update the PivotTable manually to recalculate summary data in the PivotTable report. The sales figure and Units Sold for 2015 for children's Bling style in other venues are incorrect in the original sheet. The correct values for children's Bling sneakers sold in other venues are 51 and 3315 for Units Sold 2015 and 2015 Sales, respectively. The following steps correct the typographical error in the underlying worksheet, and then update the PivotTable report.

1

- Tap or click the Sales Analysis Figures sheet tab to make it the active sheet.

- Tap or click cell E18, type **51** as the new value, and then select cell G18.

- Type **3315** in cell G18 and then press the ENTER key to change the contents of the cell (Figure 8–52).

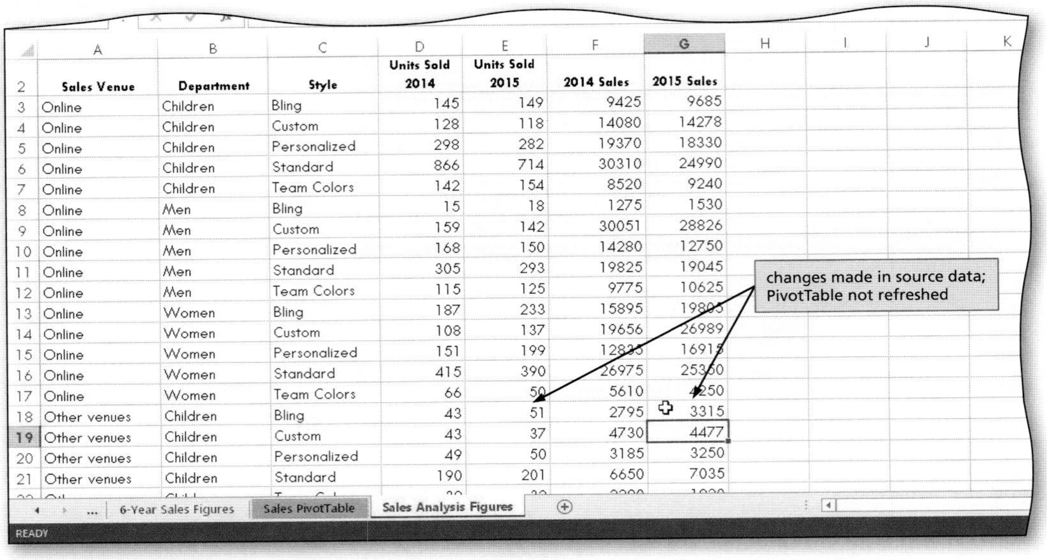

Q&A What data will this change in the PivotTable?
The changed value is for sales of Children's Bling shoes in Other venues. This change will be reflected in cells D7 and F7 in the Sales PivotTable worksheet when the update is performed.

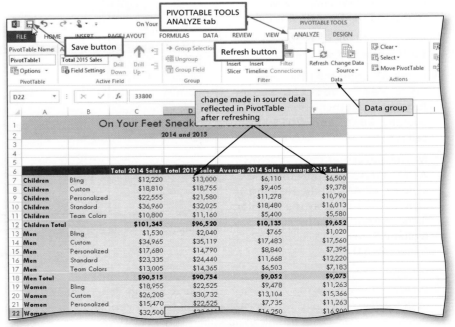

Figure 8–52

2

- Tap or click the Sales PivotTable sheet tab to make it the active sheet.

- If necessary, tap or click inside the PivotTable report to make it active.

- Tap or click the PIVOTTABLE TOOLS ANALYZE tab on the ribbon.

- Tap or click the Refresh button (PIVOTTABLE TOOLS ANALYZE tab | Data group) to update the PivotTable report to reflect the change to the underlying data.

- Tap or click the Save button on the Quick Access Toolbar to save the workbook (Figure 8–53).

Figure 8–53

Do you always have to refresh the PivotTable when you make a change to the underlying data?

PivotTables can be based on information stored in one or more worksheets or in external data sources such as Microsoft Access databases. The contents of a PivotTable are not refreshed when the data from which they are created changes. This means you must refresh the PivotTable manually when underlying data changes. If you add rows to the source data, a new PivotTable must be created to incorporate the new data. The exception to this is PivotTables built on data tables. A PivotTable built on a data table that has new rows added to the bottom of the table will automatically incorporate those new rows when you refresh the PivotTable.

Break Point: If you wish to take a break, this is a good place to do so. You can exit Excel now. To resume at a later time, run Excel, open the file called On Your Feet Sneakers Sales Analysis, and continue following the steps from this location forward.

To Create a PivotChart Report from an Existing PivotTable Report

1 CREATE LINE CHART & TRENDLINE | 2 CREATE PIVOTTABLE | 3 CHANGE LAYOUT & VIEW OF PIVOTTABLE | 4 FILTER PIVOTTABLE
5 FORMAT PIVOTTABLE | 6 CREATE PIVOTCHART | 7 CHANGE PIVOTCHART VIEW & CONTENTS | 8 ADD SLICERS

Why create a PivotChart from a PivotTable report? A PivotChart report always must be associated with a PivotTable report. The association is created in one of two ways. If you already have created a PivotTable report, you can create a PivotChart report for that PivotTable report using the PivotChart button on the PIVOTTABLE TOOLS ANALYZE tab. The following steps create a PivotChart report from the existing PivotTable report, formatting it as a 3-D clustered column chart that shows the two-year data for total sales side by side.

- If necessary, tap or click cell A7 to select it in the PivotTable report.
- Tap or click the Field List button (PIVOTTABLE TOOLS ANALYZE tab | Show group) to display the PivotTable Fields task pane.
- Tap or click the PivotChart button (PIVOTTABLE TOOLS ANALYZE tab | Tools group) to display the Insert Chart dialog box.
- Tap or click '3-D Clustered Column' in the Column chart type gallery to select the chart type (Figure 8–54).

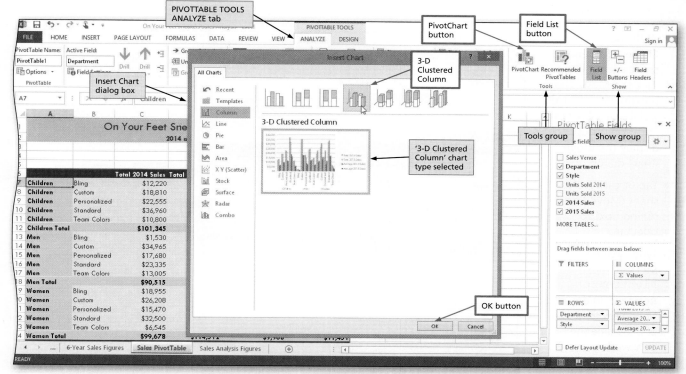

Figure 8–54

• Tap or click the
OK button (Insert
Chart dialog box)
to add the chart to
the Sales PivotTable
worksheet
(Figure 8–55).

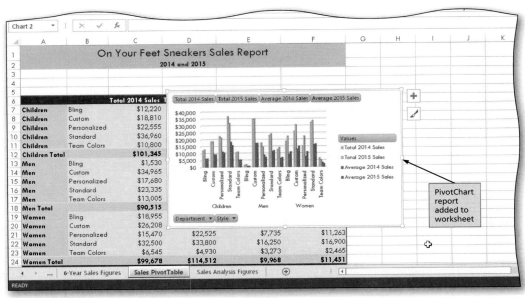

Figure 8–55

To Change the Location of a PivotChart Report and Delete Average Sales Data

1 CREATE LINE CHART & TRENDLINE | 2 CREATE PIVOTTABLE | 3 CHANGE LAYOUT & VIEW OF PIVOTTABLE | 4 FILTER PIVOTTABLE | 5 FORMAT PIVOTTABLE | 6 CREATE PIVOTCHART | **7 CHANGE PIVOTCHART VIEW & CONTENTS** | 8 ADD SLICERS

By default, a PivotChart report will be created on the same page as the associated PivotTable report. *Why move the PivotChart? Larger charts may benefit from having their own sheet to best display the content.* The following steps move the PivotChart report to a separate sheet and then change the tab color to match the tab color of the PivotTable report tab.

• With the 3-D
Clustered Column
chart selected, tap or
click the Move Chart
button (PIVOTCHART
TOOLS DESIGN tab |
Location group) to
display the Move
Chart dialog box.

• Tap or click New
sheet (Move Chart
dialog box) to
select it.

• Type **Total
Sales
PivotChart
Report** in the
New sheet text
box to name the
new worksheet
(Figure 8–56).

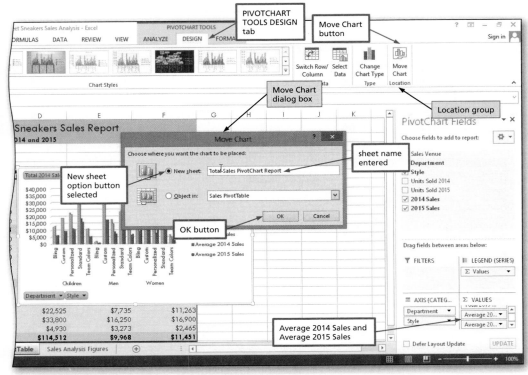

Figure 8–56

- Tap or click the OK button (Move Chart dialog box) to move the 3-D clustered column chart to the new Total Sales PivotChart Report sheet.

- Press and hold or right-click the new sheet tab, point to Tab Color on the shortcut menu to display the Tab Color submenu, and then tap or click 'Orange, Accent 2' (column 6, row 1) to change the color of the sheet tab.

- In the PivotChart Fields task pane, drag Average 2014 Sales and Average 2015 Sales out of the VALUES area to remove the average sales data from the PivotChart report and PivotTable report (Figure 8–57).

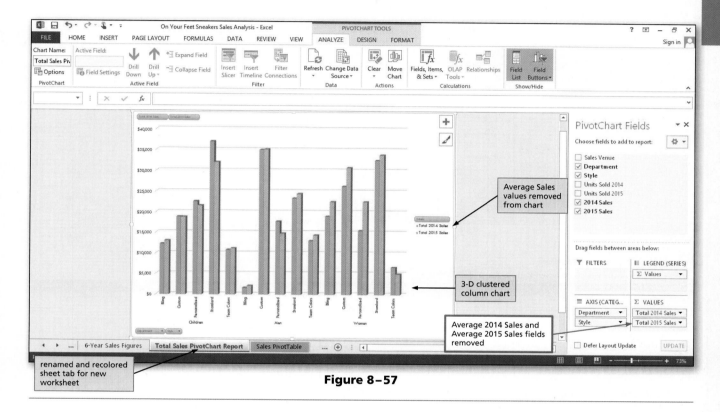

Figure 8–57

To Change the PivotChart Type and Format the Chart

1 CREATE LINE CHART & TRENDLINE | 2 CREATE PIVOTTABLE | 3 CHANGE LAYOUT & VIEW OF PIVOTTABLE | 4 FILTER PIVOTTABLE | 5 FORMAT PIVOTTABLE | 6 CREATE PIVOTCHART | 7 CHANGE PIVOTCHART VIEW & CONTENTS | 8 ADD SLICERS

Why? Selecting a chart type instead of using the default provides variety for the reader. The default chart type for a PivotChart is a clustered column chart. PivotCharts can support most chart types, except XY (scatter), stock, and bubble. The steps on the following page change the PivotChart type to 3-D cylinder, add a title to the PivotChart report, and apply formatting options to the chart.

1

- Tap or click one of the Total 2014 columns to select the data series.

- Press and hold or right-click to display the shortcut menu (Figure 8–58).

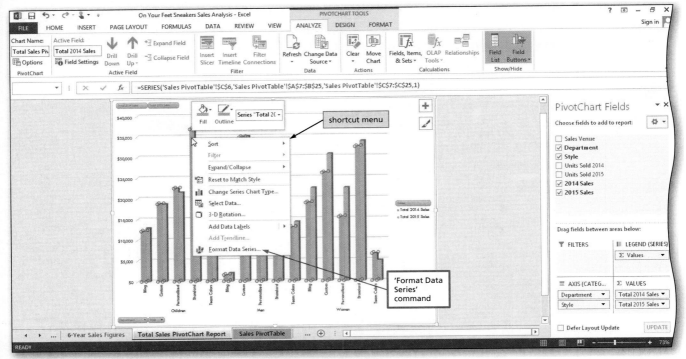

Figure 8–58

2

- Tap or click 'Format Data Series' on the shortcut menu to open the Format Data Series task pane.

- In the Column shape section, tap or click Cylinder (Figure 8–59).

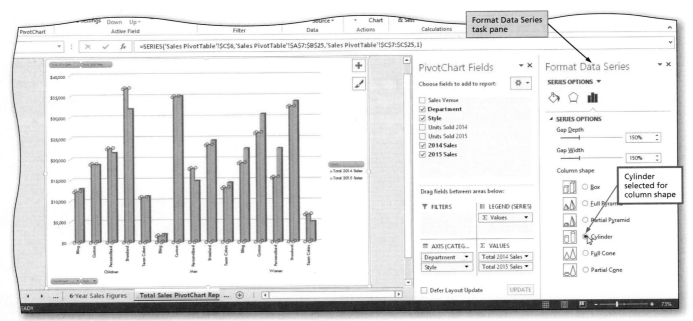

Figure 8–59

3

- Tap or click one of the 2015 columns to select the data series and then tap or click Cylinder in the Column shape section of the Format Data Series task pane.

- Tap or click the Close button to close the Format Data Series task pane.

- Tap or click the Chart Elements button and tap or click to place a check mark in the Chart Title check box.

- Drag to select the title text in the chart title placeholder.

- Type **On Your Feet Sneakers** as the first line in the chart title and then press the ENTER key to move to a new line.

- Type **Total Sales by Department and Style** as the second line in the chart title and then press the ENTER key to move to a new line.

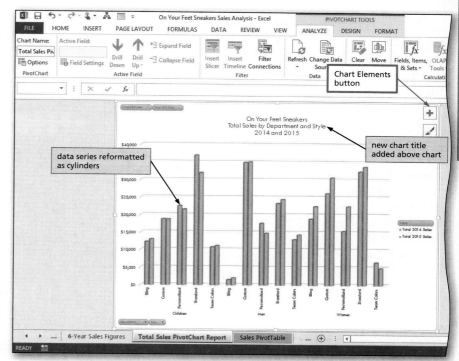

Figure 8–60

- Type **2014 and 2015** as the third line in the chart title and then tap or click anywhere on the chart to add the title to the chart (Figure 8–60).

4

- Tap or click the chart title to select it.

- Tap or click the PIVOTCHART TOOLS FORMAT tab on the ribbon.

- Tap or click the More button (PIVOTCHART TOOLS FORMAT tab | WordArt Styles group) to display the WordArt Styles gallery (Figure 8–61).

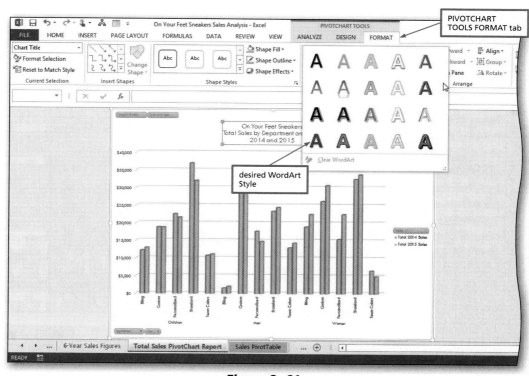

Figure 8–61

5

- Tap or click 'Pattern Fill - White, Text 2, Dark Upward Diagonal, Shadow' (column 1, row 4) in the WordArt Styles gallery to apply it to the chart title.

- Tap or click the Chart Elements arrow (PIVOTCHART TOOLS FORMAT tab | Current Selection group) to display the Chart Elements menu (Figure 8–62).

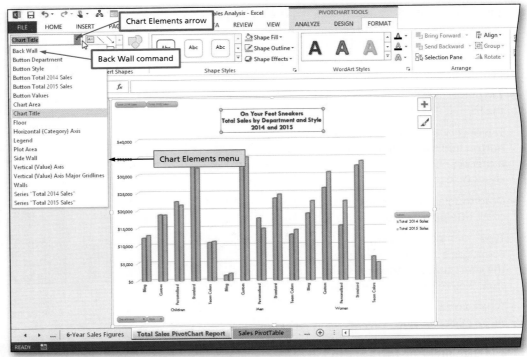

Figure 8–62

6

- Tap or click Back Wall on the Chart Elements menu to select the back wall of the chart.

- Tap or click the Shape Fill arrow (PIVOTCHART TOOLS FORMAT tab | Shape Styles group) to display the Shape Fill menu.

- Point to Gradient on the Shape Fill menu to display the Gradient submenu (Figure 8–63).

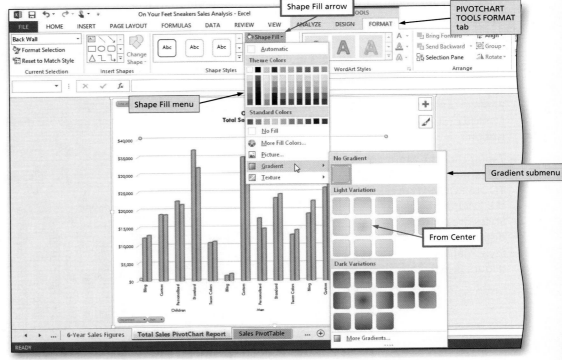

Figure 8–63

7

- Tap or click From Center in the Light Variations area to apply a gradient fill to the back wall of the chart (Figure 8–64).

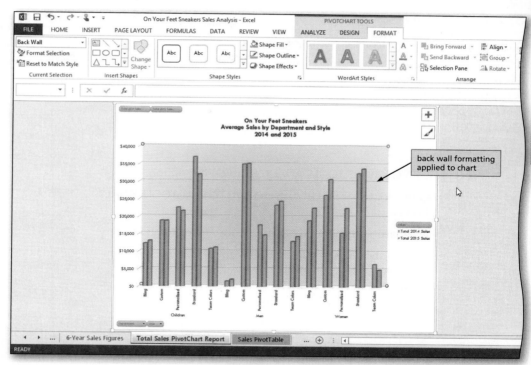

Figure 8–64

8

- Repeat Steps 6 and 7 after selecting Side Wall on the Chart Elements menu (Figure 8–65).

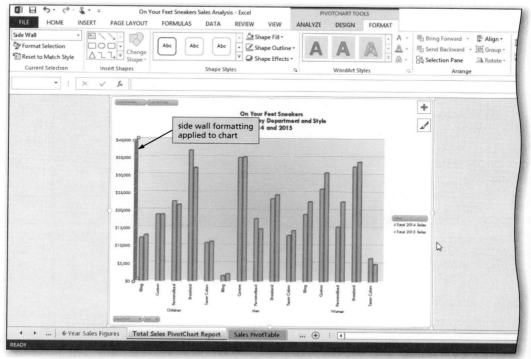

Figure 8–65

To Change the View of a PivotChart

Why change the view of a PivotChart? Changing the view of the PivotChart lets you analyze different relationships graphically. As with regular charts, when the data in a PivotTable report is changed, any PivotChart reports built upon that PivotTable report update to reflect those changes. Unique to PivotCharts, however, is that changes made to the view of the PivotChart are reflected automatically in the view of the PivotTable. The following steps change the view of the PivotChart report and then show how the change in the PivotChart causes a corresponding change in the view of its PivotTable report.

1

- Tap or click the PIVOTCHART TOOLS ANALYZE tab on the ribbon.
- If necessary, tap or click the Field List button (PIVOTCHART TOOLS ANALYZE tab | Show/Hide group) to display the PivotChart Fields task pane.
- Tap or click the Department check box in the Choose fields to add to report area to deselect the Department field.
- Place a check mark in the Sales Venue check box to select the Sales Venue field and add it to the AXIS area (Figure 8–66).

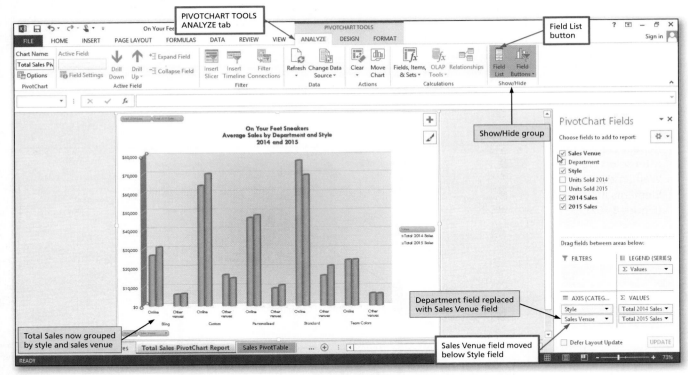

Figure 8–66

- Tap or click the Sales PivotTable sheet tab to view the changes in the corresponding PivotTable report (Figure 8–67).

Q&A What happens when the view of the PivotChart report changes? Changes in the PivotChart report are reflected automatically in the PivotTable report. Changes to category (x-axis) fields, such as Sales Venue in this case, are correspondingly made to **row fields** in the PivotTable report. Similarly, changes to series (y-axis) fields in a PivotChart report appear as changes to **column fields** in the PivotTable report.

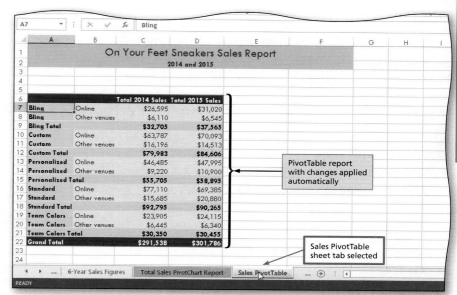

Figure 8–67

- In the PivotTable report, delete the Sales Venue field and replace it with the Department field in the AXIS area.
- If necessary, change the order of the row labels to display the data first by Department and then by Style.
- Tap or click the Total Sales PivotChart Report sheet tab to make it the active tab (Figure 8–68).

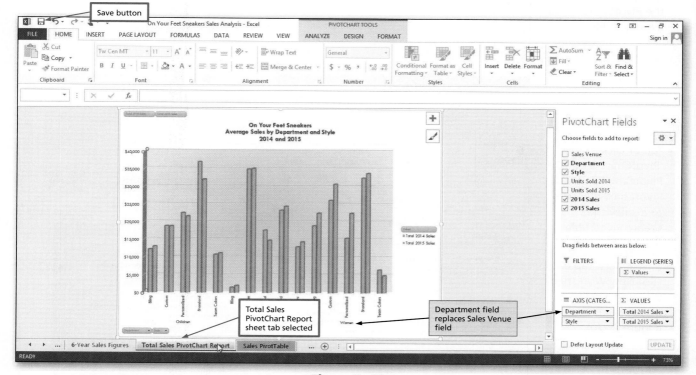

Figure 8–68

- Tap or click the Save button on the Quick Access Toolbar to save the workbook.

To Create a PivotChart Report Directly from Data

1 CREATE LINE CHART & TRENDLINE | 2 CREATE PIVOTTABLE | 3 CHANGE LAYOUT & VIEW OF PIVOTTABLE | 4 FILTER PIVOTTABLE
5 FORMAT PIVOTTABLE | 6 CREATE PIVOTCHART | **7 CHANGE PIVOTCHART VIEW & CONTENTS** | **8 ADD SLICERS**

Why? *Creating a second PivotChart and PivotTable provides the platform for pursuing multiple inquiries of the data simultaneously.* The requirements document included a request to create a second PivotChart and PivotTable that examine the average sale amount, controlling for different variables. As noted earlier, PivotChart reports are created in Excel either based on an existing PivotTable report or directly from data. The following steps create a PivotChart report and its associated PivotTable report directly from available data.

1

- Tap or click the Sales Analysis Figures sheet tab to display the worksheet.
- Tap or click INSERT on the ribbon to display the INSERT tab.
- Tap or click cell A3 to select a cell displaying sales venue data.
- Tap or click the PivotChart arrow (INSERT tab | Charts group) to display the PivotChart menu (Figure 8–69).

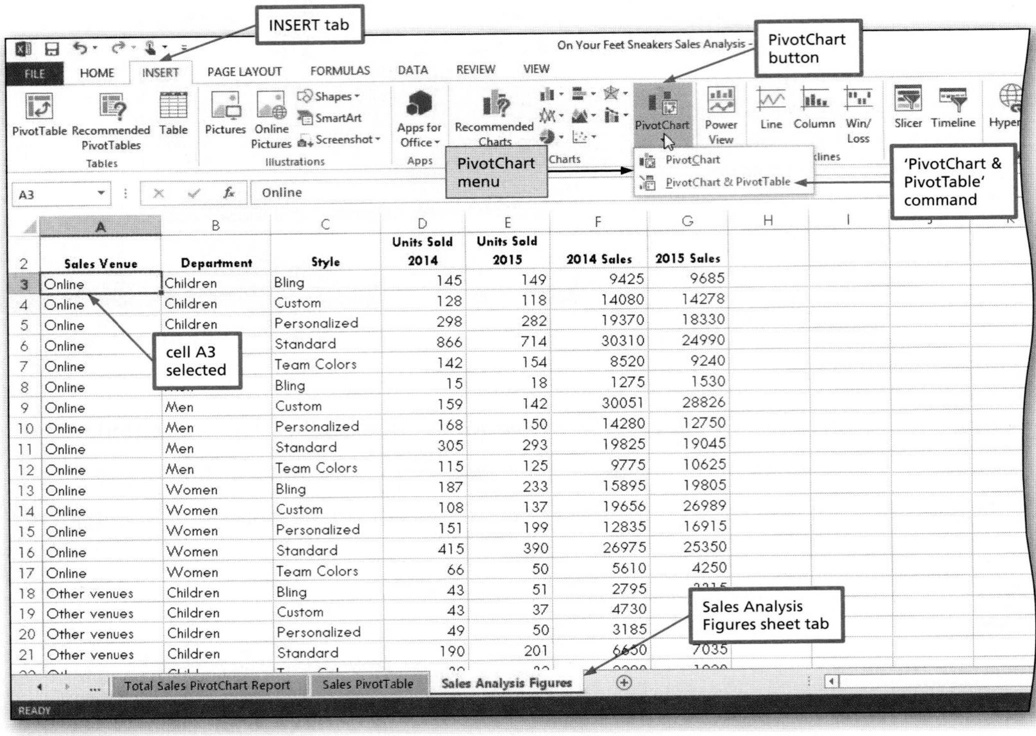

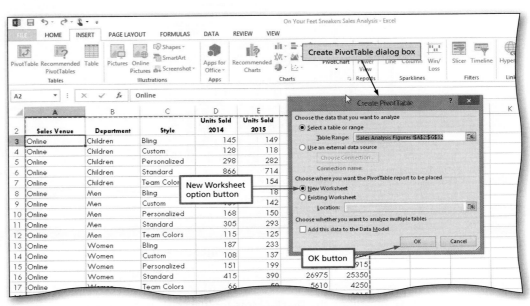

Figure 8–69

2

- Tap or click 'PivotChart & PivotTable' on the PivotChart menu to display the Create PivotTable dialog box.
- If necessary, tap or click New Worksheet (Create PivotTable dialog box) (Figure 8–70).

Figure 8–70

3

- Tap or click the OK button to add a new worksheet containing a blank PivotTable and blank PivotChart (Figure 8–71).

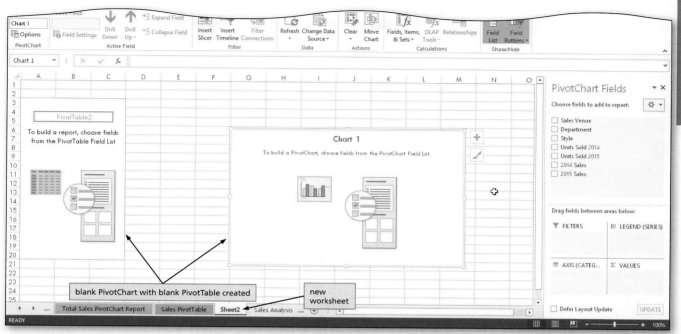

Figure 8–71

4

- Add the Department and Sales Venue fields to the AXIS area in the PivotChart Fields task pane.

- Add the 2014 Sales and 2015 Sales fields to the VALUES area in the PivotChart Fields task pane (Figure 8–72).

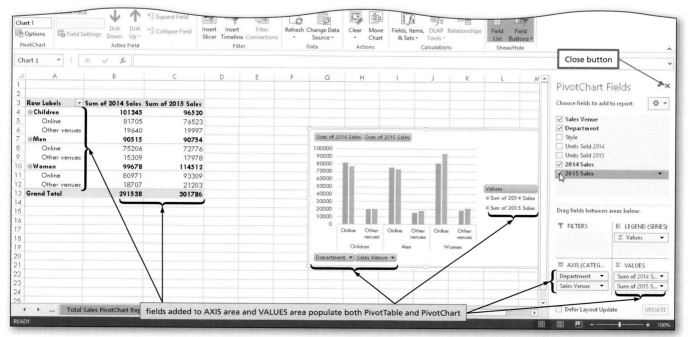

Figure 8–72

To Add a Calculated Field to a PivotTable Report

1 CREATE LINE CHART & TRENDLINE | 2 CREATE PIVOTTABLE | 3 CHANGE LAYOUT & VIEW OF PIVOTTABLE | 4 FILTER PIVOTTABLE
5 FORMAT PIVOTTABLE | 6 CREATE PIVOTCHART | 7 CHANGE PIVOTCHART VIEW & CONTENTS | 8 ADD SLICERS

Why add a calculated field? You may need to create new fields based on data in the underlying table. You would like to review average sales by department and sales venue for 2014 and 2015, but this information currently is not part of the data set with which you are working. You can, however, calculate the values you need through the use of a calculated field. A **calculated field** is a field with values not entered as data, but determined by computation involving data in other fields. In this case, Average 2014 Sale and Average 2015 Sale are new calculated fields, based on the existing values of the 2014 Sales, 2015 Sales, and Units Sold 2014 and Units Sold 2015 fields. The following steps create calculated fields that use the existing data and then use these calculated fields in the PivotTable and PivotChart reports.

1

- Rename the new sheet as Average Sale by Department.
- Tap or click the Close button to close the PivotChart Fields task pane.
- If necessary, tap or click the PivotTable to make it active.
- Tap or click the PIVOTTABLE TOOLS ANALYZE tab on the ribbon.
- Tap or click the 'Fields, Items, & Sets' button (PIVOTTABLE TOOLS ANALYZE tab | Calculations group) to display the Fields, Items, & Sets menu (Figure 8–73).

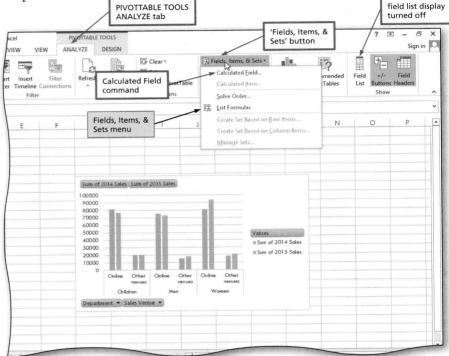

Figure 8–73

2

- Tap or click Calculated Field on the Fields, Items, & Sets menu to display the Insert Calculated Field dialog box.
- In the Name box, type **Average 2014 Sale**.
- In the Formula text box, delete the value to the right of the equal sign, in this case, 0.
- Double-tap or double-click the 2014 Sales entry in the Fields list to select it, type / (a forward slash), and then double-tap or double-click the 'Units Sold 2014' entry in the Fields list to complete the formula, which should read = '2014 Sales'/'Units Sold 2014' (Figure 8–74).

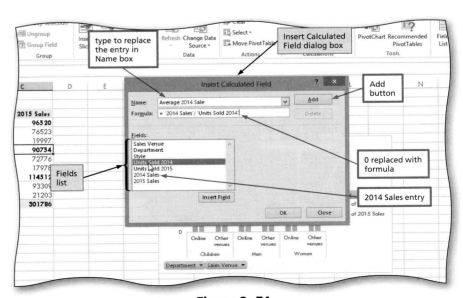

Figure 8–74

3

- Tap or click the Add button (Insert Calculated Field dialog box) to add the calculated field to the Fields list (Figure 8–75).

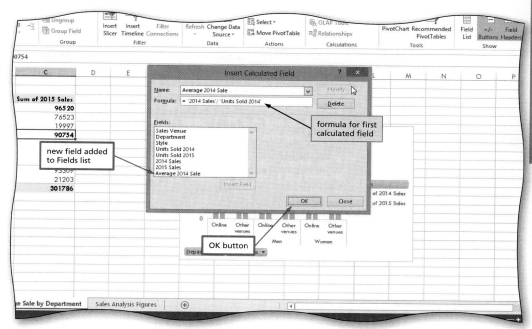

Figure 8–75

4

- Repeat Steps 2 and 3 to create a calculated field named Average 2015 Sale, calculated using 2015 Sales data rather than 2014 Sales data.

- Tap or click the OK button (Insert Calculated Field dialog box) to close the dialog box (Figure 8–76).

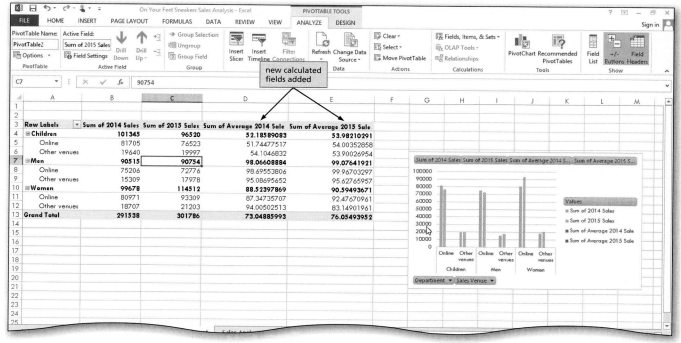

Figure 8–76

To Format the PivotTable and PivotChart

Now that you have added a calculated field, you can format the PivotTable and PivotChart so they look professional and are easy to interpret. The following steps format the PivotTable report.

1 If necessary, tap or click the Field List button (PIVOTTABLE TOOLS ANALYZE tab | Show group) to display the PivotTable Fields task pane and then tap or click the 2014 Sales check box and the 2015 Sales check box to remove these fields from the PivotTable report and the PivotChart report.

2 If necessary, tap or click cell A3, tap or click DESIGN on the ribbon to display the PIVOTTABLE TOOLS DESIGN tab, and then apply Pivot Style Medium 12 to the PivotTable.

3 Insert two blank rows above the PivotTable. In cell A1, enter the title **On Your Feet Sneakers**. In cell A2, enter the subtitle **Average Sale, 2014 and 2015**. Merge and center the text across A1:C1 and A2:C2. Apply the Title style to cell A1 and the Heading 2 style to cell A2.

4 Change the field name in cell B5 to Average Sale 2014. Change the field name in cell C5 to Average Sale 2015.

5 Apply the currency number format with 2 decimal places and the $ symbol to the Average Sale 2014 and Average Sale 2015 fields.

6 Change the column widths for columns B and C to 12.00.

7 Wrap and center the field names in cells B5 and C5.

8 Change the column width for column D to 50.

9 Use the Field List button, the +/- Buttons button, and the Field Headers button (PIVOTTABLE TOOLS ANALYZE tab | Show group) to hide the field list, the Expand/Collapse buttons, and the field headers (Figure 8–77).

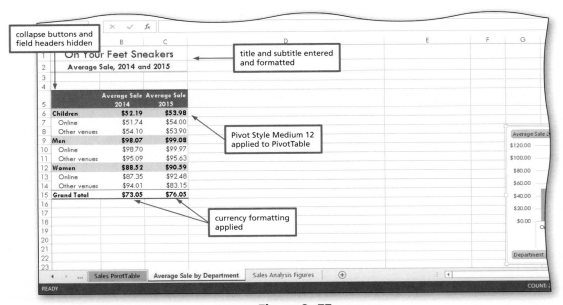

Figure 8–77

To Format the PivotChart

The following steps format the PivotChart report.

1   If necessary, tap or click in the PivotChart report to select it. Move and resize the PivotChart report so that it fills the range D1:D15. Tap or click cell E15 to deselect the PivotChart report.

2   Select the PivotChart and then apply Style 12 in the Chart Styles gallery. Use the 'Chart Quick Colors' button (PIVOTCHART TOOLS DESIGN tab | Chart Styles group) to change the colors to Color 8 in the Monochromatic area. Use the 'Add Chart Element' button (PIVOTCHART TOOLS DESIGN tab | Chart Layouts group) to position the legend at the top of the PivotChart report.

3   Tap or click the Field Buttons button (PIVOTCHART TOOLS ANALYZE tab | Show/Hide group) to hide the field buttons.

4   Save the workbook (Figure 8–78).

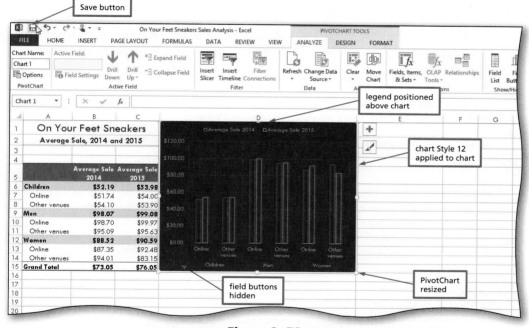

Figure 8–78

Break Point: If you wish to take a break, this is a good place to do so. You can exit Excel now. To resume at a later time, run Excel, open the file called On Your Feet Sneakers Sales Analysis, and continue following the steps from this location forward.

Working with Slicers

One of the strengths of PivotTables is that you can ask questions of the data by using filters. Being able to identify and examine subgroups is a useful analytical tool. Slicers are a visual filter used to make PivotCharts and PivotTables easier to interpret. When using filters and autofilters, the user cannot always tell which subgroups the filters and autofilters have selected, without clicking filter buttons to see the subgroups selected. With Slicers, the subgroups are immediately identifiable and can be changed with a tap or click of a button or buttons.

BTW

Certification
The Microsoft Office Specialist (MOS) program provides an opportunity for you to obtain a valuable industry credential — proof that you have the Excel 2013 skills required by employers. For more information, visit the Certification resource on the Student Companion Site located on www .cengagebrain.com. For detailed instructions about accessing available resources, visit www.cengage.com/ ct/studentdownload or contact your instructor for information about accessing the required files.

Why would you use slicers rather than row, column, or report filters?

One effective way to analyze PivotTable data is to use slicers to filter the data in more than one field. Slicers let you refine the display of data in a PivotTable. They offer the following advantages over filtering directly in a PivotTable:

- In a PivotTable, you use the filter button to specify how to filter the data, which involves a few steps. After you create a slicer, you can perform this same filtering task in one step.

- You can filter only one PivotTable at a time, whereas you can connect slicers to more than one PivotTable to filter data.

- Excel treats slicers as graphic objects, which means you can move, resize, and format them as you can any other graphic object. As graphic objects, they invite interaction.

The owner of On Your Feet Sneakers asked you to set up a PivotChart and PivotTable to provide a user-friendly way for anyone to explore the total sales data. You can use slicers to complete this task efficiently.

To Copy a PivotTable and PivotChart

To create a canvas for exploratory analysis of sales data, you first need to create a new PivotTable and a PivotChart. The following steps copy an existing PivotTable and PivotChart to a new sheet, format the PivotTable, and rename the sheet.

1 Create a copy of the Average Sale by Department worksheet and then move the copy so that it precedes the Sales Analysis Figures worksheet.

2 Rename the new sheet, Slicers.

3 Apply the Pivot Style Medium 6 style to the PivotTable.

4 Set the column widths of columns B and C to 14.00. Set the column widths of columns E and F to 17.00. If necessary, wrap the text in cells B5 and C5 and then center it. Set the font size in cell A2 to 12 point.

5 If necessary, turn off the display of field headers and +/– buttons (Figure 8–79).

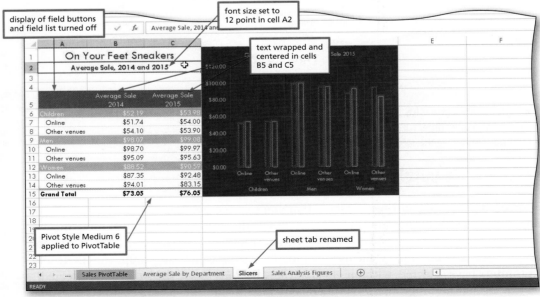

Figure 8–79

To Format the PivotChart

The following steps format the PivotChart.

1 Apply chart Style 5 to the PivotChart to format the PivotChart.

2 Use the 'Chart Quick Colors' button (PIVOTCHART DESIGN tab | Chart Styles group) to apply Color 9 in the Monochromatic area in the Chart Quick Colors gallery to the PivotChart (Figure 8–80).

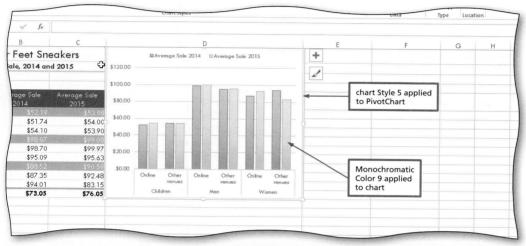

Figure 8–80

To Add Slicers to the Worksheet

1 CREATE LINE CHART & TRENDLINE | 2 CREATE PIVOTTABLE | 3 CHANGE LAYOUT & VIEW OF PIVOTTABLE | 4 FILTER PIVOTTABLE
5 FORMAT PIVOTTABLE | 6 CREATE PIVOTCHART | 7 CHANGE PIVOTCHART VIEW & CONTENTS | 8 ADD SLICERS

Why? *To analyze sales data for specific subgroups, you can use slicers instead of PivotTable filters.* The following steps show how to add a slicer that provides an easier way to filter the new PivotTable and PivotChart.

1

- If necessary, tap or click to make the PivotChart active.

- Tap or click the PIVOTCHART TOOLS ANALYZE tab on the ribbon.

- Tap or click the Insert Slicer button (PIVOTCHART TOOLS ANALYZE tab | Filter group) to display the Insert Slicers dialog box.

- Tap or click to place check marks in the Sales Venue, Department, and Style check boxes (Figure 8–81).

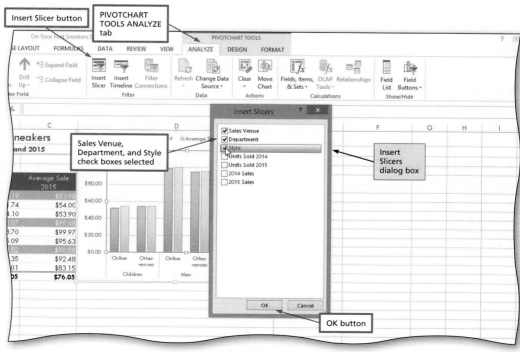

Figure 8–81

2

- Tap or click the OK button (Insert Slicers dialog box) to display the selected slicers on the worksheet (Figure 8–82).

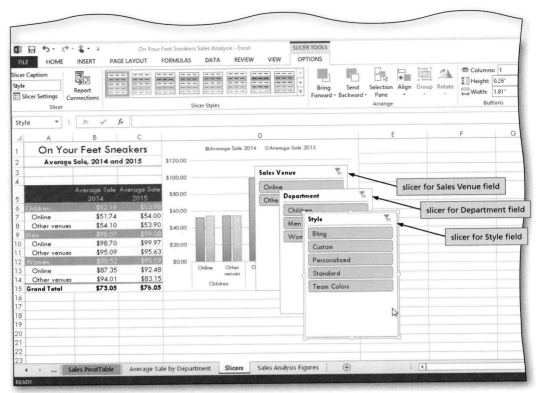

Figure 8–82

To Format Slicers

1 CREATE LINE CHART & TRENDLINE | 2 CREATE PIVOTTABLE | 3 CHANGE LAYOUT & VIEW OF PIVOTTABLE | 4 FILTER PIVOTTABLE
5 FORMAT PIVOTTABLE | 6 CREATE PIVOTCHART | 7 CHANGE PIVOTCHART VIEW & CONTENTS | **8 ADD SLICERS**

Why? *The slicers need to be moved and formatted so that they do not obscure the PivotTable or PivotChart and are easy to read and use.* The following steps move the slicers to the right of the PivotChart and then format them to fit in with the PivotTable and PivotChart styles.

1

- Tap or click the title bar of the Sales Venue slicer and then drag the Sales Venue slicer to column E.
- Use the sizing handles to adjust the length of the slicer so that it ends at the bottom of row 6, and the width of the slicer so that it ends at the right edge of column E.
- Tap or click and then drag the Department slicer to column E, locating the top of the Department slicer against the bottom of the Sales Venue slicer.
- Use the sizing handles to change the length of the Department slicer so that it ends at the bottom of row 15, and change the width of the Department slicer so that it ends at the right edge of column E.
- Tap or click and drag the Style slicer to column F, locating the upper-left corner of the slicer in the upper-left corner of cell F1.
- Use the sizing handles to adjust the length of the Style slicer so that it ends at the bottom of row 15 and the width so that it ends at the right edge of column F.
- Hold down the CTRL key and then tap or click to select all three slicers.
- Tap or click the Height box (SLICER TOOLS OPTIONS tab | Buttons group) and then set the button height to 0.4 (Figure 8–83).

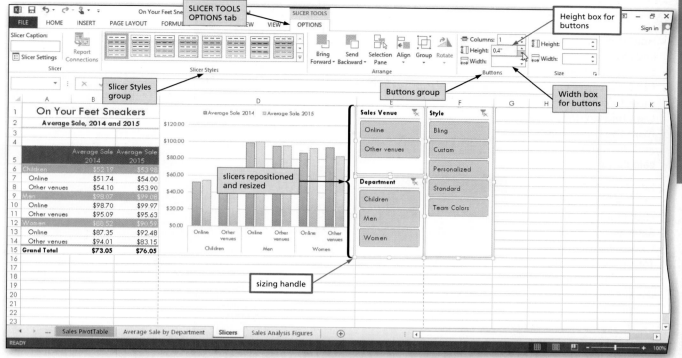

Figure 8–83

2

- Tap or click the 'Slicer Style Light 5' Slicer style (SLICER TOOLS OPTIONS tab | Slicer Styles group) to apply it to the slicers (Figure 8–84).

3

- Tap or click cell F17 to deselect the slicers.

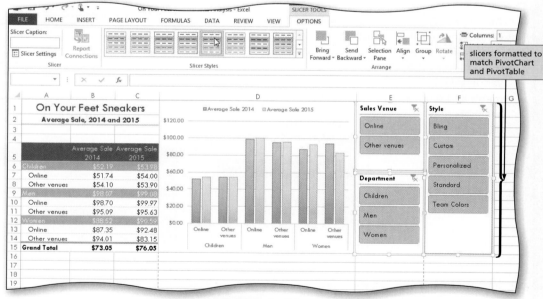

Figure 8–84

To Use the Slicers to Review Groups in the PivotTable

1 CREATE LINE CHART & TRENDLINE | 2 CREATE PIVOTTABLE | 3 CHANGE LAYOUT & VIEW OF PIVOTTABLE | 4 FILTER PIVOTTABLE
5 FORMAT PIVOTTABLE | 6 CREATE PIVOTCHART | 7 CHANGE PIVOTCHART VIEW & CONTENTS | 8 ADD SLICERS

Why use slicers? *Slicers provide you with a visual means of filtering data.* You do not need knowledge of Excel to use slicers. Instead, you tap or click the subgroups of interest. Slicers based on Row Label fields provide the same results as filters in a PivotTable. They narrow the table down to a visible subgroup or subgroups. The following steps use slicers to review average sales for different combinations of Department and Sales Venue.

1

- Hold down the CTRL key and then tap or click Children in the Department slicer to remove the Children data from the PivotTable and PivotChart calculations.

- Release the CTRL key and then tap or click Online in the Sales Venue slicer to display the data for online sales of men's and women's sneakers only (Figure 8–85).

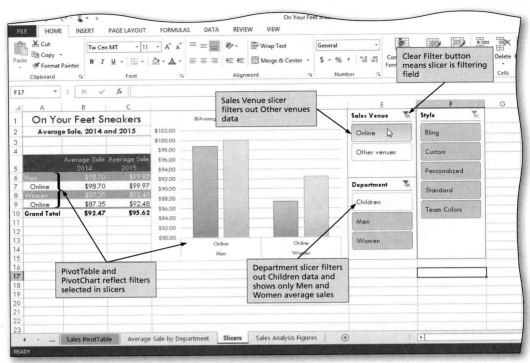

Figure 8–85

2

- Tap or click Other venues in the Sales Venue slicer to see the data for other venue sales of men's and women's sneakers only (Figure 8–86).

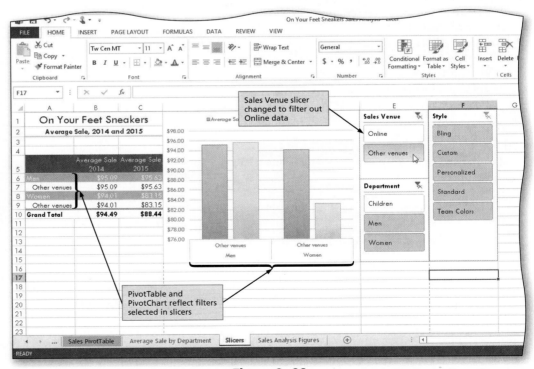

Figure 8–86

To Use the Slicers to Review Groups Not in the PivotTable

Why? *Slicers based on fields not included in the PivotTable provide the same results as report filters. They regroup and narrow the PivotTable content to groups not visible in the PivotTable.* You can use slicers to analyze influences other than those recorded in the PivotTable as possible explanations for patterns. The following steps show how to use slicers to review groups not currently included in the PivotTable.

1

- Tap or click the Clear Filter button on the Sales Venue slicer and the Department slicer to remove the filters and return the PivotTable and PivotCharts to their unfiltered states.

- Tap or click Custom in the Style slicer to see the aggregate data for the average sale of custom sneakers, broken down by Sales Venue and Department (Figure 8–87).

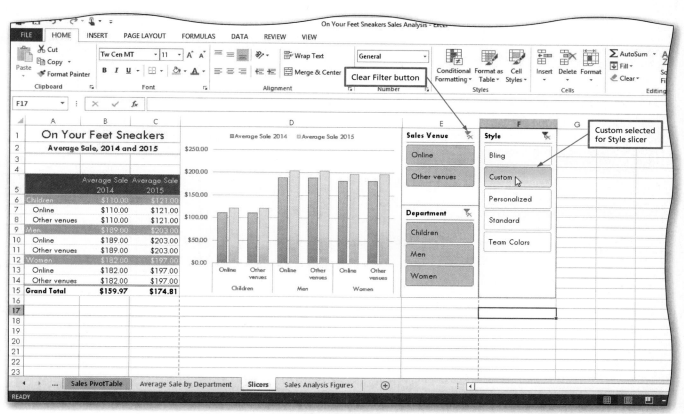

Figure 8–87

2

Experiment

- Tap or click different styles and combinations of styles to see how the aggregate data changes.

- If necessary, tap or click Custom in the Style slicer to select it, hold down the CTRL key, and then tap or click Personalized in the Style slicer to see the aggregate data for the handcrafted shoes, broken down by Sales Venue and Department (Figure 8–88).

Q&A How can I save a particular PivotTable setup?

PivotTables are dynamic by nature. To save a particular configuration, make a copy of the sheet, and use the Protect sheet command (REVIEW tab | Changes group) to keep changes from being made to the worksheet copy. You can continue to use the PivotTable on the original sheet to analyze the data.

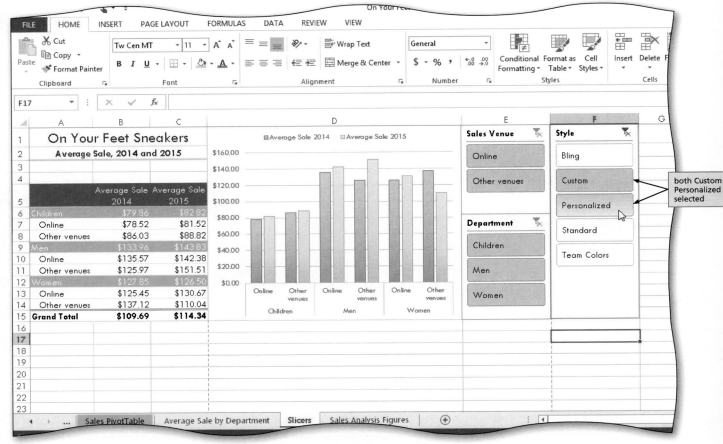

Figure 8–88

3

- Save the workbook.

BTW

Quick Reference
For a table that lists how to complete the tasks covered in this book using touch gestures, the mouse, ribbon, shortcut menu, and keyboard, see the Quick Reference Summary at the back of this book, or visit the Quick Reference resource on the Student Companion Site located on www.cengagebrain.com. For detailed instructions about accessing available resources, visit www.cengage.com/ct/studentdownload or contact your instructor for information about accessing the required files.

To Exit Excel

The project now is complete. The following steps exit Excel.

1 Tap or click the Close button on the right side of the title bar.

2 If the Microsoft Office Excel dialog box is displayed, tap or click the Don't Save button.

Chapter Summary

In this chapter, you learned how to create a trendline on a chart, and create, format, filter, and analyze interactive PivotTables and PivotCharts. The items listed below include all the new Excel skills you have learned in this chapter, with the tasks grouped by activity.

Calculated Fields and Summary Functions
Switch Summary Functions in a PivotTable (EX 499)
Add a Second Value Calculation to a PivotTable Report (EX 502)
Add a Calculated Field to a PivotTable Report (EX 520)

Create and Format Line Chart with Trendline
Create a 2-D Line Chart (EX 478)
Add a Trendline to a Chart (EX 481)
Change the Format of a Data Point (EX 483)

Create and Format PivotTables
Create a Blank PivotTable (EX 486)
Add Data to a PivotTable (EX 487)
Change the Layout of a PivotTable (EX 488)
Change the View of a PivotTable Report (EX 490)
Format a PivotTable Report (EX 497)
Customize the Display of the Field List and Field Headers in a PivotTable Report (EX 504)
Customize the Display of the Expand and Collapse Buttons in a PivotTable Report (EX 506)
Update the Contents of a PivotTable Report (EX 508)

Create and Format PivotCharts
Create a PivotChart Report from an Existing PivotTable Report (EX 509)

Change the Location of a PivotChart Report and Delete Average Sales Data (EX 510)
Change the PivotChart Type and Format a Chart (EX 511)
Change the View of a PivotChart (EX 516)
Create a PivotChart Report Directly from Data (EX 518)

Filter PivotTables
Filter a PivotTable Report Using a Report Filter (EX 491)
Filter a PivotTable Report Using Multiple Selection Criteria (EX 492)
Remove a Report Filter from a PivotTable Report (EX 494)
Filter a PivotTable Report Using the Row Label Filter (EX 494)
Remove a Row Label Filter from a PivotTable Report (EX 496)

Slicers
Add Slicers to a Worksheet (EX 525)
Format Slicers (EX 526)
Use the Slicers to Review Groups in a PivotTable (EX 527)
Use the Slicers to Review Groups Not in a PivotTable (EX 529)

What decisions will you need to make when creating your next worksheet to analyze data using trendlines, PivotCharts and PivotTables?
Use these guidelines as you complete the assignments in this chapter and create your own worksheets for evaluating and analyzing data outside of this class.

1. Identify trend(s) to analyze with a trendline.

   a) Determine data to use.

   b) Determine time period to use.

   c) Determine type and format of trendline.

2. Identify questions to ask of your data.

   a) Determine which variables to combine in a PivotTable or PivotChart.

3. Create and format PivotTables and PivotCharts.

   a) Add all fields to the field list.

   b) Use formatting features for PivotTables and PivotCharts.

4. Manipulate PivotTables and PivotCharts to analyze data.

   a) Select fields to include in PivotTables and PivotCharts.

   b) Use filters to review subsets of data.

   c) Use calculated fields and summary statistics to look at different measures of data.

   d) Create and use slicers to look at subsets of data.

CONSIDER THIS: PLAN AHEAD

How should you submit solutions to questions in the assignments identified with a ✳ symbol?

Every assignment in this book contains one or more questions identified with a ✳ symbol. These questions require you to think beyond the assigned file. Present your solutions to the questions in the format required by your instructor. Possible formats may include one or more of these options: write the answer; create a document that contains the answer; present your answer to the class; discuss your answer in a group; record the answer as audio or video using a webcam, smartphone, or portable media player; or post answers on a blog, wiki, or website.

Apply Your Knowledge

Reinforce the skills and apply the concepts you learned in this chapter.

Creating a PivotTable

Note: To complete this assignment, you will be required to use the Data Files for Students. Visit www.cengage.com/ct/studentdownload for detailed instructions or contact your instructor for information about accessing the required files.

Instructions: Run Excel. Open the document Apply 8-1 Hattie's Handbags from the Data Files for Students and then save the workbook as Apply 8-1 Hattie's Handbags Complete.

The owner of Hattie's Handbags wants you to create a PivotTable from the current inventory and then manipulate it to display different totals. Figure 8–89 shows the completed Inventory PivotTable worksheet.

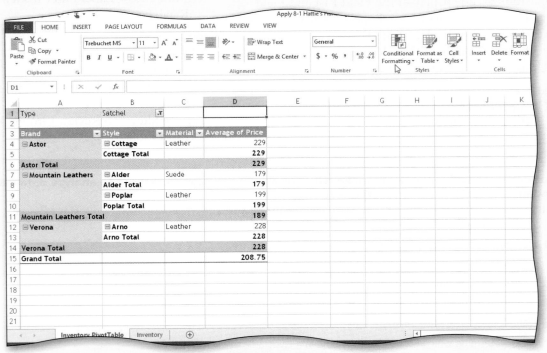

Figure 8–89

Perform the following tasks:

1. Select cell A3 and then tap or click the PivotTable button (INSERT tab | Tables group) to display the Create PivotTable dialog box. Make sure New Worksheet is selected and then tap or click the OK button.

2. Drag the Brand field from the Choose fields to add to report list to the ROWS area to add the Brand field to the PivotTable. Repeat this step for the Style, Material, and Type fields.

3. Drag the Price field from the Choose fields to add to report list to the VALUES area to add the sum of the Price field to the PivotTable.

4. Change the summary calculation for Price from Sum to Average by tapping or clicking the 'Sum of Price' button in the VALUES area of the PivotTable Fields task pane and then choosing Average from the Value Field Settings dialog box.

5. Change the PivotTable report layout to tabular.

6. Write down the averages for each brand of handbag and the overall average.

7. Tap or click the filter button in cell A3 to display the filter menu. Select only Mountain Leathers and Taylor and then tap or click the OK button. Write down the averages for the brands and the overall average.

8. Remove the Brand filter so that all data is displayed.

9. Drag the Type button in the ROWS area to the FILTERS area in the PivotTable Fields task pane to create a new field. Tap or click the filter button for the Type field, tap or click Satchel, and then tap or click the OK button. Write down the averages for the makes and the overall total.

10. Tap or click cell A4, tap or click the PivotTable Styles More button on the PIVOTTABLE TOOLS DESIGN tab, and then tap or click 'Pivot Style Medium 14' to apply the style to the PivotTable.

11. If requested by your instructor, include in cell A17 the following text: **List compiled by <yourname>**, substituting your name for <yourname>.

12. Name the sheet Inventory PivotTable. Save the workbook with the PivotTable, and then close the workbook.

13. Submit the revised document in the format specified by your instructor.

14. ✳ List two changes you would make to the PivotTable report to make it more easily interpreted by the user, and explain why you would make these changes. These changes could be to formatting, layout, or both.

Extend Your Knowledge

Extend the skills you learned in this chapter and experiment with new skills. You may need to use Help to complete the assignment.

Grouping Content in PivotTables

Note: To complete this assignment, you will be required to use the Data Files for Students. Visit www.cengage.com/ct/studentdownload for detailed instructions or contact your instructor for information about accessing the required files.

Instructions: Run Excel. Open the workbook Extend 8-1 Campus Coffee To Go from the Data Files for Students and then save the workbook using the file name, Extend 8-1 Campus Coffee To Go Complete.

Create a PivotTable and PivotChart for Campus Coffee To Go that analyzes a year's worth of sales data. Figure 8–90 on the next page shows the completed Income Review worksheet.

Continued >

Extend Your Knowledge continued

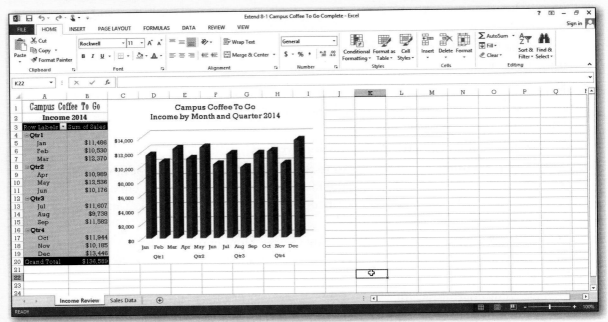

Figure 8–90

Perform the following tasks:

1. Create a PivotTable based on the sales data in Sheet1. Use Date as the ROWS field and use Sales as the VALUES field. Name the new sheet containing the PivotTable, Income Review. Change the PivotTable style to 'Pivot Style Medium 19'. Add a title and subtitle to the PivotTable, as shown in Figure 8–90, formatting cell A1 using the Title cell style and A2 using the Heading 2 cell style.

2. Use the Group Field command (PIVOTTABLE TOOLS ANALYZE tab | Group group) to group the daily sales figures by months and quarters. Format the Sum of Sales values as currency with no decimal places.

3. Create a PivotChart, and locate it on the same sheet as the PivotTable. Use the 3-D clustered column chart type, and set up the chart to have no legend. Hide the field buttons. Right-click in the chart area, choose '3-D Rotation' on the shortcut menu, and set X rotation to 100° and Y rotation to 50°. Change Chart Quick Colors to Color 17. Edit the chart title to match the title and resize the PivotChart as shown in Figure 8–90.

4. If requested by your instructor, add a worksheet header with your name and course number.

5. Preview and then print the PivotTable sheet in landscape orientation.

6. Save the workbook with the new page setup characteristics.

7. Submit the revised document in the format specified by your instructor.

8. ✳ What other chart type would you use to present this data for the user? Why would you choose that particular chart type?

Analyze, Correct, Improve

Analyze a workbook, correct all errors, and improve it.

Manipulating a Chart and Adding a Trendline

Note: To complete this assignment, you will be required to use the Data Files for Students. Visit www.cengage.com/ct/studentdownload for detailed instructions or contact your instructor for information about accessing the required files.

Instructions: Run Excel. Open the workbook Analyze 8-1 Stay Secure and then save the workbook as Analyze 8-1 Stay Secure Complete. Correct the following design and formula problems shown in Figure 8–91 so that the Revenue Totals sheet appears with an embedded chart.

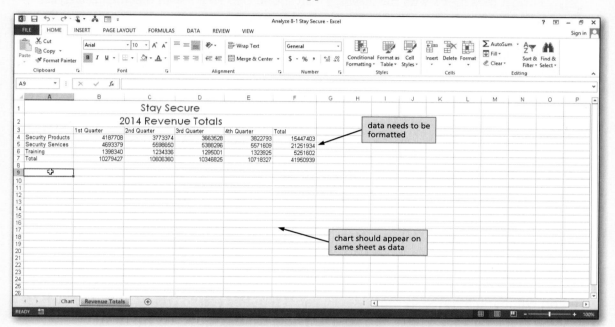

(a) Revenue Totals Sheet

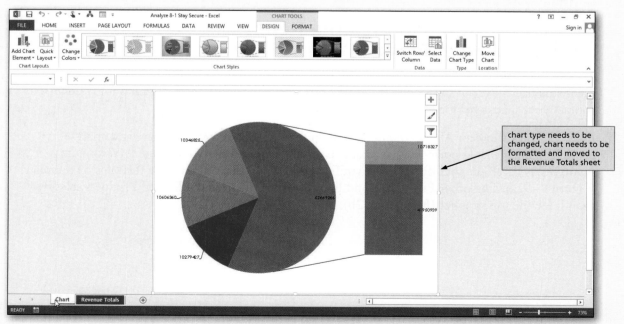

(b) Original Chart

Figure 8–91

Continued >

Analyze, Correct, Improve *continued*

1. **Correct** Change the bar of pie chart on the Chart sheet to a clustered column chart. Use the Select Data button (CHART TOOLS DESIGN tab | Data group) to correct the data range the chart is based upon so that it contains only quarterly information. Change the chart layout to Layout 5 and apply chart Style 5. Change the chart title text to match that in cells A1:A2 of the Revenue Totals worksheet. Delete the axis titles and data labels, and set the primary vertical axis to show values. Add a linear trendline to the chart. Extend the trendline by two quarters, and display the R-squared value on the chart.

2. **Improve** On the Revenue Totals worksheet, apply a fill color of 'Plum, Accent 1, Darker 25%' and a text color of 'White, Background 1' to cells A1:A2. Format cells A1:A2 with the Title cell style. Format cells A3:F3 with the Heading 3 style, and cells A7:F7 with the Total cell style. Bold cells A4:A7 and resize column A to fit. Apply a currency format with a currency symbol and no decimal places to ranges B4:F4 and B7:F7, and a currency format with no symbol and no decimal places to ranges B5:F6.

   Move the chart to the Revenue Totals worksheet, and resize it so that it fills the range A8:F27.

   If requested by your instructor, add a footer with your name and phone number in the center section.

   Save the workbook. Submit the revised document in the format specified by your instructor.

3. ✱ In this exercise, you added a forecast period to your trendline. How confident would you be using the forecast generated?

In the Labs

Design and/or create a workbook using the guidelines, concepts, and skills presented in this chapter. Labs 1 and 2, which increase in difficulty, require you to create solutions based on what you learned in the chapter; Lab 3 requires you to create a solution, which uses cloud and web technologies, by learning and investigating on your own from general guidance.

Lab 1: Creating a PivotTable Report and PivotChart Report

Note: To omplete this assignment, you will be required to use the Data Files for Students. See the inside back cover of this book for instructions on downloading the Data Files for Students, or contact your instructor for information about accessing the required files.

Problem: You work for Altar Holdings and help the financial director prepare and analyze revenue and expense reports. He has asked you to create two PivotTables and corresponding PivotCharts based on sales data. One PivotTable and PivotChart summarize the sales by Supplier (Figure 8–92a). The other PivotTable and PivotChart summarize the Digital Products sales by month for the top supplier (Figure 8–92b).

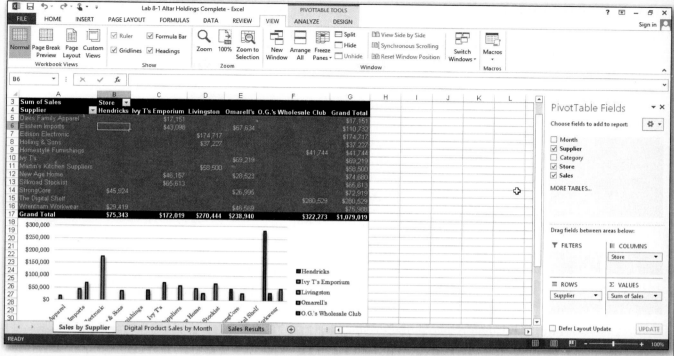

(a) Sales by Supplier

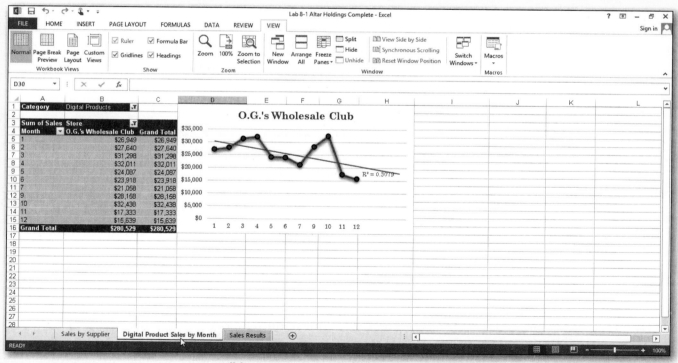

(b) Digital Products Sales by Month

Figure 8–92

In the Labs *continued*

Instructions: Perform the following tasks:

1. Open the workbook Lab 8-1 Altar Holdings from the Data Files for Students and then save the workbook using the file name, Lab 8-1 Altar Holdings Complete.

2. Using the data in the Sales Results worksheet, create the PivotTable and associated PivotChart shown in Figure 8–92a in a separate sheet in the workbook. Name the worksheet Sales by Supplier.

3. If necessary, add two blank lines above the PivotTable and then change the contents of cell A4 to Supplier and cell B3 to Store. Apply the 'Pivot Style Dark 21' style to the PivotTable. Format the values as currency values with a dollar sign and no decimal places. Apply the chart Style 14 to the PivotChart. Resize the PivotChart to cover the range A18:G35 and then hide the field buttons.

4. Create a second PivotTable and associated PivotChart, as shown in Figure 8–92b, in a separate sheet in the workbook. Name the worksheet Digital Product Sales by Month.

5. Change the contents of cell A4 to Month and cell B3 to Store. Apply the 'Pivot Style Dark 4' style to the PivotTable. Format the values as currency values with a dollar sign and no decimal places.

6. Filter the category by Digital Products. Filter the store to O.G.'s Wholesale Club.

7. Change the chart type to Line and then add a linear trendline that forecasts the trend for three more months. Add the R squared value to the trendline. Apply the chart Style 15 to the PivotChart and then hide the field buttons. Delete the legend. Resize the chart to the range D1:H16.

8. If requested by your instructor, add the text, Contact number, followed by your phone number to cell B66 of the Sales Results worksheet.

   Save the workbook. Submit the revised document in the format specified by your instructor.

9. ✳ How helpful is the monthly breakdown when analyzing sales of various products?

Lab 2: **Manipulating PivotTables and PivotCharts**

Problem: The Wordsmiths editor-in-chief has asked you to analyze the current week's billing sheet using PivotTables and PivotCharts. She wants you to create them for three scenarios: (a) the payment amount totals for hours billed, (b) the averages of the hours per region, and (c) the cost of the miscellaneous hours if they had been billable. The PivotTables and PivotCharts should appear as shown in Figure 8–93.

Instructions: Perform the following tasks:

1. Open the workbook Lab 8-2 Wordsmiths Billing from the Data Files for Students and then save the workbook using the file name, Lab 8-2 Wordsmiths Billing Complete.

2. Create the PivotTable shown in Figure 8–93a based on the data in the range A4:F26 in the Billing worksheet. Add a calculated field called Billed Amount that multiplies the hours billed by 45. Create the PivotChart shown in Figure 8–93a. Name the worksheet Billing Amounts. Change the contents of cell A3 to Regions. Apply the Pivot Style Medium 2 to the PivotTable. Format the Billed Amount values as currency values with a dollar sign and no decimal places. Format the Hours Billed with the number format. Apply the chart Style 5 to the PivotChart.

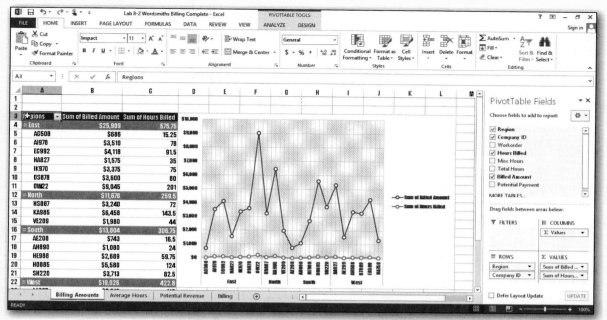

(a) Total Billed Amounts and Hours by Region

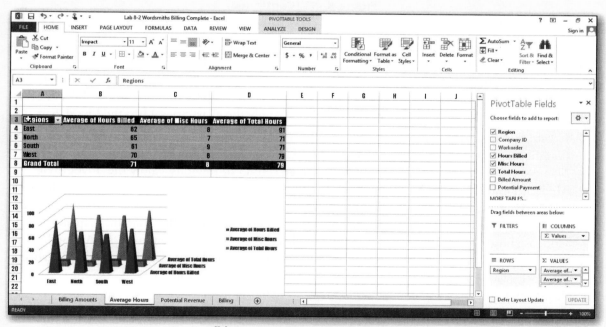

(b) Average Hours by Region

Figure 8–93

Continued >

In the Labs *continued*

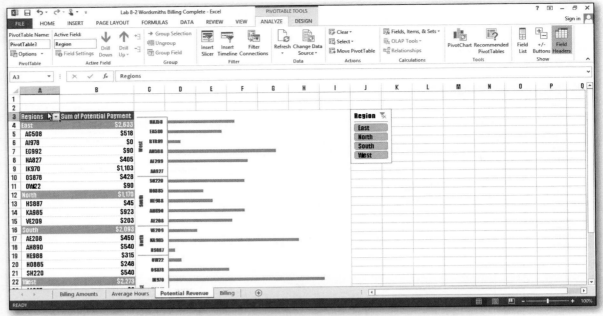

(c) Potential Revenues by Region
Figure 8–93 (Continued)

3. On a new sheet, create the PivotTable and Partial Pyramids PivotChart shown on the Average Hours sheet in Figure 8–93b on the previous page. Change the calculations to averages. Change the contents of cell A3 to Regions. Apply the 'Pivot Style Dark 4' style to the PivotTable. Format all value fields as number with no decimal places. Apply the chart Style 11 to the PivotChart.

4. Create the PivotTable shown in Figure 8–93c. Add a calculated field called Potential Payment that multiplies the miscellaneous hours by 45. Create the PivotChart shown in Figure 8–93c. Name the worksheet Potential Revenue. Change cell A3 to Regions. Apply the 'Pivot Style Medium 5' style to the PivotTable. Format the Potential Payment values as currency values with a dollar sign and no decimal places. Apply the chart Style 2 to the PivotChart and change colors to Monochromatic Color 8. Remove the legend and chart title. Hide the Expand/Collapse buttons, and close the PivotTable Fields task pane. Add a Region slicer. Apply the 'Slicer Style Light 4' to the slicer. Set button widths to .8" and button heights to .2". Set slicer size to 1" wide and 1.37" high. Position the slicer as shown in Figure 8–93c. Use the slicer to display potential payments for the eastern region only.

5. If requested by your instructor, add a worksheet header with your name and course number.

6. Select all three PivotTable sheets. With the three sheets selected, preview and then print the sheets. Save the workbook with the new page setup characteristics. Submit the revised document in the format specified by your instructor.

7. ✳ In this exercise, you have a PivotTable that can span more than one screen at a time. Did you find this a hindrance when working on the PivotTables and PivotCharts? How could you address this when setting up your PivotTables and PivotCharts?

Lab 3: Expand Your World: Cloud and Web Technologies
Creating Charts for a School District

Note: To complete this assignment, you will be required to use the Data Files for Students. Visit www.cengage.com/ct/studentdownload for detailed instructions or contact your instructor for information about accessing the required files.

Problem: You volunteer with the Northville school district. The district would like to make available for parents some summary results from the latest round of statewide testing of the students in 4th, 7th, 10th, and 12th grade. Data has been compiled for the three testing areas, Math, Science, and English, for each of the 10 schools in the district. The data includes both the average score for each grade and school combination and the test goal the various grades were charged with meeting. Assume for computation purposes that the class sizes for the schools across grades are within one or two students of each other, allowing calculation of goal averages without weighting. You have been tasked with creating a PivotTable for the school district for use on the publicly available portion of their SkyDrive. The school district would like a PivotTable that would allow parents to visit SkyDrive and, using slicers, examine the data for any school/grade combinations that are of interest to them. In addition to the PivotTable, you need to create brief instructions for visitors on how to use slicers to view combinations of grade and school.

Instructions: Perform the following tasks:

1. Open the workbook Lab 8-3 Northville School District from the Data Files for Students and then save the workbook using the file name, Lab 8-3 Northville School District Complete.

2. Create a PivotTable for the data provided. Set up the PivotTable to allow users to compare average scores and goals by school and/or grade.

3. Format the PivotTable and slicers to provide the user with a visually pleasing, easy-to-use product. You will need to decide which PivotTable elements to display, and how to display them. You also will need to make decisions about how to format various elements, taking into account color, size, default text, etc.

4. Write your brief instructions for users. You can place this guide in a group of merged cells, or you can insert a text box on the worksheet (visit Help to learn about text boxes and how to use them). You will need to make text formatting decisions to ensure that the instructions are readable and fit on the sheet with the PivotTable and slicers. Remember when setting this up that if you have content on your sheet that you need to see to set up the table, but the user does not need to see to use the PivotTable, you can hide specific rows/columns without affecting the performance of the worksheet contents. This can free up space on the worksheet for the content that needs to be visible.

5. If requested by your instructor, add a line at the bottom of your guide identifying you as the author of the guide.

6. Make decisions about which other content needs to be visible once saved on SkyDrive. Hide content as you deem appropriate prior to saving the worksheet.

7. Save the workbook on SkyDrive, and test its performance. Make any changes necessary. Submit the revised document in the format specified by your instructor.

8. ✸ Evaluate the strengths and weaknesses of this method of making information available to parents. List three concerns, and suggest how you might begin to address them.

STUDENT ASSIGNMENTS

Consider This: Your Turn

Apply your creative thinking and problem solving skills to design and implement a solution.

Note: To complete these assignments, you may be required to use the Data Files for Students. Visit www.cengage.com/ct/studentdownload for detailed instructions or contact your instructor for information about accessing the required files.

1: Budget Analysis
Personal

Part 1: You have created a table that shows your household income and expenses. You would now like to create charts to help you analyze your budget. Part of this includes identifying a trend in your spending habits. Open the workbook Your Turn 8-1 Budget Analysis from the Data Files for Students and then save the workbook using the file name, Your Turn 8-1 Household Budget Analysis Complete.

Create a chart using the expenses from the budget. Move the chart to its own sheet. Use WordArt to add a chart title of Household Expenses to the chart using Text Fill, Text Outline, and Text Effects to enhance the title. Create a chart using the cash flow data from the budget. Move the chart to its own sheet. Use WordArt to add a chart title of Cash Flow Trend to the chart, and format the title as you did on the Household Expenses chart. Add a trendline to the chart that shows trends for the next four months. Rename the chart sheets as appropriate to match their contents. Submit your assignment in the format specified by your instructor.

Part 2: In Part 1, you made choices about which type(s) of chart(s) to use to present budget data. What was the rationale behind those selections? How did the data in the Household Expenses pose a special challenge? How might you address that challenge?

2: Evaluating Employee Readiness
Professional

Your company is preparing three groups of employees for certification testing. Employees have taken a pretest to evaluate their readiness for the certification exam. The company wants to use a PivotTable to filter the data and analyze the results. Your task is to create the PivotTable and calculate the requested results.

Part 1: Open the workbook Your Turn 8-2 Certification Pretest from the Data Files for Students and then save the workbook using the file name, Your Turn 8-2 Certification Pretest Complete. Create a PivotTable on its own worksheet using Department and Pretest as row labels, and Score as three columns (summarize them using the MIN, MAX, and AVERAGE functions). Format the scores with the number format with no decimal places. Use the row filter to filter out CERT4 pretest results. Name the worksheet, Row Filter.

Create a second PivotTable on its own worksheet. Name the sheet AutoFilter. Use Pretest to create an AutoFilter. Filter the courses for the CERT1, CERT2, and CERT3 pretests. Print the worksheets and save the workbook. Submit the assignment as requested by your instructor.

Part 2: In Part 1, you created two PivotTables that present the same data in different formats. Compare and contrast these two PivotTables. List two conclusions you can make from both PivotTables, and for each table, a conclusion that is unique to that table.

3: Comparing Budget Data

Research and Collaboration

Part 1:   As part of a student task force on college affordability, you have been tasked with gathering information from five other students and working together to summarize the data you gathered. Open the Your Turn 8-3 Budget Research workbook and save as Your Turn 8-3 Budget Research Complete. Fill in with estimates or actual figures of your income and expenses information for a six-month period agreed to by your group or assigned by your instructor. Gather the group information into a single worksheet. Calculate average, minimum, and maximum values for the Income, Expense, and Cash Flow fields. Create a series of line charts for Average, Minimum, and Maximum Income; Expense; and Cash Flow. Add trendlines to the series where useful. Print the worksheets and save the workbook. Submit the assignment as requested by your instructor.

Part 2:   ☀ In Part 1, you created a series of line charts. What criteria did you use for determining whether or not to add a trendline to a particular chart?

Learn Online

Reinforce what you learned in this chapter with games, exercises, training, and many other online activities and resources.

Student Companion Site   Reinforcement activities and resources are available at no additional cost on www.cengagebrain.com. Visit www.cengage.com/ct/studentdownload for detailed instructions about accessing the resources available at the Student Companion Site.

SAM   Put your skills into practice with SAM! If you have a SAM account, go to www.cengage .com/sam2013 to access SAM assignments for this chapter.

9 | Formula Auditing, Data Validation, and Complex Problem Solving

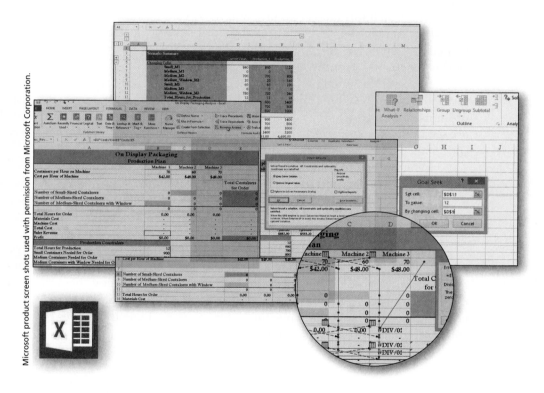

Microsoft product screen shots used with permission from Microsoft Corporation.

Objectives

You will have mastered the material in this chapter when you can:

- Use formula auditing techniques to analyze a worksheet
- Trace precedents and dependents
- Use error checking to identify and correct errors
- Add data validation rules to cells
- Use trial and error to solve a problem on a worksheet
- Use goal seeking to solve a problem

- Circle invalid data on a worksheet
- Use Solver to solve a complex problem
- Use the Scenario Manager to record and save sets of what-if assumptions
- Create a Scenario Summary report
- Create a Scenario PivotTable report
- Save a workbook for use in a previous version of Excel

9 | Formula Auditing, Data Validation, and Complex Problem Solving

Introduction

This chapter introduces you to auditing the formulas in a worksheet, validating data, and solving complex problems. **Formula auditing** allows you to examine formulas to determine which cells are referenced by those formulas and examine cells to determine which formulas are built upon those cells. Auditing the formulas in a worksheet can give you insight into how a worksheet is structured and how cells are related to each other. Formula auditing is especially helpful when presented with a workbook created by someone else.

    Data validation allows you to set cells so that the values they accept are restricted in terms of type and range of data. This feature can be set up to display prompts and error messages when users select a cell or enter invalid data. You also can use data validation to circle cells containing data that does not meet the criteria you specified.

    When trying to solve some problems, you can make an educated guess if you are familiar with the data and the structure of the workbook. This process is called **trial and error**. For simpler problems, you may find a solution using this process. For more complex problems, you might need to use software, such as Excel, to find a satisfactory solution.

    One of the tools that Excel provides to solve complex problems is **Solver**, which allows you to specify up to 200 cells that can be adjusted to find a solution to a problem. Solver also lets you place limits or constraints on allowable values for some or all of those cells. A **constraint** is a limitation on the possible values that a cell can contain. Solver will try many possible solutions to find one that solves the problem subject to the constraints placed on the data.

Project — On Display Packaging Production Plan

In previous chapters, simple what-if analyses have shown the effect of changing one value on another value of interest. This chapter introduces you to Excel tools used to solve complex problems. The worksheet in Figure 9–1a was created to determine the most cost-effective way of producing an order of containers.

    On Display Packaging produces specialty containers for various businesses. Their main income source is the production of stock containers that businesses can purchase for customization. In addition to production of stock containers, the business also handles special orders for containers using specialty materials. The company has three machines that can be used with specialty materials, including one machine that handles window insertion in containers. The three machines have differing output capacities. Machines 1 and 3 can produce 70 containers per hour, while machine 2 can produce 60 containers per hour. The worksheet in Figure 9–1a shows the details of the production requirements for the three machines, taking into account these differing output capacities. The worksheet includes machine cost and materials cost per hour. A second worksheet lists materials cost and prices for the three different types of containers.

Figure 9–1b on page EX 548 shows the details of the first solution determined by Solver. Rows 8 through 10 contain the suggested distribution of container types across the machines. Column E contains summary information. Highlighted cells represent container types that cannot be produced on a certain machine. For instance, machine 2 cannot be used to produce small containers. Row 13 shows total hours needed to produce a specific quantity of containers. Row 14 shows total materials cost for the number of containers produced. Row 15 shows the total machine cost for the number of containers produced, and Row 16 gives a total cost for materials and machine. Updating the numbers for each type of container in rows 8 through 10 results in changes in the values in rows 13 through 16. Solver has modified the values of cells in the range B8:D10 to find the best combination of containers to produce on each machine to minimize the total cost and, therefore, maximize profit. After applying a different set of order constraints, Solver determines a new solution. When Solver finishes solving a problem, you can instruct it to create an Answer Report. An **Answer Report** (Figure 9–1c on page EX 548) shows the answer that Solver found, which constraints were in place, and which values in the worksheet Solver manipulated in order to solve the problem within those constraints.

Excel's **Scenario Manager** is a what-if analysis tool that allows you to record and save different sets of what-if assumptions used to forecast the outcome of a worksheet model. This chapter shows you how to use the Scenario Manager to manage the two sets of Solver data for two scenarios involving the production of different sizes of containers. The Scenario Manager also allows you to create reports that summarize the scenarios on your worksheet. Figure 9–1d on page EX 548 shows a Scenario Summary report and Figure 9–1e on page EX 549 shows a Scenario PivotTable, each of which concisely reports the differences in the two production scenarios.

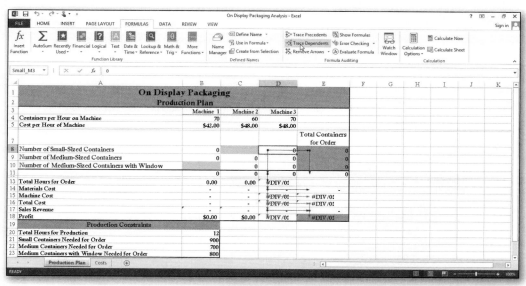

(a) Initial Worksheet

Figure 9–1 (Continued)

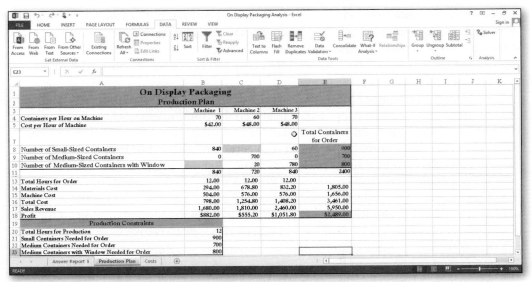

(b) First Solver Solution

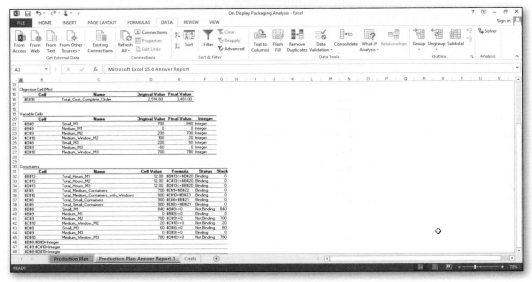

(c) Answer Report

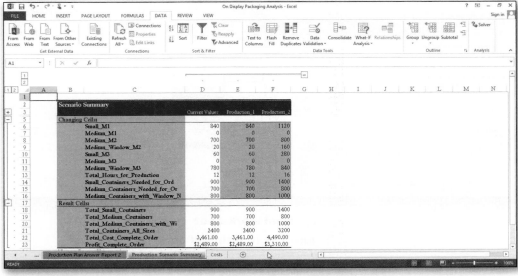

(d) Scenario Summary Report

Figure 9–1 (Continued)

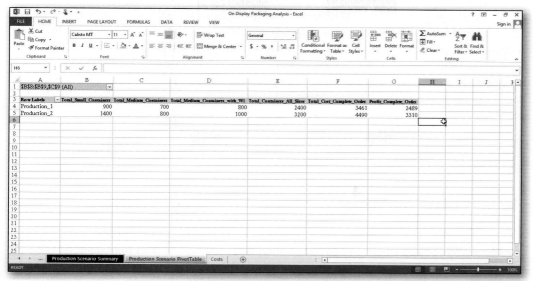

(e) Scenario PivotTable

Figure 9–1 (Continued)

Figure 9–2 illustrates the requirements document for the On Display Packaging Analysis workbook. It includes the needs, source of data, and other facts about its development.

Worksheet Title	On Display Packaging Analysis
Needs	On Display Packaging takes on special orders for containers using specialty materials, in addition to the regular production done by the company. It needs to determine for a special order the optimal distribution of production of three different types of containers across the three machines capable of producing containers using specialty materials. This special order requires production of 900 small containers, 700 medium containers, and 800 medium containers with windows. The solution should minimize total cost, to maximize potential profit. The company would like a workbook that will allow them to determine what the optimal distribution would be for other special orders. They have provided you with figures for a second special order to use to test the workbook for this.
Source of Data	Cost and price information is available in the On Display Packaging workbook on the Costs worksheet.
Calculations	All formulas are set up in the workbook. The worksheets in the workbook should be reviewed to familiarize yourself with the calculations.
Other Requirements	None.

© 2014 Cengage Learning

Figure 9–2

Roadmap

In this chapter, you will learn how to create and use the workbook shown in Figure 9–1. The following roadmap identifies general activities you will perform as you progress through this chapter:

1. ANALYZE WORKBOOK FORMULAS.

2. SET DATA VALIDATION RULES.

3. PROPOSE PROBLEM-SOLVING STRATEGIES.

4. CREATE and EVALUATE SCENARIOS.

5. FINALIZE the WORKBOOK.

BTW

The Ribbon and Screen Resolution
Excel may change how the groups and buttons within the groups appear on the ribbon, depending on the computer's screen resolution. Thus, your ribbon may look different from the ones in this book if you are using a screen resolution other than 1366 × 768.

At the beginning of step instructions throughout the chapter, you will see an abbreviated form of this roadmap. The abbreviated roadmap uses colors to indicate chapter progress: gray means the chapter is beyond that activity, blue means the task being shown is covered in that activity, and black means that activity is yet to be covered. For example, the following abbreviated roadmap indicates the chapter would be showing a task in the 2 SET DATA VALIDATION RULES activity.

1 ANALYZE WORKBOOK FORMULAS | 2 SET DATA VALIDATION RULES | 3 PROPOSE PROBLEM-SOLVING STRATEGIES
4 CREATE & EVALUATE SCENARIOS | 5 FINALIZE WORKBOOK

Use the abbreviated roadmap as a progress guide while you read or step through the instructions in this chapter.

To Run Excel and Open a Workbook

The following steps, which assume Windows 8 is running, use the Start screen or the search box to run Excel based on a typical installation. You may need to ask your instructor how to run Excel on your computer. For a detailed example of the procedure summarized below, refer to the Office and Windows chapter.

To complete these steps, you will be required to use the Data Files for Students. Visit www.cengage.com/ct/studentdownload for detailed instructions or contact your instructor for information about accessing the required files.

BTW

Quick Reference
For a table that lists how to complete the tasks covered in this book using touch gestures, the mouse, ribbon, shortcut menu, and keyboard, see the Quick Reference Summary at the back of this book, or visit the Quick Reference resource on the Student Companion Site located on www.cengagebrain.com. For detailed instructions about accessing available resources, visit www.cengage.com/ct/studentdownload or contact your instructor for information about accessing the required files.

1 Scroll the Start screen for an Excel 2013 tile. If your Start screen contains an Excel 2013 tile, tap or click it to run Excel. Otherwise, search for the Excel app using the Charms bar and then tap or click Excel 2013 in the search results.

2 Tap or click 'Open Other Workbooks' on the Excel start screen.

3 Navigate to the location of the Data Files for Students and the Excel Chapter 9 folder.

4 Double-tap or double-click the file named On Display Packaging to open it.

5 If the Excel window is not maximized, tap or click the Maximize button on its title bar to maximize the window.

6 Save the workbook with the file name, On Display Packaging Analysis.

7 If necessary, tap or click cell F23 (Figure 9–3).

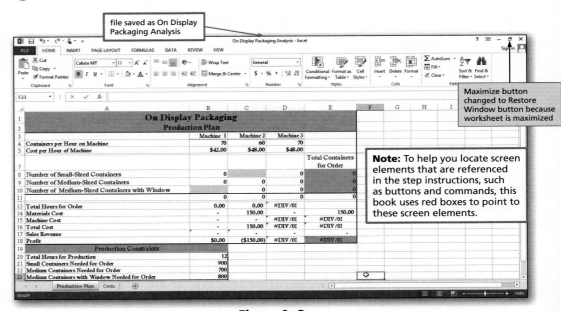

Figure 9–3

About the Production Plan Worksheet

The Production Plan worksheet shown in Figure 9–1a on page EX 547 provides information for three machines and three types of containers. Rows 4 and 5 show the hourly output and machine cost for each of the three machines. The range B8:D10 contains the optimal combination of containers produced on each machine for a particular production run, which is the information that needs to be determined in this chapter. The empty cells — cells C8 and B10 — indicate that a particular machine cannot produce a certain type of container. Rows 13 through 18 show the total hours, costs, revenues, and profits for each machine, based on the quantities listed in the range B8:D10. As cells in the range B8:D10 change, the values in the range B13:D18 are updated. The total number of containers is calculated in cells E8:E11, the total cost for the production run is calculated and shown in cell E16, and profit for the production run is shown in cell E18. The goals of the project in this chapter are (1) to produce the required number of containers for the production run without using each machine more than the number of hours shown in cell B20, while minimizing total cost, shown in cell E16.

The current worksheet displays production run constraints for the first production run scenario in the range B20:B23. As outlined in the requirements document in Figure 9–2 on page EX 549, a second production run, reflecting a larger order, must also be analyzed. The information in the range B20:B23, thus, will be modified later in the chapter to reflect the constraints associated with the larger production run.

BTW

BTWs

For a complete list of the BTWs found in the margins of this book, visit the BTW resource on the Student Companion Site located on www.cengagebrain.com. For detailed instructions about accessing available resources, visit www.cengage .com/ct/studentdownload or contact your instructor for information about accessing the required files.

Formula Auditing

Errors can be introduced into a worksheet in formulas. Formula auditing is the process of reviewing formulas for errors. Errors may be obvious, with results that indicate that a formula is incorrect. In Figure 9–3, cells D13, D15, E15, D16, E16, D18, and E18, display error codes. These errors are flagged by both the error code #DIV /0! and the error indicator, a green triangle, in the upper-left corner of those cells. Errors also may be less obvious, introduced through formulas that, while technically correct, result in unintended results in the worksheet. Error indicators with no accompanying error code, such as those found in cells B17 and B18, should be examined for these less-obvious errors. A complex worksheet should be reviewed to correct obvious errors, *and* to correct formulas that do not produce error indicators but still do not produce the intended results. You also can use formula auditing to review the formulas in a worksheet.

BTW

Q&As

For a complete list of the Q&As found in many of the step-by-step sequences in this book, visit the Q&A resource on the Student Companion Site located on www.cengagebrain .com. For detailed instructions about accessing available resources, visit www.cengage .com/ct/studentdownload or contact your instructor for information about accessing the required files.

CONSIDER THIS

How do formula auditing tools assist in the understanding of the workbook?

Tracing precedents and dependents reveals how formulas and values are related. Use Excel tools to examine the structure of the worksheet and identify where the source of an identified error is located, and to review and confirm the logic of the relationships between formulas and values. You should check to find the source of errors and to make sure that formulas have been constructed correctly. This requires a basic understanding of the necessary calculations in the worksheet.

The Formula Auditing group on the FORMULAS tab supplies several tools that you can use to analyze the formulas in a worksheet. Some tools, such as the Error Checking command, deal with identified errors. You also can use other auditing tools that provide visual cues to identify how cells in a worksheet are related to each other. **Tracer arrows** are drawn from one cell to another, identifying cells that are related to other cells through use in a formula. A tracer arrow can be drawn from a cell that appears in a formula in another cell or from a cell that contains a formula with cell references. Red tracer arrows indicate that one of the referenced cells contains an error.

A cell containing a formula that references other cells is said to have precedents. Each cell referenced in the formula is a **precedent** of the cell containing the formula. For example, in the formula C24 = C23/$B$1, cells C23 and B1 are precedents of cell C24. Cells C23 and B1 also can have precedents, and these cells would also be precedents of cell C24. Tracing precedents can highlight where a formula may be incorrect. Tracing precedents in Excel is accomplished by tapping or clicking the Trace Precedents button in the Formula Auditing group on the FORMULAS tab on the ribbon.

To Trace Precedents

1 ANALYZE WORKBOOK FORMULAS | 2 SET DATA VALIDATION RULES | 3 PROPOSE PROBLEM-SOLVING STRATEGIES
4 CREATE & EVALUATE SCENARIOS | 5 FINALIZE WORKBOOK

Why? Tracing precedents in Excel allows you to see upon which cells a particular cell is based, not only directly by the formula in the cell, but indirectly via precedents for the precedent cells. The following steps show how to trace the precedent cells for cell E14, which displays the Total Materials Cost for producing the special container order.

1

- If necessary, make Production Plan the active sheet to trace precedents in the Production Plan worksheet.

- Tap or click FORMULAS on the ribbon to display the FORMULAS tab.

- Tap or click cell E14 to make it the active cell.

- Tap or click the Trace Precedents button (FORMULAS tab | Formula Auditing group) to draw a tracer arrow across precedents of the selected cell (Figure 9–4).

How do I interpret the precedent arrows?

The arrow in Figure 9–4 has arrowheads on the traced cell, in this case cell E14. The heavy blue line through the range of cells B14:D14 indicates that all cells in the range are precedents of the traced cell, E14.

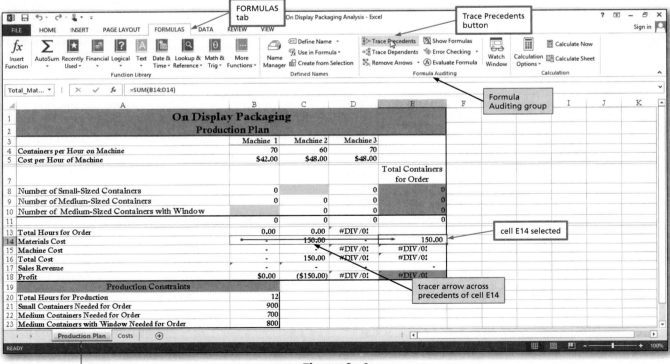

Figure 9–4

2

- Tap or click the Trace Precedents button (FORMULAS tab | Formula Auditing group) again to draw arrows indicating precedents of cells B14:D14 (Figure 9–5).

Q&A How do I interpret the new precedent arrows?
The new arrows in Figure 9–5 have arrowheads on traced cells and dots on cells that are direct precedents of the cells with arrowheads. For instance, cell B14 has a tracer arrow to it with dots in cell B8 and B9. The line is lighter than the one in the previous figure. This indicates that the cells in the range B8:B13 are not all precedents of cell B14. The precedents of cell B14 are the cells with the dots in them, cells B8 and B9. In addition, there is a black dashed line to cell B14, with a worksheet icon at the other end of it. This indicates that precedent cells exist on another worksheet.

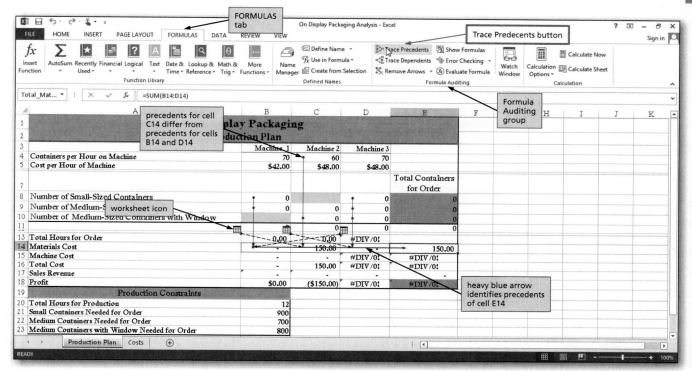

Figure 9–5

To Review Precedents
on a Different Worksheet

1 ANALYZE WORKBOOK FORMULAS | 2 SET DATA VALIDATION RULES | 3 PROPOSE PROBLEM-SOLVING STRATEGIES
4 CREATE & EVALUATE SCENARIOS | 5 FINALIZE WORKBOOK

Why? *Precedents can be located on different worksheets in the same workbook, or in different workbooks.* In Figure 9–5, the dashed precedent arrows and worksheet icons identify precedents on another worksheet. The following steps review the precedents located on a different sheet for cell C14, which has a value in the worksheet different from the surrounding cells.

1

- Tap or click cell C14 to display the formula in the formula bar (Figure 9–6).

Q&A I am having difficulty selecting cell C14. Is this cell locked? When precedent or dependent arrows are drawn through a cell, the area you can tap or click in the cell to select it is reduced. Tap or click near the boundaries of the cell in order to select it.

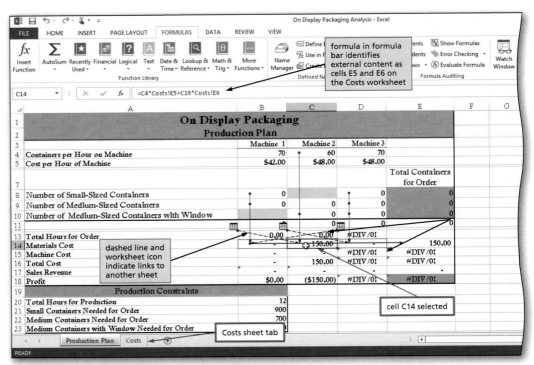

Figure 9–6

2

- Review the formula in the formula bar to identify the location of the precedent cell or cells, in this case cells E5 and E6 on the Costs worksheet.

- Tap or click the Costs sheet tab to make it the active sheet.

- Review the precedent cells to determine if the reference to them in the formula is correct as written (Figure 9–7).

Q&A What does it mean that cells E5 and E6 in the Costs worksheet are precedent cells for cell C14? In this case, it means that cell C14 contains a formula that refers to cells E5 and E6 in the Costs worksheet.

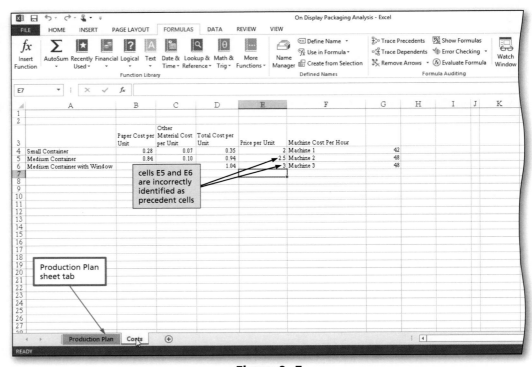

Figure 9–7

To Remove the Precedent Arrows

Why? *Reducing visual clutter makes the worksheet easier to navigate.* After reviewing the precedents of cell E14, you determine that cell C14 needs to be changed to calculate the total material cost correctly for machine 2. The following steps show how to remove the precedent arrows level by level and then correct the formula in cell C14.

1

- Tap or click the Production Plan sheet tab to make the Production Plan worksheet the active worksheet.

- Tap or click cell E14 to make it the active cell.

- Tap or click the 'Remove All Arrows' arrow (FORMULAS tab | Formula Auditing group) to display the Remove All Arrows menu (Figure 9–8).

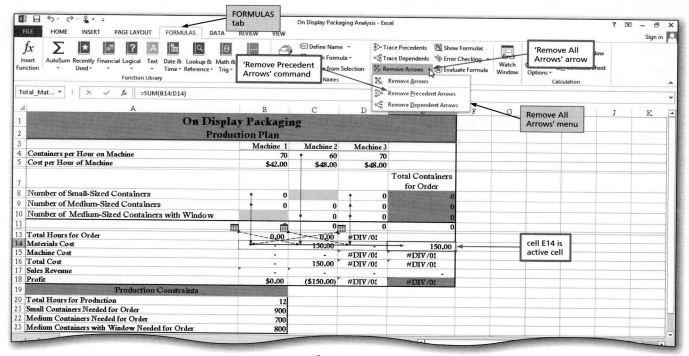

Figure 9–8

2

- Tap or click 'Remove Precedent Arrows' on the Remove All Arrows menu to remove precedent arrows linking to the Costs sheet.

- Tap or click the 'Remove All Arrows' arrow (FORMULAS tab | Formula Auditing group) again to display the Remove All Arrows menu.

- Tap or click Remove Arrows on the Remove All Arrows menu to remove the remaining tracer arrows.

- Edit the formula in cell C14 to read `=C9*Costs!D5+C10*Costs!D6` to correct the error (Figure 9–9).

Q&A Do I have to remove the precedent arrows level by level?

No. If you tap or click the 'Remove All Arrows' button instead of the 'Remove All Arrows' arrow, you remove all arrows at once.

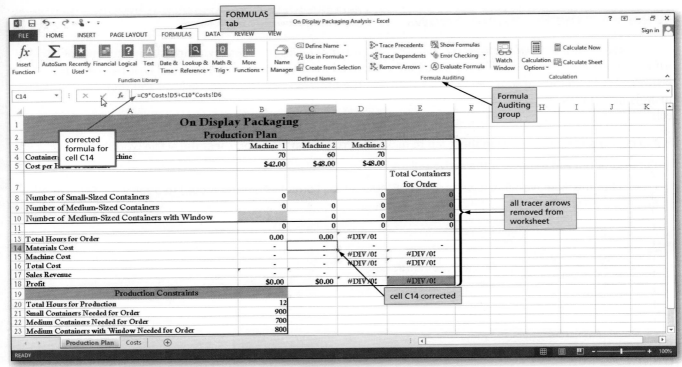

Figure 9–9

BTW

Tracing Precedents and Dependents
When all levels of precedents or dependents have been identified, Excel will sound a beep if you try to trace another level.

TO REVIEW PRECEDENTS ON A DIFFERENT WORKSHEET USING THE GO TO COMMAND

If you are using a mouse, you can use precedent arrows to navigate directly to precedents on a different worksheet or different workbook. If you choose to use this feature, you would use the following steps:

1. Double-tap or double-click on the dashed precedent arrow to display the Go To dialog box.
2. Select the cell reference to navigate to from the Go to list (Figure 9–10).
3. Tap or click the OK button (Go To dialog box) to navigate to the selected cell reference.

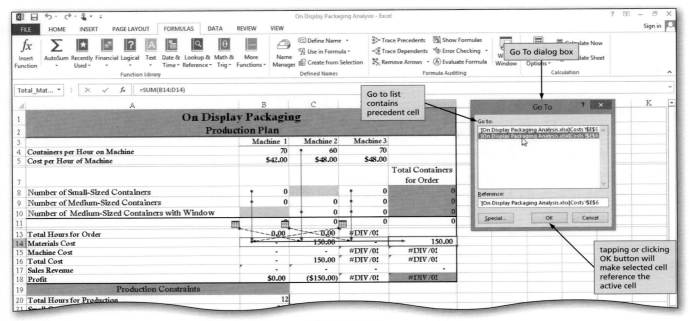

Figure 9–10

To Trace Dependents

Why? Identifying dependents highlights where changes will occur in the worksheet as a result of changing the value in the cell you are identifying as a referenced cell. A cell that references another cell is said to be a **dependent** of that referenced cell. If cell A3 contained the formula =B2/B4, cell A3 would be a dependent of cells B2 and B4. Changing the value in cell B2 or cell B4 also changes the result in the dependent cell A3. The following steps trace the dependents of cell D8, which eventually will show the optimal number of small containers to produce on machine 3.

1

- Tap or click cell D8 to make it the active cell.

- Tap or click the Trace Dependents button (FORMULAS tab | Formula Auditing group) to draw arrows to dependent cells D11, D14, D17, and E8 (Figure 9–11).

Q&A What is the meaning of the dependent arrows?
Figure 9–11 indicates that cells D11, D14, D17, and E8 directly depend on cell D8. Cell D8 is explicitly referenced in the formulas in these cells.

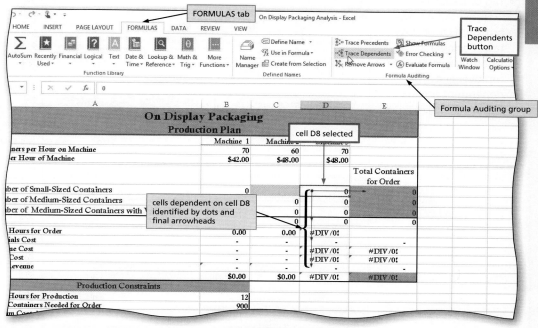

Figure 9–11

2

- Tap or click the Trace Dependents button three more times to draw arrows indicating the remaining dependents of cell D8 (Figure 9–12).

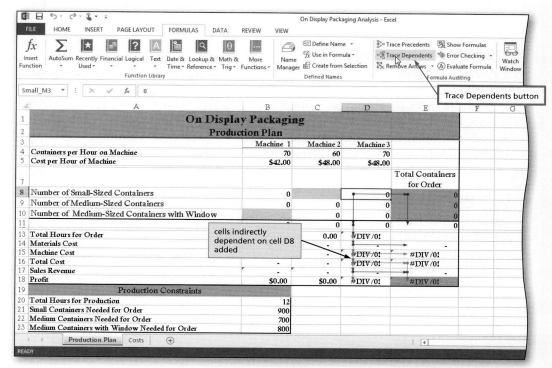

Figure 9–12

To Remove the Dependent Arrows

Why? *Once dependent cells are identified, you may want to remove the dependent arrows to clear the worksheet of extraneous content.* Tracing dependents identified the cells that depend on cell D8, which will help to correct the #DIV/0! errors, so you are finished auditing the worksheet with formula auditing. The following step clears the dependent arrows from the worksheet.

1
- Tap or click the 'Remove All Arrows' button (FORMULAS tab | Formula Auditing group) to remove all of the dependent arrows (Figure 9–13).

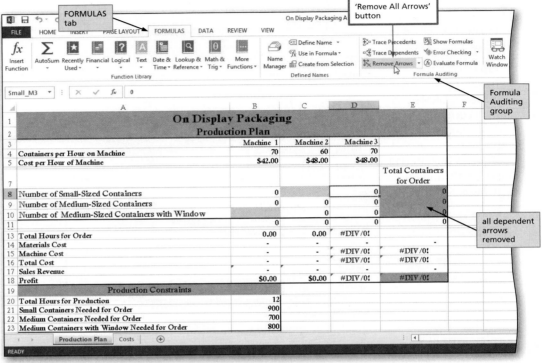

Figure 9–13

To Use Error Checking to Correct Errors

Why use error checking? *Excel can provide assistance in determining the source of errors in the worksheet.* Cells D13, D15:E16, and D18:E18 all contain error codes. Their contents indicate that these cells are in error because the formulas they contain attempt to divide a number by zero. The following steps use error checking features to find the source of these errors and correct them.

1
- Tap or click cell E18 to select it.
- Tap or click the Trace Precedents button (FORMULAS tab | Formula Auditing group) five times to identify the precedents of cell E18.
- Tap or click cell D5 to display the formula with reference to a cell on the Costs worksheet (Figure 9–14).

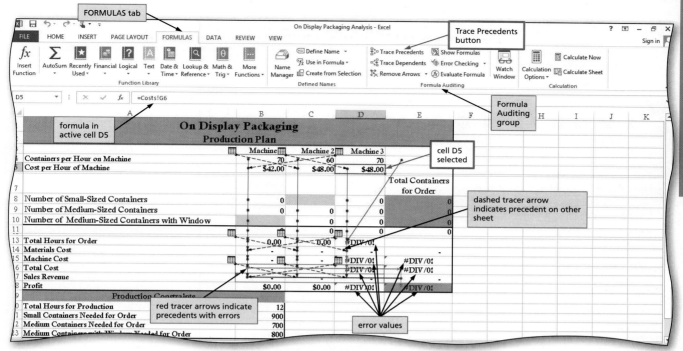

Figure 9–14

2

- Tap or click the Costs sheet tab to make Costs the active worksheet.

- Review cell G6 to determine if the reference to it in cell D5 of the Production Plan worksheet is correct.

- Make Production Plan the active sheet and then select cell E18.

- Tap or click the Error Checking button (FORMULAS tab | Formula Auditing group) to display the Error Checking dialog box (Figure 9–15).

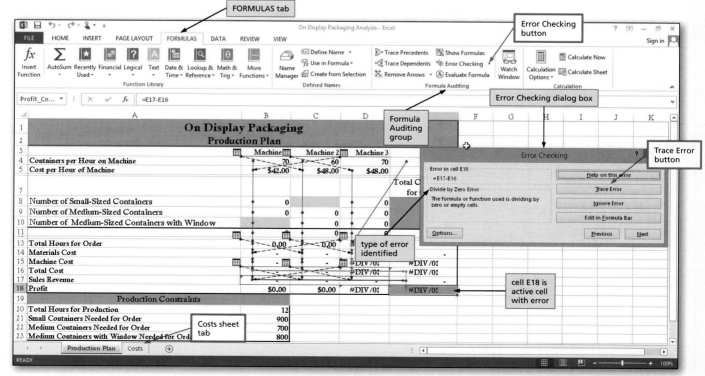

Figure 9–15

3

- Tap or click the Trace Error button (Error Checking dialog box) to highlight the precedents of the active cell, which also contain error codes (Figure 9–16).

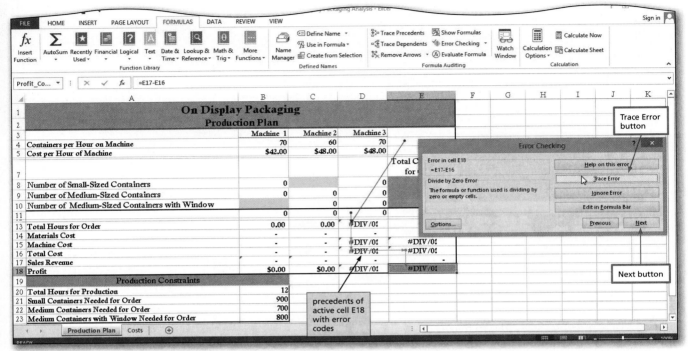

Figure 9–16

4

- Tap or click the Next button (Error Checking dialog box) to move to the next error in the workbook, found in cell D13 in this case (Figure 9–17).

Q&A

What happens when I tap or click the Next button?

Excel will move to the next cell in which it finds an error code or an error indicator. Excel moves forward through the workbook, row by row, when you tap or click the Next button, and backward through the workbook, row by row, when you tap or click the Previous button. Using the Next button here brings you to the first error in the workbook, because the workbook contains no errors after cell E18.

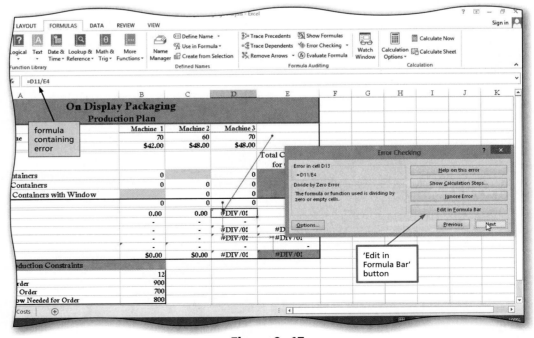

Figure 9–17

5

• Tap or click the 'Edit in Formula Bar' button (Error Checking dialog box) and edit cell D13 to read =D11/D4.

• Tap or click the Enter box in the formula bar to complete the edit of the cell (Figure 9–18).

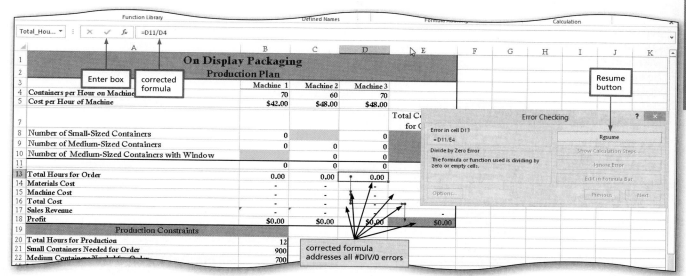

Figure 9–18

6

• Tap or click the Resume button (Error Checking dialog box) to resume checking errors.

Q&A

Why does Excel jump to cell B17 when I tap or click the Resume button?
Tapping or clicking the Resume button moves the selected cell to the next cell with an error in it if you corrected the error in the previous cell. If you did not correct the error, the selected cell would not change.

Why did cell B17, identified by error checking, not contain an error code?
This is an example of a formula that technically is correct but is flagged as a possible error because the formula references cells that are currently empty.

Excel selected cell C17 when I clicked Resume. Why?
Excel will select cell B17 if you are working on a machine with none of the default error checking options changed. If Excel selects a cell other than B17, it means that the error checking settings have been changed and Excel no longer flags empty referenced cells as possible errors.

• Edit the formula in cell B17 to read =B8*Costs!E4+B9*Costs!E5 and then tap or click the Resume button (Error Checking dialog box) to complete the edit (Figure 9–19).

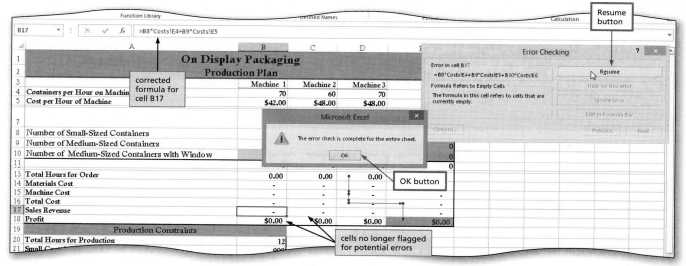

Figure 9–19

Q&A | Why did the flag in cell C17 disappear after editing the formula in cell B17?
The formula in cell C17 was originally flagged as a potential error because the formula was inconsistent with the cells on either side of it. Once the formula in cell B17 was edited, Excel no longer expects consistency because none of the three cells, B17:D17, contain formulas that are consistent with each other, so the error flag is removed.

- Tap or click the OK button in the Microsoft Excel dialog box to close the open dialog boxes.

- If necessary, tap or click the 'Remove All Arrows' button (FORMULAS tab | Formula Auditing group) to remove all of the dependent arrows (Figure 9–20).

Figure 9–20

BTW

Setting Iterative Calculation Options

In certain situations, you will want Excel to recalculate a formula that contains a circular reference, to enable Excel to converge upon an acceptable solution. Changing the Iterative Calculation option allows Excel to recalculate a formula a specified number of times after the initial circular reference error message is dismissed. To allow Excel to recalculate a formula, display the Excel Options dialog box and then tap or click the Formulas button. In the Calculation Options area, tap or click to select 'Enable Iterative Calculation'. You can specify the maximum number of iterations and the smallest amount of change acceptable between iterations. Be aware that turning on this option will slow down the worksheet due to the additional computations.

More about the Formula Auditing Group

Figure 9–21 shows some of the buttons in the Formula Auditing group on the FORMULAS tab. You already have used the Trace Precedents, Trace Dependents, and 'Remove All Arrows' buttons, which provide insight into the structure of the worksheet. You also have used the Error Checking button to check for errors throughout the worksheet. When tapped or clicked, it highlights each error in the worksheet in sequence and displays options for correcting it. When you select a cell containing an error and then tap or click the Error Checking arrow, you have two additional options. The Trace Error command highlights with red arrows the precedents of the selected cell with the error, which may point out the source of the error. The second option, Circular References, is available only when the error in the cell is a **circular reference**. When a cell contains a circular reference, it means that one of its defining values is itself. For example, if you type =B2/A2 in cell B2, you have created a circular reference. Excel displays an error message when you create a circular reference, and provides you with access to the appropriate Help topic. In complex worksheets with multiple precedent levels, these errors are not uncommon.

Table 9–1 lists common error codes identified in Excel.

Table 9–1 Common Excel Error Codes

Error Code	Description
#DIV/0!	Indicates that you have created a formula that divides a number by zero
#N/A!	Indicates that a value is not available to a formula or function
#NAME?	Indicates use of an invalid function name
#NULL!	Indicates no common cells in two ranges a formula identifies as having an intersection
#NUM!	Indicates that you used an invalid argument in a formula
#REF!	Indicates that a cell reference in a formula is not valid; it may be pointing to an empty cell, for instance
#VALUE!	Indicates that you have included nonnumeric data in a calculation

You can use three other buttons when auditing formulas. The Evaluate Formula button allows you to move through a formula step by step, which can be a useful tool when working with long, complex formulas.

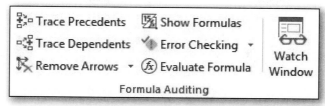

Figure 9–21

The two other buttons in the group provide you with display options for viewing the worksheet and keeping an eye on cells of interest. The Show Formulas button displays the formulas instead of values in the active worksheet. The Watch Window button opens a separate window that displays values and formulas for specific cells that you choose to monitor.

Using the Watch Window

The Watch Window (Figure 9–22a) allows you to keep an eye on cells that you have identified as being related; this allows you to observe changes to the cells even when viewing a different worksheet or workbook. You add cells to the Watch Window using the Add Watch button in the Watch Window and the Add Watch dialog box (Figure 9–22b). The Watch Window continues to show the values of watched cells even as you navigate the worksheet and the cells no longer are in view. Similarly, if you change the view to another worksheet or workbook, the Watch Window allows you to continue to monitor the cell values.

To Open the Watch Window

If you wanted to open the Watch Window, you would perform the following steps:

1. If necessary, tap or click FORMULAS on the ribbon to display the FORMULAS tab.
2. Tap or click the Watch Window button (FORMULAS tab | Formula Auditing group) to open the Watch Window (Figure 9–22a on the next page).
3. If necessary, move the Watch Window to a location where it does not obscure cells you want to observe.

To Add Cells to the Watch Window

If you wanted to add cells to the Watch Window, you would perform the following steps:

1. Tap or click the Add Watch button on the Watch Window toolbar to display the Add Watch dialog box (Figure 9–22b on the next page).
2. Select the cell or cells to be watched.
3. Tap or click the Add button (Add Watch dialog box) to add the selected cells to the Watch Window.

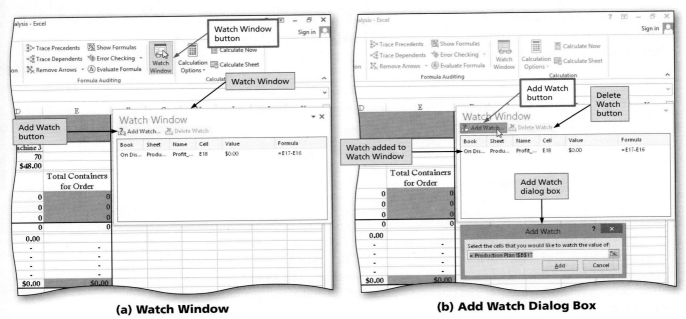

(a) Watch Window

(b) Add Watch Dialog Box

Figure 9–22

TO DELETE CELLS FROM THE WATCH WINDOW

If you wanted to delete cells from the Watch Window, you would perform the following steps:

1. In the Watch Window dialog box, tap or click the watched cell you want to stop watching.
2. Tap or click the Delete Watch button in the Watch Window to delete the selected cell from the Watch Window.

TO CLOSE THE WATCH WINDOW

If you wanted to close the Watch Window, you would perform the following step:

1. Tap or click the Close button on the Watch Window title bar to close the Watch Window.

BTW

Errors and Data Validation

Excel cannot identify cells that contain formulas that are mathematically correct, but logically incorrect, without the use of data validation rules. It is up to the user to create validation rules that restrict solutions to values that are logical.

Data Validation

When calculating formulas, some values used in calculations might not have any useful meaning for the problem at hand. For example, cells B8 and D8 in the Production Plan worksheet display the number of small containers produced. Because you cannot create a negative number of containers, only values greater than or equal to zero should be entered in cells B8 and D8. In other words, only values greater than or equal to zero are valid in cells B8 and D8. Excel provides you with tools to restrict the values that can be placed in cells to valid values. You can place restrictions on values, provide a message to the user when a cell with restrictions is selected, and create an error message that is displayed when a restricted, or invalid, value is entered.

Excel's data validation rules apply only when you enter data into the cell manually. Excel does not check the validation rules if a cell is calculated by a formula or set in a way other than direct input by the user.

How do you determine which cells need data validation rules?

When considering which cells to assign data validation rules, review the changing cells and determine which, if any, need restriction. Formulas in a cell may be mathematically possible for any values entered, but may not make sense for a range of data. In this case, validation rules need to be set to ensure that any numbers entered meet the criteria specified in the requirements document.

The types of data validation criteria you can use include any specified value, whole numbers, a value in a list (such as a text value), dates, and custom values. When using the Custom validation type, you can use a formula that evaluates to either true or false. If the value is false, users may not enter data in the cell. Suppose, for example, you have a cell that contains an employee's salary. If the salary is zero, which indicates the employee no longer is with the company, you may want to prohibit a user from entering a percentage in another cell that contains the employee's raise for the year.

To Add Data Validation to Cells

1 ANALYZE WORKBOOK FORMULAS | 2 SET DATA VALIDATION RULES | 3 PROPOSE PROBLEM-SOLVING STRATEGIES
4 CREATE & EVALUATE SCENARIOS | 5 FINALIZE WORKBOOK

Why add data validation? In the Production Plan worksheet, the number of containers produced on each machine, of each size, must be nonnegative whole numbers. The cells that need to be restricted are cells B8:B9, C9:C10, and D8:D10 because they display the number of containers produced. You can use data validation to apply these conditions and restrictions to the cells. The following steps add data validation to cells in the ranges B8:B9, C9:C10, and D8:D10.

- Select cells B8 and D8 to prepare for adding data validation rules to them.
- Tap or click DATA on the ribbon to display the DATA tab.
- Tap or click the Data Validation button (DATA tab | Data Tools group) to display the Data Validation dialog box.
- Tap or click the Allow arrow (Data Validation dialog box) to display a list of validation criteria types.
- Tap or click Whole number in the Allow list to select it as the validation criteria type.
- Tap or click the Data arrow and then tap or click 'greater than or equal to' in the Data list to select it.
- Type   0   in the Minimum box to specify that the values in the selected cells must be whole numbers greater than or equal to zero (Figure 9–23).

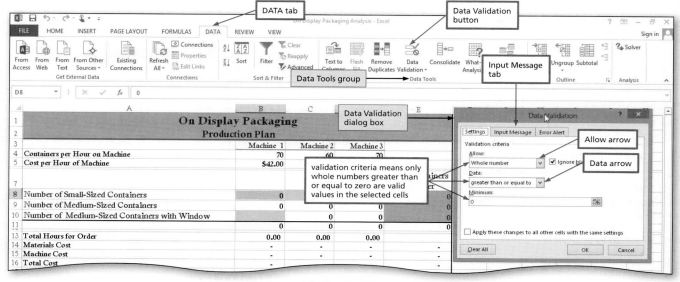

Figure 9–23

What is the purpose of the Ignore blank check box?
The Ignore blank check box should be cleared if you want to require that the user enter data in the cell. By leaving the Ignore blank check box selected, Excel allows the user to select the cell and then deselect the cell without entering data.

2

- Tap or click the Input Message tab (Data Validation dialog box) to display the options on the Input Message sheet.

- Type **Number of Small Containers** in the Title text box to enter a title for the message displayed when cell B8 or D8 is selected.

- Type **Enter the number of small containers to produce on this machine. The number must be a whole number that is greater than or equal to zero.** in the Input message text box to enter the text for the message (Figure 9–24).

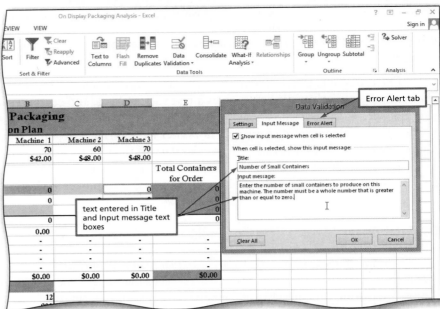

Figure 9–24

Q&A

How else can I validate data?

Excel allows several types of validation to be set in the Settings sheet (Data Validation dialog box) shown in Figure 9–23 on the previous page. Each selection in this sheet changes the type of value that Excel allows a user to enter in the cell. In the Allow list, the Any value selection allows you to enter any value, but still allows you to specify an input message for the cell. The Whole number, Decimal, Date, and Time selections permit only values of those types to be entered in the cell. The List selection allows you to specify a range that contains a list of valid values for the cell. The Text length selection allows only a certain length of text string to be entered in the cell. The Custom selection allows you to specify a formula that validates the data entered by the user.

3

- Tap or click the Error Alert tab (Data Validation dialog box) to display the Error Alert sheet.

- If necessary, tap or click the Style arrow and then tap or click Stop to select the Stop error style.

- Type **Input Error** in the Title text box to enter a title for the error message displayed if invalid data is entered in cell B8 or D8.

- Type **You must enter a whole number that is greater than or equal to zero.** in the Error message text box to enter the text for the error message (Figure 9–25).

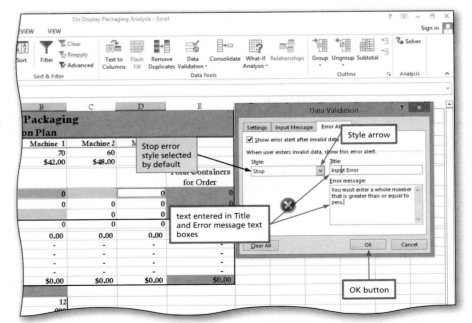

Figure 9–25

Q&A

What does the Stop error style mean?

You can select one of three types of error styles. Stop prevents users from entering invalid data in a cell. Warning displays a message that the data is invalid and lets users accept the invalid entry, edit it, or remove it. Information displays a message that the data is invalid, but still allows users to enter it.

4

- Tap or click the OK button (Data Validation dialog box) to accept the data validation settings for cells B8 and D8.

5

- Repeat Steps 1 through 4 twice, once for medium containers in cells B9:D9, and once for medium containers with windows in cells C10:D10. Tap or click the OK button after completing Step 3 each time. Use the same constraints for the values that can be entered in the cells, and make the appropriate changes for cell addresses and the text in the input message. When creating the title for the input message for cells B10:D10, use Number of Medium with Windows in order to make the title fit.

- Select cell E23 to make it the active cell.

Q&A What is the result of the validation rules just created?

If a user selects one of the cells in the ranges B8:B9, C9:C10, or D8:D10, Excel displays the input message defined in Figure 9–24. If the user enters a value that either is less than zero or is not a whole number in cells in the ranges B8:B9, C9:C10, and D8:D10, Excel displays the error message defined in Figure 9–25 and forces the user to change the value to a valid number before deselecting the cell.

Solving Complex Problems

In the On Display Packaging Analysis workbook, the problem of determining how to produce the number of containers needed within the constraints provided is not straightforward, due to the number of variables involved. You can attempt to solve the problem manually, through trial and error, or you can use an Excel tool to automate some or all of the solution. To solve the problem manually, you could try adjusting cells in the ranges B8:B9, C9:C10, and D8:D10 until the criteria for the order are met. Because so many possible combinations could meet the criteria, you could hold one or more of the variables constant that fall within the constraints, and make adjustments to the other variables to attempt to meet the rest of the criteria.

BTW

Copying Validation Rules

You can copy validation rules from one cell to other cells using the Paste Special command. Select the cell that contains the validation rules you need to copy, select the cell or cells to which you want to apply the validation rules, tap or click the Paste button arrow, and then tap or click Paste Special. In the Paste Special dialog box, below Paste, select Validation, and then tap or click the OK button (Paste Special dialog box).

How should you approach solving a complex problem?

When considering an approach to a complex problem in Excel, start with the least complex method of attempting to solve the problem. In general, the following methods can be useful in the order shown:

1. **Use trial and error** to modify the input, or changing, values in the worksheet. Use a commonsense approach, and keep in mind the range of acceptable answers to your problem. For example, the number of containers produced on a machine in this chapter should not be a negative number.

2. **Use Excel's Goal Seek feature** to have Excel automatically modify a cell's value in a worksheet in an attempt to reach a certain goal in a dependent cell.

3. **Use Excel's Solver feature** to provide Excel with all of the known rules, or constraints, of your problem as well as the goal you are seeking. Allow Solver to attempt as many different solutions to your problem as possible.

CONSIDER THIS

To Use Trial and Error to Attempt to Solve a Complex Problem

1 ANALYZE WORKBOOK FORMULAS | 2 SET DATA VALIDATION RULES | **3 PROPOSE PROBLEM-SOLVING STRATEGIES**
4 CREATE & EVALUATE SCENARIOS | 5 FINALIZE WORKBOOK

Trial and error is not making blind guesses. *Why use trial and error? With an understanding of how a worksheet is set up and how the various intervals interact, you can use this knowledge and logic to inform each subsequent trial following the first trial.* In the first trial for the On Display Packaging Analysis workbook, you will set up the production so that all the containers are manufactured on machine 3, the one machine that can manufacture all three types of containers, and then make some adjustments based on the results. The following steps illustrate the process of using trial and error to attempt to solve a complex problem.

1

- Tap or click cell D8 to make it the active cell and display the Number of Small Containers input message.

- Type 850.5 and then press the ENTER key to enter the number of small containers to produce on machine 3 and display the Input Error dialog box (Figure 9–26).

Q&A
Why does the Input Error dialog box appear after entering 850.5 in cell D8?
You set a data validation rule in cell D8 that accepts only whole numbers greater than or equal to zero. Because 850.5 is not a whole number, Excel displays the Input Error dialog box with the title and error message you specified when you set the data validation rule.

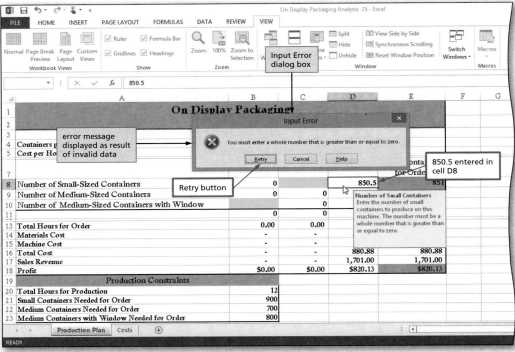

Figure 9–26

2

- Tap or click the Retry button (Input Error dialog box) to return to cell D8.

- Enter 900 in cell D8 as the number of small containers to produce on machine 3.

- Enter 700 in cell D9 as the number of medium containers to produce on machine 3.

- Enter 800 in cell D10 as the number of medium containers with windows to produce on machine 3 and then press the ENTER key.

- If necessary, press the ENTER key to update the totals in the range B13:D18 and column E (Figure 9–27).

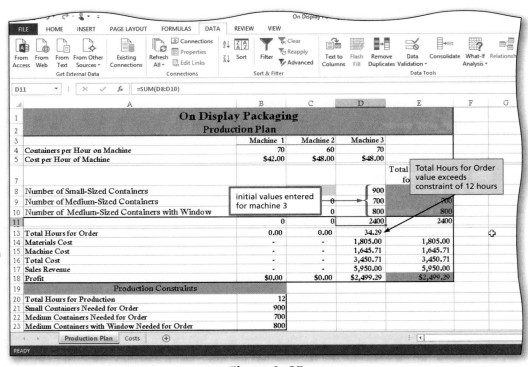

Figure 9–27

Q&A
Do the values entered in Step 2 solve the problem for machine 3?
No. Cell B20 indicates that the containers must be produced in 12 hours or less. The values entered in Step 2 mean that the containers will be manufactured in 34.29 hours on machine 3.

3

- Tap or click cell D8 to make it the active cell.

- Type **200** and then press the ENTER key to enter the number of small containers to produce on machine 3.

- Tap or click cell B8 to make it the active cell. Type **700** and then press the ENTER key to enter the number of small containers to produce on machine 1 (Figure 9–28).

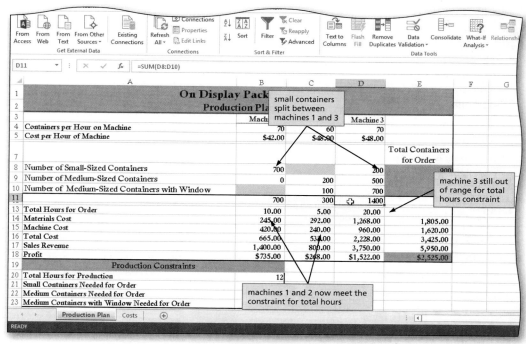

Figure 9–28

Q&A Do the values entered in Step 3 solve the problem for machine 3?

No. The values entered in Step 3 mean that the machine 3 still needs 24.29 hours for the order, which is greater than the 12-hour constraint shown in cell B20.

4

- Tap or click cell C9 to make it the active cell.

- Enter **200** as the number of medium containers to produce on machine 2.

- Enter **500** in cell D9 as the number of medium containers to produce on machine 3.

- Enter **100** in cell C10 as the number of medium containers with windows to produce on machine 2.

- Enter **700** in cell D10 as the number of medium containers with windows to produce on machine 3 (Figure 9–29).

Figure 9–29

Q&A Do the values entered in Step 4 solve the problem for all machines?

No. The manufacturing time on machine 3 still exceeds the 12-hour production constraint.

What are some problems with using trial and error?

While trial and error can be used on simple problems, it has many limitations when used to solve complex problems. The Production Plan worksheet has seven cells (B8, B9, C9, C10, D8, D9, and D10) that can be adjusted to solve the problem. Endless combinations of values could be entered in those seven cells to try to come up with a solution. Using trial and error, it is difficult to determine if a solution you reach satisfies the goal of minimizing the total cost, subject to the constraints.

To Use the Goal Seek Command to Attempt to Solve a Complex Problem

Figure 9–29 illustrates a situation where Goal Seek may help you to solve a complex problem. You know that cell D13 needs to be less than or equal to 12 hours. The formula in cell D13 is =D11/ D4, where D11 is the sum of cells D8:D10, which means that D13 depends on cells D8:D10 and cell D4. With Goal Seek, you can manipulate one of these precedent cells to find a solution for cell D13 that meets the 12-hour constraint. Goal seeking will change the value of a cell until a single criterion is met in another cell. You decide to have Goal Seek manipulate cell D9, because machine 1 has the same production capacity as machine 3 and is not currently manufacturing any medium-sized containers. Any reduction in machine 3 would produce an equal increase in machine 1 time. In doing this, you hope that the other constraints of the problem also are satisfied.

The following steps show how Goal Seek can be used to change the number of medium containers on machine 3 to keep the total hours for machine 3 at less than or equal to 12.

- If necessary, tap or click DATA on the ribbon to display the DATA tab.

- Tap or click the 'What-If Analysis' button (DATA tab | Data Tools group) to display the What-If Analysis menu (Figure 9–30).

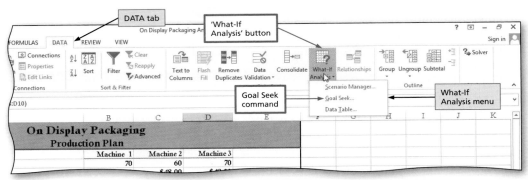

Figure 9–30

❷

- Tap or click Goal Seek on the What-If Analysis menu to display the Goal Seek dialog box.

- Type **$D$13** in the Set cell box (Goal Seek dialog box) to specify the cell that should contain the goal value.

- Tap or click the To value text box and then type **12** as the goal value.

- Tap or click the 'By changing cell' box to prepare for entering the cell containing the value to change.

- If necessary, move the Goal Seek dialog box so that cell D9 is visible on the worksheet and then tap or click cell D9 to enter its reference in the 'By changing cell' box (Figure 9–31).

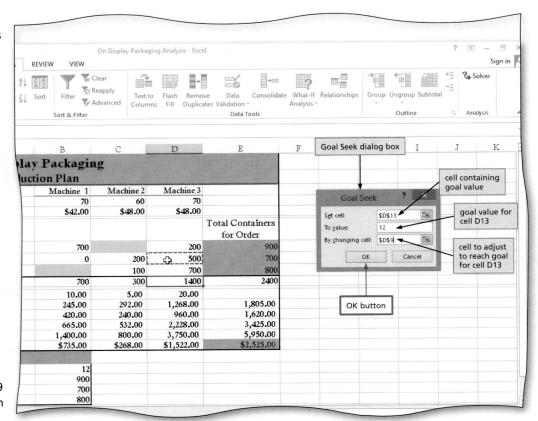

Figure 9–31

3

- Tap or click the OK button (Goal Seek dialog box) to seek the goal of 12 hours in cell D13 and display the Goal Seek Status dialog box, which indicates that goal seeking found a solution (Figure 9–32).

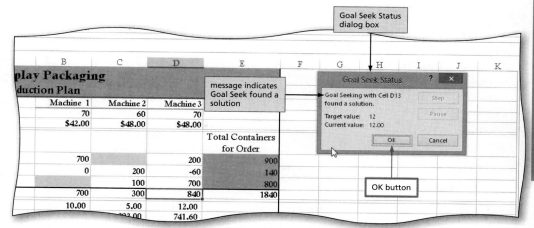

Figure 9–32

4

- Tap or click the OK button (Goal Seek Status dialog box) to close the dialog box and display the updated worksheet.

- Tap or click cell E23 to deselect any other cell (Figure 9–33).

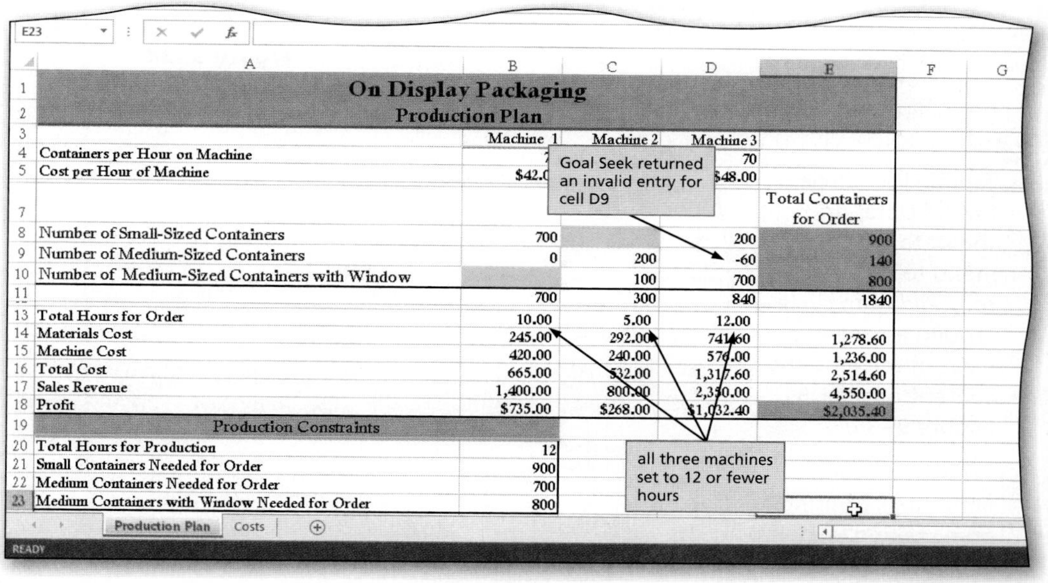

Q&A

How can cell D9 contain a negative number when data validation rules allow only numbers greater than or equal to zero?

Data validation rules are applied only to data that is entered into a cell. Entries that are the result of calculations will not produce a data validation error.

Figure 9–33

To Circle Invalid Data and Clear Validation Circles

1 ANALYZE WORKBOOK FORMULAS | 2 SET DATA VALIDATION RULES | 3 PROPOSE PROBLEM-SOLVING STRATEGIES
4 CREATE & EVALUATE SCENARIOS | 5 FINALIZE WORKBOOK

Why? *The 'Circle Invalid Data' command checks for invalid data entered as the result of a formula or automated tool, such as Goal Seek.* The previous set of steps illustrates that the data validation rules set up earlier apply only to data directly entered into a cell, not to the results of features such as Goal Seek. In this case, Goal Seek found a solution that satisfied the criteria specified for the goal, but that same solution violated the conditions specified for data validation. It is good practice to check your worksheet for invalid data periodically through use of the 'Circle Invalid Data' command. The following steps check for and circle any invalid data on the Production Plan worksheet and then clear the validation circles.

1

- Tap or click the Data Validation arrow (DATA tab | Data Tools group) to display the Data Validation menu (Figure 9–34).

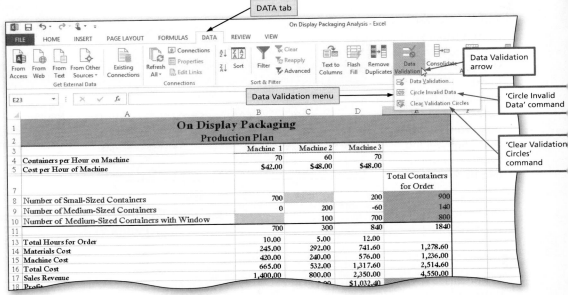

Figure 9–34

2

- Tap or click 'Circle Invalid Data' on the Data Validation menu to place a red validation circle around any invalid data, in this case the content of cell D9 (Figure 9–35).

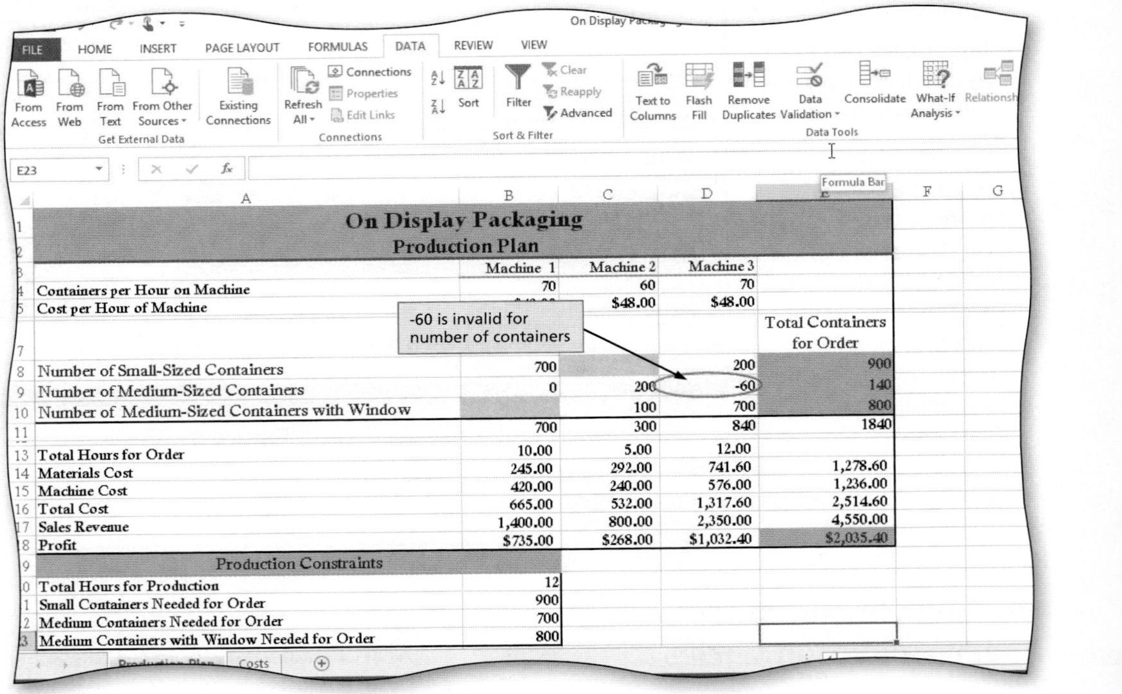

Q&A

What are some limitations of using goal seeking?
Goal seeking allows you to manipulate only one cell in order to reach a goal. In this example, to change the total number of hours on machine 3 to 12, the number of medium containers is changed to –60. Goal Seek can produce a result that is acceptable mathematically, but not logically, as is the case here.

Figure 9–35

Has the problem been solved?
No. At this point, all machines are meeting the 12-hour constraint, but not enough medium containers are being produced. Even if all production constraints were met, you still have no way of knowing whether the goal to minimize cost (cell E16) has been achieved.

- Tap or click the Data Validation arrow (DATA tab | Data Tools group) to display the Data Validation menu.

- Tap or click 'Clear Validation Circles' on the Data Validation menu to remove the red validation circle.

- If necessary, select cell E23 to deselect any other cell (Figure 9–36).

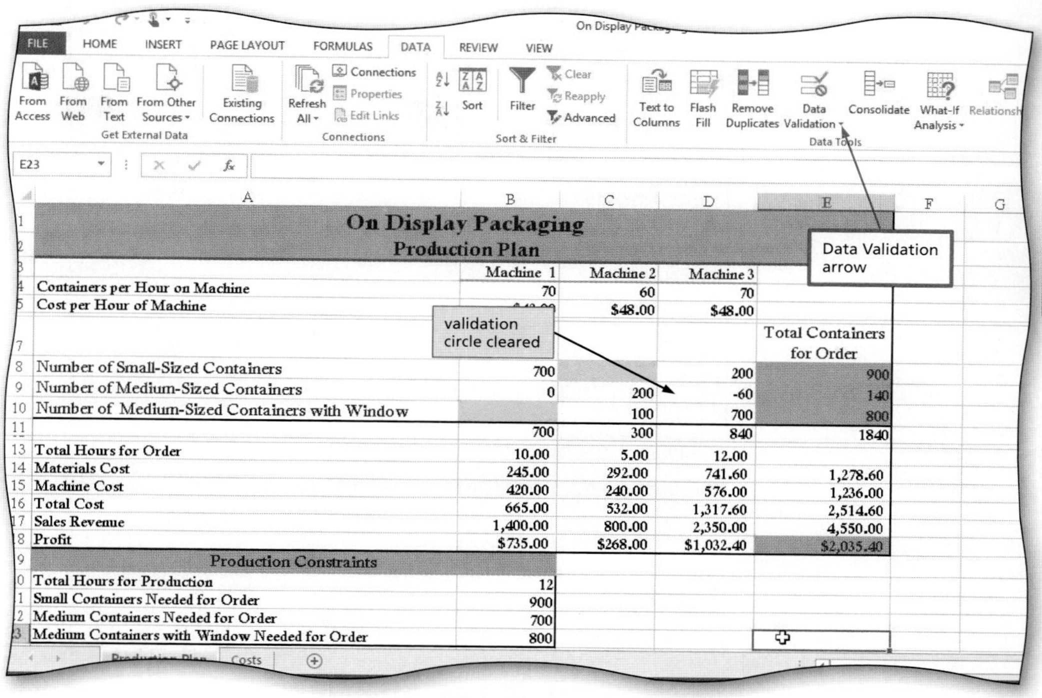

Figure 9–36

Using Solver to Solve Complex Problems

Solver allows you to solve complex problems where a number of variables can be changed in a worksheet in order to meet a goal in a particular cell. Unlike Goal Seek, Solver is not constrained to changing one cell at a time and can efficiently evaluate many combinations for a solution.

The technique Solver uses to solve a problem depends on the model that the user selects as best representing the data. Three techniques are available. For the current workbook, Solver will use a technique called linear programming to solve problems. **Linear programming** is a complex mathematical process used to solve problems that include multiple variables and the minimizing or maximizing of result values. Solver essentially tries as many possible combinations of solutions as it can. On each attempt to solve the problem, Solver checks to see if it has found a solution. The other two techniques are beyond the scope of this chapter.

Figure 9–37a shows the result of using Solver on the Production Plan worksheet. Cells in the ranges B8:B9, C9:C10, and D8:D10 are the changing cells. **Changing cells**, or **adjustable cells**, are the cells modified by Solver to solve the problem. The total cost in cell E16 is identified as the **target cell**. Solver will attempt to minimize the value of this cell by varying the values in the other changing cells, within the constraints you set. Constraints are the requirements that have been placed on certain values in the problem, as listed in the requirements document. For example, no machine should be in production for more than 12 hours. You have also been provided with a minimum mix of containers that needs to be produced in the 12-hour period.

BTW
Solver Requirements
Regardless of the technique Solver uses to solve a problem, it requires three different types of input from the user: the objective, or the result you need for the target cell; variable cells, the values that can change; and constraints, the conditions that the solution has to meet.

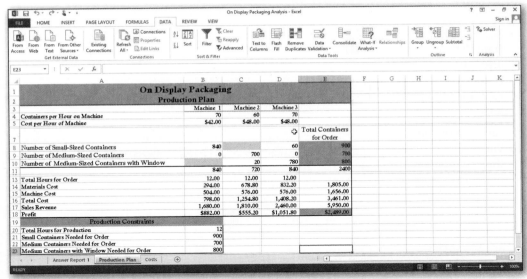

(a) Solver Result

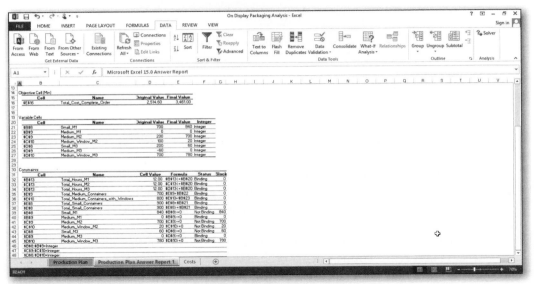

(b) Solver Answer Report

Figure 9–37

Figure 9–37b shows a Solver Answer Report. As previously discussed, an Answer Report is a worksheet summarizing a Solver calculation. It shows the answer for the target cell, the values used in the changing cells to arrive at that answer, and the constraints that were applied to the calculation. The report satisfies the requirement to document the results of the production calculation, as shown in Figure 9–2 on page EX 549.

The DATA tab on the ribbon includes the Solver button, which starts Solver.

Note: If the Solver button does not appear on the DATA tab, then you must use the Add-Ins option in the Excel Options dialog box to add it. If other add-ins, such as the Analysis ToolPak, are selected on your computer, then the DATA tab on the ribbon may appear differently than shown in this book.

The goal for Solver is to minimize the total cost of the containers produced, within the constraints set in the requirements document. The cells that can be changed by Solver to accomplish this goal are cells in the ranges B8:B9, C9:C10, and D8:D10, which contain the number of containers to produce on each machine. The constraints are summarized in Table 9–2.

Table 9–2 Constraints for Solver		
Cell or Range	**Operator**	**Constraint**
$B$8:$B$9	>=	0
$B$8:$B$9	int	integer
$C$9:$C$10	>=	0
$C$9:$C$10	int	integer
$D$8:$D$10	>=	0
$D$8:$D$10	int	integer
$E$8	=	$B$21
$E$9	=	$B$22
$E$10	=	$B$23
$B$13	<=	$B$20
$C$13	<=	$B$20
$D$13	<=	$B$20

© 2014 Cengage Learning

To Use Solver to Find the Optimal Solution to a Complex Problem

1 ANALYZE WORKBOOK FORMULAS | 2 SET DATA VALIDATION RULES | 3 PROPOSE PROBLEM-SOLVING STRATEGIES
4 CREATE & EVALUATE SCENARIOS | 5 FINALIZE WORKBOOK

Why use Solver? Solver allows Excel to evaluate multiple combinations of values for changing variables to find an optimal solution to a complex problem. The following steps show how to use Solver to find the optimal solution to solve the problem in the Production Plan worksheet within the given constraints.

1

- Tap or click the Solver button (DATA tab | Analysis group) to display the Solver Parameters dialog box.

- Tap or click the Collapse Dialog button in the Set Objective box to collapse the Solver Parameters dialog box.

- Tap or click cell E16 to set the target cell (Figure 9–38).

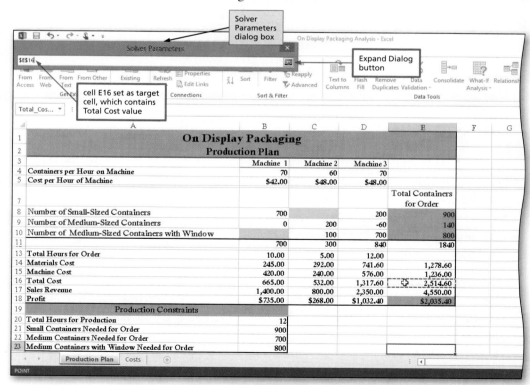

Figure 9–38

2

- Tap or click the Expand Dialog button on the right side of the collapsed Solver Parameters dialog box to expand the dialog box.

- Tap or click Min in the To area to specify that the value of the target cell should be as small as possible.

- Tap or click the Collapse Dialog button in the 'By Changing Variable Cells' box to collapse the Solver Parameters dialog box.

- If you are using a touch screen, select the range B8:B9, type   ,   (a comma), select the range C9:C10, type   ,   (a comma), and then select the range D8:D10; if you are using a mouse, select the range B8:B9, hold down the CTRL key, and then select the ranges C9:C10 and D8:D10.

- Tap or click the Expand Dialog button on the right side of the collapsed Solver Parameters dialog box to expand the dialog box (Figure 9–39).

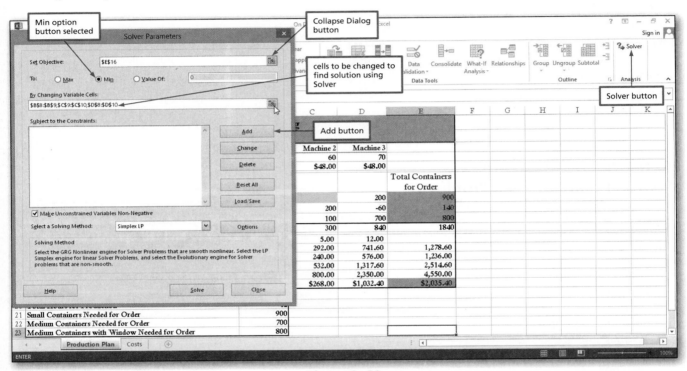

Figure 9–39

3

- Tap or click the Add button to display the Add Constraint dialog box.

- If necessary, move the Add Constraint dialog box so that the range B8:B9 is visible.

- Select the range B8:B9 to set the value of the Cell Reference box.

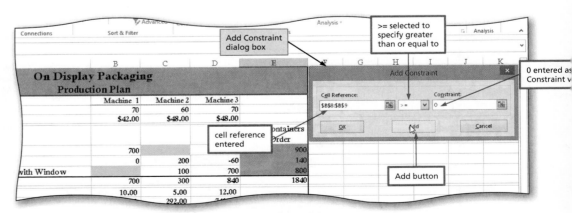

Figure 9–40

- Tap or click the middle arrow and then select >= in the list.

- Type   0   in the Constraint box to set the constraint on the cells in the range B8:B9 to be greater than or equal to 0 (Figure 9–40).

Q&A

How is the Constraint box used?
When adding constraints, as shown in Figure 9–40, Solver allows you to enter a cell reference followed by an operator. If the operator is <=, >=, or =, then you enter the constraint value in the Constraint box. The constraint can be a value or a cell reference. Other valid operators are **int**, for an integer value, or **bin**, for cells that contain only one of two values, such as yes/no or true/false.

What do the entries in the Add Constraint dialog box in Figure 9–40 mean?
The entries limit the number of containers on machine 1 (cells B8:B9) to a number greater than or equal to zero.

4

- Tap or click the Add button (Add Constraint dialog box) to add a second constraint.

- Select the range B8:B9 to set the value of the Cell Reference box.

- Tap or click the middle box arrow and then select int in the list to set a constraint on the cells in the range B8:B9 to be assigned only integer values (Figure 9–41).

Figure 9–41

5

- Tap or click the Add button (Add Constraint dialog box) to add a third constraint.

- Select the range C9:C10 to set the value of the Cell Reference box.

- Tap or click the middle box arrow and then select >= in the list.

- Type   0   in the Constraint box to set the constraint on the cells in the range C9:C10 to be greater than or equal to 0 (Figure 9–42).

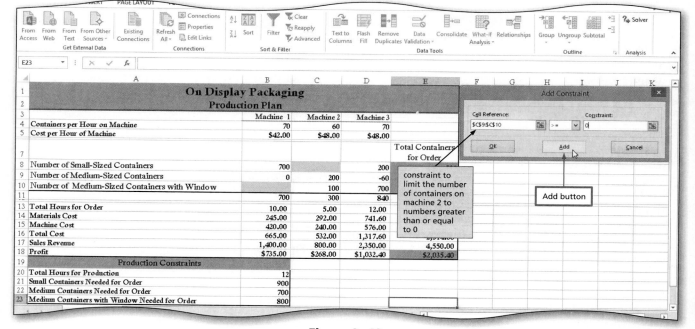

Figure 9–42

6

- Tap or click the Add button (Add Constraint dialog box) to add a fourth constraint.

- Enter the remaining constraints shown in Table 9–2 on page EX 575, beginning with the constraints for the range C9:C10.

- When finished with the final constraint, tap or click the OK button (Add Constraint dialog box) to close the dialog box and display the Solver Parameters dialog box (Figure 9–43).

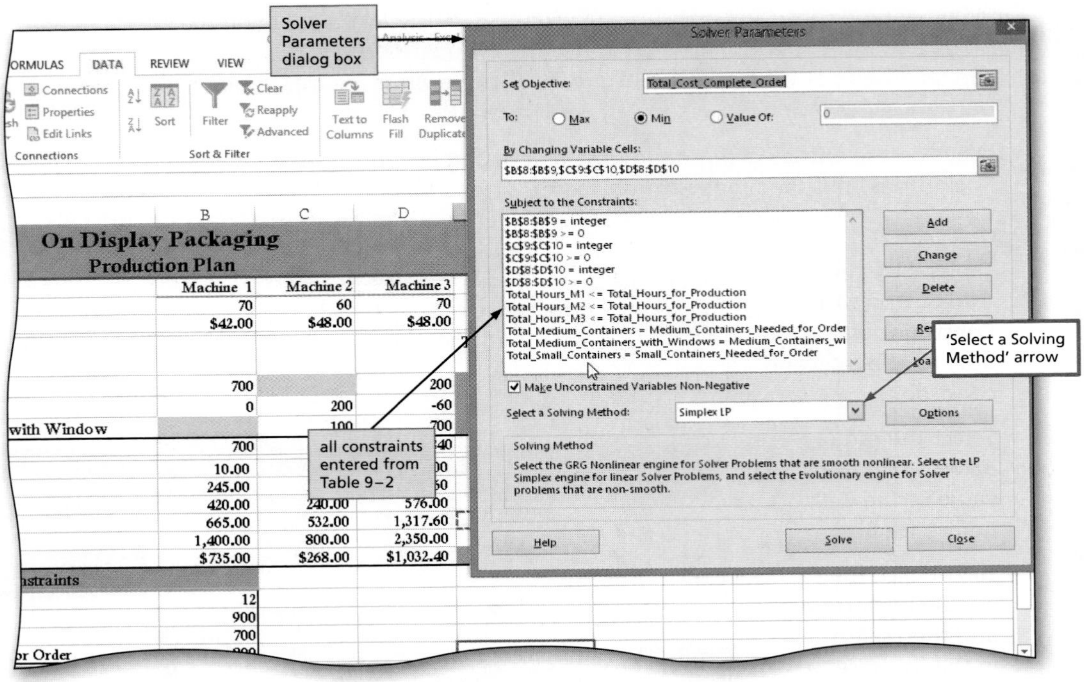

Figure 9–43

Q&A What should I do if a constraint does not match the ones shown in Figure 9–43?

Select the constraint, tap or click the Change button (Solver Parameters dialog box), and then enter the constraints as shown in Table 9–2 on page EX 575.

7

- Tap or click the 'Select a Solving Method' arrow to display a list of solving methods.

- If necessary, tap or click Simplex LP in the list to select the linear progression method (Figure 9–44).

Q&A What does Simplex LP mean?

LP stands for linear progression, and Simplex refers to the basic problem-solving method used to solve linear problems.

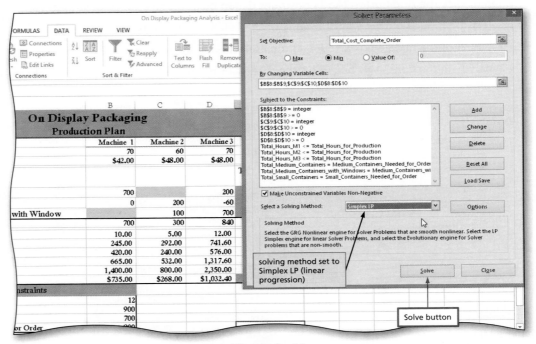

Figure 9–44

8

- Tap or click the Solve button (Solver Parameters dialog box) to display the Solver Results dialog box, indicating that Solver found a solution to the problem (Figure 9–45).

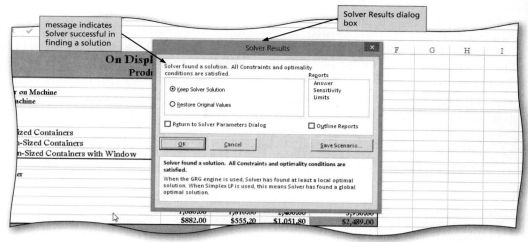

Figure 9–45

9

- Tap or click Answer in the Reports list to select the type of report to generate (Figure 9–46).

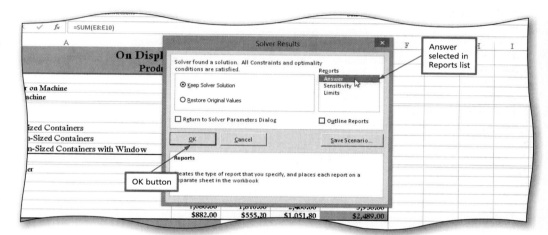

Figure 9–46

10

- Tap or click the OK button (Solver Results dialog box) to display the values found by Solver and the newly recalculated totals (Figure 9–47).

Q&A

What is the result of using Solver?
Figure 9–47 shows a solution found by Solver that both meets the constraints and minimizes the total cost of the containers produced.

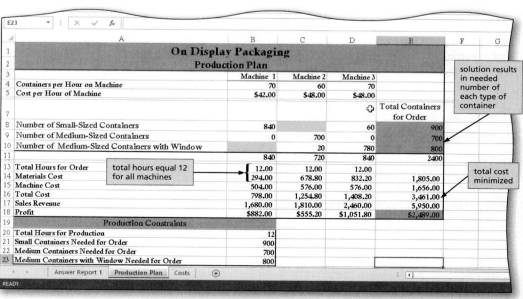

Figure 9–47

To View the Solver Answer Report

Solver generates the requested Answer Report on a separate worksheet after it finds a solution. The Solver Answer Report summarizes the problem that you have presented to Solver. It shows the original and final values of the target cell along with the original and final values of the changing cells (adjustable cells) that Solver adjusted to find the answer. Additionally, it lists all of the constraints that you imposed on Solver.

Why view the Answer Report generated by Solver? The Answer Report documents that a particular problem has been solved correctly. Because it lists all of the relevant information in a concise format, you can use the Answer Report to make certain that you have entered all of the constraints and allowed Solver to vary all the cells necessary to solve the problem. You also can use the report to reconstruct the Solver model in the future.

The following steps view the Solver Answer Report.

1

• Tap or click the Answer Report 1 sheet tab to display the Solver Answer Report (Figure 9–48).

If requested by your instructor, add the name of your hometown in cell A3, following the content already in that cell.

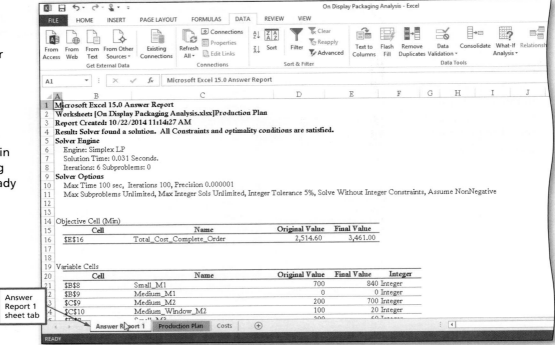

Figure 9–48

2

• Drag the Answer Report 1 sheet tab to the right of the Production Plan sheet tab to move the worksheet in the workbook.

• Double-tap or double-click the Answer Report 1 sheet tab to select the name.

• Type **Production Plan Answer Report 1** to rename the worksheet.

• Change the color of the sheet tab to 'Red, Accent 5'.

• Save the workbook.

• Tap or click the Zoom Out button on the status bar three times to set the zoom to 70%.

• Scroll down to view the remaining cells of the Answer Report (Figure 9–49).

Q&A What is shown in the Answer Report?
Figure 9–49 shows additional information about the constraints that you placed on the problem and how the constraints were used to solve the problem. Column F, the **Status column**, indicates whether the constraint was binding or not. A constraint that is **binding** is one that limited the final solution in some way. For example, the total number of hours in cell B13 in the Production Plan worksheet is binding because the solution found the maximum number required by the constraints, which is 12 hours. No more time could be allocated to production on that machine given the constraints. A constraint that is **not binding** is one that was not a limiting factor in the solution that Solver provided.

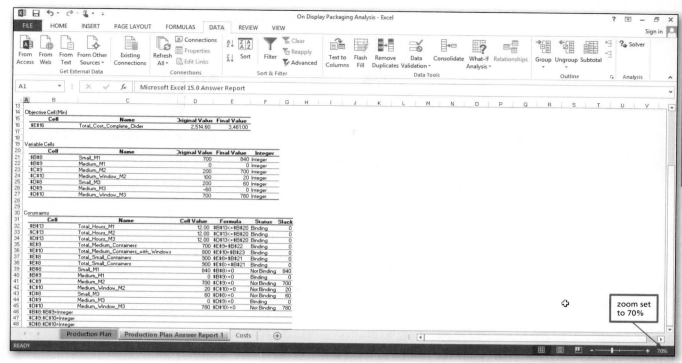

Figure 9–49

Working with Solver Methods and Options

When you selected the Simplex LP method of solving the production problem in the Solver Parameters dialog box shown in Figure 9–44 on page EX 578, you selected a linear programming method that assumes the problem to solve is a linear one. After selecting the Solver method, you can select various options to further configure the inner workings of Solver. Discussion of many of these parameters is beyond the scope of this book. Table 9–3 presents some of the more commonly used Solver options.

BTW
Viewing Other Solutions
If you want to view solutions other than the one Solver identifies as optimal, select the Show Iteration Results check box in the Solver Parameters dialog box. After each iteration, the Show Trial Solution dialog box will be displayed, and you will have the option of saving that scenario and then stopping Solver or continuing on to the next solution.

Table 9–3 Commonly Used Solver Parameters in the Solver Options Dialog Box	
Parameter	**Meaning**
Max Time	The total time that Solver should spend trying different solutions, expressed in seconds
Iterations	The number of possible answer value combinations that Solver should try
Constraint Precision	Instructs Solver how close it must come to the target value in order to consider the problem to be solved; for example, if the target value is 100 and the Tolerance is 5%, then 95 is an acceptable answer
Use Automatic Scaling	Selected by default, specifies that Solver should internally rescale values of variables, restraints, and the objective to reduce the effect of outlying values

© 2014 Cengage Learning

Excel saves the most recently used Solver parameters and options. When using Solver, three other issues must be kept in mind. First, some problems do not have solutions. The constraints may be constructed in such a way that an answer that satisfies all of the constraints cannot be found. Second, sometimes multiple answers solve the same problem. Solver does not indicate when this is the case, and you will have to use your own judgment to determine if you should continue seeking another solution. As long as you are confident that you have given Solver all of the constraints for a problem, however, all answers should be equally valid. Finally, Solver may require more time or iterations to solve the problem if it fails to find a solution.

Break Point: If you wish to take a break, this is a good place to do so. You can exit Excel now. To resume at a later time, run Excel, open the file called On Display Packaging Analysis, and continue following the steps from this location forward.

Using Scenarios and Scenario Manager to Analyze Data

Scenarios are named combinations of values that are assigned to variables in a model. These values are what-if assumptions for a model. In this chapter, each different Production Plan option being analyzed can be considered a scenario. For example, a Production Plan option requiring 900 small containers, 700 medium containers, and 800 medium containers with windows produced in 12 hours would be a scenario named Production 1. Changing the number of containers in any or all categories creates a new scenario. Each set of values in these examples represents a what-if assumption. You use the Scenario Manager to keep track of various scenarios, and produce a report detailing the what-if assumptions and results for each scenario.

The primary uses of the Scenario Manager are to:

1. Create different scenarios with multiple sets of changing cells;
2. Build summary worksheets that contain the different scenarios; or
3. View the results of each scenario on your worksheet.

CONSIDER THIS

How do you determine which cells to save in a scenario?

When considering which cells to save in a scenario, you should plan to save as few cells in a scenario as possible. Rule out cells with the following three characteristics:

1. **Cells that contain sheet title, row heading, or column heading text.** These cells are static cells.
2. **Cells that include formulas.** These cells change when their precedents change.
3. **Cells that remain constant across scenarios.** In the Production Plan worksheet, the number of containers that can be produced per hour for each machine is a constant, determined by the equipment.

You should include cells that are input cells for your model. In this example, the total number of each type of container could change from scenario to scenario. The number of each type of container produced on each machine and the number of hours available to produce them could also change from scenario to scenario. Therefore, the changing cells would be B8:B9, B20:B23, C9:C10, and D8:D10.

The next section in this chapter shows how to use the Scenario Manager for each of the three uses listed earlier. After you create the scenarios, you can instruct Excel to build the summary worksheets, including a Scenario Summary worksheet and a Scenario PivotTable worksheet.

To Save the Current Data as a Scenario

1 ANALYZE WORKBOOK FORMULAS | 2 SET DATA VALIDATION RULES | 3 PROPOSE PROBLEM-SOLVING STRATEGIES
4 CREATE & EVALUATE SCENARIOS | **5 FINALIZE WORKBOOK**

Why? *The current data on the Production Plan worksheet consists of constraints and the values that correctly solve the production problem.* These values can be saved as a scenario named Production 1 that can be accessed later or compared with other scenarios. The following steps save the current data for the Production 1 scenario using the Scenario Manager dialog box.

- Tap or click the Production Plan sheet tab to make Production Plan the active sheet.

- Tap or click the 'What-If Analysis' button (DATA tab | Data Tools group) to display the What-If Analysis menu (Figure 9–50).

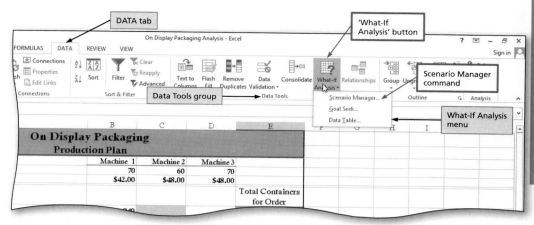

Figure 9–50

- Tap or click Scenario Manager on the What-If Analysis menu to display the Scenario Manager dialog box, which indicates that no scenarios are defined (Figure 9–51).

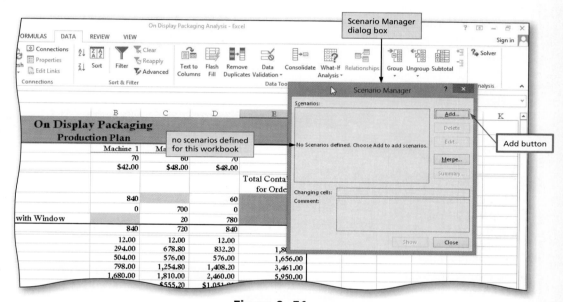

Figure 9–51

❸

- Tap or click the Add button (Scenario Manager dialog box) to prepare for adding a scenario to the workbook.

- When Excel displays the Add Scenario dialog box, type **Production_1** in the Scenario name text box to provide a name for the scenario (Figure 9–52).

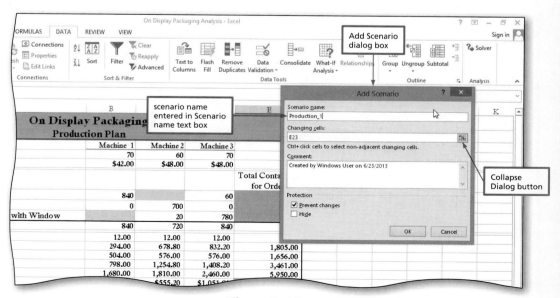

Figure 9–52

4

- Tap or click the Collapse Dialog button (Add Scenario dialog box) to collapse the dialog box.

- Select the range B8:B9, type , (a comma), and then select the ranges C9:C10, D8:D10, and B20:B23, separating each range with a comma to select the cells for the scenario, display a marquee around the selected cells, and assign the cells to the Changing cells box (Figure 9–53).

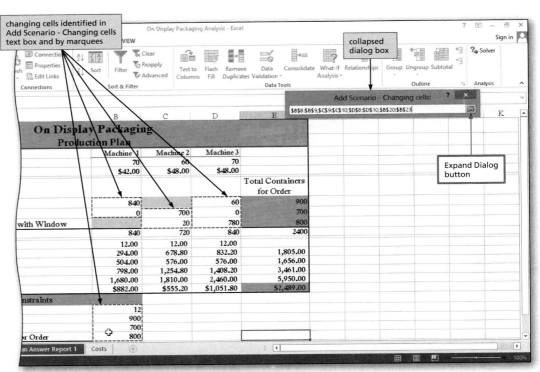

Figure 9–53

5

- Tap or click the Expand Dialog button (Add Scenario - Changing cells dialog box) to change the Add Scenario dialog box to the Edit Scenario dialog box (Figure 9–54).

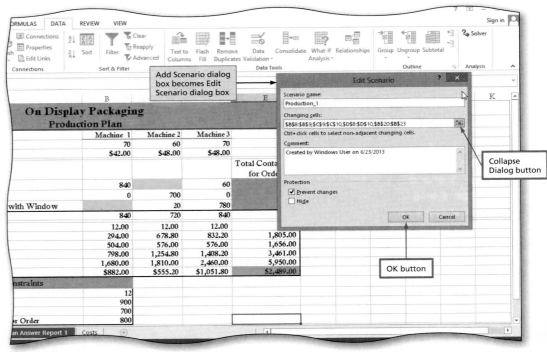

Figure 9–54

6

- Tap or click the OK button (Edit Scenario dialog box) to accept the settings in the dialog box and display the Scenario Values dialog box (Figure 9–55).

Q&A What does Excel display in the list of changing cells in the Scenario Values dialog box?
Excel displays the cells identified as changing cells in a numbered list with their current values (Figure 9–55). Names were assigned to these cells when the worksheet was created, and these are used rather than cell references in the numbered list.
The names make it easier to determine which variables are included.

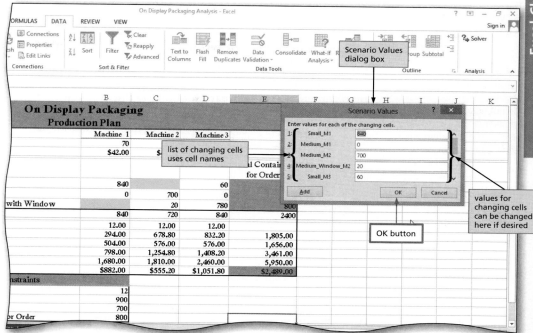

Figure 9–55

What can I do with the scenario?
After the scenario has been saved, you can recall it at any time using the Scenario Manager. In Figure 9–55, the values of the changing cells in the Scenario Values dialog box default to the current values in the worksheet. By changing the text boxes next to the cell names, you can save the scenario using values different from the current values.

7

- Tap or click the OK button (Scenario Values dialog box) to display the Scenario Manager dialog box with the Production_1 scenario selected in the Scenarios list (Figure 9–56).

8

- Tap or click the Close button (Scenario Manager dialog box) to save the Production_1 scenario in the workbook.

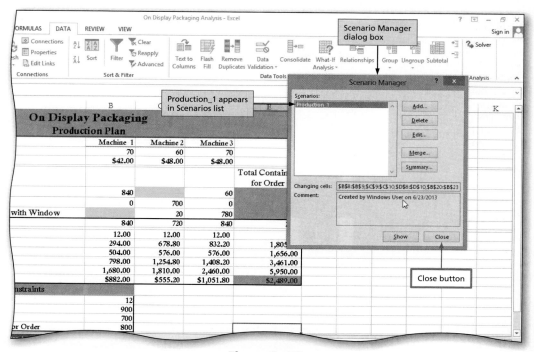

Figure 9–56

Adding Data for a New Scenario

After saving the Production_1 scenario, you can enter the data for the Production_2 scenario directly in the worksheet and then use Solver to solve the Production_2 scenario (Figure 9–57a) in the same way that you solved the Production_1 scenario. Because both scenarios are based on the same model, you do not need to reenter the constraints. The Answer Report (Figure 9–57b) meets the requirement that you create supporting documentation for your answer.

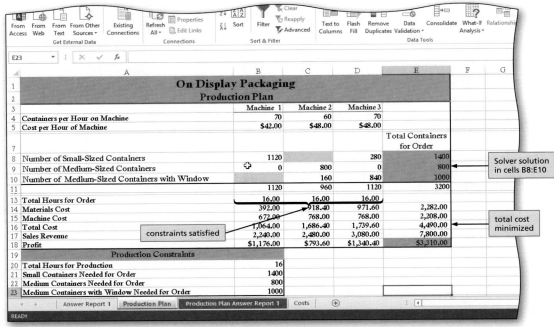

(a) Production_2 Scenario

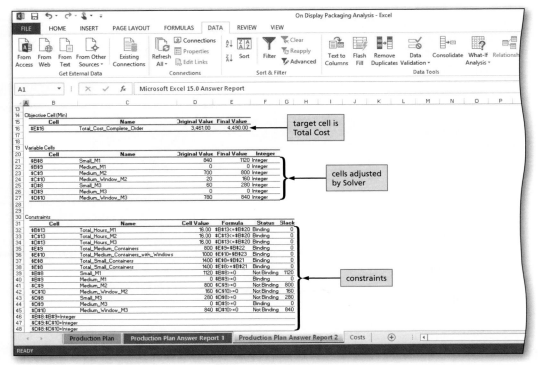

(b) Answer Report

Figure 9–57

To Add the Data for a New Scenario

The constraints for the Production_2 scenario require that at least 1,400 small containers, 800 medium containers, and 1,000 medium containers with windows be produced in 16 hours. These values must be entered into the appropriate cells before you can use Solver.

The following steps add the data for a new scenario.

1 Tap or click cell B20 and then type **16** as the maximum hours for the order.

2 Tap or click cell B21 and then type **1400** as the number of small containers.

3 Tap or click cell B22 and then type **800** as the number of medium containers.

4 Tap or click cell B23, type **1000** as the number of medium containers with windows, and then tap or click cell E23 to deselect cell B23 (Figure 9–58).

	A	B	C	D	E	F	G
					E23		
1		On Display Packaging					
2		Production Plan					
3		Machine 1	Machine 2	Machine 3			
4	Containers per Hour on Machine	70	60	70			
5	Cost per Hour of Machine	$42.00	$48.00	$48.00			
7					Total Containers for Order		
8	Number of Small-Sized Containers	840		60	900		
9	Number of Medium-Sized Containers	0	700	0	700		
10	Number of Medium-Sized Containers with Window		20	780	800		
11		840	720	840	2400		
13	Total Hours for Order	12.00	12.00	12.00			
14	Materials Cost	294.00	678.80	832.20	1,805.00		
15	Machine Cost	504.00	576.00	576.00	1,656.00		
16	Total Cost	798.00	1,254.80	1,408.20	3,461.00		
17	Sales Revenue	1,680.00	1,810.00	2,460.00	5,950.00		
18	Profit	$882.00	$555.20	$1,051.80	$2,489.00		
19	Production Constraints						
20	Total Hours for Production	16					
21	Small Containers Needed for Order	1400		data entered for new scenario			
22	Medium Containers Needed for Order	800					
23	Medium Containers with Window Needed for Order	1000					

Production Plan | Production Plan Answer Report 1 | Costs

READY

Figure 9–58

To Use Solver to Find a New Solution

1 ANALYZE WORKBOOK FORMULAS | 2 SET DATA VALIDATION RULES | 3 PROPOSE PROBLEM-SOLVING STRATEGIES
4 CREATE & EVALUATE SCENARIOS | 5 FINALIZE WORKBOOK

Why? After entering the new values, it is clear that the total number of containers shown in cells E8:E10 does not satisfy the production constraints for the Production_2 scenario. You now must use Solver to determine if a solution exists for the constraints of Production_2. The following steps use Solver to seek a solution.

1

- Tap or click the Solver button (DATA tab | Analysis group) to display the Solver Parameters dialog box with the target cell, changing cells, and constraints used with the previous scenario (Figure 9–59).

Why am I not updating the constraints?
When you set up the constraints in Solver for Production_1, you used cell references rather than actual numbers for the minimum number of each type of container. Entering the new figures in cells B20:B23 automatically updates the constraints.

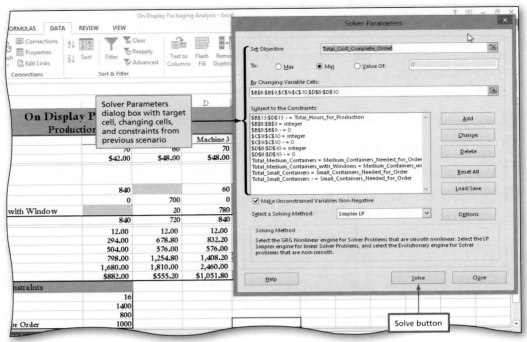

Figure 9–59

2

- Tap or click the Solve button (Solver Parameters dialog box) to solve the problem using Solver and the constraints just entered and display the Solver Results dialog box.

- Tap or click Answer in the Reports list to select a report type (Figure 9–60).

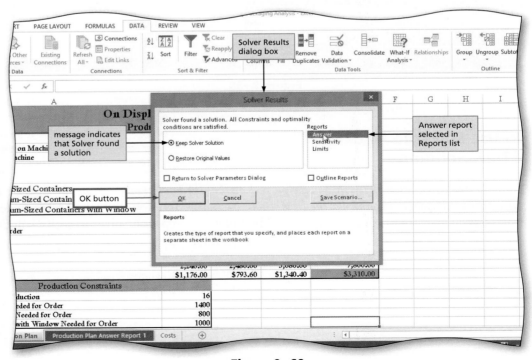

Figure 9–60

3

- Tap or click the OK button (Solver Results dialog box) to display the values found by Solver (Figure 9–61).

Q&A What did Solver accomplish?
As shown in Figure 9–61, Solver found a solution that satisfies all of the constraints and minimizes the total cost. In this new scenario, total cost will be $4,490.00.

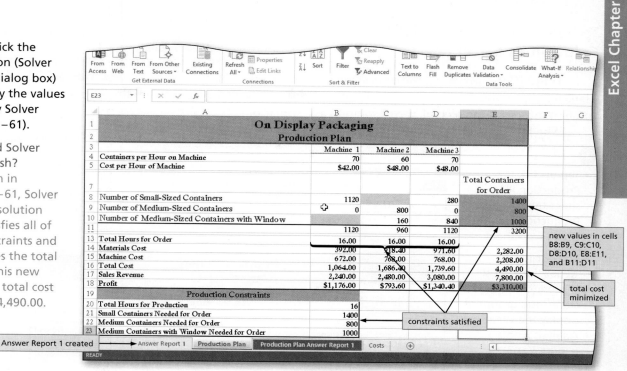

Figure 9–61

To View the Solver Answer Report for the Production_2 Solution

1 ANALYZE WORKBOOK FORMULAS | 2 SET DATA VALIDATION RULES | 3 PROPOSE PROBLEM-SOLVING STRATEGIES
4 CREATE & EVALUATE SCENARIOS | 5 FINALIZE WORKBOOK

Why? *Viewing the answer report allows you to compare the results of the Production_1 and Production_2 solutions.* The next step views the Answer Report for the Production_2 solution.

1

- Tap or click and then drag the Answer Report 1 sheet tab to the right of the Production Plan Answer Report 1 sheet tab to move the worksheet in the workbook.

- Rename the Answer Report 1 worksheet as Production Plan Answer Report 2.

- Change the sheet tab color to 'Brown, Accent 6'.

- Set the zoom to 70% and then scroll down to view the remaining cells of the Production_2 Answer Report (Figure 9–62).

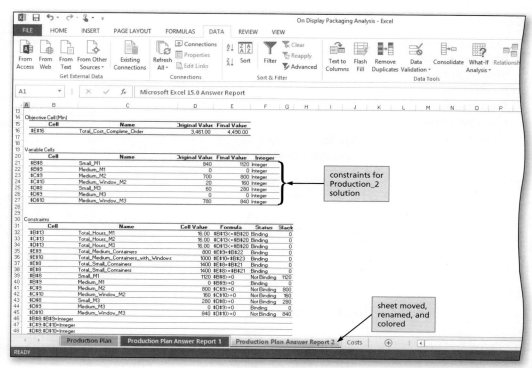

Figure 9–62

To Save the Second Solver Solution as a Scenario

Why? *With a second scenario created, you can begin to take advantage of the Scenario Manager.* The Scenario Manager allows you to compare multiple scenarios side by side. In order to use the Scenario Manager for this, you first must save the second Solver solution as a scenario.

The following steps save the second Solver solution as a scenario.

1

- Tap or click the Production Plan sheet tab to make Production Plan the active worksheet.

- Tap or click the 'What-If Analysis' button (DATA tab | Data Tools group) to display the What-If Analysis menu (Figure 9–63).

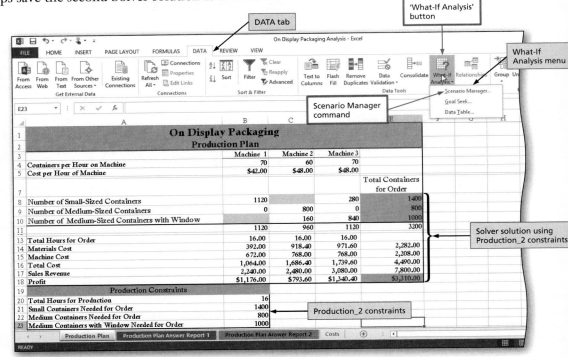

Figure 9–63

2

- Tap or click Scenario Manager on the What-If Analysis menu to display the Scenario Manager dialog box (Figure 9–64).

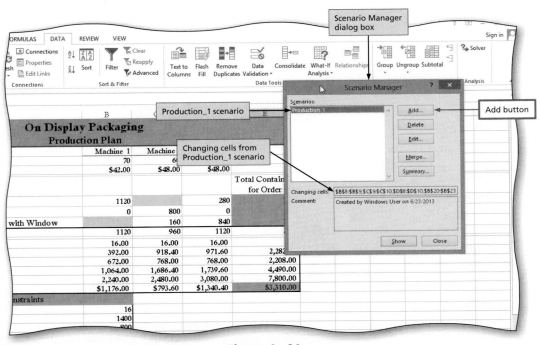

Figure 9–64

3

- Tap or click the Add button (Scenario Manager dialog box) to display the Add Scenario dialog box.

- Type **Production_2** in the Scenario name text box to name the new scenario (Figure 9–65).

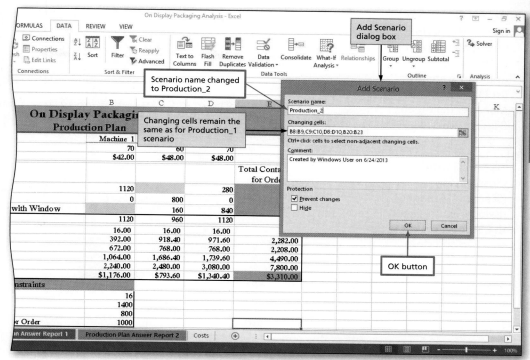

Figure 9–65

4

- Tap or click the OK button (Add Scenario dialog box) to display the Scenario Values dialog box with the current values from the worksheet (Figure 9–66).

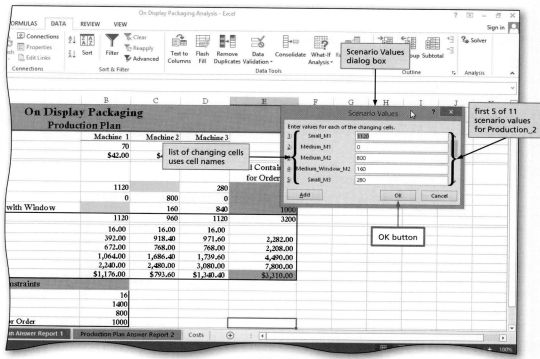

Figure 9–66

5

- Tap or click the OK button (Scenario Values dialog box) to display the updated Scenarios list in the Scenario Manager dialog box (Figure 9–67).

6

- Tap or click the Close button (Scenario Manager dialog box) to save the Production_2 scenario and close the dialog box.

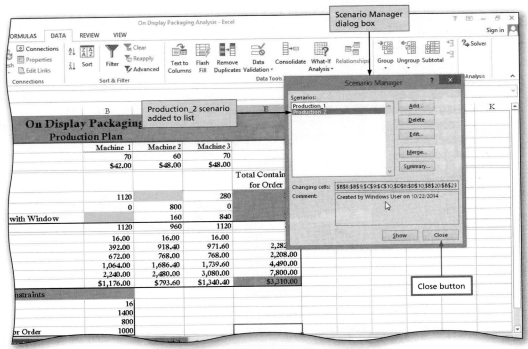

Figure 9–67

1 ANALYZE WORKBOOK FORMULAS | 2 SET DATA VALIDATION RULES | 3 PROPOSE PROBLEM-SOLVING STRATEGIES
4 CREATE & EVALUATE SCENARIOS | 5 FINALIZE WORKBOOK

To Show a Saved Scenario

Why? *You can display and review any scenario in the workbook by using the Show button in the Scenario Manager dialog box.* The following steps display the Production_1 scenario created earlier.

1

- Tap or click the 'What-If Analysis' button (DATA tab | Data Tools group) to display the What-If Analysis menu.

- Tap or click Scenario Manager on the What-If Analysis menu to display the Scenario Manager dialog box.

- Tap or click the scenario of interest, Production_1 in this case, to select it (Figure 9–68).

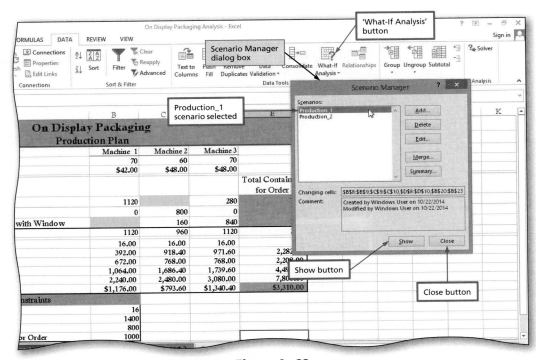

Figure 9–68

2

- Tap or click the Show button (Scenario Manager dialog box) to display the data for the selected scenario in the worksheet.

- Tap or click the Close button (Scenario Manager dialog box) to close the dialog box (Figure 9–69).

Q&A Do I have to use the Scenario Manager to switch between scenarios?
Once you have viewed two or more scenarios in a row, you can use the Undo and Redo commands to switch between them, as an alternative to using the Scenario Manager.

E23	▼	:	×	✓	fx			

	A	B	C	D	E	F	G
1	**On Display Packaging**						
2	Production Plan						
3		Machine 1	Machine 2	Machine 3			
4	Containers per Hour on Machine	70	60	70			
5	Cost per Hour of Machine	$42.00	$48.00	$48.00			
6							
7					Total Containers for Order		
8	Number of Small-Sized Containers	840		60	900		
9	Number of Medium-Sized Containers	0	700	0	700		
10	Number of Medium-Sized Containers with Window		20	780	800		
11		840	720	840	2400		
13	Total Hours for Order	12.00	12.00	12.00			
14	Materials Cost	294.00	678.80	832.20	1,805.00		
15	Machine Cost	504.00	576.00	576.00	1,656.00		
16	Total Cost	798.00	1,254.80	1,408.20	3,461.00		
17	Sales Revenue	1,680.00	1,810.00	2,460.00	5,950.00		
18	Profit	$882.00	$555.20	$1,051.80	$2,489.00		
19	Production Constraints						
20	Total Hours for Production	12					
21	Small Containers Needed for Order	900					
22	Medium Containers Needed for Order	700					
23	Medium Containers with Window Needed for Order	800					

data and solution for Production_1 scenario

Production Plan | Production Plan Answer Report 1 | Production Plan Answer Report 2 | Costs

READY

Figure 9–69

Summarizing Scenarios

You can create a Scenario Summary worksheet or a Scenario PivotTable worksheet to review and analyze various what-if scenarios when making decisions. A **Scenario Summary worksheet** generated by the Scenario Manager actually is a worksheet in outline format (Figure 9–70a) that you can print and manipulate just like any other worksheet. Chapter 6 presented skills that you can use to manipulate outline features for information presentation.

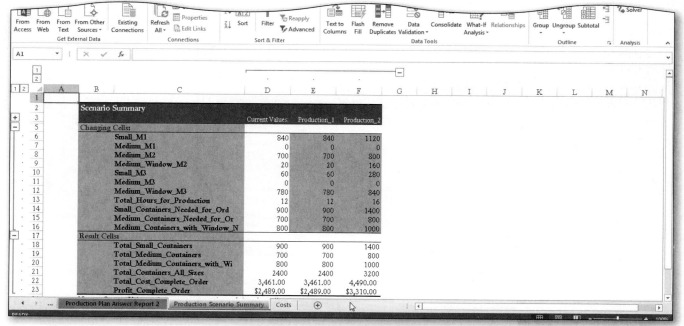

(a) Scenario Summary Worksheet

Figure 9–70 (Continued)

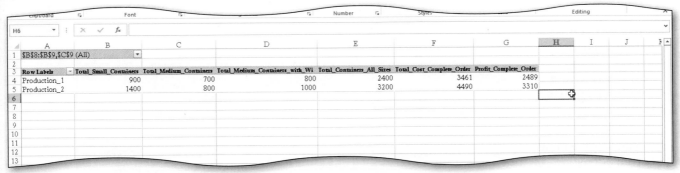

(b) Scenario PivotTable Worksheet

Figure 9–70 (Continued)

The **Scenario PivotTable worksheet** (Figure 9–70b) generated by the Scenario Manager also is a worksheet that you can print and manipulate like other worksheets. PivotTables summarize large amounts of data, and can be rearranged and regrouped to show the data in various forms. Chapter 8 presented skills that can be used to analyze summary data using PivotTables. The Scenario PivotTable worksheet allows you to compare the results of scenarios.

To Create a Scenario Summary Worksheet

1 ANALYZE WORKBOOK FORMULAS | 2 SET DATA VALIDATION RULES | 3 PROPOSE PROBLEM-SOLVING STRATEGIES
4 CREATE & EVALUATE SCENARIOS | 5 FINALIZE WORKBOOK

Why? *A Scenario Summary worksheet is a useful decision-making tool.* The Scenario Summary worksheet in Figure 9–70a shows the number of each type of container produced and total cost of the containers produced for the current worksheet values and the Production_1 and Production_2 scenarios. The optimal number of each type of container to produce on each machine calculated by Solver is shown for both production plans.

The following steps create a Scenario Summary worksheet.

- Tap or click the 'What-If Analysis' button (DATA tab | Data Tools group) to display the What-If Analysis menu.

- Tap or click Scenario Manager on the What-If Analysis menu to display the Scenario Manager dialog box (Figure 9–71).

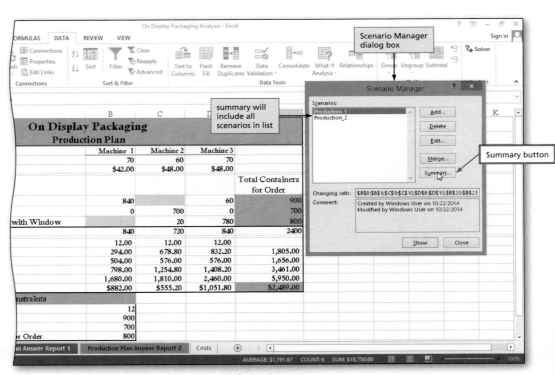

Figure 9–71

2

- Tap or click the Summary button (Scenario Manager dialog box) to display the Scenario Summary dialog box.

- Tap or click the Collapse Dialog button (Scenario Summary dialog box) and then select the cells E8:E11, E16, and E18.

- Tap or click the Expand Dialog button to return to the Scenario Summary dialog box (Figure 9–72).

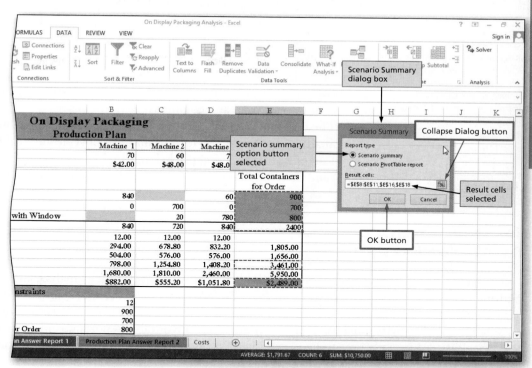

Figure 9–72

3

- Tap or click the OK button (Scenario Summary dialog box) to generate a Scenario Summary report.

- Rename the Scenario Summary worksheet as Production Scenario Summary to provide a descriptive name for the sheet.

- Change the sheet tab color to 'Gray -80%, Text 2' (row 1, column 4).

- Drag the Production Scenario Summary sheet tab to the right of the Production Plan Answer Report 2 sheet tab to move the worksheet in the workbook (Figure 9–73).

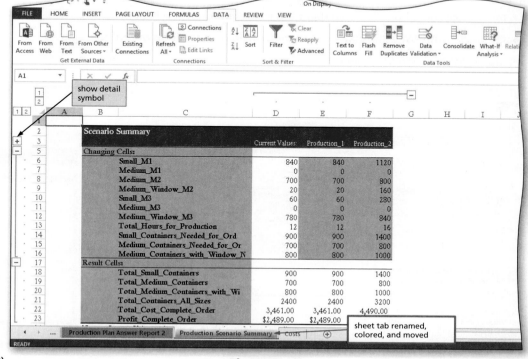

Figure 9–73

Q&A

What is shown in the Production Scenario Summary worksheet?

The Production Scenario Summary worksheet shows the results of the current values in the Production Plan worksheet and the results of any scenarios you have created. In Figure 9–73, current value results are shown in column D, and results for scenarios Production_1 and Production_2 are shown in columns E and F, respectively.

BTW
**Scenario Summary
Details**
Tapping or clicking the
show detail symbol on the
Scenario Summary worksheet
will display any information
entered in the Comments
box of the Scenario Manager
dialog box, along with
creation and modification
information.

Working with an Outlined Worksheet

As shown in Figure 9–73, Excel automatically outlines the Production Scenario Summary worksheet. The outline symbols for expanding and collapsing appear above and to the left of the worksheet. Chapter 6 provided instruction on working with outlined worksheets. You can hide or display levels of detail by using the hide detail and show detail symbols. You can also use the row- and column-level symbols to collapse or expand rows and columns.

The outline feature is especially useful when working with very large worksheets. With smaller worksheets, the feature may not provide any real benefits. You can remove an outline by tapping or clicking the Ungroup arrow (DATA tab | Outline group) and then tapping or clicking Clear Outline on the Ungroup menu.

To Create a Scenario PivotTable Worksheet

1 ANALYZE WORKBOOK FORMULAS | 2 SET DATA VALIDATION RULES | 3 PROPOSE PROBLEM-SOLVING STRATEGIES
4 CREATE & EVALUATE SCENARIOS | 5 FINALIZE WORKBOOK

Excel also can create a Scenario PivotTable report worksheet to help analyze and compare the results of multiple scenarios. ***Why create a Scenario PivotTable report worksheet?*** *A Scenario PivotTable report worksheet gives you the ability to summarize the scenario data and reorganize the rows and columns to obtain different views of the summarized data.* Manipulation and interpretation of PivotTable reports was introduced in Chapter 8. The Scenario PivotTable worksheet to be created in this chapter is shown in Figure 9–70b on page EX 594. The PivotTable summarizes the Production_1 and Production_2 scenarios and shows the result cells for the two scenarios for easy comparison.

The following steps create the Scenario PivotTable worksheet shown in Figure 9–70b.

1
- Tap or click the Production Plan sheet tab to make Production Plan the active worksheet.
- Tap or click the 'What-If Analysis' button (DATA tab | Data Tools group) to display the What-If Analysis menu.
- Tap or click Scenario Manager on the What-If Analysis menu to display the Scenario Manager dialog box (Figure 9–74).

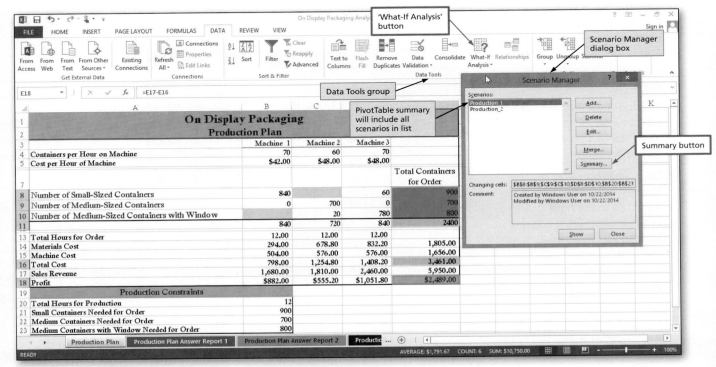

Figure 9–74

2
- Tap or click the Summary button (Scenario Manager dialog box) to display the Scenario Summary dialog box.
- Tap or click 'Scenario PivotTable report' in the Report type area (Scenario Summary dialog box) (Figure 9–75).

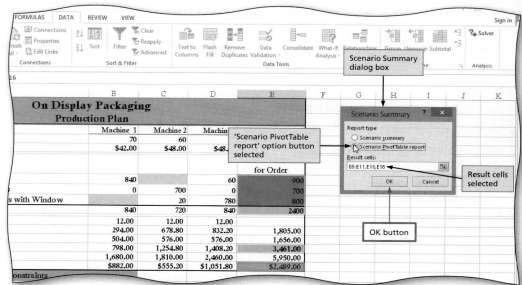

Figure 9–75

3
- Tap or click the OK button to display the Scenario PivotTable (Figure 9–76).

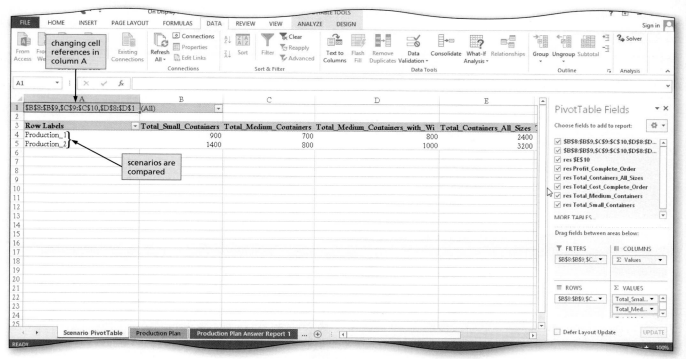

Figure 9–76

4

- Rename the Scenario PivotTable worksheet as Production Scenario PivotTable, to provide a descriptive name for the worksheet.

- Change the sheet tab color for the Production Scenario PivotTable worksheet to 'Brown, Accent 1'.

- Drag the Production Scenario PivotTable sheet tab to the right of the Production Scenario Summary sheet tab to move the worksheet in the workbook.

- Reduce the font size in row 3 to 9 point.

- Set the width of column A to 13.00.

- Set the width of columns B:G to best fit.

- If necessary, close the PivotTable Fields task pane (Figure 9–77).

Q&A How can I use the PivotTable?

After creating the PivotTable, you can treat it like any other worksheet. Thus, you can print or chart a PivotTable. If you update the data in one of the scenarios, tap or click the Refresh All button (DATA tab | Connections group) on the ribbon to update the PivotTable. If you show a scenario and merely change values on the scenario worksheet, it is not the same as changing the scenario. If you want to change the data in a scenario, you must use the Scenario Manager.

- Tap or click the Save button on the Quick Access Toolbar to save the workbook.

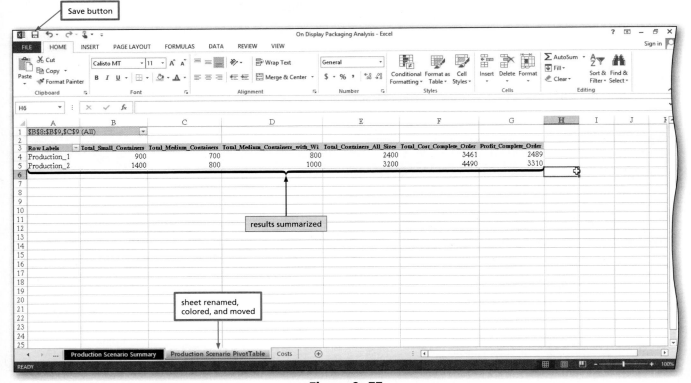

Figure 9–77

Break Point: If you wish to take a break, this is a good place to do so. You can exit Excel now. To resume at a later time, run Excel, open the file called On Display Packaging Analysis, and continue following the steps from this location forward.

Preparing a Workbook for Distribution

Excel provides several methods to protect your privacy or data that you may not want to share with others. Before distributing your workbook to others, you should consider what type of hidden information might be in your document. In previous chapters, you have learned to hide rows and columns, protect cells, protect worksheets, and protect workbooks. Other types of information may be hidden in a workbook. Excel provides a tool called the Document Inspector to inspect and report such information. You then easily can remove the hidden information or choose to leave the information in the document.

When distributing a workbook, you also should consider whether the intended recipients have the most recent version of Excel. If this is not the case, Excel allows you to save a workbook for use in previous versions of Excel, such as Excel 97-2003. When you save a workbook in the Excel 97-2003 Workbook file format, Excel will invoke the Compatibility Checker, which notifies you if any of the content of your workbook cannot be saved in that format. Additionally, the Compatibility Checker will inform you if any content will not appear the same, such as cell or chart formatting.

To Inspect a Document for Hidden and Personal Information

1 ANALYZE WORKBOOK FORMULAS | 2 SET DATA VALIDATION RULES | 3 PROPOSE PROBLEM-SOLVING STRATEGIES
4 CREATE & EVALUATE SCENARIOS | 5 FINALIZE WORKBOOK

Why? *The Document Inspector should be used before sharing a workbook publicly or when you suspect extraneous information remains in hidden rows and columns, hidden worksheets, document properties, headers and footers, or worksheet comments.*

The following steps make a copy of the On Display Packaging Analysis workbook and then inspect the copy for hidden and personal information.

- Save the workbook with the file name, On Display Packaging Analysis Distribute.

- Make Production Plan the active worksheet.

- Tap or click FILE on the ribbon to open the Backstage view (Figure 9–78).

Q&A

Why am I saving this workbook with a different file name? When preparing a workbook for distribution, you may decide to use the Document Inspector to make changes to the document. Saving the workbook with a different file name ensures that you will not lose information, and that you will have a copy of the workbook with all information for your records.

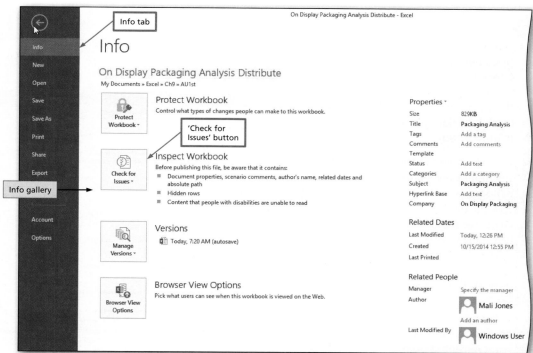

Figure 9–78

②

- Tap or click the 'Check for Issues' button in the Info gallery to display the Check for Issues menu (Figure 9–79).

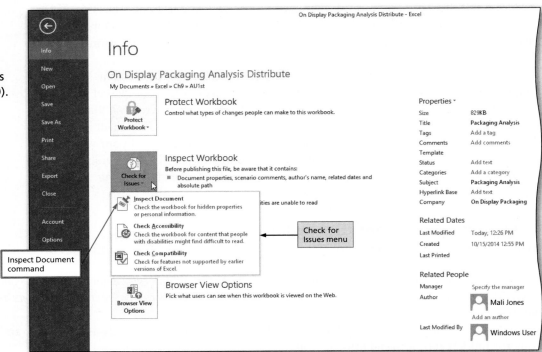

Figure 9–79

③

- Tap or click Inspect Document on the Check for Issues menu to display the Document Inspector dialog box (Figure 9–80).

 What is shown in the Document Inspector dialog box?
The Document Inspector dialog box allows you to choose which types of content to inspect. Unless you are comfortable with some items not being checked, you typically should leave all of the items selected. In Figure 9–80, the Document Inspector

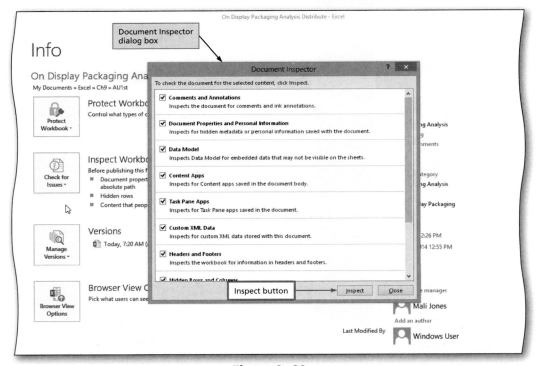

Figure 9–80

will search the document properties, which may contain your name. If you want your name or other personal information in the document properties, remove the check mark from the 'Document Properties and Personal Information' check box.

- Tap or click the Inspect button (Document Inspector dialog box) to run the Document Inspector and display its results (Figure 9–81).

Q&A What did the Document Inspector find?

The Document Inspector found document properties (Figure 9–81a) and a hidden row in the Scenario PivotTable (Figure 9–81b). The Remove All buttons in the dialog box allow you quickly to remove the items found if needed. In many instances, you may want to take notes of the results and then investigate and remedy each one separately. In the On Display Packaging Analysis Distribute workbook, all of these items found by the Document Inspector are expected and do not need to be remedied.

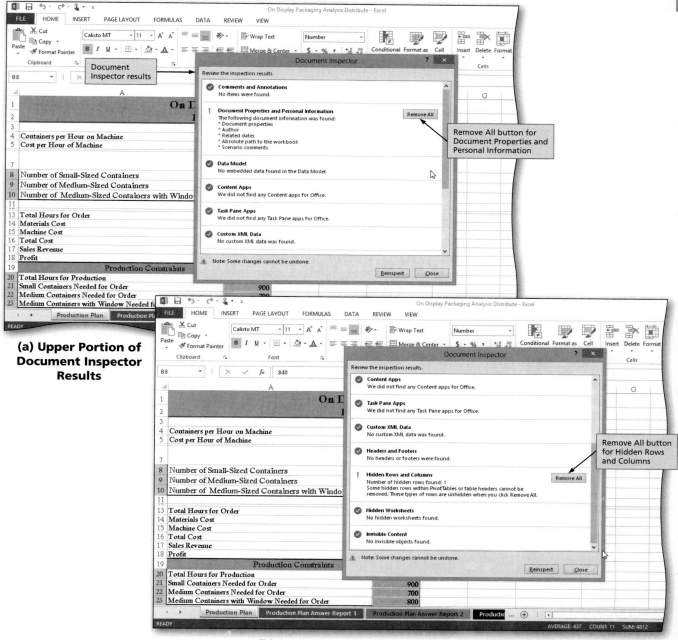

(a) Upper Portion of Document Inspector Results

(b) Lower Portion of Document Inspector Results

Figure 9–81

- Tap or click the Close button (Document Inspector dialog box) to close the dialog box.

BTW
Certification
The Microsoft Office Specialist (MOS) program provides an opportunity for you to obtain a valuable industry credential — proof that you have the Excel 2013 skills required by employers. For more information, visit the Certification resource on the Student Companion Site located on www.cengagebrain.com. For detailed instructions about accessing available resources, visit www.cengage.com/ct /studentdownload or contact your instructor for information about accessing the required files.

Information Rights Management

Information Rights Management (**IRM**) is a feature of Excel that allows you to restrict access to workbooks. With IRM, you can restrict who can view, modify, print, forward, and copy a workbook. The types of restrictions include a variety of options. For example, expiration dates for reading or modifying a workbook are available. Before using IRM, your computer first must be configured with IRM, as should the computers or mobile devices of anyone attempting to use a document that includes IRM features.

When IRM is installed properly, the Protect Workbook menu in the Info gallery in the Backstage view includes several commands for limiting access to the workbook. You can limit who can access the workbook and who can make changes to the workbook. For more information about IRM, search Excel Help using the search string, information rights management.

To Check Compatibility and Save a Workbook Using the Excel 97-2003 Workbook File Format and Mark a Workbook as Final

1 ANALYZE WORKBOOK FORMULAS | 2 SET DATA VALIDATION RULES | 3 PROPOSE PROBLEM-SOLVING STRATEGIES
4 CREATE & EVALUATE SCENARIOS | **5 FINALIZE WORKBOOK**

Why? *You occasionally need to save a workbook for use in previous versions of Excel. Each version of Excel includes varying features, so you should use the Compatibility Checker to determine if the features you use in your workbook are compatible with earlier versions of Excel.*

Before sharing a workbook with others, you can mark the workbook as being final. When another user of your workbook opens the workbook, he or she will be notified that you have marked the workbook as final. The workbook can still be edited, but only if the user taps or clicks a button to indicate that he or she wants to edit the workbook.

The following steps check the compatibility of the workbook while saving the workbook in the Excel 97-2003 Workbook file format.

1

- Tap or click FILE on the ribbon to open the Backstage view, tap or click the Save As tab in the Backstage view to display the Save As gallery, and then navigate to the location in which you want to save the workbook to display the Save As dialog box.

- Tap or click the 'Save as type' arrow (Save As dialog box) and then tap or click 'Excel 97-2003 Workbook' to select the file format (Figure 9-82).

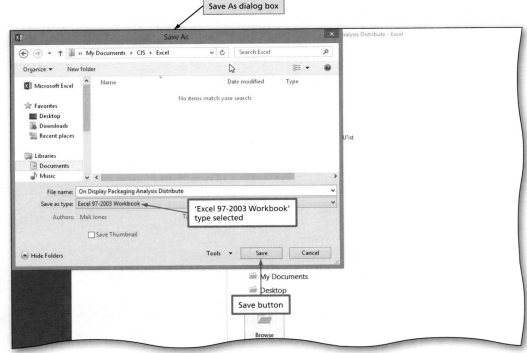

Figure 9-82

Q&A | Won't saving the file using the same name overwrite the 2013 version of the workbook?
No. The new workbook will have a file extension of .xls, while the 2013 version will have a file extension of .xlsx. You can save the workbook with a new name if you want, but it is not necessary.

2

- Tap or click the Save button (Save As dialog box) to display the Microsoft Excel - Compatibility Checker dialog box.

- Drag an edge of the dialog box to resize it so that it displays all the issues (Figure 9–83).

Q&A

What is shown in the Microsoft Excel - Compatibility Checker dialog box? The Summary column of the list of issues shows that both the PivotTable and the style used to format the PivotTable are not compatible with previous versions of Excel. While the workbook still will be saved in the Excel 97-2003 file format, the Production Scenario PivotTable will not be available as a PivotTable report. In addition, some cell formatting is unique to Excel 2013. These formats will be converted to the nearest approximation in the earlier version of Excel.

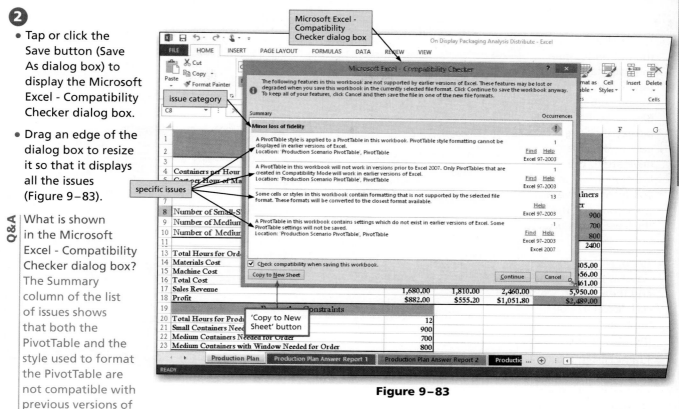

Figure 9–83

3

- Tap or click the 'Copy to New Sheet' button to create a worksheet with the compatibility information in the workbook (Figure 9–84).

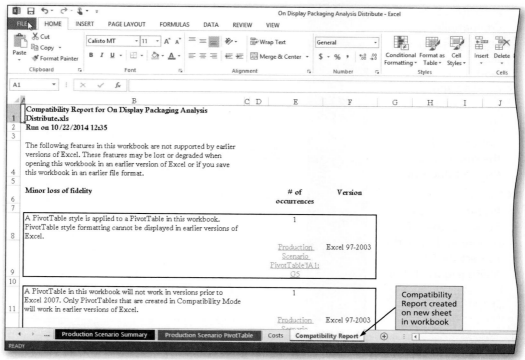

Figure 9–84

4

- Tap or click FILE on the ribbon to open the Backstage view, tap or click the Save As tab in the Backstage view to display the Save As gallery, and then navigate to the location in which you want to save the workbook to display the Save As dialog box.

- Tap or click the 'Save as type' arrow and then tap or click 'Excel 97-2003 Workbook' to select the file format.

- Tap or click the Save button (Save As dialog box) to display the Microsoft Excel - Compatibility Checker dialog box (Figure 9–85).

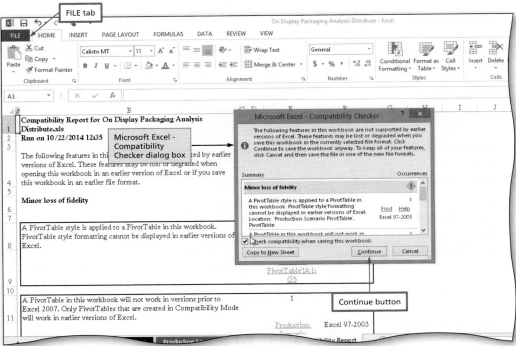

Figure 9–85

5

- Tap or click the Continue button (Microsoft Excel - Compatibility Checker dialog box) to save the workbook in the Excel 97-2003 Workbook file format.

- Tap or click FILE on the ribbon to open the Backstage view.

- Tap or click the Protect Workbook button in the Info gallery to display the Protect Workbook menu (Figure 9–86).

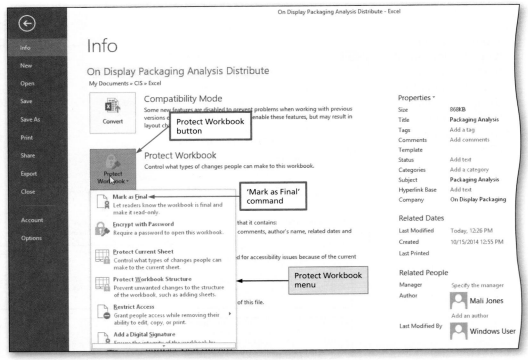

Figure 9–86

6

- Tap or click 'Mark as Final' on the Protect Workbook menu to display the Microsoft Excel dialog box (Figure 9–87).

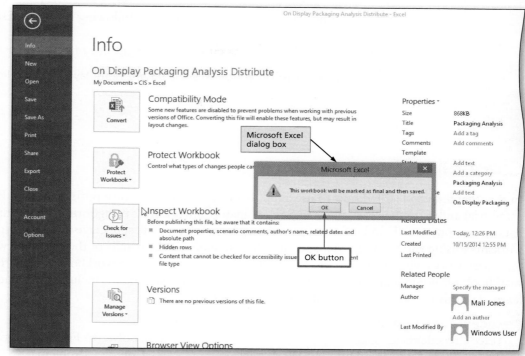

Figure 9–87

7

- Tap or click the OK button (Microsoft Excel dialog box) to indicate you want to mark the workbook as final.

- If necessary, tap or click the Continue button (Microsoft Excel - Compatibility Checker dialog box) to display the Microsoft Excel dialog box.

- Tap or click the OK button to close the Microsoft Excel dialog box and mark the workbook as final (Figure 9–88).

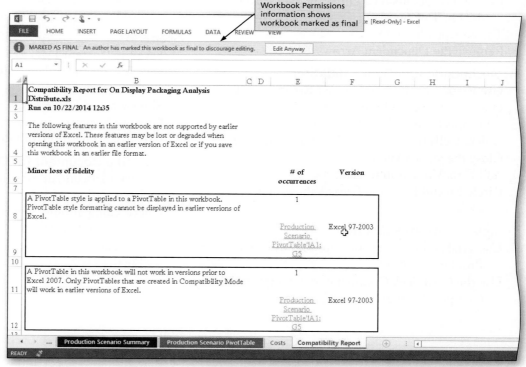

Figure 9–88

To Exit Excel

The project now is complete. The following steps exit Excel.

1 Tap or click the Close button on the right side of the title bar.

2 If the Microsoft Office Excel dialog box is displayed, tap or click the Don't Save button.

Chapter Summary

In this chapter, you learned how to use a number of techniques to solve problems using Excel, including using trial and error, goal seeking, and Solver; analyze a worksheet using formula auditing techniques; use data validation on cells and inform a user about the validation rules; manage different problems on the same worksheet using the Scenario Manager and then summarize the results of the scenarios with a Scenario Summary worksheet and a Scenario PivotTable worksheet; prepare a workbook for distribution; and save a workbook for use in a previous version of Excel. The items listed below include all the new Excel skills you have learned in this chapter, with the tasks grouped by activity.

Precedents and Dependents
Trace Precedents (EX 552)
Review Precedents on a Different Worksheet (EX 553)
Remove the Precedent Arrows (EX 555)
Review Precedents on a Different Worksheet Using the Go To Command (EX 556)
Trace Dependents (EX 557)
Remove the Dependent Arrows (EX 558)

Error Checking and Data Validation
Use Error Checking to Correct Errors (EX 558)
Open the Watch Window (EX 563)
Add Cells to the Watch Window (EX 563)
Delete Cells from the Watch Window (EX 564)
Close the Watch Window (EX 564)
Add Data Validation to Cells (EX 565)
Circle Invalid Data and Clear Validation Circles (EX 571)

Complex Problem Solving
Use Trial and Error to Attempt to Solve a Complex Problem (EX 567)
Use the Goal Seek Command to Attempt to Solve a Complex Problem (EX 570)

Solver
Use Solver to Find the Optimal Solution to a Complex Problem (EX 575)
View the Solver Answer Report (EX 580)
Use Solver to Find a New Solution (EX 587)
View the Solver Answer Report for the Production_2 Solution (EX 589)

Scenarios
Save the Current Data as a Scenario (EX 582)
Save the Second Solver Solution as a Scenario (EX 590)
Show a Saved Scenario (EX 592)
Create a Scenario Summary Worksheet (EX 594)
Create a Scenario PivotTable Worksheet (EX 596)

Preparing a Document for Distribution
Inspect a Document for Hidden and Personal Information (EX 599)
Check Compatibility and Save a Workbook Using the Excel 97-2003 Workbook File Format and Mark a Workbook as Final (EX 602)

What decisions will you need to make when creating your next worksheet to solve a complex problem?
Use these guidelines as you complete the assignments in this chapter and create your own worksheets for evaluating and analyzing data outside of this class.

1. Review and analyze workbook structure and organization.

   a) Review all formulas.

   b) Use precedent and dependent tracing to determine dependencies.

   c) Use formula auditing tools to correct formula errors.

2. Establish data validation rules.

   a) Identify changing cells.

   b) Determine data restrictions to address using data validation.

3. Determine strategies for problem solving.

   a) Use trial and error to modify input or changing values.

   b) Use Goal Seek.

   c) Use Solver to address multiple constraints and changing cells.

4. Create and store scenarios.

   a) Use the Scenario Manager to keep track of multiple scenarios.

   b) Use a Scenario Summary worksheet to present and compare multiple scenarios.

   c) Use a Scenario PivotTable report to manipulate and interpret scenario results.

5. Prepare the workbook for distribution.

   a) Inspect a workbook for hidden and personal information and update as necessary.

   b) Save a workbook in formats needed by a recipient.

   c) Check for compatibility issues in different formats.

   d) Mark a workbook as final.

How should you submit solutions to questions in the assignments identified with a ☀ symbol?
Every assignment in this book contains one or more questions identified with a ☀ symbol. These questions require you to think beyond the assigned file. Present your solutions to the questions in the format required by your instructor. Possible formats may include one or more of these options: write the answer; create a document that contains the answer; present your answer to the class; discuss your answer in a group; record the answer as audio or video using a webcam, smartphone, or portable media player; or post answers on a blog, wiki, or website.

Apply Your Knowledge

Reinforce the skills and apply the concepts you learned in this chapter.

Calculating the Bundles for a Shipment

Note: To complete this assignment, you will be required to use the Data Files for Students. Visit www.cengage.com/ct/studentdownload for detailed instructions or contact your instructor for information about accessing the required files.

Instructions: Run Excel. Open the workbook Apply 9-1 Global Textiles LLC from the Data Files for Students, and then save the workbook as Apply 9-1 Global Textiles LLC Complete.

Global Textiles LLC collects and ships textiles from various eastern and African nations for resale in North America. Bundles are shipped to the North American distribution hub in standard shipping containers with a maximum capacity of 800 cubic feet. Use Solver to find the optimal mix of bundles so that each shipment includes at least one of each type of bundle, and no more than four of Bundle 3. Maximize total profit for the shipment. Figure 9–89 on the next page shows the completed Costs and Shipping worksheet.

Continued >

Apply Your Knowledge *continued*

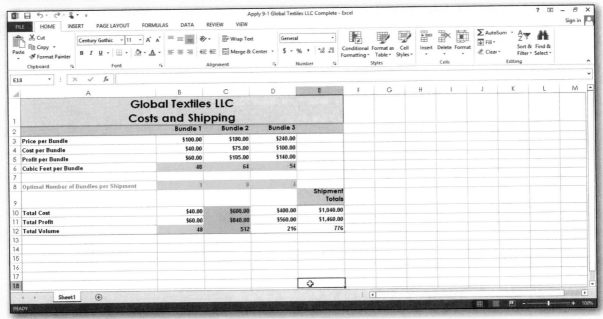

Figure 9–89

Perform the following tasks:

1. Use Solver to find a solution to the problem so that the total profit on the shipment (cell E11) is maximized. Allow Solver to change cells B8, C8, and D8. The results in cells B8, C8, and D8 should be integer values. Add constraints to Solver to limit the number of bundles to no more than four of Bundle 3, and to include at least one of each bundle type. Cell E12 should be limited to no more than 800 to accommodate the maximum volume constraint. Use the Simplex LP option in Solver.

2. Instruct Solver to create the Answer Report for your solution. Solver should find the answer as shown in Figure 9–89.

3. Trace precedents for cell E12 by tapping or clicking the Trace Precedents button (FORMULAS tab | Formula Auditing group) two times. Fill the cells identified by the precedent arrows with dots with a yellow fill color. Remove the precedent arrows. Trace dependents for cell C8 by tapping or clicking the Trace Dependents button (FORMULAS tab | Formula Auditing group) two times. Fill the cells identified by the dependent arrows with dots with an orange fill color. Remove the dependent arrows.

4. Use the Watch Window to monitor cells E10:E12. Change values in the range B8:D8 and view changes in the Watch Window. Close the Watch Window.

5. If requested by your instructor, add the following text to the end of the first line in cell A1: **(EST. <year of birth>),** replacing <year of birth> with your year of birth.

6. Save the workbook. Submit the revised workbook in the format specified by your instructor.

7. ✷ How would you adjust the constraints to further investigate maximizing total profit? Which constraints would you change, and why?

Extend Your Knowledge

Extend the skills you learned in this chapter and experiment with new skills. You may need to use Help to complete the assignment.

Working with Data Validation Rules

Note: To complete this assignment, you will be required to use the Data Files for Students. Visit www.cengage.com/ct/studentdownload for detailed instructions or contact your instructor for information about accessing the required files.

Instructions: Run Excel. Open the workbook Extend 9-1 Kidz Campz Registration.

You have been asked to create data validation rules in an Excel worksheet that calculates registration fees for Kidz Campz, a summer camp group that runs three specialty camps for two weeks each during the summer. These camps are popular and space is limited, so campers are restricted to one session per summer. Registration fees vary according to the camp selected. Kidz Campz provides some add-on services such as early drop-off and late pick-up. They also offer a discount for registrations paid in full when registering. Figure 9–90 shows the completed Camp Registration worksheet.

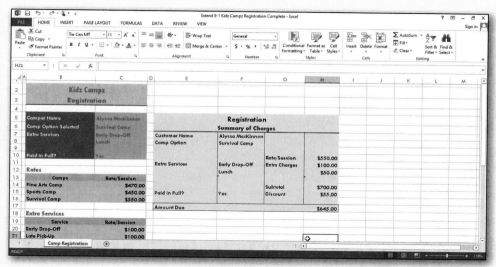

Figure 9–90

Perform the following tasks:

1. Save the workbook as Extend 9-1 Kidz Campz Registration Complete.

2. In cell C5 on the Camp Registration worksheet, enter a data validation rule that allows users to enter any value. Use the following:

   Input message title: Camper Name

   Input message: Please enter the camper's full name.

   Error alert title: Input Error

   Error message: Enter camper name

   Error alert style: Stop

Continued >

Extend Your Knowledge *continued*

3. In cell C6, enter a data validation rule that requires users to select a camp from a list. Allow users to select the data from a list of camps, which is contained in the range B14:B16. Do not allow users to leave cell C6 blank. Use the following for data validation:

   Input message title: Which Camp?

   Input message: Tap or click the arrow to the right to select the desired camp

   Error alert title: Invalid Camp

   Error message: Select Fine Arts Camp, Sports Camp, or Survival Camp from the list

   Error alert style: Stop

4. In cell C7, enter another data validation rule that allows users to select a valid entry from a list of extra services, which are included in cells B20:B22. These are optional services, so you can allow users to leave cell C7 blank. For the input message, use an appropriate title and display text that reminds users to enter the first extra service the customer needs. Choose a style of error alert considering that if users enter a service, they must select one of the three services in the list. Enter an appropriate error alert title and an error message that instructs users to select a service from the list.

5. In cell C8, enter a data validation rule that uses the custom formula =AND(C8<>C7,C8<>C9) as its validation criteria to verify that the value entered in cell C8 is not the same as the value in cell C7 or C9. For the input message, use an appropriate title and display text that reminds users to enter the second service the customer used. Choose a style of error alert considering that if users enter a second service, they must enter one of the three services not already entered. Enter an appropriate error alert title and an error message.

6. In cell C9, enter a data validation rule that uses a custom formula similar to the one you entered for cell C8. This formula, however, should verify that the value entered in cell C9 is not the same as the value in cell C7 or C8. For the input message, use an appropriate title and display text that reminds users to enter the third service the customer used. Choose an appropriate style of error, error alert title, and error message.

7. In cell C10, enter a data validation rule that instructs users to enter Yes if paying at time of registration, No if not. Do not allow users to leave cell C10 blank. Use Payment as the input message title and enter an input message that reminds users to enter Yes if paying, and No if not. Choose an appropriate style of error alert. Use Invalid Entry as the error alert title and enter an error message that instructs users to enter Yes or No.

8. Test the data validation rules by entering the following values in the specified cells. If an error message appears, tap or click the Retry button or the Cancel button and then enter valid data.

   C5: Alyssa MacKinnon

   C6: Survival Camp

   C7: Early Drop-Off

   C8: Lunch

   C9:

   C10: Yes

9. If requested by your instructor, enter the following text in cell E20: `Registered by <yourname>,` substituting your initials for <yourname>.

10. Save the workbook. Submit the revised workbook in the format specified by your instructor.

11. ❀ Cells C7:C9 used two different approaches to prompting users for information, selecting from a list or typing information based on a screen prompt. Which do you think is more effective, and why? List a weakness of the approach you feel is more effective.

Analyze, Correct, Improve

Analyze a workbook, correct all errors, and improve it.

Correcting Solver Parameters and Options

Note: To complete this assignment, you will be required to use the Data Files for Students. Visit www.cengage.com/ct/studentdownload for detailed instructions or contact your instructor for information about accessing the required files.

Instructions: Run Excel. Open the workbook Analyze 9-1 College Savings and then save it with the file name, Analyze 9-1 College Savings Complete. The workbook is used to forecast college savings for 16 years. In the situation shown in Figure 9–91, a client has $2,500 to start saving, and plans to contribute to a 529(c) account for 16 years, at which time her older of two children should start college. She estimates that from year 1 to year 12, she will earn 8% interest on the money in the account. After that, she will change the distribution of investments to a more conservative portfolio, and estimates that she will earn 6%. After her initial deposit of $2,500, she plans to contribute $4800 a year for the first year and an additional $240 a year for each year through year 16, at which time her goal is to have $200,000 in the account. At the end of year 16 she will stop contributing funds to the account and start withdrawing money for college expenses. Starting in year 17, she plans to withdraw $25,000 a year for two years, $50,000 a year for two years, and $25,000 a year for two years. These withdrawals will occur at the beginning of each year.

Correct the following problems with formulas, Solver parameters, and Solver options to achieve the results shown in Figure 9–91.

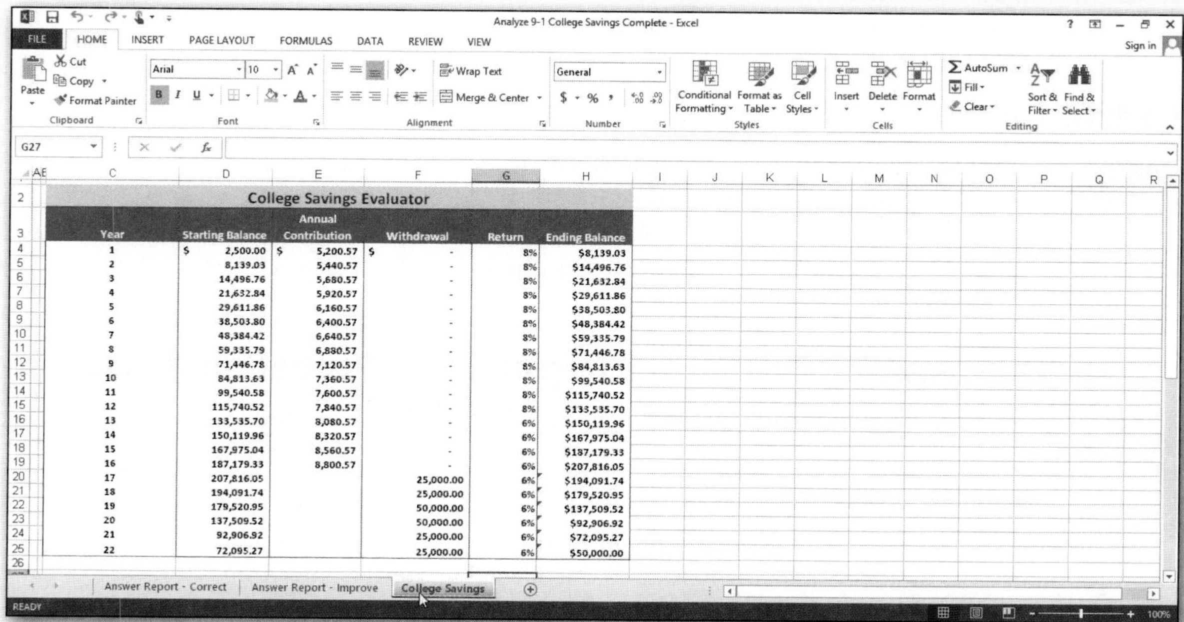

Figure 9–91

Continued >

Analyze, Correct, Improve *continued*

1. Correct

a. The formula for the ending balance in column H does not properly include the annual return on investment listed in column G. Update the formula correctly to include an annual rate of return.

b. Update the workbook to reflect the client's planned contributions, withdrawals, and her goals for interest earned outlined earlier.

c. Start Solver to view the Solver parameters for the worksheet. The Solver target is set to maximize the first annual contribution in cell E4. Change the Solver target to set cell H19 to 200,000 to reflect the client's stated goal. The changing cells should be set to change cell E4, rather than cell D4.

d. The constraints set for Solver are not necessary. Delete these constraints.

e. The solving method should be Simplex LP. Tap or click the Solve button in the Solver Parameters dialog box to run Solver. Create an answer report. Name the answer report Answer Report - Correct.

2. Improve

a. The client is interested in how she would have to change her saving plan in order to ensure that at the end of year 22 there is a $50,000 balance to provide support for graduate school, if either of her children choose to pursue graduate degrees. She will consider increasing her initial yearly contribution to a maximum of $5,400, but would prefer not to increase her initial deposit of $2,500 unless necessary. Use Solver to provide the client with an answer report outlining how her annual contribution and initial deposit would need to change in order to provide that opportunity. Name the answer report Answer Report - Improve.

b. If requested by your instructor, change the sheet tab currently named College Savings to <yourname> College Savings, replacing <yourname> with your name.

c. Save the workbook. Submit the revised document in the format specified by your instructor.

3. ✳ Can you think of another tool you could use to calculate the solution found in Step 1e? Explain why you can use this tool for the situation.

In the Labs

Design and/or create a workbook using the guidelines, concepts, and skills presented in this chapter. Labs 1 and 2, which increase in difficulty, require you to create solutions based on what you learned in the chapter; Lab 3 requires you to create a solution, which uses cloud and web technologies, by learning and investigating on your own from general guidance.

Lab 1: Creating a PivotTable Report and PivotChart Report

Note: To complete this assignment, you will be required to use the Data Files for Students. Visit www.cengage.com/ct/studentdownload for detailed instructions or contact your instructor for information about accessing the required files.

Problem: You want to select the best payback options for a debt consolidation loan you will be getting. You have created a data table to examine the effects of interest rates from 7.0% to 10.00% for a loan. You want to use Goal Seek to determine how many months it will take to pay off a loan of $22,000.00 with an interest rate of 8.5% using different monthly payment goals.

Instructions: Perform the following tasks.

1. Open the workbook Lab 9-1 Consolidation Loan from the Data Files for Students, and then save the workbook as Lab 9-1 Consolidation Loan Complete.

2. Enter a loan amount of 22,000 (cell G4), interest rate of 8.5% (cell G5), and months of 48 (cell G6) in the payment calculator portion of the workbook (Figure 9–92).

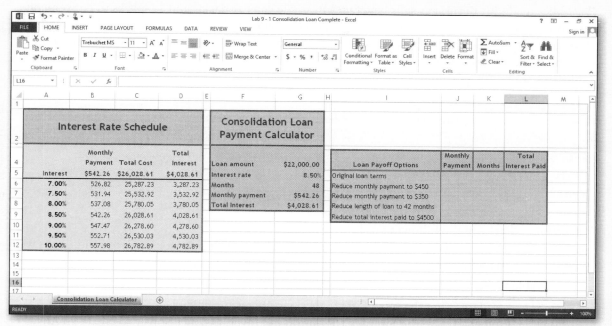

Figure 9–92

3. Enter the Monthly Payment, Months, and Total Interest Paid from the Consolidation Loan Payment Calculator in the Original loan terms row of the Loan Payoff Options table found in the range I4:L9.

4. Select cell G7 and then display the Goal Seek dialog box by tapping or clicking the 'What-If Analysis' button (DATA tab | Data Tools group) and then tapping or clicking Goal Seek on the What-If Analysis menu. Determine how many months you need to pay off the loan if you pay $450.00 per month by setting cell G7 to the value 450 and changing cell G6. Update the Loan Payoff Options table with the results of this Goal Seek.

5. Use Goal Seek to determine how many months you need to pay off the loan if you pay $350.00 per month. Update the Loan Payoff Options table with the results of this Goal Seek.

6. Reduce the loan term to 42 months and record the monthly payment and total interest paid in the Loan Payoff Options table.

7. If requested by your instructor, enter your name in cell I4, before the text Loan Payoff Options.

8. Save the workbook. Submit the revised workbook as specified by your instructor.

9. ✺ Use Goal Seek to determine the Monthly Payment and Months for the final option in the Loan Payoff Options table, row 9. Which variable did you choose to change? What other variable could you change to reach a Total Interest figure of $4,500?

Continued >

In the Labs *continued*

Lab 2: **Finding the Optimal Product Mix**

Note: To complete this assignment, you will be required to use the Data Files for Students. Visit www.cengage.com/ct/studentdownload for detailed instructions or contact your instructor for information about accessing the required files.

Problem: Aaahhhh Beverages sells beverages in single cans, 6-packs, and 12-packs to convenience and grocery stores. They are expanding to a national chain big box store where they have purchased 58 square feet of shelf space. They want to optimize the use of that shelf space to ensure that they showcase all three configurations of their product while maximizing profit as best they can. Table 9–4 shows the pertinent information for the three beverage configurations.

Table 9–4 Aaahhhh Beverages Item Information			
Item	**Display Constraints**	**Profit per Item**	**Square Feet per Item**
Single cans	50 maximum	0.08	0.0625
6-packs	30 minimum	0.45	0.4
12-packs	30 minimum	0.88	0.75

© 2014 Cengage Learning

Instructions: Perform the following tasks.

1. Open the workbook Lab 9-2 Aaahhhh Beverages on the Data Files for Students and then save the workbook with the file name, Lab 9-2 Aaahhhh Beverages Complete.

2. Use Table 9–4 to fill in the worksheet.

3. Use Solver to determine the mix of items that maximizes profit subject to the constraints shown in Table 9–4. Use the Simplex LP option in Solver. Instruct Solver to create an Answer Report if it can find a solution to the problem. Figure 9–93 shows the values Solver should find. Save the scenario as Maximize Profit 1, and rename the Answer Report containing the scenario as Maximize Profit 1.

4. If the company decides to set the maximum number of 12-Packs at 30, how would this affect the mix of items? Use Solver to determine the new mix. Instruct Solver to create an Answer Report if it can find a solution to the problem. Save the scenario as Maximize Profit 2, and rename the Answer Report containing the scenario as Maximize Profit 2.

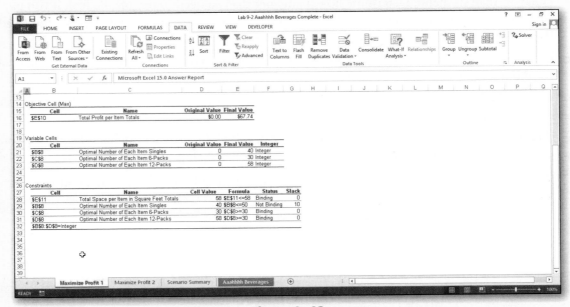

Figure 9–93

5. Create a Scenario Summary showing the two scenarios you saved in the Scenario Manager.

6. If requested by your instructor, change the name of the store in cell A2 from Big Box Store to <streetname> Store, where <streetname> is the name of a street you lived on in high school.

7. Save the workbook. Submit the revised workbook as specified by your instructor.

8. ☀ What changes would you suggest to the company to maximize profit, other than raising prices? How could you use Scenarios to make your point?

Lab 3: Expand Your World: Cloud and Web Technologies
Distributing Workbooks

Problem: You need to distribute the workbook you modified in Lab 2 to a team of colleagues at different stores who are using older versions of Excel. You are trying to determine which is the best way to distribute this workbook — by making it available on the web or by converting it to Excel 97-2003 format and sending it as an email attachment.

Instructions: Perform the following tasks.

1. Open the workbook Lab 9-2 Aaahhhh Beverages Complete and then save the workbook with the file name, Lab 9-3 Aaahhhh Beverages Complete.

2. Save the workbook in Excel 97-2003 format, with the file name, Lab 9-3 Aaahhhh Beverages Complete 2003. Save a copy of the compatibility report information on a separate sheet in this workbook.

3. Open the workbook Lab 9-2 Aaahhhh Beverages Complete and then save the workbook with the file name, Lab 9-3 Aaahhhh Beverages Complete Web. Save the file on SkyDrive, and then open it in the Excel Web App. Review the content of the workbook using the Excel Web App. Add a worksheet to the workbook, and make note of any reduced functionality of the workbook in the Web App.

4. If requested by your instructor, change the text in cell A2 to read Stock Plan, <lastname> Big Box Store, replacing <lastname> with your lastname.

5. Save the workbook. Submit the revised workbook as specified by your instructor.

6. ☀ Compare the two methods of distributing the workbooks. What are the strengths and weaknesses of each? Which would you recommend, and why?

☀ Consider This: Your Turn

Apply your creative thinking and problem solving skills to design and implement a solution.

1: Using Solver to Plan Fitness Programs
Personal/Academic

Part 1: You have started a new position at the campus health club. You have been asked to create a worksheet that personal trainers could use with their clients to determine an optimal fitness routine for weight loss. The personal trainers are interested in being able to review combinations of exercises for a client, and to vary the length of workout. The personal trainers will provide you with a list of exercises, and calories burned per 15 minutes of exercise for each entry on the list, for men and women separately.

You have explained that this is a complex problem-solving exercise, and that the best approach is to build a simple workbook to test first. Your goal is to create a test workbook using four generic fitness activities, and fictitious calorie counts per 15 minutes of activity for each of the fitness activities. Create a workbook that reflects the structure needed to solve this problem. Each 15-minute block of a particular exercise could be considered a unit of that exercise, and you would

Continued >

Consider This: Your Turn *continued*

want to solve for how many units of different types, or the same type, of exercise would give the individual the most benefit, subject to constraints. You can constrain which exercises the individual does (personal choice, medical/physical limitations, etc.) and how many units of each exercise he or she does. As indicated, you need to take gender into account. You will have different calorie counts for men and women for each unit of each activity.

Part 2: ✳ In addition to type and length of activity, what other information would you consider building into a more complex model? What are the challenges associated with introducing the information you are suggesting?

2: Scenario Summaries

Professional

Part 1: You are working with a local financial planning services company. You have been asked to create a summary of three different scenarios for car loans to illustrate the relationship between the various assumptions. Using the Consider This 9-2 Car Loan data file, create three scenarios based on three different sets of loan assumptions outlined in Table 9–5. Create a Scenario Summary worksheet that summarizes the three scenarios.

Part 2: ✳ How effective do you think this use of scenarios to be?

Table 9–5 Car Loan Scenarios			
Assumption	**Scenario 1**	**Scenario 2**	**Scenario 3**
Car	Honda Fit	Ford Escape	Toyota Prius
Price	17,490	27,000	25,455
Down Payment	3,000	3,000	3,000
Interest Rate	6.5%	7%	7%
Years	4	5	5

© 2014 Cengage Learning

3: Digital Signatures

Research and Collaboration

Part 1: More and more often, important documents are shared electronically. Security of information is a constant concern. Information Rights Management allows you to restrict access to workbooks and ensure integrity of workbooks through the use of digital signatures. Research the protections provided by Excel that are available to users on the Protect Workbook menu in the Info gallery in the Backstage view. Provide a one- to two-paragraph description of each item.

Part 2: ✳ Which items would you be most likely to use in your everyday life? Which items would you recommend to a supervisor for sharing workbooks via electronic means? What reasoning drives your choices?

Learn Online

Reinforce what you learned in this chapter with games, exercises, training, and many other online activities and resources.

Student Companion Site Reinforcement activities and resources are available at no additional cost on www.cengagebrain.com. Visit www.cengage.com/ct/studentdownload for detailed instructions about accessing the resources available at the Student Companion Site.

SAM Put your skills into practice with SAM! If you have a SAM account, go to www.cengage .com/sam2013 to access SAM assignments for this chapter.

10 | Using Macros, Controls, and Visual Basic for Applications (VBA) with Excel

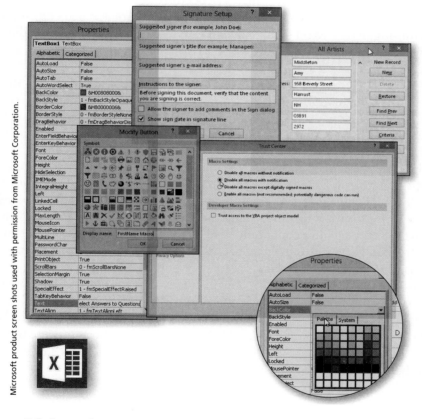

Microsoft product screen shots used with permission from Microsoft Corporation.

Objectives

You will have mastered the material in this chapter when you can:

- Use passwords to assign protected and unprotected status to a worksheet

- Use the macro recorder to create a macro

- Execute a macro and view and print code for a macro

- Customize the Quick Access Toolbar by adding a button

- Use a Data Form to add data to a worksheet

- Understand Visual Basic for Applications (VBA) code and explain event-driven programs

- Add controls such as command buttons, option buttons, and check boxes to a worksheet

- Assign properties to controls

- Review a digital signature on a workbook

10 | Using Macros and Visual Basic for Applications (VBA) with Excel

Introduction

Before a computer can take an action and produce a desired result, it must have a step-by-step description of the task to be accomplished. The step-by-step description is a series of precise instructions called a **procedure**. **Program** and **code** are other names for a procedure. The process of writing a procedure is called **computer programming**. Every Excel command and ribbon button has a corresponding procedure that the computer executes, or carries out the step-by-step instructions, when you tap or click the command or button.

Excel provides a feature for entering data when the content is straightforward text or numbers. A **data form** is created from a range of cells, and uses the column headings from that range to create the fields on the form. Data forms are particularly helpful when working with a series of columns that would otherwise require you to scroll horizontally, or when entering a large number of entries into a worksheet.

Because Excel does not have a command or button for every possible worksheet task, Microsoft has included a powerful programming language called Visual Basic for Applications. **Visual Basic for Applications (VBA)** is a programming language that allows you to customize and extend the capabilities of Excel. You also can create a macro to group together commonly used combinations of tasks, which then can be reused later. Use macros to ensure consistency in calculations, formatting, and manipulation of nonnumeric data.

In this chapter, you will learn how to create macros using a code generator called a **macro recorder**. A **macro** is a procedure composed of VBA code. It is called a macro rather than a procedure because it is created using the macro recorder. You also will learn how to add buttons to the Quick Access Toolbar and then associate these with macros. Finally, you will learn the basics of VBA, including creating a user interface, setting the properties, and writing the code.

Project — Waterfront Studios

The project in the chapter follows proper design guidelines and uses Excel to create the worksheets shown in Figure 10–1 and Figure 10–2. Waterfront Studios is part of a mill rehabilitation project that provides work and exhibition space for artists. Waterfront Studios works with a group of visual artists. The artist board of Waterfront Studios needs to keep records of the artists who are part of the cooperative. Basic information (name, address, and the last four digits of Social Security number) was provided by the artists themselves. Some information was being maintained informally by one of the artists at a previous cooperative effort in an earlier version of Excel. Figure 10–1a shows the state of the existing artist information, and Figure 10–1b shows the final layout for the information. In addition, the studio needs to develop a way to enter new artist information in a format consistent with the current layout. The studio also needs an easy-to-use interface that will allow visitors at various studio events to provide contact information for promoting other events. The interface can assume that the user has some comfort with computers, but should not assume the user has Excel knowledge. Figure 10–2 shows the user interface that will be used at studio events and the separate worksheet that contains the information gathered through the user interface.

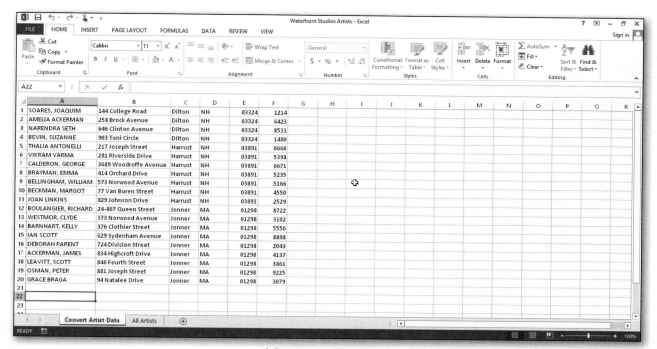

(a) Initial Worksheet

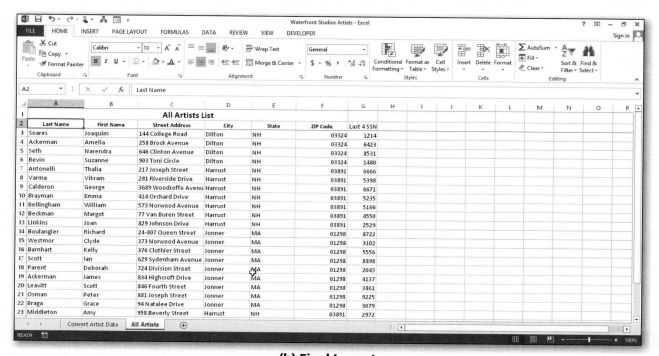

(b) Final Layout

Figure 10–1

The studio information workbooks are modified according to the following phases:

Phase 1 — Update the workbook to reformat the artist information in the artist data worksheet to a consistent layout through the use of macros. Use a data form to provide a user interface for entering new artist data.

Phase 2 — Create an area on a worksheet called Mailing List Signup (Figure 10–2) that allows a studio visitor with no Excel knowledge to enter his or her name, address, and additional information using command buttons, check boxes, and option buttons.

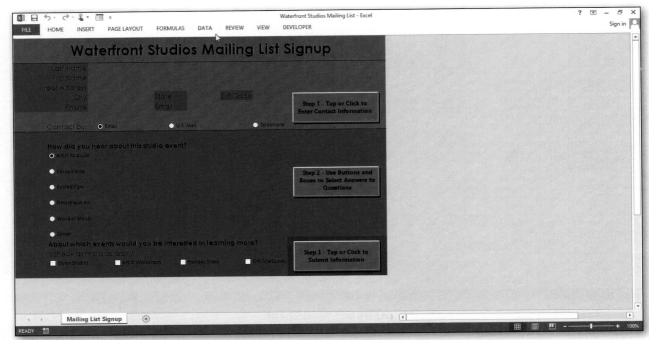

(a) User Interface

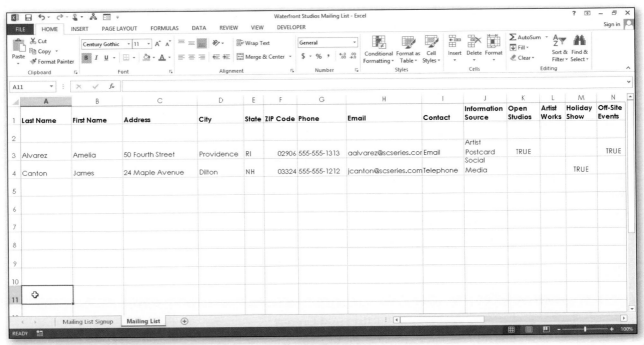

(b) Mailing List

Figure 10–2

Figure 10–3 illustrates the requirements document for the Waterfront Studios workbooks. It includes the needs, source of data, summary of format changes, and other facts about its development. The requirements document indicates that the development of the workbooks should be done in two phases, as outlined earlier. Figure 10–4 shows a rough sketch of the user interface described in the requirements document, to assist in the initial layout of the user interface in Phase 2.

Worksheet Title	Waterfront Studios Artists and Waterfront Studios Mailing List
Needs	An easy-to-use interface for the Studios' activities as follows: **Phase 1:** Use the macro recorder to create macros that reformat the artist names in the artist data worksheet so that the last name is in column A and the first name is in column B. This will require two macros. Both macros will be assigned to a key combination and one will be assigned to a button on the Quick Access Toolbar. Use a data form to add additional records. **Phase 2:** Create an area on the Mailing List Signup worksheet (Figure 10–2) that allows a patron with no Excel knowledge to enter his or her name, address, and additional information using command buttons, check boxes, and option buttons.
Source of Data	The workbook shown in Figures 10–1a and 10–1b is available in the Data Files for Students with the file name, Waterfront Studios Data. The workbook containing the base information for the workbook shown in Figures 10–2a and 10–2b is available in the Data Files for Students, with the file name Waterfront Studios Mailing Data.

© 2014 Cengage Learning

Figure 10–3

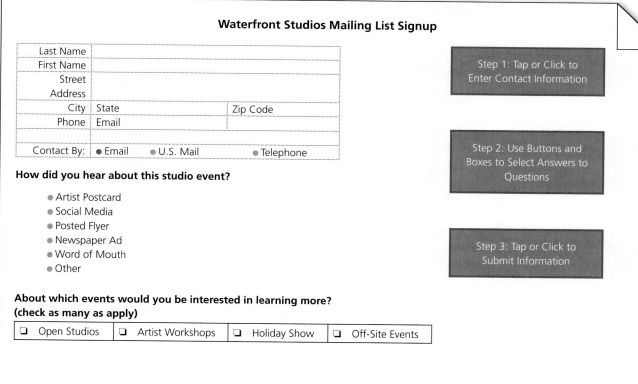

Figure 10–4

Roadmap

In this chapter, you will learn how to modify the existing Waterfront Studios Artists workbook shown in Figure 10–1 and Figure 10–2 through the use of macros, data forms, and Visual Basic for Applications. The following roadmap identifies general activities you will perform as you progress through this chapter:

1. SET PROTECTION and SECURITY.
2. WRITE MACROS.
3. CREATE the DATA FORM.
4. DESIGN the USER INTERFACE.
5. SET the CONTROL PROPERTIES.
6. WRITE the VISUAL BASIC CODE.
7. TEST the USER INTERFACE.

BTW
BTWs
For a complete list of the BTWs found in the margins of this book, visit the BTW resource on the Student Companion Site located on www.cengagebrain.com. For detailed instructions about accessing available resources, visit www.cengage.com/ct/studentdownload or contact your instructor for information about accessing the required files.

At the beginning of step instructions throughout the chapter, you will see an abbreviated form of this roadmap. The abbreviated roadmap uses colors to indicate chapter progress: gray means the chapter is beyond that activity, blue means the task being shown is covered in that activity, and black means that activity is yet to be covered. For example, the following abbreviated roadmap indicates the chapter would be showing a task in the 2 WRITE MACROS activity.

1 SET PROTECTION & SECURITY | 2 WRITE MACROS | 3 CREATE DATA FORM | 4 DESIGN USER INTERFACE
5 SET CONTROL PROPERTIES | 6 WRITE VISUAL BASIC CODE | 7 TEST USER INTERFACE

Use the abbreviated roadmap as a progress guide while you read or step through the instructions in this chapter.

To Run Excel and Open a Workbook

The following steps, which assume Windows 8 is running, use the Start screen or the search box to run Excel based on a typical installation. You may need to ask your instructor how to run Excel on your computer. For a detailed example of the procedure summarized below, refer to the Office and Windows chapter.

To complete these steps, you will be required to use the Data Files for Students. Visit www.cengage.com/ct/studentdownload for detailed instructions or contact your instructor for information about accessing the required files.

1. Scroll the Start screen for an Excel 2013 tile. If your Start screen contains an Excel 2013 tile, tap or click it to run Excel. Otherwise, search for the Excel app using the Charms bar and then tap or click Excel 2013 in the search results.

2. Tap or click 'Open Other Workbooks' on the Excel start screen.

3. Navigate to the location of the Data Files for Students and the Excel Chapter 10 folder.

4. Double-tap or double-click the file named Waterfront Studios Data to open it.

5. If the Excel window is not maximized, tap or click the Maximize button on its title bar to maximize the window.

6. Save the workbook with the file name, Waterfront Studios Artists (Figure 10–5).

BTW
The Ribbon and Screen Resolution
Excel may change how the groups and buttons within the groups appear on the ribbon, depending on the computer's screen resolution. Thus, your ribbon may look different from the ones in this book if you are using a screen resolution other than 1366 × 768.

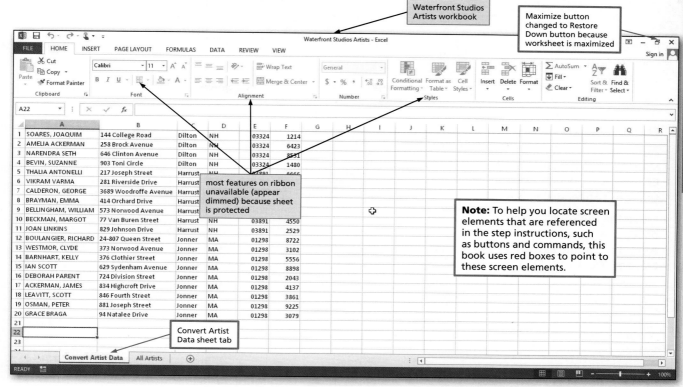

Figure 10–5

How do you familiarize yourself with a workbook created by someone else?

When you work with a workbook created by someone else, such as the Waterfront Studios Artists workbook, you should review the content and structure of the workbook before you make changes to it. You can learn more about a workbook by doing as much of the following as possible to the worksheet:

1. Press CTRL+ACCENT MARK (`) to display any formulas to gain an understanding of what formulas and functions are used in the worksheet and which cells are referenced by the formulas and functions.

2. Use Range Finder or the auditing commands to show which cells are referenced in formulas and functions. You double-tap or double-click a cell with a formula or function to activate Range Finder.

3. Check which cells are locked and which cells are unlocked. Usually all cells in a workbook are locked, except for those in which you enter data. For example, on the All Artists worksheet, only the cells in the range A3:G3 are unlocked.

4. Enter sample data and verify the results.

To Unprotect a Password-Protected Worksheet

1 SET PROTECTION & SECURITY | 2 WRITE MACROS | 3 CREATE DATA FORM | 4 DESIGN USER INTERFACE
5 SET CONTROL PROPERTIES | 6 WRITE VISUAL BASIC CODE | 7 TEST USER INTERFACE

The worksheets in the Waterfront Studio Artists workbook are protected, which restricts the changes you can make to the worksheet to unlocked cells only. You cannot make changes to locked cells, or modify the worksheet itself. *Why unprotect the worksheet? Unprotect the worksheet to allow changes to locked cells and the worksheet itself.* Recall from Chapter 4 that a password ensures that users cannot unprotect the worksheet simply by clicking the Unprotect button. The password for the worksheets in this workbook is Art15t5.

The following steps unprotect the password-protected Convert Artist Data worksheet.

①

- If necessary, tap or click the Convert Artist Data sheet tab to make it the active sheet.

- Tap or click REVIEW on the ribbon to display the REVIEW tab.

- Tap or click the Unprotect Sheet button (REVIEW tab | Changes group) to display the Unprotect Sheet dialog box.

- When the Unprotect Sheet dialog box appears, type **Art15t5** in the Password text box (Figure 10–6).

Q&A

Do any rules apply to passwords?

Yes. Passwords in Excel can contain, in any combination, letters, numbers, spaces, and symbols and can be up to 15 characters long. Passwords are case sensitive. If you decide to password-protect a worksheet, make sure you write down the password and keep it in a secure place. If you lose the password, you cannot open or gain access to the password-protected worksheet.

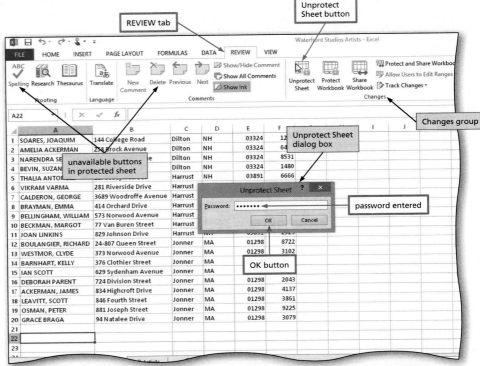

Figure 10–6

②

- Tap or click the OK button (Unprotect Sheet dialog box) to unprotect the Convert Artist Data worksheet (Figure 10–7).

Q&A

Can I work with the entire worksheet now?

Yes. With the worksheet unprotected, you can modify the contents of cells, regardless of whether they are locked or unlocked. Cells must both be locked and the worksheet protected to restrict what users can do to cell contents.

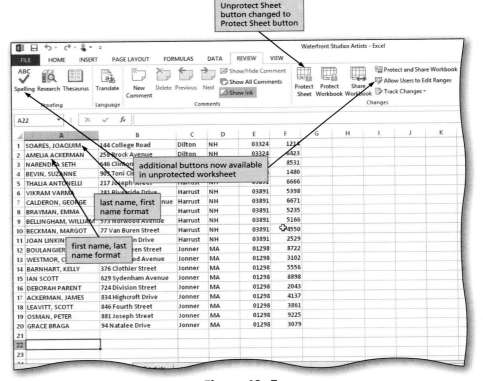

Figure 10–7

Phase 1 — Recording Macros and Assigning Them to a Toolbar Button and Keyboard Combination

The first phase of this project creates a macro to reformat the artist data so that it can be sorted more easily. Currently, the first and last names of the artists appear in column A, in all uppercase. In some instances, the first name appears first; in others, the last name appears first (Figure 10–7). The planned macros will (1) change the case from uppercase to mixed case; (2) create new columns for text manipulation; (3) split the contents of column A, placing first names in one column and last names in another column; (4) delete the columns used to manipulate text; and (5) copy the contents of the worksheet to a separate worksheet.

The purpose of these macros is to automate editing tasks that would be repetitive and time-consuming if done for each entry separately. The macros save time, but they also ensure consistency in how the artist data is organized. After the macros are created, they will be assigned to a keyboard shortcut or a button on the Quick Access Toolbar. When additional artist data is available that needs to be reformatted, it can be copied or imported into this workbook. The macros will ensure that the new artist data conforms to the format needed.

Excel includes a macro recorder that can record a series of actions and save them as a macro. The macro recorder can be turned on, during which time it records your activities, and then turned off to stop the recording. After recording a macro, you can play it back, or **execute** it, as often as you want to repeat the steps you recorded with the macro recorder.

Three steps must be taken in preparation for working with macros in Excel. The DEVELOPER tab, which by default does not appear on the ribbon, must be made available by changing an Excel option. The DEVELOPER tab on the ribbon includes commands used to work with macros. Second, a security setting in Excel must be modified to enable macros whenever you use Excel. Finally, Excel requires a workbook that includes macros to be saved as an Excel Macro-Enabled Workbook file type.

To Display the DEVELOPER Tab, Enable Macros, and Save a Workbook as a Macro-Enabled Workbook

1 SET PROTECTION & SECURITY | **2 WRITE MACROS** | **3 CREATE DATA FORM** | **4 DESIGN USER INTERFACE**
5 SET CONTROL PROPERTIES | **6 WRITE VISUAL BASIC CODE** | **7 TEST USER INTERFACE**

Why? *Before you can work with macros or Visual Basic for Applications, you need to prepare the workbook by providing access to these features.* The following steps display the DEVELOPER tab on the ribbon, enable macros, and save the workbook as a macro-enabled workbook.

- Tap or click the FILE tab on the ribbon to open the Backstage view.
- Tap or click Options in the left pane to display the Excel Options dialog box.
- Tap or click Customize Ribbon in the left pane (Excel Options dialog box) to display the Customize the Ribbon tools.
- Tap or click the Developer check box in the Main Tabs list to select the DEVELOPER tab for display on the ribbon (Figure 10–8).

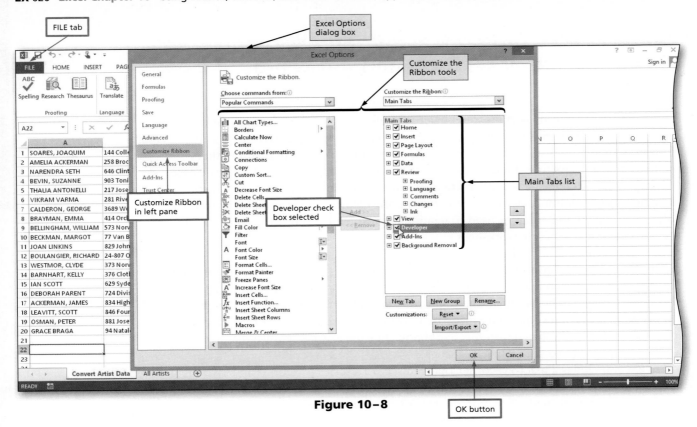

Figure 10–8

2

- Tap or click the OK button (Excel Options dialog box) to display the DEVELOPER tab on the ribbon.
- Tap or click the DEVELOPER tab to make it the active tab.
- Tap or click the Macro Security button (DEVELOPER tab | Code group) to display the Trust Center dialog box.
- Tap or click 'Enable all macros' to select the option button (Figure 10–9).

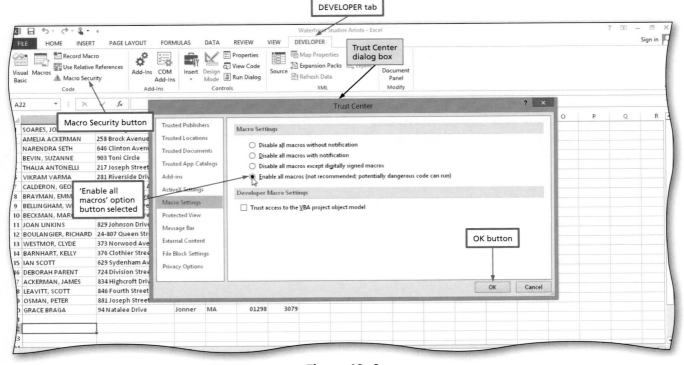

Figure 10–9

- Tap or click the OK button (Trust Center dialog box) to close the dialog box and enable macros.

- Tap or click FILE on the ribbon to open the Backstage view, tap or click the Save As tab in the Backstage view to display the Save As gallery, and then navigate to the location on which you want to save the workbook to display the Save As dialog box.

- Tap or click the 'Save as type' arrow (Save As dialog box) and then tap or click 'Excel Macro-Enabled Workbook' to select the file format (Figure 10–10).

- Tap or click the Save button (Save As dialog box) to save the workbook as an Excel Macro-Enabled Workbook file.

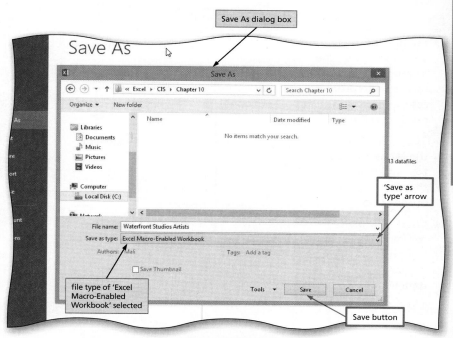

Figure 10–10

To Convert Names to Proper Case and Add Extra Columns

1 SET PROTECTION & SECURITY | 2 WRITE MACROS | 3 CREATE DATA FORM | 4 DESIGN USER INTERFACE
5 SET CONTROL PROPERTIES | 6 WRITE VISUAL BASIC CODE | 7 TEST USER INTERFACE

Why? *Proper case is more easily read than uppercase. The additional columns make it easier to manipulate the text in later steps.* The following steps insert blank columns and convert names to proper case.

- Insert a blank column to the left of column A to move the column containing the names to column B.

- Set the width of column A to 21.00 to resize the column.

- Tap or click cell A1 to select it.

- Type `=PROPER(` and then tap or click cell B1 to begin entering a formula with the PROPER function (Figure 10–11).

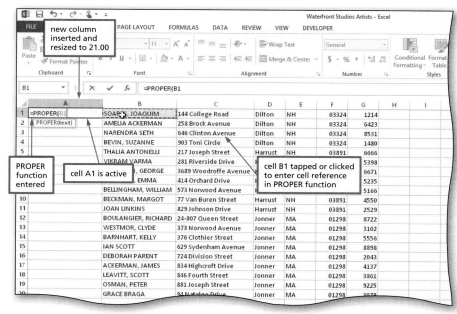

Figure 10–11

2

- Tap or click the Enter box to complete the formula, convert the name to proper case, and display the result in cell A1.

- Copy cell A1 to the range A2:A20 to convert all the names to proper case.

- Insert four blank columns to the right of column B to prepare for adding data (Figure 10–12).

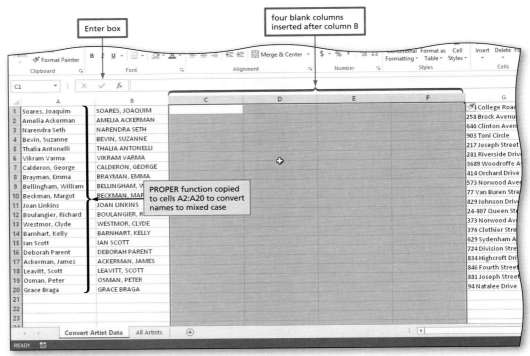

Figure 10–12

Recording Macros

A macro is created by performing a set of steps and recording the steps as they are performed. The steps and their order should be determined and rehearsed before creating the macro. When recording the macro, you perform the steps as they are recorded, so that you can confirm that the macro will do what you expect it to do.

To create the macro to reformat the artist data for Waterfront Studios, you will turn on the macro recorder and then complete the tasks outlined in Table 10–1.

Table 10–1 Planning a Macro to Reformat Names	
Step	**Task**
1	Use the LEN function in column C to determine the total number of characters in the artist name. The result of the LEN function should be displayed in column C.
2	Use the SEARCH function in column D to determine the position of the space that separates the first and last names. The result of the SEARCH function should be displayed in column D.
3	Use the RIGHT function to capture the last name. The result of the RIGHT function should be displayed in column E. Use the Paste Values command to replace the formula with a text value.
4	Use the LEFT function to capture the first name. The result of the LEFT function should be displayed in column F. Use the Paste Values command to replace the formula with a text value.
5	Stop the macro recorder.

© 2014 Cengage Learning

When you create a macro, you assign a name to it. A **macro name** can be up to 255 characters long; it can contain numbers, letters, and underscores, but it cannot contain spaces or other punctuation. The name is used later to identify the macro when you want to execute it. Executing a macro causes Excel to step through all of the recorded steps just as they were recorded. The first macro name in this project is FirstName.

When planning your macro, you must determine if you are going to select any cells using keyboard navigation. Entering a cell reference always directs the macro to that specific cell. Navigating to a cell using keyboard navigation, however, requires the use of relative cell addressing. If you will be using keyboard navigation, you must ensure that the **'Use Relative References' button** in the Code group on the DEVELOPER tab is selected so that the macro works properly.

To Record a Macro to Reformat the Artist Data Where First Name Appears First

1 SET PROTECTION & SECURITY | 2 WRITE MACROS | 3 CREATE DATA FORM | 4 DESIGN USER INTERFACE
5 SET CONTROL PROPERTIES | 6 WRITE VISUAL BASIC CODE | 7 TEST USER INTERFACE

Why? The macro uses the space between the first name and last name to differentiate the two parts of the current name entry. The following steps record the FirstName macro to separate into two different columns the first name and last name for the entries that appear as FirstName LastName in column A.

1
- If necessary, tap or click DEVELOPER on the ribbon to display the DEVELOPER tab.
- Tap or click the 'Use Relative References' button (DEVELOPER tab | Code group) so that the macro uses relative cell references when selecting cells.
- Select cell A2, the first instance of first name appearing first.
- Tap or click the Record Macro button (DEVELOPER tab | Code group) to display the Record Macro dialog box.
- When the Record Macro dialog box is displayed, type **FirstName** in the Macro name text box.
- Type **f** in the Shortcut key text box to set the shortcut key for the macro to CTRL+F.
- Make sure the 'Store macro in' box displays This Workbook and then type **This macro formats names for entries with first name appearing first.** in the Description text box (Figure 10–13).

Q&A Where are macros stored?
In the Record Macro dialog box, you can select the location to store the macro in the 'Store macro in' box. If you want a macro to be available to use in any workbook whenever you use Microsoft Excel, select Personal Macro Workbook in the Store macro in list. This selection causes the macro to be stored in the **Personal Macro Workbook**, which is part of Excel. If you tap or click New Workbook in the Store macro in list, then Excel stores the macro in a new workbook. Most macros created with the macro recorder are workbook-specific and, thus, are stored in the active workbook. Selecting This Workbook in the Store macro in list, as specified in Step 1, stores the macro in the active workbook.

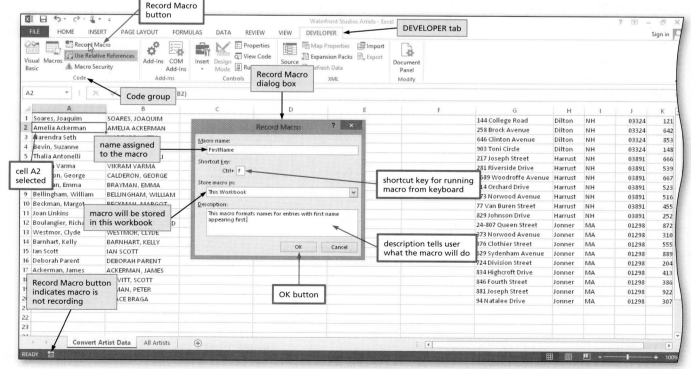

Figure 10–13

2

- Tap or click the OK button (Record Macro dialog box) to begin recording the macro and to change the Record Macro button to the Stop Recording button (Figure 10–14).

Q&A

What will be included in the macro?
Any task you perform in Excel will be part of the macro. When you are finished recording the macro, tapping or clicking the Stop Recording button on the ribbon or on the status bar ends the recording.

What is the purpose of the Record Macro button on the status bar?
You can use the Record Macro button on the status bar to start or stop recording a macro. When you are not recording a macro, this button is displayed as the Record Macro button. If you tap or click it to begin recording a macro, the button changes to become the Stop Recording button.

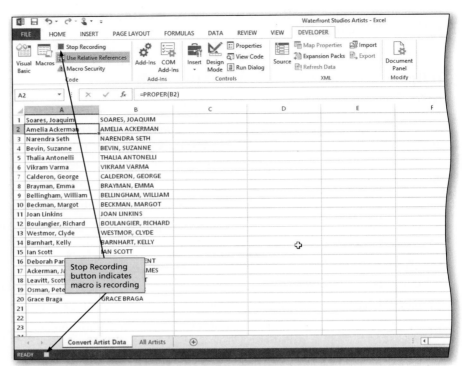

Figure 10–14

3

- Tap or click HOME on the ribbon to display the HOME tab.
- Press the RIGHT ARROW key twice to move to cell C2.
- Type **=LEN(** and then tap or click cell A2 to begin entering a formula (Figure 10–15).

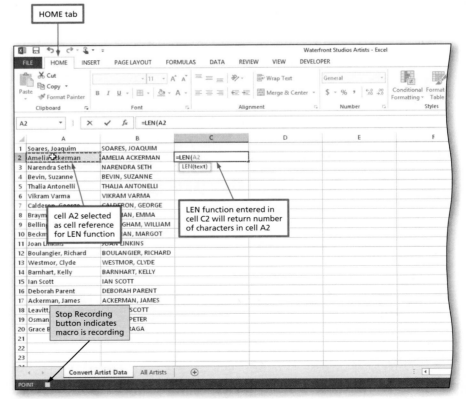

Figure 10–15

- Tap or click the Enter box in the formula bar to compute the number of characters in cell A2.
- Press the RIGHT ARROW key once to move to cell D2.
- Type **=SEARCH(" ",** and then tap or click cell A2 to begin entering a formula (Figure 10–16).

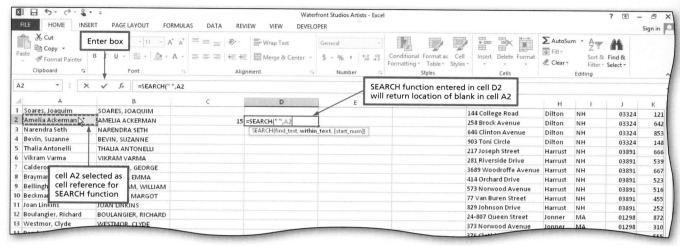

Figure 10–16

- Tap or click the Enter box in the formula bar to compute the location of the space separating the first and last names in cell A2.
- Press the RIGHT ARROW key once to move to cell E2.
- Type **=RIGHT(A2, C2-D2** and then tap or click the Enter box in the formula bar to copy the last name to cell E2 (Figure 10–17).

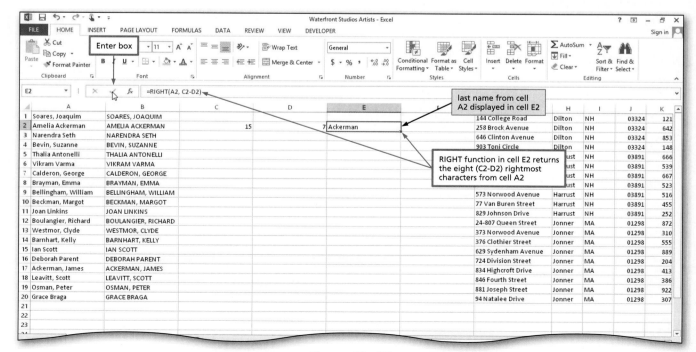

Figure 10–17

6
- Press CTRL+C to copy the cell contents.
- Tap or click the Paste arrow (HOME tab | Clipboard group) to display the Paste gallery (Figure 10–18).

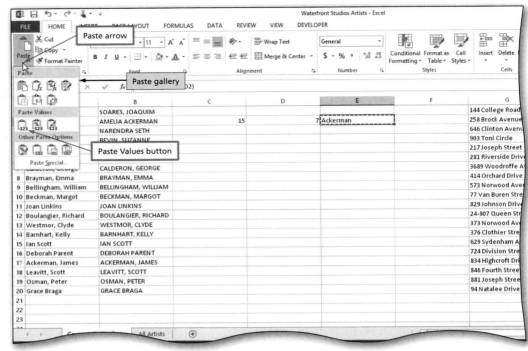

Figure 10–18

7
- Tap or click the Values (V) button in the Paste gallery to replace the RIGHT function with the text value (Figure 10–19).

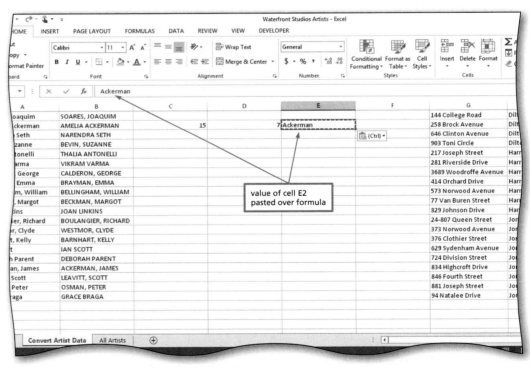

Figure 10–19

- Press the RIGHT ARROW key once to move to cell F2.
- Type =LEFT(A2, D2-1 and then tap or click the Enter box in the formula bar to copy the first name to cell F2.
- Press CTRL+C to copy the cell contents.
- Tap or click the Paste arrow (HOME tab | Clipboard group) to display a gallery of paste options.
- Tap or click Values (V) in the Paste gallery to replace the LEFT function with the text value (Figure 10–20).

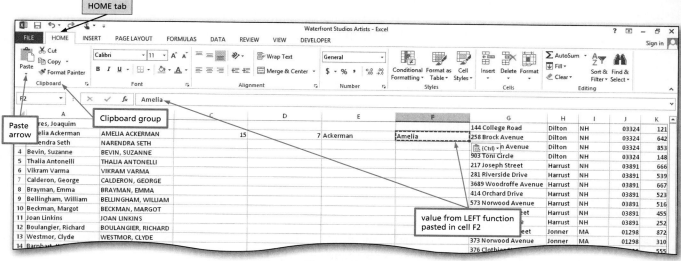

Figure 10–20

- Press the HOME key to make cell A2 the active cell.
- Press the ESC key to remove the marquee in cell F2.
- Tap or click DEVELOPER on the ribbon to display the DEVELOPER tab.
- Tap or click the Stop Recording button (DEVELOPER tab | Code group) to stop recording the worksheet activities (Figure 10–21).

Q&A

What if I make a mistake while recording the macro?

If you make a mistake while recording a macro, delete the macro and record it again. You delete a macro by tapping or clicking the View Macros button (DEVELOPER tab | Code group), tapping or clicking the name of the macro in the Macro dialog box, and then tapping or clicking the Delete button. You then can record the macro again with the same macro name.

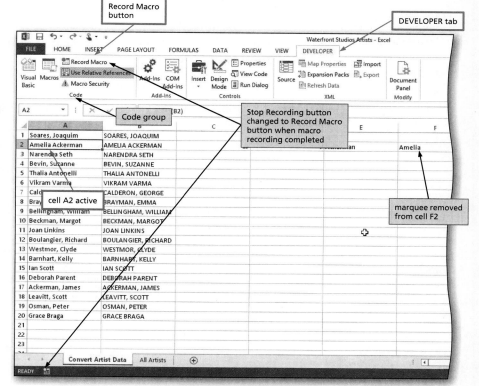

Figure 10–21

Other Ways

1. Tap or click Record Macro button (DEVELOPER tab | Code group)

BTW
Cell Selection in Macros
Before recording a macro, you should select your starting cell. If you select it after you begin recording the macro, the macro always will start in that particular cell, which will limit the macro's usefulness.

To Record a Macro to Reformat the Artist Data Where Last Name Appears First

To create the macro to reformat the artist data for Waterfront Studios Artists when the last name appears first, you will turn on the macro recorder and then complete the following tasks.

1. Use the LEN function in column C to determine the total number of characters in the artist name. The result of the LEN function should be displayed in column C.

2. Use the SEARCH function in column D to determine the position of the space that separates the first and last names. The result of the SEARCH function should be displayed in column D.

3. Use the LEFT function to capture the last name. The result of the LEFT function should be displayed in column E. Use the Paste Values command to replace the formula in column E with a text value.

4. Use the RIGHT function to capture the first name. The result of the RIGHT function should be displayed in column F. Use the Paste Values command to replace the formula in column F with a text value.

5. Stop the macro recorder.

BTW
Shortcut Keys
Macro shortcut keys take precedence over Excel's existing shortcut keys. If you assign an existing shortcut key to a macro, it no longer will work for its original purpose. For instance, assigning CTRL+C to a macro means that you no longer will be able to use that shortcut key to copy content.

To ensure consistent results, use the arrow and Home keys to navigate and the Enter box on the formula bar to enter formulas. The following steps record the LastName macro to separate into two different columns the first name and last name for the entries that appear as LastName, FirstName.

1 Select cell A1, the first instance of last name appearing first.

2 Tap or click the Record Macro button (DEVELOPER tab | Code group) to start the macro recorder to record a macro named **LastName**, with a shortcut key of CTRL+L, and a Description of **Macro splits names for entries with last name appearing first**.

3 Enter the formula **=LEN(A1)** in cell C1.

4 Enter the formula **=SEARCH(" ", A1)** in cell D1.

5 Enter the formula **=LEFT(A1, D1-2)** in cell E1. Replace the content of cell E1 with the text value, using the Paste Values command.

6 Enter the formula **=RIGHT(A1, C1-D1)** in cell F1. Replace the content of cell F1 with the text value, using the Paste Values command.

7 Press the ESC key to remove the selection marquee, make cell A1 the active cell, and then stop the Macro Recorder (Figure 10–22).

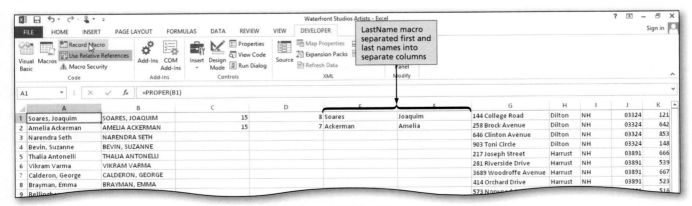

Figure 10–22

To Password-Protect the Worksheet, Save the Workbook, and Close the Workbook

The following steps protect the Convert Artist Data worksheet, save the workbook using the file name Waterfront Studios Artists, and then close the workbook.

1 Tap or click the REVIEW tab on the ribbon, and then tap or click the Protect Sheet button (REVIEW tab | Changes group). When the Protect Sheet dialog box is displayed, type `Art15t5` in the 'Password to unprotect sheet' text box and then tap or click the OK button (Protect Sheet dialog box). When the Confirm Password dialog box is displayed, type `Art15t5` and then tap or click the OK button (Confirm Password dialog box).

2 Save the workbook.

3 Tap or click the FILE tab on the ribbon and then tap or click Close in the Backstage view to close the workbook and leave Excel active.

Changing the Macro Security Level

Macros provide you with an opportunity to make certain tasks much more efficient and accurate. However, macros introduce an element of risk to your work in the form of computer viruses. A **computer virus** is a potentially damaging computer program designed to affect, or infect, your computer negatively by altering the way it works without your knowledge or permission. The increased use of networks, the Internet, and email have accelerated the spread of computer viruses.

Macros are known carriers of viruses because of the ease with which a person can add programming code to macros. To combat this menace, most computer users run antivirus programs that search for viruses and destroy them before they ever have a chance to infect the computer. In addition, Excel provides four levels of protection from macro viruses: Disable all macros without notification, Disable all macros with notification, Disable all macros except digitally signed macros, and Enable all macros. By default, the macro security level is set to Disable all macros with notification, meaning that only macros from trusted sources can be used. Trusted sources are discussed later in this chapter.

BTW

Enabling Macros
Excel remembers your decision about enabling macros. If you have enabled macros in a worksheet, Excel will not ask you about enabling them the next time you open the worksheet, but will open the worksheet with macros enabled.

To Set the Macro Security Level

1 SET PROTECTION & SECURITY | 2 WRITE MACROS | 3 CREATE DATA FORM | 4 DESIGN USER INTERFACE
5 SET CONTROL PROPERTIES | 6 WRITE VISUAL BASIC CODE | 7 TEST USER INTERFACE

Why? You should set the macro security level to provide the appropriate security for the workbook you are using. The following steps check and set the level of protection, if necessary, to Disable all macros with notification.

1

- Tap or click DEVELOPER on the ribbon to display the DEVELOPER tab.

- Tap or click the Macro Security button (DEVELOPER tab | Code group) to display the Trust Center dialog box.

- If necessary, tap or click 'Disable all macros with notification' to select the option button (Figure 10–23).

2

- Tap or click the OK button (Trust Center dialog box) to close the dialog box.

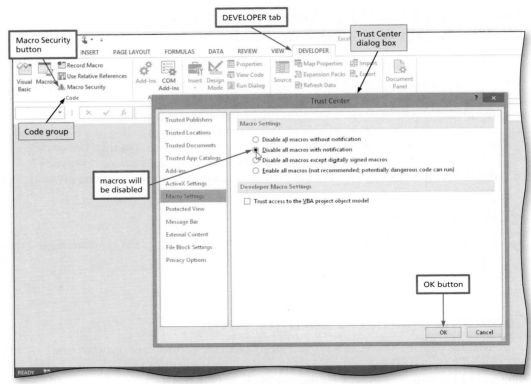

Figure 10–23

Other Ways

1. Tap or click FILE tab, tap or click Options in the left pane, tap or click Trust Center in the left pane (Excel Options dialog box), tap or click Trust Center Settings button in right pane, tap or click Macro Settings tab (Trust Center dialog box), tap or click 'Disable all macros with notification' option

---

CONSIDER THIS

How should you make decisions about macro security?

Each time you open a workbook with an associated macro and the macro security level is set to 'Disable all macros with notification', Excel displays a SECURITY WARNING bar with an Enable Content button. Tapping or clicking the Enable Content button enables the macros, which means that the code can be executed.

If you are confident of the source (author) of the workbook and macros, tap or click the Enable Content button. If you are uncertain about the reliability of the source of the workbook and macros, you can work with the macros disabled, which means that the code is not executable.

To Open a Workbook with Macros and Execute a Macro

1 SET PROTECTION & SECURITY | 2 WRITE MACROS | 3 CREATE DATA FORM | 4 DESIGN USER INTERFACE
5 SET CONTROL PROPERTIES | 6 WRITE VISUAL BASIC CODE | 7 TEST USER INTERFACE

Why? *When you open a workbook with macros, you must enable the macros in the workbook before you can use them.* The following steps open the Waterfront Studios Artists workbook and enable the macros in the workbook. The steps show how to execute the recorded macro LastName by using the shortcut keys CTRL+L established when the macro was created.

1

• With Excel active, open the Waterfront Studios Artists workbook (Figure 10–24).

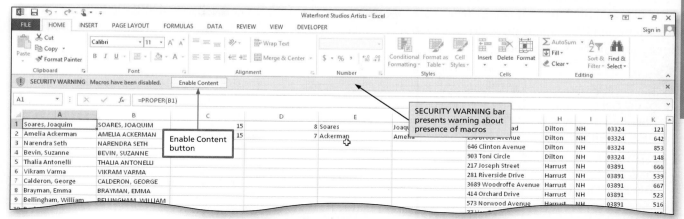

Figure 10–24

2

• Tap or click the Enable Content button in the SECURITY WARNING bar to open the workbook with macros enabled.

• Tap or click REVIEW on the ribbon to display the REVIEW tab.

• Tap or click the Unprotect Sheet button (REVIEW tab | Changes group) to unprotect the Convert Artist Data worksheet using the password, Art15t5.

• In the Convert Artist Data worksheet, tap or click cell A4 to select it.

• Press CTRL+SHIFT+L to run the LastName macro.

• Tap or click all cells in column A with names in the last name, first name format, and then run the LastName macro in each cell to format the name text in the desired format (Figure 10–25).

Q&A Should I also run the FirstName macro?
Not yet. You will run the FirstName macro shortly.

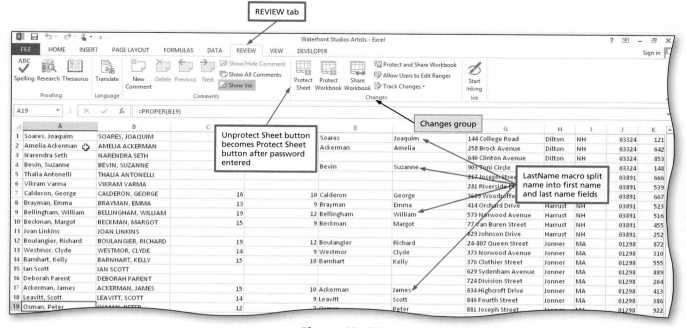

Figure 10–25

Other Ways

1. On DEVELOPER tab, tap or click View Macros button, double-tap or double-click macro name

To View and Print a Macro's VBA Code

Why? It is helpful to print out a copy of VBA code for review. Edits can be made on hard copy and then to the *actual code*. As described earlier, a macro is composed of VBA code, which is created automatically by the macro recorder. Use the **Visual Basic Editor** (**VBE**) to view and print the VBA code. The Visual Basic Editor (VBE) is used by all Office applications to enter, modify, and view VBA code. The following steps view and print the FirstName macro's VBA code.

1

- Tap or click DEVELOPER on the ribbon to display the DEVELOPER tab.

- Tap or click the View Macros button (DEVELOPER tab | Code group) to display the Macro dialog box.

- When the Macro dialog box is displayed, tap or click FirstName in the Macro name list (Figure 10–26).

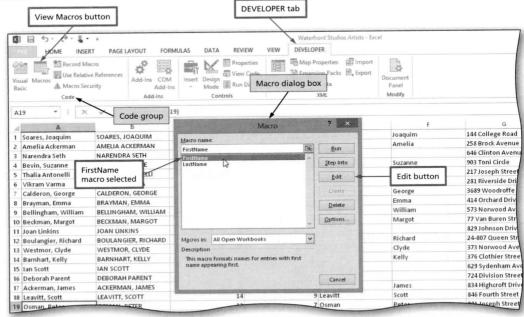

Figure 10–26

2

- Tap or click the Edit button (Macro dialog box) to display the Visual Basic Editor.

- If necessary, tap or click the Maximize button on the title bar to maximize the Visual Basic Editor window (Figure 10–27).

Q&A Can I edit the macro code?

Yes, you can edit the code in the Visual Basic Editor. For instance, if you had entered a period rather than a comma as the SEARCH argument when recording the macro, you could edit the code to modify the macro rather than rerecording the macro. After making the change(s) in the code, closing the Visual Basic Editor will save the change(s) you made automatically.

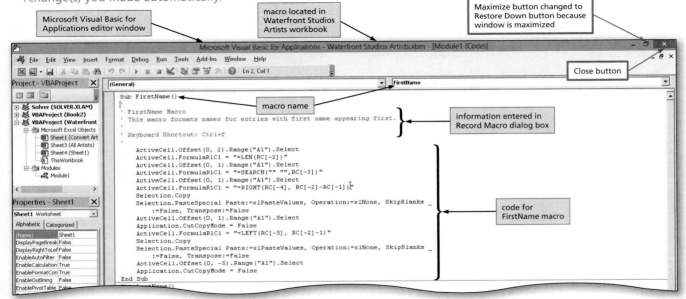

Figure 10–27

- Examine the VBA code.

- When you are finished, tap or click File on the menu bar to display the File menu (Figure 10–28).

- Tap or click Print on the File menu to display the Print - VBAProject dialog box.

- Tap or click the OK button (Print - VBAProject dialog box) to print the macro code.

- Tap or click the Close button on the right side of the title bar in the Visual Basic Editor window to close it.

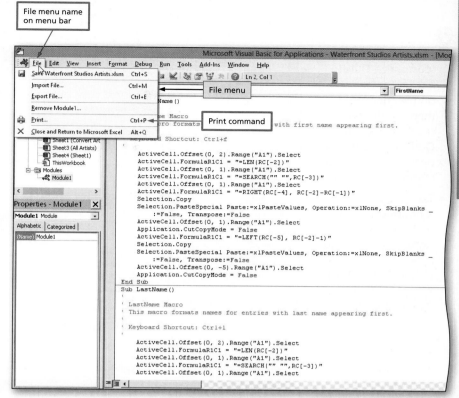

Figure 10–28

Other Ways

1. Tap or click Visual Basic button (DEVELOPER tab | Codes group)

2. Press and hold or right-click the worksheet tab, tap or click View Code on shortcut menu

3. ALT+F11

To Add a Button to the Quick Access Toolbar, Assign the Button a Macro, and Use the Button

1 SET PROTECTION & SECURITY | 2 WRITE MACROS | 3 CREATE DATA FORM | 4 DESIGN USER INTERFACE
5 SET CONTROL PROPERTIES | 6 WRITE VISUAL BASIC CODE | 7 TEST USER INTERFACE

Why? For macros you use often, adding a button provides you with easy access to the macro. You can add as many buttons as you want to the Quick Access Toolbar. You also can select an icon for the buttons you add. The following steps add a button to the Quick Access Toolbar, change the button image, assign the FirstName macro to the button, and then use the button to reformat the artist data for Waterfront Studios when the first name appears first.

- Press and hold or right-click anywhere on the Quick Access Toolbar to display the shortcut menu (Figure 10–29).

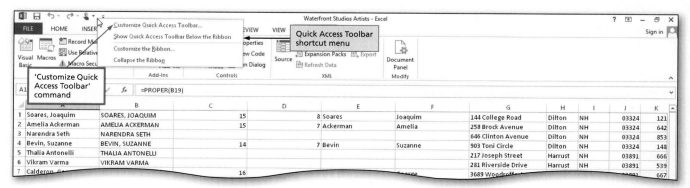

Figure 10–29

- Tap or click 'Customize Quick Access Toolbar' on the shortcut menu to display the Customize the Quick Access Toolbar options in the Excel Options dialog box.

- Tap or click the 'Choose commands from' arrow in the right pane to display a list of commands to add to the Quick Access Toolbar (Figure 10–30).

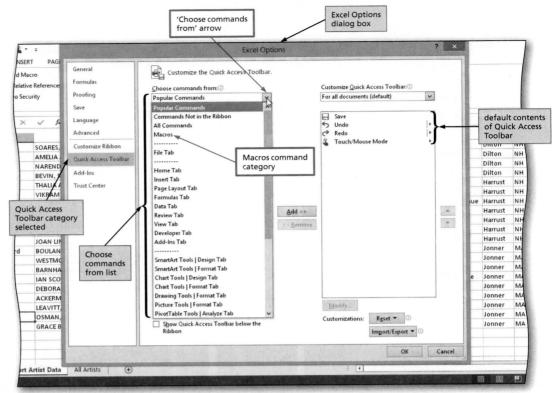

Figure 10–30

- Tap or click Macros in the Choose commands from list to display a list of macros.

- Tap or click FirstName in the Macros list to select it.

- Tap or click the Add button (Excel Options dialog box) to add the FirstName macro to the Customize Quick Access Toolbar list (Figure 10–31).

Q&A How can I delete the buttons that I add to the Quick Access Toolbar?

You can reset the Quick Access Toolbar to its installation default by tapping or clicking the Reset button in the Customize Quick Access Toolbar options in the Excel Options dialog box. If you share a computer with others, you should reset the Quick Access Toolbar before you exit Excel.

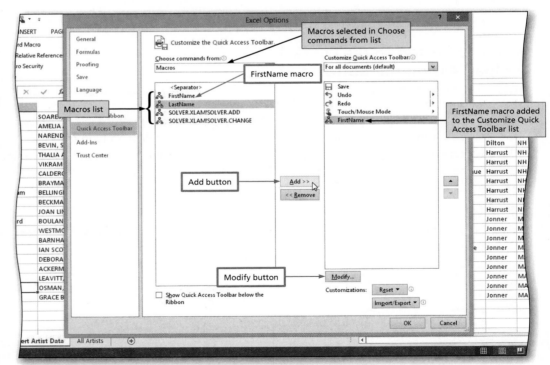

Figure 10–31

4

- Tap or click the Modify button to display the Modify Button dialog box.

- Type **FirstName Macro** in the Display name text box (Figure 10–32).

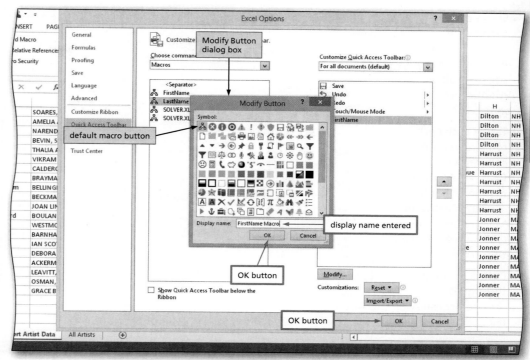

Figure 10–32

5

- Tap or click the OK button (Modify Button dialog box) to modify the display name of the button.

- Tap or click the OK button (Excel Options dialog box) to close the dialog box.

- Point to the FirstName Macro button on the Quick Access Toolbar to display the ScreenTip for the button (Figure 10–33).

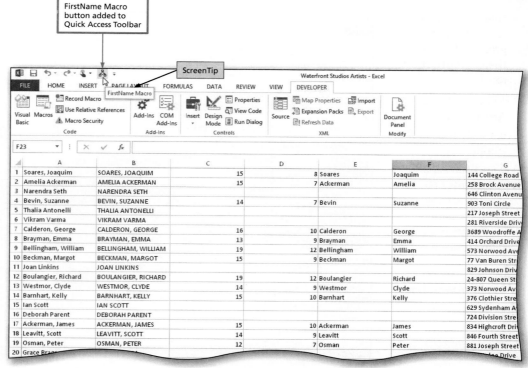

Figure 10–33

6

- Select cell A3 and then tap or click the FirstName Macro button on the Quick Access Toolbar to run the FirstName macro.

- Tap or click each remaining entry in column A with the first name appearing first and then tap or click the FirstName Macro button on the Quick Access Toolbar to run the macro.

- Delete columns A through D and then select cell A1 (Figure 10–34).

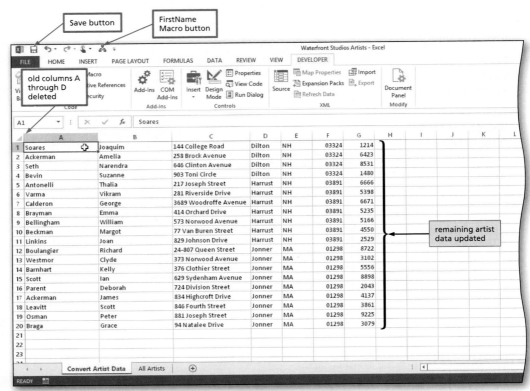

Figure 10–34

7

- Select the range A1:G20, and then press CTRL+C to copy the contents of the range.

- Tap or click the All Artists sheet tab to make it the active sheet.

- Select cell A3 and then press CTRL+V to paste the converted artist data into the All Artists worksheet (Figure 10–35).

8

- Save the workbook.

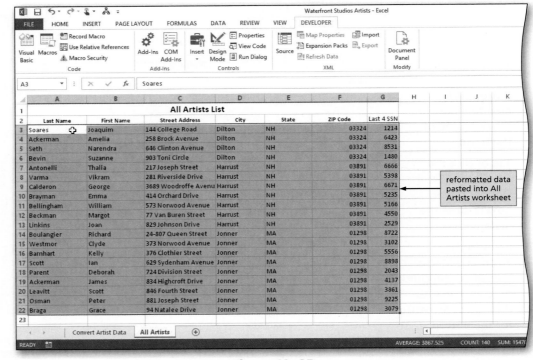

Figure 10–35

To Use a Data Form to Enter Additional Records

Why create a data form? *Created from the worksheet column headings, a data form provides the user with a simple interface to enter data in the worksheet.* It is a straightforward method for entering additional records without having to navigate the worksheet. The following steps create a data form and use it to enter additional records to the All Artists worksheet.

- Press and hold or right-click anywhere on the Quick Access Toolbar to display the shortcut menu.

- Tap or click 'Customize Quick Access Toolbar' on the shortcut menu to display the Quick Access Toolbar options in the Excel Options dialog box.

- Tap or click the 'Choose commands from' arrow to display a list of commands to add to the Quick Access Toolbar.

- Tap or click 'Commands Not in the Ribbon' in the Choose commands from list to display a list of commands that currently do not appear on the ribbon.

- Scroll down to Form in the list, tap or click Form to select it, and then tap or click the Add button (Excel Options dialog box) to add the Form command to the Customize Quick Access Toolbar list (Figure 10–36).

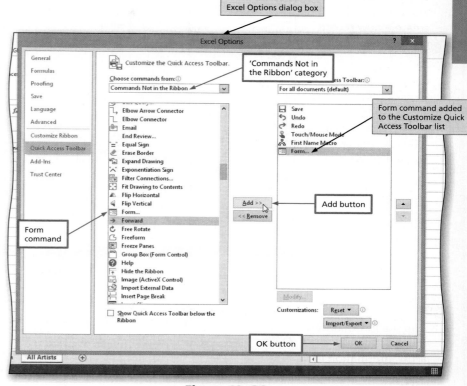

Figure 10–36

- Tap or click the OK button (Excel Options dialog box) to close the dialog box.

- If necessary, tap or click cell A3 to select a cell in the row immediately below the column headings.

- Tap or click the Form button on the Quick Access Toolbar to open the All Artists data form.

- Tap or click the New button in the All Artists form to create a new record. Enter the information for the first artist in Table 10–2 on page EX 645 into the form. You can use the TAB key, the mouse, or touch gestures (taps) to move from field to field (Figure 10–37).

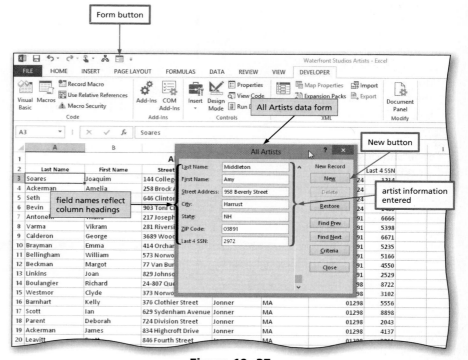

Figure 10–37

3

- Tap or click the New button in the All Artists data form to add the information you just entered to the All Artists worksheet and to create a new record (Figure 10–38).

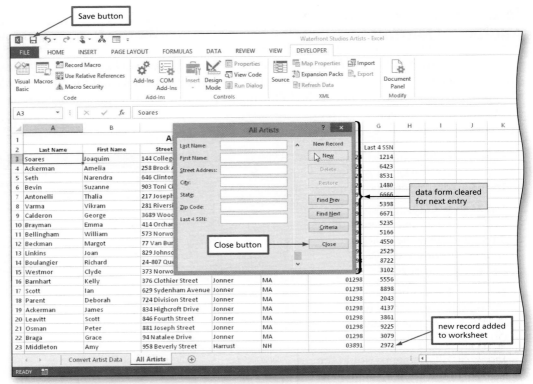

Figure 10–38

4

- Add the information for the remaining artist information in Table 10–2, creating a new record for each artist. Tap or click the Close button (All Artists data form) after completing the data entry. Scroll down to review the new records (Figure 10–39).

5

- Save and close the workbook.

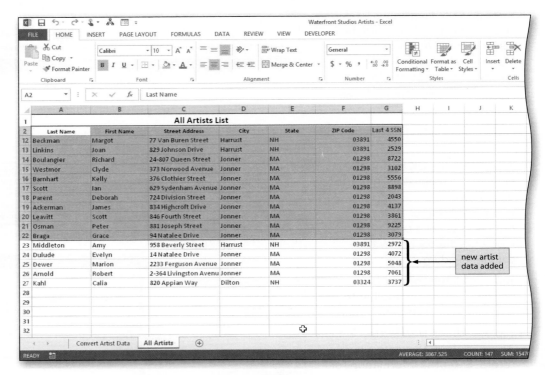

Figure 10–39

Table 10–2 New Artist Data						
Last Name	**First Name**	**Street Address**	**City**	**State**	**Zip Code**	**Last 4 SSN**
Middleton	Amy	958 Beverly Street	Harrust	NH	03891	2972
Dulude	Evelyn	14 Natalee Drive	Jonner	MA	01298	4072
Dewer	Marion	2233 Ferguson Avenue	Jonner	MA	01298	5048
Arnold	Robert	2-364 Livingston Avenue	Jonner	MA	01298	7061
Kahl	Calia	820 Appian Way	Dilton	NH	03324	3737

© 2014 Cengage Learning

Break Point: If you wish to take a break, this is a good place to do so. You can exit Excel now. To resume at a later time, run Excel, and continue following the steps from this location forward.

Phase 2 — Creating a Mailing List Data Entry Screen Automating the Mailing List Data Entry

The Waterfront Studios project up to now has been concerned with working with data that has already been entered, and entering data using a form. Macros were used to edit the existing data consistently. New data was entered using a data form created from existing column headings. At times you may need to provide a method of entering data to people with little or no knowledge of Excel, who might not know what cells to select or how to navigate the worksheet. Phase 2 calls for creating a user interface that can be used by patrons to sign up for the Studios mailing list. Figure 10–40 on the next page shows the approach that will be used to create the user interface, and how the Mailing List Signup worksheet will look when complete. When a user clicks the 'Tap or Click to Enter Contact Information' command button, it will trigger Excel to display a series of input dialog boxes to collect contact information. The remaining data (preferred method of communication, source of information about event, and event interest) will be entered using check boxes and option buttons to help reduce input errors that can be caused by mistyped data. Multiple check boxes can be selected for event interests. Unlike check boxes, option buttons restrict users to one selection per worksheet or group, in this case to one preferred method of contact and one source of information. By having all data entry done through controls and input dialog boxes, protecting the workbook before using it to gather data will limit user interaction to those controls and dialog boxes.

Figure 10–41 on page EX 647 shows the gallery of controls available to use in constructing a user interface.

Two types of controls are used to create the user interface: form controls and ActiveX controls. Form controls and ActiveX controls look identical in the gallery. They do have functional differences, however, that can help determine which one is the best choice for an object. Form controls require no knowledge of VBA to use. You can assign an Excel macro directly to a form control, allowing the macro to be run with a simple tap or click. Form controls also allow you to reference cells easily and use Excel functions and expressions to manipulate data. You can customize their appearance at a rudimentary level.

ActiveX controls provide great flexibility in terms of their design. They have extensive properties that can be used to customize their appearance. ActiveX controls cannot be assigned an Excel macro directly. The macro code must be part of the VBA code for the control.

In this project, you will use form controls for the check box and option button controls because of their ease of use and the ability to use Excel functions with no additional code. You will use ActiveX controls for the command button and text box

BTW
Certification
The Microsoft Office Specialist (MOS) program provides an opportunity for you to obtain a valuable industry credential — proof that you have the Excel 2013 skills required by employers. For more information, visit the Certification resource on the Student Companion Site located on www .cengagebrain.com. For detailed instructions about accessing available resources, visit www.cengage.com /ct/studentdownload or contact your instructor for information about accessing the required files.

Step 1 — Create the User Interface

Step 2 — Set the Properties

Step 3 — Write the VBA Code

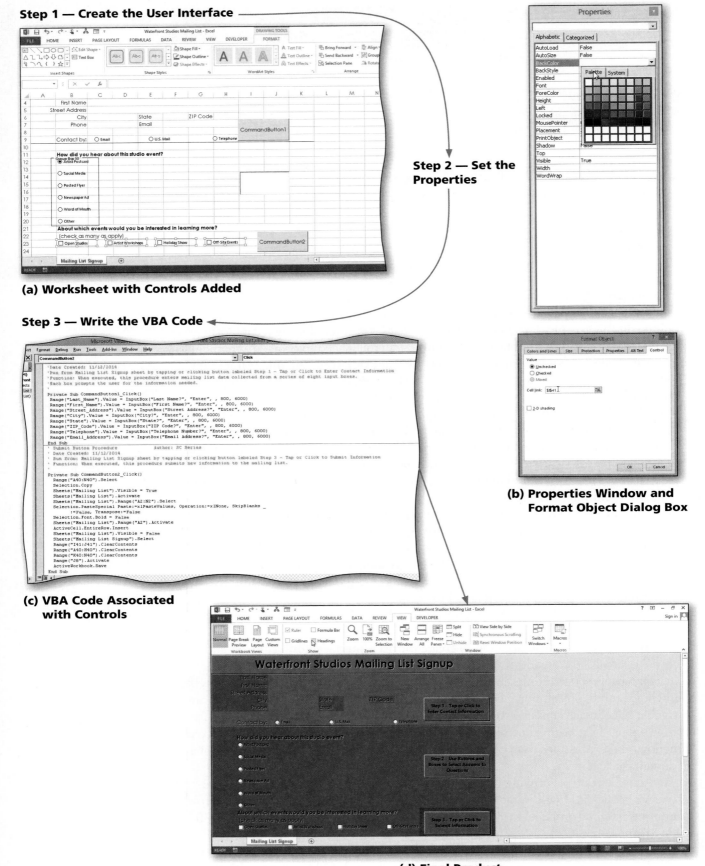

(a) Worksheet with Controls Added

(b) Properties Window and Format Object Dialog Box

(c) VBA Code Associated with Controls

(d) Final Product

Figure 10–40

Figure 10–41

controls to provide a more visually appealing interface than would be possible using form controls.

The option button controls will be used with the Excel INDEX function to record the single selections for two entries: the patron's preferred method of contact and how patrons heard about the studio. The control itself returns a number indicating which option button was selected. The INDEX function matches that selection to a list and returns the entry in the list. This allows the workbook to contain entries such as Telephone, Email, and U.S. Mail, rather than values that the control returns such as 1, 2, and 3. The INDEX function makes use of the named ranges, Contact and 'Information_Source', found in Column W of the Mailing List Signup worksheet. These named ranges are placed in column W to keep them out of sight but still on the same worksheet as the user interface.

Finally, the user interface records input in two places. It temporarily records input in row 40 of the Mailing List Signup worksheet, out of sight when the user interface is visible. Using an ActiveX control, the input is copied from this temporary recording place to a hidden worksheet, Mailing List.

To Open a Workbook and Unprotect a Worksheet

The following steps open the workbook Waterfront Studios Mailing Data, apply a theme and color theme, and save the workbook.

1 Open the Waterfront Studios Mailing Data workbook from the Data Files for Students.

2 Unprotect the worksheet using the password Art15t5.

3 Apply the Ion theme to the workbook.

4 Apply the Blue Warm color theme to the workbook.

5 Save the workbook as a macro-enabled workbook, using the file name Waterfront Studios Mailing List.

To Format Name and Address Fields

The following steps format the title, subtitle, name, and address fields.

1 Merge and center the ranges A1:K2.

2 Format the title in cell A1 to 24 point, bold.

3 Middle-align the text in cell A1.

④ Set column B to a width of 10.75, and right-align the contents of cells B3:B9.

⑤ Merge the range B11:F11, and apply bold to the cells.

⑥ Merge the range B21:H21, and apply bold to the cells.

⑦ Merge ranges C3:H3, C4:H4, C5:H5, C6:D6, C7:D7, and F7:H7.

⑧ Apply a bottom border to ranges A2:K2 and A9:K9 and then select cell L20 (Figure 10–42).

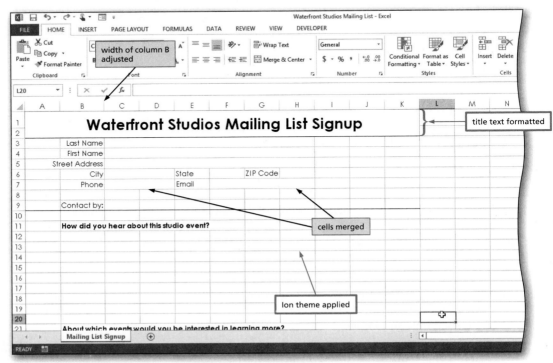

Figure 10–42

To Add Form Controls to a Worksheet

1 SET PROTECTION & SECURITY | 2 WRITE MACROS | 3 CREATE DATA FORM | 4 DESIGN USER INTERFACE
5 SET CONTROL PROPERTIES | 6 WRITE VISUAL BASIC CODE | 7 TEST USER INTERFACE

Why? *You will use form controls rather than macros here to make the final interface one that someone not familiar with Excel will be able to use.* The following steps create the form controls, but do not position them exactly in the locations shown in Figure 10–41a, which will be done later in the chapter.

1

- Tap or click DEVELOPER on the ribbon to display the DEVELOPER tab.

- Tap or click the Insert Controls button (DEVELOPER tab | Controls group) to display the Controls gallery (Figure 10–43).

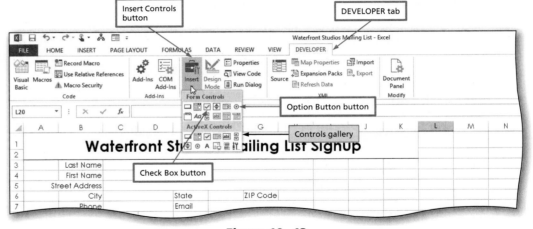

Figure 10–43

2

- Tap or click the Option Button button in the Form Controls area in the Controls gallery.

- Drag the pointer to place the control in the location shown in Figure 10–44.

Q&A The option button I added looks different. It uses the same Ion theme font as used in the rest of the worksheet. What should I do?
You probably selected the Option Button control in the ActiveX Controls area of the Controls gallery. Tap or click the option button control, press the DELETE key, and then repeat Steps 1 and 2.

My option button has more label text showing. Is that incorrect?
The amount of text visible is determined by the size of the control. Dragging through a larger space on the worksheet will result in more label text being displayed. You can adjust this by resizing the control.

Figure 10–44

3

- Repeat Step 2 to place eight additional option buttons, as shown in Figure 10–45.

Q&A What if I add a control in error?
You can delete a control by pressing and holding or right-clicking the control and selecting Cut on the shortcut menu.

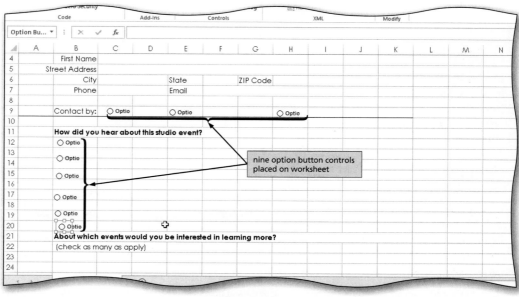

Figure 10–45

4

- Tap or click the Insert Controls button (DEVELOPER tab | Controls group) to display the Controls gallery.

- Tap or click the Check Box button in the Form Controls area in the Controls gallery.

- If you are using touch, drag using your finger or the stylus so that the control is displayed, as shown in Figure 10–46.

- If you are using a mouse, drag using the pointer so that the control is displayed, as shown in Figure 10–46.

Q&A Why is the check box control in Figure 10–46 named Check Box 10? Excel assigns a name to each control, using the type of control as the first part of the name and an incremented number as the second part. This is the first check box control added to the workbook but the tenth control of any type, and it is therefore assigned the name, Check Box 10.

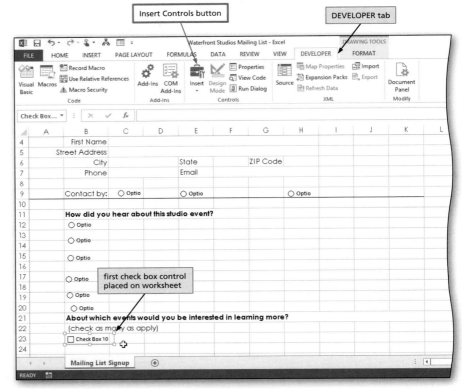

Figure 10–46

5

- Repeat Step 4 to place three additional check box buttons, as shown in Figure 10–47.

Q&A What if I placed the control incorrectly?
If you want to reposition a control, select the control and then drag it to its new location. If you are using touch, you will find this easier to do if you zoom in first before selecting and dragging.

The check box is not the size I need it to be. What can I do?
Check boxes are resized easily. The check boxes here will be resized after the captions are changed later in this chapter.

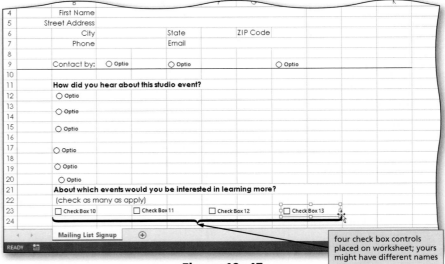

Figure 10–47

Other Ways

1. Select control, tap or click Copy button (HOME tab | Clipboard group), tap or click Paste button (HOME tab | Clipboard group)

2. Press and hold or right-click control, tap or click Copy on shortcut menu, press and hold or right-click worksheet, tap or click Paste on shortcut menu

3. Select control, press CTRL+C to copy, press CTRL+V to paste

To Group Option Buttons in a User Interface

Why? *With form controls, only one of the option buttons on the form can be selected unless the option buttons are grouped. When grouped, one option button per group can be selected.* Use the group box form control to group one set of the option buttons together. The following steps first create the group box form control, and then group option buttons inside it.

1

- Tap or click the Insert Controls button (DEVELOPER tab | Controls group) to display the Controls gallery (Figure 10–48).

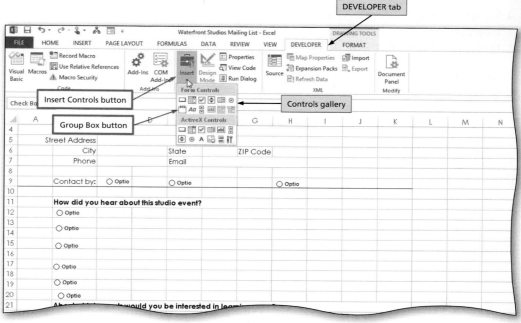

Figure 10–48

2

- Tap or click the Group Box button in the Form Controls area in the Controls gallery.

- If you are using touch, use your finger or a stylus to drag so that the group box control is displayed, as shown in Figure 10–49.

- If you are using a mouse, drag the pointer so that the group box control is displayed, as shown in Figure 10–49.

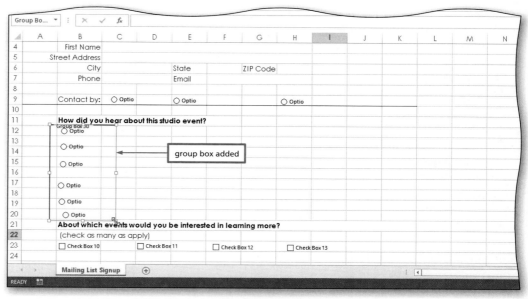

Figure 10–49

Q&A

How accurate does the group box have to be?

The option button controls need to be completely enclosed in the group box control in order for it to work correctly.

I do not like the outline of the box around the option buttons. What can I do?

You can make the box outline invisible using VBA code. You add this later, when you associate code with the control.

To Add a Command Button Control to the Worksheet

Why? *A command button control can have Visual Basic code associated with it that accomplishes more complex actions than a macro or a form button can accommodate.* The following steps add command button controls to the worksheet.

1
- Tap or click the Insert Controls button (DEVELOPER tab | Controls group) to display the Controls gallery (Figure 10–50).

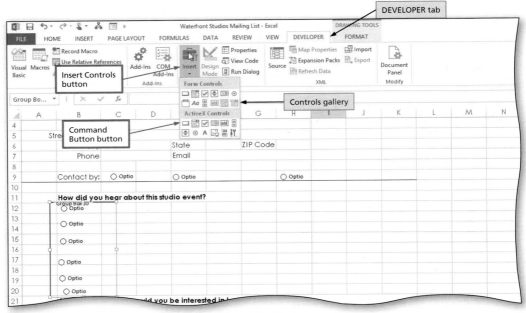

Figure 10–50

2
- Tap or click the Command Button button in the ActiveX Controls area of the Controls gallery (column 1, row 1 of ActiveX area) to switch to Design mode.

- If you are using touch, use your finger or a stylus to drag from the upper-left corner of cell I7 through the lower-right corner of cell J9.

- If you are using a mouse, move the pointer (a crosshair) to the upper-left corner of cell I7, and then drag the pointer through the lower-right corner of cell J9 (Figure 10–51).

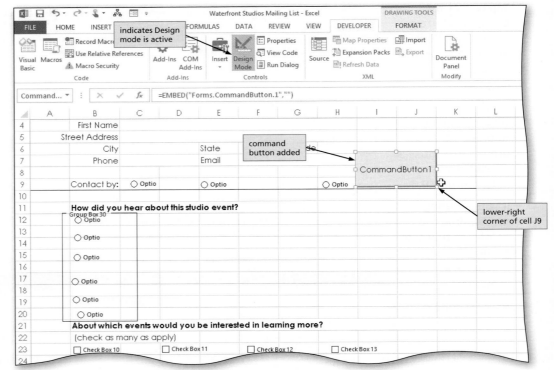

Figure 10–51

Excel Chapter 10

3

- Repeat Steps 1 and 2 to add a second command button in the location shown in Figure 10–52.

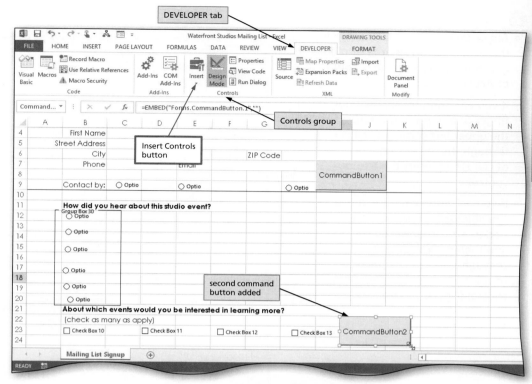

Figure 10–52

To Add a Text Box Control to the Worksheet

1 SET PROTECTION & SECURITY | 2 WRITE MACROS | 3 CREATE DATA FORM | 4 DESIGN USER INTERFACE
5 SET CONTROL PROPERTIES | 6 WRITE VISUAL BASIC CODE | 7 TEST USER INTERFACE

Why? *A text box control can be used to impart information in a user interface.* The following steps add a text box control to the worksheet.

1

- Tap or click the Insert Controls button (DEVELOPER tab | Controls group) to display the Controls gallery (Figure 10–53).

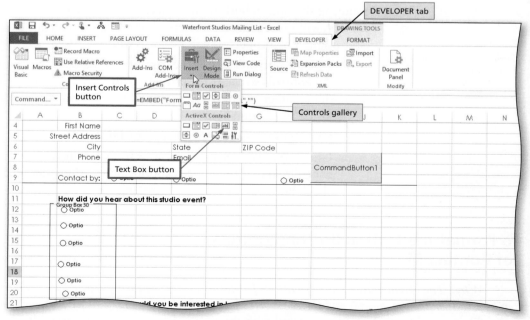

Figure 10–53

2

- Tap or click the Text Box button in the ActiveX Controls area of the Controls gallery (column 5, row 1 of ActiveX area).

- If you are using touch, use your finger or a stylus to drag from the upper-left corner of cell I14 through the lower-right corner of cell J16 to insert the text box control.

- If you are using a mouse, move the pointer (a crosshair) to the upper-left corner of cell I14, and then drag the pointer through the lower-right corner of cell J16 to insert the text box control (Figure 10–54).

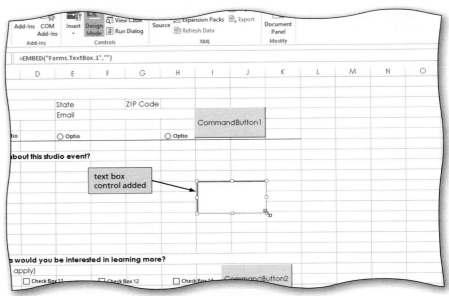

Figure 10–54

Setting Form Control Properties

Each form control available in the Controls gallery has many **properties**, or characteristics, that can be set to determine the control's appearance and behavior. You set these properties using the Format Control dialog box, which can be accessed either by pressing and holding or right-clicking the form control and selecting Format Control from the shortcut menu, or by selecting the control and tapping or clicking the Properties button (DEVELOPER tab | Controls group) on the ribbon.

The next step is to set the properties for the 13 form controls in the user interface. The 13 controls best can be seen by referring to Figure 10–40d and counting the option buttons and check boxes. The group box, while technically a form control, will not be formatted here. The three ActiveX controls will be formatted at a later point. The properties will be set as follows:

1. **Option buttons** — Set the captions to match those in Figure 10–40d. Resize the controls so that the entire caption shows. Align and horizontally distribute the Contact by controls. Align and vertically distribute the option buttons inside the Group box.

2. **Group box** — Hide the group box border.

3. **Check boxes** — Set the captions to match those in Figure 10–40d. Resize the controls so that the entire caption shows. Align and horizontally distribute the check box controls.

To Format the Option Button Controls for Contact Method

1 SET PROTECTION & SECURITY | 2 WRITE MACROS | 3 CREATE DATA FORM | 4 DESIGN USER INTERFACE
5 SET CONTROL PROPERTIES | 6 WRITE VISUAL BASIC CODE | 7 TEST USER INTERFACE

Why? *The option button controls must be formatted to identify their purpose for the user. Other formatting options can be used to make the controls and the worksheet upon which they are found easier and more pleasant to use.* The following steps change the text associated with the option button controls, resize the controls, and align and distribute the controls.

1

- Press and hold or right-click the first option button control in the Contact by area to display the shortcut menu (Figure 10–55).

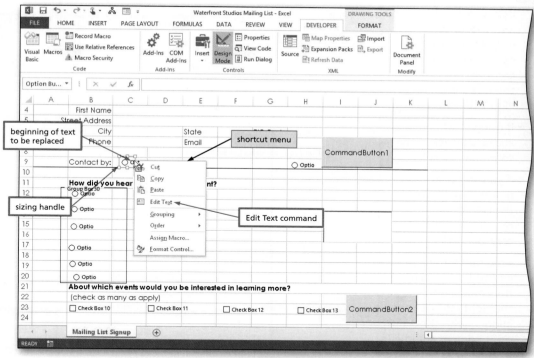

Figure 10–55

2

- Tap or click Edit Text on the shortcut menu so that you can edit the control text.

- Delete the text in the control and type **Email** to replace the text.

- Resize the control so that it just encloses the new text (Figure 10–56).

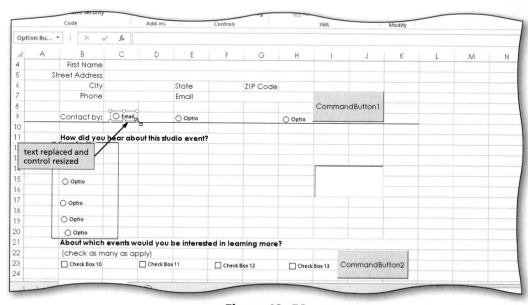

Figure 10–56

- Repeat Steps 1 and 2 to resize and rename the other two contact controls, naming them as shown in Figure 10–57.

- If using touch, press and hold the Telephone control to select it.

- If you are using a mouse, hold down the CTRL key and click the Telephone control to select it.

- Hold down the ALT key and then drag the control until the right edge is aligned with the right edge of column H (Figure 10–57).

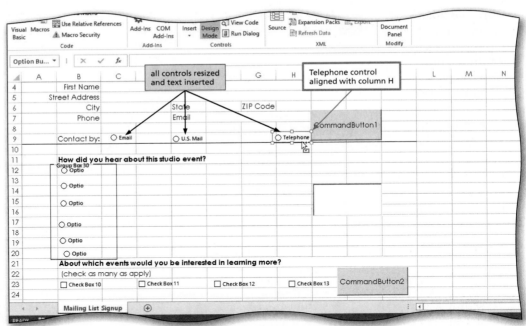

Figure 10–57

Q&A Why do not I have the ALT key on my on-screen keyboard?
You may not have the full virtual keyboard enabled. To enable it, select PC Settings in the Charms bar, choose General Settings, and then tap or click to turn on the 'Make standard keyboard layout available' option.

- Hold down the CTRL key and then tap or click the other two controls to select all three option button controls.

- Tap or click DRAWING TOOLS FORMAT on the ribbon to display the DRAWING TOOLS FORMAT tab.

- Tap or click the Shape Height box up arrow (DRAWING TOOLS FORMAT tab | Size group) to increase the shape height to 0.2".

- Tap or click the Align Objects button (DRAWING TOOLS FORMAT tab | Arrange group) to display the alignment options (Figure 10–58).

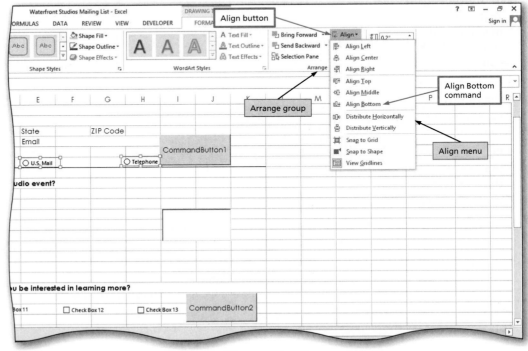

Figure 10–58

- Tap or click Align Bottom on the Arrange menu to align the three controls along their bottom borders.

- Tap or click the Align Objects button again (DRAWING TOOLS FORMAT tab | Arrange group) to display the alignment options.

- Tap or click Distribute Horizontally on the Arrange menu to space the three controls evenly between columns C and H (Figure 10–59).

Q&A

How can I make the controls stand out more?
You can format the controls with borders and fill colors to make them stand out from the background. Choose Format Control on the shortcut menu and use the Color and Lines sheet in the Format Object dialog box to apply colors and patterns.

Can I make the controls a specific size?
Size of controls can also be set using the Format Control command on the shortcut menu.

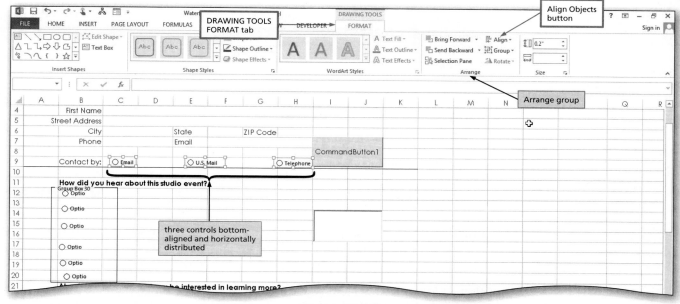

Figure 10–59

To Format the Group Box Controls

The following steps format the option buttons in the group box control.

1. Select each of the six option buttons in the group box in turn and edit the text to match the text in Figure 10–60 on the next page.

2. Move the top option button so that its upper-left corner aligns with the upper-left corner of cell B12, and move the bottom option button so that its lower-left corner aligns with the lower-left corner of cell B20.

3. Select all six controls, and using the Shape Height and Shape Width boxes (DRAWING TOOLS FORMAT tab | Size group), set the control height to 0.2" and the shape width to 1.1".

4. With the six controls still selected, using the Align button (DRAWING TOOLS FORMAT tab | Arrange group), apply the Align Left and Distribute Vertically formats to the group.

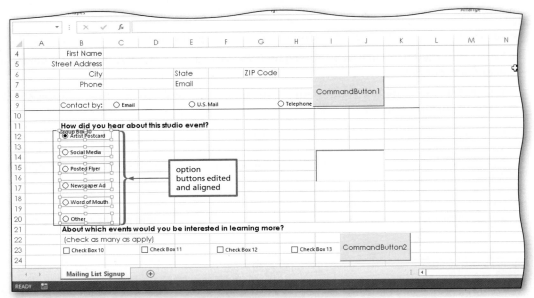

Figure 10–60

To Format the Check Box Controls

The check box controls are formatted in the same fashion as the option button controls. The following steps format and align the check box controls.

1 Select each of the four check box buttons in turn and edit the text to match the text in Figure 10–61.

2 Move the leftmost check box button so that its upper-left corner aligns with the upper-left corner of cell B23, and move the rightmost check box button so that its upper-right corner aligns with the upper-right corner of cell H23.

3 Select all four controls, and using the Shape Height and Shape Width boxes (DRAWING TOOLS FORMAT tab | Size group), set the control height to 0.2" and the shape width to 1.2".

4 Select all four controls, and using the Align button (DRAWING TOOLS FORMAT tab | Arrange group), apply the Align Top and Distribute Horizontally formats to the group (Figure 10–61).

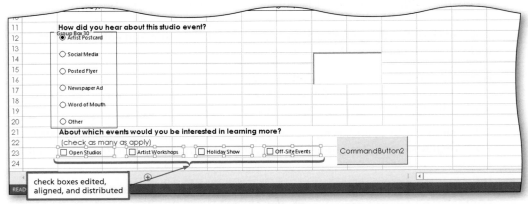

Figure 10–61

Setting ActiveX Control Properties

Like with form controls, each ActiveX control available in the Controls gallery has many properties that can be set to determine the control's appearance and behavior. You set these properties in Design mode, entered into using the Design button in the Controls group on the DEVELOPER tab on the ribbon. This will open the Properties dialog box where the control properties can be set or edited.

The user interface contains three ActiveX controls, two command buttons, and a text box. These will need to be formatted to match the final controls in Figure 10–41d.

To Format the Command Button and Text Box Controls

1 SET PROTECTION & SECURITY | 2 WRITE MACROS | 3 CREATE DATA FORM | 4 DESIGN USER INTERFACE

5 SET CONTROL PROPERTIES | 6 WRITE VISUAL BASIC CODE | 7 TEST USER INTERFACE

Why? *Format the command button and text box controls to provide instructions to the user and to make them visually prominent.* The command button and text box controls are formatted using the Properties window. The following steps set the properties for the command button and text box controls.

1

- Select the two command button controls and the text box control to prepare for setting their properties.

- Tap or click the Control Properties button (DEVELOPER tab | Controls group) to open the Properties window.

- Tap or click the BackColor property to display the BackColor arrow.

- Tap or click the BackColor arrow to display the BackColor tabs.

- Tap or click the Palette tab to display the colors on that tab (Figure 10–62).

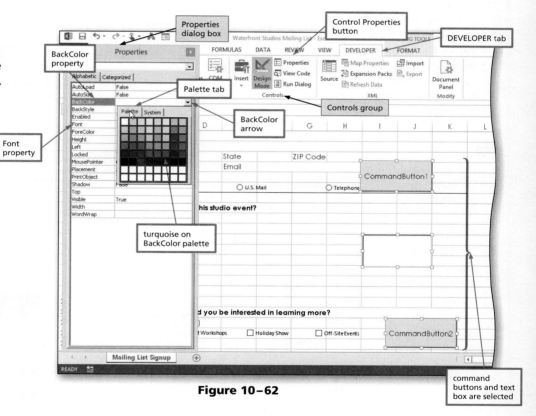

Figure 10–62

2

- Tap or click turquoise (column 6, row 5) to add a turquoise background to the command buttons.

- Tap or click the Font property to display the ellipsis button.

- Tap or click the ellipsis button to display the Font dialog box.

- Tap or click Segoe UI in the Font list, 10 in the Size list, and Bold in the Font style list to use the 10 point bold Segoe UI font on the command buttons and in the text box (Figure 10–63).

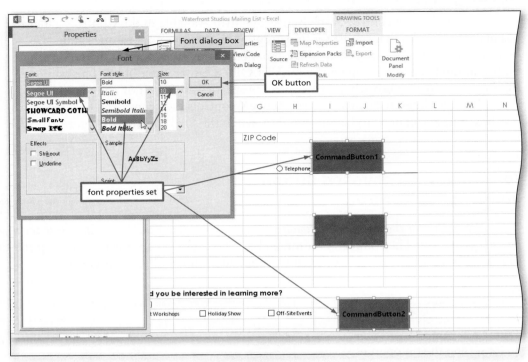

Figure 10–63

3

- Tap or click the OK button (Font dialog box) to apply this font to the text in the controls.

- Set the WordWrap and Shadow properties to True.

- Set Height to 50.25 and Width to 140.25 (Figure 10–64).

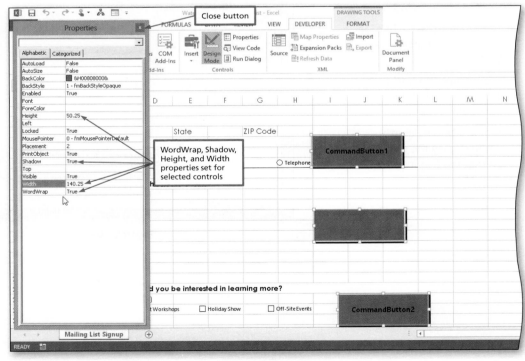

Figure 10–64

- Tap or click the Close button to close the Properties window.

- Select the command button controls individually, open the Properties window, and set the Caption property to the text shown in Figure 10–65.

- Select the text box to prepare for entering properties for the control.

- Set the Multiline property to True so that users can enter more than one line of text.

- Set Text to the text shown in the text box in Figure 10–65.

- Set Special Effect to 1 - fmSpecialEffect Raised to format the control.

Experiment

- Set Special Effect to different options to see the effect on the control. Set to 1 - fmSpecialEffect Raised when finished.

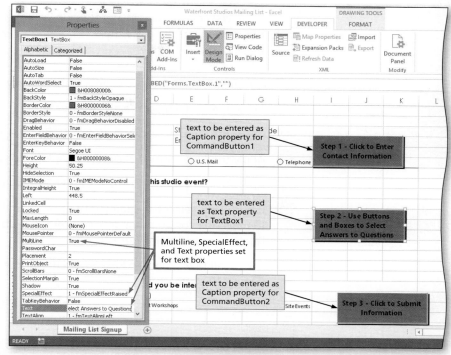

Figure 10–65

- Close the Properties window.

- Select the command buttons and the text box and use the Align button (DRAWING TOOLS FORMAT tab | Arrange group) to apply the Align Right and Distribute Vertically formats to the group. With the three controls still selected, use the arrow keys to move the controls as a group to the final locations shown in Figure 10–66.

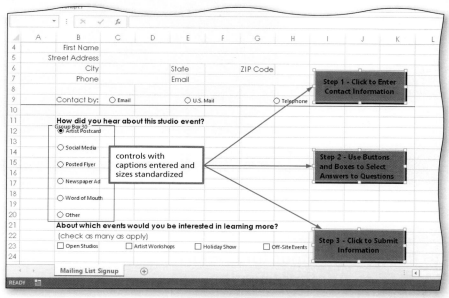

Figure 10–66

To Add Fill Color to the Worksheet

The last step in formatting the worksheet is to add fill colors to differentiate different sections of the worksheet. The following steps add fill colors to the worksheet.

1 Apply the Blue, Accent 3, Lighter 80% fill color to the entire worksheet.

2 Apply the Dark Purple, Text 2, Lighter 40% fill color to cell A1.

3 Apply the Blue, Accent 2, Darker 25% fill color to cells A3:K10.

4 Apply the Blue, Accent 3, Darker 25% fill color to cells A3:B7, E6:E7, G6, and A10:K24.

5 Apply the Blue-Gray, Accent 1, Darker 25% fill color to cells I21:K24.

6 If necessary, select the command buttons and the text box and use the arrow keys to move the controls as a group to center the bottom command button in the range I21:K24, as shown in Figure 10–67.

7 Select cell M24. Zoom to 80% to see the whole formatted section of the worksheet (Figure 10–67).

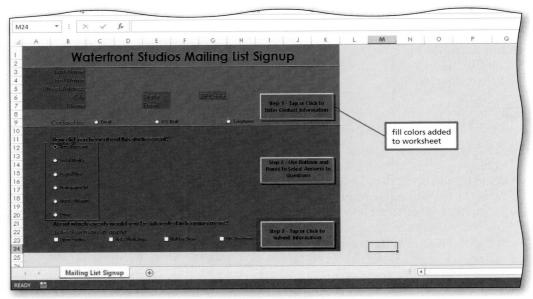

Figure 10–67

To Record User Input for Contact Method to Another Location on the Worksheet

Why? *User input needs to be recorded in another location on the worksheet in preparation for copying it to a permanent location on another worksheet.* The following steps record the user input for contact information to another place on the worksheet.

1

- Zoom to 100%.

- Press and hold or right-click the Email option button control to display the shortcut menu.

- Tap or click Format Control to display the Format Object dialog box.

- If necessary, tap or click the Control tab (Format Object dialog box) to display the Control sheet.

- Enter **$I$41** in the Cell link box to enter the identity of the option button selected in cell I41 (Figure 10–68).

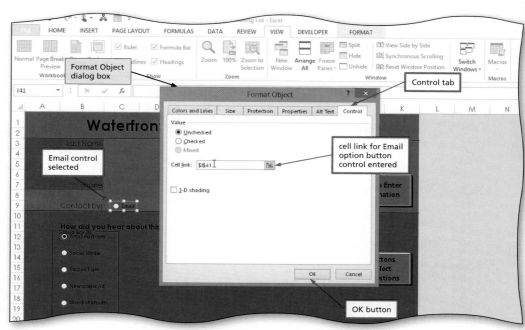

Figure 10–68

2

- Tap or click the OK button (Format Control dialog box) to close the dialog box.

- Tap or click cell I40 to make it the active cell.

- Enter **=INDEX(contact,$I$41)** to return text rather than numbers in row 40 (Figure 10–69).

Q&A

How does the INDEX function work here?

You were introduced to the INDEX function in Chapter 6. In this instance, the INDEX function looks at the value in cell I41, which identifies which option button was selected, and returns the entry associated with that value from the named range contact. The named range contact is found in column W in this worksheet.

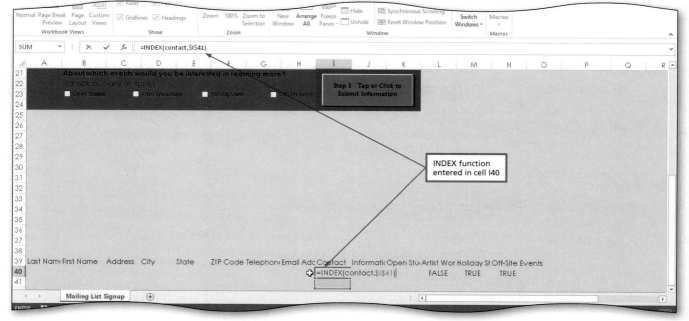

Figure 10–69

To Record User Input for the Group Box Controls

The following steps record the user input for the information source in another place on the worksheet.

1 Press and hold or right-click the Artist Postcard option button control and then click Format Control on the shortcut menu. If necessary, tap or click the Control tab and then enter `$J$41` in the Cell link box (Format Control dialog box).

2 Make cell J40 the active cell. Enter `=INDEX(information_source,$J$41)` to return text from the named range information_source rather than numbers in row 40 (Figure 10–70).

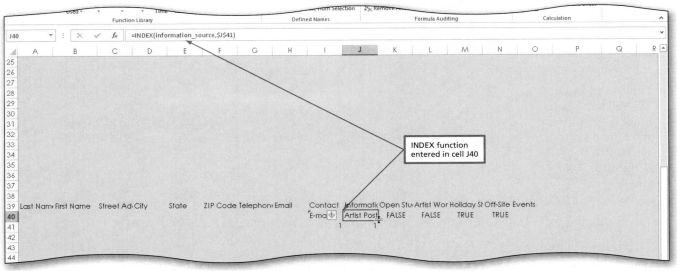

Figure 10–70

To Record User Input for the Check Box Controls

The following steps record the user input for the check boxes at another place on the worksheet.

1 Select the Open Studios Check Box control. Use the shortcut menu to display the Format Control dialog box. In the Cell link box (Format Control dialog box, Control tab), type `$K$40` to record user input.

2 Tap or click the OK button (Format Control dialog box).

3 Repeat Steps 1 and 2 for each of the remaining three check box controls, using cells L40 through N40 for the cell links.

To Assign Names to Cells

The following steps assign names to cells and enter necessary references. The lists of cell names and references are found in Tables 10–3 and 10–4.

1 Select the range A39:H40 and use the 'Create from Selection' button (FORMULAS tab | Defined Names group) to assign the names in cells A39:H39 to the cells A40:H40.

2 Enter the cell references listed in Table 10–4 into the appropriate cells.

Table 10–3 Cell Names	
Cell	**Name**
A40	Last_Name
B40	First_Name
C40	Street_Address
D40	City
E40	State
F40	Zip_Code
G40	Telephone
H40	Email_Address

© 2014 Cengage Learning

Table 10–4 Cell References	
Cell	**Reference**
C3	=A40
C4	=B40
C5	=C40
C6	=D40
F6	=E40
H6	=F40
C7	=G40
F7	=H40

© 2014 Cengage Learning

Writing Code for a Command Button

Using the Controls gallery to insert a command button control into a worksheet inserts an object only. To have the button take action when a user clicks it, you must write VBA code that directs the events in the worksheet after the command button is tapped or clicked.

The next step is to write and then enter the procedure that will execute when the user taps or clicks the 'Step 1 - Tap or Click to Enter Contact Information' button. Code is entered in the Visual Basic Editor, which is accessed from the DEVELOPER tab on the ribbon. The Visual Basic Editor is a separate window from the window containing the worksheet.

When you trigger the event that executes a procedure, such as tapping or clicking a button, Excel steps through the Visual Basic statements one at a time, beginning at the top of the procedure. The statements should reflect the steps you want Excel to take, in the exact order in which they should occur. An **event-driven program** includes procedures that are executed when the specific actions taken by the user or other events occur.

After you determine what you want the procedure to do, write the VBA code on paper, creating a table similar to Table 10–5. Test the code before you enter it in the Visual Basic Editor, by stepping through the instructions one at a time yourself. As you do so, think about how the procedure affects the worksheet. This process is called **desk checking**, and it is an important part of the development process.

BTW
Printing VBA Code
Some people find it easier to review and edit code by working with a printout. To print out VBA code while using the Visual Basic Editor, tap or click File on the menu bar and then tap or click Print on the File menu.

Should you document your code?
Yes. Use comments to document each procedure. This will help you remember its purpose at a later date or help somebody else understand its purpose. In Table 10–5, the first five lines are comments. **Comments** begin with the word Rem (short for Remark) or an apostrophe ('). Comments have no effect on the execution of a procedure; they simply provide information about the procedure, such as name, creation date, and function. Comments can be placed at the beginning before the Sub statement, in between lines of code, or at the end of a line of code, as long as each comment begins with an apostrophe ('). It is good practice to place comments containing overall documentation and information at the beginning, before the Sub statement.

CONSIDER THIS

To Enter the Command Button
Procedures Using the Visual Basic Editor

1 SET PROTECTION & SECURITY | 2 WRITE MACROS | 3 CREATE DATA FORM | 4 DESIGN USER INTERFACE
5 SET CONTROL PROPERTIES | 6 WRITE VISUAL BASIC CODE | **7 TEST USER INTERFACE**

Why use the Visual Basic Editor? To enter a procedure, you use the Visual Basic Editor. To activate the Visual Basic Editor, Excel must be in Design mode. To activate the Visual Basic Editor, tap or click the Design Mode button (DEVELOPER tab | Controls group) to switch Excel to Design mode, select a control, and then tap or click the View Code button (DEVELOPER tab | Controls group).

The Visual Basic Editor is a full-screen editor, which allows you to enter a procedure by typing the lines of VBA code as if you were using word processing software. At the end of each line, you press the ENTER key or use the DOWN ARROW key to move to the next line. If you make a mistake in a statement, you can use the arrow keys and the DELETE or BACKSPACE key to correct it. You also can move the insertion point to previous lines to make corrections.

The following steps activate the Visual Basic Editor and create the procedure for the Step 1 button.

1
- With the Step 1 button selected and Excel in Design mode, tap or click the View Code button (DEVELOPER tab | Controls group) to display the Microsoft Visual Basic Editor.

Q&A Do I need to maximize the Microsoft Visual Basic Editor window?
Yes. If necessary, double-tap or double-click the title bar to maximize the Visual Basic Editor window.

- Tap or click the Object arrow at the top of the window and then tap or click CommandButton1 in the Alphabetical list.

- Enter the VBA code shown in Table 10–5 (Figure 10–71).

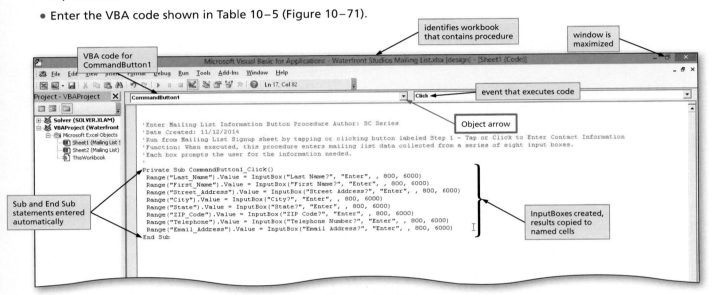

Figure 10–71

Table 10–5 Enter Mailing List Information Button Procedure	
Line	Statement
1	' Enter Mailing List Information Button Procedure Author: SC Series
2	' Date Created: 11/12/2014
3	' Run from: Mailing List Signup sheet by tapping or clicking button labeled Step 1 — Tap or Click to Enter Contact Information
4	' Function: When executed, this procedure enters contact information for mailing list.
5	'
6	Private Sub CommandButton1_Click()
7	Range("Last_Name").Value = InputBox("Last Name?", "Enter", , 800, 6000)
8	Range("First_Name").Value = InputBox("First Name?", "Enter", , 800, 6000)
9	Range("Street_Address").Value = InputBox("Street Address?", "Enter", , 800, 6000)
10	Range("City").Value = InputBox("City?", "Enter", , 800, 6000)
11	Range("State").Value = InputBox("State?", "Enter", , 800, 6000)
12	Range("ZIP_Code").Value = InputBox("Zip Code?", "Enter", , 800, 6000)
13	Range("Telephone").Value = InputBox("Telephone number?", "Enter", , 800, 6000)
14	Range("Email_Address").Value = InputBox("Email Address?", "Enter", , 800, 6000)
15	End Sub

2

• Repeat Step 1 for the Step 3 button (CommandButton2) using the VBA code shown in Table 10–6 (Figure 10–72). If requested by your instructor, enter your place of birth following the entry on Line 2 in Table 10–6.

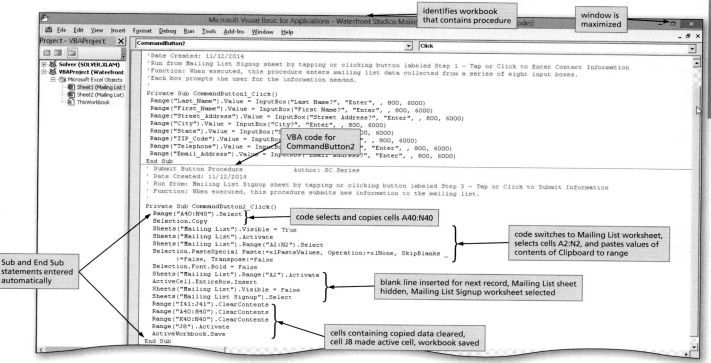

Figure 10–72

Table 10–6 Submit Button Procedure

Line	Statement
1	' Submit Button Procedure Author: SC Series
2	' Date Created: 11/12/2014
3	' Run from: Mailing List Signup sheet by tapping or clicking button labeled Step 3 — Tap or Click to Submit Information.
4	' Function: When executed, this procedure submits new information to the mailing list.
5	'
6	Private Sub CommandButton2_Click()
7	Range("A40:O40").Select
8	Selection.Copy
9	Sheets("Mailing List").Visible = True
10	Sheets("Mailing List").Activate
11	Sheets("Mailing List").Range("A2:N2").Select
12	Selection.PasteSpecial Paste:=xlPasteValues, Operation:=xlNone, SkipBlanks _
13	:=False, Transpose:=False, Selection.Font.Bold = False
14	Sheets("Mailing List").Range("A2").Activate
15	ActiveCell.EntireRow.Insert
16	Sheets("Mailing List").Visible = False
17	Sheets("Mailing List Signup").Select
18	Range("I41:J41").ClearContents
19	Range("A40:H40").ClearContents
20	Range("K40:N40").ClearContents
21	Range("J8").Activate
22	ActiveWorkbook.Save
23	End Sub

To Remove the Outline from the Group Control

Why? *Removing the outline from the group control will result in a more visually pleasing user interface.* Removing the outline requires a line of VBA code. You will enter this in the Immediate window in the VBE. The Immediate window often is used for debugging and executing statements during design. As its name suggests, code entered in this window is executed immediately upon exiting the VBE. The following step removes the outline from the group control.

- If necessary, switch to the Visual Basic Editor.

- Press CTRL+G to open the Immediate window.

- Type **activesheet. groupboxes. visible = false** and then press the ENTER key to remove the box from around the group control (Figure 10–73).

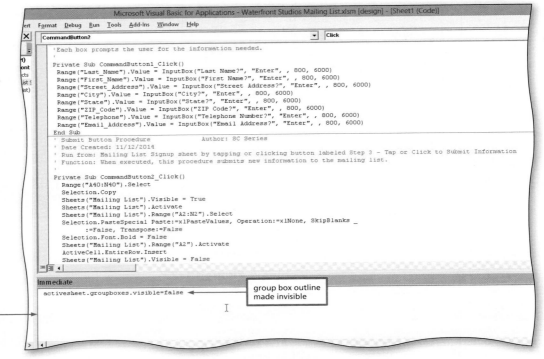

Figure 10–73

To Prepare and Protect the Worksheet and Save the Workbook

Why? *You are removing the ribbon from view and protecting the worksheet to restrict what the user can do in this worksheet.* The VBA code is complete. Before closing the Visual Basic Editor, you should verify your code by comparing it again with the content of Tables 10–5 and 10–6 on pages EX 666–667. The following steps close the Visual Basic Editor window, exit Design mode, prepare and protect the worksheet, and save the workbook.

- Close the Visual Basic Editor window.

- If necessary, when the Excel window is visible, tap or click the Design Mode button (DEVELOPER tab | Controls group) to exit Design mode.

- Tap or click FILE on the ribbon to open the Backstage view.

- Tap or click Options to display the Excel Options dialog box.

- Tap or click Advanced in the left pane (Excel Options dialog box) to display the advanced options.

- Scroll to the Display options for this worksheet area in the right pane and then, if necessary, tap or click the 'Show page breaks' and 'Show a zero in cells that have zero value' check boxes to remove the check marks (Figure 10–74).

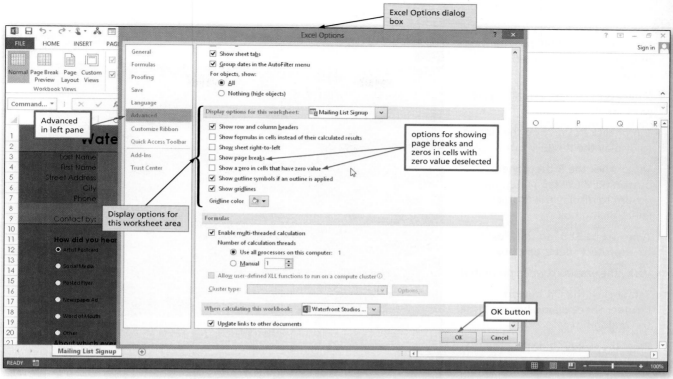

Figure 10-74

2

• Tap or click the OK button to close the dialog box.

• Tap or click VIEW on the ribbon to display the VIEW tab.

• Tap or click the View Gridlines, Formula Bar, and Headings check boxes (VIEW tab | Show group) to remove the check marks (Figure 10–75).

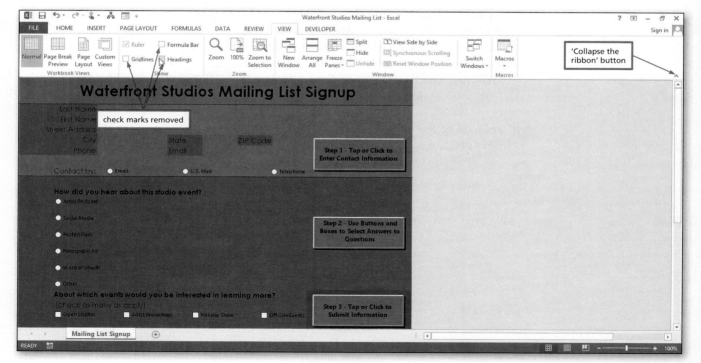

Figure 10-75

- Tap or click the 'Collapse the ribbon' button on the ribbon to collapse the ribbon.

- If necessary, hide the Mailing List worksheet.

- Tap or click REVIEW on the ribbon to display the REVIEW tab.

- Tap or click the Protect Sheet button (REVIEW tab | Changes group) to display the Protect Sheet dialog box.

- Type **Art15t5** in the 'Password to unprotect sheet' text box.

- Verify the password when prompted.

- Tap or click the OK button (Protect Sheet dialog box) to close the dialog box.

- Press the F5 key to display the Go To dialog box.

- Enter **J8** and then press the ENTER key to make cell J8 the active cell.

- Tap or click the Save button on the Quick Access Toolbar to save the workbook (Figure 10–76).

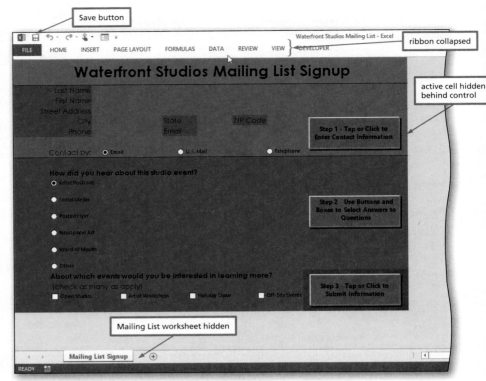

Figure 10–76

To Test the Controls in the New Member Signup Sheet

The final step is to test the controls in the Mailing List Signup sheet. The following steps test the controls using the following test data:

Canton, James, 24 Maple Avenue, Dilton, NH, 03324, 555-555-1212, jcanton@scseries.com, Telephone, Social Media, Holiday Show.

Alvarez, Amelia, 50 Fourth Street, Providence, RI, 02906, 555-555-1313, aalvarez@scseries.com, Email, Artist Postcard, Open Studios, Off-Site Events.

1 For each of the records above, using the command buttons, enter the data, following prompts, and submit the data.

2 Unhide the Mailing List sheet, and confirm that the records copied correctly (Figure 10–77).

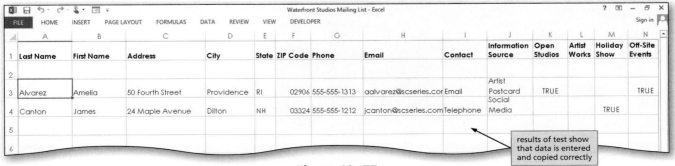

Figure 10–77

3 Hide the Mailing List sheet again.

4 Save the file.

To Reset the Quick Access Toolbar and Ribbon and Exit Excel

The following steps reset the Quick Access Toolbar in order to remove the FirstName button; remove the DEVELOPER tab from the ribbon; restore the ribbon, headings, and formula bar; and exit Excel.

1 Press and hold or right-click anywhere on the Quick Access Toolbar and then tap or click Customize Quick Access Toolbar on the shortcut menu.

2 When the Excel Options dialog box is displayed, tap or click the Reset button and then tap or click 'Reset all customizations' on the Reset menu. Tap or click the Yes button in the Microsoft Office dialog box and then tap or click the OK button to close the Excel Options dialog box.

3 Tap or click the 'Ribbon Display Options' button (shown in Figure 10–77) and then tap or click 'Show Tabs and Commands' on the Ribbon Display Options menu to reset the ribbon.

4 Tap or click the Formula Bar and Headings check boxes (VIEW tab | Show group) to show row and column headings and the formula bar.

5 Tap or click the Close button on the right side of the title bar.

6 If the Microsoft Excel dialog box is displayed, tap or click the Don't Save button.

BTW

Q&As

For a complete list of the Q&As found in many of the step-by-step sequences in this book, visit the Q&A resource on the Student Companion Site located on www.cengagebrain.com. For detailed instructions about accessing available resources, visit www.cengage.com /ct/studentdownload or contact your instructor for information about accessing the required files.

Digital Signatures

Some users prefer to attach a digital signature to verify the authenticity of a document. A **digital signature** is an electronic, encrypted, and secure stamp of authentication on a document. This signature confirms that the file originated from the signer (file developer) and that it has not been altered.

A digital signature may be visible or invisible. In either case, the digital signature references a digital certificate. A **digital certificate** is an attachment to a file or email message that vouches for its authenticity, provides secure encryption, or supplies a verifiable signature. Many users who receive files enable the macros based on whether they are digitally signed by a developer on the user's list of trusted sources.

You can obtain a digital certificate from a commercial **certificate authority**, from your network administrator, or you can create a digital signature yourself. A digital certificate you create yourself is not issued by a formal certification authority. Thus, signed macros using such a certificate are referred to as **self-signed projects**. Certificates you create yourself are considered unauthenticated and still will generate a warning when opened if the security level is set to very high, high, or medium. Many users, however, consider self-signed projects safer to open than those with no certificates at all.

To Add a Signature Box and Digital Signature to a Workbook

After adding a digital signature, Excel will display the digital signature whenever the document is opened. If you wanted to add a digital signature to an Excel workbook, you would perform the following steps.

1. Open the Waterfront Studios Mailing List workbook and then unprotect the worksheet using the password of Art15t5.

2. Tap or click the INSERT tab on the ribbon and then tap or click the 'Add a Signature Line' button in the Text group. If a Microsoft Excel dialog box appears, tap or click the OK button.

3. When the Signature Setup dialog box appears, type your name in the Suggested signer text box and then tap or click the OK button to add the signature box to the workbook (Figure 10–78).

4. When Excel adds the signature box to the workbook, press and hold or right-click anywhere in the signature box and then tap or click Sign on the shortcut menu. If you have a digital ID in place, proceed to Step 5. If you do not have a digital ID in place, tap or click the OK button to get a digital ID and then proceed with Step 5.

5. When the Sign dialog box appears, type your name in the signature box or tap or click the Select Image link to select a file that contains an image of your signature.

6. Tap or click the Sign button (Sign dialog box) to digitally sign the document.

Figure 10–78

If you do not have any digital certificates on your computer when you tap or click the Sign command in Step 4, you will be prompted in the Microsoft Excel dialog box to obtain or create a new digital certificate. You can choose to create a certificate online with a service provider recommended by Microsoft by tapping or clicking the 'Signature Services from the Office Marketplace' button. By doing so, other users can authenticate the signature on your workbooks because the certificate is available online. This alternative, however, may require payment.

TO REVIEW A DIGITAL SIGNATURE ON A WORKBOOK

A **file digital signature** is a digital signature that is displayed when you email a document from Excel. Excel will display the digital signature whenever the document is opened. When you open a digitally signed document, Excel displays a message announcing the signature on the status bar while the file opens. After the file is opened, Excel displays a certification icon on the status bar. You can tap or click the icon to find out who digitally signed the document. The word, (Signed), also appears on the title bar in parentheses, indicating the document is signed digitally. If you wanted to review a digital signature on an Excel workbook, you would perform the following steps.

1. Tap or click the FILE tab on the ribbon to open the Backstage view. If necessary, tap or click the Info tab and then tap or click View Signatures to open the Signatures task pane.

BTW
Quick Reference
For a table that lists how to complete the tasks covered in this book using touch gestures, the mouse, ribbon, shortcut menu, and keyboard, see the Quick Reference Summary at the back of this book, or visit the Quick Reference resource on the Student Companion Site located on www.cengagebrain.com. For detailed instructions about accessing available resources, visit www.cengage.com /ct/studentdownload or contact your instructor for information about accessing the required files.

2. Select a name from the Valid signature list in the Signature task pane and then tap or click the button arrow next to the name. When the shortcut menu appears, tap or click Signature Details.

3. When you are finished reviewing the certificate, tap or click the Close button in the Signature Details dialog box and then close the workbook without saving it.

Chapter Summary

In this chapter, you learned how to unprotect and protect a worksheet and workbook using a password. In Phase 1, you learned how to record a macro and assign it to a button on the Quick Access Toolbar. You also learned how to create a data form from column headings and use it to enter data. In Phase 2, you learned how to create a user interface made up of command button controls, check box controls, and option button controls; set properties for those controls using the Properties window; write VBA code for the controls; and add and review a digital signature on a workbook. The items listed below include all the new Excel skills you have learned in this chapter, with the tasks grouped by activity.

Set Protection and Security
Set the Macro Security Level to Medium (EX 635)
Unprotect a Password-Protected Worksheet (EX 623)
Add a Signature Box to a Workbook (EX 671)
Add a Digital Signature to a Workbook (EX 671)
Review a Digital Signature on a Workbook (EX 672)

Write Macros
Add a Button to the Quick Access Toolbar, Assign the Button a Macro, and Use the Button (EX 639)
Convert Names to Proper Case and Add Extra Columns (EX 627)
Display the DEVELOPER tab, Enable Macros, and Save a Workbook as a Macro-Enabled Workbook (EX 625)
Open a Workbook with Macros and Execute a Macro (EX 636)
Record a Macro to Reformat the Artist Data Where First Name Appears First (EX 629)
View and Print a Macro's VBA Code (EX 638)

Create the Data Form
Use a Data Form to Enter Additional Records (EX 643)

Design the User Interface
Add a Command Button Control to the Worksheet (EX 652)
Add Form Controls to a Worksheet (EX 648)
Group Option Buttons in a User Interface (EX 651)

Set the Control Properties
Format the Command Button and Text Box Controls (EX 659)
Format the Option Button Controls for Contact Method (EX 654)
Record User Input for Contact Method to Another Location on the Worksheet (EX 662)

Write the Visual Basic Code
Enter the Command Button Procedures Using the Visual Basic Editor (EX 665)
Remove the Outline from the Group Control (EX 668)

What decisions will you need to make when using macros and/or controls in a worksheet?

Use these guidelines as you complete the assignments in this chapter and create your own worksheets for evaluating and analyzing data outside of this class.

1. Set security and protection for the workbook. Workbooks containing macros or controls must be macro-enabled.

2. Determine the actions you want to automate, and create a macro. The steps and their order should be determined and rehearsed before creating the macro.

3. Create a data form. If you will be adding records to a simple worksheet, consider creating a data form.

4. Design a user interface. Excel provides several types of controls, such as buttons, text boxes, and check boxes, which you can use in a user interface. Which controls you use for each task is determined by the type of data the control is used to enter.

5. Set control properties. The properties that you set give meaning and limitations to the user regarding the control's use.

6. Write the Visual Basic code. When a user interacts with a control, such as tapping or clicking a button, Visual Basic code that is associated with that action is executed.

7. Test the user interface. The final step in creating a user interface is to test it to prove that the interface behaves as designed and as a user expects.

CONSIDER THIS: PLAN AHEAD

CONSIDER THIS

How should you submit solutions to questions in the assignments identified with a ✳ symbol?
Every assignment in this book contains one or more questions identified with a ✳ symbol. These questions require you to think beyond the assigned file. Present your solutions to the questions in the format required by your instructor. Possible formats may include one or more of these options: write the answer; create a document that contains the answer; present your answer to the class; discuss your answer in a group; record the answer as audio or video using a webcam, smartphone, or portable media player; or post answers on a blog, wiki, or website.

Apply Your Knowledge

Reinforce the skills and apply the concepts you learned in this chapter.

Creating a Macro and Assigning It to a Button

Note: To complete this assignment, you will be required to use the Data Files for Students. Visit www.cengage.com/ct/studentdownload for detailed instructions or contact your instructor for information about accessing the required files.

Instructions: Run Excel. Open the workbook Apply 10 – 1 Avia Salon from the Data Files for Students and then save the workbook as an Excel Macro-Enabled Workbook file type using the file name, Apply 10 – 1 Avia Salon Complete.

In the following steps, you create a macro to add a column to a worksheet, assign the macro to a button on the Quick Access Toolbar, and then execute the macro. Figure 10 – 79 shows the completed worksheet.

Figure 10–79

Perform the following tasks:

1. If the DEVELOPER tab is not displayed on the ribbon, tap or click the FILE tab to open the Backstage view, tap or click Options in the left pane to display the Excel Options dialog box, tap or click Customize Ribbon, tap or click the Developer check box in the Customize the Ribbon area, and then tap or click the OK button.

2. Create a macro that adds a column before the Total column by doing the following:

   a. Tap or click the Record Macro button (DEVELOPER tab | Code group).

   b. When the Record Macro dialog box appears, name the macro, AddColumn, assign the keyboard shortcut CTRL+N, store the macro in this workbook, enter your name in the Description box, and then tap or click the OK button (Record Macro dialog box) to start the macro recording process.

   c. Select cell C3, tap or click the Insert Cells arrow (HOME tab | Cells group) and then tap or click the 'Insert Sheet Columns' button from the Insert Cells menu.

   d. Select cell C6, sum the cell range C4:C5, set the column width to 15, and then tap or click the Stop Recording button (DEVELOPER tab | Code group).

3. In the newly added column, enter **Nail Services** in cell C3, **12060** in cell C4, and **7400** in cell C5.

4. Tap or click the View Macros button (DEVELOPER tab | Code group) to display the Macro dialog box. Run the AddColumn macro to add a column. Enter the following data: **Makeup Services, 8400,** and **2740.** Tap or click the View Macros button (DEVELOPER tab | Code group) again, select the AddColumn macro (Macro dialog box), and then tap or click the Edit button (Macro dialog box). When the Visual Basic Editor displays the macro, tap or click File on the menu bar and then tap or click Print on the File menu. Click OK in the Print – VBA Project dialog box, and then close the VBA window.

5. Press and hold or right-click anywhere on the Quick Access Toolbar and then tap or click 'Customize Quick Access Toolbar' on the shortcut menu. When the Excel Options dialog box is displayed, tap or click the 'Choose commands from' arrow and tap or click Macros. Tap or click AddColumn, tap or click the Add button, and then tap or click the OK button to close the Excel Options dialog box.

6. Run the macro as follows:

   a. Tap or click the AddColumn button on the Quick Access Toolbar and then enter **Facial Services, 22455,** and **10235** for the column values.

   b. Press CTRL+SHIFT+N and then enter **Other Aesthetics, 14,115,** and **7,500** for the column values.

7. Protect the worksheet using the password, b3au!y.

8. If requested by your instructor, add the following text to the end of the text in cell A1: **(EST. <year of birth>),** replacing <year of birth> with your year of birth.

9. Press and hold or right-click the AddColumn button on the Quick Access Toolbar and then tap or click 'Remove from Quick Access Toolbar' on the shortcut menu.

10. Save the workbook. Submit the revised workbook in the format specified by your instructor.

11. ✸ How would using the 'Use Relative References' button when recording your macro change how you insert columns using the AddColumn macro?

Extend Your Knowledge

Extend the skills you learned in this chapter and experiment with new skills. You may need to use Help to complete the assignment.

Creating and Using a Start-Up Macro

Note: To complete this assignment, you will be required to use the Data Files for Students. Visit www.cengage.com/ct/studentdownload for detailed instructions or contact your instructor for information about accessing the required files.

Instructions: Run Excel. Open the workbook Extend 10-1 Northborough Hockey (Figure 10–80) from the Data Files for Students. You will create a macro that runs when the workbook is opened. The macro sorts the top scorers by last name, and first name, and then formats goals scored greater than 30.

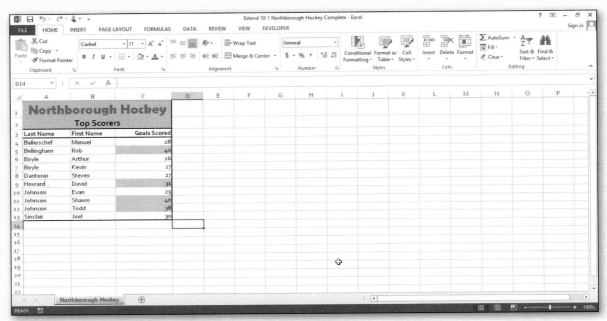

Figure 10–80

Perform the following tasks:

1. Save the workbook as an Excel Macro-Enabled Workbook file type using the file name, Extend 10-1 Northborough Hockey Complete. If the DEVELOPER tab is not displayed on the ribbon, tap or click the FILE tab, tap or click Options in the left pane, tap or click Customize Ribbon, tap or click the Developer check box in the Customize the Ribbon area, and then tap or click the OK button (Excel Options dialog box).

2. Create a macro that sorts the players by last name and first name and highlights goals scored greater than 30 by doing the following:

   a. Use Help to determine the name to give a macro so that it will run automatically when this workbook is opened.

   b. Run the Macro Recorder, use the name you found in Help as your macro name, store the macro in this workbook, enter your name in the Description box, and then tap or click the OK button (Record Macro dialog box) to start the macro recording process.

c. Select cell range A4:C13, sort by Last Name and then by First Name, select cell range C4:C13, apply conditional formatting to highlight cells with goals scored greater than 30 with a light red fill, select a cell outside the range A1:C13, and then stop the macro recorder.

3. Undo the changes to the workbook to return it to unsorted, unhighlighted columns. Save the workbook. Close the workbook.

4. Open the Extend 10-1 Northborough Hockey Complete workbook. If necessary, enable content so that the macro runs. Save the workbook.

5. Print both the worksheet and VBA code. Print the formulas version of the worksheet.

6. If requested by your instructor, edit the macro to include the name of the high school you attended in 10th grade in the description of the macro. You should edit it in the Visual Basic Editor.

7. Save the workbook and submit the revised workbook as specified by your instructor.

8. ✳ You can set a macro in Excel to run when a particular workbook is opened or when Excel is run. Suggest an example of the latter that you would consider setting up on your own computer.

Analyze, Correct, Improve

Analyze a workbook, correct all errors, and improve it.

Changing Properties and Correcting Visual Basic Code

Note: To complete this assignment, you will be required to use the Data Files for Students. Visit www.cengage.com/ct/studentdownload for detailed instructions or contact your instructor for information about accessing the required files.

Instructions: Run Excel. Open the workbook Analyze 10-1 Loan Calculator. Enable the content by tapping or clicking the Enable Content button on the SECURITY WARNING bar and then save it with the file name, Analyze 10-1 Loan Calculator Complete. The workbook is used to calculate different savings outcomes. Figure 10–81a shows the final desired form of the calculator, and Figure 10–81b shows the underlying Visual Basic code that contains errors.

Correct the following problems with properties and Visual Basic code to achieve the results shown in Figure 10–81.

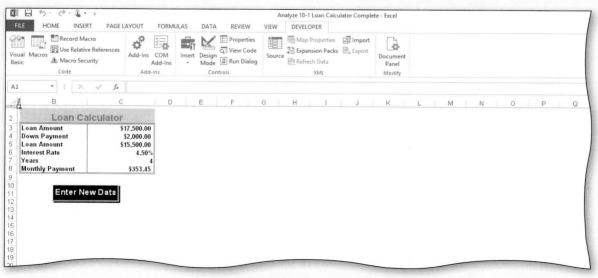

(a) Finished Loan Calculator

Figure 10–81

Continued >

Analyze, Correct, Improve *continued*

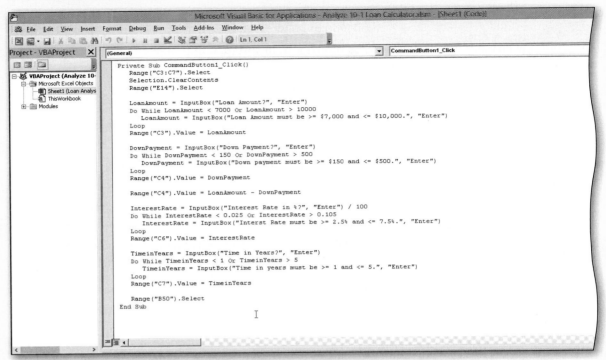

```
Private Sub CommandButton1_Click()
    Range("C3:C7").Select
    Selection.ClearContents
    Range("E14").Select

    LoanAmount = InputBox("Loan Amount?", "Enter")
    Do While LoanAmount < 7000 Or LoanAmount > 10000
        LoanAmount = InputBox("Loan Amount must be >= $7,000 and <= $10,000.", "Enter")
    Loop
    Range("C3").Value = LoanAmount

    DownPayment = InputBox("Down Payment?", "Enter")
    Do While DownPayment < 150 Or DownPayment > 500
        DownPayment = InputBox("Down payment must be >= $150 and <= $500.", "Enter")
    Loop
    Range("C4").Value = DownPayment

    Range("C4").Value = LoanAmount - DownPayment

    InterestRate = InputBox("Interest Rate in %?", "Enter") / 100
    Do While InterestRate < 0.025 Or InterestRate > 0.105
        InterestRate = InputBox("Interst Rate must be >= 2.5% and <= 7.5%.", "Enter")
    Loop
    Range("C6").Value = InterestRate

    TimeinYears = InputBox("Time in Years?", "Enter")
    Do While TimeinYears < 1 Or TimeinYears > 5
        TimeinYears = InputBox("Time in years must be >= 1 and <= 5.", "Enter")
    Loop
    Range("C7").Value = TimeinYears

    Range("B50").Select
End Sub
```

(b) Code with Errors

Figure 10–81

1. Correct

a. If the DEVELOPER tab is not displayed on the ribbon, tap or click the FILE tab to open the Backstage view, tap or click Options in the left pane, tap or click Customize Ribbon in the left pane (Excel Options dialog box), tap or click the Developer check box in the Main Tabs list, and then tap or click the OK button.

b. Add a caption on the command button to match the caption in Figure 10–81a.

c. Move the command button to the location shown in Figure 10–81a.

d. Turn off the gridline display in the worksheet.

e. Open the Visual Basic Editor to view the code associated with CommandButton1.

f. Check the cell references in the code for the input boxes. (*Hint:* Look at the Range statements.) Make corrections as necessary so that input supplied by the user in an input box is entered into the correct cell in the calculator.

g. Correct the code to prompt for the following ranges in the input boxes: Loan Amount between $7,000 and $18,000, Down Payment between $1,500 and $5,000, Interest Rate between 2.5 and 7.5, and Time in Years between 2 and 5 years.

h. Correct the code to select cell C15 before exiting the procedure.

2. Improve

a. Tap or click the View Code button (DEVELOPER tab | Controls group). Add comments before the first line of code. Include a procedure title, your name, date, and the purpose of the procedure.

b. Add comments to explain what is happening before each input in the code. The comment should identify the input box and add any other information you feel would be helpful for documenting the code.

c. If requested by your instructor, change the sheet tab to include your mother's maiden name prior to the text, Loan Analysis.

d. Enter Design mode and change the command button properties to reflect the image in Figure 10-81a. Shadow should be True, BackColor should be black, and ForeColor should be white.

e. Exit Design mode. Tap or click the 'Enter New Data' button and enter the following loan data: Loan Amount = $17,500; Down Payment = $2,000; Interest Rate = 4.5; Years = 4. The monthly payment in cell C8 should equal $353.45. Enter additional data that tests the limits of acceptable loan data.

f. Disable macros using the Macro Security button (DEVELOPER tab | Code group).

g. Print both the worksheet and Visual Basic code.

h. Save the workbook. Submit the revised document in the format specified by your instructor.

3. ❁ How might you change the content of the input boxes to better direct the user?

In the Labs

Design and/or create a workbook using the guidelines, concepts, and skills presented in this chapter. Labs 1 and 2, which increase in difficulty, require you to create solutions based on what you learned in the chapter; Lab 3 requires you to create a solution, which uses cloud and web technologies, by learning and investigating on your own from general guidance.

Lab 1: **Automating a Savings Calculator**

Note: To complete this assignment, you will be required to use the Data Files for Students. Visit www.cengage.com/ct/studentdownload for detailed instructions or contact your instructor for information about accessing the required files.

Problem: Community Credit advises customers how to reach various financial goals, including savings goals. The savings calculator shows how much money can be saved during a 12-month time period, given a monthly deposit amount, an initial deposit, and an interest rate. You have been asked to automate the entry of savings data into the calculator.

Part 1 Instructions: Perform the following tasks:

1. Run Excel. If the DEVELOPER tab is not displayed on the ribbon, tap or click the FILE tab to open the Backstage view, tap or click Options in the left pane, tap or click Customize Ribbon in the left pane (Excel Options dialog box), tap or click the Developer check box in the Customize the Ribbon area, and then tap or click the OK button.

2. To enable macros, tap or click the Macro Security button (DEVELOPER tab | Code group). When the Trust Center dialog box is displayed, tap or click 'Enable all macros' and then tap or click the OK button.

3. Open the Lab 10-1 Community Credit workbook from the Data Files for Students and then save the workbook as an Excel Macro-Enabled Workbook file type using the file name, Lab 10-1 Part 1 Community Credit Complete.

4. Tap or click the Insert Controls button (DEVELOPER tab | Controls group) and then tap or click Command Button in the ActiveX Controls area. Draw the button in row 20, as shown in Figure 10–82a.

Continued >

In the Labs *continued*

5. With the command button control selected, tap or click the Properties button (Developer tab | Controls group). Change the following properties: (a) Caption = Enter Savings Data; (b) Font = Lucida Sans, 9 pt.; (c) PrintObject = False; and (d) WordWrap = True. Close the Properties window.

6. With the command button control selected, press and hold or right-click the button and select View Code. Enter the procedure shown in Figure 10–82b. Check your code carefully.

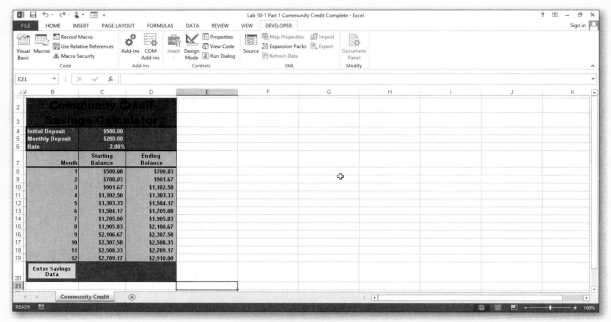

(a) Savings Calculator

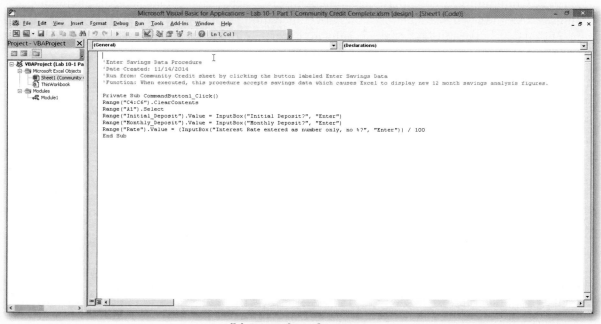

(b) Procedure for Entry

Figure 10–82

7. Close the Visual Basic Editor window. Tap or click the Design Mode button (DEVELOPER tab | Controls group) to exit Design mode.

8. If requested by your instructor, change the sheet tab to include your month and day of birth following the text, Community Credit.

9. Use the newly created button to display the savings analysis for the following data and then print the worksheet for each data set: (a) Initial Deposit = $2,500; Monthly Deposit = $150; Rate = 2.5%; (b) Initial Deposit = $500; Monthly Deposit = $200; Rate = 2.0%.

10. Print the worksheet and then print the Visual Basic code.

11. To disable macros, tap or click the Macro Security button (DEVELOPER tab | Code group). When the Trust Center dialog box is displayed, tap or click 'Disable all macros with notification' and then tap or click the OK button.

12. Protect the worksheet using the password, Community.

13. Save the workbook. Submit the revised document in the format specified by your instructor.

Part 2 Instructions: Perform the following tasks to add a macro to the workbook and add a button to the Quick Access Toolbar that executes the macro:

1. Run Excel. Open the workbook Lab 10-1 Part 1 Community Credit Complete and then save the workbook as an Excel Macro-Enabled Workbook file type using the file name, Lab 10-1 Part 2 Community Credit Complete.

2. Unprotect the worksheet using the password, Community.

3. Tap or click the Insert Controls button (DEVELOPER tab | Controls group) and then tap or click Button (column 1, row 1) in the Form Controls area. Draw a button beside the Enter Data button, as shown in Figure 10–83 on the next page. If the Assign Macro dialog box opens, tap or click Cancel to close it.

4. Press and hold or right-click the new button and select Edit Text from the shortcut menu. Change the button text to, Copy Results. Change the font to Lucida Sans, 9 pt. Bold the text. (*Hint:* You will need to select the text and use the Bold button on the HOME tab.)

5. Enter Design mode and then select both command buttons. On the DRAWING TOOLS FORMAT tab, set the height to 0.4", the width to 1.2" and top-align the buttons.

6. Exit Design mode.

7. Create a macro that copies the savings calculator values to a new worksheet by doing the following:

   a. Tap or click the Record Macro button (DEVELOPER tab | Code group). When the Record Macro dialog box is displayed, name the macro, CopyResults; assign the shortcut key CTRL+SHIFT+V; add your name in the Description box; and store the macro in this workbook. Tap or click the OK button (Record Macro dialog box) to start the macro recording process.

   b. Copy the cell range A4:D19, insert a new worksheet, and paste the values and source formatting to the cell range A4:D19. With the cells on the new sheet still selected, use the 'Keep Source Column Widths (W)' button in the Paste gallery to keep the column widths on the new sheet the same widths as those on the source sheet. Tap or click the Stop Recording button (DEVELOPER tab | Code group).

8. Make the Community Credit worksheet the active sheet and then press the ESC key to remove the marquee. Assign the macro CopyResults to the Copy Results button.

Continued >

In the Labs *continued*

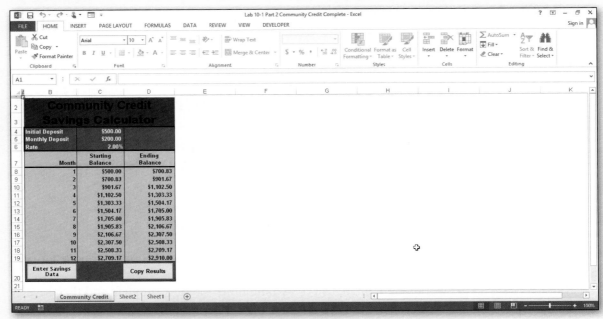

Figure 10–83

9. Test the Copy Results button. Print the created worksheet.

10. To disable macros, tap or click the Macro Security button (DEVELOPER tab | Code group). When the Trust Center dialog box is displayed, tap or click 'Disable all macros with notification' and then tap or click the OK button.

11. Protect the worksheet using the password, Community.

12. Save the workbook. Submit the revised document in the format specified by your instructor.

13. ✹ What might you add to the CopyResults macro to make the use of the workbook more straightforward for an inexperienced Excel user?

Lab 2: **Automating a Projected Income Workbook**

Note: To complete this assignment, you will be required to use the Data Files for Students. Visit www.cengage.com/ct/studentdownload for detailed instructions or contact your instructor for information about accessing the required files.

Problem: You have been asked to complete the task of automating the Projected Income Statement workbook, as shown in Figure 10–84. You need to finish setting up a user interface to automate the data entry in cells D4 (Units Sold), D5 (Price per Unit), D14 (Material Cost per Unit), and D16 (Manufacturing Cost per Unit). All other cells in the worksheet use formulas. This automation is partially completed. You will utilize the completed content, Excel Help, and the following instructions to complete the project.

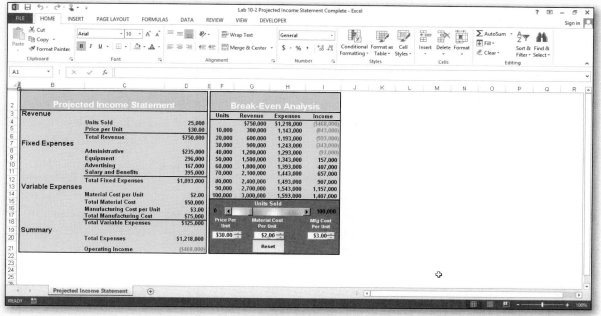

Figure 10–84

Instructions:

1. Open the workbook Lab 10-2 Projected Income Statement on the Data Files for Students and then save the workbook with the file name, Lab 10-2 Projected Income Statement Complete.

2. Unprotect the worksheet using the password, Break3v3n.

3. If the DEVELOPER tab is not displayed on the ribbon, tap or click the FILE tab to open the Backstage view, tap or click Options in the left pane, tap or click Customize Ribbon in the left pane (Excel Options dialog box), tap or click the Developer check box in the Customize the Ribbon area, and then tap or click the OK button.

4. To enable macros, tap or click the Macro Security button (DEVELOPER tab | Code group) and when the Trust Center dialog box is displayed, tap or click 'Enable all macros' and then tap or click the OK button.

5. Tap or click the Name Manager button (FORMULAS tab | Defined Names group) and then review the named cells. You will make use of some of these names later in the exercise.

6. The worksheet contains three spin button controls, which will be used to enter in Price per Unit, Material Cost per Unit, and Manufacturing Cost per Unit. Each of these three spin button controls have two labels associated with the spin button control. One, which appears above the spin button control, identifies the control. The second, which appears to the left of the spin control, shows the current value of the item of interest. One of these spin controls, for Price per Unit, has been fully set up. Enter Design mode and then view the properties for this spin control and the two associated labels. All the set properties also are identified in Table 10–7. Based on your review and the information in Table 10–7, set the properties for the remaining spin controls and their associated labels.

Continued >

In the Labs *continued*

7. The worksheet contains a scroll bar control, which will be used to enter Units Sold. This control has three labels associated with it, one which identifies the control, and two which indicate the minimum and maximum values for Units Sold. The code is already in the workbook, but the properties have not been set. Set the properties for this control and the three labels according to the values in Table 10–7. Save the workbook.

8. Use formatting tools to adjust the size and alignment of the controls to reflect the layout in Figure 10–84. Remember that you can select multiple controls at once using the CTRL key, and apply certain formats to multiple controls at the same time.

9. Open the Visual Basic editor window and review the code that has been entered so far for this workbook. Review the code for setting up the Price per Unit spin control and associated labels. Notice how the named cell, Price_per_Unit, is assigned the value set using the spin control named spnPrice. Follow the same logic and use the control names in Table 10–7 to complete the code for the Material Cost per Unit and Manufacturing Cost per Unit spin controls and associated labels, and the Units Sold scroll bar and associated labels. Make use of comments to document your work. The Price per Unit spin button assigns a value to cell D5. The Material Cost per Unit spin button should assign a value to cell D14. The Mfg Cost per Unit spin button should assign a value to cell D16.

10. Enter the Reset Button procedure, which sets the Units Sold scroll bar (scrUnitsSold) to 25000, the Price per Unit spin button (spnPrice) to 3000, the Material Cost per Unit spin button (spnMaterialCost) to 200, and the Mfg Cost per Unit spin button (spnMfgCost) to 300. It should select cell A1 as its last action. This procedure has been started, but needs to be completed.

11. Close the Visual Basic Editor window. Tap or click the Design Mode button (DEVELOPER tab | Controls group) to exit Design mode.

12. Protect the worksheet using the password, Break3v3n.

13. Use the newly designed user interface to determine the operating income for the following projections and then print the worksheet for each data set: (a) Units Sold = 75,000; Price per Unit = $25.00; Material Cost per Unit = $2.50; and Manufacturing Cost per Unit = $3.70; (b) Units Sold = 34,000; Price per Unit = $42.00; Material Cost per Unit = $13.50; and Manufacturing Cost per Unit = $8.30. The Operating Income in cell D21 for (a) is $317,000 and for (b) is ($406,200).

14. Print the worksheet. Print the procedure. Save the workbook.

15. To disable macros, tap or click the Macro Security button on the DEVELOPER tab on the ribbon. When the Trust Center dialog box is displayed, tap or click 'Disable all macros with notification' and then tap or click the OK button.

16. Save the workbook. Submit the revised document in the format specified by your instructor.

17. ✸ How might you change the properties of the spin button controls and the scroll bar controls to make them more efficient?

Table 10–7 Controls and Properties

Control	Name	Caption	Font	Text Align	Word Wrap	Special Effect	Max	Min	Small Chg/ Large Chg	Back Color
0 Label		0	White, 10-point bold	Center						Gray
Units Sold Label		Units Sold	White, 10-point bold	Center						Gray
100,000 Label		100,000	White, 10-point bold	Center						Gray
Units Sold Scroll Bar	scrUnitsSold						100000	0	100/1000	
Price per Unit Label		Price per Unit	White, 8-point bold	Center	True					Gray
Price per Unit Spin Button	spnPrice						9999	0	10	
Price per Unit Spin Button Label	lblPrice	$30.00	10-point bold	Right		Sunken				
Material Cost per Unit Label		Material Cost per Unit	White, 8-point bold	Center	True					Gray
Material Cost per Unit Spin Button	spnMaterialCost						9999	0	10	
Material Cost per Unit Spin Button Label	lblMaterialCost	$2.00	10-point bold	Right		Sunken				
Mfg Cost per Unit Label		Mfg Cost per Unit	White, 8-point bold	Center	True					Gray
Mfg Cost per Unit Spin Button	spnMfgCost						9999	0	10	
Mfg Cost per Unit Spin Button Label	lblMfgCost	$3.00	10-point bold	Right		Sunken				
Reset Button	btnReset	Reset	Black, 8-point bold							Inactive Border

Lab 3: Expand Your World: Cloud and Web Technologies
Preparing Surveys

Problem: You have been asked to create a survey related to either education or employment to illustrate how to use controls in Excel to create a survey accessible to anyone with basic computer skills.

Instructions: Perform the following tasks:

1. Run a browser and navigate to http://www.surveymonkey.com. Search the site for an example of a survey in either education or employment that you can render using Excel controls. Surveymonkey.com has many survey templates that will be more than adequate for your needs. The survey that you select should contain at least 10 questions. Save the web address and print a copy of the survey.

Continued >

In the Labs *continued*

2. Run Excel and open a blank workbook. Using the skills you learned in this chapter, create a survey that includes the questions from the survey you found on SurveyMonkey.com. You should use more than one type of control in creating your survey.

3. Write either a macro or a procedure to collect the entered data each time the survey is completed and store it on a separate, hidden worksheet.

4. Use worksheet protection and formatting to set up your survey so that a user can answer questions but not gain access to the hidden worksheet or areas on the current worksheet outside of the survey. Make sure to document in your code how you accomplished this.

5. Save the file and submit it in the format specified by your instructor.

6. ✻ Did you use ActiveX controls, form controls, or a combination of both in your survey? For two of your controls, explain why you chose one type of control over the other and one benefit of using the other type of control.

✻ Consider This: Your Turn

Apply your creative thinking and problem solving skills to design and implement a solution.

1: Calculating Home Equity Loans

Personal

Part 1: You volunteer with a local community group that provides home owners with information about using the equity in their homes to finance home improvements. You have created a loan calculator, and would like to automate it for use by other volunteers. Open the workbook Consider 10-1 Home Equity Loan Calculator from the Data Files for Students and then save the workbook as an Excel Macro-Enabled Workbook file type using the file name, Consider 10-1 Home Equity Loan Calculator Complete. Add a Home Equity Loan button that prompts for and accepts the values in cells C3, C4, and C5. The procedure associated with the Home Equity Loan button on the worksheet should validate the loan amount, interest rate, and years as follows: (a) the loan amount must be between $15,000 and $80,000 inclusive; (b) the interest rate must be between 3.25% and 5.75% inclusive; and (c) the years must be between 3 and 20 inclusive. Print the procedure. Create and enter two sets of valid test data. Print the worksheet for each set. Save the workbook. Submit the assignment as requested by your instructor.

Part 2: ✻ How suitable is this format for the loan calculator? How could you meet the challenges associated with entering the interest rate in a format that is easy for the user?

2: Scenario Summaries

Professional

Part 1: You have been asked to generate a first draft of a five-question customer satisfaction survey. The five questions can be found in the Consider 10-2 Survey workbook on the Questions worksheet. Open the Consider 10-2 Survey workbook and save it as a macro-enabled workbook named Consider 10-2 Survey Complete. On a new worksheet, create a draft of a survey that would be done via phone, with the company surveyor entering the results in the Excel workbook. The surveyor should be able to use a button or command to record the results of each survey to a third worksheet. Use test data to make sure your survey worksheet is operational.

Part 2: ✻ If you had to restrict yourself to one type of control, which would it be, and why?

3: Automating Printing Tasks

Research and Collaboration

Part 1:   You work as part of a two-person team on a research project. Your roles are complementary, but very different. You both need to access and edit a single worksheet. You need to print out the formulas version of the worksheet in landscape orientation, while your teammate needs to print out the values version of the worksheet in portrait orientation, scaled to fit on one page. Create macros for each of these printing needs. Make sure that each macro resets the Page Setup options before terminating. Execute the macros. Print the worksheet and macros. Save the workbook. Submit the assignment as requested by your instructor.

Part 2:   ✹ What method would you use for accessing the macros? You can use keyboard shortcuts, buttons, or run the macros from the Macro dialog box. Explain why you selected a particular method.

Learn Online

Reinforce what you learned in this chapter with games, exercises, training, and many other online activities and resources.

Student Companion Site   Reinforcement activities and resources are available at no additional cost on www.cengagebrain.com. Visit www.cengage.com/ct/studentdownload for detailed instructions about accessing the resources available at the Student Companion Site.

SAM   Put your skills into practice with SAM! If you have a SAM account, go to www.cengage .com/sam2013 to access SAM assignments for this chapter.

11 | Collaboration Features for Workbooks

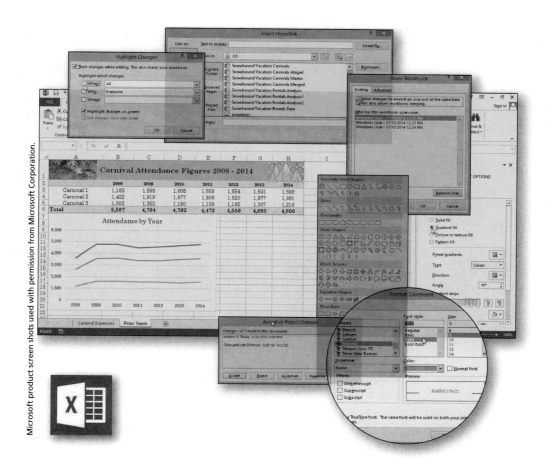

Microsoft product screen shots used with permission from Microsoft Corporation.

Objectives

You will have mastered the material in this chapter when you can:

- Explain sharing and collaboration techniques
- Insert, edit, and delete a comment
- Review all comments in a workbook
- Format a worksheet background
- Track changes and share a workbook
- Accept and reject tracked changes made to a workbook

- Turn off tracked changes
- Distribute a workbook through email
- Add and edit hyperlinks in a worksheet
- Compare and merge workbooks
- Save a custom view of a worksheet
- Add and format pictures and shapes
- Enhance charts and sparklines
- Save a workbook as a PDF file

11 | Collaboration Features for Workbooks

Introduction

In today's business environment, colleagues are as likely to be in the next state as in the next office. Excel allows you to share and collaborate with others through a variety of features, depending on your resources and preferences and the resources and preferences of those with whom you are collaborating. In this chapter, you will learn how to use the collaboration features in Excel to gather input from multiple users, by a variety of methods, to update and enhance an Excel workbook.

To allow several people to view and change a workbook at the same time, a user can **share** the workbook. Excel also has the capability to **track changes** to a workbook by marking who changed what data, in which cell, and when. **Comments**, or descriptions, which do not regularly appear as part of the worksheet data, can be added to the workbook to alert the recipients to special information and then later can be edited or deleted. Workbooks that have been saved and copied to others also can be compared and merged. **Comparing** workbooks allows users to view and scroll worksheets side by side and visually search the worksheets for differences. **Merging** allows users to bring together copies of workbooks that others have worked on independently. You also will learn how to save a **custom view** of a worksheet, which enables each user to view the worksheet in a familiar manner, even if other users alter the appearance or layout of a worksheet.

Project — Snowbound Vacation Rentals Analysis

Snowbound Vacation Rentals is a new venture, formed from three small vacation rental businesses that recently have merged. The new business now will manage vacation rentals in three contiguous resort communities in the Adirondack Mountains in New York State. The real estate portfolios of the original three businesses were complementary, targeting three different markets with some overlap in units. The plan is to reduce overhead through economies of scale and to increase revenues through a rental portfolio that provides more flexibility to the rental agent due to increased units and more opportunities to move clients into an upgraded property when those in the originally requested price range are full. The new business was formed at the end of the 2013/2014 season, and final figures still are being gathered as the season is wrapped up. The owners have decided to review rental data for the last two seasons. The owners will use the collaborative features in Excel to exchange and update rental data. The initial worksheet shared among the owners contains queries about initial rental data provided (Figure 11–1a). The final version of that worksheet reflects a series of decisions by the owners about content and presentation, corrections to the data, and includes a background image, hyperlink, and watermark (Figure 11–1b). In addition, the owners are planning for the three carnivals they participate in, for the 2014/2015 season. They will add hyperlinks and formatting to a worksheet containing expense estimates for the carnivals (Figure 11–1c on page EX 692), and add chart formatting, sparklines, a manipulated image, and shapes to a worksheet containing attendance data for the carnivals (Figure 11–1d on page EX 692).

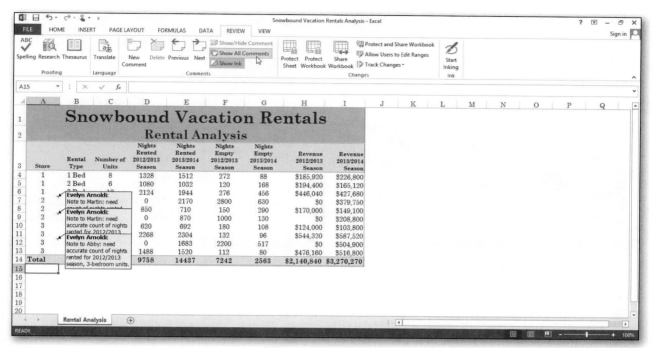

(a) Initial Worksheet

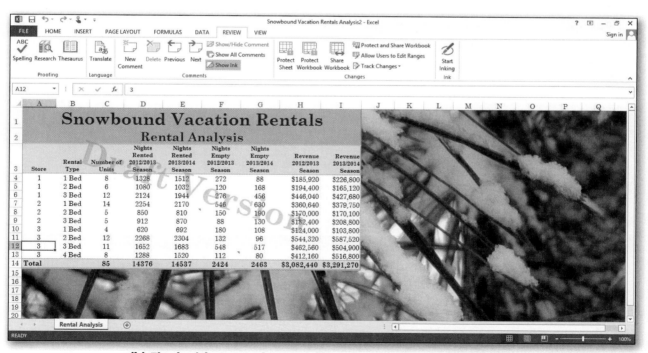

(b) Final with Corrections, Background Image, and Watermark

Figure 11–1 (Continued)

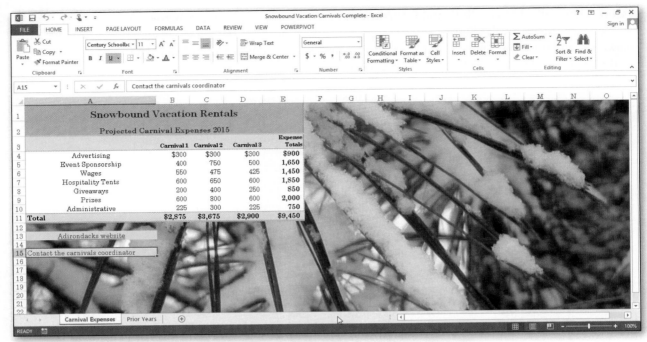

(c) Carnival Projected Expenses with Hyperlinks

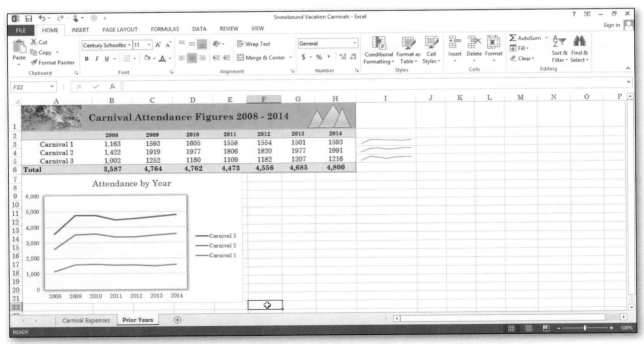

(d) Carnival Attendance Sheet with Image and Shapes Added to Heading

Figure 11–1 (Continued)

Figure 11–2 illustrates the requirements document for the Snowbound Vacation Rentals Analysis worksheet and the Snowbound Vacation Carnivals. It includes the needs, source of data, calculations, and other facts about the worksheets' development.

Worksheet Title	Snowbound Vacation Rentals Analysis and Snowbound Vacation Carnivals
Needs	• Update rental data based on feedback from property managers. • Set up worksheet for sharing via email. It should be sent out to the two property managers in a form that will allow for merging of edits into a single workbook. Changes should be able to be identified by who made them, in case questions arise. • Add a background image and a watermark to the rental data worksheet. • Add hyperlinks for the Adirondacks website and an email contact to the carnivals workbook. • Add a version of the background image from the rental worksheet to the heading of the carnivals worksheet. • Add a draft of the business logo (three mountains) to the heading of the carnivals worksheet.
Source of Data	Initial data is provided in the Data Files for Students.
Calculations	None.

© 2014 Cengage Learning

Figure 11–2

Roadmap

In this chapter, you will learn how to create and use the workbook shown in Figure 11–1. The following roadmap identifies general activities you will perform as you progress through this chapter:

1. USE COMMENTS.
2. ADD BACKGROUND and WATERMARK.
3. TRACK CHANGES.
4. USE SHARED WORKBOOKS.
5. SAVE CUSTOM VIEWS.
6. ADD and EDIT HYPERLINKS.
7. ADD CHARTS and SHAPES.

At the beginning of step instructions throughout the chapter, you will see an abbreviated form of this roadmap. The abbreviated roadmap uses colors to indicate chapter progress: gray means the chapter is beyond that activity, blue means the task being shown is covered in that activity, and black means that activity is yet to be covered. For example, the following abbreviated roadmap indicates the chapter would be showing a task in the 3 TRACK CHANGES activity.

1 USE COMMENTS | 2 ADD BACKGROUND & WATERMARK | 3 TRACK CHANGES | 4 USE SHARED WORKBOOKS
5 SAVE CUSTOM VIEWS | 6 ADD & EDIT HYPERLINKS | 7 ADD CHARTS & SHAPES

Use the abbreviated roadmap as a progress guide while you read or step through the instructions in this chapter.

To Run Excel and Open a Workbook

The following steps, which assume Windows 8 is running, use the Start screen or the search box to run Excel based on a typical installation. You may need to ask your instructor how to run Excel on your computer. For a detailed example of the procedure summarized below, refer to the Office and Windows chapter.

To complete these steps, you will be required to use the Data Files for Students. Visit www.cengage.com/ct/studentdownload for detailed instructions or contact your instructor for information about accessing the required files.

BTW

**The Ribbon and
Screen Resolution**
Excel may change how the
groups and buttons within
the groups appear on the
ribbon, depending on the
computer's screen resolution.
Thus, your ribbon may look
different from the ones in
this book if you are using a
screen resolution other than
1366 × 768.

① Scroll the Start screen for an Excel 2013 tile. If your Start screen contains an Excel 2013 tile, tap or click it to run Excel. Otherwise, search for the Excel app using the Charms bar and then tap or click Excel 2013 in the search results.

② Tap or click 'Open Other Workbooks' on the Excel start screen.

③ Navigate to the location of the Data Files for Students and the Excel Chapter 11 folder.

④ Double-tap or double-click the file named Snowbound Vacation Rentals Data to open it.

⑤ If the Excel window is not maximized, tap or click the Maximize button on its title bar to maximize the window.

⑥ Save the workbook with the file name, Snowbound Vacation Rentals Analysis (Figure 11–3).

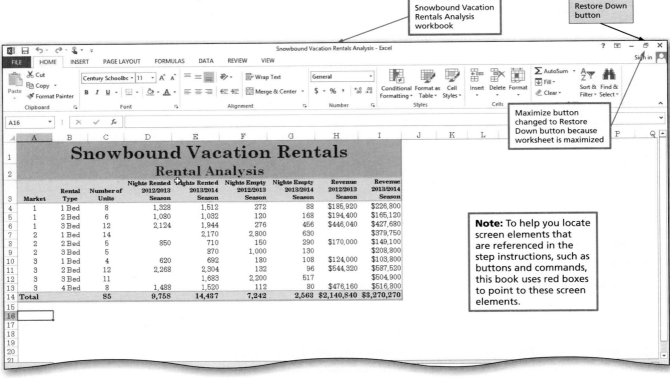

Figure 11–3

BTW

BTWs
For a complete list of the
BTWs found in the margins
of this book, visit the BTW
resource on the Student
Companion Site located on
www.cengagebrain.com. For
detailed instructions about
accessing available resources,
visit www.cengage.com/
ct/studentdownload or
contact your instructor for
information about accessing
the required files.

About the Snowbound Vacation Rentals Analysis Worksheet

As shown in Figure 11–3, the Snowbound Vacation Rentals Analysis worksheet is incomplete in terms of data. Before sending this worksheet out to gather data, you will add comments to the worksheet specifying what you need from coworkers.

Gathering Feedback Using Comments

Comments are the electronic version of sticky notes or annotations in the margin. They can request additional information or clarification of existing information. Comments can provide direction to the reader about how to interpret content or describe what type of content to add. You can add comments to a cell in a worksheet. Once added, you can edit, format, move, copy, or resize them. You can choose to show comments in a worksheet, to display only a comment indicator, or to hide comments. Comments work well when multiple people are collaborating and commenting on a worksheet. Comments added by each user are identified by a name in the comment, set by the user.

Depending on the nature of the comments, you may decide to delete some or all comments after reading them and making edits to the worksheet, if appropriate.

To Add Comments to a Worksheet

1 USE COMMENTS | 2 ADD BACKGROUND & WATERMARK | 3 TRACK CHANGES | 4 USE SHARED WORKBOOKS
5 SAVE CUSTOM VIEWS | 6 ADD & EDIT HYPERLINKS | 7 ADD CHARTS & SHAPES

Why? *Comments in Excel can be used to remind the user of material that needs to be added or updated.* The Sales Analysis worksheet in the Snowbound Vacation Rentals Analysis workbook has some missing data. The following steps add comments to the worksheet in cells A7, A9, and A12.

1

• Press and hold or right-click cell A7 to display the shortcut menu (Figure 11–4).

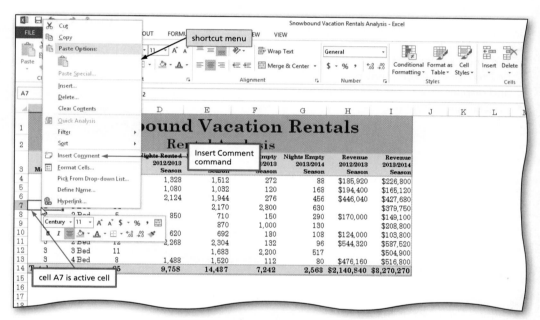

Figure 11–4

2

• Tap or click Insert Comment on the shortcut menu to open a comment box next to the selected cell and display a comment indicator in the cell (Figure 11–5).

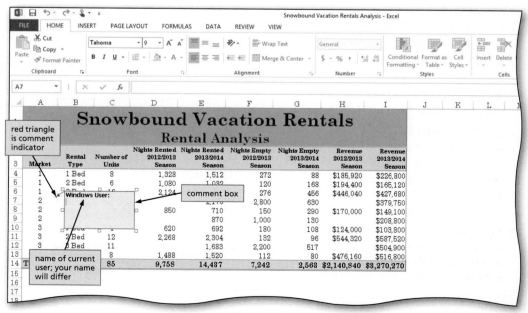

Figure 11–5

3

- Enter the text **Note to Martin - need count of nights rented for 2012/2013 season, 1-bedroom units.** in the comment box (Figure 11–6).

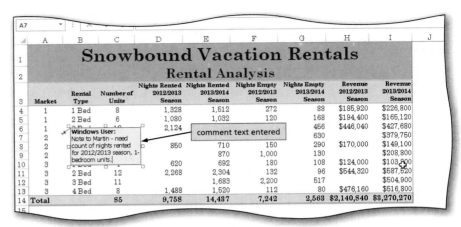

Figure 11–6

4

- Tap or click outside the comment box to close the comment box and display only the red comment indicator in cell A7 (Figure 11–7).

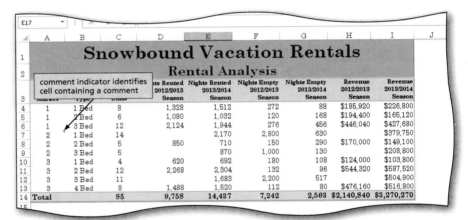

Figure 11–7

5

- Enter a comment in cell A9 with the text **Note to Martin - need accurate count of nights rented for 2012/2013 season, 3-bedroom units.**

- Tap or click outside the comment box to close the comment box and display only the red comment indicator in cell A9.

- Enter a comment in cell A12 with the text **Note to Abby - need accurate count of nights rented for 2012/2013 season, 3-bedroom units.**

- Tap or click outside the comment box to close the comment box and display only the red comment indicator in cell A12 (Figure 11–8).

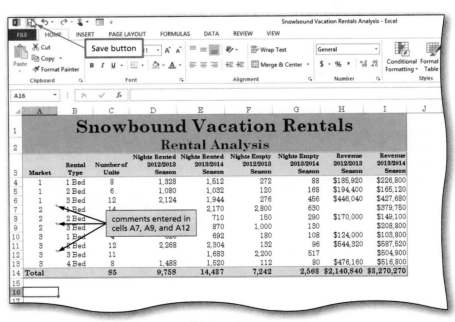

Figure 11–8

- Tap or click the Save button on the Quick Access Toolbar to save the workbook.

Other Ways

1. Tap or click 'Insert a Comment' button (REVIEW tab | Comments group) 2. Press SHIFT+F2

To Display All Comments on a Worksheet

1 USE COMMENTS | 2 ADD BACKGROUND & WATERMARK | 3 TRACK CHANGES | 4 USE SHARED WORKBOOKS
5 SAVE CUSTOM VIEWS | 6 ADD & EDIT HYPERLINKS | 7 ADD CHARTS & SHAPES

Why? While editing the worksheet, you may find it helpful to have comments visible. The comments currently are hidden. The following step makes all comments visible.

- Tap or click REVIEW on the ribbon to display the REVIEW tab.

- Tap or click the 'Show All Comments' button (REVIEW tab | Comments group) to show all comments in the workbook (Figure 11–9).

Q&A

What if I want to hide all comments? The 'Show All Comments' button is a toggle. Tapping or clicking it once shows all comments; tapping or clicking it a second time hides all comments.

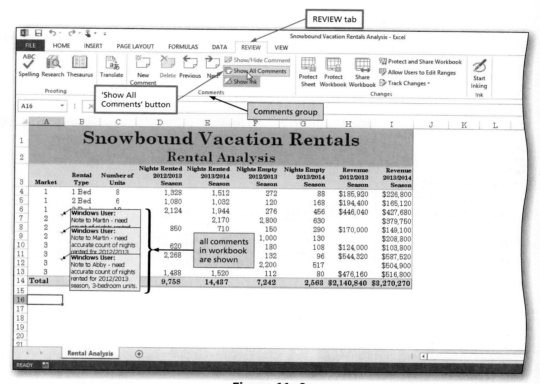

Figure 11–9

To Edit Comments on a Worksheet

1 USE COMMENTS | 2 ADD BACKGROUND & WATERMARK | 3 TRACK CHANGES | 4 USE SHARED WORKBOOKS
5 SAVE CUSTOM VIEWS | 6 ADD & EDIT HYPERLINKS | 7 ADD CHARTS & SHAPES

Why? After adding comments to a worksheet, you may need to edit them to add or change information. The steps on the next page edit the comment in cell A7.

1

● Press and hold or right-click cell A7 to display the shortcut menu (Figure 11–10).

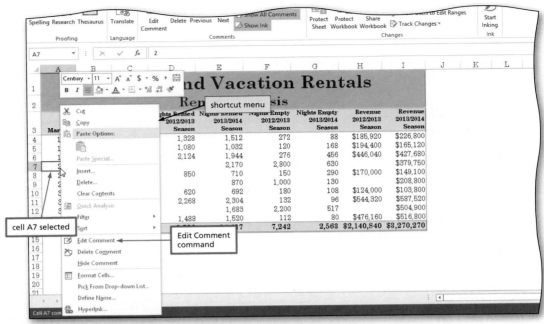

Figure 11–10

2

● Tap or click Edit Comment on the shortcut menu to open the comment for editing (Figure 11–11).

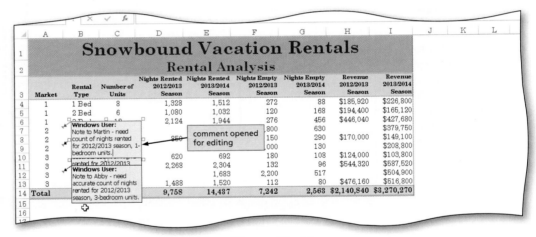

Figure 11–11

3

● Change the comment by adding the word, accurate, between the words, need and count, so that the text reads as follows: Note to Martin - need accurate count of nights rented for 2012/2013 season, 1-bedroom units. (Figure 11–12).

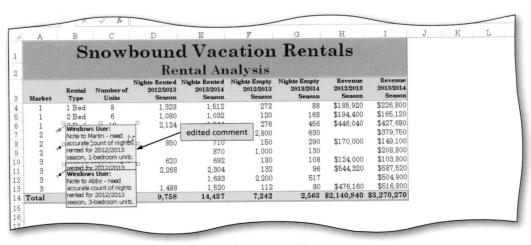

Figure 11–12

4

- Tap or click cell A16 to complete the editing.

- Tap or click the 'Show All Comments' button (REVIEW tab | Comments group) to hide all comments in the workbook (Figure 11–13).

Q&A How can I quickly read a hidden comment in a worksheet?
Point to a comment indicator to display the related comment.

Can I edit a hidden comment?
Yes. The Edit Comment command can be accessed whether the comment is hidden or visible.

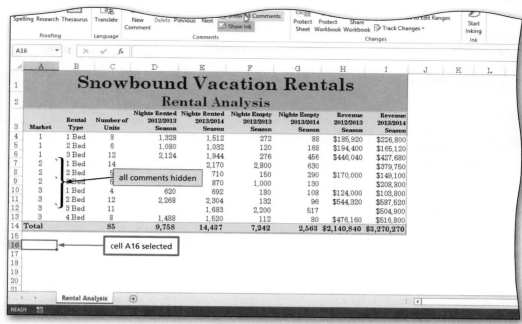

Figure 11–13

To Format Comments on a Worksheet

1 USE COMMENTS | 2 ADD BACKGROUND & WATERMARK | 3 TRACK CHANGES | 4 USE SHARED WORKBOOKS
5 SAVE CUSTOM VIEWS | 6 ADD & EDIT HYPERLINKS | 7 ADD CHARTS & SHAPES

Why format a comment? *You may want to change the appearance of a particular comment to make it stand out from other comments.* The following steps format the comment text in cell A7.

1

- Tap or click cell A7 to make active the cell containing the comment to format.

- Tap or click the Edit Comment button (REVIEW tab | Comments group) to open the comment for editing.

- Select the comment text to prepare for formatting it.

- Press and hold or right-click the selected comment text to display the shortcut menu (Figure 11–14).

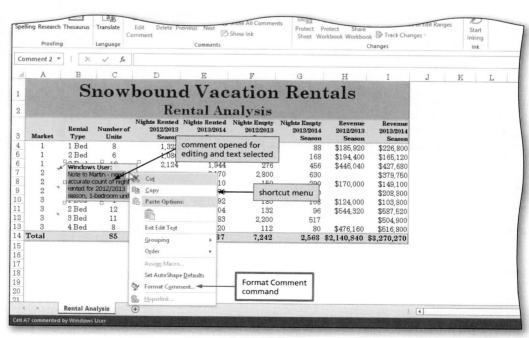

Figure 11–14

2

- Tap or click Format Comment on the shortcut menu to display the Format Comment dialog box.

- Change the comment text to red and bold (Figure 11–15).

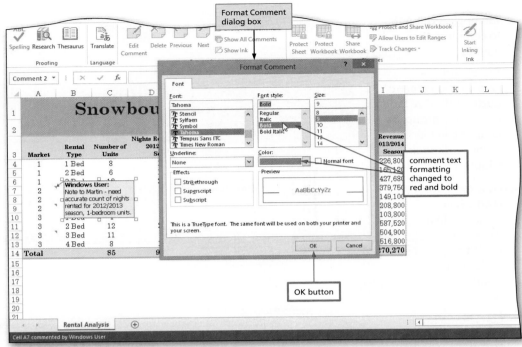

Figure 11–15

3

- Tap or click the OK button (Format Comment dialog box) to apply the selected formatting to the comment text. Use the sizing handles to resize the comment box as necessary so that all the text is visible.

- Tap or click cell A7 to deselect the comment text and then point to cell A7 to display the formatted comment (Figure 11–16).

Q&A Can I print comments?
Yes. You can print comments where they appear on the

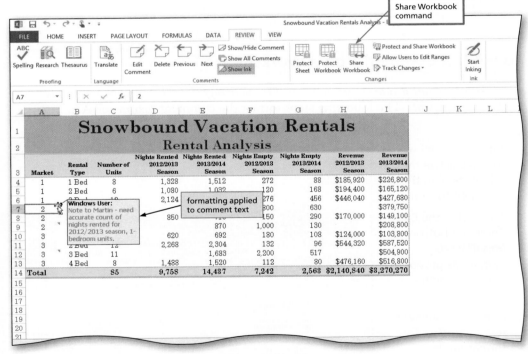

Figure 11–16

worksheet by displaying all comments and then printing the sheet. You can print a list of comments separately using the Sheet tab in the Page Setup dialog box. To do so, tap or click the Page Setup Dialog Box Launcher (PAGE LAYOUT tab | Page Setup group), tap or click the Sheet tab (Page Setup dialog box), tap or click the Comments arrow, and then tap or click 'At end of sheet' in the Comments list.

Worksheet Backgrounds and Watermarks

After a workbook functions in the manner in which it was designed, final touches can be added to the worksheets in the workbook to make them more attractive and easy to use. **Worksheet backgrounds** allow an image to be specified for use as a background image, or watermark, behind the data in cells of a worksheet. A **watermark** is faded text overlaid on the worksheet, used to convey something about the state of the worksheet, often an indicator of status, such as Draft or Confidential.

BTW1
Copying Comments
You can copy comments from one cell to other cells using the Paste Special command. Select the cell that contains the comment you need to copy, tap or click the Copy button (HOME tab | Clipboard group), select the cell or cells to which you want to apply the comment, tap or click the Paste arrow, and then tap or click Paste Special. In the Paste Special dialog box, in the As list, select Comments, and then tap or click the OK button.

To Format a Worksheet Background

1 USE COMMENTS | 2 ADD BACKGROUND & WATERMARK | 3 TRACK CHANGES | 4 USE SHARED WORKBOOKS
5 SAVE CUSTOM VIEWS | 6 ADD & EDIT HYPERLINKS | 7 ADD CHARTS & SHAPES

Excel allows an image to be used as a worksheet background. *Why format a worksheet background? Worksheet backgrounds can provide visual appeal to a worksheet, allowing for a corporate logo or other identifying image to serve as the background for an entire worksheet.*

The following steps add an image as a worksheet background to the Snowbound Vacation Rentals Analysis worksheet.

1

- Tap or click PAGE LAYOUT on the ribbon to display the PAGE LAYOUT tab.

- Tap or click the Background button (PAGE LAYOUT tab | Page Setup group) to display the Insert Pictures window (Figure 11–17).

 Why do I have additional locations listed in my Insert Pictures window?
If you are logged in to your Microsoft account, you will have additional, cloud-based locations listed.

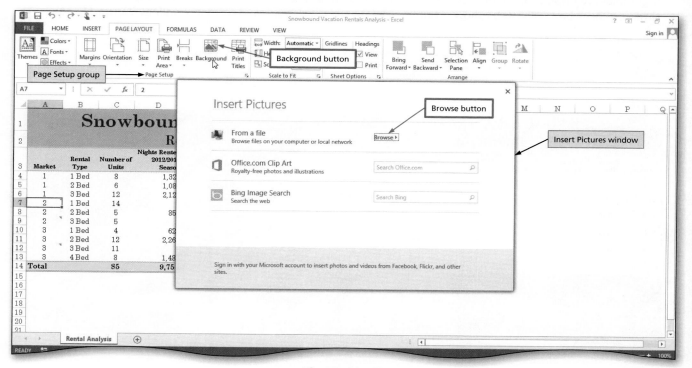

Figure 11–17

2

- Tap or click the Browse button in the From a file area, navigate to the location of the Data Files for Students, and then select the snowtrees image file (Figure 11–18).

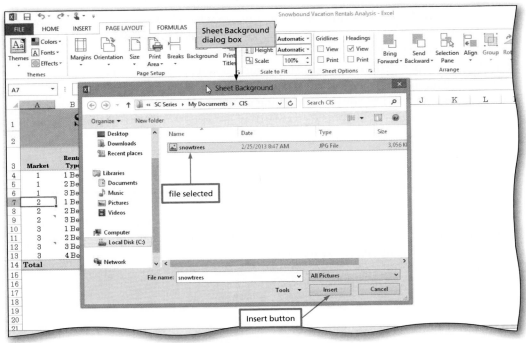

Figure 11–18

3

- Tap or click the Insert button (Sheet Background dialog box) to display the image as the worksheet background.

- If gridlines are displayed, tap or click VIEW on the ribbon to display the VIEW tab and then tap or click the View Gridlines check box (VIEW tab | Show group) to remove the check mark and turn off gridlines (Figure 11–19).

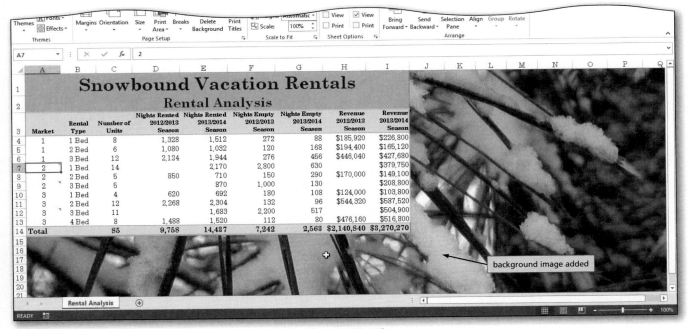

Figure 11–19

4

- Save the workbook.

To Add a Watermark to a Worksheet

Why? *A watermark can be used to provide a reminder to the user. In this case, it will remind the users that the worksheet contains draft content.* Excel does not have a watermark function, but you can use WordArt to mimic one. The following steps add a watermark to the worksheet.

- Tap or click the INSERT tab on the ribbon and then tap or click the Insert WordArt button (INSERT tab | Text group) to display the Insert WordArt gallery (Figure 11–20).

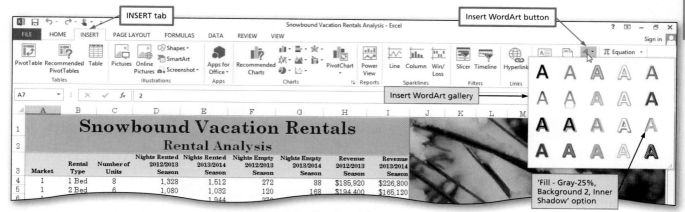

Figure 11–20

2

- Tap or click 'Fill - Gray-25%, Background 2, Inner Shadow' to insert a new WordArt object.

- If using touch with a stylus, point to the border of the WordArt object, and when the pointer changes to a four-headed arrow, drag the WordArt object to the center of the worksheet content, as shown in Figure 11–21.

- If using touch with a touch screen, press CTRL on the on-screen keyboard and then drag the WordArt object to the center of the worksheet content, as shown in Figure 11–21.

- If using a mouse, point to the border of the WordArt object, and when the pointer changes to a four-headed arrow, drag the WordArt object to the center of the worksheet content, as shown in Figure 11–21.

- Select the text in the WordArt object and then type `Draft Version` as the watermark text.

- With the WordArt text selected, press and hold or right-click the WordArt object to display a shortcut menu (Figure 11–21).

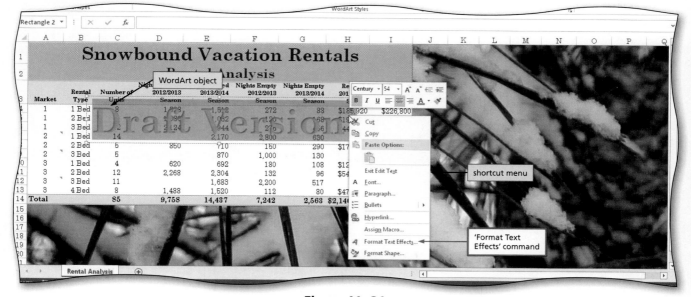

Figure 11–21

- Tap or click 'Format Text Effects' on the shortcut menu to open the Format Shape task pane.

- If necessary, tap or click the TEXT OPTIONS tab in the Format Shape task pane.

- If necessary, tap or click the 'Text Fill & Outline' button and then, if necessary, tap or click the TEXT FILL arrow to expand the TEXT FILL section.

- Set the Transparency slider to 80% to change the transparency of the Word Art (Figure 11–22).

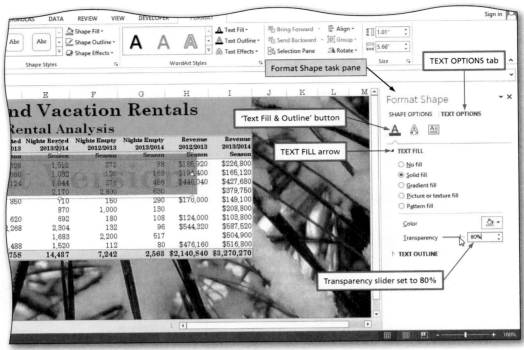

Figure 11–22

- Tap or click the Close button in the Format Shape task pane to close it.

- With the WordArt object still selected, drag the rotation handle until the orientation of the WordArt object appears as shown in Figure 11–23.

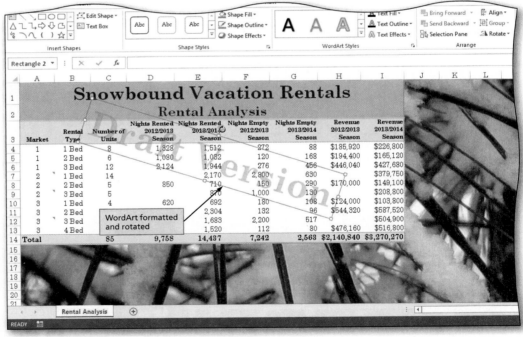

Figure 11–23

Collaborating and Tracking Changes on a Workbook

The next steps in the project are to share the workbook and then turn on features to track changes.

If others need to edit a workbook or suggest changes, Excel provides three ways to collaborate. **Collaborating** means working together on a document in cooperation with other Excel users.

The first option is to **distribute** the workbook to others, physically on storage media, through email using the Share gallery in the Backstage view, or via Windows Live SkyDrive. In the Share gallery, the document can be embedded as part of the email message, or the file can be sent as an email attachment, which allows recipients of the email message to open the file if Excel is installed on their computer or mobile device.

A second option is to collaborate by **sharing** the workbook using the Sharing feature in Excel. Sharing involves more than simply giving another user a copy of a file; it allows multiple people to work independently on the same workbook at the same time if they are in a networked environment. Sharing a workbook puts restrictions on the types of edits a user can make, which provides a degree of control over the editing process that distributing the workbook does not. If users are not in a networked environment, workbook sharing allows them to work on the workbook in turn, while keeping track of who was responsible for the various edits. In a nonnetworked environment, having several people work consecutively on a shared workbook provides the original user with the control over what types of edits can be performed.

A third option is to collaborate interactively with other people through discussion threads or online meetings. The use of SharePoint Services with Microsoft Office 2013 allows people at different sites to share and exchange files.

BTW
Q&As
For a complete list of the Q&As found in many of the step-by-step sequences in this book, visit the Q&A resource on the Student Companion Site located on www.cengagebrain.com. For detailed instructions about accessing available resources, visit www.cengage.com/ct/studentdownload or contact your instructor for information about accessing the required files.

CONSIDER THIS

How do I choose the appropriate option?

The option you choose should reflect the needs of the project. You can take into account the need for reviewer privacy, the required turnaround for the collaborative feedback, and the resources available to the people who are providing you with feedback.

Sharing can be turned on for a workbook using the Share Workbook button on the REVIEW tab. When workbook sharing is enabled, a number of Excel features — merging cells, deleting worksheets, changing or removing passwords, using scenarios, creating data tables, modifying macros, using data validation, and creating PivotTables — are disabled for the workbook. For this reason, the time when a workbook is shared should be limited; further, sharing should be used only for the purpose of reviewing and modifying the contents of worksheet data.

When a workbook is shared with other users, changes made and saved by the other users are visible only when you attempt to save changes. When Excel recognizes that another user has modified a shared workbook, Excel displays a dialog box indicating that the workbook has been updated with changes saved by other users; you then can review and accept or reject their work. If both you and another user change the same cell, Excel displays a Resolve Conflicts dialog box when the workbook is saved. The dialog box lists the conflicting changes and provides options to choose which change to accept in the workbook.

To Share and Collaborate on a Workbook

Why? *Sharing a workbook can provide you with a timely, interactive editing process with colleagues.* The following steps turn on sharing for the Snowbound Vacation Rentals Analysis workbook and then allow collaboration with another user in a networked environment to make changes to the workbook.

1

- Tap or click REVIEW on the ribbon to display the REVIEW tab.

- Tap or click the Share Workbook button (REVIEW tab | Changes group) to display the Share Workbook dialog box.

- When Excel displays the Share Workbook dialog box, tap or click the 'Allow changes by more than one user at the same time' check box to insert a check mark (Figure 11–24).

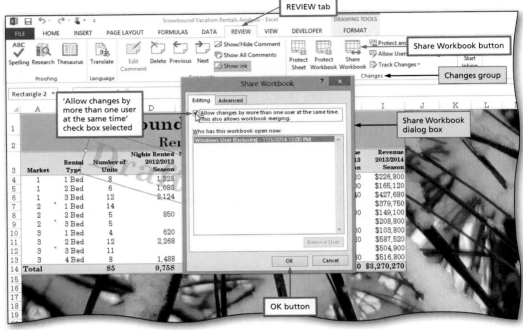

Figure 11–24

Q&A What is shown in the Share Workbook dialog box?
The 'Allow changes by more than one user at the same time' check box is selected, indicating that the workbook should be shared. The Who has this workbook open now list in the Share Workbook dialog box lists all users who currently have a copy of the workbook open.

2

- Tap or click the OK button (Share Workbook dialog box) to share the workbook with other users.

- When Excel displays the Microsoft Excel dialog box, tap or click the OK button to save and then share the workbook (Figure 11–25).

Q&A How do I know when the workbook is being shared?
The text "[Shared]" appears on the title bar next to the file name, indicating that the workbook is being shared.

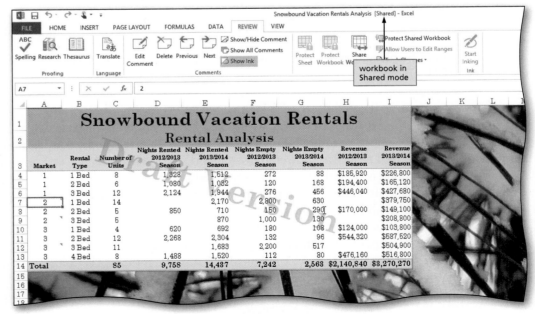

Figure 11–25

❸

- If possible, have a classmate open a second copy of the workbook.
- With a second copy of the workbook open, tap or click the Share Workbook button (REVIEW tab | Changes group) to display the Share Workbook dialog box, which lists all users who currently have the workbook open (Figure 11–26).

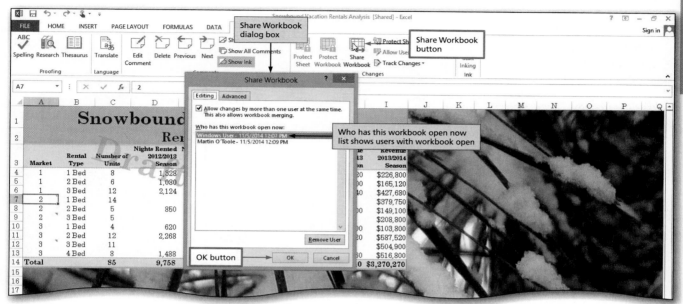

Figure 11–26

❹

- Tap or click the OK button (Share Workbook dialog box) to close the dialog box.
- Ask the second workbook user to tap or click cell D7, enter **2254** as the new value, and then save the workbook.
- In your copy of the workbook, tap or click the Save button on the Quick Access Toolbar to display the Microsoft Excel dialog box indicating that the workbook has been updated with changes saved by another user (Figure 11–27).

Q&A Must I save the workbook before I am notified of another user's changes?
Yes. Until the workbook is saved, Excel provides no indication that another user has changed the shared workbook. To prohibit another user from saving additional updates to the workbook, tap or click the user name in the Share Workbook dialog box and then tap or click the Remove User button.

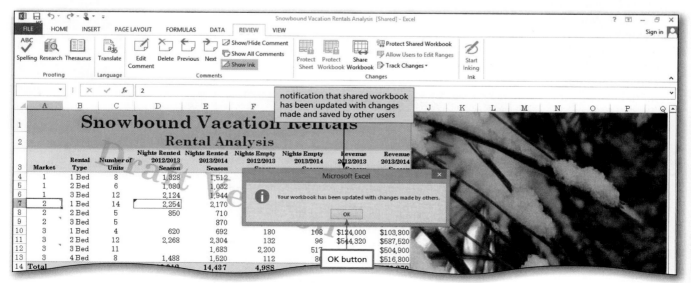

Figure 11–27

5

- Tap or click the OK button (Microsoft Excel dialog box) to close the dialog box.

- Point to the triangle in cell D7 to display the comment that identifies the other user's changes (Figure 11–28).

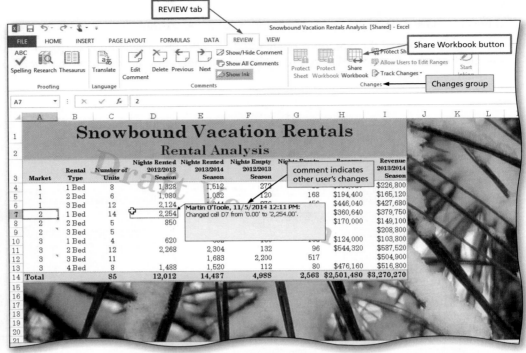

Figure 11–28

6

- Ask the second user of the workbook to close the workbook.

- Tap or click the Share Workbook button (REVIEW tab | Changes group) to display the Share Workbook dialog box.

- When Excel displays the Share Workbook dialog box, click the 'Allow changes by more than one user at the same time' check box to remove the check mark (Figure 11–29).

Q&A

How long are changes kept?
The changes made to a workbook are called the change history. When a workbook is shared, Excel keeps the changes made for 30 days unless you set the change history to a different number of days. To increase the length of time, select the Advanced tab in the Share Workbook dialog box, and set 'Keep change history for' to the desired interval.

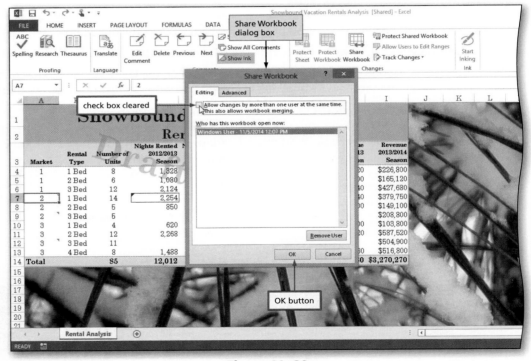

Figure 11–29

7

- Tap or click the OK button (Share Workbook dialog box) to stop sharing the workbook (Figure 11–30).

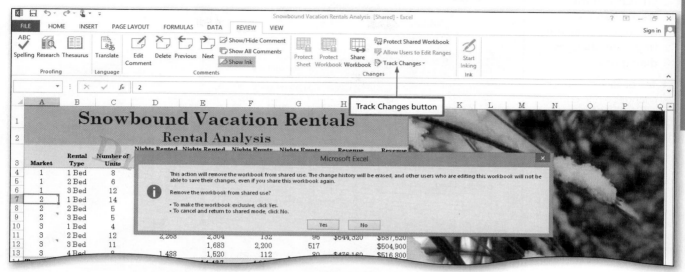

Figure 11–30

8

- If Excel displays the Microsoft Excel dialog box asking whether the workbook should be removed from shared use, tap or click the Yes button (shown in Figure 11 - 30).

To Turn on Track Changes

1 USE COMMENTS | 2 ADD BACKGROUND & WATERMARK | 3 TRACK CHANGES | 4 USE SHARED WORKBOOKS
5 SAVE CUSTOM VIEWS | 6 ADD & EDIT HYPERLINKS | 7 ADD CHARTS & SHAPES

Why track changes? Tracking changes when working collaboratively keeps a record of the changes that others make to a workbook. Tracking changes means that Excel, through the Track Changes command, will display the edited cells with a comment indicating who made the change, when the change was made, and what the original value was of the cell that was changed. If either tracking or sharing is enabled, Excel enables the other by default. The following steps turn on track changes.

1

- Tap or click the Track Changes button (REVIEW tab | Changes group) to display the Track Changes menu (Figure 11–31).

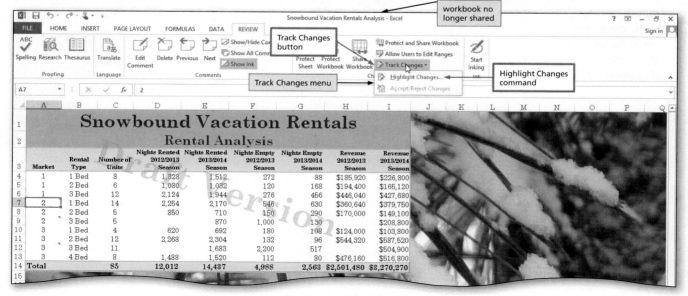

Figure 11–31

2

- Tap or click Highlight Changes on the Track Changes menu to display the Highlight Changes dialog box.

- Tap or click the 'Track changes while editing. This also shares your workbook.' check box to insert a check mark.

- If necessary, tap or click all of the check boxes in the Highlight which changes area to clear them (Figure 11–32).

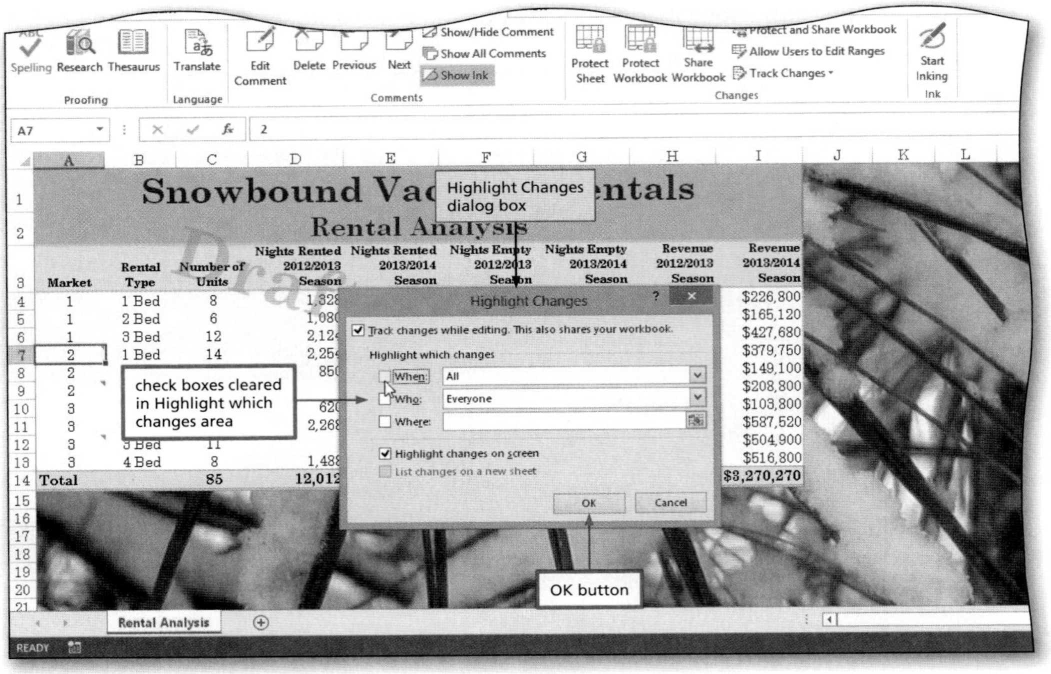

Q&A What is the purpose of clearing the check marks?

Tapping or clicking the 'Track changes while editing. This also shares your workbook.' check box enables track changes and shares the workbook. The When, Who, and Where check boxes play no role when track changes first is enabled.

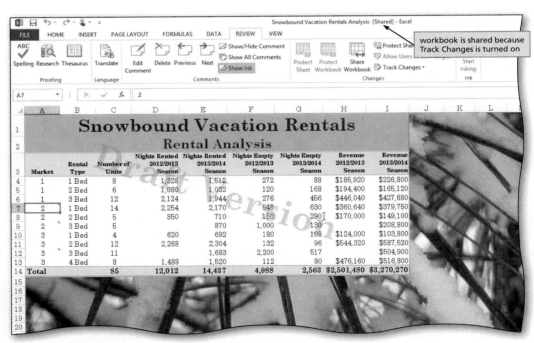

Figure 11–32

3

- Tap or click the OK button (Highlight Changes dialog box) to close the dialog box.

- If a Microsoft Excel dialog box appears, tap or click the OK button (Microsoft Excel dialog box) to save, share, and track changes in the workbook (Figure 11–33).

Q&A What is the change history, and how can it be protected?

Excel keeps a change history with each shared workbook. In the case of a shared workbook in which changes should be tracked, Excel provides a way for users to make data entry changes, but does not allow them to modify the change history. To protect the change history associated with a shared workbook, tap or click the Protect Shared Workbook button (REVIEW tab | Changes group). When Excel displays the Protect Shared Workbook dialog box, tap or click 'Sharing with track changes' to select it and then tap or click the OK button. After a shared workbook is protected, no one can unprotect or change it except the owner.

Figure 11–33

To Distribute a Workbook by Email

Why distribute by email? *You may need to have a workbook reviewed by someone who does not share network access with you.* You can send a shared workbook using email. The recipient can make changes; when he or she sends the workbook back to you for review, his or her changes will be tagged just as they would be if the recipient opened the workbook on the network. The following steps save the workbook and send it by email.

1

- With Excel active, tap or click FILE on the ribbon to open the Backstage view.

- Tap or click the Share tab to display the Share gallery.

- Tap or click the Email button to display the Email options in the right pane (Figure 11–34).

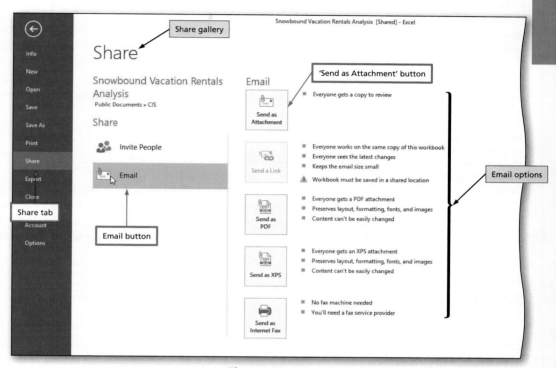

Figure 11–34

2

- Tap or click the 'Send as Attachment' button to open an email message with the workbook as an attachment (Figure 11–35).

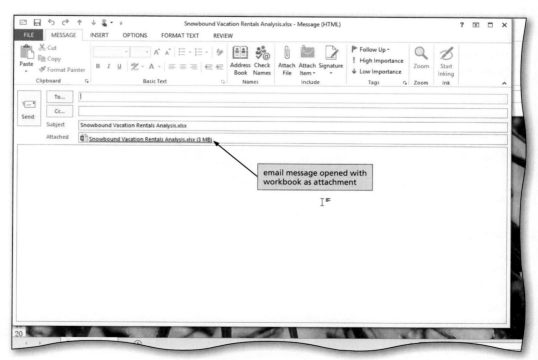

Figure 11–35

- Fill in the To: line, add any message you want to send, and then tap or click the Send button to send the message with attached workbook.

- Close the Snowbound Vacation Rentals Analysis workbook.

Distributing a Workbook via SkyDrive

You can use SkyDrive to distribute workbooks so that you do not need to send email messages with attachments. Just as with sharing via email, colleagues can make changes, and then save the workbook on SkyDrive for review. Saving on SkyDrive to distribute workbooks does not need to differ from saving on SkyDrive when saving your own files. You do need to make the workbook available to others by saving it in an accessible location on SkyDrive.

Reviewing Tracked Changes

Instead of writing suggestions and changes on a printed draft copy and sending it to the person in charge of a workbook, Excel's track changes feature allows users to enter suggested changes directly in the workbook. The owner of the workbook then looks through each change and makes a decision about whether to accept it.

To Open a Workbook and Review Tracked Changes

1 USE COMMENTS | 2 ADD BACKGROUND & WATERMARK | 3 TRACK CHANGES | 4 USE SHARED WORKBOOKS
5 SAVE CUSTOM VIEWS | 6 ADD & EDIT HYPERLINKS | 7 ADD CHARTS & SHAPES

After others have reviewed a workbook, it usually is returned to the owner. When track changes is enabled for a workbook, the file, when returned to the owner, will contain other users' changes, corrections, and comments. **Why review tracked changes?** *The owner of the workbook then can review those changes and make decisions about whether to accept the changes.* A workbook named Snowbound Vacation Rentals Analysis1, which includes tracked changes from other users to the Snowbound Vacation Rentals Analysis workbook, is saved on the Data Files for Students. The following steps use this workbook to illustrate reviewing tracked changes.

- With Excel active, open the file Snowbound Vacation Rentals Analysis1 from the Data Files for Students.

- If necessary, tap or click the Enable Editing button on the Protected View bar to open the workbook for editing.

- Tap or click REVIEW on the ribbon to display the REVIEW tab.

- Tap or click the Track Changes button (REVIEW tab | Changes group) to display the Track Changes menu (Figure 11–36).

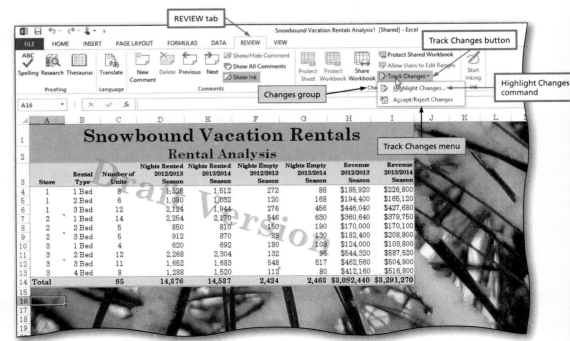

Figure 11–36

2

- Tap or click Highlight Changes on the Track Changes menu to display the Highlight Changes dialog box.

- When Excel displays the Highlight Changes dialog box, tap or click the When check box to remove the check mark and have Excel highlight all changes (Figure 11–37).

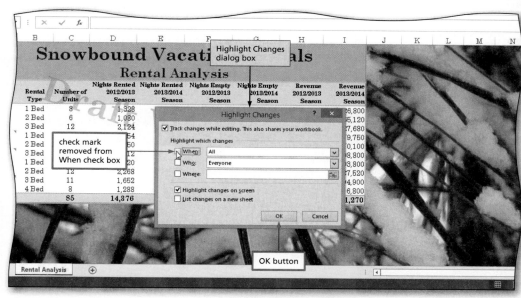

Q&A What is the purpose of clearing the check mark(s)?

Clearing the check mark from the When check box indicates that all changes in the change history should be available for review. Excel can track three categories of changes in the change history. The When check box allows you to specify the time from which you want to review changes. The Who check box allows you to specify individual users from whom to review changes. The Where check box allows you to specify a range of cells to check for changes.

When would I select the When, Who, and Where check boxes?

You would select these check boxes when you want to highlight only some changes, such as those made since you last saved or those made by everyone except you.

Figure 11–37

3

- Tap or click the OK button (Highlight Changes dialog box) to close the dialog box.

- Point to cell D9 to display a comment box with information about the change made to the cell D9 (Figure 11–38).

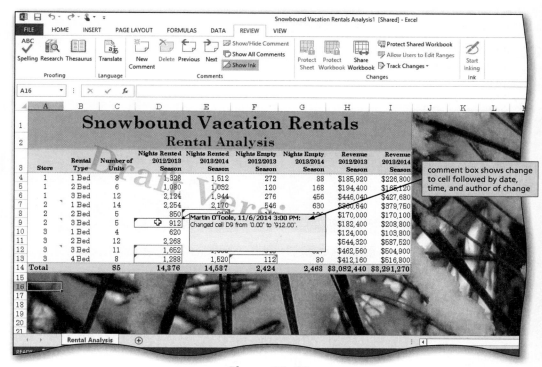

Figure 11–38

4

- Tap or click the Track Changes button (REVIEW tab | Changes group) to display the Track Changes menu (Figure 11–39).

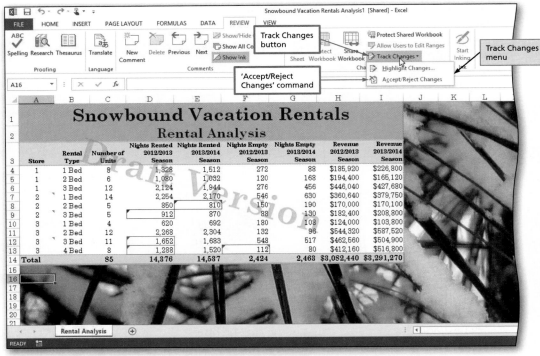

Figure 11–39

5

- Tap or click 'Accept/ Reject Changes' on the Track Changes menu to display the Select Changes to Accept or Reject dialog box.

- If necessary, tap or click all check boxes to clear them, indicating that all changes in the change history file should be reviewed (Figure 11–40).

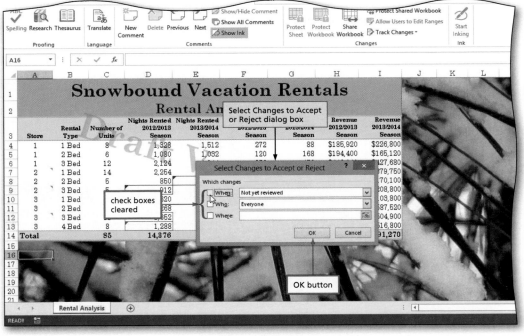

Figure 11–40

6

- Tap or click the OK button (Select Changes to Accept or Reject dialog box) to display the first tracked change (Figure 11–41).

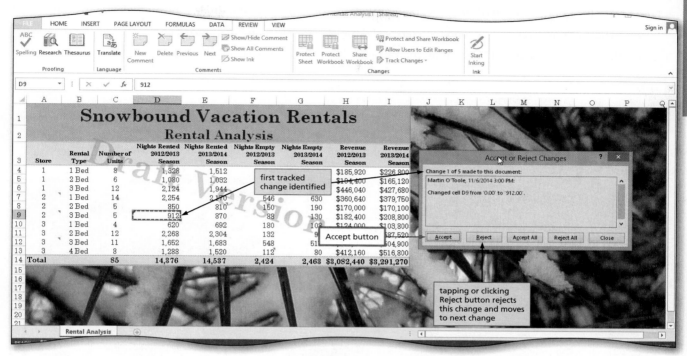

Figure 11–41

7

- Tap or click the Accept button (Accept or Reject Changes dialog box) to accept the change to the cell.
- As Excel displays each change in the Accept or Reject Changes dialog box, tap or click the Accept button until the dialog box closes (Figure 11–42).

Q&A Could I tap or click the Accept All button to accept all remaining changes?
Yes, though you cannot review changes when you tap or click the Accept All button.

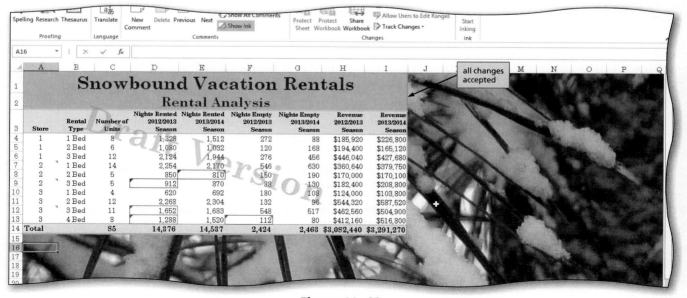

Figure 11–42

8

- Tap or click the 'Show All Comments' button (REVIEW tab | Comments group) to display all comments in the worksheet.
- Press and hold or right-click cell A7 and then tap or click Delete Comment on the shortcut menu to delete the comment.
- Press and hold or right-click cell A9 and then tap or click Delete Comment on the shortcut menu to delete the comment.
- Press and hold or right-click cell A12 and then tap or click Delete Comment on the shortcut menu to delete the comment.
- Resize the comment for cell F13 so that all the text is visible (Figure 11–43).

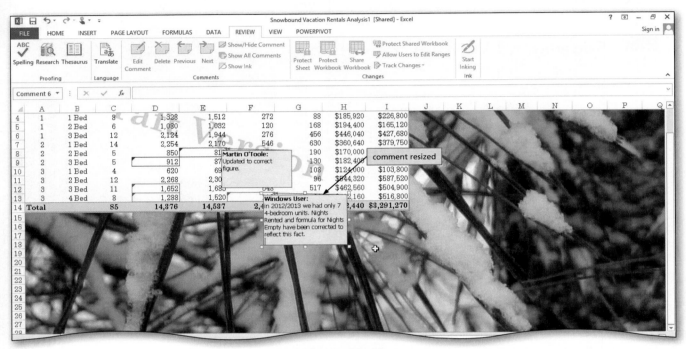

Figure 11–43

9

- Tap or click the 'Show All Comments' button (REVIEW tab | Comments group) to hide the remaining comments.

Other Ways
1. Tap or click Delete Comment button (REVIEW tab | Comments group)

To Save the Workbook with a New File Name

You have made several modifications to the workbook since you last saved it. Thus, you should save it again. The following steps save the workbook again using a new file name.

1 Tap or click FILE on the ribbon to display the Backstage view, and then tap or click Save As to display the Save As dialog box.

2 Type `Snowbound Vacation Rentals Analysis2` in the File name text box.

3 Tap or click the Save button (Save As dialog box) to save the workbook with the new file name.

To Turn Off Track Changes

Why? *When workbook sharing is enabled, Excel denies access to a number of features. Turning off track changes, which also turns off sharing and saves the workbook, provides access to those features again.* The workbook is saved as an **exclusive workbook**, one that is not shared and can be opened only by a single user. The following steps turn off track changes and make the workbook exclusive.

1

- Tap or click the Track Changes button (REVIEW tab | Changes group) to display the Track Changes menu.

- Tap or click Highlight Changes on the Track Changes menu to display the Highlight Changes dialog box.

- Tap or click the 'Track changes while editing' check box to remove the check mark (Figure 11–44).

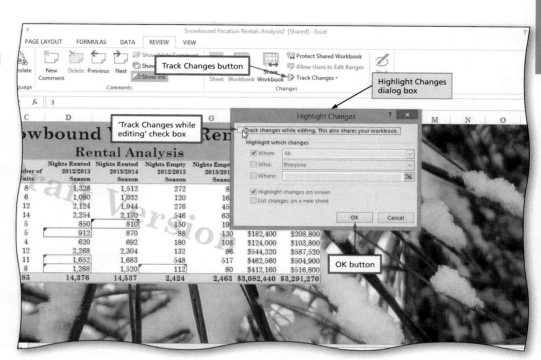

Figure 11–44

2

- Tap or click the OK button (Highlight Changes dialog box) to close the dialog box, turn off track changes, and display the Microsoft Excel dialog box asking if the workbook should be made exclusive (Figure 11–45).

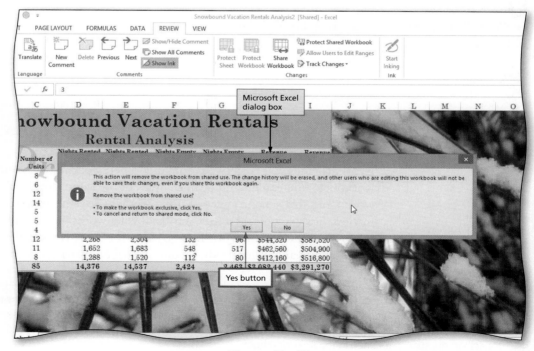

Figure 11–45

3

- Tap or click the Yes button to make the workbook exclusive (Figure 11–46).

Q&A | What happens when track changes is disabled?
| When track changes is disabled, sharing is disabled as well. At the same time, Excel erases the change history. The workbook automatically is resaved as an exclusive workbook, which is not shared and can be opened only by a single user.

| How do I know that the workbook is an exclusive workbook?
| The text, [Shared], no longer is displayed on the title bar.

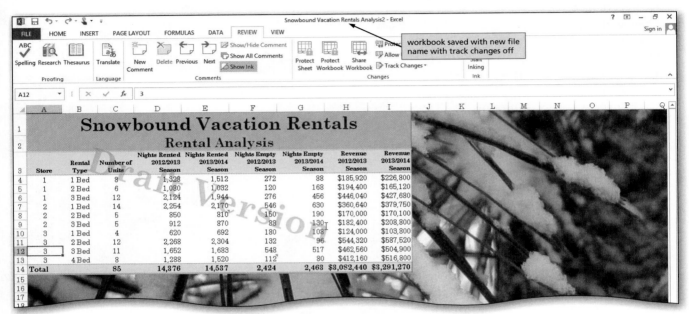

Figure 11–46

4

- Close all open workbooks, but keep Excel running.

Break Point: If you wish to take a break, this is a good place to do so. You can exit Excel now. To resume at a later time, run Excel, and continue following the steps from this location forward.

Comparing and Merging Workbooks

Excel provides you with two commands when working with multiple versions of a workbook. You can open multiple copies of the same workbook and move through the workbooks in a synchronized manner so that the same area of each workbook is always in view. For example, as a user scrolls down a worksheet, Excel automatically updates the view of the second worksheet to show the same rows as the first worksheet. This functionality allows for a side-by-side, visual comparison of two workbooks.

Why would I want to compare workbooks side by side instead of just merging them?
When working with multiple copies of the same workbook, you can be faced with a situation where the same cell can contain different values in the various copies of the workbook. Careful review and evaluation is necessary to ensure that the correct value for cells in question is retained in the final workbook.

In the case of multiple copies of a workbook, Excel provides the capability to merge multiple copies into a single workbook. This feature requires you to do some preparation. To merge the changes from one or more workbooks into another, all workbooks must satisfy the following requirements:

- The original workbook must be shared before making copies, and each workbook must be a copy of the same workbook.

- When copies of the workbook are made, track changes or sharing must be enabled, so that the change history of the workbook is kept.

- Tapping or clicking the Share Workbook button on the REVIEW tab displays a dialog box with a tab for recording the number of days to record the change history. Shared workbooks must be merged within that time period.

- If the workbooks have been assigned passwords, all workbooks involved in the merge must have the same password.

- Each copy of the workbook must have a different file name.

When all of the copies of the workbook are available on your hard disk, USB drive, SkyDrive, or other storage medium, you can use the 'Compare and Merge Workbooks' command to merge the workbooks. When Excel merges the workbooks, both data and comments are merged, so that if comments are recorded, they appear one after another in a given cell's comment box. If Excel cannot merge the workbooks, information from one workbook still can be incorporated into another by copying and pasting the information from one workbook to another.

Can merging workbooks destroy any of my existing data?
When merging workbooks, it is good practice to keep a backup copy of the files to be merged. Merging workbooks can overwrite data.

CONSIDER THIS

To Compare Workbooks

1 USE COMMENTS | 2 ADD BACKGROUND & WATERMARK | 3 TRACK CHANGES | 4 USE SHARED WORKBOOKS
5 SAVE CUSTOM VIEWS | 6 ADD & EDIT HYPERLINKS | 7 ADD CHARTS & SHAPES

Snowbound Vacation Rentals plans to participate in three winter carnivals in the 2014/2015 season. Proposed carnival expenditures are saved in a workbook that has been shared and copied to two other members of the staff for review. Because two different users — Abigail and Martin — modified the separate workbooks, the workbooks must be merged. *Why compare workbooks?* *Before merging the workbooks, they can be compared visually to note the changes made by different users.* The following steps open the Snowbound Vacation Carnivals and Snowbound Vacation Carnivals Abigail workbooks and compare the workbooks side by side.

- Open the file Snowbound Vacation Carnivals from the Data Files for Students.

- If the file opens in a maximized state, tap or click the workbook's Restore Down button to resize the window.

- Open the file Snowbound Vacation Carnivals Abigail from the Data Files for Students.

- If the file opens in a maximized state, click the workbook's Restore Down button to resize the window.

- Tap or click VIEW on the ribbon to display the VIEW tab (Figure 11–47 on the next page).

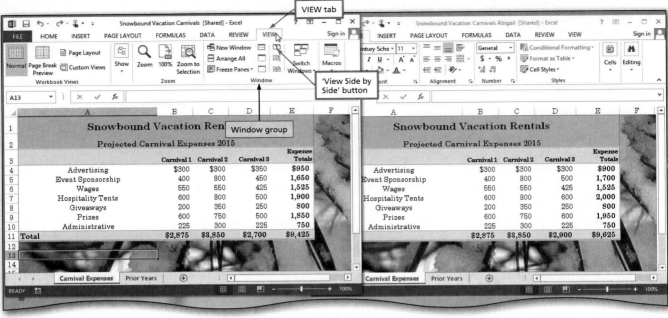

Figure 11-47

2

- Tap or click the 'View Side by Side' button (VIEW tab | Window group) to display the workbooks side by side.

Q&A | How should the workbooks be arranged after tapping or clicking the 'View Side by Side' button?
Depending on how previous Excel windows were arranged on your computer, the workbooks may appear next to each other left-to-right, or with one window above the other.

- Use the scroll bar in the active window to scroll the Snowbound Vacation Carnivals worksheet (Figure 11-48).

Q&A | What happens when I scroll the worksheet?
Because the Synchronous Scrolling button is selected, both worksheets scroll at the same time so that you can make a visual comparison of the workbooks.

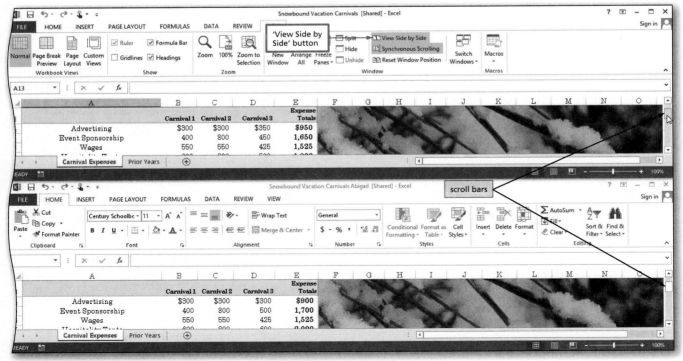

Figure 11-48

- Tap or click the 'View Side by Side' button (VIEW tab | Window group) again to display the windows separately and turn off synchronous scrolling.
- Tap or click the workbook's Close Window button to close the Snowbound Vacation Carnivals Abigail workbook.
- If Excel displays a Microsoft Excel dialog box, click the No button.
- Tap or click the Maximize button in the Snowbound Vacation Carnivals window to maximize the window.

To Merge Workbooks

1 USE COMMENTS | 2 ADD BACKGROUND & WATERMARK | 3 TRACK CHANGES | 4 USE SHARED WORKBOOKS
5 SAVE CUSTOM VIEWS | 6 ADD & EDIT HYPERLINKS | 7 ADD CHARTS & SHAPES

Why? When multiple users have made changes to copies of a workbook, merging can be more efficient and accurate than copying changes over to a single workbook. After the initial review, the next step is to merge the two workbooks changed by Abigail and Martin into the original Snowbound Vacation Carnivals workbook. All three of the workbooks are shared. The following steps merge the workbooks containing changes from Abigail and Martin with the original workbook, Snowbound Vacation Carnivals.

- Make a backup copy of the Snowbound Vacation Carnivals workbook in a different location.
- Tap or click the 'Customize Quick Access Toolbar' arrow next to the Quick Access Toolbar and then tap or click More Commands on the Customize Quick Access Toolbar menu to display the Excel Options dialog box.
- Select All Commands in the Choose commands from list.
- Scroll to the 'Compare and Merge Workbooks' command in the list on the left and then tap or click it.
- Tap or click the Add button (Excel Options dialog box) to add the 'Compare and Merge Workbooks' command to the list on the right side of the dialog box (Figure 11–49).

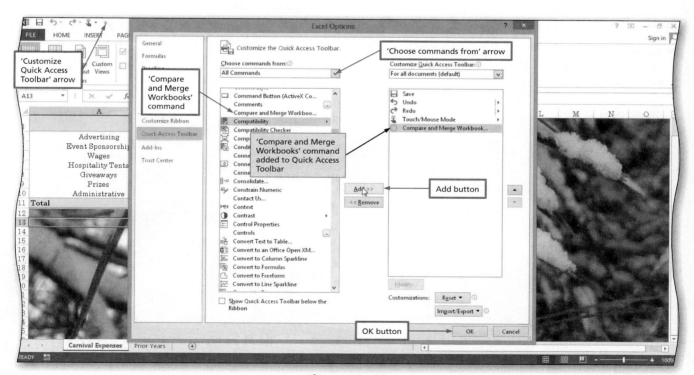

Figure 11–49

2

- Tap or click the OK button to add the 'Compare and Merge Workbooks' button to the Quick Access Toolbar.
- Tap or click the 'Compare and Merge Workbooks' button on the Quick Access Toolbar to display the Select Files to Merge Into Current Workbook dialog box.

Q&A | Why is my 'Compare and Merge Workbooks' button gray?
The workbook must be shared before you can use the 'Compare and Merge Workbooks' button. Check to make sure your workbook is shared.

- Navigate to the save location of the files (in this case, the Excel folder in the CIS 101 folder [or your class folder] on the USB flash drive).

- Tap or click 'Snowbound Vacation Carnivals Abigail', hold down the SHIFT key, and then tap or click 'Snowbound Vacation Carnivals Martin' to select both files (Figure 11–50).

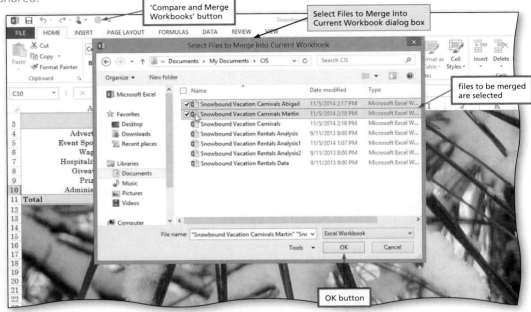

Figure 11–50

3

- Tap or click the OK button (Select Files to Merge Into Current Workbook dialog box) to merge the workbooks (Figure 11–51).

Q&A | What is the result of the merge?
The workbooks have been merged, and the Snowbound Vacation Carnivals worksheet reflects the changes from Abigail and Martin. If Abigail and Martin had changed a common cell with different values, Excel would have displayed a prompt, asking which change to keep in the merged workbook.

How do I undo changes?
Merged changes cannot be undone. Make sure you make a copy of your files before you perform the merge.

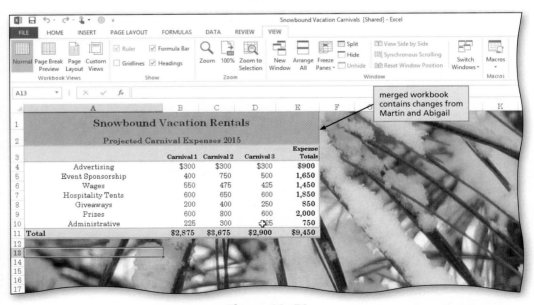

Figure 11–51

To Turn Off Workbook Sharing and Save the Workbook

Why? *Turn off workbook sharing once the workbooks have been merged to have access to all of Excel's features.* The following steps turn off workbook sharing so that the data can be manipulated.

- Tap or click REVIEW on the ribbon to display the REVIEW tab.

- Tap or click the Share Workbook button (REVIEW tab | Changes group) to display the Share Workbook dialog box.

- If necessary, tap or click the 'Allow changes by more than one user at the same time' check box to remove the check mark (Figure 11–52).

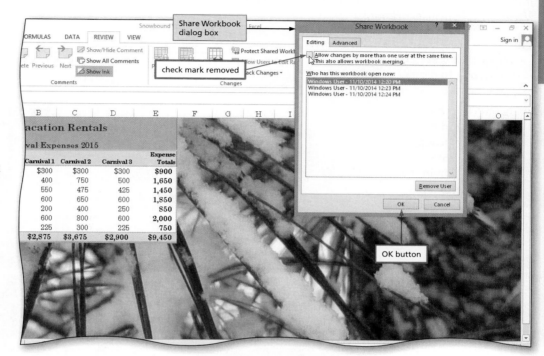

Figure 11–52

- Tap or click the OK button (Share Workbook dialog box) to turn off workbook sharing.

- If Excel displays the Microsoft Excel dialog box, tap or click the Yes button.

- Save the workbook with the file name, Snowbound Vacation Carnivals Merged.

Saving Custom Views

After a workbook functions in the manner in which it was designed, final touches can be added to the worksheets in the workbook to make them more attractive and easy to use. Custom views allow certain layout and printing characteristics of a workbook to be saved and then used later.

When a custom view of a workbook is saved, Excel stores information about the window size of the workbook and print settings that have been applied to the workbook at the time it is saved. Because of this, the workbook should be changed to have the desired layout and print settings before saving a custom view of a workbook. Each custom view that is created includes a name. The Custom Views button on the VIEW tab is used to save, delete, and show custom views. When a user saves a view, Excel also stores the name of the current worksheet. When a user shows a view by tapping or clicking the Show button in the Custom Views dialog box, Excel switches to the worksheet that was active in the workbook when the workbook view was saved.

To Save a Custom View of a Workbook

Why save a custom view? If a workbook requires that you customize certain layout and printing settings to use it effectively, saving a custom view allows you to save those settings with the workbook. Whenever the workbook is opened, it will be opened with those settings active. The following steps create and save a custom view of the Snowbound Vacation Carnivals workbook.

1

- Tap or click VIEW on the ribbon to display the VIEW tab.

- Tap or click the Zoom button (VIEW tab | Zoom group) and select 75% magnification in the Zoom dialog box (Figure 11–53).

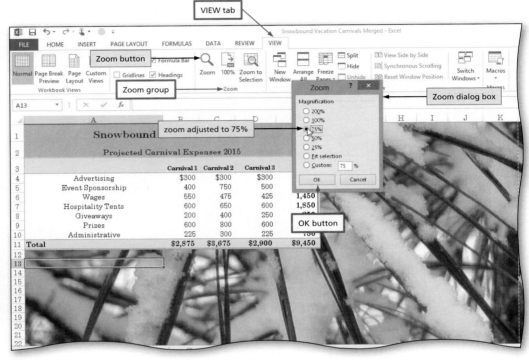

Figure 11–53

2

- Tap or click the OK button (Zoom dialog box) to set the zoom to 75%.

- Tap or click the Custom Views button (VIEW tab | Workbook Views group) to display the Custom Views dialog box (Figure 11–54).

Q&A Why does my list of views differ?
The views listed will reflect the authors of any open documents and any users signed in to Windows.

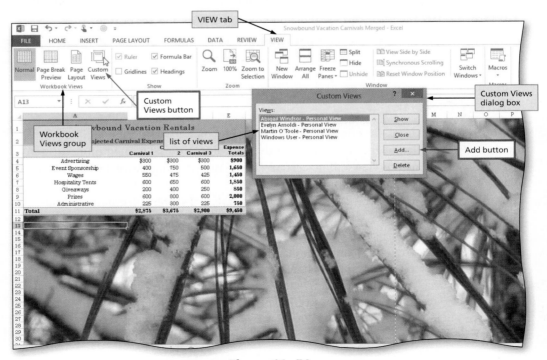

Figure 11–54

- Tap or click the Add button (Custom Views dialog box) to display the Add View dialog box.

- Type **Carnival Expenses** in the Name text box to provide a name for the custom view (Figure 11–55).

- Tap or click the OK button (Add View dialog box) to close the dialog box.

- Tap or click the 100% button (VIEW tab | Zoom group) to set the zoom to 100%.

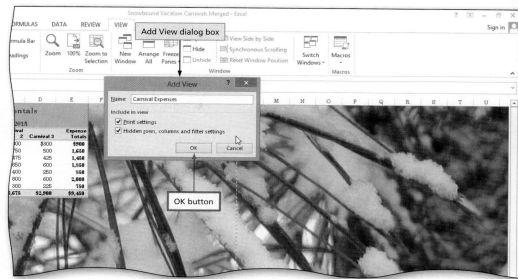

Figure 11–55

- Tap or click the Custom Views button (VIEW tab | Workbook Views group) to display the Custom Views dialog box.

- Tap or click Carnival Expenses in the Views list and then tap or click the Show button (Custom Views dialog box) to display the Carnival Expenses view, which includes a zoom to 75%.

- Tap or click the 100% button (VIEW tab | Zoom group) to set the zoom to 100%.

Q&A
Can I delete a view?
Yes. To delete views, use the Delete button in the Custom Views dialog box shown in Figure 11–54.

To Add a Hyperlink to a Webpage

1 USE COMMENTS | 2 ADD BACKGROUND & WATERMARK | 3 TRACK CHANGES | 4 USE SHARED WORKBOOKS
5 SAVE CUSTOM VIEWS | 6 ADD & EDIT HYPERLINKS | 7 ADD CHARTS & SHAPES

Why? *Hyperlinks can be used to direct the user to an outside information source.* You need to add a hyperlink that will take readers to the Adirondacks website, where they can review various events and opportunities, including winter carnivals. The following steps add a hyperlink to a cell in the worksheet.

- Press and hold or right-click cell A13 and then tap or click Hyperlink on the shortcut menu to display the Insert Hyperlink dialog box.

- If necessary, tap or click 'Existing File or Web Page' in the Link to bar (Figure 11–56).

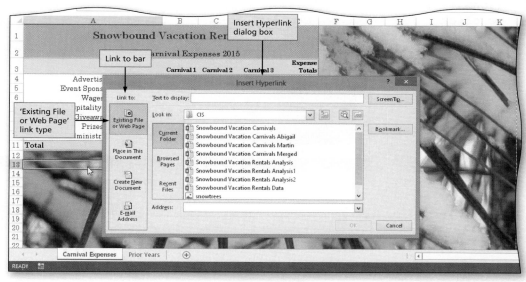

Figure 11–56

- Type `http://` `visitadirondacks` `.com` in the Address text box to provide the website address.

- Tap or click the 'Text to display' text box, delete any existing text, and then type **Adirondacks** **website** to provide display text for the hyperlink (Figure 11–57).

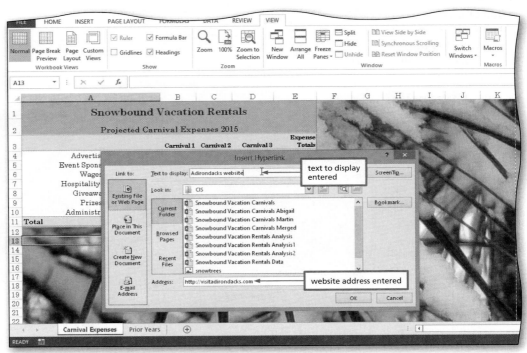

Figure 11–57

③

- Tap or click the ScreenTip button (Insert Hyperlink dialog box) to display the Set Hyperlink ScreenTip dialog box.

- Type `Tap or` `click to` `go to the` `Adirondacks` `website. Tap` `or click` `the + beside` `Attractions to` `find the link` `for Carnivals.` in the 'ScreenTip text' text box to provide a ScreenTip (Figure 11–58).

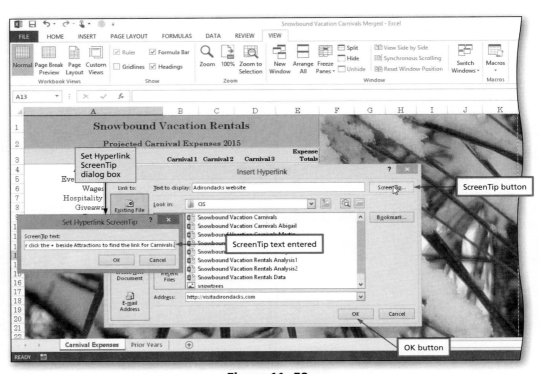

Figure 11–58

Q&A

Why not include a link to the carnivals webpage?

Links to pages off the main page often change. Providing a link to the main page with instructions for navigating is less likely to result in a broken link than providing the direct link to the carnivals page.

- Tap or click the OK button (Set Hyperlink ScreenTip dialog box) to close the dialog box.

- Tap or click the OK button (Insert Hyperlink dialog box) to close the dialog box and display the hyperlink in the worksheet (Figure 11–59).

- Tap or click the link to ensure that it is working.

- Close the browser window.

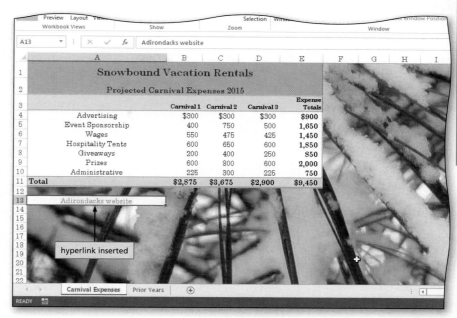

Figure 11–59

Other Ways

1. Tap or click 'Add a Hyperlink' button (INSERT tab | Links group)   2. Press CTRL+K

To Add a Hyperlink to an Email Address

1 USE COMMENTS | 2 ADD BACKGROUND & WATERMARK | 3 TRACK CHANGES | 4 USE SHARED WORKBOOKS
5 SAVE CUSTOM VIEWS | 6 ADD & EDIT HYPERLINKS | 7 ADD CHARTS & SHAPES

Why? *You can use a hyperlink to provide the user with an easy way to contact via email an individual related to the worksheet content.* You need to add a hyperlink that allows readers to contact the carnivals coordinator by email. The following steps add a hyperlink to an email address.

1

- Press and hold or right-click cell A15 and then tap or click Hyperlink on the shortcut menu to display the Insert Hyperlink dialog box.

- Tap or click E-mail Address in the Link to bar to update the Insert Hyperlink dialog box with fields related to email.

- Type `EvelynArnoldi@ snowboundvacations.com` in the E-mail address text box to enter an email address.

- Drag through the text in the 'Text to display' text box to select it and then type `Contact the carnivals coordinator` to provide the display text (Figure 11–60).

Q&A Why not fill in the Subject text box?
Any text entered in the Subject text box will appear automatically in the subject line of any email messages initiated using this link. You do not have to fill in this text box. Leaving this blank allows users to determine the subject of their email messages.

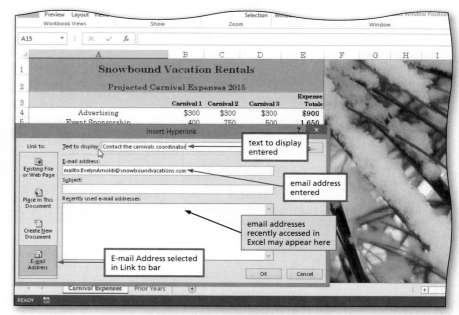

Figure 11–60

2

- Tap or click the ScreenTip button (Insert Hyperlink dialog box) to display the Set Hyperlink ScreenTip dialog box.

- Type **Tap or click to contact the carnivals coordinator.** as the ScreenTip text (Figure 11–61).

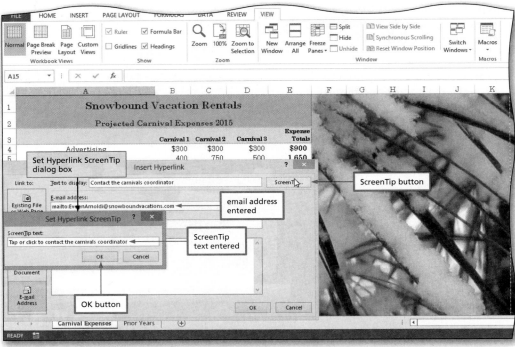

Figure 11–61

3

- Tap or click the OK button (Set Hyperlink ScreenTip dialog box) to close the dialog box.

- Tap or click the OK button (Insert Hyperlink dialog box) to close the dialog box and display the email hyperlink in the worksheet (Figure 11–62).

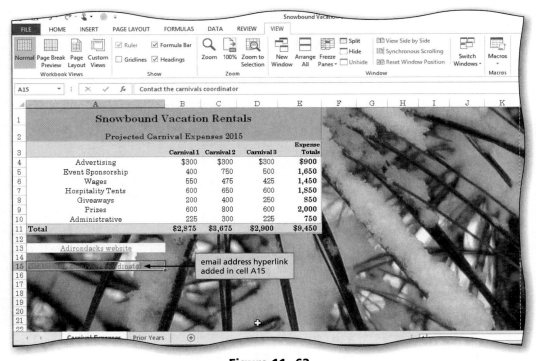

Figure 11–62

To Format the Hyperlinks

1 USE COMMENTS | 2 ADD BACKGROUND & WATERMARK | 3 TRACK CHANGES | 4 USE SHARED WORKBOOKS
5 SAVE CUSTOM VIEWS | 6 ADD & EDIT HYPERLINKS | **7 ADD CHARTS & SHAPES**

Why? *You can change the formatting of the hyperlinks and their cells to match the look of your worksheet.* The following steps change the formatting of the hyperlinks.

1

- Tap or click HOME on the ribbon to display the HOME tab.

- Tap or click the Cell Styles button (HOME tab | Styles group) to display the Cell Styles gallery.

- Press and hold or right-click the Hyperlink cell style to display the shortcut menu (Figure 11–63).

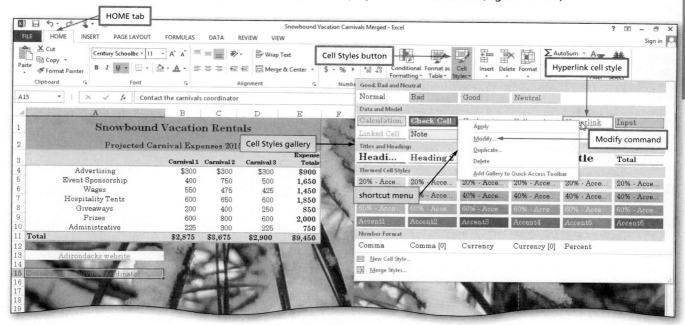

Figure 11–63

2

- Tap or click Modify on the shortcut menu to display the Style dialog box.

- Tap or click the Format button (Style dialog box) to display the Format Cells dialog box.

- If necessary, tap or click the Font tab, tap or click the Color button, and then tap or click 'Lavender, Accent 1, Darker 50%' (column 5, row 6) (Format Cells dialog box).

- Tap or click the Fill tab and then tap or click the lavender option in column 5, row 2 in the Background Color gallery (Figure 11–64).

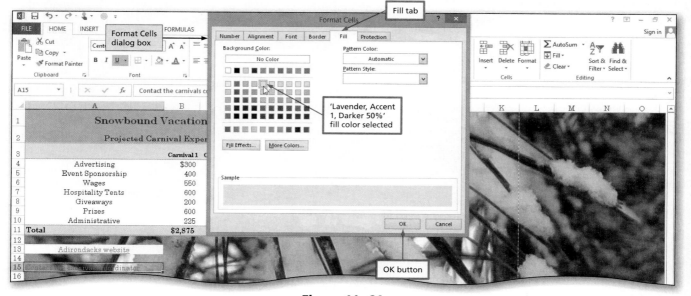

Figure 11–64

3

- Tap or click the OK button (Format Cells dialog box) to close the dialog box.
- Tap or click the OK button (Style dialog box) to apply the hyperlink style to the hyperlinks (Figure 11–65).

Q&A Why is only the second hyperlink formatted?
You tested the first hyperlink in a previous step, so it now is formatted with the Followed Hyperlink style.

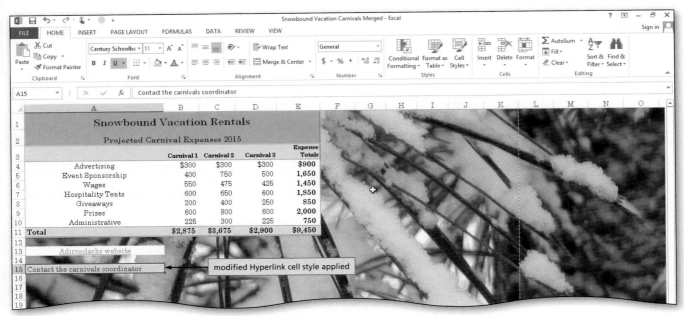

Figure 11–65

4

- Repeat Steps 1 through 3 for the Followed Hyperlink style in the Cell Styles gallery (Figure 11–66).

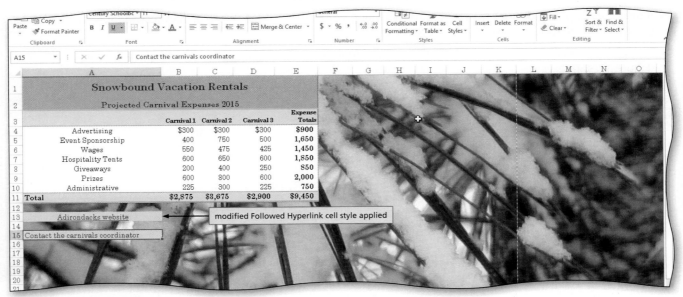

Figure 11–66

To Edit the Hyperlinks

Why? You can edit hyperlinks after they have been inserted in a worksheet to keep information current. You decide to change the email address to the coordinator address. The following steps edit the email address in the hyperlink.

- Press and hold or right-click cell A15 and then click Edit Hyperlink on the shortcut menu to display the Edit Hyperlink dialog box.

- Change the E-mail address entry in the dialog box to `mailto:coordinator@snowboundvacations.com` (Figure 11–67).

Q&A Why does the E-mail address entry now include "mailto:"?
The mailto: prefix is a standard prefix for email hyperlinks, which Excel adds automatically.

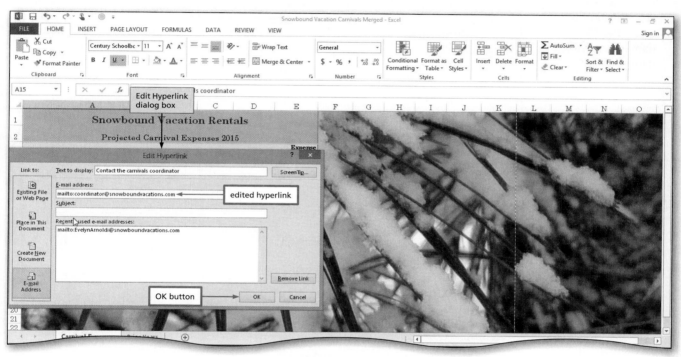

Figure 11–67

- Tap or click the OK button (Edit Hyperlink dialog box) to save the hyperlink with the new email address.

Q&A What if I want to delete a hyperlink rather than edit it?
You can delete a hyperlink by selecting Remove Hyperlink on the shortcut menu. You can also remove the hyperlink using the Remove Hyperlink button (Edit Hyperlink dialog box).

To Add a Picture to a Worksheet

Why? Pictures can be used to create continuity across worksheets and workbooks. The steps on the next page add a smaller version of the worksheet background from the Carnival Expenses worksheet to the Prior Years worksheet heading.

1

- Make the Prior Years worksheet the active worksheet.

- Select cell A1.

- Tap or click the From File button (INSERT tab | Illustrations group) to open the Insert Picture dialog box.

- Navigate to the Data Files for Students and then select the file named, snowtrees (Figure 11–68).

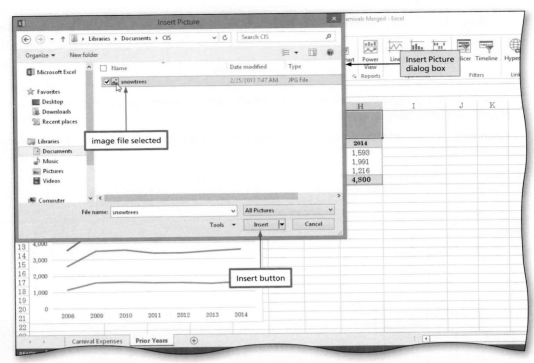

Figure 11–68

2

- Tap or click the Insert button (Insert Picture dialog box) to insert the image.

- Use the sizing handles to reduce and adjust the picture to the size shown in Figure 11–69.

Q&A

I cannot see all the sizing handles. How do I resize the image?

You can zoom out if necessary to see all the sizing handles and make the initial picture size reduction. Remember to zoom in to 100% after the initial resizing.

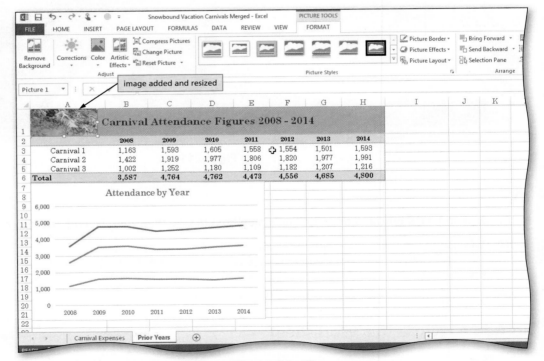

Figure 11–69

To Add Shapes to a Worksheet

Why? *You can use drawing capabilities in Excel, such as inserting shapes, to create your own logos and other images. The following steps use shapes to create a logo placeholder in the worksheet heading.*

1
- Tap or click the Shapes button (INSERT tab | Illustrations group) to display the Shapes gallery (Figure 11–70).

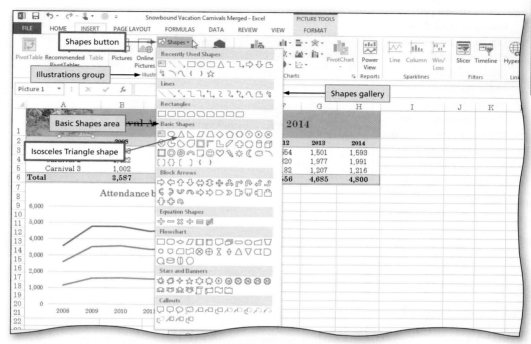

Figure 11–70

2
- Tap or click the Isosceles Triangle shape in the Basic Shapes area to close the Shapes gallery and change the pointer to a crosshair.

- Drag the crosshair pointer to draw a triangle in the worksheet heading (Figure 11–71).

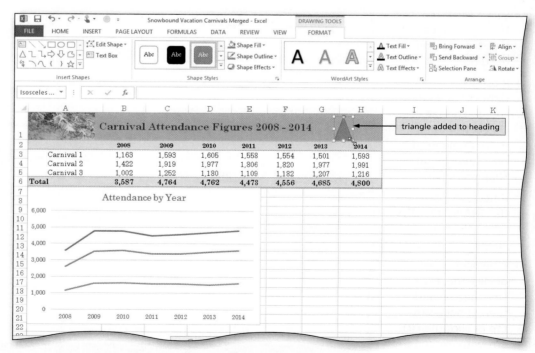

Figure 11–71

- Tap or click the Copy
button (HOME tab |
Clipboard group)
to make a copy
of the shape just
inserted, and then
tap or click the Paste
button (HOME tab |
Clipboard group)
twice to insert two
more triangles in
the worksheet. Use
the sizing handles to
resize the triangles
and move them to
a pattern similar to
that in Figure 11–72.

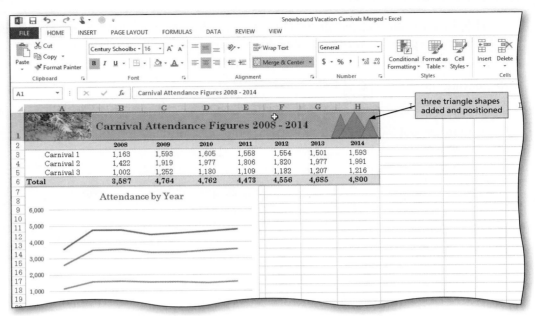

Figure 11–72

To Change a Shape Fill and Outline

1 USE COMMENTS | 2 ADD BACKGROUND & WATERMARK | 3 TRACK CHANGES | 4 USE SHARED WORKBOOKS
5 SAVE CUSTOM VIEWS | 6 ADD & EDIT HYPERLINKS | 7 ADD CHARTS & SHAPES

Why? Consider modifying various formatting features of shapes to enhance the appearance of the image you create.
The following steps change the outline and fill of the shapes added to the worksheet heading.

- Select the three
triangle shapes
in the worksheet
heading.

- Press and hold or
right-click and then
choose Format
Object from the
shortcut menu to
open the Format
Shape task pane.

- If necessary, select
the SHAPE OPTIONS
tab in the Format
Shape task pane.

- If necessary, tap
or click the 'Fill &
Line' button and
then, if necessary,
tap or click the FILL
arrow to expand the
FILL section.

- Select Gradient fill to
change the fill of the shapes
to a gradient (Figure 11–73).

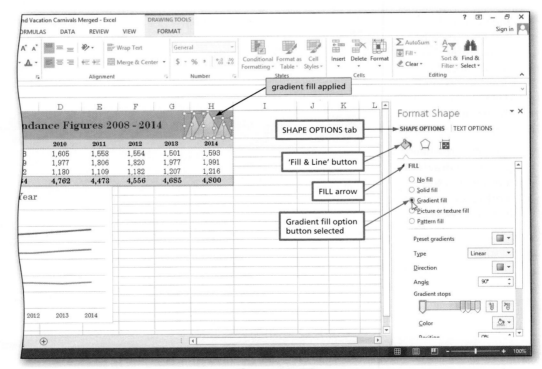

Figure 11–73

2

- Tap or click the FILL arrow to collapse the FILL section and then tap or click the LINE arrow to expand the LINE section.

- Change the Width to 1 pt and the Dash type to Square Dot (Figure 11–74).

3

- Close the Format Shape task pane and then tap or click cell F22 to deselect the shapes.

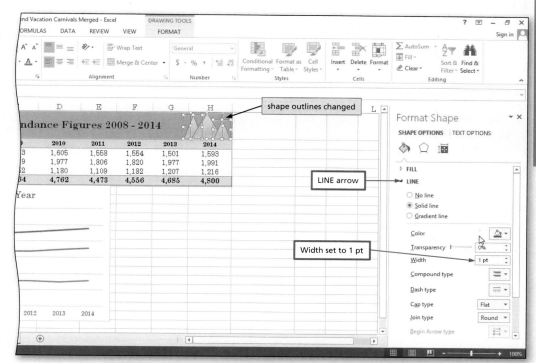

Figure 11–74

To Add a Legend to a Chart

1 USE COMMENTS | 2 ADD BACKGROUND & WATERMARK | 3 TRACK CHANGES | 4 USE SHARED WORKBOOKS
5 SAVE CUSTOM VIEWS | 6 ADD & EDIT HYPERLINKS | **7 ADD CHARTS & SHAPES**

Why? *With line charts containing multiple lines, a legend is necessary for the reader to be able to understand the chart information.* The following steps add a legend to the chart.

1

- Tap or click anywhere in the chart to select it.

- Tap or click the Chart Elements button to display the CHART ELEMENTS gallery. Point to Legend to display an arrow and then tap or click the arrow to display the Legend fly-out menu (Figure 11–75).

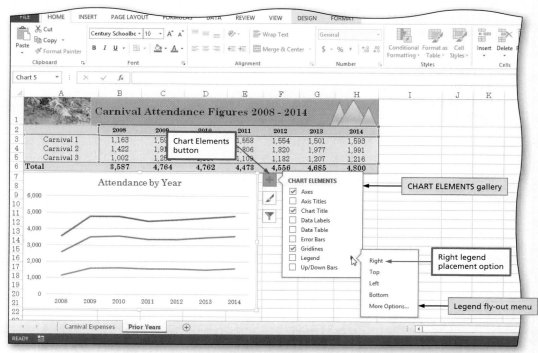

Figure 11–75

2

- Tap or click Right on the Legend flyout menu to add a legend to the right of the chart.

- Tap or click the Chart Elements button to close the gallery (Figure 11–76).

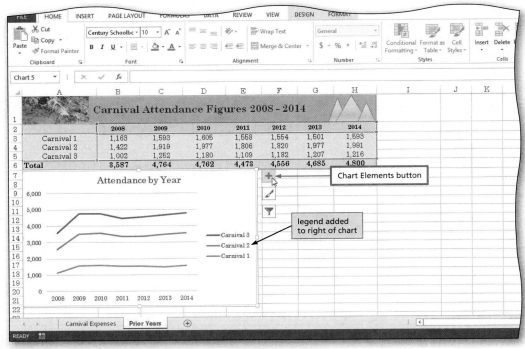

Figure 11–76

To Add a Shadow to a Chart Element

1 USE COMMENTS | 2 ADD BACKGROUND & WATERMARK | 3 TRACK CHANGES | 4 USE SHARED WORKBOOKS
5 SAVE CUSTOM VIEWS | 6 ADD & EDIT HYPERLINKS | 7 ADD CHARTS & SHAPES

Why? Shadows and other design features can add depth and a more professional look to your charts. The following steps add a shadow to the plot area of the chart.

1

- Tap or click anywhere in the plot area to select it.

- Press and hold or right-click the plot area to display a shortcut menu (Figure 11–77).

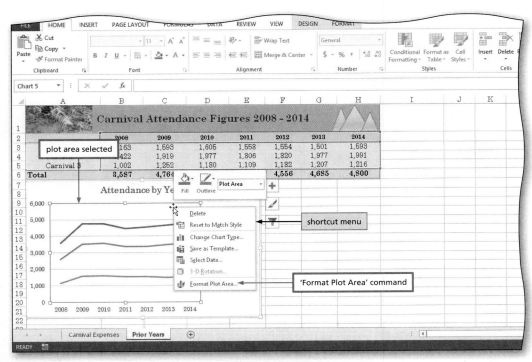

Figure 11–77

2

- Tap or click 'Format Plot Area' on the shortcut menu to open the Format Plot Area task pane.

- If necessary, tap or click the Effects button in the Format Plot Area task pane to select it, and then tap or click the SHADOW arrow to expand the SHADOW section.

- Tap or click the SHADOW button to display the Shadow gallery (Figure 11–78).

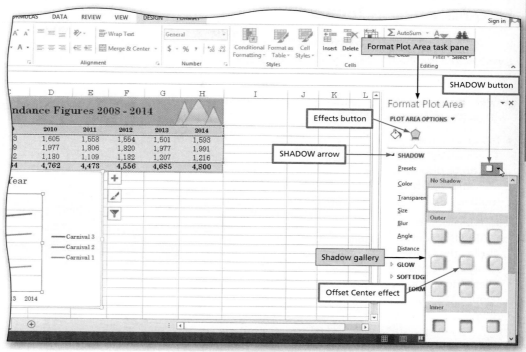

Figure 11–78

3

- Tap or click Offset Center in the Outer area to apply a shadow effect to the plot area of the chart.

- Close the Format Plot Area task pane and then tap or click cell F22 to deselect the plot area (Figure 11–79).

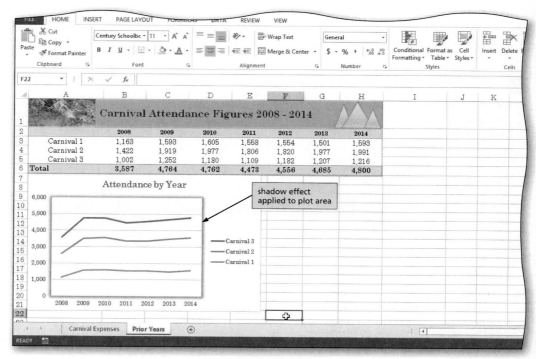

Figure 11–79

To Add Sparklines Using the Quick Analysis Toolbar

Why? Sparklines provide charts immediately beside the data that creates them, allowing for easy comparison of numerical and graphical data. The following steps add sparkline charts for attendance figures.

1
- Select the range B3:H5.
- Tap or click the 'Quick Analysis Lens' button to display the Quick Analysis toolbar.
- Tap or click the SPARKLINES tab to display the Quick Analysis buttons related to sparklines (Figure 11–80).

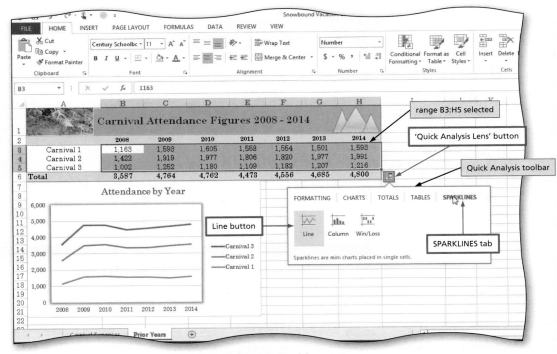

Figure 11–80

2
- Tap or click Line to insert sparklines in cells I3:I5.
- Tap or click cell F22 to deselect the cells containing the sparkline charts (Figure 11–81).

3
- Save the file with the file name, Snowbound Vacation Carnivals Complete.

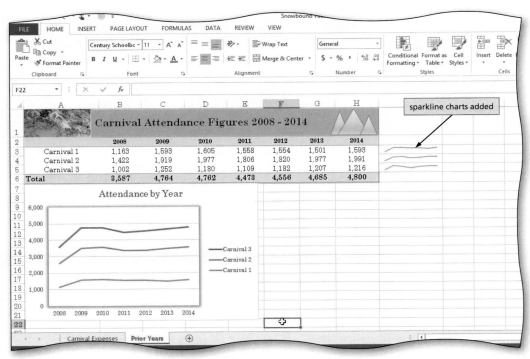

Figure 11–81

Collaborating with Users Who Do Not Use Excel 2013

It is not unusual to need to collaborate with others who are using different versions of software, or different software entirely, to do their work. It is not unheard of to find different versions of software being used within the same company. When collaborating with others, be sure to spend time evaluating how your collaborators will be working with the workbooks you create. The results of this evaluation will inform decisions you make about how to save files and distribute them.

In instances where people are working with earlier versions of software, or different software, you need to provide them with the workbook in a format that they can use.

To Save a Workbook in an Earlier Version of Excel

If someone is using an earlier version of Excel, you can save the workbook in that earlier format. You should be aware that some features in Excel 2013 are not compatible with earlier versions of the software. In cases where you have used one of these features, Excel will use the most compatible features of the earlier version of the software whenever possible. The following steps save the workbook in an earlier version of Excel.

1 Tap or click the FILE tab to open the Backstage view.

2 Tap or click Save As and then tap or click the Browse button to display the Save As dialog box.

3 Tap or click the 'Save as type' arrow to display a list of file types.

4 Tap or click 'Excel 97-2003 Workbook' in the Save as type list to select the appropriate file type.

5 Tap or click the Save button (Save As dialog box) to save the workbook in an earlier version of Excel.

6 When the Microsoft Excel - Compatibility Checker dialog box is displayed, tap or click the 'Copy to New Sheet' button to create a copy of the compatibility report (Figure 11–82).

7 After reviewing the compatibility report, save it as an Excel 97-2003 workbook, tapping or clicking the Continue button (Microsoft Excel - Compatibility Checker dialog box) to complete the save process.

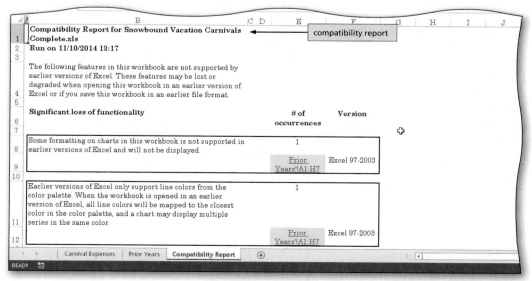

Figure 11–82

To Save a Workbook as a PDF File

The following steps save the workbook as a PDF file in preparation for distribution.

1 Tap or click the FILE tab to display the Backstage view.

2 Tap or click Save As and then tap or click the Browse button to display the Save As dialog box.

3 Tap or click the 'Save as type' arrow to display a list of file types.

4 Tap or click PDF in the Save as type list to select the appropriate file type.

5 Tap or click the Save button (Save As dialog box) to save the workbook as a PDF file.

6 If necessary, exit Adobe Reader or Adobe Acrobat.

Importing and Exporting XML Data for Collaboration

XML is an increasingly popular format for sharing data. **XML** stands for **Extensible Markup Language**, which is a language that is used to encapsulate data and a description of the data in a single text file, or **XML file**. **Tags** are used in XML files to describe data items, which are called **elements**. XML files typically have a file extension of .xml. Industry organizations and companies create standard XML file layouts and tags to describe commonly used types of data.

Excel is capable of importing and exporting XML in a variety of layouts, as long as the XML file is described by a schema. A **schema** is a special type of XML file used to describe the layout of data in other XML files. A schema describes what information an XML file should contain, the order in which the elements should appear, the values allowed for each element, and a variety of other information. A schema file typically is sent from a technical source, such as a programmer or a person in a company's information technology department.

Before importing XML data into a worksheet or exporting XML data from a worksheet, the schema file that describes the format of the XML file to import must be added to a workbook. When a schema is added to a workbook, the schema is called an **XML map** in Excel.

With an XML map, an import area can be created on a worksheet by dragging elements from the XML map to cells in a worksheet. When the XML data is imported, it is imported as a table. To attach an XML map to a workbook, you first must display the DEVELOPER tab on the ribbon as described in Chapter 10 on page EX 625. The XML group is displayed on the DEVELOPER tab. Tap or click the Source button (DEVELOPER tab | XML group) to open the XML Source task pane. Tap or click the XML Maps button and then tap or click the Add button (XML Maps dialog box). You then can navigate to the location of the schema file that was provided to you and drag and drop XML elements to your worksheet to create the XML map. When your XML map is complete, tap or click the Import button (DEVELOPER tab | XML group) to begin the process of importing an XML file. After importing the XML data, you often may need to convert the table to a range because, as stated earlier, XML data always is imported as a table.

To Exit Excel

The project is complete. The following steps restore the Quick Access Toolbar to its original state and exit Excel.

1 Press and hold or right-click the 'Compare and Merge Workbooks' button on the Quick Access Toolbar and then select 'Remove from Quick Access Toolbar' on the shortcut menu to remove the 'Compare and Merge Workbooks' button from the Quick Access Toolbar.

2 Tap or click the Close button on the right side of the title bar.

3 If the Microsoft Office Excel dialog box is displayed, tap or click the Don't Save button.

Chapter Summary

In this chapter, you learned how to use comments to give feedback, edit, format and delete comments, share workbooks and track changes, distribute workbooks by email, compare and merge workbooks, save a custom view of a workbook, format a worksheet background, add pictures and shapes to a worksheet, and save a file to different formats to facilitate collaboration. The items listed below include all the new Excel skills you have learned in this chapter, with the tasks grouped by activity.

Use Comments
Add Comments to a Worksheet (EX 695)
Display All Comments on a Worksheet (EX 697)
Edit Comments on a Worksheet (EX 697)
Format Comments on a Worksheet (EX 699)

Track Changes
Turn On Track Changes (EX 709)
Open a Workbook and Review Tracked
　Changes (EX 712)
Turn Off Track Changes (EX 717)

Add Hyperlinks
Add a Hyperlink to a Webpage (EX 725)
Add a Hyperlink to an Email Address (EX 727)
Format the Hyperlinks (EX 728)
Edit the Hyperlinks (EX 731)

Format Worksheets and Workbooks
Format a Worksheet Background (EX 701)
Add a Watermark to a Worksheet (EX 703)

Save a Custom View of a Workbook (EX 724)
Save a Workbook as a PDF File (EX 740)

Format Charts
Add a Legend to a Chart (EX 735)
Add a Shadow to a Chart Element (EX 736)
Add Sparklines Using the Quick Analysis
　Menu (EX 738)

Use Shapes
Add Shapes to a Worksheet (EX 733)
Change a Shape Fill and Outline (EX 734)

Share Workbooks
Share and Collaborate on a Workbook (EX 706)
Distribute a Workbook by Email (EX 711)
Compare Workbooks (EX 719)
Merge Workbooks (EX 721)
Turn Off Workbook Sharing and Save the
　Workbook (EX 723)

What decisions will you need to make when using Excel to collaborate with others?
Use these guidelines as you complete the assignments in this chapter and create your own worksheets for collaborating with others outside of this class.

1. Determine the audience and the purpose behind the collaboration.

2. Determine the options available for collaboration.

3. Prepare workbook(s) for distribution.

4. Evaluate changes made by colleagues.

    a) With a single distributed workbook, use Track Changes and Accept/Reject changes.

    b) With multiple workbooks, use Compare and Merge and then Accept/Reject changes.

5. Add worksheet enhancements.

    a) Add worksheet background, watermark, and shapes as appropriate.

    b) Enhance charts if appropriate.

How should you submit solutions to questions in the assignments identified with a ✳ symbol?
Every assignment in this book contains one or more questions identified with a ✳ symbol. These questions require you to think beyond the assigned file. Present your solutions to the questions in the format required by your instructor. Possible formats may include one or more of these options: write the answer; create a document that contains the answer; present your answer to the class; discuss your answer in a group; record the answer as audio or video using a webcam, smartphone, or portable media player; or post answers on a blog, wiki, or website.

Apply Your Knowledge

Reinforce the skills and apply the concepts you learned in this chapter.

Working with Comments and Tracked Changes
Note: To complete this assignment, you will be required to use the Data Files for Students. Visit www.cengage.com/ct/studentdownload for detailed instructions or contact your instructor for information about accessing the required files.

Instructions: Run Excel. Open the workbook Apply 11-1 Amber Workshop Expenses from the Data Files for Students and then save the workbook using the file name, Apply 11-1 Amber Workshop Expenses Complete.

Figure 11–83 shows the initial workbook. You need to make changes based on comments, create a worksheet showing the history of tracked changes, and accept/reject tracked changes.

Perform the following tasks:
1. If necessary, share the workbook. Tap or click the Track Changes button (REVIEW tab | Changes group) and then tap or click Highlight Changes on the Track Changes menu. Clear the three check boxes in the Highlight which changes area. Tap or click the 'List changes on a new sheet' check box to place a check mark in the check box. Tap or click the OK button. Print the History worksheet.

2. In the Amber Workshop Expenses worksheet, tap or click the Track Changes button (REVIEW tab | Changes group) and then tap or click 'Accept/Reject Changes' on the Track Changes menu. Clear the When check box and then click the OK button. Reject the change to cell B6. Accept the other change.

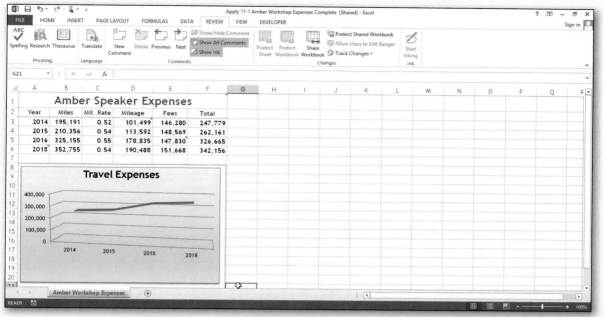

Figure 11–83

3. Tap or click the 'Show All Comments' button (REVIEW tab | Comments group). Make the changes as indicated in the comments. Delete the comments and then print the worksheet.

4. If requested by your instructor, add a comment to cell A2 noting your date of birth.

5. Save the workbook and then exit Excel.

6. Submit the assignment as requested by your instructor.

7. ✳ You can review changes made to the worksheet either by generating the History worksheet or by reviewing the comments added to the worksheet by the Highlight Changes command. Which method of reviewing changes do you prefer, and why?

Extend Your Knowledge

Extend the skills you learned in this chapter and experiment with new skills. You may need to use Help to complete the assignment.

Consolidating Worksheets by Category

Note: To complete this assignment, you will be required to use the Data Files for Students. Visit www.cengage.com/ct/studentdownload for detailed instructions or contact your instructor for information about accessing the required files.

Instructions: Run Excel. Open the workbook Extend 11-1 M&W Gourmet from the Data Files for Students and then save the workbook using the file name, Extend 11-1 M&W Gourmet Complete.

   Modify the workbook so that it consolidates data from existing worksheets. The data in the worksheets have the same column and row labels (Figure 11–84).

Continued >

Extend Your Knowledge *continued*

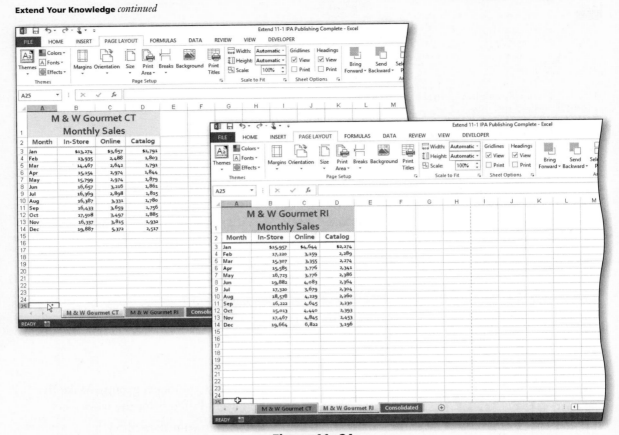

Figure 11–84

Perform the following tasks.

1. Select the M&W Gourmet CT worksheet. Select the range A2:D14 and name the range CT.

2. Select the M&W Gourmet RI worksheet. Select the range A2:D14 and name the range RI.

3. Insert a blank worksheet. Name the worksheet Consolidated and color the tab blue. Copy the range A1:D1 from the M&W Gourmet RI worksheet and then paste it to the range A1:D1 on the Consolidated worksheet. Change the background color of the range to Light Blue from the Standard Colors area in the background color palette. Change M&W Gourmet RI Monthly Sales in cell A1 to M&W Gourmet Consolidated Monthly Sales.

4. Select cell A2. Tap or click the Consolidate button (DATA tab | Data Tools group). In the Consolidate dialog box, type   CT   in the Reference text box and then tap or click the Add button (Consolidate dialog box). Type   RI   in the Reference text box, and then tap or click the Add button. Tap or click the Top row and Left column check boxes to insert check marks. Tap or click the OK button (Consolidate dialog box) to consolidate the worksheets. Use Paste Special to copy the formatting and column widths for the ranges A2:D2 and A3:D14 from either state worksheet to the consolidated worksheet.

5. If requested by your instructor, change RI to the abbreviation for the state in which you were born.

6. Print the consolidated worksheet.

7. Save the workbook. Submit the assignment as requested by your instructor.

8. ✸ How does consolidation differ from copying and pasting content from one worksheet to another? How does it differ from using Compare and Merge?

Analyze, Correct, Improve

Analyze a workbook, correct all errors, and improve it.

Preparing and Sharing a Workbook

Note: To complete this assignment, you will be required to use the Data Files for Students. Visit www.cengage.com/ct/studentdownload for detailed instructions or contact your instructor for information about accessing the required files.

Instructions: Run Excel. Open the workbook Analyze 11-1 QuikCarts from the Data Files for Students and then save the workbook using the file name, Analyze 11-1 QuikCarts Complete.

The workbook is going to be shared among team members; however, several editing and formatting items have to be resolved before sharing because the changes cannot be made after the file is shared. After making the changes, you will share the workbook. The completed QuikCarts worksheet is shown in Figure 11–85.

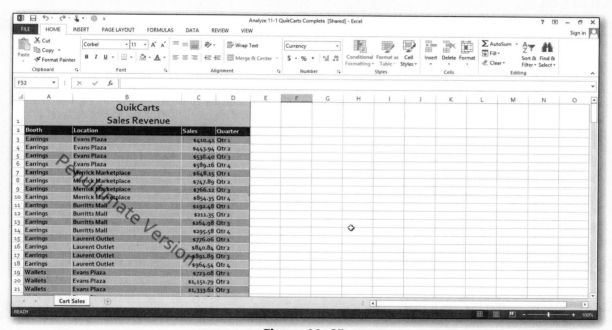

Figure 11–85

1. Correct

a. Merge and center the cell range A1:D1.

b. If requested by your instructor, add a comment to cell B2 listing your name and birthdate.

c. Review all comments in the worksheet, and make corrections as necessary. Two of the comments should remain in the worksheet, as noted. Delete all the rest of the comments after completing the corrections.

2. Improve

a. Add a watermark to the worksheet using WordArt. Use Fill - Black, Text 1, Shadow from the WordArt gallery. Use the text Penultimate Version for the WordArt, set the font size to 36, and the transparency to 75%. Place as shown in the figure.

b. Tap or click the Protect Workbook button (REVIEW tab | Changes group). Set the password to **cartsales** for the workbook.

Continued >

Analyze, Correct, Improve *continued*

    c. Tap or click the Share Workbook button (REVIEW tab | Changes group). Tap or click the 'Allow changes by more than one user at the same time' check box to place a check mark in it. Tap or click the OK button (Share Workbook dialog box) to share the workbook.

    d. Print the worksheet.

    e. Save the workbook. Submit the revised workbook in the format specified by your instructor.

3. ✸ If you had been in charge of setting up this workbook, would you have used comments or track changes as the method for updating content? Explain your choice.

In the Labs

Design and/or create a workbook using the guidelines, concepts, and skills presented in this chapter. Labs 1 and 2, which increase in difficulty, require you to create solutions based on what you learned in the chapter; Lab 3 requires you to create a solution, which uses cloud and web technologies, by learning and investigating on your own from general guidance.

Lab 1: **Merging Workbooks**

Note: To complete this assignment, you will be required to use the Data Files for Students. Visit www.cengage.com/ct/studentdownload for detailed instructions or contact your instructor for information about accessing the required files.

Problem: As the collegewide lab director, you have created a workbook using the time sheets from the lab assistants and have shared the workbook with the lab managers who made their own copies. They have sent their copies back with their changes to the timesheet data for the various lab assistants from the West, East, and Central locations of Eastbrook Cole University. Olivia, Emrys, and Robert are floating lab managers who oversee the three labs. You now need to merge their changes into one workbook. The result of the merge is shown in Figure 11–86.

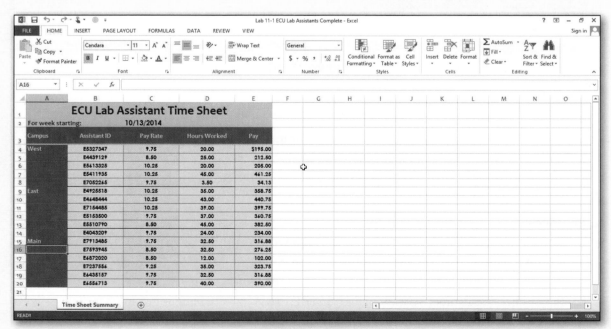

Figure 11–86

Instructions: Perform the following tasks:

1. Open the workbook Lab 11-1 ECU Lab Assistants from the Data Files for Students and then save the workbook using the file name, Lab 11-1 ECU Lab Assistants Complete.

2. If necessary, add the 'Compare and Merge Workbooks' button to the Quick Access Toolbar. Use the 'Compare and Merge Workbooks' button to merge the workbooks Lab 11-1 ECU Lab Assistants Emrys, Lab 11-1 ECU Lab Assistants Olivia, and Lab 11-1 ECU Lab Assistants Robert into Lab 11-1 ECU Lab Assistants Complete.

3. In the Lab 11-1 ECU Lab Assistants Complete workbook, tap or click the Track Changes button (REVIEW tab | Changes group) and then tap or click 'Accept/Reject Changes' on the Track Changes menu. If necessary, clear the When check box and then click OK (Select Changes to Accept or Reject dialog box). For cells C7 and C9, accept Emrys' changes, for cell D5, accept Olivia's change. For cell C8, accept Robert's changes. For cells C18 and D20, accept the original value. Accept all other changes.

4. Turn off sharing so that the workbook is exclusive.

5. If requested by your instructor, add a comment to cell A3 with your date of birth.

6. Print the worksheet. Save the workbook and submit the assignment in the format requested by your instructor.

7. ✸ What do you see as the disadvantages of comparing and merging as compared with using comments exclusively for updating content?

Lab 2: Merging Sales Data and Working with Charts and Backgrounds

Note: To complete this assignment, you will be required to use the Data Files for Students. Visit www.cengage.com/ct/studentdownload for detailed instructions or contact your instructor for information about accessing the required files.

Problem: You work for Jones Motorcycle Rentals. You have been asked to merge revenue data from the three sectors where the motorcycles are rented. After you have merged the data, you will save a version in a previous version of Excel for sharing with your supervisor, who has Excel 2003.

Part 1: Instructions: Perform the following tasks.

1. Run Excel. Open the Lab 11-2 Jones Motorcycle Rentals workbook from the Data Files for Students and then save the workbook using the file name, Lab 11-2 Jones Motorcycle Rentals Complete.

2. If necessary, add the 'Compare and Merge Workbooks' button to the Quick Access Toolbar. Use the 'Compare and Merge Workbooks' button to merge the workbooks Lab 11-2 Jones Motorcycle Rentals Sector 2 and Lab 11-2 Jones Motorcycle Rentals Sector 3 into Lab 11-2 Jones Motorcycle Rentals Complete. Turn off sharing so that the workbook is exclusive (Figure 11–87).

3. Enhance the chart by adding an appropriate chart title and additional formatting, such as a shadow to the plot area.

4. Add a worksheet background that reflects the company's products and services. (*Hint:* After tapping or clicking the Background button (PAGE LAYOUT Tab | Page Setup group), use the search term, motorcycle, in Office.com Clip Art in the Insert Pictures window.) Make any additional formatting changes to the page that you think are necessary once you have placed your background image.

Continued >

In the Labs *continued*

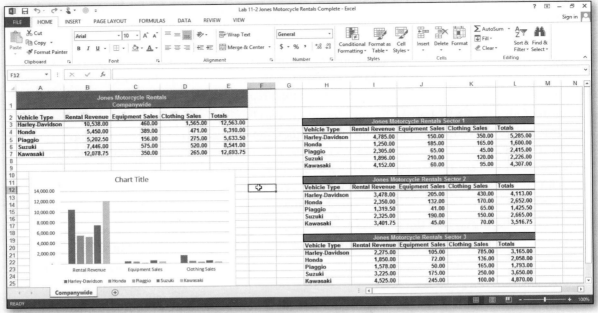

Figure 11–87

5. If requested by your instructor, add a comment to cell A11 with the name of your hometown in it.

6. Print the worksheet. Save the workbook and submit the assignment as requested by your instructor.

Instructions Part 2: Perform the following tasks to save the workbook in Excel 2003 format.

1. If necessary, open Lab 11-2 Jones Motorcycle Rentals Complete.

2. Save the workbook with a file name of Lab 11-2 Jones Motorcycle Rentals Complete 2003 and a file type of Excel 97-2003 Workbook. After reviewing the Compatibility Checker results, tap or click the Continue button (Compatibility Checker dialog box) to save the workbook.

3. Submit the assignment as requested by your instructor.

4. ✵ What formatting changes did you make to the worksheet to accommodate the image you used as a background?

Lab 3: Routing Workbooks, Tracking Changes, and Inserting Comments

Note: To complete this assignment, you will be required to use the Data Files for Students. Visit www.cengage.com/ct/studentdownload for detailed instructions or contact your instructor for information about accessing the required files.

Problem: You are a teaching assistant for a professor who is teaching an IT (Information Technology) Honors class. You have been asked to verify the project grades for student projects. Four graduate students function as project leaders for the projects and provide grades for each student's project performance.

Instructions: Perform the following tasks.

1. Open the Lab 11-3 IT Honors Project workbook from the Data Files for Students and then save the workbook using the file name, Lab 11-3 IT Honors Project Complete.

2. Add a comment to cell D5. Type **I entered an 89 for this project score. Can you verify this score?** for the comment text.

3. Track changes to the workbook. Tap or click the Track Changes button (REVIEW tab | Changes group), and then tap or click Highlight Changes on the Track Changes menu. Tap or click the 'Track changes while editing' check box and then clear the three check boxes in the Highlight which changes area.

4. Send the workbook to two classmates by tapping or clicking the Share tab (FILE tab), tapping or clicking the 'Send Using E-mail' button, and then tapping or clicking 'Send as Attachment'. Select the email addresses of two classmates and then enter **IT Honors Project Verification** in the Subject text box. Enter appropriate message text in the Message text box, requesting that each classmate add comments to at least one cell and change the contents of two cells and then send the message.

5. Ask a classmate to send the workbook to you as an email attachment. When you receive the email message, print it. Add a comment to at least one cell and then change the contents of at least three cells before sending the workbook to the next recipient.

6. When you receive your workbook after it has been sent to all recipients, tap or click the Track Changes button (REVIEW tab | Changes group) and then tap or click 'Accept/Reject Changes' on the Track Changes menu. Reject two changes and accept all the others.

7. In the Comments group on the REVIEW tab, tap or click the 'Show All Comments' button.

8. Submit the assignment as requested by your instructor.

9. ✸ You completed this project using email to share material. You also could have completed this project using SkyDrive to share material. Which would be your preference, and why?

✸ Consider This: Your Turn

Apply your creative thinking and problem solving skills to design and implement a solution.

1: Merging Workbooks and Reviewing Changes

Personal/Academic

Part 1: Barrymore College Art Gallery has several targeted fund-raising drives. During the October fund-raising drive at the university, a computer error occurred that caused the file to become corrupt. After reconstructing the latest donation records from paper receipts, you have been asked to compare the two worksheets containing reconstructed data against the master worksheet to ensure that all information has been updated.

Open the workbook CT 11-1 Barrymore College from the Data Files for Students and then save the workbook using the file name, CT 11-1 Barrymore College Complete. Review the Fundraising worksheet, which lists donations made to the Barrymore College Art Gallery fund.

Continued >

Consider This: Your Turn *continued*

Merge the workbooks CT 11-1 Barrymore College - Justin and CT 11-1 Barrymore College - Flores into the CT 11-1 Barrymore College Complete workbook. Highlight and review the changes that your fund-raising managers Justin and Flores made to the workbook. Accept all the changes and then turn off sharing so that the workbook is exclusive. In cell D13, insert the label, Subtotals. In cell E13, calculate the sum of the donations made to date. Format the label and results using the Total cell style. Print the worksheet and save the workbook. Submit the assignment as requested by your instructor.

Part 2: ✳ How likely is it that you would use a collaborative feature of Excel like this with colleagues? What are the drawbacks to such an approach that might make you not consider this?

2: Using Commenting and Track Changes to Evaluate Report Differences

Professional

Part 1: Open the workbook CT 11-2 First Thing Couriers from the Data Files for Students and then save the workbook using the file name, CT 11-2 First Thing Couriers Complete. You have reports for two years for First Thing Couriers that contain discrepancies for actual recorded hours by position. You have been charged with identifying discrepancies and then gathering information to better understand these discrepancies. Use the collaborative features of Excel to design a strategy for gathering information and presenting it. Use Position titles rather than names for any comments or requests that are to be directed to a particular person. You should prepare a workbook or workbooks containing the collaborative content needed to gather information. In the workbook (or workbooks), insert a new sheet named Instructions. Insert a text box on this sheet and use it to describe how you would use your workbook(s) to gather and present the information requested. Save the workbook. Submit the assignment as requested by your instructor.

Part 2: ✳ Identify an alternative approach in Excel to this task, and explain why you chose the method you did over this alternative.

3: Commenting and Sharing a Fitness Schedule

Research and Collaboration

Part 1: Open the workbook CT 11-3 Family Fitness from the Data Files for Students and then save the workbook using the file name, CT 11-3 Family Fitness Complete. For a fitness goal, you and your family have joined a local gym. Using emailed information about your family's hours spent at the gym in four categories, you have created a workbook. You now want to add comments and then share the workbook and send it to your family. Add a comment asking what they think of the title of the worksheet. For your mother, father, and siblings (Betty, Lee, and Tony), add comments asking them to review the hours and adjust them accordingly. Ask them to add comments for changes they would suggest in the setup of the workbook. Add a hyperlink in cell A10 to a website that provides information about fitness benefits of various types of fitness. Format the hyperlink to make it visually appealing. Apply any additional formatting you think is needed to integrate the hyperlink with the rest of the worksheet content. Share the workbook. Save the workbook. Submit the assignment as requested by your instructor.

Part 2: ✳ How likely is it that you would use a collaborative feature of Excel like this with family? What are the drawbacks to such an approach that might make you not consider this?

Learn Online

Reinforce what you learned in this chapter with games, exercises, training, and many other online activities and resources.

Student Companion Site Reinforcement activities and resources are available at no additional cost on www.cengagebrain.com. Visit www.cengage.com/ct/studentdownload for detailed instructions about accessing the resources available at the Student Companion Site.

SAM Put your skills into practice with SAM! If you have a SAM account, go to www.cengage .com/sam2013 to access SAM assignments for this chapter.

8 | Macros, Navigation Forms, and Control Layouts

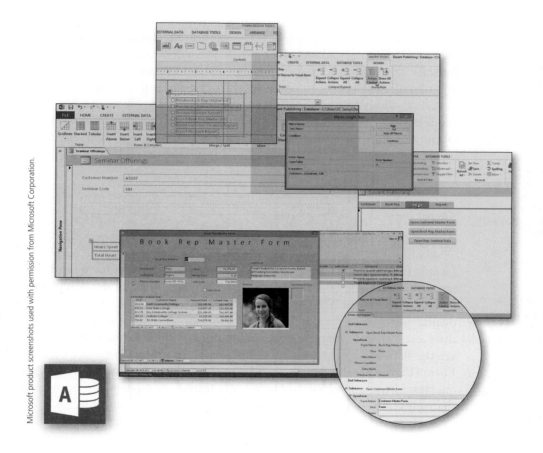

Objectives

You will have mastered the material in this project when you can:

- Create and modify macros and submacros
- Create a menu form with command buttons
- Create a menu form with an option group
- Create a macro for the option group
- Use an IF statement in a macro
- Create datasheet forms
- Create user interface (UI) macros
- Create navigation forms
- Add tabs to a navigation form
- Create data macros
- Create and remove control layouts
- Use the ARRANGE tab to modify control layouts on forms and reports

8 | Macros, Navigation Forms, and Control Layouts

Introduction

BTW

Q&As

For a complete list of the Q&As found in many of the step-by-step sequences in this book, visit the Q&A resource on the Student Companion Site located on www.cengagebrain.com. For detailed instructions about accessing available resources, visit www.cengage.com/ct/studentdownload or contact your instructor for information about accessing the required files.

BTW

BTWs

For a complete list of the BTWs found in the margins of this book, visit the BTW resource on the Student Companion Site located on www.cengagebrain.com. For detailed instructions about accessing available resources, visit www.cengage.com/ct/studentdownload or contact your instructor for information about accessing the required files.

BTW

Macros

A macro is a series of commands used to automate repeated tasks. You can create macros in other Office apps, such as Word and Excel.

In this chapter, you will learn how to create and test macros that open forms and that preview reports and export reports. You will create a menu form with command buttons as well as a menu form with an **option group**, which is an object that enables you to make a selection by choosing the option button corresponding to your choice. You also will create and use user interface (UI) macros in forms. Bavant Publishing requires a navigation form that will allow users to open forms and reports simply by tapping or clicking appropriate tabs and buttons. You will learn about the use of data macros for ensuring that updates to the database are valid. Finally, you will learn how to use control layouts on forms and reports.

Project — Macros, Navigation Forms, and Control Layouts

Bavant Publishing would like its users to be able to access forms and reports by simply tapping or clicking tabs and buttons, rather than by using the Navigation Pane. A **navigation form** like the one shown in Figure 8–1a is a form that includes tabs to display forms and reports. This navigation form contains several useful features. With the Customer tab selected, you can tap or click the customer number on any row to see the data for the selected customer displayed in the Customer View and Update Form (Figure 8–1b). The form does not appear in a tabbed sheet, the way tables, queries, forms, and reports normally do. Rather, it appears as a **pop-up form**, a form that stays on top of other open objects, even when another object is active.

Tapping or clicking the Book Rep tab displays book rep data. As with customers, tapping or clicking the book rep number on any record displays data for that rep in a pop-up form.

Tapping or clicking the Forms tab in the Bavant Publishing navigation form displays buttons for each of the available forms (Figure 8–1c). You can open the desired form by tapping or clicking the appropriate button. Tapping or clicking the Reports tab displays an option group for displaying reports (Figure 8–1d). You can preview or export any of the reports one at a time by tapping or clicking the corresponding option button. Bavant plans to use the navigation form because they believe it will improve the user-friendliness of the database, thereby improving employee satisfaction and efficiency.

Before creating the navigation form, Bavant will create **macros**, which are collections of actions designed to carry out specific tasks. To perform the actions in a macro, you run the macro. When you run a macro, Access will execute the various steps, called **actions**, in the order indicated by the macro. You run the navigation form macros by tapping or clicking certain buttons in the form.

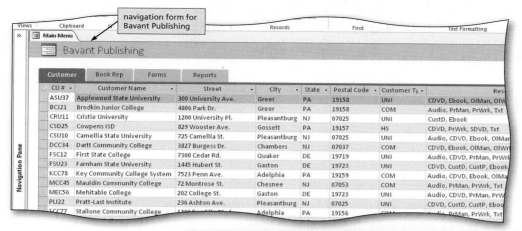

Figure 8–1 (a) Navigation Form

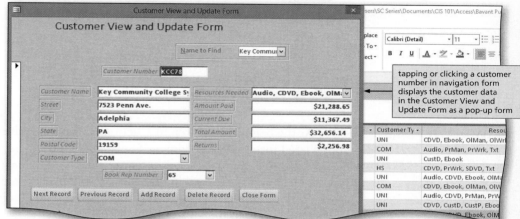

Figure 8–1 (b) Pop-Up Form Displaying Customer Data

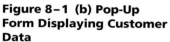

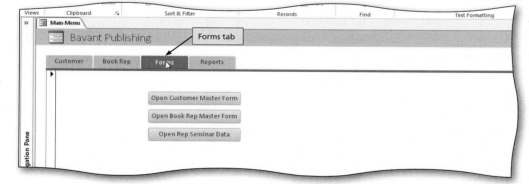

Figure 8–1 (c) Forms Tab

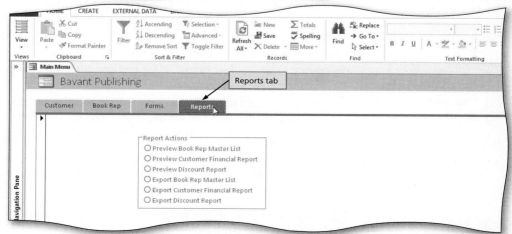

Figure 8–1 (d) Reports Tab

Bavant also will create another type of macro, a data macro. A **data macro** is a special type of macro that enables you to add logic to table events such as adding, changing, or deleting data. You typically use data macros to ensure data validity.

Roadmap

BTW
Touch and Pointers
Remember that if you are using your finger on a touch screen, you will not see the pointer.

In this chapter, you will learn how to create and use the navigation form shown in Figure 8–1 on the previous page. The following roadmap identifies general activities you will perform as you progress through this chapter:

1. Create and modify a MACRO WITH SUBMACROS
2. Create a menu form with COMMAND BUTTONS
3. Create a menu form with an OPTION GROUP
4. Create a MACRO FOR the OPTION GROUP
5. Create DATASHEET FORMS
6. Create USER INTERFACE (UI) MACROS
7. Create a NAVIGATION FORM
8. Create a DATA MACRO

BTW
On-Screen Keyboard
To display the on-screen touch keyboard, tap the Touch Keyboard button on the Windows taskbar. When finished using the touch keyboard, tap the X button on the touch keyboard to close the keyboard.

At the beginning of step instructions throughout the chapter, you will see an abbreviated form of this roadmap. The abbreviated roadmap uses colors to indicate chapter progress: gray means the chapter is beyond that activity; blue means the task being shown is covered in that activity, and black means that activity is yet to be covered. For example, the following abbreviated roadmap indicates the chapter would be showing a task in the 3 OPTION GROUP activity.

1 MACRO WITH SUBMACROS | 2 COMMAND BUTTONS | 3 OPTION GROUP | 4 MACRO FOR OPTION GROUP
5 DATASHEET FORMS | 6 USER INTERFACE MACROS | 7 NAVIGATION FORM | 8 DATA MACRO

Use the abbreviated roadmap as a progress guide while you read or step through the instructions in this chapter.

To Run Access

BTW
The Ribbon and Screen Resolution
Access may change how the groups and buttons within the groups appear on the ribbon, depending on the computer's screen resolution. Thus, your ribbon may look different from the ones in this book if you are using a screen resolution other than 1366 × 768.

If you are using a computer to step through the project in this chapter and you want your screens to match the figures in this book, you should change your screen's resolution to 1366 × 768. For information about how to change a computer's resolution, refer to the Office and Windows chapter at the beginning of this book.

The following steps, which assume Windows is running, use the Start screen or the search box to run Access based on a typical installation. You may need to ask your instructor how to run Access on your computer. For a detailed example of the procedure summarized below, refer to the Office and Windows chapter.

1 Scroll the Start screen for an Access 2013 tile. If your Start screen contains an Access 2013 tile, tap or click it to run Access; if the Start screen does not contain the Access 2013 tile, proceed to the next step to search for the Access app.

2 Swipe in from the right edge of the screen or point to the upper-right corner of the screen to display the Charms bar and then tap or click the Search charm on the Charms bar to display the Search menu.

3 Type **Access** as the search text in the Search text box and watch the search results appear in the Apps list.

4 Tap or click Access 2013 in the search results to run Access.

To Open a Database from Access

The following steps open the Bavant Publishing database from the location you specified when you first created it (for example, the Access folder in the CIS 101 folder). For a detailed example of the procedure summarized below, refer to the Office and Windows chapter at the beginning of this book.

1 Tap or click FILE on the ribbon to open the Backstage view, if necessary.

2 If the database you want to open is displayed in the Recent list, tap or click the file name to open the database and display the opened database in the Access window; then skip to Step 7. If the database you want to open is not displayed in the Recent list or if the Recent list does not appear, tap or click Open Other Files to display the Open Gallery.

3 If the database you want to open is displayed in the Recent list in the Open gallery, tap or click the file name to open the database and display the opened database in the Access window; then skip to Step 7.

4 Tap or click Computer, SkyDrive, or another location in the left pane and then navigate to the location of the database to be opened (for example, the Access folder in the CIS 101 folder).

5 Tap or click Bavant Publishing to select the database to be opened.

6 Tap or click the Open button (Open dialog box) to open the selected file and display the opened database in the Access window.

7 If a Security Warning appears, tap or click the Enable Content button.

BTW
Touch Screen Differences
The Office and Windows interfaces may vary if you are using a touch screen. For this reason, you might notice that the function or appearance of your touch screen differs slightly from this chapter's presentation.

Creating and Using Macros

Similar to other Office apps, Access allows you to create and use macros. A macro consists of a series of actions that Access performs when the macro is run. When you create a macro, you specify these actions. Once you have created a macro, you can simply run the macro, and Access will perform the various actions you specified. For example, the macro might open a form in read-only mode, a mode where changes to the data are prohibited. Another macro might export a report as a PDF file. You can group related macros into a single macro, with the individual macros existing as submacros within the main macro.

How do you create macros? How do you use them?
You create a macro by entering a specific series of actions in a window called the Macro Builder window. Once a macro is created, it exists as an object in the database, and you can run it from the Navigation Pane by pressing and holding or right-clicking the macro and then tapping or clicking Run on the shortcut menu. Macros also can be associated with buttons on forms. When you tap or click the corresponding button on the form, Access will run the macro. Whether a macro is run from the Navigation Pane or from a form, the effect is the same: Access will execute the actions in the order in which they occur in the macro.

CONSIDER THIS

In this chapter, you will create macros for a variety of purposes. As you enter actions, you will select them from a list presented to you by the Macro Builder. The names of the actions are self-explanatory. The action to open a form, for example, is OpenForm. Thus, it is not necessary to memorize the specific actions that are available.

To Begin Creating a Macro

The following steps begin creating a macro. *Why? Once you have created the macro, you will be able to add the appropriate actions.*

1

- If necessary, close the Navigation Pane.

- Display the CREATE tab (Figure 8–2).

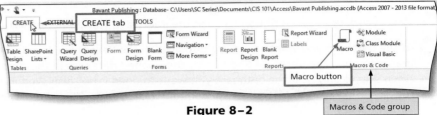

Figure 8–2

2

- Tap or click the Macro button (CREATE tab | Macros & Code group) to create a new macro.

- Tap or click the Action Catalog button (MACRO TOOLS DESIGN tab | Show/Hide group) if necessary to display the action catalog (Figure 8–3).

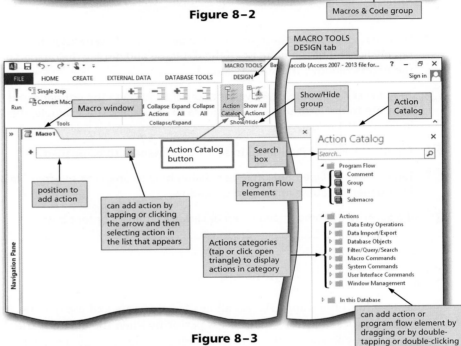

Figure 8–3

The Macro Builder Window

You create a macro by adding actions in the macro window, shown in Figure 8–3. You can add actions by tapping or clicking the Add New Action arrow and selecting the desired action from the list of possible actions. You can also use the Action Catalog, which is a list of macro actions organized by type. If the Action Catalog does not appear, tap or click the Action Catalog button (MACRO TOOLS DESIGN tab | Show/Hide group) to display it. You can add an action by double-tapping or double-clicking the action in the Action Catalog or by dragging it.

Access arranges the available actions in categories. To see the actions in a category, tap or click the **expand indicator** (the open triangle) in front of the category. The actions will appear and the expand indicator will change to a solid triangle. To hide the actions in a category, tap or click the solid triangle.

CONSIDER THIS

How can you find an action if you are not sure which category contains the action?

You can search the list by typing in the Search box. Access will then reduce the list of actions displayed to only those actions whose names or descriptions contain the text you have typed.

Many actions require additional information, called the **arguments** of the action. For example, if the action is OpenForm, Access needs to know which form is to be opened. You indicate the form to be opened by setting the value of the Form Name argument to the desired form. If the value for the Form Name argument for the OpenForm action is Rep Seminar Data, then Access will open the Rep Seminar Data form when it executes this action.

Actions can have more than one argument. For example, in addition to the Form Name argument, the OpenForm action also has a Data Mode argument. If the value of the Data Mode argument is Read Only, then the form will be opened in read-only mode, which indicates users will be able to view but not change data. When you select an action, the arguments will appear along with the action, and you can make any necessary changes to them.

In the forms you will create later in this chapter, you need macros for opening the Rep Seminar Data form as read-only (to prevent updates), opening the Book Rep Master Form, opening the Customer Master Form, previewing the Book Rep Master List, previewing the Customer Financial Report, previewing the Discount Report, exporting the Book Rep Master List as a PDF file, exporting the Customer Financial Report as a PDF file, and exporting the Discount Report as a PDF file. You could create nine separate macros to accomplish these tasks. A simpler way, however, is to make each of these a submacro within a single macro. You can run a submacro just as you can run a macro.

You will create a macro called Forms and Reports that contains these nine submacros. Table 8–1 shows the submacros. Submacros can contain many actions, but each one in this table includes only a single action. For each submacro, the table gives

BTW

Converting a Macro to VBA Code
If you want to use many of the resources provided by Windows or communicate with another Windows app, you will need to convert any macros to VBA (Visual Basic for Applications) code. To convert a macro to VBA code, open the macro in Design view and tap or click the 'Convert Macros to Visual Basic' button (MACRO TOOLS DESIGN tab | Tools group). When the Convert Macro dialog box appears, select the appropriate options, and then tap or click Convert.

BTW

Saving a Macro as a VBA Module
You can save a macro as a VBA module using the Save Object As command in Backstage view. Open the macro in Design view, tap or click FILE on the ribbon to open Backstage view, and then tap or click Save As. When the Save As gallery appears, tap or click Save Object As in the File Types area, and then tap or click the Save As button. When the Save As dialog box appears, tap or click Module in the As text box and then tap or click the OK button.

Table 8–1 Forms and Reports Macro

Submacro	Action	Arguments to be Changed
Open Rep Seminar Data		
	OpenForm	Form Name: Rep Seminar Data Data Mode: Read Only
Open Book Rep Master Form		
	OpenForm	Form Name: Book Rep Master Form
Open Customer Master Form		
	OpenForm	Form Name: Customer Master Form
Preview Book Rep Master List		
	OpenReport	Report Name: Book Rep Master List View: Print Preview
Preview Customer Financial Report		
	OpenReport	Report Name: Customer Financial Report View: Print Preview
Preview Discount Report		
	OpenReport	Report Name: Discount Report View: Print Preview
Export Book Rep Master List		
	ExportWithFormatting	Object Type: Report Object Name: Book Rep Master List Output Format: PDF Format (*.pdf)
Export Customer Financial Report		
	ExportWithFormatting	Object Type: Report Object Name: Customer Financial Report Output Format: PDF Format (*.pdf)
Export Discount Report		
	ExportWithFormatting	Object Type: Report Object Name: Discount Report Output Format: PDF Format (*.pdf)

the action, those arguments that need to be changed, and the values you need to assign to those arguments. If an argument is not listed, then you do not need to change the value from the default value that is assigned by Access.

To Add an Action to a Macro

1 MACRO WITH SUBMACROS | 2 COMMAND BUTTONS | 3 OPTION GROUP | 4 MACRO FOR OPTION GROUP
5 DATASHEET FORMS | 6 USER INTERFACE MACROS | 7 NAVIGATION FORM | 8 DATA MACRO

To continue creating the Forms and Reports macro, enter the actions in the Macro Builder. In these steps, you will enter actions by double-tapping or double-clicking the action in the Action Catalog. *Why? The actions in the Action Catalog are organized by function, making it easier to locate the action you want.* Access will add the action to the Add New Action box. If there is more than one Add New Action box, you need to ensure that the one where you want to add the action is selected before you double-tap or double-click.

The following steps add the first action. They also make the necessary changes to any arguments. Finally, the steps save the macro.

1

• Double-tap or double-click the Submacro element from the Program Flow section of the Action Catalog to add a second submacro and then type **Open Rep Seminar Data** as the name of the submacro (Figure 8–4).

Q&A How can I tell the purpose of the various actions?
If necessary, expand the category containing the action so that the action appears. Point to the action. An expanded ScreenTip will appear, giving you a description of the action.

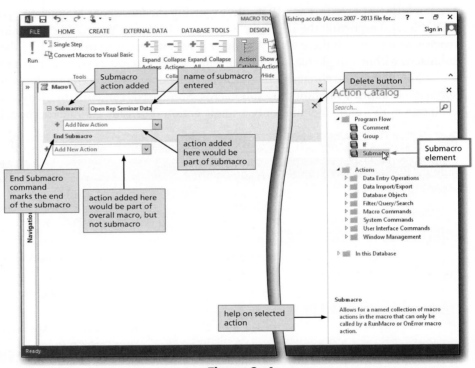

Figure 8–4

- Tap or click the expand indicator for the Database Objects category of actions to display the actions within the category.

- Double-tap or double-click the OpenForm action to add it to the submacro (Figure 8–5).

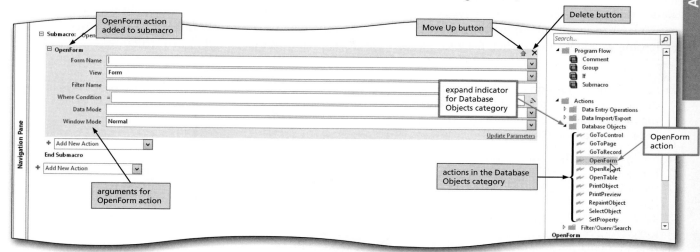

Figure 8–5

Q&A | What should I do if I add an action in the wrong position? What should I do if I add the wrong action?

If you add an action in the wrong position, use the Move Up or Move Down buttons to move it to the correct position. If you added the wrong action, tap or click the Delete button to delete the action, and then fix the error by adding the correct action.

- Tap or click the drop-down arrow for the Form Name argument and then select Rep Seminar Data as the name of the form to be opened.

- Tap or click the drop-down arrow for the Data Mode argument and then select Read Only to specify that users cannot change the data in the form (Figure 8–6).

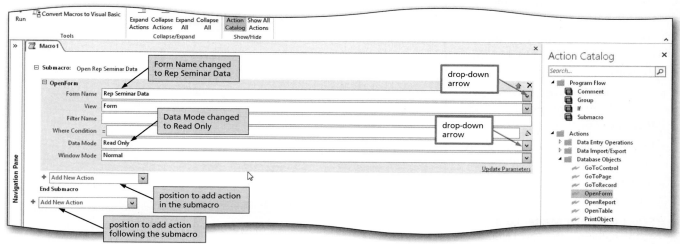

Figure 8–6

Q&A | What is the effect of the other Data Mode options?

Add allows viewing records and adding new records, but not updating records. Edit allows viewing records, adding new records, and updating existing records.

- Tap or click the Save button on the Quick Access Toolbar, type **Forms and Reports** as the name of the macro, and then tap or click the OK button to save the macro.

To Add More Actions to a Macro

To complete the macro, you need to add the additional actions shown in Table 8–1 on page AC 479. You add the additional actions just as you added the first action. Initially, Access displays all the actions you have added with their arguments clearly visible. After you have added several actions, you might want to collapse some or all of the actions. **Why?** *It makes it easier to get an overall view of your macro.* You can always expand any action later to see details concerning the arguments. The following steps add additional actions to a macro, collapsing existing actions when necessary to provide a better view of the overall macro structure.

1

- Point to the minus sign (-) in front of the OpenForm action and then tap or click the minus sign to collapse the action (Figure 8–7).

Q&A Could I also use the buttons on the ribbon?

Yes, you can use the buttons in the Collapse/Expand group on the MACRO TOOLS DESIGN tab. Tap or click the Expand Actions button to expand the selected action, or tap or click the Collapse Actions button to collapse the selected action. You can expand all actions at once by tapping or clicking the Expand All button, or you can collapse all actions at once by tapping or clicking the Collapse All button.

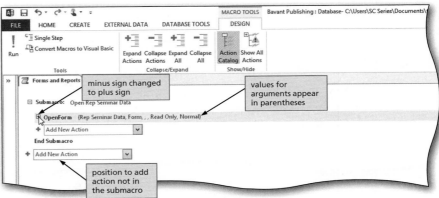

Figure 8–7

2

- Double-tap or double-click the Submacro element from the Program Flow section of the Action Catalog to add a submacro and then type **Open Book Rep Master Form** as the name of the submacro.

- Double-tap or double-click the OpenForm action to add it to the submacro.

- Tap or click the drop-down arrow for the Form Name argument and then select Book Rep Master Form.

- In a similar fashion, add the Open Customer Master Form submacro.

- Add the OpenForm action to the submacro.

- Select Customer Master Form as the value for the Form Name argument (Figure 8–8).

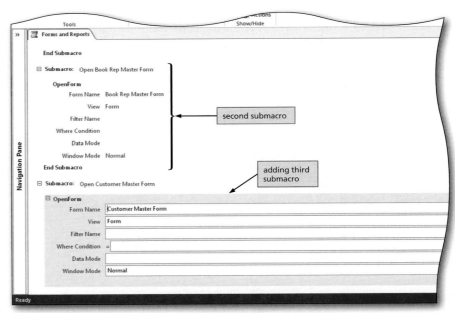

Figure 8–8

Q&A Do I have to change the values of any of the other arguments?
No. The default values that Access sets are appropriate.

- For each of the three submacros, point to the minus sign in front of the submacro and then tap or click the minus sign to collapse the submacro.

- Add a submacro named Preview Book Rep Master List.

- Add the OpenReport action to the macro.

- Select Book Rep Master List as the report name.

- Select Print Preview as the view (Figure 8–9).

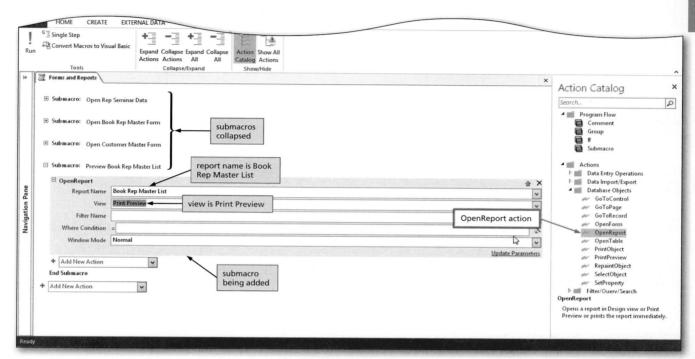

Figure 8–9

- Collapse the Preview Book Rep Master List submacro.

- Add the Preview Customer Financial Report submacro. Include the action described in Table 8–1 on page AC 479. The report name is Customer Financial Report and the view is Print Preview.

- Add the Preview Discount Report submacro. Include the action described in Table 8–1. The report name is Discount Report and the view is Print Preview.

- Collapse the Preview Customer Financial Report and Preview Discount Report submacros.

- Collapse the Database Objects category and then expand the Data Import/Export category.

- Add a submacro called Export Book Rep Master List.

- Add the ExportWithFormatting action, which will export and maintain any special formatting in the process.

- Tap or click the drop-down arrow for the Object Type argument to display a list of possible object types (Figure 8–10 on the next page).

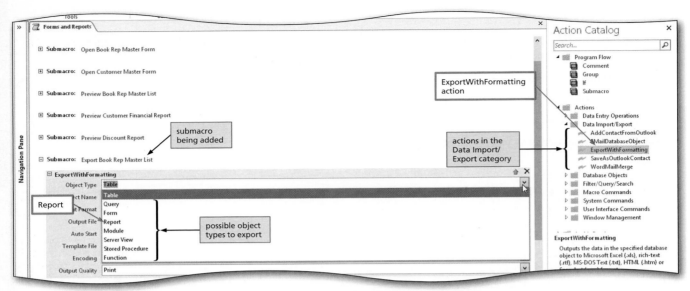

Figure 8–10

- Tap or click Report in the list to indicate that Access is to export a report.
- Tap or click the drop-down arrow for the Object Name argument and select Book Rep Master List as the object name.
- Tap or click the drop-down arrow for the Output Format argument and then select PDF Format (*.pdf) as the Output Format to export the report in PDF format (Figure 8–11).

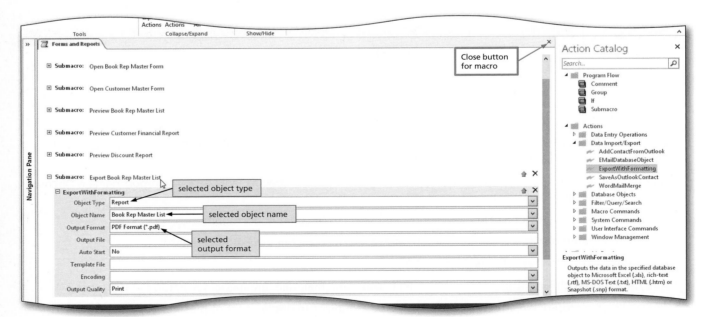

Figure 8–11

- Add the Export Customer Financial Report submacro and the action from Table 8–1 on page AC 479.
- Include the action described in Table 8–1 and select Customer Financial Report as the report name.

- Select PDF Format (*.pdf) as the Output Format to export the report in PDF format.
- Add the Export Discount Report submacro.
- Select Discount Report as the report name.
- Select PDF Format (*.pdf) as the Output Format to export the report in PDF format.
- Save the macro.
- Close the macro by tapping or clicking its Close button, shown in Figure 8–11.

Opening Databases Containing Macros

It is possible that a macro stored in a database can contain a computer virus. By default, Access disables macros when it opens a database and displays a Security Warning. If the database comes from a trusted source and you are sure that it does not contain any macro viruses, tap or click the Enable Content button. You can make adjustments to Access security settings by tapping or clicking FILE on the ribbon to open the Backstage view, and then tapping or clicking Options to display the Access Options dialog box, tapping or clicking Trust Center, tapping or clicking Trust Center Settings, and then tapping or clicking Macro Settings.

Errors in Macros

Macros can contain errors. The macro may abort. It might open the wrong table or produce a wrong message. If you have problems with a macro, you can **single-step the macro**, that is, proceed through a macro a step at a time in Design view.

Figure 8–12 shows a macro open in Design view. This macro first has an action to open the Customer table in Datasheet view in Read Only mode. It then changes the view to Print Preview. Next, it opens the Customer table in Datasheet view, this time in Edit mode. Finally, it opens the Rep-Customer Query in Datasheet view in Edit mode. The macro in the figure is a common type of macro that opens several objects at once. To open all these objects, the user only has to run the macro. Unfortunately, this macro contains an error. The name of the Customer table is written as "Customers" in the second OpenTable action.

BTW

Viewing VBA Code
You can view VBA code that is attached to a form or report. To do so, open the form or report in Design view and tap or click the View Code button (REPORT DESIGN TOOLS DESIGN tab | Tools group) for reports or (FORM DESIGN TOOLS DESIGN tab | Tools group) for forms.

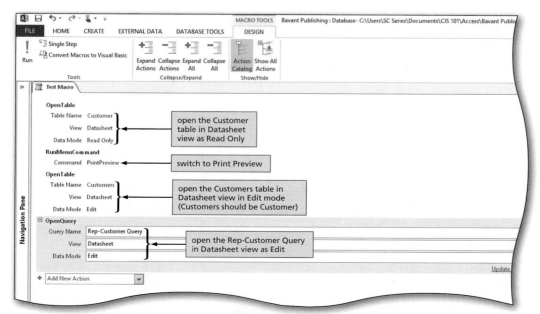

Figure 8–12

To run this macro in single-step mode, you first would tap or click the Single Step button (MACRO TOOLS DESIGN tab | Tools group). You next would tap or click the Run button (MACRO TOOLS DESIGN tab | Tools group) to run the macro. Because you tapped or clicked the Single Step button, Access would display the Macro Single Step dialog box (Figure 8–13). The dialog box shows the action to be executed and the values of the various arguments. You can tap or click the Step button to proceed to the next step.

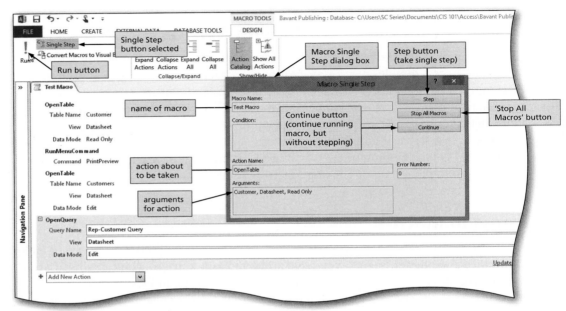

Figure 8–13

With this macro, after you tapped or clicked the Step button twice, you would arrive at the screen shown in Figure 8–14. Access is about to execute the OpenTable command. The arguments are Customers, Datasheet, and Edit. At this point, you might spot the fact that "Customers" is misspelled. It should be "Customer." If so, you could tap or click the 'Stop All Macros' button and then make the necessary changes.

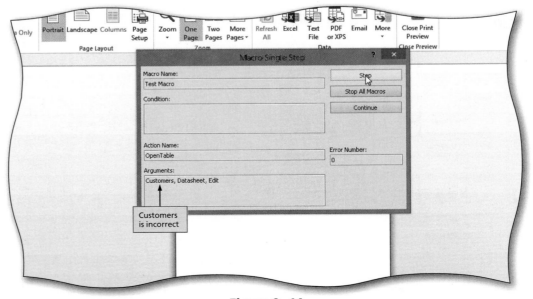

Figure 8–14

If you instead tap or click the Step button, the misspelled name will cause the macro to abort. Access would display the appropriate error message in the Microsoft Access dialog box (Figure 8–15). This error indicates that Access could not find the object named Customers. Armed with this knowledge, you can tap or click the OK button, stop the macro, and then make the necessary change.

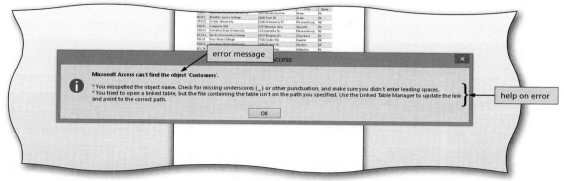

Figure 8–15

You do not need to step through a macro to discover the error. You can simply run the macro, either by tapping or clicking the Run button (MACRO TOOLS DESIGN tab | Tools group) with the macro open, or by pressing and holding or right-clicking the macro in the Navigation Pane and tapping or clicking Run. In either case, Access will run the macro until it encounters the error. When it does, it will display the same message shown in Figure 8–15. Just as with stepping through the macro, you would tap or click the OK button, stop the macro, and then make the necessary change.

> **Break Point:** If you wish to stop working through the chapter at this point, you can resume the project later by starting Access, opening the database called Bavant Publishing, and continuing to follow the steps from this location forward.

Creating and Using a Navigation Form

Figure 8–1a on page AC 475 showed a navigation form for Bavant Publishing. A **navigation form** is a form that contains a **navigation control**, a control that can display a variety of forms and reports. Like the form in Figure 8–1, navigation controls contain tabs. Tapping or clicking the tab displays the corresponding form or report. The tabs can be arranged across the top and/or down the sides.

You only can include forms and reports on the tabs; you cannot include either tables or queries. The navigation form in Figure 8–1, however, appears to have a tab corresponding to the Customer table. There is a technique you can use to make it appear as though the navigation form contains tables or queries. You create a datasheet form based on the table or query. Figure 8–1 actually shows a datasheet form based on the Customer table and does not show the Customer table itself.

Before creating the navigation form, you have some other forms to create. For example, you might want the users to be able to tap or click a tab in the navigation form and then choose from a list of forms or reports. Figure 8–16 on the next page shows a list of forms presented as buttons; the user would tap or click the button for the desired form. Tapping or clicking the Open Customer Master Form button, for example, would display the Customer View and Update Form as shown in Figure 8–17 on the next page.

BTW
Navigation Forms
A navigation form often is used as a switchboard or main page for a database to reduce clutter and target the most commonly used database objects. A navigation form contains a navigation control and a subform control. After you create a navigation form, you can use the Navigation Where Clause property associated with a navigation control to automatically apply a filter.

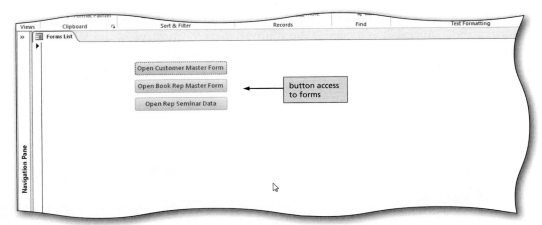

Figure 8–16

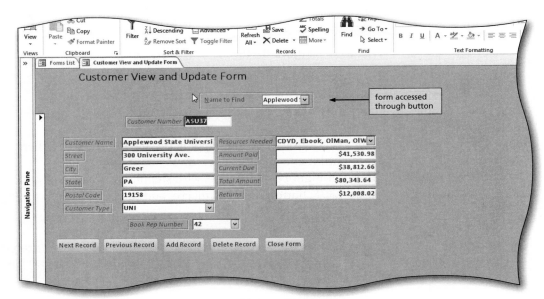

Figure 8–17

To implement options like these, you create blank forms and add either the command buttons or the option group. You then include the form you have created in the navigation form. When users tap or click the corresponding tab, Access displays the form and users can then tap or click the appropriate button.

To Create a Menu Form Containing Command Buttons

1 MACRO WITH SUBMACROS | 2 COMMAND BUTTONS | 3 OPTION GROUP | 4 MACRO FOR OPTION GROUP
5 DATASHEET FORMS | 6 USER INTERFACE MACROS | 7 NAVIGATION FORM | 8 DATA MACRO

Why? *A menu form in which you make a selection by clicking the appropriate command button provides a convenient way to select a desired option.* You can create a menu form by adding command buttons to the form, just as you added command buttons to the form in Chapter 7 on pages AC 428 through AC 430. The following steps use this technique to create a menu form with three buttons: Open Customer Master Form, Open Book Rep Master Form, and Open Rep Seminar Data. The actions assigned to each button will run a macro that causes the desired action to occur. For example, the action for the Open Customer Master Form button will run the Open Customer Master Form submacro, which in turn will open the Customer Master Form.

The following steps create a form in Design view and then add the necessary buttons.

1

- Display the CREATE tab.

- Tap or click the Form Design button (CREATE tab | Forms group) to create a blank form in Design view.

- If a field list appears, tap or click the 'Add Existing Fields' button (FORM DESIGN TOOLS DESIGN tab | Tools group) to remove the field list.

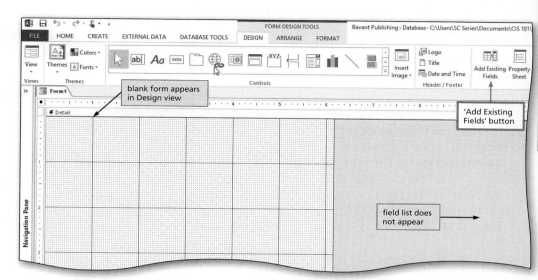

Figure 8–18

- If a property sheet appears, tap or click the Property Sheet button (FORM DESIGN TOOLS DESIGN tab | Tools group) to remove the property sheet (Figure 8–18).

2

- Make sure the 'Use Control Wizards' button is selected.

- Tap or click the Button tool (FORM DESIGN TOOLS DESIGN tab | Controls group) and move the pointer to the approximate position shown in Figure 8–19.

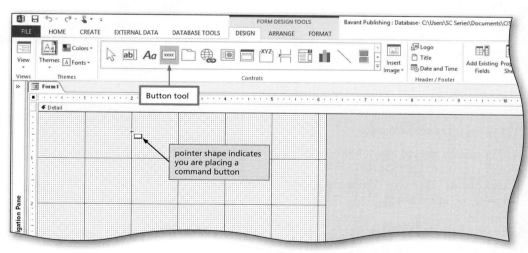

Figure 8–19

3

- Tap or click the position shown in Figure 8–19 to display the Command Button Wizard dialog box.

- Tap or click Miscellaneous in the Categories box, and then tap or click Run Macro in the Actions box (Figure 8–20).

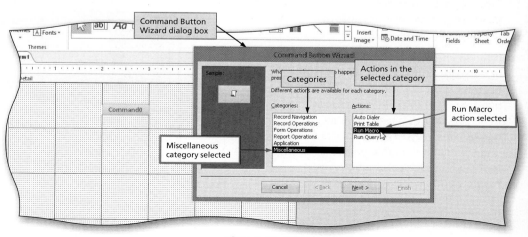

Figure 8–20

- Tap or click the Next button to display the next screen in the wizard.
- Tap or click Forms and Reports. Open Customer Master Form to select the macro to be run (Figure 8–21).

Q&A What does this notation mean?
The portion before the period is the macro and the portion after the period is the submacro. Thus, this notation means the Open Customer Master Form submacro within the Forms and Reports macro.

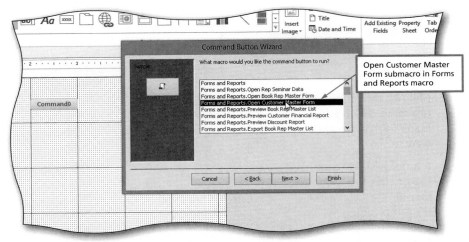

Figure 8–21

- Tap or click the Next button to display the next Command Button Wizard screen.
- Tap or click the Text option button.

Q&A What is the purpose of these option buttons?
Choose the first option button to place text on the button. You then can specify the text to be included or accept the default choice. Choose the second option button to place a picture on the button. You then can select a picture.

- If necessary, delete the default text and then type **Open Customer Master Form** as the text (Figure 8–22).

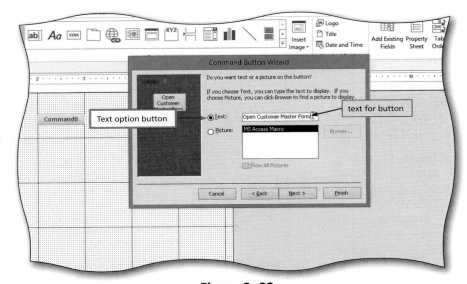

Figure 8–22

- Tap or click the Next button.
- Type **Open_Customer_Master_Form** as the name of the button (Figure 8–23).

Q&A Why do you include the underscores in the name of the button?
If you are working with macros or VBA, you cannot have spaces in names. One way to avoid spaces and still make readable names is to include underscores where you would normally have had spaces. Thus, Open Customer Master Form becomes Open_Customer_Master_Form.

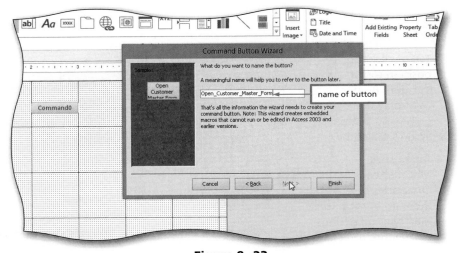

Figure 8–23

7

- Tap or click the Finish button to finish specifying the button.

- Use the techniques in Steps 2 through 6 to place the Open Book Rep Master Form button below the Open Customer Master Form button. The only difference is that the macro to be run is the Open Book Rep Master Form submacro, the text is Open Book Rep Master Form, and the name of the button is Open_Book_Rep_Master_Form.

- Use the techniques in Steps 2 through 6 to place the Open Rep Seminar Data button below the Open Book Rep Master Form

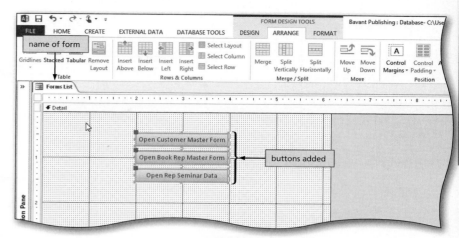

Figure 8–24

button. The only difference is that the macro to be run is the Open Rep Seminar Data submacro, the text is Open Rep Seminar Data, and the name of the button is Open_Rep_Seminar_Data.

- Adjust the size and spacing of the buttons to approximately match those in Figure 8–24, using the ARRANGE tab, if necessary.

- Save the form using the name, Forms List.

Q&A How can I test the buttons to make sure the macros work?
Press and hold or right-click the Forms List form in the Navigation Pane and tap or click Open. Tap or click each of the buttons on the form. If there are errors in any of the macros, open the macro in the Macro Builder window and correct the errors.

Experiment

- Test each of the buttons on the form. Ensure that the correct form opens. If there are errors, correct the corresponding macro.

8

- Close the form.

Option Groups

You might find it useful to allow users to make a selection from some predefined options by including an option group. An **option group** is a rectangle containing a collection of option buttons. To select an option, you simply tap or click the corresponding option button. Figure 8–25 on the next page shows a list of reports presented in an option group where the user would tap or click the desired option button. Notice that the user could tap or click an option button to preview a report. The user could tap or click a different option button to export the report as a PDF file. Tapping or clicking the Preview Book Rep Master List option button, for example, would display a preview of the Book Rep Master List (Figure 8–26 on the next page). Tapping or clicking the Close Print Preview button would return you to the option group.

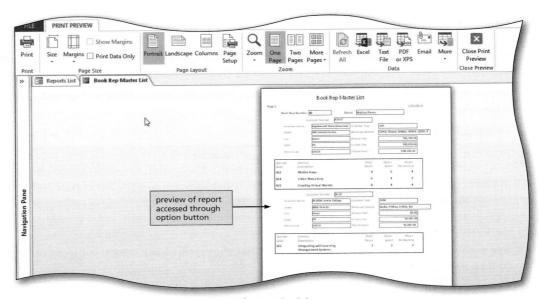

Figure 8–25

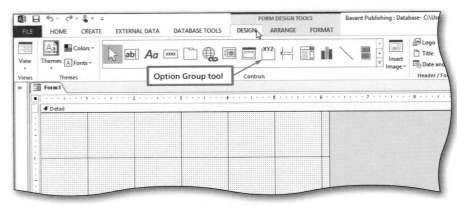

Figure 8–26

To Create a Menu Form Containing an Option Group

1 MACRO WITH SUBMACROS | 2 COMMAND BUTTONS | 3 OPTION GROUP | 4 MACRO FOR OPTION GROUP
5 DATASHEET FORMS | 6 USER INTERFACE MACROS | 7 NAVIGATION FORM | 8 DATA MACRO

The form you are creating will contain an option group called Form Options. *Why? The option group allows users to select an option button to indicate either a report to preview or a report to export.*

The following steps use the Option Group tool to create the Form Options option group.

• Display the CREATE tab.

• Tap or click the Form Design button (CREATE tab | Forms group) to create a blank form in Design view.

• If a field list appears, tap or click the 'Add Existing Fields' button (FORM DESIGN TOOLS DESIGN tab | Tools group) to remove the field list (Figure 8–27).

Figure 8–27

2

- Tap or click the Option Group tool (FORM DESIGN TOOLS DESIGN tab | Controls group) and then move the pointer to the approximate position shown in Figure 8–28.

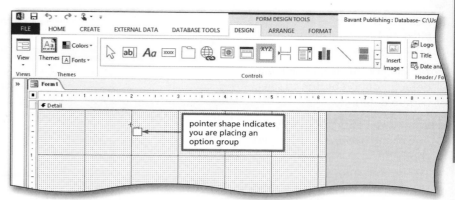

Figure 8–28

3

- Tap or click the position shown in Figure 8–28 to place an option group and start the Option Group Wizard (Figure 8–29).

Q&A The Option Group Wizard did not start for me. What should I do?
You must not have had the 'Use Control Wizards' button selected. With the option group selected, press the DELETE key to delete the option group. Select the 'Use Control Wizards' button, and then add the option group a second time.

- Type **Preview Book Rep Master List** in the first row of label names and press the DOWN ARROW key.

- Type **Preview Customer Financial Report** in the second row of label names and press the DOWN ARROW key.

- Type **Preview Discount Report** in the third row of label names and press the DOWN ARROW key.

- Type **Export Book Rep Master List** in the fourth row of label names and press the DOWN ARROW key.

- Type **Export Customer Financial Report** in the fifth row of label names and press the DOWN ARROW key.

- Type **Export Discount Report** in the sixth row of label names (Figure 8–30).

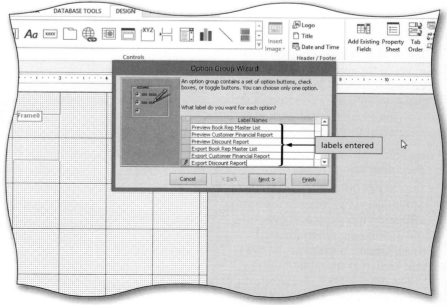

Figure 8–29

Figure 8–30

4

- Tap or click the Next button to move to the next Option Group Wizard screen.

- Tap or click the 'No, I don't want a default.' option button to select it (Figure 8–31).

Q&A What is the effect of specifying one of the options as the default choice?
The default choice will initially be selected when you open the form. If there is no default choice, no option will be selected.

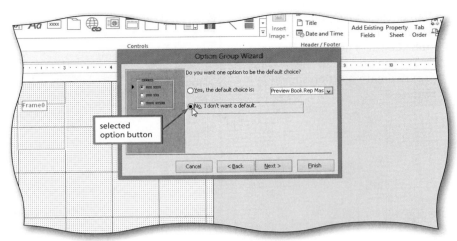

Figure 8–31

5

- Tap or click the Next button to move to the next Option Group Wizard screen and then verify that the values assigned to the labels match those shown in Figure 8–32.

Q&A How do I use the values that I have assigned?
You can use them in macros or VBA. You will use them in a macro later in this chapter.

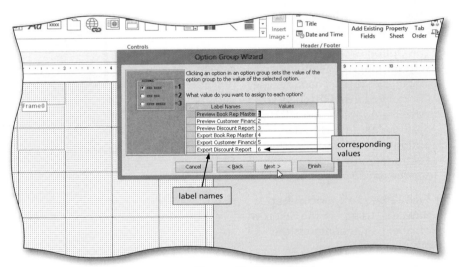

Figure 8–32

6

- Tap or click the Next button to move to the next Option Group Wizard screen, and then ensure that Option buttons is selected as the type of control and Etched is selected as the style (Figure 8–33).

🔍 Experiment

- Tap or click different combinations of types and styles to see the effects on the samples shown in the dialog box. When finished, select Option buttons as the type and Etched as the style.

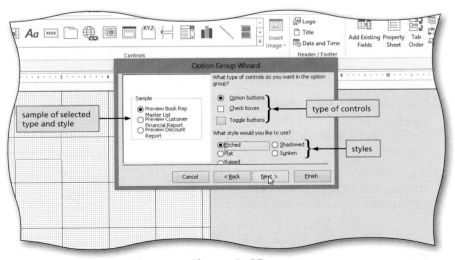

Figure 8–33

7
- Tap or click the Next button to move to the next Option Group Wizard screen and then type **Report Actions** as the caption.
- Tap or click the Finish button to complete the addition of the option group (Figure 8–34).

8
- Save the form using the name, Reports List.

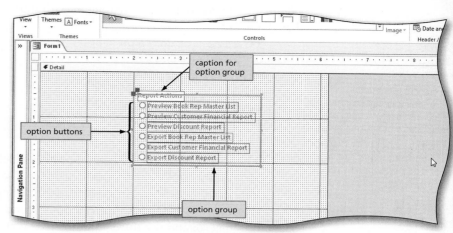

Figure 8–34

Using an If Statement

You will create a macro that will take appropriate action when the user updates the option group, that is, when the user taps or clicks an option button in the group. The macro will run the appropriate submacro, depending on which option the user has selected.

Because the specific actions that the macro will perform depend on the option button the user selects, the macro will contain conditions. The conditions will determine which action should be taken. If the user selects the first option button, Access should run the Preview Book Rep Master List submacro. If, on the other hand, the user selects the second option button, Access should instead run the Preview Customer Financial Report submacro. For each of the six possible option buttons a user can select, Access should run a different submacro.

To instruct Access to perform different actions based on certain conditions, the macro will contain an If statement. The simplest form of an If statement is:

```
If condition Then
  action
End If
```

If the condition is true, Access will take the indicated action. If the condition is false, no action will be taken. For example, the condition could be that the user selects the first option button, and the action could be to run the Book Rep Master List submacro. No action would be taken if the user selects any other button.

Another form of the If statement contains an Else clause. This form is:

```
If condition Then
  first action
Else
  second action
End If
```

If the condition is true, the first action is taken; if the condition is false, the second action is taken. For example, the condition could be that the user selects option button 1; the first action could be to run the Preview Book Rep Master List submacro, and the second action could be to run the Preview Customer Financial Report submacro. If the user selects option button 1, Access would run the Preview Book Rep Master list submacro. If the user selects any other option button, Access would run the

Preview Customer Financial Report submacro. Because there are six option buttons, the macro needs to use an If statement with multiple Else Ifs. This type of If statement has the form:

```
If first condition Then
  first action
Else If second condition Then
  second action
Else If third condition Then
  third action
End If
```

The first condition could be that the user selects the first option button; the second condition could be that the user selects the second option button; and the third condition could be that the user selects the third option button. The first action could be that Access runs the first submacro; the second action could be that it runs the second submacro; and the third could be that it runs the third submacro. This would work, except that in this case there are six option buttons and six submacros. For six conditions, as required in this macro, the If statement will contain five Else Ifs. The If statement along with the five Else Ifs will collectively contain six conditions: one to test if the user selected option 1, one for option 2, one for option 3, one for option 4, one for option 5, and one for option 6.

To Create a Macro with a Variable for the Option Group

1 MACRO WITH SUBMACROS | 2 COMMAND BUTTONS | 3 OPTION GROUP | **4 MACRO FOR OPTION GROUP**
5 DATASHEET FORMS | 6 USER INTERFACE MACROS | 7 NAVIGATION FORM | 8 DATA MACRO

The following steps begin creating the macro and add an action to set a variable to the desired value. *Why? The expression that contains the option number is [Forms]![Customer Master Form]![Form_Options]. Because this expression is fairly lengthy, the macro will begin by setting a temporary variable to this expression. A* **variable** *is a named location in computer memory. You can use a variable to store a value that you can use later in the macro. You will assign the name Optno (short for option number) as the variable name for the expression. This location can contain a value, in this case, the option number on the form. In each of the conditions, you can then use Optno rather than the full expression.*

- With the option group selected, display a property sheet.
- If necessary, tap or click the All tab.
- Change the name of the option group to Form_Options (Figure 8–35).

Q&A

Why this name?
The name Form_Options reflects the fact that these are options that control the action that will be taken on this form. The underscore keeps the name from containing a space.

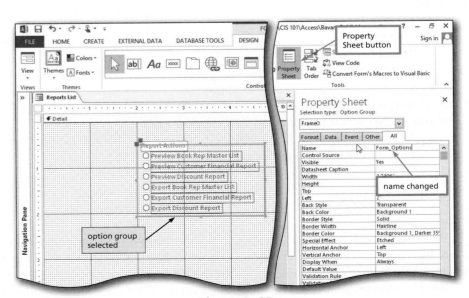

Figure 8–35

- Tap or click the After Update property.
- Tap or click the Build button to display the Choose Builder dialog box (Figure 8–36).

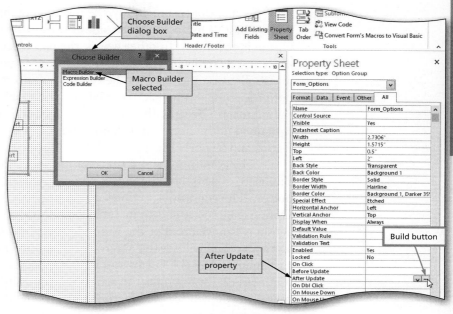

Figure 8–36

- With Macro Builder selected in the Choose Builder dialog box, tap or click the OK button to create a macro.
- If necessary, tap or click the Action Catalog button (MACRO TOOLS DESIGN tab | Show/Hide group) to display the Action Catalog.
- If necessary, collapse the Data Import/Export category.
- Expand the Macro Commands action category.
- Double-tap or double-click the SetTempVar action in the Action Catalog to add the SetTempVar action to the macro.
- Enter **Optno** as the value for the Name argument.
- Enter **[Form_Options]** as the value for the Expression argument (Figure 8–37).

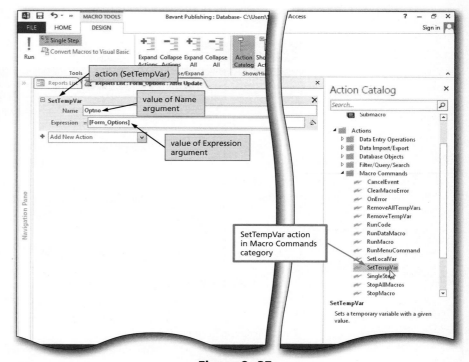

Figure 8–37

How can Access make it easier to enter values for arguments?

Access helps you in three ways. First, if you point to the argument, Access will display a description of the argument. Second, many arguments feature a drop-down list, where you can display the list and then select the desired value. Finally, if you begin typing an expression, a feature called IntelliSense will suggest possible values that start with the letters you have already typed and that are appropriate in the context of what you are typing. If you see the value you want in the list, you can simply tap or click it to select the value.

CONSIDER THIS

Macro for Option Group

As mentioned previously, the macro contains six conditions. The first is [TempVars]! [Optno]=1, which simply means the value in the temporary variable Optno is equal to 1. In other words, the user selected the first option button. The action associated with this condition is RunMacro. The argument is the name of the macro. Because the macro to be run is a submacro, the name of the macro includes both the name of the macro containing the submacro, a period, and then the name of the submacro. Because the submacro to be run is Preview Book Rep Master List and is contained in the Forms and Reports macro, the value of the Macro Name argument is Forms and Reports.Preview Book Rep Master List.

The conditions and actions for options 2 through 6 are similar to the first submacro. The only difference is which submacro is associated with each option button. The conditions, actions, and arguments that you will change for the Form_Options macro are shown in Table 8–2. If the option number is 1, for example, the action is RunMacro. For the RunMacro action, you will change the Macro Name argument. You will set the Macro Name argument to the Preview Book Rep Master List submacro in the Forms and Reports macro. On the other hand, if the option number is 2, for example, the action is again RunMacro. If the option number is 2, however, you will set the Macro Name argument to the Preview Customer Financial Report submacro in the Forms and Reports macro. Similar actions take place for the other possible values for the Optno variable, that is, for option buttons 3-6. Because the temporary variable, Optno, is no longer needed at the end of the macro, the macro concludes with the RemoveTempVar command to remove this variable.

Table 8–2 Macro for After Update Property of the Option Group		
Condition	**Action**	**Arguments to be Changed**
	SetTempVar	Name: Optno Expression: [Form_Options]
If [TempVars]![Optno]=1		
	RunMacro	Macro Name: Forms and Reports.Preview Book Rep Master List
Else If [TempVars]![Optno]=2		
	RunMacro	Macro Name: Forms and Reports.Preview Customer Financial Report
Else If [TempVars]![Optno]=3		
	RunMacro	Macro Name: Forms and Reports.Preview Discount Report
Else If [TempVars]![Optno]=4		
	RunMacro	Macro Name: Forms and Reports.Export Book Rep Master List
Else If [TempVars]![Optno]=5		
	RunMacro	Macro Name: Forms and Reports.Export Customer Financial Report
Else If [TempVars]![Optno]=6		
	RunMacro	Macro Name: Forms and Reports.Export Discount Report
End If		
	RemoveTempVar	Name: Optno

To Add Actions to the Form Options Macro

The following steps add the conditions and actions to the Form_Options macro. **Why?** *The macro is not yet complete. Adding the conditions and actions will complete the macro.*

- Double-tap or double-click the If element from the Program Flow section of the Action Catalog to add an If statement to the submacro and then type   `[TempVars]![Optno]=1`   as the condition in the If statement.

- With the Macro Commands category expanded, double-tap or double-click RunMacro to add the RunMacro action.

- Tap or click the drop-down arrow for the Macro Name argument and select the Preview Book Rep Master List submacro within the Forms and Reports macro as the value for the argument (Figure 8–38).

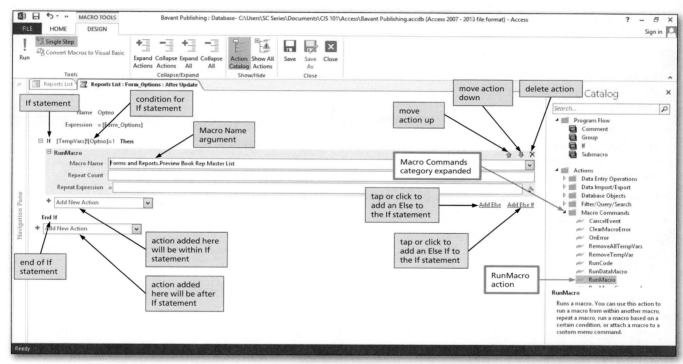

Figure 8–38

Q&A What should I do if I add an action in the wrong position? What should I do if I add the wrong action?
If you add an action in the wrong position, use the Move Up or Move Down buttons to move it to the correct position. If you added the wrong action, tap or click the Delete button to delete the action, and then fix the error by adding the correct action.

- Tap or click Add Else If to add an Else If clause to the If statement.

- Add the conditions and actions associated with options 2, 3, 4, 5, and 6 as described in Table 8–2, and specify the arguments for the actions. Tap or click Add Else If after adding each action except for the last one.

Q&A Do I have to enter all these actions? They seem to be very similar to the ones associated with option 1.
You can copy and paste the action for option 1. Press and hold or right-click the action to select it and display a shortcut menu. Tap or click Copy on the shortcut menu. Press and hold or right-click the action just above where you want to insert the selected action and then tap or click Paste. If the new action is not inserted in the correct position, select the new action and then tap or click either the Move Up or Move Down buttons to move it to the correct location. Once the action is in the correct location, you can make any necessary changes to the arguments.

- Add the RemoveTempVar action and argument after the end of the If statement, as shown in Figure 8–39.

- Enter **Optno** as the name of the TempVar to remove.

Do I need to remove the temporary variable?
Technically, no. In fact, if you plan to use this temporary variable in another macro and want it to retain the value you assigned in this macro, you would definitely not remove it. If you do not plan to use it elsewhere, it is a good idea to remove it, however.

3

- Tap or click the Save button (MACRO TOOLS DESIGN tab | Close group) to save the macro.

- Tap or click the Close button (MACRO TOOLS DESIGN tab | Close group) to close the macro and return to the form.

- Close the property sheet, save the form, and close the form.

How can I test the option group to make sure the macros work?
Press and hold or right-click the Reports List form in the Navigation Pane and tap or click Open. Tap or click each of the buttons in the option group. If there are errors in any of the macros, open the macro in the Macro Builder window and correct the errors.

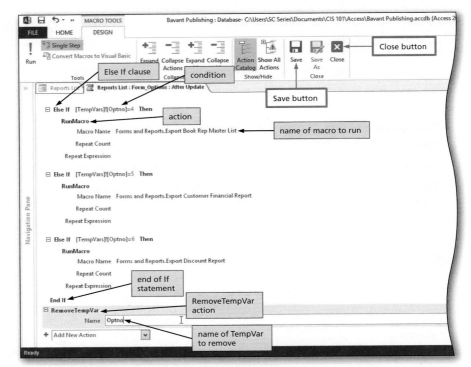

Figure 8–39

Experiment

- Test each of the buttons in the option group. If you do not preview or export the correct report, correct the error in the corresponding macro. If you get an error indicating that the section width is greater than the page width, you have an error in the corresponding report. Correct the error using the instructions on pages AC 485 through AC 487.

Break Point: If you wish to stop working through the chapter at this point, you can resume the project at a later time by starting Access, opening the database called Bavant Publishing, and continuing to follow the steps from this location forward.

User Interface (UI) Macros

A **user interface (UI) macro** is a macro that is attached to a user interface object, such as a command button, an option group, or a control on a form. The macro you just created for the option group is thus a UI macro, as were the macros you attached to command buttons. A common use for UI macros is to associate actions with the tapping or clicking of a control on a form. In the Customer form shown in Figure 8–40, for example, if you tap or click the customer number on the row in the datasheet where the customer number is CRU11, Access displays the data for that customer in a pop-up form (Figure 8–41), that is, a form that stays on top of other open objects, even when another object is active.

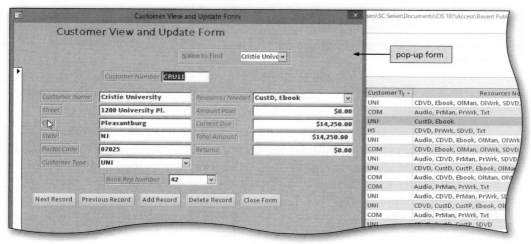

Figure 8–40

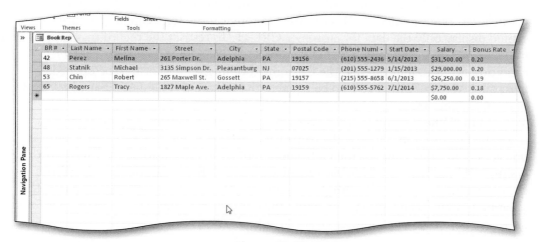

Figure 8–41

Similarly, in the Book Rep form shown in Figure 8–42, for example, if you tap or click the book rep number on the row in the datasheet where the book rep number is 65, Access displays the data for that book rep in a pop-up form (Figure 8–43 on the next page).

Figure 8–42

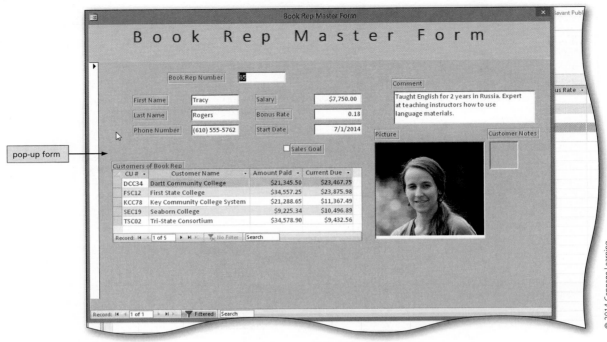

Figure 8–43

BTW
Distributing a Document
Instead of printing and distributing a hard copy of a document, you can distribute the document electronically. Options include sending the document by email; posting it on cloud storage (such as SkyDrive) and sharing the file with others; posting it on a social networking site, blog, or other website; and sharing a link associated with an online location of the document. You also can create and share a PDF or XPS image of the document, so that users can view the file in Acrobat Reader or XPS Viewer instead of in Access.

Recall that you can only use forms and reports for the tabs in a navigation form, yet the Customer tab appears to display the Customer table in Datasheet view. You can make it appear as though you are displaying the Customer table in Datasheet view by creating a datasheet form that you will call Customer. You will create a UI macro in this Customer datasheet form. The UI macro that will be associated with the tapping or clicking of the customer number on some record in the Customer form will display the selected customer in the Customer Master Form.

To display the Customer Master Form, the UI macro will use the OpenForm action. You must set the Form Name argument of the OpenForm action to the actual name of the form to be opened, Customer Master Form. (Customer View and Update Form is just the form caption.) Bavant wants to prevent the user from updating data using this form, so the Data Mode argument is set to Read Only. The form should appear as a pop-up, which you accomplish by setting the value of the Window Mode argument to Dialog.

The form should display only the record that the user selected. If the user taps or clicks customer number CRU11 in the Customer form, for example, the form should display only the data for customer CRU11. To restrict the record that appears in the form, you include the Where Condition argument in the UI macro. The condition needs to indicate that the Customer Number in the form to be opened, Customer Master Form, needs to be equal to the Customer Number the user selected in the Customer form.

In the Where Condition, you can simply refer to a control in the form to be opened by using its name. If the name has spaces, you must enclose it in square brackets. Thus, the name for the Customer Number in the Customer Master Form is simply [Customer Number]. To reference a control that is part of any other form, the expression must include both the name of the form and the name of the control, separated by an exclamation point. Thus, the Customer Number in the Customer form would be [Customer]![Customer Number]. This declaration works correctly when you are programming a macro that simply opens the Customer form. However, when you associate the Customer form with a tab in the navigation form, the Customer form becomes a subform, which requires modification to the expression. This means that a form that works correctly when you open the form may not work correctly when the form is assigned to a tab in a navigation form. A safer approach avoids these issues by using a temporary variable.

Table 8–3 shows the UI macro for the Customer form. It is associated with the On Click event for the Customer Number control. When a user taps or clicks a Customer Number, the UI macro will display the data for the selected customer in the Customer Master Form. The main function of the macro is to open the appropriate form using the OpenForm action.

Table 8–3 UI Macro Associated with On Tap or Click Event in the Customer Form		
Condition	**Action**	**Arguments to be Changed**
	SetTempVar	Name: CN Expression: [Customer Number]
	OpenForm	Form Name: Customer Master Form Where Condition: [Customer Number]=[TempVars]![CN] Data Mode: Read Only Window Mode: Dialog
	RemoveTempVar	Name: CN

© 2014 Cengage Learning

In the macro shown in Table 8–3, the first action, SetTempVar, assigns the temporary variable CN to the Customer Number. The two arguments are Name, which is set to CN, and Expression, which is set to [Customer Number]. The CN temporary variable refers to the Customer Number in the Customer form; recall that the completed macro will open the Customer form. You then can use that temporary variable in the Where Condition argument. The expression is thus [Customer Number]=[TempVars]![CN]. The [Customer Number] portion refers to the Customer Number in the Customer Master Form. The [TempVars]![CN] portion is the temporary variable that has been set equal to the Customer Number in the Customer form.

The macro ends by removing the temporary variable.

Table 8–4 shows the macro for the Book Rep form, which is very similar to the macro for the Customer form.

Table 8–4 UI Macro Associated with On Tap or Click Event in the Book Rep Form		
Condition	**Action**	**Arguments to be Changed**
	SetTempVar	Name: BN Expression: [Book Rep Number]
	OpenForm	Form Name: Book Rep Master Form Where Condition: [Book Rep Number]=[TempVars]![BN] Data Mode: Read Only Window Mode: Dialog
	RemoveTempVar	Name: BN

© 2014 Cengage Learning

To Create Datasheet Forms

The following steps create two datasheet forms, one for the Customer table and one for the Book Rep table. *Why? The datasheet forms enable the Customer and Book Rep tables to appear to be displayed in Datasheet view, while satisfying the restriction that tables cannot be used on the tabs in a navigation form.*

- Open the Navigation Pane and select the Customer table.

- Display the CREATE tab and then tap or click the More Forms button (CREATE tab | Forms group) to display the More Forms gallery (Figure 8–44).

- Tap or click Datasheet to create a datasheet form.

- Save the form using the name, Customer.

Q&A Is it acceptable to use the same name for the form as for the table?
Yes. In this case, you want it to appear to the user that the Customer table is open in Datasheet view. One way to emphasize this fact is to use the same name as the table.

What is the difference between this form, Customer, and the form named Customer Form?
The Customer Form is a simple form that displays only one record at a time. The form you just created displays the data in a datasheet.

- Use the same technique to create a datasheet form named Book Rep for the Book Rep table.

- Close both forms.

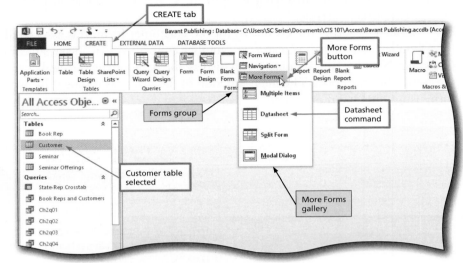

Figure 8–44

To Create UI Macros for the Datasheet Forms

The following steps create the UI macro for the Customer table shown in Table 8–3 on the previous page and the UI macro for the Book Rep table shown in Table 8–4 on the previous page. *Why? The UI macros will cause the appropriate pop-up forms to appear as a result of tapping or clicking the appropriate position on the forms.*

- Open the Customer form and then close the Navigation Pane.

- Tap or click the Customer Number (CU #) heading to select the Customer Number column in the datasheet.

- If necessary, tap or click the Property sheet button (FORM TOOLS DATASHEET tab | Tools group) to display a property sheet.

- Tap or click the Event tab to display only event properties.

Q&A Why tap or click the Event tab? Why not just use the All tab as we have before?
You can always use the All tab; however, if you know the category that contains the property in which you are interested, you can greatly reduce the number of properties that Access will display by tapping or clicking the tab for that category. That gives you fewer properties to search through to find the property you want. Whether you use the All tab or one of the other tabs is strictly a matter of personal preference.

- Tap or click the On Click event and then tap or click the Build button (the three dots) to display the Choose Builder dialog box (Figure 8–45).

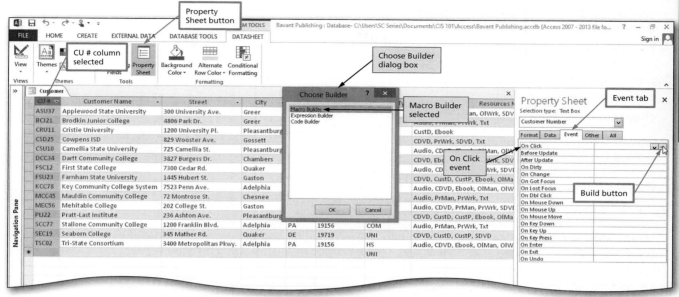

Figure 8–45

 2

- Tap or click the OK button (Choose Builder dialog box) to display the Macro Builder window.

- Add the SetTempVar action to the macro, enter `CN` as the value for the Name argument, and enter `[Customer Number]` as the value for the Expression argument.

- Add the OpenForm action to the macro, select Customer Master Form as the value for the Form Name argument, leave the value of the View argument set to Form, enter `[Customer Number]=[TempVars]![CN]` as the value for the Where Condition argument, select Read Only as the value for the Data Mode argument, and select Dialog as the value for the Window Mode argument.

Q&A What does this expression mean?

The portion before the equal sign, [Customer Number], refers to the Customer Number in the form just opened, that is, in the Customer Master Form. The portion to the right of the equal sign, [TempVars]![CN], is the temporary variable that was set equal to the Customer Number on the selected record in the Customer form. This Where Condition guarantees that the record displayed in the Customer Master Form will be the record with the same Customer Number as the one selected in the Customer form.

- Add the RemoveTempVar action to the macro and enter `CN` as the value for the Name argument (Figure 8–46).

Q&A Why do you need to remove the temporary variable?

Technically, you do not. It has fulfilled its function, however, so it makes sense to remove it at this point.

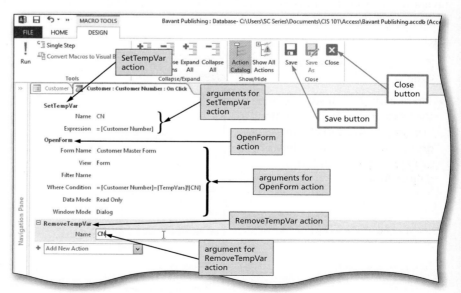

Figure 8–46

- Tap or click the Save button (MACRO TOOLS DESIGN tab | Close group) to save the macro.

- Tap or click the Close button (MACRO TOOLS DESIGN tab | Close group) to close the macro and return to the form design.

- Close the property sheet.

- Save the form by tapping or clicking the Save button on the Quick Access Toolbar and then close the form.

- Use the techniques in Steps 1 through 3 to create a UI macro for the Book Rep table called Book Rep, referring to Table 8–4 for the actions. Create the macro shown in Figure 8–47 associated with tapping or clicking the Book Rep Number (BR #) column.

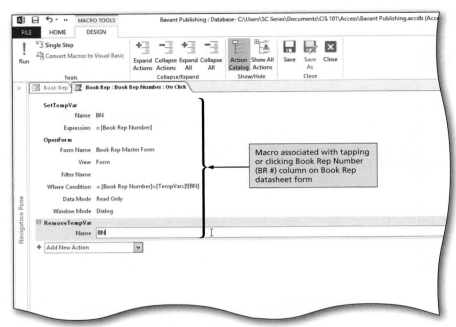

Figure 8–47

- Tap or click the Save button (MACRO TOOLS DESIGN tab | Close group) to save the macro.

- Tap or click the Close button (MACRO TOOLS DESIGN tab | Close group) to close the macro and return to the datasheet form.

- Close the property sheet.

- Save the form by tapping or clicking the Save button on the Quick Access Toolbar and then close the form.

To Create a Navigation Form

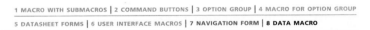

You now have all the forms you need to include in the navigation form. The following steps create the navigation form using horizontal tabs. *Why? Horizontal tabs are common on navigation forms and are easy to use.* The steps then save the form and change the title.

- If necessary, open the Navigation Pane.

- Tap or click the CREATE tab and then tap or click the Navigation button (CREATE tab | Forms group) to display the gallery of available navigation forms (Figure 8–48).

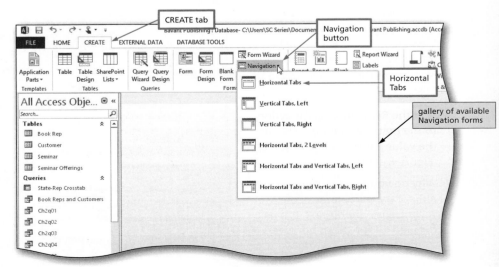

Figure 8–48

- Tap or click Horizontal Tabs in the gallery to create a form with a navigation control in which the tabs are arranged horizontally in a single row.

- If a field list appears, tap or click the 'Add Existing Fields' button (FORM LAYOUT TOOLS DESIGN tab | Tools group) to remove the field list (Figure 8–49).

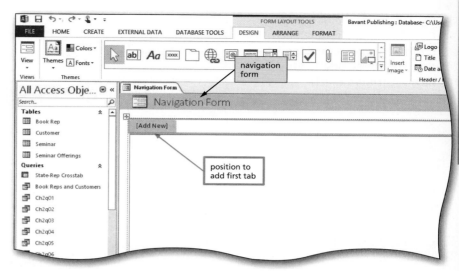

Figure 8–49

- Save the form using the name, Main Menu.

- Tap or click the form title twice: once to select it and the second time to produce an insertion point.

- Erase the current title and then type **Bavant Publishing** as the new title (Figure 8–50).

- Save the form.

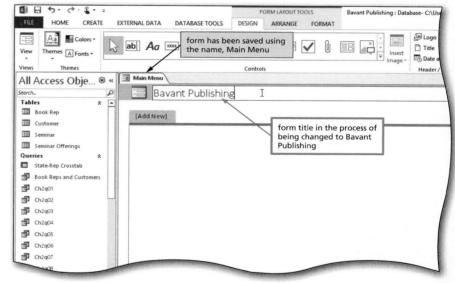

Figure 8–50

To Add Tabs to a Navigation Form

1 MACRO WITH SUBMACROS | 2 COMMAND BUTTONS | 3 OPTION GROUP | 4 MACRO FOR OPTION GROUP
5 DATASHEET FORMS | 6 USER INTERFACE MACROS | 7 **NAVIGATION FORM** | 8 DATA MACRO

To add a form or report to a tab in a navigation form, be sure the Navigation Pane is open and then drag the form or report to the desired tab. As a result, users can display that form or report by tapping or clicking the tab. For the Bavant Publishing navigation form, you will drag four forms to the tabs. The Customer form is a datasheet form that appears to display the Customer table open in Datasheet view. Similarly, the Book Rep form is a datasheet form that appears to display the Book Rep table open in Datasheet view. The Forms List form contains three buttons users can tap or click to display the form of their choice. Finally, the Reports List form contains an option group users can use to select a report to preview or export. The steps on the next page add the tabs to the navigation form. They also change the name of the Forms List and Reports List tabs. *Why? The names of the tabs do not have to be the same as the name of the corresponding forms. By changing them, you can often make tabs more readable.*

- Scroll down in the Navigation Pane so that the form named Customer appears, and then drag the form to the position to add a new tab (Figure 8–51).

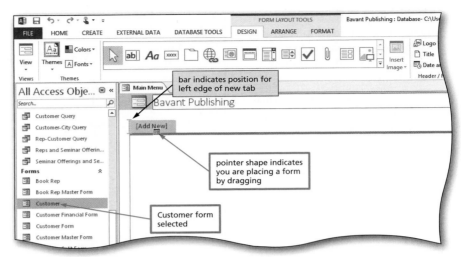

Figure 8–51

- Release your finger or the left mouse button to add the Customer form as the first tab.

- Drag the Book Rep form to the position to add a new tab (Figure 8–52).

Q&A What should I do if I made a mistake and added a form or report to the wrong location? You can rearrange the tabs by dragging them. Often, the simplest way to correct a mistake is to tap or click the Undo button to reverse your most recent action, however. You can also choose to simply close the form without saving it and then start over.

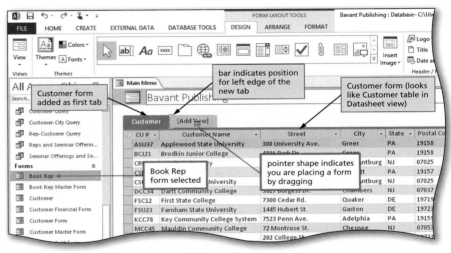

Figure 8–52

- Release your finger or the left mouse button to add the Book Rep form as the second tab.

- Using the techniques illustrated in Steps 1 and 2, add the Forms List form as the third tab and the Reports List form as the fourth tab (Figure 8–53).

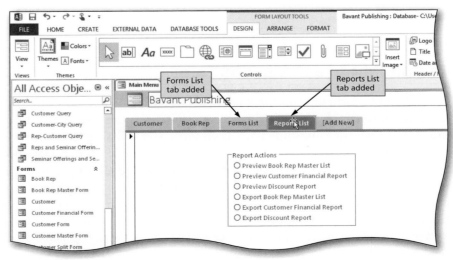

Figure 8–53

4

- Tap or click the Forms List tab twice: once to select it and the second time to produce an insertion point.

- Change the name from Forms List to Forms.

- In a similar fashion, change the name of the Reports List tab from Reports List to Reports (Figure 8–54).

Q&A

I created these two forms using the names Forms List and Reports List. Now I have changed the names to Forms and Reports. Why not call them Forms and Reports in the first place, so I would not have to rename the tabs?

Because the words, forms and reports, have specific meaning in Access, you cannot use these names. Thus, you needed to use some other names, like Forms List and Reports List. Because tabs are not database objects, you can rename them to be any name you want.

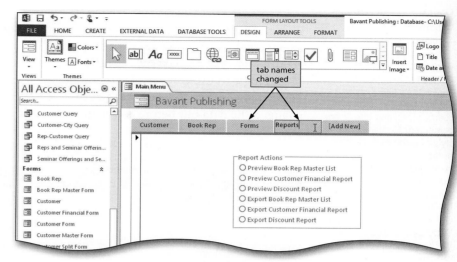

Figure 8–54

5

- Save the Main Menu form.

- Close the form.

- If requested to do so by your instructor, rename the Main Menu form as LastName Main Menu where LastName is your last name.

Using a Navigation Form

The Main Menu navigation form is complete and ready for use. To use the navigation form, press and hold or right-click the form in the Navigation Pane, and then tap or click Open on the shortcut menu. The Main Menu form then will appear with the first tabbed object (see Figure 8–1 on page AC 475). To display the other forms, simply tap or click the appropriate tab.

How do you determine the organization of the navigation form?

Once you decide you want a navigation form, you need to decide how to organize the form.

Determine which tasks should be accomplished by having the user tap or click tabs or buttons in the navigation form. Which forms should be opened? Which reports should be opened? Are there any tables or queries that you need to be able to open in the navigation form? If so, you must create forms for the tables or queries.

Determine any special requirements for the way the tasks are to be performed. When a form is opened, should a user be able to edit data, or should the form open as read-only? Should a report be exported or simply viewed on the screen?

Determine how to group the various tasks. Should forms or reports simply be assigned to the tabs in the navigation form? Should they be grouped as buttons on a menu form? Should they be placed as options within an option group? (For consistency, you would usually decide on one of these approaches and use it throughout. In this chapter, one menu form uses command buttons, and the other uses an option group simply to illustrate both approaches.) As far as the navigation form is concerned, is a single set of horizontal tabs sufficient, or would you also like vertical tabs? Would you like two rows of horizontal tabs?

 CONSIDER THIS

BTW
Quick Styles for Controls
To make a navigation form more visually appealing, you can change the style of a command button and/or tabs. Quick styles change how the different colors, fonts, and effects are combined. To change the style of a command button or tab, open the navigation form in Layout view. Select the controls or controls for which you want to change the style and tap or click Quick Styles. When the Quick Styles gallery appears, select the desired style. You also can change the style of a control in Design view.

Data Macros

A data macro is a special type of macro that is associated with specific table-related events, such as updating a record in a table. The possible events are Before Change, Before Delete, After Insert, After Update, and After Delete. Data macros allow you to add logic to these events. For example, the data macro shown in Table 8–5 is associated with the Before Change event, the event that occurs after the user has changed the data but before the change is actually made in the database.

Table 8–5 Data Macro for Before Change Event		
Condition	**Action**	**Arguments to Be Changed**
If [Hours Spent]>[Total Hours]		
	SetField	Name: [Hours Spent] Value: [Total Hours]
Else If [Hours Spent]<0		
	SetField	Name: [Hours Spent] Value: 0
End If		

BTW
Data Macros
Data macros are similar to SQL triggers. You attach logic to record or table events and any forms and code that update those events inherit the logic. Data macros are stored with the table.

This macro will examine the value in the Hours Spent field in the Seminar Offerings table. If the user's update would cause the value in the Hours Spent field to be greater than the value in the Total Hours field, the macro will change the value in the Hours Spent field so that it is equal to the value in the Total Hours field. Likewise, if the update would cause the value in the Hours Spent field to be less than zero, the macro will set the value in the Hours Spent field to 0. These changes take place after the user has made the change on the screen but before Access commits the change to the database, that is, before the data in the database is actually changed.

There are other events to which you can assign data macros. The actions in a data macro associated with the Before Delete event will take place after a user has indicated that he or she wants to delete a record, but before the record actually is removed from the database. The actions in a macro associated with the After Insert event will take place immediately after a record physically is added to the database. The actions in a macro associated with the After Update event will take place immediately after a record physically is changed in the database. The actions in a macro associated with the After Delete event will take place immediately after a record physically is removed from the database.

To Create a Data Macro

1 MACRO WITH SUBMACROS | 2 COMMAND BUTTONS | 3 OPTION GROUP | 4 MACRO FOR OPTION GROUP
5 DATASHEET FORMS | 6 USER INTERFACE MACROS | 7 NAVIGATION FORM | **8 DATA MACRO**

The following steps create the data macro in Table 8–5, a macro that will be run after a user makes a change to a record in the Seminar Offerings table, but before the record is updated in the database. *Why? Bavant Publishing management wants to prevent users from entering invalid data into the database.*

1

- Open the Seminar Offerings table in Datasheet view and close the Navigation Pane.

- Display the TABLE TOOLS TABLE tab (Figure 8–55).

Q&A

What is the meaning of the events in the Before Events and After Events groups?

Actions in macros associated with the Before events will occur after the user has taken action to change or delete a record, but before the change or deletion is made permanent in the database. Actions in macros associated with the After Events will occur after the corresponding update has been made permanent in the database.

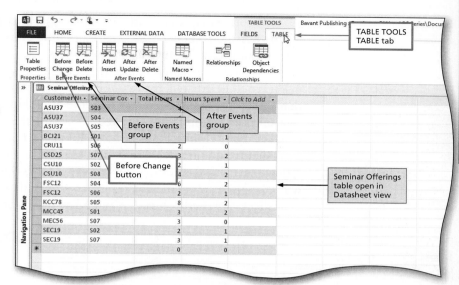

Figure 8–55

2

- Tap or click the Before Change button (TABLE TOOLS TABLE tab | Before Events group).

- Create the macro shown in Figure 8–56.

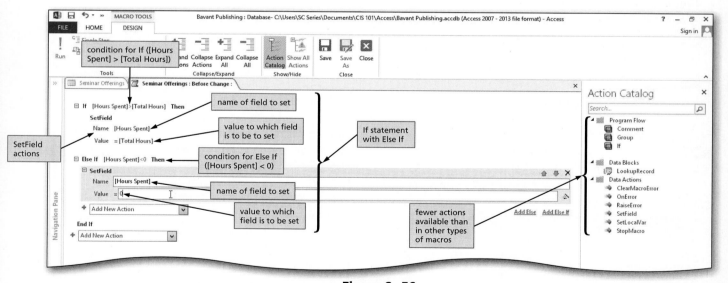

Figure 8–56

Q&A

What happened to all the actions that were in the list? In the previous macros we created, there seemed to be many more actions available.

There are only certain actions that make sense in data macros. Only those actions appear. The list of actions that appear is much smaller in a data macro than in other macros.

3

- Save the macro.

- Close the macro.

- Save and close the Seminar Offerings table.

Using a Table that Contains a Data Macro

If you update a table that contains a data macro, the actions in the data macro will be executed whenever the corresponding event takes place. If the data macro corresponds to the Before Change event, the actions will be executed after the user has changed the data, but before the change is saved in the database. With the data macro you just created, for example, if a user attempts to change the data in such a way that the Hours Spent is greater than the Total Hours (Figure 8–57), as soon as the user takes an action that would require saving the record, Access makes Hours Spent equal to Total Hours (Figure 8–58). Likewise, if a user attempts to set Hours Spent to a negative number (Figure 8–59), as soon as the user takes an action that would require saving the record, Access will set Hours Spent to 0 (Figure 8–60). This change will take place automatically, regardless of whether the user changes the values in Datasheet view, with a form, in an update query, or in any other fashion.

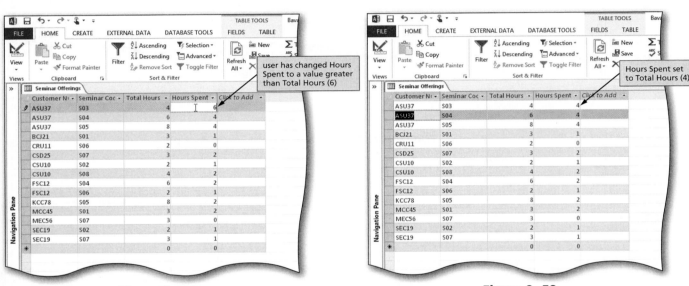

Figure 8–57

Figure 8–58

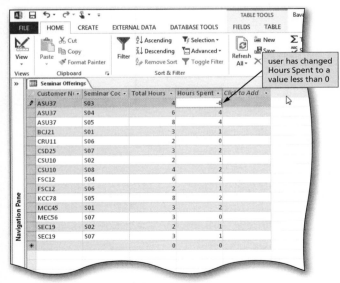

Figure 8–59

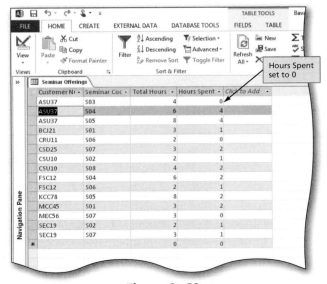

Figure 8–60

Break Point: If you wish to stop working through the chapter at this point, you can resume the project at a later time by starting Access, opening the database called Bavant Publishing, and continuing to follow the steps from this location forward.

Using Control Layouts on Forms and Reports

In earlier chapters, you worked with control layouts in forms and reports. In a control layout, the data is aligned either horizontally or vertically. The two types of layouts are stacked layouts, which are most commonly used in forms, and tabular layouts, which are most commonly used in reports (Figure 8–61).

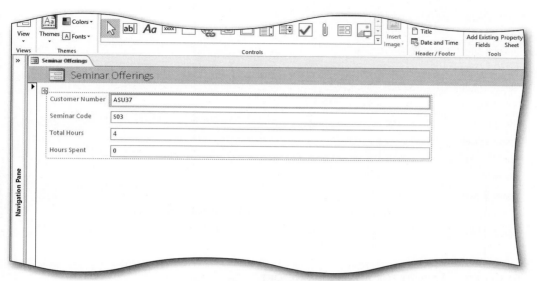

Figure 8–61 (a) Stacked Layout

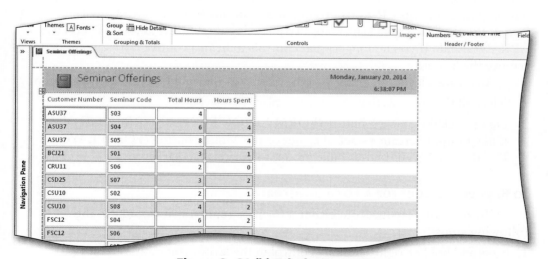

Figure 8–61 (b) Tabular Layout

In working with control layouts, there are many functions you can perform using the FORM LAYOUT TOOLS ARRANGE tab. You can insert rows and columns, delete rows and columns, split and merge cells, and move rows. You also can change margins, which affects spacing within cells, and padding, which affects spacing between rows and columns. You can split a layout into two layouts and move layouts. Finally, you can anchor controls so that they maintain the same distance between the control and the anchor position as the form or report is resized. Table 8–6 on the next page gives descriptions of the functions available on the FORM LAYOUT TOOLS ARRANGE tab.

Table 8–6 ARRANGE Tab	
Button	**Enhanced ScreenTip**
Gridlines	Gridlines.
Stacked	Create a layout similar to a paper form with labels to the left of each field.
Tabular	Create a layout similar to a spreadsheet with labels across the top and data in columns below the labels.
Insert Above	Insert above.
Insert Below	Insert below.
Insert Left	Insert left.
Insert Right	Insert right.
Select Layout	Select layout.
Select Column	Select column.
Select Row	Select row.
Merge	Merge cells.
Split Vertically	Split the selected layout into two rows.
Split Horizontally	Split the selected layout into two columns.
Move Up	Move up.
Move Down	Move down.
Control Margins	Specify the location of information displayed within the control.
Control Padding	Set the amount of spacing between controls and the gridlines of a layout.

© 2014 Cengage Learning

BTW
Change the Shape of a Control
Command buttons and tabs have a default shape. For example, both command buttons and tabs have a rounded rectangle shape as the default shape. You can change the shape of a button or tab control on a navigation form. To do so, open the navigation form in Layout view. Select the controls or controls for which you want to change the shape and tap or click Change Shape. When the Change Shape gallery appears, select the desired shape. You also can change the shape of a command button or tab in Design view.

TO CREATE A LAYOUT FOR A FORM OR REPORT

If you create a form using the Form button (CREATE tab | Forms group), Access automatically creates a stacked layout. If you create a report using the Report button (CREATE tab | Reports group), Access automatically creates a tabular layout. In other cases, you can create a layout using the FORM LAYOUT TOOLS ARRANGE tab. If you no longer want controls to be in a control layout, you can remove the layout.

To create a layout in either a form or report, you would use the following steps.

1. Select all the controls that you want to place in a layout.

2. Tap or click the Stacked button (FORM LAYOUT TOOLS ARRANGE tab | Table group) to create a stacked layout or the Tabular button (FORM LAYOUT TOOLS ARRANGE tab | Table group) to create a tabular layout.

TO REMOVE A LAYOUT FOR A FORM OR REPORT

To remove a layout from either a form or report, you would use the following steps.

1. Press and hold or right-click any control in the layout you want to remove to produce a shortcut menu.

2. Point to Layout on the shortcut menu and then tap or click Remove Layout on the submenu to remove the layout.

Using Undo

When making changes with the FORM LAYOUT TOOLS ARRANGE tab buttons, it is not uncommon to make a change that you did not intend. Sometimes taking appropriate action to reverse the change can prove difficult. If so, remember that you can undo the change by tapping or clicking the Undo button on the Quick

Access Toolbar. It is also a good idea to save your work frequently. That way, you can always close the form or report without saving. When you reopen the form or report, it will not have any of your most recent changes.

TO INSERT A ROW

You can insert a blank row either above or below a selected row (Figure 8–62). You can then fill in the row by either typing a value or dragging a field from a field list. In a similar fashion, you can insert a blank column either to the left or right of a selected column.

You would use the following steps to insert a blank row.

1. Select any control in the row above or below where you want to insert a new row.

2. Tap or click the Select Row button (FORM LAYOUT TOOLS ARRANGE tab | Rows & Columns group) to select the row.

3. Tap or click the Insert Above button (FORM LAYOUT TOOLS ARRANGE tab | Rows & Columns group) to insert a blank row above the selected row or the Insert Below button (FORM LAYOUT TOOLS ARRANGE tab | Rows & Columns group) to insert a blank row below the selected row.

BTW

PivotTables and PivotCharts
PivotTable view and PivotChart view have been discontinued in Access 2013. To create a PivotChart or PivotTable, create a new workbook in the Microsoft Excel app, tap or click the From Access button (DATA tab | Get External Data group) and follow the directions in the Select Data Source dialog box to import an Access table. You then can use the PivotTable and PivotChart features of Excel.

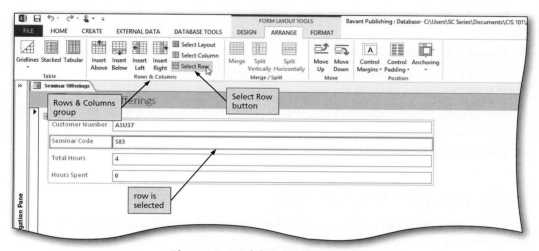

Figure 8–62 (a) Selecting a Row

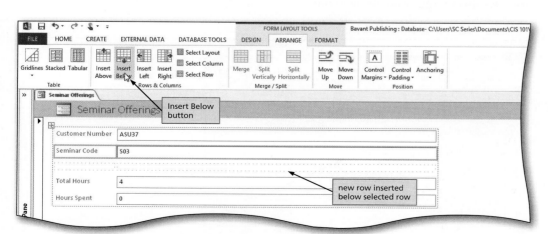

Figure 8–62 (b) Inserting a Row

As you have seen earlier in the text, you also can insert a row containing a field by simply dragging the field from the field list to the desired location.

TO INSERT A COLUMN

You would use the following steps to insert a new column.

1. Select any control in the column to the right or left of where you want to insert a new column.
2. Tap or click the Select Column button (FORM LAYOUT TOOLS ARRANGE tab | Rows & Columns group) to select the column.
3. Tap or click the Insert Left button (FORM LAYOUT TOOLS ARRANGE tab | Rows & Columns group) to insert a blank column to the left of the selected column or the Insert Right button (FORM LAYOUT TOOLS ARRANGE tab | Rows & Columns group) to insert a blank column to the right of the selected column.

TO DELETE A ROW

You can delete any unwanted row or column from a control layout. You would use the following steps to delete a row.

1. Tap or click any control in the row you want to delete.
2. Tap or click Select Row (FORM LAYOUT TOOLS ARRANGE tab | Rows & Columns group).
3. Press the DELETE key to delete the row.

TO DELETE A COLUMN

You would use the following steps to delete a column.

1. Tap or click any control in the column you want to delete.
2. Tap or click Select Column (FORM LAYOUT TOOLS ARRANGE tab | Rows & Columns group).
3. Press the DELETE key to delete the column.

Splitting and Merging Cells

You can split a cell into two cells either horizontally, as shown in Figure 8–63, or vertically. You can then enter contents into the new cell. For example, in Figure 8–63, you could type text into the new cell that gives information about customer numbers. You can also merge two cells into one.

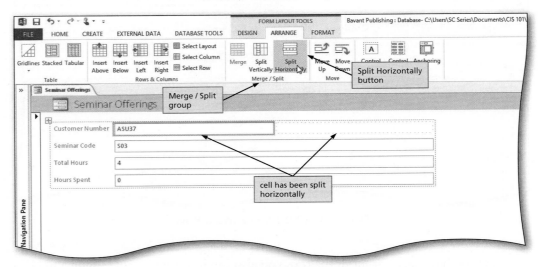

Figure 8–63

TO SPLIT A CELL

To split a cell, you would use the following steps.

1. Tap or click the cell to be split.
2. Tap or click the Split Vertically button (FORM LAYOUT TOOLS ARRANGE tab | Merge / Split group) to split the selected cell vertically or the Split Horizontally button (FORM LAYOUT TOOLS ARRANGE tab | Merge / Split group) to split the selected cell horizontally.

TO MERGE CELLS

You would use the following steps to merge cells.

1. Select the first cell to be merged.
2. While holding down the CTRL key, tap or click all the other cells to be merged.
3. Tap or click the Merge button (FORM LAYOUT TOOLS ARRANGE tab | Merge / Split group) to merge the cells.

Moving Cells

You can move a cell in a layout by dragging it to its new position. Most often, however, you will not want to move individual cells, but rather whole rows (Figure 8–64). You can move a row by selecting the row and then dragging it to the new position or you can use the Move buttons on the FORM LAYOUT TOOLS ARRANGE tab.

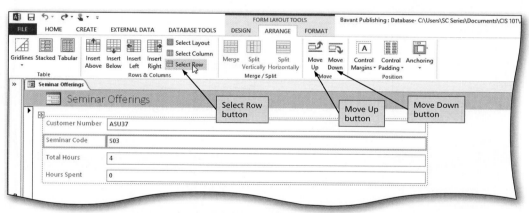

Figure 8–64 (a) Row Selected

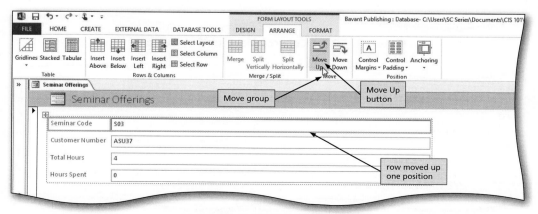

Figure 8–64 (b) Row Moved

To Move Rows Using the Move Buttons

You would use the following steps to move a row.

1. Select any cell in the row to be moved.
2. Tap or click the Select Row button (FORM LAYOUT TOOLS ARRANGE tab | Rows & Columns group) to select the entire row.
3. Tap or click the Move Up button (FORM LAYOUT TOOLS ARRANGE tab | Move group) to move the selected row up one row or the Move Down button (FORM LAYOUT TOOLS ARRANGE tab | Move group) to move the selected row down one row.

Margins and Padding

You can change the spacing within a layout by changing the control margins and the control padding. The control margins, which you change with the Control Margins button, affect the spacing around the text inside a control. Figure 8–65 shows the various options as well as samples of two of the options.

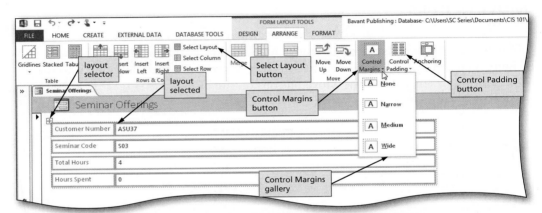

Figure 8–65 (a) Changing Control Margins

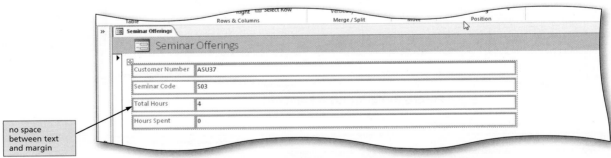

Figure 8–65 (b) Control Margins Set to None

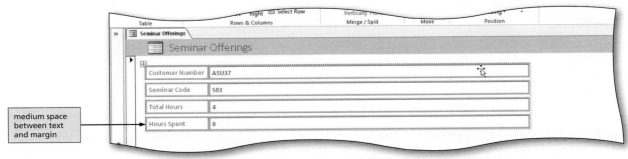

Figure 8–65 (c) Control Margins Set to Medium

The control padding, which you change with the Control Padding button, affects the spacing around the outside of a control. The options are the same as those for control margins. Figure 8–66 shows samples of two of the options.

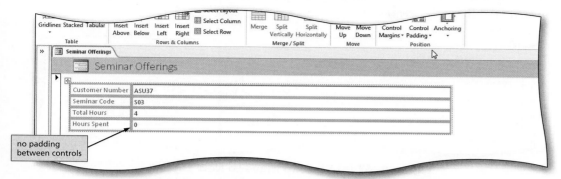

Figure 8–66 (a) Control Padding Set to None

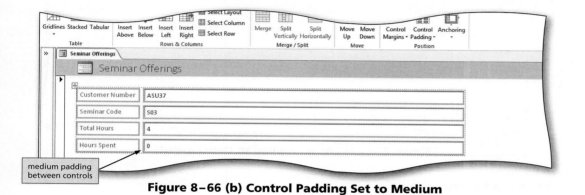

Figure 8–66 (b) Control Padding Set to Medium

To Change Control Margins

You would use the following steps to change a control's margins.

1. Select any cell in the layout.
2. Tap or click the Select Layout button (FORM LAYOUT TOOLS ARRANGE tab | Rows & Columns group) to select the entire layout. (You also can select the layout by tapping or clicking the layout selector.)
3. Tap or click the Control Margins button (FORM LAYOUT TOOLS ARRANGE tab | Position group) to display the available margin settings.
4. Tap or click the desired margin setting.

To Change Control Padding

You would use the following steps to change control padding.

1. Select the layout.
2. Tap or click the Control Padding button (FORM LAYOUT TOOLS ARRANGE tab | Position group) to display the available padding settings.
3. Tap or click the desired padding setting.

Although you can make the margin and padding changes for individual controls, it is much more common to do so for the entire layout. Doing so gives a uniform appearance to the layout.

Splitting a Layout

You can split a single control layout into two separate layouts (Figure 8–67) and then modify each layout separately. They can be moved to different locations and formatted differently.

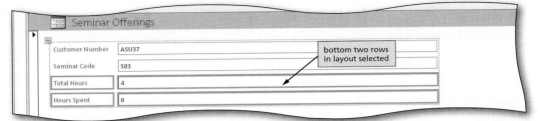

Figure 8–67 (a) Rows to Move to New Layout

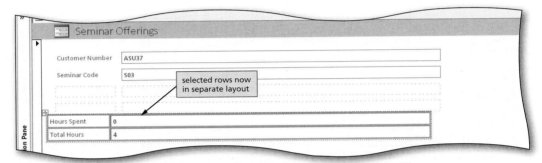

Figure 8–67 (b) Rows Moved to New Layout

TO SPLIT A LAYOUT

To split a layout, you would use the following steps.

1. Select all the cells that you want to move to a new layout.
2. Tap or click the Stacked button (FORM LAYOUT TOOLS ARRANGE tab | Table group) to place the cells in a stacked layout or the Tabular button (FORM LAYOUT TOOLS ARRANGE tab | Table group) to place the cells in a tabular layout.

Moving a Layout

You can move a control layout to a different location on the form (Figure 8–68).

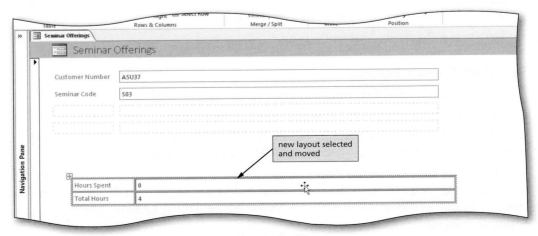

Figure 8–68

To Move a Layout

You would use the following steps to move a layout.

1. Tap or click any cell in the layout to be moved and then tap or click the Select Layout button (FORM LAYOUT TOOLS ARRANGE tab | Rows & Columns group) to select the layout.

2. Drag the layout to the new location.

Anchoring Controls

The Anchoring button allows you to tie (anchor) controls to a section or to other controls so that they maintain the same distance between the control and the anchor position as the form is resized. To anchor the controls you have selected, you use the Anchoring gallery (Figure 8–69).

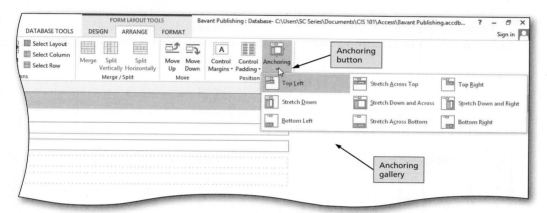

Figure 8–69

The Top Left, Top Right, Bottom Left, and Bottom Right options anchor the control in the indicated position on the form. The other five operations also stretch the controls in the indicated direction.

To Anchor Controls

You would use the following steps to anchor controls.

1. Select the control or controls to be anchored.

2. Tap or click the Anchoring button (FORM LAYOUT TOOLS ARRANGE tab | Position group) to produce the Anchoring gallery.

3. Select the desired Anchoring option from the Anchoring gallery.

The best way to see the effect of anchoring is to display objects in overlapping windows rather than tabbed documents. With overlapping windows, you can resize the object by dragging the border of the object. Anchored objects keep their same relative position (Figure 8–70 on the next page).

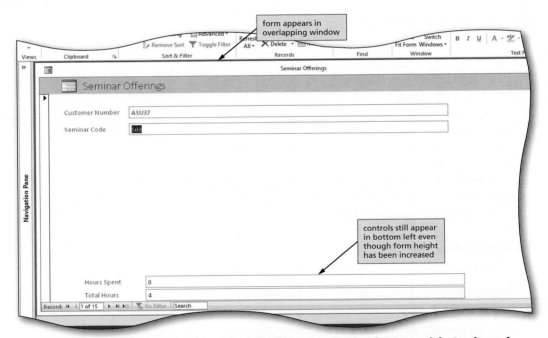

Figure 8–70 (a) Overlapping Windows Showing Form with Anchored Controls

Figure 8–70 (b) Overlapping Window Showing Resized Form with Anchored Controls

BTW

Overlapping Windows

When you display objects in overlapping windows, each database object appears in its own windows. When multiple objects are open, these windows overlap each other. By default, Access 2013 displays database objects in a single pane separated by tabs.

If you want to display objects in overlapping windows, you have to modify the appropriate Access option.

TO DISPLAY OBJECTS IN OVERLAPPING WINDOWS

You would use the following steps to overlap windows.

1. Tap or click FILE on the ribbon to open the Backstage view.

2. Tap or click Options to display the Access Options dialog box.

3. Tap or click Current Database to display the Current Database options.

4. In the Application Options area, tap or click the Overlapping Windows option button.

5. Tap or click the OK button to close the Access Options dialog box.

6. For the changes to take effect, you will need to close and then reopen the database. You use a similar process to return to displaying objects in tabbed documents.

TO DISPLAY OBJECTS IN TABBED DOCUMENTS

You would use the following steps to display tabbed documents.

1. Tap or click FILE on the ribbon to open the Backstage view.

2. Tap or click Options to display the Access Options dialog box.

3. Tap or click Current Database to display the Current Database options.

4. In the Application Options area, tap or click the Tabbed Documents option button.

5. Tap or click the OK button to close the Access Options dialog box.

6. For the changes to take effect, you will need to close and then reopen the database.

To Sign Out of a Microsoft Account

If you are signed in to a Microsoft account and are using a public computer or otherwise wish to sign out of your Microsoft account, you should sign out of the account from the Account gallery in the Backstage view before exiting Access. Signing out of the account is the safest way to make sure that nobody else can access SkyDrive files or settings stored in your Microsoft account. The following steps sign out of a Microsoft account from Access. For a detailed example of the procedure summarized below, refer to the Office and Windows chapter at the beginning of this book.

1 If you wish to sign out of your Microsoft account, tap or click FILE on the ribbon to open the Backstage view and then tap or click the Account tab to display the Account gallery.

2 Tap or click the Sign out link, which displays the Remove Account dialog box. If a Can't remove Windows accounts dialog box appears instead of the Remove Account dialog box, click the OK button and skip the remaining steps.

Q&A Why does a Can't remove Windows accounts dialog box appear?
If you signed in to Windows using your Microsoft account, then you also must sign out from Windows, rather than signing out from within Access. When you are finished using Windows, be sure to sign out at that time.

3 Tap or click the Yes button (Remove Account dialog box) to sign out of your Microsoft account on this computer.

Q&A Should I sign out of Windows after signing out of my Microsoft account?
When you are finished using the computer, you should sign out of your account for maximum security.

4 Tap or click the Back button in the upper-left corner of the Backstage view to return to the database.

To Exit Access

The following steps exit Access.

1 Tap or click the Close button on the right side of the title bar to exit Access.

2 If a Microsoft Access dialog box appears, tap or click the Yes button to save any changes made to the object since the last save.

BTW
Certification
The Microsoft Office Specialist (MOS) program provides an opportunity for you to obtain a valuable industry credential — proof that you have the Access 2013 skills required by employers. For more information, visit the Certification resource on the Student Companion Site located on www.cengagebrain.com. For detailed instructions about accessing available resources, visit www.cengage.com/ct/studentdownload or contact your instructor for information about accessing the required files.

BTW
Quick Reference
For a table that lists how to complete the tasks covered in this book using touch gestures, the mouse, ribbon, shortcut menu, and keyboard, see the Quick Reference Summary at the back of this book, or visit the Quick Reference resource on the Student Companion Site located on www.cengagebrain.com. For detailed instructions about accessing available resources, visit www.cengage.com/ct/studentdownload or contact your instructor for information about accessing the required files.

Chapter Summary

In this chapter you have learned to create and use macros; create a menu form that uses command buttons for the choices; create a menu form that uses an option group for the choices; create a macro that implements the choices in the option group; create datasheet forms that utilize user interface macros; create a navigation form; add tabs to a navigation form; and create data macros. You also learned to use control layouts.

Data Macro Creation
Create a Data Macro (AC 510)

Datasheet Form Creation
Create Datasheet Forms (AC 504)

Displaying Objects
Display Objects in Overlapping Windows (AC 522)
Display Objects in Tabbed Documents (AC 522)

Layouts, Use
Create a Layout for a Form or Report (AC 514)
Remove a Layout for a Form or Report (AC 514)
Insert a Row (AC 515)
Insert a Column (AC 516)
Delete a Row (AC 516)
Delete a Column (AC 516)
Split a Cell (AC 517)
Merge Cells (AC 517)
Move Rows Using the Move Buttons (AC 518)
Change Control Margins (AC 519)
Change Control Padding (AC 519)
Split a Layout (AC 520)

Move a Layout (AC 521)
Anchor Controls (AC 521)

Macro Creation
Begin Creating a Macro (AC 478)
Add an Action to a Macro (AC 480)
Add More Actions to a Macro (AC 482)
Create a Macro with a Variable for the Option Group (AC 496)
Add Actions to the Form Options Macro (AC 499)
Create UI Macros for the Datasheet Forms (AC 504)

Menu Form Creation
Create a Menu Form Containing Command Buttons (AC 488)
Create a Menu Form Containing an Option Group (AC 492)

Navigation Form Creation
Create a Navigation Form (AC 506)
Add Tabs to a Navigation Form (AC 507)

CONSIDER THIS: PLAN AHEAD

What decisions will you need to make when creating your own macros and navigation forms?

Use these guidelines as you complete the assignments in this chapter and create your own macros and navigation forms outside of this class.

1. Determine when it would be beneficial to automate tasks in a macro.

   a. Are there tasks involving multiple steps that would be more conveniently accomplished by running a macro than by carrying out all the individual steps? For example, opening a form in read-only mode could be accomplished conveniently through a macro.

   b. Are there tasks that are to be performed when the user taps or clicks buttons on a menu form?

   c. Are there tasks to be performed when a user taps or clicks a control on a form?

   d. Are there tasks to be performed when a user updates a table? These tasks can be placed in a macro that can be run when the button is tapped or clicked.

2. Determine whether it is appropriate to create a navigation form.

   a. If you want to make it easy and convenient for users to perform a variety of tasks just by tapping or clicking tabs and buttons, consider creating a navigation form.

   b. You can associate the performance of the various tasks with the tabs and buttons in the navigation form.

3. Determine the organization of the navigation form.

   a. Determine the various tasks that need to be performed by tapping or clicking tabs and buttons.

   b. Decide the logical grouping of the tabs and buttons.

CONSIDER THIS

How should you submit solutions to questions in the assignments identified with a ✳ symbol?
Every assignment in this book contains one or more questions identified with a ✳ symbol. These questions require you to think beyond the assigned database. Present your solutions to the questions in the format required by your instructor. Possible formats may include one or more of these options: write the answer; create a document that contains the answer; present your answer to the class; discuss your answer in a group; record the answer as audio or video using a webcam, smartphone, or portable media player; or post answers on a blog, wiki, or website.

Apply Your Knowledge

Reinforce the skills and apply the concepts you learned in this chapter.

Creating UI Macros and a Navigation Form

Note: To complete this assignment, you will be required to use the Data Files for Students. Visit www.cengage.com/ct/studentdownload for detailed instructions or contact your instructor for information about accessing the required files.

Instructions: Start Access. Open the Apply Natural Products database. Natural Products is a company that distributes cleaning supplies, hand lotions, soaps, and other items that are eco-friendly. The company markets to retail stores, fitness centers, salons, and spas.

Perform the following tasks:

1. Create a datasheet form for the Customer table and name the form Customer. Create a UI macro for the Customer form. When a user taps or clicks a customer number on a row in the datasheet form, the Customer Master Form should appear in a pop-up form.

2. Create a datasheet form for the Sales Rep table and name the form Sales Rep. Create a UI macro for the Sales Rep form. When a user taps or clicks a sales rep number on a row in the datasheet form, the Sales Rep Master Form should appear in a pop-up form.

3. Create the navigation form shown in Figure 8–71. The purpose of the form is to display the two datasheet forms in the database as horizontal tabs. Name the form Datasheet Forms Menu and change the title to Natural Products Navigation Form.

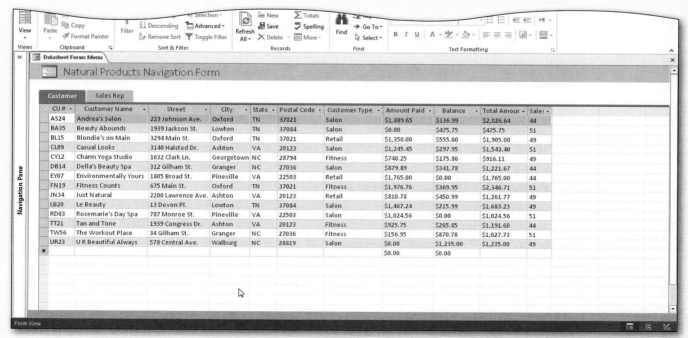

Figure 8–71

Continued >

Apply Your Knowledge *continued*

4. If requested to do so by your instructor, open the Sales Rep datasheet form and change the first and last names of sales rep 44 to your first and last name.

5. Submit the revised database in the format specified by your instructor.

6. ✳ How could you add the Sales Rep Order Data form to the navigation form?

Extend Your Knowledge

Extend the skills you learned in this chapter and experiment with new skills. You may need to use Help to complete the assignment.

Modifying Navigation Forms

Note: To complete this assignment, you will be required to use the Data Files for Students. Visit www.cengage.com/ct/studentdownload for detailed instructions or contact your instructor for information about accessing the required files.

Instructions: Start Access. Open the Extend Corporate Training database. Corporate Training provides training on Microsoft Office apps to commercial businesses.

Perform the following tasks:

1. Open the Main Menu form in Design view and change the theme for this object only to Organic. Expand the size of the form header and add the current date to the form header. Add a command button to the form header that closes the form. Save the changes and close the form.

2. Open the Reports List form in Design view. Select the Report Actions label, and change the font weight to semi-bold and the special effect to raised. You may need to enlarge the label slightly. Select all the option buttons and use the Size/Space menu to adjust the labels to be the same width as the widest label. Select the option group and change the special effect to Shadowed. Change the theme colors to Green. Change the background color of the form to White, Background 1, Darker 5%. Save the changes to the form.

3. Open the Forms List form in Design view and make the same changes that you made to the Reports List form. Save the changes to the form.

4. Convert the Forms and Reports macro to Visual Basic code.

5. Open the Main Menu navigation form in Layout view. Change the shapes of the Forms tab and the Reports tab to Snip Single Corner Rectangle.

6. If requested to do so by your instructor, add a label to the form header for the Main Menu form with your first and last name.

7. Submit the revised database in the format specified by your instructor.

8. ✳ Why would you convert a macro to Visual Basic code?

Analyze, Correct, Improve

Analyze a database, correct all errors, and improve the design.

Correcting Macro Errors and Improving a Navigation Form

Note: To complete this assignment, you will be required to use the Data Files for Students. Visit www.cengage.com/ct/studentdownload for detailed instructions or contact your instructor for information about accessing the required files.

Instructions: Start Access and open the Analyze Consignment database from the Data Files for Students. Analyze Consignment is a database maintained by the Friends group of the local animal shelter. The Friends group manages a consignment store and uses the monies raised to help the animal shelter. The store manager has asked you to correct some errors in macros and to improve the navigation form.

Perform the following tasks:

1. Correct The store manager created a datasheet form for the Seller table and a UI macro that should open the Seller Master Form when a seller code is selected. When she tries to run the macro, she receives the error message shown in Figure 8–72.

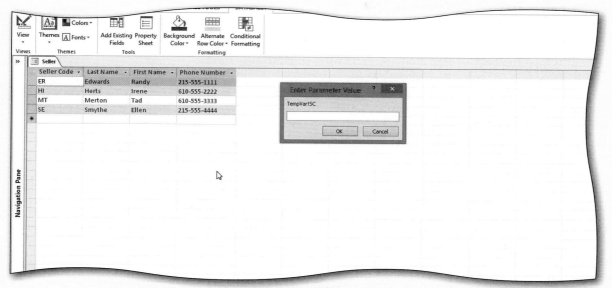

Figure 8–72

Also, she inadvertently selected the XPS exporting format instead of PDF in the two export report submacros that she created.

2. Improve The Forms and Reports form has an option group for forms and an option group for reports that appear side by side. The manager prefers these option groups to appear vertically, one above the other, with the Forms option group appearing at the top. The title on the navigation form could be improved by changing it from Main Menu to Friends Consignment.

3. ✴ Why do you think the name of the navigation form is Main Menu? Is there another name that would more accurately describe the purpose of the navigation form?

In the Labs

Design, create, modify, and/or use a database following the guidelines, concepts, and skills presented in this chapter. Labs are listed in order of increasing difficulty. Labs 1 and 2, which increase in difficulty, require you to create solutions based on what you learned in the chapter; Lab 3 requires you to create a solution, which uses cloud and web technologies, by learning and investigating on your own from general guidance.

Lab 1: Creating Macros and a Navigation Form for the Technology Services Database

Note: To complete this assignment, you will be required to use the Data Files for Students. Visit www.cengage.com/ct/studentdownload for detailed instructions or contact your instructor for information about accessing the required files.

Continued >

In the Labs *continued*

Problem: Technology Services provides information technology services to local businesses and service organizations. The services include backup and recovery, troubleshooting, software and hardware upgrades, and web hosting. The company would like an easy way to access the various tables, forms, and reports included in the database. This would make the database easier to maintain and update.

Instructions: Perform the following tasks:

1. Open the Lab 1 Technology Services database and create a macro named Forms and Reports that will include submacros to perform the following tasks:

   a.   Open the Service Rep Request Data form in read-only mode.
   b.   Open the Service Rep Master Form.
   c.   Open the Client Master Form.
   d.   Preview the Service Rep Master List.
   e.   Preview the Client Financial Report.
   f.   Preview the Client Discount Report.
   g.   Export the Service Rep Master List in PDF format.
   h.   Export the Client Financial Report in PDF format.
   i.   Export the Client Discount Report in PDF format.

2. Create the menu form shown in Figure 8–73. The command buttons should use the macros you created in Step 1 to open the three forms.

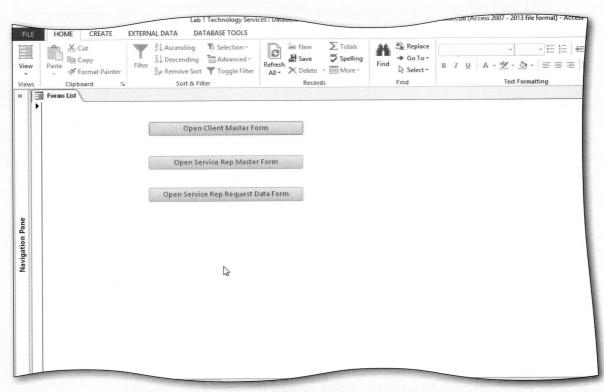

Figure 8–73

3. Create the menu form shown in Figure 8–74. The option group should use the macros you created in Step 1 to preview and export the three reports.

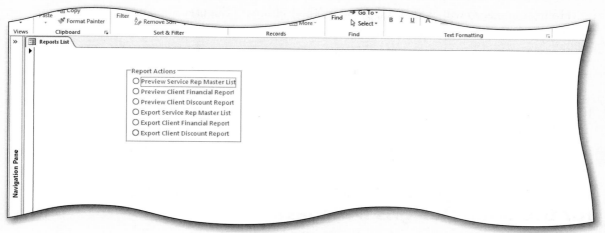

Figure 8–74

4. Create a datasheet form for the Client table and name the form Client. Create an IU macro for the Client form. When a user taps or clicks a client number on a row in the datasheet, the Client Master Form should appear in a pop-up form.

5. Create a datasheet form for the Service Rep table and name the form Service Rep. Create an IU macro for the Service Rep form. When a user taps or clicks a service rep number on a row in the datasheet, the Service Rep Master Form should appear in a pop-up form.

6. Create the navigation form shown in Figure 8–75 for the Technology Services database. Use the same design for your navigation form as the one illustrated in this chapter. For example, the Client tab should display the Client form you created in Step 4, and the Service Rep tab should display the Service Rep form you created in Step 5. The Forms tab should display the Forms List form you created in Step 2, and the Reports tab should display the Reports List form you created in Step 3.

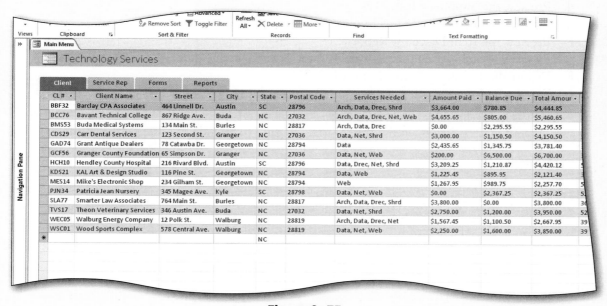

Figure 8–75

Continued >

In the Labs *continued*

7. Create a data macro for the Service Requests table. The macro will examine the value in the Hours Spent field. If the user's update would cause the value to be greater than the Total Hours, the macro will change the value to Total Hours. If the user's update would cause the value to be less than 0, the macro will change the value to 0.

8. If requested to do so by your instructor, add your name to the title for the Main Menu navigation form.

9. Submit the revised database in the format specified by your instructor.

10. ✸ In this exercise, you have created both command buttons and option groups to run macros. Which do you prefer? Why?

Lab 2: Creating Macros and a Navigation Form for the Team Designs Database

Problem: Team Designs is a company that supplies customized clothing and accessories to sports teams. The company purchases these items from suppliers at wholesale prices and adds the team's design. The final item price is determined by marking up the wholesale price and adding a fee that is based on the complexity of the design. The company would like an easy way to access the various tables, forms, and reports included in the database. This would make the database easier to maintain and update.

Note: To complete this assignment, you will be required to use the Data Files for Students. Visit www.cengage.com/ct/studentdownload for detailed instructions or contact your instructor for information about accessing the required files.

Instructions: Perform the following tasks:

1. Open the Lab 2 Team Designs database and create a macro named Forms and Reports that will include submacros to perform the following tasks:

   a. Open the Supplier Orders Data form in read-only mode.
   b. Open the Supplier Master Form.
   c. Open the Item Master Form.
   d. Preview the Supplier Master List.
   e. Preview the Inventory Status Report.
   f. Preview the Item Discount Report.
   g. Export the Supplier Master List in XPS format.
   h. Export the Inventory Status Report in XPS format.
   i. Export the Item Discount Report in XPS format.

2. Create the menu form shown in Figure 8–76. The command buttons should use the macros you created in Step 1 to open the three forms. Be sure to include the title on the form.

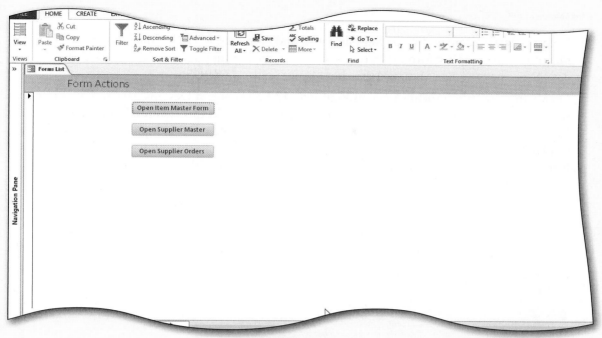

Figure 8–76

3. Create the menu form shown in Figure 8–77. The command buttons should use the macros you created in Step 1 to preview and export the three reports. Be sure to include the title on the form.

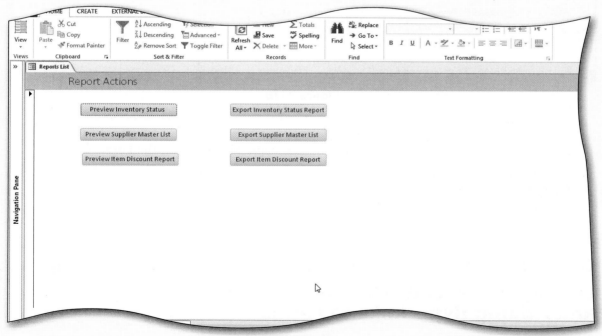

Figure 8–77

4. Create a datasheet form for the Item table and name the form Item. Create an IU macro for the Item form. When a user taps or clicks an item number on a row in the datasheet, the Item Master Form should appear in a pop-up form.

Continued >

In the Labs *continued*

5. Create a datasheet form for the Supplier table and name the form Supplier. Create an IU macro for the Supplier form. When a user taps or clicks a supplier code on a row in the datasheet, the Supplier Master Form should appear in a pop-up form.

6. Create the navigation form shown in Figure 8–78 for the Team Designs database. Use the same design for your navigation form as the one illustrated in this chapter. For example, the Item tab should display the Item form you created in Step 4, and the Supplier tab should display the Supplier form you created in Step 5. The Forms tab should display the Forms List form you created in Step 2, and the Reports tab should display the Reports List form you created in Step 3.

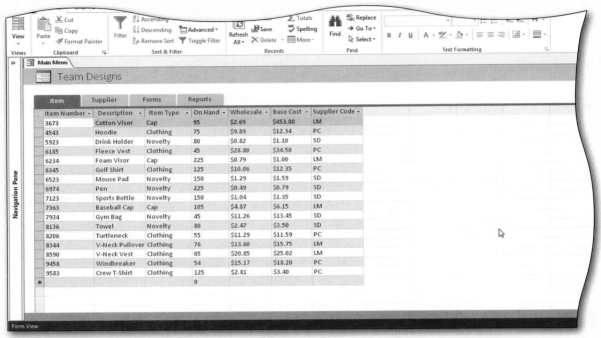

Figure 8–78

7. If requested to do so by your instructor, add your name to the title for the Forms List form.

8. Submit the revised database in the format specified by your instructor.

9. ✳ In this exercise, you exported reports in XPS format. How would you create a macro to export the Item table in Excel format?

Lab 3: Expand Your World: Cloud and Web Technologies
Linking an Excel Workbook, Adding an Image, and Adding Hyperlinks to Forms

Problem: Energy Savings is an organization that provides energy saving devices. The organization has created macros and a navigation form but would like to link a workbook containing residential energy statistics and add a hyperlink to a form.

Note: To complete this assignment, you will be required to use the Data Files for Students. Visit www.cengage.com/ct/studentdownload for detailed instructions or contact your instructor for information about accessing the required files.

Instructions: Perform the following tasks:

1. Open your browser and navigate to the U. S. Energy Information Administration website, www.eia.gov/consumption/residential/data/2009/. Select the Consumption & Expenditures tab, and then select By End Uses. Download the expenditure workbook for the region of the country where you live. If you do not live in one of those regions, download the workbook for the United States.

2. Open the Lab 3 Energy Savings database from the Data Files for Students and link the workbook you downloaded to the database.

3. Access the office.com website or any other website containing royalty-free images and search for an energy-related image suitable for a navigation form.

4. Open the navigation form in Design view and add the image to the form header. Add a hyperlink to the main U.S. Energy Information Administration website to the form header.

5. Save your changes.

6. Submit the revised database in the format specified by your instructor.

7. ✸ Which workbook did you download and link? What image did you choose for the navigation form? Why did you make those choices?

✸ Consider This: Your Turn

Apply your creative thinking and problem solving skills to design and implement a solution.

1: Creating Macros and a Navigation Form for the Fine Crafts Database
Personal/Academic

Note: To complete this assignment, you will be required to use the Data Files for Students. Visit www.cengage.com/ct/studentdownload for detailed instructions or contact your instructor for information about accessing the required files.

Part 1:   You attend a university that is renowned for its school of arts and crafts. Students who major in arts and crafts can sell their work through an agreement with the university bookstore. For your senior capstone project, you have created a database in which to store data about the craft items for sale and the students who created the items. You now need to add macros and a navigation form to make the database easier to use.

Open the Your Turn 1 Fine Crafts database from the Data Files for Students. Then, use the concepts and techniques presented in this chapter to perform each of the following tasks:

a. Create a macro that includes submacros to open the two forms: Item Master Form and Student Master Form in Read-Only mode. The macro also should include submacros to preview and export three reports in PDF format: Crafts for Sale, Item Sale Report, and Items by Student.

b. Create a menu form for the two forms and a menu form for the three reports. Use an option group for each form and include a descriptive title on each form.

c. Create a datasheet form for the Item table and name the form Item. Create a UI macro for the Item form. When a user taps or clicks an item number on a row in the datasheet form, the Item Master Form should appear in a pop-up form in Edit mode.

d. Create a datasheet form for the Student table and name the form Student. Create a UI macro for the Student form. When a user taps or clicks a student code on a row in the datasheet form, the Student Master Form should appear in a pop-up form in Edit mode.

e. Create a navigation form for the Fine Crafts database. Use the same design for your navigation form as that shown in Figure 8–1a on page AC 475. Include the Item form, the Student form, the menu form for the forms, and the menu form for the reports.

Submit your assignment in the format specified by your instructor.

Continued >

Consider This: Your Turn *continued*

Part 2: ✸ You made several decisions while in this assignment, including creating option groups. What was the rationale behind your decisions? Do you think it is necessary to have a title on the option group menu forms? Why or why not?

2: Creating Macros and a Navigation Form for the Landscaping Services Database
Professional

Note: To complete this assignment, you will be required to use the Data Files for Students. Visit www.cengage.com/ct/studentdownload for detailed instructions or contact your instructor for information about accessing the required files.

Part 1: Landscaping Services is a local company that provides landscaping and lawn maintenance services to commercial customers, such as businesses, homeowner's associations, and schools. You work part-time for the company while attending college. The owner, Carol Williams has asked you to create macros and a navigation form to make the database easier to use.

Open the Your Turn 2 Landscaping Services database from the Data Files for Students. Then, use the concepts and techniques presented in this chapter to perform the following tasks:

a. Create a macro that includes submacros to open the Customer Master Form, the Supervisor Master Form, and the Supervisor Request Data form. The macro should also include submacros to preview and export in XPS format the Customer Financial Report, the Supervisor Master Report, and the Customers by Supervisor report.

b. Create a menu form for the forms and a menu form for the reports. Use command buttons for each form and include a descriptive title on each form.

c. Create a datasheet form for the Customer table and name the form Customer. Create a user interface macro for the Customer form. When a user taps or clicks a customer number on a row in the datasheet form, the Customer Master Form should appear in a pop-up form.

d. Create a datasheet form for the Supervisor table and name the form Supervisor. Create a UI macro for the Supervisor form. When a user taps or clicks a supervisor number on a row in the datasheet form, the Supervisor Master Form should appear in a pop-up form.

e. Create a data macro for the Customer Requests table. The macro will examine the value in the Hours Spent field. If the user's update would cause the value to be greater than the Total Hours, the macro will change the value to Total Hours. If the user's update would cause the value to be less than 0, the macro will change the value to 0.

f. Create a navigation form for the Landscaping Services database. Use the same design for your navigation form as that shown in Figure 8–1a on page AC 475. Include the Customer form, the Supervisor form, and the menu forms you created in Step b.

Submit your assignment in the format specified by your instructor.

Part 2: ✸ You made several decisions while completing this assignment, including creating a macro to open a pop-up form. What was the rationale behind your decisions? The window mode to open a form as a pop-up form is Dialog. What would be the effect if the form opened in Normal mode?

3: Understanding Navigation Forms and Control Layouts
Research and Collaboration

Part 1: Before you begin this assignment, save the Bavant Publishing database as your team name database. For example, if your team is the Fab Four, then name the database Fab Four. Use the database for this assignment. Create a blog, a Google document, or a Word document on the SkyDrive on which to store the team's research findings and observations for this assignment.

a. In this project, you created a navigation form with horizontal tabs. Create additional navigation forms using a different tab arrangement. Compare the arrangements and as a team vote on which navigation form arrangement you prefer. Record your vote and your reason in your blog or other shared document.

b. Open the Customer Form in Layout view. Use the ARRANGE tab to create a form that has the City, State, and Postal Code on one row. Record which features on the ARRANGE tab you used in your blog or other shared document.

c. Create a new workbook in Microsoft Excel. Import the Customer table in Excel and use the recommended PivotTable feature to create a PivotTable for the Customer table. Create a PivotChart from the same data.

Submit your assignment in the format specified by your instructor.

Part 2: ✷ You made several decisions while completing this assignment, including changing the arrangement of a navigation form. What was the rationale behind your decisions? Which navigation form best suits the database and why?

Learn Online

Reinforce what you learned in this chapter with games, exercises, training, and many other online activities and resources.

Student Companion Site   Reinforcement activities and resources are available at no additional cost on www.cengagebrain.com. Visit www.cengage.com/ct/studentdownload for detailed instructions about accessing the resources available at the Student Companion Site.

SAM   Put your skills into practice with SAM Projects! SAM Projects for this chapter can be found online. If you have a SAM account, go to www.cengage.com/sam2013 to access SAM assignments for this chapter.

9 | Administering a Database System

Microsoft product screenshots used with permission from Microsoft Corporation.

Objectives

You will have mastered the material in this project when you can:

- Convert a database to and from earlier versions of Access
- Use the Table Analyzer, Performance Analyzer, and Documenter
- Create custom categories and groups in the Navigation Pane
- Use table, database, and field properties
- Create indexes
- Enable and use automatic error checking

- Create custom data type parts
- Create a database for a template
- Create a custom template
- Encrypt a database and set a password
- Lock a database and split a database
- Create a custom web app
- Create custom views for a web app

9 | Administering a Database System

BTW

Q&As
For a complete list of the Q&As found in many of the step-by-step sequences in this book, visit the Q&A resource on the Student Companion Site located on www.cengagebrain.com. For detailed instructions about accessing available resources, visit www.cengage.com/ct/studentdownload or contact your instructor for information about accessing the required files.

Introduction

Administering a database system is an important activity that has many facets. Going far beyond the simple updating of a database, administration activities improve the usability, accessibility, security, and efficiency of the database.

Project — Administering a Database System

Bavant Publishing realizes the importance of database administration, that is, the importance of administering its database system properly. Making a database available on the web using a web app (Figure 9–1) is part of this activity. The Clients and Recruiters database shown in Figure 9–1 is a database that contains information about a recruiting agency that specializes in placing health science professionals. The recruiting agency is a division in a company in which Bavant recently acquired a controlling interest. Figure 9–1a shows the Recruiter table selected in List view. Not only does the data about the recruiter appear on the screen, but data concerning the clients of the selected recruiter does as well. Figure 9–1b shows the Client table selected in By City view, which has grouped the clients by City. Clients in the selected city, Berridge in this case, appear on the screen. Tapping or clicking an individual client causes all the data for the client to appear as shown in Figure 9–1c.

BTW

BTWs
For a complete list of the BTWs found in the margins of this book, visit the BTW resource on the Student Companion Site located on www.cengagebrain.com. For detailed instructions about accessing available resources, visit www.cengage.com/ct/studentdownload or contact your instructor for information about accessing the required files.

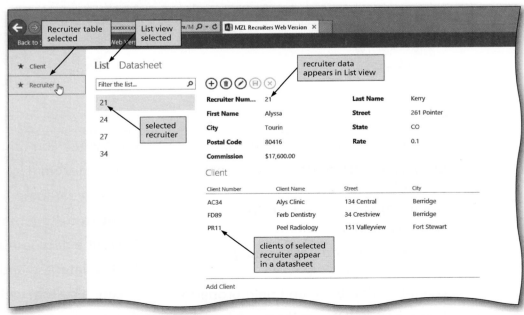

Figure 9–1 (a) Recruiter Table Shown in Web App

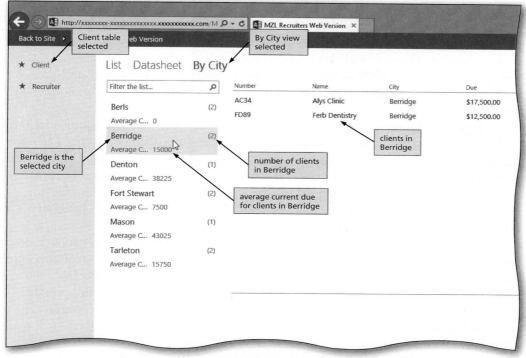

Figure 9–1 (b) Client Table Shown in Web App

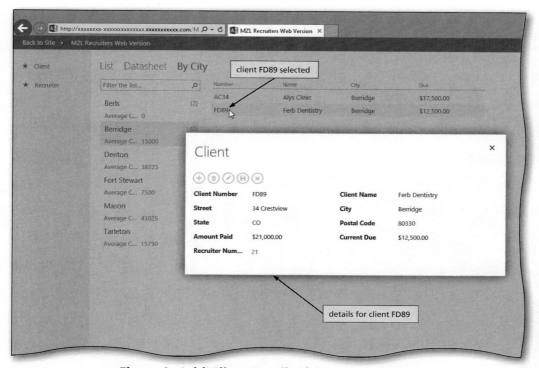

Figure 9–1 (c) Client Details Shown in Web App

Another important activity in administering databases is the creation of custom templates, application parts, and data type parts. **Application parts** and **data type parts** are templates included in Access that you can add to your database to extend its functionality. Tapping or clicking an application part adds to your database a predetermined collection of objects such as tables, queries, forms, reports, and/or macros. Tapping or clicking a data type part adds a predetermined collection of fields to a table.

Figure 9–2 illustrates the range of activities involved in database administration, including the conversion of an Access database to an earlier version of Access. Database administration usually includes such activities as analyzing tables for potential problems, analyzing performance to see if changes could make the system perform more efficiently, and documenting the various objects in the database. It can include creating custom categories and groups in the Navigation Pane as well as changing table and database properties. It also can include the use of field properties in such tasks as creating a custom input mask and allowing zero-length strings. It can include the creation of indexes to speed up retrieval. The inclusion of automatic error checking is part of the administration of a database system. Understanding the purpose of the Trust Center is critical to the database administration function. Another important area of database administration is the protection of the database. This protection includes locking the database through the creation of an ACCDE file to prevent unauthorized changes from being made to the VBA source code or to the design of forms and reports. Splitting the database into a front-end and a back-end database is another way to protect the functionality and efficiency of a database.

Figure 9–2

© 2014 Cengage Learning

Roadmap

In this chapter, you will learn how to perform a variety of database administration tasks. The following roadmap identifies general activities you will perform as you progress through this chapter:

1. Learn how to CONVERT a DATABASE
2. Use tools to ANALYZE AND DOCUMENT a database
3. Customize the NAVIGATION PANE
4. Use CUSTOM PROPERTIES AND create INDEXES
5. Create a CUSTOM DATA PART
6. Create a CUSTOM TEMPLATE
7. ENCRYPT, LOCK, AND SPLIT a database
8. Learn how to create a CUSTOM WEB APP
9. Learn how to create CUSTOM VIEW in a web app

At the beginning of step instructions throughout the chapter, you will see an abbreviated form of this roadmap. The abbreviated roadmap uses colors to indicate chapter progress: gray means the chapter is beyond that activity; blue means the task being shown is covered in that activity, and black means that activity is yet to be covered. For example, the following abbreviated roadmap indicates the chapter would be showing a task in the 3 NAVIGATION PANE activity.

1 CONVERT DATABASE | 2 ANALYZE & DOCUMENT | **3 NAVIGATION PANE** | 4 CUSTOM PROPERTIES & INDEXES
5 CUSTOM DATA PART | 6 CUSTOM TEMPLATE | 7 ENCRYPT LOCK & SPLIT | 8 CUSTOM WEB APP | 9 CUSTOM VIEW

Use the abbreviated roadmap as a progress guide while you read or step through the instructions in this chapter.

To Run Access

If you are using a computer to step through the project in this chapter and you want your screens to match the figures in this book, you should change your screen's resolution to 1366 × 768. For information about how to change a computer's resolution, refer to the Office and Windows chapter at the beginning of this book.

The following steps, which assume Windows is running, use the Start screen or the search box to run Access based on a typical installation. You may need to ask your instructor how to run Access on your computer. For a detailed example of the procedure summarized below, refer to the Office and Windows chapter.

1 Scroll the Start screen for an Access 2013 tile. If your Start screen contains an Access 2013 tile, tap or click it to run Access; if the Start screen does not contain the Access 2013 tile, proceed to the next step to search for the Access app.

2 Swipe in from the right edge of the screen or point to the upper-right corner of the screen to display the Charms bar, and then tap or click the Search charm on the Charms bar to display the Search menu.

3 Type `Access` as the search text in the Search text box and watch the search results appear in the Apps list.

4 Tap or click Access 2013 in the search results to run Access.

BTW
Touch Screen Differences
The Office and Windows interfaces may vary if you are using a touch screen. For this reason, you might notice that the function or appearance of your touch screen differs slightly from this chapter's presentation.

BTW
The Ribbon and Screen Resolution
Access may change how the groups and buttons within the groups appear on the ribbon, depending on the computer's screen resolution. Thus, your ribbon may look different from the ones in this book if you are using a screen resolution other than 1366 x 768.

To Open a Database from Access

BTW
**Distributing
a Document**
Instead of printing and
distributing a hard copy of a
document, you can distribute
the document electronically.
Options include sending the
document via email; posting
it on cloud storage (such as
SkyDrive) and sharing the
file with others; posting it
on a social networking site,
blog, or other website; and
sharing a link associated
with an online location of
the document. You also can
create and share a PDF or
XPS image of the document,
so that users can view the
file in Acrobat Reader or XPS
Viewer instead of in Access.

The following steps open the Bavant Publishing database from the location you specified when you first created it (for example, the Access folder in the CIS 101 folder). For a detailed example of the procedure summarized below, refer to the Office and Windows chapter at the beginning of this book.

1 Tap or click FILE on the ribbon to open the Backstage view, if necessary.

2 If the database you want to open is displayed in the Recent list, tap or click the file name to open the database and display the opened database in the Access window; then skip to Step 7. If the database you want to open is not displayed in the Recent list or if the Recent list does not appear, tap or click Open Other Files to display the Open Gallery.

3 If the database you want to open is displayed in the Recent list in the Open gallery, tap or click the file name to open the database and display the opened database in the Access window; then skip to Step 7.

4 Tap or click Computer, SkyDrive, or another location in the left pane and then navigate to the location of the database to be opened (for example, the Access folder in the CIS 101 folder).

5 Tap or click Bavant Publishing to select the database to be opened.

6 Tap or click the Open button (Open dialog box) to open the selected file and display the opened database in the Access window.

7 If a Security Warning appears, tap or click the Enable Content button.

Converting Databases

BTW
**Maintaining Backward
Compatibility**
If you plan to share your
database with users who may
have an earlier version of
Access, be sure to maintain
backward compatibility.
Do not include multivalued
fields, attachment fields,
or calculated fields in your
database design. For example,
if there is a calculation that
is used frequently, create a
query with the calculated field
and use the query as the basis
for forms and reports rather
than adding the field to the
table design.

Access 2007, Access 2010, and Access 2013 all use the same file format, the .accdb format. The format is usually referred to as the Access 2007 file format. Thus, in Access 2013, you can use any database created in Access 2007. You should be aware of the following changes in Access 2013:

1. Unlike previous versions, Access 2013 does not support PivotTables or PivotCharts.
2. The Text data type is now Short Text and the Memo data type is now Long Text.
3. Smart Tags are no longer supported.
4. Replication is no longer available.

To convert an Access 2007 database to an earlier version, the database cannot contain any features that are specific to Access 2007, 2010, or 2013. These include attachments, multivalued fields, offline data, or links to external files not supported in earlier versions of Access. They also include objects published to the web, data macros, and calculated columns. Provided the database does not contain such features, you can convert the database by tapping or clicking the Save As tab in the Backstage view (Figure 9–3). You then can choose the appropriate format.

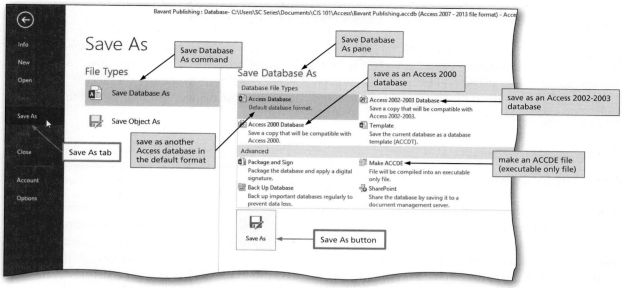

Figure 9–3

To Convert an Access 2007–2013 Database to an Earlier Version

1 CONVERT DATABASE | 2 ANALYZE & DOCUMENT | 3 NAVIGATION PANE | 4 CUSTOM PROPERTIES & INDEXES
5 CUSTOM DATA PART | 6 CUSTOM TEMPLATE | 7 ENCRYPT LOCK & SPLIT | 8 CUSTOM WEB APP | 9 CUSTOM VIEW

Specifically, to convert an Access 2007–2013 database to an earlier version, you would use the following steps.

1 With the database to be converted open, tap or click FILE on the ribbon to open the Backstage view.

2 Tap or click the Save As tab.

3 With the Save Database As command selected, tap or click the desired format, and then tap or click the Save As button.

4 Type the name you want for the converted database, select a location in which to save the converted database, and tap or click the Save button.

To Convert an Access 2000 or 2002–2003 Database to an Access 2013 Database

1 CONVERT DATABASE | 2 ANALYZE & DOCUMENT | 3 NAVIGATION PANE | 4 CUSTOM PROPERTIES & INDEXES
5 CUSTOM DATA PART | 6 CUSTOM TEMPLATE | 7 ENCRYPT LOCK & SPLIT | 8 CUSTOM WEB APP | 9 CUSTOM VIEW

To convert an Access 2000 or Access 2002–2003 database to the default database format for Access 2013, you open the database in Access 2013. Initially, the database is open in compatibility mode, where features that are new to Access 2013 and that cannot easily be displayed or converted are disabled. In this mode, the database remains in its original format. If you want to convert it so that you can use it in Access 2013, you use the Access Database command on the Backstage view. Once the database is converted, the disabled features will be enabled. You will no longer be able to share the database with users of Access 2000 or Access 2002–2003, however.

Specifically, to convert an Access 2000 or 2002–2003 database to the default database format for Access 2013, you would use the following steps.

1. With the database to be converted open, tap or click FILE on the ribbon to open the Backstage view.

2. Tap or click the Save As tab.

3. With the Save Database As command selected, tap or click Access Database and then tap or click the Save As button.

4. Type the name you want for the converted database, select a location, and tap or click the Save button.

BTW

Saving Databases to External Locations
You also can save a database to an external location such as SkyDrive, and to any portable storage device, such as a USB flash drive. To do so, select the desired external location or portable storage device when you browse to specify a location for your database.

BTW

Exporting XML Data
Database administration also may include responsibility for exchanging data between dissimilar systems or apps. Extensible Markup Language (XML) is a data interchange standard for describing and delivering data on the web. With XML, you can describe both the data and the structure (schema) of the data. You can export tables queries, forms, or reports. To export a database object, select the object and tap or click the XML File button (EXTERNAL DATA tab | Export group). Select the appropriate options in the Export XML dialog box.

BTW
Creating Databases in Older Formats
To create a database in an older format, create a database and browse to select a location for the database, then tap or click the Save As Type arrow in the File New Database dialog box, and select either 2002–2003 format or 2000 format.

Microsoft Access Analysis Tools

Microsoft Access has a variety of tools that are useful in analyzing databases. Analyzing a database gives information about how the database functions and identifies opportunities for improving functionality. You can use the Access analysis tools to analyze tables and database performance, and to create detailed documentation.

To Use the Table Analyzer

1 CONVERT DATABASE | 2 ANALYZE & DOCUMENT | 3 NAVIGATION PANE | 4 CUSTOM PROPERTIES & INDEXES
5 CUSTOM DATA PART | 6 CUSTOM TEMPLATE | 7 ENCRYPT LOCK & SPLIT | 8 CUSTOM WEB APP | 9 CUSTOM VIEW

Access contains a Table Analyzer tool that performs three separate functions. This tool can analyze tables while looking for potential redundancy (duplicated data). The Table Analyzer also can analyze performance and check for ways to make queries, reports, or forms more efficient. Then the tool will make suggestions for possible changes. The final function of the analyzer is to produce detailed documentation describing the structure and content of the various tables, queries, forms, reports, and other objects in the database.

The following steps use the Table Analyzer to examine the Customer table for **redundancy**, or duplicated data. *Why? Redundancy is one of the biggest potential sources of problems in a database.* If redundancy is found, the Table Analyzer will suggest ways to split the table in order to eliminate the redundancy.

- Open the Bavant Publishing database.
- If necessary, close the Navigation Pane.
- Display the DATABASE TOOLS tab (Figure 9–4).

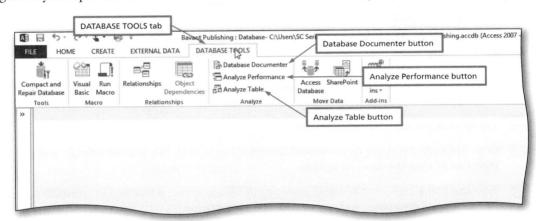

Figure 9–4

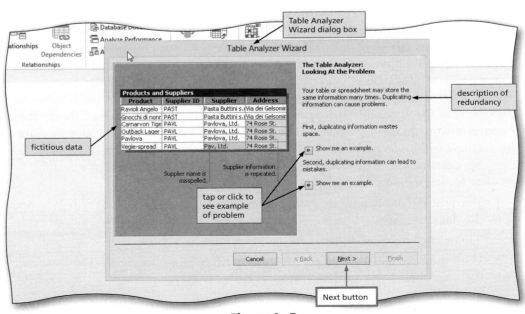

- Tap or click the Analyze Table button (DATABASE TOOLS tab | Analyze group) to display the Table Analyzer Wizard dialog box (Figure 9–5).

Q&A
Where did the data in the figure come from? It does not look like my data. The data is fictitious. It is just intended to give you an idea of what the data might look like.

Figure 9–5

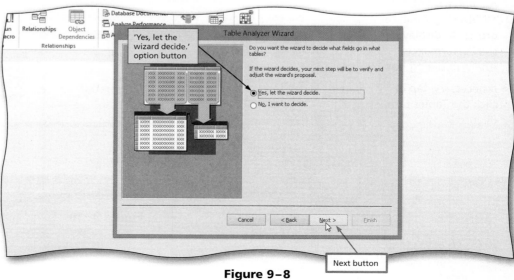

3

- Tap or click the Next button to display the next Table Analyzer Wizard screen (Figure 9–6).

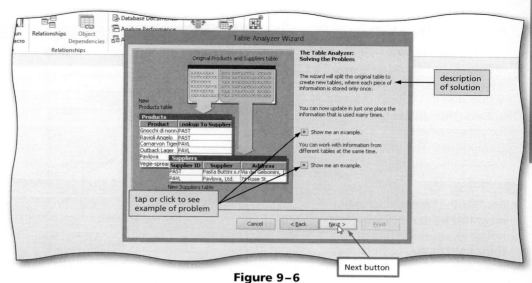

description of solution

tap or click to see example of problem

Next button

Figure 9–6

4

- Tap or click the Next button to display the next Table Analyzer Wizard screen.

- Select the Customer table (Figure 9–7).

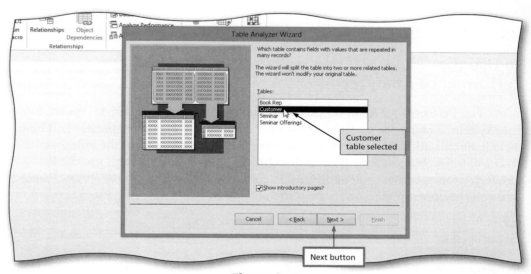

Customer table selected

Next button

Figure 9–7

5

- Tap or click the Next button.

- Be sure the 'Yes, let the wizard decide.' option button is selected (Figure 9–8) to let the wizard determine what action to take.

'Yes, let the wizard decide.' option button

Next button

Figure 9–8

6

- Tap or click the Next button to run the analysis (Figure 9–9).

Q&A

I do not really want to put the city, state, and postal code in a different table, even though I realize that this data does appear to be duplicated. Do I have to follow this advice?
Certainly not. This is only a suggestion.

7

- Because the type of duplication identified by the analyzer does not pose a problem, tap or click the Cancel button to close the analyzer.

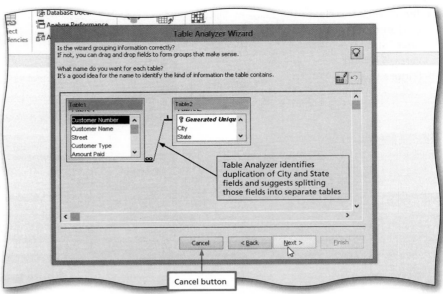

Figure 9–9

To Use the Performance Analyzer

1 CONVERT DATABASE | 2 ANALYZE & DOCUMENT | 3 NAVIGATION PANE | 4 CUSTOM PROPERTIES & INDEXES
5 CUSTOM DATA PART | 6 CUSTOM TEMPLATE | 7 ENCRYPT LOCK & SPLIT | 8 CUSTOM WEB APP | 9 CUSTOM VIEW

The Performance Analyzer examines the database's tables, queries, reports, forms, and other objects in your system, looking for ways to improve the efficiency of database operations. These improvements could include modifications to the way data is stored, as well as changes to the indexes created for the system. (You will learn about indexes later in this chapter.) The following steps use the Performance Analyzer. *Why?* *The Performance Analyzer will identify possible areas for improvement in the Bavant Publishing database. Users then can determine whether to implement the suggested changes.*

1

- Tap or click the Analyze Performance button, shown in Figure 9–4 on page AC 544, (DATABASE TOOLS tab | Analyze group) to display the Performance Analyzer dialog box.

- If necessary, tap or click the Tables tab (Figure 9–10).

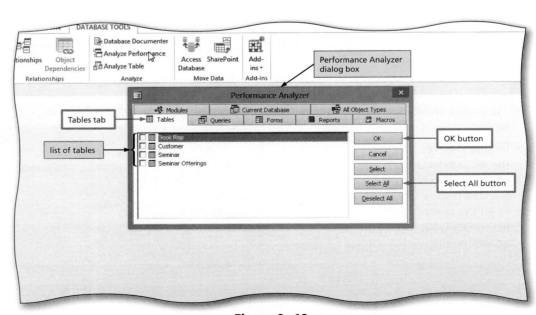

Figure 9–10

- Tap or click the Select All button to select all tables.

- Tap or click the OK button to display the results (Figure 9–11).

Q&A What do the results mean?

Because both fields contain only numbers, Access is suggesting that you might improve the efficiency of the table by changing the data types of the fields to Long Integer. As the icon in front of the suggestions indicates, this is simply an idea — something to consider. For these particular fields, Short Text is a better type, however, so you should ignore this suggestion.

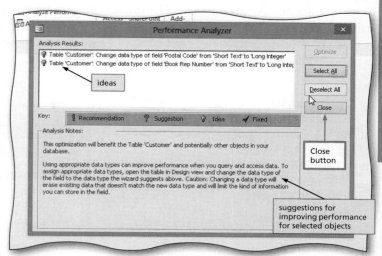

Figure 9–11

❸

- Tap or click the Close button to finish working with the Performance Analyzer.

To Use the Database Documenter

The Database Documenter allows you to produce detailed documentation of the various tables, queries, forms, reports, and other objects in your database. Documentation is required by many organizations. It is used for backup, disaster recovery, and planning for database enhancements. Figure 9–12 shows a portion of the documentation for the Customer table. The complete documentation is much lengthier than the one shown in the figure.

C:\Users\SC Series\Documents\CIS 101\Access\Bavant Publishing.accdb Monday, March 16, 2015

Table: Customer Page: 1

Columns

Name Type Size

Customer Number Short Text 5
Customer Name Short Text 30
Street Short Text 25
City Short Text 20
State Short Text 2
Postal Code Short Text 5

Customer Type Short Text 255
RowSource: "HS";"COM";"UNI"
RowSourceType: Value List
ValidationRule: ="HS" Or ="COM" Or ="UNI"
ValidationText: Must be HS, COM, or UNI
Resources Needed 4
RowSource: "Audio";"CDVD";"CustD";"CustP";"Ebook";"OlMan";"OlWrk";"PrMan";" PrWrk";"SDVD";"Txt"
RowSourceType: Value List

Amount Paid Currency 8

Current Due Currency 8

Total Amount Currency (Calculated) 8

Expression: [Amount Paid]+[Current Due]

Returns Currency 8

ValidationRule: >=0 And <=30000
ValidationText: Must be at least $0.00 and at most $30,000.00
Book Rep Number Short Text   2

Figure 9–12

Notice that the documentation of the Customer Type field contains the row source associated with the Lookup information for the field. The documentation for both the Customer Type and Returns fields contains validation rules and validation text.

The following steps use the Database Documenter. *Why? The Database Documenter is the easiest way to produce detailed documentation for the Customer table.*

- Tap or click the Database Documenter button, shown in Figure 9–4 on page AC 544 (DATABASE TOOLS tab | Analyze group), to display the Documenter dialog box.

- If necessary, tap or click the Tables tab and then tap or click the Customer check box to specify documentation for the Customer table (Figure 9–13).

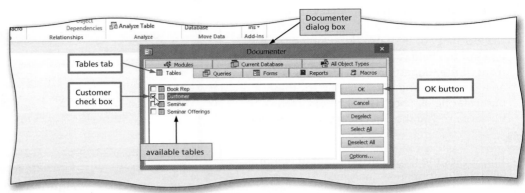

Figure 9–13

- Tap or click the OK button to produce a preview of the documentation (Figure 9–14).

Q&A What can I do with this documentation? You could print it by tapping or clicking the Print button (PRINT PREVIEW tab | Print group). You could create a PDF or XPS file containing the documentation by tapping or clicking the PDF or XPS button (PRINT PREVIEW tab | Data group) and following the directions. You could create a Word (RTF) file by tapping or clicking the More button (PRINT PREVIEW tab | Data group), and then tapping or clicking Word and following the directions. Whatever option you choose, you may need to use this documentation later if you make changes to the database design.

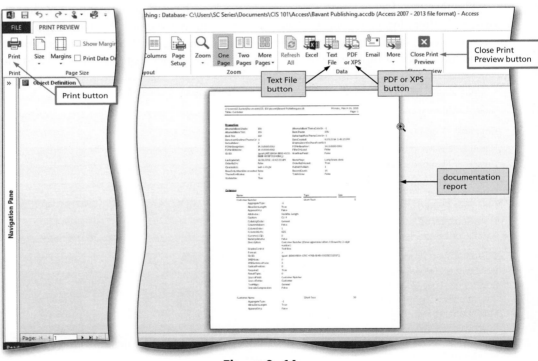

Figure 9–14

- Tap or click the Close Print Preview button (PRINT PREVIEW tab | Close Preview group) to close the preview of the documentation.

Experiment

- Try other options within the Database Documenter to see the effect of your choice on the documentation produced. Each time, close the preview of the documentation.

Navigation Pane Customization

You already have learned how to customize the Navigation Pane by selecting the category and the filter as well as how to use the Search Bar to restrict the items that appear in the Navigation Pane. You also can create custom categories and groups that you can use to categorize the items in the database in ways that are most useful to you.

To Create Custom Categories and Groups

1 CONVERT DATABASE | **2** ANALYZE & DOCUMENT | **3** NAVIGATION PANE | **4** CUSTOM PROPERTIES & INDEXES
5 CUSTOM DATA PART | **6** CUSTOM TEMPLATE | **7** ENCRYPT LOCK & SPLIT | **8** CUSTOM WEB APP | **9** CUSTOM VIEW

You can create custom categories in the Navigation Pane. You can further refine the objects you place in a category by adding custom groups to the categories. *Why? Custom groups allow you to tailor the Navigation Pane for your own specific needs.* The following steps create a custom category called Financial Items. They then add two custom groups, Detailed and Summary, to the Financial Items category.

- If necessary, display the Navigation Pane.
- Press and hold or right-click the Navigation Pane title bar to display a shortcut menu (Figure 9–15).

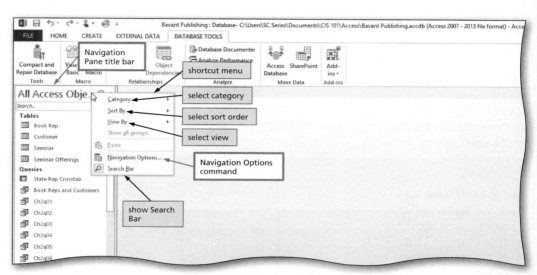

Figure 9–15

- Tap or click the Navigation Options command on the shortcut menu to display the Navigation Options dialog box (Figure 9–16).

Q&A
What else could I do with the shortcut menu?
You could select a category, select a sort order, or select how to view the items within the Navigation Pane.

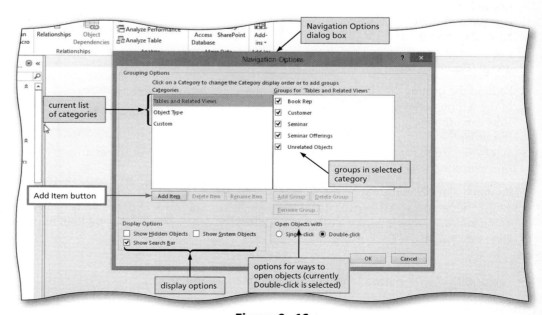

Figure 9–16

• Tap or click the Add Item button to add a new category (Figure 9–17).

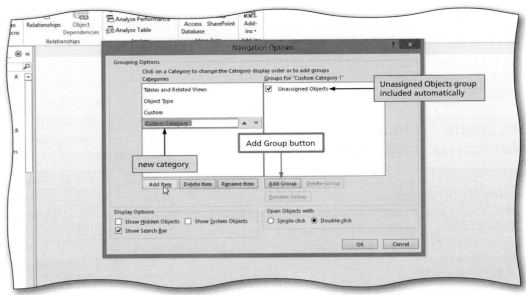

Figure 9–17

• Type **Financial Items** as the name of the category.

• Tap or click the Add Group button to add a group and then type **Detailed** as the name of the group.

• Tap or click the Add Group button to add a group and then type **Summary** as the name of the group (Figure 9–18).

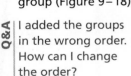

I added the groups in the wrong order. How can I change the order?

Select the group that is in the wrong position. Tap or click the Up or Down arrows to move the group to the correct location.

If I made a mistake in creating a new category, how can I fix it?

Select the category that is incorrect. If the name is wrong, tap or click the Rename Item button and change the name appropriately. If you do not want the category, tap or click the Delete Item button to delete the category and then tap or click the OK button.

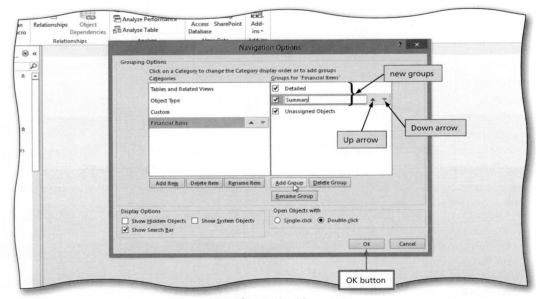

Figure 9–18

• Tap or click the OK button to create the new category and groups.

To Add Items to Groups

Once you have created new groups, you can add existing items to the new groups. The following steps add items to the Summary and Detailed groups in the Financial Items category. *Why? These items are all financial in nature.*

● Tap or click the Navigation Pane arrow to produce the Navigation Pane menu (Figure 9–19).

◄ | Do I have to tap or click the
Q&A | arrow?
No. If you prefer, you can tap or click anywhere in the title bar for the Navigation Pane. Tapping or clicking arrows is a good habit, however, because there are many situations where you must tap or click the arrow.

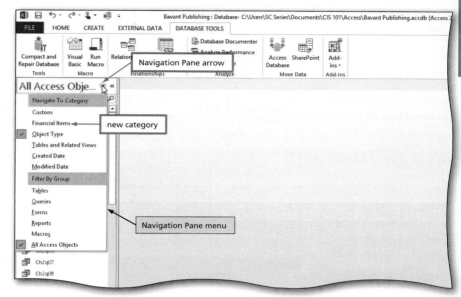

Figure 9–19

● Tap or click the Financial Items category to display the groups within the category. Because you created the Detailed and Summary groups but did not assign items, the table objects all appear in the Unassigned Objects area of the Navigation Pane.

● Press and hold or right-click State-Rep Crosstab to display the shortcut menu.

● Point to the 'Add to group' command on the shortcut menu to display the list of available groups (Figure 9–20).

◄ | I did not create an Unassigned
Q&A | Objects group. Where did it come from?
Access creates the Unassigned Objects group automatically. Until you add an object to one of the groups you created, it will be in the Unassigned Objects group.

What is the purpose of the New Group on the submenu?
You can create a new group using this submenu. This is an alternative to using the Navigation Options dialog box. Use whichever approach you find most convenient.

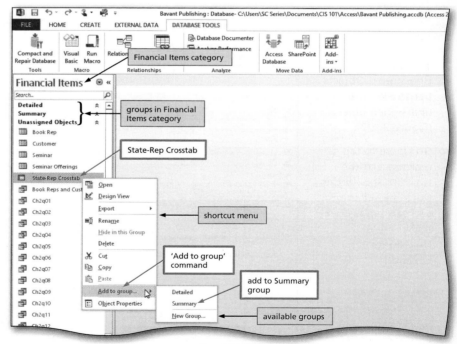

Figure 9–20

3

- Tap or click Summary to add the State-Rep Crosstab to the Summary group.

- Using the same technique, add the items shown in Figure 9–21 to the Detailed and Summary groups.

Q&A
What is the symbol that appears in front of the items in the Detailed and Summary groups?
It is the link symbol. You actually do not add an object to your group. Rather, you create a link to the object. In practice, you do not have to worry about this. The process for opening an object in one of your custom groups remains the same.

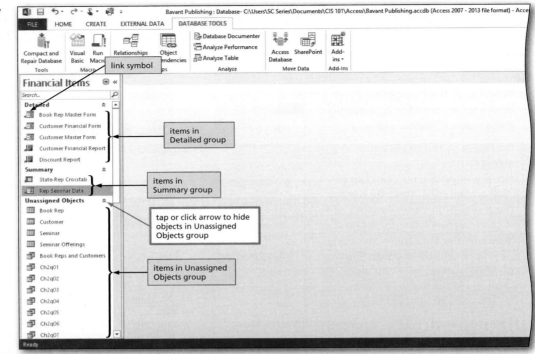

Figure 9–21

4

- Tap or click the arrow in the Unassigned Objects bar to hide the unassigned objects (Figure 9–22).

Q&A
Do I have to tap or click the arrow?
No. Just as with the Navigation Pane, you can tap or click anywhere in the Unassigned Objects bar.

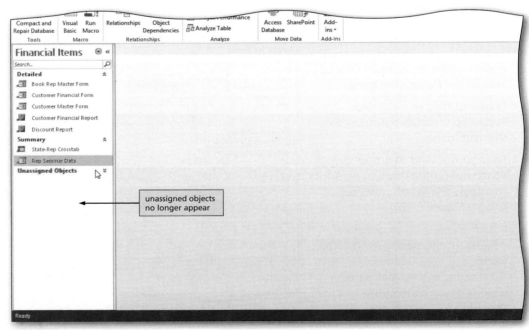

Figure 9–22

Break Point: If you wish to stop working through the chapter at this point, you can close Access now. You can resume the project at a later time by starting Access, opening the Bavant Publishing database, and continuing to follow the steps from this location forward.

What issues do you consider in determining the customization of the Navigation Pane?
The types of issues to consider are the following:

• Would a new category be useful?

• If so, are there new groups that would be useful to include in the new category?

• If you have created a new category and new groups, which items should be included in the new groups, and which should be left uncategorized?

Table and Database Properties

You can assign properties to tables. For example, you could assign a validation rule and validation text to an entire table. You also can assign properties to the database, typically for documentation purposes.

To Create a Validation Rule for a Table

1 CONVERT DATABASE | 2 ANALYZE & DOCUMENT | 3 NAVIGATION PANE | 4 CUSTOM PROPERTIES & INDEXES

5 CUSTOM DATA PART | 6 CUSTOM TEMPLATE | 7 ENCRYPT LOCK & SPLIT | 8 CUSTOM WEB APP | 9 CUSTOM VIEW

Previously, you created validation rules that applied to individual fields within a table. Some, however, apply to more than one field. In the Seminar Offerings table, you created a macro that would change the value of the Hours Spent field in such a way that it could never be greater than the Total Hours field. You also can create a validation rule that ensures this will never be the case; that is, the validation rule would require that the hours spent must be less than or equal to the total hours. To create a validation rule that involves two or more fields, you need to create the rule for the table using the table's Validation Rule property. The following steps create a table validation rule. **Why?** *This rule involves two fields, Hours Spent and Total Hours.*

• If necessary, tap or click the arrow for Unassigned Objects to display those objects in the Navigation Pane.

• Open the Seminar Offerings table in Design view and close the Navigation Pane.

• Tap or click the Property Sheet button (TABLE TOOLS DESIGN tab | Show/Hide group) to display the table's property sheet.

• Tap or click the Validation Rule property and type [Hours Spent]<=[Total Hours] as the validation rule.

• Tap or click the Validation Text property and type **Hours spent cannot exceed total hours** as the validation text (Figure 9–23).

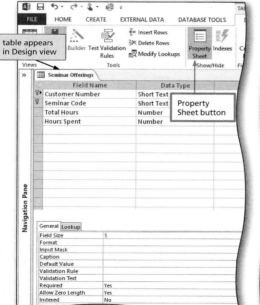
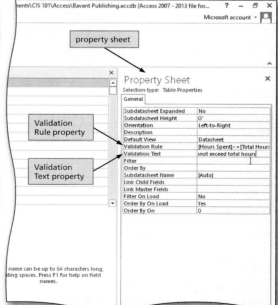

Figure 9–23

Q&A | Could I use the Expression Builder to create the validation rule?
Yes. Use whichever method you find the most convenient.

● Close the property sheet.

● Tap or click the Save button on the Quick Access Toolbar to save the validation rule and the validation text.

● When asked if you want to test existing data, tap or click the No button.

● Close the Seminar Offerings table.

To Create Custom Properties

1 CONVERT DATABASE | 2 ANALYZE & DOCUMENT | 3 NAVIGATION PANE | 4 CUSTOM PROPERTIES & INDEXES

5 CUSTOM DATA PART | 6 CUSTOM TEMPLATE | 7 ENCRYPT LOCK & SPLIT | 8 CUSTOM WEB APP | 9 CUSTOM VIEW

In addition to the general database property categories, you also can use custom properties. *Why? You can use custom properties to further document your database in a variety of ways. If you have needs that go beyond the custom properties, you can create your own original or unique properties.* The following steps **populate** the Status custom property; that is, they set a value for the property. In this case, they set the Status property to Live Version, indicating this is the live version of the database. If the database were still in a test environment, the property would be set to Test Version. The steps also create and populate a new property, Production, that represents the date the database was placed into production.

● Tap or click FILE on the ribbon to open the Backstage view.

● Ensure the Info tab is selected (Figure 9–24).

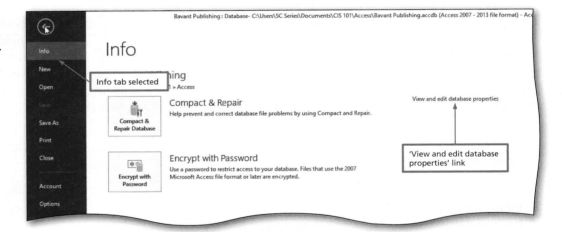

Figure 9–24

● Tap or click the 'View and edit database properties' link to display the Bavant Publishing .accdb Properties dialog box.

● Tap or click the Custom tab.

● Scroll down in the Name list so that Status appears, and then tap or click Status.

● If necessary, tap or click the Type arrow to set the data Type to Text.

● Tap or click the Value box and type **Live Version** as the value to create the custom category (Figure 9–25).

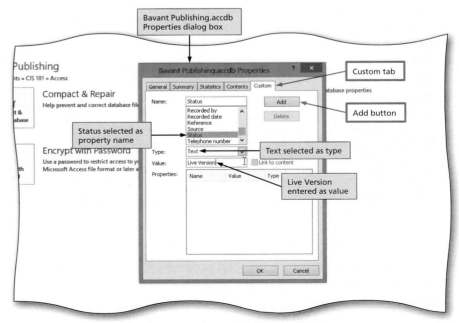

Figure 9–25

- Tap or click the Add button to add the property.
- Type **Production** in the Name box.
- If requested to do so by your instructor, type your first and last name in the Name box.
- Select Date as the Type.
- Type **03/03/2015** as the value (Figure 9–26) to indicate that the database went into production on March 3, 2015.

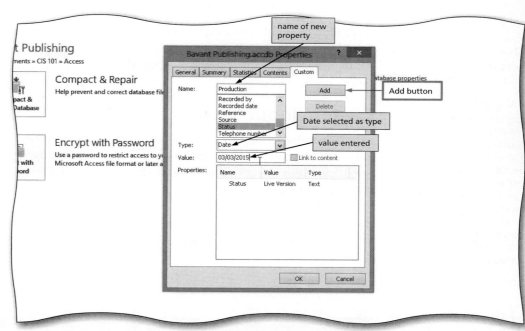

Figure 9–26

- Tap or click the Add button to add the property (Figure 9–27).

Q&A What if I add a property that I decide I do not want?

You can delete it. To do so, tap or click the property you no longer want and then tap or click the Delete button.

- Tap or click the OK button to close the Bavant Publishing .accdb Properties dialog box.

Q&A How do I view these properties in the future?

The same way you created them. Tap or click FILE on the ribbon, tap or click the Info tab, and then tap or click the 'View and edit database properties' link. Tap or click the desired tab to see the properties you want.

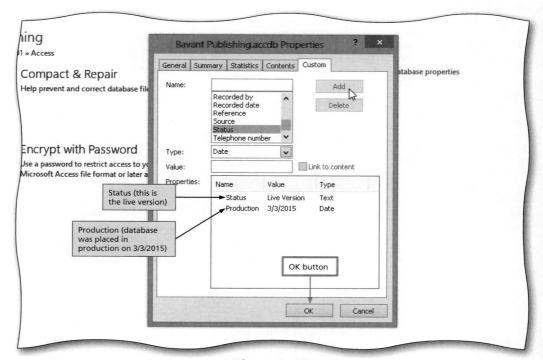

Figure 9–27

Special Field Properties

BTW
Changing Data Formats
To create custom data formats, enter various characters in the Format property of a table field. The characters can be placeholders (such as 0 and #), separators (such as periods and commas), literal characters, and colors. You can create custom formats for short text, date, number, and currency fields. Date, number, and currency fields also include a number of standard data formats.

Each field in a table has a variety of field properties available. Recall that field properties are characteristics of a field. Two special field properties, the Custom Input Mask property and the Allow Zero Length property, are described in this section.

Custom Input Masks

One way to help users enter data using a certain format is to use an input mask. You already have used the Input Mask Wizard to create an input mask. Using the wizard, you can select the input mask that meets your needs. This often is the best way to create the input mask.

If the input mask you need to create is not similar to any in the list provided by the wizard, you can create a custom input mask by entering the appropriate characters as the value for the Input Mask property. In doing so, you use the symbols from Table 9–1.

BTW
Table Descriptions
To add a description for a table, press and hold or right-click the table in the Navigation Pane and then tap or click Table Properties on the shortcut menu. When the Properties dialog box for the table appears, enter the description in the Description property and then tap or click the OK button. To enter a description for a table in Design view, tap or click the Property Sheet button, and then enter a description in the Description property on the property sheet (see Figure 9-23 on page AC 553).

Table 9–1 Input Mask Symbols

Symbol	Type of Data Accepted	Data Entry Optional
0	Digits 0 through 9 without plus (+) or minus (-) sign are accepted. Positions left blank appear as zeros.	No
9	Digits 0 through 9 without plus (+) or minus (-) sign are accepted. Positions left blank appear as spaces.	Yes
#	Digits 0 through 9 with plus (+) or minus (-) sign are accepted. Positions left blank appear as spaces.	Yes
L	Letters A through Z are accepted.	No
?	Letters A through Z are accepted.	Yes
A	Letters A through Z or digits 0 through 9 are accepted.	No
a	Letters A through Z or digits 0 through 9 are accepted.	Yes
&	Any character or a space is accepted.	No
C	Any character or a space is accepted.	Yes
<	Symbol converts any letter entered to lowercase.	Does not apply
>	Symbol converts any letter entered to uppercase.	Does not apply
!	Characters typed in the input mask fill it from left to right.	Does not apply
\	Character following the slash is treated as a literal in the input mask.	Does not apply

© 2014 Cengage Learning

For example, to indicate that customer numbers must consist of three letters followed by two numbers, you would enter LLL99. The Ls in the first three positions indicate that the first three positions must be letters. Using L instead of a question mark indicates that the users are required to enter these letters. If you had used the question mark, they could leave these positions blank. The 9s in the last two positions indicate that the users can enter only digits 0 through 9. Using 9 instead of 0 indicates that they could leave these positions blank; that is, they are optional. Finally, to ensure that any letters entered are displayed as uppercase, you would use the > symbol at the beginning of the input mask. The complete mask would be >LLL99.

To Create a Custom Input Mask

1 CONVERT DATABASE | 2 ANALYZE & DOCUMENT | 3 NAVIGATION PANE | 4 CUSTOM PROPERTIES & INDEXES
5 CUSTOM DATA PART | 6 CUSTOM TEMPLATE | 7 ENCRYPT LOCK & SPLIT | 8 CUSTOM WEB APP | 9 CUSTOM VIEW

The following step creates a custom input mask for the Customer Number field. *Why? None of the input masks in the list meet the specific needs for the Customer Number field.*

- Open the Navigation Pane, open the Customer table in Design view, and then close the Navigation Pane.

- With the Customer Number field selected, tap or click the Input Mask property, and then type `>LLL99` as the value (Figure 9–28).

Q&A

What is the difference between the Format property and the Input Mask property?
The Format property ensures that data is displayed consistently, for example, always in uppercase. The Input Mask property controls how data is entered.

What is the effect of this input mask?
From this point on, anyone entering a customer number will be restricted to letters in the first three positions and numeric digits in the last two. Further, any letters entered in the first three positions will be displayed as uppercase.

In Figure 9–28, the Customer Number field has both a custom input mask and a format. Is this a problem?
Technically, you do not need both. When the same field has both an input mask and a format, the format takes precedence. Because the format specified for the Customer Number field is the same as the input mask (uppercase), it will not affect the data.

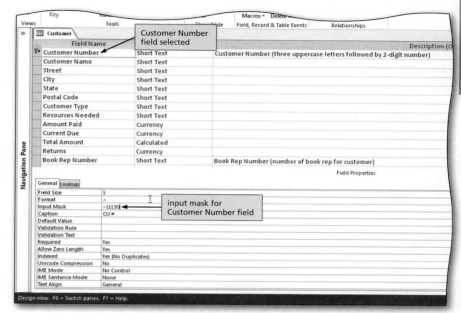

Figure 9–28

To Allow Zero Length

1 CONVERT DATABASE | 2 ANALYZE & DOCUMENT | 3 NAVIGATION PANE | 4 CUSTOM PROPERTIES & INDEXES
5 CUSTOM DATA PART | 6 CUSTOM TEMPLATE | 7 ENCRYPT LOCK & SPLIT | 8 CUSTOM WEB APP | 9 CUSTOM VIEW

You can use zero-length strings to distinguish data that does not exist from data that is unknown. *Why? Entering a zero-length string is not the same as leaving the field blank.* For example, in the Book Rep table, you may want to set the Required property for the Comment field to Yes, so that users do not forget to enter a comment. If the user forgets to enter a comment, Access will display an error message and not add the record until the user enters a comment. If, on the other hand, there are certain reps for whom no comment is appropriate, users can enter a **zero-length string** — a string that contains no characters — and Access will accept the record without generating an error message. To enter a zero-length string, you type two quotation marks with no space in between (""). If you enter a zero-length string into a Short Text or Long Text field whose Required property is set to Yes, Access will not report an error.

If you want to ensure that data is entered in the field and a zero-length string is not appropriate, you can set the Required property to Yes and the Allow Zero Length property to No. The steps on the next page set the Allow Zero Length property for the Customer Name field to No. (The Required property already has been set to Yes.)

1

- Tap or click the row selector for the Customer Name field to select the field.

- Tap or click the Allow Zero Length property and then tap or click the arrow that appears to display a menu.

- Tap or click No in the menu to change the value of the Allow Zero Length property from Yes to No (Figure 9–29).

Q&A Could I just type the word, No?
Yes. In fact, you could type the letter, N, and Access would complete the word, No. Use whichever technique you prefer.

2

- Save your changes and tap or click the No button when asked if you want to test existing data.

- Close the table.

Q&A What is the effect of this change?
If the value for the Allow Zero Length property is set to No, an attempt to enter a zero-length string ("") will result in an error message.

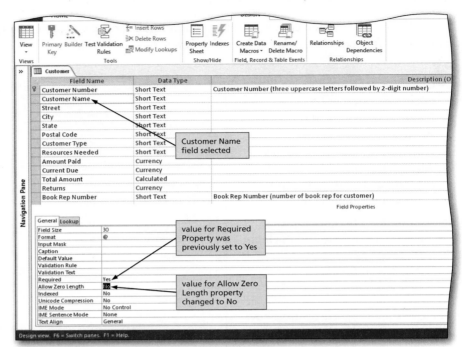

Figure 9–29

Creating and Using Indexes

BTW

Indexes
The most common structure for high-performance indexes is called a B-tree. It is a highly efficient structure that supports very rapid access to records in the database as well as a rapid alternative to sorting records. Virtually all systems use some version of the B-tree structure.

You already are familiar with the concept of an index. The index in the back of a book contains important words or phrases along with a list of pages on which the given words or phrases can be found. An **index** for a table is similar. An index is a database object that is created based on a field or combination of fields. An index on the Customer Name field, for example, would enable Access to rapidly locate a record that contains a particular customer name. In this case, the items of interest are customer names instead of keywords or phrases, as is the case in the back of this book. The field or fields on which the index is built is called the **index key**. Thus, in the index on customer names, the Customer Name field is the index key.

Each name occurs in the index along with the number of the record on which the corresponding customer is located. Further, the names appear in the index in alphabetical order, so Access can use this index to rapidly produce a list of customers alphabetized by customer name.

Another benefit of indexes is that they provide an efficient way to order records. That is, if the records are to appear in a certain order in a database object, Access can use an index instead of physically having to rearrange the records in the database. Physically rearranging the records in a different order can be a very time-consuming process.

To gain the benefits of an index, you first must create one. Access automatically creates an index on some special fields. If, for example, a table contains a field called Postal Code, Access would create an index for this field automatically. You must create any other indexes you determine would improve database performance, indicating the field or fields on which the index is to be built.

Although the index key usually will be a single field, it can be a combination of fields. For example, you might want to sort records by amount paid within customer type. In other words, the records are ordered by a combination of fields: Customer Type and Amount Paid. An index can be used for this purpose by using a combination of fields for the index key. In this case, you must assign a name to the index. It is a good idea to assign a name that represents the combination of fields. For example, an index whose key is the combination of the Customer Type and Amount Paid fields might be called TypePaid.

BTW

Changing Default Sort Order
To display the records in a table in an order other than the primary key (the default sort order), use the Order By property on the table's property sheet (see Figure 9-23 on page AC 553).

How Access Uses Indexes

You can create indexes in Access automatically. If you request that data be sorted in a particular order and Access determines that an index is available that it can use to make the process efficient, it will do so automatically. If no index is available, it still will sort the data in the order you requested; it will just take longer than with the index.

Similarly, if you request that Access locate a particular record that has a certain value in a particular field, Access will use an index if an appropriate one exists. If not, it will have to examine each record until it finds the one you want.

To Create a Single-Field Index

1 CONVERT DATABASE | 2 ANALYZE & DOCUMENT | 3 NAVIGATION PANE | **4 CUSTOM PROPERTIES & INDEXES**
5 CUSTOM DATA PART | 6 CUSTOM TEMPLATE | 7 ENCRYPT LOCK & SPLIT | 8 CUSTOM WEB APP | 9 CUSTOM VIEW

The following steps create a single-field index on the Customer Name field. *Why? This index will make finding customers based on their name more efficient than it would be without the index. It also will improve the efficiency of sorting by customer name.*

- Open the Navigation Pane, open the Customer table in Design view, and then close the Navigation Pane.

- Select the Customer Name field.

- Tap or click the Indexed property box in the Field Properties pane to select the property.

- Tap or click the down arrow that appears to display the Indexed list (Figure 9–30).

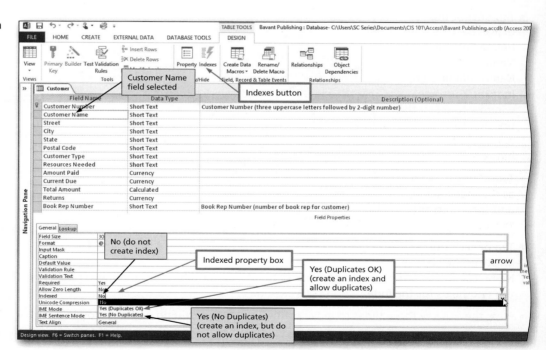

Figure 9–30

2

- Tap or click Yes (Duplicates OK) in the list to specify that duplicates are to be allowed.

To Create a Multiple-Field Index

Creating **multiple-field indexes** — that is, indexes whose key is a combination of fields — involves a different process than creating single-field indexes. To create multiple-field indexes, you will use the Indexes button, enter a name for the index, and then enter the combination of fields that make up the index key. The following steps create a multiple-field index on the combination of Customer Type and Amount Paid. *Why? Bavant needs to sort records on the combination of Customer Type and Amount Paid and wants to improve the efficiency of this sort.* The steps assign this index the name TypePaid.

- Tap or click the Indexes button, shown in Figure 9–30 on the previous page, (TABLE TOOLS DESIGN tab | Show/Hide group) to display the Indexes: Customer window (Figure 9–31).

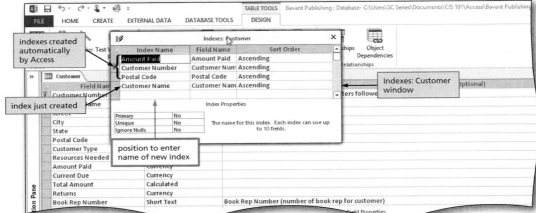

Figure 9–31

- Tap or click the blank row (the row below Customer Name) in the Index Name column in the Indexes: Customer window to select the position to enter the name of the new index.

- Type **TypePaid** as the index name, and then press the TAB key.

- Tap or click the arrow in the Field Name column to produce a list of fields in the Customer table, and then select Customer Type to enter the first of the two fields for the index.

- Press the TAB key three times to move to the Field Name column on the following row.

- Select the Amount Paid field in the same manner as the Customer Type field (Figure 9–32).

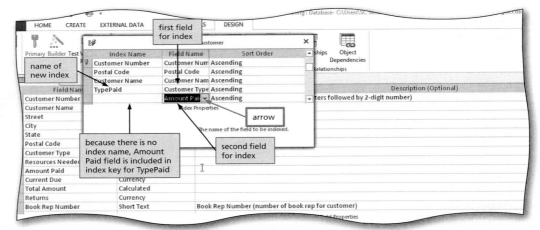

Figure 9–32

❸

- Close the Indexes: Customer window by tapping or clicking its Close button.

- Tap or click the Save button on the Quick Access Toolbar to save your changes.

- Close the Customer table.

How do you determine when to use an index?

An index improves efficiency for sorting and finding records. On the other hand, indexes occupy space on your disk. They also require Access to do extra work. Access must keep current all the indexes that have been created. The following guidelines help determine how and when to use indexes to their fullest advantage.

Create an index on a field (or combination of fields) if one or more of the following conditions are present:

1. The field is the primary key of the table. (Access creates this index automatically.)

2. The field is the foreign key in a relationship you have created.

3. You frequently will need your data to be sorted on the field.

4. You frequently will need to locate a record based on a value in this field.

Because Access handles condition 1 automatically, you only need to concern yourself about conditions 2, 3, and 4. If you think you will need to see customer data arranged in order of current due amounts, for example, you should create an index on the Current Due field. If you think you will need to see the data arranged by amount paid within customer type, you should create an index on the combination of the Customer Type field and the Amount Paid field. Similarly, if you think you will need to find a customer given the customer's name, you should create an index on the Customer Name field.

Automatic Error Checking

Access can automatically check for several types of errors in forms and reports. When Access detects an error, it warns you about the existence of the error and provides you with options for correcting it. The types of errors that Access can detect and correct are shown in Table 9–2.

BTW

Touch and Pointers
Remember that if you are using your finger on a touch screen, you will not see the pointer.

BTW

On-Screen Keyboard
To display the on-screen touch keyboard, tap the Touch Keyboard button on the Windows taskbar. When finished using the touch keyboard, tap the X button on the touch keyboard to close the keyboard.

Table 9–2 Types of Errors	
Error Type	**Description**
Unassociated label and control	A label and control are selected and are not associated with each other.
New unassociated labels	A newly added label is not associated with any other control.
Keyboard shortcut errors	A shortcut key is invalid. This can happen because an unassociated label has a shortcut key, there are duplicate shortcut keys assigned, or a blank space is assigned as a shortcut key.
Invalid control properties	A control property is invalid. For example, the property contains invalid characters.
Common report errors	The report has invalid sorting or grouping specifications, or the report is wider than the page size.

© 2014 Cengage Learning

To Enable Error Checking

1 CONVERT DATABASE | 2 ANALYZE & DOCUMENT | 3 NAVIGATION PANE | 4 CUSTOM PROPERTIES & INDEXES
5 CUSTOM DATA PART | 6 CUSTOM TEMPLATE | 7 ENCRYPT LOCK & SPLIT | 8 CUSTOM WEB APP | 9 CUSTOM VIEW

Why? *For automatic error checking to take place, it must be enabled.* The steps on the next page ensure that error checking is enabled and that errors are found and reported.

1

- Tap or click FILE on the ribbon and then tap or click the Options tab to display the Access Options dialog box.

- Tap or click Object Designers to display the options for creating and modifying objects.

- Scroll down so that the Error checking area appears.

- Ensure the 'Enable error checking' check box is checked (Figure 9–33).

Q&A

What is the purpose of the other check boxes in the section?

All the other check boxes are checked, indicating that Access will perform all the various types of automatic error checking that are possible. If there were a particular type of error checking that you would prefer to skip, you would remove its check mark before tapping or clicking the OK button.

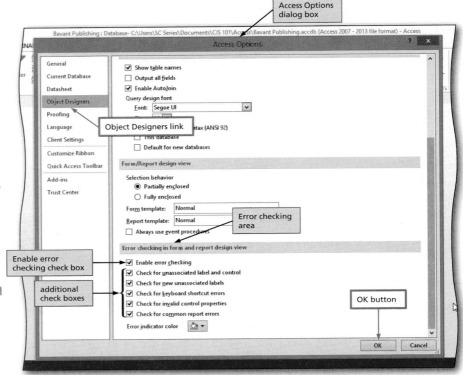

Figure 9–33

2

- Tap or click the OK button to close the Access Options dialog box.

Error Indication

With error checking enabled, if an error occurs, a small triangle called an **error indicator** appears in the appropriate field or control. For example, you could change the label for Book Rep Number in the Customer View and Update Form to include an ampersand (&) before the letter, N, making it a keyboard shortcut for this control. This would be a problem because N is already a shortcut for Name to Find. If this happens, an error indicator appears in both controls in which N is the keyboard shortcut, as shown in Figure 9–34.

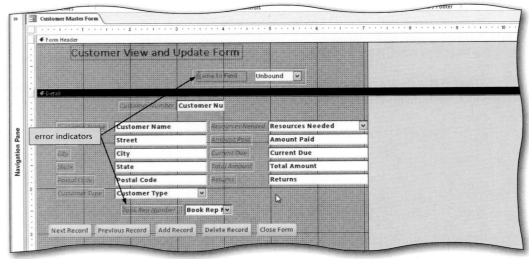

Figure 9–34

Selecting a control containing an error indicator displays an 'Error Checking Options' button. Tapping or clicking the 'Error Checking Options' button produces the 'Error Checking Options' menu, as shown in Figure 9–35. The first line in the menu is simply a statement of the type of error that occurred, and the second is a description of the specific error. The Change Caption command gives a submenu of the captions that can be changed. The 'Edit Caption Property' command allows you to change the caption directly and is the simplest way to correct this error. The 'Help on This Error' command gives help on the specific error that occurred. You can choose to ignore the error by using the Ignore Error command. The final command, 'Error Checking Options', allows you to change the same error checking options shown in Figure 9–33.

BTW
Freezing Fields
The Freeze Fields command allows you to place a column or columns in a table on the left side of the table. As you scroll to the right, the column or columns remain visible. To freeze a column or columns, select the column(s) in Datasheet view, press and hold or right-click and tap or click Freeze Fields on the shortcut menu. To unfreeze fields, tap or click the 'Unfreeze All Fields' command on the shortcut menu. When you freeze a column, Access considers it a change to the layout of the table. When you close the table, Access will ask you if you want to save the changes.

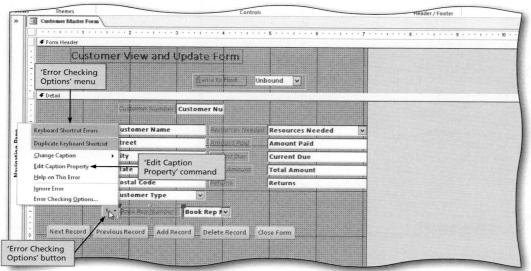

Figure 9–35

The simplest way to fix this error is to edit the caption property. Tapping or clicking the 'Edit Caption Property' command produces a property sheet with the Caption property highlighted. You then could change the Caption property to make another letter the shortcut key. For example, you could make the letter, B, the shortcut key by typing `&Book Rep Number` as the entry.

Data Type Parts

Access contains data type parts that are available on the More Fields gallery. Some data type parts, such as the Category part, consist of a single field. Others, such as the Address part, consist of multiple fields. To insert all the fields in the part into your table, all you need to do is tap or click the part. In addition to the parts provided by Access, you can create your own parts.

To Create Custom Data Parts

1 CONVERT DATABASE | 2 ANALYZE & DOCUMENT | 3 NAVIGATION PANE | 4 CUSTOM PROPERTIES & INDEXES
5 CUSTOM DATA PART | 6 CUSTOM TEMPLATE | 7 ENCRYPT LOCK & SPLIT | 8 CUSTOM WEB APP | 9 CUSTOM VIEW

To create data parts in the Quick Start category from existing fields, you select the desired field or fields and then select the Save Selection as New Data Type command in the More Fields gallery. If you select multiple fields, the fields must be adjacent.

Bavant has decided that combining several address-related fields into a single data part would make future database updates easier. The following steps create a Quick Start field consisting of the Last Name, First Name, Street, City, State, and Postal Code fields in the Book Rep table. *Why? Once you have created this Quick Start field, users can add this collection of fields to a table by simply tapping or clicking the Quick Start field.*

- Open the Navigation Pane, open the Book Rep table in Datasheet view, and then close the Navigation Pane.

- Tap or click the column heading for the Last Name field to select the field.

- Hold the SHIFT key down and tap or click the column heading for the Postal Code field to select all the fields from the Last Name field to the Postal Code field.

- Display the TABLE TOOLS FIELDS tab.

- Tap or click the More Fields button (TABLE TOOLS FIELDS tab | Add & Delete group) to display the More Fields gallery (Figure 9–36).

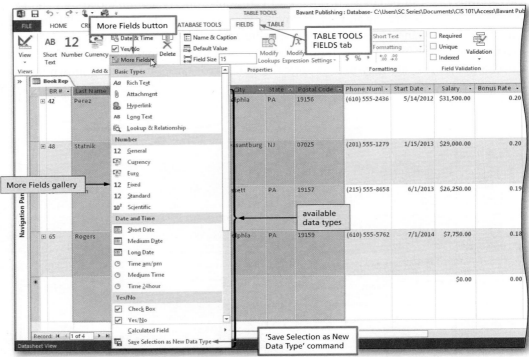

Figure 9–36

- Tap or click 'Save Selection as New Data Type' to display the Create New Data Type from Fields dialog box.

- Enter **Name-Address** as the name.

- Enter **Last Name, First Name, Street, City, State, and Postal Code** as the description.

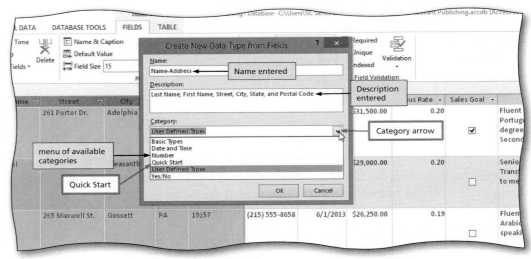

Figure 9–37

Q&A

What is the purpose of the description?
When a user points to the Quick Start field you created, a ScreenTip will appear containing the description you entered.

- Tap or click the Category arrow to display a list of available categories (Figure 9–37).

3

- Tap or click Quick Start to indicate the new data type will be added to the Quick Start category.

Q&A What is the difference between the Quick Start and User Defined Types category?

If you select the Quick Start category, the data type you create will be listed among the Quick Start data types that are part of Access. If you select the User Defined Types category, the data type you create will be in a separate category containing only those data types you create. In either case, however, tapping or clicking the data type will produce the same result.

- Tap or click the OK button (Create New Data Type from Fields dialog box) to save the data type.

- When Access indicates that your template (that is, your Quick Start field) has been saved, tap or click the OK button (Microsoft Access dialog box).

- Close the table.

- If necessary, tap or click No when asked if you want to save the changes to the layout of the table.

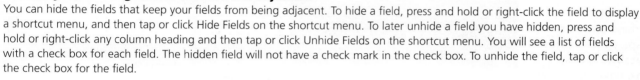

CONSIDER THIS

How do you rearrange fields that are not adjacent?

You can hide the fields that keep your fields from being adjacent. To hide a field, press and hold or right-click the field to display a shortcut menu, and then tap or click Hide Fields on the shortcut menu. To later unhide a field you have hidden, press and hold or right-click any column heading and then tap or click Unhide Fields on the shortcut menu. You will see a list of fields with a check box for each field. The hidden field will not have a check mark in the check box. To unhide the field, tap or click the check box for the field.

Templates

You have worked with Access templates in previous chapters. You can use a template to create a complete database application containing tables, forms, queries, and other objects. There are many templates available for Access.

You can create your own template from an existing database. To do so, you must first ensure that you have created a database with all the characteristics you want in your template. In this chapter, the database you create will have two tables, a query, two single-item forms, two datasheet forms that use macros, and a navigation form that will serve as the main menu. In addition, the navigation form will be set to appear automatically whenever you open the database. Once you have incorporated all these features, you will save the database as a template. From that point on, anyone can use your template to create a new database. The database that is created will incorporate all the same features as your original database.

Later in this chapter, you will create a web app, which is a database that anyone can use through a browser. The easiest way to create the tables for the web app is to import them from an existing database. You will use your template to create such a database. While the queries and forms that are part of the template will not be included in the web app, the tables will.

Access enforces some restrictions to tables used in web apps, so the tables in your template should adhere to these restrictions, as follows:

- While you can change the name of the default autonumber primary key, you cannot change its data type. If you have a text field that you want to be the primary key, the best you can do is to specify that the field must be both required and unique.

- You cannot create relationships as you can do with a typical database. Rather, any relationships must be specified through lookup fields.

To Create a Desktop Database

The following steps create the Clients and Recruiters **desktop database**, that is, a database designed to run on a personal computer. *Why? This database will become the basis for a template.*

- Tap or click FILE on the ribbon to open the Backstage view.

- Tap or click the New tab.

- Tap or click the 'Blank desktop database' button.

- Type **Clients and Recruiters** as the name of the database file.

- Tap or click the Browse button to display the File New Database dialog box, navigate to the desired save location (for example, the Access folder in the CIS 101 folder), and then tap or click the OK button to return to the Backstage view (Figure 9–38).

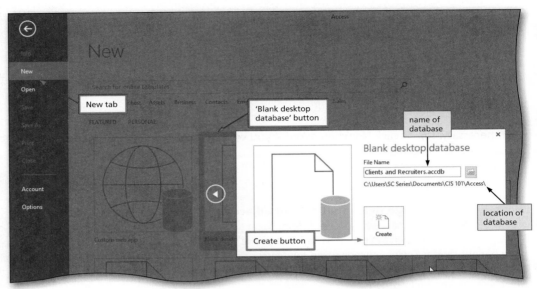

Figure 9–38

- Tap or click the Create button to create the database (Figure 9–39).

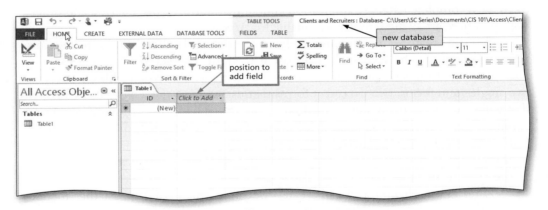

Figure 9–39

To Add Fields to the Table

The tables will have an autonumber ID field as the primary key. *Why? You will later import the tables in this database to a web app, and tables in a web app must have an autonumber field as a primary key.* In addition, the field that normally would be the primary key will be designated both required and unique, two characteristics of the primary key.

The following steps add the Recruiter Number, Last Name, First Name, Street, City, State, Postal Code, Rate, and Commission to a table. The Rate field is a Number field and the Commission field is a Currency field.

The steps designate the Recruiter Number field as both required and unique. They add the Last Name, First Name, Street, City, State, and Postal Code as a single operation by using the Quick Start field created earlier. After adding the fields, they save the table using the name, Recruiter. They also change the field size for the Rate field, a Number field, to Single so that the field can contain decimal places.

1

- Tap or click the Click to Add column heading and select Short Text as the data type.

- Type **Recruiter Number** as the field name.

- Tap or click the white space below the field name to complete the change of the name. Tap or click the white space a second time to select the field.

- Change the field size to 2.

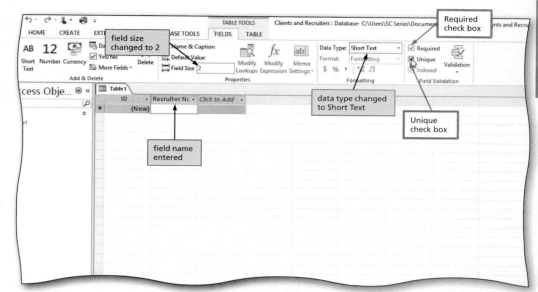

Figure 9–40

- Tap or click the Required check box (TABLE TOOLS FIELDS tab | Field Validation group) to make the field a required field.

- Tap or click the Unique check box (TABLE TOOLS FIELDS tab | Field Validation group) so that Access will ensure that values in the field are unique (Figure 9–40).

2

- Tap or click under the Click to Add column heading to produce an insertion point in the next field.

- Tap or click the More Fields button (TABLE TOOLS FIELDS tab | Add & Delete group) to display the More Fields menu (Figure 9–41).

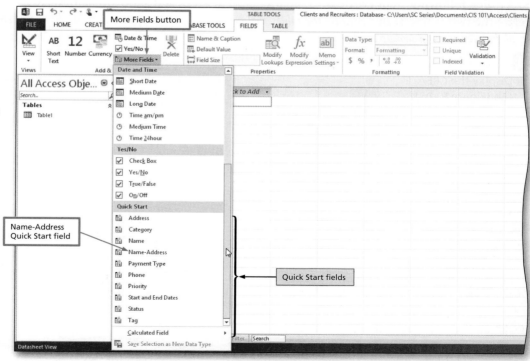

Figure 9–41

● Tap or click the
Name-Address Quick
Start field that you
created earlier to
add the Last Name,
First Name, Street,
City, State, and
Postal Code fields
(Figure 9–42).

● Add the Rate and
Commission fields
as the last two
fields. The Rate field
has the Number
data type and the
Commission field has
the Currency data
type.

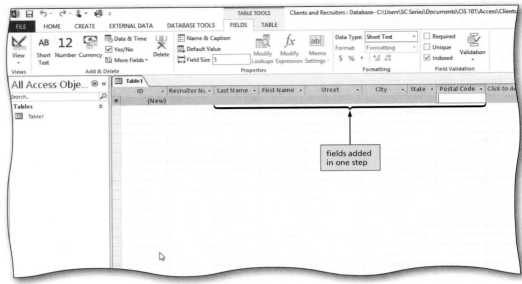

Figure 9–42

● Save the table, assigning `Recruiter` as the table name.

● Switch to Design view, select the Number field, and change the field size to Single so that the Rate field can include
decimal places.

● Save and close the table.

To Create a Second Table

1 CONVERT DATABASE | 2 ANALYZE & DOCUMENT | 3 NAVIGATION PANE | 4 CUSTOM PROPERTIES & INDEXES
5 CUSTOM DATA PART | 6 CUSTOM TEMPLATE | 7 ENCRYPT LOCK & SPLIT | 8 CUSTOM WEB APP | 9 CUSTOM VIEW

The following steps create the Client table. The steps add a lookup field for Recruiter Number to
relate the two tables. *Why? Because the tables will be used in a web app, the relationship between the tables needs to be
implemented using a lookup field.*

● Display the CREATE
tab (Figure 9–43).

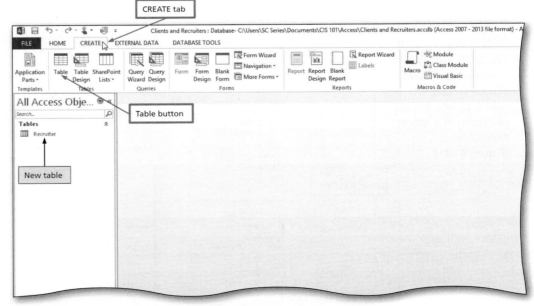

Figure 9–43

2

- Tap or click the Table button (CREATE tab | Tables group) to create a new table.

- Tap or click the 'Click to Add' column heading and select Short Text as the data type.

- Type **Client Number** as the field name.

- Tap or click the white space below the field name to complete the change of the name. Tap or click the white space a second time to select the field.

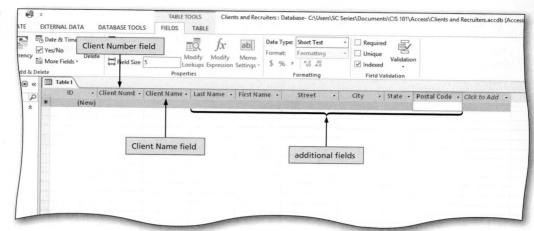

Figure 9–44

- Change the field size to 5.

- Tap or click the Required check box (TABLE TOOLS FIELDS tab | Field Validation group) to make the field a required field.

- Tap or click the Unique check box (TABLE TOOLS FIELDS tab | Field Validation group) so that Access will ensure that values in the field are unique.

- In a similar fashion, add the Client Name field and change the field size to 30. Do not check the Required or Unique check boxes.

- Tap or click under the 'Click to Add' column heading to produce an insertion point in the next field.

- Tap or click the More Fields button (TABLE TOOLS FIELDS tab | Add & Delete group) to display the More Fields menu (see Figure 9–41 on page AC 567).

- Tap or click the Name-Address Quick Start field that you added earlier to add the Last Name, First Name, Street, City, State, and Postal Code fields (Figure 9–44).

3

- Press and hold or right-click the Last Name field to produce a shortcut menu, and then tap or click Delete Field to delete the field.

- Press and hold or right-click the First Name field to produce a shortcut menu, and then tap or click Delete Field to delete the field.

- Add the Amount Paid and Current Due fields. Both fields have the Currency data type.

- Save the table, assigning Client as the table name.

- Scroll, if necessary, so that the 'Click to Add' column appears on your screen.

- Tap or click the 'Click to Add' column heading to display a menu of available data types (Figure 9–45).

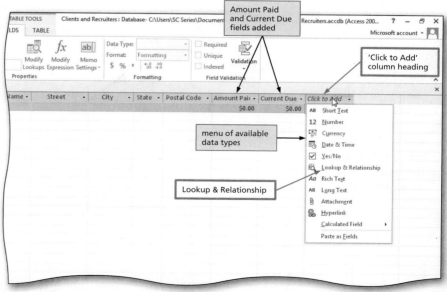

Figure 9–45

- Tap or click Lookup & Relationship to display the Lookup Wizard dialog box (Figure 9–46).

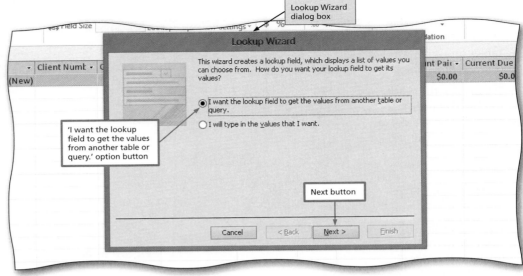

Figure 9–46

- Tap or click the Next button to display the next Lookup Wizard screen, and then tap or click the Recruiter table to select it so that you can add a lookup field for the Recruiter Number to the Client table (Figure 9–47).

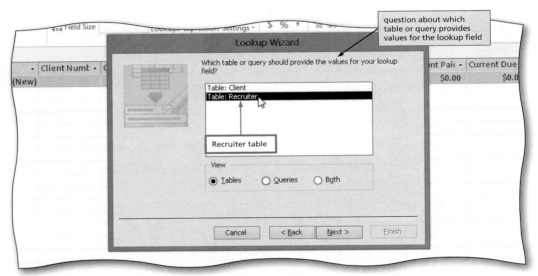

Figure 9–47

- Tap or click the Next button, and then select the Recruiter Number, First Name, and Last Name fields for the columns in the lookup field (Figure 9–48).

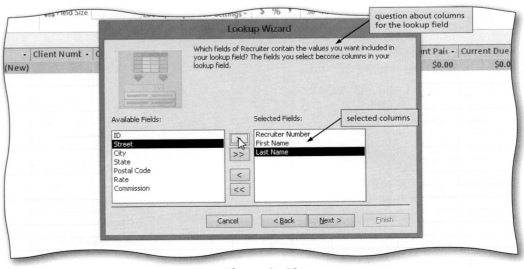

Figure 9–48

- Tap or click the Next button, select the Recruiter Number field for the sort order, and then tap or click the Next button again. (Figure 9–49).

Q&A
I see the ID field listed when I am selecting the Recruiter Number field for the sort order. Did I do something wrong?
No. Access automatically included the ID field.

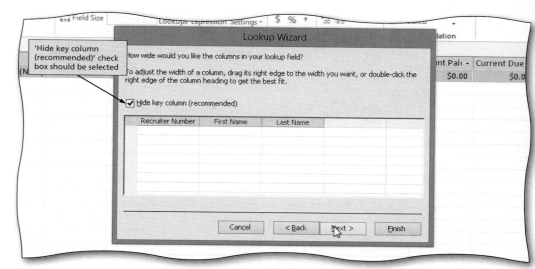

Figure 9–49

- Ensure the 'Hide key column (recommended)' check box is selected, and then tap or click the Next button.

- Type **Recruiter Number** as the label for the lookup field.

- Tap or click the 'Enable Data Integrity' check box to select it (Figure 9–50).

Q&A
What is the effect of selecting Enable Data Integrity?
Access will enforce referential integrity for the Recruiter Number. That is, Access will not allow a recruiter number in a client record that does not match the number of a recruiter in the Recruiter table.

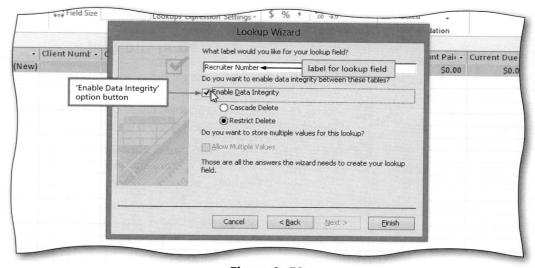
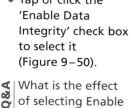

Figure 9–50

- Tap or click the Finish button to add the lookup field.

- Save the table.

- Close the table.

To Import the Data

Now that the tables have been created, you need to add data to them. You could enter the data, or if the data is already in electronic form, you could import the data. The data for the Recruiter and Client tables are included in the Data Files for Students as text files. The steps on the next page import the data.

1. With the Clients and Recruiters database open, display the EXTERNAL DATA tab, and then tap or click the Text File button (EXTERNAL DATA tab | Import & Link group) to display the Get External Data - Text File dialog box.

2. Tap or click the Browse button (Get External Data - Text File dialog box) and select the location of the files to be imported (for example, the Access folder in the CIS 101 folder).

3. Select the Recruiter text file and then tap or click the Open button.

4. Select the 'Append a copy of records to the table' option button, select the Recruiter table, and then tap or click the OK button.

5. Be sure the Delimited option button is selected, and then tap or click the Next button.

6. Be sure the Comma option button is selected, tap or click the Next button, and then tap or click the Finish button.

7. Tap or click the Close button to close the Get External Data – Text File dialog box without saving the import steps.

8. Use the technique shown in Steps 1 through 7 to import the Client text file into the Client table.

To Create a Query Relating the Tables

The following steps create a query that relates the Client and Recruiter tables.

1. Display the CREATE tab and then tap or click the Query Design button (CREATE tab | Queries group) to create a new query.

2. Tap or click the Client table, tap or click the Add button, tap or click the Recruiter table, tap or click the Add button, and then tap or click the Close button to close the Show Table dialog box.

3. Double-tap or double-click the Client Number, Client Name, and Recruiter Number fields from the Client table. Double-tap or double-click the First Name and Last Name fields from the Recruiter table to add the fields to the design grid.

4. Tap or click the Save button on the Quick Access Toolbar to save the query, type `Client-Recruiter Query` as the name of the query, and then tap or click the OK button.

5. Close the query.

Creating Forms

There are several types of forms that need to be created for this database. The Client and Recruiter detail forms show a single record at a time. The Client, Recruiter, and Client-Recruiter Query forms are intended to look like the corresponding table or query in Datasheet view. Finally, the main menu is a navigation form.

To Create Single-Item Forms

The following steps create two single-item forms, that is, forms that display a single record at a time. The first form, called Client Details, is for the Client table. The second form is for the Recruiter table and is called Recruiter Details.

1 Select the Client table in the Navigation Pane and then display the CREATE tab.

2 Tap or click the Form button (CREATE tab | Forms group) to create a single-item form for the Client table.

3 Tap or click the Save button on the Quick Access Toolbar and then type `Client Details` as the name of the form, click the OK button (Save As dialog box) to save the form, and then close the form.

4 Select the Recruiter table, display the CREATE tab, and then tap or click the Form button (CREATE tab | Forms group) to create a single-item form for the Recruiter table.

5 Save the form, using `Recruiter Details` as the form name.

6 Close the form.

To Create Datasheet Forms

1 CONVERT DATABASE | 2 ANALYZE & DOCUMENT | 3 NAVIGATION PANE | 4 CUSTOM PROPERTIES & INDEXES
5 CUSTOM DATA PART | 6 CUSTOM TEMPLATE | 7 ENCRYPT LOCK & SPLIT | 8 CUSTOM WEB APP | 9 CUSTOM VIEW

The following steps create two datasheet forms, that is, forms that display the data in the form of a datasheet. *Why? These forms enable you to make it appear that you are displaying datasheets in a navigation form; recall that navigation forms can display only forms.* The first form is for the Client table and is also called Client. The second is for the Recruiter table and is also called Recruiter. The steps also create macros that will display the data for a selected record in a single-item form, as you did in Chapter 8 on pages AC 504 through AC 507.

1

- Select the Client table and then display the CREATE tab.

- Tap or click the More Forms button (CREATE tab | Forms group) to display the More Forms menu (Figure 9–51).

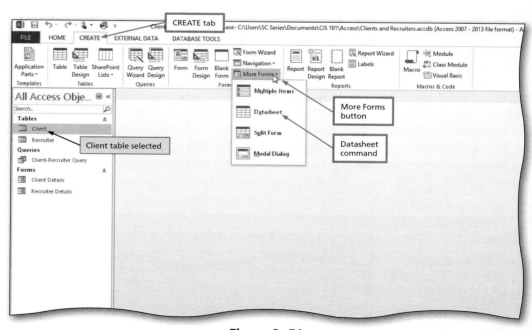

Figure 9–51

- Tap or click
  Datasheet to create
  a datasheet form for
  the Client table.

- Tap or click the Save
  button on the Quick
  Access Toolbar and
  then accept Client
  as the default name
  of the form.

- Tap or click the
  column heading for
  the ID field to select
  the field.

- Display the property
  sheet and tap or
  click the Event tab to
  display only the
  event properties
  (Figure 9–52).

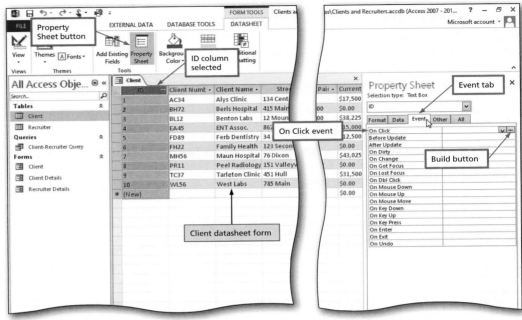

Figure 9–52

- Tap or click the Build
  button (the three
  dots) for the On
  Click event and then
  use the techniques
  on pages AC 504
  through AC 507 in
  Chapter 8 to enter
  the macro shown in
  Figure 9–53.

4

- Tap or click the Save
  button (MACRO
  TOOLS DESIGN tab |
  Close group) to save
  the macro and then
  tap or click the Close
  button to close the
  macro.

- Close the property
  sheet.

- Save the Client
  datasheet form and
  then close the form.

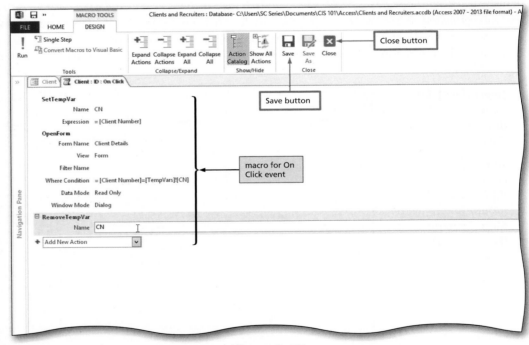

Figure 9–53

⑤

• Use the techniques in Steps 1 and 2 to create a datasheet form for the Recruiter table. Use `Recruiter` as the name for the form. The macro for the On Click event for the ID field is shown in Figure 9–54.

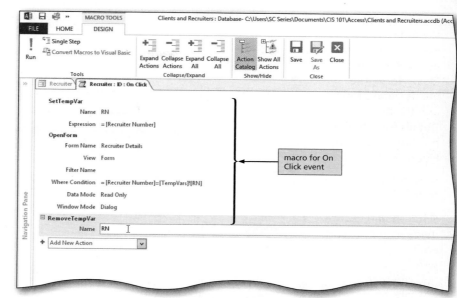

Figure 9–54

⑥

• Save and close the macro.

• Close the property sheet.

• Save and close the form.

⑦

• Select the Client-Recruiter Query.

• Create a datasheet form for the Client-Recruiter Query. Save the form, using `Client-Recruiter Query` as the form name.

• Close the Client-Recruiter Query form.

 Experiment

• Test each of the macros by tapping or clicking the client number in the Client form or the recruiter number in the Recruiter form. Ensure that the correct form opens. If there are errors, correct the corresponding macro. When finished, close any form you have opened.

To Create a Navigation Form

1 CONVERT DATABASE | 2 ANALYZE & DOCUMENT | 3 NAVIGATION PANE | 4 CUSTOM PROPERTIES & INDEXES
5 CUSTOM DATA PART | 6 CUSTOM TEMPLATE | 7 ENCRYPT LOCK & SPLIT | 8 CUSTOM WEB APP | 9 CUSTOM VIEW

The following steps create a navigation form containing a single row of horizontal tabs. The steps save the form using the name, Main Menu. *Why? This form is intended to function as a menu.* The steps change the form title and add the appropriate tabs.

①

• Display the CREATE tab and then tap or click the Navigation button (CREATE tab | Forms group) to show the menu of available navigation forms.

• Tap or click Horizontal Tabs in the menu to create a form with a navigation control in which the tabs are arranged in a single row, horizontally.

• If a field list appears, tap or click the 'Add Existing Fields' button (FORM LAYOUT TOOLS DESIGN tab | Tools group) to remove the field list.

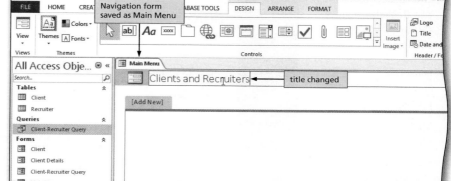

Figure 9–55

• Save the navigation form, using Main Menu as the form name.

• Tap or click the form title twice, once to select it and the second time to produce an insertion point.

• Erase the current title and then type `Clients and Recruiters` as the new title (Figure 9–55).

2

- One at a time, drag the Client form, the Recruiter form, the Client-Recruiter Query form, the Client Details form, and the Recruiter Details form to the positions shown in Figure 9–56.

- Save and close the form.

 What should I do if I made a mistake and added a form to the wrong location? You can rearrange the tabs by dragging. Often, the simplest way to correct a mistake is to tap or click the Undo button to reverse your most recent action, however. You also can choose to simply close the form without saving it and then start over.

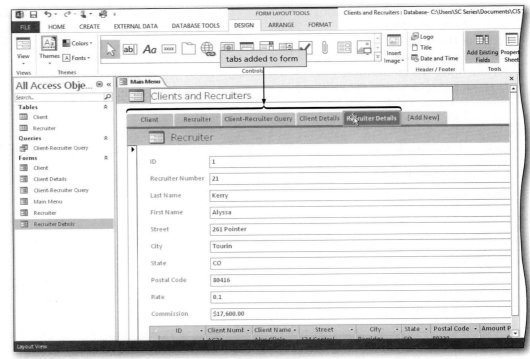

Figure 9–56

To Select a Startup Form

1 CONVERT DATABASE | 2 ANALYZE & DOCUMENT | 3 NAVIGATION PANE | 4 CUSTOM PROPERTIES & INDEXES
5 CUSTOM DATA PART | 6 CUSTOM TEMPLATE | 7 ENCRYPT LOCK & SPLIT | 8 CUSTOM WEB APP | 9 CUSTOM VIEW

If the database includes a navigation form, it is common to select the navigation form as a **startup form,** which launches when the user opens the database. *Why? Designating the navigation form as a startup form ensures that the form will appear automatically when a user opens the database.* The following steps designate the navigation form as a startup form.

1

- Tap or click FILE on the ribbon to display the Backstage view (Figure 9–57).

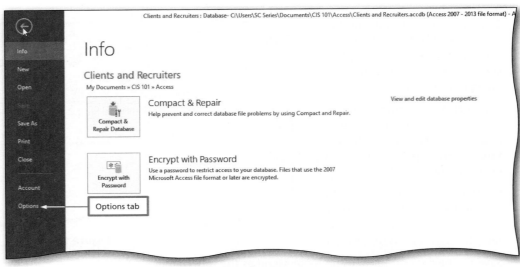

Figure 9–57

- Tap or click the Options tab.

- Tap or click Current Database (Access Options dialog box) to select the options for the current database.

- Tap or click the Display Form arrow to display the list of available forms.

- Tap or click Main Menu to select it as the form that will automatically be displayed whenever the database is opened (Figure 9–58).

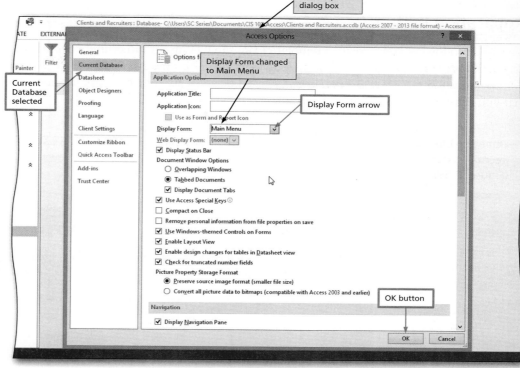

Figure 9–58

- Tap or click the OK button (Access Options dialog box) to save your changes.

- Tap or click the OK button (Microsoft Access dialog box) when Access displays a message indicating that you must close and reopen the database for the change to take effect.

- Close the database.

Break Point: If you wish to stop working through the chapter at this point, you can close Access now. You can resume the project at a later time by starting Access, and continuing to follow the steps from this location forward.

Templates

An Access **template** is a file that contains the elements needed to produce a specific type of complete database. You can select a template when you create a database. The resulting database will contain all the tables, queries, forms, reports, and/or macros included in the template. In addition, with some templates, the resulting database also might contain data.

Some templates are also available as **application parts**. Application parts are very similar to templates in that selecting a single application part can create tables, queries, forms, reports, and macros. The difference is you select a template when you first create a database, whereas you select an application part after you have already created a database. The objects (tables, queries, forms, reports, and macros) in the application part will be added to any objects you already have created.

Access provides a number of templates representing a variety of types of databases. You also can create your own template from an existing database. When you create a template, you can choose to create an application part as well. When creating templates and application parts, you can also include data if desired.

BTW
Templates and Application Parts
By default, user-created templates and application parts are stored in the C:\Users*user name*\AppData\Roaming\Microsoft\Templates\Access folder.

To Create a Template and Application Part

The following steps create a template from the Clients and Recruiters database. *Why? The Clients and Recruiters database now contains all the tables, queries, and forms you want in the template. You then will be able to use the template when you want to create similar databases.* The steps also create an application part from the database so that you can reuse the parts in other databases.

- Open the Clients and Recruiters database (Figure 9–59).

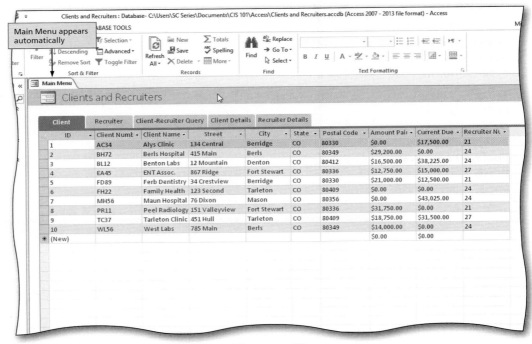

Figure 9–59

- Close the Main Menu form.
- Open the Backstage view.
- Tap or click the Save As tab.
- Tap or click the Template button in the Save Database As area to indicate you are creating a template (Figure 9–60).

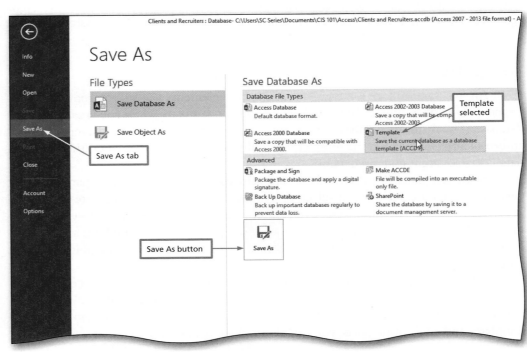

Figure 9–60

3

- Tap or click the Save As button to display the Create New Template from This Database dialog box.

- Type **Clients and Recruiters** as the name for the new template.

- Type **Database of clients and recruiters with navigation form menu.** as the description.

- Tap or click the Application Part check box to indicate that you also want to create an application part.

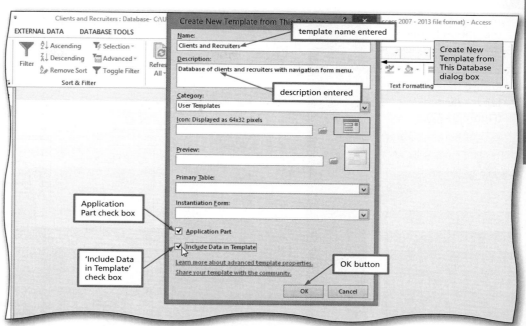

Figure 9–61

- Tap or click the 'Include Data in Template' check box to indicate you want to include the data in the database as part of the template (Figure 9–61).

Q&A Why include data?
Anytime a user creates a database using the template, the database automatically will include data. This enables the users to see what any reports, forms, or queries look like with data in them. Once the users have the reports, forms, and queries the way they want them, they can delete all this data. At that point, they can begin adding the real data to the database.

4

- Tap or click the OK button (Create New Template from This Database dialog box) to create the template.

- When Access indicates that the template has been successfully saved, tap or click the OK button (Microsoft Access dialog box).

To Use the Template

1 CONVERT DATABASE | 2 ANALYZE & DOCUMENT | 3 NAVIGATION PANE | 4 CUSTOM PROPERTIES & INDEXES
5 CUSTOM DATA PART | 6 CUSTOM TEMPLATE | 7 ENCRYPT LOCK & SPLIT | 8 CUSTOM WEB APP | 9 CUSTOM VIEW

You can use the Clients and Recruiters template just as you would use any other template, such as the Blank database template you previously used. The only difference is that, after tapping or clicking the New tab in the Backstage view, you need to tap or click the PERSONAL link. **Why?** *The PERSONAL link displays any templates you created and lets you select the template you want.*

The steps on the next page use the template created earlier to create the MZL Recruiters database. Later in the chapter, you will learn how to use this database to import tables to a web app.

1

- Tap or click FILE on the ribbon to open the Backstage view, if necessary.

- Ensure that the New tab is selected (Figure 9–62).

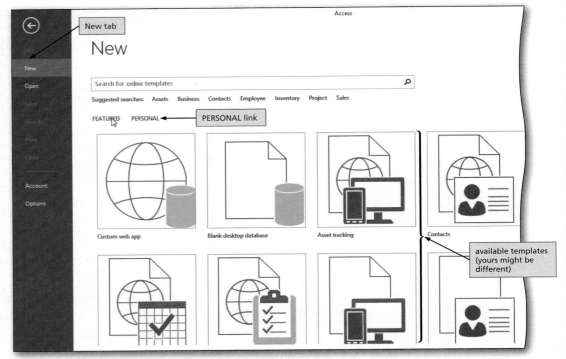

Figure 9–62

2

- Tap or click the PERSONAL link to display the templates you have created (Figure 9–63).

3

- Tap or click the 'Clients and Recruiters' template that you created earlier.

- Type **MZL Recruiters** as the name of the database and then navigate to the location of the database to be opened (for example, the Access folder in the CIS 101 folder).

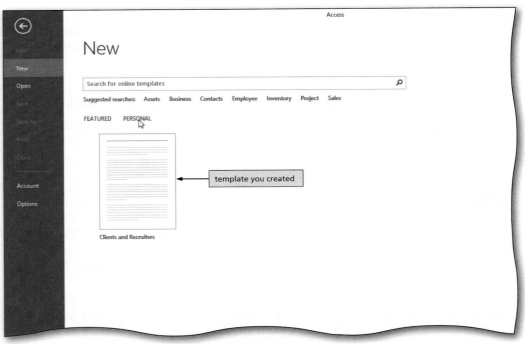

Figure 9–63

- Tap or click the Create button to create the database from the template.

- Close the database.

Note: Unless your instructor indicates otherwise, you are strongly encouraged to simply read the material in this chapter from this point on without carrying out any operations. If you decide to try it for yourself, it is important to make a backup copy of your database and store it in a secure location before performing the operation. That way, if something damages your database or you can no longer access your database, you still can use the backup copy. In addition, for the material on web apps, you must have access to a SharePoint 2013 site.

Using an Application Part

To use the application part you created, you first need to create a database. After doing so, you tap or click the Application Parts button (CREATE tab | Templates group) to display the Application Parts menu (Figure 9–64).

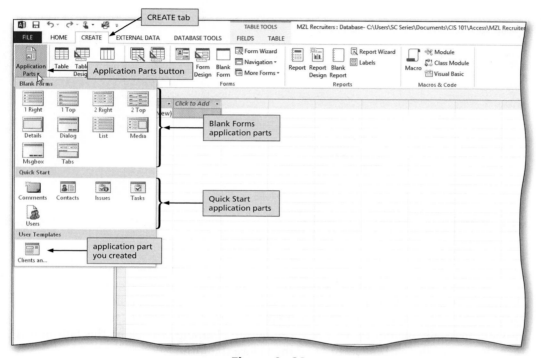

Figure 9–64

You then can tap or click the application part you created, which will be located in the User Templates section of the Application Parts menu. If you have any open objects, Access will indicate that "all open objects must be closed before instantiating this application part" and ask if you want Access to close all open objects. After you tap or click the Yes button, Access will add all the objects in the Application part to the database. If you already had created other objects in the database, they still would be included.

1 CONVERT DATABASE | 2 ANALYZE & DOCUMENT | 3 NAVIGATION PANE | 4 CUSTOM PROPERTIES & INDEXES
5 CUSTOM DATA PART | 6 CUSTOM TEMPLATE | 7 ENCRYPT LOCK & SPLIT | 8 CUSTOM WEB APP | 9 CUSTOM VIEW

TO USE THE APPLICATION PART

Specifically, to use the application part created earlier, you would use the following steps.

1. Create or open the database for which you want to use the application part.
2. Display the CREATE tab and then tap or click the Application Parts button (CREATE tab | Templates group).
3. Tap or click the application part to be added.
4. If Access indicates that open objects must be closed, tap or click the Yes button.

Blank Forms Application Parts

Blank Forms application parts (see Figure 9–64 on the previous page) represent a way to create certain types of forms (Figure 9–64). To do so, you click the Application Parts button to display the gallery of application part styles, and then tap or click the desired type of form, for example, 1 Right. Access then creates a form with the desired characteristics and assigns it a name. It does not open the form, but you can see the form in the Navigation Pane (Figure 9–65).

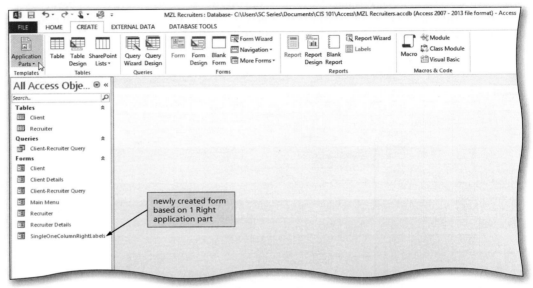

Figure 9–65

You can modify the form by opening the form in Layout or Design view (Figure 9–66). This form automatically creates a Save button. Tapping or clicking this button when you are using the form will save changes to the current record. The form also automatically includes a Save & Close button. Tapping or clicking this button will save changes to the current record and then close the form.

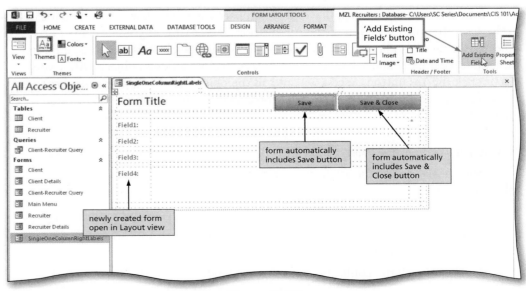

Figure 9–66

To add the specific fields you want to the form, display a field list. You then can drag a field onto the form while holding down the CTRL key (Figure 9–67). Once you have added the field, you can change the corresponding label by tapping or clicking the label to select it, tapping or clicking the label a second time to produce an insertion point, and then making the desired change.

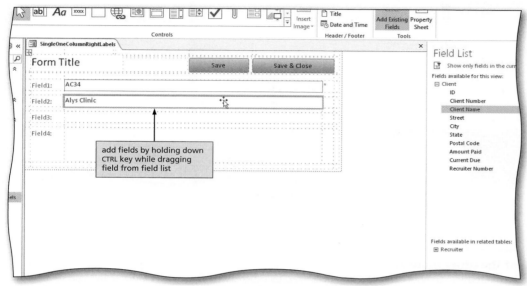

Figure 9–67

Encrypting a Database

Encrypting refers to the storing of data in the database in an encoded, or encrypted, format. Anytime a user stores or modifies data in the encrypted database, the database management system (DBMS) will encode the data before actually updating the database. Before a legitimate user retrieves the data using the DBMS, the data will be decoded. The whole encrypting process is transparent to a legitimate user; that is, he or she is not even aware it is happening. If an unauthorized user attempts to bypass all the controls of the DBMS and get to the database through a utility program or a word processor, however, he or she will be able to see only the encoded, and unreadable, version of the data. In Access, you encrypt a database and set a password as part of the same operation.

BTW
Encryption and Passwords
Encryption helps prevent unauthorized use of an Access database. Consider using encryption when the database contains sensitive data, such as medical records or employee records. Passwords should be eight or more characters in length. The longer the length of the password and the more random the characters, the more difficult it is for someone to determine. Use a combination of uppercase and lowercase letters as well as numbers and special symbols when you create a password. Make sure that you remember your password. If you forget it, there is no method for retrieving it. You will be unable to open the encrypted database.

1 CONVERT DATABASE | 2 ANALYZE & DOCUMENT | 3 NAVIGATION PANE | 4 CUSTOM PROPERTIES & INDEXES
5 CUSTOM DATA PART | 6 CUSTOM TEMPLATE | 7 ENCRYPT LOCK & SPLIT | 8 CUSTOM WEB APP | 9 CUSTOM VIEW

TO OPEN A DATABASE IN EXCLUSIVE MODE

To encrypt a database and set a password, the database must be open in exclusive mode; that is, no other user can access the database in any way. To open a database in exclusive mode, you use the Open arrow (Figure 9–68 on the next page) rather than simply tapping or clicking the Open button.

To open a database in exclusive mode, you would use the following steps.

1. If necessary, close any open databases.
2. Tap or click Open in the Backstage view to display the Open dialog box.
3. Tap or click Computer, then tap or click Browse.
4. Navigate to the location of the database to be opened.
5. Tap or click the name of the database to be opened.
6. Tap or click the Open arrow to display the Open button menu.
7. Tap or click Open Exclusive to open the database in exclusive mode.

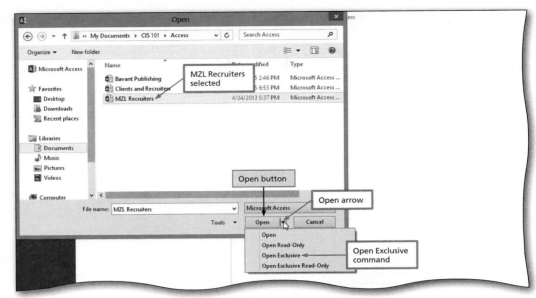

Figure 9–68

What is the purpose of the other modes?

The Open option opens the database in a mode so that it can be shared by other users. Open Read-Only allows you to read the data in the database, but not update the database.

Encrypting a Database with a Password

If you wanted to encrypt the database with a password, you would open the Backstage view (Figure 9–69).

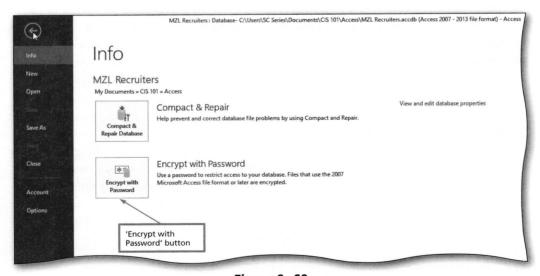

Figure 9–69

You then would select 'Encrypt with Password' and enter the password you have chosen in both the Password text box and Verify text box (Figure 9–70).

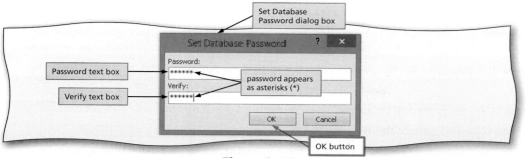

Figure 9–70

TO ENCRYPT A DATABASE WITH A PASSWORD

1 CONVERT DATABASE | 2 ANALYZE & DOCUMENT | 3 NAVIGATION PANE | 4 CUSTOM PROPERTIES & INDEXES
5 CUSTOM DATA PART | 6 CUSTOM TEMPLATE | **7 ENCRYPT LOCK & SPLIT** | **8 CUSTOM WEB APP** | **9 CUSTOM VIEW**

With the database open in exclusive mode, you would use the following steps to encrypt the database with a password.

1. Tap or click FILE on the ribbon to open the Backstage view and ensure the Info tab is selected.
2. Tap or click the 'Encrypt with Password' button to display the Set Database Password dialog box.
3. Type the desired password in the Password text box in the Set Database Password dialog box.
4. Press the TAB key and then type the password again in the Verify text box.
5. Tap or click the OK button to encrypt the database and set the password.
6. If you get a message indicating that row level locking will be ignored, tap or click the OK button.
7. Close the database.

Is the password case sensitive?

Yes, you must enter the password using the same case you used when you created it.

Opening a Database with a Password

When you open a database that has a password, you will be prompted to enter your password in the Password Required dialog box. Once you have done so, tap or click the OK button. Assuming you have entered your password correctly, Access then will open the database.

Decrypting a Database and Removing a Password

If the encryption and the password no longer are necessary, you can decrypt the database and remove the password. The button to encrypt a database with a password has changed to Decrypt Database (Figure 9–71).

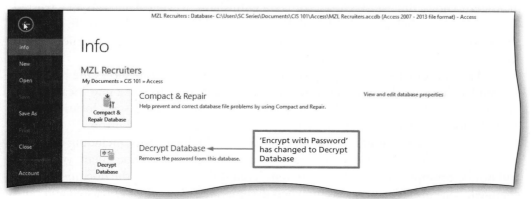

Figure 9–71

CONSIDER THIS

To Decrypt the Database and Remove the Password

To decrypt a database that you have previously encrypted and remove the password, you would use the following steps.

1. Open the database to be decrypted in exclusive mode, entering your password when requested.
2. Open the Backstage view and ensure the Info tab is selected.
3. Tap or click the Decrypt Database button to display the Unset Database Password dialog box.
4. Type the password in the Password dialog box.
5. Tap or click the OK button to remove the password and decrypt the database.
6. Close the database.

The Trust Center

The Trust Center is a feature within Access where you can set security options and also find the latest information on technology related to privacy, safety, and security. To use the Trust Center, you tap or click FILE on the ribbon and then tap or click the Options tab to display the Access Options dialog box. You then tap or click Trust Center to display the Trust Center content (Figure 9–72). You then would tap or click the 'Trust Center Settings' button to display the Trust Center dialog box in which you can make changes in the following categories.

BTW
Security
Security is the prevention of unauthorized access to a database. Within an organization, the database administrator determines the types to access individual users can have to the database. Various government rules and regulations, such as the Sarbannes-Oxley Act (SOX) and the Health Insurance Portability and Accountability Act (HIPPA), require database administrators to have strict security procedures in place to protect data from unauthorized users.

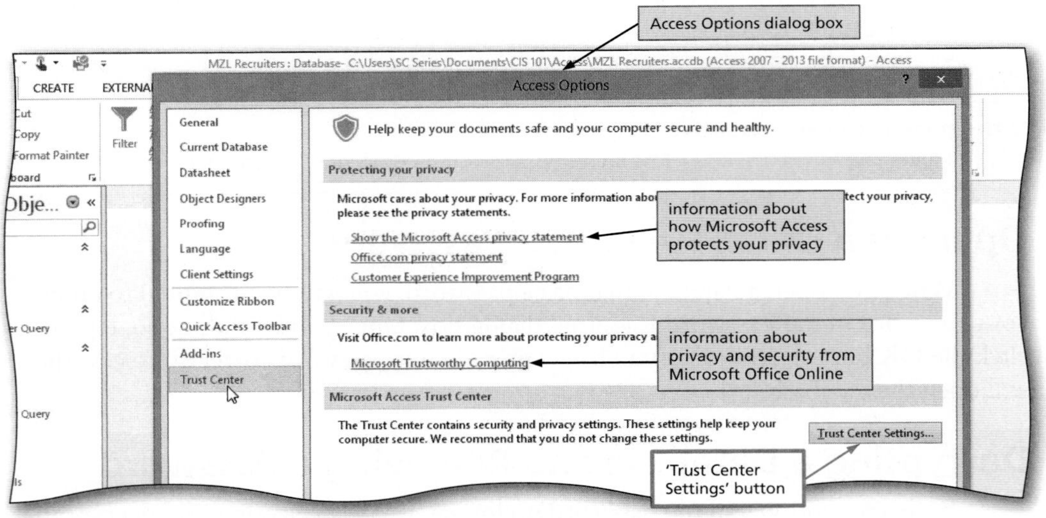

Figure 9–72

Trusted Publishers. Tapping or clicking Trusted Publishers in the Trust Center dialog box shows the list of trusted software publishers. To view details about a trusted publisher, tap or click the publisher and then tap or click the View button. To remove a trusted publisher from the list, tap or click the publisher and then tap or click the Remove button. Users may also add trusted publishers.

Trusted Locations. Tapping or clicking Trusted Locations shows the list of trusted locations on the Internet or within a user's network. To add a new location, tap or click the 'Add new location' button. To remove or modify an existing location, tap or click the location and then tap or click the Remove or the Modify button.

Trusted Documents. You can designate certain documents, including database, Word, Excel, and other files, as trusted. When opening a trusted document, you will not be prompted to enable the content, even if the content of the document has changed. You should be very careful when designating a document as trusted and only do so when you are absolutely sure the document is from a trusted source.

Add-ins. Add-ins are additional programs that you can install and use within Access. Some come with Access and are typically installed using the Access Setup program. Others can be purchased from other vendors. Tapping or clicking Add-ins gives you the opportunity to specify restrictions concerning Add-ins.

ActiveX Settings. When you use ActiveX controls within an Office app, Office prompts you to accept the controls. The ActiveX settings allow you to determine the level of prompting from Office.

Macro Settings. Macros written by other users have the potential to harm your computer; for example, a macro could spread a virus. The Trust Center uses special criteria, including valid digital signatures, reputable certificates, and trusted publishers, to ensure a macro is safe. If the Trust Center discovers a macro that is potentially unsafe, it will take appropriate action. The action the Trust Center takes depends on the Macro Setting you have selected. Tapping or clicking Macro Settings enables you to select or change this setting.

Message Bar. Tapping or clicking Message Bar lets you choose whether the message bar should appear when content has been blocked.

Privacy Options. Tapping or clicking Privacy Options lets you set security settings to protect your personal privacy.

Managing Add-ins. You can manage add-ins by opening the Backstage view, tapping or clicking Options, and then tapping or clicking Add-ins. You can view details concerning existing add-ins. You also can manage existing add-ins or add new ones by selecting the add-in category in the Manage box and then tapping or clicking the Go button to start the Add-in Manager. You also can start the Add-in Manager by tapping or clicking DATABASE TOOLS on the ribbon to display the DATABASE TOOLS tab and then tapping or clicking the Add-ins button.

Locking a Database

By **locking** a database, you can prevent users from viewing or modifying VBA code in your database or from making changes to the design of forms or reports while still allowing them to update records. When you lock the database, Access changes the file name extension from .accdb to .accde. To do so, you would use the Make ACCDE command shown in Figure 9–3 on page AC 543.

TO CREATE A LOCKED DATABASE (ACCDE FILE)

1 CONVERT DATABASE | 2 ANALYZE & DOCUMENT | 3 NAVIGATION PANE | 4 CUSTOM PROPERTIES & INDEXES

5 CUSTOM DATA PART | 6 CUSTOM TEMPLATE | 7 ENCRYPT LOCK & SPLIT | 8 CUSTOM WEB APP | 9 CUSTOM VIEW

To lock a database, you would use the following steps.

1. With the database open, tap or click FILE on the ribbon to open the Backstage view.
2. Tap or click the Save As tab.
3. Tap or click Make ACCDE in the Advanced area.
4. Tap or click the Save As button.
5. In the Save As dialog box, indicate a location and name for the ACCDE file.
6. Tap or click the Save button in the Save As dialog box to create the file.

Using the Locked Database

You use an ACCDE file just as you use the databases with which you now are familiar, with two exceptions. First, you must select ACCDE files in the 'Files of type' box when opening the file. Second, you will not be able to modify any source code or change the design of any forms or reports. If you pressed and held or right-clicked the Client Form, for example, you would find that the Design View command on the shortcut menu is dimmed, as are many other commands (Figure 9–73).

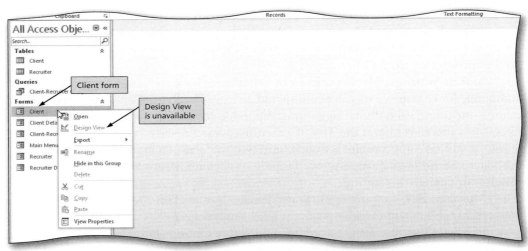

Figure 9–73

It is very important that you save your original database in case you ever need to make changes to VBA code or to the design of a form or report. You cannot use the ACCDE file to make such changes, nor can you convert the ACCDE file back to the ACCDB file format.

Record Locking

You can indicate how records are to be locked when multiple users are using a database at the same time. To do so, tap or click FILE on the ribbon, tap or click the Options tab, and then tap or click Client Settings. Scroll down so that the Advanced area appears on the screen (Figure 9–74).

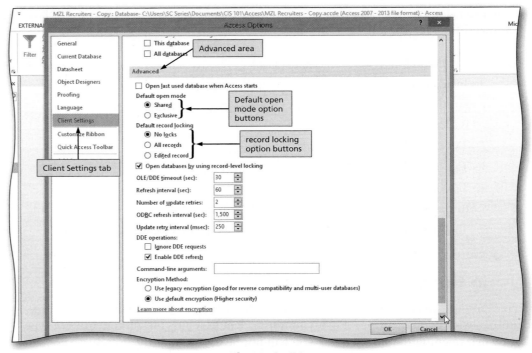

Figure 9–74

If you wanted the default open mode to be exclusive (only one user can use the database at a time) rather than shared (multiple users can simultaneously use the database), you could tap or click the Exclusive option button. You also can select the approach you want for record locking by tapping or clicking the appropriate record locking option button. The possible approaches to record locking are shown in Table 9–3.

Table 9–3 Record Locking Approaches	
Locking Type	**Description**
No locks	When you edit a record, Access will not lock the record. Thus, other users also could edit the same record at the same time. When you have finished your changes and attempt to save the record, Access will give you the option of overwriting the other user's changes (not recommended), copying your changes to the clipboard, or canceling your changes.
All records	All records will be locked as long as you have the database open. No other user can edit or lock the records during this time.
Edited record	When you edit a record, Access will lock the record. When other users attempt to edit the same record, they will not be able to do so. Instead, they will see the locked record indicator.

© 2014 Cengage Learning

Database Splitting

You can **split** a database into two databases, one called the **back-end database** containing only the table data, and another database called the **front-end database** containing the other objects. Only a single copy of the back-end database can exist, but each user could have his or her own copy of the front-end database. Each user would create the desired custom reports, forms, and other objects in his or her own front-end database, thereby not interfering with any other user.

Splitting a Database

When splitting a database, the database to be split must be open. In the process, you will identify a name and location for the back-end database that will be created by the Access splitter. In the process, you would display the Database Splitter dialog box (Figure 9–75).

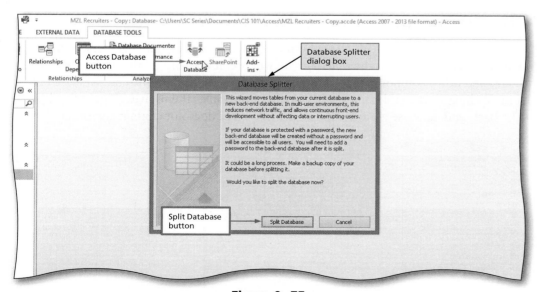

Figure 9–75

You also would have to select a location for the back-end database (Figure 9–76 on the next page). Access assigns a name to the back-end database that ends with an underscore and the letters, be. You can override this name if you prefer.

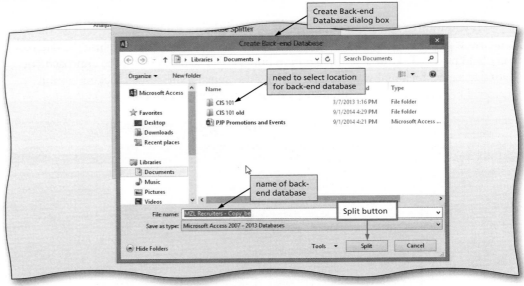

Figure 9–76

1 CONVERT DATABASE | 2 ANALYZE & DOCUMENT | 3 NAVIGATION PANE | 4 CUSTOM PROPERTIES & INDEXES
5 CUSTOM DATA PART | 6 CUSTOM TEMPLATE | 7 ENCRYPT LOCK & SPLIT | 8 CUSTOM WEB APP | 9 CUSTOM VIEW

TO SPLIT THE DATABASE

To split a database, you would use the following steps.

1. Open the database to be split.
2. Display the DATABASE TOOLS tab.
3. Tap or click the Access Database button (DATABASE TOOLS tab | Move Data group) to display the Database Splitter dialog box.
4. Tap or click the Split Database button to display the Create Back-end Database dialog box.
5. Either accept the file name Access suggests or change it to the one you want.
6. Select a location for the back-end database.
7. Tap or click the Split button to split the database.
8. Tap or click the OK button to close the dialog box reporting that the split was successful.

The Front-End and Back-End Databases

The database now has been split into separate front-end and back-end databases. The front-end database is the one that you will use; it contains all the queries, reports, forms, and other components from the original database. The front-end database only contains links to the tables, however, instead of the tables themselves (Figure 9–77). The back-end database contains the actual tables but does not contain any other objects.

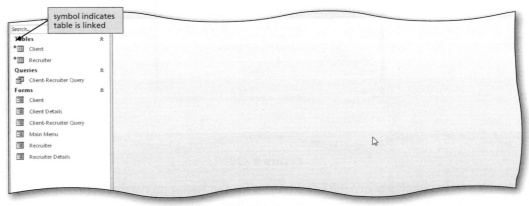

Figure 9–77

Web Apps

A **web app** is a database that you use in a web browser. You do not need to have Access installed to use the web app. You design and modify the web app using Access 2013, but users do not need Access 2013 to use the web app. To create or use a web app, you need a SharePoint server to host the web app. There are three typical ways of getting access to a SharePoint server. If your company has a SharePoint server using the full version of SharePoint 2013, you could use that. You also could purchase an Office 365 subscription plan that includes SharePoint. Finally, you could get SharePoint 2013 hosting from some other company.

Access provides a specific interface for creating web apps. When you create web apps, Access restricts some of the available database features. Tables in web apps must have AutoNumber fields as the primary key. Relationships between tables must be accomplished through lookup fields. Web apps viewed in a browser consist solely of a collection of related tables and various views of those tables. List view, which is similar to Form view, and Datasheet view are automatically included. You can define additional summary views that group data on selected fields.

BTW
Web Apps
Wep apps replace Access web databases, which were a feature of Access 2010. In Access 2013, you create web apps where the data and database objects are stored in SQL Server or a Windows Azure SQL Database.

Creating Web Apps

You can create custom web apps, in which you will indicate the specific tables and fields you want to include. Alternatively, you can select one of the web app templates. In either case, you must enter a name for your app as well as a web location for the app (Figure 9–78).

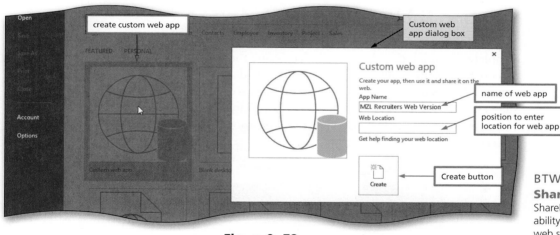

Figure 9–78

BTW
SharePoint 2013
SharePoint offers users the ability to store data on the web so that access to that data can be shared across a network. It is essentially a storage location that can be accessed collaboratively. No special software is required on the client side. SharePoint 2013 allows users to share calendars, blogs, wikis, surveys, document libraries and task lists.

TO CREATE A WEB APP   1 CONVERT DATABASE | 2 ANALYZE & DOCUMENT | 3 NAVIGATION PANE | 4 CUSTOM PROPERTIES & INDEXES
5 CUSTOM DATA PART | 6 CUSTOM TEMPLATE | 7 ENCRYPT LOCK & SPLIT | **8 CUSTOM WEB APP** | **9 CUSTOM VIEW**

To create a web app, you would use the following steps.

1. Tap or click either 'Custom web app' to create a web app of your own design or one of the web app templates to create a web app matching the template.

2. Enter a descriptive name for the web app.

3. If you see a list of available locations for the web app, you can select one of the locations. If not, or if none of the available locations is appropriate, enter the URL that points to your SharePoint site.

4. Tap or click the Create button to create the web app.

5. If requested, enter the User ID and password for your SharePoint site and click the Sign In button to finish creating the web app on your SharePoint site.

Figure 9–79 shows the result of creating a custom web app called MZL Recruiters Web Version.

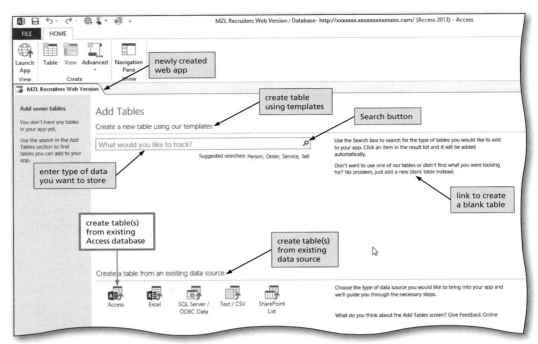

Figure 9–79

Creating Tables for the Web App

There are three ways of creating the tables for the web app. You can use a template, in which case Access will determine the fields to be included in the table. You can create a blank table and then enter the fields and data types yourself. Finally, if you have an Access database or other existing data source that contains the desired tables, such as the MZL Recruiters database, you can import the data. In importing the data, you would need to identify the name and location of the file that contains the desired data (Figure 9–80).

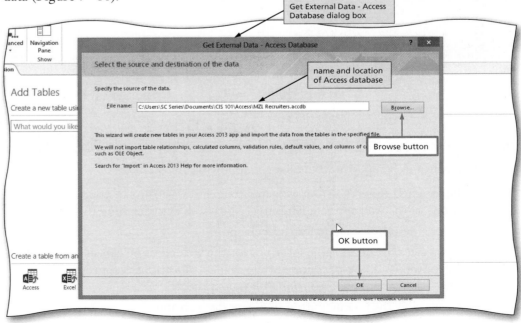

Figure 9–80

After identifying the file containing the tables, you would be presented with a list of tables in that file (Figure 9–81). You could select individual tables in the list or select all the tables by tapping or clicking the Select All button. Once you have made your selection, you would tap or click the OK button to import the data.

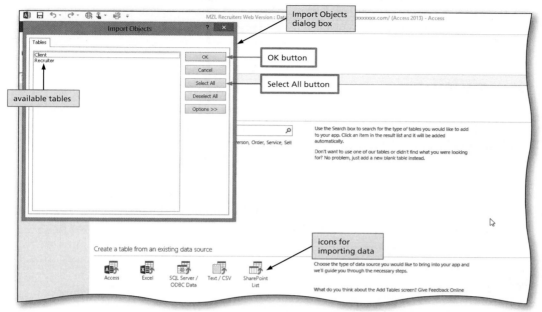

Figure 9–81

1 CONVERT DATABASE | 2 ANALYZE & DOCUMENT | 3 NAVIGATION PANE | 4 CUSTOM PROPERTIES & INDEXES
5 CUSTOM DATA PART | 6 CUSTOM TEMPLATE | 7 ENCRYPT LOCK & SPLIT | **8 CUSTOM WEB APP** | **9 CUSTOM VIEW**

TO CREATE TABLES BY IMPORTING DATA

To import data from an existing source such as an Access database, you would use the following steps.

1. Tap or click the icon for the type of data to import.
2. Browse to the location of the data to import and select the file to import.
3. Tap or click the OK button.
4. Select the tables to import. If you want to import all the tables in the data source, tap or click the Select All button.
5. Tap or click the OK button to import the data.

TO CREATE TABLES FROM TEMPLATES

Access provides templates to assist in the creation of tables. To create a table for a web app from a template, you would use the following steps.

1. Enter the type of object for which you will be storing data (for example, Customers), and tap or click the Search button.
2. When Access presents a list of options, tap or click the option that best fits your needs.

TO CREATE BLANK TABLES

You can create a blank table for the web app and then enter the names, data types, and other characteristics of the fields in Design view just as you have created other tables. To create a blank table, you would use the following step.

1. Tap or click the 'add a new blank table' link to create the table and display the table in Design view.

The Rate field has a special field size, Single, which is necessary to display decimal places. If you create the Recruiter table as a blank table in a web app, do you still have the option to change the field size to Single?

Not exactly. The possible field sizes for Number fields are slightly different when you create a web app than when you create a desktop database. The possibilities are Whole Number (no decimal places), Fixed-point number (6 decimal places), and Floating-point number (variable decimal places). If you import a table from a desktop database in which you have set the field size to Single, Access will automatically assign the field the Floating-point number field size, which is appropriate.

Using Views

Figure 9–82 shows the web app with the two tables created during the import process. The Client table currently is selected. The web app offers two views, List view and Datasheet view. List view, in which the data appears as a form, currently is selected. Figure 9–82 shows the appearance of the view, not the actual data. You will see the data when you run the app.

To make changes to the way the table appears in List view, you would tap or click the floating Edit button, which appears in the middle of the list.

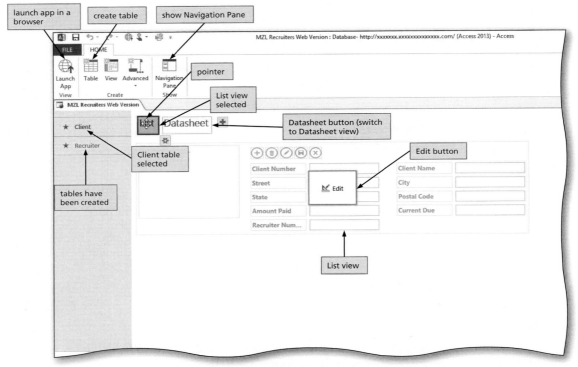

Figure 9–82

If you tap or click the Edit button, you will be able to edit the view (Figure 9–83). Editing the view allows you to change the appearance of the view, not the underlying data. The process is similar to modifying the layout of a form in either Layout or Design view. You can display a field list as shown in the figure by tapping or clicking the 'Add Existing Fields' button. You can add a field by dragging it from the field list into the desired location in the view. You can delete an existing field by tapping or clicking the field, and then pressing the DELETE key. You can move fields within the list by dragging them to the desired location. You also can tap or click a field and then tap or click the Formatting button to display the FORMATTING menu. Using that menu, you can display a tooltip for the field, choose whether the field is visible, or choose whether the field is enabled.

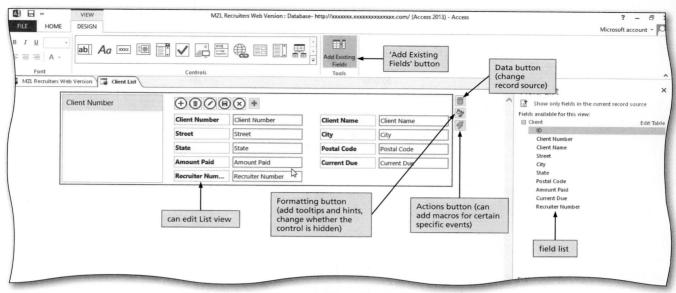

Figure 9–83

If you tap or click the Datasheet view button for the same table, you will see the Datasheet view for the table, which is similar to viewing the normal Datasheet view you see when working with a desktop database (Figure 9–84).

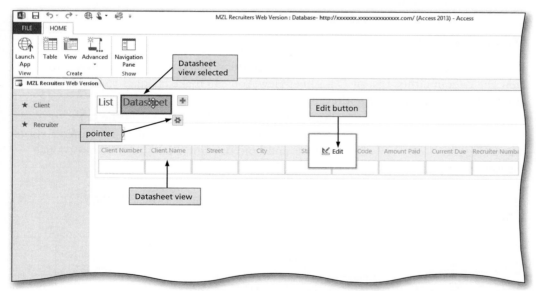

Figure 9–84

Just as with List view, you can tap or click the floating Edit button to be able to edit the view (Figure 9–85 on the next page). You can then use the same techniques as when editing List view to make any desired changes.

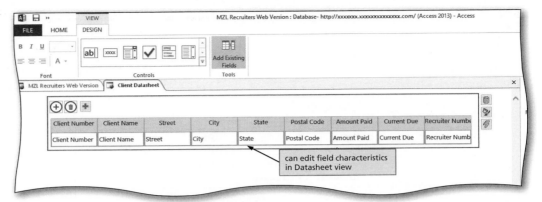

Figure 9–85

TO EDIT VIEWS

To edit a view, you would use the following steps.

1. Tap or click the table whose view you want to edit.

2. Tap or click the view to edit.

3. Tap or click the Edit button.

4. When finished editing, tap or click the Close button for the view you are editing.

5. Tap or click the Yes button to save your changes. Tap or click the No button if you do not want to save your changes.

Viewing Data

When you later run the app, you will see the actual data in the database. You can view the data in either List or Datasheet view. You can make changes to the data, which are immediately available to other users.

You also can view the data from within Access. To do so, select the table you want to view and tap or click the Settings/Action button to display the Settings/Action menu (Figure 9–86). You also can press and hold or right-click the table to produce the same menu.

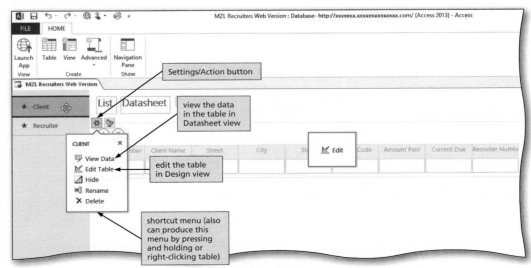

Figure 9–86

If you tap or click View Data on the Settings/Action menu, you will see the data in Datasheet view (Figure 9–87). You can both view and change the data.

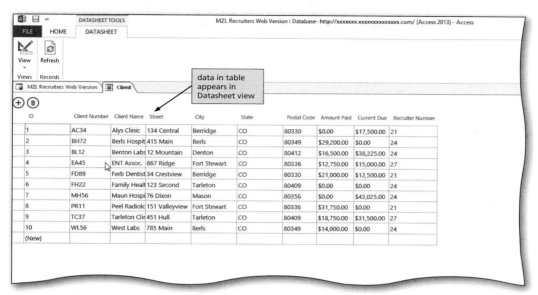

Figure 9–87

TO VIEW DATA

To view or update the data in a table from Access, you would use the following steps.

1. Tap or click the table containing the data you want to view or update.
2. Tap or click the Settings/Action button.
3. Tap or click View Data on the Settings/Action menu.

You also can modify the design of a table using the Settings/Action button. To do so, you would tap or click Edit Table rather than View Data. You then would see the table displayed in Design view (Figure 9–88). You can make changes to the table design similar to how you updated other tables in Design view.

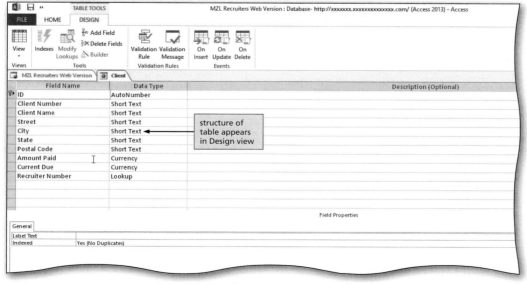

Figure 9–88

TO CHANGE THE DESIGN OF A TABLE

To view or modify the design of a table, you would use the following steps.

1. Tap or click the table whose design you want to view or update.
2. Tap or click the Settings/Action button.
3. Tap or click Edit Table on the Settings/Action menu.

CONSIDER THIS

What is the purpose of the other commands on the Settings/Action menu?

If you select Hide, the selected table will not appear when you run the app. If you hide a table, you can later select Unhide, in which case it will once again appear. You can rename a table by selecting Rename and delete the table by selecting Delete.

Creating an Additional View

You can create additional views that then are included in the app. To do so, tap or click the 'Add New View' button (Figure 9–89) to display the ADD NEW VIEW dialog box. You also can tap or click the View button (HOME tab | Create group) to display the dialog box. Figure 9–89 also shows the list of available view types. The available types are List Details (List view), Datasheet, Summary, and Blank. You already have seen List and Datasheet views. You will see how to create a Summary view later in this chapter. A Blank view allows you to create a view from scratch, similar to using a blank form.

In the ADD NEW VIEW dialog box, you enter a name for the view, select the View Type, and then select the record source. The record source can be either a table or a query.

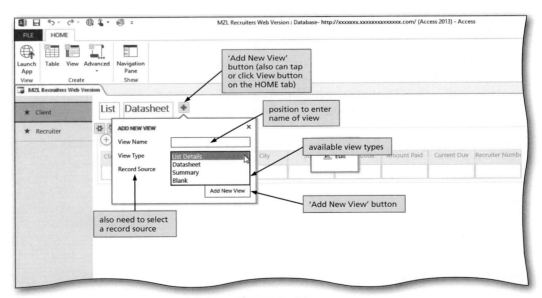

Figure 9–89

TO CREATE AN ADDITIONAL VIEW

To create an additional view, you would use the following steps.

1. Tap or click the 'Add New View' button.
2. Enter a name for the view.
3. Tap or click the View Type arrow to display the menu of available view types.

4. Tap or click the desired view type.

5. Tap or click the Record Source arrow to display a list of the available tables and queries.

6. Tap or click the desired table or query.

7. Tap or click the 'Add New View' button to create the new view.

Creating Additional Objects

You can create tables by tapping or clicking the Table button (HOME tab | Create group). You then will see the same screen you saw earlier (Figure 9–79 on page AC 592). You then have the same three options for creating tables: You can create the table using a template, create a blank table, or import a table from an existing data source.

You can create other objects, such as queries, by tapping or clicking the Advanced button (HOME tab | Create group) to produce the Advanced menu (Figure 9–90). The Advanced menu gives you options for creating queries, blank views, blank List views, blank Datasheet views, and various types of macros.

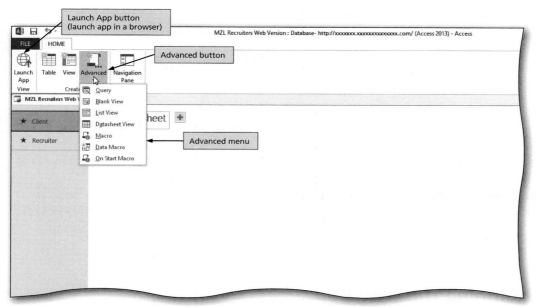

Figure 9–90

To use any of the blank views, you can place fields in the view by dragging the field from a field list, just as you have done in previous chapters with forms and reports. Creating macros uses the same process you have seen earlier. However, creating macros in the web app does limit some of the available options. Creating a query in the web app also is similar to the process you used to create queries earlier; the design grid used in the web app is similar to that used in Access (Figure 9–91 on the next page). As with macros, creating queries in the web app limits some of the options, but the options that are present function in the manner you expect. Once you have created a query, you can use it as the record source for a view.

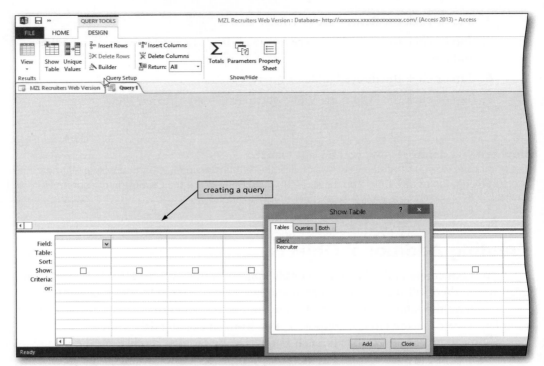

Figure 9-91

TO CREATE ADDITIONAL OBJECTS

To create an additional object, you would use the following steps.

1. To create a table, tap or click the Table button (HOME tab | Create group), and then indicate whether you will create the table using a template, create a blank table, or import a table from an existing data source.

2. To create another type of object, tap or click the Advanced button (HOME tab | Create group) to display the Advanced menu, and then select the type of object to create.

How can you see the additional objects you have created?

You can only see them in the Navigation Pane. To display the Navigation Pane, tap or click the Navigation Pane button (HOME tab | Show group).

CONSIDER THIS

Running the Web App

You run the web app in a browser. You can do so from Access by tapping or clicking the Launch App button (HOME tab | View group). You then will see the web app in your browser (Figure 9–92). On the left side of the screen, you see the list of tables in the app. At anytime, one of the tables will be selected. In the figure, the Client table is currently selected.

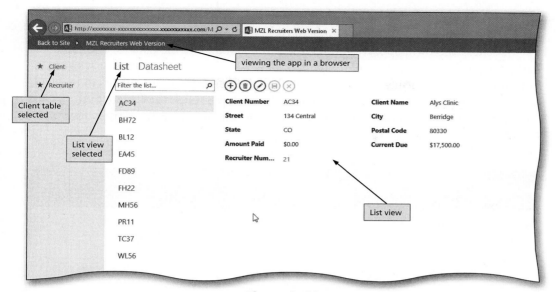

Figure 9–92

Is Launch the same as Run?

Yes. They are different words for the same operation.

CONSIDER THIS

The available views for the selected table are displayed at the top of the screen. There are currently two views, List view and Datasheet view. List view is currently selected. The list view for the table as well as a list of key values, in this case, client numbers, are displayed in the center area of the screen.

TO RUN AN APP FROM ACCESS

1 CONVERT DATABASE | **2** ANALYZE & DOCUMENT | **3** NAVIGATION PANE | **4** CUSTOM PROPERTIES & INDEXES
5 CUSTOM DATA PART | **6** CUSTOM TEMPLATE | **7** ENCRYPT LOCK & SPLIT | **8** CUSTOM WEB APP | **9** CUSTOM VIEW

To run an app from Access, the app must be open. Assuming it is, you would use the following step to run the app.

1. Click the Launch App button (HOME tab | View group) to run the app.

To display a table in Datasheet view, first be sure the desired table is selected. Next, tap or click the Datasheet link. The table will appear in Datasheet view (Figure 9–93).

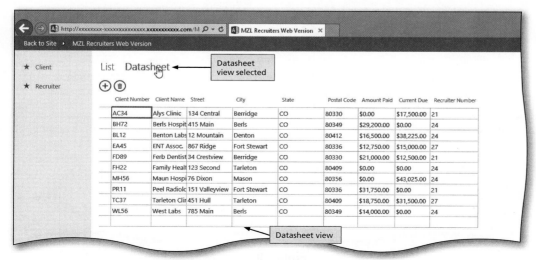

Figure 9–93

If you tap or click the List link, the table again will appear in List view (Figure 9–94). You can tap or click one of the client numbers on the left and the data for that client then will appear on the screen. You can update the data for the client currently on the screen, add a new client, or delete a client. To do so, tap or click the button for the desired action. If you tap or click the Add button, the form will be blank and you can type the data for the new client. If you tap or click the Delete button, you will be asked to confirm the deletion. If you do, the client currently on the screen will be deleted.

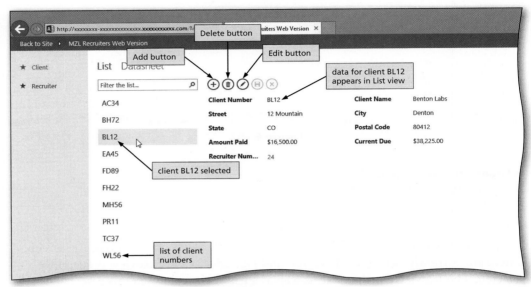

Figure 9–94

If you tap or click the Edit button, the buttons change slightly (Figure 9–95). The Add, Delete, and Edit buttons are dimmed whereas the Save and Cancel buttons are not. After making a change, such as the change of the state as shown in the figure, you can tap or click the Save button to save the change or the Cancel button to cancel the change.

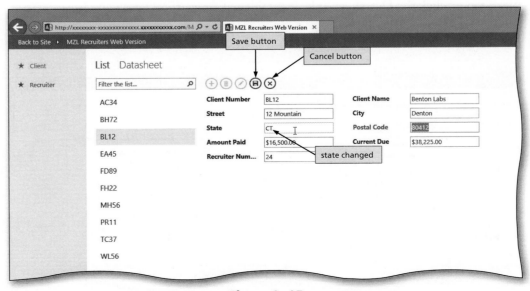

Figure 9–95

You also can update data in Datasheet view. To add a record, tap or click the Add button and type the contents of the new record. To delete a record, tap or click anywhere in the record, tap or click the Delete button, and then confirm the deletion. To edit a record, tap or click in the field to be changed and make the desired change.

TO UPDATE DATA USING A WEB APP

To update data using a web app, you would use the following steps after running the app.

1. Tap or click the table to be updated.

2. Tap or click either the List link to select List view or the Datasheet link to select Datasheet view.

3. To add a record in Datasheet view, tap or click the Add button, enter the contents of the record, and press the TAB key after entering the final field. To add in List view, tap or click the Add button, enter the contents of the record, and tap or click the Save button.

4. To delete a record in either view, select the record to be deleted, click the Delete button, and then confirm the deletion.

5. To edit a record in Datasheet view, tap or click the field to be changed and make the necessary change. As soon as you leave the record, the change will automatically be saved. To edit a record in List view, select the record to be edited, tap or click the Edit button, make the change, and then tap or click the Save button.

Showing a Relationship in List View

If you view the "one" table in a one-to-many relationship in List view, you will see the corresponding records in the "many" table appear in a datasheet. Figure 9–96 shows the Recruiter table appearing in List view. The data for the selected recruiter appears in List view. The clients of the selected recruiter appear in a datasheet just below the data for the recruiter. Note that this is the only way to see the relationship. Viewing the "one" table in Datasheet view will not show the relationship, nor will viewing the "many" table in either view.

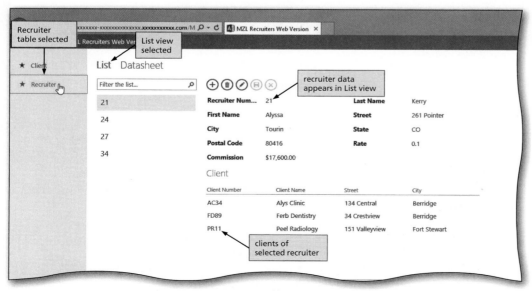

Figure 9–96

Running a Web App from a Browser

To run a web app, you navigate to your SharePoint site and simply run the app. You do not have to run Access, open the app, and then run the app. It is not even necessary to have Access on your computer. You can run the app directly from your browser.

1 CONVERT DATABASE | 2 ANALYZE & DOCUMENT | 3 NAVIGATION PANE | 4 CUSTOM PROPERTIES & INDEXES

5 CUSTOM DATA PART | 6 CUSTOM TEMPLATE | 7 ENCRYPT LOCK & SPLIT | **8 CUSTOM WEB APP** | **9 CUSTOM VIEW**

To Run a Web App from a Browser

To run a web app from a browser, you would use the following steps.

1. Type the URL for your SharePoint site and press ENTER.
2. When requested, type your user name and password.
3. Tap or click the OK button to display the contents of your SharePoint site.
4. Tap or click the desired web app to run the app.

Customizing a Web App

You can customize a web app from within Access. If you are running the app in a browser, you launch Access by tapping or clicking the Settings button to display the 'Customize in Access' command (Figure 9–97) and then tapping or clicking the 'Customize in Access' command.

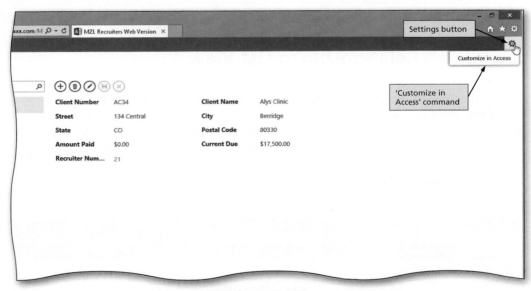

Figure 9–97

1 CONVERT DATABASE | 2 ANALYZE & DOCUMENT | 3 NAVIGATION PANE | 4 CUSTOM PROPERTIES & INDEXES

5 CUSTOM DATA PART | 6 CUSTOM TEMPLATE | 7 ENCRYPT LOCK & SPLIT | 8 CUSTOM WEB APP | **9 CUSTOM VIEW**

To Customize a Web App

To customize a web app that you are running in a browser, you would use the following steps.

1. Tap or click the Settings button.
2. Tap or click the 'Customize in Access' command.

Adding a Summary View

One of the ways you can customize a web app is to add an additional view, such as a Summary view. After selecting the table for which you want to add the view, you use the 'Add New View' button to select Summary as the view type and select the record source table (Figure 9–98).

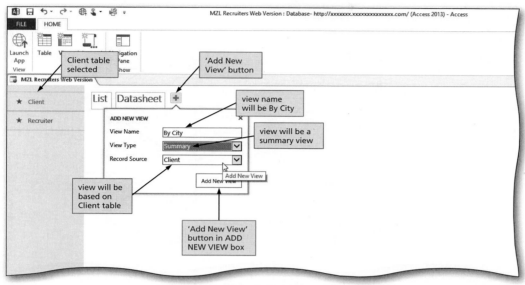

Figure 9–98

Tapping or clicking the 'Add New View' button in the ADD NEW VIEW dialog box again creates the view. You can edit the view using the EDIT button. Then, you can use the Data button to display the DATA box, where you indicate Group By field, Sort Order, Calculation Field, and Calculation Type (Figure 9–99).

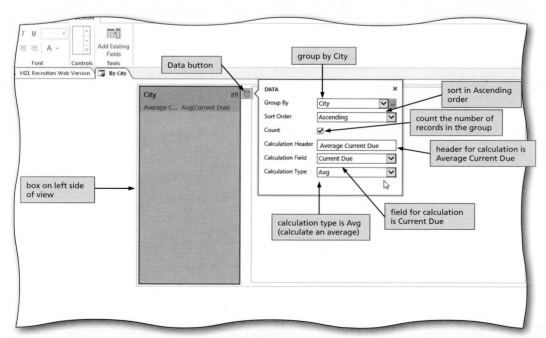

Figure 9–99

By tapping or clicking the box on the right and then tapping or clicking the Data button, you can enter up to four fields to be displayed and optionally display captions for the fields. Specifying the popup view determines the view that will appear as a popup when the user taps or clicks a specific record and will give additional information about that record. The final step is to enter the sort order (Figure 9–100).

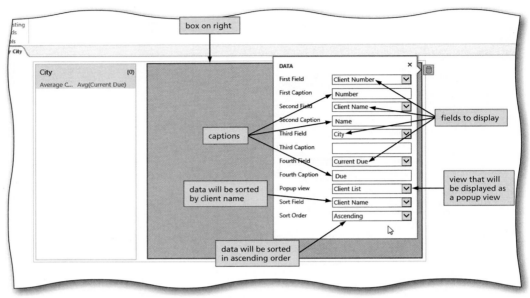

Figure 9–100

After closing the view and saving the changes, you can run the app by tapping or clicking the Launch App button, being sure the appropriate table is selected. You tap or click the new view to test the view, and then close the view (Figure 9–101).

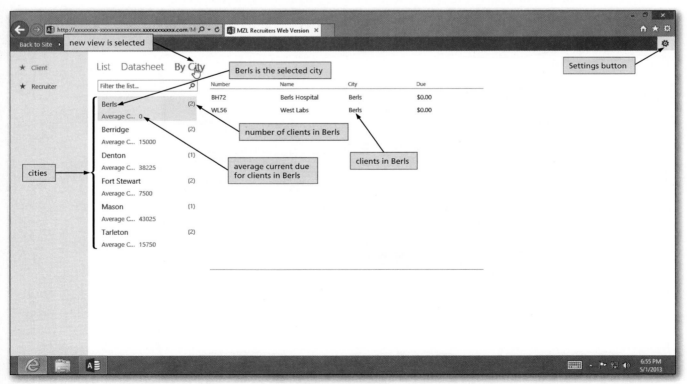

Figure 9–101

If you select another value in the left-hand column, all the corresponding records will now appear in the right column (Figure 9–102).

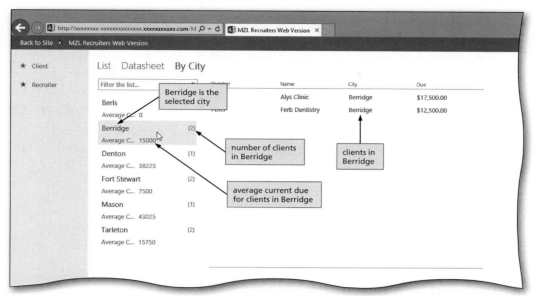

Figure 9–102

Select one of the records in the group to display details concerning that record in a popup view (Figure 9–103).

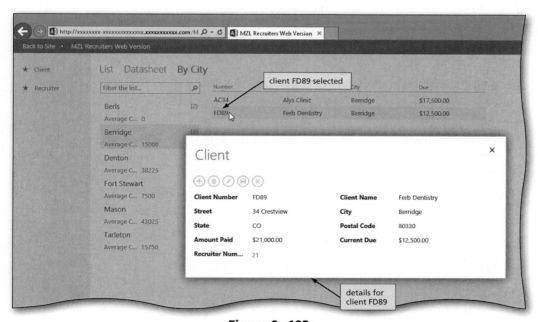

Figure 9–103

TO CREATE A SUMMARY VIEW

1 CONVERT DATABASE | 2 ANALYZE & DOCUMENT | 3 NAVIGATION PANE | 4 CUSTOM PROPERTIES & INDEXES

5 CUSTOM DATA PART | 6 CUSTOM TEMPLATE | 7 ENCRYPT LOCK & SPLIT | 8 CUSTOM WEB APP | 9 CUSTOM VIEW

To create a Summary view, you would use the following steps.

1. Tap or click the table for which you want to add the view and then tap or click the 'Add New View' button to display the ADD NEW VIEW box.

2. Enter a name for the view, select Summary as the view type, and select the table that will be the record source.

3. Tap or click the 'Add New View' button (ADD NEW VIEW dialog box) to create the view.

4. Tap or click the Edit button to edit the view.

5. Tap or click the box on the left side of the view and then tap or click the Data button to display the DATA box.

6. Enter the Group By field, sort order, whether you want a count displayed, the header for the calculation, the field for the calculation, and the calculation type (average or sum).

7. Close the DATA box, tap or click the box on the right, and then tap or click its Data button.

8. Enter up to four fields to be displayed. You can optionally enter captions for any of the fields.

9. Enter the popup view.

10. Enter the sort order.

11. Close the view and tap or click the Yes button when asked if you want to save your changes.

To Sign Out of a Microsoft Account

If you are signed in to a Microsoft account and are using a public computer or otherwise wish to sign out of your Microsoft account, you should sign out of the account from the Account gallery in the Backstage view before exiting Access. Signing out of the account is the safest way to make sure that nobody else can access SkyDrive files or settings stored in your Microsoft account. The following steps sign out of a Microsoft account from Access. For a detailed example of the procedure summarized below, refer to the Office and Windows chapter at the beginning of this book.

1 If you wish to sign out of your Microsoft account, tap or click FILE on the ribbon to open the Backstage view and then tap or click the Account tab to display the Account gallery.

2 Tap or click the Sign out link, which displays the Remove Account dialog box. If a Can't remove Windows accounts dialog box appears instead of the Remove Account dialog box, click the OK button and skip the remaining steps.

Q&A Why does a Can't remove Windows accounts dialog box appear?
If you signed in to Windows using your Microsoft account, then you also must sign out from Windows, rather than signing out from within Access. When you are finished using Windows, be sure to sign out at that time.

3 Tap or click the Yes button (Remove Account dialog box) to sign out of your Microsoft account on this computer.

Q&A Should I sign out of Windows after signing out of my Microsoft account?
When you are finished using the computer, you should sign out of your account for maximum security.

4 Tap or click the Back button in the upper-left corner of the Backstage view to return to the database.

To Exit Access

The following steps exit Access.

1 Tap or click the Close button on the right side of the title bar to exit Access.

2 If a Microsoft Access dialog box appears, tap or click the Yes button to save any changes made to the object since the last save.

Chapter Summary

In this chapter you have learned to convert Access databases to and from earlier versions; use Microsoft Access tools to analyze and document an Access database; add custom categories and groups to the Navigation Pane; use table and database properties; use field properties to create a custom input mask; allow zero-length strings; create indexes; use automatic error checking; create custom data parts; create and use templates and application parts; encrypt a database and set a password; understand the Trust Center; lock a database; split a database; create and run a web app; customize a web app. The following list includes all the new Access skills you have learned in this chapter.

Data Parts
Create Custom Data Parts (AC 563)

Database, Creation for Template
Create a Desktop Database (AC 566)
Add Fields to the Table (AC 566)
Create a Second Table (AC 568)
Create Datasheet Forms (AC 573)
Create a Navigation Form (AC 575)
Select a Startup Form (AC 576)

Database Conversion
Convert an Access 2007-2013 Database to an Earlier Version (AC 543)
Convert an Access 2000 or 2002-2003 Database to an Access 2013 Database (AC 543)

Database Tools
Use the Table Analyzer (AC 544)
Use the Performance Analyzer (AC 546)
Use the Database Documenter (AC 547)

Encryption
Open a Database in Exclusive Mode (AC 583)
Encrypt a Database with a Password (AC 585)
Decrypt the Database and Remove the Password (AC 586)

Groups
Create Custom Categories and Groups (AC 549)
Add Items to Groups (AC 551)

Indexes
Create a Single-Field Index (AC 559)
Create a Multiple-Field Index (AC 560)

Objects in Web Apps
Edit Views (AC 596)
View Data (AC 597)
Change the Design of a Table (AC 598)
Create an Additional View (AC 598)
Create Additional Objects (AC 600)
Create a Summary View (AC 607)

Properties
Create Custom Properties (AC 554)
Create a Custom Input Mask (AC 557)
Allow Zero Length (AC 557)
Enable Error Checking (AC 561)

Special Database Operations
Create a Locked Database (ACCDE File) (AC 587)
Split the Database (AC 590)

Templates
Create a Template and Application Part (AC 578)
Use the Template (AC 579)
Use the Application Part (AC 581)

Validation
Create a Validation Rule for a Table (AC 553)

Web Apps
Create a Web App (AC 591)
Create Tables by Importing Data (AC 593)
Create Tables from Templates (AC 593)
Create Blank Tables (AC 593)
Run an App from Access (AC 601)
Update Data Using a Web App (AC 603)
Run a Web App from a Browser (AC 604)
Customize a Web App (AC 604)

What decisions will you need to make when administering your own databases?

Use these guidelines as you complete the assignments in this chapter and administer your own databases outside of this class.

1. **Determine whether a database needs to able to be shared over the web.**

   a. Do you have users who would profit from being able to access a database over the web? If so, you will need to create a web app, which requires you to have access to a SharePoint server.

   b. Determine the tables that should be in the web app.

   c. Determine the views of the tables that should be included in the web app.

2. **Determine whether you should create any templates, application parts, or data type parts.**

   a. Is there a particular combination of tables, queries, forms, reports, and/or macros that you would like to enable users to easily include in their databases? If so, you could create a template and an application part containing the specific objects you want them to be able to include.

   b. Is there a particular collection of fields that you would like to enable users to include in a table with a single click? If so, you could create a data type part containing those fields.

3. **Determine whether a database needs to be converted to or from an earlier version.**

   a. Do users of a previous version of Access need to be able to use the database? If so, you will need to be sure the database does not contain any features that would prevent it from being converted.

   b. Do you use a database that was created in an earlier version of Access that you would like to use in Access 2013? If so, you can convert the database for use in Access 2013.

4. **Determine when to analyze and/or document the database.**

   a. Once you create a database, you should use the table and performance analyzers to determine if any changes to the structure are warranted.

   b. You also should document the database.

5. **Determine the most useful way to customize the Navigation Pane.**

   a. Would it be helpful to have custom categories and groups?

   b. What objects should be in the groups?

   c. Would it be helpful to restrict the objects that appear to only those whose names contain certain characters?

6. **Determine any table-wide validation rules.**

   a. Are there any validation rules that involve more than a single field?

7. **Determine any custom database properties.**

   a. Are there properties that would be helpful in documenting the database and are not included in the list of database properties you can use?

8. **Determine indexes.**

   a. Examine retrieval and sorting requirements to determine possible indexes. Indexes can make both retrieval and sorting more efficient.

9. **Determine whether the database should be encrypted.**

   a. If you need to protect the security of the database's contents, you strongly should consider encryption.

   b. As part of the process, you also will set a password.

10. **Determine whether the database should be locked.**

    a. Should users be able to change the design of forms, reports, and/or macros?

11. **Determine whether the database should be split.**

    a. It is often more efficient to split the database into a back-end database, which contains only the table data, and a front-end database, which contains other objects, such as queries, forms, and reports.

How should you submit solutions to questions in the assignments identified with a ✳ symbol?

Every assignment in this book contains one or more questions identified with a ✳ symbol. These questions require you to think beyond the assigned database. Present your solutions to the questions in the format required by your instructor. Possible formats may include one or more of these options: write the answer; create a document that contains the answer; present your answer to the class; discuss your answer in a group; record the answer as audio or video using a webcam, smartphone, or portable media player; or post answers on a blog, wiki, or website.

Apply Your Knowledge

Reinforce the skills and apply the concepts you learned in this chapter.

Administering the Natural Products Database

Note: To complete this assignment, you will be required to use the Data Files for Students. Visit www.cengage.com/ct/student download for detailed instructions or contact your instructor for information about accessing the required files.

Instructions: Start Access. Open the Apply Natural Products database that you modified in Chapter 8. If you did not use this database, contact your instructor for information about accessing the required database.

Perform the following tasks:

1. Open the Customer table in Design view and create an index that allows duplicates on the Customer Name field. Zero-length strings should not be allowed in the Customer Name field.

2. Create a custom input mask for the Customer Number field. The first two characters of the customer number must be uppercase letters and the last two characters must be numerical digits.

3. Create an index on the combination of Customer Type and Amount Paid. Name the index TypePaid.

4. Save the changes to the Customer table.

5. Use the Database Documenter to produce detailed documentation for the Customer Orders table. Export the documentation to a Word RTF file. (*Hint*: See the Q&A on page AC 548.) Change the name of the file to LastName_Documentation.rtf where LastName is your last name.

6. Use the Table Analyzer to analyze the table structure of the Customer table. Open the rtf file that you created in Step 5 and record the results of the analysis at the end of the file.

7. Use the Performance Analyzer to analyze all the tables in the database. Report the results of your analysis in your rtf file.

8. Populate the Status property for the database with the value Apply Natural Products.

9. If requested to do so by your instructor, populate the Status property with your first and last name.

10. Create a custom property with the name, Due Date. Use Date as the type and enter the current date as the value.

11. Submit the revised Apply Natural Products database and the rtf file in the format specified by your instructor.

12. ✹ Can you convert the Apply Natural Products to an Access 2002-2003 database? Why or Why not?

Extend Your Knowledge

Extend the skills you learned in this chapter and experiment with new skills. You may need to use Help to complete the assignment.

Note: To complete this assignment, you will be required to use the Data Files for Students. Visit www.cengage.com/ct/studentdownload for detailed instructions or contact your instructor for information about accessing the required files.

Instructions: Start Access. Open the Extend Reuse Restore database. The Extend Reuse Restore database contains information about a used furnishings store owned and operated by college students.

Continued >

Extend Your Knowledge *continued*

Perform the following tasks:

1. Change the Current Database options to ensure that the Main Menu opens automatically.

2. Currently, when you open the Items table in Datasheet view, the table is ordered by Item Number. Change the property for the table so the table is in order by Description. (*Hint*: See the BTW on page AC 559).

3. Customize the Navigation Pane by adding a custom category called Reuse Store. Then add two custom groups, Current and Reduced, to the Reuse Store category.

4. Add the Item Master Form and Available Items Report to the Current group. Add the Item Sale Report, the Reduced Price Report, and the Seller and Items Query to the Reduced group.

5. Add the Address Quick Start field to the Seller table. Move the Phone Number field so that it follows the Country Region field. Save the changes to the table.

6. If requested to do so by your instructor, add a table description to the Seller table that includes your first and last name.

7. Submit the revised database in the format specified by your instructor.

8. ✻ What advantages are there to listing items by Description rather than by Item Number?

Analyze, Correct, Improve

Analyze a database, correct all errors, and improve the design.

Correcting Table Design Errors

Note: To complete this assignment, you will be required to use the Data Files for Students. Visit www.cengage.com/ct/studentdownload for detailed instructions or contact your instructor for information about accessing the required files.

Instructions: Start Access and open the Analyze Maintenance database. The database contains data about a local business that provides maintenance and repairs.

Perform the following tasks:

1. Correct   The owner created an input mask for the Customer Number, which is shown in Figure 9–104. The input mask does not work correctly. It allows a user to input a customer number that does not include letters. The customer number must be two uppercase letters followed by two numbers. (*Hint*: There are two reasons that the input mask does not work.) The owner also added the index shown in Figure 9–104 but she gets an error message when she tries to save the table. Create the input mask and the index correctly. If requested to do so by your instructor, change the first and last name for the worker with Worker Number 102 to your first and last name.

2. Improve   One of the employees for the company has agreed to help maintain the database on his own time, but he only has Access 2003. Save the database in the 2002-2003 format as Analyze Maintenance_02_03 so the employee can use it.

3. ✻ What were the two input mask errors in this database?

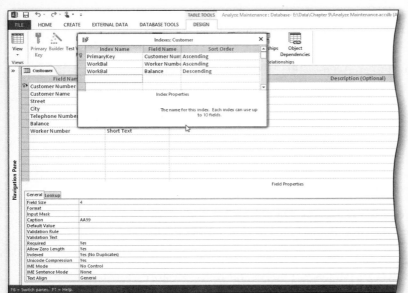

Figure 9–104

In the Labs

Design, create, modify, and/or use a database following the guidelines, concepts, and skills presented in this chapter. Labs are listed in order of increasing difficulty. Labs 1 and 2, which increase in difficulty, require you to create solutions based on what you learned in the chapter; Lab 3 requires you to create a solution, which uses cloud and web technologies, by learning and investigating on your own from general guidance.

Lab 1: Administering the Technology Services Database

Note: To complete this assignment, you will be required to use the Data Files for Students. Visit www.cengage.com/ct/studentdownload for detailed instructions or contact your instructor for information about accessing the required files.

Problem: Technology Services has determined a number of database administration tasks that need to be done. These include creating indexes and custom input masks, adding table and database properties, creating a template, and splitting a database.

Instructions: Perform the following tasks:

1. Start Access and open the Lab 1 Technology Services database you modified in Chapter 8. If you did not use this database, contact your instructor for information about accessing the required database.

2. Open the Service Requests table in Datasheet view and add the Quick Start Status field to the end of the table. In Datasheet view, assign the value Not Started to all requests where the Hours Spent is 0. Assign the value In Progress to all other requests. You do not need to use a query.

3. Open the Service Requests table in Design view and create a validation rule that ensures that the value in the Hours Spent field is less than or equal to the value in the Total Hours field.

4. Open the Client table in Design view and create custom input masks for the following fields: Client Number, State, Postal Code, and Service Rep Number. The Client Number field should consist of three uppercase letters followed by two numbers. The State field should contain two uppercase letters. Both the Postal Code and Service Rep Number fields only can contain numbers.

5. Create an index on the Client Name field that allows duplicates.

6. Change the options to ensure that the Main Menu form is displayed automatically when a user opens the database.

7. Save the Lab 1 Technology Services database as a template with data but not as an application part. Create a new database from the Lab 1 Technology Services template. Name the database Lab 1 Technology New. Split the Lab 1 Technology New database.

8. If requested to do so by your instructor, open the front-end database, open the Forms List in Layout view, and add a title with your first and last name.

9. Submit the revised databases in the format specified by your instructor.

10. ✺ In this exercise, you split a database into a front-end and a back-end. Why would you split a database?

Lab 2: Administering the Team Designs Database

Problem: Team Designs has determined a number of database administration tasks that need to be done. These include creating indexes and custom input masks, adding table and database properties, and creating a locked database.

Note: To complete this assignment, you will be required to use the Data Files for Students. Visit www.cengage.com/ct/studentdownload for detailed instructions or contact your instructor for information about accessing the required files.

Continued >

In the Labs *continued*

Instructions: Perform the following tasks:

1. Start Access and open the Lab 2 Team Designs database you modified in Chapter 8. If you did not use this database, contact your instructor for information about accessing the required database.

2. Open the Item table in Design view and add a validation rule that ensures that the wholesale price always is less than the base cost of an item. Include validation text.

3. Create an index on the combination of item type and description. Name the index TypeDesc.

4. Do not allow zero-length strings for the Description field.

5. Create custom input masks for the Item Number and the Supplier Code fields.

6. Save the changes to the table design.

7. In Datasheet view, add the Address Quick Start field to the Supplier table following the Supplier Name field. Delete the Attachments field.

8. If requested to do so by your instructor, change the Supplier Name for Supplier Code LM to your last name and change the phone to your phone number.

9. Rename the Main Menu form object in the Navigation Pane as Team Designs Menu.

10. Change the Current Database options to ensure that the Team Designs Menu opens automatically.

11. Create a locked database.

12. Submit the revised database and the locked database in the format specified by your instructor.

13. ✹ Why would you lock a database?

Lab 3: Expand Your World: Cloud and Web Technologies Sharing Access Databases

Problem: There are many ways to share an Access database. Some ways require each user to have Microsoft Access installed on their computer, while others do not. The method you select depends on factors such as need and available resources.

Instructions: Perform the following tasks:

1. Create a blog, a Google document, or a Word document on the SkyDrive on which to store your findings.

2. Use the web to search for different ways to share an Access database, such as Bavant Publishing, with others. Be sure to note any specific resources needed, such as an Access database or a SharePoint server, and provide examples of different reasons for sharing a database such as Bavant Publishing. Record your findings in your blog, Google document, or Word document, being sure to appropriately reference your sources.

3. Save your Bavant Publishing database to the SkyDrive. What happens when you open your database on the SkyDrive?

4. Submit the assignment in the format specified by your instructor.

5. ✹ Based on your research, what method would you choose to share your Access databases?

Consider This: Your Turn

Apply your creative thinking and problem solving skills to design and implement a solution.

1: Creating a Template for the Fine Crafts Database
Personal/Academic

Note: To complete this assignment, you will be required to use the Data Files for Students. Visit www.cengage.com/ct/studentdownload for detailed instructions or contact your instructor for information about accessing the required files.

Part 1: Your instructor has asked you to create a template from your database and then create a database that could be used as the basis for a web app. Open the Your Turn 1 Fine Crafts database you used in Chapter 8. If you did not use this database, contact your instructor for information about accessing the required database. Use the concepts and techniques presented in this chapter to perform each of the following tasks:

a. Create a Quick Start data type that includes all fields in the Item table except Total Value and Student Code. Save the data type as Basic Item Data.

b. Create a Quick Start data type that includes all fields in the Student table except the Picture and Biography fields. Save the data type as Basic Student Data.

c. Create a new desktop database named Students and Crafts.

d. Create a Student table using the Basic Student Data Quick Start data type. Student Code should be both required and unique. ID is the first field in the table.

e. Create an Item table using the Basic Item Data Quick Start data type. Item Number should be both required and unique. ID is the first field in the table. Add the Student Code field to the Item table as a Lookup & Relationship data type. Be sure to enable data integrity.

f. Import the Student.txt file into the Student table and the Item.txt table into the Item table. Because there is a relationship between the Student table and the Item table; be sure to import the Student table first.

g. Create a query that joins the Student and Item tables. Include the Student Code, First Name, Last Name, Item Number, Description, Price, and On Hand fields. Save the query as Students and Items.

h. Create single-item forms for the Student and Item tables. Name these forms Student Details and Item Details.

i. Create datasheet forms for the Student and Item tables. Include an On Click macro in each form that opens the respective Details form.

j. Create a datasheet form for the Students and Items query.

k. Create a navigation form similar to the one shown in Figure 9–59 on page AC 578. Include the datasheet forms and the detail forms.

l. Create a template and an application part for this database. Name the template Students and Crafts and include data in the template.

m. Create a new database named First Name Last Name Crafts where First Name and Last Name are your first and last name using the template you created in Step l.

n. If you have access to SharePoint and you have your instructor's permission, create a web app using the database you created in Step m.

Submit your assignment in the format specified by your instructor.

Part 2: ✺ You made several decisions while completing this assignment. What was the rationale behind your decisions?

2: Administering the Landscaping Services Database

Professional

Note: To complete this assignment, you will be required to use the Data Files for Students. Visit www.cengage.com/ct/studentdownload for detailed instructions or contact your instructor for information about accessing the required files.

Part 1: The owner of the landscaping company has asked you to perform a number of administration tasks. Open the Your Turn 2 Landscaping Services database you used in Chapter 8. If you did not use this database, contact your instructor for information about accessing the required database. Use the concepts and techniques presented in this chapter to perform each of the following tasks.

a. Change the Current Database options to ensure that the Main Menu opens automatically.

b. Open the Customer table in Design view and add custom input masks for the Customer Number and Postal Code fields. Create an index for the Customer Name field that allows duplicates. Do not allow zero-length strings for the Customer Name field.

Continued >

Consider This: Your Turn *continued*

   c. Open the Supervisor table in Design view and create an index named LastFirst on the last name and the first name.

   d. Open the Customer Requests table in Design view and create a validation rule to ensure that Hours Spent are less than or equal to Total Hours.

   e. Open the Customer Requests table in Datasheet view and add the Quick Start Priority field to the table. Assign a High priority to requests for customers B10 and S11. Assign a Low priority to the request for customer T16. All other requests have a Normal priority.

   f. Populate the Editor custom database property with your first and last name.

   g. Use the 1 Right Blank Forms application part to create a form for the Service Requests table. Include all fields except Priority on the form. Change the title and the name of the form to Service Requests.

Submit your assignment in the format specified by your instructor.

Part 2: ☀ You made several decisions while completing this project, including using an application part to create a form. What was the rationale behind your decisions? Would you use an application part to create another form? Why or why not?

3: Understanding Database Administration Tasks
Research and Collaboration

Part 1: Before you begin this assignment, save the Bavant Publishing database as your team name database. For example, if your team is the Fab Four, then name the database Fab Four. Use the re-named database for this assignment. For each of the tasks listed below, perform the task and record the outcome. Create a blog, a Google document, or a Word document on the SkyDrive on which to store the team's results and observations for this assignment.

   a. Create an earlier version of the database (Access 2003 or previous version).

   b. Use the Table Analyzer on every table in the database.

   c. Use the Performance Analyzer on all database objects.

   d. Encrypt the database and set a password.

   e. Decrypt the database.

   f. Change macro settings.

   g. Change privacy options.

   h. Determine which add-ins are available for Access.

   i. Change error checking options.

Submit your assignment in the format specified by your instructor.

Part 2: ☀ You made several decisions while completing this assignment. What was the rationale behind your decisions? Were you able to create an earlier version of the database? Why or why not?

Learn Online

Reinforce what you learned in this chapter with games, exercises, training, and many other online activities and resources.

Student Companion Site Reinforcement activities and resources are available at no additional cost on www.cengagebrain.com. Visit www.cengage.com/ct/studentdownload for detailed instructions about accessing the resources available at the Student Companion Site.

SAM Put your skills into practice with SAM Projects! SAM Projects for this chapter can be found online. If you have a SAM account, go to www.cengage.com/sam2013 to access SAM assignments for this chapter.

10 | Using SQL

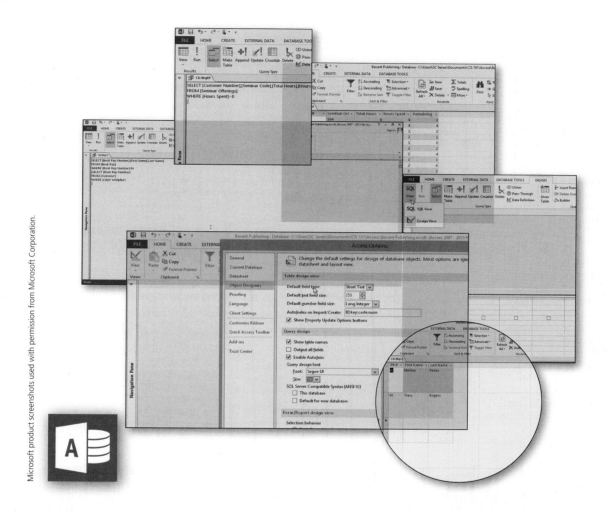

Microsoft product screenshots used with permission from Microsoft Corporation.

Objectives

You will have mastered the material in this project when you can:

- Understand the SQL language and how to use it
- Change the font or font size for queries
- Create SQL queries
- Include fields in SQL queries
- Include simple and compound criteria in SQL queries
- Use computed fields and built-in functions in SQL queries

- Sort the results in SQL queries
- Use aggregate functions in SQL queries
- Group the results in SQL queries
- Join tables in SQL queries
- Use subqueries
- Compare SQL queries with Access-generated SQL
- Use INSERT, UPDATE, and DELETE queries to update a database

10 | Using SQL

Introduction

BTW

Q&As

For a complete list of the Q&As found in many of the step-by-step sequences in this book, visit the Q&A resource on the Student Companion Site located on www.cengagebrain.com. For detailed instructions about accessing available resources, visit www.cengage.com/ct/studentdownload or contact your instructor for information about accessing the required files.

The language called **SQL (Structured Query Language)** is a very important language for querying and updating databases. It is the closest thing to a universal database language, because the vast majority of database management systems, including Access, use it in some fashion. Although some users will be able to do all their queries through the query features of Access without ever using SQL, those in charge of administering and maintaining the database system should be familiar with this important language. You also can use Access as an interface to other database management systems, such as SQL Server. Using or interfacing with SQL Server requires knowledge of SQL. Virtually every DBMS supports SQL.

Project — Using SQL

Bavant Publishing wants to be able to use the extended data management capabilities available through SQL. As part of becoming familiar with SQL, Bavant would like to create a wide variety of SQL queries.

BTW

BTWs

For a complete list of the BTWs found in the margins of this book, visit the BTW resource on the Student Companion Site located on www.cengagebrain.com. For detailed instructions about accessing available resources, visit www.cengage.com/ct/studentdownload or contact your instructor for information about accessing the required files.

Similar to creating queries in Design view, SQL provides a way of querying relational databases. In SQL, however, instead of making entries in the design grid, you type commands into SQL view to obtain the desired results, as shown in Figure 10–1a. You then can click the View button to view the results just as when you are creating queries in Design view. The results for the query in Figure 10–1a are shown in Figure 10–1b.

Figure 10–1 (a) Query in SQL

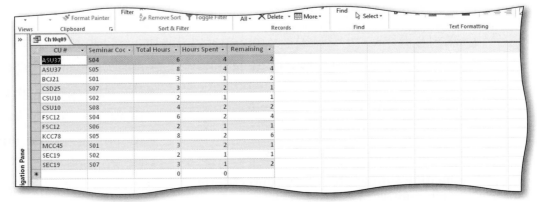

Figure 10–1 (b) Results

Roadmap

In this chapter, you will learn how to create and use SQL queries like the one shown in Figure 10–1. The following roadmap identifies general activities you will perform as you progress through this chapter:

1. Create a query in SQL VIEW
2. Use SIMPLE CRITERIA in a query
3. Use COMPOUND CRITERIA in a query
4. SORT RESULTS of a query
5. GROUP RESULTS of a query
6. JOIN TABLES in a query
7. USE a SUBQUERY in a query
8. UPDATE DATA with a query

At the beginning of step instructions throughout the chapter, you will see an abbreviated form of this roadmap. The abbreviated roadmap uses colors to indicate chapter progress: gray means the chapter is beyond that activity; blue means the task being shown is covered in that activity, and black means that activity is yet to be covered. For example, the following abbreviated roadmap indicates the chapter would be showing a task in the 3 COMPOUND CRITERIA activity.

1 SQL VIEW | 2 SIMPLE CRITERIA | 3 COMPOUND CRITERIA | 4 SORT RESULTS
5 GROUP RESULTS | 6 JOIN TABLES | 7 USE SUBQUERY | 8 UPDATE DATA

Use the abbreviated roadmap as a progress guide while you read or step through the instructions in this chapter.

To Run Access

If you are using a computer to step through the project in this chapter and you want your screens to match the figures in this book, you should change your screen's resolution to 1366 × 768. For information about how to change a computer's resolution, refer to the Office and Windows chapter at the beginning of this book.

The following steps, which assume Windows is running, use the Start screen or the search box to run Access based on a typical installation. You may need to ask your instructor how to run Access on your computer. For a detailed example of the procedure summarized below, refer to the Office and Windows chapter.

1 Scroll the Start screen for an Access 2013 tile. If your Start screen contains an Access 2013 tile, tap or click it to run Access; if the Start screen does not contain the Access 2013 tile, proceed to the next step to search for the Access app.

2 Swipe in from the right edge of the screen or point to the upper-right corner of the screen to display the Charms bar and then tap or click the Search charm on the Charms bar to display the Search menu.

3 Type `Access` as the search text in the Search text box and watch the search results appear in the Apps list.

4 Tap or click Access 2013 in the search results to run Access.

To Open a Database from Access

The following steps open the Bavant Publishing database from the location you specified when you first created it (for example, the Access folder in the CIS 101 folder). For a detailed example of the procedure summarized below, refer to the Office and Windows chapter at the beginning of this book.

1 Tap or click FILE on the ribbon to open the Backstage view, if necessary.

2 If the database you want to open is displayed in the Recent list, tap or click the file name to open the database and display the opened database in the Access window; then skip to Step 7. If the database you want to open is not displayed in the Recent list or if the Recent list does not appear, tap or click Open Other Files to display the Open Gallery.

3 If the database you want to open is displayed in the Recent list in the Open gallery, tap or click the file name to open the database and display the opened database in the Access window; then skip to Step 7.

4 Tap or click Computer, SkyDrive, or another location in the left pane and then navigate to the location of the database to be opened (for example, the Access folder in the CIS 101 folder).

5 Tap or click Bavant Publishing to select the database to be opened.

6 Tap or click the Open button (Open dialog box) to open the selected file and display the opened database in the Access window.

7 If a Security Warning appears, tap or click the 'Enable Content' button.

SQL Background

In this chapter, you query and update a database using the language called **SQL (Structured Query Language)**. Similar to using the design grid in the Access Query window, SQL provides users with the capability of querying a relational database. Because SQL is a language, however, you must enter **commands** to obtain the desired results, rather than completing entries in the design grid. SQL uses commands to update tables and to retrieve data from tables. The commands that are used to retrieve data are usually called **queries**.

SQL was developed under the name SEQUEL at the IBM San Jose research facilities as the data manipulation language for IBM's prototype relational model DBMS, System R, in the mid-1970s. In 1980, it was renamed SQL to avoid confusion with an unrelated hardware product called SEQUEL. Most relational DBMSs, including Microsoft Access and Microsoft SQL Server, use a version of SQL as a data manipulation language.

Some people pronounce SQL by pronouncing the three letters, that is, "ess-que-ell." It is very common, however to pronounce it as the name under which it was developed originally, that is, "sequel."

To Change the Font Size

You can change the font and/or the font size for queries using the Options button in the Backstage view and then Object Designers in the list of options in the Access Options dialog box. There usually is not a compelling reason to change the font, unless there is a strong preference for some other font. It often is worthwhile to change the font size, however. ***Why?*** *With the default size of 8, the queries can be hard to read. Increasing the font size to 10 can make a big difference.* The following steps change the font size for queries to 10.

- Tap or click FILE on the ribbon to open the Backstage view.

- Tap or click Options to display the Access Options dialog box.

- Tap or click Object Designers to display the Object Designer options.

- In the Query design area, tap or click the Size box arrow, and then tap or click 10 in the list to change the size to 10 (Figure 10–2).

- Tap or click the OK button to close the Access Options dialog box.

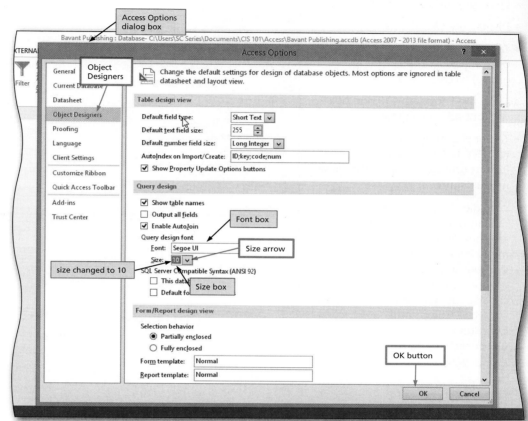

Figure 10–2

SQL Queries

When you query a database using SQL, you type commands in a blank window rather than filling in the design grid. When the command is complete, you can view your results just as you do with queries you create using the design grid.

BTW

Touch and Pointers
Remember that if you are using your finger on a touch screen, you will not see the pointer.

To Create a New SQL Query

You begin the creation of a new **SQL query**, which is a query expressed using the SQL language, just as you begin the creation of any other query in Access. The only difference is that you will use SQL view instead of Design view. *Why? SQL view enables you to type SQL commands rather than making entries in the design grid.* The following steps create a new SQL query.

1

- Close the Navigation Pane.

- Display the CREATE tab.

- Tap or click the Query Design button (CREATE tab | Queries group) to create a query.

- Close the Show Table dialog box without adding any tables.

- Tap or click the View arrow (QUERY TOOLS DESIGN tab | Results group) to display the View menu (Figure 10–3).

 Why did the icon on the View button change to SQL, and why are there only two items on the menu instead of the usual five? Without any tables selected, you cannot view any results. You only can use the normal Design view or SQL view. The change in the icon indicates that you could simply tap or click the button to transfer to SQL view.

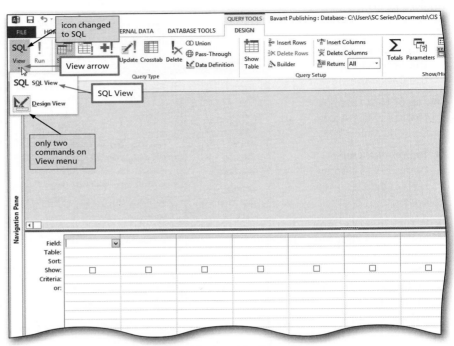

Figure 10–3

2

- Tap or click SQL View on the View menu to view the query in SQL view (Figure 10–4).

 What happened to the design grid?
In SQL view, you specify the queries by typing SQL commands rather than making entries in the design grid.

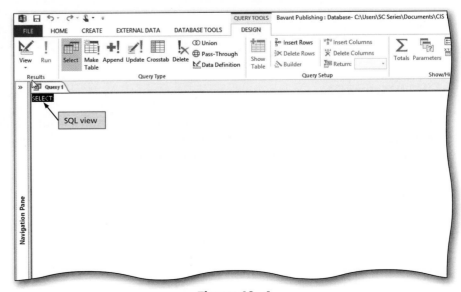

Figure 10–4

SQL Commands

The basic form of SQL expressions is quite simple: SELECT-FROM-WHERE. The command begins with a **SELECT clause**, which consists of the word, SELECT, followed by a list of those fields you want to include. The fields will appear in the results in the order in which they are listed in the expression. Next, the command contains a **FROM clause**, which consists of the word, FROM, followed by a list of the table or tables involved in the query. Finally, there is an optional **WHERE clause**, which consists of the word, WHERE, followed by any criteria that the data you want to retrieve must satisfy. The command ends with a semicolon (;), which in this text will appear on a separate line.

SQL has no special format rules for placement of terms, capitalization, and so on. One common style is to place the word FROM on a new line, and then place the word WHERE, when it is used, on the next line. This style makes the commands easier to read. It also is common to show words that are part of the SQL language in uppercase and others in a combination of uppercase and lowercase. Because it is a common convention, and necessary in some versions of SQL, you will place a semicolon (;) at the end of each command.

Microsoft Access has its own version of SQL that, unlike some other versions of SQL, allows spaces within field names and table names. There is a restriction, however, to the way such names are used in SQL queries. When a name containing a space appears in SQL, it must be enclosed in square brackets. For example, Customer Number must appear as [Customer Number] because the name includes a space. On the other hand, City does not need to be enclosed in square brackets because its name does not include a space. For consistency, all names in this text are enclosed in square brackets. Thus, the City field would appear as [City] even though the brackets technically are not required by SQL.

BTW

Context-Sensitive Help in SQL
When you are working in SQL view, you can obtain context-sensitive help on any of the keywords in your query. To do so, tap or click anywhere in the word about which you wish to obtain help and press F1.

BTW

Entering Field Names
Be sure to enclose field names in square brackets. If you accidentally use parentheses or curly braces, Access will display a syntax error (missing operator) message.

To Include Only Certain Fields

1 SQL VIEW | 2 SIMPLE CRITERIA | 3 COMPOUND CRITERIA | 4 SORT RESULTS
5 GROUP RESULTS | 6 JOIN TABLES | 7 USE SUBQUERY | 8 UPDATE DATA

To include only certain fields in a query, list them after the word, SELECT. If you want to list all rows in the table, you do not include the word, WHERE. *Why? If there is no WHERE clause, there is no criterion restricting which rows appear in the results. In that case, all rows will appear.* The steps on the next page create a query for Bavant Publishing that will list the number, name, amount paid, and current due amount of all customers.

1

- Type **SELECT [Customer Number],[Customer Name],[Amount Paid],[Current Due]** as the first line of the command, and then press the ENTER key.

Q&A
What is the purpose of the SELECT clause?
The SELECT clause indicates the fields that are to be included in the query results. This SELECT clause, for example, indicates that the Customer Number, Customer Name, Amount Paid, and Current Due fields are to be included.

- Type **FROM [Customer]** as the second line to specify the source table, press the ENTER key, and then type a semicolon (**;**) on the third line.

Q&A
What is the purpose of the FROM clause?
The FROM clause indicates the table or tables that contain the fields used in the query. This FROM clause indicates that all the fields in this query come from the Customer table.

- Tap or click the View button (QUERY TOOLS DESIGN tab | Results group) to view the results (Figure 10–5).

Q&A
My screen displays a dialog box that asks me to enter a parameter value. What did I do wrong?
You typed a field name incorrectly. Tap or click Cancel to close the dialog box and then correct your SQL statement.

Why does CU # appear as the column heading for the Customer Number field?
This is the caption for the field. If the field has a special caption defined, Access will use the caption rather than the field name. You will learn how to change this later in this chapter.

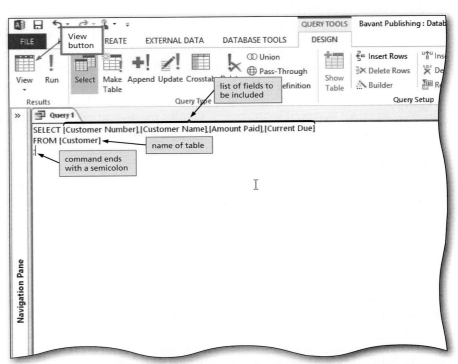

Figure 10–5 (a) Query to List the Customer Number, Customer Name, Amount Paid, and Current Due for All Customers

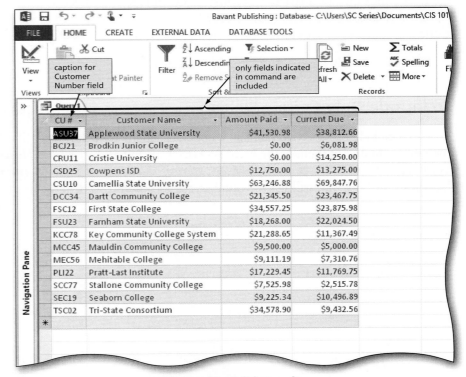

Figure 10–5 (b) Results

2

- Tap or click the Save button on the Quick Access Toolbar, type **Ch10q01** as the name in the Save As dialog box, and tap or click the OK button to save the query as Ch10q01.

To Prepare to Enter a New SQL Query

1 SQL VIEW | 2 SIMPLE CRITERIA | 3 COMPOUND CRITERIA | 4 SORT RESULTS
5 GROUP RESULTS | 6 JOIN TABLES | 7 USE SUBQUERY | 8 UPDATE DATA

To enter a new SQL query, you could close the window, tap or click the No button when asked if you want to save your changes, and then begin the process from scratch. A quicker alternative is to use the View menu and then select SQL View. ***Why?*** *You will be returned to SQL view with the current command appearing. At that point, you could erase the current command and then enter a new one. If the next command is similar to the previous one, however, it often is simpler to modify the current command instead of erasing it and starting over.* The following step shows how to prepare to enter a new SQL query.

1

- Tap or click the View arrow (HOME tab | Views group) to display the View menu (Figure 10–6).
- Tap or click SQL View to return to SQL view.

Q&A Could I just tap or click the View button, or do I have to tap or click the arrow?
Because the icon on the button is not the icon for SQL view, you must tap or click the arrow.

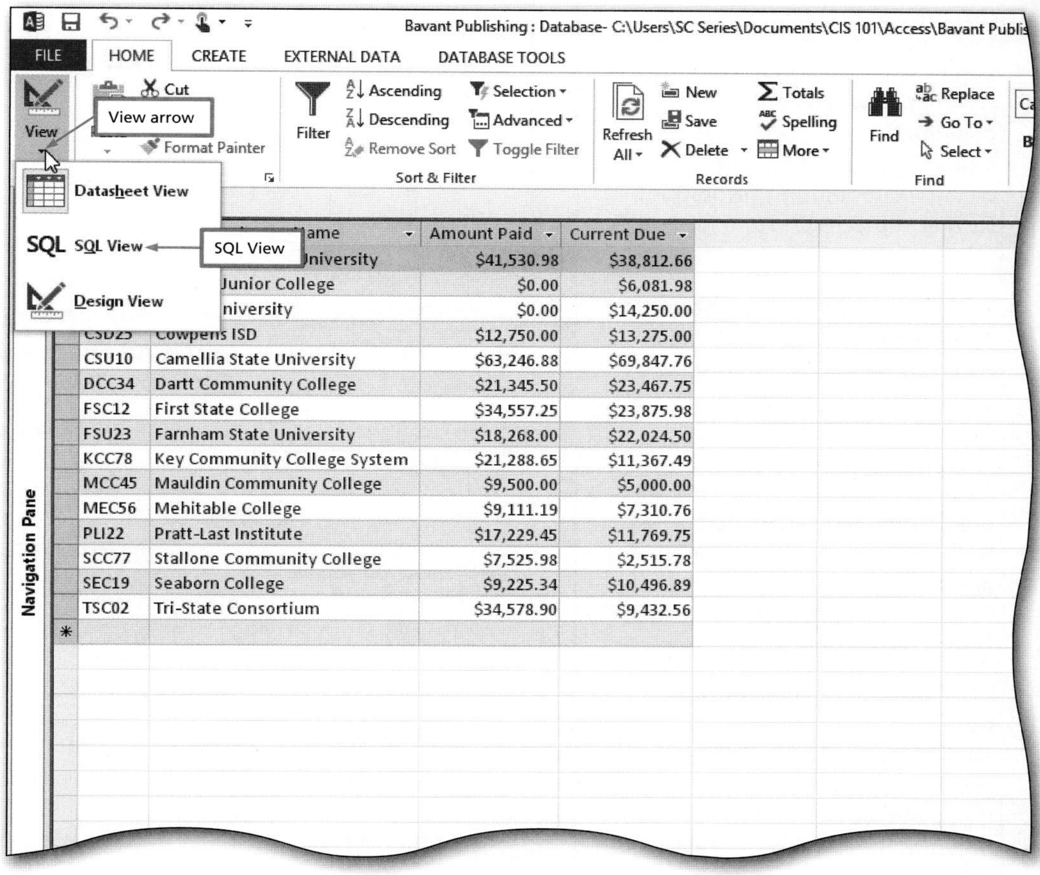

Figure 10–6

To Include All Fields

1 SQL VIEW | 2 SIMPLE CRITERIA | 3 COMPOUND CRITERIA | 4 SORT RESULTS
5 GROUP RESULTS | 6 JOIN TABLES | 7 USE SUBQUERY | 8 UPDATE DATA

To include all fields, you could use the same approach as in the previous steps, that is, list each field in the Customer table after the word, SELECT. There is a shortcut, however. Instead of listing all the field names after SELECT, you can use the asterisk (*) symbol. ***Why?*** *Just as when working in the design grid, the asterisk symbol represents all fields.* This indicates that you want all fields listed in the order in which you described them to the system during data definition. The steps on the next page list all fields and all records in the Customer table.

1

- Delete the current command, type **SELECT *** as the first line of the command, and then press the ENTER key.

- Type **FROM [Customer]** as the second line, press the ENTER key, and type a semicolon (**;**) on the third line.

- View the results (Figure 10–7).

Can I use copy and paste commands when I enter SQL commands?

Yes, you can use copy and paste as well as other editing techniques, such as replacing text.

2

- Tap or click FILE on the ribbon to open the Backstage view, tap or click the Save As tab to display the Save As gallery, tap or click Save Object As in the File Types area, then tap or click the Save As button to display the Save As dialog box, type **Ch10q02** as the name for the saved query, and tap or click the OK button to save the query as Ch10q02 and return to the query.

Can I just tap or click the Save button on the Quick Access Toolbar as I did when I saved the previous query?

If you did, you would replace the previous query with the version you just created. Because you want to save both the previous query and the new one, you need to save the new version with a different name. To do so, you must use Save Object As, which is available through the Backstage view.

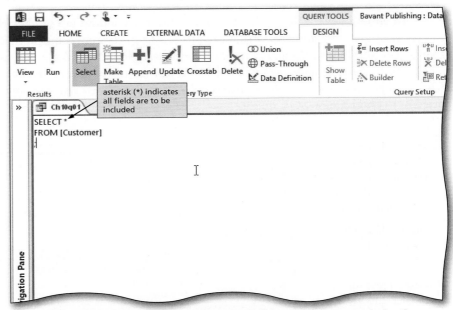

Figure 10–7 (a) Query to List All Fields and All Records in the Customer Table

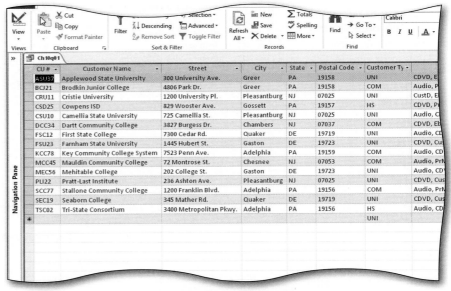

Figure 10–7 (b) Results

To Use a Criterion Involving a Numeric Field

To restrict the records to be displayed, include the word WHERE followed by a criterion as part of the command. If the field involved is a numeric field, you simply type the value. In typing the number, you do not type commas or dollar signs. *Why? If you enter a dollar sign, Access assumes you are entering text. If you enter a comma, Access considers the criterion invalid.* The following steps create a query to list the customer number and name of all customers whose returns amount is $0.00.

- Return to SQL view and delete the current command.

- Type `SELECT [Customer Number],[Customer Name]` as the first line of the command.

- Type `FROM [Customer]` as the second line.

- Type `WHERE [Returns]=0` as the third line, and then type a semicolon (;) on the fourth line.

Q&A | What is the purpose of the WHERE clause?
The WHERE clause restricts the rows to be included in the results to only those that satisfy the criteria included in the clause. With this WHERE clause, for example, only those rows on which Returns is equal to 0 will be included.

- View the results (Figure 10–8).

Q&A | On my screen, the customers are listed in a different order. Did I do something wrong?
No. The order in which records appear in a query result is random unless you specifically order the records. You will see how to order records later in this chapter.

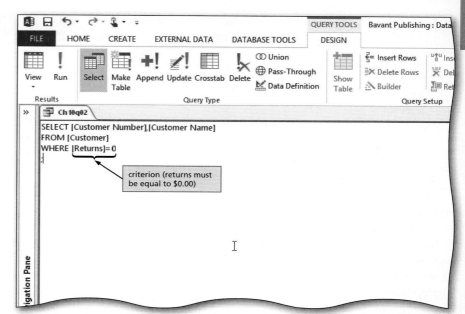

Figure 10–8 (a) Query to List the Customer Number and Customer Name for Those Customers Where Returns is Equal to 0

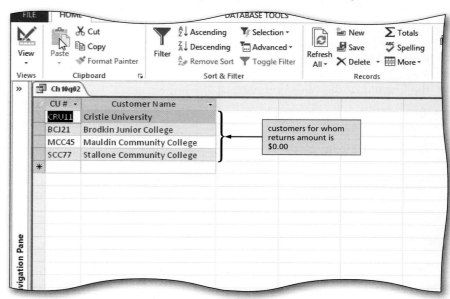

Figure 10–8 (b) Results

2

- Save the query as Ch10q03.

BTW
SQL Standards
The International Standards Organization (ISO) and the American National Standards Institute (ANSI) recognize SQL as a standardized language. Different relational database management systems may support the entire set of standardized SQL commands or only a subset.

Simple Criteria

The criterion following the word WHERE in the preceding query is called a simple criterion. A **simple criterion** has the form: field name, comparison operator, then either another field name or a value. The possible comparison operators are shown in Table 10–1.

Table 10–1 Comparison Operators	
Comparison Operator	**Meaning**
=	equal to
<	less than
>	greater than
<=	less than or equal to
>=	greater than or equal to
<>	not equal to

© 2014 Cengage Learning

To Use a Comparison Operator

**1 SQL VIEW | 2 SIMPLE CRITERIA | 3 COMPOUND CRITERIA | 4 SORT RESULTS
5 GROUP RESULTS | 6 JOIN TABLES | 7 USE SUBQUERY | 8 UPDATE DATA**

In the following steps, Bavant Publishing uses a comparison operator to list the customer number, customer name, amount paid, and current due for all customers whose amount paid is greater than $20,000. *Why? A comparison operator allows you to compare the value in a field with a specific value or with the value in another field.*

- Return to SQL view and delete the current command.

- Type `SELECT [Customer Number],[Customer Name],[Amount Paid],[Current Due]` as the first line of the command.

- Type `FROM [Customer]` as the second line.

- Type `WHERE [Amount Paid]>20000` as the third line, and then type a semicolon (`;`) on the fourth line.

- View the results (Figure 10–9).

- Save the query as Ch10q04.

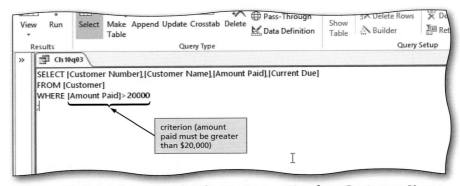

Figure 10–9 (a) Query to List the Customer Number, Customer Name, Amount Paid, and Current Due for Those Customers Where Amount Paid is Greater than $20,000

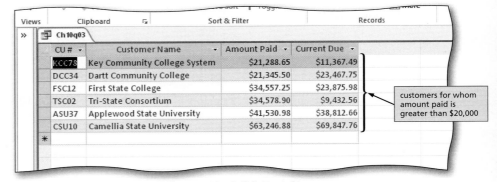

Figure 10–9 (b) Results

To Use a Criterion Involving a Text Field

If the criterion involves a text field, the value must be enclosed in quotation marks. *Why? Unlike when you work in the design grid, Access will not insert the quotation marks around text data for you in SQL view. You need to include them.* The following example lists the customer number and name of all of Bavant Publishing's customers located in Adelphia, that is, all customers for whom the value in the City field is Adelphia.

- Return to SQL view, delete the current command, and type `SELECT [Customer Number],[Customer Name]` as the first line of the command.

- Type `FROM [Customer]` as the second line.

- Type `WHERE [City]='Adelphia'` as the third line and type a semicolon (;) on the fourth line.

- View the results (Figure 10–10).

Q&A Could I enclose the text field value in double quotation marks instead of single quotation marks?
Yes. It is usually easier, however, to use single quotes when entering SQL commands.

2

- Save the query as Ch10q05.

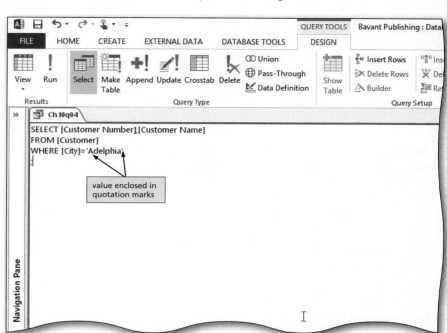

Figure 10–10 (a) Query to List the Customer Number and Customer Name for Those Customers Whose City is Adelphia

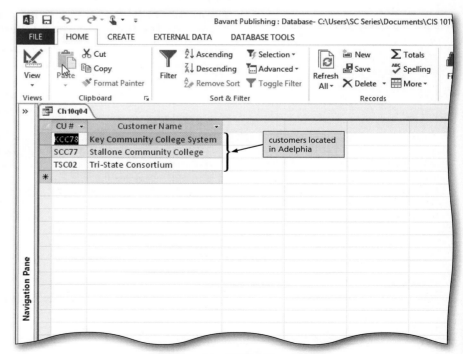

Figure 10–10 (b) Results

To Use a Wildcard

In most cases, the conditions in WHERE clauses involve exact matches, such as retrieving rows for each customer located in the city of Adelphia. In some cases, however, exact matches do not work. *Why? You might only know that the desired value contains a certain collection of characters.* In such cases, you use the LIKE operator with a wildcard symbol.

Rather than testing for equality, the LIKE operator uses one or more wildcard characters to test for a pattern match. One common wildcard in Access, the **asterisk** (*), represents any collection of characters. Thus, G* represents the letter, G, followed by any string of characters. Another wildcard symbol is the question mark (?), which represents any individual character. Thus T?m represents the letter, T, followed by any single character, followed by the letter, m, such as in Tim or Tom.

The following steps use a wildcard to display the customer number and name for every customer of Bavant Publishing whose city begins with the letter, G.

- Return to SQL view, delete the previous query, and type `SELECT [Customer Number],[Customer Name],[City]` as the first line of the command.
- Type `FROM [Customer]` as the second line.
- Type `WHERE [City] LIKE 'G*'` as the third line and type a semicolon (;) on the fourth line.
- View the results (Figure 10–11).

2
- Save the query as Ch10q06.

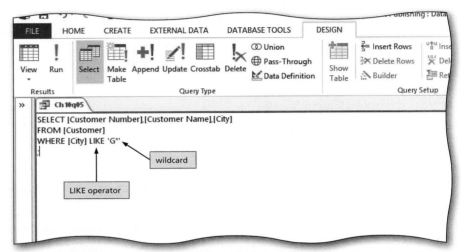

Figure 10–11 (a) Query to List the Customer Number, Customer Name, and City for Those Customers Whose City Begins with the Letter G

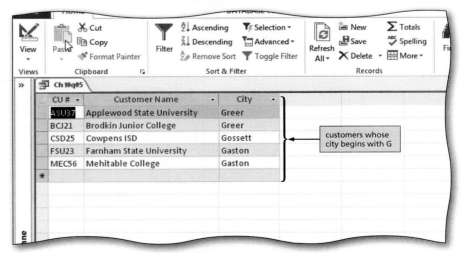

Figure 10–11 (b) Results

Break Point: If you wish to stop working through the chapter at this point, you can close Access now. You can resume the project later by starting Access, opening the database called Bavant Publishing, creating a new query in SQL view, and continuing to follow the steps from this location forward.

Compound Criteria

You are not limited to simple criteria in SQL. You also can use compound criteria. **Compound criteria** are formed by connecting two or more simple criteria using AND, OR, and NOT. When simple criteria are connected by the word AND, all the simple criteria must be true in order for the compound criterion to be true. When simple criteria are connected by the word OR, the compound criterion will be true whenever any of the simple criteria are true. Preceding a criterion by the word NOT reverses the truth or falsity of the original criterion. That is, if the original criterion is true, the new criterion will be false; if the original criterion is false, the new one will be true.

BTW
Wildcards
Other implementations of SQL do not use the asterisk (*) and question mark (?) wildcards. In SQL for Oracle and for SQL Server, the percent sign (%) is used as a wildcard to represent any collection of characters. In Oracle and SQL Server, the WHERE clause shown in Figure 10–11 on page AC 630 would be WHERE [City] LIKE `G%'.

To Use a Compound Criterion Involving AND

1 SQL VIEW | 2 SIMPLE CRITERIA | 3 COMPOUND CRITERIA | 4 SORT RESULTS
5 GROUP RESULTS | 6 JOIN TABLES | 7 USE SUBQUERY | 8 UPDATE DATA

The following steps use a compound criterion. **Why?** *A compound criterion allows you to impose multiple conditions.* In particular, the steps enable Bavant to display the number and name of those customers located in Greer who have a returns amount of $0.00.

- Return to SQL view, delete the previous query, and type `SELECT [Customer Number],[Customer Name]` as the first line of the command.

- Type `FROM [Customer]` as the second line.

- Type `WHERE [City]='Greer'` as the third line.

- Type `AND [Returns]=0` as the fourth line and type a semicolon (**;**) on the fifth line.

Q&A What is the purpose of the AND clause?
The AND clause indicates that there are multiple criteria, all of which must be true. With this AND clause, only rows on which BOTH City is Greer AND Returns is 0 will be included.

- View the results (Figure 10–12).

- Save the query as Ch10q07.

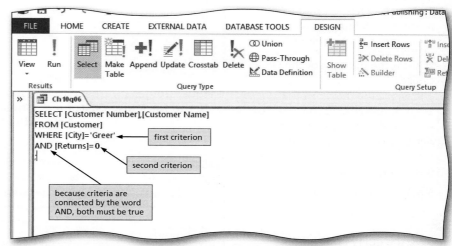

Figure 10–12 (a) Query to List the Customer Number and Customer Name for Those Customers Whose City is Greer and Whose Returns Amount is Equal to $0

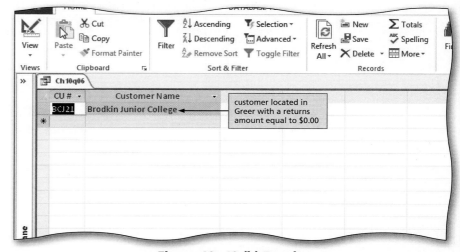

Figure 10–12 (b) Results

AC 632 **Access Chapter 10** Using SQL

1 SQL VIEW | 2 SIMPLE CRITERIA | 3 COMPOUND CRITERIA | 4 SORT RESULTS
5 GROUP RESULTS | 6 JOIN TABLES | 7 USE SUBQUERY | 8 UPDATE DATA

To Use a Compound Criterion Involving OR

The following steps use a compound criterion involving OR to enable Bavant Publishing to display the customer number and name of those customers located in Greer or for whom the returns amount is $0.00. *Why? In an OR criterion only one of the individual criteria needs to be true in order for the record to be included in the results.*

- Return to SQL view, delete the previous query, and type `SELECT [Customer Number],[Customer Name]` as the first line of the command.

- Type `FROM [Customer]` as the second line.

- Type `WHERE [City]='Greer'` as the third line.

- Type `OR [Returns]=0` as the fourth line and type a semicolon (;) on the fifth line.

Q&A What is the purpose of the OR clause?

The OR clause indicates that there are multiple criteria, only one of which needs to be true. With this AND clause, those rows on which EITHER City is Greer OR Returns is 0 (or both) will be included.

- View the results (Figure 10–13).

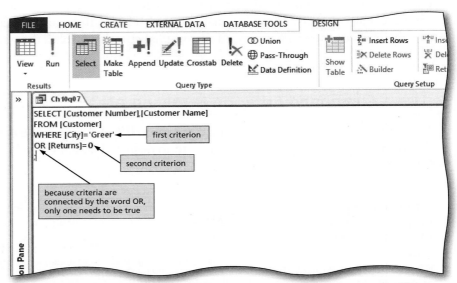

Figure 10–13 (a) Query to List the Customer Number and Customer Name for Those Customers Whose City is Greer or Whose Returns Amount is Equal to $0

- Save the query as Ch10q08.

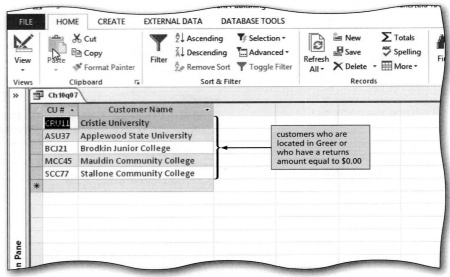

Figure 10–13 (b) Results

To Use NOT in a Criterion

Why? *You can negate any criterion by preceding the criterion with the word NOT.* The following steps use NOT in a criterion to list the numbers and names of the customers of Bavant Publishing not located in Greer.

 1

- Return to SQL view and delete the previous query.

- Type `SELECT [Customer Number],[Customer Name],[City]` as the first line of the command.

- Type `FROM [Customer]` as the second line.

- Type `WHERE NOT [City]='Greer'` as the third line and type a semicolon (`;`) on the fourth line.

- View the results (Figure 10–14).

2

- Save the query as Ch10q09.

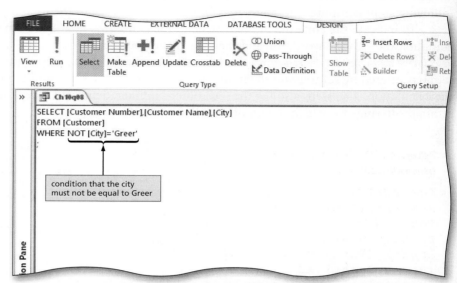

Figure 10–14 (a) Query to List the Customer Number, Customer Name, and City for Those Customers Whose City is not Greer

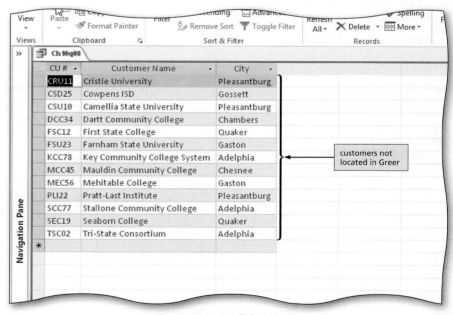

Figure 10–14 (b) Results

To Use a Computed Field

Just as with queries created in Design view, you can include fields in queries that are not in the database, but that can be computed from fields that are. Such a field is called a **computed** or **calculated field**. Computations can involve addition (+), subtraction (-), multiplication (*), or division (/). The query in the following steps computes the hours remaining, which is equal to the total hours minus the hours spent.

To indicate the contents of the new field (the computed field), you can name the field by following the computation with the word, AS, and then the name you want to assign the field. *Why? Assigning the field a descriptive name makes the results much more readable.* The following steps calculate the hours remaining for each seminar offered by subtracting the hours spent from the total hours and then assigning the name Remaining to the calculation. The steps also list the Customer Number, Seminar Code, Total Hours, and Hours Spent for all seminar offerings for which the number of hours spent is greater than 0.

- Return to SQL view and delete the previous query.
- Type **SELECT [Customer Number],[Seminar Code],[Total Hours],[Hours Spent],[Total Hours]-[Hours Spent] AS [Remaining]** as the first line of the command.
- Type **FROM [Seminar Offerings]** as the second line.
- Type **WHERE [Hours Spent]>0** as the third line and type a semicolon on the fourth line.
- View the results (Figure 10–15).

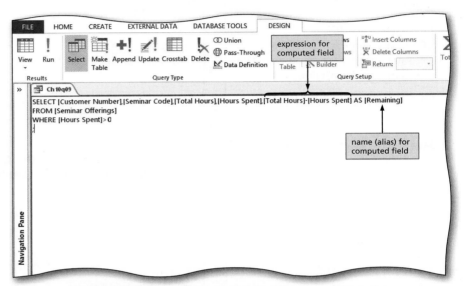

Figure 10–15 (a) Query to list the Customer Number, Seminar Code, Hours Spent, and Hours Remaining for Those Seminar Offerings on Which Hours Spent is Greater than 0

- Save the query as Ch10q10.

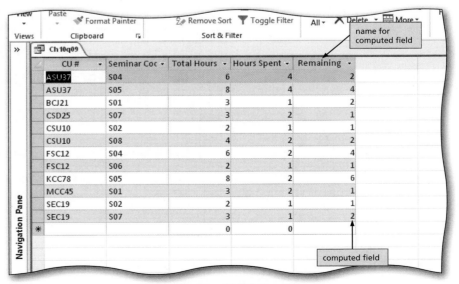

Figure 10–15 (b) Results

Sorting

Sorting in SQL follows the same principles as when using Design view to specify sorted query results, employing a sort key as the field on which data is to be sorted. SQL uses major and minor sort keys when sorting on multiple fields. By following a sort key with the word DESC with no comma in between, you can specify descending sort order. If you do not specify DESC, the data will be sorted in ascending order.

To sort the output, you include an **ORDER BY clause**, which consists of the words ORDER BY followed by the sort key. If there are two sort keys, the major sort key is listed first. Queries that you construct in Design view require that the major sort key is to the left of the minor sort key in the list of fields to be included. In SQL, there is no such restriction. The fields to be included in the query are in the SELECT clause, and the fields to be used for sorting are in the ORDER BY clause. The two clauses are totally independent.

BTW
SELECT clause
When you enter field names in a SELECT clause, you do not need to enter a space after the comma. Access inserts a space after the comma when you save the query and close it. When you re-open the query in SQL view, a space will appear after each comma that separates fields in the SELECT clause.

To Sort the Results on a Single Field

1 SQL VIEW | 2 SIMPLE CRITERIA | 3 COMPOUND CRITERIA | 4 SORT RESULTS
5 GROUP RESULTS | 6 JOIN TABLES | 7 USE SUBQUERY | 8 UPDATE DATA

The following steps list the customer number, name, amount paid, current due, and book rep number for all customers sorted by customer name. *Why? Bavant Publishing wants this data to appear in alphabetical order by customer name.*

- Return to SQL view and delete the previous query.

- Type `SELECT [Customer Number],[Customer Name], [Amount Paid],[Current Due],[Book Rep Number]` as the first line of the command.

- Type `FROM [Customer]` as the second line.

- Type `ORDER BY [Customer Name]` as the third line and type a semicolon (;) on the fourth line.

Q&A

What is the purpose of the ORDER BY clause?

The ORDER BY clause indicates that the results of the query are to be sorted by the indicated field or fields. This ORDER BY clause, for example, would cause the results to be sorted by Customer Name.

- View the results (Figure 10–16).

- Save the query as Ch10q11.

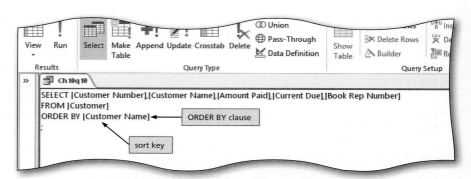

Figure 10–16 (a) Query to List the Customer Number, Customer Name, Amount Paid, Current Due, and Book Rep Number for All Customers with the Results Sorted by Customer Name

CU #	Customer Name	Amount Paid	Current Due	BR #
ASU37	Applewood State University	$41,530.98	$38,812.66	42
BCJ21	Brodkin Junior College	$0.00	$6,081.98	42
CSU10	Camellia State University	$63,246.88	$69,847.76	53
CSD25	Cowpens ISD	$12,750.00	$13,275.00	53
CRU11	Cristie University	$0.00	$14,250.00	42
DCC34	Dartt Community College	$21,345.50	$23,467.75	65
FSU23	Farnham State University	$18,268.00	$22,024.50	42
FSC12	First State College	$34,557.25	$23,875.98	65
KCC78	Key Community College System	$21,288.65	$11,367.49	65
MCC45	Mauldin Community College	$9,500.00	$5,000.00	53
MEC56	Mehitable College	$9,111.19	$7,310.76	42
PLI22	Pratt-Last Institute	$17,229.45	$11,769.75	53
SEC19	Seaborn College	$9,225.34	$10,496.89	65
SCC77	Stallone Community College	$7,525.98	$2,515.78	42
TSC02	Tri-State Consortium	$34,578.90	$9,432.56	65

rows sorted by customer name

Figure 10–16 (b) Results

To Sort the Results on Multiple Fields

The following steps list the customer number, name, amount paid, current due, and book rep number for all customers. The data is to be sorted on multiple fields. ***Why?*** *Bavant wants the data to be sorted by amount paid within book rep number. That is, the data is to be sorted by book rep number. In addition, within the group of customers that have the same rep number, the data is to be sorted further by amount paid.* To accomplish this sort, the Book Rep Number field is the major (primary) sort key and the Amount Paid field is the minor (secondary) sort key.

1

- Return to SQL view and delete the previous query.

- Type `SELECT [Customer Number],[Customer Name],[Amount Paid],[Current Due],[Book Rep Number]` as the first line of the command.

- Type `FROM [Customer]` as the second line.

- Type `ORDER BY [Book Rep Number],[Amount Paid]` as the third line and type a semicolon (;) on the fourth line.

- View the results (Figure 10–17).

 Experiment

- Try reversing the order of the sort keys to see the effect. Also, try to specify descending order for one or both of the sort keys. In each case, view the results to see the effect of your choice. When finished, return to the original sorting order for both fields.

2

- Save the query as Ch10q12.

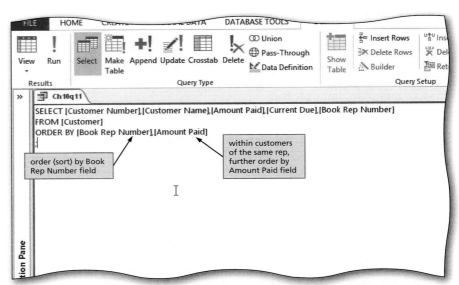

Figure 10–17 (a) Query to List the Customer Number, Customer Name, Amount Paid, Current Due, and Book Rep Number for All Customers with Results Sorted by Book Rep Number and Amount Paid

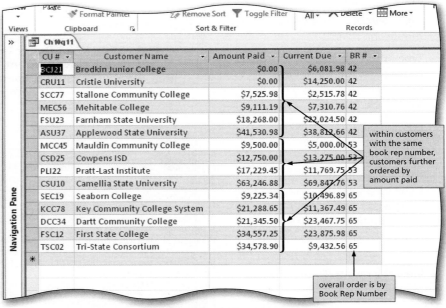

Figure 10–17 (b) Results

To Sort the Results in Descending Order

Why? *To show the results in high-to-low rather than low-to-high order, you sort in descending order.* To sort in descending order, you follow the name of the sort key with the DESC operator. The following steps list the customer number, name, amount paid, current due, and book rep number for all customers. Bavant wants the data to be sorted by descending current due within book rep number. That is, within the customers having the same rep number, the data is to be sorted further by current due in descending order.

1

- Return to SQL view and delete the previous query.

- Type `SELECT [Customer Number],[Customer Name],[Amount Paid],[Current Due],[Book Rep Number]` as the first line of the command.

- Type `FROM [Customer]` as the second line.

- Type `ORDER BY [Book Rep Number],[Current Due] DESC` as the third line and type a semicolon (;) on the fourth line.

 Do I need a comma between [Current Due] and DESC?
No. In fact, you must not use a comma. If you did, SQL would assume that you want a field called DESC. Without the comma, SQL knows that the DESC indicates that the sort on the [Current Due] field is to be in descending order.

- View the results (Figure 10–18).

2

- Save the query as Ch10q13.

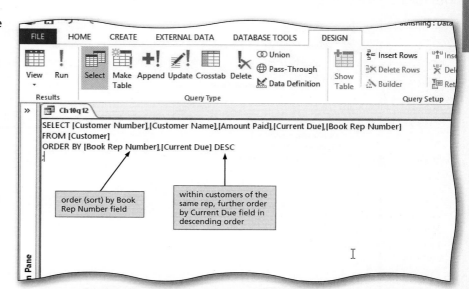

Figure 10–18 (a) Query to List the Customer Number, Customer Name, Amount Paid, Current Due, and Book Rep Number for All Customers with Results Sorted by Book Rep Number and Descending Current Due

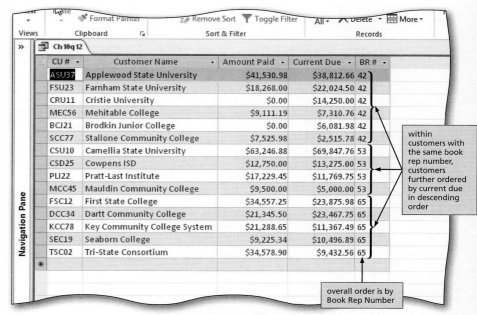

Figure 10–18 (b) Results

To Omit Duplicates When Sorting

When you sort data, duplicates normally are included. For example, the query in Figure 10–19 sorts the customer numbers in the Seminar Offerings table. Because any customer can be offered many seminars at a time, customer numbers can be included more than once. Bavant does not find this useful and would like to eliminate these duplicate customer numbers. To do so, use the DISTINCT operator in the query. *Why? The DISTINCT operator eliminates duplicate values in the results of a query.* To use the operator, you follow the word DISTINCT with the field name in parentheses.

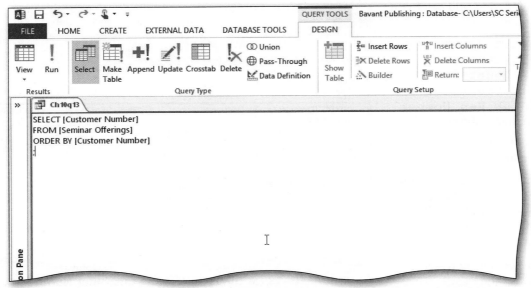

Figure 10–19 (a) Query to List the Customer Numbers in the Seminar Offerings Table Sorted by Customer Number

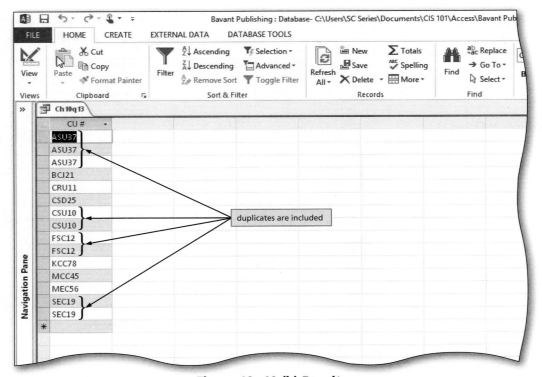

Figure 10–19 (b) Results

The following steps display the customer numbers in the Seminar Offerings table in customer number order, but with any duplicates removed.

- Return to SQL view and delete the previous query.

- Type **SELECT DISTINCT([Customer Number])** as the first line of the command.

- Type **FROM [Seminar Offerings]** as the second line.

- Type **ORDER BY [Customer Number]** as the third line and type a semicolon (**;**) on the fourth line.

- View the results (Figure 10–20).

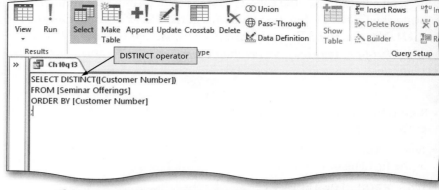

Figure 10–20 (a) Query to List the Customer Numbers in the Seminar Offerings Table Sorted by Customer Number Ensuring That No Customer Number is Listed More Than Once

2

- Save the query as Ch10q14. Return to the query.

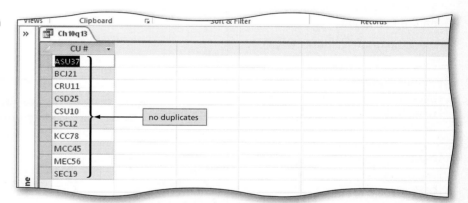

Figure 10–20 (b) Results

How do you determine sorting when creating a query?

Examine the query or request to see if it contains words such as *order* or *sort* that would imply that the order of the query results is important. If so, you need to sort the query.

Determine whether data is to be sorted. Examine the requirements for the query looking for words like *sorted by*, *ordered by*, *arranged by*, and so on.

Determine sort keys. Look for the fields that follow sorted by, ordered by, or any other words that signify sorting. If the requirements for the query include the phrase, ordered by customer name, then Customer Name is a sort key.

If there is more than one sort key, determine which one will be the major sort key and which will be the minor sort key. Look for words that indicate which field is more important. For example, if the requirements indicate that the results are to be ordered by amount paid within book rep number, Book Rep Number is the more important sort key.

Break Point: If you wish to stop working through the chapter at this point, you can close Access now. You can resume the project later by starting Access, opening the database called Bavant Publishing, creating a new query in SQL view, and continuing to follow the steps from this location forward.

To Use a Built-In Function

SQL has built-in functions, also called aggregate functions, to perform various calculations. Similar to the functions you learned about in Chapter 2, these functions in SQL are COUNT, SUM, AVG, MAX, and MIN, respectively. Bavant uses the following steps to determine the number of customers assigned to rep number 42 by using the COUNT function with an asterisk (*). ***Why use an asterisk rather than a field name when using the COUNT function?*** *You could select a field name, but that would be cumbersome and imply that you were just counting that field. You really are counting records. It doesn't matter whether you are counting names or street addresses or anything else.*

1

- Return to SQL view and delete the previous query.

- Type `SELECT COUNT(*)` as the first line of the command.

- Type `FROM [Customer]` as the second line.

- Type `WHERE [Book Rep Number]='42'` as the third line and type a semicolon (;) on the fourth line.

- View the results (Figure 10–21).

Why does Expr1000 appear in the column heading of the results? Because the field is a computed field, it does not have a name. Access assigns a generic expression name. You can add a name for the field by including the AS clause in the query, and it is good practice to do so.

2

- Save the query as Ch10q15.

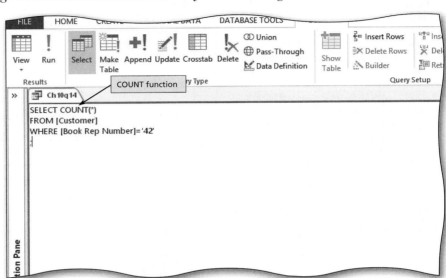

Figure 10–21 (a) Query to Count the Number of Customers Whose Book Rep Number is 42

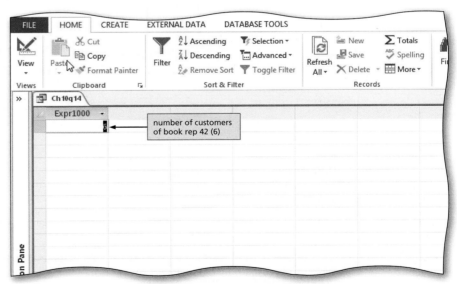

Figure 10–21 (b) Results

To Assign a Name to the Results of a Function

Bavant Publishing would prefer to have a more meaningful name than Expr1000 for the results of counting customer numbers. ***Why?*** *The default name of Expr1000 does not describe the meaning of the calculation.* Fortunately, just as you can assign a name to a calculation that includes two fields, you can assign a name to the results of a function. To do so, follow the expression for the function with the word AS and then the name to be assigned to the result. The following steps assign the name, Customer Count, to the expression in the previous query.

- Return to SQL view and delete the previous query.

- Type `SELECT COUNT(*) AS [Customer Count]` as the first line of the command.

- Type `FROM [Customer]` as the second line.

- Type `WHERE [Book Rep Number]='42'` as the third line and type a semicolon (;) on the fourth line.

- View the results (Figure 10–22).

2

- Save the query as Ch10q16.

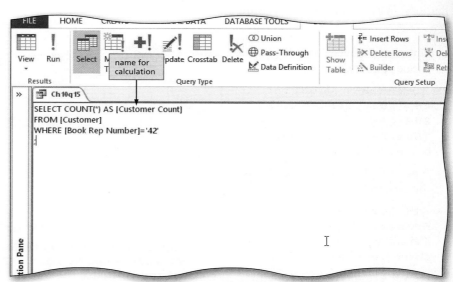

Figure 10–22 (a) Query to Count the Number of Customers Whose Book Rep Number is 42 With Results Called Customer Count

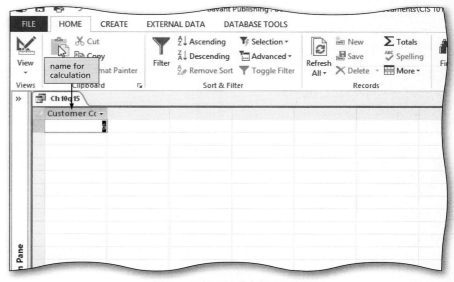

Figure 10–22 (b) Results

To Use Multiple Functions in the Same Command

There are two differences between COUNT and SUM, other than the obvious fact that they are computing different statistics. First, in the case of SUM, you must specify the field for which you want a total, instead of an asterisk (*); second, the field must be numeric. ***Why?*** *If the field is not numeric, it does not make sense to calculate a sum. You could not calculate a sum of names or addresses, for example.* The following steps use both the COUNT and SUM functions to count the number of customers whose book rep number is 42 and calculate the sum (total) of their amounts paid. The steps use the word AS to name COUNT(*) as Customer Count and to name SUM([Amount Paid]) as Sum Paid.

- Return to SQL view and delete the previous query.

- Type `SELECT COUNT(*) AS [Customer Count], SUM([Amount Paid]) AS [Sum Paid]` as the first line of the command.

- Type `FROM [Customer]` as the second line.

- Type `WHERE [Book Rep Number]='42'` as the third line and type a semicolon (;) on the fourth line.

- View the results (Figure 10–23).

Experiment

- Try using the other functions in place of SUM. In each case, view the results to see the effect of your choice. When finished, once again select SUM.

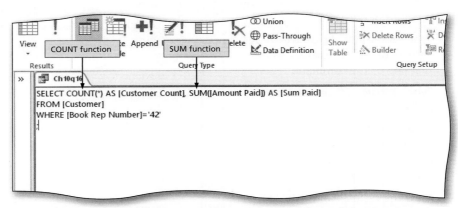

Figure 10–23 (a) Query to Count the Number of Customers Whose Book Rep Number is 42 With Results Called Customer Count and Calculate the Sum of Amount Paid With Results Called Sum Paid

- Save the query as Ch10q17.

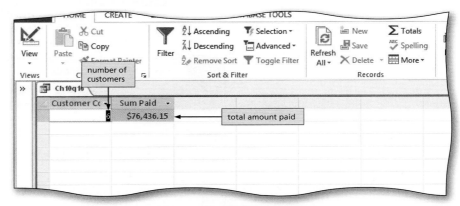

Figure 10–23 (b) Results

The use of AVG, MAX, and MIN is similar to SUM. The only difference is that a different statistic is calculated.

Grouping

Recall that grouping means creating groups of records that share some common characteristic. When you group rows, any calculations indicated in the SELECT command are performed for the entire group.

To Use Grouping

Bavant Publishing wants to calculate the totals of the Amount Paid field, called Sum Paid, and the Current Due field, called Sum Due, for the customers of each rep. To calculate the totals, the command will include the calculations, SUM([Amount Paid]) and SUM([Current Due]). To get totals for the customers of each rep, the command also will include a **GROUP BY clause**, which consists of the words, GROUP BY, followed by the field used for grouping, in this case, Book Rep Number. *Why? Including GROUP BY Book Rep Number will cause the customers for each rep to be grouped together; that is, all customers with the same book rep number will form a group. Any statistics, such as totals, appearing after the word SELECT will be calculated for each of these groups.* Using GROUP BY does not mean that the information will be sorted.

The following steps use the GROUP BY clause to produce the results Bavant wants. The steps also rename the total amount paid as Sum Paid and the total current due as Sum Due by including appropriate AS clauses; finally, the steps sort the records by book rep number.

- Return to SQL view and delete the previous query.

- Type **SELECT [Book Rep Number], SUM([Amount Paid]) AS [Sum Paid], SUM([Current Due]) AS [Sum Due]** as the first line of the command.

- Type **FROM [Customer]** as the second line.

- Type **GROUP BY [Book Rep Number]** as the third line.

Q&A What is the purpose of the GROUP BY clause?
The GROUP BY clause causes the rows to be grouped by the indicate field. With this GROUP BY clause, the rows will be grouped by Book Rep Number.

- Type **ORDER BY [Book Rep Number]** as the fourth line and type a semicolon (**;**) on the fifth line.

- View the results (Figure 10–24).

2

- Save the query as Ch10q18.

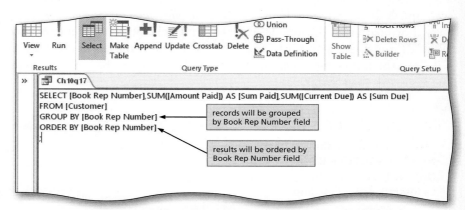

Figure 10–24 (a) Query to Group Records by Book Rep Number and List the Book Rep Number, the Sum of Amount Paid, and the Sum of Current Due

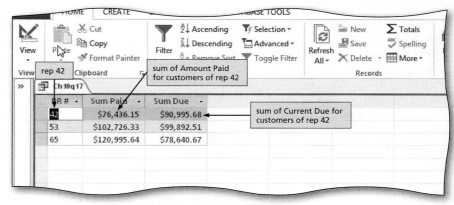

Figure 10–24 (b) Results

Grouping Requirements

When rows are grouped, one line of output is produced for each group. The only output that SQL can display is statistics that are calculated for the group or fields whose values are the same for all rows in a group. For example, when grouping rows by book rep number as in the previous query, it is appropriate to display the book rep number, because the number in one row in a group must be the same as the number in any other row in the group. It is appropriate to display the sum of the Amount Paid and Current Due fields because they are statistics calculated for the group. It would not be appropriate to display a customer number, however, because the customer number varies on the rows in a group; the rep is associated with many customers. SQL would not be able to determine which customer number to display for the group. SQL will display an error message if you attempt to display a field that is not appropriate, such as the customer number.

To Restrict the Groups that Appear

1 SQL VIEW | 2 SIMPLE CRITERIA | 3 COMPOUND CRITERIA | 4 SORT RESULTS
5 GROUP RESULTS | 6 JOIN TABLES | 7 USE SUBQUERY | 8 UPDATE DATA

In some cases, Bavant Publishing may want to display only certain groups. For example, management may want to display only those reps for whom the sum of the current due amounts are greater than $90,000.00. This restriction does not apply to individual rows, but instead to groups. You cannot use a WHERE clause to accomplish this restriction. *Why? WHERE applies only to rows, not groups.*

Fortunately, SQL provides the **HAVING clause**, which functions with groups similarly to the way WHERE functions with rows. The HAVING clause consists of the word HAVING followed by a criterion. It is used in the following steps, which restrict the groups to be included to those on which the sum of the current due is greater than $90,000.00.

- Return to SQL view.

- Tap or click the beginning of the fourth line (ORDER BY [Book Rep Number]) and press the ENTER key to insert a new blank line.

- Tap or click the beginning of the new blank line, and then type **HAVING SUM([Current Due])>90000** as the new fourth line.

Q&A What is the purpose of the HAVING clause?
The HAVING clause restricts the groups that will be included to only those satisfying the indicated criteria. With this clause, only groups on which the sum of the current due amount is greater than 90000 will be included.

- View the results (Figure 10–25).

- Save the query as Ch10q19.

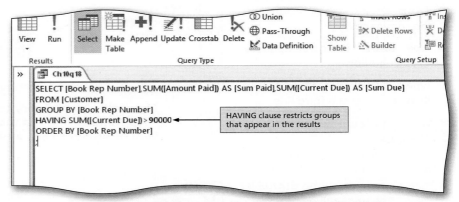

Figure 10–25 (a) Query to Restrict the Results of The Previous Query to Only Those Groups For Which the Sum of Current Due is More Than $90,000

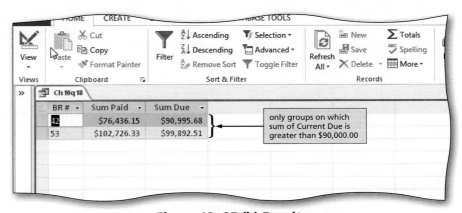

Figure 10–25 (b) Results

How do you determine grouping when creating a query?

Examine the query or request to determine whether records should be organized by some common characteristic.

Determine whether data is to be grouped in some fashion. Examine the requirements for the query to see if they contain individual rows or information about groups of rows.

Determine the field or fields on which grouping is to take place. By which field is the data to be grouped? Look to see if the requirements indicate a field along with several group calculations.

Determine which fields or calculations are appropriate to display. When rows are grouped, one line of output is produced for each group. The only output that can appear are statistics that are calculated for the group or fields whose values are the same for all rows in a group. For example, it would make sense to display the rep number, because all the customers in the group have the same rep number. It would not make sense to display the customer number, because the customer number will vary from one row in a group to another. SQL could not determine which customer number to display for the group.

Break Point: If you wish to stop working through the chapter at this point, you can close Access now. You can resume the project later by starting Access, opening the database called Bavant Publishing, creating a new query in SQL view, and continuing to follow the steps from this location forward.

Joining Tables

Many queries require data from more than one table. Just as with creating queries in Design view, SQL should provide a way to **join** tables, that is, to find rows in two tables that have identical values in matching fields. In SQL, this is accomplished through appropriate criteria following the word WHERE.

If you want to list the customer number, name, book rep number, first name of the rep, and last name of the rep for all customers, you need data from both the Customer and Book Rep tables. The Book Rep Number field is in both tables, the Customer Number field is only in the Customer table, and the First Name and Last Name fields are only in the Book Rep Table. You need to access both tables in your SQL query, as follows:

1. In the SELECT clause, you indicate all fields you want to appear.
2. In the FROM clause, you list all tables involved in the query.
3. In the WHERE clause, you give the criterion that will restrict the data to be retrieved to only those rows included in both of the two tables, that is, to the rows that have common values in matching fields.

BTW

Inner Joins
A join that compares the tables in the FROM clause and lists only those rows that satisfy the condition in the WHERE clause is called an inner join. SQL has an INNER JOIN clause. You could replace the query shown in Figure 10–26a on page AC 646 with FROM [Customer] INNER JOIN [Book Rep] ON [Customer]. [Book Rep Number]=[Book Rep].[Book Rep Number] to get the same results as shown in Figure 10–26b.

Qualifying Fields

There is a problem in indicating the matching fields. The matching fields are both called Book Rep Number. There is a field in the Customer table called Book Rep Number, as well as a field in the Book Rep Table called Book Rep Number. In this case, if you only enter Book Rep Number, it will not be clear which table you mean. It is necessary to **qualify** Book Rep Number, that is, to specify to which field in which table you are referring. You do this by preceding the name of the field with the name of the table, followed by a period. The Book Rep Number field in the Customer table, for example, is [Customer].[Book Rep Number].

Whenever a query is potentially ambiguous, you must qualify the fields involved. It is permissible to qualify other fields as well, even if there is no confusion. For example, instead of [Customer Name], you could have typed [Customer].[Customer Name] to indicate the Customer Name field in the Customer table. Some people prefer to qualify all fields, and this is not a bad approach. In this text, you only will qualify fields when it is necessary to do so.

BTW

Qualifying Fields
There is no space on either side of the period that is used to separate the table name from the field name. Adding a space will result in an error message.

To Join Tables

Bavant Publishing wants to list the customer number, customer name, book rep number, first name of the rep, and last name of the rep for all customers. The following steps create a query to join the tables. *Why? The data comes from two tables.* The steps also order the results by customer number.

1

- Return to SQL view and delete the previous query.

- Type `SELECT [Customer Number],[Customer Name],[Customer].[Book Rep Number],[First Name],[Last Name]` as the first line of the command.

- Type `FROM [Customer], [Book Rep]` as the second line.

Q&A Why does the FROM clause contain more than one table?
The query involves fields from both tables.

- Type `WHERE [Customer].[Book Rep Number]=[Book Rep].[Book Rep Number]` as the third line.

Q&A What is the purpose of the WHERE clause?
The WHERE clause specifies that only rows on which the rep numbers match are to be included. In this case, the rep number in the Customer table ([Customer].[Book Rep Number]) must be equal to the rep number in the Book Rep table ([Book Rep].[Book Rep Number]).

- Type `ORDER BY [Customer Number]` as the fourth line and type a semicolon (;) on the fifth line.

- View the results (Figure 10–26).

2

- Save the query as Ch10q20.

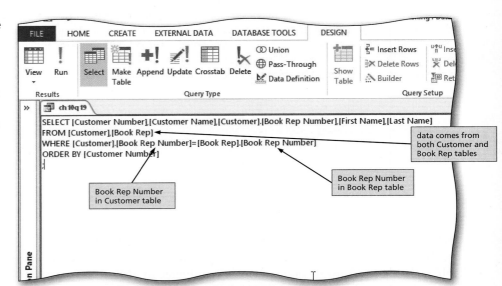

Figure 10–26 (a) Query to List the Customer Number, Customer Name, Book Rep Number, First Name, and Last Name for All Customers

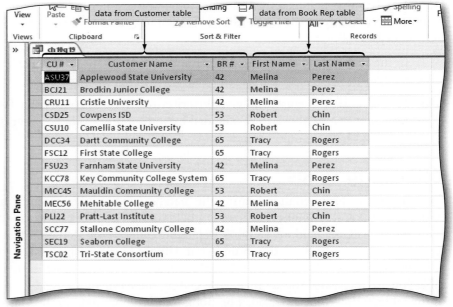

Figure 10–26 (b) Results

To Restrict the Records in a Join

You can restrict the records to be included in a join by creating a compound criterion. The compound criterion will include the criterion necessary to join the tables along with a criterion to restrict the records. The criteria will be connected with AND. *Why? Both the criterion that determines the records to be joined and the criterion to restrict the records must be true.*

Bavant would like to modify the previous query so that only reps whose start date is prior to May 1, 2014, are included. The following steps modify the previous query appropriately. The date is enclosed between number signs (#), which is the date format used in the Access version of SQL.

- Return to SQL view.
- Tap or click the end of line 1.
- Type **, [Start Date]** to add the Start Date field to the SELECT clause.
- Tap or click immediately prior to the ORDER BY clause.
- Type **AND [Start Date]<#5/1/2014#** and press the ENTER key.

Q&A
Could I use other formats for the date in the criterion?
Yes. You could type #May 1, 2014# or #1-May-2014#.

- View the results (Figure 10–27).

2

- Save the query as Ch10q21.

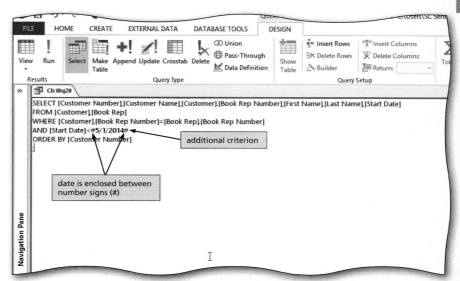

Figure 10–27 (a) Query to Restrict the Results of Previous Query to Only Those Customers Whose Start Date is Before 5/1/2014

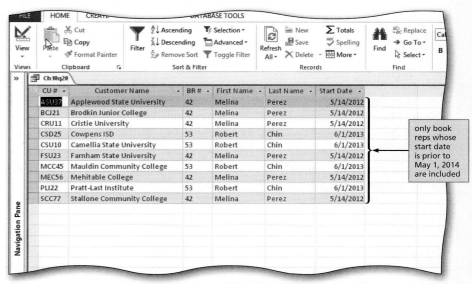

Figure 10–27 (b) Results

Aliases

When tables appear in the FROM clause, you can give each table an **alias**, or an alternative name, that you can use in the rest of the statement. You create an alias by typing the name of the table, pressing the SPACEBAR, and then typing the name of the alias. No commas or periods are necessary to separate the two names.

You can use an alias for two basic reasons: for simplicity or to join a table to itself. Figure 10–28 shows the same query as in Figure 10–27 on the previous page, but with the Customer table assigned the letter, C, as an alias and the Book Rep table assigned the letter, B. The query in Figure 10–28 is less complex. Whenever you need to qualify a field name, you can use the alias. Thus, you only need to type B.[Book Rep Number] rather than [Book Rep].[Book Rep Number].

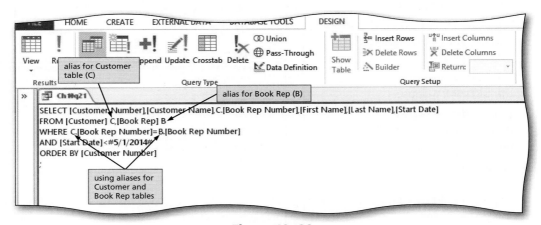

Figure 10–28

To Join a Table to Itself

1 SQL VIEW | 2 SIMPLE CRITERIA | 3 COMPOUND CRITERIA | 4 SORT RESULTS
5 GROUP RESULTS | 6 JOIN TABLES | 7 USE SUBQUERY | 8 UPDATE DATA

The other use of aliases is in joining a table to itself. An example of this type of join would enable Bavant to find customer numbers and names for every pair of customers located in the same city. One such pair, for example, would be customer KCC78 (Key Community College System) and customer SCC77 (Stallone Community College) because both customers are located in the same city (Adelphia). Another example would be customer KCC78 (Key Community College System) and customer TSC02 (Tri-State Consortium) because both customers are also located in the same city (Adelphia). Finally, because both SCC77 and TSC02 are located in the same city (Adelphia), there would be a third pair: SCC77 (Stallone Community College) and TSC02 (Tri-State Consortium).

If there were two Customer tables in the database, Bavant could obtain the results they want by simply joining the two Customer tables and looking for rows where the cities were the same. Even though there is only one Customer table, you actually can treat the Customer table as two tables in the query by creating two aliases. You would change the FROM clause to:

```
FROM [CUSTOMER] F, [CUSTOMER] S
```

SQL treats this clause as a query of two tables. The clause assigns the first Customer table the letter, F, as an alias. It also assigns the letter, S, as an alias for the Customer table. The fact that both tables are really the single Customer table is not a problem. The following steps assign two aliases (F and S) to the Customer table and list the customer number and customer name of both customers as well as the city in which both are located. The steps also include a criterion to ensure F.[Customer Number] < S.[Customer Number]. **Why?** *If you did not include this criterion, the query would contain four times as many results. On the first row in the results, for example, the first customer number is ASU37 and the second is BCJ21. Without this criterion, there would be a row on which both the first and second customer numbers are ASU37, a row on which both are BCJ21, and a row on which the first is BCJ21 and the second is ASU37. This criterion only selects the one row on which the first customer number (ASU37) is less than the second customer number (BCJ21).*

1

- Return to SQL view and delete the previous query.

- Type **SELECT F.[Customer Number],F.[Customer Name],S.[Customer Number],S.[Customer Name],F.[City]** as the first line of the command to select the fields to display in the query result.

- Type **FROM [Customer] F,[Customer] S** as the second line to create the aliases for the first and second Customer tables.

- Type **WHERE F.[City]=S.[City]** as the third line to indicate that the cities in each table must match.

- Type **AND F.[Customer Number]<S.[Customer Number]** as the fourth line to indicate that the customer number from the first table must be less than the customer number from the second table, and then type a semicolon (**;**) on the fifth line.

- View the results (Figure 10–29).

2

- Save the query as Ch10q22.

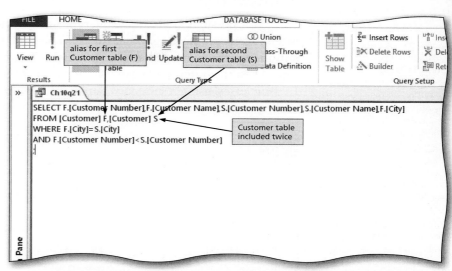

Figure 10–29 (a) Query to List the Customer Name and Customer Number For Pairs of Customers Located in the Same City

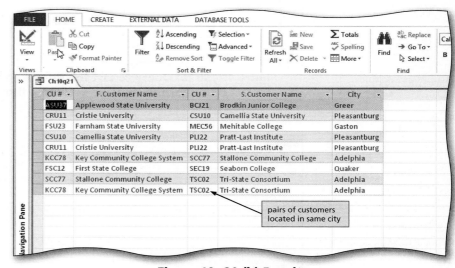

Figure 10–29 (b) Results

How do you determine criteria when creating a query?

Examine the query or request to determine any restrictions or conditions that records must satisfy to be included in the results.

Determine the fields involved in the criteria. For any criterion, determine the fields that are included. Determine the data types for these fields. If the criterion uses a value that corresponds to a Text field, enclose the value in single quotation marks. If the criterion uses a date, enclose the value between number signs (for example, #4/15/2014#).

Determine comparison operators. When fields are being compared to other fields or to specific values, determine the appropriate comparison operator (equals, less than, greater than, and so on). If a wildcard is involved, then the query will use the LIKE operator.

Determine join criteria. If tables are being joined, determine the fields that must match.

Determine compound criteria. If more than one criterion is involved, determine whether all individual criteria are to be true, in which case you will use the AND operator, or whether only one individual criterion needs to be true, in which case you will use the OR operator.

BTW
Union, Pass-Through, and Data Definition Queries
There are three queries that cannot be created in Design view. When you tap or click the button on the ribbon for any of these three queries in Design view, the SQL view window opens. The Union query combines fields from more than one table into one query result set. The Pass-Through query enables you to send SQL commands directly to ODBC (Open Database Connectivity) databases using the ODBC database's SQL syntax. The Data Definition query allows you to create or alter database tables or create indexes in Access directly.

Subqueries

It is possible to place one query inside another. You will place the query shown in Figure 10–30 inside another query. When you have done so, it will be called a **subquery**, which is an inner query, contained within parentheses, that is evaluated first. Then the outer query can use the results of the subquery to find its results. In some cases, using a subquery can be the simplest way to produce the desired results, as illustrated in the next set of steps.

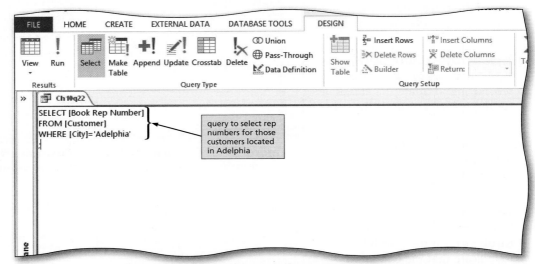

Figure 10–30 (a) Query to List the Book Rep Number For All Records In The Customer Table on Which the City is Adelphia

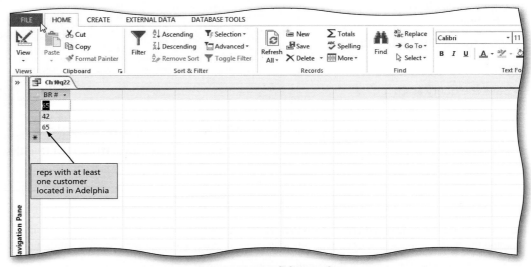

Figure 10–30 (b) Results

CONSIDER THIS

Why does book rep 65 appear twice?
The Bavant Publishing database includes two customers whose city is Adelphia and whose book rep number is 65. This is not a problem because in the next query it is only important what numbers are included, not how many times they appear. If you wanted the numbers only to appear once, you would use the order the results by Book Rep Number and use the DISTINCT operator.

To Use a Subquery

The following steps use the query shown in Figure 10–30 as a subquery. *Why? Bavant Publishing can use this query to select rep numbers for those reps who have at least one customer located in Adelphia.* After the subquery is evaluated, the outer query will select the rep number, first name, and last name for those reps whose rep number is in the list produced by the subquery.

①

- Return to SQL view and delete the previous query.

- Type **SELECT [Book Rep Number],[First Name],[Last Name]** as the first line of the command.

- Type **FROM [Book Rep]** as the second line.

- Type **WHERE [Book Rep Number] IN** as the third line.

- Type **(SELECT [Book Rep Number]** as the fourth line.

- Type **FROM [Customer]** as the fifth line.

- Type **WHERE [City]='Adelphia')** as the sixth line and type a semicolon (**;**) on the seventh line.

- View the results (Figure 10–31).

②

- Save the query as Ch10q23.

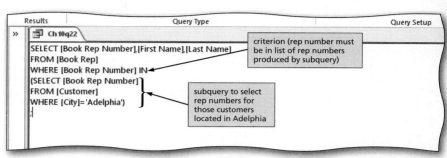

Figure 10–31 (a) Query to List Book Rep Number, First Name, and Last Name for All Book Reps Who Represent At Least One Customer Located in Adelphia

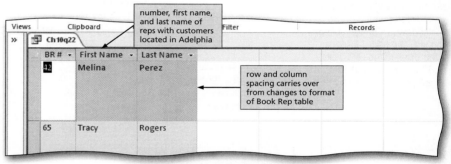

Figure 10–31 (b) Results

Using an IN Clause

The query in Figure 10–31 uses an IN clause with a subquery. You also can use an IN clause with a list as an alternative to an OR criterion when the OR criterion involves a single field. For example, to find customers whose city is Adelphia, Gaston, or Greer, the criterion using IN would be City IN ('Adelphia', 'Gaston', 'Greer'). The corresponding OR criterion would be City='Adelphia' OR City= 'Gaston' OR City= 'Greer'. The choice of which one to use is a matter of personal preference.

You also can use this type of IN clause when creating queries in Design view. To use the criterion in the previous paragraph, for example, include the City field in the design grid and enter the criterion in the Criteria row.

BTW

BETWEEN Operator
The BETWEEN operator allows you to search for a range of values in one field. For example, to find all customers whose amount paid is between $20,000.00 and $30,000.00, the WHERE clause would be WHERE [Amount Paid] BETWEEN 20000 AND 30000.

Comparison with Access-Generated SQL

When you create a query in Design view, Access automatically creates a corresponding SQL query that is similar to the queries you have created in this chapter. The Access query shown in Figure 10–32 on the next page, for example, was created in Design view and includes the Customer Number and Customer Name fields. The City field has a criterion (Greer), but the City field will not appear in the results.

BTW

Outer Joins

Sometimes you need to list all the rows from one of the tables in a join, regardless of whether they match any rows in the other table. For example, you can perform a join on the Customer and Seminar Offerings table but display all customers — even the ones without seminar offerings. This type of join is called an outer join. In a left outer join, all rows from the table on the left (the table listed first in the query) will be included regardless of whether they match rows from the table on the right (the table listed second in the query). Rows from the right will be included only if they match. In a right outer join, all rows from the table on the right will be included regardless of whether they match rows from the table on the left. The SQL clause for a left outer join is LEFT JOIN and the SQL clause for a right outer join is RIGHT JOIN.

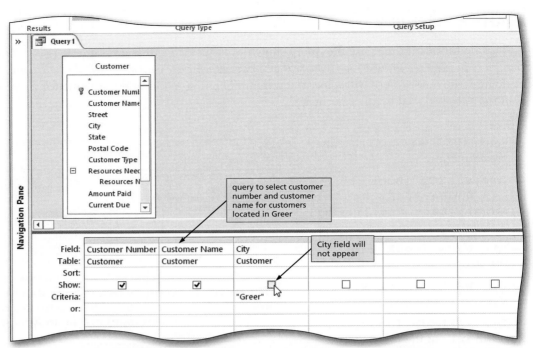

Figure 10–32 (a) Query to List the Customer Number and Customer Name for all Customers Whose City is Greer

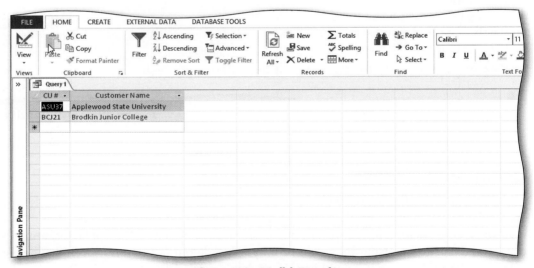

Figure 10–32 (b) Results

The SQL query that Access generates in correspondence to the Design view query is shown in Figure 10–33. The query is very similar to the queries you have entered, but there are three slight differences. First, the Customer.[Customer Number] and Customer.[Customer Name] fields are qualified, even though they do not need to be; only one table is involved in the query, so no qualification is necessary. Second, the City field is not enclosed in square brackets. The field legitimately is not enclosed in square brackets because there are no spaces or other special characters in the field name. Finally, there are extra parentheses in the criteria.

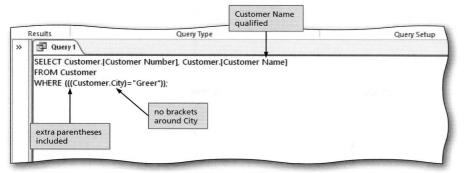

Figure 10–33

Both the style used by Access and the style you have been using are legitimate. The choice of style is a personal preference.

Updating Data through SQL

Although SQL is often regarded as a language for querying databases, it also contains commands to update databases. You can add new records, update existing records, and delete records.

To Use an INSERT Command

1 SQL VIEW | 2 SIMPLE CRITERIA | 3 COMPOUND CRITERIA | 4 SORT RESULTS
5 GROUP RESULTS | 6 JOIN TABLES | 7 USE SUBQUERY | **8 UPDATE DATA**

You can add records to a table using the SQL INSERT command. The command consists of the words INSERT INTO followed by the name of the table into which the record is to be inserted. Next is the word VALUE, followed by the values for the fields in the record. Values for Text fields must be enclosed within quotation marks. Why? *Just as you needed to type the quotation marks when you used text data in a criterion, you need to do the same when you use text values in an INSERT INTO command.* The following steps add a record that Bavant Publishing wants to add to the Seminar Offerings table. The record is for customer BCJ21 and Seminar S06, and indicates that the seminar will be offered for a total of 2 hours, of which 0 hours already have been spent.

- If necessary, return to SQL view and delete the existing query.

- Type **INSERT INTO [Seminar Offerings]** as the first line of the command.

Q&A What is the purpose of the INSERT INTO clause?
The clause indicates the table into which data is to be inserted.

- Type **VALUES** as the second line.

- Type **('BCJ21','S06',2,0)** as the third line and type a semicolon (;) on the fourth line (Figure 10–34).

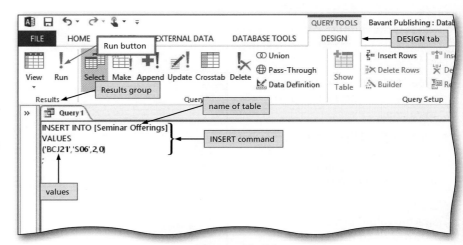

Figure 10–34

Q&A What is the purpose of the VALUES clause?
The VALUES clause, which typically extends over two lines, indicates the values that are to be inserted into a new record in the table. For readability, it is common to place the word VALUES on one line and the actual values on a separate line.

● Run the query by tapping or clicking the Run button (QUERY TOOLS DESIGN tab | Results group).

● When Access displays a message indicating the number of records to be inserted (appended), tap or click the Yes button to insert the records.

Q&A I tapped or clicked the View button and did not get the message. Do I need to tap or click the Run button?
Yes. You are making a change to the database, so you must tap or click the Run button, or the change will not be made.

How can I see if the record was actually inserted?
Use a SELECT query to view the records in the Seminar Offerings table.

● Save the query as Ch10q24.

To Use an UPDATE Command

1 SQL VIEW | 2 SIMPLE CRITERIA | 3 COMPOUND CRITERIA | 4 SORT RESULTS
5 GROUP RESULTS | 6 JOIN TABLES | 7 USE SUBQUERY | **8 UPDATE DATA**

You can update records in SQL by using the UPDATE command. The command consists of UPDATE, followed by the name of the table in which records are to be updated. Next, the command contains one or more SET clauses, which consist of the word SET, followed by a field to be updated, an equal sign, and the new value. The SET clause indicates the change to be made. Finally, the query includes a WHERE clause. ***Why?*** *When you execute the command, all records in the indicated table that satisfy the criterion will be updated.* The following steps use the SQL UPDATE command to perform an update requested by Bavant Publishing. Specifically, they change the Hours Spent to 1 on all records in the Seminar Offerings table on which the customer number is BCJ21 and the seminar code is S06. Because the combination of the Customer Number and Seminar Code fields is the primary key, only one record will be updated.

● Delete the existing query.

● Type **UPDATE [Seminar Offerings]** as the first line of the command.

Q&A What is the purpose of the UPDATE clause?
The UPDATE clause indicates the table to be updated. This clause indicates that the update is to the Seminar Offerings table.

● Type **SET [Hours Spent]=1** as the second line.

Q&A What is the purpose of the SET clause?
The SET clause indicates the field to be changed as well as the new value. This SET clause indicates that the hours spent is to be set to 1.

● Type **WHERE [Customer Number]='BCJ21'** as the third line.

● Type **AND [Seminar Code]='S06'** as the fourth line and type a semicolon (**;**) on the fifth line (Figure 10–35).

Q&A Do I need to change a field to a specific value such as 1?
No. You could use an expression. For example, to add $100 to the Current Due amount, the SET clause would be SET [Current Due]=[Current Due]+100.

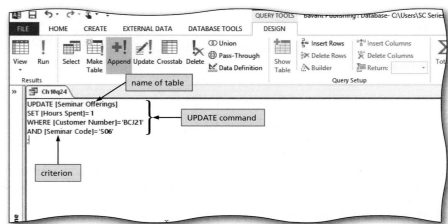

Figure 10–35

- Run the query.

- When Access displays a message indicating the number of records to be updated, tap or click the Yes button to update the records.

Q&A
How can I see if the update actually occurred?
Use a SELECT query to view the records in the Seminar Offerings table.

- Save the query as Ch10q25.

To Use a DELETE Command

1 SQL VIEW | 2 SIMPLE CRITERIA | 3 COMPOUND CRITERIA | 4 SORT RESULTS
5 GROUP RESULTS | 6 JOIN TABLES | 7 USE SUBQUERY | 8 UPDATE DATA

You can delete records in SQL using the DELETE command. The command consists of DELETE FROM, followed by the name of the table from which records are to be deleted. Finally, you include a WHERE clause to specify the criteria. **Why?** *When you execute the command, all records in the indicated table that satisfy the criterion will be deleted.* The following steps use the SQL DELETE command to delete all records in the Seminar Offerings table on which the customer number is BCJ21 and the seminar code is S06, as Bavant Publishing has requested. Because the combination of the Customer Number and Seminar Code fields is the primary key, only one record will be deleted.

- Delete the existing query.

- Type **DELETE FROM [Seminar Offerings]** as the first line of the command.

Q&A
What is the purpose of the DELETE clause?
The DELETE clause indicates the table from which records will be deleted. This DELETE clause indicates that records will be deleted from the Seminar Offerings table.

- Type **WHERE [Customer Number]='BCJ21'** as the second line.

- Type **AND [Seminar Code]='S06'** as the third line and type a semicolon (;) on the fourth line (Figure 10–36).

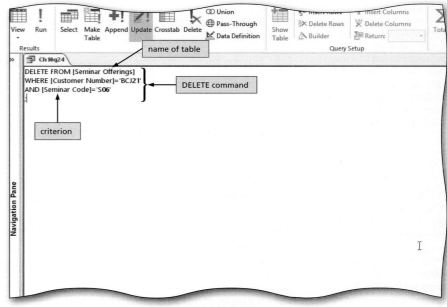

Figure 10–36

- Run the query.

- When Access displays a message indicating the number of records to be deleted, tap or click the Yes button to delete the records.

Q&A
How can I see if the deletion actually occurred?
Use a SELECT query to view the records in the Seminar Offerings table.

- Save the query as Ch10q26.

- Close the query.

CONSIDER THIS

How do you determine any update operations to be performed?
Examine the database to determine if records must be added, updated, and/or deleted.

Determine INSERT operations. Determine whether new records need to be added. Determine to which table they should be added.

Determine UPDATE operations. Determine changes that need to be made to existing records. Which fields need to be changed? Which tables contain these fields? What criteria identify the rows that need to be changed?

Determine DELETE operations. Determine which tables contain records that are to be deleted. What criteria identify the rows that need to be deleted?

To Restore the Font Size

BTW
Certification
The Microsoft Office Specialist (MOS) program provides an opportunity for you to obtain a valuable industry credential — proof that you have the Access 2013 skills required by employers. For more information, visit the Certification resource on the Student Companion Site located on www .cengagebrain.com. For detailed instructions about accessing available resources, visit www.cengage.com/ ct/studentdownload or contact your instructor for information about accessing the required files.

Earlier you changed the font size from its default setting of 8 to 10 so the SQL queries would be easier to read. Unless you prefer to retain this new setting, you should change the setting back to the default. The following steps restore the font size to its default setting.

1 Tap or click FILE on the ribbon to open the Backstage view.

2 Tap or click Options to display the Access Options dialog box.

3 If necessary, tap or click Object Designers to display the Object Designer options.

4 In the Query design area, tap or click the Size box arrow, and then tap or click 8 in the list that appears to change the size back to 8.

5 Tap or click the OK button to close the Access Options dialog box.

To Sign Out of a Microsoft Account

BTW
Quick Reference
For a table that lists how to complete the tasks covered in this book using touch gestures, the mouse, ribbon, shortcut menu, and keyboard, see the Quick Reference Summary at the back of this book, or visit the Quick Reference resource on the Student Companion Site located on www.cengagebrain.com. For detailed instructions about accessing available resources, visit www.cengage .com/ct/studentdownload or contact your instructor for information about accessing the required files.

If you are signed in to a Microsoft account and are using a public computer or otherwise wish to sign out of your Microsoft account, you should sign out of the account from the Account gallery in the Backstage view before exiting Access. Signing out of the account is the safest way to make sure that nobody else can access SkyDrive files or settings stored in your Microsoft account. The following steps sign out of a Microsoft account from Access. For a detailed example of the procedure summarized below, refer to the Office and Windows chapter at the beginning of this book.

1 If you wish to sign out of your Microsoft account, tap or click FILE on the ribbon to open the Backstage view and then tap or click the Account tab to display the Account gallery.

2 Tap or click the Sign out link, which displays the Remove Account dialog box. If a Can't remove Windows accounts dialog box appears instead of the Remove Account dialog box, click the OK button and skip the remaining steps.

Q&A Why does a Can't remove Windows accounts dialog box appear?
If you signed in to Windows using your Microsoft account, then you also must sign out from Windows, rather than signing out from within Access. When you are finished using Windows, be sure to sign out at that time.

3 Tap or click the Yes button (Remove Account dialog box) to sign out of your Microsoft account on this computer.

Q&A Should I sign out of Windows after signing out of my Microsoft account?
When you are finished using the computer, you should sign out of your account for maximum security.

4 Tap or click the Back button in the upper-left corner of the Backstage view to return to the database.

To Exit Access

The following steps exit Access.

1 Tap or click the Close button on the right side of the title bar to exit Access.

2 If a Microsoft Access dialog box appears, tap or click the Yes button to save any changes made to the object since the last save.

Chapter Summary

In this chapter you have learned to create SQL queries; include fields in a query; use criteria involving both numeric and text fields as well as use compound criteria; use computed fields and rename the computation; sort the results of a query; use the built-in functions; group records in a query and also restrict the groups that appear in the results; join tables and restrict the records in a join; and use subqueries. You looked at the SQL that is generated automatically by Access. Finally, you used the INSERT, UPDATE, and DELETE commands to update data. The items listed below include all the new Access skills you have learned in this chapter.

Compound Criteria
Use a Compound Criterion Involving AND (AC 631)
Use a Compound Criterion Involving OR (AC 632)
Use NOT in a Criterion (AC 633)

Display Change
Change the Font Size (AC 621)

Field Selection
Include Only Certain Fields (AC 623)
Include All Fields (AC 625)
Use a Computed Field (AC 634)

Functions
Use a Built-In Function (AC 640)
Assign a Name to the Results of a Function (AC 641)
Use Multiple Functions in the Same Command (AC 642)

Grouping
Use Grouping (AC 643)
Restrict the Groups that Appear (AC 644)

Joining Tables
Join Tables (AC 646)
Restrict the Records in a Join (AC 647)
Join a Table to Itself (AC 648)

Query Creation
Create a New SQL Query (AC 622)
Prepare to Enter a New SQL Query (AC 625)

Simple Criteria
Use a Criterion Involving a Numeric Field (AC 627)
Use a Comparison Operator (AC 628)
Use a Criterion Involving a Text Field (AC 629)
Use a Wildcard (AC 630)

Sort Results
Sort the Results on a Single Field (AC 635)
Sort the Results on Multiple Fields (AC 636)
Sort the Results in Descending Order (AC 637)
Omit Duplicates When Sorting (AC 638)

Subqueries
Use a Subquery (AC 651)

Updates
Use an INSERT Command (AC 653)
Use an UPDATE Command (AC 654)
Use a DELETE Command (AC 655)

CONSIDER THIS: PLAN AHEAD

What decisions will you need to make when creating your own SQL queries?

Use these guidelines as you complete the assignments in this chapter and create your own queries outside of this class.

1. **Select the fields for the query.**
   a. Examine the requirements for the query you are constructing to determine which fields are to be included.

2. **Determine which table or tables contain these fields.**
   a. For each field, determine the table in which it is located.

3. **Determine criteria.**
   a. Determine any criteria that data must satisfy to be included in the results.
   b. If there are more than two tables in the query, determine the criteria to be used to ensure the data matches correctly.

4. **Determine sort order.**
   a. Is the data to be sorted in some way?
   b. If so, by what field or fields is it to be sorted?

5. **Determine grouping.**
   a. Is the data to be grouped in some way?
   b. If so, by what field is it to be grouped?
   c. Identify any calculations to be made for the group.

6. **Determine any update operations to be performed.**
   a. Determine whether rows need to be inserted, changed, or deleted.
   b. Determine the tables involved.

CONSIDER THIS

How should you submit solutions to questions in the assignments identified with a ✳ symbol?

Every assignment in this book contains one or more questions identified with a ✳ symbol. These questions require you to think beyond the assigned database. Present your solutions to the questions in the format required by your instructor. Possible formats may include one or more of these options: write the answer; create a document that contains the answer; present your answer to the class; discuss your answer in a group; record the answer as audio or video using a webcam, smartphone, or portable media player; or post answers on a blog, wiki, or website.

Apply Your Knowledge

Reinforce the skills and apply the concepts you learned in this chapter.

Using Criteria, Joining Tables, and Sorting in SQL Queries

Note: To complete this assignment, you will be required to use the Data Files for Students. Visit www.cengage.com/ct/studentdownload for detailed instructions or contact your instructor for information about accessing the required files.

Instructions: Start Access. Open the Apply Natural Products database that you used in Apply Your Knowledge in Chapter 9 on page AC 611. (If you did not complete the exercise, see your instructor for a copy of the database.) Use SQL to query the Apply Natural Products database.

Perform the following tasks:
1. Find all customers whose customer type is Salon. Display all fields in the query result. Save the query as AYK Step 1 Query.

2. Find all customers whose amount paid amount or balance amount is $0.00. Display the Customer Number, Customer Name, Amount Paid, and Balance fields in the query result. Save the query as AYK Step 2 Query.

3. Find all customers in the Customer table who are not located in TN. Display the Customer Number, Customer Name, and State in the query result. Save the query as AYK Step 3 Query.

4. Display the Customer Number, Customer Name, Sales Rep Number, First Name, and Last Name for all customers. Sort the records in ascending order by sales rep number and customer number. Save the query as AYK Step 4 Query.

5. Display the Sales Rep Number, First Name, Last Name, and Salary YTD for all sales reps whose Salary YTD amount is greater than $15,000. Save the query as AYK Step 5 Query.

6. If requested to do so by your instructor, rename the AYK Step 5 Query as Last Name Query where Last Name is your last name.

7. Submit the revised database in the format specified by your instructor.

8. ✸ What WHERE clause would you use if you wanted to find all customers who lived in cities beginning with the letter G?

Extend Your Knowledge

Extend the skills you learned in this chapter and experiment with new skills. You may need to use Help to complete the assignment.

Using Wildcards, Special Operators, and Subqueries

Note: To complete this assignment, you will be required to use the Data Files for Students. Visit www.cengage.com/ct/studentdownload for detailed instructions or contact your instructor for information about accessing the required files.

Instructions: Start Access. Open the Extend Personal Training database. Personal Training is a small company that offers personal fitness training and customized workouts. Use SQL to answer the following queries.

Perform the following tasks:
1. Find all clients where the client's first name is either Alex or Alec. Display the Client Number, First Name, Last Name, and Address fields in the query result. Save the query as EYK Step 1 Query.

2. Find all clients who live in Fort Mill or Indian Land. Use the IN operator. Display the Client Number, First Name, Last Name, and City fields in the query result. Save the query as EYK Step 2 Query.

3. Find all clients whose amount paid amount is greater than or equal to $400.00 and less than or equal to $500.00. Use the BETWEEN operator. Display the Client Number, First Name, Last Name, and Amount Paid fields in the query result. Save the query as EYK Step 3 Query.

4. Use a subquery to find all trainers whose clients are located in Ballantyne. Display the Trainer Number, First Name, and Last Name fields in the query result. Save the query as EYK Step 4 Query.

5. If requested to do so by your instructor, rename the EYK Step 4 Query as First Name City Query where First Name is your first name and City is the city where you currently reside.

6. Submit the revised database in the format specified by your instructor.

7. ✸ What WHERE clause would you use to find the answer to Step 2 without using the IN operator?

Analyze, Correct, Improve

Analyze a database, correct all errors, and improve the design.

Correcting SQL Errors and Improving a Query Result

Note: To complete this assignment, you will be required to use the Data Files for Students. Visit www.cengage.com/ct/studentdownload for detailed instructions or contact your instructor for information about accessing the required files.

Instructions: Start Access and open the Analyze Metro Couriers database. Metro Couriers is a local company that provides courier services to business organizations in the metro area of a large city.

Continued >

Analyze, Correct, Improve *continued*

Perform the following tasks:

1. Correct The owner created the SQL query shown in Figure 10–37 but when he viewed the query results, there were 36 records and he knows that is not correct. Also, the query results did not sort correctly. The results should be sorted by ascending courier number and then by descending balance. Open the Analyze Courier Query in SQL view, correct the errors, and then save the query with the same name.

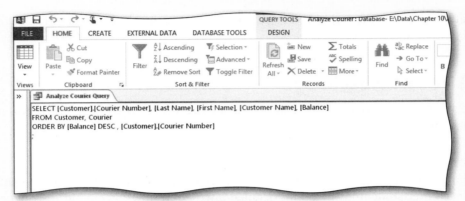

Figure 10–37

2. Improve The owner also created a SQL query to total customer balances for each courier. The query results are shown in Figure 10–38. The owner does not understand why Expr1001 is displayed as the column heading for the total balances. He has asked you to add a more meaningful name for the calculation. Open the Analyze Grouping Query in SQL view, improve the query, and then save the query with the same name. If requested to do so by your instructor, rename the query as Analyze Last Name Query where Last Name is your last name. Submit the revised database in the format specified by your instructor.

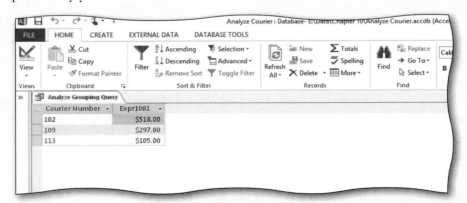

Figure 10–38

3. ✷ Why does the query shown in Figure 10–37 return 36 results?

In the Labs

Design, create, modify, and/or use a database following the guidelines, concepts, and skills presented in this chapter. Labs are listed in order of increasing difficulty. Labs 1 and 2, which increase in difficulty, require you to create solutions based on what you learned in the chapter; Lab 3 requires you to create a solution, which uses cloud and web technologies, by learning and investigating on your own from general guidance.

Lab 1: Querying the Technology Services Database Using SQL

Note: Use the database modified in Lab 1 of Chapter 9 on page AC 613 for this assignment, or see your instructor for information on accessing the required files.

Problem: Technology Services wants to learn more about SQL and has determined a number of questions it wants SQL to answer. You must obtain answers to the questions using SQL.

Instructions: Perform the following tasks:

1. Start Access. Open the Lab 1 Technology Services database and create a new query in SQL view. Find all clients who are located in the city of Austin. Include the Client Number, Client Name, and City in the query results. Save the query as ITL 1 Step 1 Query.

2. Find all clients located in North Carolina (NC) with an amount paid amount greater than $3,000.00. Include the Client Number, Client Name, and Amount Paid fields in the query results. Save the query as ITL 1 Step 2 Query.

3. Find all clients whose names begin with the letter W. Include the Client Number, Client Name, and City fields in the query result. Save the query as ITL 1 Step 3 Query.

4. List all cities in descending order. Each city should appear only once. Save the query as ITL 1 Step 4 Query.

5. Display the client number, client name, service rep number, first name, and last name for all clients. Sort the results in ascending order by service rep number and client number. Save the query as ITL 1 Step 5 Query.

6. List the average balance due amount grouped by service rep number. Name the average balance as Average Balance. Save the query as ITL 1 Step 6 Query.

7. Find the client number, name, and city for every pair of clients who are located in the same city. Save the query as ITL 1 Step 7 Query.

8. Find the client numbers, names, and service rep numbers for all clients that have service requests. Use the alias S for the Service Requests table and C for the Client table. Each client should appear only once in the results. Save the query as ITL 1 Step 8 Query.

9. Use a subquery to find all service reps whose clients are located in Georgetown. Save the query as ITL 1 Step 9 Query.

10. Find the average balance due amount for service rep 52. Save the query as ITL 1 Step 10 Query.

11. If requested to do so by your instructor, open the Service Rep table and change the first and last name for service rep 52 to your first and last name.

12. Submit the revised database in the format specified by your instructor.

13. ✴ What WHERE clause would you use to find all records where one of the resources needed was DATA?

Lab 2: Querying the Team Designs Database Using SQL

Problem: Team Designs wants to learn more about SQL and has determined a number of questions it wants SQL to answer. You must obtain answers to the questions using SQL.

Note: Use the database modified in Lab 2 of Chapter 9 on page AC 613 for this assignment, or see your instructor for information on accessing the required files.

Instructions: Perform the following tasks.

1. Start Access and open the Lab 2 Team Designs database. Using SQL, find all records in the Item table where the difference between the base cost of an item and the wholesale price is

Continued >

STUDENT ASSIGNMENTS

In the Labs *continued*

greater than $2.00. Display the item number, description, wholesale price, and base cost in the query result. Save the query as ITL 2 Step 1 Query.

2. Display the item number, description, and difference (base cost – wholesale cost) for all items. Name the computed field Markup. Save the query as ITL 2 Step 2 Query.

3. Find all items where the description begins with the letter, F. Include the item number and description in the query result. Save the query as ITL 2 Step 3 Query.

4. Display the supplier name, item number, description, and base cost for all items where the number on hand is greater than 100. Sort the results in ascending order by supplier name and description. Save the query as ITL 2 Step 4 Query.

5. Find the average wholesale price by supplier. Name the computed field Avg Wholesale. Include the supplier code in the result. Save the query as ITL 2 Step 5 Query.

6. Find the total number of reordered items in the Reorder table. Name the computed field Total Ordered. Include the item number in the result. Save the query as ITL 2 Step 6 Query.

7. Add the following record to the Reorder table.

Item Number	Date Ordered	Number Ordered
6345	10/9/2014	8

Save the query to add the record as ITL 2 Step 7 Query.

8. If requested to do so by your instructor, rename the ITL 2 Step 7 Query as LastName Reorder Query where LastName is your last name.

9. Update the Number Ordered field to 12 for those records where the Item Number is 6345. Save the query to update the records as ITL 2 Step 9 Query.

10. Delete all records from the Reorder table where the Item Number is 6345. Save the query to delete the records as ITL 2 Step 10 Query.

11. Submit the revised database in the format specified by your instructor.

12. ✳How would you write a SQL query for Step 9 if the instructions were to increment the number ordered by 4?

Lab 3: Expand Your World: Cloud and Web Technologies Using SQL on the Web

Problem: Many SQL tutorials are available on the web. One site, www.w3schools.com/sql/, has an online SQL editor that allows you to edit SQL commands and then run the commands. You will use this editor to create and run queries.

Note: For each SQL statement that you create and run, use the * to select all fields in the table. Copy the SQL statement and the number of results retrieved to your blog, Google document, or Word document.

Instructions: Perform the following tasks:

1. Create a blog, a Google document, or a Word document on the SkyDrive on which to store your SQL statements and the number of results obtained from the query.

2. Access the www.w3schools.com/sql/ website and spend some time becoming familiar with the tutorial and how it works.

3. Create a query to find all records in the OrderDetails table where the ProductID is 14 and the Quantity is less than 15.

4. Create a query to find all records in the Customers table where the City begins with the letter M. (*Hint*: Use the percent symbol (%), not the asterisk, in this query.)

5. Create a query to find all records in the Employees table where the birth date of the employee is before January 1, 1960. (*Hint*: View all the records in the table first to determine how dates are stored.)

6. Submit the document containing your statements and results in the format specified by your instructor.

7. ✳ What differences did you notice between the online SQL editor and Access SQL? Which one would you prefer to use? Why?

Consider This: Your Turn

Apply your creative thinking and problem solving skills to design and implement a solution.

1: Querying the Fine Crafts Database Using SQL
Personal/Academic

Instructions: Open the Fine Crafts database you modified in Chapter 9 on page AC 614. If you did not modify this database, contact your instructor for information about accessing the required files.

Part 1:   Use the concepts and techniques presented in this chapter to create queries using SQL for the following. Save each query using the format CT 1 Step x Query where x is the step letter.

   a.   Find the item number and description of all items that contain the word, Stool.
   b.   Find the item number, description, price, and number on hand for all items where the price is less than $50.00 and the number on hand is less than 5.
   c.   Calculate the total price (price * on hand) of each item available for sale. Show the item number, description, and total price.
   d.   Find the students who made each item. Show the student's first name and last name as well as the item number, description, price, and on hand.
   e.   Modify the query you created in Step d to restrict retrieval to those items with a price less than $20.00.
   f.   Find the average price amount grouped by student code.

Submit your assignment in the format specified by your instructor.

Part 2:   ✳ You made several decisions while creating the queries in this assignment. What was the rationale behind your decisions? How could you modify the query in Step e to find items with a price between $20.00 and $40.00?

2: Creating Queries for the Landscaping Services Database Using SQL
Professional

Instructions: Open the Landscaping Services database you modified in Chapter 9 on page AC 615. If you did not modify this database, contact your instructor for information about accessing the required files.

Part 1:   Use the concepts and techniques presented in this chapter to create queries using SQL for the following. Save each query using the format CT 2 Step x Query where x is the step letter.

   a.   Find the names of all customers who have the letters, comm, in their customer name.
   b.   Find the totals of the amount paid and the balance amounts for all customers.
   c.   Find all supervisors who started before 1/1/2013. Show the supervisor first name, last name, and start date.
   d.   Find the supervisor for each customer. List the supervisor number, first name, last name, customer number, and customer name. Assign aliases to the Customer and Supervisor tables. Sort the results in ascending order by supervisor number and customer number.
   e.   Restrict the records retrieved in Step d above to only those records where the balance is greater than $800.00.

Continued >

Consider This: Your Turn *continued*

 f. Find the average balance amount grouped by supervisor number.

 g. Restrict the records retrieved in Step f to only those groups where the average balance amount is greater than $700.00.

 h. List the customer number, customer name, service code, service description, and hours spent for all service requests. Sort the results by customer number and service code.

Submit your assignment in the format specified by your instructor.

Part 2: ✺ You made several decisions while doing this assignment. What was the rationale behind your decisions? How could you modify the query in Step h to find only those customers where hours spent is equal to zero?

3: Understanding Advanced SQL Commands
Research and Collaboration

Note: To complete this assignment, you will be required to use the Data Files for Students. Visit www.cengage.com/ct/studentdownload for detailed instructions or contact your instructor for information about accessing the required files.

Part 1: Before you begin this assignment, download the Your Turn 3 Courier Services database from the Data Files for students and rename the database as your team name database. For example, if your team is the Fab Four, then name the database Fab Four. Use the database for this assignment. For this assignment you will create several SQL queries for the Courier Services database. Your team may need to use Help or research SQL commands on the web to complete the assignment. Create the following queries:

 a. List the courier number, customer number, service code, and service fee for all weekly services provided to customers.

 b. Find the number and name of all customers who had a service performed at 10:00 a.m. on any day of the week.

 c. Add a new service to the Services Offered table. The service is Food Delivery, the charge is $8.00, and the service code is 06.

 d. Update the fees for all services by adding $1.50 to the current service fees.

 e. Find the five customers with the highest balances. (*Hint*: You will need to add a new clause to your SQL command.)

Submit your assignment in the format specified by your instructor.

Part 2: ✺ You made several decisions while doing this assignment. What was the rationale behind your decisions? What resources did you use to help you create the SQL commands for this assignment?

Learn Online

Reinforce what you learned in this chapter with games, exercises, training, and many other online activities and resources.

Student Companion Site Reinforcement activities and resources are available at no additional cost on www.cengagebrain.com. Visit www.cengage.com/ct/studentdownload for detailed instructions about accessing the resources available at the Student Companion Site.

SAM Put your skills into practice with SAM Projects! SAM Projects for this chapter can be found online. If you have a SAM account, go to www.cengage.com/sam2013 to access SAM assignments for this chapter.

11 | Database Design

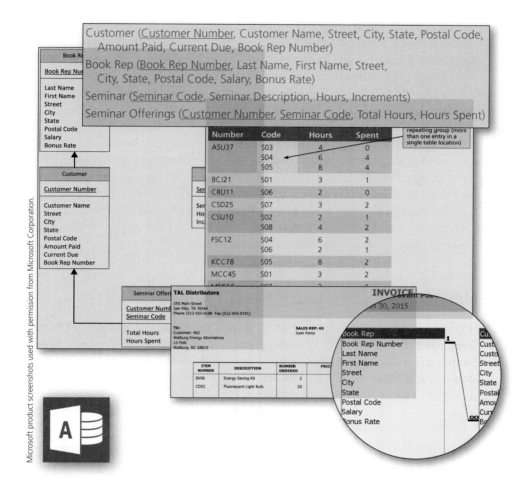

Microsoft product screenshots used with permission from Microsoft Corporation.

Objectives

You will have mastered the material in this chapter when you can:

- Understand the terms entity, attribute, and relationship

- Understand the terms relation and relational database

- Understand functional dependence and identify when one column is functionally dependent on another

- Understand the term primary key and identify primary keys in tables

- Design a database to satisfy a set of requirements

- Convert an unnormalized relation to first normal form

- Convert tables from first normal form to second normal form

- Convert tables from second normal form to third normal form

- Understand how to represent the design of a database using diagrams

11 | Database Design

Introduction

This chapter presents a method for determining the tables and fields necessary to satisfy a set of requirements. **Database design** is the process of determining the particular tables and fields that will comprise a database. In designing a database, you must identify the tables in the database, the fields in the tables, the primary keys of the tables, and the relationships between the tables.

The chapter begins by examining some important concepts concerning relational databases and then presents the design method. To illustrate the process, the chapter presents the requirements for the Bavant Publishing database. It then applies the design method to those requirements to produce the database design. The chapter applies the design method to a second set of requirements, which are requirements for a company called TAL Distributors. It next examines normalization, which is a process that you can use to identify and fix potential problems in database designs. The chapter concludes by explaining how to use a company's policies and objectives — which are typically addressed in existing documentation — to plan and design a database. Finally, you will learn how to represent a database design with a diagram.

Project — Design a database

This chapter expands on the database design guidelines presented in Chapter 1 beginning on page AC 58. Without a good understanding of database design, you cannot use a database management system such as Access effectively. In this chapter, you will learn how to design two databases by using the database design process shown in Figure 11–1.

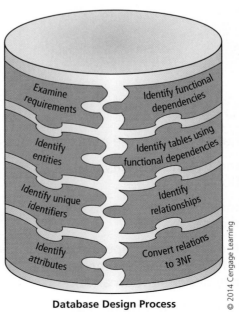

Database Design Process

Figure 11–1

You will design a database for Bavant Publishing that is similar to the database you have used in the previous chapters. You also will design a database for TAL Distributors, a distributor of energy-saving and water-conservation devices.

Entities, Attributes, and Relationships

Working in the database environment requires that you be familiar with some specific terms and concepts. The terms *entity*, *attribute*, and *relationship* are fundamental when discussing databases. An **entity** is like a noun: it is a person, place, thing, or event. The entities of interest to Bavant Publishing, for example, are such things as book reps, customers, and seminars. The entities that are of interest to a college include students, faculty, and classes; a real estate agency is interested in buyers, sellers, properties, and agents; and a used car dealer is interested in vehicles, customers, salespeople, and manufacturers. When creating a database, an entity is represented as a table.

An **attribute** is a property of an entity. The term is used here exactly as it is used in everyday English. For the entity *person*, for example, the list of attributes might include such things as eye color and height. For Bavant Publishing, the attributes of interest for the entity *customer* are such things as name, address, city, and so on. For the entity *faculty* at a school, the attributes would be such things as faculty number, name, office number, phone, and so on. For the entity *vehicle* at a car dealership, the attributes are such things as the vehicle identification number, model, price, year, and so on. In databases, attributes are represented as the fields in a table or tables.

A **relationship** is an association between entities. There is an association between book reps and customers, for example, at Bavant Publishing. A book rep is associated with all of his or her customers, and a customer is associated with the one book rep to whom the customer is assigned. Technically, you say that a book rep is *related* to all of his or her customers, and a customer is *related* to his or her book rep.

The relationship between book reps and customers is an example of a one-to-many relationship because one book rep is associated with many customers, but each customer is associated with only one book rep. In this type of relationship, the word *many* is used in a way that is different from everyday English; it might not always mean a large number. In this context, for example, the term *many* means that a book rep might be associated with *any* number of customers. That is, one book rep can be associated with zero, one, or more customers.

There also is a relationship between customers and seminars. Each customer can be offered many seminars, and each seminar can be offered to many customers. This is an example of a many-to-many relationship.

How does a relational database handle entities, attributes of entities, and relationships between entities? Entities and attributes are fairly simple. Each entity has its own table; in the Bavant Publishing database, there is one table for book reps, one table for customers, and so on. The attributes of an entity become the columns in the table. In the table for customers, for example, there is a column for the customer number, a column for the customer name, and so on.

What about relationships? Relationships are implemented through matching fields. One-to-many relationships, for example, are implemented by including matching fields in the related tables. Book reps and customers are related, for example, by including the Book Rep Number field in both the Book Rep table and the Customer table.

Many-to-many relationships are implemented through an additional table that contains matching fields for both of the related tables. Customers and Seminars are related, for example, through the Seminar Offerings table. Both the Customer table and the Seminar Offerings table contain Customer Number fields. In addition, both the Seminar and the Seminar Offerings table contain Seminar Code fields.

BTW

Systems Analysis
The determination of database requirements is part of a process known as systems analysis. A systems analyst interviews users, examines existing and proposed documents, investigates current procedures, and reviews organizational policies to determine exactly the type of data needs the database must support.

BTW

Entities
Bavant Publishing could include many other entities in a database, such as entities for employees, textbooks, and authors. The decisions on which entities to include are part of the process of determining database requirements based on user needs.

Relational Databases

A relational database is a collection of tables similar to the tables for Bavant Publishing that appear in Figure 11–2. In the Bavant Publishing database, the Customer table contains information about the customers to which Bavant Publishing provides foreign language textbooks (Figure 11–2a). Note that, for simplification purposes, the tables in the figure do not include all the fields of the final Bavant database in Chapter 10.

Customer

Customer Number	Customer Name	Street	City	State	Postal Code	Amount Paid	Current Due	Book Rep Number
ASU37	Applewood State University	300 University Ave.	Greer	PA	19158	$41,530.98	$38,812.66	42
BCJ21	Brodkin Junior College	4806 Park Dr.	Greer	PA	19158	$0.00	$6,081.98	42
CRU11	Cristie University	1200 University Pl.	Pleasantburg	NJ	07025	$0.00	$14,250.00	42
CSD25	Cowpens ISD	829 Wooster Ave.	Gossett	PA	19157	$12,750.00	$13,275.00	53
CSU10	Camellia State University	725 Camellia St.	Pleasantburg	NJ	07025	$63,246.88	$69,847.76	53
DCC34	Dartt Community College	3827 Burgess Dr.	Chambers	NJ	07037	$21,345.50	$23,467.75	65
FSC12	First State College	7300 Cedar Rd.	Quaker	DE	19719	$34,557.25	$23,875.98	65
FSU23	Farnham State University	1445 Hubert St.	Gaston	DE	19723	$18,268.00	$22,024.50	42
KCC78	Key Community College System	7523 Penn Ave.	Adelphia	PA	19159	$21,288.65	$11,367.49	65
MCC45	Mauldin Community College	72 Montrose St.	Chesnee	NJ	07053	$9,500.00	$5,000.00	53
MEC56	Mehitable College	202 College St.	Gaston	DE	19723	$9,111.19	$7,310.76	42
PLI22	Pratt-Last Institute	236 Ashton Ave.	Pleasantburg	NJ	07025	$17,229.45	$11,769.75	53
SCC77	Stallone Community College	1200 Franklin Blvd.	Adelphia	PA	19156	$7,525.98	$2,515.78	42
SEC19	Seaborn College	345 Mather Rd.	Quaker	DE	19719	$9,225.34	$10,496.89	65
TSC02	Tri-State Consortium	3400 Metropolitan Pkwy.	Adelphia	PA	19156	$34,578.90	$9,432.56	65

Figure 11–2 (a) Customer Table

Bavant assigns each customer to a specific book rep. The Book Rep table contains information about the reps to whom these customers are assigned (Figure 11–2b).

Book Rep

Book Rep Number	Last Name	First Name	Street	City	State	Postal Code	Salary	Bonus Rate
42	Perez	Melina	261 Porter Dr.	Adelphia	PA	19156	$31,500.00	0.20
48	Statnik	Michael	3135 Simpson Dr.	Pleasantburg	NJ	07025	$29,000.00	0.20
53	Chin	Robert	265 Maxwell St.	Gossett	PA	19157	$26,250.00	0.19
65	Rogers	Tracy	1827 Maple Ave.	Adelphia	PA	19159	$7,750.00	0.18

Figure 11–2 (b) Book Rep Table

The Seminar table lists the specific seminars that the reps at Bavant Publishing offer to their customers (Figure 11–2c). Each seminar has a code and a description. The table also includes the number of hours for which the seminar usually is offered and the seminar's increments, that is, the standard time blocks, in which the seminar usually is offered. The first row, for example, indicates that seminar S01 is Integrating with Learning Management Systems. The seminar typically is offered in 1-hour increments for a total of 3 hours.

Seminar			
Seminar Code	**Seminar Description**	**Hours**	**Increments**
S01	Integrating with Learning Management Systems	3	1
S02	Using Web-based Technologies and Tools	2	1
S03	Mobile Apps	4	2
S04	Video Podcasting	6	2
S05	Creating Virtual Worlds	8	2
S06	Clickers in the Classroom	2	1
S07	Online Seminar Strategies	3	1
S08	Using Social Networking	4	2

Figure 11–2 (c) Seminar Table

The Seminar Offerings table contains a customer number, a seminar code, the total number of hours for which the seminar is scheduled, and the number of hours the customer has already spent in the seminar (Figure 11–2d). The first record shows that customer number ASU37 currently has scheduled seminar S03. The seminar is scheduled for 4 hours, of which no hours have currently been spent. The total hours is usually the same as the number of hours indicated for the seminar in the Seminar table, but it can differ.

BTW
Relationships
One-to-one relationships also can occur but they are not common. To implement a one-to-one relationship, treat it as a one-to-many relationship. You must determine which table will be the one table and which table will be the many table. To do so, consider what may happen in the future. In the case of one project that has one employee assigned to it, more employees could be added. Therefore, the project table would be the one table and the employee table would be the many table.

© 2014 Cengage Learning

Seminar Offerings			
Customer Number	**Seminar Code**	**Total Hours**	**Hours Spent**
ASU37	S03	4	0
ASU37	S04	6	4
ASU37	S05	8	4
BCJ21	S01	3	1
CRU11	S06	2	0
CSD25	S07	3	2
CSU10	S02	2	1
CSU10	S08	4	2
FSC12	S04	6	2
FSC12	S06	2	1
KCC78	S05	8	2
MCC45	S01	3	2
MEC56	S07	3	0
SEC19	S02	2	1
SEC19	S07	3	1

© 2014 Cengage Learning

Figure 11–2 (d) Seminar Offerings Table

The formal term for a table is relation. If you study the tables shown in Figure 11–2 on the previous page, you might see that there are certain restrictions you should place on relations. Each column in a table should have a unique name, and entries in each column should match this column name. For example, in the Postal Code column, all entries should in fact *be* postal codes. In addition, each row should be unique. After all, if two rows in a table contain identical data, the second row does not provide any information that you do not already have. In addition, for maximum flexibility, the order in which columns and rows appear in a table should be immaterial. Finally, a table's design is less complex if you restrict each position in the table to a single entry, that is, you do not permit multiple entries, often called **repeating groups,** in the table. These restrictions lead to the following definition:

A **relation** is a two-dimensional table in which:

1. The entries in the table are single-valued; that is, each location in the table contains a single entry.
2. Each column has a distinct name, technically called the *attribute name*.
3. All values in a column are values of the same attribute; that is, all entries must correspond to the column name.
4. Each row is distinct; that is, no two rows are identical.

Figure 11–3a shows a table with repeating groups, which violates Rule 1. Figure 11–3b shows a table in which two columns have the same name, which violates Rule 2. Figure 11–3c shows a table in which one of the entries in the Seminar Description column is not a seminar description, which violates Rule 3. Figure 11–3d shows a table with two identical rows, which violates Rule 4.

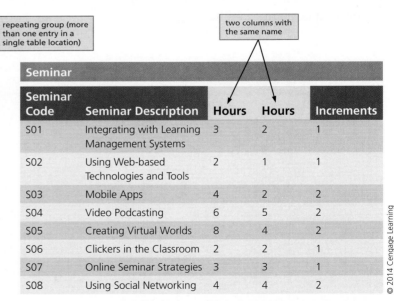

Seminar Offerings

Customer Number	Seminar Code	Total Hours	Hours Spent
ASU37	S03	4	0
	S04	6	4
	S05	8	4
BCJ21	S01	3	1
CRU11	S06	2	0
CSD25	S07	3	2
CSU10	S02	2	1
	S08	4	2
FSC12	S04	6	2
	S06	2	1
KCC78	S05	8	2
MCC45	S01	3	2
MEC56	S07	3	0
SEC19	S02	2	1
	S07	3	1

repeating group (more than one entry in a single table location)

© 2014 Cengage Learning

Figure 11–3 (a) Seminar Offerings Table Violation of Rule 1 – Table Contains Repeating Groups

two columns with the same name

Seminar

Seminar Code	Seminar Description	Hours	Hours	Increments
S01	Integrating with Learning Management Systems	3	2	1
S02	Using Web-based Technologies and Tools	2	1	1
S03	Mobile Apps	4	2	2
S04	Video Podcasting	6	5	2
S05	Creating Virtual Worlds	8	4	2
S06	Clickers in the Classroom	2	2	1
S07	Online Seminar Strategies	3	3	1
S08	Using Social Networking	4	4	2

© 2014 Cengage Learning

Figure 11–3 (b) Seminar Table Violation of Rule 2 – Each Column has a Distinct Name

Seminar			
Seminar Code	**Seminar Description**	**Hours**	**Increments**
S01	Integrating with Learning Management Systems	3	1
S02	Using Web-based Technologies and Tools	2	1
S03	7@!	4	2
S04	Video Podcasting	6	2
S05	Creating Virtual Worlds	8	2
S06	Clickers in the Classroom	2	1
S07	Online Seminar Strategies	3	1
S08	Using Social Networking	4	2

value does not correspond to column name; that is, it is not a seminar description

© 2014 Cengage Learning

Figure 11–3 (c) Seminar Table Violation of Rule 3 – All Entries in a Column Must Correspond to the Column Name

Seminar			
Seminar Code	**Seminar Description**	**Hours**	**Increments**
S01	Integrating with Learning Management Systems	3	1
S02	Using Web-based Technologies and Tools	2	1
S03	Mobile Apps	4	2
S03	Mobile Apps	4	2
S04	Video Podcasting	6	2
S05	Creating Virtual Worlds	8	2
S06	Clickers in the Classroom	2	1
S07	Online Seminar Strategies	3	1
S08	Using Social Networking	4	2

identical rows

© 2014 Cengage Learning

Figure 11–3 (d) Seminar Table Violation of Rule 4 – Each Row is Distinct

In addition, in a relation, the order of columns is immaterial. You can view the columns in any order you want. The order of rows is also immaterial. You can view the rows in any order you want.

A **relational database** is a collection of relations. Rows in a table (relation) often are called **records** or **tuples**. Columns in a table (relation) often are called **fields** or **attributes**. Typically, the terms *record* and *field* are used in Access.

To depict the structure of a relational database, you can use a commonly accepted shorthand representation: you write the name of the table and then within parentheses list all of the fields in the table. Each table should begin on a new line. If the entries in the table occupy more than one line, the entries that appear on the next line should be indented so it is clear that they do not constitute another table. Using this method, you would represent the Bavant Publishing database as in Figure 11–4.

Customer (Customer Number, Customer Name, Street, City, State, Postal Code, Amount Paid, Current Due, Book Rep Number)
Book Rep (Book Rep Number, Last Name, First Name, Street, City, State, Postal Code, Salary, Bonus Rate)
Seminar (Seminar Code, Seminar Description, Hours, Increments)
Seminar Offerings (Customer Number, Seminar Code, Total Hours, Hours Spent)

Figure 11–4

The Bavant Publishing database contains some duplicate field names. For example, the Book Rep Number field appears in *both* the Book Rep table *and* the Customer table. This duplication of names can lead to possible confusion. If you write Book Rep Number, it is not clear to which Book Rep Number field you are referring.

When duplicate field names exist in a database, you need to indicate the field to which you are referring. You do so by writing both the table name and the field name, separated by a period. You would write the Book Rep Number field in the Customer table as Customer.Book Rep Number and the Book Rep Number field in the Book Rep table as Book Rep.Book Rep Number. Technically, when you combine a field name with a table name, you say that you **qualify** the field names. It is *always* acceptable to qualify field names, even if there is no possibility of confusion. If confusion may arise, however, it is *essential* to qualify field names.

Functional Dependence

In the Bavant Publishing database (Figure 11–2 on page AC 668), a given customer number in the database will correspond to a single customer because customer numbers are unique. Thus, if you are given a customer number in the database, you could find a single name that corresponds to it. No ambiguity exists. The database terminology for this relationship between customer numbers and names is that Customer Number determines Customer Name, or, equivalently, that Customer Name is functionally dependent on Customer Number. Specifically, if you know that whenever you are given a value for one field, you will be able to determine a single value for a second field, the first field is said to **determine** the second field. In addition, the second field is said to be **functionally dependent** on the first.

There is a shorthand notation that represents functional dependencies using an arrow. To indicate that Customer Number determines Customer Name, or, equivalently, that Customer Name is functionally dependent on Customer Number, you would write Customer Number → Customer Name. The field that precedes the arrow determines the field that follows the arrow.

If you were given a city and asked to find a single customer's name, you could not do it. Given Greer as the city, for example, you would find two customer names, Applewood State University and Brodkin Junior College (Figure 11–5). Formally, you would say the City does *not* determine Customer Name, or that Customer Name is *not* functionally dependent on City.

BTW
Functional Dependence
To help identify functional dependencies, ask yourself the following question. If you know a unique value for an attribute, do you know the unique values for another attribute? For example, when you have three attributes — Book Rep Number, Last Name, and First Name — and you know a unique value for Book Rep Number, do you also know a unique value for Last Name and First Name? If so, then Last Name and First Name are functionally dependent on Book Rep Number.

CONSIDER THIS

In the Book Rep table, is Last Name functionally dependent on Book Rep Number?
Yes. If you are given a value for Book Rep Number, for example 42, you will always find a *single* last name, in this case Perez, associated with it.

In the Customer table, is Customer Name functionally dependent on Book Rep Number?
No. A given Book Rep Number occurs on multiple rows. Book Rep Number 42, for example, occurs on a row on which the Customer Name is Applewood State University. It also occurs on a row on which the Customer Name is Brodkin Junior College. Thus, rep number 42 is associated with more than one customer name.

city is Greer; name is
Applewood State University

Customer

Customer Number	Customer Name	Street	City	State	Postal Code	Amount Paid	Current Due	Book Rep Number
ASU37	Applewood State University	300 University Ave.	Greer	PA	19158	$41,530.98	$38,812.66	42
BCJ21	Brodkin Junior College	4806 Park Dr.	Greer	PA	19158	$0.00	$6,081.98	42
CRU11	Cristie University	1200 University Pl.	Pleasantburg	NJ	07025	$0.00	$14,250.00	42
CSD25	Cowpens ISD	829 Wooster Ave.	Gossett	PA	19157	$12,750.00	$13,275.00	53
CSU10	Camellia State University	725 Camellia St.	Pleasantburg	NJ	07025	$63,246.88	$69,847.76	53
DCC34	Dartt Community College		hambers	NJ	07037	$21,345.50	$23,467.75	65
FSC12	First State College	7300 Cedar Rd.	Quaker	DE	19719	$34,557.25	$23,875.98	65
FSU23	Farnham State University	1445 Hubert St.	Gaston	DE	19723	$18,268.00	$22,024.50	42
KCC78	Key Community College System	7523 Penn Ave.	Adelphia	PA	19159	$21,288.65	$11,367.49	65
MCC45	Mauldin Community College	72 Montrose St.	Chesnee	NJ	07053	$9,500.00	$5,000.00	53
MEC56	Mehitable College	202 College St.	Gaston	DE	19723	$9,111.19	$7,310.76	42
PLI22	Pratt-Last Institute	236 Ashton Ave.	Pleasantburg	NJ	07025	$17,229.45	$11,769.75	53
SCC77	Stallone Community College	1200 Franklin Blvd.	Adelphia	PA	19156	$7,525.98	$2,515.78	42
SEC19	Seaborn College	345 Mather Rd.	Quaker	DE	19719	$9,225.34	$10,496.89	65
TSC02	Tri-State Consortium	3400 Metropolitan Pkwy.	Adelphia	PA	19156	$34,578.90	$9,432.56	65

city is also Greer, but name is Brodkin Junior College (same city, but different customer name)

Figure 11–5

© 2014 Cengage Learning

In the Seminar Offerings table, is Hours Spent functionally dependent on Customer Number?
No. There is a row, for example, on which the Customer Number is ASU37 and the Hours Spent is 0. There is another row on which the Customer Number is ASU37 but the Hours Spent is 4, a different number.

In the Seminar Offerings table, is Hours Spent functionally dependent on Seminar Code?
No. There is a row, for example, on which the Seminar Code is S04 and the Hours Spent is 4. There is another row on which the Seminar Code is S04 but the Hours Spent is 2, a different number.

On which fields is the Hours Spent functionally dependent?
To determine a value for Hours Spent, you need both a Customer Number and a Seminar Code. In other words, Hours Spent is functionally dependent on the combination, formally called the **concatenation**, of Customer Number and Seminar Code. That is, given a Customer Number *and* a Seminar Code, you can find a single value for Hours Spent.

On which fields is the Total Hours functionally dependent?
Because the Total Hours for a given seminar can vary from one customer to another, Total Hours is also functionally dependent on the combination of Customer Number and Seminar Code.

On which fields would the Total Hours be functionally dependent if every time a seminar was scheduled, the Total Hours had to be the same as the number of hours given in the Seminar table?
In that case, to determine Total Hours, you would only need to know the Seminar Code. Thus, Total Hours would be functionally dependent on Seminar Code.

Primary Key

The **primary key** of a table is the field or minimum collection of fields — the fewest number of fields possible — that uniquely identifies a given row in that table. In the Book Rep table, the rep's number uniquely identifies a given row. Any rep number appears on only one row of the table. Thus, Book Rep Number is the primary key. Similarly, Customer Number is the primary key of the Customer table, and Seminar Code is the primary key of the Seminar table.

Is the Customer Number field the primary key for the Seminar Offerings table?
No, because it does not functionally determine either Total Hours or Hours Spent.

Is the Seminar Code field the primary key for the Seminar Offerings table?
No, because, like Customer Number, it does not functionally determine either Total Hours or Hours Spent.

What is the primary key of the Seminar Offerings table?
The primary key is the combination of the Customer Number and Seminar Code fields. You can determine all other fields from this combination. Further, neither the Customer Number nor the Seminar Code alone has this property.

Is the combination of the Seminar Code and Seminar Description fields the primary key for the Seminar table?
No. Although it is true that you can determine all fields in the Seminar table by this combination, Seminar Code alone also has this property. The Seminar Code field is the primary key.

The primary key provides an important way of distinguishing one row in a table from another. In the shorthand representation, you underline the field or collection of fields that comprise the primary key for each table in the database. Thus, the complete shorthand representation for the Bavant Publishing database is shown in Figure 11–6.

Customer (<u>Customer Number</u>, Customer Name, Street, City, State, Postal Code, Amount Paid, Current Due, Book Rep Number)

Book Rep (<u>Book Rep Number</u>, Last Name, First Name, Street, City, State, Postal Code, Salary, Bonus Rate)

Seminar (<u>Seminar Code</u>, Seminar Description, Hours, Increments)

Seminar Offerings (<u>Customer Number</u>, <u>Seminar Code</u>, Total Hours, Hours Spent)

Figure 11–6

BTW
Candidate Keys
According to the definition of a candidate key, a Social Security number is a legitimate primary key. Many databases use a person's Social Security number as a primary key. However, many institutions and organizations are moving away from using Social Security numbers because of privacy issues. Instead, many institutions and organizations use unique student numbers or employee numbers as primary keys.

Occasionally, but not often, there might be more than one possibility for the primary key. For example, if the Bavant Publishing database included the rep's Social Security number in the Book Rep table, either the rep number or the Social Security number could serve as the primary key. In this case, both fields are referred to as candidate keys. Similar to a primary key, a **candidate key** is a field or combination of fields on which all fields in the table are functionally dependent. Thus, the definition for primary key really defines candidate key as well. There can be many candidate keys, although having more than one is very rare. By contrast, there is only one primary key. The remaining candidate keys are called **alternate keys**.

Database Design

This section presents a specific database design method, based on a set of requirements that the database must support. The section then presents a sample of such requirements and illustrates the design method by designing a database to satisfy these requirements.

Design Process

The following is a method for designing a database for a set of requirements.

1. Examine the requirements and identify the entities, or objects, involved. Assign names to the entities. The entities will become tables. If, for example, the design involves the entities departments and employees, you could assign the names, Department and Employee. If the design involves the entities customers, orders, and parts, you could assign the names, Customer, Orders, and Part.

> **NOTE:** The word, Order, has special meaning in SQL. If you use it for the name of a table, you will not be able to use SQL to query that table. A common approach to avoid this problem is to make the name plural. That is the reason for choosing Orders rather than Order as the name of the table.

2. Identify a unique identifier for each entity. For example, if one of the entities is parts, you would determine what it takes to uniquely identify each individual part. In other words, what enables the organization to distinguish one part from another? For a part entity, it may be Item Number. For a customer entity, it may be Customer Number. If there is no such unique identifier, it is a good idea to add one. Perhaps the previous system was a manual one where customers were not assigned numbers, in which case this would be a good time to add Customer Numbers to the system. If there is no natural candidate for a primary key, you can add an AutoNumber field, which is similar to the ID field that Access adds automatically when you create a new table.

3. Identify the attributes for all the entities. These attributes will become the fields in the tables. It is possible that more than one entity has the same attribute. At Bavant Publishing, for example, customers and reps both have the attributes of street address, city, state, and postal code. To address this duplication, you can follow the name of the attribute with the corresponding entity in parentheses. Thus, Street (Customer) would be the street address of a customer, whereas Street (Book Rep) would be the street address of a rep.

4. Identify the functional dependencies that exist among the attributes.

5. Use the functional dependencies to identify the tables. You do this by placing each attribute with the attribute or minimum combination of attributes on which it is functionally dependent. The attribute or attributes on which all other attributes in the table are dependent will be the primary key of the table. The remaining attributes will be the other fields in the table. Once you have determined all the fields in the table, you can assign an appropriate name to the table.

6. Determine and implement relationships among the entities. The basic relationships are one-to-many and many-to-many.

One-to-many. You implement a one-to-many relationship by including the primary key of the "one" table as a foreign key in the "many" table. A **foreign key** is a field in one table whose values are required to match the primary key of another table. In the one-to-many relationship between book reps and customers, for example, you include the primary key of the Book Rep Table, Book Rep Number, as a foreign key in the Customer table. You may already have included this field in the earlier steps. If so, you simply would designate it to be a foreign key. If you had not added it already, you would need to add it at this point, designating it as a foreign key.

Many-to-many. A many-to-many relationship is implemented by creating a new table whose primary key is the combination of the keys of the original tables. To implement the many-to-many relationship between customers and seminars, for example, you would create a table whose primary key is the combination of Customer Number and Seminar Code, which are the primary keys of the original tables. Both of the fields that make up the primary key of the new table will be foreign keys also. The Customer Number field, for example, will be a foreign key required to match the primary key of the Customer table. Similarly, the Seminar Code field will be a foreign key required to match the primary key of the Seminar table.

You already may have identified such a table in the earlier steps, in which case, all you need to do is to be sure you have designated each portion of the primary key as a foreign key that is required to match the primary key of the appropriate table. If you have not, you would add the table at this point. The primary key will consist of the primary keys from each of the tables to be related. If there are any attributes that depend on the combination of fields that make up the primary key, you need to include them in this table. (*Note:* There may not be any other fields that are dependent on this combination. In that case, there will be no fields besides the fields that make up the primary key.)

The following sections illustrate the design process by designing the database for Bavant Publishing. The next section gives the requirements that this database must support, and the last section creates a database design based on those requirements.

Requirements for the Bavant Publishing Database

Systems analysts have examined the needs and organizational policies at Bavant Publishing and have determined that the Bavant Publishing database must support the following requirements:

1. For a customer, Bavant needs to maintain the customer number, name, street address, city, state, postal code, amount paid, and the amount that is currently due. They also need the total amount, which is the sum of the amount already paid and the current amount due.

2. For a book rep, store the rep number, last name, first name, street address, city, state, postal code, salary paid, and bonus rate.

3. For a seminar, store the seminar code, seminar description, hours, and increments. In addition, for each offering of the seminar, store the number of the customer for whom the seminar is offered, the total number of hours planned for the offering of the seminar, and the number of hours already spent in the seminar. The total hours may be the same as the normal number of hours for the seminar, but it need not be. This gives Bavant the flexibility of tailoring the offering of the seminar to the specific needs of the customer.

4. Each customer has a single rep to which the customer is assigned. Each rep may be assigned many customers.

5. A customer may be offered many seminars and a seminar may be offered to many customers.

Design of the Bavant Publishing Database

The following represents the application of the design method for the Bavant Publishing requirements.

1. There appear to be three entities: customers, reps, and seminars. Reasonable names for the corresponding tables are Customer, Book Rep, and Seminar, respectively.

2. The unique identifier for customers is the customer number. The unique identifier for reps is the rep number. The unique identifier for seminars is the seminar code. Reasonable names for the unique identifiers are Customer Number, Book Rep Number, and Seminar Code, respectively.

3. The attributes are:

> **Customer Number**
> **Customer Name**
> **Street (Customer)**
> **City (Customer)**
> **State (Customer)**
> **Postal Code (Customer)**
> **Amount Paid**
> **Current Due**
> **Book Rep Number**
> **Last Name**
> **First Name**
> **Street (Book Rep)**
> **City (Book Rep)**
> **State (Book Rep)**
> **Postal Code (Book Rep)**
> **Salary**
> **Bonus Rate**
> **Seminar Code**

> Seminar Description
>
> Hours
>
> Increments
>
> Total Hours
>
> Hours Spent

Remember that parentheses after an attribute indicate the entity to which the attribute corresponds. Thus, Street (Customer) represents the street address of a customer in a way that distinguishes it from Street (Book Rep), which represents the street address of a rep.

CONSIDER THIS

Why is Total Amount not included?

Total Amount, which is Amount Paid plus Current Due, can be calculated from other fields. You can perform this calculation in queries, forms, and reports. Thus, there is no need to include it as a field in the Customer table. Further, by including it, you introduce the possibility of errors in the database. For example, if Amount Paid is $5,000, Current Due is $2,000, yet you set Total Amount equal to $8,000, you have an error. You also need to be sure to change Total Amount appropriately whenever you change either Amount Paid or Current Due. If it is not stored, but rather calculated when needed, you avoid all these problems.

If including the Total Amount field is not appropriate, why did we include the Total Amount field in the Customer table in Chapter 3?

Access allows calculated fields. Rather than storing a value, you simply indicate the calculation. Access will calculate the value when needed. This approach avoids the above problems, so you actually could include the field. Often, however, you still will decide not to include it. If you plan to use another database management system, for example, an earlier version of Access, you should not include it. In addition, if you are using Access but plan to use the database with SQL Server, you should not include it.

4. The functional dependencies among the attributes are:

> **Customer Number → Customer Name, Street (Customer), City (Customer), State (Customer), Postal Code (Customer), Amount Paid, Current Due, Book Rep Number**
>
> **Book Rep Number → Last Name, First Name, Street (Book Rep), City (Book Rep), State (Book Rep), Postal Code (Book Rep), Salary, Bonus Rate**
>
> **Seminar Code → Seminar Description, Hours, Increments**
>
> **Customer Number, Seminar Code → Total Hours, Hours Spent**

CONSIDER THIS

Why is Total Hours listed with Customer Number and Seminar Code rather than just with Seminar Code?

If the total hours were required to be the same as the number of hours for the seminar, then it indeed would be listed with Seminar Code because it would not vary from one customer to another. Because Bavant wants the flexibility of tailoring the number of hours for which a particular seminar is offered to the specific needs of the customer, Total Hours also is dependent on Customer Number.

The customer's name, street address, city, state, postal code, amount paid, and current due are dependent only on customer number. Because a customer has a single rep, the rep number is dependent on customer number as well. The rep's last name, first name, street address, city, state, postal code, salary, and bonus rate are dependent only on Book Rep Number. A seminar description, the number of hours for the seminar, and the increments in which the seminar is offered are dependent only on seminar code. The total hours for a particular seminar offering as well as the hours already spent are dependent on the combination of customer number and seminar code.

5. The shorthand representation for the tables is shown in Figure 11–7.

Customer (<u>Customer Number</u>, Customer Name, Street, City, State, Postal Code, Amount Paid, Current Due, Book Rep Number)

Book Rep (<u>Book Rep Number</u>, Last Name, First Name, Street, City, State, Postal Code, Salary, Bonus Rate)

Seminar (<u>Seminar Code</u>, Seminar Description, Hours, Increments)

Seminar Offerings (<u>Customer Number</u>, <u>Seminar Code</u>, Total Hours, Hours Spent)

Figure 11–7

6. The following are the relationships between the tables:

a. The Customer and Book Rep tables are related using the Book Rep Number fields, which is the primary key of the Book Rep table. The Book Rep Number field in the Customer table is a foreign key.

b. The Customer and Seminar Offerings tables are related using the Customer Number fields, which is the primary key of the Customer table. The Customer Number field in the Seminar Offerings table is a foreign key.

c. The Seminar and Seminar Offerings tables are related using the Seminar Code fields, which is the primary key of the Seminar table. The Seminar Code field in the Seminar Offerings table is a foreign key.

CONSIDER THIS

Does a many-to-many relationship exist between customers and seminars?
Yes. The Seminar Offerings table is precisely the table that will implement a many-to-many relationship between customers and seminars. You identified this table as part of the database design process. If you had not, you would need to add it at this point.

In the Seminar Offerings table, the primary key consists of two fields, Customer Number and Seminar Code. There are two additional fields, Total Hours and Hours Spent. What if the design requirements did not require these additional fields? Would we still need the Seminar Offerings table?
Yes, because this table implements the many-to-many relationship between customers and seminars. It is perfectly legitimate for the table that implements a many-to-many relationship to contain no columns except the two columns that constitute the primary key.

In the Seminar Offerings table, the primary key consists of two fields, Customer Number and Seminar Code. Does the Customer Number field have to come first?
No. The Seminar Code could have come first just as well.

NOTE: In the shorthand representation for the table containing the primary key, represent the foreign key by using the letters FK, followed by an arrow, followed by the name of the table containing the primary key. For example, to indicate that the Book Rep Number in the Customer table is a foreign key that must match the primary key of the Book Rep table, you would write FK Book Rep Number → Book Rep.

The shorthand representation for the tables and foreign keys is shown in Figure 11–8. It is common to list a table containing a foreign key after the table that contains the corresponding primary key, when possible. Thus, in the figure, the Book Rep table has been moved so that it comes before the Customer table.

Book Rep (Book Rep Number, Last Name, First Name, Street, City, State, Postal Code, Salary, Bonus Rate)

Customer (Customer Number, Customer Name, Street, City, State, Postal Code, Amount Paid, Current Due, Book Rep Number)
FK Book Rep Number → Book Rep

Seminar (Seminar Code, Seminar Description, Hours, Increments)

Seminar Offerings (Customer Number, Seminar Code, Total Hours, Hours Spent)
FK Customer Number → Customer
FK Seminar Code → Seminar

Figure 11–8

TAL Distributors

The management of TAL Distributors, a distributor of energy-saving and water-conservation items, has determined that the company's rapid growth requires a database to maintain customer, order, and inventory data. With the data stored in a database, management will be able to ensure that the data is current and more accurate. In addition, managers will be able to obtain answers to their questions concerning the data in the database easily and quickly, with the option of producing a variety of reports.

Requirements for the TAL Distributors Database

A system analyst has interviewed users and examined documents at TAL Distributors, and has determined that the company needs a database that will support the following requirements:

1. For a sales rep, store the rep's number, last name, first name, street address, city, state, postal code, total commission, and commission rate.
2. For a customer, store the customer's number, name, street address, city, state, postal code, balance owed, and credit limit. These customers are businesses, so it is appropriate to store a single name, rather than first name and last name as you would if the customers were individuals. Additional fields you need to store are the number, last name, and first name of the sales rep representing this customer. The analyst also has determined that a sales rep can represent many customers, but a customer must have exactly one sales rep. In other words, one sales rep must represent each customer; a customer cannot be represented by zero or more than one sales rep.
3. For a part, store the part's number, description, units on hand, the category the part is in, and the price.

4. For an order, store the order number, order date, the number and name of the customer placing the order, and the number of the sales rep representing that customer. For each line item within an order, store the part's number and description, the number ordered, and the quoted price. The analyst also obtained the following information concerning orders:

   a. There is only one customer per order.

   b. On a given order, each part is listed only as a single line item. For example, part DR93 cannot appear on multiple lines within the same order.

   c. The quoted price might differ from the actual price in cases in which the sales rep offers a discount for a certain part on a specific order.

Design of the TAL Distributors Database

The following steps apply the design process to the requirements for TAL Distributors to produce the appropriate database design:

1. Assign entity names. There appear to be four entities: reps, customers, parts, and orders. The names assigned to these entities are Rep, Customer, Part, and Orders, respectively.

2. Determine unique identifiers. From the collection of entities, review the data and determine the unique identifier for each entity. For the Rep, Customer, Part, and Orders entities, the unique identifiers are the rep number, the customer number, the item number, and the order number, respectively. These unique identifiers are named Rep Number, Customer Number, Item Number, and Order Number, respectively.

3. Assign attribute names. The attributes mentioned in the first requirement all refer to sales reps. The specific attributes mentioned in the requirement are the sales rep's number, last name, first name, street address, city, state, postal code, total commission, and commission rate. Assigning appropriate names to these attributes produces the following list:

   Rep Number

   Last Name

   First Name

   Street

   City

   State

   Postal Code

   Commission

   Rate

The attributes mentioned in the second requirement refer to customers. The specific attributes are the customer's number, name, street address, city, state, postal code, balance, and credit limit. The requirement also mentions the number, first name, and last name of the sales rep representing this customer. Assigning appropriate names to these attributes produces the following list:

   Customer Number

   Customer Name

   Street

   City

   State

BTW

Line Items

A line item is a unit of information that appears on its own line. For example, when you purchase groceries, each grocery item appears on its own line. Line items also can be referred to as order line items or item detail lines.

Postal Code

Balance

Credit Limit

Rep Number

Last Name

First Name

Do you need to include the last name and first name of a sales rep in the list of attributes for the second requirement?
There is no need to include them in this list, because they both can be determined from the sales rep number and already are included in the list of attributes determined by Rep Number. They will be removed in a later step.

There are attributes named Street, City, State, and Postal Code for sales reps as well as attributes named Street, City, State, and Postal Code for customers. To distinguish these attributes in the final collection, the name of the attribute is followed by the name of the corresponding entity. For example, the street for a sales rep is Street (Rep) and the street for a customer is Street (Customer).

The attributes mentioned in the third requirement refer to parts. The specific attributes are the part's number, description, units on hand, category, and price. Assigning appropriate names to these attributes produces the following list:

Item Number

Description

On Hand

Category

Price

The attributes mentioned in the fourth requirement refer to orders. The specific attributes include the order number, order date, the number and name of the customer placing the order, and the number of the sales rep representing the customer. Assigning appropriate names to these attributes produces the following list:

Order Number

Order Date

Customer Number

Customer Name

Rep Number

The statement concerning orders indicates that there are specific attributes to be stored for each line item within the order. These attributes are the item number, description, the number ordered, and the quoted price. If the quoted price must be the same as the price, you simply could call it Price. According to requirement 4c, however, the quoted price might differ from the price. Thus, you must add the quoted price to the list. Assigning appropriate names to these attributes produces the following list:

Item Number

Description

Number Ordered

Quoted Price

The complete list grouped by entity is as follows:

Rep

   Rep Number

   Last Name

   First Name

   Street (Rep)

   City (Rep)

   State (Rep)

   Postal Code (Rep)

   Commission

   Rate

Customer

   Customer Number

   Customer Name

   Street (Customer)

   City (Customer)

   State (Customer)

   Postal Code (Customer)

   Balance

   Credit Limit

   Rep Number

   Last Name

   First Name

Part

   Item Number

   Description

   On Hand

   Category

   Price

Orders

   Order Number

   Order Date

   Customer Number

   Customer Name

   Rep Number

For line items within an order:

   Order Number

   Item Number

   Description

   Number Ordered

   Quoted Price

4. Identify functional dependencies. The fact that the unique identifier for sales reps is the Rep Number gives the following functional dependencies:

Rep Number → Last Name, First Name, Street (Rep), City (Rep), State (Rep), Postal Code (Rep), Commission, Rate

The fact that the unique identifier for customers is the Customer Number gives the following preliminary list of functional dependencies:

Customer Number → Customer Name, Street (Customer), City (Customer), State (Customer), Postal Code (Customer), Balance, Credit Limit, Rep Number, Last Name, First Name

The fact that the unique identifier for parts is the Item Number gives the following functional dependencies:

Item Number → Description, On Hand, Category, Price

The fact that the unique identifier for orders is the Order Number gives the following functional dependencies:

Order Number → Order Date, Customer Number, Customer Name, Rep Number

Do you need to include the name of a customer and the number of the customer's rep in the list of attributes determined by the order number?
There is no need to include the customer name and the rep number in this list because you can determine them from the customer number, and they already are included in the list of attributes determined by customer number. They will be removed in the next step.

The final attributes to be examined are those associated with the line items within the order: Item Number, Description, Number Ordered, and Quoted Price.

Why are Number Ordered and Quoted Price not included in the list of attributes determined by the Order Number?
To uniquely identify a particular value for Number Ordered or Quoted Price, Order Number alone is not sufficient. It requires the combination of Order Number and Item Number.

The following shorthand representation indicates that the combination of Order Number and Item Number functionally determines Number Ordered and Quoted Price:

Order Number, Item Number → Number Ordered, Quoted Price

Does Description need to be included in this list?
No, because Description can be determined by the Item Number alone, and it already appears in the list of attributes dependent on the Item Number.

The complete list of functional dependencies with appropriate revisions is as follows:

Rep Number → Last Name, First Name, Street (Rep), City (Rep), State (Rep), Postal Code (Rep), Commission, Rate

Customer Number → Customer Name, Street (Customer), City (Customer), State (Customer), Postal Code (Customer), Balance, Credit Limit, Rep Number

Item Number → Description, On Hand, Category, Price

Order Number → Order Date, Customer Number

Order Number, Item Number → Number Ordered, Quoted Price

5. Create the tables. Using the functional dependencies, you can create tables with the attribute(s) to the left of the arrow being the primary key and the items to the right of the arrow being the other fields. For tables corresponding to those entities identified in Step 1, you simply can use the name you already determined. Because you did not identify any entity that had a unique identifier that was the combination of Order Number and Item Number, you need to assign a name to the table whose primary key consists of these two fields. Because this table represents the individual line items within an order, the name Line Item is a good choice. The final collection of tables is shown in Figure 11–9.

Rep (<u>Rep Number</u>, Last Name, First Name, Street, City, State, Postal Code, Commission, Rate)

Customer (<u>Customer Number</u>, Customer Name, Street, City, State, Postal Code, Balance, Credit Limit, Rep Number)

Part (<u>Item Number</u>, Description, On Hand, Category, Price)

Orders (<u>Order Number</u>, Order Date, Customer Number)

Line Item (<u>Order Number</u>, <u>Item Number</u>, Number Ordered, Quoted Price)

Figure 11–9

6. Identify relationships.
   a. The Customer and Rep tables are related using the Rep Number fields. The Rep Number field in the Rep table is the primary key. The Rep Number field in the Customer table is a foreign key.
   b. The Orders and Customer tables are related using the Customer Number fields. The Customer Number field in the Customer table is the primary key. The Customer Number field in the Orders table is a foreign key.
   c. The Line Item and Orders tables are related using the Order Number fields. The Order Number field in the Orders table is the primary key. The Order Number field in the Line Item table is a foreign key.
   d. The Line Item and Part tables are related using the Item Number fields. The Item Number field in the Part table is the primary key. The Item Number field in the Line Item table is a foreign key.

Does a many-to-many relationship exist between orders and parts?
Yes. The Line Item table is precisely the table that will implement a many-to-many relationship between orders and parts. You identified this table as part of the database design process. If you had not, you would need to add it at this point.

In the Line Item table, the primary key consists of two fields, Order Number and Item Number. There are two additional fields, Number Ordered and Quoted Price. What if the design requirements did not require these additional fields? Would we still need the Line Item table?

Yes, because this table implements the many-to-many relationship between orders and parts. It is perfectly legitimate for the table that implements a many-to-many relationship to contain only the two columns that constitute the primary key.

The shorthand representation for the tables and foreign keys is shown in Figure 11–10.

Rep (<u>Rep Number</u>, Last Name, First Name, Street,
  City, State, Postal Code, Commission, Rate)

Customer (<u>Customer Number</u>, Customer Name, Street,
  City, State, Postal Code, Balance, Credit Limit,
  Rep Number)
  FK Rep Number → Rep

Part (<u>Item Number</u>, Description, On Hand, Category, Price)

Orders (<u>Order Number</u>, Order Date, Customer Number)
  FK Customer Number → Customer

Line Item (<u>Order Number</u>, <u>Item Number</u>, Number Ordered,
  Quoted Price)
  FK Order Number → Orders
  FK Item Number → Part

Figure 11–10

Sample data for the TAL Distributors database is shown in Figure 11–11.

Rep Table

Rep Number	Last Name	First Name	Street	City	State	Postal Code	Commission	Rate
20	Kaiser	Valerie	624 Randall	Georgetown	NC	28794	$2,542.50	0.05
35	Hull	Richard	532 Jackson	Kyle	SC	28797	$3,216.00	0.07
65	Perez	Juan	1626 Taylor	Byron	SC	28795	$2,487.00	0.05

Customer Table

Customer Number	Customer Name	Street	City	State	Postal Code	Balance	Credit Limit	Rep Number
148	Al's Hardware Store	2837 Greenway	Oxford	TN	37021	$2,550.00	$7,500.00	20
282	Brookings Direct	3827 Devon	Ashton	VA	20123	$431.50	$2,500.00	35
356	Ferguson's	382 Wildwood	Georgetown	NC	28794	$2,785.00	$7,500.00	65
408	The Energy Shop	1828 Raven	Granger	NC	27036	$1,285.25	$5,000.00	35
462	Walburg Energy Alternatives	12 Polk	Walburg	NC	28819	$1,412.00	$2,500.00	65
524	Kline's	838 Ridgeland	Oxford	TN	37021	$3,762.00	$7,500.00	20
608	Conservation Foundation	372 Oxford	Ashton	VA	20123	$106.00	$5,000.00	65
687	CleanPlanet	282 Evergreen	Lowton	TN	37084	$2,851.00	$5,000.00	35
725	Patricia Jean's Home Center	282 Columbia	Walburg	NC	28819	$248.00	$7,500.00	35
842	The Efficient Home	28 Lakeview	Pineville	VA	22503	$4,221.00	$7,500.00	20

Figure 11–11

Orders Table

Order Number	Order Date	Customer Number
12608	4/5/2015	148
12610	4/5/2015	356
12613	4/6/2015	408
12614	4/6/2015	282
12617	4/8/2015	608
12619	4/8/2015	148
12623	4/8/2015	608

Item Table

Item Number	Description	On Hand	Category	Price
AT94	Air Deflector	50	General	$5.45
BV06	Energy Saving Kit	45	Energy	$42.75
CD52	Fluorescent Light Bulb	65	Energy	$4.75
DL71	Low Flow Shower Head	21	Water	$8.75
DR93	Smoke Detector	38	General	$6.10
DW11	Retractable Clothesline	12	General	$13.25
FD21	Water Conservation Kit	22	Water	$13.45
KL62	Toilet Tank Water Saver	32	Water	$3.35
KT03	Programmable Thermostat	8	Energy	$34.25
KV29	Windows Insulator Kit	19	Energy	$4.95

© 2014 Cengage Learning

Line Item Table

Order Number	Item Number	Number Ordered	Quoted Price
12608	AT94	11	$5.45
12610	DR93	5	$6.10
12610	DW11	3	$12.50
12613	KL62	10	$3.35
12614	KT03	6	$33.00
12617	BV06	2	$40.25
12617	CD52	20	$4.25
12619	DR93	12	$6.00
12623	KV29	8	$4.95

© 2014 Cengage Learning

Figure 11–11 (continued)

Normalization

After you create your database design, you should analyze it using a process called **normalization** to make sure the design is free of potential update, redundancy, and consistency problems. This process also supplies methods for correcting these problems.

The normalization process involves converting tables into various types of **normal forms**. A table in a particular normal form possesses a certain desirable set of properties. Several normal forms exist, the most common being first normal form (1NF), second normal form (2NF), and third normal form (3NF). The forms create a progression in which a table that is in 1NF is better than a table that is not in 1NF;

a table that is in 2NF is better than one that is in 1NF; and so on. The goal of normalization is to take a table or collection of tables and produce a new collection of tables that represents the same information but is free of problems.

First Normal Form

A table that contains a **repeating group**, or multiple entries for a single row, is called an **unnormalized table**. Recall from the definition of relation that an unnormalized table actually violates the definition of relation.

Removal of repeating groups is the starting point in the goal of having tables that are as free of problems as possible. In fact, in most database management systems, tables cannot contain repeating groups. A table (relation) is in **first normal form (1NF)** if it does not contain repeating groups.

In designing a database, you may have created a table with a repeating group. For example, you might have created a Seminar Offerings table in which the primary key is the Customer Number and there is a repeating group consisting of Seminar Code, Total Hours, and Hours Spent. In the example, each customer appears on a single row and Seminar Code, Total Hours, and Hours Spent are repeated as many times as necessary for each customer (Figure 11–12).

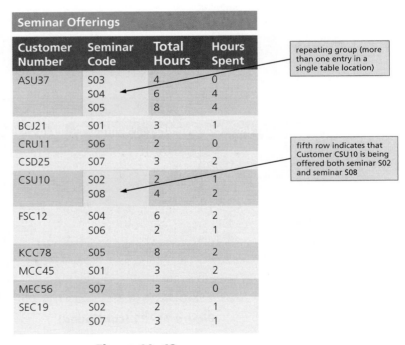

Figure 11–12

In the shorthand representation, you represent a repeating group by enclosing the repeating group within parentheses. The shorthand representation for the Seminar Offerings table from Figure 11–12 is shown in Figure 11–13.

Seminar Offerings (<u>Customer Number</u>, (Seminar Code, Total Hours, Hours Spent))

Figure 11–13

Conversion to First Normal Form

Figure 11–14 shows the normalized version of the table. Note that the fifth row of the unnormalized table (Figure 11–12) indicates that customer CSU10 currently is being offered both seminar S02 and seminar S08. In the normalized table, this information is represented by *two* rows, the seventh and the eighth. The primary key for the unnormalized Seminar Offerings table was the Customer Number only. The primary key for the normalized table now is the combination of Customer Number and Seminar Code.

Seminar Offerings			
Customer Number	Seminar Code	Total Hours	Hours Spent
ASU37	S03	4	0
ASU37	S04	6	4
ASU37	S05	8	4
BCJ21	S01	3	1
CRU11	S06	2	0
CSD25	S07	3	2
CSU10	S02	2	1
CSU10	S08	4	2
FSC12	S04	6	2
FSC12	S06	2	1
KCC78	S05	8	2
MCC45	S01	3	2
MEC56	S07	3	0
SEC19	S02	2	1
SEC19	S07	3	1

seventh row indicates that Customer CSU10 is being offered seminar S02

eighth row indicates that Customer CSU10 is being offered seminar S08

© 2014 Cengage Learning

Figure 11–14

In general, when converting a non-1NF table to 1NF, the primary key typically will include the original primary key concatenated with the key of the repeating group, that is, the field that distinguishes one occurrence of the repeating group from another within a given row in the table. In this case, Seminar Code is the key to the repeating group and thus becomes part of the primary key of the 1NF table.

To convert the table to 1NF, remove the parentheses enclosing the repeating group and expand the primary key to include the key to the repeating group. The shorthand representation for the resulting table is shown in Figure 11–15. Notice that the primary key is now the combination of the Customer Number field and the Seminar Code field.

Seminar Offerings (<u>Customer Number</u>, <u>Seminar Code</u>, Total Hours, Hours Spent)

Figure 11–15

Second Normal Form

Even though the following table is in 1NF, problems may exist that will cause you to want to restructure the table. In the database design process, for example, you might have created the Seminar Offerings table shown in Figure 11–16.

Seminar Offerings (<u>Customer Number</u>, Customer Name, <u>Seminar Code</u>, Seminar Description, Total Hours, Hours Spent)

Figure 11–16

This table contains the following functional dependencies:

Customer Number → Customer Name

Seminar Code → Seminar Description

Customer Number, Seminar Code → Total Hours, Hours Spent

This notation indicates that Customer Number alone determines Customer Name; Seminar Code alone determines Seminar Description, but it requires *both* a Customer Number *and* a Seminar Code to determine either Total Hours or Hours Spent. Figure 11–17 shows a sample of this table.

description of seminar S05 occurs more than once

Seminar

Customer Number	Customer Name	Seminar Code	Seminar Description	Total Hours	Hours Spent
ASU37	Applewood State University	S03	Mobile Apps	4	0
ASU37	Applewood State University	S04	Video Podcasting	6	4
ASU37	Applewood State University	S05	Creating Virtual Worlds	8	4
BCJ21	Brodkin Junior College	S01	Integrating with Learning Management Systems	3	1
CRU11	Cristie University	S06	Clickers in the Classroom	2	0
CSD25	Cowpens ISD	S07	Online Course Strategies	3	2
CSU10	Camellia State University	S02	Using Web-based Technologies and Tools	2	1
CSU10	Camellia State University	S08	Using Social Networking	4	2
FSC12	First State College	S04	Video Podcasting	6	2
FSC12	First State College	S06	Clickers in the Classroom	2	1
KCC78	Key Community College System	S05	Creating Virtual Worlds	8	2
MCC45	Mauldin Community College	S01	Integrating with Learning Management Systems	3	2
MEC56	Mehitable College	S07	Online Course Strategies	3	0
SEC19	Seaborn College	S02	Using Web-based Technologies and Tools	2	1
SEC19	Seaborn College	S07	Online Course Strategies	3	1

name of customer FSC12 occurs more than once

Figure 11–17

© 2014 Cengage Learning

The name of a specific customer, FSC12 for example, occurs multiple times in the table, as does the description of a seminar. This redundancy causes several problems. It is certainly wasteful of space, but that is not nearly as serious as some of the other problems. These other problems are called **update anomalies**, and they fall into four categories:

1. **Update.** A change to the name of customer FSC12 requires not one change to the table, but several: you must change each row in which FSC12 appears. This certainly makes the update process much more cumbersome; it is more complicated logically and takes longer to update.

2. **Inconsistent data.** There is nothing about the design that would prohibit customer FSC12 from having two or more different names in the database. The first row, for example, might have First State College as the name, whereas the second row might have First Statewide College.

3. **Additions.** There is a real problem when you try to add a new seminar and its description to the database. Because the primary key for the table consists of both Customer Number and Seminar Code, you need values for both of these to add a new row. If you have a customer to add but there are so far no seminars scheduled for it, what do you use for a Seminar Code? The only solution would be to make up a placeholder Seminar Code and then replace it with a real Seminar Code once the customer requests a seminar. Certainly this is not an acceptable solution.

4. **Deletions.** In Figure 11–17, if you delete seminar S01 from the database, you would need to delete all rows on which the Seminar Code is S01. In the process, you will delete the only row on which customer MCC45 appears, so you also would *lose* all the information about customer MCC45. You no longer would know that the name of customer MCC45 is Mauldin Community College.

These problems occur because there is a field, Customer Name, that is dependent on only a Customer Number, which is just a portion of the primary key. There is a similar problem with Seminar Description, which depends only on the Seminar Code, not the complete primary key. This leads to the definition of second normal form. Second normal form represents an improvement over first normal form because it eliminates update anomalies in these situations. In order to understand second normal form, you need to understand the term, nonkey field.

A field is a **nonkey field**, also called a **nonkey attribute**, if it is not a part of the primary key. A table (relation) is in **second normal form (2NF)** if it is in first normal form and no nonkey field is dependent on only a portion of the primary key.

Note that if the primary key of a table contains only a single field, the table is automatically in second normal form. In that case, there could not be any field dependent on only a portion of the primary key.

Conversion to Second Normal Form

To correct the problems, convert the table to a collection of tables in second normal form. Then name the new tables. The following is a method for performing this conversion.

1. Take each subset of the set of fields that make up the primary key and begin a new table with this subset as its primary key. The result of applying this step to the Seminar Offerings table is shown in Figure 11–18.

(Customer Number,
(Seminar Code,
(Customer Number, Seminar Code,

Figure 11–18

2. Place each of the other fields with the appropriate primary key; that is, place each one with the minimal collection of fields on which it depends. The result of applying this step to the Seminar Offerings table is shown in Figure 11–19 on the next page.

(<u>Customer Number</u>, Customer Name)

(<u>Seminar Code</u>, Seminar Description)

(<u>Customer Number</u>, <u>Seminar Code</u>, Total Hours, Hours Spent)

Figure 11–19

3. Give each of these new tables a name that is descriptive of the meaning of the table, such as Customer, Seminar, and Seminar Offerings.

Figure 11–20 shows samples of the tables.

Customer	
Customer Number	**Customer Name**
ASU37	Applewood State University
BCJ21	Brodkin Junior College
CRU11	Cristie University
CSD25	Cowpens ISD
CSU10	Camellia State University
DCC34	Dartt Community College
FSC12	First State College
FSU23	Farnham State University
KCC78	Key Community College System
MCC45	Mauldin Community College
MEC56	Mehitable College
PLI22	Pratt-Last Institute
SCC77	Stallone Community College
SEC19	Seaborn College
TSC02	Tri-State Consortium

name of Customer FSC12 occurs only once

© 2014 Cengage Learning

Seminar	
Seminar Code	**Seminar Description**
S01	Integrating with Learning Management Systems
S02	Using Web-based Technologies and Tools
S03	Mobile Apps
S04	Video Podcasting
S05	Creating Virtual Worlds
S06	Clickers in the Classroom
S07	Online Course Strategies
S08	Using Social Networking

description of seminar S05 occurs only once

© 2014 Cengage Learning

Figure 11–20

Seminar Offerings			
Customer Number	Seminar Code	Total Hours	Hours Spent
ASU37	S03	4	0
ASU37	S04	6	4
ASU37	S05	8	4
BCJ21	S01	3	1
CRU11	S06	2	0
CSD25	S07	3	2
CSU10	S02	2	1
CSU10	S08	4	2
FSC12	S04	6	2
FSC12	S06	2	1
KCC78	S05	8	2
MCC45	S01	3	2
MEC56	S07	3	0
SEC19	S02	2	1
SEC19	S07	3	1

© 2014 Cengage Learning

Figure 11–20 (continued)

The new design eliminates the update anomalies. A customer name occurs only once for each customer, so you do not have the redundancy that you did in the earlier design. Changing the name of a customer is now a simple process involving a single change. Because the name of a customer occurs in a single place, it is not possible to have multiple names for the same customer in the database at the same time.

To add a new customer, you create a new row in the Customer table, and thus there is no need to have a seminar offering already scheduled for that customer. In addition, deleting seminar S01 has nothing to do with the Customer table and, consequently, does not cause customer MCC45 to be deleted. Thus, you still have its name, Mauldin Community College, in the database. Finally, you have not lost any information in the process.

Can I reconstruct the data in the original design from the data in the new design?
Yes. The following SQL query would produce the data in the form shown in Figure 11–17 on page AC 690:

```
SELECT [Customer].[Customer Number], [Customer Name],
   [Seminar].[Seminar Code], [Seminar Description],
   [Total Hours], [Hours Spent]
FROM [Customer],[Seminar],[Seminar Offerings]
WHERE [Customer].[Customer Number]=
   [Seminar Offerings].[Customer Number]
AND [Seminar].[Seminar Code]=
   [Seminar Offerings].[Seminar Code];
```

CONSIDER THIS

Third Normal Form

BTW

3NF
The definition given for third normal form is not the original definition. This more recent definition, which is preferable to the original, is often referred to as Boyce-Codd normal form (BCNF) when it is important to make a distinction between this definition and the original definition. This text does not make such a distinction but will take this to be the definition of third normal form.

Problems still can exist with tables that are in 2NF, as illustrated in the Customer table whose shorthand representation is shown in Figure 11–21.

Customer (<u>Customer Number</u>, Customer Name, Street, City, State, Postal Code, Amount Paid, Current Due, Book Rep Number, Last Name, First Name)

Figure 11–21

The functional dependencies in this table are:

Customer Number → Customer Name, Street, City, State, Postal Code, Amount Paid, Current Due, Book Rep Number

Book Rep Number → Last Name, First Name

As these dependencies indicate, Customer Number determines all the other fields. In addition, Book Rep Number determines Last Name and First Name.

Because the primary key of the table is a single field, the table is automatically in second normal form. As the sample of the table shown in Figure 11–22 demonstrates, however, this table has problems similar to those encountered earlier, even though it is in 2NF. In this case, it is the last name and first name of a rep that can occur many times in the table; see rep 42, Melina Perez, for example. (Note that the three dots represent fields that do not appear due to space considerations.)

Customer

Customer Number	Customer Name	...	Amount Paid	Current Due	Book Rep Number	Last Name	First Name
ASU37	Applewood State University	...	$41,530.98	$38,812.66	42	Perez	Melina
BCJ21	Brodkin Junior College	...	$0.00	$6,081.98	42	Perez	Melina
CRU11	Cristie University	...	$0.00	$14,250.00	42	Perez	Melina
CSD25	Cowpens ISD	...	$12,750.00	$13,275.00	53	Chin	Robert
CSU10	Camellia State University	...	$63,246.88	$69,847.76	53	Chin	Robert
DCC34	Dartt Community College	...	$21,345.50	$23,467.75	65	Rogers	Tracy
FSC12	First State College	...	$34,557.25	$23,875.98	65	Rogers	Tracy
FSU23	Farnham State University	...	$18,268.00	$22,024.50	42	Perez	Melina
KCC78	Key Community College System	...	$21,288.65	$11,367.49	65	Rogers	Tracy
MCC45	Mauldin Community College	...	$9,500.00	$5,000.00	53	Chin	Robert
MEC56	Mehitable College	...	$9,111.19	$7,310.76	42	Perez	Melina
PLI22	Pratt-Last Institute	...	$17,229.45	$11,769.75	53	Chin	Robert
SCC77	Stallone Community College	...	$7,525.98	$2,515.78	42	Perez	Melina
SEC19	Seaborn College	...	$9,225.34	$10,496.89	65	Rogers	Tracy
TSC02	Tri-State Consortium	...	$34,578.90	$9,432.56	65	Rogers	Tracy

name of rep 42 occurs more than once

Figure 11–22

This redundancy results in the same set of problems described previously with the Seminar Offerings table. In addition to the problem of wasted space, you have similar update anomalies, as follows:

1. **Updates.** A change to the name of a rep requires not one change to the table, but several changes. Again the update process becomes very cumbersome.

2. **Inconsistent data.** There is nothing about the design that would prohibit a rep from having two different names in the database. On the first row, for example, the name for rep 42 might read Melina Perez, whereas on the third row (another row on which the rep number is 42), the name might be Melina Gomez.

3. **Additions.** In order to add rep 59, whose name is Mary Simpson, to the database, she must have at least one customer. If she has not yet been assigned any customers, either you cannot record the fact that her name is Mary Simpson, or you have to create a fictitious customer for her to represent. Again, this is not a desirable solution to the problem.

4. **Deletions.** If you were to delete all the customers of rep 42 from the database, then you also would lose all information concerning rep 42.

These update anomalies are due to the fact that Book Rep Number determines Last Name and First Name, but Book Rep Number is not the primary key. As a result, the same Book Rep Number and consequently the same Last Name and First Name can appear on many different rows.

You have seen that 2NF is an improvement over 1NF, but to eliminate 2NF problems, you need an even better strategy for creating tables in the database. Third normal form provides that strategy.

Before looking at third normal form, you need to become familiar with the special name that is given to any field that determines another field, like Book Rep Number in the Customer table. Any field or collection of fields that determines another field is called a **determinant**. Certainly the primary key in a table is a determinant. Any candidate key is a determinant as well. (Remember that a candidate key is a field or collection of fields that could function as the primary key.) In this case, Book Rep Number is a determinant, but it certainly is not a candidate key for the Customer table shown in Figure 11–22, and that is the problem.

A table is in **third normal form** (3NF) if it is in second normal form and if the only determinants it contains are candidate keys.

Conversion to Third Normal Form

You now have identified the problem with the Customer table: it is not in 3NF. You need a way to correct the deficiency in the Customer table and in all tables having similar deficiencies. Such a method follows.

First, for each determinant that is not a candidate key, remove from the table the fields that depend on this determinant, but do not remove the determinant. Next, create a new table containing all the fields from the original table that depend on this determinant. Finally, make the determinant the primary key of this new table.

In the Customer table, for example, Last Name and First Name are removed because they depend on the determinant Book Rep Number, which is not a candidate key. A new table is formed, consisting of Book Rep Number as the primary key, Last Name, and First Name. Specifically, you would replace the Customer table in Figure 11–22 with the two tables shown in Figure 11–23 on the next page.

Customer (<u>Customer Number</u>, Customer Name, Street, City, State, Postal Code, Amount Paid, Current Due, Book Rep Number)

Book Rep (<u>Book Rep Number</u>, Last Name, First Name)

Figure 11–23

Figure 11–24 shows samples of the tables.

Customer

Customer Number	Customer Name	...	Amount Paid	Current Due	Book Rep Number
ASU37	Applewood State University	...	$41,530.98	$38,812.66	42
BCJ21	Brodkin Junior College	...	$0.00	$6,081.98	42
CRU11	Cristie University	...	$0.00	$14,250.00	42
CSD25	Cowpens ISD	...	$12,750.00	$13,275.00	53
CSU10	Camellia State University	...	$63,246.88	$69,847.76	53
DCC34	Dartt Community College	...	$21,345.50	$23,467.75	65
FSC12	First State College	...	$34,557.25	$23,875.98	65
FSU23	Farnham State University	...	$18,268.00	$22,024.50	42
KCC78	Key Community College System	...	$21,288.65	$11,367.49	65
MCC45	Mauldin Community College	...	$9,500.00	$5,000.00	53
MEC56	Mehitable College	...	$9,111.19	$7,310.76	42
PLI22	Pratt-Last Institute	...	$17,229.45	$11,769.75	53
SCC77	Stallone Community College	...	$7,525.98	$2,515.78	42
SEC19	Seaborn College	...	$9,225.34	$10,496.89	65
TSC02	Tri-State Consortium	...	$34,578.90	$9,432.56	65

© 2014 Cengage Learning

name of rep 42 occurs only once

Book Rep

Book Rep Number	Last Name	First Name
42	Perez	Melina
48	Statnik	Michael
53	Chin	Robert
65	Rogers	Tracy

© 2014 Cengage Learning

Figure 11–24

This design corrects the previously identified problems. A rep's name appears only once, thus avoiding redundancy and making the process of changing a rep's name a very simple one. With this design, it is not possible for a rep to have two different names in the database. To add a new rep to the database, you add a row in the Book Rep table; it is not necessary to have a pre-existing customer for the rep. Finally, deleting all the customers of a given rep will not remove the rep's record from the Book Rep table, so you retain the rep's name; all the data in the original table can be reconstructed from the data in the new collection of tables. All previously mentioned problems indeed have been solved.

Can I reconstruct the data in the original design from the data in the new design?
Yes. The following SQL query would produce the data in the form shown in Figure 11–22 on page AC 694:

```
SELECT [Customer Number], [Customer Name], [Street],
    [City], [State], [Postal Code], [Amount Paid],
    [Current Due], [Customer].[Book Rep Number],
    [Last Name], [First Name]
FROM [Customer],[Book Rep]
WHERE [Customer].[Book Rep Number]=
    [Book Rep].[Book Rep Number];
```

Special Topics

In addition to knowing how to design a database and how to normalize tables, there are two other topics with which you should be familiar. First, you may be given a requirement for a database in the form of a document the database must be capable of producing, for example, an invoice. In addition, you should know how to represent your design with a diagram.

Obtaining Information from Existing Documents

Existing documents often can furnish helpful information concerning the database design. You need to know how to obtain information from the document that you then will use in the design process. An existing document, like the invoice for the company named TAL Distributors shown in Figure 11–25 on the next page, often will provide the details that determine the tables and fields required to produce the document.

The first step in obtaining information from an existing document is to identify and list all fields and give them appropriate names. You also need to understand the business policies of the organization. For example, in the order shown in Figure 11–25, the information on TAL Distributors is preprinted on the form, and it is not necessary to describe the company. The following is a list of the fields you can determine from the invoice shown in Figure 11–25.

> **Order Number**
> **Order Date**
> **Customer Number**
> **Customer Name**
> **Street (Customer)**
> **City (Customer)**
> **State (Customer)**
> **Postal Code (Customer)**
> **Rep Number**
> **Last Name (Rep)**
> **First Name (Rep)**
> **Item Number**
> **Description**
> **Number Ordered**
> **Price**
> **Total**
> **Order Total**

BTW
Existing Documents
Other examples of existing documents would be purchase orders, procedure manuals, organizational policy manuals, inventory lists, and so on.

TAL Distributors

INVOICE

555 Main Street
San Rita, TX 78364
Phone (512-555-0190 Fax (512-555-0191)

ORDER: 12617
DATE: APRIL 15, 2015

TO:
Customer: 462
Walburg Energy Alternatives
12 Polk
Walburg, NC 28819

SALES REP: 65
Juan Perez

ITEM NUMBER	DESCRIPTION	NUMBER ORDERED	PRICE	TOTAL
BV06	Energy Saving Kit	2	40.25	80.50
CD52	Fluorescent Light Bulb	20	4.25	85.00
		TOTAL		165.50

Make all checks payable to TAL Distributors
Total due in 15 days. Overdue accounts subject to a service charge of 1% per month.

Thank you for your business!

Figure 11–25

Next, you need to identify functional dependencies. If the document you are examining is unfamiliar to you, you may have difficulty determining the dependencies and may need to get all the information directly from the user. On the other hand, you often can make intelligent guesses based on your general knowledge of the type of document you are studying. You may make mistakes, of course, and these should be corrected when you interact with the user. After initially determining the functional dependencies, you may discover additional information. The following are possible initial functional dependencies:

> **Customer Number → Customer Name, Street (Customer), City (Customer), State (Customer), Postal Code (Customer), Rep Number, Last Name (Rep), First Name (Rep)**
>
> **Item Number → Description, Price**
>
> **Order Number → Order Date, Customer Number, Order Total**
>
> **Order Number, Item Number → Number Ordered, Price, Total**

You may find, for example, that the price for a particular item on an order need not be the same as the standard price for the item. If that is the case, Price and Total are functionally dependent on the combination of Order Number and Item Number, not just Item Number alone. You also may decide to change the field name to Quoted Price to indicate the fact that it can vary from one order to another.

For the same reasons that you did not include Total Amount in the Bavant Publishing database, you probably would not want to include either Total or Order Total. Both can be computed from other data. The other correction that you should make to the functional dependencies is to realize that the last name and first name of a rep depend on the data in the Rep Number field.

Given these corrections, a revised list of functional dependencies might look like the following:

> **Rep Number → Last Name, First Name**
>
> **Customer Number → Customer Name, Street (Customer), City (Customer), State (Customer), Postal Code (Customer), Rep Number**
>
> **Item Number → Description, Price**
>
> **Order Number → Order Date, Customer Number**
>
> **Order Number, Item Number → Number Ordered, Quoted Price**

After you have determined the preliminary functional dependencies, you can begin determining the tables and assigning fields. You could create tables with the determinant — the field or fields to the left of the arrow — as the primary key and with the fields to the right of the arrow as the remaining fields. This would lead to the following initial collection of tables shown in Figure 11–26.

Rep (<u>Rep Number</u>, Last Name, First Name)

Customer (<u>Customer Number</u>, Customer Name, Street, City, State, Postal Code, Rep Number)

Part (<u>Item Number</u>, Description)

Orders (<u>Order Number</u>, Order Date, Customer Number)

OrderLine (<u>Order Number</u>, <u>Item Number</u>, Number Ordered, Quoted Price)

Figure 11–26

Adding the foreign key information produces the shorthand representation shown in Figure 11–27.

Rep (<u>Rep Number</u>, Last Name, First Name)

Customer (<u>Customer Number</u>, Customer Name, Street, City, State, Postal Code, Rep Number)
   FK Rep Number → Rep

Part (<u>Item Number</u>, Description)

Orders (<u>Order Number</u>, Order Date, Customer Number)
   FK Customer Number → Customer

OrderLine (<u>Order Number</u>, <u>Item Number</u>, Number Ordered, Quoted Price)
   FK Order Number → Orders
   FK Item Number → Part

Figure 11–27

BTW
Merging Entities
When you merge entities, do not assume that the merged entities will be in 3NF. Apply normalization techniques to convert all entities to 3NF.

BTW
Certification
The Microsoft Office Specialist (MOS) program provides an opportunity for you to obtain a valuable industry credential — proof that you have the Access 2013 skills required by employers. For more information, visit the Certification resource on the Student Companion Site located on www .cengagebrain.com. For detailed instructions about accessing available resources, visit www.cengage.com/ ct/studentdownload or contact your instructor for information about accessing the required files.

At this point, you would need to verify that all the tables are in third normal form. If any are not in 3NF, you need to convert them. If you had not determined the functional dependency of Last Name and First Name on Rep Number earlier, for example, you would have had Last Name and First Name as fields in the Customer table. These fields were dependent on Rep Number, making Rep Number a determinant that is not a primary key, violating third normal form. Once you converted that table to 3NF, you would have the tables shown in Figure 11–27.

You already may have created some tables in your database design. For example, you may have obtained financial data on customers from the Accounting department. If so, you would need to merge the tables in Figure 11–27 with those tables you already created. To merge tables, you combine tables that have the same primary key. The new table contains all the fields in either individual table and does not repeat fields that are present in both tables. Figure 11–28, for example, illustrates the merging of two tables that both have the Customer Number field as the primary key. In addition to the primary key, the result contains the Customer Name and Rep Number fields, which are included in both of the original tables; the Street, City, State, and Postal Code fields, which are only in the first table; and the Balance and Credit Limit fields, which are only in the second table. The order in which you decide to list the fields is immaterial.

Merging

Customer (<u>Customer Number</u>, Customer Name, Street, City, State, Postal Code, Rep Number)

and

Customer (<u>Customer Number</u>, Customer Name, Balance, Credit Limit, Rep Number)

gives

Customer (<u>Customer Number</u>, Customer Name, Street, City, State, Postal Code, Balance, Credit Limit, Rep Number)

Figure 11–28

Diagrams for Database Design

You now have seen how to represent a database design as a list of tables, fields, primary keys, and foreign keys. It is often helpful to also be able to represent a database design with a diagram. If you already have created the database and relationships in Access, the Relationships window and Relationships report provide a helpful diagram of the design. Figure 11–29 shows the Access Relationship diagram and report for the Bavant Publishing database. In these diagrams, rectangles represent tables. The fields in the table are listed in the corresponding rectangle with a key symbol appearing in front of the primary key. Relationships are represented by lines with the "one" end of the relationship represented by the number, 1, and the "many" end represented by the infinity symbol (∞).

BTW
Quick Reference
For a table that lists how to complete the tasks covered in this book using touch gestures, the mouse, ribbon, shortcut menu, and keyboard, see the Quick Reference Summary at the back of this book, or visit the Quick Reference resource on the Student Companion Site located on www.cengagebrain.com. For detailed instructions about accessing available resources, visit www.cengage.com/ct/studentdownload or contact your instructor for information about accessing the required files.

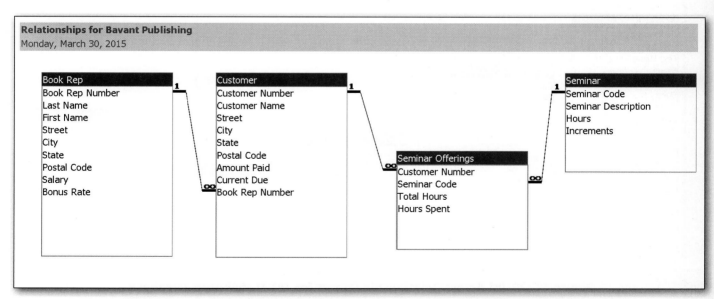

Figure 11–29 (a) Access Relationship Diagram for Bavant Publishing Database

Figure 11–29 (b) Access Relationship Report for Bavant Publishing Database

Figure 11–30 shows the Access Relationship diagram and report for the TAL Distributors database.

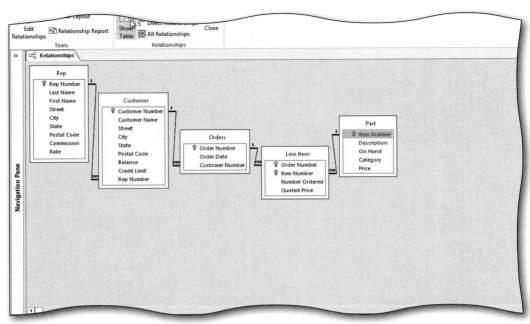

Figure 11–30 (a) Access Relationship Diagram for TAL Distributors Database

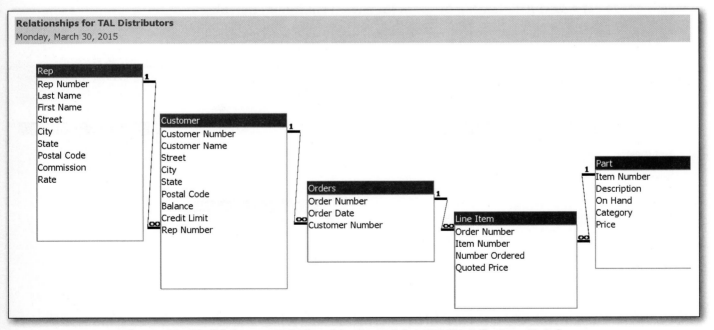

Figure 11–30 (b) Access Relationship Report for TAL Distributors Database

Another popular option for diagramming a database design is the **entity-relationship diagram (ERD)**. Figure 11–31 shows a sample ERD for the Bavant Publishing database. In this type of diagram, rectangles represent the tables. The primary key is listed within the table above a line. Below the line are the other fields in the table. The arrow goes from the rectangle that represents the many part of the relationship to the one part of the relationship.

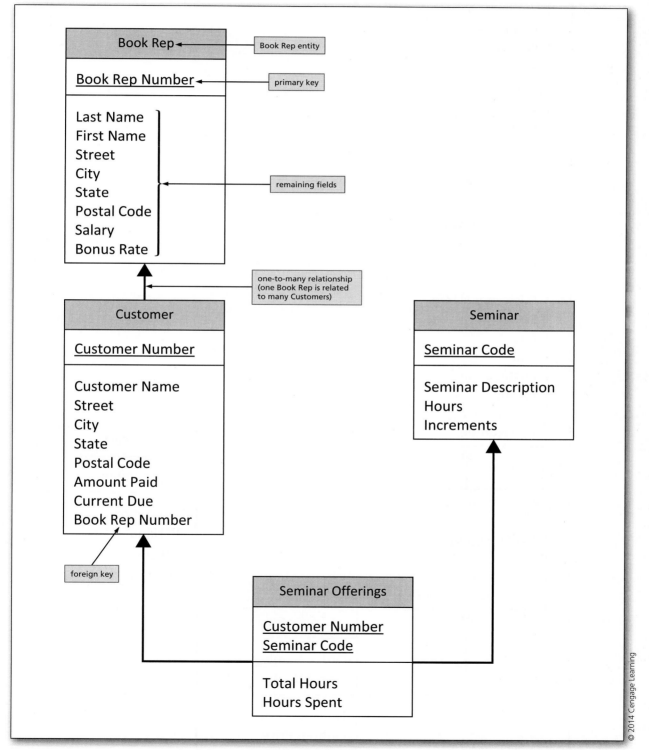

Figure 11–31

Figure 11–32 shows a similar diagram for the TAL Distributors database.

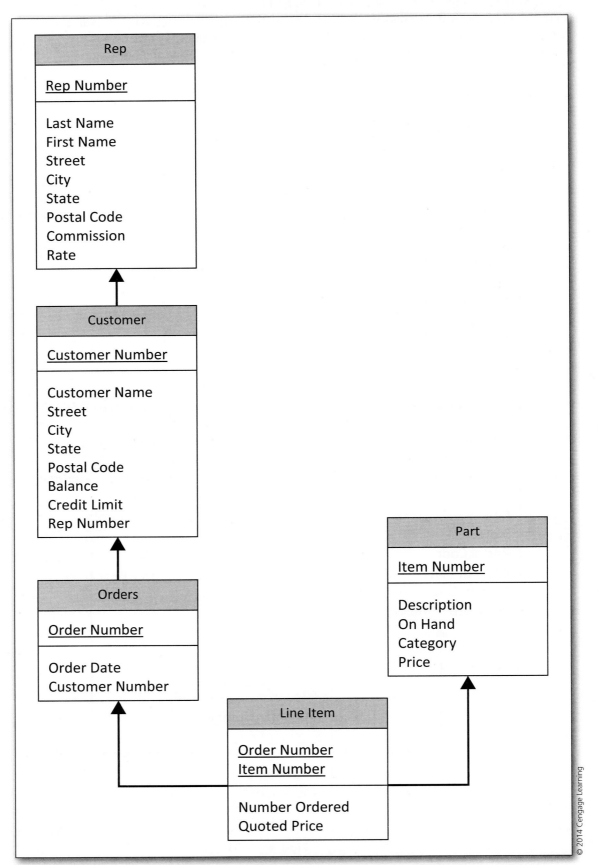

Figure 11–32

There are many options for such diagrams. Some options include more detail than shown in the figure. You can include, for example, such details as data types and indexes. Other options have less detail, showing only the name of the table in the rectangle, for example. There are also other options for the appearance of the lines representing relationships.

Chapter Summary

In this chapter, you have learned the following concepts.

1. An entity is a person, place, thing, or event. An attribute is a property of an entity. A relationship is an association between entities.

2. A relation is a two-dimensional table in which the entries in the table are single-valued, each column has a distinct name, all values in a column are values of the same attribute (that is, all entries must correspond to the column name), and each row is distinct.

3. In a relation, the order of columns is immaterial. You can view the columns in any order you want. The order of rows is also immaterial. You can view the rows in any order you want.

4. A relational database is a collection of relations.

5. Rows in a table (relation) often are called records or tuples. Columns in a table (relation) often are called fields or attributes. Typically, the terms *record* and *field* are used in Access.

6. If you know that whenever you are given a value for one field, you will be able to determine a single value for a second field, then the first field is said to determine the second field. In addition, the second field is said to be functionally dependent on the first.

7. The primary key of a table is the field or minimum collection of fields that uniquely identifies a given row in that table.

8. The following is a method for designing a database for a set of requirements.

   a. Examine the requirements and identify the entities (objects) involved. Assign names to the entities.
   b. Identify a unique identifier for each entity.
   c. Identify the attributes for all the entities. These attributes will become the fields in the tables.
   d. Identify the functional dependencies that exist among the attributes.
   e. Use the functional dependencies to identify the tables.
   f. Identify any relationships between tables by looking for matching fields where one of the fields is a primary key. The other field then will be a foreign key. In the shorthand representation for the table containing the primary key, represent the foreign key by using the letters FK, followed by an arrow, followed by the name of the table containing the primary key.

9. A table (relation) is in first normal form (1NF) if it does not contain repeating groups.

10. To convert a table to 1NF, remove the parentheses enclosing the repeating group and expand the primary key to include the key to the repeating group.

11. A field is a nonkey field (also called a nonkey attribute) if it is not a part of the primary key. A table (relation) is in second normal form (2NF) if it is in first normal form and no nonkey field is dependent on only a portion of the primary key.

12. To convert a table to 2NF, take each subset of the set of fields that make up the primary key and begin a new table with this subset as its primary key. Place each of the other fields with the appropriate primary key; that is, place each one with the minimal collection of fields on which it depends. Give each of these new tables a name that is descriptive of the meaning of the table.

13. Any field (or collection of fields) that determines another field is called a determinant. A table is in third normal form (3NF) if it is in second normal form and if the only determinants it contains are candidate keys.

14. To convert a table to 3NF, for each determinant that is not a candidate key, remove from the table the fields that depend on this determinant, but do not remove the determinant. Create a new table containing all the fields from the original table that depend on this determinant and make the determinant the primary key of this new table.

15. An entity-relationship diagram (ERD) is a diagram used to represent database designs. In ERDs, rectangles represent tables and lines between rectangles represent one-to-many relationships between the corresponding tables. You also can diagram a database design by using the Access relationship window.

How should you submit solutions to questions in the assignments identified with a ✸ symbol?

Every assignment in this book contains one or more questions identified with a ✸ symbol. These questions require you to think beyond the assigned database. Present your solutions to the questions in the format required by your instructor. Possible formats may include one or more of these options: write the answer; create a document that contains the answer; present your answer to the class; discuss your answer in a group; record the answer as audio or video using a webcam, smartphone, or portable media player; or post answers on a blog, wiki, or website.

Apply Your Knowledge

Reinforce the skills and apply the concepts you learned in this chapter.

Understanding Keys and Normalization

Instructions: Answer the following questions in the format specified by your instructor.

1. Figure 11–33 contains sample data for a Book table. Use this figure to answer the following:

   a. Is the table in first normal form (1NF)? Why or why not?
   b. Is the table in second normal form (2NF)? Why or why not?
   c. Is the table in third normal form (3NF)? Why or why not?
   d. Identify candidate keys for the table.

Book				
ISBN	**Book Code**	**Title**	**Publisher Code**	**Publisher Name**
0-7895-1344-7	0180	The Stranger	BP	Bavant Publishing
0-8967-1544-8	079X	Second Sight	SB	Science Books
1-1234-2334-5	1351	Travel Mysteries	MP	Mysterious Press
1-4188-3635-4	3350	Dawn	BP	Bavant Publishing

Figure 11–33

2. Figure 11–34 contains sample data for books and stores. In discussing the data with users, you find that book codes — but not titles — uniquely identify books and that location names uniquely identify store location. Multiple book stores can stock the same book.

   a. Convert the data in Figure 11–34 into a relation in first normal form (1NF) using the shorthand representation used in this chapter.
   b. Identify all functional dependencies using the notation demonstrated in this chapter.

3. ✸ Using only the data in Figure 11–33, how could you identify the entities and attributes that would be the starting point for a database design?

Book				
Book Code	**Title**	**Location Name**	**Address**	**Number of Copies**
0180	The Stranger	Phil Downtown	Georgetown	2
		Phil Brentwood	Brentwood	1
079X	Second Sight	Phil Downtown	Georgetown	4
		Phil Brentwood	Brentwood	3
		Phil Eastshore	Georgetown	5

Figure 11–34

Extend Your Knowledge

Extend the skills you learned in this chapter and experiment with new skills. You may need to use Help to complete the assignment.

Modifying a Database Design and Understanding Diagrams

Instructions: Answer the following questions in the format specified by your instructor.

1. Using the shorthand representation illustrated in this chapter, indicate the changes you would need to make to the Bavant Publishing database design shown in Figure 11–8 on page AC 680 in order to support the following requirements:

   a.   A customer does not necessarily work with one book rep but can work with several book reps.
   b.   Hours and Total Hours do not vary based on customer.

2. Using the shorthand representation illustrated in this chapter, indicate the changes you would need to make to the TAL Distributors database design shown in Figure 11–10 on page AC 686 to support the following requirements.

   a.   The price for a part does not change but is the same for all customers.
   b.   TAL also needs to keep track of the wholesale cost of a part.

3. Use the Access Relationship Report for the JMS TechWizards database shown in Figure 11–35 to answer the following:

   a.   Identify the foreign keys in the Work Orders table.
   b.   What is the purpose of the Work Orders table?
   c.   What is the primary key of the Work Orders table?

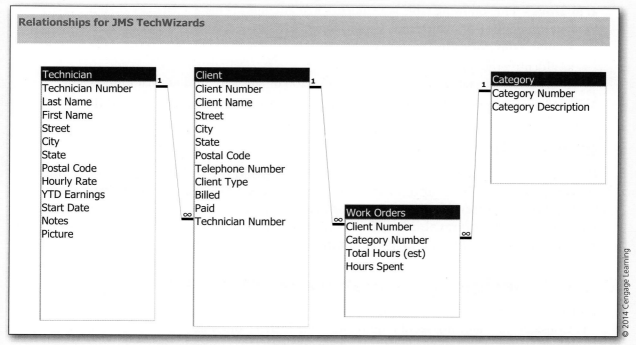

Figure 11–35

4. ✳ TAL Distributors has decided to add its suppliers to the database. One supplier can supply many items but an item has only one supplier. What changes would you need to make to the database design for TAL Distributors?

Analyze, Correct, Improve

Analyze a database, correct all errors, and improve the design.

Correcting a Database Design

Instructions: Answer the following questions in the format specified by your instructor.

1. Correct List four relational characteristics that are violated in the Book table shown in Figure 11–36.

Book			
Date	**Book Code**	**Number Ordered**	**Date**
04/06/2015	0180	11	04/01/2015
04/06/2015	0189	1	04/09/2015
	0378	1	Friday
04/07/2015	0808	3	04/13/2015
04/07/2015	1382	4	04/12/2015
	2226	2	$23.95
04/07/2015	0808	3	04/13/2015
04/08/2015	7559	2	04/15/2015
04/09/2015	9883	5	04/15/2015

© 2014 Cengage Learning

Figure 11–36

2. Improve The following table is a student's first attempt to create a database design:
Student (<u>StudentID</u>, StudentName, CreditHours, AdvisorID, AdvisorName, (CourseID, CourseName, Grade))

   a. Identify the functional dependencies.
   b. Convert this table to an equivalent collection of tables in third normal form (3NF).

3. ✺ What assumptions did you need to make to convert the Student relation to 3NF?

In the Labs

Design, create, modify, and/or use a database following the guidelines, concepts, and skills presented in this chapter. Labs are listed in order of increasing difficulty. Labs 1 and 2, which increase in difficulty, require you to create solutions based on what you learned in the chapter; Lab 3 requires you to create a solution, which uses cloud and web technologies, by learning and investigating on your own from general guidance.

Lab 1: Designing a Database for Metro Couriers

Instructions: Answer the following questions in the format specified by your instructor.
  1. Consider the following set of requirements for Metro Couriers:
    a. For each courier, the company keeps track of the courier's name (first name and last name), courier's address (street, city, state, postal code), courier's driver license number, and mobile telephone number.
    b. For each motorbike, the company keeps track of a unique motorbike ID number, motorbike license number, and motorbike model.
    c. A courier can be assigned to more than one motorbike. A motorbike will have multiple couriers but only one courier at a time.

2. Based on these requirements, do the following:

   a. Identify and list the entities and attributes of those entities.

   b. Identify and list the functional dependencies.

   c. Create a set of 3NF relations using the shorthand notation given in the chapter. Be sure to identify all primary and foreign keys appropriately.

3. Submit your database design in the format specified by your instructor.

4. ✳ Metro Couriers wants to add the customers it serves to the database. One customer can be serviced by many couriers and one courier can service many customers. What entities would you need to add to the database design?

Lab 2: Normalizing a Patient Relation

Instructions: Answer the following questions in the format specified by your instructor.

Consider the following relation:

> Patient (Patient#, PatientName, BalanceDue, DentistID, DentistName, ServiceCode, ServiceDesc, ServiceFee, ServiceDate)

This is a relation concerning data about patients of dentists at a dental clinic and the services the dentists perform for their patients. The following dependencies exist in Patient:

> Patient# → PatientName, BalanceDue, DentistID, DentistName
> DentistID → DentistName
> ServiceCode → ServiceDesc, ServiceFee
> Patient#, DentistID, ServiceCode → ServiceDate

1. Convert Patient to 1NF based on the functional dependencies given.

2. Convert to a set of relations in 3NF.

3. ✳ The database design needs to include an attribute for the date of the patient's last visit. In what table would you place this attribute?

Lab 3: Expand Your World: Cloud and Web Technologies Database Models

Instructions: There are several websites that provide examples of database models, such as www .databaseanswers.org/data_models/index.htm. These models provide a good starting point for creating your own database design.

1. Create a blog, a Google document, or a Word document on the SkyDrive on which to store your assignment.

2. Open your browser and access www.databaseanswers.org/data_models/index.htm or another website of your choice.

3. Browse the different database models and select one in which you have an interest.

4. In your own words, create a scenario for which the database model would work. Study the model to see if you would need to modify it to make it applicable to your scenario. If changes are necessary, document the required modifications.

5. ✳ Why did you select the model that you did? How easy was it to understand the entities, attributes, and relationships? Were the relations in 3NF?

Consider This: Your Turn

Apply your creative thinking and problem solving skills to design and implement a solution.

1: Designing a Community Center Sports Program Database
Personal/Academic

Instructions: You have been hired as an intern at the local community center. The center has a number of sports programs for youth. You have been asked to create a database to keep track of the programs and the youths who participate in these sports activities. Use the concepts and techniques presented in this chapter to design a database to meet the following requirements:

Part 1: The Community Center database must support the following requirements:

1. For an activity, store its number and name, for example, 013, Track. Each activity has a cost associated with it.

   a. For a participant, store his or her number, first name, and last name as well as the name, home telephone number, and cell telephone number of the parent or guardian primarily responsible for the participant.

   b. One participant can enroll in many activities, and one activity can include many participants. One parent/guardian can have many participants.

   Based on these requirements:

   a. Identify and list the entities and attributes of those entities.

   b. Identify and list the functional dependencies.

   c. Create a set of 3NF relations using the shorthand notation given in the chapter. Be sure to identify all primary keys and foreign keys appropriately.

Submit your database design in the format specified by your instructor.

Part 2: ☀ You made several decisions while designing this database. What was the rationale behind your decisions? Are there other requirements that would have been helpful to you in the design process?

2: Designing a Mobile Dog Groomers Database
Professional

Part 1: You have just started a mobile dog grooming business. You want to create a database to keep track of your customers and their dogs. Use the concepts and techniques presented in this chapter to design a database to meet the following requirements:

1. The Mobile Dog Groomers database must support the following requirements:

   a. For each dog, list the dog ID, dog name, breed name (for example, Standard Poodle, mixed breed, Collie, and so on), size (large, medium, small), gender, frequency of grooming (monthly, weekly, quarterly), owner's first name and last name, home telephone number, mobile telephone number.

   b. For each owner/customer, list the customer ID, the customer's first and last name, address (street, city, state, postal code), home telephone number, mobile telephone number, and amount paid.

   c. The database also must store the grooming cost of each dog. The grooming cost depends on both the dog and the customer.

A dog belongs to only one breed, but a breed can have many dogs. An owner/customer also can have many dogs.

2. Based on these requirements:

   a. Identify and list the entities and the attributes of those entities.

   b. Identify and list the functional dependencies.

   c. Create a set of 3NF relations using the shorthand notation given in this chapter. Be sure to identify all primary keys and foreign keys appropriately.

Submit your database design in the format specified by your instructor.

Part 2: ✳ You made several decisions while designing this database. What was the rationale behind your decisions? Are there other requirements that would have been helpful to you in the design process?

3: Understanding Normalization

Research and Collaboration

Part 1: Create a blog, a Google document, or a Word document on the SkyDrive on which to store your research findings and results for this assignment.

This chapter discussed the concept of normalization and applied the normalization process to a database. Three normal forms were identified. Many database designers also recognize a fourth normal form (4NF). Use the web to research 4NF, and then apply the normalization techniques for 4NF to the databases used in this chapter. Decide whether all relations are in 4NF. If a relation is not in 4NF, convert the database to 4NF.

Submit your assignment in the format specified by your instructor.

Part 2: ✳ You made several decisions while designing this database. What was the rationale behind your decisions? How important do you think it is to ensure that all relations in a database are in 4NF?

Learn Online

Reinforce what you learned in this chapter with games, exercises, training, and many other online activities and resources.

Student Companion Site   Reinforcement activities and resources are available at no additional cost on www.cengagebrain.com. Visit www.cengage.com/ct/studentdownload for detailed instructions about accessing the resources available at the Student Companion Site.

SAM   Put your skills into practice with SAM Projects! SAM Projects for this chapter can be found online. If you have a SAM account, go to www.cengage.com/sam2013 to access SAM assignments for this chapter.

4 | Creating and Managing Tasks with Outlook

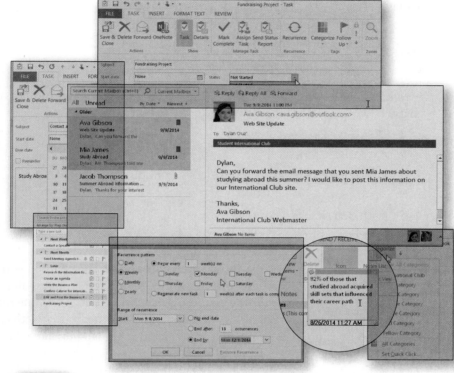

Objectives

You will have mastered the material in this chapter when you can:

- Create a new task
- Create a task with a status
- Create a task with a priority
- Create a task with a reminder
- Create a recurring task
- Categorize a task
- Configure Quick Clicks
- Categorize email messages

- Update a task
- Attach a file to a task
- Assign a task
- Forward a task
- Send a status report
- Print tasks
- Create a note
- Change the view of notes

4 | Creating and Managing Tasks with Outlook

This introductory chapter covers features and functions common to creating and managing tasks in Outlook 2013.

Roadmap

In this chapter, you will learn how to perform basic contact tasks. The following roadmap identifies general activities you will perform as you progress through this chapter:

1. CREATE a NEW TASK
2. CATEGORIZE a TASK
3. CATEGORIZE an EMAIL MESSAGE
4. ASSIGN a TASK
5. PRINT a TASK
6. CREATE AND USE NOTES

At the beginning of step instructions throughout the chapter, you will see an abbreviated form of this roadmap. The abbreviated roadmap uses colors to indicate chapter progress: gray means the chapter is beyond that activity, blue means the task being shown is covered in that activity, and black means that activity is yet to be covered. For example, the following abbreviated roadmap indicates the section would be about assigning a task.

1 CREATE NEW TASK | 2 CATEGORIZE TASK | 3 CATEGORIZE EMAIL MESSAGE
4 ASSIGN TASK | 5 PRINT TASK | 6 CREATE AND USE NOTES

Use the abbreviated roadmap as a progress guide while you read or step through the instructions in this chapter.

Introduction to Outlook Tasks

Whether you are keeping track of your school assignments that are due next week or the action items that your boss needs completed as soon as possible, you can use Outlook tasks to manage your to-do list by generating a checklist and tracking activities. Instead of keeping a paper list of the things you need to do, you can use Outlook to combine your various tasks into one list that has reminders and tracking. A **task** is an item that you create in Outlook to track until its completion. A **to-do item** is any Outlook item such as a task, an email message, or a contact that has been flagged for follow-up later.

Creating and managing tasks in Outlook allows you to keep track of projects, which might include school assignments, work responsibilities, or personal activities. Using a task, you can record information about a project such as start date, due date, status, priority, and percent complete. Outlook also can remind you about the task so that you do not forget to complete it. If you are managing a project, for example, you can assign tasks to people so that everyone can complete their portion of the project.

Project — Managing Tasks

People and businesses create tasks to keep track of projects that are important to them or their organizations. Tasks can be categorized and monitored to ensure that all projects are completed in a timely fashion. You can track one-time tasks as well as tasks that recur over a period of time. You also can prioritize tasks so that you can decide which ones must be completed first.

The project in this chapter follows general guidelines and uses Outlook to create the task list shown in Figure 4–1. The task list in the Dylan Chapter 4 mailbox includes tasks that are organized using class, personal, and project team categories.

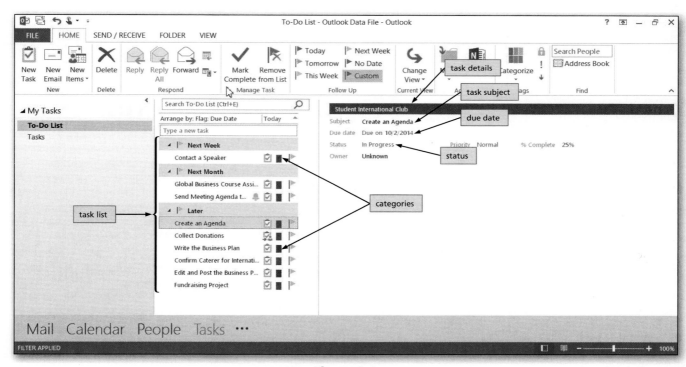

Figure 4–1

Creating a Task

The first step in creating a task for your to-do list is to open the Tasks category in Outlook. After you create a list of tasks, you can sync your tasks across multiple devices such as your smartphone and laptop, staying up to date and improving your productivity.

BTW
The Ribbon and Screen Resolution
Outlook may change how the groups and buttons within the groups appear on the ribbon, depending on the computer's screen resolution. Thus, your ribbon may look different from the ones in this book if you are using a screen resolution other than 1366 × 768.

What advantages does an Outlook task list provide beyond a basic to-do list?

Many business employees use an Outlook task list to detail their hours, business expenses, and mileage. Instead of jotting down how many hours you worked on Thursday to report later, remembering the tolls paid on a business trip, or how many miles you must list on your expense report, you can store this information in a task. When it is time to turn in your work hours or expense report, you can easily retrieve the details from your task list.

To-Do List Window

For an introduction to Windows 8 and instruction about how to perform basic Windows 8 tasks, read the Office 2013 and Windows 8 chapter at the beginning of this book, where you can learn how to resize windows, change screen resolution, create folders, move and rename files, use Windows Help, and much more.

The To-Do List – Outlook Data File window shown in Figure 4–2 includes a variety of features to help you manage your tasks. It contains many elements similar to the windows in other Office programs, as well as some that are unique to Outlook. The main elements of the To-Do List window are the Navigation Pane, the To-Do list pane, and the Preview pane. The My Tasks folder in the Navigation Pane displays the To-Do list link and Tasks folder. Clicking the To-Do list link displays the tasks in the To-Do list view, and tapping or clicking Tasks displays the tasks in the task folder in Simple List view.

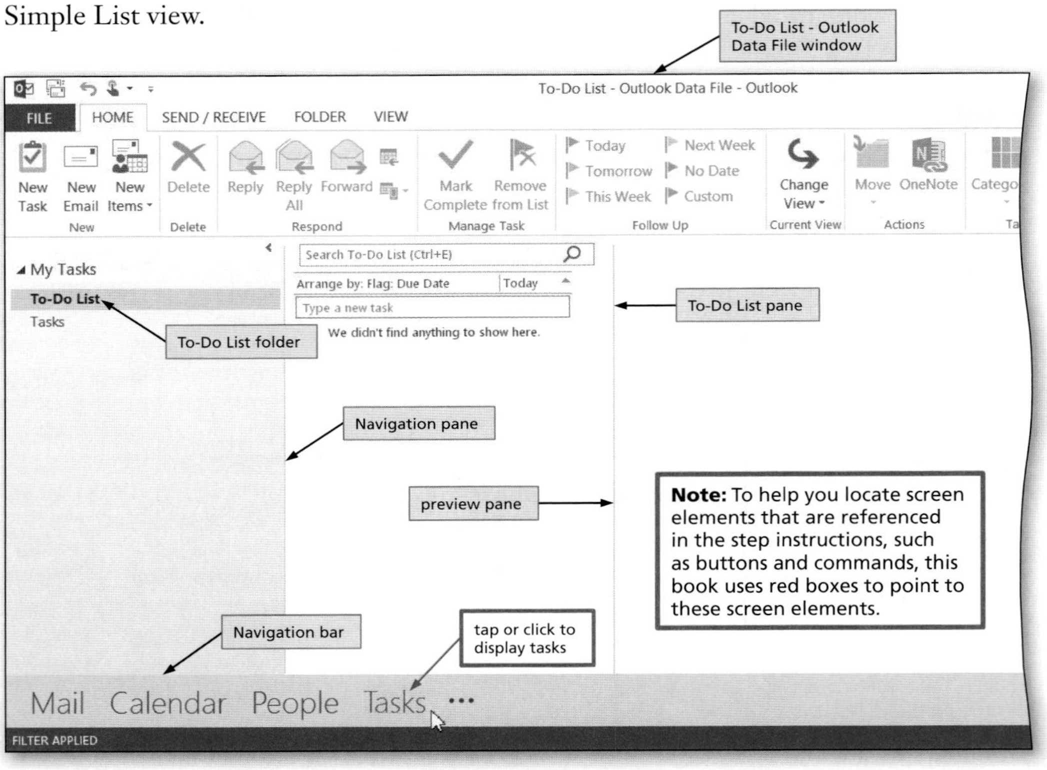

Figure 4–2

To Run Outlook

One of the few differences between Windows 7 and Windows 8 occurs in the steps to run Outlook. If you are using Windows 7, click the Start button, type Outlook in the 'Search programs and files' box, click Outlook 2013, and then, if necessary, maximize the Outlook window.

If you are using a computer to step through the project in this chapter and you want your screens to match the figures in this book, you should change your screen's resolution to 1366 × 768. For information about how to change a computer's resolution, refer to the Office and Windows chapter at the beginning of this book.

The following steps, which assume Windows is running, use the Search text box to run Outlook based on a typical installation. You may need to ask your instructor how to run Outlook on your computer. For a detailed example of the procedure summarized below, refer to the Office 2013 and Windows 8 chapter.

① Swipe in from the right edge of the screen or point to the upper-right corner of the screen to display the Charms bar.

② Tap or click the Search charm on the Charms bar to display the Search menu.

③ Type `Outlook` as the search text in the Search text box and watch the search results appear in the Apps list.

④ Tap or click Outlook 2013 in the search results to run Outlook.

⑤ If the Outlook window is not maximized, tap or click the Maximize button on its title bar to maximize the window.

Creating a To-Do List

The first step in creating a To-Do list is to select a folder for storing your tasks. By default, Outlook stores tasks in the Tasks folder, but you also can create a personal folder in which to store your tasks, using the technique presented in Chapter 2. In this chapter, you will create tasks in the Tasks folder.

To Create a New Task

**1 CREATE NEW TASK | 2 CATEGORIZE TASK | 3 CATEGORIZE EMAIL MESSAGE
4 ASSIGN TASK | 5 PRINT TASK | 6 CREATE AND USE NOTES**

Dylan Cruz, the student president of the International Club, would like to create a task list to keep track of what is going on in the club and in his own classes. To start, Dylan plans to create the first task, which is to contact a speaker for the club in October at least a month before the meeting so that he does not forget to complete the task. The following steps create a new task. *Why? To stay organized, you should keep Outlook tasks to make sure you complete all the items on your to-do list.*

①

- Open the Dylan Chapter 4.pst Outlook Data File from the Data Files for Students for Chapter 4.

- Tap or click Tasks (shown in Figure 4–2) on the Navigation Bar to display the Outlook Tasks.

- Tap or click the New Task button (HOME tab | New group) to display the Untitled – Task window (Figure 4–3).

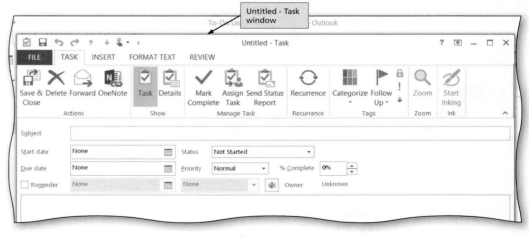

Figure 4–3

Why is my screen different? My Untitled – Task window does not have the two buttons named Assign Task and Send Status Report in the Manage Task group as shown in Figure 4–3.

If you do not have an email account connected to Outlook (covered in Chapter 1), you will not have these two buttons.

The New Task button does not appear on the HOME tab. What should I do?

Click the New Items button (HOME tab | New group), and then click Task. Now the New Task button should appear on the HOME tab.

2

- Type **Contact a Speaker** in the Subject text box to enter a subject for the task.
- Type **Study Abroad program speaker for the October meeting** in the task body area to enter a description for the task (Figure 4–4).

Q&A Why did the title of the Task window change after I entered the subject?
As soon as you enter the subject, Outlook updates the Task window title to reflect the information you entered. The task is not saved, however; only the window title is updated.

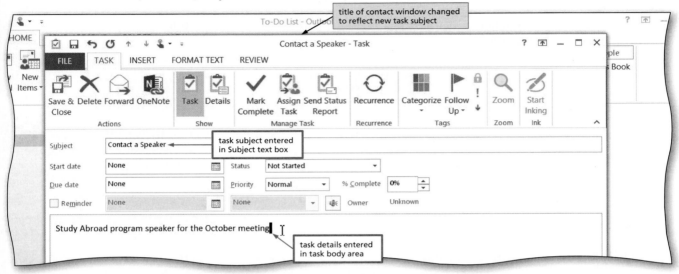

Figure 4–4

3

- Tap or click the Start date Calendar button to display a calendar for the current month (Figure 4–5).

Q&A Why does my calendar display a different month?
Depending on the actual calendar month, your current month may be different.

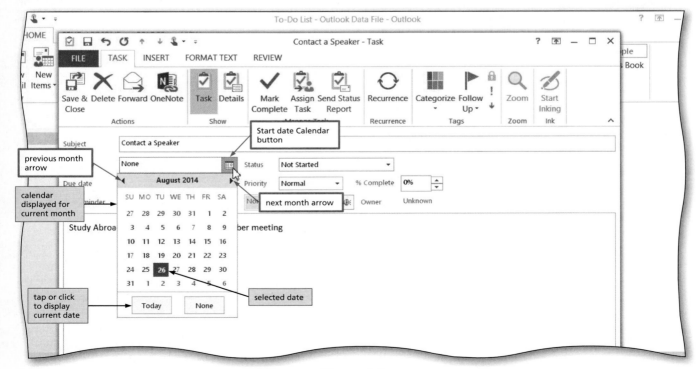

Figure 4–5

- If necessary, tap or click the next month arrow or previous month arrow an appropriate number of times to advance to September 2014.

- Tap or click 5 to select Fri 9/5/2014 as the start date (Figure 4–6).

Q&A Why did the due date change?
If you enter a start date, the due date automatically changes to match the start date. You can change the due date if needed.

Can I just type the date?
Yes, you can type the date. Using the calendar allows you to avoid potential errors due to typing mistakes.

What if September 2014 is in the past?
If September 2014 is in the past, tap or click the previous month arrow an appropriate number of times until you reach September 2014.

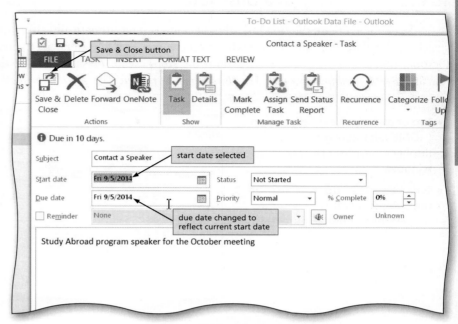

Figure 4–6

- Tap or click the Save & Close button (TASK tab | Actions group) (shown in Figure 4–6) to save the task and close the Task window (Figure 4–7).

Q&A My tasks are displayed in an arrangement different from the one in Figure 4–7. What should I do?
Tap or click the Change View button or the More button (HOME tab | Current View group), and then click To-Do List.

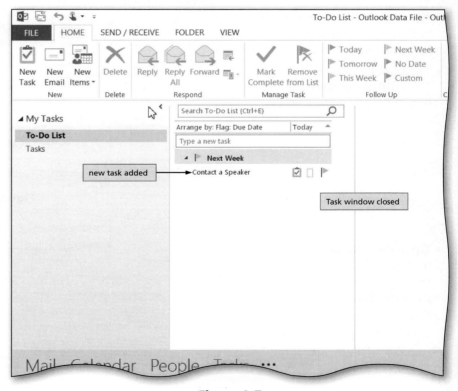

Figure 4–7

Other Ways

1. Press CTRL+N

To Create a Task with a Due Date

When you create the first task, the due date is set automatically after you enter the start date. If you have a specific due date, you can enter it when you create a task. Dylan needs to create a meeting agenda before the October meeting on October 2. The following steps create a task with a due date. *Why? You can quickly add a specific due date to set a deadline for a task. You also can sort by the due date, placing the most urgent tasks at the top of your list.*

- Tap or click the New Task button (HOME tab | New group) to display the Untitled – Task window.

- Type **Create an Agenda** in the Subject text box to enter a subject for the task (Figure 4–8).

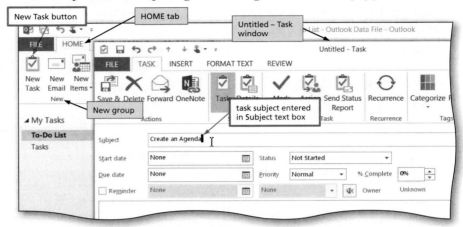

Figure 4–8

- Tap or click the Due date Calendar button to display a calendar for the current month.

- Tap or click the next month arrow button an appropriate number of times to advance to October 2014.

- Tap or click 2 to select Thu 10/2/2014 as the due date (Figure 4–9).

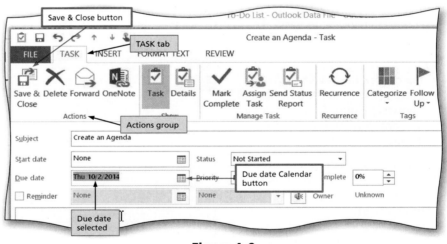

Figure 4–9

- Tap or click the Save & Close button (TASK tab | Actions group) to save the task and close the Task window (Figure 4–10).

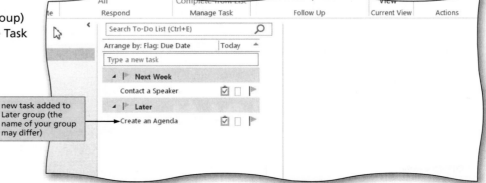

Figure 4–10

To Create a Task with a Status

Dylan is planning a fundraising project for the International Club that will be presented at the November meeting on 11/6/2014. Outlook allows you to assign a status to any task you create. You can assign one of five status indicators: Not Started, In Progress, Completed, Waiting on someone else, and Deferred. Dylan has already started working on the fundraising project ideas, so the task status should be set to In Progress. The following steps create a task with a status. *Why? You can reflect your current progress by changing the status of a task.*

1

- Tap or click the New Task button (HOME tab | New group) to display the Untitled – Task window.

- Type **Fundraising Project** in the Subject text box to enter a subject for the task.

- Tap or click the Due date Calendar button to display a calendar for the current month.

- Tap or click the next month arrow button an appropriate number of times to advance to November 2014.

- Tap or click 6 to select Thu 11/6/2014 as the due date (Figure 4–11).

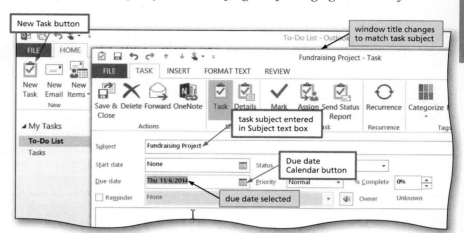

Figure 4–11

2

- Tap or click the Status box arrow to display the status options (Figure 4–12).

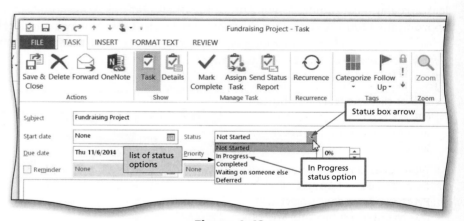

Figure 4–12

3

- Tap or click In Progress to change the status of the task (Figure 4–13).

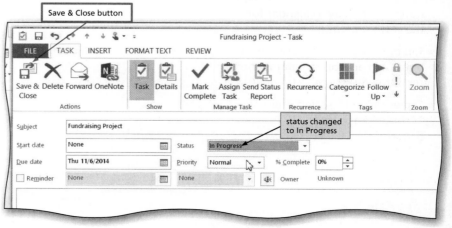

Figure 4–13

- Tap or click the Save & Close button (TASK tab | Actions group) to save the task and close the Task window (Figure 4–14).

Figure 4–14

To Create a Task with a Priority

1 CREATE NEW TASK | 2 CATEGORIZE TASK | 3 CATEGORIZE EMAIL MESSAGE
4 ASSIGN TASK | 5 PRINT TASK | 6 CREATE AND USE NOTES

As you itemize your work, Outlook can organize each task by setting priorities to reflect its importance. Dylan is hosting an International Food Festival on October 19 and needs to confirm the catering details at least five days in advance. As you enter the task in Outlook, you should set a high priority for this event as appropriate. Outlook allows for three priority levels: Low, Normal, and High. The following steps set the priority of a task. *Why? Using the built-in priority feature, you can later sort according to the importance of the task so you can determine how best to focus your time.*

- Tap or click the New Task button (HOME tab | New group) to display the Untitled – Task window.

- Type **Confirm Caterer for International Food Festival** in the Subject text box to enter a subject for the task.

- Tap or click the Due date Calendar button to display a calendar for the current month.

- Tap or click the next month arrow button an appropriate number of times to advance to October 2014.

- Tap or click 14 to select Tue 10/14/2014 as the due date (Figure 4–15).

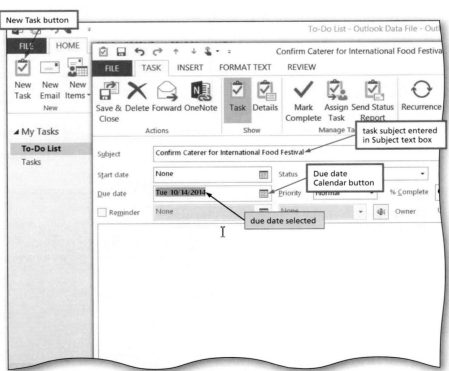

Figure 4–15

• Tap or click the Priority box arrow to display the priority options (Figure 4–16).

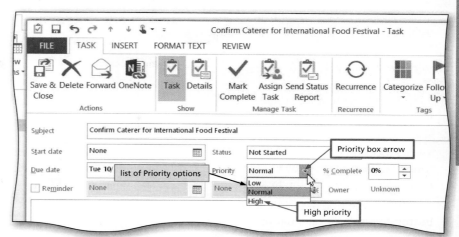

Figure 4–16

• Tap or click High to set the priority (Figure 4–17).

4

• Tap or click the Save & Close button (TASK tab | Actions group) to save the task and close the Task window.

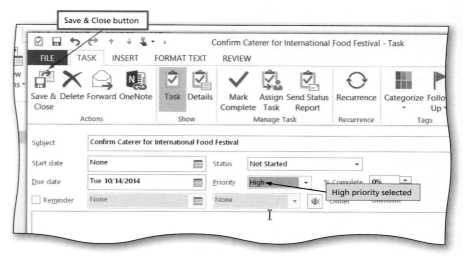

Figure 4–17

CONSIDER THIS

Can a manager in a business team assign tasks in Outlook to keep track of what work the team has completed?

Outlook provides an easy way for managers to assign tasks. For example, a manager might want to receive status reports and updates on the progress of a task. If the person who is assigned a task rejects it, the manager can reassign the task to someone else and set a high priority for the task.

To Create a Task with a Reminder

1 CREATE NEW TASK | 2 CATEGORIZE TASK | 3 CATEGORIZE EMAIL MESSAGE
4 ASSIGN TASK | 5 PRINT TASK | 6 CREATE AND USE NOTES

When you are busy with classes, a task reminder is helpful to ensure that you complete a project. Mr. Thompson, the faculty advisor, has asked Dylan to send the October meeting agenda to him by the end of September. *Why? By adding a reminder to a task, Outlook can remind you about the task automatically.* Reminders can be set before the task is actually due so you will have enough time to complete the task. The following steps add a task and set the reminder option for a week before the task is due.

- Tap or click the New Task button (HOME tab | New group) to display the Untitled – Task window.
- Type **Send Meeting Agenda to Mr. Thompson** in the Subject text box to enter a subject for the task.
- Type **October International Club agenda** in the task body area to enter a description for the task.
- Tap or click the Due date Calendar button to display a calendar for the current month.
- Tap or click the next month arrow an appropriate number of times to advance to September 2014.
- Tap or click 30 to select Tue 9/30/2014 as the due date (Figure 4–18).

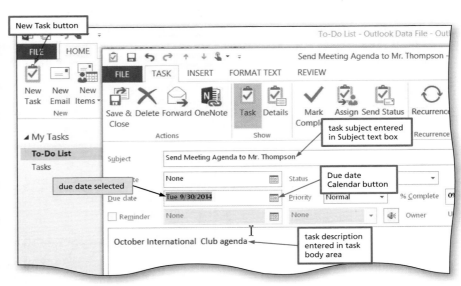

Figure 4–18

- Tap or click the Reminder check box to insert a check mark, enable the Reminder boxes, and configure Outlook to display a reminder (Figure 4–19).

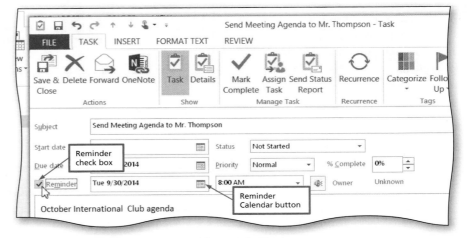

Figure 4–19

- Tap or click the Reminder Calendar button to display a calendar for September.
- Tap or click 23 to select Tue 9/23/2014 as the Reminder date (Figure 4–20).

Q&A

Can I change the time that Outlook displays the reminder? Yes. When you set a reminder, Outlook automatically sets the time for the reminder to 8:00 AM. You can change the time by tapping or clicking the Reminder box arrow and then selecting a time. You also can use the Outlook Options dialog box to change the default time to whatever time you desire.

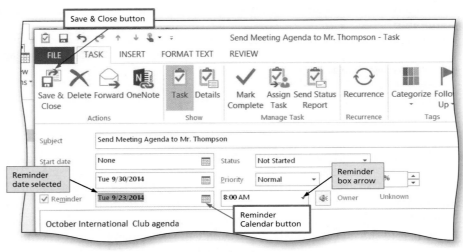

Figure 4–20

4

- Tap or click the Save & Close button (TASK tab | Actions group) to save the task and close the Task window (Figure 4–21).

Q&A How does Outlook remind me of a task?

If you selected a reminder for a task, Outlook displays the Task window for the task at the specified time. If you used the Sound icon to set an alarm for the reminder, Outlook also plays the sound when it displays the Task window.

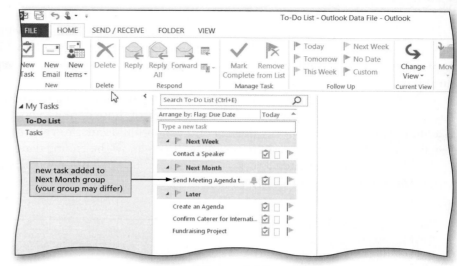

new task added to Next Month group (your group may differ)

Figure 4–21

To Create More Tasks

1 CREATE NEW TASK | 2 CATEGORIZE TASK | 3 CATEGORIZE EMAIL MESSAGE
4 ASSIGN TASK | 5 PRINT TASK | 6 CREATE AND USE NOTES

Dylan has additional tasks related to his studies. These include three tasks regarding a project in his business course to develop a business plan. The first task is to research the information for the business plan. An additional task is to write the business plan document. He also needs a task for editing and posting the business plan assignment.

Table 4–1 displays the business plan tasks with their due dates. The following step creates these remaining tasks in the Task window. *Why? By adding academic tasks to your list, an item that requires attention will not be overlooked.*

Table 4–1 Additional Tasks

Subject	Due Date
Research the Information for the Business Plan	10/1/2014
Write the Business Plan	10/8/2014
Edit and Post the Business Plan	10/15/2014

© 2014 Cengage Learning

1

- Tap or click the New Task button (HOME tab | New group) to display the Untitled – Task window.

- Enter the subject in the Subject text box for the first task in Table 4–1.

- Tap or click the Due date Calendar button to display a calendar for the current month, and then select the due date for the task as shown in Table 4–1.

- Tap or click the Save & Close button (TASK tab | Actions group) to save the task and close the Task window.

- Repeat the actions in bullets 1 through 4 for the two remaining tasks in Table 4–1 (Figure 4–22).

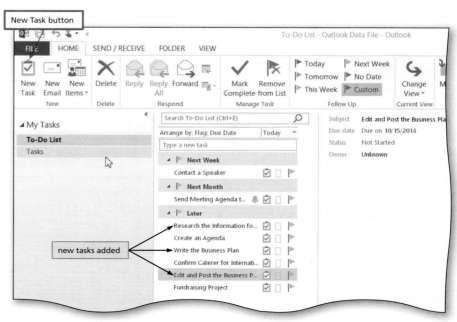

New Task button

new tasks added

Figure 4–22

To Create a Recurring Task

So far, the tasks you created had a specific date for completion. Sometimes, a task occurs repeatedly until the due date. For example, Dylan has a weekly assignment due in his Global Business course on Mondays from September 8 until December 1. The task will be considered complete on December 1, but it occurs every week until then.

When you create a task, Outlook allows you to specify if it is a recurring task. You can select whether the task recurs daily, weekly, monthly, or yearly. For each of those options, you can provide specifics. For example, if it is a monthly task, you can specify the day of the month it occurs. You also can choose to have a task automatically regenerate itself to keep the task from ending. If you know the ending date, you can specify the exact end date.

The following steps add a recurring weekly task. **Why?** *When you have a task that occurs at regular intervals, you should set a recurring task to keep you informed.*

- Tap or click the New Task button (HOME tab | New group) to display the Untitled – Task window.

- Type **Global Business Course Assignment** in the Subject text box to enter a subject for the task.

- Type **Submit assignment online** in the task body area to enter a description for the task.

- Tap or click the Start date Calendar button to display a calendar for the current month.

- Tap or click the next month arrow button an appropriate number of times to advance to September 2014.

- Tap or click 8 to select Mon 9/8/2014 as the start date (Figure 4–23).

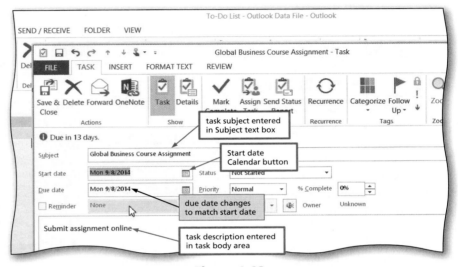

Figure 4–23

- Tap or click the Recurrence button (TASK tab | Recurrence group) to display the Task Recurrence dialog box (Figure 4–24).

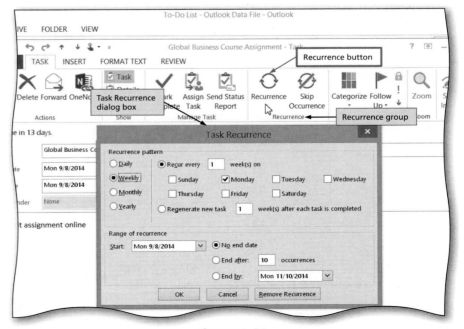

Figure 4–24

- Tap or click the End by option button to select it.

- Tap or click the End by box arrow to display a calendar.

- If necessary, tap or click the next month arrow button an appropriate number of times to advance to December 2014.

- Tap or click 1 to select Mon 12/1/2014 as the End by date (Figure 4–25).

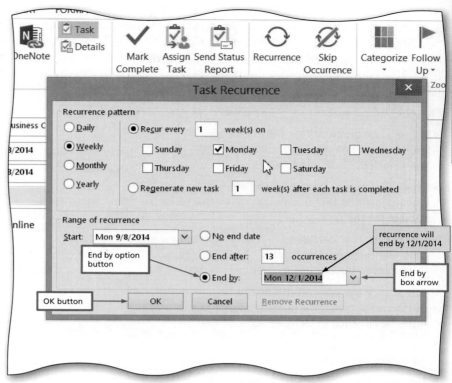

Figure 4–25

- Tap or click the OK button (Task Recurrence dialog box) to accept the recurrence settings (Figure 4–26).

- Tap or click the Save & Close button (TASK tab | Actions group) to save the task and close the Task window.

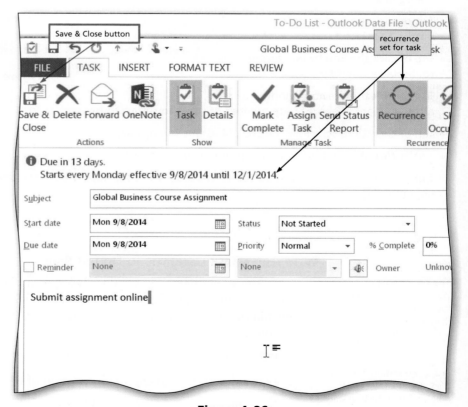

Figure 4–26

To Create Another Recurring Task

As part of Dylan's role as the president of the International Club, a recurring task is necessary for collecting the donations for the International Red Cross. He and his team plan to collect the donations from the donation bins placed around campus every Saturday from October 4 until November 22.

The following step adds another recurring task. *Why? When you have a task that occurs at regular intervals, you should add it as a recurring task to keep you informed.*

1

- Tap or click the New Task button (HOME tab | New group) to display the Untitled – Task window.

- Type `Collect Donations` in the Subject text box to enter a subject for the task.

- Tap or click the Start date Calendar button to display a calendar for the current month.

- Tap or click the next month arrow button an appropriate number of times to advance to October 2014.

- Tap or click 4 to select Sat 10/4/2014 as the start date.

- Tap or click the Recurrence button (TASK tab | Recurrence group) to display the Task Recurrence dialog box.

- Tap or click the End by option button to select it.

- Tap or click the End by box arrow to display a calendar.

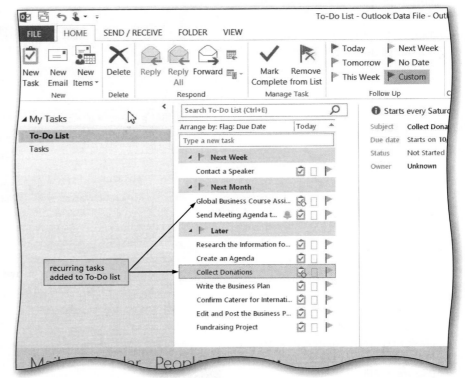

Figure 4–27

- Tap or click the previous month arrow button an appropriate number of times to return to November 2014.

- Tap or click 22 to select Sat 11/22/2014 as the End by date.

- Tap or click the OK button to accept the recurrence settings.

- Tap or click the Save & Close button (TASK tab | Actions group) to save the task and close the Task window (Figure 4–27).

To Add a Task Using the To-Do List Pane

You sometimes need to add a task quickly. You can do this using the To-Do List Pane. The To-Do List Pane lets you create quick tasks that normally are due the day you add them. If you wanted to add a task using the To-Do List Pane, you would use the following steps.

1. Tap or click the 'Type a new task' box to select the text box.

2. Type a description to enter a description of the task.

3. Press the ENTER key to finish adding the task and display it in the To-Do list with the current date.

Categorizing Tasks

Outlook allows you to categorize email messages, contacts, tasks, and calendar items so that you can identify which ones are related to each other as well as quickly identify the items by their color. In Chapter 2 of this text, color categories were used to organize calendar items. In the same way, you can color-categorize tasks to organize and manage different types of tasks.

Six color categories are available by default, but you also can create your own categories and select one of 25 colors to associate with them. After you create a category, you can set it as a Quick Click. The **Quick Click** category is the category applied by default when you tap or click an item's category column in the To-Do list pane. For example, the default Quick Click category is the red category. If you tapped or clicked a task's category column in the To-Do list pane, the red category automatically is assigned to it.

To Create a New Category

1 CREATE NEW TASK | 2 CATEGORIZE TASK | 3 CATEGORIZE EMAIL MESSAGE
4 ASSIGN TASK | 5 PRINT TASK | 6 CREATE AND USE NOTES

Why? *Custom categories can organize tasks listed in Outlook.* The first category you want to create is for International Club tasks. You intend to use the International Club category for all tasks that are related to the International Club at Raven College. To create a category, select a task and then create the category. Outlook applies the category to the selected task. After you create a category, apply it to other tasks as necessary. The following steps create a color category and apply it to a task.

1

- Tap or click the Contact a Speaker task to select it.

- Tap or click the Categorize button (HOME tab | Tags group) to display the Categorize menu (Figure 4–28).

Q&A Why do I have to select the Contact a Speaker task?
To activate the Categorize button, you first need to select a task or group of tasks.

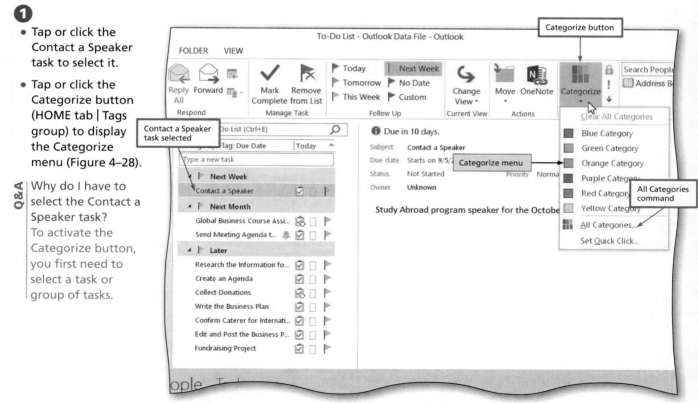

Figure 4–28

BTW

Q&As

For a complete list of the Q&As found in many of the step-by-step sequences in this book, visit the Q&A resource on the Student Companion Site located on www.cengagebrain.com. For detailed instructions about accessing available resources, visit www.cengage.com/ct/studentdownload or contact your instructor for information about accessing the required files.

2

- Tap or click All Categories to display the Color Categories dialog box (Figure 4–29).

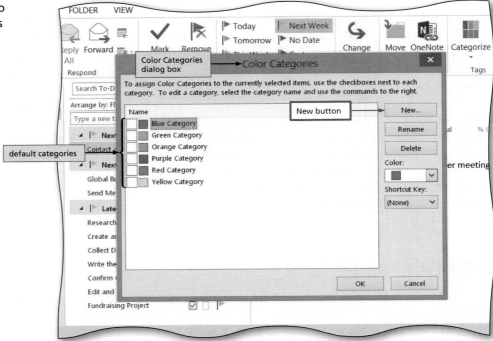

Figure 4–29

3

- Tap or click the New button (Color Categories dialog box) to display the Add New Category dialog box (Figure 4–30).

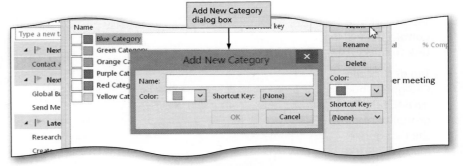

Figure 4–30

4

- Type **International Club** in the Name text box to enter a name for the category.

- Tap or click the Color box arrow to display a list of colors (Figure 4–31).

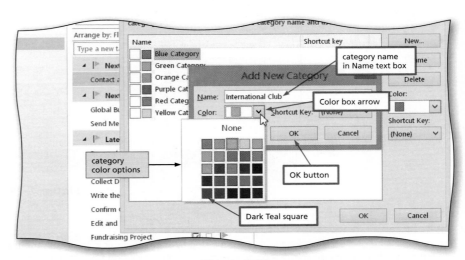

Figure 4–31

5

- Tap or click the Dark Teal square (column 1, row 5) to select a category color.

- Tap or click the OK button (Add New Category dialog box) to create the new category and display it in the Color Categories dialog box (Figure 4–32).

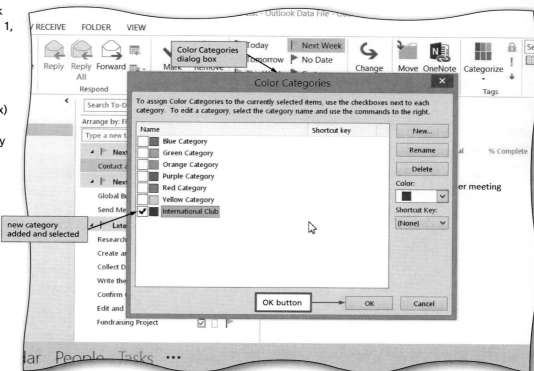

Figure 4–32

6

- Tap or click the OK button (Color Categories dialog box) to assign the Contact a Speaker task to the International Club category (Figure 4–33).

Figure 4–33

BTW

BTWs

For a complete list of the BTWs found in the margins of this book, visit the BTW resource on the Student Companion Site located on www.cengagebrain.com. For detailed instructions about accessing available resources, visit www.cengage.com/ct/studentdownload or contact your instructor for information about accessing the required files.

To Categorize a Task

After creating a category, you can apply other tasks that are related to that category. *Why? You can easily identify all the tasks for a specific category by using color categories.* The following steps assign a task to an existing color category.

1

- Tap or click the Create an Agenda task to select it.
- Tap or click the Categorize button (HOME tab | Tags group) to display the Categorize menu (Figure 4–34).

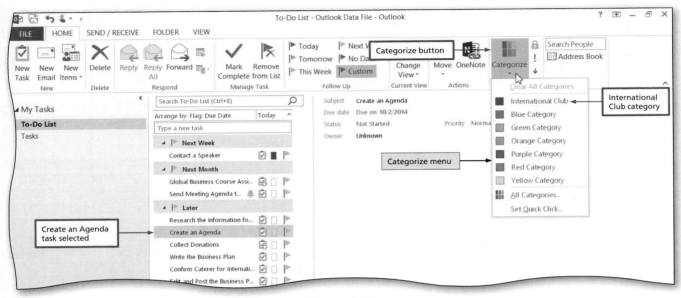

Figure 4–34

2

- Tap or click International Club to assign the Create an Agenda task to that category (Figure 4–35).

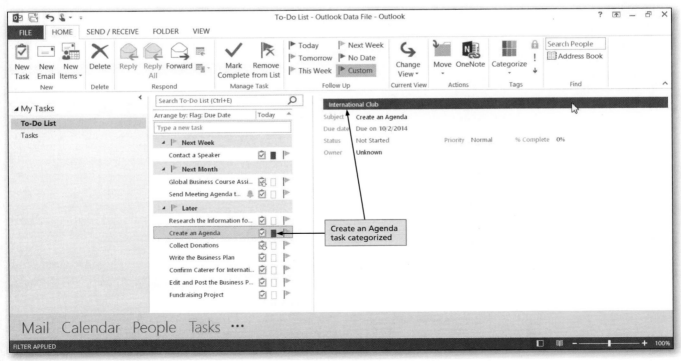

Figure 4–35

To Categorize Multiple Tasks

1 CREATE NEW TASK | 2 CATEGORIZE TASK | 3 CATEGORIZE EMAIL MESSAGE
4 ASSIGN TASK | 5 PRINT TASK | 6 CREATE AND USE NOTES

Outlook allows you to categorize multiple tasks at the same time. All of the course-related tasks can be assigned to a new category called Course Work. The tasks to assign to the Course Work category include the three business plan assignments and the Global Business course tasks.

The following steps create the Course Work category and apply it to the course-related tasks. *Why? As a student, you can view a single category to locate all of your assignments.*

1

- Select the Research the Information for the Business Plan, Write the Business Plan, Edit and Post the Business Plan, and the Global Business Course Assignment tasks.

- Tap or click the Categorize button (HOME tab | Tags group) to display the Categorize menu (Figure 4–36).

How do I select more than one task?
Tap or click the first task, press and hold the CTRL key, and then tap or click the other tasks to select them.

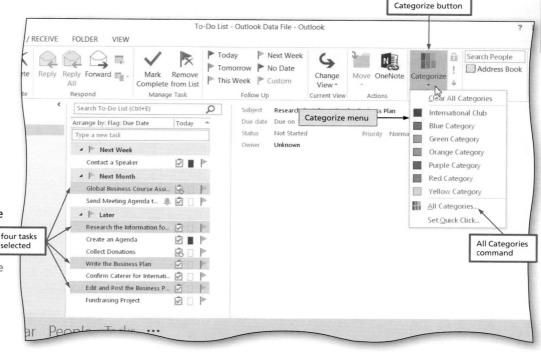

Figure 4–36

2

- Tap or click All Categories to display the Color Categories dialog box.

- Tap or click the New button (Color Categories dialog box) to display the Add New Category dialog box (Figure 4–37).

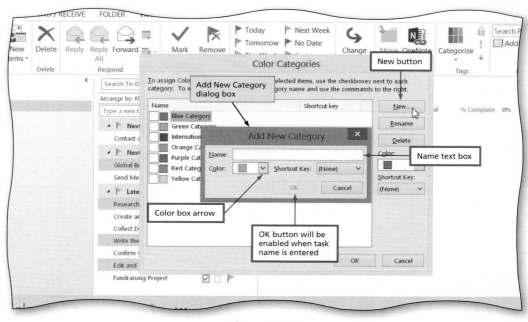

Figure 4–37

3

- Type **Course Work** in the Name text box to enter a name for the category.
- Tap or click the Color box arrow to display a list of colors.
- Click the Dark Red square (column 1, row 4) to select the category color.
- Tap or click the OK button (Add New Category dialog box) to create the Course Work category (Figure 4–38).

Figure 4–38

4

- Tap or click the OK button (Color Categories dialog box) to assign the selected tasks to a category (Figure 4–39).

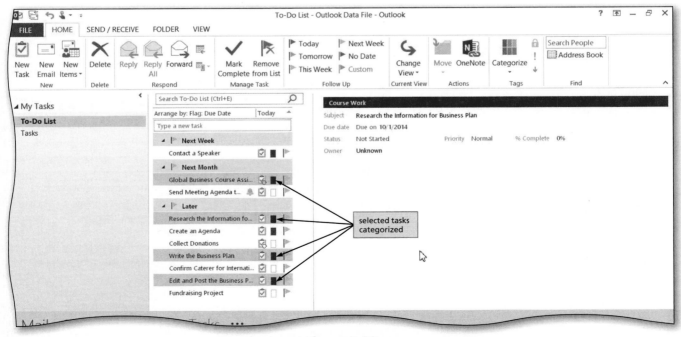

Figure 4–39

To Categorize Remaining Tasks

1 CREATE NEW TASK | 2 CATEGORIZE TASK | 3 CATEGORIZE EMAIL MESSAGE
4 ASSIGN TASK | 5 PRINT TASK | 6 CREATE AND USE NOTES

Now that you know how to categorize multiple tasks at once, you decide to categorize the remaining tasks by assigning them to the International Club category. The following steps categorize the remaining tasks. *Why? When you sort by category, you will be able to view at a glance what tasks need completion in each of the facets of your life.*

1

- Select the Create an Agenda, Collect Donations, Fundraising Project, Confirm Caterer for International Food Festival, and Send Meeting Agenda to Mr. Thompson tasks.

- Tap or click the Categorize button (HOME tab | Tags group) to display the Categorize menu.

- Tap or click International Club to categorize the selected tasks (Figure 4–40).

Figure 4–40

To Rename a Category

1 CREATE NEW TASK | 2 CATEGORIZE TASK | 3 CATEGORIZE EMAIL MESSAGE
4 ASSIGN TASK | 5 PRINT TASK | 6 CREATE AND USE NOTES

After categorizing the project tasks, Dylan decides to change the name of the International Club category to the Student International Club category. The following steps rename a color category. *Why? By renaming the color categories, you can assign names that are meaningful to you.*

1

- Tap or click the Categorize button (HOME tab | Tags group) to display the Categorize menu.

- Tap or click All Categories to display the Color Categories dialog box (Figure 4–41).

Q&A
Do the category tasks have to be selected before renaming the category?
No, any task can be selected. When you change the name, Outlook will update every task in that category.

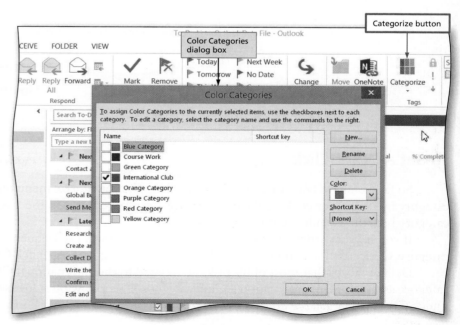

Figure 4–41

2

- Tap or click the International Club category to select it.

- Tap or click the Rename button (Color Categories dialog box) to select the category name for editing.

- Type **Student International Club** and then press the ENTER key to change the category name (Figure 4–42).

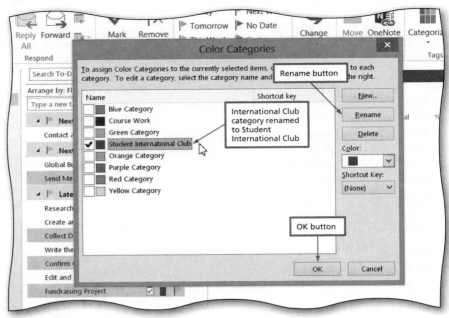

Figure 4–42

3

- Tap or click the OK button (Color Categories dialog box) to apply the changes (Figure 4–43).

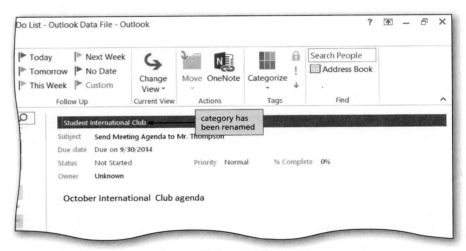

Figure 4–43

To Set a Quick Click

1 CREATE NEW TASK | 2 CATEGORIZE TASK | 3 CATEGORIZE EMAIL MESSAGE
4 ASSIGN TASK | 5 PRINT TASK | 6 CREATE AND USE NOTES

So far, you have been categorizing tasks using the Categorize menu options. You could assign a task to a category by tapping or clicking the category box next to each task in the To-Do list pane. If you tap or click the category box, the default category is applied.

If you have a particular category that you know you will use frequently, you can set it as the default category. Outlook allows you to do this by setting the category as a Quick Click.

Dylan realizes that most of his tasks are related to the International Club, so he decides to set the default category as the Student International Club category. The following steps assign the default category using a Quick Click. **Why?** *You can assign a frequently used color category (Quick Click category) by selecting it as your default color category.*

- Tap or click the Categorize button (HOME tab | Tags group) to display the Categorize menu (Figure 4–44).

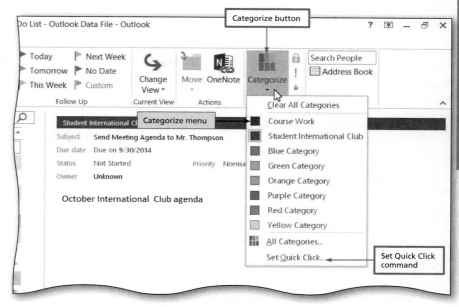

Figure 4–44

- Tap or click Set Quick Click to display the Set Quick Click dialog box.
- Tap or click the category button to display the list of categories (Figure 4–45).

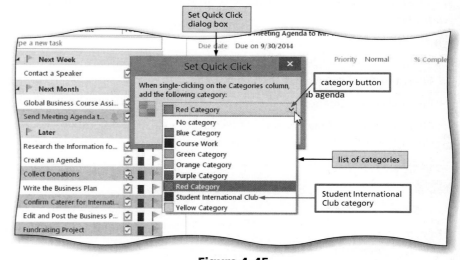

Figure 4–45

- Tap or click Student International Club to set it as the Quick Click category (Figure 4–46).

- Tap or click the OK button (Set Quick Click dialog box) to apply the changes.

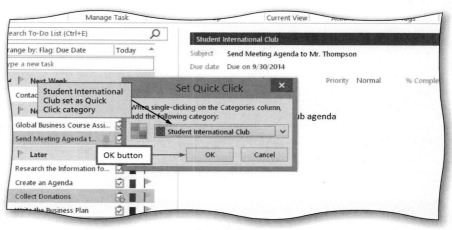

Figure 4–46

Break Point: If you wish to take a break, this is a good place to do so. To resume at a later time, continue to follow the steps from this location forward.

BTW
Copying and Moving Tasks
If you want to move or copy an existing task to another folder, select the task, and then click the Move button (HOME tab | Move group). Click the Other Folder command if you want to move the task, or click the Copy to Folder command if you want to copy the task. Next, select the folder to which you want to move or copy the task, and then click the OK button.

Categorizing Email Messages

Recall that you can use categories with email messages, contacts, tasks, and calendar items. Any category you create for a task then can be used for your email messages. Categorizing your email messages allows you to create a link between them and other related items in Outlook. By looking at the category, you quickly can tell which Outlook items go together.

To Categorize an Email Message

1 CREATE NEW TASK | 2 CATEGORIZE TASK | 3 **CATEGORIZE EMAIL MESSAGE**
4 ASSIGN TASK | 5 PRINT TASK | 6 CREATE AND USE NOTES

Dylan received a couple of email messages from members of the International Club. These email messages can be assigned to the Student International Club category. The following steps categorize email messages. *Why? Color categories can be assigned to email messages, enabling you to quickly identify them and associate them with related tasks.*

1
- Tap or click the Mail button in the Navigation Pane to switch to your Inbox.
- Select the Ava Gibson and Mia James email messages.
- Tap or click the Categorize button (HOME tab | Tags group) to display the Categorize menu (Figure 4–47).

Q&A What should I do if my Inbox is not displayed?
Tap or click the Inbox folder in the Navigation Pane to view the mailbox.

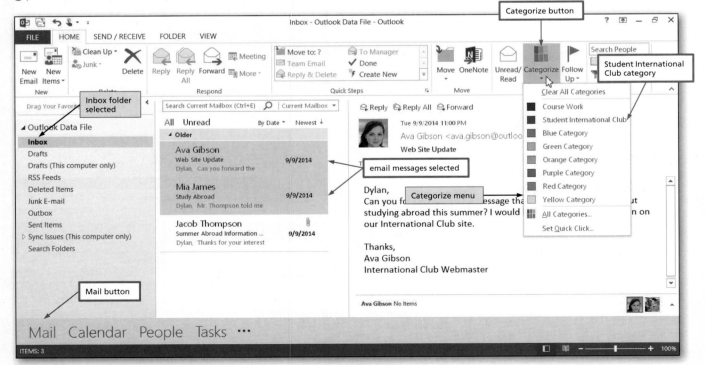

Figure 4–47

2

- Tap or click Student International Club to assign the selected email messages to the Student International Club category (Figure 4–48).

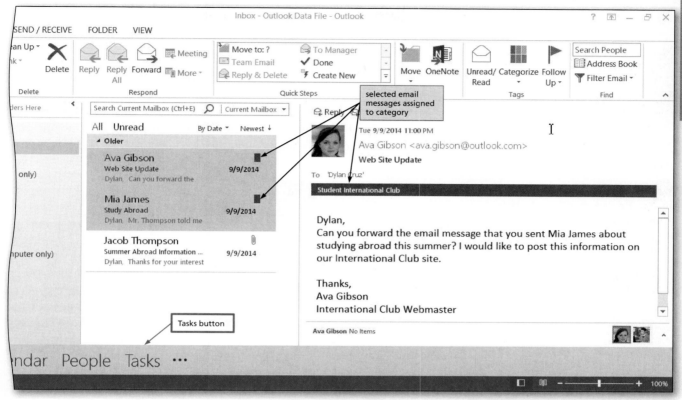

Figure 4–48

Managing Tasks

After creating one or more tasks in your To-Do list, you can perform maintenance on your tasks to manage them. Maintenance can include marking tasks complete when you finish them, updating them, assigning some of them to other people, adding attachments to them, and even removing them. Outlook allows you to manage your tasks and modify them as necessary while you are tracking them.

People sometimes create a To-Do list and never look at it again. To make the best use of your To-Do list, you should review it often to identify tasks that can be marked as complete, removed, or updated. For example, when you email the agenda for the meeting to Mr. Thompson, mark the task as complete. That way, you will not have to remember later whether you completed the assignment.

When you are working on a project with others, you sometimes may want to assign tasks to them. Outlook allows you to assign tasks to other people and still monitor the tasks. When a task has been assigned to another person, that person can accept or reject the task. If the task is rejected, it comes back to you. If it is accepted, the task belongs to that person to complete. When you assign a nonrecurring task, you can retain a copy and request a status report when the task is completed. If the task is a recurring task, you cannot retain a copy, but can request a status report when the task is completed.

BTW
Outlook Help
At any time while using Outlook, you can find answers to questions and display information about various topics through Outlook Help. Used properly, this form of assistance can increase your productivity and reduce your frustrations by minimizing the time you spend learning how to use Outlook. For instruction about Outlook Help and exercises that will help you gain confidence in using it, read the Office and Windows chapter at the beginning of this book.

Can you assign tasks to others within a business or club setting?

In the professional world, you typically work on projects as a member of a group or team. As you organize the large and small tasks required to complete the project, you can assign each task to members of your team and track the progress of the entire project.

1 CREATE NEW TASK | 2 CATEGORIZE TASK | 3 CATEGORIZE EMAIL MESSAGE
4 ASSIGN TASK | 5 PRINT TASK | 6 CREATE AND USE NOTES

To Update a Task

The November International Club meeting has been moved so the fundraising project task is due on November 13 instead of on November 6. The following steps change the due date for a task. *Why? As tasks change, be sure to update the due dates of your tasks.*

 1

- Tap or click the Tasks button in the Navigation Pane (shown in Figure 4–48) to display the To-Do list.

- Double-tap or double-click the Fundraising Project task to display the Fundraising Project – Task window (Figure 4–49).

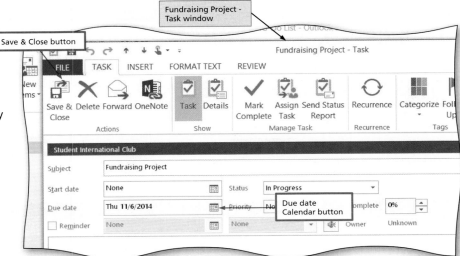

Figure 4–49

 2

- Tap or click the Due date Calendar button to display a calendar for November.

- Tap or click 13 to select Thu 11/13/2014 as the due date.

- Tap or click Save & Close (TASK tab | Actions group) to save the changes (Figure 4–50).

Q&A How do I change the task name only?

Tap or click the task name in the task list to select it, and then tap or click it again to edit the name.

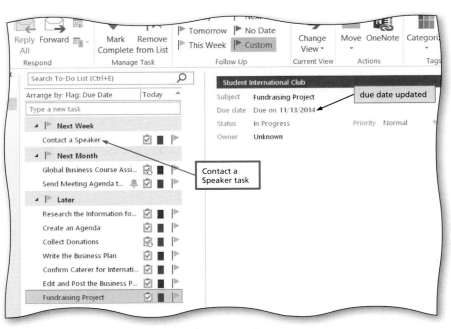

Figure 4–50

To Attach a File to a Task

Outlook allows you to attach a file to a task. *Why? This is helpful if you want quick access to information when you are looking at a task.* Jacob Thompson has emailed you a Study Abroad flyer, which you already have saved to your computer. You decide that you should attach it to the Contact a Speaker task so that you can share the flyer with the speaker. The following steps attach a document to a task.

1

- Double-tap or double-click the Contact a Speaker task (shown in Figure 4–50) to display the Contact a Speaker - Task window.

- Tap or click INSERT on the ribbon to display the INSERT tab (Figure 4–51).

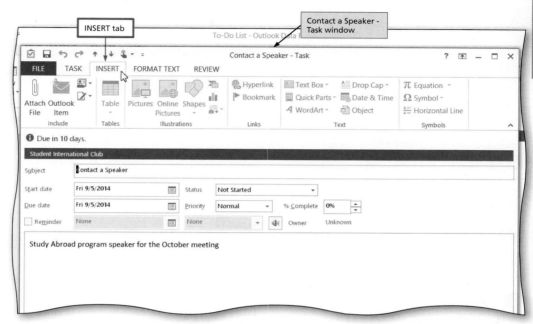

Figure 4–51

2

- Tap or click the Attach File button (INSERT tab | Include group) to display the Insert File dialog box.

- If necessary, navigate to the folder containing the data files for this chapter (in this case, the Chapter 04 folder in the Outlook folder in the Data Files for Students folder).

- Tap or click Study Abroad (Word document) to select the file to attach (Figure 4–52).

Figure 4–52

- Tap or click the
Insert button (Insert
File dialog box)
to attach the file
(Figure 4–53).

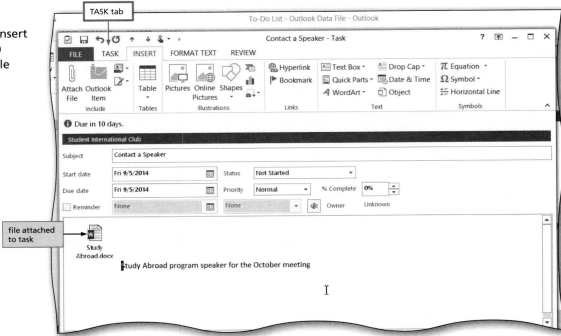

Figure 4–53

- Tap or click TASK
on the ribbon
to display the
TASK tab.

- Tap or click Save &
Close (TASK tab |
Actions group) to
save the changes
(Figure 4–54).

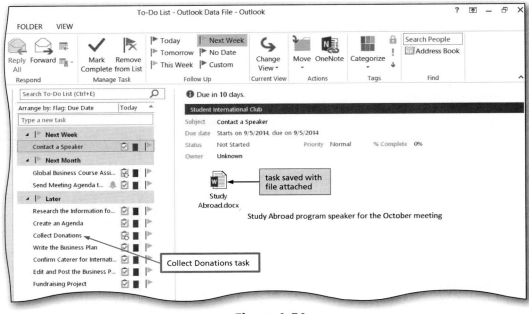

Figure 4–54

To Assign a Task

1 CREATE NEW TASK | 2 CATEGORIZE TASK | 3 CATEGORIZE EMAIL MESSAGE
4 ASSIGN TASK | 5 PRINT TASK | 6 CREATE AND USE NOTES

In addition to creating your own tasks, you can create tasks to assign to others. Ava Gibson has
volunteered to collect the International Red Cross donations. To assign a task, you first create the task, and then
send it as a task request to someone. *Why? You can assign a task to someone else while ensuring that you retain a copy
of the task and receive a status report once the task is completed.* The following steps assign a task.

1

- Double-tap or double-click the Collect Donations task (shown in Figure 4–54) to display the Collect Donations - Task window (Figure 4–55).

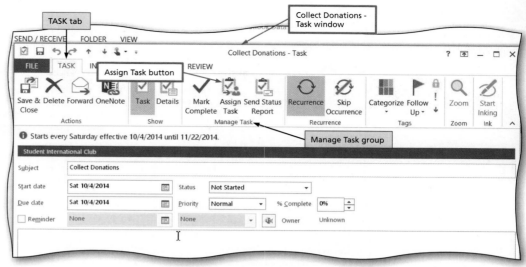

Figure 4–55

2

- Tap or click the Assign Task button (TASK tab | Manage Task group) to display the Assign Task options (Figure 4–56).

Q&A Why is my window missing the Assign Task button? To follow the steps in the Assign Tasks section of this chapter, you need to set up an email account in Outlook as shown in Chapter 1.

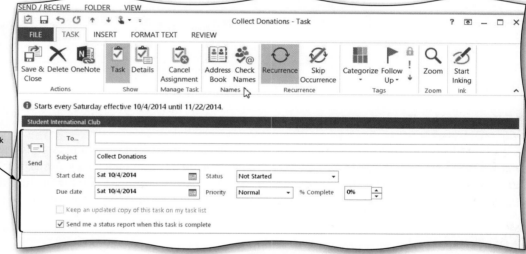

Figure 4–56

3

- Type **ava. gibson@ outlook.com** in the To text box to enter a recipient (Figure 4–57).

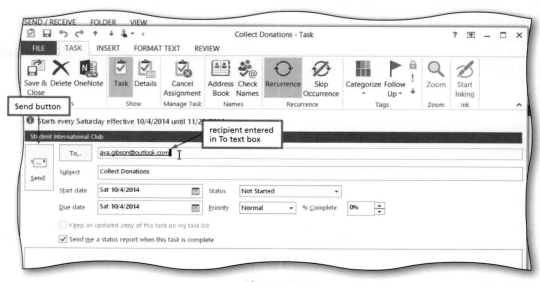

Figure 4–57

4

- Tap or click the Send button (shown in Figure 4–57) to send the task to Ava Gibson (Figure 4–58).

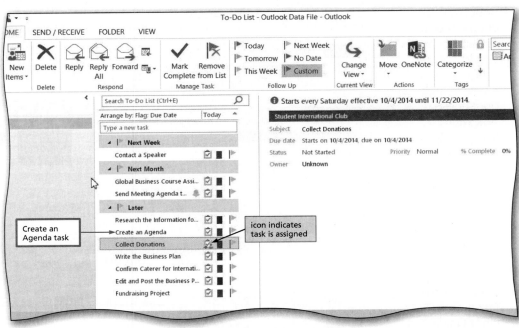

Figure 4–58

To Forward a Task

1 CREATE NEW TASK | 2 CATEGORIZE TASK | 3 CATEGORIZE EMAIL MESSAGE
4 ASSIGN TASK | 5 PRINT TASK | 6 CREATE AND USE NOTES

In addition to assigning a task to a person, you can forward a task to a person. *Why? When you forward a task, you are forwarding a copy of the task to the person who can add it to their To-Do list for tracking.* Mia James has agreed to assist you in creating the agenda for the October meeting task. By forwarding the task to Mia, the task appears on her to-do list and she can track it on her own. The following steps forward a task.

1

- Double-tap or double-click the Create an Agenda task (shown in Figure 4–58) to display the Create an Agenda – Task window (Figure 4–59).

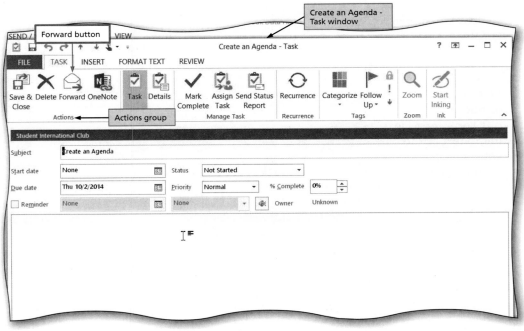

Figure 4–59

2

- Tap or click the Forward button (TASK tab | Actions group) to display the FW: Create an Agenda – Message (HTML) window (Figure 4–60).

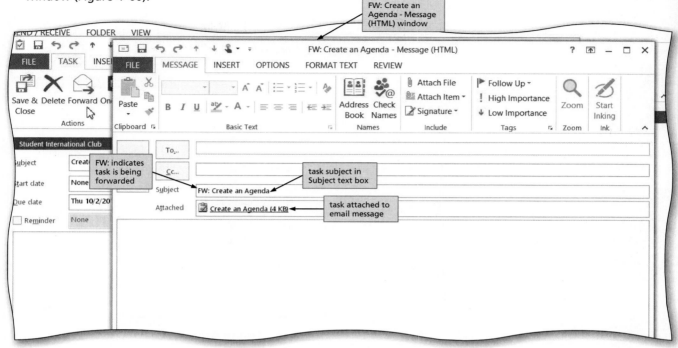

Figure 4–60

3

- Type **mia.james@outlook.com** in the To text box to enter a recipient.

- Type **Attached is the agenda task for you to add to your to-do list.** in the message body area to enter a message.

- Press the ENTER key two times and then type **Dylan** to complete the message (Figure 4–61).

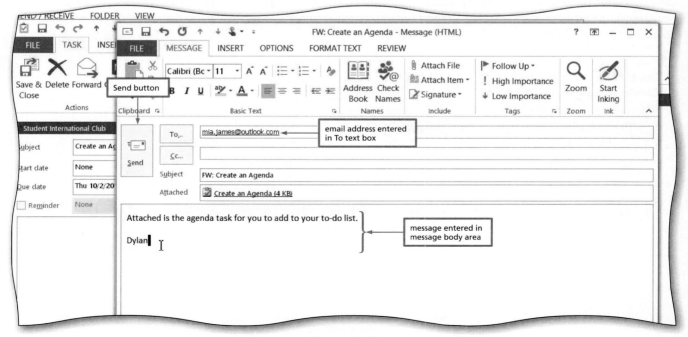

Figure 4–61

- Tap or click the Send button to forward the task to Mia James (Figure 4–62).

Figure 4–62

To Send a Status Report

1 CREATE NEW TASK | 2 CATEGORIZE TASK | 3 CATEGORIZE EMAIL MESSAGE
4 ASSIGN TASK | 5 PRINT TASK | 6 CREATE AND USE NOTES

While a task is in progress, you can send status reports to other people. The status reports indicate the status and completion percentage of the task. Mr. Jacob Thompson has requested that he be kept informed about the agenda for the October meeting. Dylan has completed 25 percent of the work and wants to inform him that the task is in progress. The following steps create and send a status report. *Why? If you have been assigned a task, you can submit a status report at some point prior to completion of the task. This could be used to detail why the task has not been completed or why the task needs to be amended.*

- Double-tap or double-click the Create an Agenda task to display the Create an Agenda - Task window.

- Tap or click the Status box arrow to display a status list.

- Tap or click In Progress to change the status of the task (Figure 4–63).

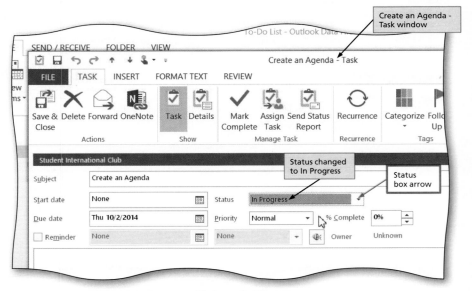

Figure 4–63

● Tap or click the Up arrow to change the % Complete to 25% (Figure 4–64).

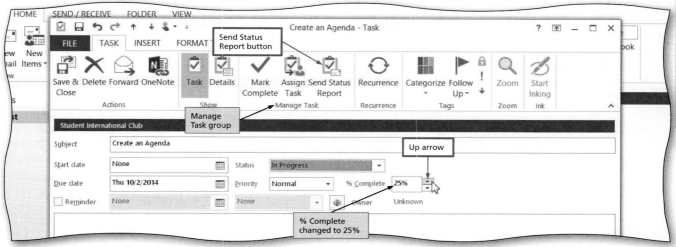

Figure 4–64

● Tap or click the Send Status Report button (TASK tab | Manage Task group) to display the Task Status Report: Create an Agenda - Message (Rich Text) window.

● Type `jacob.thompson@outlook.com` in the To text box to enter a recipient.

● Type **`Mr. Thompson,`**   and then press the ENTER key two times in the message body area to enter the greeting line of the message.

● Type **`Here is my first update on this task.`**   in the message.

● Press the ENTER key two times, and then type **`Dylan`**   to complete the message (Figure 4–65).

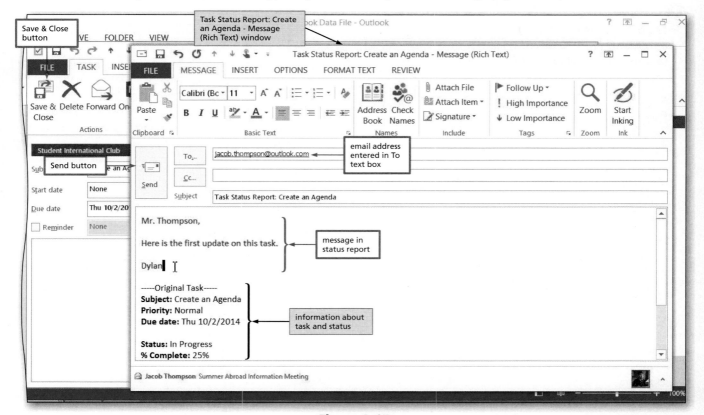

Figure 4–65

4

- Tap or click the Send button to send the status report to Jacob Thompson.
- Tap or click the Save & Close button (TASK tab | Actions group) to save the changes to the task (Figure 4–66).

Figure 4–66

To Mark a Task Complete

1 CREATE NEW TASK | 2 CATEGORIZE TASK | 3 CATEGORIZE EMAIL MESSAGE
4 ASSIGN TASK | 5 PRINT TASK | 6 CREATE AND USE NOTES

When you accomplish a task, you should mark it as complete so that you know it is finished. You have just completed the research for the business plan. *Why? You can mark a task as complete so that you no longer have to worry about it.* The following steps mark a task as complete.

1

- Tap or click the Research the Information for the Business Plan task to select it (Figure 4–67).

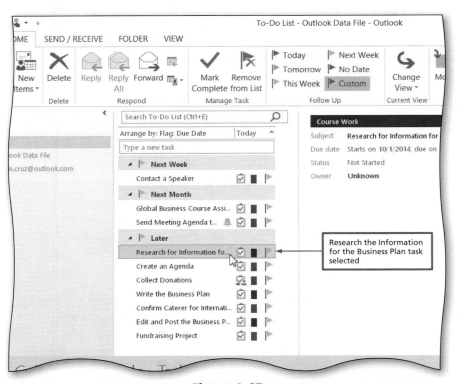

Figure 4–67

②

- Tap or click the Mark Complete button (HOME tab | Manage Task group) to mark the Research the Information for the Business Plan task as completed (Figure 4–68).

Q&A

Why was the Research the Information for the Business Plan task removed from the To-Do list? Once you mark a task as complete, Outlook removes it from the To-Do list and places it in the Completed list. You can see the Completed list by changing your view to Completed using the Change View button (HOME tab | Current View group).

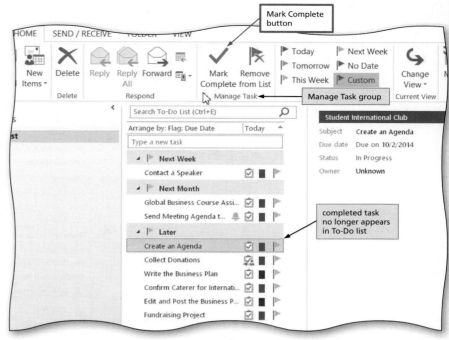

Figure 4–68

To Remove a Task

You sometimes may need to remove a task. **Why?** *When you remove a task, it no longer is displayed in your To-Do List.* For example, the Student International Club has decided to remove the Fundraising Project task until the club has time to promote the project. The following steps remove a task.

①

- Tap or click the Fundraising Project task to select it (Figure 4–69).

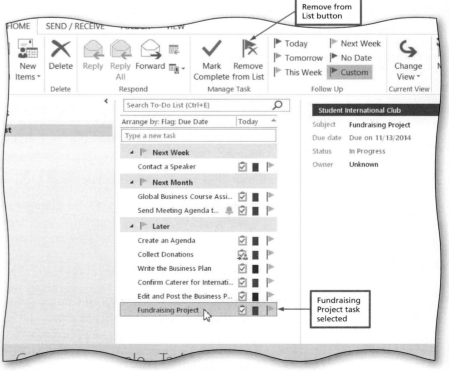

Figure 4–69

2

- Tap or click the Remove from List button (HOME tab | Manage Task group) to remove the task (Figure 4–70).

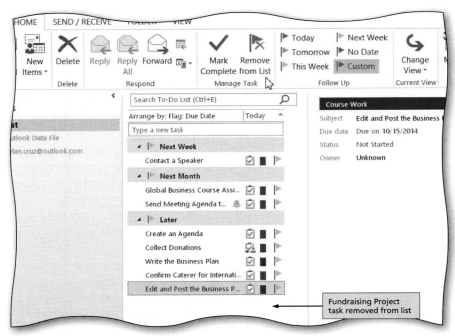

Figure 4–70

---

1 CREATE NEW TASK | 2 CATEGORIZE TASK | 3 CATEGORIZE EMAIL MESSAGE
4 ASSIGN TASK | 5 PRINT TASK | 6 CREATE AND USE NOTES

TO DELETE A CATEGORY

When you no longer need a category, you can delete it. Deleting a category removes the category from the category list but not from the tasks that already have been assigned to it. If you wanted to delete a category, you would use the following steps.

1. Tap or click a task within the category that you would like to delete.

2. Tap or click the Categorize button (HOME tab | Tags group) to display the Categorize menu.

3. Tap or click All Categories to display the Color Categories dialog box.

4. Tap or click the category that you want to delete to select it.

5. Tap or click the Delete button (Color Categories dialog box) to delete the color category.

6. Tap or click the Yes button (Microsoft Outlook dialog box) to confirm the deletion.

7. Tap or click the OK button (Color Categories dialog box) to close the dialog box.

BTW
Touch Screen Differences
The Office and Windows interfaces may vary if you are using a touch screen. For this reason, you might notice that the function or appearance of your touch screen differs slightly from this chapter's presentation.

Choosing Display and Print Views

When working with tasks, you can change the view to see your tasks better. For instance, you can view your tasks as a detailed list, simple list, priority list, or a complete list. Change the view of your tasks to fit your current needs. For example, if you want to see tasks listed according to their priority (High, Normal, or Low), you can display the tasks in the Prioritized view. You also can print tasks in a summarized list or include the details for each task.

To Change the Task View

Tasks can be displayed in different customized view layouts. *Why? If you would like to see the total picture of what you have to accomplish, the Detailed view provides all the task details, including task subject, status, due date, and categories.* By displaying tasks in Detailed view, you can view all tasks, including completed tasks. The following steps change the view to Detailed view.

1

- Tap or click the Change View button (HOME tab | Current View group) to display the Change View gallery (Figure 4–71).

Q&A The Change View button does not appear on my HOME tab. What should I do?
Tap or click the More button (HOME tab | Current View group) to display the Change View gallery.

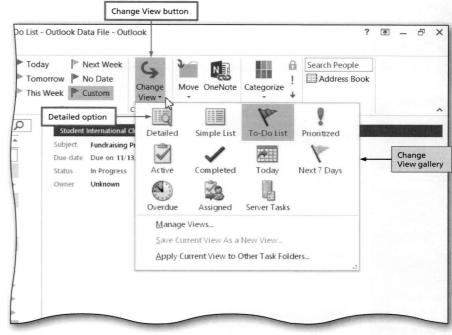

Figure 4–71

2

- Tap or click Detailed to change the view (Figure 4–72).

🔍 **Experiment**

- Tap or click the other views in the Current View gallery to view the tasks in other arrangements. When you are finished, tap or click Detailed to return to Detailed view.

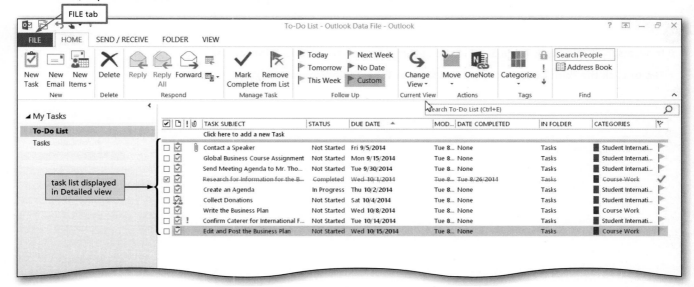

Figure 4–72

To Print Tasks

If you need to print your tasks, Outlook provides printing options based upon the view and tasks you have selected. For example, in the To-Do List view, you can select a single task and print in Table Style or Menu Style. In Detailed view, which is the current view, you can print only in Table Style. The following steps print the tasks using Table Style. *Why? Sometimes it is easier to print a To-Do list to view at any time when you are not working at your computer.*

1
- Tap or click FILE on the ribbon to open the Backstage view.
- Tap or click the Print tab in the Backstage view to display the Print gallery (Figure 4–73).

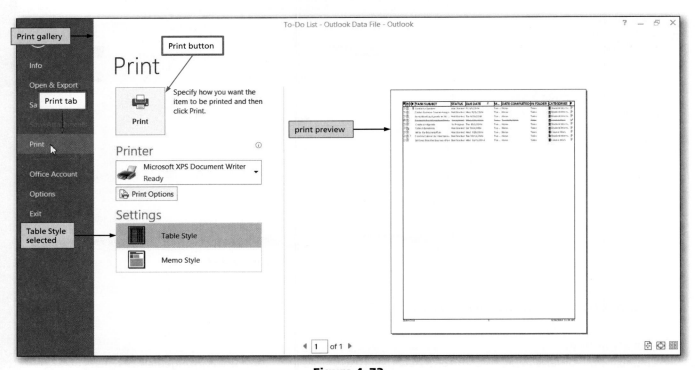

Figure 4–73

2
- If necessary, tap or click Table Style in the Settings section to select a print format.
- Tap or click the Print button to print the tasks in Table Style (Figure 4–74).

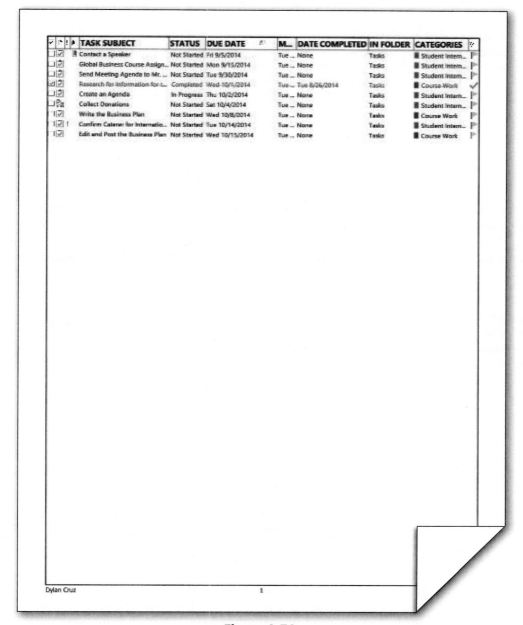

Figure 4–74

Using Notes

Outlook allows you to create the equivalent of paper notes using the Notes feature. Use notes to record ideas, spur-of-the-moment questions, and even words that you would like to recall or use at a later time. You can leave notes open on the screen while you continue using Outlook, or you can close them and view them in the Notes window. The Notes window contains the Navigation Pane and Notes Pane.

CONSIDER THIS

Can I use the Outlook Notes as sticky notes?

Notes are the electronic equivalent of yellow paper sticky notes. You can jot down notes for the directions that you find online to your interview, for example, or write questions that you want to remember to ask.

To Create a Note

1 CREATE NEW TASK | 2 CATEGORIZE TASK | 3 CATEGORIZE EMAIL MESSAGE
4 ASSIGN TASK | 5 PRINT TASK | 6 CREATE AND USE NOTES

Why? *A note can save a reminder from a phone conversation, information you find online for future reference, or even a grocery list.* As Dylan was surfing the web, he came across some information that he would like to share at the next club meeting. When text is entered into a note, it is saved automatically with the last modified date shown at the bottom of the note; therefore, you do not have to tap or click a Save button. The following steps create a note reminder.

1

- Tap or click the Navigation Options button (three dots) on the Navigation bar to display the Navigation Options menu (Figure 4–75).

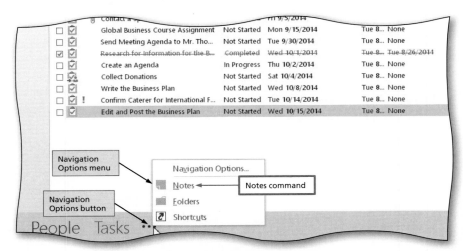

Figure 4–75

2

- Tap or click Notes to open the Notes – Outlook Data File – Outlook window.

- Tap or click the New Note button (HOME tab | New group) to display a new blank note (Figure 4–76).

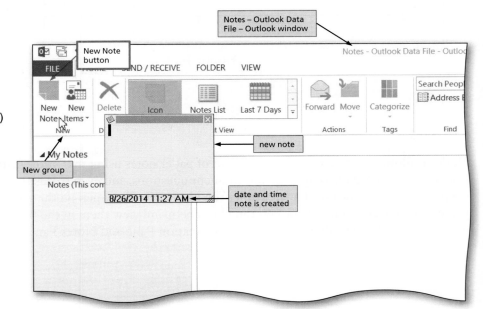

Figure 4–76

3

- Type **82% of those that studied abroad acquired skill sets that influenced their career path** as the note text to enter a note (Figure 4–77).

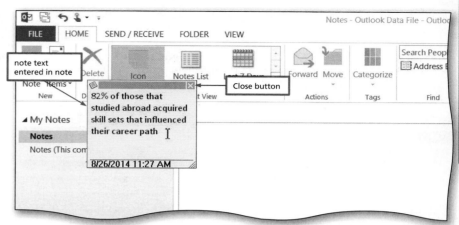

Figure 4–77

4

- Tap or click the Close button to save and close the note (Figure 4–78).

Q&A

Why is my Notes view different from Figure 4–78?

There are three basic Notes views: Icon, Notes List, and Last 7 Days. In Figure 4–78, the note is displayed in Icon view. To switch to Icon view, tap or click the Icon button (HOME tab | Current View group).

Can I print notes?

Yes. First, select the note(s) you want to print. To select multiple notes, hold the CTRL key while tapping or clicking the notes to print. Next, tap or click the FILE tab to open the Backstage view, tap or click the Print tab, and then tap or click the Print button.

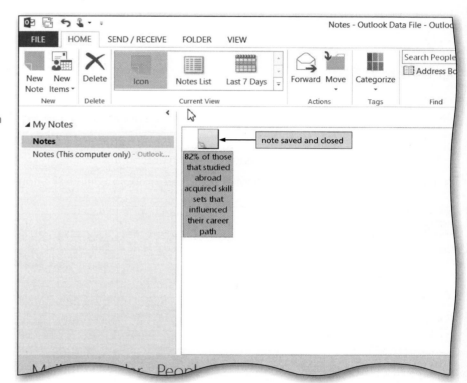

Figure 4–78

Other Ways

1. Press CTRL+SHIFT+N

To Change the Notes View

1 CREATE NEW TASK | 2 CATEGORIZE TASK | 3 CATEGORIZE EMAIL MESSAGE
4 ASSIGN TASK | 5 PRINT TASK | 6 CREATE AND USE NOTES

Why? *You would like to display your notes as a list instead in the sticky note layout.* As with tasks, you can change the view of your notes. You decide to change your notes view to Notes List. The following step changes the view to Notes List view.

1

- Tap or click the Notes List button (HOME tab | Current View group) to change the view to Notes List (Figure 4–79).

Experiment

- Tap or click the other views in the Current View group to view the notes in other arrangements. When you are finished, tap or click Notes List to return to Notes List view.

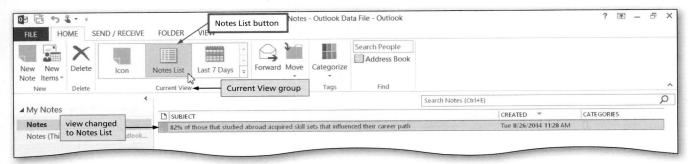

Figure 4–79

To Delete a Note

1 CREATE NEW TASK | 2 CATEGORIZE TASK | 3 CATEGORIZE EMAIL MESSAGE
4 ASSIGN TASK | 5 PRINT TASK | 6 CREATE AND USE NOTES

Why? *When you no longer need a note, you should delete it.* After sharing the note about studying abroad at the club meeting, you decide to delete the note because you no longer need it. The following step deletes a note.

1

- If necessary, tap or click the note about studying abroad to select it.

- Tap or click the Delete button (HOME tab | Delete group) to delete the note (Figure 4–80).

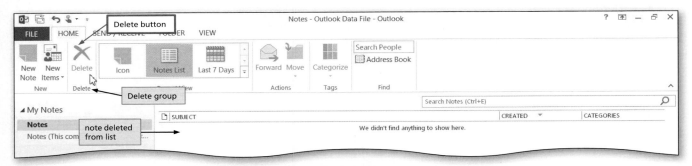

Figure 4–80

To Exit Outlook

This project now is complete. The following steps exit Outlook. For a detailed example of the procedure summarized below, refer to the Office 2013 and Windows 8 chapter at the beginning of this book.

1 If you have a note or task open, tap or click the Close button on the right side of the title bar to close the window.

2 Tap or click the Close button on the right side of the title bar to exit Outlook.

Chapter Summary

In this chapter, you have learned how to use Outlook to create a task, categorize tasks, categorize email messages, manage tasks, print tasks, create notes, and print notes. The items listed below include all the new Outlook skills you have learned in this chapter with the tasks grouped by activity.

Creating a Task
Create a New Task (OUT 181)
Create a Task with a Due Date (OUT 184)
Create a Task with a Status (OUT 185)
Create a Task with a Priority (OUT 186)
Create a Task with a Reminder (OUT 187)
Create More Tasks (OUT 189)
Create a Recurring Task (OUT 190)
Create Another Recurring Task (OUT 192)

Categorizing Tasks
Create a New Category (OUT 193)
Categorize a Task (OUT 196)
Categorize Multiple Tasks (OUT 197)
Categorize Remaining Tasks (OUT 199)
Rename a Category (OUT 199)
Set a Quick Click (OUT 200)

Categorizing Email Messages
Categorize an Email Message (OUT 202)

Managing Tasks
Update a Task (OUT 204)
Attach a File to a Task (OUT 205)
Assign a Task (OUT 206)
Forward a Task (OUT 208)
Send a Status Report (OUT 210)
Mark a Task Complete (OUT 212)
Remove a Task (OUT 213)

Choosing Display and Print Views
Change the Task View (OUT 215)
Print Tasks (OUT 216)

Using Notes
Create a Note (OUT 218)
Change the Notes View (OUT 219)
Delete a Note (OUT 220)

CONSIDER THIS

Consider This: Plan Ahead

What decisions will you need to make when creating tasks, categorizing email messages, choosing views, and using notes in the future?

A. Create Tasks:

1. Determine what projects you want to track. People use tasks to keep track of the projects that are most important to them.

2. Determine the information you want to store for a task. For any task, you can store basic information, add attachments, and add detailed instructions.

B. Categorize Tasks and Email Messages:

1. Plan categories for tasks. To identify and group tasks and other Outlook items easily, assign the items to categories.

2. Assign emails to the same categories as tasks.

C. Manage Tasks:

1. Determine which tasks may need to be assigned to others.

D. Choose Display and Print Views:

1. Determine the preferred way to view the tasks to find the information you are seeking.

2. Determine how you want to view your tasks.

E. Use Notes:

1. Determine what reminder notes would assist you.

BTW
Quick Reference
For a table that lists how to complete the tasks covered in this book using touch gestures, the mouse, ribbon, shortcut menu, and keyboard, see the Quick Reference Summary at the back of this book, or visit the Quick Reference resource on the Student Companion Site located on www.cengagebrain.com. For detailed instructions about accessing available resources, visit www.cengage.com/ct/studentdownload or contact your instructor for information about accessing the required files.

STUDENT ASSIGNMENTS

CONSIDER THIS

How should you submit solutions to questions in the assignments identified with a ✲ symbol?
Every assignment in this book contains one or more questions identified with a ✲ symbol. These questions require you to think beyond the assigned file. Present your solutions to the questions in the format required by your instructor. Possible formats may include one or more of these options: write the answer; create a document that contains the answer; present your answer to the class; discuss your answer in a group; record the answer as audio or video using a webcam, smartphone, or portable media player; or post answers on a blog, wiki, or website.

Apply Your Knowledge

Reinforce the skills and apply the concepts you learned in this chapter.

Editing a Task List

Note: To complete this assignment, you will be required to use the Data Files for Students. Visit www.cengage.com/ct/studentdownload for detailed instructions or contact your instructor for information about accessing the required files.

Instructions: Start Outlook. Import the Apply Your Knowledge 4–1 Tasks file from the Data Files for Students folder into Outlook. The Apply Your Knowledge 4–1 Tasks file contains tasks for Dr. Tom Nodori. Many of the tasks have changed and some are incomplete. You need to revise the tasks and then create categories for them. Then, you will print the resulting task list (Figure 4–81).

Figure 4–81

Perform the following tasks:

1. Display the Apply Your Knowledge 4–1 Tasks folder in the Outlook To-Do List window.

2. Change the due date of the Microsoft Office 2013 Seminar task to February 19, 2015.

3. Change the due date of the Seminar Banquet task to February 20, 2015. In the Task body, type **Closing banquet for all speakers and attendees.**

4. Change the task name of CIS 315 to CIS 202. Configure the task as a recurring task that occurs every Tuesday and Thursday from January 6, 2015 until April 30, 2015.

5. Make CIS 201 a recurring task that occurs every Wednesday from January 7, 2015 until April 29, 2015.

6. Make CIS 101 a recurring task that occurs every Monday, Wednesday, and Saturday from January 5, 2015 until May 2, 2015.

7. Create two color categories. Name the first one Spring Classes and the second one Seminars. Use the colors of your choice.

8. Categorize CIS 101, CIS 201, and CIS 202 using the Spring Classes category. Categorize the Microsoft Office 2013 Seminar and Seminar Banquet tasks using the Seminars category.

9. Print the final task list, as shown in Figure 4–81, and then submit it in the format specified by your instructor.

10. Export the Apply Your Knowledge 4–1 Tasks folder to a USB flash drive and then delete the folder from the hard disk.

11. ✳ What task categories would you create to categorize the tasks in your personal life?

Extend Your Knowledge

Extend the skills you learned in this chapter and experiment with new skills. You may need to use Help to complete the assignment.

Creating Notes

Note: To complete this assignment, you will be required to use the Data Files for Students. Visit www.cengage.com/ct/studentdownload for detailed instructions or contact your instructor for information about accessing the required files.

Instructions: Start Outlook. Import the Extend Your Knowledge 4–1 Notes file from the Data Files for Students folder into Outlook. The Extend Your Knowledge 4–1 Notes file has no notes. You will create new notes, categorize the notes, and then print the notes.

Perform the following tasks:

1. Use Help to learn about customizing notes.

2. Display the Extend Your Knowledge 4–1 Notes folder in the Outlook Notes window.

3. Create the following notes:

   - Send an email message to Dr. Johnson about upcoming appointment
   - Remember to review new website design
   - Apply for passport
   - Review newsletter
   - Ask supervisor for website content
   - Set up secondary email account to handle work email messages

4. Select the Apply for passport note, and then create a color category named Critical. Use a color of your choosing.

Continued >

Extend Your Knowledge *continued*

5. Categorize the notes about the website using a new "Website" category. Use a color of your choosing.

6. Categorize the remaining notes using a new "Upcoming" category. Use a color of your choosing.

7. Replace "Dr. Johnson" in the "Send an email message to Dr. Johnson about upcoming appointment" note with the name of your favorite teacher.

8. Change the view to Notes List. Print the notes in Table Style, as shown in Figure 4–82, and then submit them in the format specified by your instructor.

9. Export the Extend Your Knowledge 4–1 Notes folder to a USB flash drive and then delete the folder from the hard disk.

10. ✺ When is it appropriate to create a note instead of creating a task?

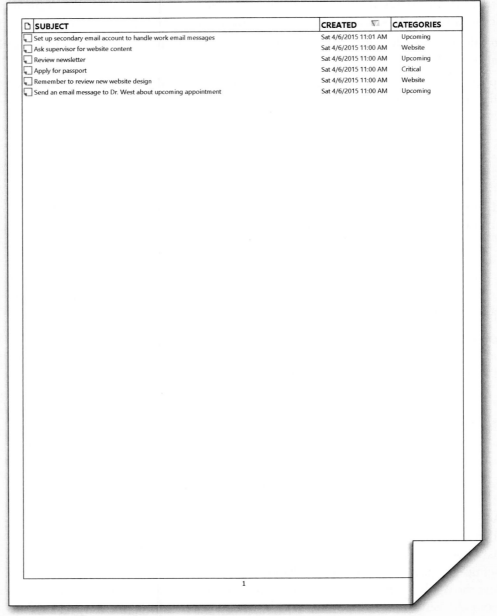

SUBJECT	CREATED	CATEGORIES
Set up secondary email account to handle work email messages	Sat 4/6/2015 11:01 AM	Upcoming
Ask supervisor for website content	Sat 4/6/2015 11:00 AM	Website
Review newsletter	Sat 4/6/2015 11:00 AM	Upcoming
Apply for passport	Sat 4/6/2015 11:00 AM	Critical
Remember to review new website design	Sat 4/6/2015 11:00 AM	Website
Send an email message to Dr. West about upcoming appointment	Sat 4/6/2015 11:00 AM	Upcoming

1

Figure 4–82

Analyze, Correct, Improve

Analyze tasks and correct all errors and/or improve tasks.

Correcting Tasks and Task Groups

Note: To complete this assignment, you will be required to use the Data Files for Students. Visit www.cengage.com/ct/studentdownload for detailed instructions or contact your instructor for information about accessing the required files.

Instructions: Start Outlook. Import the Analyze 4–1 Tasks file from the Data Files for Students folder into Outlook. While reviewing your Outlook tasks, you realize that you created several tasks incorrectly, failed to add a task, and categorized some tasks inappropriately. You will identify and open the incorrect tasks, edit them so that they reflect the correct information, add the missing task, apply the right categories, and then save all changes. You also will print the tasks (Figure 4–83).

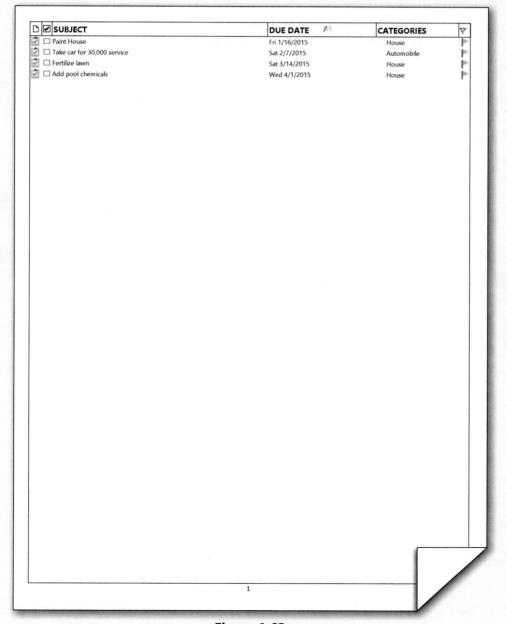

	SUBJECT	DUE DATE	CATEGORIES	
	☐ Paint House	Fri 1/16/2015	House	
	☐ Take car for 30,000 service	Sat 2/7/2015	Automobile	
	☐ Fertilize lawn	Sat 3/14/2015	House	
	☐ Add pool chemicals	Wed 4/1/2015	House	

1

Figure 4–83

Continued >

Analyze, correct, improve *continued*

Perform the following tasks:

1. Correct While creating your tasks in Outlook, you inadvertently specified the incorrect year for the due date of each task. In your task list, change the due date for each task so that the year is 2015 instead of 2014.

2. Improve Add other information to each task, including an appropriate start date, category, status, reminder, and priority.

3. ❋ When might you want to set a priority for your tasks?

In the Labs

Design, create, modify, and/or use tasks and notes using the guidelines, concepts, and skills presented in this chapter. Labs are listed in order of increasing difficulty.

Lab 1: **Creating Departmental Tasks**

Problem: You are an assistant for the Information Technology (IT) department at Cometins Pharmaceuticals. Your team is working on upgrading staff computers and will use Microsoft Outlook to keep track of all tasks. Table 4–2 lists the regular tasks and Table 4–3 lists the recurring tasks for the IT department. Enter the tasks into the To-Do list. The task list you create will look like the one in Figure 4–84.

Perform the following tasks:
1. Create a Tasks folder named Lab 4–1 Tasks.
2. Create the regular tasks in the Lab 4–1 Tasks folder using the information listed in Table 4–2.

Table 4–2 Information Technology Tasks

Task	Start Date	Due Date	Status	Priority
Back up data	3/6/2015	3/13/2015	In Progress	Normal
Remove old computers	3/13/2015	3/27/2015		Normal
Install new computers	3/27/2015	4/17/2015		High
Test new computers	4/17/2015	4/24/2015		High
Restore backed up data	4/24/2015	5/8/2015		Normal

© 2014 Cengage Learning

3. Create the recurring tasks in the Lab 4–1 Tasks folder using the information listed in Table 4–3.

Table 4–3 Information Technology Recurring Tasks

Task	Start Date	Due Date	Recurrence
Perform software updates	5/12/2015	5/9/2017	Monthly, second Tuesday
Perform virus scans	5/8/2015	5/19/2017	Weekly, Fridays

© 2014 Cengage Learning

4. Create a color category called Maintenance, using a color of your choice. Classify the Perform software updates and Perform virus scans tasks using the Maintenance category.

5. Create a color category called Computer Upgrades, using a color of your choice. Categorize all tasks with this category.

6. Print the Lab 4–1 Tasks list in Table Style, and then submit it in a format specified by your instructor (Figure 4–84).

7. Export the Lab 4–1 Tasks folder to your USB flash drive and then delete the folder from the hard disk.

8. ✳ Why is it a good idea to include as much detail as possible in each task?

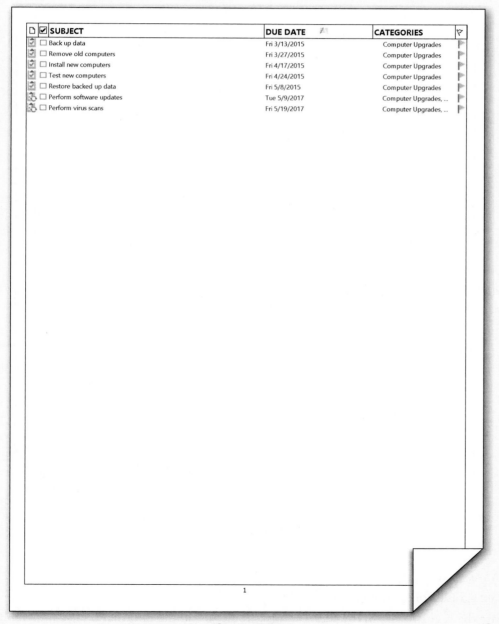

	☑ SUBJECT	DUE DATE	CATEGORIES	
	☐ Back up data	Fri 3/13/2015	Computer Upgrades	
	☐ Remove old computers	Fri 3/27/2015	Computer Upgrades	
	☐ Install new computers	Fri 4/17/2015	Computer Upgrades	
	☐ Test new computers	Fri 4/24/2015	Computer Upgrades	
	☐ Restore backed up data	Fri 5/8/2015	Computer Upgrades	
	☐ Perform software updates	Tue 5/9/2017	Computer Upgrades, ...	
	☐ Perform virus scans	Fri 5/19/2017	Computer Upgrades, ...	

1

Figure 4–84

Continued >

Lab 2: **Creating an Ice Cream Store Task List**

Problem: You are the owner of Great Licks Ice Cream Heaven and decide to enter your various tasks into Outlook for your first year of business. You need to create a list of all your tasks and categorize them appropriately (Figure 4–85).

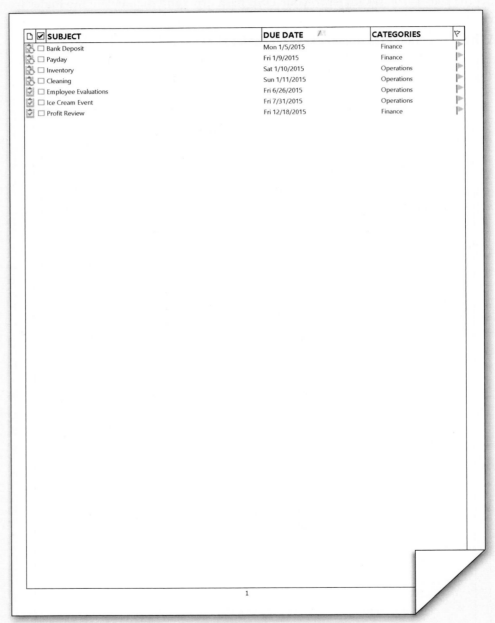

	SUBJECT	DUE DATE	CATEGORIES	
	Bank Deposit	Mon 1/5/2015	Finance	
	Payday	Fri 1/9/2015	Finance	
	Inventory	Sat 1/10/2015	Operations	
	Cleaning	Sun 1/11/2015	Operations	
	Employee Evaluations	Fri 6/26/2015	Operations	
	Ice Cream Event	Fri 7/31/2015	Operations	
	Profit Review	Fri 12/18/2015	Finance	

Figure 4–85

Perform the following tasks:

1. Create a Tasks folder named Lab 4–2 Tasks.

2. Create the regular tasks in the Lab 4–2 Tasks folder using the information listed in Table 4–4.

Table 4–4 Great Licks Tasks					
Task	**Task Body**	**Due Date**	**Status**	**Priority**	**Reminder**
Employee Evaluations	Conduct annual reviews	6/26/2015	In Progress	Normal	6/19/2015
Ice Cream Event	Free samples at sports complex	7/31/2015	In Progress	Normal	
Profit Review	First year profit review	12/18/2015		High	12/11/2015

© 2014 Cengage Learning

3. Create the recurring tasks in the Lab 4–2 Tasks folder using the information listed in Table 4–5.

Table 4–5 Great Licks Recurring Tasks			
Task	**Due Date**	**Task Body**	**Recurrence**
Bank Deposit	1/5/2015	First Trust of America Bank	Weekly, Monday, Wednesday, Friday
Payday	1/9/2015	Process direct deposit	Weekly, Friday
Inventory	1/10/2015	Weekly inventory control	Weekly, Saturday
Cleaning	1/11/2015	Cleaning by Spotless Interiors, Inc.	Weekly, Sunday

© 2014 Cengage Learning

4. Categorize the Bank Deposit, Payday, and Profit Review tasks as Finance by creating a new color category.

5. Categorize the remaining tasks as Operations by creating a new color category.

6. Print the tasks in Table Style, and then submit the task list in the format specified by your instructor.

7. ✺ Why is it a good idea to update the status of a task as it changes?

Lab 3: Expand Your World: Cloud and Web Technologies

Problem: Outlook.com allows you to enter and maintain a task list from any computer with a web browser and an Internet connection. You are to use Outlook.com to create a task list for Johnston Hills Photography using the information in Table 4–6. You have six events coming up in the next month and want to create the tasks along with the reminders for them. You also want to create notes to remind you about how to prepare for each event.

Figure 4–86

Continued >

In the Labs *continued*

Part 1 Perform the following tasks:

1. Start your web browser and navigate to outlook.com.

2. Sign in to outlook.com. If necessary, sign up for a new account.

3. View the calendar.

4. Create the tasks shown in Table 4–6.

Table 4–6 Johnston Hills Photography Tasks

Event	Due Date	Time	Reminder Type	Reminder Time	Priority
Tagleo Wedding	May 2, 2015	6:00PM	Email	2 weeks before	High
Lipton Bar Mitzvah	May 9, 2015	12:00PM	Email	2 weeks before	High
A-1 Electronics Annual Dinner	May 15, 2015	7:00PM	Email	1 week before	Normal
Jacobs Birthday Party	May 16, 2015	3:00PM	Email	2 days before	Low
East Ridge Class Reunion	May 30, 2015	6:30PM	Email	1 week before	Normal

© 2014 Cengage Learning

5. When you have finished adding the tasks, share the calendar with your instructor. Your instructor should be able to view the details on your calendar, but should not be able to edit anything. If you have additional items on your calendar that you do not want to share with your instructor, contact your instructor and determine an alternate way to submit this assignment.

6. ✳ When would you want to add your tasks to Outlook.com instead of using Microsoft Outlook? Is there a way to automatically get your tasks in Microsoft Outlook to appear in your Outlook.com account?

✳ Consider This: Your Turn

Apply your creative thinking and problem solving skills to design and implement a solution.

Note: To complete this assignment, you will be required to use the Data Files for Students. Visit www.cengage.com/ct/studentdownload for detailed instructions or contact your instructor for information about accessing the required files.

1: Create Study Group Tasks

Academic

Part 1: Use the concepts and techniques presented in this chapter to create tasks for a study group using the information in Table 4–7. You are in charge of your study group, which consists of students who are taking Introduction to Computer Information Systems (CIS 114) and Computers in Society (CIS 211) classes. You are charged with creating tasks for the major tests in each class. Using Table 4–7, create the tasks as shown. Categorize the tasks based upon the Class column. Print the final list of tasks, and then submit it in the format specified by your instructor.

Table 4–7 Study Group Tasks			
Class	**Deliverable Name**	**Due Date**	**Chapters Covered**
CIS 101	Assignment 1	9/18/2015	1–4
CIS 101	Assignment 2	11/6/2015	5–8
CIS 101	Assignment 3	12/11/2015	6–12
CIS 114	Semester Project	12/15/2015	1–12
CIS 211	Exam 1	9/14/2015	1–5
CIS 211	Exam 2	10/26/2015	6–10
CIS 211	Final Exam	12/21/2015	1–10

© 2014 Cengage Learning

Part 2: ✹ You made several decisions when creating the task list in this assignment, such as how to store the information about each task. What was the rationale behind each of these decisions?

2: Create a Team List

Professional

Part 1: After attending a professional development event, you now have several bits of information that you would like to create as notes in Outlook, so that later on you can use the ideas from the event with the rest of your managers and staff. You have created a list of items you want to use as your notes, which is shown in Table 4–8. You indicate which notes will be used for managers and which notes will be used for staff members in the Audience column. Create the notes and categorize them appropriately. Print the notes list and submit it in the format specified by your instructor.

Table 4–8 Event Notes	
Note	**Audience**
Motivate employees	Managers
Customers are always right	Staff
Everyone shares responsibility	Managers
Document customer purchasing habits	Managers
Maintain a positive attitude at all times	Managers, Staff
Develop relationships with customers	Staff

© 2014 Cengage Learning

Part 2: ✹ You made several decisions when creating the notes in this assignment, such as what to type for each note and how to categorize the notes. What was the rationale behind each of these decisions?

3: Creating and Assigning Tasks

Research and Collaboration

Part 1: Your Introduction to Computer Information Systems instructor has assigned a term paper to be completed by a team of three people. Each person in the team is responsible for researching one computer manufacturer and writing about the company's history, products currently offered, and a roadmap for the future. After each team member performs adequate research and writes his or her part of the paper, he or she will send it to another team member for a peer review. After all team members have performed a peer review, they will finalize their content and send it to you to compile into one document and prepare it for submission. Using Outlook, each team member should create tasks for the work they will have to perform on the term paper (for example, research, writing the first draft, sending for peer review, performing a peer review, finalizing content,

Continued >

STUDENT ASSIGNMENTS

Consider This: Your Turn *continued*

compiling into one master document, preparing for submission, and submitting the paper). Add as much information to the tasks as possible, such as the start date, due date, priority, status, and percent complete. Categorize the tasks appropriately. Then, assign the peer review task to the team member who will be performing a review on your content. Finally, send a status report to all team members showing how much of each task you currently have completed. Submit the task list in a format specified by your instructor.

Part 2: ✳ You have made several decisions while creating the task list in this assignment, such as which tasks to create, what details to add to each task, and how to categorize each task. What was the rationale behind each of these decisions?

Learn Online

Reinforce what you learned in this chapter with games, exercises, training, and many other online activities and resources.

Student Companion Site Reinforce chapter terms and concepts using review questions, flash cards, practice tests, and interactive learning games, such as a crossword puzzle. These and other online activities and resources are available at no additional cost on www.cengagebrain.com. Visit www.cengage.com/ct/studentdownload for detailed instructions about accessing the resources available at the Student Companion Site.

5 | Customizing Outlook

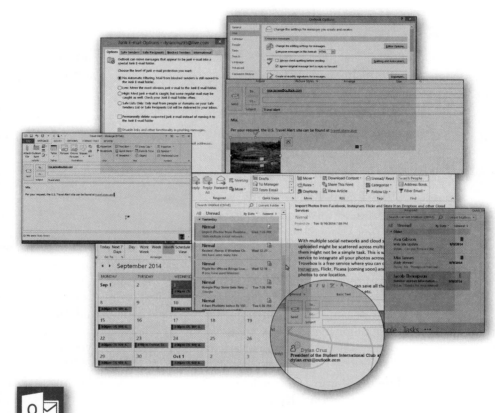

Objectives

You will have mastered the material in this chapter when you can:

- Add another email account
- Insert Quick Parts in email messages
- Insert hyperlinks in email messages
- Insert images in email messages
- Create a search folder
- Set the default message format
- Create an email signature
- Format a signature

- Assign signatures
- Customize personal stationery
- Configure junk email options
- Create rules
- Configure AutoArchive settings
- Adjust calendar settings
- Subscribe to a news feed

5 | Customizing Outlook

This chapter covers features and functions common to customizing Outlook 2013.

Roadmap

In this chapter, you will learn how to perform basic customizing tasks. The following roadmap identifies general activities you will perform as you progress through this chapter:

1. CUSTOMIZE EMAIL MESSAGES
2. CUSTOMIZE SIGNATURES and STATIONERY
3. MANAGE JUNK EMAIL FILTERS
4. CONFIGURE RULES
5. CHANGE CALENDAR OPTIONS
6. ADD a NEWS FEED

At the beginning of step instructions throughout the chapter, you will see an abbreviated form of this roadmap. The abbreviated roadmap uses colors to indicate chapter progress: gray means the chapter is beyond that activity, blue means the task being shown is covered in that activity, and black means that activity is yet to be covered. For example, the following abbreviated roadmap indicates the section would be about configuring rules.

> 1 CUSTOMIZE EMAIL MESSAGES | 2 CUSTOMIZE SIGNATURES & STATIONERY | 3 MANAGE JUNK EMAIL FILTERS
> 4 CONFIGURE RULES | 5 CHANGE CALENDAR OPTIONS | 6 ADD NEWS FEED

Use the abbreviated roadmap as a progress guide while you read or step through the instructions in this chapter.

Introduction to Customizing Outlook

Outlook provides many options for customizing your experience when working with email messages, calendars, and other items. From creating custom email signatures to adjusting how the workweek is displayed in your calendar, you can make Outlook fit your requirements so that you can use it more efficiently. For example, a rule is a command that tells Outlook how to process an email message. Using rules, you quickly can categorize or flag your email messages as they arrive so that you can identify at a glance which ones you first want to address. You can change the fonts and colors that are used by default as well. Outlook's customization options can help you become more productive.

Project — Adding a New Email Account and Customizing Options

People often have more than one email account. In fact, some people have more than they can remember. Outlook allows you to manage multiple email accounts. That way, you can read your email messages from all accounts without needing to use several email programs such as one for a Microsoft email account, another for a Gmail account, and a third for a school email account.

The project in this chapter follows general guidelines and uses Outlook to add a new email account and customize Outlook options, as shown in Figure 5–1.

(a) New email account

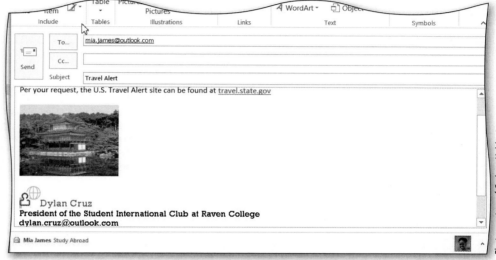

(b) Signature and stationery

Photo courtesy of Corinne Hoisington

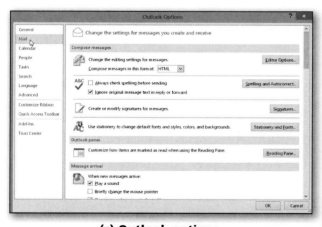

(c) Outlook options

(d) Customized calendar

Figure 5–1

Adding New Email Accounts

As you learned in Chapter 1, when setting up an email account, you need to know basic information such as the email address and password. For example, in Figure 5–2, the first mailbox is displayed as Outlook Data File (Dylan Chapter 5.pst). The second mailbox displayed in Figure 5–2 is an additional Internet-based email account named dylancruz95@live.com.

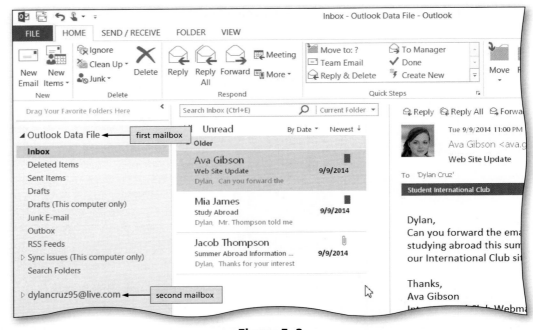

Figure 5–2

After you install Outlook, the Auto Account Setup feature runs and helps you to set up the first email account that Outlook manages. You can add another account and then use Outlook to manage two or more mailboxes.

Depending on your instructor's preferences and your email services, you can perform the steps in this chapter by opening an Outlook data file provided with the book and by adding a new email account to Outlook. Before you can add a new email account in Outlook, you must have an account set up with an email service provider that is different from any other account already set up in Outlook. For example, you might have a Microsoft account that provides email service. If you have not configured this account in Outlook, you can complete the steps in this chapter to do so.

To add a new account, you use the Add Account option in the Backstage view, which lets you add an account using the Add Account dialog box. If you want to add an account and change advanced settings, you should use the Account Settings dialog box instead.

CONSIDER THIS

My work email address requires additional information to set up my account. Where do I place this server information?

For the work email account you plan to add, make sure you know the account properties and settings before you start to add the account. Gather the following information: type of account, such as email, text messaging, or fax mail; your name, email address, and password; server information, including account type and the addresses of incoming and outgoing mail servers. You typically receive the server information from the IT staff at your place of employment. If additional server information is needed, tap or click Manual setup or additional server types when you create an account to add this information.

To Run Outlook

If you are using a computer to step through the project in this chapter and you want your screens to match the figures in this book, you should change your screen's resolution to 1366 × 768. For information about how to change a computer's resolution, refer to the Office 2013 and Windows 8 chapter at the beginning of this book.

The following steps, which assume Windows 8 is running, use the Search text box to run Outlook based on a typical installation. You may need to ask your instructor how to run Outlook on your computer. For a detailed example of the procedure summarized below, refer to the Office 2013 and Windows 8 chapter.

1 Swipe in from the right edge of the screen or point to the upper-right corner of the screen to display the Charms bar.

2 Tap or click the Search charm on the Charms bar to display the Search menu.

3 Type `Outlook` as the search text in the Search text box and watch the search results appear in the Apps list.

4 Tap or click Outlook 2013 in the search results to run Outlook.

5 If the Outlook window is not maximized, tap or click the Maximize button on its title bar to maximize the window.

To Add an Email Account

Dylan has a second email address that he dedicates to mailing lists. Dylan uses a second email account (dylancruz95@live.com) within Outlook so that he can manage both his primary and secondary email accounts. To follow all the steps within this chapter, an additional email account is necessary.

If you choose to add an email account to Outlook, you would use the following steps. If you are performing these steps on your computer, enter the name, email address, and password for an email account you own but have not yet added to Outlook.

1. Tap or click the FILE tab and then tap or click Add Account.
2. Tap or click the Your Name text box and then type your first and last name to associate your name with the account.
3. Tap or click the E-mail Address text box and then type your full email address to associate your email address with the account.
4. Tap or click the Password text box and then type your password to verify the password to your email account.
5. Tap or click the Retype Password text box and then type your password again to confirm your password.
6. Tap or click the Next button to configure your account settings and sign in to your mail server.
7. Tap or click the Finish button to add the secondary email account.
8. Tap or click the new email account to select it.

One of the few differences between Windows 7 and Windows 8 occurs in the steps to run Outlook. If you are using Windows 7, click the Start button, type Outlook in the 'Search programs and files' box, click Outlook 2013, and then, if necessary, maximize the Outlook window. For a summary of the steps to run Outlook in Windows 7, refer to the Quick Reference located at the back of this book.

For an introduction to Office and instruction about how to perform basic tasks in Office apps, read the Office and Windows chapter at the beginning of this book, where you can learn how to run an application, use the ribbon, save a file, open a file, exit an application, use Help, and much more.

BTW
Multiple Email Accounts
If you have multiple email accounts configured in Outlook, you can decide which email account to use each time you compose and send a new email message. To select the account from which to send the email message, click the From button in the Untitled – Message window, and then click the desired email account.

BTW
**Touch Screen
Differences**
The Office and Windows
interfaces may vary if you are
using a touch screen. For this
reason, you might notice that
the function or appearance
of your touch screen differs
slightly from this chapter's
presentation.

Customizing Email Messages

No matter what type of message you are composing in Outlook, whether business or personal, you always can find a way to add your unique style. With a variety of features such as background colors, graphics, designs, hyperlinks, and custom signatures, your email message starts as a blank, generic canvas and becomes an attractive, memorable communication.

To Add a Hyperlink to an Email Message

1 CUSTOMIZE EMAIL MESSAGES | 2 CUSTOMIZE SIGNATURES & STATIONERY | 3 MANAGE JUNK EMAIL FILTERS
4 CONFIGURE RULES | 5 CHANGE CALENDAR OPTIONS | 6 ADD NEWS FEED

Mia James asked Dylan to send her the web address of the travel advisory page that the U.S. Department of State maintains. Mia is planning to study abroad this summer, and wants to check the web page for advice about locations she will visit. Dylan can send her the web address as a hyperlink in an email message. *Why? Outlook automatically formats hyperlinks so that recipients can use them to access a website directly.* To follow the link, the recipient can double-tap or hold down the CTRL key and click the hyperlink, which is formatted as blue, underlined text by default. The following steps add a hyperlink within an email message.

- If the Dylan Chapter 5.pst Outlook Data File is not open in Outlook, click Outlook Data File in the Navigation Pane to display its contents.

- Tap or click the New Email button (HOME tab | New group) to open the Untitled – Message (HTML) window.

- Type **mia.james@outlook.com** in the To text box to enter the email address of the recipient.

- Tap or click the Subject text box, and then type **Travel Alert** to enter the subject line.

- Press the TAB key to move the insertion point into the message area (Figure 5–3).

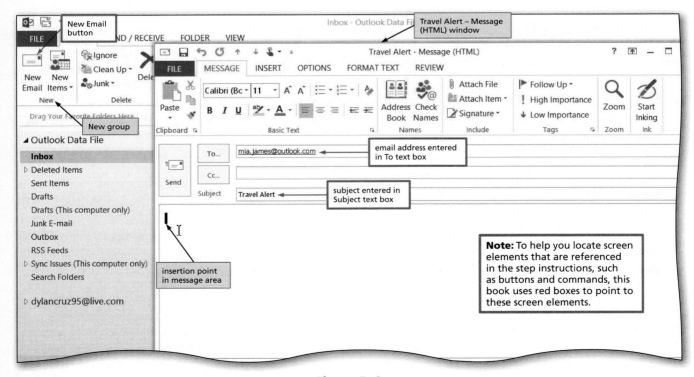

Figure 5–3

- Type **Mia,** as the greeting line and then press the ENTER key twice to insert a blank line between the greeting line and the message text.

- Type **Per your request, the U.S. Travel Alert site can be found at** and then press the SPACEBAR to enter the message text.

- Tap or click INSERT on the ribbon to display the INSERT tab (Figure 5–4).

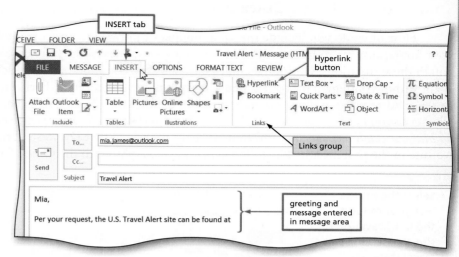

Figure 5–4

- Tap or click the Hyperlink button (INSERT tab | Links group) to open the Insert Hyperlink dialog box.

- In the Address box, type **travel.state.gov** to enter a hyperlink to a web address (Figure 5–5).

Q&A Why do I not have to type the http:// part of the web address? When you insert a hyperlink, Outlook does not require the hypertext transfer protocol (http) portion of the address.

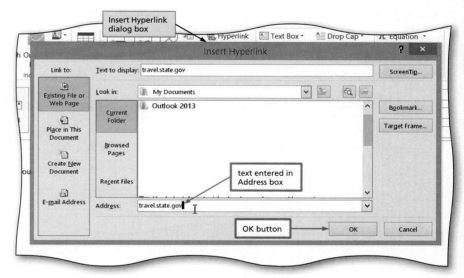

Figure 5–5

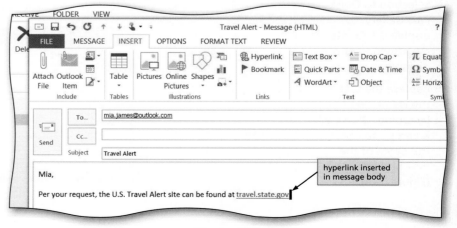

- Tap or click the OK button to insert the hyperlink in the message body (Figure 5–6).

Figure 5–6

Other Ways

1. Press CTRL+K

To Create and Insert Quick Parts

How often do you include the same snippet or phrase in your correspondence, such as directions to your home, answers to frequently answered questions, or even the full name of a school or business? To assist you in these situations, Outlook includes **Quick Parts**, common building blocks that can be recycled and used again within your email messages. The first step in creating a Quick Part is to select the content that you want to reuse. After naming the contents and saving them to the Quick Part gallery, you can use the Quick Parts whenever you need to repeat that phrase. *Why? Quick Parts allow you to save pieces of content to reuse them easily within your email messages.* Several students have requested that Dylan send them the link to the travel alert website in the past month. The following steps save a phrase to the Quick Parts gallery.

1
- Select the phrase 'Per your request, the U.S. Travel Alert site can be found at travel.state.gov'.

- Tap or click the Quick Parts button (INSERT tab | Text group) to display the Quick Parts list of options (Figure 5–7).

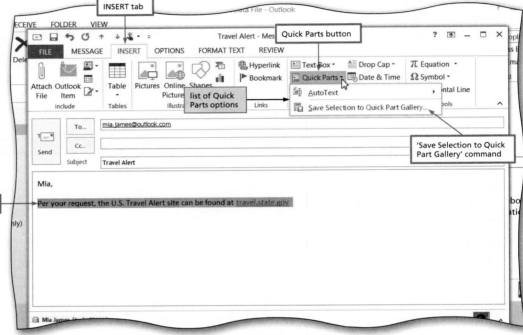

Figure 5–7

2
- Tap or click 'Save Selection to Quick Part Gallery' to display the Create New Building Block dialog box.

- Replace the text in the Name text box by typing **Travel Alert** to change the name of the new building block (Figure 5–8).

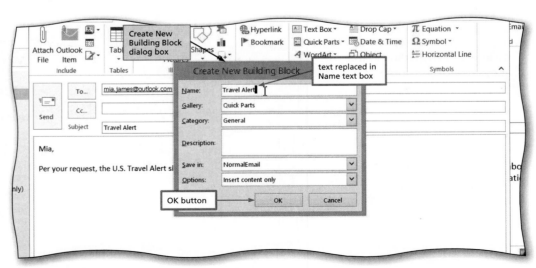

Figure 5–8

3

- Tap or click the OK button (Create New Building Block dialog box) to add the Travel Alert Building Block to the Quick Parts gallery (Figure 5–9).

 Experiment

- Tap or click the Quick Parts button (INSERT tab | Text group) to display a list of Quick Parts options. Tap or click Travel Alert to insert the building block into the email message. When you are finished, tap or click the Undo button on the Quick Access Toolbar to remove the travel alert text.

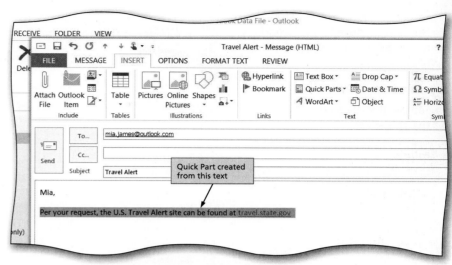

Figure 5–9

To Insert an Image into an Email Message

1 CUSTOMIZE EMAIL MESSAGES | 2 CUSTOMIZE SIGNATURES & STATIONERY | 3 MANAGE JUNK EMAIL FILTERS
4 CONFIGURE RULES | 5 CHANGE CALENDAR OPTIONS | 6 ADD NEWS FEED

As you learned in Chapter 1, you can attach files to an email message, including image files. Outlook also provides the ability to insert an image directly within the message body of an email message. *Why? The recipient can quickly view the image without downloading an attachment or saving the picture on their computer.* Dylan would like to add a recent picture from his study abroad experience in Japan. The picture is available with the Data Files for Students for Chapter 05. The following steps insert an image into an email message.

1

- Tap or click after the travel.state.gov web address, and then press the ENTER key twice to move the insertion point to a new line.

- Tap or click the Pictures button (INSERT tab | Illustrations group) to display the Insert Picture dialog box.

- Navigate to the file location, in this case, the Chapter 05 folder in the Outlook folder provided with the Data Files for Students.

- Tap or click Japan to select the photo of Japan (Figure 5–10).

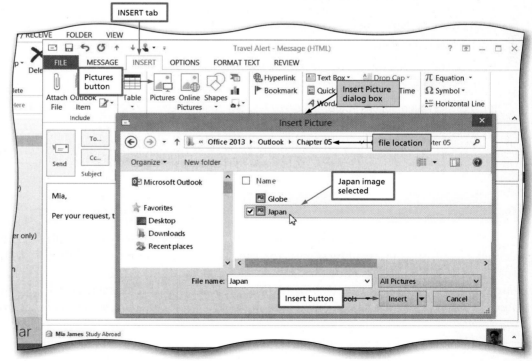

Figure 5–10

2
- Tap or click the Insert button (shown in Figure 5–10) to add an image to the message body (Figure 5–11).

3
- Tap or click the Save button on the Quick Access Toolbar to save the email message in the Drafts folder.
- Close the Travel Alert – Message (HTML) window.

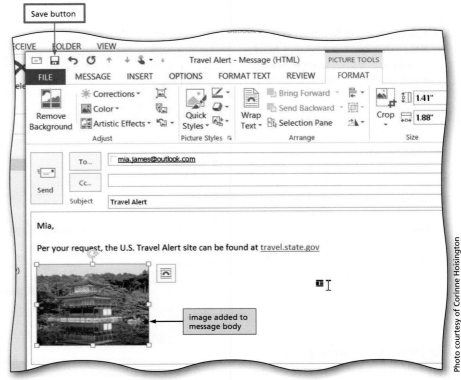

Figure 5–11

CONSIDER THIS

Can I use Outlook to allow a message recipient to vote, such as when I want to poll club members for their preferred speaker for our next event?

When composing a message, you can configure voting options by using the Properties dialog box. For example, you can choose to use voting buttons as well as request delivery and read receipts. To configure voting options:

1. While composing a message, tap or click OPTIONS on the ribbon to display the OPTIONS tab.

2. Tap or click the Use Voting Buttons button (OPTIONS tab | Tracking group) to display a list of options.

3. Tap or click Custom to display the Properties dialog box.

4. Select voting options in the Voting and Tracking options area.

5. Tap or click the Close button to close the Properties dialog box.

To Search Using Advanced Find

1 CUSTOMIZE EMAIL MESSAGES | 2 CUSTOMIZE SIGNATURES & STATIONERY | 3 MANAGE JUNK EMAIL FILTERS
4 CONFIGURE RULES | 5 CHANGE CALENDAR OPTIONS | 6 ADD NEWS FEED

At the top of the message pane is the **Instant Search** text box, which displays search results based on any matching words in your email messages. You can use the options on the SEARCH TOOLS SEARCH tab to broaden or narrow the scope of your search using the Advanced Find features. For example, Dylan would like to search for messages that have attachments. The following steps use instant search with Advanced Find features to locate email messages with attachments. *Why? Using Advanced Find, you can quickly search for an email with an attachment.*

1

- If necessary, select your Inbox, and then tap or click the Instant Search text box to display the SEARCH TOOLS SEARCH tab (Figure 5–12).

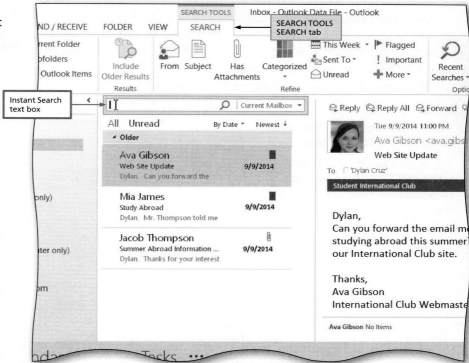

Figure 5–12

2

- Tap or click the Has Attachments button (SEARCH TOOLS SEARCH tab | Refine group) to display email messages with attachments (Figure 5–13).

3

- Tap or click the Close Search button (shown in Figure 5–13) to display the Inbox messages without the search criteria.

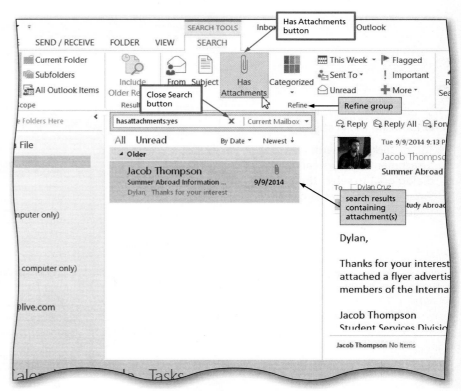

Figure 5–13

To Create a New Search Folder

Use search folders to gather email messages and other items into a folder based on search criteria. For example, Dylan wants to place messages with attachments into a separate search folder. You might want to create other search folders to view all messages that you have not read yet or to combine messages from a specific person. The following steps create a new search folder for email messages with attachments. *Why? By using search folders, you can better manage large amounts of email.*

1

- Tap or click FOLDER on the ribbon to display the FOLDER tab.

- Tap or click the New Search Folder button (FOLDER tab | New group) to display the New Search Folder dialog box (Figure 5–14).

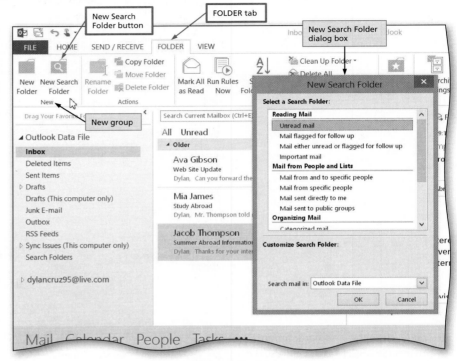

Figure 5–14

2

- Scroll down to view the Organizing Mail category.

- Tap or click 'Mail with attachments' (New Search Folder dialog box) to select the type of email to store in a search folder (Figure 5–15).

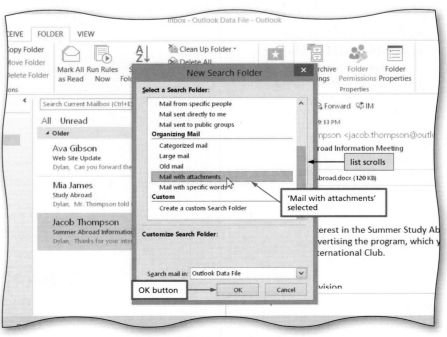

Figure 5–15

● Tap or click the OK button (New Search Folder dialog box) to create a new search folder that searches for and collects email messages with attachments (Figure 5–16).

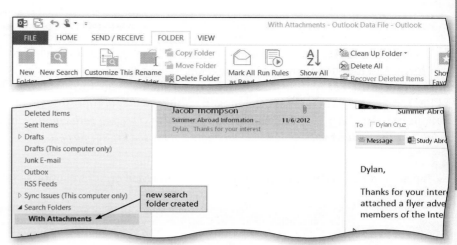

Figure 5–16

To Display Outlook Options

1 CUSTOMIZE EMAIL MESSAGES | 2 CUSTOMIZE SIGNATURES & STATIONERY | 3 MANAGE JUNK EMAIL FILTERS

4 CONFIGURE RULES | 5 CHANGE CALENDAR OPTIONS | 6 ADD NEWS FEED

Why? *To customize your Outlook email with default settings such as the message format, you use the Outlook Options dialog box.* The following step displays the Outlook Options dialog box.

● Tap or click FILE on the ribbon to open the Backstage view.

● Tap or click the Options tab in the Backstage view to display the Outlook Options dialog box (Figure 5–17).

What options can I set in the General category?

The General category allows you to customize the user interface by enabling the Mini Toolbar and Live Preview, and changing the ScreenTip style and Theme. You also can personalize Microsoft Outlook by specifying your user name and initials. The Start up options allow you to specify whether Outlook should be the default program for email, contacts, and calendar.

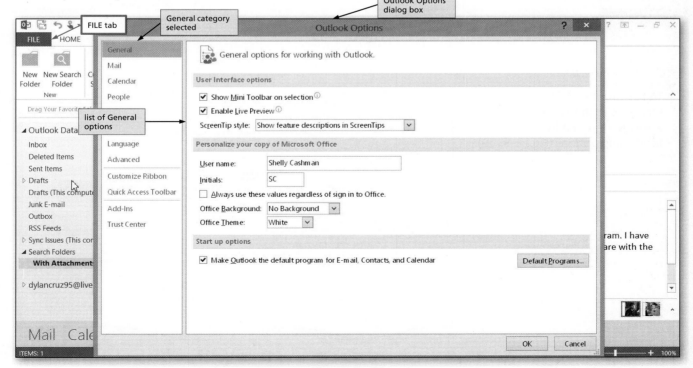

Figure 5–17

To Set the Message Format

Email messages can be formatted as HTML, Plain Text, or Rich Text. As you learned in Chapter 1, you can format an individual email message using one of these message formats. To make sure that all your email messages use the HTML format by default, set the message format in the Outlook Options dialog box. The HTML message format allows the most flexibility when composing email messages. The following steps set the default message format to HTML. *Why? Instead of changing each email message to a different format, you can set a default in the Outlook options. All new messages display the default format.*

1

• Tap or click Mail in the Category list to display the Mail options (Figure 5–18).

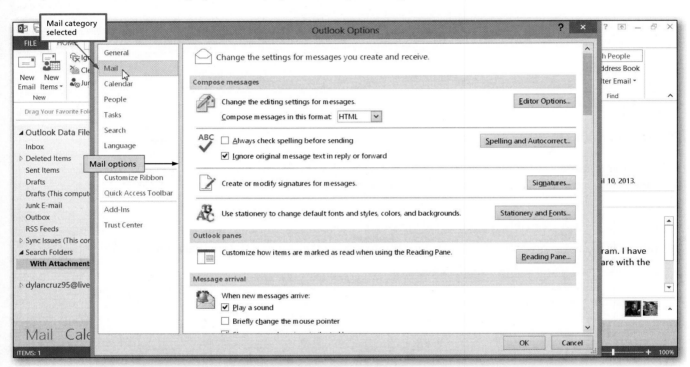

Figure 5–18

2

• Tap or click the 'Compose messages in this format' box arrow to display a list of formatting options (Figure 5–19).

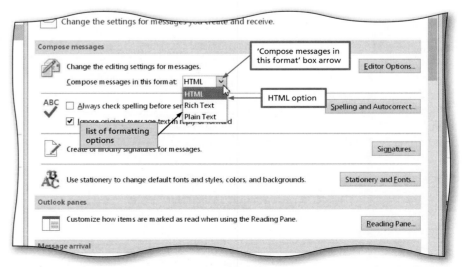

Figure 5–19

Outlook Chapter 5

3

- If necessary, tap or click HTML to set the default message format to HTML (Figure 5–20).

Q&A

What if HTML already is selected as the default message format?
Depending on who set up Outlook, the default message format already might be HTML. In that case, you can skip Step 3.

What if I want to choose a different format?
When you display the available message formats, choose the type you want to use. For example, if you want all new email messages to be in the Plain Text format, tap or click the Plain Text option.

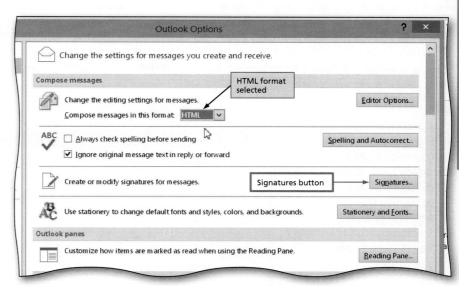

Figure 5–20

CONSIDER THIS

Can I sort my email messages by conversation instead of by date, which is the default setting?
Yes, you can sort by conversation if you prefer to sort your email messages by their subject field grouped by conversation. To sort by conversation:

1. Tap or click VIEW on the ribbon to display the VIEW tab.

2. Tap or click the Show as Conversations (VIEW tab | Messages group) to select Show as Conversations.

Your Inbox is re-sorted, linking email messages in the same conversation together. Individual messages that do not belong to a conversation will look the same as before, while those involved in conversations will have a white triangle on the upper-left part of the message header.

Creating Signatures and Stationery

You can configure Outlook to add signatures to your email messages automatically. A **signature** is similar to a closing set of lines in a formal letter. It can include your full name, job title, email address, phone number, company information, and logo. You even can include business cards in your signature.

If you have more than one email account, you need to select the account for which you want to create the signature. You can create the signature while you are creating an email message or you can use the Outlook Options dialog box at any other time. If you create the signature while writing an email message, you have to apply the signature to the email message, because Outlook will not insert it automatically. If you create a signature using the Outlook Options dialog box, it is added automatically to all subsequent messages.

Besides adding signatures to your email messages, you can customize the **stationery**, which determines the appearance of your email messages, including background, fonts, and colors. You can pick fonts to use in the email message text, or you can select a theme or stationery design and apply that to your email messages.

BTW
Q&As
For a complete list of the Q&As found in many of the step-by-step sequences in this book, visit the Q&A resource on the Student Companion Site located on www.cengagebrain.com. For detailed instructions about accessing available resources, visit www.cengage.com/ct/studentdownload or see the inside back cover of this book.

BTW
BTWs
For a complete list of the BTWs found in the margins of this book, visit the BTW resource on the Student Companion Site located on www.cengagebrain.com. For detailed instructions about accessing available resources, visit www.cengage.com/ct/studentdownload or see the inside back cover of this book.

To Create an Email Signature

An email signature provides a consistent closing to every email message without requiring you to retype signature lines repeatedly. Dylan would like to create an email signature named School that includes his name, title, and email address. The following steps create an email signature. *Why? An email signature provides your contact information in a condensed format, typically two to four lines.*

1

- Tap or click the Signatures button (Outlook Options dialog box) (shown in Figure 5–20) to display the Signatures and Stationery dialog box (Figure 5–21).

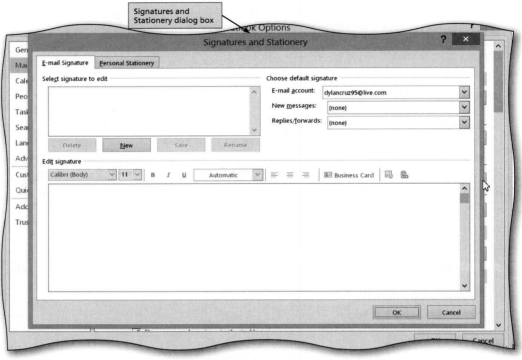

Figure 5–21

2

- Tap or click the New button (Signatures and Stationery dialog box) to display the New Signature dialog box (Figure 5–22).

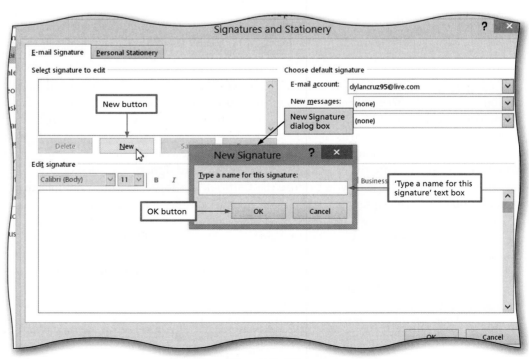

Figure 5–22

- Type **School** in the 'Type a name for this signature' text box to enter a name for the signature.

- Tap or click the OK button (shown in Figure 5–22) to name the signature (Figure 5–23).

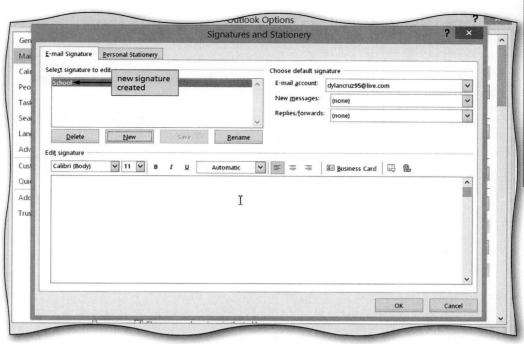

Figure 5–23

To Format an Email Signature

1 CUSTOMIZE EMAIL MESSAGES | 2 CUSTOMIZE SIGNATURES & STATIONERY | 3 MANAGE JUNK EMAIL FILTERS
4 CONFIGURE RULES | 5 CHANGE CALENDAR OPTIONS | 6 ADD NEWS FEED

The email message signature will include Dylan's name, title, and email address. In addition, he wants to use a format that suits him. The format of the signature should be attractive, but maintain a professional, clean appearance. The following steps format and add the text for the signature. *Why? An email signature should convey the impression you are trying to make. A company might require employees to use a certain email signature when communicating with customers to create a consistent look.*

- Tap or click the Font box arrow (Signatures and Stationery dialog box) to display a list of fonts (Figure 5–24).

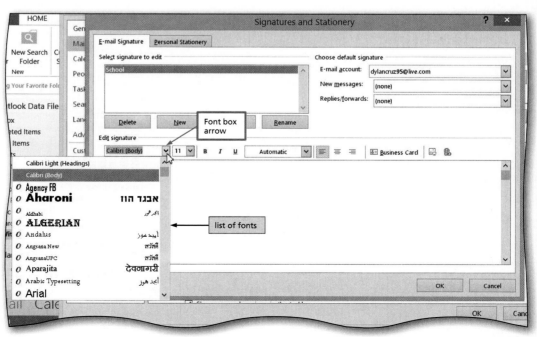

Figure 5–24

- Scroll down until Rockwell is visible, and then tap or click Rockwell to select the font.
- Tap or click the Font Size box arrow to display a list of font sizes (Figure 5–25).

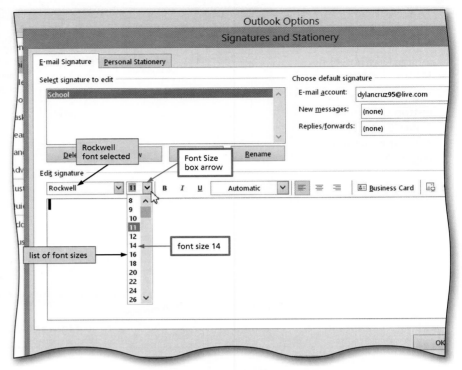

Figure 5–25

- Tap or click 14 to change the font size.
- Tap or click the Font Color box arrow to display a list of colors (Figure 5–26).

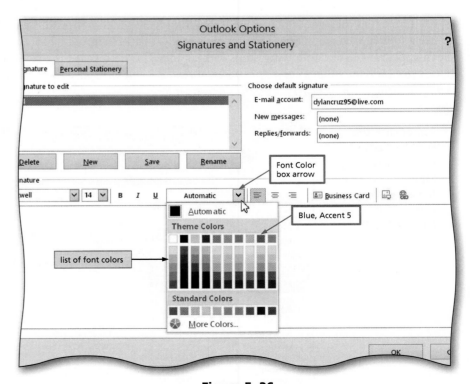

Figure 5–26

• Tap or click Blue, Accent 5 (first row, ninth column) to change the font color.

• Type **Dylan Cruz** in the signature body to enter the first line of the signature.

• Tap or click the Font Color box arrow to display a list of colors.

• Tap or click Automatic to change the font color to automatic, which is black (Figure 5–27).

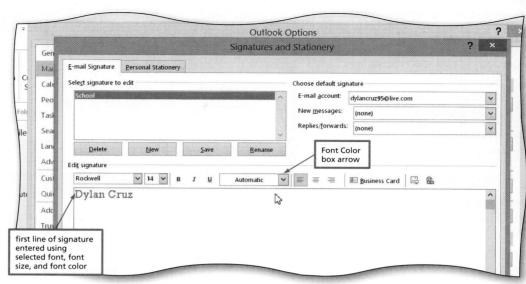

Figure 5–27

• Press the ENTER key and then tap or click the Font Size box arrow to display a list of font sizes.

• Tap or click 12 to change the font size.

• Type **President of the Student International Club at Raven College** in the signature body to enter the second line of the signature.

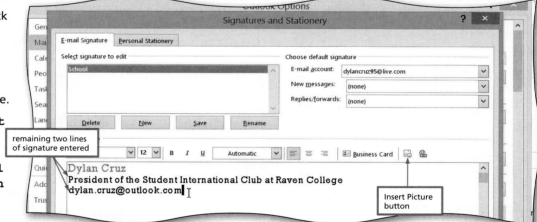

Figure 5–28

• Press the ENTER key and then type **dylan.cruz@outlook.com** in the signature body to enter the third line of the signature (Figure 5–28).

To Add an Image to an Email Signature

1 CUSTOMIZE EMAIL MESSAGES | 2 CUSTOMIZE SIGNATURES & STATIONERY | 3 MANAGE JUNK EMAIL FILTERS
4 CONFIGURE RULES | 5 CHANGE CALENDAR OPTIONS | 6 ADD NEWS FEED

You can add an image such as a photo or logo to your signature to create visual appeal. Dylan would like to add the Student International Club logo in the signature. The picture is available in the Data Files for Students for Chapter 5. The following steps add a logo image to a signature and save the changes. *Why? Adding a logo can promote brand or organization identity.*

1

- Move the insertion point to the beginning of the first line of the signature text.

- Tap or click the Insert Picture button (Signatures and Stationery dialog box) to display the Insert Picture dialog box.

- Navigate to the file location, in this case, the Chapter 05 folder in the Outlook folder provided with the Data Files for Students.

- Tap or click Globe to select the Globe logo (Figure 5–29).

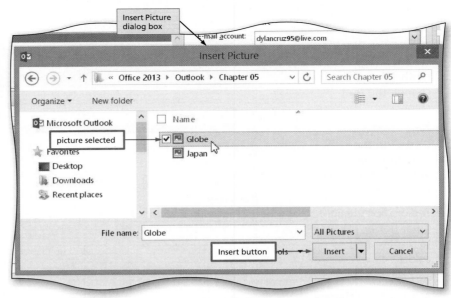

Figure 5–29

2

- Tap or click the Insert button (Insert Picture dialog box) (shown in Figure 5–29) to insert the image into the signature (Figure 5–30).

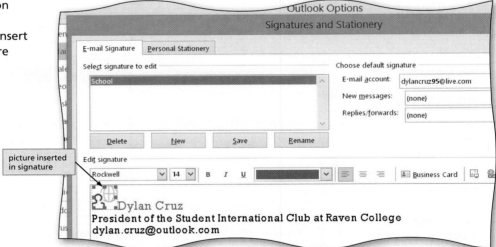

Figure 5–30

3

- Tap or click the Save button (Signatures and Stationery dialog box) to save the changes to the signature (Figure 5–31).

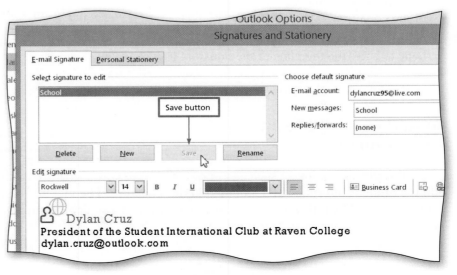

Figure 5–31

To Configure Signature Options

After creating a signature, you need to assign it to an email account. You can associate the signature with as many accounts as you want. When working with an account, you can set two default signatures: one for new messages and one for replies and forwards. Dylan wants to apply his signature for new messages to his email account named dylancruz95@live.com (select your own account). The following steps set the default signature for new messages. If you are completing these steps on a personal computer, your email account must be set up in Outlook (see Chapter 1) to be able to select an email account to apply the signature. ***Why?*** *By associating a signature with a particular email account, your signature automatically appears at the bottom of new messages.*

1

- Tap or click the E-mail account box arrow to display a list of accounts.

- Tap or click your email account, in this case dylancruz95@live .com, to select the email account (Figure 5–32).

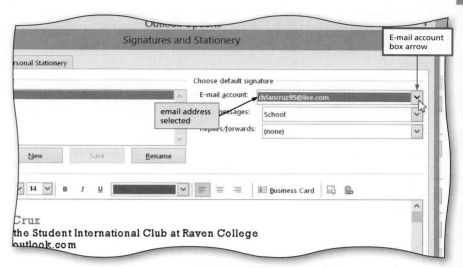

Figure 5–32

2

- Tap or click the New messages box arrow to display a list of signatures.

- Tap or click School to make it the default signature for new messages (Figure 5–33).

 Q&A

How do I place a signature in all messages including replies and forwards?

Tap or click the Replies/forwards box arrow and then tap or click School to make it the default signature for all message replies and forwards.

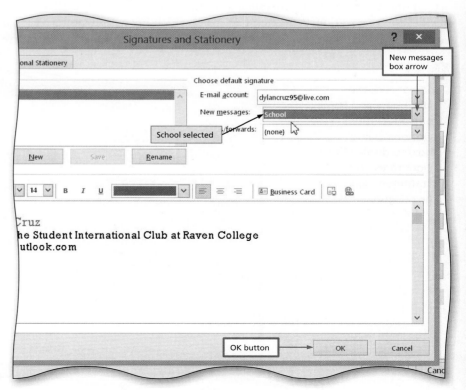

Figure 5–33

• Tap or click the OK button (Signatures and Stationery dialog box) to save the changes to the signature settings, close the Signatures and Stationery dialog box, and return to the Outlook Options dialog box (Figure 5–34).

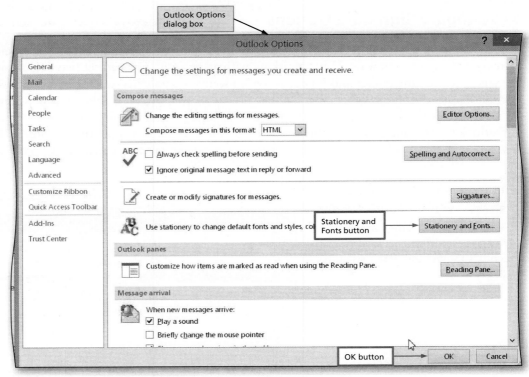

Figure 5–34

To Customize Stationery

1 CUSTOMIZE EMAIL MESSAGES | 2 CUSTOMIZE SIGNATURES & STATIONERY | 3 MANAGE JUNK EMAIL FILTERS
4 CONFIGURE RULES | 5 CHANGE CALENDAR OPTIONS | 6 ADD NEWS FEED

Outlook provides backgrounds and patterns for email message stationery and offers themes, which are sets of unified design elements, such as fonts, bullets, colors, and effects that you can apply to messages. Dylan decides to use a stationery named Compass, which fits with his international interests. The following steps customize the email message stationery. **Why?** *Stationery provides a distinctive look for your email messages.*

1

• Tap or click the Stationery and Fonts button (Outlook Options dialog box) to display the Signatures and Stationery dialog box (Figure 5–35).

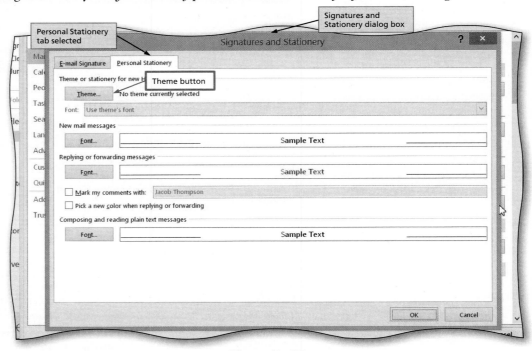

Figure 5–35

2

- Tap or click the Theme button (Signatures and Stationery dialog box) to display the Theme or Stationery dialog box (Figure 5–36).

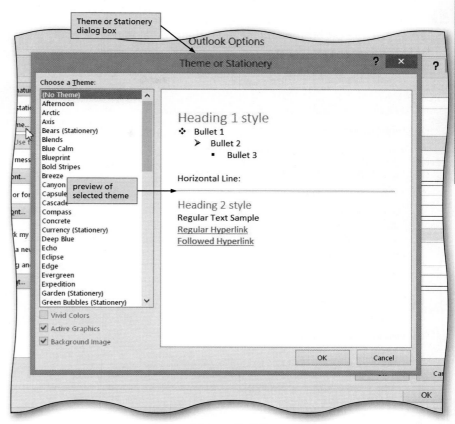

Figure 5–36

3

- Tap or click Compass to select it and display a preview of its formats (Figure 5–37).

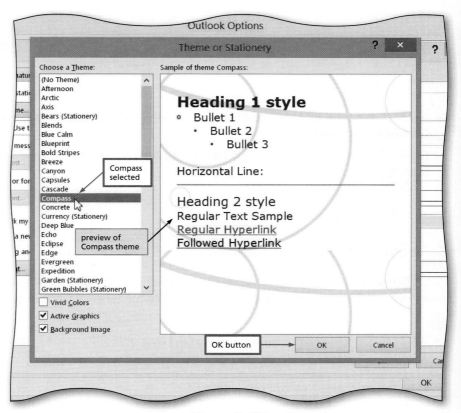

Figure 5–37

- Tap or click the OK button (Theme or Stationery dialog box) to apply the theme to the stationery (Figure 5–38).

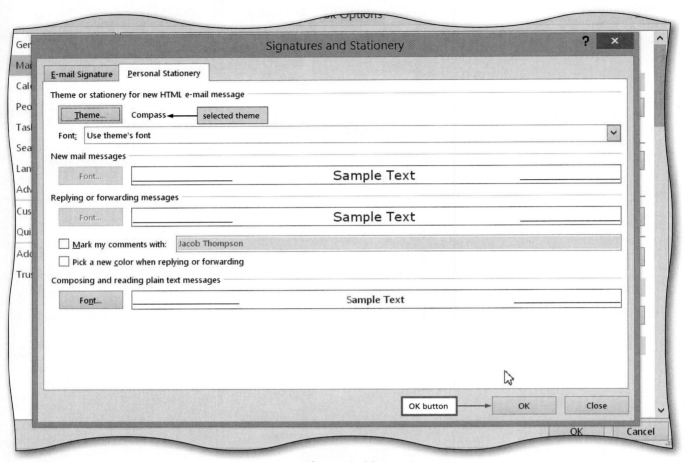

Figure 5–38

- Tap or click the OK button (Signatures and Stationery dialog box) to save the theme settings and return to the Outlook Options dialog box.

- Tap or click the OK button (Outlook Options dialog box) (shown in Figure 5–34 on page OUT 254) to close the Outlook Options dialog box.

To Preview Message Changes

1 CUSTOMIZE EMAIL MESSAGES | 2 CUSTOMIZE SIGNATURES & STATIONERY | 3 MANAGE JUNK EMAIL FILTERS
4 CONFIGURE RULES | 5 CHANGE CALENDAR OPTIONS | 6 ADD NEWS FEED

Why? *You want to preview the changes you made to your email signature and stationery and see how they look in an email message.* The following steps display a new email message without sending it.

1

- Tap or click the New Email button (HOME tab | New group) to create a new email message (Figure 5–39).

2

- Close the email message without sending it.

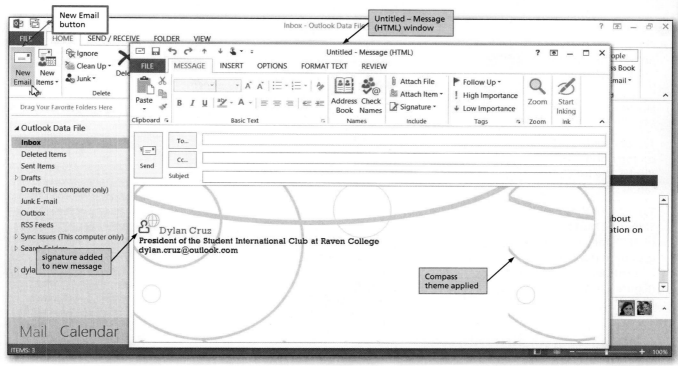

Figure 5–39

To Assign Signatures to a Single Email Message

1 CUSTOMIZE EMAIL MESSAGES | 2 CUSTOMIZE SIGNATURES & STATIONERY | 3 MANAGE JUNK EMAIL FILTERS
4 CONFIGURE RULES | 5 CHANGE CALENDAR OPTIONS | 6 ADD NEWS FEED

If you use multiple email accounts, you can set a signature for each account or you can apply a signature to an individual email message. Dylan still needs to send the email about the travel alert to Mia and wants to apply the School signature to that message, which is now stored in the Drafts folder. *Why? Instead of assigning your email address to one signature, you may want to create different signatures and apply a signature to individual emails before you send them.* The following steps assign a signature to a single email message.

1

- Tap or click the Drafts folder in the Navigation Pane to display the message header for the Travel Alert email message in the message list.

- Double-tap or double-click the Travel Alert message header in the messages pane to open the Travel Alert – Message (HTML) window (Figure 5–40).

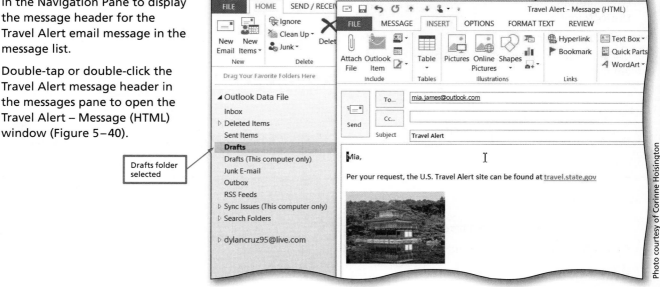

Figure 5–40

Photo courtesy of Corinne Hoisington

2

- Place the insertion point to the right of the Japan image and then press the ENTER key to move to the next line.

- Tap or click INSERT on the ribbon to display the INSERT tab.

- Tap or click the Signature button (INSERT tab | Include group) to display a list of signatures (Figure 5–41).

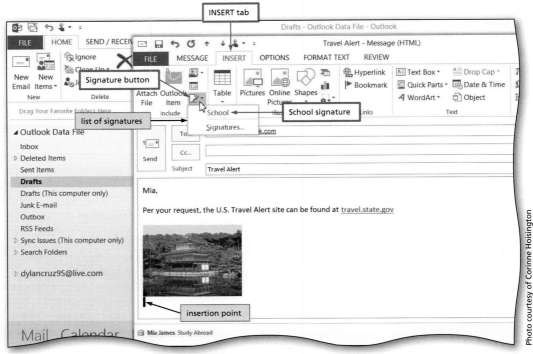

Figure 5–41

Photo courtesy of Corinne Hoisington

3

- Tap or click School to add the School signature to the email message body (Figure 5–42).

4

- Tap or click the Save button on the Quick Access Toolbar to save the email message in the Drafts folder.

- Tap or click the Close button to close the email message.

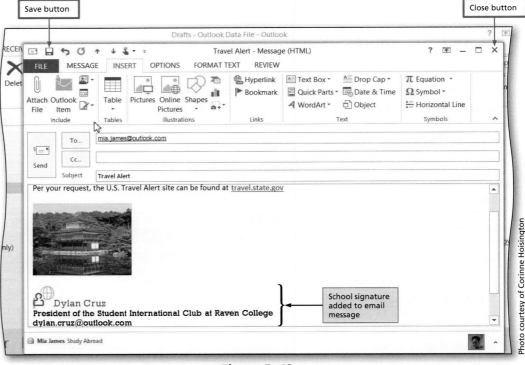

Figure 5–42

Photo courtesy of Corinne Hoisington

Break Point: If you wish to take a break, this is a good place to do so. To resume at a later time, continue to follow the steps from this location forward.

Managing Junk Email Options

As you learned in Chapter 1, junk email is bulk email, spam, or other unwanted email messages. Outlook uses a filter to control the amount of junk email you receive. The junk email filter evaluates incoming messages and sends to the Junk E-mail folder those messages that meet the criteria for junk email. You can use the Junk button in the Delete group on the HOME tab to override the default criteria when viewing email messages by deciding to block the sender, never block the sender, never block the sender's domain, or never block a group or mailing list.

Using the Junk E-mail Options dialog box, you can change even more settings (Figure 5 – 43). Table 5 – 1 describes the options you can adjust using the Junk E-mail Options dialog box.

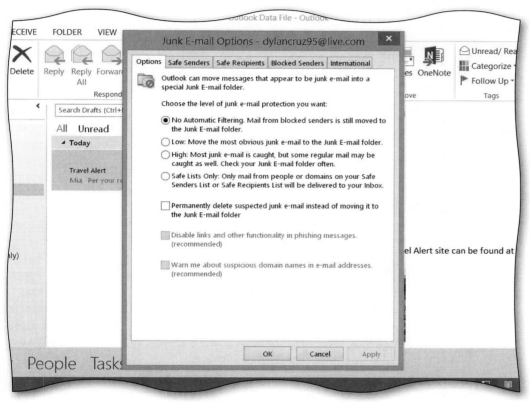

Figure 5–43

Table 5–1 Junk Email Options	
Tab	**Description**
Options	Allows you to choose the level of protection (No Automatic Filtering, Low, High, Safe Lists Only), as well as set whether junk email is deleted, links are disabled in phishing messages, and warnings are provided for suspicious domain names.
Safe Senders	Permits the specification of safe e-mail addresses and domains. Email messages from the listed email addresses and domains will not be treated as junk email.
Safe Recipients	Specifies that email messages sent to email addresses or domains in the safe recipient list will not be treated as junk email.
Blocked Senders	Allows you to manage your list of blocked email addresses and domains.
International	Manages which domains and encodings you would like to block based on languages used.

© 2014 Cengage Learning

BTW

Junk Email
It usually is a good idea to check your Junk E-mail folder regularly to make sure no items are labeled as junk inadvertently. If, after clicking the Junk E-mail folder, you find an email message that is not junk, select the email message, click the Junk button (HOME tab | Delete group), click Not Junk, and then click the OK button.

To Add a Domain to the
Safe Senders List

The junk email filter in Outlook is turned on by default, providing a protection level that is set to Low. This level is designed to catch only the most obvious junk email messages. Dylan feels that too many incoming messages from Microsoft are being sent to his Junk E-mail folder. Microsoft.com can be added to the Safe Sender list, which adjusts the filter sensitivity of Outlook, so the messages are sent to the Inbox instead of the Junk E-mail Folder. If you are completing these steps on a personal computer, your email account must be set up in Outlook (see Chapter 1) to be able to select an email account to configure the junk email options. The following steps configure the junk email options for an email account. *Why? The Junk E-mail Folder helps to sort out relevant email messages from junk mail.*

- Tap or click your personal email account (in this case, dylancruz95@live.com) in the Navigation Pane to select the mailbox (Figure 5–44).

Q&A Why did I have to select the email account?
To change junk email options for an account, the account first should be selected. If you selected a different mailbox, you would have changed junk email settings for that account.

Figure 5–44

- Tap or click the Junk button (HOME tab | Delete group) to display the Junk options (Figure 5–45).

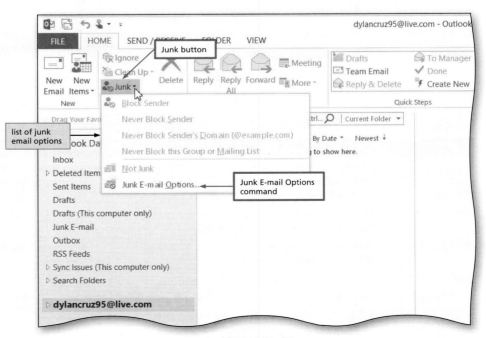

Figure 5–45

3

• Tap or click Junk E-mail Options to display the Junk E-mail Options dialog box (Figure 5–46).

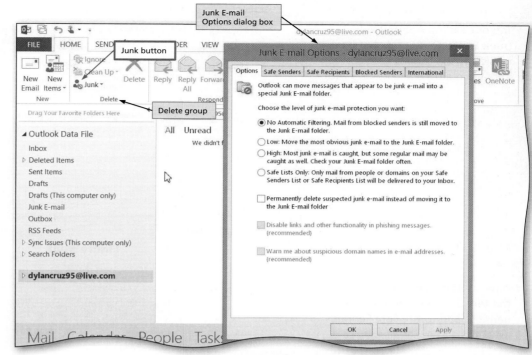

Figure 5–46

4

• Tap or click the Safe Senders tab (Junk E-mail Options dialog box) to display the Safe Senders options (Figure 5–47).

Figure 5–47

5

- Tap or click the Add button (Junk E-mail Options dialog box) to display the 'Add address or domain' dialog box (Figure 5–48).

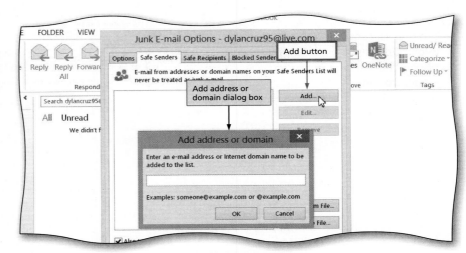

Figure 5–48

6

- Type `@Microsoft.com` in the text box to enter a domain name to add to the Safe Sender's list (Figure 5–49).

Q&A

Do I have to type the @ symbol? Although Outlook recommends that you type the @ symbol to indicate a domain name, you can omit the symbol. In that case, you leave it up to Outlook to determine if your entry is a domain name or email address. Most of the time, Outlook interprets the entry correctly; however, to be certain, type the @ symbol.

Figure 5–49

7

- Tap or click the OK button (Add address or domain dialog box) to add the domain to the Safe Senders List (Figure 5–50).

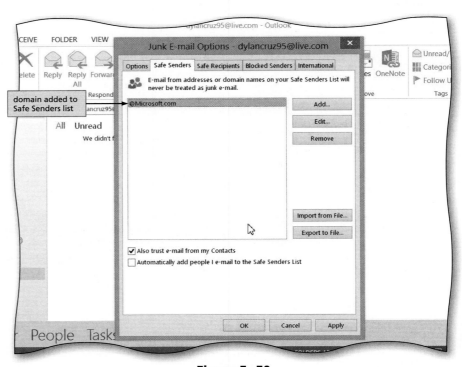

Figure 5–50

To Block a Specific Email Address

Why? *You may want to block a specific email address or domain to prevent people or companies from sending you messages you do not want to receive.* Dylan has received multiple unwanted emails from the following email address: getrich2@live.com. He considers these messages as junk email. The following steps block a specific email address using the junk filters.

- Tap or click the Blocked Senders tab (Junk E-mail Options dialog box) to display the Blocked Senders options.

- Tap or click the Add button (Junk E-mail Options dialog box) to display the 'Add address or domain' dialog box.

- Type **getrich2@live .com** in the text box to enter the domain name to add to the Blocked Sender's list (Figure 5–51).

2

- Tap or click the OK button (Add address or domain dialog box) to add the domain to the Blocked Senders List.

- Tap or click the OK button (Junk E-mail Options dialog box) to close the Junk E-mail Options dialog box.

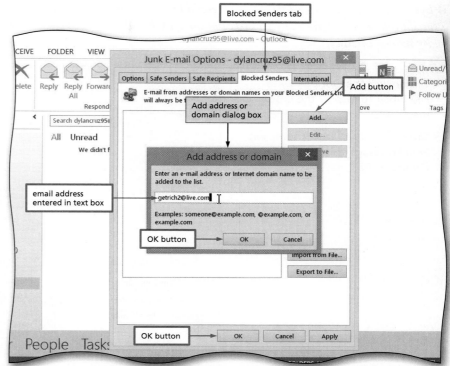

Figure 5–51

Working with Rules

To further automate the processing of email messages in Outlook, you can create rules. A **rule** is a set of instructions that tells Outlook how to handle email messages in your mailbox. You can create rules that apply to email messages you have received and those you send. For example, you can specify that email messages from a particular user be categorized automatically or placed in a specified folder. You can create rules from a template or from scratch based on conditions you specify. Rules apply to an email account, not a single folder or file. If you are working with a data file instead of an email account, you cannot create rules.

To simplify the process of creating rules, Outlook provides a Rules Wizard, which presents a list of conditions for selecting an email message and then lists actions to take with messages that meet the conditions. If necessary, you also can specify exceptions to the rule. For example, you can move certain messages to a specified folder unless they are sent with high importance.

To Create a New Rule

Dylan would like to create a rule to flag all email messages from your faculty advisor, Jacob Thompson, for follow-up. This way, he easily can remember to follow up with Mr. Thompson on important tasks. If you are completing these steps on a personal computer, your email account must be set up in Outlook so that you can select an email account to create a rule. The following steps create a rule that automatically flags email messages. *Why?* *Rules help you file and follow up on email messages. For example, your instructor can create a rule for messages from a specific course section, such as CIS 101. You can set CIS 101 in the Subject line to be flagged for follow-up and moved to a folder named Literacy.*

- Tap or click the Outlook Data File Inbox to display the Inbox messages.
- Tap or click the Jacob Thompson email message to select it (Figure 5–52).

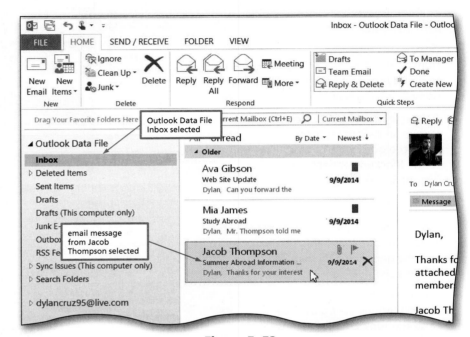

Figure 5–52

❷

- Tap or click the Rules button (HOME tab | Move group) to display a list of rule options (Figure 5–53).

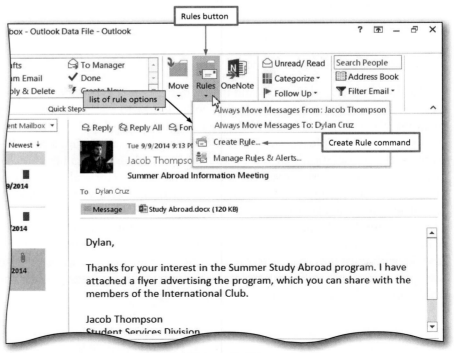

Figure 5–53

3

- Tap or click the Create Rule command to display the Create Rule dialog box (Figure 5–54).

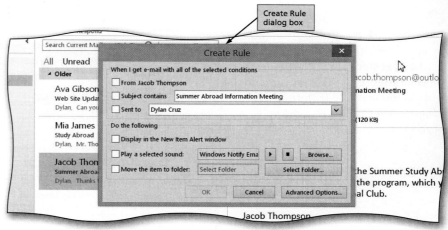

Figure 5–54

4

- Tap or click the 'From Jacob Thompson' check box to select it (Figure 5–55).

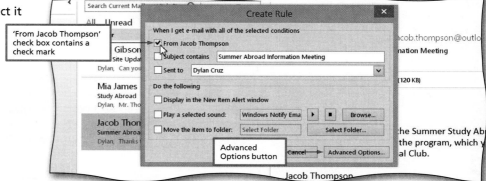

Figure 5–55

5

- Tap or click the Advanced Options button (Create Rule dialog box) to display the Rules Wizard dialog box (Figure 5–56).

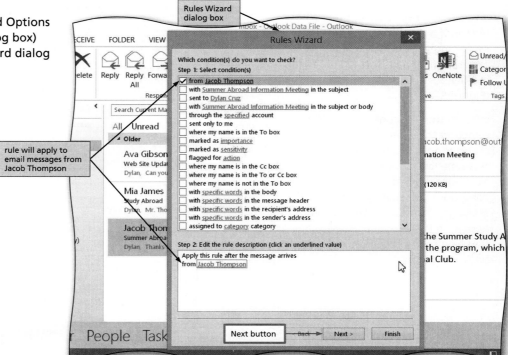

Figure 5–56

6

- Tap or click the Next button (Rules Wizard dialog box) to continue to the next step, where you specify one or more actions to take with a selected message (Figure 5–57).

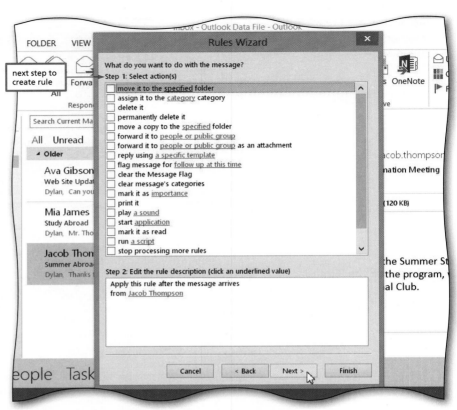

Figure 5–57

7

- Tap or click the 'flag message for follow up at this time' check box to select it.

- If necessary, tap or click the Yes button if a dialog box opens informing you that the rule you are creating can never be edited in previous versions of Outlook (Figure 5–58).

Q&A What is the effect of selecting the 'flag message for follow up at this time' check box? Messages that meet the conditions you specify, in this case, messages from Jacob Thompson, appear in the message list with a flag icon to indicate they need to be followed up.

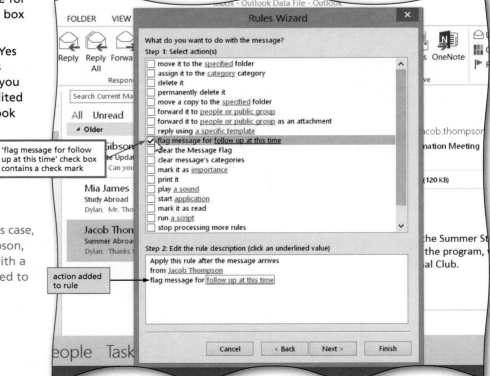

Figure 5–58

8

- Tap or click the 'follow up at this time' link in the Step 2 area to display the Flag Message dialog box (Figure 5–59).

For what purposes can I use the Flag Message dialog box?

You can flag a message for follow up (the default) or for other options, including For Your Information, No Response Necessary, and Reply. You also can specify when to follow up: Today (the default), Tomorrow, This Week, Next Week, No Date, or Complete.

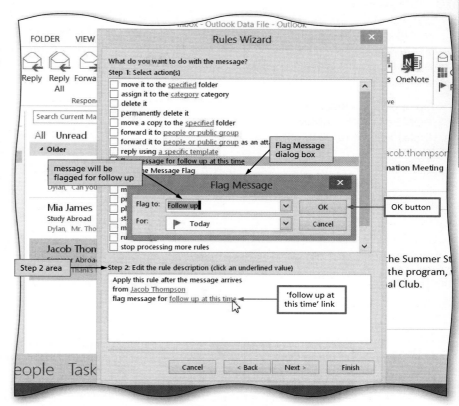

Figure 5–59

9

- Tap or click the OK button (Flag Message dialog box) to accept the default settings and return to the Rules Wizard dialog box (Figure 5–60).

10

- Tap or click the Finish button (Rules Wizard dialog box) to save the rule.

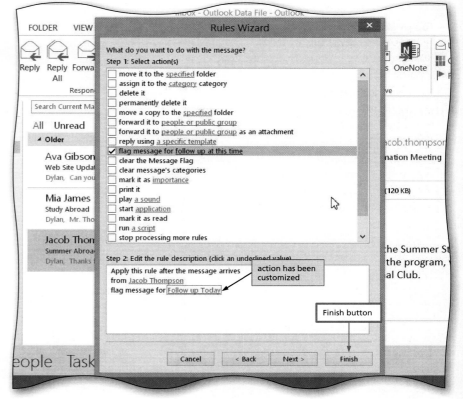

Figure 5–60

To Run Rules

Rules that you create run for all incoming email messages received after you create the rule. *Why? If you want to apply rules to email messages that you already received, you use the Rules and Alerts dialog box.* The following steps run the newly created rule.

1

- Tap or click the Rules button (HOME tab | Move group) to display a list of rule options (Figure 5–61).

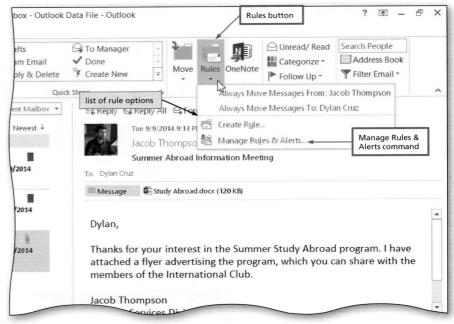

Figure 5–61

2

- Tap or click the Manage Rules & Alerts command to display the Rules and Alerts dialog box (Figure 5–62).

Q&A After I create a rule, can I modify it?

Yes. To modify an existing rule, select the rule you want to modify, tap or click the Change Rule button, and then tap or click the Edit Rule Settings command. Next, make the desired changes in the Rules Wizard. Tap or click the Finish button after making all necessary changes.

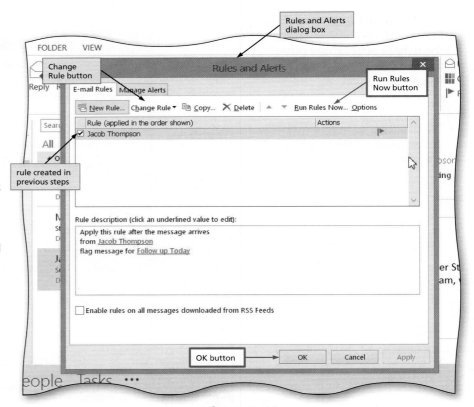

Figure 5–62

3

- Tap or click the Run Rules Now button (Rules and Alerts dialog box) to display the Run Rules Now dialog box.

- Tap or click the Jacob Thompson check box to select it and specify the rule that will run.

- Tap or click the Run Now button (Run Rules Now dialog box) to run the rule (Figure 5–63).

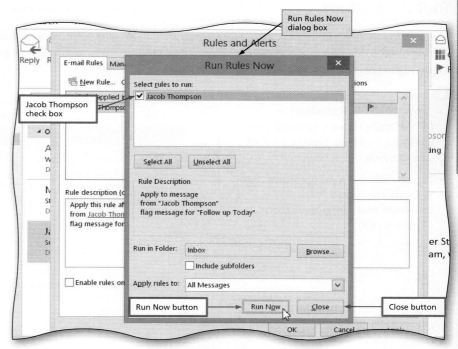

Figure 5–63

4

- Tap or click the Close button (Run Rules Now dialog box) to close the Run Rules Now dialog box.

- Tap or click the OK button (Rules and Alerts dialog box) (shown in Figure 5–62) to close the Rules and Alerts dialog box (Figure 5–64).

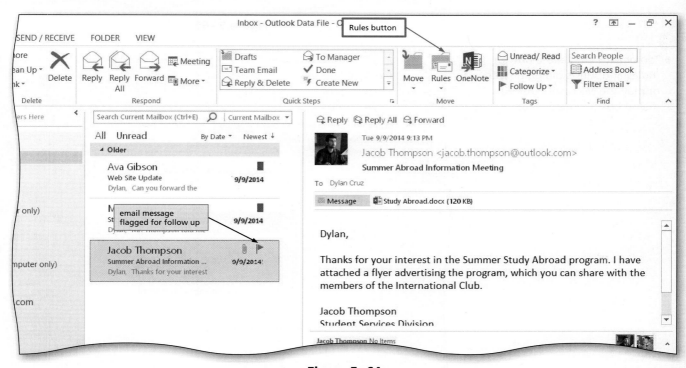

Figure 5–64

To Delete a Rule

Why? When you no longer need a rule, you should delete it. After further consideration, you decide that you do not need to flag all email messages from your faculty advisor; therefore, you decide to delete the rule. The following steps delete a rule.

- Tap or click the Rules button (HOME tab | Move group) (shown in Figure 5–64) to display a list of rule options.

- Tap or click the Manage Rules & Alerts command to display the Rules and Alerts dialog box (Figure 5–65).

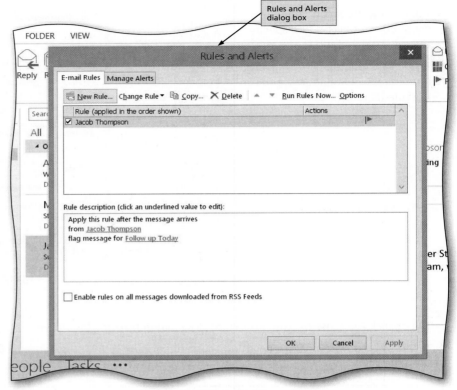

Figure 5–65

- Tap or click the Delete button (Rules and Alerts dialog box) to display the Microsoft Outlook dialog box (Figure 5–66).

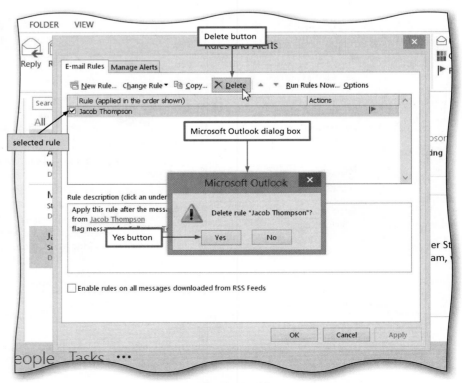

Figure 5–66

❸

- Tap or click the Yes button (Microsoft Outlook dialog box) to delete the Jacob Thompson rule (Figure 5–67).

❹

- Tap or click the OK button (Rules and Alerts dialog box) to close the Rules and Alerts dialog box.

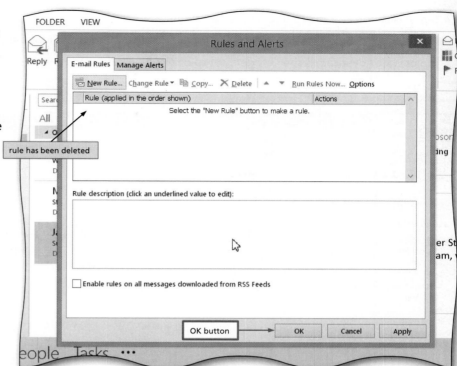

Figure 5–67

TO SET UP AUTOMATIC REPLIES

Outlook provides a quick way to set up automatic replies for when you may be away from your email account, such as when you are out of the office; however, your email account must support automatic replies using Microsoft Exchange. If you wanted to set up automatic replies, you would use the following steps.

1. Tap or click the FILE tab to display the Backstage view.
2. If necessary, tap or click Info in the Backstage view to display account information.
3. Tap or click Automatic Replies to display the Automatic Replies dialog box.
4. Tap or click 'Send automatic replies' to turn on automatic replies.
5. Change the Start time to select the day and time for the automatic replies to start.
6. Change the End time to select the day and time for the automatic replies to stop.
7. Select Inside My Organization and enter an email message for email messages to be sent inside your organization.
8. Select Outside My Organization and enter an email message for email messages to be sent outside your organization.
9. Tap or click OK to save the rule for automatic replies.

BTW

Cleanup Tools
In addition to archiving email messages, Outlook provides cleanup tools to help control the size of your mailbox. To access the various cleanup tools, display the Backstage view, click the Info tab, if necessary, click the Cleanup Tools button, and then click the desired cleanup tool you want to access.

To Set AutoArchive Settings

1 CUSTOMIZE EMAIL MESSAGES | 2 CUSTOMIZE SIGNATURES & STATIONERY | 3 MANAGE JUNK EMAIL FILTERS

4 CONFIGURE RULES | 5 CHANGE CALENDAR OPTIONS | 6 ADD NEWS FEED

Why? *You can have old items in Outlook automatically transferred to a storage file. Items are only considered old after a certain number of days that you specify.* Dylan decides that he should back up the email messages in his email account. By default, when AutoArchive is turned on, Outlook archives messages every 14 days. The following steps turn on AutoArchive.

1

- Tap or click the FILE tab to display the Backstage view.
- Tap or click Options in the Backstage view to display the Outlook Options dialog box.
- Tap or click Advanced in the Category list to display the Advanced options (Figure 5–68).

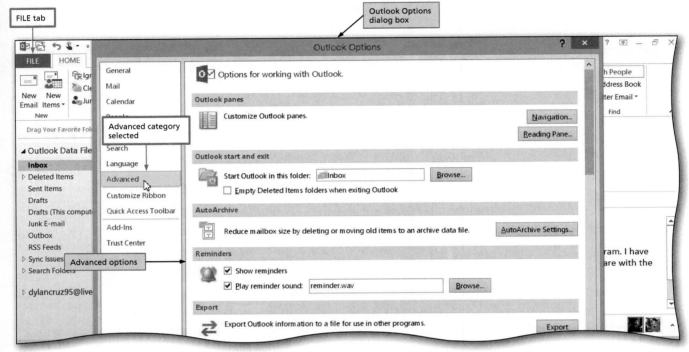

Figure 5–68

2

- Tap or click the AutoArchive Settings button (Outlook Options dialog box) to display the AutoArchive dialog box (Figure 5–69).

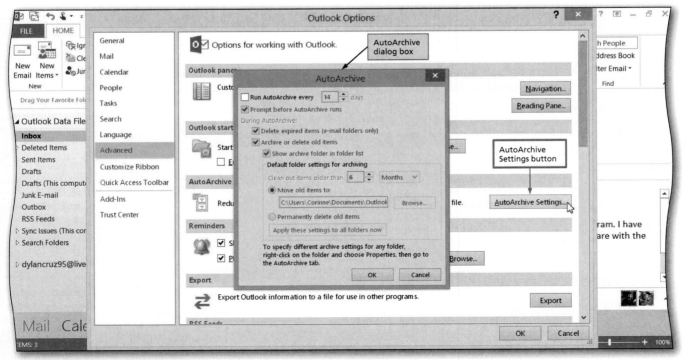

Figure 5–69

3

- Tap or click the 'Run AutoArchive every' check box to select it and enable AutoArchive (Figure 5–70).

4

- Tap or click the OK button (AutoArchive dialog box) to close the AutoArchive dialog box.

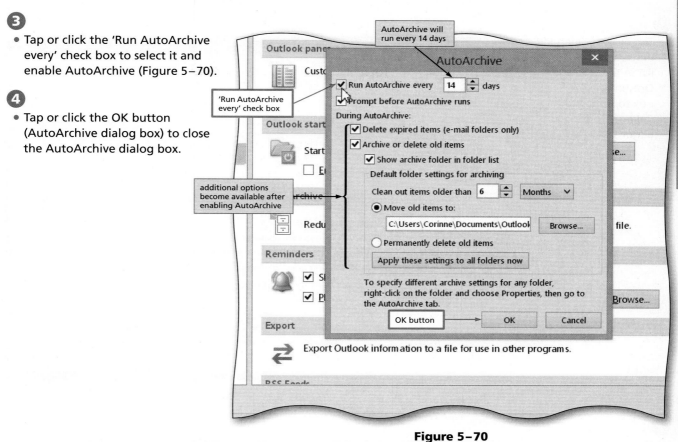

Figure 5–70

Customizing the Calendar

You can customize the Calendar to better suit your needs. For example, you can select the days of your workweek and set the displayed time range to reflect the start and end times of your workday. You also can change the default reminder time from 15 minutes to any other interval, such as five minutes or a half-hour. Other Calendar options you can customize include the calendar font and current time zone.

BTW
Advanced Options
In addition to the various Outlook options presented in this chapter, Outlook allows users to view and change advanced options. To access the advanced options, open the Outlook Options dialog box and then click Advanced in the Category list.

To Change the Work Time on the Calendar

1 CUSTOMIZE EMAIL MESSAGES | 2 CUSTOMIZE SIGNATURES & STATIONERY | 3 MANAGE JUNK EMAIL FILTERS
4 CONFIGURE RULES | 5 CHANGE CALENDAR OPTIONS | **6 ADD NEWS FEED**

Dylan would like to customize the work time on the Calendar so that it reflects his work schedule. He normally works from 8:30 AM to 5:00 PM on Mondays, Wednesdays, Fridays, and Saturdays. The following steps change the Calendar settings to match the work schedule and make Monday the first day of the week. *Why? By default, the Calendar Work Week is set for Monday through Friday, but you can select which days comprise your workweek.*

- Tap or click Calendar in the Category list in the Outlook Options dialog box to display the Calendar options (Figure 5–71).

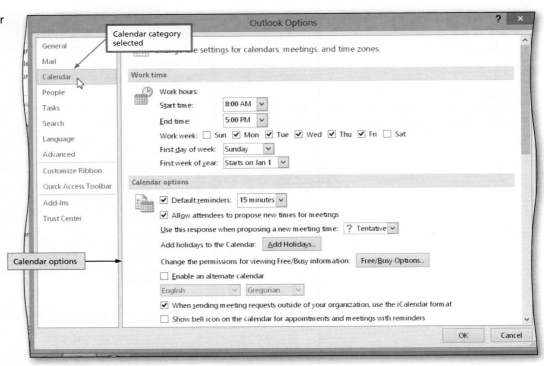

Figure 5–71

- Tap or click the Start time box arrow to display a list of start times.

- Select 8:30 AM to change the start time.

- Tap or click the End time box arrow to display a list of end times.

- Select 4:30 PM to change the end time (Figure 5–72).

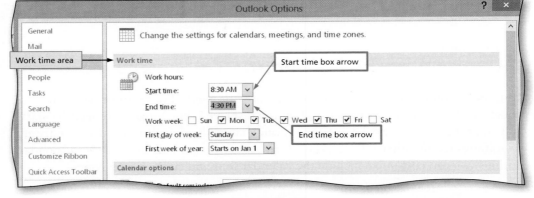

Figure 5–72

- Tap or click the Tue check box to deselect it.

- Tap or click the Thu check box to deselect it.

- Tap or click the Sat check box to select it (Figure 5–73).

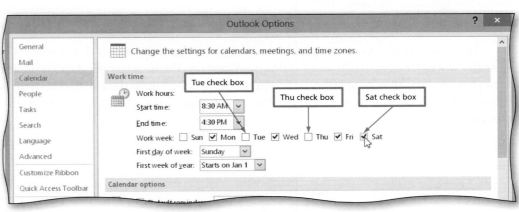

Figure 5–73

- Tap or click the 'First day of week' box arrow to display a list of days.
- Tap or click Monday to change the first day of the week to Monday (Figure 5–74).

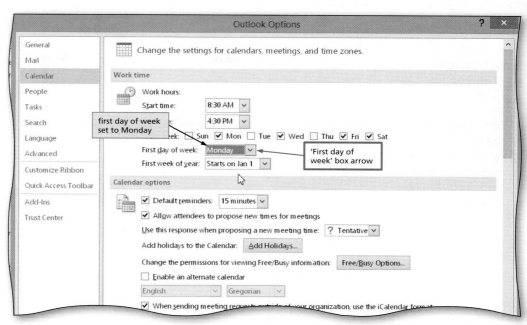

Figure 5–74

To Change the Time for Calendar Reminders

1 CUSTOMIZE EMAIL MESSAGES | 2 CUSTOMIZE SIGNATURES & STATIONERY | 3 MANAGE JUNK EMAIL FILTERS
4 CONFIGURE RULES | 5 CHANGE CALENDAR OPTIONS | 6 ADD NEWS FEED

To further customize the Outlook calendar, Dylan would like to increase the time for reminders to 30 minutes. The following step changes the time for reminders. *Why? By default, the Calendar reminders are set for 15 minutes prior to an appointment or meeting.*

- Tap or click the Default reminders box arrow to display a list of times.
- Tap or click 30 minutes to select it as the default time for reminders (Figure 5–75).

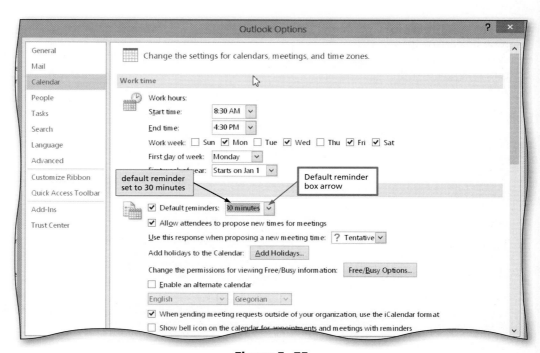

Figure 5–75

To Change the Time Zone Setting

Why? *When you travel, your time zone may change and your calendar should be updated. If you change the time zone setting in Calendar, Outlook updates your appointments to display the new time zone when you arrive.* Dylan is participating in the Study Abroad program this summer in Madrid, Spain, and needs to change the time zones accordingly. The following steps change the time zone.

- Scroll down until the Time zones settings are visible in the Outlook Options dialog box (Figure 5–76).

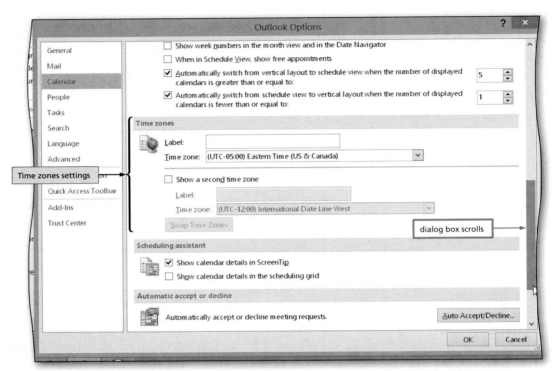

Figure 5–76

- Tap or click the Time zone box arrow to display a list of time zones (Figure 5–77).

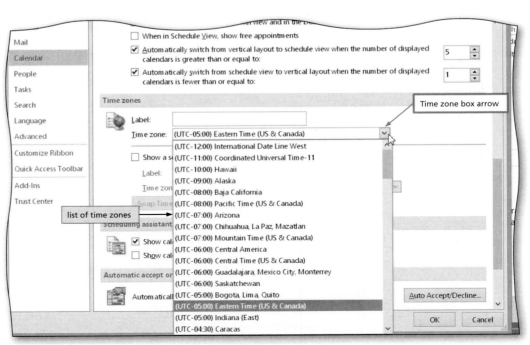

Figure 5–77

3

• Slide or scroll and then tap or click (UTC+01:00) Brussels, Copenhagen, Madrid, Paris to select the time zone (Figure 5–78).

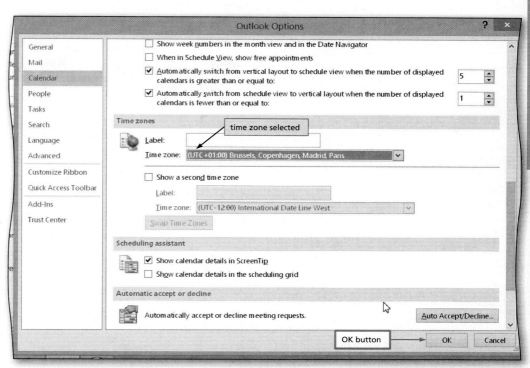

Figure 5–78

4

• Tap or click the OK button (Outlook Options dialog box) to close the Outlook Options dialog box.

• Tap or click the Calendar button in the Navigation Pane to display the Calendar to view the changes (Figure 5–79).

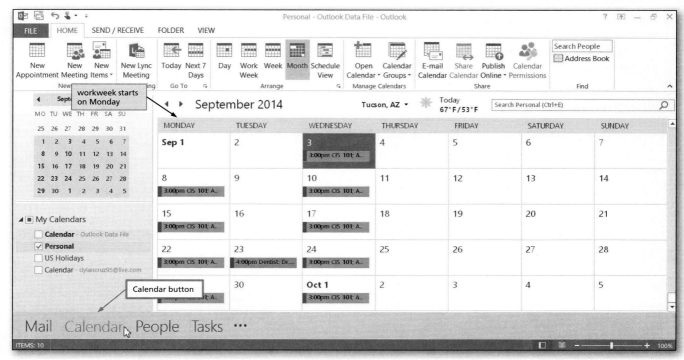

Figure 5–79

Working with RSS Feeds

Really Simple Syndication (RSS) is a way for content publishers to make news, blogs, and other content available to subscribers. RSS feeds typically are found on news websites, political discussion boards, educational blogs, and other sites that frequently update their content. For example, the CNN website contains two RSS feeds that allow people to view top stories and recent stories in one convenient location. If you frequently visit websites that offer RSS feeds, you quickly can review the feed content of all the websites in a simple list in your browser by subscribing to their RSS feeds, without having to first navigate to each individual site.

If you want to use Outlook to read the feed, you can add the RSS feed to your account using the Account Settings dialog box. Outlook creates an easy way to manage and work with your RSS feed. Some accounts let you access the feeds from your web browser if they are using a common feeds folder; however, not all accounts allow for this.

To Subscribe to an RSS Feed

1 CUSTOMIZE EMAIL MESSAGES | 2 CUSTOMIZE SIGNATURES & STATIONERY | 3 MANAGE JUNK EMAIL FILTERS
4 CONFIGURE RULES | 5 CHANGE CALENDAR OPTIONS | 6 ADD NEWS FEED

Dylan subscribes to several RSS feeds in his web browser. To view the feed using Outlook, he needs to set up an RSS feed called Life Rocks 2.0 from http://www. nirmaltv.com/feed/. The following steps subscribe to an RSS feed and display the messages. *Why?* *The benefit of displaying an RSS feed in Outlook is the ability to combine feeds from multiple web sources in one place. You no longer have to visit different websites for news, weather, blogs, and other information.*

1

- Tap or click the Mail button in the Navigation bar to display the mailboxes in the Navigation Pane.

- Press and hold or right-click the RSS Feeds folder in the Navigation Pane to display a shortcut menu (Figure 5–80).

Q&A What should I do if an RSS Feeds folder does not appear in Dylan's mailbox?
Press and hold or right-click the RSS Feeds folder in a different mailbox on your computer.

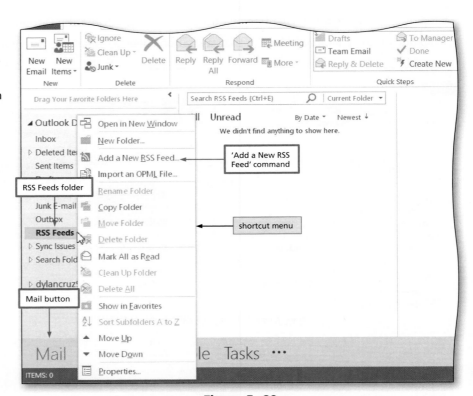

Figure 5–80

2

• Tap or click the Add a New RSS Feed command to display the New RSS Feed dialog box (Figure 5–81).

Figure 5–81

3

• Type `http://www .nirmaltv.com/feed/` in the text box to enter the address of an RSS feed (Figure 5–82).

Figure 5–82

4

• Tap or click the Add button (New RSS Feed dialog box) to add the RSS feed to the RSS Feeds folder.

• Tap or click the Yes button (Microsoft Outlook dialog box) to confirm you want to add the RSS feed (Figure 5–83).

Experiment

• Tap or click the different messages to see what has been posted in the RSS Feeds folder.

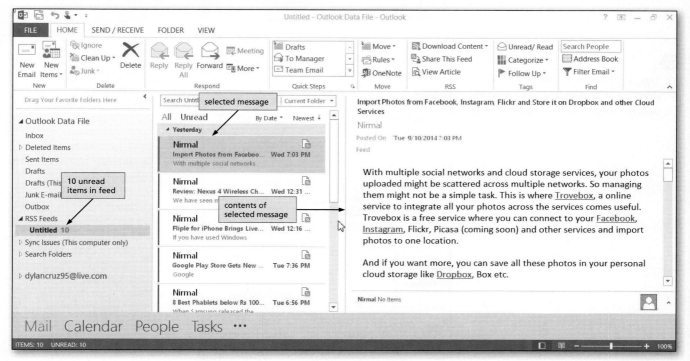

Figure 5–83

To Delete an RSS Feed

Why? When you no longer need to use an RSS feed, you should delete it so that you do not have unwanted messages in your account. The following steps delete an RSS feed.

- Press and hold or right-click the Untitled folder below the RSS Feeds folder in the Navigation Pane to display a shortcut menu (Figure 5–84).

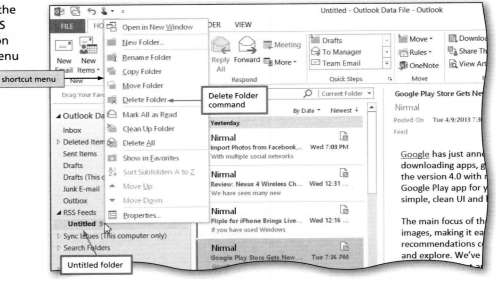

Figure 5–84

- Tap or click the Delete Folder command to display the Microsoft Outlook dialog box (Figure 5–85).

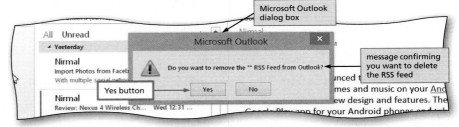

Figure 5–85

- Tap or click the Yes button (Microsoft Outlook dialog box) to delete the RSS Feed (Figure 5–86).

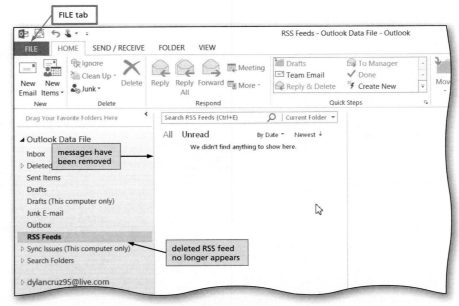

Figure 5–86

To Reset the Time Zone Setting

Why? You should change the time zone back to your original time zone before quitting *Outlook*. The following steps reset the time zone.

1 If necessary, tap or click the FILE tab to open the Backstage view, and then tap or click Options to display the Outlook Options dialog box.

2 Tap or click Calendar, and then scroll down until the Time zones settings are visible in the Outlook Options dialog box.

3 Tap or click the Time zone box arrow to display a list of time zones.

4 Tap or click your time zone to select the time zone.

To Exit Outlook

This project now is complete. The following steps exit Outlook. For a detailed example of the procedure summarized below, refer to the Office 2013 and Windows 8 chapter at the beginning of this book.

1 If you have an appointment open, tap or click the Close button on the right side of the title bar to close the Contact window.

2 Tap or click the Close button on the right side of the title bar to exit Outlook.

BTW
Quick Reference
For a table that lists how to complete the tasks covered in this book using touch gestures, the mouse, ribbon, shortcut menu, and keyboard, see the Quick Reference Summary at the back of this book, or visit the Quick Reference resource on the Student Companion Site located on www.cengagebrain.com. For detailed instructions about accessing available resources, visit www.cengage.com/ct/studentdownload or see the inside back cover of this book.

Chapter Summary

In this chapter, you have learned how to add another email account, customize Outlook options, add signatures and stationery, manage the junk email filter, create rules, customize calendar options, and add RSS Feeds. The items listed below include all the new Outlook skills you have learned in this chapter with the tasks grouped by activity.

Customizing Email Messages
Add an Email Account (OUT 237)
Add a Hyperlink to an Email Message (OUT 238)
Create and Insert Quick Parts (OUT 240)
Insert an Image into an Email Message (OUT 241)
Search Using Advanced Find (OUT 242)
Create a New Search Folder (OUT 243)
Set the Message Format (OUT 246)

Creating Signatures and Stationery
Create an Email Signature (OUT 248)
Format an Email Signature (OUT 249)
Add an Image to an Email Signature (OUT 251)
Configure Signature Options (OUT 253)
Customize Stationery (OUT 254)
Preview Message Changes (OUT 256)
Assign Signatures to a Single Message (OUT 257)

Managing Junk Email Options
Add a Domain to the Safe Senders List (OUT 260)
Block a Specific Email Address (OUT 263)

Working with Rules
Create a New Rule (OUT 264)
Run Rules (OUT 268)
Delete a Rule (OUT 270)
Set AutoArchive Settings (OUT 271)

Customizing the Calendar
Change the Work Time on the Calendar (OUT 273)
Change the Time for Calendar Reminders (OUT 275)
Change the Time Zone Settings (OUT 276)

Working with RSS Feeds
Subscribe to an RSS Feed (OUT 278)
Delete an RSS Feed (OUT 280)

CONSIDER THIS: PLAN AHEAD

What decisions will you need to make when customizing email messages, adding signatures and stationery, managing junk email options, working with rules, customizing the calendar, and adding RSS feeds in the future?

A. Customize Email Messages:

1. Determine which options you want to customize.
2. Determine the information to include in your signature.
3. Determine the layout that you would like for stationery.

B. Managing Junk Email Options:

1. Determine which domains should be placed on the Safe Senders list.
2. Determine which specific email addresses should be placed on the Blocked Senders list.

C. Working with Rules:

1. Plan rules to use with your email messages.
2. Determine how you would like your email messages to be processed.

D. Customizing the Calendar:

1. Determine the calendar settings you need.

E. Adding RSS Feeds:

1. Determine what news feeds you would like to use.

CONSIDER THIS

How should you submit solutions to questions in the assignments identified with a ❈ symbol?

Every assignment in this book contains one or more questions identified with a ❈ symbol. These questions require you to think beyond the assigned file. Present your solutions to the questions in the format required by your instructor. Possible formats may include one or more of these options: write the answer; create a document that contains the answer; present your answer to the class; discuss your answer in a group; record the answer as audio or video using a webcam, smartphone, or portable media player; or post answers on a blog, wiki, or website.

Apply Your Knowledge

Reinforce the skills and apply the concepts you learned in this chapter.

Creating a Signature

Instructions: Start Outlook. You will be using the Signatures and Stationery dialog box (Figure 5–87) to create a signature to use when you send email messages to others.

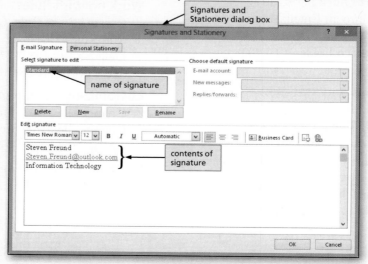

Figure 5–87

Perform the following tasks:

1. Display the Outlook Options dialog box. Tap or click Mail and then tap or click the Signatures button to display the Signatures and Stationery dialog box.

2. Tap or click the New button to create a signature. Type `standard` as the name of the signature.

3. Change the font to Times New Roman and the font size to 12.

4. On three lines, enter the following information: your name, your email address, and your major.

5. Set the signature to apply to new messages, replies, and forwards.

6. Tap or click the Personal Stationery tab and then tap or click the Theme button.

7. Select the Ice theme as your stationery.

8. Accept the changes in the dialog boxes and then create a new email message addressed to your instructor to display your new signature and stationery.

9. Submit the email message in the format specified by your instructor.

10. ✻ Why is it a good idea to configure Outlook to include a signature in outgoing email messages?

Extend Your Knowledge

Extend the skills you learned in this chapter and experiment with new skills. You may need to use Help to complete the assignment.

Adding a Second Email Account to Microsoft Outlook

Instructions: You are going to add a second email account to Microsoft Outlook so that you can send and receive email messages from two accounts. If you do not already have another email account to add to Microsoft Outlook, sign up for a free account using a service such as Outlook. com, Gmail, or Yahoo!. Once you create the account, you will add the email account to Outlook using the Add Account Wizard shown in Figure 5–88, and then send an email to your instructor.

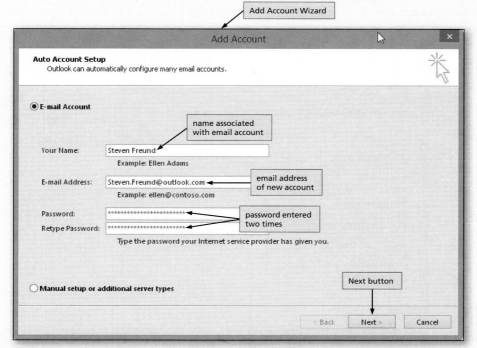

Figure 5–88

Continued >

Extend Your Knowledge *continued*

Perform the following tasks:

1. If necessary, navigate to a free email service and sign up for a free email account.

2. Start Outlook and display the Backstage view.

3. If necessary, tap or click the Info tab to display the Info gallery.

4. Tap or click the Add Account button to display the first dialog box in the Add Account Wizard.

5. Enter the desired information for the email account you are adding, including your name, email address, and password.

6. Tap or click the Next button to instruct Outlook to automatically configure the account. If Outlook is unable to configure the account automatically, you may need to manually configure the account settings.

7. When the account has been configured successfully, tap or click the Finish button.

8. Open a new email message addressed to your instructor stating that you have configured a new email account in Outlook. Send the email message to your instructor using the account you have just configured.

9. ✳ In what circumstances is it helpful to have multiple email accounts configured in Microsoft Outlook?

Analyze, Correct, Improve

Analyze the Outlook configuration and correct all errors and/or improve the configuration.

Copying and Modifying a Signature

Instructions: Start Outlook. Your boss has informed you that it is not acceptable to send business-related email messages without an approved company signature and an appropriate theme. Figure 5–89 shows an example of an email signature used by one of your coworkers. You will modify the signature to reflect your information and then change the default theme for your email messages.

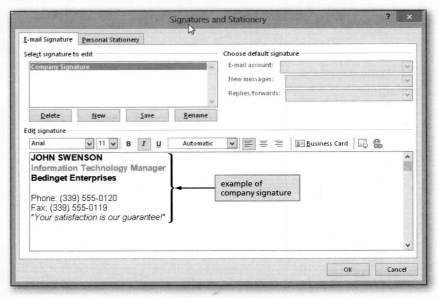

Figure 5–89

Perform the following tasks:

1. Correct Review the signature used in Figure 5–89. Change the name in the signature to reflect your name, update the title to one of your choosing, and change the phone number to your phone number (you may use a fictitious phone number if you are not comfortable including yours). Save the signature and configure it to be included with all new email messages, as well as forwarded messages and replies.

2. Improve Change the color, font, and font size of your name in the signature so that it stands out from the other information in the signature. Next, choose an appropriate theme for your email messages. If necessary, make additional changes to the font color you used in the signature to make sure it is readable with the new theme.

3. ✸ Why might businesses want all employees to use consistent signatures? Have you ever received an email message without sufficient contact information in the signature? If so, how did you obtain the information you needed?

In the Labs

Design, create, modify, and/or use signatures and rules using the guidelines, concepts, and skills presented in this chapter. Labs are listed in order of increasing difficulty.

Lab 1: **Creating Custom Signatures**

Problem: You communicate with both professors and other students via email. Your professors ask students to clearly identify themselves in email messages, but you do not want to include the same information in email messages you send to your friends. Instead, you want to include your nickname and cell phone number in your email signature. You will create two signatures: one to use when you send email messages to your professors, and another for email messages you send to friends. You will use the Signatures and Stationery dialog box to create the signatures (Figure 5–90).

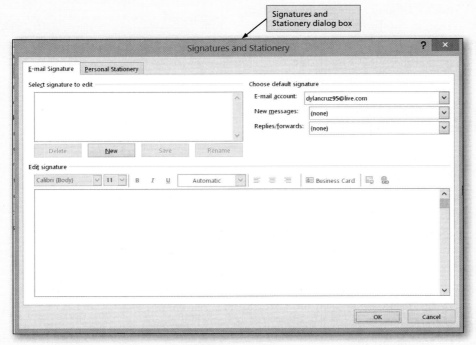

Figure 5–90

Continued >

In the Labs *continued*

Perform the following tasks:

1. Display the Outlook Options dialog box. Tap or click Mail and then tap or click the Signatures button to display the Signatures and Stationery dialog box.

2. Tap or click the New button to create a signature. Type `Academic` as the name of the signature.

3. Change the font to Arial and the font size to 14.

4. On three lines, enter the following information: your name, the name of your school, the classes in which you are enrolled, and your email address.

5. Using the Academic signature, send an email message to your instructor. The email message should specify that the signature is the Academic signature.

6. Display the Outlook Options dialog box. Tap or click Mail and then tap or click the Signatures button to display the Signatures and Stationery dialog box.

7. Tap or click the New button to create a signature. Type `Personal` as the name of the signature.

8. Change the font to Comic Sans MS, the font size to 16, and the font color to one of your choosing.

9. On three lines, enter the following information: your name, your phone number, and your email address.

10. Using the Personal signature, send an email message to a friend. The email message should specify that the signature is the Personal signature.

11. ✸ Do you think it is easier to switch back and forth between different signatures or manually type signature information individually into each email message? Why?

Lab 2: **Configuring Junk Email**

Problem: You occasionally find email messages you want to read in the Junk E-mail folder for your Outlook email account. You also receive spam from a certain email address. You want to use the Junk E-mail Options dialog box (Figure 5–91) to make sure you receive email messages from some senders, while blocking email messages from another sender.

Perform the following tasks:

1. In Outlook, display the Junk E-mail Options dialog box.

2. Tap or click the Safe Senders tab.

3. Add CNN.com to the Safe Senders list. Write down what is displayed in the Safe Senders list.

4. Tap or click the Safe Recipients tab. Add ewhite173@gmail.com to the Safe Recipients list. Write down what is displayed in the Safe Recipients list.

Figure 5–91

5. Tap or click the Blocked Senders tab. Add @crazyedigames.com to the Blocked Senders list. Write down what is displayed in the Blocked Senders list.

6. Submit what you have recorded in the format specified by your instructor.

7. ☀ What other domains and email addresses might you add to the Safe Senders list? What are some examples of other domains and email addresses you might add to the Blocked Senders list?

Lab 3: Expand Your World: Cloud and Web Technologies

Problem: RSS feeds are web technologies that can deliver up-to-date content directly to Outlook. You want to add an RSS feed from CNN.com so that you can view technology news in Outlook (Figure 5–92).

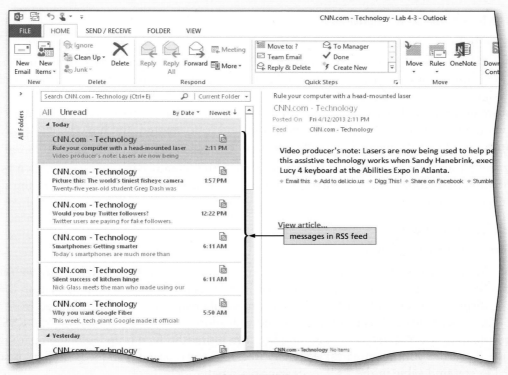

Figure 5–92

Perform the following tasks:

1. Run your browser and navigate to CNN.com.

2. Navigate to the page on the CNN.com website that displays the list of available RSS feeds.

3. Select and copy the web address for the Technology RSS feed.

4. In Outlook, press and hold or right-click the RSS Feeds folder (or the feeds folder for your email account) and then display the New RSS Feed dialog box.

5. Paste the web address from Step 3 into the text box.

6. Add the feed to Outlook.

7. Open the first RSS message.

8. Print the message and then submit it in the format specified by your instructor.

9. ☀ What other RSS feeds might you find useful to include in Microsoft Outlook?

Consider This: Your Turn

Apply your creative thinking and problem solving skills to design and implement a solution.

1: Create Rules
Academic

Part 1: For three of the classes you are currently taking, create email folders for each class. Create rules to move messages related to the classes to the appropriate class email folder. Write a rule for one class that flags messages for follow-up the following week. Write down the rules and then submit your work in the format specified by your instructor.

Part 2: ❋ You made several decisions when creating the rules in this exercise, such as which folders to create and how to set up the rule to identify to which class an email message belongs. What was the rationale behind each of these decisions?

2: Create a Company Signature
Professional

Part 1: Your supervisor has asked you to create an email signature to be used in all outgoing email communication from company employees. He has not given you specifics about what should be in the signature, but you do know that it is important to provide useful information. Create a new signature in Outlook that will be used as the company's standard signature, and determine which information to include in the signature, how it should be formatted, and how the items in the signature should be arranged. Then, send an email to your instructor that contains the signature.

Part 2: ❋ You made several decisions when creating the signature in this exercise, such as what information to include, how to format the signature, and how to arrange the items in the signature. What was the rationale behind each of these decisions?

3: Subscribe to Feeds
Research and Collaboration

Part 1: Your instructor has assigned teams of three people to search for and identify websites that contain RSS feeds. Your team should search for RSS feeds providing useful information that you want to display in Microsoft Outlook. Each team member should locate an RSS feed from at least five different websites and record the name and web address of the site containing the RSS feed, the information the RSS feed contains, and how often the RSS feed is updated. Compare the list with the lists from your teammates. Were any RSS feeds or types of RSS feeds similar? If so, which ones? Do you find value in the RSS feeds your teammates identified?

Part 2: ❋ You made several decisions when searching for RSS feeds in this exercise, such as where to search for the RSS feeds and which types of RSS feeds would be useful to include in Outlook. What was the rationale behind each of these decisions?

Learn Online

Reinforce what you learned in this chapter with games, exercises, training, and many other online activities and resources.

Student Companion Site Reinforce chapter terms and concepts using review questions, flash cards, practice tests, and interactive learning games, such as a crossword puzzle. These and other online activities and resources are available at no additional cost on www.cengagebrain.com. Visit www.cengage.com/ct/studentdownload for detailed instructions about accessing the resources available at the Student Companion Site.

Capstone Project 1: Starrs Mountain Resort

The Capstone Project consists of an integrated, comprehensive set of problems related to a single scenario. Students apply concepts and skills presented in this book to create solutions to the problems using Word, PowerPoint, Excel, Access, and Outlook.

Starrs Mountain Resort in Starrs, Vermont offers a variety of winter sports activities such as downhill skiing, snowboarding, cross-country skiing, and snowshoeing. As an intern at the resort, you work closely with the resort's general manager, Julie Wilson.

Note: To complete this assignment, you will be required to use the Data Files for Students. Visit www.cengage.com/ct/studentdownload for detailed instructions or contact your instructor for information about accessing the required files.

Word Capstone Project 1

Creating a Memo with a Chart and an Online Form

Problem: Starrs Mountain Resort is getting ready for ski season. Julie Wilson has asked you to create some documents and forms that the resort can use in the upcoming months. These documents include a memo with a table and a chart and a template for an online form. Julie also asked you to work with the rental center to create a document that can be used as a rental equipment checklist.

Instructions Part 1: Create the memo shown in Figure 1–1 on the next page that Julie can send to new resort associates. Start Word and open the Cap 1 Memo Draft document from the Data File for Students. Start Excel and open the Cap 1 Revenue Information workbook from the Data File for Students. Link the Excel worksheet to the memo, then center and autofit the contents of the linked table as shown in Figure 1–1. Break the link to the worksheet and close the Excel app.

Create the chart shown in Figure 1–1. Be sure to remove the extra data series from the worksheet. Apply Style 12 to the chart and change the Chart Quick Colors to Color 2. Add primary minor vertical gridlines to the chart. Change the chart title to that shown in Figure 1–1. Format the vertical axis so that the revenue categories are listed in the same order on the chart as they are in the table. The values for the horizontal axis should appear at the bottom of the chart and the legend should appear at the top. Adjust the legend by removing the check mark from the 'Show the legend without overlapping the chart' check box and move it so that it rests on top of the vertical lines. Add a Blue, Accent 1, Darker 25% shape outline with a weight of 1½ pt. Apply a Shadow, Offset Center shape effect. If requested to do so by your instructor, replace the text, RESORT ASSOCIATE, with your first and last names.

Save the document using the file name, Cap 1 Ski Revenue Memo. Submit the document in the format specified by your instructor.

Instructions Part 2: The manager of the rental shop, Steve Chastain, asked you to create a rental equipment outline. He wants to develop the outline into a reference document that employees can use. You created an initial outline and sent it to Steve for review. He made several changes using the Track Changes feature of Word and also included comments. Open the Cap 1 Checklist with

Word Capstone Project 1 *continued*

INTEROFFICE MEMORANDUM

TO: RESORT ASSOCIATE
FROM: JULIE WILSON
SUBJECT: FINANCIAL OVERVIEW
DATE: OCTOBER 20, 2014

Welcome to Starrs Mountain Resort! All of us are excited about the upcoming winter season. If the long-range weather forecasts are accurate, it should be great. Below is a table and chart that summarize our revenues from last season as well as our projected revenues for the coming season. During the 2013 season, the resort had 29,495 skier visits. Revenues for 2014 are based on an estimated 35,240 skier visits.

2013 Actual and 2014 Projected Ski Revenues

Revenue Category	Actual 2013	Projected 2014
Season Passes	$ 209,633	$ 230,596
Ticket Sales	$ 859,014	$ 1,098,071
Lessons	$ 106,104	$ 127,652
Racing	$ 23,958	$ 26,354
Parks and Pipes	$ 85,901	$ 87,846
Rentals	$ 32,444	$ 38,765

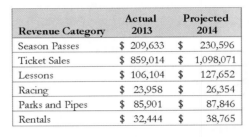

shape outline: Blue, Accent 1, Darker 25% with a weight of 1½ pt; Shadow, Offset Center shape effect

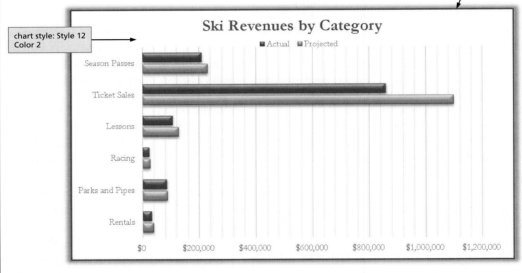

chart style: Style 12 Color 2

Figure 1–1

Comments document and switch to Outline view. Make the changes to the document suggested by Steve. Accept all changes, delete Steve's comments, and disable tracked changes. Collapse the Payment Method item and the items under Adult and Child. The revised checklist is shown in Figure 1–2. If requested to do so by your instructor, add your name in parentheses to the end of the first line of the document.

Save the revised document as Cap 1 Rental Equipment Checklist Revised. Submit the document in the format specified by your instructor.

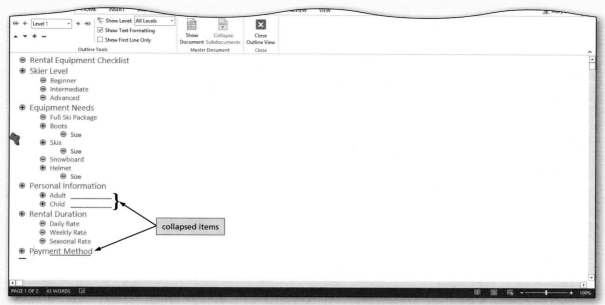

Figure 1–2

Instructions Part 3: Julie Wilson has asked you to create a template for an online form to determine which equipment storage options are most popular with the skiers. Create a new document in Word and save the file as a Word template with the name Cap 1 Equipment Storage Survey. Change the paper size for the template to 8.5 inches wide by 4.75 inches tall. Change the top margin to .25 and the bottom margin to 0. Change the left and right margins to .5. Change the theme colors to Blue Warm and the theme font to Gill Sans MT. Change the page color to Blue, Accent 2, Lighter 80%.

Enter and format the resort title, tag line, and form title as shown in Figure 1–3. Insert the picture from the Office.com website. Use the search text, skier, to find the picture. Resize the picture to 40% of its original size and move it to the position shown in Figure 1–3. Apply the Soft Edge Oval picture style. Enter the instructions above the data entry area.

Figure 1–3

Continued >

In the data entry area, enter the labels as shown in Figure 1–3 on the previous page and the content controls as follows: First Name and Last Name are plain text controls in a 2 × 1 table. Storage option is a drop-down list control with these choices: Coin-Operated Locker, Basket Room, Stor-A-Ski, Seasonal Locker, Repair Center, and None. Types is a check box content control and Why is a plain text control.

Edit the placeholder text of all content controls to match Figure 1–3. Change the properties of the content controls so that each contains a title and has locking set so that the content control cannot be deleted. Format the placeholder text with subtle emphasis.

Enter the line below the data entry area as shown in Figure 1–3. Draw a rectangle around the data entry area. Change the shape style of the rectangle to Subtle Effect - Gray-50%, Accent 6. If requested to do so by your instructor, replace Starrs in the title with your last name. Protect the form. Do not use a password. Hide the DEVELOPER tab.

Save the form again. Submit the document in the format specified by your instructor.

Instructions Part 4:   Open the template you created in Part 3 and save it as a macro-enabled template with the file name, Cap 1 Equipment Storage Survey with Macros. Show the DEVELOPER tab and unprotect the template. Change the document theme to Droplet. Delete the clip art on the form and modify the formats of the resort name, resort tag line, and user instructions as shown in Figure 1–4. Change the page color to the white marble texture fill effect.

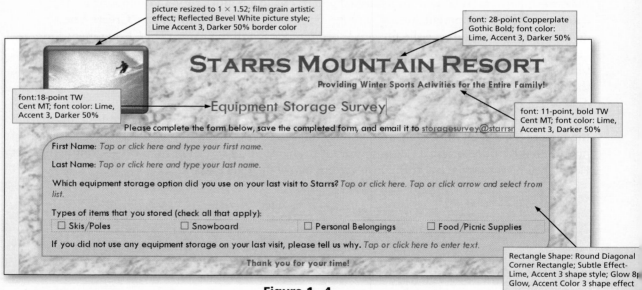

Figure 1–4

In the 2 × 1 table containing the First Name and Last Name content controls, convert the table to text. Be sure the rectangle covers the entire data entry area. Change the style for the email address so that the text is displayed in the theme color, Lime, Accent 3, Darker 50%. Change the font color of the placeholder text and the thank you line at the end of the survey to Lime, Accent 3, Darker 50%.

Change the shape of the rectangle to Round Diagonal Corner Rectangle. Change the shape style to Subtle Effect-Lime, Accent 3. Apply the Lime 8 pt Glow effect, and Accent Color 3 shape effect.

Insert the clip art from the Office.com website. Use the search text, skier, to find the clip art. Resize the picture to 1" × 1.52" and move it to the position shown in Figure 1–4. Apply the film grain artistic effect with the Reflected Bevel White picture style. Change the border color to Lime Accent 3, Darker 50%.

Record a macro that hides the formatting marks and the rulers. Name it HideScreenElements and assign it the shortcut key ALT+H. Run the macro to test it. Protect the form.

Save the form again and submit it in the format specified by your instructor.

PowerPoint Capstone Project

Customizing a Template, Modifying a Presentation, and Using Outside Content

Problem: Julie Wilson and other resort associates often must prepare presentations for groups and for special events. Julie has asked you to prepare some basic presentations that can be reused and modified.

Instructions Part 1:   Julie has asked you to create a custom template that can be used to advertise family events and other special activities at the resort. The template that you will create consists of a slide master, title slide, title and content slide, and blank slide, and is shown in Figure 1–5. Create a new presentation and save the presentation as Cap 1 Starrs Custom Template. Display the presentation in Slide Master view and change the theme to Droplet. Change the theme colors to Blue Warm. Customize the theme fonts, selecting Copperplate Gothic Bold as the Heading font and Corbel as the body font. Give the new theme the name, Starrs. Apply Style 6 as the Background Style as shown in Figure 1–5a.

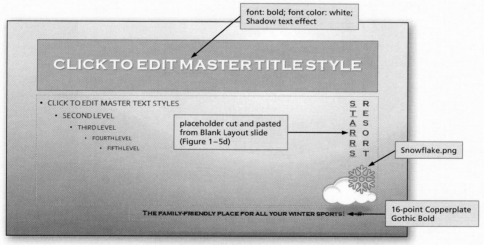

(a) Slide Master

(b) Title Slide Layout

Figure 1–5

Continued >

PowerPoint Capstone Project 1 *continued*

(c) Title and Content Layout

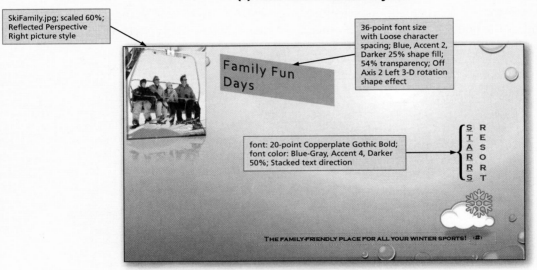

(d) Blank Layout
Figure 1–5 (Continued)

Delete the date placeholder in the slide footer and move the content footer placeholder to the position shown in Figure 1–5a on the previous page. Add the text shown in Figure 1–5a to the content footer placeholder. Ensure that the page number does not appear on the title slide. Change the font for the content footer placeholder and the slide number to Copperplate Gothic Bold with a font size of 16.

Insert the Snowflake.png picture from the Data File for Students as a background graphic into the slide master and position it as shown in Figure 1–5a. On the slide master's title placeholder, change the font color to bold, white, and apply the Shadow text effect.

In the Overview pane, select the Blank Layout slide and add the Starrs Resort placeholder shown in Figure 1–5d. The placeholder has a Stacked text direction with 20-point Copperplate Gothic Bold font and font color of Blue-Gray, Accent 4, Darker 50%. Because this placeholder should appear on all slides, cut and paste the placeholder into the slide master.

On the Blank Layout slide, insert the SkiFamily.jpg picture from the Data File for Students. Scale the image to 60% and position it as shown in Figure 1–5d. Apply the Reflected Perspective Right picture style. Add a text box with the text, Family Fun Days, to the slide. Change the font size to 36 point and the character spacing to Loose. Apply the Blue, Accent 2, Darker 25% shape fill color to the text box and increase the transparency to 54%. Apply an Off Axis 2 Left 3-D rotation shape effect to the text box and position it as shown in Figure 1–5d.

Rename the slide master as Starrs and rename the Blank Layout slide as Family Fun Days. Delete all slides except the four slides shown in Figure 1–5. If requested to do so by your instructor, add your name to the footer content placeholder.

Save the presentation as a template with the name Cap 1 Starrs Custom Template and submit it in the format specified by your instructor.

Instructions Part 2:   Snowshoeing continues to increase in popularity as a winter sport. Julie Wilson has asked you to prepare a short presentation that presents snowshoeing basics. Open the Cap 1 Snowshoe presentation from the Data File for Students and modify the presentation to create the presentation shown in Figure 1–6.

Add the text box shown in Figure 1–6a to Slide 1. Change the font color of the text to Black, Background 1, Lighter 15%. Apply a Square Dot dashed outline with a 3-pt weight and Aqua, Accent 1, Darker 50% outline color. Apply the Glow, Green, 18-pt glow, Accent Color 4 shape effect. Format the text with the Fill – Dark Green, Background 2, Inner Shadow WordArt style and increase the font size to 36. Set the text box as the default text box so that the same formatting will appear in the remaining slides. Position the text box as shown in Figure 1–6a.

(a) Slide 1

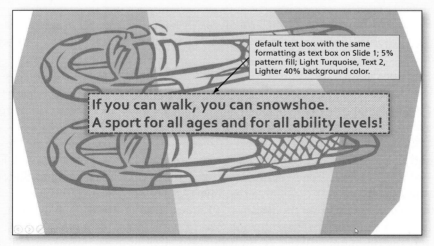

(b) Slide 2

Figure 1–6

Continued >

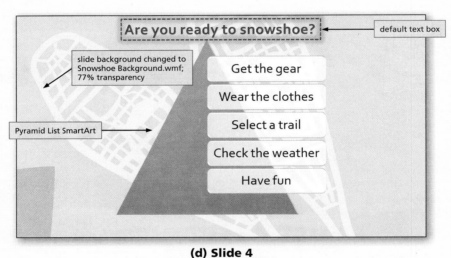

(c) Slide 3

(d) Slide 4

Figure 1–6 (Continued)

Add the text box shown in Figure 1–6b on the previous page to Slide 2. Apply a 5% pattern fill with a Light Turquoise, Text 2, Lighter 40% background color. Position the text box as shown in Figure 1–6b.

Add the text box shown in Figure 1–6c to Slide 3. Center the text box using the align feature. Convert the WordArt paragraphs to a SmartArt Target List. Reorder the shapes so that Footwear precedes Clothing. Demote the socks bullet and the thermal underwear bullets. Change the SmartArt layout to the Vertical Block List shown in Figure 1–6c.

Change the slide background for Slide 4 to a snowshoe background as shown in Figure 1–6d. The background image, Snowshoe Background.wmf is in the Data File for Students. Format the background with a 77% transparency. Add the text box shown in Figure 1–6d to Slide 4. Center the text box using the align feature. Change the SmartArt layout to a Pyramid List.

Apply the Dissolve transition to all slides. If requested to do so by your instructor, replace the text, For Fun and Fitness, in the text box on Slide 1 with your first and last names. Save the presentation as Cap 1 Snowshoe Basics. Submit the presentation in the format specified by your instructor.

Instructions Part 3: Julie would like a presentation that includes some statistics concerning snowshoeing. Open the Cap 1 Snowshoe Facts Draft presentation and modify this presentation as shown in Figure 1–7. Do not make any changes to Slide 1 (Figure 1–7a).

no changes

(a) Slide 1

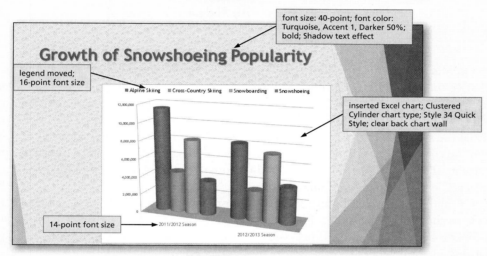

font size: 40-point; font color: Turquoise, Accent 1, Darker 50%; bold; Shadow text effect

legend moved; 16-point font size

inserted Excel chart; Clustered Cylinder chart type; Style 34 Quick Style; clear back chart wall

14-point font size

(b) Slide 2

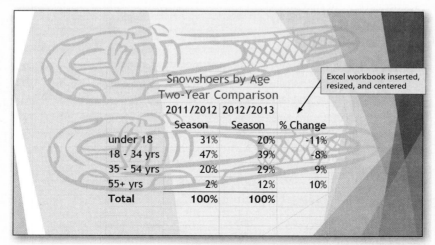

Excel workbook inserted, resized, and centered

(c) Slide 3

Figure 1–7

Continued >

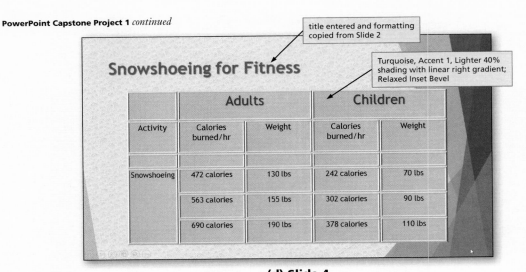

(d) Slide 4

Figure 1–7 (Continued)

On Slide 2, add the title shown in Figure 1–7b on the previous page. Change the font size to 40; change the font color to Turquoise, Accent 1, Darker 50%; bold the title; and apply the Shadow text effect. Insert an Excel chart from the Cap 1 Snowshoe Popularity workbook, which is included in the Data Files for Students. Resize the chart to 5.5" wide × 7.55" high. Align the chart to the center of the slide and to the bottom of the slide. Switch the rows and columns in the chart, and change the chart type to Clustered Cylinder. Move the legend to the top of the chart and change the font size to 16. Change the font size of the horizontal axis to 14. Apply the Style 34 Quick Style to the chart. Clear the Chart Wall fill.

On Slide 3, shown in Figure 1–7c on the previous page, insert the Cap 1 Age Demographics Excel worksheet on to the slide. The workbook is in the Data Files for Students. Be sure to link the worksheet to the presentation. If necessary, resize the worksheet to 5.5" high × 7.27" wide. Center the worksheet. The worksheet contains two incorrect percentages. Edit the worksheet and replace the 18% in the 2011/2012 Season column with 20%. Replace the 4% in the same column with 2%.

On Slide 4, enter the title text shown in Figure 1–7d and use the Format Painter to copy the formatting from the Slide 2 title to Slide 4. Draw a table that has six rows and five columns. Erase columns and rows as necessary to create the format shown in Figure 1–7d. Enter the data for the table. Change the width of column 1 to 1.83". Distribute columns 2 through 5 evenly. Distribute rows 4 through 6 evenly. Change the height of row 3 to .5". Change the height of rows 1 and 2 to 1". Center the text in the table and center the table horizontally on the slide. Apply Turquoise, Accent 1, Lighter, 40% shading with a linear right gradient. Apply a Relaxed Inset Bevel to the table.

Apply the Wipe transition to all slides. If requested to do so by your instructor, add your name to the title slide. Save the presentation as Cap 1 Snowshoe Facts Completed and submit the presentation in the format specified by your instructor.

Excel Capstone Project 1

Working with Trendlines, PivotTables, PivotCharts, Goal Seek, Scenario Manager, and Macros

Problem: Julie Wilson wants to analyze skier visit data from past years. The resort knows that skiers come from all over the country to ski at Starrs, and management wants to create a marketing campaign to market resort timeshares to skiers from the Northeast and MidAtlantic regions. To help Julie, you will create a trendline chart, PivotTable, and PivotChart. The resort also needs to make some business decisions regarding the purchase of an additional shuttle bus to transport skiers from offsite lodging and parking lots to the ski slopes. Finally, Julie would like to automate some tasks associated with tracking equipment rentals.

Instructions Part 1: Open the Cap 1 Starrs Skier Visitor Data workbook from the Data Files for Students. Create a 2-D line chart with data markers using the data on the 5-Year Visitor Data worksheet. Move the chart to a new sheet and name the sheet as Trendline Chart. Change the title on the chart to that shown in Figure 1–8. Change the font size for the title to 18. Add a linear trendline to the chart. Extend the trendline by two years and display the R-squared value on the chart. Increase the size of the 2011 data point to 16 and apply the Dark Red color to the data point. Apply the Damask theme to the workbook and change the theme colors to Blue Warm. Move the Trendline Chart sheet so that it follows the 5-Year Visitor Data worksheet.

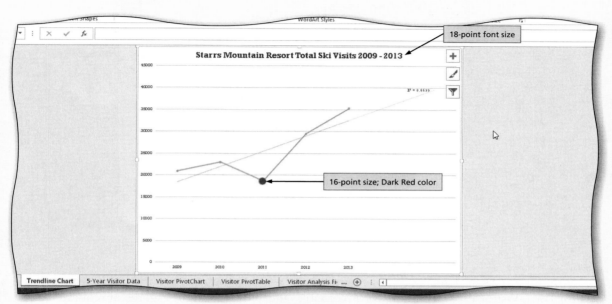

Figure 1–8

Using the Visitor Analysis Figures, create the PivotTable shown in Figure 1–9. Onsite means the visitor stayed at the resort. Offsite means the visitor stayed somewhere else or was a daytripper. Use Pivot Style Dark 3 as the PivotTable Style and format the numbers with thousands separators and no decimal places. Insert two rows at the top of the PivotTable and add a title and subtitle as shown in Figure 1–9. Format cell A1 with the Title style and cell A2 with the Heading 4 Style. Merge and center the title and subtitle. Apply the Light Blue 2, Background fill color. Be sure to filter the PivotTable for only those visitors from the Northeast. Name the worksheet as Visitor PivotTable.

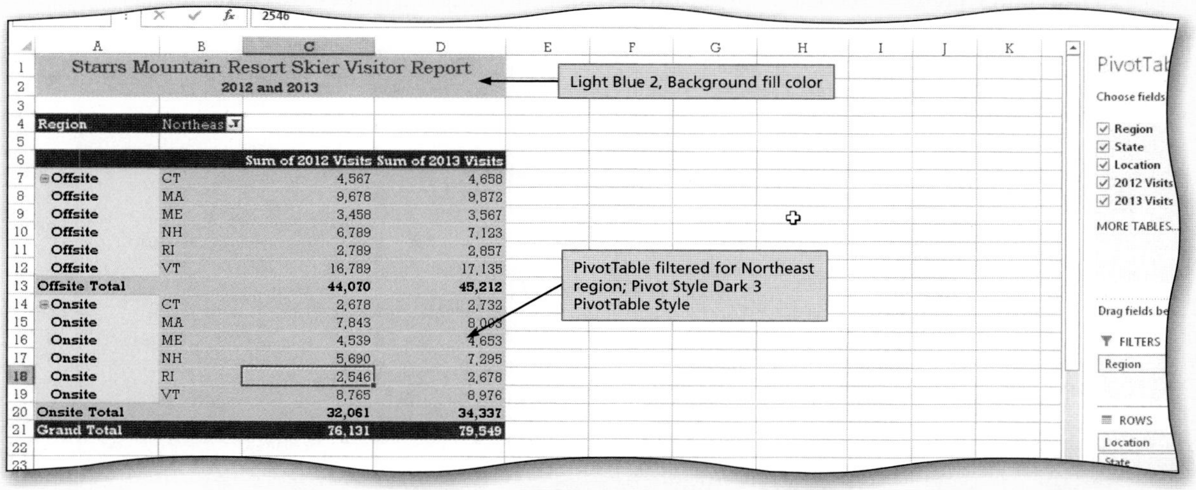

Figure 1–9

Continued >

Excel Capstone Project 1 *continued*

Create the associated 3-D Clustered Column PivotChart shown in Figure 1–10. Apply chart Style 3 to the chart and change the chart colors to Color 2. Change the chart title to that shown in Figure 1–10. Change the title font size to 16. Format the data series as cylinders. Add a back wall to the chart and format with a gradient shape fill of Lime, Accent 1, Lighter 40%. Name the worksheet as Visitor PivotChart.

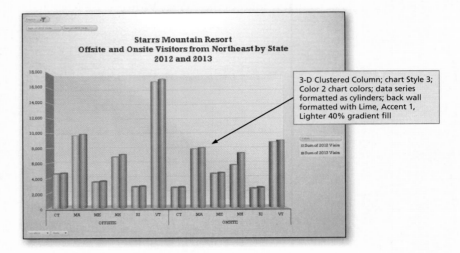

Figure 1–10

Reorder the sheets to appear in the following order (left to right): Trendline Chart, 5-Year Visitor Data, Visitor PivotChart, Visitor PivotTable, and Visitor Analysis Figures. If requested to do so by your instructor, rename the 5-Year Visitor Data worksheet as First Name Last Name Data where First Name and Last Name are your first and last names. Save the workbook as Cap 1 Visitor Analysis. Submit the workbook in the format specified by your instructor.

Instructions Part 2: Last year's visitors to the resort complained of long lines for shuttle bus service from offsite locations. Julie has a quote for a new 24-passenger shuttle bus and would like to purchase the bus through a bank loan. Open the Cap 1 Shuttle Bus Data file from the Data Files for Students. Change the theme to Droplet. Enter a loan amount of $59,990, interest rate of 4.5% and months of 36 in the workbook. Use Goal Seek to determine the length of the loan if monthly payments are $1,250.00. Record the number of months in cell K10 as shown in Figure 1–11. Use Goal Seek again to determine the length of the loan if monthly payments are $1,500.00.

Starrs Mountain Resort

Interest Rate Schedule				Loan Payment Calculator	
	Monthly Payment	Total Cost	Total Interest	Shuttle Bus	
Interest	$1,500.00	$65,117.60	$5,127.60	Loan amount	$59,990.00
4.00%	1,486.58	64,534.85	4,544.85	Interest rate	4.50%
4.50%	1,500.00	65,117.60	5,127.60	Months	43
5.00%	1,513.50	65,703.59	5,713.59	Monthly payment	$1,500.00
5.50%	1,527.07	66,292.82	6,302.82		
6.00%	1,540.72	66,885.29	6,895.29	Number of months with a monthly payment of $1,250 –>	
6.50%	1,554.44	67,480.98	7,490.98		
7.00%	1,568.24	68,079.90	8,089.90		

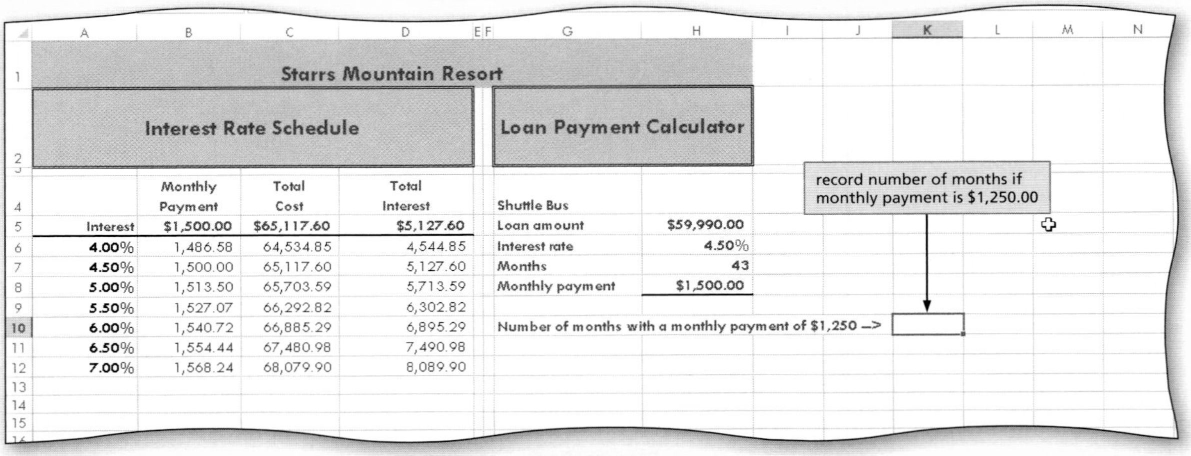

Figure 1–11

If requested to do so by your instructor, replace the contents of cell A1 with your first and last name. Save the workbook as Cap 1 Shuttle Bus Loan Calculator. Submit the workbook in the format specified by your instructor.

Instructions Part 3:   Similar to many other ski resorts, Starrs Mountain sells resort timeshares. Julie Wilson has asked you to determine the impact of raising commissions for the resort sales team from 4% to 6%. To accommodate the potential increase, the resort needs to increase the markup at which they sell the timeshares. Currently, the markup is 12%. If the resort increases the price, they probably will sell fewer timeshares. Create and compare three scenarios for the new commission rate and projected timeshare sales based on three potential price markups.

Open the Cap 1 Starrs Resort Timeshares Data workbook and create a validation rule for the number of timeshares sold. Only integer data can be entered in the cell. Then, create the following scenarios:

1. 65 timeshares are sold with a markup of 14% and a commission rate of 6%

2. 60 timeshares are sold with a markup of 16% and a commission rate of 6%

3. 56 timeshares are sold with a markup of 17% and a commission rate of 6%

Create the Scenario PivotTable report shown in Figure 1–12 showing the three scenarios saved in the Scenario Manager. Create the Scenario Summary Report shown in Figure 1–13 showing the three scenarios saved in the Scenario Manager.

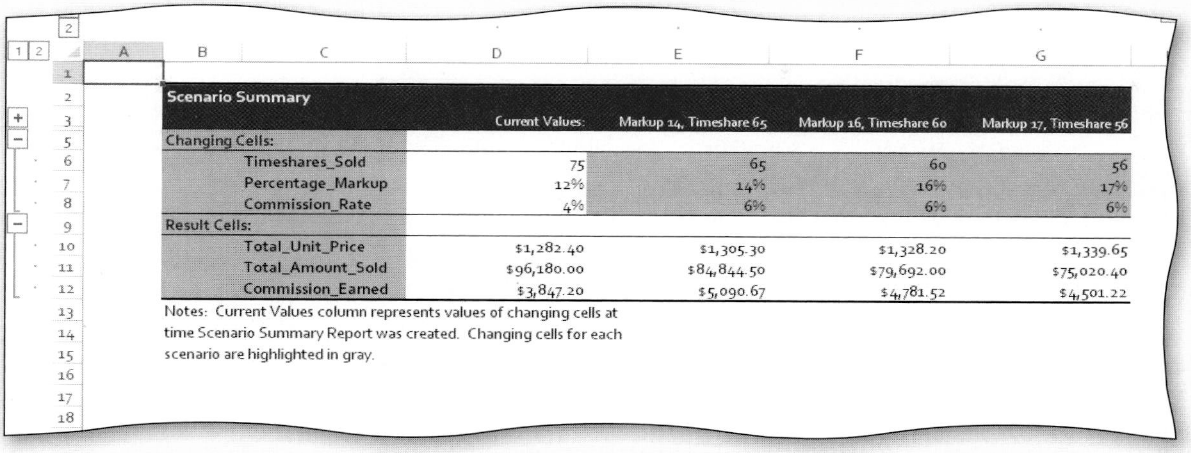

		Current Values:	Markup 14, Timeshare 65	Markup 16, Timeshare 60	Markup 17, Timeshare 56
Scenario Summary					
Changing Cells:					
Timeshares_Sold		75	65	60	56
Percentage_Markup		12%	14%	16%	17%
Commission_Rate		4%	6%	6%	6%
Result Cells:					
Total_Unit_Price		$1,282.40	$1,305.30	$1,328.20	$1,339.65
Total_Amount_Sold		$96,180.00	$84,844.50	$79,692.00	$75,020.40
Commission_Earned		$3,847.20	$5,090.67	$4,781.52	$4,501.22

Notes: Current Values column represents values of changing cells at
time Scenario Summary Report was created. Changing cells for each
scenario are highlighted in gray.

Figure 1–12

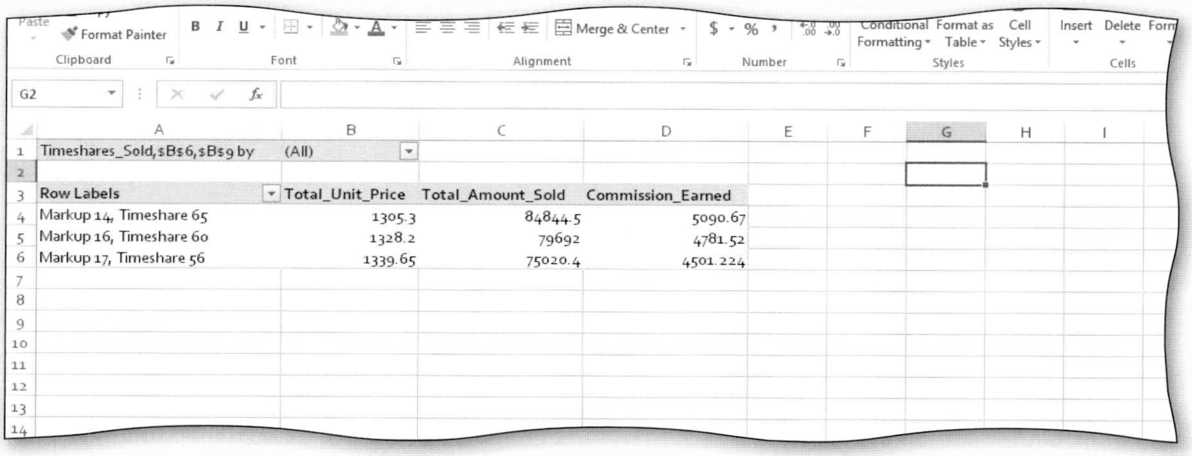

Row Labels	Total_Unit_Price	Total_Amount_Sold	Commission_Earned
Markup 14, Timeshare 65	1305.3	84844.5	5090.67
Markup 16, Timeshare 60	1328.2	79692	4781.52
Markup 17, Timeshare 56	1339.65	75020.4	4501.224

Timeshares_Sold,$B$6,$B$9 by   (All)

Figure 1–13

Continued >

Excel Capstone Project 1 *continued*

If requested to do so by your instructor, rename the October Commissions worksheet as First Name Last Name Commissions where First Name and Last Name are your first and last names. Save the workbook as Cap 1 Starrs Resort Timeshares Scenarios and submit the workbook in the format specified by your instructor.

Instructions Part 4: The rental center would like a simple workbook that they can use to track equipment rentals on a weekly basis. Open the Cap 1 Starrs Rental Data workbook from the Data Files for Students. Display the DEVELOPER tab on the ribbon. Select cell B4 and record a macro that formats the cell with the Accounting format. Name the macro AccFormat, assign the shortcut key CTRL+C, store the macro in the workbook, and if requested to do so by your instructor, enter your name in the Description box. Use the shortcut key to run the macro in cell B6. Add the macro to the Quick Access Toolbar and then use the command to run the macro in cells C4, C6, D4, and D6. Remove the AccFormat macro from the Quick Access Toolbar.

Create a macro that adds a column before column C, sums the cell range C4:C5, and sets the column width to 18. Name the macro AddColumn, assign the shortcut key CTRL+N, store the macro in this workbook, and add a description for the macro. In the newly added column, enter the data shown in Figure 1–14 for Snowshoes. Add a command button form control to the worksheet in the position shown in Figure 1–14. Assign the AddColumn macro to the command button. Use the command button to add another column to the worksheet and enter the data for Ski Only as shown in Figure 1–14.

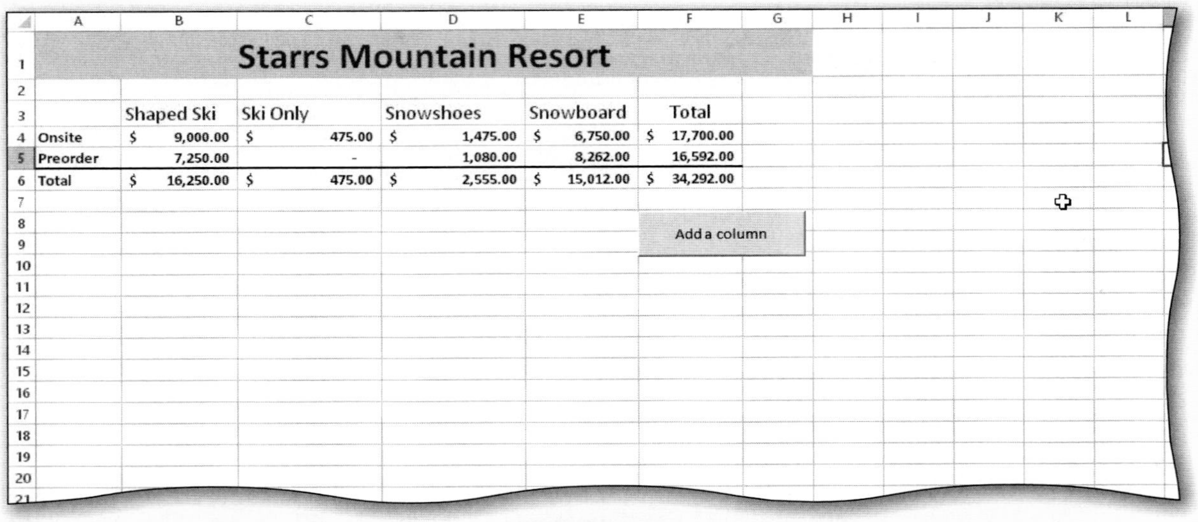

Figure 1–14

Save the workbook as a macro-enabled workbook with the name Cap 1 Starrs Rental Macro Complete and submit the workbook in the format specified by your instructor.

Access Capstone Project 1

Creating Macros and Navigation Forms for the Starrs Apparel Database

Problem: Similar to other ski resorts, Starrs supplies equipment and apparel for various winter sports; guests of the resort can purchase or rent what they need. Inventory for these items is handled through the Rental Center. In addition, Starrs also sells clothing and novelty items in its gift shop, equipment barn, and restaurants. Starrs maintains a database of these items. Julie Wilson has asked you to modify the database to make it easier to maintain and update.

Instructions Part 1: Open the Cap 1 Starrs Apparel database from the Data File for Students and create a macro named Forms and Reports that will include submacros to perform the following tasks:

a. Open the Supplier Master Form
b. Open the Item Master Form
c. Preview the Supplier Master List
d. Preview the Inventory Status Report
e. Export the Supplier Master List in PDF format
f. Export the Inventory Status Report in PDF format

Create the menu form shown in Figure 1–15. The command buttons should use the macros you created to open the two forms. Create the menu form shown in Figure 1–16. The option group should use the macros you created to preview and export the two reports. Change the background color of the forms to light gray (Column 1, Row 2 on the color palette).

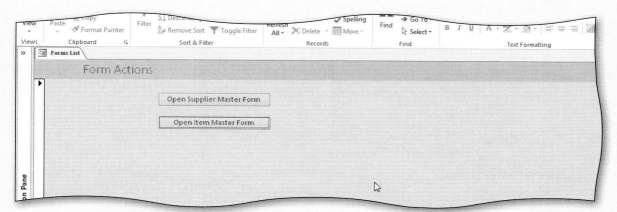

Figure 1–15

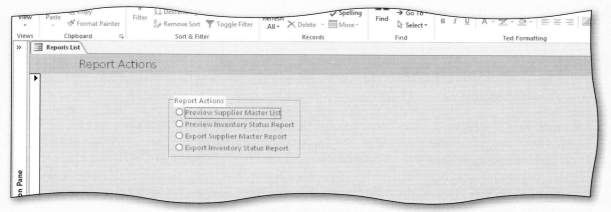

Figure 1–16

Create a datasheet form for the Item table and name the form Item. Create a UI macro for the Item form. When a user taps or clicks an item number on a row from the Datasheet, the Item Master Form should appear in a pop-up form. Create a datasheet form for the Supplier table and name the form Supplier. Create a UI macro for the Supplier form. When a user taps or clicks a supplier code on a row from the Datasheet, the Supplier Master Form should appear in a pop-up form.

Continued >

Create the navigation form shown in Figure 1–17. The navigation form has a left vertical layout. The form name is Starrs Main Menu and the title of the form is Starrs Apparel. The Item tab should display the Item datasheet form and the Supplier tab should display the Supplier datasheet form. The Forms tab should display the form shown in Figure 1–15 on the previous page. The Reports tab should display the form shown in Figure 1–16 on the previous page.

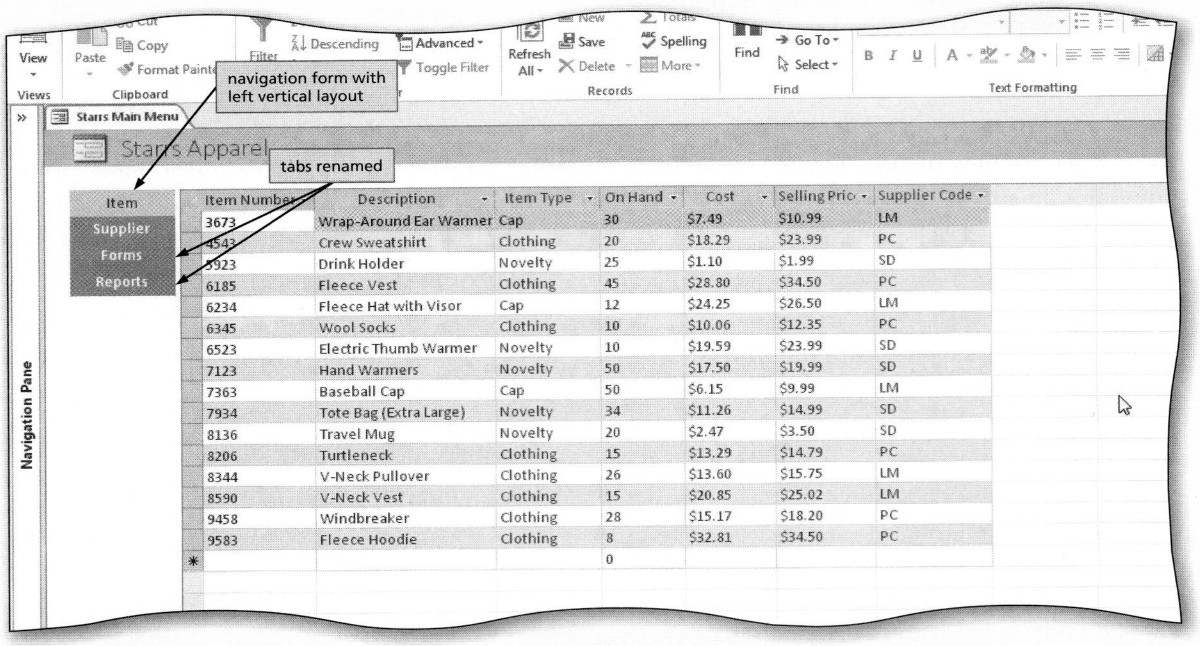

Figure 1–17

Instructions Part 2: Julie would like to improve the data entry process by adding some validation rules, input masks, and indexes to the database. Create a custom input mask for the Item Number field in the Item and Reorder tables. Create a custom input mask for the Supplier Code field in the Item and Supplier tables. Do not allow zero-length strings in the Description and Supplier Name fields. Create an index on the combination of item type and description and name the index TypeDesc.

Change the Current Database options to ensure that the navigation form opens automatically. Add the Priority Quick Start field to the end of the Reorder table.

Instructions Part 3: Because of the large volume of sales and rentals, the Rental Center is considering moving from Access to SQL Server, which is a database management system that can handle large amounts of data. Julie would like to gain some understanding of SQL to help in the decision-making process. She has asked you to create five queries in SQL that will illustrate some of the features of SQL. Create the following queries for Julie. Save each query using a format similar to the following: SQL Query a, SQL Query b, and so on.

a. Display the item number, description, and inventory value (on hand * cost) for all items. Name the computed field Inventory Value.

b. Find all items where the description includes the word, fleece. Include the item number and description in the result.

c. Display the supplier name, item number, description, and selling price for all items where the number on hand is greater than 30. Sort the results in ascending order by supplier name and description.

d. Find the average cost by supplier. Name the computed field Avg Cost. Include the supplier code in the result.

e. Display the item number, description, number on hand, and selling price for all items where the selling price is under $15.00 and the number on hand is fewer than 15.

If requested to do so by your instructor, change the supplier name for supplier code LM to your first and last name. Save your changes to the database and submit the database in the format specified by your instructor.

Instructions Part 4: Julie is concerned that relying on one supplier for a particular item could result in inventory shortages. How would the current database design for Starrs Apparel need to change if more than one supplier supplied the same item? Use the database design shorthand representation to list the complete database design for Starrs given this change. Submit the design in the format specified by your instructor.

Outlook Capstone Project 1

Creating and Managing Tasks for Starrs Mountain Resort

Problem: Starrs recently purchased a computerized ski lift maintenance software system. The system will help Starrs schedule maintenance tasks, maintain accurate inventory records, and perform other tasks necessary to keep the ski lifts operating efficiently and safely. There are a number of tasks involved with the installation of the new system and you will use Outlook to keep track of these tasks.

Instructions Part 1: Create a Tasks folder named Ski Lift Tasks. Create regular tasks in this folder using the information listed in Table 1–1. Create recurring tasks using the information listed in Table 1–2. Submit the Ski Lift Tasks in the format specified by your instructor.

Table 1–1 Ski Lift Tasks				
Task	**Start Date**	**Due Date**	**Status**	**Priority**
Install new computers	10/20/2014	10/22/2014		High
Train associates	10/6/2014	11/3/2014	In progress	High
Install software	10/23/2014	10/23/2014		High
Test new system	10/27/2014	10/31/2014		High
Recycle old computers	10/17/2014	12/15/2014		Low

© 2014 Cengage Learning

Table 1–2 Ski Lift Recurring Tasks			
Task	**Start Date**	**Due Date**	**Recurrence**
Run maintenance reports	11/3/2014	11/1/2017	Weekly, Fridays
Perform software updates	12/10/2014	12/10/2017	Monthly, second Wednesday

© 2014 Cengage Learning

Instructions Part 2: You are using Outlook on a daily basis and realize it would be more professional to create a custom signature that reflects your position at Starrs. Create a signature named Starrs and change the font to Arial and the font size to 14. On three lines, enter the following information: your name, Starrs Mountain Resort, and your email address. Set the signature to apply to new messages, replies, and forwards. Select the Ice theme as your personal stationery. Send a message to your instructor to display your new signature and stationery.

Submit the email message in the format specified by your instructor.

Continued >

Outlook Capstone Project 1 *continued*

CRITICAL THINKING

How should you submit solutions to questions in the assignments identified with a symbol?

Every assignment in this book contains one or more questions identified with a symbol. These questions require you to think beyond the assigned database. Present your solutions to the questions in the format required by your instructor. Possible formats may include one or more of these options: write the answer; create a document that contains the answer; present your answer to the class; discuss your answer in a group; record the answer as audio or video using a webcam, smartphone, or portable media player; or post answers on a blog, wiki, or website.

1. You created a memo that linked an Excel worksheet to the Word document. What other methods could you use to incorporate an Excel worksheet in a Word document?

2. What are the advantages to creating and using a custom template for an organization such as Starrs? Are there any disadvantages?

3. What is the purpose of the Recommended PivotTables button? Could you have used the button to create the PivotTable in Figure 1–9 on page CAP 11?

4. Why is the primary key for the Reorder table in the Starrs Apparel database composed of both Item Number and Reorder Date?

5. What other information would you include in a custom signature for a business, such as Starrs?

Capstone Project 2: TechConnections

The Capstone Project consists of an integrated, comprehensive set of problems related to a single scenario. Students apply concepts and skills presented in this book to create solutions to the problems using Word, PowerPoint, Excel, Access, and Outlook.

TechConnections provides information technology training workshops for organizations and individuals. The workshops deliver training in Microsoft Office and other IT topics. TechConnections employs trainers who work with clients to determine training needs and then conduct training. The company is known for targeting training to specific business needs. You are doing an internship at TechConnections and work for the Manager of Training Services, Phil Maris.

Note: To complete this assignment, you will be required to use the Data Files for Students. Visit www.cengage.com/ct/studentdownload for detailed instructions or contact your instructor for information about accessing the required files.

Word Capstone Project 2

Creating a Reference Document, Modifying an Online Survey, Creating Macros
Problem: Phil has asked you to create a reference document that provides an Overview of Office 365. He also would like to modify an online survey that attendees complete after a class.

Instructions Part 1: Open the Cap 2 Office 365 Draft from the Data Files for Students. Save the document with the file name, Cap 2 Office 365 Subdocument. Change the theme to Slate.

Add a screenshot for Office365.com after the last sentence of the document. Then, add the following captions to the figures: first figure - Figure 1: Office 2013 and Office 365 Feature Comparison; second figure - Figure 2: Lync Communications Program; third figure - Figure 3: Office 365 Website. Replace the three occurrences of XX in the document with cross-references to the figure showing labels and numbers only.

Insert an Ion Sidebar 2 text box on the first page. Enter the text shown in Figure 2 – 1 in the text box. Format the second question the same as the first. On the next page, insert another Ion Sidebar 2 text box and delete the contents of the second text box. Link the two boxes together. Resize each text box so that each one contains just one question and answer. Move the first text box to the top of the first page and the second text box to the bottom of the second page.

Mark the following entries in the document: Outlook, Click-to-Run, Office on Demand, and Lync Web Apps as index entries. If there is more than one entry, mark only the first occurrence. Save and close the document.

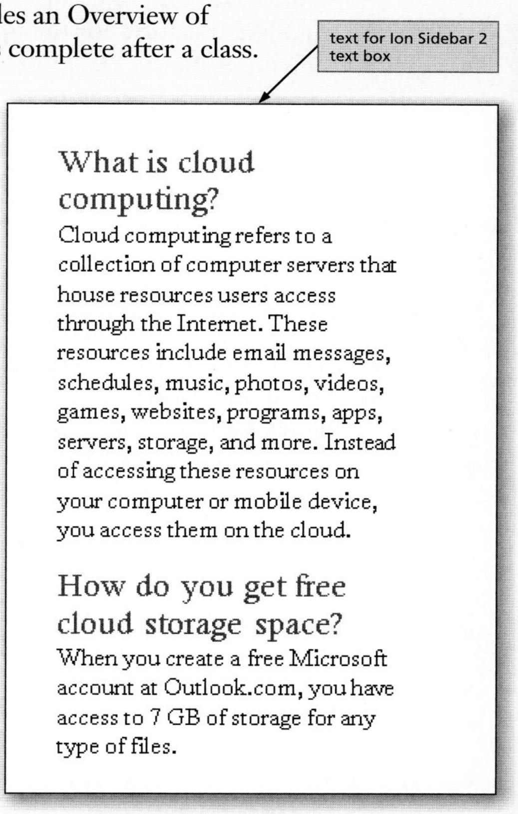

text for Ion Sidebar 2 text box

What is cloud computing?

Cloud computing refers to a collection of computer servers that house resources users access through the Internet. These resources include email messages, schedules, music, photos, videos, games, websites, programs, apps, servers, storage, and more. Instead of accessing these resources on your computer or mobile device, you access them on the cloud.

How do you get free cloud storage space?

When you create a free Microsoft account at Outlook.com, you have access to 7 GB of storage for any type of files.

Figure 2–1

Create a new document and change the theme to Slate. In Outline view, type `Copyright 2015` as the first line formatted as Body Text. Type `TechConnections` as the second line formatted as Body Text. Add two more lines containing the headings `Table of Figures` and `Index`. Insert a next page section break between each line. Save the master document with the name Cap 2 Office 365 Reference Document.

Between the Copyright line and Table of Figures heading, insert the subdocument named Cap 2 Office 365 Subdocument. Be sure that the subdocument and the master document are in the same directory.

In Print Layout view, create a cover page by inserting the Ion (Light) style cover page. Use the following information on the cover page: title – Office 365 Overview; subtitle – CLOUD COMPUTING; author – use your name. Format the copyright page with a vertical alignment of Justified. Insert a blank page between the copyright page and the heading, Office 365 Overview.

Create a table of contents on the blank page using the Distinctive style, right-aligned page numbers, and dots for leader characters. At the end of the document, create a table of figures. Use the Formal format with right-aligned page numbers and dots for leader characters. Build an index for the document. Use the Formal format in two columns with right-aligned page numbers.

Beginning on the fourth page (with the heading, Office 365 Overview), create a footer. Insert the Banded page number style. The cover page, copyright page, and table of contents should not contain the footer.

Delete Figure 2 and the reference to the figure in the preceding paragraph. The sentence that previously began "As shown in Figure 2," should now begin with "You can . . . .". Update the table of contents, cross references, List of Figures, and Index. A miniature version of the finished document is shown in Figure 2–2.

Save the document and submit the document in the format specified by your instructor.

Instructions Part 2: In the next few months, TechConnections will teach several workshops on Office 2013. Phil has a survey form that has been used previously for workshops. He has asked you to update this form for the upcoming workshops. Open the Cap 2 TechConnections Survey 2010 template from the Data Files for Students and unprotect the template.

Change the theme to Slate and change the page color to Tan, Accent 3, Lighter, 40%. Change the text, IT Training, to Office 2013 Training, as shown in Figure 2–3 on page CAP 22. Change the shape fill color of the rectangle to Tan, Accent 3, Lighter 80%. Add a Circle Bevel shape effect. Change the font color of the email link and the last sentence (Thank you) to Brown, Accent 1, Darker 25%.

Replace the computer images with the tablet image from the Data Files for Students. Group the images together and change the color to Brown, Accent Color 1 Dark.

Change the labels for the Check Box content control to those shown on Figure 2–3. Change the Title property for each Check Box content control to match the corresponding labels. Replace the values in the Drop-Down List area of the Course content control with the values shown in Figure 2–4 on page CAP 22. Move the Access item so that it appears after Excel in the list.

Save the survey template as Cap 2 TechConnections Survey 2015. If requested to do so by your instructor, replace the email address on the form with your own email address. Protect the modified template. Submit the form in the format specified by your instructor.

Instructions Part 3: Phil has asked you to add two macros to the online survey form. Open the Cap 2 TechConnections Survey 2015 template that you previously modified and unprotect the document. Record a macro that hides the formatting marks and rulers. Name it HideScreenElements and assign it to a button. Test the macro button and then delete the button from the Quick Access Toolbar. Create an automatic macro called AutoNew using the macro recorder. The macro should change the view to page width. Edit the AutoNew macro so that it also hides the DEVELOPER tab. Protect the form.

Save the template as a macro-enabled template with the name Cap 2 TechConnections Survey 2015 macro. Submit the template in the format specified by your instructor.

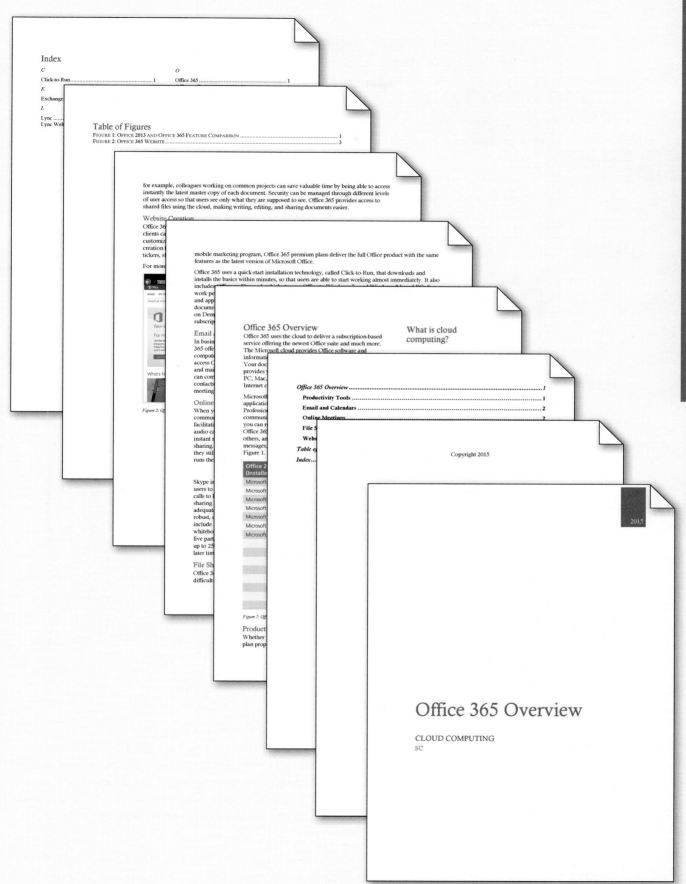

Index

Table of Figures

for example, colleagues working on common projects can save valuable time by being able to access instantly the latest master copy of each document. Security can be managed through different levels of user access so that users see only what they are supposed to see. Office 365 provides access to shared files using the cloud, making writing, editing, and sharing documents easier.

Website Creation

Office 36
clients ca
customiz
creation
tickers, s

For more

mobile marketing program, Office 365 premium plans deliver the full Office product with the same features as the latest version of Microsoft Office.

Office 365 uses a quick-start installation technology, called Click-to-Run, that downloads and installs the basics within minutes, so that users are able to start working almost immediately. It also
includes

work pe
and app
docume
on Dem
subscrip

Email a
In busin
365 offe
comput
access O
and mai
can com
contacts
meeting

Office 365 Overview
Office 365 uses the cloud to deliver a subscription-based service offering the newest Office suite and much more. The Microsoft cloud provides Office software and informati
Your doc
provides
PC, Mac,
Internet c

What is cloud computing?

Online
When y
commu
facilitati
audio ca
instant r
sharing.
they still
runs the

Microsoft
applicatio
Professio
communi
you can r
Office 365
others, an
messages,
Figure 1.

Copyright 2015

Skype is
users to
calls to
sharing
adequat
robust,
include
whitebo
five par
up to 25
later tim

File Sh
Office 36
difficult

Figure 1: Of

Product
Whether
plan prop

Office 365 Overview

CLOUD COMPUTING
SC

2015

Figure 2–2

Continued >

Word Capstone Project 2 *continued*

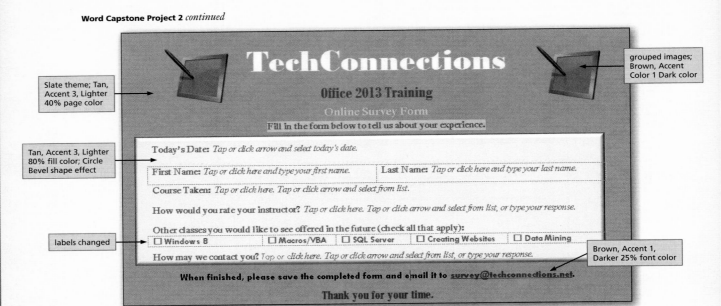

Figure 2–3

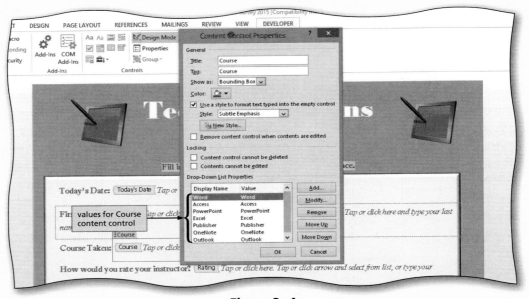

Figure 2–4

PowerPoint Capstone Project 2

Organizing Slides, Creating a Photo Album, and Creating a Postcard

Problem: TechConnections has a new client, a small travel agency that specializes in adventure tours with a maximum of 10 people per tour. Previously, the client used the services of a marketing company to prepare presentations and brochures. The travel agency would like to learn how to create their own presentations to showcase their tour destinations. One of your colleagues recently returned from a trip to Ecuador and suggested that you use her photos to create a presentation that can be used for the PowerPoint training sessions.

Instructions Part 1: Open the Cap 2 Ecuador presentation from the Data Files for Students. Select Slide 1 (Figure 2–5a), create a new Slide 2 that is a duplicate of Slide 1, change the layout to Section Header, and then change the artistic effect for each picture on the slide to Cement. Create two new slides that are duplicates of Slide 2. Add the titles shown in Figures 2–5b, 2–5c, and 2–5d on the next page to Slides 2, 3, and 4. Format the titles as 60-point Broadway font, Shadow text effect, Gold, Accent 4, Lighter 40% font color. Position the titles as shown on the slides. There are now 18 slides in the presentation.

(a) Title Slide

(b) Section Slide Equator (new Slide 2)

(c) Section Slide Amazon

Figure 2–5

Continued >

PowerPoint Capstone Project 2 *continued*

60-point Broadway font; Shadow text effect; Gold, Accent 4, Lighter 40% font color; section title

Courtesy of Mary Last

(d) Section Slide Galapagos
Figure 2–5 (Continued)

Move Slide 3 so that it follows the slides for the Equator. The Equator slides have a gold background. Move Slide 4 so that it follows the slides for the Amazon. The Amazon slides have a green background. Add a section break between Slides 1 and 2. Add another section break before the Amazon slides and another section break before the Galapagos slides. Rename the four sections as Ecuador Travel, Equator, Amazon, and Galapagos. Reorder the sections as shown in Figure 2–6.

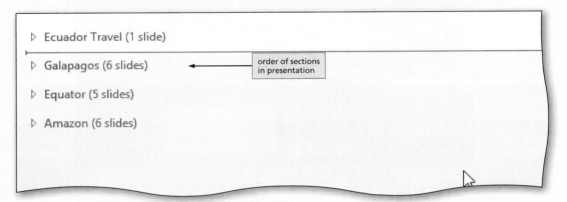

▷ Ecuador Travel (1 slide)

▷ Galapagos (6 slides) ← order of sections in presentation

▷ Equator (5 slides)

▷ Amazon (6 slides)

Figure 2–6

Create a custom slide show that includes Slide 1 and all slides in the Galapagos section. Name the custom show as Cap 2 Galapagos Favorites. Copy the custom slide show and edit the copy by moving Slide 6 so that it follows Slide 3. Rename the copy as Cap 2 Galapagos Favorites Reordered.

Save the presentation using the file name, Cap 2 Ecuador Travel and submit the file in the format specified by your instructor.

Instructions Part 2: Your colleague gave you some wonderful photos of Galapagos birds. Create a new photo album and add the bird photos from the Data Files for Students. Move the Pelican, Heron, and Greater Flamingo photos to positions 9, 10, and 11 respectively. Move the Magnificent Frigate birds photo above the Magnificent Frigate bird and baby and move the Nazca Boobie birds photo above the Nazca Boobie bird and chicks. Select the Magnificent Frigate birds photo and increase the brightness by tapping or clicking the Increase Brightness button two times. For the same photo, increase the contrast by tapping or clicking the Increase Contrast button two times. Change the layout so that only one picture appears on a slide, add a simple white frame as the frame layout, and change the theme to Slice. Add a caption below all pictures and create the photo album.

Edit the photo album to change the frame style to rounded rectangle. Add a text box to the album and position the text box as Slide 1, and then update the photo album.

Apply the Wind transition effect to all slides with a 3-second duration. Change the title and subtitle text on Slide 1 as shown in Figure 2–7a. Increase the font size of the subtitle to 48 point, change the character spacing to very loose, and the font color to white. If requested to do so by your instructor, add your name to the subtitle.

On Slide 2, enter the text shown in Figure 2–7b. Replace the word, baby, in the caption on Slide 7 with the word, chick.

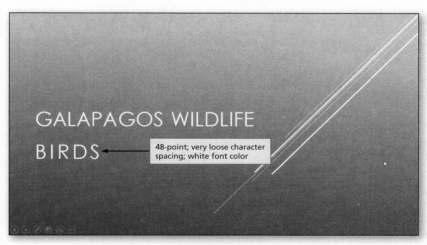

(a) Slide 1

(b) Slide 2

Figure 2–7

Save the presentation as Cap 2 Galapagos Birds Photo Album and submit the photo album in the format specified by your instructor.

Instructions Part 3: The travel agency would like to create invitations for travel talks. Open the Cap 2 Galapagos Giant Tortoise presentation from the Data Files for Students and change the size of the slide to 5" × 7" with a portrait orientation. Add a second text box below the picture and

Continued >

enter the text shown in Figure 2–8. Use Cooper Black font with a 20-point font size for the first text box and an 18-point font size for the second text box. Move the text boxes and image to match that shown in Figure 2–8. If requested to do so by your instructor, replace the text in the bottom text box with your name.

Save the presentation as Cap 2 Galapagos Giant Tortoise Invitation and submit it in the format specified by your instructor.

Figure 2–8

Excel Capstone Project 2

Working with PivotTables, PivotCharts, Slicers, Solver, and Macros

Problem: Telton-Edwards manufactures turf care products for both the commercial and retail markets. The company, a client of TechConnections, needs some help with Excel. Marketing would like to create a PivotTable and PivotChart to analyze sales data. Production needs some help with scheduling production of its mowers. Phil has asked you to prepare some sample worksheets using data and information that Telton-Edwards has provided.

Instructions Part 1: Open the Cap 2 TechConnections PivotTable Data workbook from the Data Files for Students and create a blank PivotTable report. Add the Product field to the ROWS area and then add the Sales Associate field to the ROWS area. Add the 2014 Sales field and the 2015 Sales field to the VALUES area. Change the layout of the report to Tabular and repeat all item labels.

Filter the table by State and select MI as the filter criterion. Drag the Product field from the ROW area to the FILTERS area. Drag the State field from the FILTERS area to the ROWS area. Filter the table for leaf blowers and trimmers. Remove all filters. Use a filter for the State ROWS field to filter records for IN and IL only, then remove the filter.

Remove the Sales Associate field from the PivotTable and add the Product field to the ROWS area.

Rename Sheet1 as Sales PivotTable and change the tab color to Orange, Accent 2, Darker 25%. Format the PivotTable with Pivot Style Dark 3 PivotTable style. Format the Sales values as currency with 0 decimal places.

The PivotTable currently displays the sum of the 2014 sales and 2015 sales. Change the summary function to display the average of 2014 sales and 2015 sales. Add the total value calculations for 2014 and 2015 sales, change the field headers, and format the values as currency with 0 decimal places as shown in Figure 2–9. Add the title and subtitle shown in Figure 2–9. Change the font color to Orange, Accent 2, Darker 50%. Apply the Title style to the title and the Heading 4 style to the subtitle. Apply the Orange, Accent 2, Lighter 80% fill color. Save the workbook as Cap 2 TechConnections Sales PivotTable Report.

State	Product	Total 2014 Sales	Total 2015 Sales	Average 2014 Sales	Average 2015 Sales
IL	Leaf Blower	$9,375	$14,610	$3,125	$4,870
IL	Shredder/Vac	$21,925	$18,440	$7,308	$6,147
IL	Trimmer	$13,150	$17,630	$4,383	$5,877
IL Total		$44,450	$50,680	$4,939	$5,631
IN	Leaf Blower	$18,600	$20,675	$6,200	$6,892
IN	Shredder/Vac	$26,900	$26,570	$8,967	$8,857
IN	Trimmer	$17,600	$20,690	$5,867	$6,897
IN Total		$63,100	$67,935	$7,011	$7,548
MI	Leaf Blower	$23,900	$22,550	$7,967	$7,517
MI	Shredder/Vac	$22,850	$28,050	$7,617	$9,350
MI	Trimmer	$32,575	$32,875	$10,858	$10,958
MI Total		$79,325	$83,475	$8,814	$9,275
OH	Leaf Blower	$25,800	$24,300	$8,600	$8,100
OH	Shredder/Vac	$25,500	$31,000	$8,500	$10,333
OH	Trimmer	$36,500	$34,200	$12,167	$11,400
OH Total		$87,800	$89,500	$9,756	$9,944
Grand Total		$274,675	$291,590	$7,630	$8,100

Telton-Edwards Sales Report — 2014 and 2015

Pivot Style Dark 3 PivotTable style; numbers formatted as currency with 0 decimal places

Figure 2–9

Create a 3-D Clustered Column PivotChart for the PivotTable and move the chart to a new sheet. Name the sheet Sales PivotChart Report and change the tab color of the sheet to Gold, Accent 4, Darker 25%. Remove the average sales data from the PivotChart report and the PivotTable report. Format the data series as cylinders. Add the chart title shown in Figure 2–10 and change the font color to Orange, Accent 2, Darker 50% and bold the title. Move the Product field before the State field in the ROWS area. Save the workbook as Cap 2 TechConnections Sales PivotChart Report.

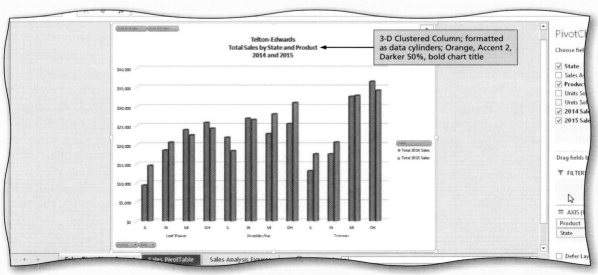

Figure 2–10

Continued >

Excel Capstone Project 2 *continued*

Display the Sales Analysis Figures worksheet, change the value in cell D3 to 9, change the value in cell F3 to 2250, and refresh the PivotTable.

Calculate the average sale for 2014 (2014 sales/units sold 2014) and the average sale for 2015. Change the field names for the calculated fields to those shown in Figure 2–11. Format the average sale fields as Currency with 2 decimal places. Change the subtitle for the worksheet to that shown in Figure 2–11. Remove the 2014 Sales and 2015 Sales fields from the PivotTable. Change the width of column A to 16 pixels. Change the report layout so that item labels do not repeat.

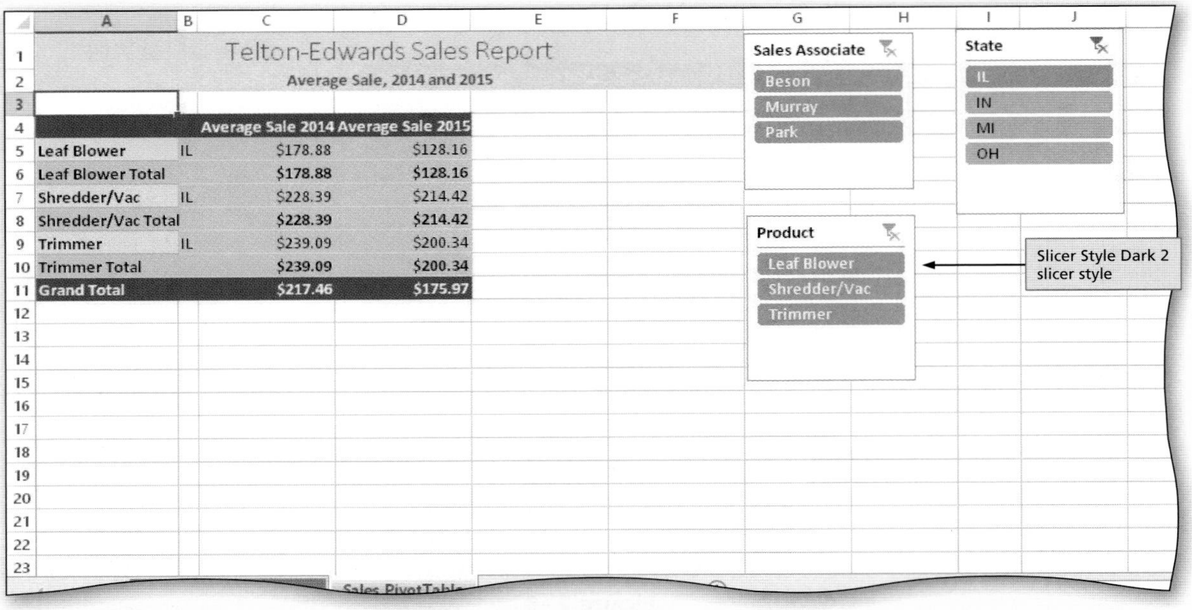

Figure 2–11

Add slicers for the State, Product, and Sales Associate fields and resize the slicers as shown in Figure 2–11. Change the button height for the three slicers to .2 and the button width to 1.3. Apply the Slicer Style Dark 2 style to the slicers. Use the State slicer to filter the PivotTable for IL. If requested to do so by your instructor, enter your name in cell A3. Save the workbook as Cap 2 TechConnections Sales PivotTable Slicer Report.

Submit the three workbooks in the format specified by your instructor.

Instructions Part 2:   Telton-Edwards would like to use Solver to schedule production of its mowers. The company produces four types of mowers and each type requires a different amount of labor input and a different amount of materials to produce a single mower. Telton-Edwards would like to determine the best mix of mowers to produce based on the amount of labor and materials available for a given week. Sales of electric and power lawn mowers are declining, so Telton-Edwards wants to produce a maximum of 25 of each of these units per week. The company wants to produce a maximum of 70 of each of the two styles of riding tractors.

Open the Cap 2 TechConnections Solver Data workbook and use Solver to determine the mix of products that maximizes the number of units produced in a week. The total number of labor hours available for the week is 5,800 and $60,000 worth of material is available. Use the Assume Linear Model option and instruct Solver to create an Answer Report if it finds a solution to the problem. Figure 2–12 shows the values Solver should find. Rename the Answer Report as Production Schedule Report and change its tab color to Brown, Accent 4, Darker 25%.

	A	B	C	D	E	F	G
2		**Telton-Edwards**					
3		**Production Planning**					
4		Electric Lawn Mower	Power Lawn Mower	Riding Garden Tractor	Riding Lawn Tractor		
5	Hours of Labor per Unit	34	45	50	69		
6	Cost of Material per Unit	$132	$216	$547	$653		
7						Totals	
8	Units to Manufacture	25	25	35	30	115	
9							
10	Total Hours for the Week	850	1,125	1,755	2,070	5,800	
11	Total Cost of Material for the Week	$3,300	$5,400	$19,200	$19,590	$47,490	
12							
13							
14							
15							

Figure 2–12

If requested to do so by your instructor, add your name to the text in cell A2 on the Production Planning worksheet. Save the workbook as Cap 2 TechConnections Solver Solution. Submit the workbook in the format specified by your instructor.

Instructions Part 3: Harrison National Bank, a TechConnections client, currently uses a loan calculator to assist bank customers requesting loans. The bank would like to automate the process of calculating monthly payments. Phil has asked you to automate the loan data entry process.

Open the Cap 2 TechConnections Loan Calculator from the Data Files for Students and save the workbook as a macro-enabled workbook using the file name, Cap 2 TechConnections Loan Calculator Automated. If necessary, add the DEVELOPER tab to the ribbon and change the macro settings to enable all macros. Before creating the macro to automate the data entry, you need to review the formulas in the worksheet. Select cell H8 and trace the precedents and the dependents for the cell. Trace the precedents for cell D5. Review the formulas and the values and then remove the arrows.

Add the command button ActiveX control to the worksheet in the position shown in Figure 2–13. Change the following properties for the button: (a) Caption = Enter Loan Data; (b) Font = 11-pt, bold, Calisto MT; (c) PrintObject = False; (d) WordWrap = True. Enter the procedure shown in Table 2–1 on the next page in the VBA code window. Check your code carefully.

	A	B	C	D	EF	G	H	I	J	K	L
1		**Harrison National Bank**									
2		**Interest Rate Schedule**				**Loan Payment Calculator**					
3											
4		Monthly Payment	Total Cost	Total Interest		Used Car					
5	Interest	$383.64	$18,414.75	$1,423.75		Loan amount	$16,991.00				
6	4.00%	383.64	18,414.75	1,423.75		Interest rate	4.00%				
7	4.50%	387.45	18,597.79	1,606.79		Months	48				
8	5.00%	391.29	18,781.95	1,790.95		Monthly payment	$383.64				
9	5.50%	395.15	18,967.24	1,976.24							
10	6.00%	399.03	19,153.64	2,162.64							
11	6.50%	402.94	19,341.16	2,350.16							
12	7.00%	406.87	19,529.79	2,538.79							
13											
14											
15											
16											
17		Enter Loan Data			←	location for ActiveX control					
18											

Figure 2–13

Continued >

Excel Capstone Project 2 *continued*

Table 2–1 Enter Loan Data Button Procedure

Line	Statement
1	'Enter Loan Data Procedure
2	'Date Created: 2/2/2015
3	'Tap or click the Enter Loan Data button on the Loan Calculator worksheet to enter new loan data.
4	
5	Private Sub CommandButton1_Click()
6	Range("G4,H5:H7").ClearContents
7	Range("A1").Select
8	Range("Loan_Purpose").Value = InputBox("Loan Purpose?", "Enter")
9	Range("Loan_Amount").Value = InputBox("Loan Amount Needed?", "Enter")
10	Range("Interest_Rate").Value = (InputBox("Interest Rate entered as a number only, no%", "Enter")) / 100
11	Range("Months").Value = InputBox("Number of Months?", "Enter")
12	
13	End Sub

Use the Enter Loan Data command button to display monthly payments for the following data: (a) Loan Purpose = Used Car; (b) Loan Amount = $16,991; (c) Interest Rate = 4.00%; (d) Months = 48. Change the macro settings to 'Disable all macros with notification'. Protect the worksheet using the password, Harrison. Save the workbook again, close the workbook, and submit the workbook in the format specified by your instructor.

Open the Cap 2 TechConnections Loan Calculator Automated workbook and unprotect the workbook using the password, Harrison. Enable all macros and, if necessary, add the DEVELOPER tab to the ribbon. Draw a command button using the Button Form Control (not the ActiveX control) in the position shown in Figure 2–14. Assign a macro to the button that copies the loan calculator values to a new worksheet. Use the name copyresults for the macro and store the macro in this workbook. The macro should copy the cell range A4:H12 to a new worksheet, paste the values and source formatting to cell range A4:H12, and keep the source column widths. Change the caption for the command button to Copy Results and bold the text. Select both buttons and set the height to .5" and the width to 1.0" and top align the buttons. Apply the Brown, Accent 1, Lighter 80% fill color to the cell range A16:D18. Remove the gridlines from the workbook.

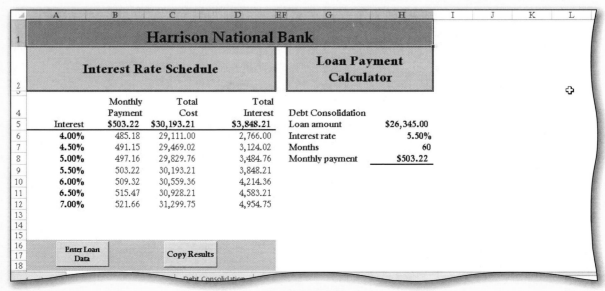

Figure 2–14

Use the Enter Loan Data command button to display monthly payments for the following data: (a) Loan Purpose = Debt Consolidation; (b) Loan Amount = $26,345; (c) Interest Rate = 5.50%; (d) Months = 60. Use the Copy Results button to copy the results to a new worksheet. Rename Sheet 1 as Used Car and rename Sheet 2 as Debt Consolidation. If requested to do so by your instructor, rename the Loan Calculator worksheet with your first and last name.

Save the workbook as a macro-enabled workbook with the name Cap 2 TechConnections Loan Calculator Automated Copyresults and protect the workbook using the password, Harrison. Submit the workbook in the format specified by your instructor.

Access Capstone Project 2

Macros, Navigation Forms, Database Administration, Using SQL, and Database Design

Problem: TechConnections has contracts with several businesses and organizations that require training and/or information technology help on a regular basis. TechConnections stores the data about these clients in a database. Phil Maris has asked you to modify the database to make it easier to maintain and update.

Instructions Part 1: Open the Cap 2 TechConnections database from the Data Files for Students and create a macro named Forms and Reports that will include submacros to perform the following tasks:

a. Open the Client Update Form

b. Open the Trainer Master Form

c. Open the Trainer Class Data form in read-only mode

d. Preview the Client Financial Report

e. Preview the Clients by Trainer Report

f. Preview Trainer Master List

g. Export the Client Financial Report in PDF format

h. Export the Clients by Trainer Report in PDF format

i. Export the Trainer Master List in PDF format

Create the menu forms shown in Figure 2–15 and 2–16 on the next page. The option group on the Forms List form should use the macros you created to open the three forms. The option group on the Reports List form should use the macros you created to preview and export the three reports. Bold the label for the option group on each form.

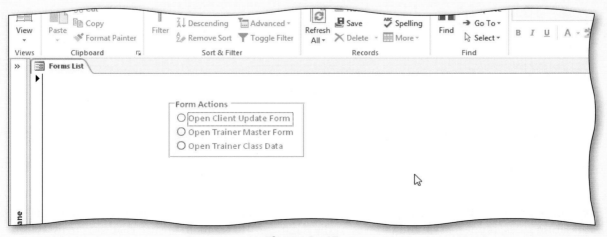

Figure 2–15

Continued >

Access Capstone Project 2 *continued*

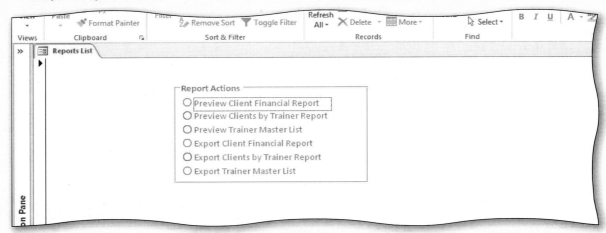

Figure 2–16

Create a datasheet form for the Client table and name the form Client. Create a UI macro for the Client form. When a user taps or clicks a client number on a row in the datasheet, the Client Update Form should appear in a pop-up form. Create a datasheet form for the Trainer table and name the form Trainer. Create a UI macro for the Trainer form. When a user taps or clicks a trainer number on a row in the datasheet, the Trainer Master Form should appear in a pop-up form.

Create the navigation form shown in Figure 2–17. The navigation form has a Horizontal Tabs layout. The form name is Main Menu and the title of the form is TechConnections. The Trainer tab should display the Trainer datasheet form and the Client tab should display the Client datasheet form. The Forms tab should display the form shown in Figure 2–15 on the previous page. The Reports tab should display the form shown in Figure 2–16.

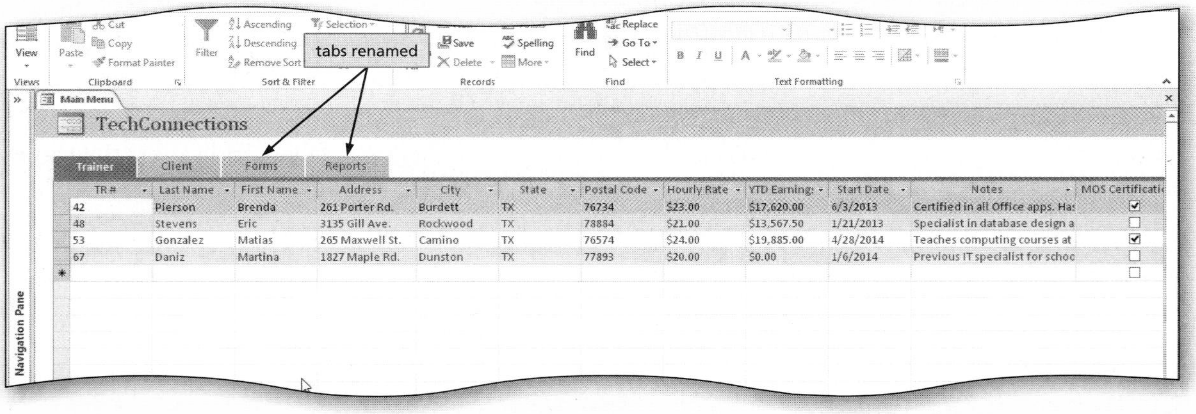

Figure 2–17

Create a data macro for the Class Offerings table. The macro will examine the value in the Hours Spent field. If the user's update would cause the value to be greater than the Total Hours, the macro will change the value to Total Hours. If the user's update would cause the value to be less than 0, the macro will change the value to 0.

Instructions Part 2: Phil would like to improve the data entry process by adding some additional validation rules, input masks, and indexes to the database. He wants to ensure that the client number field in the Client and Class Offerings table always contains two uppercase letters followed by two numeric digits. Also, he noticed that errors are occurring because text is being entered in the Postal Code field in the Client table instead of numbers. In addition, empty strings should not be allowed in the Client Name field. An index on the Client Name field and an index on the combination of the client type and client name would speed retrieval. Make these changes to the database for Phil.

Phil also would like the Main Menu navigation form to appear when the database is opened. He also would like to populate the Status database property with the value, Current Version, and create a custom property named Backup Date with a data type of Date. Populate the Backup Date property with the current date. If requested to do so by your instructor, populate the Status property with your own name as the value.

Add a validation rule to the Class table. The rule should ensure that the value in the Increments field is equal to or less than the value in the Hours field. Save the changes to the design of the table.

Instructions Part 3:   Phil wants you to learn more about SQL so you can handle some additional assignments for TechConnections. He has created several questions that he would like you to answer using SQL. Create the queries and save each query using a format similar to the following: SQL Query a, SQL Query b, and so on.

a. Display the Client Number, Client Name, Amount Paid, and Current Due amounts for all clients located in cities that start with the letter C.

b. Display the Client Number, Client Name, Amount Paid, and Current Due amounts for all clients with a current due amount of $0.00 and an amount paid amount of $0.00.

c. Display the Client Number, Client Name, and the Total Amount (the sum of current due and amount paid) for all clients.

d. Display the Client Number and Client Name for all clients with a client type other than MAN.

e. Display the Trainer Number, Last Name, Client Number, Client Name, and Amount Paid fields for all clients whose client type is MAN. Sort the records in ascending order by trainer number and client number.

f. In which cities does TechConnections have clients? List each city only once in alphabetical order.

g. How many clients are assigned to trainer number 48?

h. What is the total amount paid amount and total current due amount for all clients grouped by trainer? Assign Sum Paid and Sum Due as the names for calculations.

Save your changes to the database and submit the database in the format specified by your instructor.

Instructions Part 4:   TechConnections is growing, and management now has difficulty assigning a single trainer to a client. Phil needs the flexibility of being able to assign multiple trainers to various clients based on specialties and skills. After reviewing records for class offerings, he also believes the total hours in the Class Offerings table and the hours in the Class table always should be the same. Use the database design shorthand representation to list the complete database design for TechConnections given these two changes. Submit the design in the format specified by your instructor.

Outlook Capstone Project 2

Creating Tasks, Notes, and Custom Signatures

Problem: TechConnections partners with the library on a volunteer basis to offer classes to the public at little or no cost. Phil Maris is pleased with the work you are doing at TechConnections. He knows you are interested in either IT training or teaching after graduation and has asked if you would like to teach a workshop on online job resources at the local library. Courses are designed

Continued >

to help the unemployed and underemployed improve their computer skills. Because so many companies require job applicants to submit resumes online and complete online applications, the library has asked for a class on the topic.

Instructions Part 1: You need to create a list of all your tasks for the workshop and categorize them appropriately. Create a Tasks folder named Workshop Tasks. Create the tasks in the Workshop Tasks folder using the information listed in Table 2–2. Create a category named Class Preparation with a new color category and include the following tasks: Research online job resources, Organize presentation, and Create handouts. Categorize the remaining tasks as Administrative by creating a new color category. If requested to do so by your instructor, rename the Administrative category as your first and last name. Print the tasks in Table Style, and then submit the task list in the format specified by your instructor.

Table 2–2 Workshop Tasks

Task	Start Date	Due Date	Status	Priority
Meet with library manager		2/5/2105	Deferred	Normal
Check library facilities		2/20/2015	Not Started	Normal
Prepare workshop registration form		2/4/2015	Completed	Normal
Research online job resources	2/2/2015	2/16/2015	In Progress	High
Organize presentation	2/2/2015	2/19/2015	Not Started	High
Create handouts	2/2/2015	2/20/2015	Not Started	High
Contact attendees		2/20/2015	Not Started	Low

© 2014 Cengage Learning

You have decided on a topic for your library workshop. Collect relevant information as notes in Outlook. Some of these notes refer to questions you want to ask attendees prior to the workshop and others are items to research for the workshop. You indicate which notes are for research and which notes are for attendees in the Purpose column. Create the notes shown in Table 2–3 and categorize them appropriately. Print the notes list and submit in the format specified by your instructor.

Table 2–3 Workshop Notes

Note	Purpose
Do attendees have an email account?	Attendees
What resources does library offer?	Research
Do attendees have a resume?	Attendees
What listings are online for local jobs?	Research

© 2014 Cengage Learning

Instructions Part 2: Because you will be communicating with the library manager and others about the workshop, you want to create a signature that will identify you clearly as an employee of TechConnections rather than as a student intern. Create two signatures, one to use when you send email messages to other colleagues at TechConnections and another for email messages you send about the workshop. Name one signature as Intern and the other signature as Workshop. For the Intern signature, change the font to Arial and the font size to 14. On three lines, enter the following information, your name, the name of your school, and your telephone number. For the Workshop signature, change the font to Verdana and the font size to 12. On three lines, enter the following information, your name, TechConnections, and your email address. Using the Intern signature, send an email message to your professor. The email message should specify that the signature is the Intern signature.

CRITICAL THINKING

How should you submit solutions to questions in the assignments identified with a ❋ symbol?
Every assignment in this book contains one or more questions identified with a ❋ symbol. These questions require you to think beyond the assigned database. Present your solutions to the questions in the format required by your instructor. Possible formats may include one or more of these options: write the answer; create a document that contains the answer; present your answer to the class; discuss your answer in a group; record the answer as audio or video using a webcam, smartphone, or portable media player; or post answers on a blog, wiki, or website.

1. What are the advantages to linking text boxes?

2. In the Ecuador presentation, you created three new slides (duplicates of the title slide) and used these slides as section headers. How did this help when creating sections for the presentation?

3. What changes would you need to make to Solver if Telton-Edwards wanted to produce a maximum of 35 electric lawn mowers a week?

4. Why do you think the name of the navigation form is Main Menu? What other name would more accurately describe the purpose of the navigation form?

5. Why might businesses want all employees to use consistent signatures on email messages?

Capstone Project 3: Cloud and Web Technologies

The Capstone Project consists of an integrated, comprehensive set of problems related to a single scenario. Students apply concepts and skills presented in this book to create solutions to the problems using Word, PowerPoint, Excel, Access, and Outlook. In this project, you will use cloud and web technologies to create a solution.

Note: To complete this assignment, you will be required to use the Data Files for Students. Visit www.cengage.com/ct/studentdownload for detailed instructions or contact your instructor for information about accessing the required files.

Note: To complete this assignment, you will need to sign in to your Microsoft account, upload files to SkyDrive, use the Office Web apps, and use outlook.com. You also will create a blog account.

Problem: Starrs Mountain Resort is looking forward to a great ski season. Because you know you will be busy with other tasks once the season gets under way, you decide to do a little advance planning using web tools and desktop applications.

Word Instructions: You want to use a blog to communicate upcoming special events to two groups: resort associates and resort visitors. To post communications on a blog, you need to create a blog account on the web. Many blogging accounts are available at no cost. Research blogging services on the web, select one, and set up an account. Examples of blogging services are: Blogger, SharePoint blog, Telligent Community, TypePad, and WordPress. Register your blog account in Word and create the blog post shown in Figure 3–1. If requested to do so by your instructor, add your name to the blog post. Publish the blog post. If you do not want to create a blog account, create the blog post and save it to SkyDrive or other storage location. Submit the blog post in the format specified by your instructor.

The resort lodging manager has asked if you can create a printed survey that can be included with the lodging bill. Because this document will be printed, you decide to see if there are any survey templates for Word. Run the desktop version of Word and search for the term, survey, in the templates search box. Select the Hotel accommodation survey template and modify the template by changing the theme to Droplet and the theme colors to Blue Warm. Replace the word Hotel in the title with Starrs Resort. Replace the word hotel in the survey table with resort. Search the web to find a suitable image for the survey and insert it in the Your Logo Here placeholder. Format the image appropriately. Add a Draft watermark. If requested to do so by your instructor, add a header with your name in the header. Save the survey as Cap 3 Sample Resort Survey and submit the document in the format specified by your instructor.

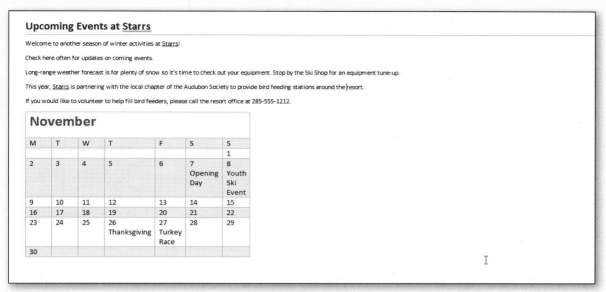

Figure 3–1

PowerPoint Instructions: While at the resort, you are using a mobile device or computer that does not have the PowerPoint app installed, but has Internet access. You remember that you need to add two slides to a PowerPoint presentation on snowshoeing. Run a browser. Navigate to the Office Web Apps website and sign in to your SkyDrive account. Create a PowerPoint presentation using the PowerPoint web app and name the presentation Cap 3 Where to Snowshoe.

Use the Title and Content layout and create a SmartArt graphic using the Vertical Box List design. Enter the text shown in Figure 3–2. Insert another slide with the Title and Content layout and enter For More Information as the title. Use your favorite search engine to find three websites that contain more information about snowshoeing. Add the website addresses to Slide 2 as hyperlinks with descriptive text. Exit the PowerPoint web app.

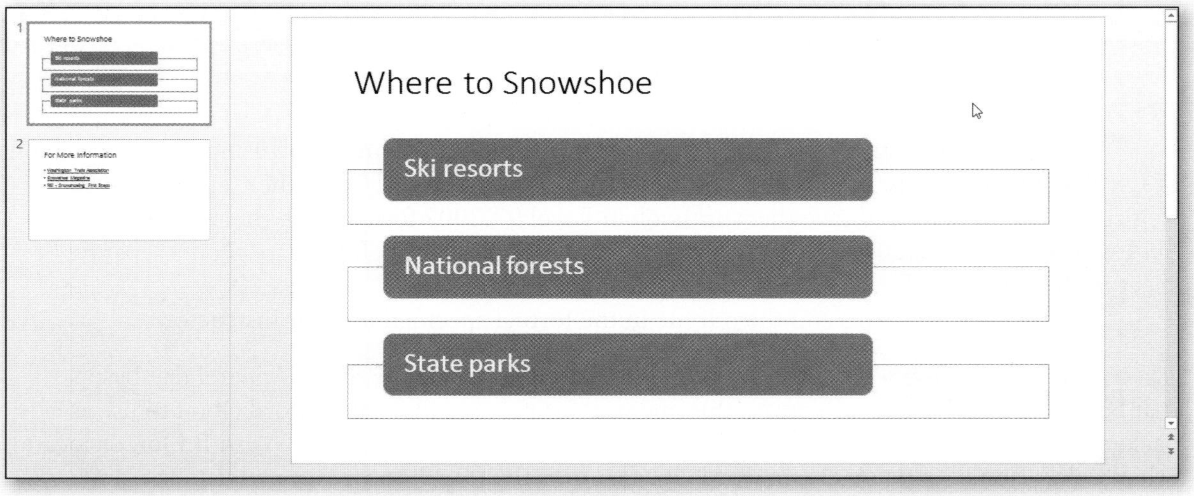

Figure 3–2

In the PowerPoint desktop app, open the Cap 3 More About Snowshoeing presentation from the Data Files for Students. Insert the two slides from the Cap 3 Where to Snowshoe presentation as Slides 4 and 5. Use the Format Painter to format the titles on Slides 4 and 5 to match the format of the title on Slide 2. Change the SmartArt style to a Vertical Picture List. Search the web to find images appropriate to the text and insert the pictures into the SmartArt graphic. On Slide 5, change the font size of the bulleted text to 40 point.

Save the presentation as Cap 3 More About Snowshoeing Finished and submit the presentation in the format specified by your instructor.

Excel Instructions: Starrs is having a Youth Ski Event and you need to maintain a registration sheet for the event. Run the desktop version of Excel and search for sports in the templates search box. Select the Sport sign-up sheet form template and modify the template by changing the theme and theme colors to coordinate with the other Starrs files. Replace the labels in rows 2 and 3 with ones appropriate for a youth ski event at Starrs. Add text in row 4 to illustrate how data should be entered in the table. Add a column with the heading, Age. Replace the I can volunteer column heading with Registration Fee Paid. Delete all data, leaving only the labels and column headings as shown in Figure 3 – 3. Search online to find an image of a child skier and insert the image in place of the Logo text box. Save the workbook as Cap 3 Ski Event Registration. Export the form as a pdf file.

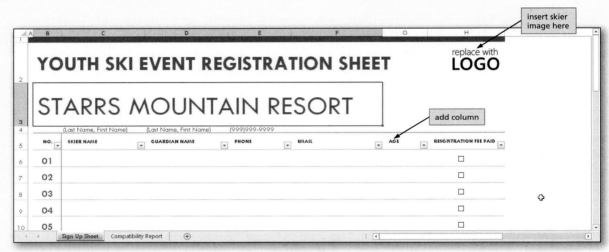

Figure 3–3

You would like to distribute this workbook to colleagues who might be using an older version of Excel and may want to modify the workbook for their own needs. Open the Cap 3 Ski Event Registration workbook and save the workbook in Excel 97-2003 format with the file name, Cap 3 Ski Event Registration 2003. Save a copy of the compatibility report information on a separate sheet in the Cap 3 Ski Event Registration workbook.

Submit the workbooks and the pdf file in the format specified by your instructor.

Access Instructions: You would like to create an opening form for the Starrs Apparel database that has some visual appeal. To create this opening form, you will create a word cloud to use as a background image on the form. Visit a website such as Tagxedo, Wordle, or Word It Out, or locate other websites that help you create word clouds. Open the Cap 3 Starrs Apparel database and create a word cloud that uses the descriptions in the Item table. Experiment with different colors and shapes. Save the word cloud image. Create a new form for the database, add the word cloud as a background image, and then add a label for the form. Coordinate the colors of the label with the colors of the word cloud. Figure 3 – 4 provides an example of an appropriate title and a word cloud image using a cloud shape. Change the Current Database options to ensure that this new form opens automatically.

Submit the database in the format specified by your instructor.

Figure 3–4

Outlook Instructions: Starrs has a number of events planned to coincide with the opening weeks of ski season. You want to use outlook.com to keep track of these events. Open your Microsoft account at outlook.com and create a new calendar named Starrs Mountain Resort. Add the tasks and descriptions shown in Table 3 – 1 to the calendar. When you have finished adding the tasks, share the calendar with your instructor. Your instructor should be able to view the details on your calendar but should not be able to edit anything.

Table 3–1 Special Events for Starrs Mountain Resort

Event	Due Date	Time	Reminder Type	Reminder Time	Priority	Description
Ski and Board Swap	October 25, 2014	9:00 AM	Email	1 week before	High	Community event in shuttle parking lot
Opening Day	November 7, 2014	9:00 AM	Email	2 weeks before	High	First day of skiing
Youth Ski Event	November 8, 2014	1:00 PM	Email	2 weeks before	High	Benefit for the community scholarship fund
Turkey Race	November 27, 2014	10:00 AM	Email	1 week before	High	Thanksgiving snowshoe race
Winter Job Fair	December 15, 2014	None	Email	2 weeks before	Normal	Recruit for holiday season

CRITICAL THINKING

How should you submit solutions to questions in the assignments identified with a symbol?
Every assignment in this book contains one or more questions identified with a ✳ symbol. These questions require you to think beyond the assigned database. Present your solutions to the questions in the format required by your instructor. Possible formats may include one or more of these options: write the answer; create a document that contains the answer; present your answer to the class; discuss your answer in a group; record the answer as audio or video using a webcam, smartphone, or portable media player; or post answers on a blog, wiki, or website.

1. Which blog service did you select and why? Do you think a blog enhances a company's presence on the web? Why or why not?

2. What is the purpose of the compatibility report that Excel produces when you save a workbook in 2003 format? What did this report tell you about the Cap 3 Ski Event Registration workbook?

3. Which SmartArt features that are available in the PowerPoint desktop app are not available in the PowerPoint web app?

4. Why would a company such as Starrs want to create an opening form for a database such as the splash screen shown in Figure 3–4 on the previous page?

5. When would you want to add your tasks to Outlook.com instead of using Microsoft Outlook?

Index

Quick Reference Summary

Microsoft Word 2013 Quick Reference Summary

Task	Page Number	Ribbon	Other On-Screen Element	Shortcut Menu	Keyboard Shortcut
Accessibility Checker	WD 722	FILE tab | Info tab, 'Check for Issues' button, Check Accessibility			
Alternative Text, Add to Graphics	WD 723	Format Shape Dialog Box Launcher (PICTURE TOOLS FORMAT tab | Picture Styles group or DRAWING TOOLS FORMAT tab or SMARTART TOOLS FORMAT tab or CHART TOOLS FORMAT tab | Shape Styles group), 'Layout & Properties' button (Format Picture, Format Shape, or Format Chart Area task pane), ALT TEXT section in task pane		Format Picture, Format Shape, Format Object, or Format Chart Area on shortcut menu Touch mode: 'Show Context Menu' button on mini toolbar, Format Picture, Format Shape, Format Object, or Format Chart Area on shortcut menu	
Alternative Text, Add to Tables	WD 723	Table Properties button (TABLE TOOLS LAYOUT tab | Table group), Alt Text tab (Table Properties dialog box)		Table Properties Touch mode: 'Show Context Menu' button on mini toolbar, Table Properties on shortcut menu, Alt Text tab (Table Properties dialog box)	
Artistic Effect	WD 700	Artistic Effects button (PICTURE TOOLS FORMAT tab | Adjust group)			
Background, Remove	WD 699	Remove Background button (PICTURE TOOLS FORMAT tab | Adjust group), adjust marking lines, 'Close Background Removal and Keep Changes' button (BACKGROUND REMOVAL tab | Close group)			
Blank Page, Insert	WD 572	'Add a Blank Page' button (INSERT tab | Pages group)			
Blog, Create Blank Document for Posting	WD 521	Blog post thumbnail (FILE tab | New tab), Create button			
Blog, Display in Browser	WD 525	Home Page button (BLOG POST tab | Blog group)			

Microsoft Word 2013 Quick Reference Summary *(continued)*

Task	Page Number	Ribbon	Other On-Screen Element	Shortcut Menu	Keyboard Shortcut
Blog, Open Existing Post	WD 526	Open Existing button (BLOG POST tab | Blog group)			
Blog, Register Account	WD 520	Manage Accounts button (BLOG POST tab | Blog group), New (Blog Accounts dialog box)			
Blog Post, Publish	WD 525	Publish button (BLOG POST tab | Blog group)			
Bookmark, Add	WD 594	'Insert a Bookmark' button (INSERT tab | Links group)			
Bookmark, Go To	WD 595	'Insert a Bookmark' button (INSERT tab | Links group), tap or click bookmark name (Bookmark dialog box)			F5, Bookmark (Find and Replace dialog box)
Bulleted List, Change Symbol Format	WD 559	Bullets arrow (HOME tab | Paragraph group)			
Bullets, Change Font Attributes	WD 560	Bullets arrow (HOME tab | Paragraph group), 'Define New Bullet'			
Bullets, Change Level	WD 560	Bullets arrow (HOME tab | Paragraph group), 'Change List Level'			
Caption, Add	WD 544	Insert Caption button (REFERENCES tab | Captions group)			
Caption, Edit	WD 583		locate caption, edit as desired		
Character Attribute, Advanced	WD 690	Font Dialog Box Launcher (HOME tab | Font group), Advanced tab (Font dialog box)			
Character Style, Create	WD 690	Styles Dialog Box Launcher (HOME tab | Styles group), Manage Styles button in Styles task pane, New Style button (Manage Styles dialog box)			
Chart, Add Data Series	WD 509	Select Data button (CHART TOOLS DESIGN tab | Data group), Add button (Select Data Source dialog box)	Drag sizing handle to include desired series		
Chart, Add Element	WD 511	'Add Chart Element' button (CHART TOOLS DESIGN tab | Chart Layouts group)			
Chart, Add Outline	WD 515	Chart Elements arrow (CHART TOOLS FORMAT tab | Current Selection group), Chart Area, Shape Outline button (CHART TOOLS FORMAT tab | Shape Styles group)			
Chart, Apply Style	WD 509	Select chart, tap or click desired style (CHART TOOLS DESIGN tab | Chart Styles group)	Chart Styles button attached to chart, STYLE tab		

Microsoft Word 2013 Quick Reference Summary *(continued)*

Task	Page Number	Ribbon	Other On-Screen Element	Shortcut Menu	Keyboard Shortcut
Chart, Change Colors	WD 510	'Chart Quick Colors' button (CHART TOOLS DESIGN tab | Chart Styles group)	Chart Styles button attached to chart, COLOR tab		
Chart, Change Type	WD 516	'Change Chart Type' button (CHART TOOLS DESIGN tab | Type group)			
Chart, Edit Element	WD 512	Chart Elements arrow (CHART TOOLS FORMAT tab | Current Selection group)	Tap or click element to select		
Chart, Format Element	WD 512	Chart Elements arrow (CHART TOOLS FORMAT tab | Current Selection group), select from list, tap or click Chart Elements button			
Chart, Remove Data Series	WD 508	Select Data button (CHART TOOLS DESIGN tab | Data group), Remove button (Select Data Source dialog box)	Drag sizing handle to include desired series		
Chart Table	WD 505	'Add a Chart' button (INSERT tab | Illustrations group)			
Combine Revisions from Multiple Authors	WD 494	Compare button (REVIEW tab | Compare group), Combine			
Comment, Delete	WD 488	Delete Comment button (REVIEW tab | Comments group)		Delete Comment Touch mode: 'Show Context Menu' button on mini toolbar, Delete Comment on shortcut menu	
Comment, Insert	WD 478	'Insert a Comment'button (REVIEW tab | Comments group)			CTRL+ALT+M
Comment, Reply To	WD 481	'Insert a Comment' button (REVIEW tab | Comments group)	Reply button in selected comment		CTRL+ALT+M
Comments, Delete All	WD 489	Delete Comment arrow (REVIEW tab | Comments group), 'Delete All Comments in Document'			
Comments, Locate Reviewer	WD 498	Find arrow (HOME tab | Editing group), Go To, Comment			CTRL+G, Comment
Comments, Mark as Done	WD 489			'Mark Comment Done' Touch mode: 'Show Context Menu' button on mini toolbar, 'Mark Comment Done' on shortcut menu	
Comments, View	WD 488	NextComment button (REVIEW tab | Comments group)			
Compare and Merge	WD 492	Compare button (REVIEW tab | Compare group), Original document or Revised document			
Compare Documents	WD 493	Compare button (REVIEW tab | Compare group)			

Microsoft Word 2013 Quick Reference Summary *(continued)*

Task	Page Number	Ribbon	Other On-Screen Element	Shortcut Menu	Keyboard Shortcut
Compress Picture	WD 558	Compress Pictures button (PICTURE TOOLS FORMAT tab | Adjust group)			
Concordance File, Create	WD 586	Insert Index button (REFERENCES tab | Index group), AutoMark button (Index dialog box)			
Content Control, Change Properties	WD 630	Control Properties button (DEVELOPER tab | Controls group)			
Content Control, Check Box, Insert	WD 638	'Check Box Content Control' button (DEVELOPER tab | Controls group)			
Content Control, Combo Box, Insert	WD 642	'Combo Box Content Control' button (DEVELOPER tab | Controls group)			
Content Control, Date Picker, Insert	WD 645	'Date Picker Content Control' button (DEVELOPER tab | Controls group)			
Content Control, Drop-Down List, Insert	WD 634	'Drop-Down List Content Control' button (DEVELOPER tab | Controls group)			
Content Control, Edit Placeholder Text	WD 628	Design Mode button (DEVELOPER tab | Controls group)			
Content Control, Plain Text, Insert	WD 627	'Plain Text Content Control' button (DEVELOPER tab | Controls group)			
Content Control, Rich Text, Insert	WD 640	'Rich Text Content Control' button (DEVELOPER tab | Controls group)			
Cover Page	WD 568	'Add a Cover Page' button (INSERT tab | Pages group)			
Create New Document Based on Template	WD 658	FILE tab | New tab	Double-click or double-tap file in File Explorer		
Cross-Reference, Create	WD 545	'Insert Cross-reference' button (INSERT tab | Links group)			
Cross-Reference, Update Manually	WD 547				Select cross-reference, CTRL+F9
Customize Status Bar	WD 482			Tap or click item on Customize Status Bar menu	
Date Field, Insert	WD 685	'Explore Quick Parts' button (INSERT tab | Text group), Field			
Default Font Settings, Modify	WD 689	Font Dialog Box Launcher (HOME tab | Font group), 'Set As Default' button (Font dialog box)			
Default Font Settings, Reset	WD 690		In File Explorer, locate Normal.dotm file, rename as oldnormal.dotm, run Word		

Microsoft Word 2013 Quick Reference Summary *(continued)*

Task	Page Number	Ribbon	Other On-Screen Element	Shortcut Menu	Keyboard Shortcut
Delete Unsaved (Draft Version) Documents	WD 560	Manage Versions button (FILE tab | Info tab), 'Delete All Unsaved Documents'			
DEVELOPER Tab, Show/Hide	WD 626	FILE tab | Options, Customize Ribbon, Developer check box (Word Options dialog box)			
Digital Signature	WD 718	Protect Document button (FILE tab | Info tab), 'Add a Digital Signature'			
Document Properties, Custom	WD 684	FILE tab | Info tab, Properties button, Advanced Properties, Custom tab (Document Properties dialog box)			
Document Properties, Insert	WD 684	'Explore Quick Parts' button (INSERT tab | Text group), Document Property, tap or click property			
Draft View	WD 593	Draft View button (VIEW tab | Views group)			
Draw Rectangle	WD 648	'Draw a Shape' button (INSERT tab | Illustrations group)			
Drawing Canvas	WD 698	'Draw a Shape' button (INSERT tab | Illustrations group), 'New Drawing Canvas' in Draw a Shape gallery			
Editing Restrictions	WD 715	FILE tab | Info tab, Protect Document button, 'Allow only this type of editing in the document' check box in Restrict Editing task pane, 'No changes (Read only)'			
Embed Excel Worksheet in Word Document	WD 502	Copy button (HOME tab | Clipboard group); Paste arrow (HOME tab | Clipboard group), Paste Special, Paste option button (Paste Special dialog box) Touch mode: Copy button (HOME tab | Clipboard group), Copy; Paste arrow (HOME tab | Clipboard group), Paste Special, Paste option button (Paste Special dialog box)			
Field, Delete	WD 686	Select field, Cut button (HOME tab | Clipboard group)	Select field, DELETE	Cut Touch mode: Cut button on mini toolbar	
Field, Edit	WD 686			Edit Field	

Microsoft Word 2013 Quick Reference Summary *(continued)*

Task	Page Number	Ribbon	Other On-Screen Element	Shortcut Menu	Keyboard Shortcut
Field Formats, Custom	WD 687	'Explore Quick Parts' button (INSERT tab | Text group), Field, Field Code button (Field dialog box), Options button, select format, 'Add to Field' button			
Footers, Alternating	WD 589	'Add a Footer' button (INSERT tab | Header & Footer group), Edit Footer, deselect 'Link to Previous' button (HEADER & FOOTER DESIGN tab | Navigation group), 'Different Odd & Even Pages' check box (HEADER & FOOTER DESIGN tab | Options group)			
Format, Find	WD 576	Find arrow (HOME tab | Editing group), Advanced Find			CTRL+F
Go to Heading Using Navigation Pane	WD 581	'Open the Navigation Pane' check box (VIEW tab | Show group), HEADINGS tab in Navigation Pane			
Go To Object	WD 547	Find arrow (HOME tab | Editing group), Go To			CTRL+G
Graphic, Change Order	WD 622	Bring Forward or Send Backward arrows (PICTURE TOOLS FORMAT tab | Arrange group)			
Graphic, Link to Webpage	WD 595	'Add a Hyperlink' button (INSERT tab | Links group), enter web address in Address text box			
Graphic, Send behind Text	WD 650	Wrap Text button (DRAWING TOOLS FORMAT tab | Arrange group)	Layout Options button attached to graphic, Behind Text	Wrap Text	
Group Objects	WD 705	Select objects, Group Objects button (DRAWING TOOLS FORMAT tab | Arrange group), Group			
Gutter Margin	WD 592	Adjust Margins button (PAGE LAYOUT tab | Page Setup group), Custom Margins			
Header and Footer, Change Default Margin	WD 592	'Header Position from Top' or 'Header Position from Bottom' box (HEADER & FOOTER TOOLS DESIGN tab | Position group)			
Header and Footer, Different First Page	WD 594	'Different First Page' check box (HEADER & FOOTER TOOLS DESIGN tab | Options group)			
Highlight Text	WD 652	'Text Highlight Color' arrow (HOME tab | Font group)			
Hyperlink, Insert	WD 596	'Add a Hyperlink' button (INSERT tab | Links group)			

Microsoft Word 2013 Quick Reference Summary (continued)

Task	Page Number	Ribbon	Other On-Screen Element	Shortcut Menu	Keyboard Shortcut
Index, Build	WD 585	Insert Index button (REFERENCES tab | Index group)			
Index, Change Format	WD 588	Insert Index button (REFERENCES tab | Index group), change settings (Index dialog box)			
Index, Delete	WD 589		Drag through field code, DELETE		
Index, Update	WD 588	Update Index button (REFERENCES tab | Index group)			
Index Entry, Delete	WD 587		Select field, DELETE		
Index Entry, Edit	WD 587		Locate field, change text inside quotation marks		
Index Entry, Mark	WD 549	Mark Entry button (REFERENCES tab | Index group)			ALT+SHIFT+X
Index Entry, Mark Multiple	WD 551	Mark Entry button (REFERENCES tab | Index group), Mark button (Mark Index Entry dialog box)			
Language, Set for Proofing Tools	WD 722	Language button (REVIEW tab | Language group), 'Set Proofing Language'			
Language, Set Preferences	WD 722	Language button (REVIEW tab | Language group), Language Preferences			
Layout Options, Advanced	WD 574	FILE tab | Options, Advanced (Word Options dialog box)			
Link, Break	WD 503			'Linked Worksheet Object', Links, Break Link button (Links dialog box)	CTRL+SHIFT+F9
Link Excel Worksheet to Word Document	WD 501	Copy button (HOME tab | Clipboard group); Paste arrow (HOME tab | Clipboard group), 'Link & Keep Source Formatting' Touch mode: Copy button (HOME tab | Clipboard group), Copy; Paste arrow (HOME tab | Clipboard group), 'Link & Keep Source Formatting'			
Link Form to Database	WD 661	FILE tab | Save As, Tools button (Save As dialog box), Save Options on Tools menu, Advanced (Word Options dialog box), 'Save form data as delimited text file' check box			
Linked Object, Edit	WD 503			'Linked Worksheet Object', Edit Link	
Macro, Automatic	WD 713	Record Macro button (DEVELOPER tab | Code group), type macro name (Record Macro dialog box)			

Microsoft Word 2013 Quick Reference Summary *(continued)*

Task	Page Number	Ribbon	Other On-Screen Element	Shortcut Menu	Keyboard Shortcut
Macro, Copy from One Template or Document to Another	WD 720	View Macros button (DEVELOPER tab | Code group or VIEW tab | Macros group), Organizer button (Macros dialog box)			
Macro, Delete	WD 709	View Macros button (DEVELOPER tab | Code group), Delete button (Macros dialog box)			
Macro, Edit VBA Code	WD 715	View Macros button (DEVELOPER tab | Code group), select macro to be edited (Macros dialog box), Edit button			
Macro, Record	WD 707	Record Macro button (DEVELOPER tab | Code group)			ALT+F8, Create button (Macros dialog box)
Macro, Rename	WD 721	View Macros button (DEVELOPER tab | Code group or VIEW tab | Macros group), Organizer button (Macros dialog box), select macro, Rename button (Organizer dialog box)			
Macro, Run	WD 709	View Macros button (DEVELOPER tab | Code group or VIEW tab | Macros group), select macro name (Macros dialog box), tap or click Run button			Press assigned shortcut key; or press ALT+F8, select macro name (Macros dialog box), tap or click Run button
Macro-Enabled Document, Create	WD 677	FILE tab | Save tab, 'Save as type' arrow (Save As dialog box), 'Word Macro-Enabled Document'			
Macro-Enabled Template, Save	WD 677	FILE tab | Save As tab, 'Save as type' arrow (Save As dialog box), 'Word Macro-Enabled Template'			
Macro Settings, Specify	WD 679	Macro Security button (DEVELOPER tab | Code group), select 'Disable all macros with notification' option button (Trust Center dialog box)			
Mark as Final	WD 492	Protect Document button (FILE tab | Info tab), 'Mark as Final'			
Markups, Print	WD 487	FILE tab | Print tab, Settings area			
Markups, Show All	WD 487	'Display for Review' arrow (REVIEW tab | Tracking group), All Markup			
Markups and Comments, Change Display	WD 484	Show Markup button (REVIEW tab | Tracking group), Balloons			
Master Document, Expand	WD 566	Expand Subdocuments button (OUTLINING tab | Master Document group)			

Microsoft Word 2013 Quick Reference Summary *(continued)*

Task	Page Number	Ribbon	Other On-Screen Element	Shortcut Menu	Keyboard Shortcut
Metadata, Remove	WD 722	'Check for Issues' button (FILE tab | Info tab), Inspect Document, Remove All button			
Microsoft Graph	WD 517	Object button (INSERT tab | Text group), Create New tab (Object dialog box), 'Microsoft Graph Chart'			
Native Format, Open Files	WD 718	Browse button (FILE tab | Open tab), file type arrow (Open dialog box)			
Outline View	WD 562	Outline View button (VIEW tab | Views group)			
Outline View, Add Entries	WD 562	'Demote to Body Text' button (OUTLINING tab | Outline Tools group) or 'Promote to Heading 1' button (OUTLINING tab | Outline Tools group)			
Outline View, Exit	WD 567	'Close Outline View' button (OUTLINING tab | Close group)			
Outline View, Show First Line Only	WD 564	'Show First Line Only' check box (OUTLINING tab | Outline Tools group)			
Page Color	WD 618	Page Color button (DESIGN tab | Page Background group)			
Page Color, Add Pattern Fill Effect	WD 619	Page Color button (DESIGN tab | Page Background group), Fill Effects			
Page Color, Fill Effect	WD 693	Page Color button (DESIGN tab | Page Background group), Fill Effects, Texture tab (Fill Effects dialog box)			
Page Color, Remove	WD 694	Page Color button (DESIGN tab | Page Background group), No Color			
Paper Size, Change	WD 615	'Choose Page Size' button (PAGE LAYOUT tab | Page Setup group)			
Paragraph Spacing, Change in Document	WD 551	Paragraph Spacing button (DESIGN tab | Document Formatting group)			
Password-Protect Document	WD 657	Restrict Editing button (DEVELOPER tab | Protect group), 'Yes, Start Enforcing Protection' button in Restrict Editing task pane, type password (Start Enforcing Protection dialog box)			
Picture, Save in Other Format	WD 558			'Save as Picture', 'Save as type' arrow (File Save dialog box)	
Print Scaling	WD 593	FILE tab | Print tab, Settings area in Print gallery, 'Scale to Paper Size'			

Microsoft Word 2013 Quick Reference Summary *(continued)*

Task	Page Number	Ribbon	Other On-Screen Element	Shortcut Menu	Keyboard Shortcut
Protect Form	WD 655	Restrict Editing button (DEVELOPER tab | Protect group), select 'Allow only this type of editing in the document' check box, 'Yes Start Enforcing Protection' button in Restrict Editing task pane			
Protected View	WD 541	FILE tab | Options, Trust Center (Word Options dialog box), 'Trust Center Settings' button, Protected View			
Quick Access Toolbar, Add Command/ Macro	WD 710	'Customize Quick Access Toolbar' button on Quick Access Toolbar, More commands, select command (Word Options dialog box), Add button		'Customize Quick Access Toolbar', More commands, select command (Word Options dialog box), Add button	
Quick Access Toolbar, Delete Buttons	WD 712			Right-click button, 'Remove from Quick Access Toolbar' Touch mode: Press and hold button, 'Remove from Quick Access Toolbar'	
Quick Table	WD 523	'Add a Table' button (INSERT tab | Tables group), Quick Tables			
Recover Unsaved (Draft Version) Documents	WD 560	FILE tab | Open tab, 'Recover Unsaved Documents' button in Recent Documents list			
Replace Formats	WD 578	Replace button (HOME tab | Editing group), Format button (Find and Replace dialog box)			
Restrict Editing to Tracked Changes or Comments or No Edits	WD 656	Restrict Editing button (DEVELOPER tab | Protect group), select 'Allow only this type of editing in the document' check box in Restrict Editing task pane, 'Yes, Start Enforcing Protection' button			
Restrict Formatting	WD 656	Restrict Editing button (DEVELOPER tab | Protect group), select 'Limit formatting to a selection of styles' check box in Restrict Editing task pane, Settings link (Formatting Restrictions dialog box), 'Yes, Start Enforcing Protection' button			
Reviewer Information, Change	WD 480	Change Tracking Options Dialog Box Launcher (REVIEW tab | Tracking group), 'Change User Name' button (Track Changes dialog box)			

Microsoft Word 2013 Quick Reference Summary *(continued)*

Task	Page Number	Ribbon	Other On-Screen Element	Shortcut Menu	Keyboard Shortcut
Reviewing Task Pane	WD 484	Reviewing Pane arrow (REVIEW tab | Tracking group)			
Ribbon, Collapse	WD 616	'Collapse the Ribbon' button (HOME tab)			
Ribbon, Expand	WD 616	'Pin the ribbon' button (HOME tab)			
Save as Template	WD 613	'Change File Type' (FILE tab | Export tab), Template			F12, Word Template
Schema, Attach	WD 727	Document Template button (DEVELOPER tab | Templates group), XML Schema tab (Templates and Add-ins dialog box), Add Schema button, select schema, Open button (Add Schema dialog box)			
Schema, Delete	WD 727	Document Template button (DEVELOPER tab | Templates group), XML Schema tab (Templates and Add-ins dialog box), Schema Library button, select schema, Delete Schema button (Schema Library dialog box)			
Screenshot, Insert	WD 542	'Take a Screenshot' button (INSERT tab | Illustrations group)			
Scroll Documents Side by Side	WD 518	'View Side by Side' button (VIEW tab | Window group)			
Shadow, Add to Shape	WD 652	Shape Effects button (DRAWING TOOLS FORMAT tab | Shape Styles group), Shadow			
Shadow, Change Color	WD 652	Shape Effects button (DRAWING TOOLS FORMAT tab | Shape Styles group), Shadow, Shadow Options			
Shadow Shape Effect, Apply	WD 696	Shape Effects button (DRAWING TOOLS FORMAT tab | Shape Styles group), Shadow, Shadow Options			
Shape, Change	WD 694	Edit Shape button (DRAWING TOOLS FORMAT tab | Insert Shapes group), Change Shape			
Shape, Fill with Picture	WD 697	Shape Fill arrow (DRAWING TOOLS FORMAT tab | Shape Styles group), Picture			
Shape, Format	WD 651	Shape Fill arrow, Shape Outline arrow, or Shape Effects arrow (DRAWING TOOLS FORMAT tab | Shape Styles group)			

Microsoft Word 2013 Quick Reference Summary *(continued)*

Task	Page Number	Ribbon	Other On-Screen Element	Shortcut Menu	Keyboard Shortcut
Shortcut Key, Assign to a Style	WD 689	Styles Dialog Box Launcher (HOME tab | Styles group), tap or click style arrow, Modify, Format button (Modify Style dialog box), Shortcut key		Press and hold or right-click style name in Styles gallery, tap or click style arrow, Modify, Format button (Modify Style dialog box), Shortcut key	
Signature Line	WD 719	'Add a Signature Line' button (INSERT tab | Text group)			
Style, Copy from One Template or Document to Another	WD 719	Styles Dialog Box Launcher (HOME tab | Styles group), Manage Styles button in Styles task pane, Import/Export button (Manage Styles dialog box)			
Style, Delete	WD 720	Styles Dialog Box Launcher (HOME tab | Styles group), Manage Styles button in Styles task pane, Import/Export button (Manage Styles dialog box), select style, Delete button			
Style, Display Hidden	WD 688	Styles Dialog Box Launcher (HOME tab | Styles group), Manage Styles button in Styles task pane, Edit tab (Manage Styles dialog box)			
Style, Modify Using Styles Task Pane	WD 687	Styles Dialog Box Launcher (HOME tab | Styles group), select style in Styles task pane, Modify			
Style, Rename	WD 720	Styles Dialog Box Launcher (HOME tab | Styles group), Manage Styles button in Styles task pane, Import/Export button (Manage Styles dialog box), select style, Rename button			
Subdocument, Convert to Part of Master Document	WD 566	Remove Subdocument button (OUTLINING tab | Master Document group)			
Subdocument, Insert	WD 564	Insert Subdocument button (OUTLINING tab | Master Document group)			
Table, Add Title	WD 723	Table Properties button (TABLE TOOLS LAYOUT tab | Table group), Alt Text tab (Table Properties dialog box)		Table Properties, Alt Text tab (Table Properties dialog box)	
Table, Control Layout	WD 623	'Add a Table' button (INSERT tab | Tables group)			
Table, Convert to Text	WD 682	'Convert to Text' button (TABLE TOOLS LAYOUT tab | Data group)			

Microsoft Word 2013 Quick Reference Summary (continued)

Task	Page Number	Ribbon	Other On-Screen Element	Shortcut Menu	Keyboard Shortcut
Table of Authorities, Build	WD 725	'Insert Table of Authorities' button (REFERENCES tab | Table of Authorities group)			
Table of Authorities, Change Format	WD 726	'Insert Table of Authorities' button (REFERENCES tab | Table of Authorities group), change desired settings/formats (Table of Authorities dialog box)			
Table of Authorities, Update	WD 725	Update Table of Authorities' button (REFERENCES tab | Table of Authorities group)			F9
Table of Contents, Change Format	WD 580	'Table of Contents' button (REFERENCES tab | Table of Contents group), 'Custom Table of Contents'			
Table of Contents, Change Style Formatting	WD 583	'Table of Contents' button (REFERENCES tab | Table of Contents group), Modify button			
Table of Contents, Change Style Level	WD 583	'Table of Contents' button (REFERENCES tab | Table of Contents group), Options button			
Table of Contents, Create	WD 573	'Table of Contents' button (REFERENCES tab | Table of Contents group)			
Table of Contents, Delete	WD 573	'Table of Contents' button (REFERENCES tab | Table of Contents group), 'Remove Table of Contents'			
Table of Contents, Retain Formatting when Adding Text	WD 578	Add Text button (REFERENCES tab | Table of Contents group), select level on Add Text menu			
Table of Contents, Update Entire	WD 579	Update Table button (REFERENCES tab | Table of Contents group)	Update Table button attached to table, 'Update entire table' (Update Table of Contents dialog box)		F9
Table of Contents, Update Page Numbers	WD 575	Update Table button (REFERENCES tab | Table of Contents group)	Update Table button attached to table, OK button (Update Table of Contents dialog box)		F9
Table of Figures, Change Format	WD 583	'Table of Figures Dialog' button (REFERENCES tab | Captions group)			

Microsoft Word 2013 Quick Reference Summary *(continued)*

Task	Page Number	Ribbon	Other On-Screen Element	Shortcut Menu	Keyboard Shortcut
Table of Figures, Create	WD 582	'Table of Figures Dialog' button (REFERENCES tab | Captions group)			
Table of Figures, Update	WD 583	'Update Table of Figures' button (REFERENCES tab | Captions group), 'Update entire table' (Update Table of Figures dialog box)			F9
Text Box, 3-D Effect	WD 704	Shape Effects button (DRAWING TOOLS FORMAT tab | Shape Styles group), '3-D Rotation'		Format Shape, TEXT OPTIONS tab (Format Shape task pane), Text Effects button	
Text Box, Change Shape Outline	WD 704	Shape Styles gallery (DRAWING TOOLS FORMAT tab | Shape Styles group)		Format Shape, LINE tab (Format Shape task pane)	
Text Box, Draw	WD 701	'Choose a Text Box' button (INSERT tab | Text group), 'Draw Text Box'			
Text Box, Insert Sidebar	WD 552	'Choose a Text Box' button (INSERT tab | Text group)			
Text Box, Link	WD 556	Create Link button (DRAWING TOOLS FORMAT tab | Text group)			
Text Direction, Change	WD 702	Text Direction button (DRAWING TOOLS FORMAT tab | Text group)		Format Shape, TEXT OPTIONS tab (Format Shape task pane)	
Theme, Reset	WD 680	Themes button (DESIGN tab | Themes group), 'Reset to Theme from Template' in Themes gallery			
Theme, Save	WD 680	Themes button (DESIGN tab | Themes group), 'Save Current Theme' in Themes gallery			
Theme, Set as Default	WD 618	'Set as Default' button (DESIGN tab | Document Formatting group)			
Theme Color, Customize	WD 653	Theme Colors button (DESIGN tab | Document Formatting group), Customize Colors			
Track Changes, Enable/Disable	WD 483	Track Changes button (REVIEW tab | Tracking group)	Track Changes indicator on status bar		CTRL+SHIFT+E
Tracked Changes, Accept/Reject All	WD 491	'Accept and Move to Next' arrow (REVIEW tab | Changes group), 'Accept All Changes' or 'Reject and Move to Next' arrow, 'Reject All Changes'			

Microsoft Word 2013 Quick Reference Summary *(continued)*

Task	Page Number	Ribbon	Other On-Screen Element	Shortcut Menu	Keyboard Shortcut
Tracked Changes, Review	WD 489	Next Change button (REVIEW tab | Changes group)		Tap or click desired command on shortcut menu Touch mode: 'Show Context Menu' button on mini toolbar tap or click desired command on shortcut	
Tracked Changes, Show Single Reviewer	WD 497	Show Markup button (REVIEW tab | Tracking group), Specific People			
Tracked Changes, Simple Markup	WD 486	'Display for Review' arrow (REVIEW tab | Tracking group), Simple Markup			
Tracking Options, Change	WD 491	Change Tracking Options Dialog Box Launcher (REVIEW tab | Tracking group), Advanced Options button (Track Changes Options dialog box)			
Ungroup Objects	WD 706	Select objects, Group Objects button (DRAWING TOOLS FORMAT tab | Arrange group), Ungroup			
Unprotect Document	WD 678	Restrict Editing button (DEVELOPER tab | Protect group), Stop Protection button in Restrict Editing task pane			
Vertical Alignment	WD 571	Page Setup Dialog Box Launcher (PAGE LAYOUT tab | Page Setup group), Vertical alignment arrow (Page Setup dialog box)			
Wildcards, Replace Text or Formatting Using	WD 578	Replace button (HOME tab | Styles group), More button			
XML Format, Save Document In	WD 726	FILE tab | Save As, 'Save as type' arrow (Save as dialog box), 'Word XML Document'			

Microsoft PowerPoint 2013 Quick Reference Summary

Task	Page Number	Mouse	Ribbon	Other On-Screen Areas	Shortcut Menu	Keyboard Shortcut
Accessibility, Check for Issues	PPT 614		'Check for Issues' button (FILE tab | Info tab), Check Accessibility			
Character Spacing, Change	PPT 495		Character Spacing button (HOME tab | Font group); Font dialog box launcher (HOME tab |Font Group), Character Spacing tab (Font dialog box)		Font, Character Spacing tab	

Microsoft PowerPoint 2013 Quick Reference Summary

Task	Page Number	Mouse	Ribbon	Other On-Screen Areas	Shortcut Menu	Keyboard Shortcut
Chart, Align	PPT 633		Align button (DRAWING TOOLS FORMAT tab | Arrange group)			
Chart, Apply Style	PPT 636		More button (CHART TOOLS DESIGN tab | Chart Styles group)	Chart Style button (paintbrush icon) on right side of chart area		
Chart, Change Colors	PPT 637		'Change Colors' button (CHART TOOLS DESIGN tab | Chart Styles group)	Chart Style button (paintbrush icon on right side of chart area), COLOR tab		
Chart, Change Type	PPT 635		'Change Chart Type' button (CHART TOOLS DESIGN tab | Type group)			
Chart, Copy from Excel	PPT 631		(In Excel) Copy button (HOME tab | Clipboard group), switch to PowerPoint, Paste arrow (HOME tab | Clipboard group), 'Use Destination Theme & Link Data'		Copy (in Excel), Paste (in PowerPoint)	
Chart, Display Gridlines	PPT 636		'Add Chart Element' button (CHART TOOLS DESIGN tab | Chart Layouts group), Gridlines			
Chart, Display and Format Axis Titles	PPT 638		'Add Chart Element' button (CHART TOOLS DESIGN tab | Chart Layouts group), Axis Titles	Chart Elements button (plus icon on right side of chart area), Axis Titles check box		
Chart, Edit Data	PPT 642		Edit Data button (CHART TOOLS DESIGN tab | Data group)			
Chart, Exclude Data	PPT 636			Chart Filters button (funnel icon on right side of chart area)		
Chart, Format Background	PPT 641		Current Selection arrow, Walls (CHART TOOLS FORMAT tab | Current Selection group), Format Selection button		Format Walls	
Chart, Format Legend	PPT 639		Current Selection arrow, Legend (CHART TOOLS FORMAT tab | Current Selection group), Format Selection button	Chart Elements button (plus icon on right side of chart area), Legend arrow	Format Legend	
Chart, Move Legend	PPT 639		Add Chart Element button (CHART TOOLS DESIGN tab | Chart Layouts group), Legend arrow	Chart Elements button (plus icon on right side of chart area), Legend arrow	Format Legend, Legend Position	
Chart, Switch Rows and Columns	PPT 634		Switch Row/Column button (CHART TOOLS DESIGN tab | Data group)			
Custom Slide Show, Create	PPT 680		In Normal view, 'Custom Slide Show' button (SLIDE SHOW tab | Start Slide Show group), Custom Shows, New			

Microsoft PowerPoint 2013 Quick Reference Summary *(continued)*

Task	Page Number	Mouse	Ribbon	Other On-Screen Areas	Shortcut Menu	Keyboard Shortcut
Custom Slide Show, Edit	PPT 682		Normal view, 'Custom Slide Show' button (SLIDE SHOW tab | Start Slide Show group), Custom Shows, select show, Edit			
Embedded File, Edit	PPT 608	Double-click embedded object to open source program		Double-tap embedded object to open source program	Document Object, Edit	
Excel Worksheet, Edit Linked	PPT 629	Double-click linked worksheet to edit		Double-tap linked worksheet to edit		
Excel Worksheet, Insert Linked	PPT 626			Object button (INSERT tab | Text group), 'Create from file', browse to Excel file		
File with Graphics and Text, Insert	PPT 606		Insert Object button (INSERT tab | Text group), 'Create from file', browse to file			
Fill Color, Apply to Slide	PPT 515		Format Background button (DESIGN tab | Customize group), FILL section (Format Background pane)		Format Background, FILL section (Format Background pane)	
Fill Color, Set Transparency	PPT 515		Format Background (DESIGN tab | Customize group), FILL section (Format Background pane), Transparency slider		Format Background, FILL area (Format Background pane), Transparency slider	
Font, Embed in Presentation	PPT 630		Tools button (FILE tab | Save As tab, Save As dialog box), Save Options, 'Embed fonts in the file'			
Grayscale, Print in	PPT 685		Color button (FILE tab, Print tab), Grayscale			
Gridlines, Display	PPT 636		Gridlines check box (VIEW tab | Show group)			
Handout Master, Use	PPT 504 PPT 520		Handout Master button (VIEW tab | Master Views group)			
Handout, Create by Exporting File to Microsoft Word	PPT 582		'Create Handouts in Microsoft Word' button (HOME tab | Handouts group); or Create Handouts button (FILE tab | Export tab)			
Line, Change Weight or Color	PPT 573		Shape Outline arrow (DRAWING TOOLS FORMAT tab | Shape Styles group), Weight or choose color			
Line, Draw	PPT 572		Shapes arrow (DRAWING TOOLS FORMAT tab | Insert Shapes group)			

Microsoft PowerPoint 2013 Quick Reference Summary *(continued)*

Task	Page Number	Mouse	Ribbon	Other On-Screen Areas	Shortcut Menu	Keyboard Shortcut
Line, Set Formatting as Default	PPT 574				Set as Default Line	
Master View	PPT 480		Slide Master button (VIEW tab | Master Views group)			
Master View, Close	PPT 510		'Close Master View' button (NOTES MASTER tab | Close group)			
Narration, Preview	PPT 705		In Normal view, select sound icon on slide, Play button (AUDIO TOOLS PLAYBACK tab | Preview group)			
Narration, Record	PPT 705		'Record Slide Show' arrow (SLIDE SHOW tab | Set Up group), 'Start Recording from Beginning' or 'Start Recording from Current Slide', 'Narrations and laser pointer' check box (Record Slide Show dialog box), Start Recording button (Record Slide Show dialog box), End Show			
Notes Master, Use	PPT 507 PPT 521		'View Notes Master' button (VIEW tab | Master Views group)			
Pattern Fill, Apply to Slide	PPT 516		Format Background button (DESIGN tab | Customize group), FILL section (Format Background pane) Pattern fill		Format Background, FILL section (Format Background pane), Pattern fill	
Permissions, Restrict	PPT 707		Protect Presentation button (FILE tab, Info tab), Restrict Access			
Photo Album, Add Captions Below All Pictures	PPT 691		Photo Album dialog box, 'Captions below ALL pictures' check box			
Photo Album, Add Theme	PPT 691		Photo Album dialog box, Browse button in Album Layout area			
Photo Album, Change Layout	PPT 690		Photo Album dialog box, Picture Layout arrow			
Photo Album, Create	PPT 692		Create button (Photo Album dialog box)			
Photo Album, Create Black and White Images	PPT 694		'New Photo Album' arrow (INSERT tab | Images group), 'ALL pictures black and white' check box (Edit Photo Album dialog box), Update			
Photo Album, Edit	PPT 692		'New Photo Album' arrow (INSERT tab | Images group), 'Edit Photo Album'			

Microsoft PowerPoint 2013 Quick Reference Summary *(continued)*

Task	Page Number	Mouse	Ribbon	Other On-Screen Areas	Shortcut Menu	Keyboard Shortcut
Photo Album, Reorder Pictures	PPT 687		Photo Album dialog box, select photo, Move Up or Move Down button			
Photo Album, Start and Add Pictures	PPT 685		'New Photo Album' button (INSERT tab | Images group)			
Photo Album Image, Adjust Brightness	PPT 689		Photo Album dialog box, Increase Brightness or Decrease Brightness button			
Photo Album Image, Adjust Contrast	PPT 689		Photo Album dialog box, Increase Contrast or Decrease Contrast button			
Photo Album Image, Adjust Rotation	PPT 688		Photo Album dialog box, 'Rotate Left 90°' or 'Rotate Right 90°' button			
Picture, Change	PPT 551		Change Picture button (PICTURE TOOLS FORMAT tab | Adjust group)		Change Picture	
Picture, Rotate	PPT 498	Drag rotation handle	Rotate button (PICTURE TOOLS FORMAT tab | Arrange group)		Format Object, 3-D ROTATION	
Picture Presentation, Save as	PPT 584		'Change File Type' (FILE tab | Export tab), 'PowerPoint Picture Presentation'			
Presentation, Display Multiple Windows Simultaneously	PPT 701		With multiple presentations open, Cascade button or Arrange All button (VIEW tab | Window group)			
Presentation, Email from within PowerPoint	PPT 705		Email button (FILE tab | Share tab), 'Send as Attachment'			
Presentation, Show with Manual Timing	PPT 680		'Set Up Slide Show' button (SLIDE SHOW tab | Set Up group), Manually (Advance slides area)			
Presenter View, Use	PPT 710		'Use Presenter View' check box (SLIDE SHOW tab | Monitors group)			
Research Pane, Use to Find Information	PPT 696		Research button (REVIEW tab | Proofing group)			
Resolution, Set for Slideshow	PPT 708		'Set Up Slide Show' button (SLIDE SHOW tab | Set Up group), Resolution arrow (Set Up Show dialog box)			
Ribbon, Customize	PPT 579		Customize Ribbon (FILE tab, Options tab)			
Ribbon, Reset	PPT 585		Reset button (FILE tab, Options tab), Customize Ribbon, Reset			

Microsoft PowerPoint 2013 Quick Reference Summary *(continued)*

Task	Page Number	Mouse	Ribbon	Other On-Screen Areas	Shortcut Menu	Keyboard Shortcut
Section, Create Break	PPT 673		In Slide Sorter view, Section button (HOME tab | Slides group), Add Section		In Slide Sorter view, tap where break desired, tap Add Section	
Section, Rename	PPT 676		Section button (HOME tab | Slides group), Rename Section		Rename Section	
Sections, Collapse or Expand	PPT 678		Section button (HOME tab | Slides group), Collapse All or Expand All		Collapse All or Expand All	
Sections, Reorder	PPT 678	Drag section name			Move Section Up or Move Section Down	
Selection, Print	PPT 710		'Print All Slides' button, Print Selection (FILE tab, Print tab)			
Shape, Apply Fill	PPT 568		Shape Fill arrow (DRAWING TOOLS FORMAT tab | Shape Styles group)		Format Shape, Fill icon (Format Shape pane)	
Shape, Set Formatting as Default	PPT 577				Set as Default Shape	
Shape, Subtract	PPT 570		Merge Shapes button (DRAWING TOOLS FORMAT tab | Insert Shapes group), Subtract			
Shape Fill, Increase Transparency	PPT 487		Drawing Dialog Box Launcher (HOME tab | Drawing group), Format Shape dialog box, Transparency slider			
Shapes, Merge	PPT 571		Merge Shapes button (DRAWING TOOLS FORMAT tab | Insert Shapes group), Union			
Slide, Set Up Custom Size	PPT 699		Slide Size button (DESIGN tab | Customize group), 'Slides sized for' arrow, Custom			
Slide Layout, Delete	PPT 502		Delete button (HOME tab | Slides group)		Delete Layout	DELETE
Slide Master, Delete Slide Layout	PPT 502		Delete button (SLIDE MASTER tab | Edit Master group)		Delete Layout	DELETE
Slide Master, Insert Placeholder	PPT 489		Insert Placeholder arrow (SLIDE MASTER tab | Master Layout group)			
Slide Master, Apply Slide and Font Themes	PPT 481		Themes button (SLIDE MASTER tab | Edit Theme group)			
Slide Master, Delete, Move, and Add Text to Footer	PPT 485		Slide Master button (VIEW tab | Master Views group), 'Header & Footer' button (INSERT tab | Text group)			

Microsoft PowerPoint 2013 Quick Reference Summary *(continued)*

Task	Page Number	Mouse	Ribbon	Other On-Screen Areas	Shortcut Menu	Keyboard Shortcut
Slide Master, Display	PPT 480		Slide Master button (VIEW tab | Master Views group)			
Slide Master, Format Background and Apply a Quick Style	PPT 484		Background Styles button (SLIDE MASTER tab | Background group)			
Slide Master, Hide and Unhide Background Graphics	PPT 499		'Hide/Unhide Background Graphics' check box (SLIDE MASTER tab | Background group)			
Slide Master, Insert a Background Graphic	PPT 488		Insert Picture button (INSERT tab | Images group)			
Slide Master, Save as a Template	PPT 510		Save as type arrow (FILE tab, Save As tab), PowerPoint Template			
Slide Master and Slide Layout, Rename	PPT 500		Rename button (SLIDE MASTER tab | Edit Master group)			
Slide Orientation, Change	PPT 699		Slide Size button (DESIGN tab | Customize group), 'Custom Slide Size'			
Slide Show, Present Online	PPT 707		Present Online arrow (SLIDE SHOW tab | Start Slide Show group), 'Office Presentation Service'			
Slide Sorter View	PPT 672		Slide Sorter button (VIEW tab | Presentation Views group)	Slide Sorter view button in taskbar		
Slides, Insert with a Section Layout	PPT 669		Slide Layout button (HOME tab | Slides group), Section Header layout		Layout, Section Header	
SmartArt, Add Shape	PPT 558		Add Shape arrow (SMARTART TOOLS DESIGN tab | Create Graphic group)			
SmartArt, Change Layout	PPT 557		More button (SMARTART TOOLS DESIGN tab | Layouts group)			
SmartArt, Convert to Text or Shapes	PPT 563 PPT 565		Convert button (SMARTART TOOLS DESIGN tab | Reset group)			
SmartArt, Remove Shape	PPT 558				Delete	select shape, DELETE

Microsoft PowerPoint 2013 Quick Reference Summary *(continued)*

Task	Page Number	Mouse	Ribbon	Other On-Screen Areas	Shortcut Menu	Keyboard Shortcut
SmartArt, Resize Graphic	PPT 559 PPT 560		Smaller or Larger button (SMARTART TOOLS FORMAT tab | Shapes group); or enter desired settings in Height and Width boxes (SMARTART TOOLS FORMAT tab | Size group)		Size and Position, SIZE area (Format Shape pane)	
SmartArt Bullet, Add	PPT 557		Add Bullet button (SMARTART TOOLS DESIGN tab | Create Graphic group			
SmartArt Bullet Level, Promote or Demote	PPT 555 PPT 556		Promote or Demote button (SMARTART TOOLS DESIGN tab | Create Graphic group)			
SmartArt Shapes, Reorder	PPT 554		Move Up or Move Down button (SMARTART TOOLS DESIGN tab | Create Graphic group)			
Table, Add Cell Effects	PPT 621		Effects button (TABLE TOOLS DESIGN tab | Table Styles group)			
Table, Add Gradient Fill	PPT 621		Shading arrow (TABLE TOOLS DESIGN tab | Table Styles group), Gradient			
Table, Add Hyperlink	PPT 644		Hyperlink button (INSERT tab | Links group)		Hyperlink	
Table, Add Shading	PPT 620		Shading arrow (TABLE TOOLS DESIGN tab | Table Styles group)			
Table, Align	PPT 625		Align button (TABLE TOOLS LAYOUT tab | Arrange group)			
Table, Distribute Rows	PPT 622		Distribute Rows button (TABLE TOOLS LAYOUT tab | Cell Size group)			
Table, Draw	PPT 610		Table button (INSERT tab | Tables group), Draw Table, drag pencil pointer			
Table, Resize Columns and Rows	PPT 623	Drag column or row borders	Table Row Height or Table Column Width boxes (TABLE TOOLS LAYOUT tab | Cell Size group)			
Table, Split Columns or Rows	PPT 617		Split Cells button (TABLE TOOLS LAYOUT tab | Merge group)		Split Cells	
Table Line, Erase	PPT 615		Table Eraser button (TABLE TOOLS DESIGN tab | Draw Borders group), click line to erase			

Microsoft PowerPoint 2013 Quick Reference Summary *(continued)*

Task	Page Number	Mouse	Ribbon	Other On-Screen Areas	Shortcut Menu	Keyboard Shortcut
Table Rows and Columns, Draw	PPT 611 PPT 613		Draw Table button (TABLE TOOLS DESIGN tab | Draw Borders group), drag pencil pointer			
Template, Open and Save as Presentation	PPT 512		Computer button (FILE tab | Open tab), Custom Office Templates, then Save As tab (FILE tab), 'Save as type', PowerPoint Presentation			
Text, Change Direction	PPT 492		Text Direction button (HOME tab | Paragraph group)			
Text Box, Align	PPT 550		Align button (DRAWING TOOLS FORMAT tab | Arrange group)			
Text Box, Apply a Gradient Fill	PPT 549		Shape Fill arrow (DRAWING TOOLS FORMAT tab | Shape Styles group), Gradient fill (Format Shape pane)		Format Shape, FILL section (Format Shape pane), Gradient fill	
Text Box, Apply a Pattern Fill	PPT 547		Shape Fill arrow (DRAWING TOOLS FORMAT tab | Shape group), Gradient, More Gradients, Pattern fill (Format Shape pane)		Format Shape, FILL section (Format Shape pane), Pattern fill	
Text Box, Apply an Effect	PPT 544		Shape Effects button (DRAWING TOOLS FORMAT tab | Shape Styles group)			
Text Box, Apply Fill	PPT 496		Shape Fill arrow (HOME tab | Drawing group)		Format Shape, FILL pane	
Text Box, Apply Picture	PPT 561		Shape Fill arrow (DRAWING TOOLS FORMAT tab | Shape Styles group), Picture		Format Shape, FILL section (Format Shape pane), Picture or texture fill	
Text Box, Change Internal Margin	PPT 497		Shape Styles dialog box launcher (DRAWING TOOLS FORMAT tab | Shape Styles group), Format Shape pane, TEXT BOX options		Format Shape, TEXT OPTIONS	
Text Box, Change Outline Weight, Color, or Style	PPT 542 PPT 543 PPT 544		Shape Outline button arrow (DRAWING TOOLS FORMAT tab | Shape Styles group), choose Weight, color, or Dashes			
Text Box, Rotate	PPT 498	Drag rotation handle	Rotate button (DRAWING TOOLS FORMAT tab | Arrange group)		Format Shape, Effects icon, 3-D ROTATION	
Text Box, Set Formatting as the Default	PPT 545				Set as Default Text Box	
Text File, Import	PPT 607		Object button (INSERT tab | Text group), 'Create from file', browse to .txt file			

Microsoft PowerPoint 2013 Quick Reference Summary *(continued)*

Task	Page Number	Mouse	Ribbon	Other On-Screen Areas	Shortcut Menu	Keyboard Shortcut
Theme Font, Customize	PPT 482		Theme Fonts button (SLIDE MASTER tab | Background group)			
Video, Create from Presentation	PPT 708		'Create a Video' button (FILE tab, Export tab)			
Video File, Compress	PPT 704		Compress Media button (FILE tab, Info tab), Media Size and Performance area, select quality			
View, Change to Color/ Grayscale	PPT 694		Color or Grayscale button (VIEW tab | Color/Grayscale group)			
WordArt, Convert to SmartArt	PPT 553				Convert to SmartArt	
Worksheet, Align	PPT 628		Align button (DRAWING TOOLS FORMAT tab | Arrange group)			

Microsoft Excel 2013 Quick Reference Summary

Task	Page Number	Ribbon	Other On-Screen Element	Shortcut Menu	Keyboard Shortcut
2-D Line Chart, Create	EX 478	'Insert Line Chart' button (INSERT tab | Charts group)	'Quick Analysis Lens' button, Charts tab		
Background, Format	EX 701	Background button (PAGE LAYOUT tab | Page Setup group)			
Chart, Add Legend	EX 735		Chart Elements button on chart, Legend		
Chart, Add Shadow	EX 736			'Format Plot Area', Effects button in Format Plot Area task pane	
Command Button Procedure, Enter	EX 665	View Code button (DEVELOPER tab | Controls group), Object arrow, enter VBA code			
Command Button, Add	EX 652	Insert Controls button (DEVELOPER tab | Controls group)			
Comment, Add	EX 695	'Insert a Comment' button (REVIEW tab | Comments group)		Insert Comment	SHIFT+F2
Comment, Format	EX 699	Edit Comment button (REVIEW tab | Comments group)		Edit Comment	

Microsoft Excel 2013 Quick Reference Summary

Task	Page Number	Ribbon	Other On-Screen Element	Shortcut Menu	Keyboard Shortcut
Comments, Display	EX 697	'Show All Comments' button (REVIEW tab | Comments group)			
Comments, Edit	EX 697			Edit Comment	
Comments, Hide	EX 697	'Show All Comments' button (REVIEW tab | Comments group)			
Comments, Print	EX 700	Page Setup Dialog Box Launcher (PAGE LAYOUT tab | Page Setup group), Comments arrow (Sheet tab in Page Setup Dialog box)			
Compare Workbooks	EX 719	'View Side by Side' button (VIEW tab | Window group)			
Control(s), Format	EX 659	Select control(s), Control Properties button (DEVELOPER tab | Controls group)			
Custom View, Save	EX 724	Custom Views button (VIEW tab | Workbook Views group)			
Data Point, Change Format	EX 483			Select data point, 'Format Data Point', 'Fill & Line button (Format Data Point task pane), MARKER	
Data Validation	EX 565	Data Validation button (DATA tab | Data Tools group)			
Dependent Arrows, Remove	EX 558	'Remove All Arrows' button (FORMULAS tab | Formula Auditing group)			
Dependents, Trace	EX 557	Trace Dependents button (FORMULAS tab | Formula Auditing group)			
DEVELOPER Tab, Display	EX 625	Options (FILE tab), Customize Ribbon (Excel Options Dialog box)			
Digital Box/ Signature, Add	EX 671	'Add a Signature Line' button (INSERT tab | Text group)			
Digital Signature, Review	EX 672	View Signatures (FILE tab | Info tab)			
Distribute Workbook by Email	EX 711	Email button (FILE tab | Share tab), 'Send as Attachment' button			
Error Checking	EX 558	Error Checking button (FORMULAS tab | Formula Auditing group), Trace Error button (Error Checking dialog box)			

Microsoft Excel 2013 Quick Reference Summary *(continued)*

Task	Page Number	Ribbon	Other On-Screen Element	Shortcut Menu	Keyboard Shortcut
Form Controls	EX 648	Insert Controls button (DEVELOPER tab | Controls group)			
Goal Seek	EX 570	'What-If Analysis' button (DATA tab | Data Tools group), Goal Seek			
Group Control, Remove Outline	EX 668				In VBE, press CTRL+G
Group Option Buttons	EX 651	Insert Controls button (DEVELOPER tab | Controls group)			
Hyperlink, Add	EX 725	'Add a Hyperlink' button (INSERT tab | Links group)		Hyperlink	CTRL+K
Hyperlink, Delete	EX 731			Remove Hyperlink	
Hyperlink, Edit	EX 731			Edit Hyperlink	
Hyperlink, Format	EX 728	Cell Styles button (HOME tab | Styles group)			
Inspect Document	EX 599	'Check for Issues button (FILE tab | Info tab), Inspect Document			
Iterative Calculation	EX 562	Formulas button (Excel options dialog box), 'Enable Iterative Calculations'			
Macro VBA Code, View	EX 638	View Macros button (DEVELOPER tab | Code group)		View Code	ALT+F11
Macro, Assign Button on Quick Access Toolbar	EX 639			'Customize Quick Access Toolbar', 'Choose commands from' arrow (Excel Options dialog box), Macros, Add button	
Macro, Execute	EX 637	Enable Content button (SECURITY WARNING bar), Unprotect Sheet button (REVIEW tab | Changes group)			
Macro, Record	EX 629	Record Macro button (DEVELOPER tab | Code group)			
Macro, Set Security Level	EX 635	Macro Security button (DEVELOPER tab | Code group), 'Disable all macros with notification' option button			
Macros, Enable	EX 625	Macro Security button (DEVELOPER tab | Code group)			

Microsoft Excel 2013 Quick Reference Summary *(continued)*

Task	Page Number	Ribbon	Other On-Screen Element	Shortcut Menu	Keyboard Shortcut
Mark as Final	EX 602	Protect Workbook button (FILE tab | Info gallery), 'Mark as Final'			
Merge Workbooks	EX 721	FILE tab | Options, 'Compare and Merge Workbooks' button (Excel Options dialog box)	'Customize Quick Access Toolbar', 'Choose commands from' arrow (Excel Options dialog box), All Commands, add 'Compare and Merge Workbooks' button		
Picture, Add to Worksheet	EX 731	From File button (INSERT tab | Illustrations group)			
PivotChart Report, Create Directly from Data	EX 518	PivotChart arrow (INSERT tab | Charts group), 'PivotChart & PivotTable)			
PivotChart, Change View	EX 516	Select/deselect check box(es) (PivotChart Fields task pane)			
PivotChart, Create Report from PivotTable Report	EX 509	PivotChart button (PIVOTTABLE TOOLS ANALYZE tab | Tools group)			
PivotTable Report, Add Calculated Field	EX 520	'Fields, Items, & Sets' button (PIVOTTABLE TOOLS ANALYZE tab | Calculations group)			
PivotTable Report, Display Field List/Header	EX 504	Field List or Field Headers button (PIVOTTABLE TOOLS ANALYZE tab | Show group)			
PivotTable Report, Expand Collapse Buttons	EX 506			Expand/Collapse	
PivotTable Report, Filter Using Row Label Filter	EX 494		Filter button in desired cell, select/deselect desired check boxes		
PivotTable Report, Update Contents	EX 508	Refresh button (PIVOTTABLE TOOLS ANALYZE tab | Data group)			
PivotTable Report, Use a Report Filter	EX 491		Drag field from Choose field to add to report area to FILTERS area (PivotTable Fields task pane)		
PivotTable, Add Data	EX 487		Drag field(s) from Choose fields to add to report area		
PivotTable, Change Layout	EX 488	Report Layout button (PIVOTTABLE TOOLS DESIGN tab | Layout group)			
PivotTable, Change View	EX 490		Drag button in ROWS area (PivotTable Fields task pane)		
PivotTable, Create	EX 486	PivotTable button (INSERT tab | Tables group)		Quick Analysis	

Microsoft Excel 2013 Quick Reference Summary (continued)

Task	Page Number	Ribbon	Other On-Screen Element	Shortcut Menu	Keyboard Shortcut
PivotTable, Remove Report Filter	EX 494		Drag button out of PivotTable Fields task pane		
PivotTable, Switch Summary Functions	EX 499			'Summarize Values By'	
Precedent Arrows, Remove	EX 555	'Remove All Arrows' button (FORMULAS tab | Formula Auditing group)			
Precedents, Review on Different Worksheet	EX 556		Double-tap or double-click dashed precedent arrow, select cell reference in Go to list (Go To dialog box)		
Precedents, Trace	EX 552	Trace Precedents button (FORMULAS tab | Formula Auditing group)			
Proper Case, Convert Names To	EX 627		Type = **proper** in cell, tap or click Enter box in formula bar		
Quick Access Toolbar, Reset	EX 671	FILE tab | Options, Reset button (Excel Options dialog box)			
Save as Excel 97-2003 Workbook File Format	EX 602	FILE tab | Save As tab, 'Save as type' arrow			
Scenario PivotTable Worksheet, Create	EX 596	'What-If Analysis' button (DATA tab | Data Tools group, Scenario Manager, Summary button (Scenario Manager dialog box)			
Scenario, Save As	EX 582	'What-If Analysis' button (DATA tab | Data Tools group), Scenario Manager, Add button (Scenario Manager dialog box)			
Shape, Add	EX 733	Shapes button (INSERT tab | Illustrations group)			
Share/Collaborate on Workbook	EX 706	Share Workbook button (REVIEW tab | Changes group)			
Slicer, Add	EX 525	Insert Slicer button (PIVOTCHART TOOLS ANALYZE tab | Filter group)			
Solver	EX 575	Solver button (DATA tab | Analysis group)			
Solver Answer Report, View	EX 580		Tap or click sheet tab containing report		
Text Box Control, Add	EX 653	Insert Controls button (DEVELOPER tab | Controls group)			

Microsoft Excel 2013 Quick Reference Summary *(continued)*

Task	Page Number	Ribbon	Other On-Screen Element	Shortcut Menu	Keyboard Shortcut
Track Changes	EX 709	Track Changes button (REVIEW tab | Changes group)			
Track Changes, Review	EX 712	Track Changes button (REVIEW tab | Changes group), Highlight Changes			
Track Changes, Turn Off	EX 717	Track Changes button (REVIEW tab | Changes group), Highlight Changes, remove check mark from 'Track changes while editing' check box			
Trendline, Add to Chart	EX 481	'Add Chart Element' button (CHART TOOLS DESIGN tab | Chart Layouts group), Trendline		Add Trendline	
Unprotect Password-Protected Worksheet	EX 623	Unprotect Sheet button (REVIEW tab | Changes group)			
Validation Circles	EX 571	Data Validation arrow (DATA tab | Data Tools group)			
Validation Rules, Copy	EX 567	Select cell, Paste arrow (HOME tab | Clipboard group), Paste Special, Validation (Paste Special dialog box)			
Watch Window, Add Cells	EX 563	Add Watch button (FORMULAS tab | Formula Auditing group), select cell to watch			
Watch Window, Close	EX 564		Close button on Watch Window title bar		
Watch Window, Delete Cells	EX 564		Tap or click watched cell, Delete Watch button in Watch Window		
Watch Window, Open	EX 563	Watch Window button (FORMULAS tab | Formula Auditing group)			
Watermark	EX 703	Insert WordArt button (INSERT tab | Text group)			

Microsoft Access 2013 Quick Reference Summary

Task	Page Number	Ribbon	Other On-Screen Areas	Shortcut Menu	Keyboard Shortcut
Control Margins, Change in Layout	AC 519	Select any cell, Select Layout button (FORM LAYOUT TOOLS ARRANGE tab | Rows & Columns group), Control Margins button, select desired margin setting			
Control Padding, Change in Layout	AC 519	Select layout, Control Padding button (FORM LAYOUT TOOLS ARRANGE tab | Position group), select desired padding setting			

Microsoft Access 2013 Quick Reference Summary

Task	Page Number	Ribbon	Other On-Screen Areas	Shortcut Menu	Keyboard Shortcut
Controls, Anchor	AC 521	Select controls to anchor, Anchoring button (FORM LAYOUT TOOLS ARRANGE tab | Position group), select desired option			
Convert Earlier Access Database to Access 2013	AC 543		With database to be converted open, tap or click FILE for backstage view, Save As tab, select Save Database As command, tap or click Access Database		
Custom Categories and Groups, Create	AC 549			Press and hold or right-click Navigation Pane title bar, Navigation Options command, Add Item button, specify category and group names, OK button	
Custom Input Mask, Create	AC 557		In Design view, select field for mask, select Input Mask property, enter mask		
Custom Properties, Create	AC 554		In Backstage view, select Info tab, tap or click 'View and edit database properties'		
Data Macro, Create	AC 510	TABLE TOOLS TABLE tab, Before Change button, enter macro code			
Data Parts, Create	AC 563	Select fields to include, tap or click More Fields button (TABLE TOOLS FIELDS tab | Add & Delete group), tap or click 'Save Selection as New Data Type'			
Database Documenter, Use	AC 548	Database Documenter button (DATABASE TOOLS tab | Analyze group)			
Database, Convert to Earlier Version of Access	AC 543		With database to be converted open, tap or click FILE for Backstage view, Save As tab, select desired format, with Save Database As selected, tap or click Save As button		
Datasheet Forms, Create	AC 504, AC 573	More Forms button (CREATE tab | Forms group), tap or click Datasheet			
Desktop Database, Create	AC 566		In Backstage view, tap or click New tab, 'Blank desktop database' button, enter name for database, Browse button, navigate to storage location, OK button		
Encrypt a Database with Password	AC 584		In Backstage view, select Info tab, tap or click 'Encrypt with Password' button		

Microsoft Access 2013 Quick Reference Summary *(continued)*

Task	Page Number	Ribbon	Other On-Screen Areas	Shortcut Menu	Keyboard Shortcut
Error Checking, Enable	AC 561		In Backstage view, tap or click Options tab, tap or click Object Designers, select 'Enable error checking' check box		
Items, Add to Groups	AC 551		Navigation Pane arrow, tap or click category, press and hold or right-click object, point to 'Add to Group,' select desired group		
Layout, Create	AC 514	Select all controls to include in layout, FORM LAYOUT TOOLS ARRANGE tab, Stacked button or Tabular button			
Layout, Delete Column	AC 516	Select column, Select Column button (FORM LAYOUT TOOLS ARRANGE tab | Rows & Columns group), DELETE key			
Layout, Delete Row	AC 516	Select row (FORM LAYOUT TOOLS ARRANGE tab | Rows & Columns group), Select Row button, DELETE key			
Layout, Insert Column	AC 516	Select column (FORM LAYOUT TOOLS ARRANGE tab | Rows & Columns group), Select Column button, tap or click Insert Left or Insert Right button			
Layout, Insert Row	AC 515	Select row (FORM LAYOUT TOOLS ARRANGE tab | Rows & Columns group), Select Row button, tap or click Insert Above or Insert Below button			
Layout, Merge Cells	AC 517	Select cells to merge, Merge button (FORM LAYOUT TOOLS ARRANGE tab | Merge/Split group)			
Layout, Move	AC 521	Select any cell in layout, Select Layout button (FORM LAYOUT TOOLS ARRANGE tab | Rows & Columns group), drag layout to new position			
Layout, Remove	AC 514		Press and hold or right-click control in layout, point to Layout, tap or click Remove Layout		
Layout, Split	AC 520	Select cells to move to new layout, Stacked button (FORM LAYOUT TOOLS ARRANGE tab | Table group)			
Layout, Split Cell	AC 517	Select cell, Split Vertically button (FORM LAYOUT TOOLS ARRANGE tab | Merge/Split group) or Split Horizontally button (FORM LAYOUT TOOLS ARRANGE tab | Merge/Split group)			
Lock Database	AC 587		With database to lock open, tap or click FILE tab to switch to Backstage view, tap or click Save As tab, tap or click Make ACCDE, tap or click Save As button		
Macro, Add Action	AC 480		Double-tap or double-click Submacro element in Action Catalog, enter actions in Macro Builder		

Microsoft Access 2013 Quick Reference Summary *(continued)*

Task	Page Number	Ribbon	Other On-Screen Areas	Shortcut Menu	Keyboard Shortcut
Macro, Create	AC 478	Macro button (CREATE tab | Macros & Code group), Action Catalog button			
Menu Form with Command Buttons, Create	AC 488	Form Design button (CREATE tab | Forms group), remove field list and property sheet if necessary, with 'Use Control Wizards' button selected, tap or click Button tool (FORM DESIGN TOOLS DESIGN tab | Controls group), tap or click form to display Command Button Wizard dialog box			
Menu Form with Option Group, Create	AC 492	Form Design button (CREATE tab | Forms group), remove field list and property sheet if necessary, with 'Use Control Wizards' button selected, tap or click Option Group tool (FORM DESIGN TOOLS DESIGN tab | Controls group), tap or click form to display Option Group Wizard dialog box			
Multiple-Field Index, Create	AC 560		Indexes button (TABLE TOOLS DESIGN tab | Show/Hide group), click blank row in Indexes: (*Table*) window		
Navigation Form, Create	AC 506, AC 575	Navigation button (CREATE tab | Forms group), tap or click Horizontal Tabs			
Objects, Display in Overlapping Windows	AC 522		In Backstage view, Options, Current Database, Overlapping Windows option button		
Objects, Display in Tabbed Documents	AC 523		In Backstage view, Options, Current Database, Tabbed Documents option button		
Performance Analyzer, Use	AC 546	Analyze Performance button (DATABASE TOOLs tab | Analyze group)			
Rows, Move using Move Buttons	AC 581	Select cell in row to move, Select Row button (FORM LAYOUT TOOLS ARRANGE tab | Rows & Columns group), Move Up or Move Down buttons			
Single-Field Index, Create	AC 559		In Design view, select field, change Indexed field property to Yes		
Split a Database	AC 590	With database to split open, tap or click Access Database button (DATABASE TOOLS tab | Move Data group), tap or click Split Database button			
Startup Form, Select	AC 576		In Backstage view, tap or click Options tab, Current Database, Display Form arrow, Main Menu		
Summary View, Create in Web Apps	AC 607		Select table, 'Add New View' button		
Table Analyzer, Use	AC 544		Analyze Table button (DATABASE TOOLS tab | Analyze group)		

Microsoft Access 2013 Quick Reference Summary *(continued)*

Task	Page Number	Ribbon	Other On-Screen Areas	Shortcut Menu	Keyboard Shortcut
Table, Create by Importing Data	AC 593		Select icon for type of data to import, select file to import, tap or click OK button, select tables to import, tap or click OK button		
Table, Create from Template	AC 593		Enter type of data that will be stored, tap or click Search button, select template from search results		
Template and Application Part, Create	AC 578		In Backstage view, tap or click Save As tab, tap or click Template button, tap or click Save As button		
Template, Use	AC 579		In Backstage view, select New tab, tap or click PERSONAL link, tap or click template from which to create database, enter name for new database, tap or click Create button		
Update Data using Web App	AC 603		With app running, select table to update, select desired view, tap or click Add button, enter data for record, tap or click Save button		
User Interface Macros, Create	AC 504		Select object, display property sheet, Event tab, On Click event, Build button, OK button, add SetTempVar action to macro, enter Name and Expression argument values		
Validation Rule for Table, Create	AC 553		In Design view, tap or click Property Sheet button (TABLE TOOLS DESIGN tab | Show/Hide group), tap or click Validation Rule property, enter rule		
View Data in Web Apps	AC 597		Select table, tap or click Settings/Action button, tap or click View Data		
Views, Edit in Web Apps	AC 596		Select table, select view to edit, tap or click Edit button		
Web App, Create	AC 591		In Backstage view, click 'Custom web app,' enter app name, select a storage location, tap or click Create button		
Web App, Customize	AC 604	Tap or click Settings button, tap or click 'Customize in Access' command			
Web App, Run from Access	AC 601	With app open, click Launch App button (HOME tab | View group)			
Zero Length, Allow	AC 557		Select field, tap or click Zero Length property, change Allow Zero Length field property value to yes		

Microsoft Outlook 2013 Quick Reference Summary

Task	Page Number	Touch Gesture	Ribbon	Other On-Screen Area	Shortcut Menu	Keyboard Shortcut
Add Email Account	OUT 237		FILE tab | click Add Account button			
Add Image to Email Signature	OUT 251			Insert Picture button (Signatures and Stationery dialog box)		
Add RSS Feed	OUT 278	Press and hold RSS Feeds folder, tap Add a New RSS Feed			Right-click RSS Feeds folder, click Add a New RSS Feed	
Assign Task	OUT 206		Assign Task button (TASK tab | Manage Task group)			
Assign Theme to Stationery	OUT 255			Stationery and Fonts button (Outlook Options dialog box), Theme button (Signatures and Stationery dialog box)		
Attach Outlook Item to Task	OUT 205		Outlook Item button (INSERT tab | Include group)			
Attachment, Add to Task	OUT 203		Attach File button (INSERT tab | Include group)			
AutoArchive Settings, Configure	OUT 271		FILE tab | Options tab, Advanced category, click AutoArchive Settings button (Outlook Options dialog box)			
Automatic Replies, Set Up	OUT 271		FILE tab | Info tab, click Automatic Replies			
Calendar, Change Time Zone for	OUT 276		FILE tab | Options tab, Calendar category, Time zone box arrow (Outlook Options dialog box)			
Calendar Options, Set	OUT 273		FILE tab | Options tab, Calendar category (Outlook Options dialog box)			
Categorize Email Message	OUT 202	Press and hold email message's category column, tap category	Categorize button (HOME tab | Tags group)		Right-click email message's category column, click category	

Microsoft Outlook 2013 Quick Reference Summary *(continued)*

Task	Page Number	Touch Gesture	Ribbon	Other On-Screen Area	Shortcut Menu	Keyboard Shortcut
Categorize Multiple Tasks	OUT 197		Select tasks, click Categorize button (HOME tab | Tags group)		Select tasks, right-click one task's category column, click All Categories	
Categorize Task	OUT 196		Click task, click Categorize button (HOME tab | Tags group)		Right-click task's category column, click All Categories	
Category, Create	OUT 193		Categorize button (HOME tab | Tags group)			
Category, Delete	OUT 214			Delete button (Color Categories dialog box)		
Category, Rename	OUT 199		Click Categorize button (HOME tab | Tags group), click All Categories, click category, click Rename		Right-click task's category column, click All Categories, select category, click Rename button	
Change Notes View	OUT 220		Notes List (HOME tab | Current View group)			
Change Task View	OUT 216		Change View button (HOME tab | Current View group)			
Change Work Time on Calendar	OUT 273		FILE tab | Options tab | Calendar category, options in Work time area (Outlook Options dialog box)			
Configure Junk Email Options	OUT 259		Junk button (HOME tab | Delete group)			
Create Category	OUT 186		Categorize button (HOME tab | Tags group)			
Create Email Signature	OUT 248		FILE tab | Options tab| Mail category | click Signatures button (Outlook Options dialog box)			
Create Note	OUT 218		New Note (HOME tab | New group)			CTRL+N

Microsoft Outlook 2013 Quick Reference Summary *(continued)*

Task	Page Number	Touch Gesture	Ribbon	Other On-Screen Area	Shortcut Menu	Keyboard Shortcut
Create Recurring Task	OUT 183		New Task button (HOME tab | New group), click Recurrence button (TASK tab | Recurrence group)			
Create Rule	OUT 265		Rules button (HOME tab | Move group)			
Create Task with Priority	OUT 179		New Task button (HOME tab | New group), click Priority box arrow			
Create Task with Reminder	OUT 180		New Task button (HOME tab | New group), click Reminder check box, click Reminder date box arrow			
Create Task with Status	OUT 177		New Task button (HOME tab | New group), click Status box arrow			
Custom Date, Flag Email Message with	OUT 199		Follow Up button (HOME tab | Tags group), click Custom		Right-click email's flag column, click Custom	
Customize Stationery	OUT 254		FILE tab | Options tab, Mail category, click Stationery and Fonts button (Outlook Options dialog box)			
Default Message Format, Set	OUT 246		FILE tab | Options tab, Mail category, click Compose messages in this format box arrow (Outlook Options dialog box)			
Delete Category	OUT 213			Delete button (Color Categories dialog box)		
Delete Note	OUT 221		Delete button (HOME tab | Delete group)			
Delete Rule	OUT 270		Rules button (HOME tab | Move group), click Manage Rules and Alerts, click Delete button (Rules and Alerts dialog box)			
Delete Task	OUT 212		Remove from List button (HOME tab | Manage Task group) or Display task, click Delete button (HOME tab | Delete group)		Right-click task, click Delete	DELETE
Display Outlook Options	OUT 245		FILE tab | Options tab			
Email Account, Add	OUT 237		FILE tab | Add Account			

Microsoft Outlook 2013 Quick Reference Summary *(continued)*

Task	Page Number	Touch Gesture	Ribbon	Other On-Screen Area	Shortcut Menu	Keyboard Shortcut
Email Address, Block	OUT 263		Blocked Senders tab (Junk E-mail Options dialog box), click Add button			
Email Message, Categorize	OUT 202		Categorize button (HOME tab | Tags group)		Right-click email message's category column, click category	
Email Message, Categorize Using OUT Quick Click	OUT 198			Click category column for email message		
Email Message, Flag for Follow-Up	OUT 198		Follow Up button (HOME tab | Tags group)		Right-click email's flag column, click option	
Email Message, Flag with Custom Date	OUT 199		Follow Up button (HOME tab | Tags group), click Custom		Right-click email's flag column, click Custom	
Email Signature, Create	OUT 248		FILE tab | Options tab, Mail category, Signatures button (Outlook Options dialog box)			
Email Signature, Format	OUT 249			Formatting options (Signatures and Stationery dialog box)		
File, Attach to Task	OUT 203		Attach File button (INSERT tab | Include group)			
Flag Email Message for Follow-Up	OUT 198	Press and hold email's flag column, tap option	Follow Up button (HOME tab | Tags group)		Right-click email's flag column, click option	
Flag Email Message with Custom Date	OUT 199	Press and hold email's flag column, tap Custom	Follow Up button (HOME tab | Tags group), click Custom		Right-click email's flag column, click Custom	
Format Email Signature	OUT 249			Formatting options (Signatures and Stationery dialog box)		
Forward Task	OUT 208		Forward button (TASK tab | Actions group)			CTRL+F
Hyperlink, Add to Email Message	OUT 238		Select text, click Hyperlink button (INSERT tab | Links group)			CTRL+K
Image, Add to Email Message	OUT 241		Pictures button (INSERT tab | Illustrations group)			

Task	Page Number	Touch Gesture	Ribbon	Other On-Screen Area	Shortcut Menu	Keyboard Shortcut
Image, Add to Email Signature	OUT 252			Insert Picture button (Signatures and Stationery dialog box)		
Item, Attach to Task	OUT 205		Outlook Item button (INSERT tab | Include group)			
Junk Email Options, Configure	OUT 259		Junk button (HOME tab | Delete group)			
Mark Task as Complete	OUT 211		Mark Complete button (HOME tab | Manage Task group)		Right-click task, click Mark Complete	
Message Format, Set Default	OUT 246		FILE tab | Options tab, Mail category, click Compose messages in this format box arrow			
Multiple Tasks, Categorize	OUT 190		Select tasks, click Categorize button (HOME tab | Tags group)		Select tasks, right-click one task's category column, click All Categories	
Note, Create	OUT 218		New Note (HOME tab | New group)			CTRL+SHIFT+N
Note, Delete	OUT 220		Delete button (HOME tab | Delete group)			
Notes View, Change	OUT 219		Notes List button (HOME tab | Current View group)			
Options for Junk Email, Configure	OUT 259		Junk button (HOME tab | Delete group)			
Outlook Item, Attach to Task	OUT 205		Outlook Item button (INSERT tab | Include group)			
Outlook Options, Display	OUT 245		FILE tab | Options tab			
Print Tasks	OUT 217		FILE tab | Print tab, click Print button			
Priority, Create Task with	OUT 179		New Task button (HOME tab | New group), click Priority box arrow			
Quick Click, Set	OUT 200		Categorize button (HOME tab | Tags group), click Set Quick Click		Right-click task's category column, click Set Quick Click	
Quick Click, Use to Categorize Email Message	OUT 198			Click category column for email message		

Microsoft Outlook 2013 Quick Reference Summary *(continued)*

Task	Page Number	Touch Gesture	Ribbon	Other On-Screen Area	Shortcut Menu	Keyboard Shortcut
Quick Parts, Create	OUT 240		Quick Parts button (INSERT tab | Text group)			
Recurring Task, Create	OUT 183		New Task button (HOME tab | New group), click Recurrence button (TASK tab | Recurrence group)			
Reminder, Create Task with	OUT 180		New Task button (HOME tab | New group), click Reminder check box, click Reminder date box arrow			
Remove Task	OUT 212		Remove from List button (HOME tab | Manage Task group) or Display task, click Delete button (HOME tab | Delete group)		Right-click task, click Delete	DELETE
Rename Category	OUT 193		Click Categorize button (HOME tab | Tags group), click All Categories, click category, click Rename		Right-click task's category column, click All Categories, select category, click Rename button	
RSS Feed, Delete	OUT 280	Press and hold RSS feed, tap Delete Folder			Right-click RSS feed, click Delete Folder	
RSS Feed, Subscribe to	OUT 278	Press and hold RSS Feeds folder, tap Add a New RSS Feed			Right-click RSS Feeds folder, click Add a New RSS Feed	
Rule, Create	OUT 264		Rules button (HOME tab | Move group), click Create Rule			
Rule, Delete	OUT 270		Rules button (HOME tab | Move group), click Manage Rules and Alerts, click Delete button (Rules and Alerts dialog box)			
Rule, Run	OUT 268		Rules button (HOME tab | Move group), click Manage Rules and Alerts, click Run Rules Now button (Rules and Alerts dialog box)			

Microsoft Outlook 2013 Quick Reference Summary *(continued)*

Task	Page Number	Touch Gesture	Ribbon	Other On-Screen Area	Shortcut Menu	Keyboard Shortcut
Run Rule	OUT 268		Rules button (HOME tab | Move group), click Manage Rules and Alerts, click Run Rules Now button (Rules and Alerts dialog box)			
Safe Senders List, Add Domain to	OUT 260		Junk button (HOME tab | Delete group), click Junk E-mail Options, click Safe Senders tab, click Add button			
Search, Refine	OUT 243		Click Search Contacts text box, click More button (SEARCH TOOLS SEARCH tab | Refine group), click property			CTRL+E
Search, Use Instant Search	OUT 243	Tap Instant Search text box		Click Instant Search text box		
Search Folder, Create	OUT 244		New Search Folder button (FOLDER tab | New group)			
Send Status Report	OUT 209		Send Status Report button (TASK tab | Manage Task group)			
Set Default Message Format	OUT 246		FILE tab | Options tab, Mail category, Compose messages in this format box arrow (Outlook Options dialog box)			
Set Junk Email Options	OUT 259		Junk button (HOME tab | Delete group)			
Set Quick Click	OUT 195		Categorize button (HOME tab | Tags group), click Set Quick Click		Right-click task's category column, click Set Quick Click	
Signature, Add Image to	OUT 251			Insert Picture button (Signatures and Stationery dialog box)		
Signature, Assign to Single Email Message	OUT 252		Open message, click Signature button (INSERT tab | Include group)			
Signature, Create for Email	OUT 248		FILE tab | Options tab, Mail category, click Signatures button (Outlook Options dialog box)			
Signature, Format	OUT 249			Font box arrow (Signatures and Stationery dialog box)		
Signature Options, Set	OUT 253			Select settings (Signatures and Stationery dialog box)		

Microsoft Outlook 2013 Quick Reference Summary (continued)

Task	Page Number	Touch Gesture	Ribbon	Other On-Screen Area	Shortcut Menu	Keyboard Shortcut
Stationery, Assign Theme to	OUT 255			Stationery and Fonts button (Outlook Options dialog box), Theme button (Signatures and Stationery dialog box)		
Stationery, Customize	OUT 254		FILE tab	Options tab, Mail category, click Stationery and Fonts button (Outlook Options dialog box)			
Status, Create Task with	OUT 177		New Task button (HOME tab | New group), click Status box arrow			
Status Report, Send	OUT 210		Send Status Report button (TASK tab | Manage Task group)			
Subscribe to RSS Feed	OUT 278	Press and hold RSS Feeds folder, tap Add a New RSS Feed			Right-click RSS Feeds folder, click Add a New RSS Feed	
Task, Add with To-Do List Pane	OUT 192	Tap 'Type a new task' box, enter description		Click 'Type a new task' box, enter description		
Task, Assign	OUT 206		Assign Task button (TASK tab | Manage Task group)			
Task, Attach File to	OUT 205		Attach File button (INSERT tab | Include group)			
Task, Categorize	OUT 196		Click task, click Categorize button (HOME tab | Tags group)		Right-click task's category column, click All Categories	
Task, Create	OUT 181		New Task button (HOME tab | New group)			
Task, Create Recurring	OUT 190		New Task button (HOME tab | New group), Recurrence button (TASK tab | Recurrence group)			
Task, Create with Due Date	OUT 184		New Task button (HOME tab | New group), click Due date box arrow			

Microsoft Outlook 2013 Quick Reference Summary *(continued)*

Task	Page Number	Touch Gesture	Ribbon	Other On-Screen Area	Shortcut Menu	Keyboard Shortcut
Task, Create with Priority	OUT 186		New Task button (HOME tab | New group), click Priority box arrow			
Task, Create with Reminder	OUT 187		New Task button (HOME tab | New group), click Reminder check box, click Reminder date box arrow			
Task, Create with Status	OUT 185		New Task button (HOME tab | New group), click Status box arrow			
Task, Forward	OUT 208		Forward button (TASK tab | Actions group)			CTRL+F
Task, Mark Complete	OUT 212		Mark Complete button (HOME tab | Manage Task group)		Right-click task, click Mark Complete	
Task, Print	OUT 216		FILE tab | Print tab, select style, click Print button			
Task, Remove	OUT 213		Remove from List button (HOME tab | Manage Task group) or Display task, click Delete button (HOME tab | Delete group)		Right-click task, click Delete	DELETE
Task, Send Status Report for	OUT 209		Send Status Report button (TASK tab | Manage Task group)			
Task, Update	OUT 204	Double-tap task		Double-click task		
Task View, Change	OUT 215		Change View button (HOME tab | Current View group)			
Tasks, Print	OUT 217		FILE tab | Print tab, click Print button			
Theme, Assign to Stationery	OUT 255			Stationery and Fonts button (Outlook Options dialog box), Theme button (Signatures and Stationery dialog box)		
Time Zone, Change in Calendar	OUT 276		FILE tab | Options tab, Calendar category, click Time zone box arrow (Outlook Options dialog box)			
Update Task	OUT 202			Double-click task		
Work Time, Change on Calendar	OUT 273		FILE tab | Options tab, Calendar category (Outlook Options dialog box)			

Important Notes for Windows 7 Users

The screen shots in this book show Microsoft Office 2013 running in Windows 8. If you are using Microsoft Windows 7, however, you still can use this book because Office 2013 runs virtually the same way on both platforms. You will encounter only minor differences if you are using Windows 7. Read this section to understand the differences.

Dialog Boxes

If you are a Windows 7 user, the dialog boxes shown in this book will look slightly different than what you see on your screen. Dialog boxes for Windows 8 have a title bar with a solid color, and the dialog box name is centered on the title bar. Beyond these superficial differences in appearance, however, the options in the dialog boxes across both platforms are the same. For instance, Figures 1 and 2 show the Font dialog box in Windows 7 and the Font dialog box in Windows 8.

Figure 1 Font Dialog Box in Windows 7

Figure 2 Font Dialog Box in Windows 8

Alternate Steps for Running an App in Windows 7

Nearly all of the steps in this book work exactly the same way for Windows 7 users; however, running an app (or program/application) requires different steps for Windows 7. The following steps show how to run an app in Windows 7.

Running an App (or Program/Application) Using Windows 7

1. Click the Start button on the taskbar to display the Start menu.
2. Click All Programs and then click the Microsoft Office 2013 folder (Figure 3).
3. If necessary, click the name of the folder containing the app you want to run.
4. Click the name of the app you want to run (such as Excel 2013).

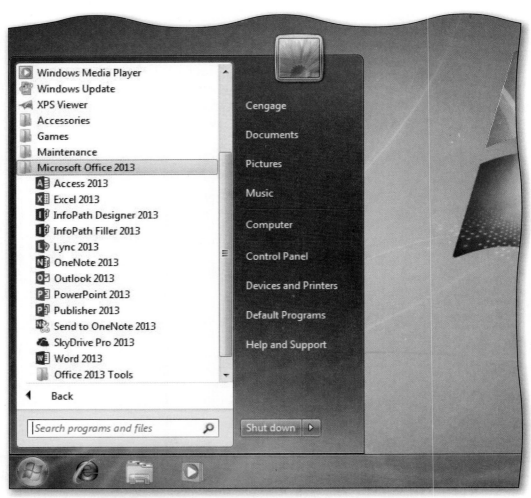

Figure 3   Running an App Using the Windows 7 Start Menu